The Management of Strategy

Concepts and Cases

9th Edition

The Management of Strategy

Concepts and Cases

9th Edition

R. Duane Ireland
Texas A&M University

Robert E. Hoskisson
Rice University

Michael A. Hitt
Texas A&M University

SOUTH-WESTERN
CENGAGE Learning™

Australia • Brazil • Japan • Korea • Mexico • Singapore • Spain • United Kingdom • United States

SOUTH-WESTERN
CENGAGE Learning™

The Management of Strategy: Concepts and Cases, Ninth Edition

R. Duane Ireland, Robert E. Hoskisson, and Michael A. Hitt

VP/Editorial Director:
Jack W. Calhoun

Editor-in-Chief:
Melissa Acuna

Senior Acquisitions Editor:
Michele Rhoades

Director of Development:
John Abner

Senior Editorial Assistant:
Ruth Belanger

Marketing Manager:
Nathan Anderson

Senior Marketing Communications Manager:
Jim Overly

Marketing Coordinator:
Suellen Ruttkay

Content Project Manager:
Jacquelyn K Featherly

Media Editor:
Rob Ellington

Senior Manufacturing Coordinator:
Sandee Milewski

Production House/Compositor:
Cadmus Communications

Senior Art Director:
Tippy McIntosh

B/W Image:
iStockphoto.com/JoLin

Color Image:
Shutterstock Images / Evok20

For product information and technology assistance, contact us at
Cengage Learning Customer & Sales Support, 1-800-354-9706

For permission to use material from this text or product,
submit all requests online at **www.cengage.com/permissions**
Further permissions questions can be emailed to
permissionrequest@cengage.com

ExamView® and ExamView Pro® are registered trademarks of FSCreations, Inc. Windows is a registered trademark of the Microsoft Corporation used herein under license. Macintosh and Power Macintosh are registered trademarks of Apple Computer, Inc. used herein under license.

Library of Congress Control Number: 2009938971

International Student Edition ISBN 13: 978-0-538-75319-7
International Student Edition ISBN 10: 0-538-75319-6

Cengage Learning International Offices

Asia
cengageasia.com
tel: (65) 6410 1200

Australia/New Zealand
cengage.com.au
tel: (61) 3 9685 4111

Brazil
cengage.com.br
tel: (011) 3665 9900

India
cengage.co.in
tel: (91) 11 30484837/38

Latin America
cengage.com.mx
tel: +52 (55) 1500 6000

UK/Europe/Middle East/Africa
cengage.co.uk
tel: (44) 207 067 2500

Represented in Canada by Nelson Education, Ltd.
nelson.com
tel: (416) 752 9100 / (800) 668 0671

For product information: **www.cengage.com/international**
Visit your local office: **www.cengage.com/global**
Visit our corporate website: **www.cengage.com**

Availability of resources may differ by region. Check with your local Cengage Learning representative for details.

Printed in Canada
2 3 4 5 6 7 13 12 11 10

To my entire family
I love each of you dearly and remain so grateful for your incredibly strong support and encouragement over the years. Your words and deeds have indeed showed me how to "keep my good eye to the sun and my blind eye to the dark."
—R. DUANE IRELAND

To my wonderful grandchildren (Mara, Seth, Roselyn, Ian, Abby, Madeline, Joseph, and Nadine), who are absolutely amazing and light up my life.
—ROBERT E. HOSKISSON

To Ashlyn and Aubrey
Your smiles are like sunshine—they brighten my day.
—MICHAEL A. HITT

Brief Contents

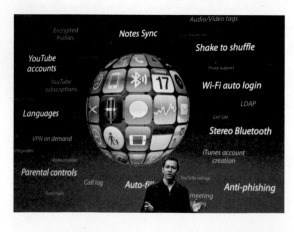

Part 2: Formulation of Strategic Actions   87

4: Business-Level Strategy   88

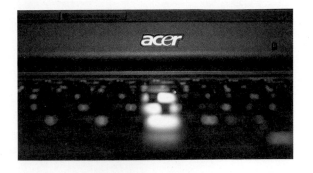

5: Competitive Rivalry and Dynamics   116

6: Corporate-Level Strategy   140

7: Strategic Acquisition and Restructuring   166

8: Global Strategy   192

**Opening Case: Entry Into China by Foreign Firms and
Chinese Firms Reaching for Global Markets   193**

Part 3: Implementation of Strategic Actions   247

11: Structure and Controls with Organizations   276

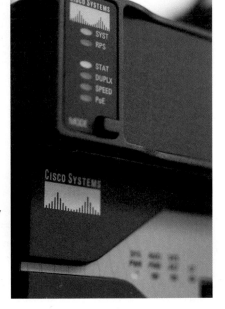

12: Leadership Implications for Strategy   306

Case Studies

Our goal in writing each edition of this book is to present a new, up-to-date standard for explaining the strategic management process. To reach this goal with the 9th edition of our market-leading text, we again present you with an intellectually rich yet thoroughly practical analysis of strategic management.

With each new edition, we are challenged and invigorated by the goal of establishing a new standard for presenting strategic management knowledge in a readable style. To prepare for each new edition, we carefully study the most recent academic research to ensure that the strategic management content we present to you is highly current and relevant for use in organizations. In addition, we continuously read articles appearing in many different business publications (e.g., *Wall Street Journal, BusinessWeek, Fortune, Financial Times,* and *Forbes,* to name a few); we do this to identify valuable examples of how companies are actually using the strategic management process. Though many of the hundreds of companies we discuss in the book will be quite familiar to you, some companies will likely be new to you as well. One reason for this is that we use examples of companies from around the world to demonstrate how globalized business has become. To maximize your opportunities to learn as you read and think about how actual companies use strategic management tools, techniques, and concepts (based on the most current research), we emphasize a lively and user-friendly writing style.

Several *characteristics* of this 9th edition of our book will enhance your learning opportunities:

■ This book presents you with the most comprehensive and thorough coverage of strategic management that is available in the market.

■ The research used in this book is drawn from the "classics" as well as the most recent contributions to the strategic management literature. The historically significant "classic" research provides the foundation for much of what is known about strategic management; the most recent contributions reveal insights about how to effectively use strategic management in the complex, global business environment in which most firms operate while trying to outperform their competitors. Our book also presents you with many up-to-date or recent examples of how firms use the strategic management tools, techniques, and concepts developed by leading researchers. Indeed, this book is strongly application oriented and presents you, our readers, with a vast number of examples and applications of strategic management concepts, techniques, and tools. In this edition, for example, we examine more than 600 companies to describe the use of strategic management. Collectively, no other strategic management book presents you with the *combination* of useful and insightful *research* and *applications* in a wide variety of organizations as does this text. Company examples range from the large U.S.-based firms such as Amazon.com, Wal-Mart, IBM, Johnson & Johnson,

Availability of resources may differ by region. Check with your local Cengage Learning representative for details.

Hershey, Hewlett Packard, Dell, PepsiCo, and Cisco to major foreign-based firms such as Toyota, Nokia, British Petroleum, Ryanair, Volkswagon, and Huawei. We also include examples of successful younger and newer firms such as Dylan's Candy Bar, Facebook, Honest Tea, MySpace, Yandex and Sun Tech Power and middle-sized family-owned firms such as Sargento Foods.

- We carefully *integrate* two of the most popular and well-known theoretical concepts in the strategic management field: industrial-organization economics and the resource-based view of the firm. Other texts usually emphasize one of these two theories (at the cost of explaining the other one to describe strategic management). However, such an approach is incomplete; research and practical experience indicate that both theories play a major role in understanding the linkage between strategic management and organizational success. No other book integrates these two theoretical perspectives effectively to explain the strategic management process and its application in all types of organizations.

- We use the ideas of prominent scholars (e.g., Raphael [Raffi] Amit, Kathy Eisenhardt, Don Hambrick, Constance [Connie] Helfat, Ming-Jer Chen, Michael Porter, C. K. Prahalad, Richard Rumelt, Ken Smith, David Teece, Michael Tushman, Oliver Williamson, and many younger, emerging scholars such as Rajshree Agarwal, Gautam Ahuja, Javier Gimeno, Amy Hillman, Michael Lennox, Yadong Luo, Jeff Reuer, Mary Tripsas, and Maurizio Zollo [along with numerous others] to shape the discussion of *what* strategic management is. We describe the practices of prominent executives and practitioners (e.g., Mike Duke, Jeffrey Immelt, Steven Jobs, Gianfranco Lanci, Indra Nooyi, and many others) to help us describe *how* strategic management is used in many types of organizations.

- We, the authors of this book, are also active scholars. We conduct research on different strategic management topics. Our interest in doing so is to contribute to the strategic management literature and to better understand how to effectively apply strategic management tools, techniques, and concepts to increase organizational performance. Thus, our own research is integrated in the appropriate chapters along with the research of numerous other scholars, some of which are noted above.

In addition to our book's *characteristics,* there are some specific *features* of this 9th edition that we want to highlight for you:

- **New Opening Cases and Strategic Focus Segments.** We continue our tradition of providing all-new Opening Cases and Strategic Focus segments. In addition, new company-specific examples are included in each chapter. Through all of these venues, we present you with a wealth of examples of how actual organizations, most of which compete internationally as well as in their home markets, use the strategic management process to outperform rivals and increase their performance.

- **24 All-New Cases** with an effective mix of organizations headquartered or based in the United States and a number of other countries. Many of the cases have full financial data (the analyses of which are in the Case Notes that are available to instructors). These timely cases present active learners with opportunities to apply the strategic management process and understand organizational conditions and contexts and to make appropriate recommendations to deal with critical concerns.

- **All New Video Case Exercises** are now included in the end-of-chapter material for each chapter and are directly connected to the textbook's Fifty Lessons video collection. These engaging exercises demonstrate for students how the concepts they are learning actually connect to the ideas and actions of the interesting individuals and companies highlighted in the videos.

- **New and Revised Experiential Exercises** to support individuals' efforts to understand the use of the strategic management process. These exercises place active learners in a variety of situations requiring application of some part of the strategic management process.

Availability of resources may differ by region. Check with your local Cengage Learning representative for details.

- **Strategy Right Now** is used in each chapter to highlight companies that are effectively using a strategic management concept examined in the chapter or to provide additional coverage of a particular topic. In **Chapter 5,** for example, Wal-Mart's offering of financial services tailored to its customers' needs, such as the MoneyCard, is discussed in the context of competition among the big box retailers. In **Chapter 13,** the explosion of social media and networking, in particular Twitter, is examined in detail. This feature is a valuable tool for readers to quickly identify how a firm is effectively using a strategic management tool, technique, or concept. We follow up with the most current research and information about these firms by using Cengage Learning's Business & Company Resource Center (BCRC). Links to specific current news articles related to these companies and topics can be found on our website (www.cengage.com/international). Whenever you see the Strategy Right Now icon in the text, you will know that current research is available from the BCRC links posted to our website.

- **An Exceptional Balance** between current research and up-to-date applications of it in actual organizations. The content has not only the best research documentation but also the largest amount of effective real-world examples to help active learners understand the different types of strategies organizations use to achieve their vision and mission.

- **Access to Harvard Business School (HBS) Cases.** We have developed a set of assignment sheets and AACSB International assessment rubrics to accompany 10 of the best selling HBS cases. Instructors can use these cases and the accompanying set of teaching notes and assessment rubrics to formalize assurance of learning efforts in the capstone Strategic Management/Business Policy course.

- **Lively, Concise Writing Style** to hold readers' attention and to increase their interest in strategic management.

- **Continuing, Updated Coverage** of vital strategic management topics such as competitive rivalry and dynamics, strategic alliances, mergers and acquisitions, international strategies, corporate governance, and ethics. Also, we continue to be the only book in the market with a separate chapter devoted to strategic entrepreneurship.

- **Full four-color** format to enhance readability by attracting and maintaining readers' interests.

To maintain current and up-to-date content, new concepts are explored in the 9th edition.

In **Chapter 2**, we added the physical environment as the seventh segment of the general environment. The discussion of the physical environment emphasizes the importance of sustainability. Sustainability has become a "watchword" at many companies such as Honest Tea and Dell. For example, Dell has a goal of having a carbon neutral footprint. This discussion is integrated with the explanation in **Chapter 4** of how firms are developing a "green" strategy that is a core part of their competitive strategy. Wal-Mart is investing significant capital and effort to be a "green" firm, as are other firms such as Procter & Gamble and Target. We describe the actions a number of firms are taking regarding the physical environment in one of the Strategic Focus segments in **Chapter 2.**

In **Chapter 6**, we explore a new strategic trend also caused by the global economic crisis. While many firms downscoped in the late 1980s and 1990s because of the performance problems caused by over-diversification, the economic recession has served as a catalyst for a new trend of diversification to help firms spread their risk across several markets (to avoid bankruptcy). In **Chapter 7,** we expand our discussion of cross-border acquisitions. In fact, cross-border acquisitions remain quite popular during the global economic crisis, largely because of the number of firms in financial trouble that have under-valued assets as a result. Chinese firms have become especially active, which is discussed in detail in **Chapter 7** with special emphasis in a Strategic Focus segment. **Chapter 8** includes new content exampling emerging international firms from China (Sun Tech Power in commercial solar power and ZTE and Huawei in network equipment) and Russia (Yandex, a competitor to Google).

In **Chapter 10,** we added content related to the new actions and policies that deal with corporate governance. For example, the U.S. Securities and Exchange Commission (SEC) has implemented some new policies providing for closer oversight of companies' financial dealings. The SEC has also developed new rules to allow owners with large stakes to propose new directors. These new rules are likely to shift the balance even more in favor of outside and independent members of companies' boards of directors. We inserted a new section into this chapter to explain corporate governance in China. As a major new global economic power with several of the world's largest firms, corporate governance in China has become an important issue. Interestingly, many of the new corporate governance practices implemented in Chinese companies resemble governance practices in the United States.

In **Chapter 13**, we explain how innovation has become highly important for firms to compete effectively in global markets. As such, there have been major drives to increase the innovativeness of firms in the United States and China. The importance of innovation has been heightened by the emphasis on sustainability (developing "greener" products—see **Chapters 2 and 4**) and by the growing demand from customers that companies provide them with "excellent" value in the form of the goods or services they are making and selling (see **Chapter 2**).

Supplements

Instructors

New Expanded Instructor Case Notes – To better reflect the varying approaches to teaching and learning via cases, the 9th edition offers a rich selection of case note options:

    Basic Case Notes – Each of the 30 cases in the 9th edition is accompanied by a succinct case note designed for ease of use while also providing the necessary background and financial data for classroom discussion.

    Presentation Case Notes – For a selection of 13 cases from the 9th edition, a full set of PowerPoint slides has been developed for instructors to effectively use in class, containing key illustrations and other case data.

    Rich Assessment Case Notes – Introduced in the 8th edition, these expanded case notes provide details about 13 additional cases from prior editions that are available on the textbook website. These expanded case notes include directed assignments, financial analysis, thorough discussion and exposition of issues in the case, and an assessment rubric tied to AACSB International assurance of learning standards that can be used for grading each case.

Instructor's Resource Manual The Instructor's Resource Manual, organized around each chapter's knowledge objectives, includes teaching ideas for each chapter and how to reinforce essential principles with extra examples. This support product includes lecture outlines, detailed answers to end-of-chapter review questions, instructions for using each chapter's experiential exercises and video cases, and additional assignments. Available on the Product Support Website.

Availability of resources may differ by region. Check with your local Cengage Learning representative for details.

Certified Test Bank Thoroughly revised and enhanced, test bank questions are linked to each chapter's knowledge objectives and are ranked by difficulty and question type. We provide an ample number of application questions throughout, and we have also retained scenario-based questions as a means of adding in-depth problem-solving questions. With this edition, we introduce the concept of certification, whereby another qualified academic has proofread and verified the accuracy of the test bank questions and answers. The test bank material is also available in computerized ExamView™ format for creating custom tests in both Windows and Macintosh formats. Available on the Product Support Website.

ExamView™ Computerized testing software contains all of the questions in the certified printed test bank. This program is an easy-to-use test-creation software compatible with Microsoft Windows. Instructors can add or edit questions, instructions, and answers, and select questions by previewing them on the screen, selecting them randomly, or selecting them by number. Instructors can also create and administer quizzes online, whether over the Internet, a local area network (LAN), or a wide area network (WAN).

Video Case Program. A collection of 13 new videos from Fifty Lessons have been selected for the 9th edition, and directly connected Video Case exercises have been included in the end-of-chapter material of each chapter. These new videos are a comprehensive and compelling resource of management and leadership lessons from some of the world's most successful business leaders. In the form of short and powerful videos, these videos capture leaders' most important learning experiences. They share their real-world business acumen and outline the guiding principles behind their most important business decisions and their career progression.

PowerPoint® An all-new PowerPoint presentation, created for the 9th edition, provides support for lectures, emphasizing key concepts, key terms, and instructive graphics. Slides can also be used by students as an aid to note-taking. Available on the Product Support Website.

Product Support Website (www.cengage.com/international) Our Product Support Website contains all ancillary products for instructors as well as the financial analysis exercises for both students and instructors.

The Business & Company Resource Center (BCRC) Put a complete business library at your students' fingertips! This premier online business research tool allows you and your students to search thousands of periodicals, journals, references, financial data, industry reports, and more. This powerful research tool saves time for students—whether they are preparing for a presentation or writing a reaction paper. You can use the BCRC to quickly and easily assign readings or research projects. Visit http://www.cengage.com/bcrc to learn more about this indispensable tool. For this text in particular, BCRC will be especially useful in further researching the companies featured in the text's 24 cases. We've also included BCRC links for the Strategy Right Now feature on our website, as well as in the Cengage NOW product.

Student Premium Companion Site The new optional student premium website features text-specific resources that enhance student learning by bringing concepts to life. Dynamic interactive learning tools include online quizzes, flashcards, PowerPoint slides, learning games, and more, helping to ensure your students come to class prepared! Ask your Cengage Learning sales representative for more details.

Students

Financial analyses of some of the cases are provided on our Product Support Website for both students and instructors. Researching financial data, company data, and industry data is made easy through the use of our proprietary database, the Business & Company Resource Center. Students are sent to this database to be able to quickly gather data needed for financial analysis.

Make It Yours – Custom Case Selection

Cengage Learning is dedicated to making the educational experience unique for all learners by creating custom materials that best suit your course needs. With our Make It Yours program, you can easily select a unique set of cases for your course from providers such as Harvard Business School Publishing, Darden, and Ivey. See http://www.custom.cengage.com/makeityours/hitt9e for more details.

Acknowledgments

We express our appreciation for the excellent support received from our editorial and production team at South-Western. We especially wish to thank Michele Rhoades, our Senior Acquisitions Editor; John Abner, our Development Editor; Nate Anderson, our Marketing Manager; and Jaci Featherly, our Content Project Manager. We are grateful for their dedication, commitment, and outstanding contributions to the development and publication of this book and its package of support materials.

We are highly indebted to the reviewers of the 8th edition in preparation for this current edition:

Erich Brockmann
University of New Orleans

Scott Elston
Iowa State University

Carol Jacobson
Purdue University

Consuelo M. Ramirez
University of Texas at San Antonio

Deepak Sethi
Old Dominion University

Len J. Trevino
Washington State University

Marta Szabo White
Georgia State University

Diana J. Wong-MingJi
Eastern Michigan University

Bruce H. Charnov
Hofstra University

Susan Hansen
University of Wisconsin-Platteville

Frank Novakowski
Davenport University

Manjula S. Salimath
University of North Texas

Manisha Singal
Virginia Tech

Edward Ward
Saint Cloud State University

Michael L Williams
Michigan State University

Wilson Zehr
Concordia University

Finally, we are very appreciative of the following people for the time and care that went into preparing the supplements to accompany this edition:

Charles Byles
Virginia Commonwealth University

Richard H. Lester
Texas A&M University

Paul Friga
University of North Carolina

Paul Mallette
Colorado State University

Kristi L. Marshall

R. Duane Ireland
Robert E. Hoskisson
Michael A. Hitt

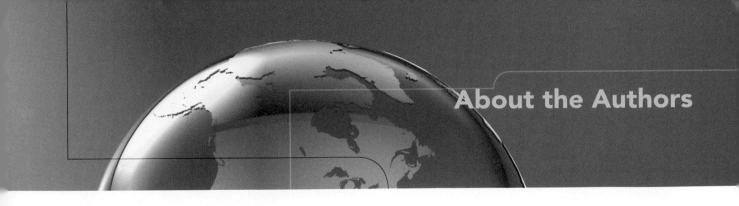

R. Duane Ireland

R. Duane Ireland is a Distinguished Professor and holds the Foreman R. and Ruby S. Bennett Chair in Business from the Mays Business School, Texas A&M University where he previously served as head of the management department. He teaches strategic management courses at all levels (undergraduate, masters, doctoral, and executive). He has over 175 publications including more than a dozen books. His research, which focuses on diversification, innovation, corporate entrepreneurship, and strategic entrepreneurship, has been published in a number of journals, including *Academy of Management Journal, Academy of Management Review, Academy of Management Executive, Administrative Science Quarterly, Strategic Management Journal, Journal of Management, Strategic Entrepreneurship Journal, Human Relations, Entrepreneurship Theory and Practice, Strategic Entrepreneurship Journal, Journal of Business Venturing,* and *Journal of Management Studies,* among others. His recently published books include *Understanding Business Strategy,* 2nd edition (South-Western Cengage Learning, 2009), *Entrepreneurship: Successfully Launching New Ventures,* 3rd edition (Prentice-Hall, 2010), and *Competing for Advantage,* 2nd edition (South-Western, 2008). He is serving or has served as a member of the editorial review boards for a number of journals, including *Academy of Management Journal, Academy of Management Review, Academy of Management Executive, Journal of Management, Strategic Enterprenurship Journal, Journal of Business Venturing, Entrepreneurship Theory and Practice, Journal of Business Strategy,* and *European Management Journal.* He is the current editor of the *Academy of Management Journal.* He has completed terms as an associate editor for *Academy of Management Journal,* as an associate editor for *Academy of Management Executive,* and as a consulting editor for *Entrepreneurship Theory and Practice.* He has co-edited special issues of *Academy of Management Review, Academy of Management Executive, Journal of Business Venturing, Strategic Management Journal, Journal of High Technology and Engineering Management,* and *Organizational Research Methods* (forthcoming). He received awards for the best article published in *Academy of Management Executive* (1999) and *Academy of Management Journal* (2000). In 2001, his co-authored article published in *Academy of Management Executive* won the Best Journal Article in Corporate Entrepreneurship Award from the U.S. Association for Small Business & Entrepreneurship (USASBE).

He is a Fellow of the Academy of Management and is a 21st Century Entrepreneurship Research Scholar. He served a three-year term as a Representative-at-Large member of the Academy of Management's Board of Governors. He received the 1999 Award for Outstanding Intellectual Contributions to Competitiveness Research from the American Society for Competitiveness and the USASBE Scholar in Corporate Entrepreneurship Award (2004).

Robert E. Hoskisson

Robert E. Hoskisson is the George R. Brown Chair of Strategic Management at the Jesse H. Jones Graduate School of Business, Rice University. He received his Ph.D. from the University of California-Irvine. Professor Hoskisson's research topics focus on corporate governance, acquisitions and divestitures, corporate and international diversification, corporate entrepreneurship, privatization, and cooperative strategy. He teaches courses in corporate and international strategic management, cooperative strategy, and strategy consulting, among others. Professor Hoskisson's research has appeared in over 120 publications, including articles in the *Academy of Management Journal, Academy of Management Review, Strategic Management Journal, Organization Science, Journal of Management, Journal of International Business Studies, Journal of Management Studies, Academy of Management Perspectives, Academy of Management Executive, California Management Review,* and 26 co-authored books. He is currently an associate editor of the *Strategic Management Journal* and a consulting editor for the *Journal of International Business Studies,* as well as serving on the Editorial Review board of the *Academy of Management Journal.* Professor Hoskisson has served on several editorial boards for such publications as the *Academy of Management Journal* (including consulting editor and guest editor of a special issue), *Journal of Management* (including associate editor), *Organization Science, Journal of International Business Studies* (consulting editor), *Journal of Management Studies* (guest editor of a special issue) and *Entrepreneurship Theory and Practice.* He has co-authored several books including *Understanding Business Strategy,* 2nd Edition (South-Western Cengage Learning, 2009), *Competing for Advantage,* 2nd edition (South-Western, 2008), and *Downscoping: How to Tame the Diversified Firm* (Oxford University Press, 1994).

He has an appointment as a Special Professor at the University of Nottingham and as an Honorary Professor at Xi'an Jiao Tong University. He is a Fellow of the Academy of Management and a charter member of the Academy of Management Journals Hall of Fame. He is also a Fellow of the Strategic Management Society. In 1998, he received an award for Outstanding Academic Contributions to Competitiveness, American Society for Competitiveness. He also received the William G. Dyer Distinguished Alumni Award given at the Marriott School of Management, Brigham Young University. He completed three years of service as a representative at large on the Board of Governors of the Academy of Management and currently is on the Board of Directors of the Strategic Management Society.

Michael A. Hitt

Michael A. Hitt is a Distinguished Professor and holds the Joe B. Foster Chair in Business Leadership at Texas A&M University. He received his Ph.D. from the University of Colorado. He has more than 260 publications including 26 co-authored or co-edited books and was cited as one of the 10 most-cited scholars in management over a 25-year period in an article published in the 2008 volume of the *Journal of Management.*

Some of his books are *Downscoping: How to Tame the Diversified Firm* (Oxford University Press, 1994); *Mergers and Acquisitions: A Guide to Creating Value for Stakeholders* (Oxford University Press, 2001); *Competing for Advantage,* 2nd edition (South-Western, 2008); and *Understanding Business Strategy,* 2nd edition (South-Western Cengage Learning, 2009). He is co-editor of several books including the following: *Managing Strategically in an Interconnected World* (1998); *New Managerial Mindsets: Organizational Transformation and Strategy Implementation* (1998); *Dynamic*

Strategic Resources: Development, Diffusion, and Integration (1999); *Winning Strategies in a Deconstructing World* (John Wiley & Sons, 2000); *Handbook of Strategic Management* (2001); *Strategic Entrepreneurship: Creating a New Integrated Mindset* (2002); *Creating Value: Winners in the New Business Environment* (Blackwell Publishers, 2002); *Managing Knowledge for Sustained Competitive Advantage* (Jossey-Bass, 2003); *Great Minds in Management: The Process of Theory Development* (Oxford University Press, 2005), and *The Global Mindset* (Elsevier, 2007). He has served on the editorial review boards of multiple journals, including the *Academy of Management Journal, Academy of Management Executive, Journal of Applied Psychology, Journal of Management, Journal of World Business,* and *Journal of Applied Behavioral Sciences.* Furthermore, he has served as consulting editor and editor of the *Academy of Management Journal.* He is currently a co-editor of the *Strategic Entrepreneurship Journal.* He is the current past president of the Strategic Management Society and is a past president of the Academy of Management.

He is a Fellow in the Academy of Management and in the Strategic Management Society. He received an honorary doctorate from the Universidad Carlos III de Madrid and is an Honorary Professor and Honorary Dean at Xi'an Jiao Tong University. He has been acknowledged with several awards for his scholarly research and he received the Irwin Outstanding Educator Award and the Distinguished Service Award from the Academy of Management. He has received best paper awards for articles published in the *Academy of Management Journal, Academy of Management Executive,* and *Journal of Management.*

Case Title	Manu-facturing	Service	Consumer Goods	Food/Retail	High Tech-nology	Internet	Transportation/Communication	International Perspective	Social/Ethical Issues	Industry Perspective
Biovail			•		•			•	•	
Wal-Mart Stores				•				•	•	
Room and Board				•					•	
Alibaba		•				•		•		
eBay, Inc.		•			•	•		•		•
Boeing	•							•		•
Motorola, Inc.	•		•					•		•
Southwest Airlines		•					•			•
Apple Computer, Inc.	•	•			•	•	•			•
Blockbuster			•	•		•				•
South Beauty Group		•		•				•		
Cinemaplex		•		•						•
JetBlue		•					•	•		•
Dell	•		•		•	•				•
Home Depot		•		•				•		
Henkel	•		•					•		
Citibank		•			•	•		•		
Nucor	•						•	•		•
Baidu		•				•		•		
TNK-BP	•							•		
The New York Times Company		•				•	•			•
Tesco versus Sainsbury's			•	•				•		
Under Armour		•						•		•
Barclays		•						•		
United Airlines		•					•	•		•
Netflix		•		•						
Oasis Hong Kong Airlines		•					•	•		
Nintendo			•		•	•		•		•
Pro Clean		•		•						

Case Title	1	2	3	4	5	6	7	8	9	10	11	12	13
Biovail								●		●	●	●	
Wal-Mart Stores	●	●	●	●									
Room and Board			●	●					●			●	●
Alibaba				●		●		●			●		
eBay, Inc.	●				●	●			●				●
Boeing				●	●			●	●				
Motorola, Inc.		●		●		●	●					●	●
Southwest Airlines		●	●	●	●							●	●
Apple Computer, Inc.			●	●	●				●				●
Blockbuster			●		●	●	●						
South Beauty Group	●	●		●								●	●
Cinemaplex		●	●	●	●				●				
JetBlue		●		●	●								
Dell		●		●	●						●	●	
Home Depot				●	●							●	
Henkel			●	●			●	●			●		
Citibank		●	●	●				●	●		●		
Nucor		●	●	●	●						●	●	
Baidu			●		●			●					
TNK-BP		●				●	●	●		●			
The New York Times Company	●	●		●					●			●	
Tesco versus Sainsbury's					●	●	●	●					
Under Armour	●		●	●				●				●	●
Barclays	●	●	●			●						●	
United Airlines		●		●				●	●				
Netflix		●	●		●							●	
Oasis Hong Kong Airlines		●	●	●				●					
Nintendo		●	●	●				●			●		
Pro Clean		●	●	●								●	●

The Management of Strategy
Concepts and Cases

9th Edition

CHAPTER 1

Strategic Management and Competitiveness

Studying this chapter should provide you with the strategic management knowledge needed to:

1. Define strategic competitiveness, strategy, competitive advantage, above-average returns, and the strategic management process.

2. Describe the competitive landscape and explain how globalization and technological changes shape it.

3. Use the industrial organization (I/O) model to explain how firms can earn above-average returns.

4. Use the resource-based model to explain how firms can earn above-average returns.

5. Describe vision and mission and discuss their value.

6. Define stakeholders and describe their ability to influence organizations.

7. Describe the work of strategic leaders.

8. Explain the strategic management process.

MCDONALD'S CORPORATION: FIRING ON ALL CYLINDERS WHILE PREPARING FOR THE FUTURE

Currently on a "tear," McDonald's ability to create value for its stakeholders (such as customers, shareholders, and employees) during the challenging times of the global recession that started roughly in early 2008 and continued throughout 2009 is indeed impressive. As one indicator of the quality of its performance, consider the fact that during 2008, McDonald's and Wal-Mart were the only two Dow Jones Industrial Average stocks to end the year with a gain.

With one of the world's most recognized brand names, mid-2009 found McDonald's operating roughly 32,000 restaurants in 118 countries. The largest fast-food restaurant chain in the world, McDonald's sales revenue was $70.7 billion in 2008, up from $64.1 billion the year before. The chain serves over 58 million customers daily. McDonald's dominates the quick-service restaurant industry in the United States, where its revenue is several times larger than Burger King and Wendy's, its closest competitors.

McDonald's impressive performance as the first decade of the twenty-first century came to a close suggests that the firm is effectively implementing its strategy. (We define *strategy* in this chapter as an integrated and coordinated set of commitments and actions designed to exploit core competencies and gain a competitive advantage.) However, the picture for McDonald's was much less positive in 2003. In that year, some analysts concluded that McDonald's "looked obsolete" as it failed to notice changes in its customers' interests and needs. The fact that the company reported its first-ever quarterly loss in 2003 and the decline in its stock price from roughly $48 per share to $13 per share suggested that McDonald's was becoming less competitive. However, by mid-2009 things had changed dramatically for McDonald's. Its "stock was trading at nearly $60, same-store sales (had) grown for the 56th straight month and the company (could) boast of having achieved double-digit operating-income growth during the onset of the financial crisis." How was this dramatic turnaround achieved?

Caro/Alamy

McDonalds restaurant in Berlin, Germany. McDonalds is the largest fast-food restaurant chain in the world, operating in 118 countries.

After examining their firm's deteriorating situation in 2003, McDonald's strategic leaders decided to change its corporate-level strategy and to take different actions to implement its business-level strategy. From a business-level strategy perspective (we discuss business-level strategies in Chapter 4), McDonald's decided to focus on product innovations and upgrades of its existing properties instead of continuing to rapidly expand the number of units while relying almost exclusively on the core products it had sold for many years as the source of its sales revenue. From a corporate-level perspective (corporate-level strategies are discussed in Chapter 6), McDonald's decided to become less diversified. To reach this objective, the firm disposed of its interests in the Chipotle Mexican Grill restaurant concept and the Boston Market chain and sold its minority interest in Prêt a Manger as well. Operationally, McDonald's starting listening carefully to its customers, who were demanding value for their dollars and convenience as well as healthier products. One analyst describes McDonald's responses to what it was hearing from its customers this way: "McDonald's eliminated the super size option, offered more premium salads and chicken sandwiches and provided greater value options. It also initiated better training for employees, extended hours of service and redesigned stores to appeal to younger consumers." In part, these actions were taken to capitalize on an ever-increasing number of consumers who were becoming and remain today very conscious about their budgets.

However, as McDonald's experiences in the early 2000s indicate, corporate success is never guaranteed. The likelihood of a company being successful in the long term increases when strategic leaders continually evaluate the appropriateness of their firm's strategies as well as actions being taken to implement them. Given this, and in light of its decision in 2003 to continuously offer innovative food items to customers, McDonald's added McCafe coffee bars to all of its U.S. locations in 2009. McDonald's coffee drinks create value for customers by giving them high-quality drinks at prices that often are lower than those of competitors such as Starbucks. A Southern-style chicken sandwich was also added to the firm's line of chicken-based offerings. Allowing customers to order from in-store kiosks is an example of an action the firm recently took to create more convenience for customers. The firm continues upgrading its existing stores and in anticipation of a global economic recovery, is buying prime real estate in Europe "… on the cheap as a result of the overall downturn in construction spending." This real estate is the foundation for McDonald's commitment to add 1,000 new European locations in the near future. Thus, McDonald's strategic leaders appear to be committed to making decisions today to increase the likelihood that the firm will be as successful in the future as it was in the last years of the twenty-first century's first decade.

Sources: J. Adamy, 2009, McDonald's seeks way to keep sizzling, *Wall Street Journal*, http;://www.wsj.com, March 10; M. Arndt, 2009, McDonald's keeps gaining, *BusinessWeek*, http://www.businessweek.com, April 22; M. Cavallaro, 2009, Still lovin' the Golden Arches, *Forbes*, http://www.forbes.com, March 6; S. Dahle, 2009, McDonald's loves your recession, *Forbes*, http://www.forbes.com, February 17; D. Patnaik & P. Mortensen, 2009, The secret of McDonald's recent success, *Forbes*, http://www.forbes.com, February 4; M. Peer, 2009, Double-edge dollar at McDonald's, *Forbes*, http://www.forbes.com, January 26; A. Raghavan, 2009, McDonald's European burger binge, *Forbes*, http://www.forbes.com, January 23; P. Ziobro, 2009, McDonald's pounds out good quarter, *Wall Street Journal*, http://www.wsj.com, April 23; 2009, McDonald's Corp., Standard & Poor's Stock Report, http://www.standardandpoors.com, April 23.

As we see from the Opening Case, McDonald's was quite successful in 2008 and 2009, outperforming Burger King and Wendy's, its two main rivals. McDonald's performance during this time period suggests that it is highly competitive (something we call a condition of *strategic competitiveness*) as it earned *above-average returns*. All firms, including McDonald's, use the strategic management process (see Figure 1.1) as the foundation for the commitments, decisions, and actions they will take when pursuing strategic competitiveness and above-average terms. The strategic management process is fully explained in this book. We introduce you to this process in the next few paragraphs.

Strategic competitiveness is achieved when a firm successfully formulates and implements a value-creating strategy. A **strategy** is an integrated and coordinated set of commitments and actions designed to exploit core competencies and gain a competitive advantage. When choosing a strategy, firms make choices among competing alternatives as the pathway for deciding how they will pursue strategic competitiveness.[1] In this sense, the chosen strategy indicates what the firm *will do* as well as what the firm *will not do*.

As explained in the Opening Case, McDonald's sold its interests in other food concepts (e.g., Boston Market) in order to focus on developing new products and upgrading existing facilities in its portfolio of McDonald's restaurants around the globe.[2] Thus, McDonald's strategic leaders decided that the firm *would* pursue product innovations and that it *would not* remain involved with additional food concepts such as Boston Market and Chipotle. In-N-Out Burger, the privately held, 232-unit restaurant chain with locations in only Arizona and California, focuses on product quality and will not take any action with the potential to reduce the quality of its food items.[3] A firm's strategy also demonstrates how it differs from its competitors. Recently, Ford Motor Company devoted efforts to explain to stakeholders how the company differs from its competitors. The main idea is that Ford claims that it is "greener" and more technically advanced than its competitors, such as General Motors and Chrysler Group LLC (an alliance between Chrysler and Fiat SpA).[4]

A firm has a **competitive advantage** when it implements a strategy competitors are unable to duplicate or find too costly to try to imitate.[5] An organization can be confident

Strategic competitiveness is achieved when a firm successfully formulates and implements a value-creating strategy.

A **strategy** is an integrated and coordinated set of commitments and actions designed to exploit core competencies and gain a competitive advantage.

A firm has a **competitive advantage** when it implements a strategy competitors are unable to duplicate or find too costly to try to imitate.

Figure 1.1 The Strategic Management Process

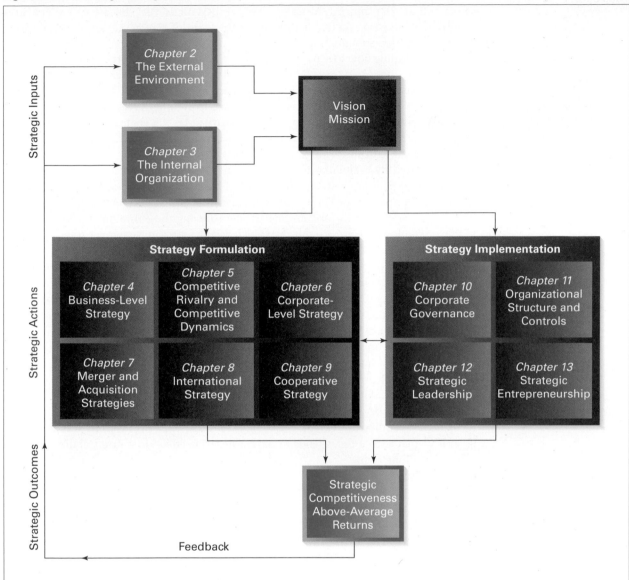

that its strategy has resulted in one or more useful competitive advantages only after competitors' efforts to duplicate its strategy have ceased or failed. In addition, firms must understand that no competitive advantage is permanent.[6] The speed with which competitors are able to acquire the skills needed to duplicate the benefits of a firm's value-creating strategy determines how long the competitive advantage will last.[7]

Above-average returns are returns in excess of what an investor expects to earn from other investments with a similar amount of risk. **Risk** is an investor's uncertainty about the economic gains or losses that will result from a particular investment.[8] The most successful companies learn how to effectively manage risk. Effectively managing risks reduces investors' uncertainty about the results of their investment.[9] Returns are often measured in terms of accounting figures, such as return on assets, return on equity, or return on sales. Alternatively, returns can be measured on the basis of stock market returns, such as monthly returns (the end-of-the-period stock price minus the beginning stock price, divided by the beginning stock price, yielding a percentage return). In smaller, new venture firms, returns are

Above-average returns are returns in excess of what an investor expects to earn from other investments with a similar amount of risk.

Risk is an investor's uncertainty about the economic gains or losses that will result from a particular investment.

sometimes measured in terms of the amount and speed of growth (e.g., in annual sales) rather than more traditional profitability measures[10] because new ventures require time to earn acceptable returns (in the form of return on assets and so forth) on investors' investments.[11]

Understanding how to exploit a competitive advantage is important for firms seeking to earn above-average returns.[12] Firms without a competitive advantage or that are not competing in an attractive industry earn, at best, average returns. **Average returns** are returns equal to those an investor expects to earn from other investments with a similar amount of risk. In the long run, an inability to earn at least average returns results first in decline and, eventually, failure. Failure occurs because investors withdraw their investments from those firms earning less-than-average returns.

After carefully evaluating its deteriorating performance and options, Circuit City decided in 2009 to liquidate its operation.[13] (Linens 'n Things, Bombay Co., Mervyn's LLC., and Sharper Image Corp. also liquidated in 2009, suggesting the difficulty of the competitive environment for consumer retailers during the economic downturn.) Prior to the liquidation decision, Circuit City filed for bankruptcy in November 2008. However, because the firm could not find a buyer and could not reach a deal with an investor as the means of gaining access to the financial capital it needed to successfully emerge from bankruptcy, it had no choice other than to liquidate. Here is how then-acting CEO James Marcum described Circuit City's situation and liquidation decision: "We are extremely disappointed by this outcome. We were unable to reach an agreement with our creditors and lenders to structure a going-concern transaction in the limited timeframe available, and so this is the only possible path for our company."[14]

As we explain in the Strategic Focus, stiff competition from Best Buy and mistakes made when implementing its strategy are the primary causes of Circuit City's failure and subsequent disappearance from the consumer electronics retail sector. Commenting about errors made at Circuit City, one analyst said, "This company made massive mistakes."[15] Additionally, Circuit City's focus on short-term profits likely was a problem as well in that such a focus tends to have a negative effect on a firm's ability to create value in the long term.[16]

Best Buy was performing well following Circuit City's demise. However, as we noted above, there are no guarantees of permanent success. This is true for McDonald's, even considering its excellent current performance, and for Best Buy. Although Best Buy clearly outperformed Circuit City, its primary direct rival for many years, the firm now faces a strong competitive challenge from Wal-Mart.[17] In order to deal with this challenge Best Buy is positioning itself as the provider of excellent customer service while selling high-end products with new interactive features. Additionally, the firm is rapidly expanding its private-label electronics business. In this business, Best Buy is using "…the mountains of customer feedback it collects from its stores to make simple innovations to established electronic gadgetry."[18] In contrast, Wal-Mart is positioning itself in the consumer electronics segment as the low-price option and seeks to sell its increasing breadth of consumer electronics products to a larger number of the more than 100 million customers who shop in its stores weekly.[19]

The **strategic management process** (see Figure 1.1) is the full set of commitments, decisions, and actions required for a firm to achieve strategic competitiveness and earn above-average returns. The firm's first step in the process is to analyze its external environment and internal organization to determine its resources, capabilities, and core competencies—the sources of its "strategic inputs." With this information, the firm develops its vision and mission and formulates one or more strategies. To implement its strategies, the firm takes actions toward achieving strategic competitiveness and above-average returns. Effective strategic actions that take place in the context of carefully integrated strategy formulation and implementation efforts result in positive outcomes. This dynamic strategic management process must be maintained as ever-changing markets

Average returns are returns equal to those an investor expects to earn from other investments with a similar amount of risk.

The **strategic management process** is the full set of commitments, decisions, and actions required for a firm to achieve strategic competitiveness and earn above-average returns.

CIRCUIT CITY: A TALE OF INEFFECTIVE STRATEGY IMPLEMENTATION AND FIRM FAILURE

When Circuit City announced on January 16, 2009, that it was out of options and that liquidation was the only viable course of action for it to take, the firm employed approximately 34,000 people to operate its 567 stores in the United States and was the second largest consumer electronics retailer in the United States. What caused Circuit City's failure? As we'll see, it appears that poor implementation of the firm's strategy was a key factor leading to the firm's demise.

Circuit City's genesis was in 1949, when Samuel S. Wurtzel opened the first Wards Company retail store in Richmond, Virginia. A television and home appliances retailer, Wards had a total of four stores in Richmond in 1959. The firm became public in 1961 and earned $246 million in revenue in 1983. Between 1969 and 1982, Wards grew by acquiring numerous electronics retailers across the United States. In 1984, the company's name was changed to Circuit City and the firm was listed on the New York Stock Exchange. Revenue growth continued, reaching $2 billion in 1990. Circuit City established CarMax, a retail venture selling used vehicles, in 1993. After some initial challenges, CarMax become quite successful. In 2002, Circuit City announced that in order to focus on its core retail consumer electronics business, it would spin off its CarMax subsidiary into a separate publicly traded company. By late 2008, the firm was in serious trouble; as a result, 155 stores were closed and 17 percent of its workforce was laid off.

With hindsight, we see that in the 1990s Circuit City was complacent and rather ineffective in its intense competition with Best Buy, its chief rival. Alan Wurtzel, the son of the firm's founder and a former Circuit City CEO, supports this position, saying that Circuit City "… didn't take the threat from Best Buy seriously enough and at some points was too focused on short-term profit rather than long-term value."

Among the actions Best Buy took during the 1990s to compete against Circuit City was to establish larger stores in superior locations. Circuit City's commitment to focus on short-term profits prevented the firm's leaders from being acutely aware of the value these new stores created for Best Buy. This short-term focus led to what turned out to be some

Ramin Talaie/CORBIS

A large "going out of business" sign hangs over a Circuit City store in Downtown Brooklyn. All of the electronics retailer's stores were closed by the end of March 2009, laying off more than 30,000 workers.

highly damaging decisions, such as the one to lay off thousands of its veteran, higher-paid employees, including sales personnel. These salespeople, who were earning attractive commissions because of their productivity, were replaced with lower-paid, less-experienced personnel. Circuit City leaders thought that sales would not suffer as a result of this decision. According to an analyst, "They (sales) did, and the damage to revenue—and Circuit City's reputation—was never undone."

In addition to concentrating on finding ways to reduce costs rather than find ways to create more value for customers, some believe that Circuit City made other mistakes while implementing its strategy. For example, the failure to effectively manage its inventory diminished the firm's ability to pay its existing debts in a timely manner and to keep its stores stocked with the latest, most innovative products. Poor customer service is another mistake. Of course, the decision to lay off the highest-paid (and most productive) employees immediately reduced the firm's ability to effectively serve customers. It is very hard for a firm to achieve strategic competitiveness and earn above-average returns when it fails to successfully implement its strategy.

Sources: E. Gruenwedel, 2009, Best Buy, Wal-Mart winners in Circuit City shuttering, *Home Media Magazine*, http://www.homemediamagazine.com, January 19; 2009, Best Buy Co. Inc., *Standard & Poor's Stock Report*, http://www.standardandpoors.com, April 18; 2009, Circuit City to liquidate U.S. stores, *MSNBC.com*, http://www.msnbc.com, January 16; S. Cranford, 2008, Circuit City: Schoonover's brand disconnect, *Seeking Alpha*, http://www.seekingalpha.com, February 17; A. Hamilton, 2008, Why Circuit City busted, while Best Buy boomed, *Time*, http://www.time.com, November 11.

and competitive structures are coordinated with a firm's continuously evolving strategic inputs.[20]

In the remaining chapters of this book, we use the strategic management process to explain what firms do to achieve strategic competitiveness and earn above-average returns. These explanations demonstrate why some firms consistently achieve competitive success while others fail to do so.[21] As you will see, the reality of global competition is a critical part of the strategic management process and significantly influences firms' performances.[22] Indeed, learning how to successfully compete in the globalized world is one of the most significant challenges for firms competing in the current century.[23]

Several topics will be discussed in this chapter. First, we describe the current competitive landscape. This challenging landscape is being created primarily by the emergence of a global economy, globalization resulting from that economy, and rapid technological changes. Next, we examine two models that firms use to gather the information and knowledge required to choose and then effectively implement their strategies. The insights gained from these models also serve as the foundation for forming the firm's vision and mission. The first model (the industrial organization or I/O model) suggests that the external environment is the primary determinant of a firm's strategic actions. Identifying and then competing successfully in an attractive (i.e., profitable) industry or segment of an industry are the keys to competitive success when using this model.[24] The second model (resource-based) suggests that a firm's unique resources and capabilities are the critical link to strategic competitiveness.[25] Thus, the first model is concerned primarily with the firm's external environment while the second model is concerned primarily with the firm's internal organization. After discussing vision and mission, direction-setting statements that influence the choice and use of strategies, we describe the stakeholders that organizations serve. The degree to which stakeholders' needs can be met increases when firms achieve strategic competitiveness and earn above-average returns. Closing the chapter are introductions to strategic leaders and the elements of the strategic management process.

The Competitive Landscape

The fundamental nature of competition in many of the world's industries is changing. The reality is that financial capital is scarce and markets are increasingly volatile.[26] Because of this, the pace of change is relentless and ever-increasing. Even determining the boundaries of an industry has become challenging. Consider, for example, how advances in interactive computer networks and telecommunications have blurred the boundaries of the entertainment industry. Today, not only do cable companies and satellite networks compete for entertainment revenue from television, but telecommunication companies are moving into the entertainment business through significant improvements in fiber-optic lines.[27] Partnerships among firms in different segments of the entertainment industry further blur industry boundaries. For example, MSNBC is co-owned by NBC Universal and Microsoft. In turn, General Electric owns 80 percent of NBC Universal while Vivendi owns the remaining 20 percent.[28]

There are other examples of fundamental changes to competition in various industries. For example, many firms are looking for the most profitable and interesting way to deliver video on demand (VOD) online besides cable and satellite companies. Raketu, a voice over the Internet protocol (VoIP) phone service in the United Kingdom, is seeking to provide customers with a social experience while watching the same entertainment on a VOD using a chat feature on its phone service.[29] Raketu's vision is to "… bring together communications, information and entertainment into one service, to remove the complexities of how people communicate with one another, make a system that is contact centric, and to make it fun and easy to use."[30] In addition, the competitive possibilities and challenges for more "traditional" communications companies that are suggested by social networking sites such as Facebook, MySpace, and Friendster appear to be endless.[31]

Other characteristics of the current competitive landscape are noteworthy. Conventional sources of competitive advantage such as economies of scale and huge advertising budgets are not as effective as they once were in terms of helping firms earn above-average returns. Moreover, the traditional managerial mind-set is unlikely to lead a firm to strategic competitiveness. Managers must adopt a new mind-set that values flexibility, speed, innovation, integration, and the challenges that evolve from constantly changing conditions.[32] The conditions of the competitive landscape result in a perilous business world, one where the investments that are required to compete on a global scale are enormous and the consequences of failure are severe.[33] Effective use of the strategic management process reduces the likelihood of failure for firms as they encounter the conditions of today's competitive landscape.

Hypercompetition is a term often used to capture the realities of the competitive landscape. Under conditions of hypercompetition, assumptions of market stability are replaced by notions of inherent instability and change.[34] Hypercompetition results from the dynamics of strategic maneuvering among global and innovative combatants.[35] It is a condition of rapidly escalating competition based on price-quality positioning, competition to create new know-how and establish first-mover advantage, and competition to protect or invade established product or geographic markets.[36] In a hypercompetitive market, firms often aggressively challenge their competitors in the hopes of improving their competitive position and ultimately their performance.[37]

Several factors create hypercompetitive environments and influence the nature of the current competitive landscape. The emergence of a global economy and technology, specifically rapid technological change, are the two primary drivers of hypercompetitive environments and the nature of today's competitive landscape.

The Global Economy

A **global economy** is one in which goods, services, people, skills, and ideas move freely across geographic borders. Relatively unfettered by artificial constraints, such as tariffs, the global economy significantly expands and complicates a firm's competitive environment.[38]

Interesting opportunities and challenges are associated with the emergence of the global economy.[39] For example, Europe, instead of the United States, is now the world's largest single market, with 700 million potential customers. The European Union and the other Western European countries also have a gross domestic product that is more than 35 percent higher than the GDP of the United States.[40] "In the past, China was generally seen as a low-competition market and a low-cost producer. Today, China is an extremely competitive market in which local market-seeking MNCs [multinational corporations] must fiercely compete against other MNCs and against those local companies that are more cost effective and faster in product development. While it

A **global economy** is one in which goods, services, people, skills, and ideas move freely across geographic borders.

General Electric received a $300 million contract from China to supply turbines and compression gear that will propel natural gas from the nation's remote north-western regions to booming eastern cities such as Shanghai.

is true that China has been viewed as a country from which to source low-cost goods, lately, many MNCs, such as P&G [Procter and Gamble], are actually net exporters of local management talent; they have been dispatching more Chinese abroad than bringing foreign expatriates to China."[41] India, the world's largest democracy, has an economy that also is growing rapidly and now ranks as the fourth largest in the world.[42] Many large multinational companies are also emerging as significant global competitors from these emerging economies.[43]

The statistics detailing the nature of the global economy reflect the realities of a hypercompetitive business environment and challenge individual firms to think seriously about the markets in which they will compete. Consider the case of General Electric (GE). Although headquartered in the United States, GE expects that as much as 60 percent of its revenue growth between 2005 and 2015 will be generated by competing in rapidly developing economies (e.g., China and India). The decision to count on revenue growth in developing countries instead of in developed countries such as the United States and European nations seems quite reasonable in the global economy. In fact, according to an analyst, what GE is doing is not by choice but by necessity: "Developing countries are where the fastest growth is occurring and more sustainable growth."[44] Based on its analyses of world markets and their potential, GE estimates that by 2024, China will be the world's largest consumer of electricity and will be the world's largest consumer and consumer-finance market (business areas in which GE competes). GE is making strategic decisions today, such as investing significantly in China and India, in order to improve its competitive position in what the firm believes are becoming vital geographic sources of revenue and profitability.

The March of Globalization

Globalization is the increasing economic interdependence among countries and their organizations as reflected in the flow of goods and services, financial capital, and knowledge across country borders.[45] Globalization is a product of a large number of firms competing against one another in an increasing number of global economies.

In globalized markets and industries, financial capital might be obtained in one national market and used to buy raw materials in another one. Manufacturing equipment bought from a third national market can then be used to produce products that are sold in yet a fourth market. Thus, globalization increases the range of opportunities for companies competing in the current competitive landscape.[46]

Wal-Mart, for instance, is trying to achieve boundary-less retailing with global pricing, sourcing, and logistics. Through boundary-less retailing, the firm seeks to make the movement of goods and the use of pricing strategies as seamless among all of its international operations as has historically been the case among its domestic stores. The firm is pursuing this type of retailing on an evolutionary basis. For example, most of Wal-Mart's original international investments were in Canada and Mexico, because it was easier for the firm to apply its global practices in countries that are geographically close to its home base, the United States. Because of the success it has had in proximate international markets, Wal-Mart is now seeking boundary-less retailing across its operations in countries such as Argentina, Brazil, Chile, China, Japan, and the United Kingdom. (The importance of Wal-Mart's international operations is indicated by the fact that the firm is divided into three divisions: Wal-Mart, Sam's Club, and International.[47])

Firms experiencing and engaging in globalization to the degree Wal-Mart is must make culturally sensitive decisions when using the strategic management process.

Additionally, highly globalized firms must anticipate ever-increasing complexity in their operations as goods, services, people, and so forth move freely across geographic borders and throughout different economic markets.

Overall, it is important for firms to understand that globalization has led to higher levels of performance standards in many competitive dimensions, including those of quality, cost, productivity, product introduction time, and operational efficiency. In addition to firms competing in the global economy, these standards affect firms competing on a domestic-only basis. The reason is that customers will purchase from a global competitor rather than a domestic firm when the global company's good or service is superior. Because workers now flow rather freely among global economies, and because employees are a key source of competitive advantage, firms must understand that increasingly, "the best people will come from … anywhere."[48] Firms must learn how to deal with the reality that in the competitive landscape of the twenty-first century, only companies capable of meeting, if not exceeding, global standards typically have the capability to earn above-average returns.

Although globalization does offer potential benefits to firms, it is not without risks. Collectively, the risks of participating outside of a firm's domestic country in the global economy are labeled a "liability of foreignness."[49]

One risk of entering the global market is the amount of time typically required for firms to learn how to compete in markets that are new to them. A firm's performance can suffer until this knowledge is either developed locally or transferred from the home market to the newly established global location.[50] Additionally, a firm's performance may suffer with substantial amounts of globalization. In this instance, firms may overdiversify internationally beyond their ability to manage these extended operations.[51] The result of overdiversification can have strong negative effects on a firm's overall performance.

Thus, entry into international markets, even for firms with substantial experience in the global economy, requires effective use of the strategic management process. It is also important to note that even though global markets are an attractive strategic option for some companies, they are not the only source of strategic competitiveness. In fact, for most companies, even for those capable of competing successfully in global markets, it is critical to remain committed to and strategically competitive in both domestic and international markets by staying attuned to technological opportunities and potential competitive disruptions that innovations create.[52]

Technology and Technological Changes

Technology-related trends and conditions can be placed into three categories: technology diffusion and disruptive technologies, the information age, and increasing knowledge intensity. Through these categories, technology is significantly altering the nature of competition and contributing to unstable competitive environments as a result of doing so.

Technology Diffusion and Disruptive Technologies

The rate of technology diffusion, which is the speed at which new technologies become available and are used, has increased substantially over the past 15 to 20 years. Consider the following rates of technology diffusion:

> *It took the telephone 35 years to get into 25 percent of all homes in the United States. It took TV 26 years. It took radio 22 years. It took PCs 16 years. It took the Internet 7 years.*[53]

Perpetual innovation is a term used to describe how rapidly and consistently new, information-intensive technologies replace older ones. The shorter product life cycles resulting from these rapid diffusions of new technologies place a competitive premium on being able to quickly introduce new, innovative goods and services into the marketplace.[54]

In fact, when products become somewhat indistinguishable because of the widespread and rapid diffusion of technologies, speed to market with innovative products may be the primary source of competitive advantage (see Chapter 5).[55] Indeed, some argue that the global economy is increasingly driven by or revolves around constant innovations. Not surprisingly, such innovations must be derived from an understanding of global standards and global expectations in terms of product functionality.[56]

Another indicator of rapid technology diffusion is that it now may take only 12 to 18 months for firms to gather information about their competitors' research and development and product decisions.[57] In the global economy, competitors can sometimes imitate a firm's successful competitive actions within a few days. In this sense, the rate of technological diffusion has reduced the competitive benefits of patents. Today, patents may be an effective way of protecting proprietary technology in a small number of industries such as pharmaceuticals. Indeed, many firms competing in the electronics industry often do not apply for patents to prevent competitors from gaining access to the technological knowledge included in the patent application.

Disruptive technologies—technologies that destroy the value of an existing technology and create new markets[58]—surface frequently in today's competitive markets. Think of the new markets created by the technologies underlying the development of products such as iPods, PDAs, WiFi, and the browser. These types of products are thought by some to represent radical or breakthrough innovations.[59] (We talk more about radical innovations in Chapter 13.) A disruptive or radical technology can create what is essentially a new industry or can harm industry incumbents. Some incumbents though, are able to adapt based on their superior resources, experience, and ability to gain access to the new technology through multiple sources (e.g., alliances, acquisitions, and ongoing internal research).[60]

The Information Age

Dramatic changes in information technology have occurred in recent years. Personal computers, cellular phones, artificial intelligence, virtual reality, massive databases, and multiple social networking sites are a few examples of how information is used differently as a result of technological developments. An important outcome of these changes is that the ability to effectively and efficiently access and use information has become an important source of competitive advantage in virtually all industries. Information technology advances have given small firms more flexibility in competing with large firms, if that technology can be efficiently used.[61]

Both the pace of change in information technology and its diffusion will continue to increase. For instance, the number of personal computers in use in the United States is expected to reach 278 million by 2010. The declining costs of information technologies and the increased accessibility to them are also evident in the current competitive landscape. The global proliferation of relatively inexpensive computing power and its linkage on a global scale via computer networks combine to increase the speed and diffusion of information technologies. Thus, the competitive potential of information technologies is now available to companies of all sizes throughout the world, including those in emerging economies.

The Internet is another technological innovation contributing to hypercompetition. Available to an increasing number of people throughout the world, the Internet provides an infrastructure that allows the delivery of information to computers in any location. Access to the Internet on smaller devices such as cell phones is having an ever-growing impact on competition in a number of industries. However, possible changes to Internet Service Providers' (ISPs) pricing structures could affect the rate of growth of Internet-based applications. In mid-2009, ISPs such as Time Warner Cable and Verizon were "… trying to convince their customers that they should pay for their service based on how much data they download in a month."[62] Users downloading or streamlining high-definition movies, playing video games online, and so forth would be affected the most if ISPs were to base their pricing structure around total usage.

Increasing Knowledge Intensity

Knowledge (information, intelligence, and expertise) is the basis of technology and its application. In the competitive landscape of the twenty-first century, knowledge is a critical organizational resource and an increasingly valuable source of competitive advantage.[63] Indeed, starting in the 1980s, the basis of competition shifted from hard assets to intangible resources. For example, "Wal-Mart transformed retailing through its proprietary approach to supply chain management and its information-rich relationships with customers and suppliers."[64] Relationships with customers and suppliers are an example of an intangible resource.

Knowledge is gained through experience, observation, and inference and is an intangible resource (tangible and intangible resources are fully described in Chapter 3). The value of intangible resources, including knowledge, is growing as a proportion of total shareholder value in today's competitive landscape.[65] The probability of achieving strategic competitiveness is enhanced for the firm that realizes that its survival depends on the ability to capture intelligence, transform it into usable knowledge, and diffuse it rapidly throughout the company.[66] Therefore, firms must develop (e.g., through training programs) and acquire (e.g., by hiring educated and experienced employees) knowledge, integrate it into the organization to create capabilities, and then apply it to gain a competitive advantage.[67] In addition, firms must build routines that facilitate the diffusion of local knowledge throughout the organization for use everywhere that it has value.[68] Firms are better able to do these things when they have strategic flexibility.

Strategic flexibility is a set of capabilities used to respond to various demands and opportunities existing in a dynamic and uncertain competitive environment. Thus, strategic flexibility involves coping with uncertainty and its accompanying risks.[69] Firms should try to develop strategic flexibility in all areas of their operations. However, those working within firms to develop strategic flexibility should understand that the task is not easy, largely because of inertia that can build up over time. A firm's focus and past core competencies may actually slow change and strategic flexibility.[70]

To be strategically flexible on a continuing basis and to gain the competitive benefits of such flexibility, a firm has to develop the capacity to learn. In the words of John Browne, former CEO of British Petroleum: "In order to generate extraordinary value for shareholders, a company has to learn better than its competitors and apply that knowledge throughout its businesses faster and more widely than they do."[71] Continuous learning provides the firm with new and up-to-date sets of skills, which allow it to adapt to its environment as it encounters changes.[72] Firms capable of rapidly and broadly applying what they have learned exhibit the strategic flexibility and the capacity to change in ways that will increase the probability of successfully dealing with uncertain, hypercompetitive environments.

The I/O Model of Above-Average Returns

From the 1960s through the 1980s, the external environment was thought to be the primary determinant of strategies that firms selected to be successful.[73] The industrial organization (I/O) model of above-average returns explains the external environment's dominant influence on a firm's strategic actions. The model specifies that the industry or segment of an industry in which a company chooses to compete has a stronger influence on performance than do the choices managers make inside their organizations.[74] The firm's performance is believed to be determined primarily by a range of industry properties, including economies of scale, barriers to market entry, diversification, product differentiation, and the degree of concentration of firms in the industry.[75] We examine these industry characteristics in Chapter 2.

Strategic flexibility is a set of capabilities used to respond to various demands and opportunities existing in a dynamic and uncertain competitive environment.

Grounded in economics, the I/O model has four underlying assumptions. First, the external environment is assumed to impose pressures and constraints that determine the strategies that would result in above-average returns. Second, most firms competing within an industry or within a segment of that industry are assumed to control similar strategically relevant resources and to pursue similar strategies in light of those resources. Third, resources used to implement strategies are assumed to be highly mobile across firms, so any resource differences that might develop between firms will be short-lived. Fourth, organizational decision makers are assumed to be rational and committed to acting in the firm's best interests, as shown by their profit-maximizing behaviors.[76] The I/O model challenges firms to find the most attractive industry in which to compete. Because most firms are assumed to have similar valuable resources that are mobile across companies, their performance generally can be increased only when they operate in the industry with the highest profit potential and learn how to use their resources to implement the strategy required by the industry's structural characteristics.[77]

The five forces model of competition is an analytical tool used to help firms find the industry that is the most attractive for them. The model (explained in Chapter 2) encompasses several variables and tries to capture the complexity of competition. The five forces model suggests that an industry's profitability (i.e., its rate of return on invested capital relative to its cost of capital) is a function of interactions among five forces: suppliers, buyers, competitive rivalry among firms currently in the industry, product substitutes, and potential entrants to the industry.[78]

Firms use the five forces model to identify the attractiveness of an industry (as measured by its profitability potential) as well as the most advantageous position for the firm to take in that industry, given the industry's structural characteristics.[79] Typically, the model suggests that firms can earn above-average returns by producing either standardized goods or services at costs below those of competitors (a cost leadership strategy) or by producing differentiated goods or services for which customers are willing to pay a price premium (a differentiation strategy). (The cost leadership and product differentiation strategies are discussed in Chapter 4.) The fact that "…the fast food industry is becoming a 'zero-sum industry' as companies' battle for the same pool of customers"[80] suggests that McDonald's is competing in a relatively unattractive industry. However, as described in the Opening Case, by focusing on product innovations and enhancing existing facilities while buying properties outside the United States at attractive prices as the foundation for selectively building new stores, McDonald's is positioned in the fast food (or quick-service) restaurant industry in a way that allows it to earn above-average returns.

As shown in Figure 1.2, the I/O model suggests that above-average returns are earned when firms are able to effectively study the external environment as the foundation for identifying an attractive industry and implementing the appropriate strategy. Companies that develop or acquire the internal skills needed to implement strategies required by the external environment are likely to succeed, while those that do not are likely to fail. Hence, this model suggests that returns are determined primarily by external characteristics rather than by the firm's unique internal resources and capabilities.

Research findings support the I/O model, in that approximately 20 percent of a firm's profitability is explained by the industry in which it chooses to compete. However, this research also shows that 36 percent of the variance in firm profitability can be attributed to the firm's characteristics and actions.[81] These findings suggest that the external environment and a firm's resources, capabilities, core competencies, and competitive advantages (see Chapter 3) all influence the company's ability to achieve strategic competitiveness and earn above-average returns.

As shown in Figure 1.2, the I/O model considers a firm's strategy to be a set of commitments and actions flowing from the characteristics of the industry in which the firm has decided to compete. The resource-based model, discussed next, takes a different view of the major influences on a firm's choice of strategy.

Figure 1.2 The I/O Model of Above-Average Returns

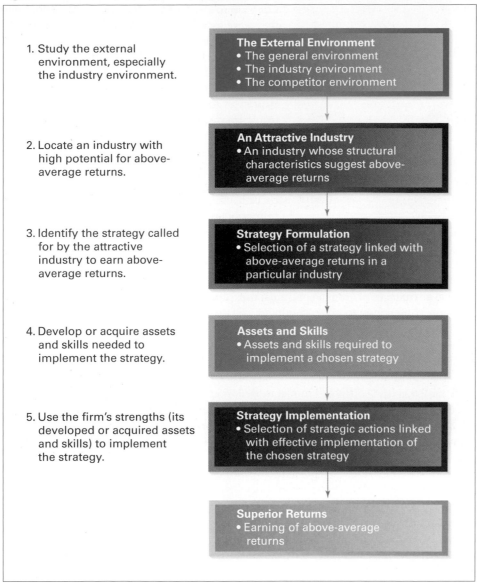

1. Study the external environment, especially the industry environment.

The External Environment
- The general environment
- The industry environment
- The competitor environment

2. Locate an industry with high potential for above-average returns.

An Attractive Industry
- An industry whose structural characteristics suggest above-average returns

3. Identify the strategy called for by the attractive industry to earn above-average returns.

Strategy Formulation
- Selection of a strategy linked with above-average returns in a particular industry

4. Develop or acquire assets and skills needed to implement the strategy.

Assets and Skills
- Assets and skills required to implement a chosen strategy

5. Use the firm's strengths (its developed or acquired assets and skills) to implement the strategy.

Strategy Implementation
- Selection of strategic actions linked with effective implementation of the chosen strategy

Superior Returns
- Earning of above-average returns

The Resource-Based Model of Above-Average Returns

The resource-based model assumes that each organization is a collection of unique resources and capabilities. The *uniqueness* of its resources and capabilities is the basis of a firm's strategy and its ability to earn above-average returns.[82]

Resources are inputs into a firm's production process, such as capital equipment, the skills of individual employees, patents, finances, and talented managers. In general, a firm's resources are classified into three categories: physical, human, and organizational capital. Described fully in Chapter 3, resources are either tangible or intangible in nature.

Individual resources alone may not yield a competitive advantage.[83] In fact, resources have a greater likelihood of being a source of competitive advantage when they are formed into a capability. A **capability** is the capacity for a set of resources to perform a task or an activity in an integrative manner. Capabilities evolve over time and must be managed

Resources are inputs into a firm's production process, such as capital equipment, the skills of individual employees, patents, finances, and talented managers.

A **capability** is the capacity for a set of resources to perform a task or an activity in an integrative manner.

Best Buy as well as many other companies collect extensive data about their customers' buying behavior and preferences to make better business decisions.

dynamically in pursuit of above-average returns.[84] **Core competencies** are resources and capabilities that serve as a source of competitive advantage for a firm over its rivals. Core competencies are often visible in the form of organizational functions. For example, we noted earlier that Best Buy is processing the extensive amount of data it has about its customers to identify private-label consumer electronic products it can produce to meet customers' needs. Best Buy relies on its strong customer service and information technology capabilities to spot ways to do this.

According to the resource-based model, differences in firms' performances across time are due primarily to their unique resources and capabilities rather than the industry's structural characteristics. This model also assumes that firms acquire different resources and develop unique capabilities based on how they combine and use the resources; that resources and certainly capabilities are not highly mobile across firms; and that the differences in resources and capabilities are the basis of competitive advantage.[85] Through continued use, capabilities become stronger and more difficult for competitors to understand and imitate. As a source of competitive advantage, a capability "should be neither so simple that it is highly imitable, nor so complex that it defies internal steering and control."[86]

The resource-based model of superior returns is shown in Figure 1.3. This model suggests that the strategy the firm chooses should allow it to use its competitive advantages in an attractive industry (the I/O model is used to identify an attractive industry).

Not all of a firm's resources and capabilities have the potential to be the foundation for a competitive advantage. This potential is realized when resources and capabilities are valuable, rare, costly to imitate, and nonsubstitutable.[87] Resources are *valuable* when they allow a firm to take advantage of opportunities or neutralize threats in its external environment. They are *rare* when possessed by few, if any, current and potential competitors. Resources are *costly to imitate* when other firms either cannot obtain them or are at a cost disadvantage in obtaining them compared with the firm that already possesses them. And they are *nonsubstitutable* when they have no structural equivalents. Many resources can either be imitated or substituted over time. Therefore, it is difficult to achieve and sustain a competitive advantage based on resources alone.[88] When these four criteria are met, however, resources and capabilities become core competencies.

As noted previously, research shows that both the industry environment and a firm's internal assets affect that firm's performance over time.[89] Thus, to form a vision and mission, and subsequently to select one or more strategies and to determine how to implement them, firms use both the I/O and the resource-based models.[90] In fact, these models complement each other in that one (I/O) focuses outside the firm while the other (resource-based) focuses inside the firm. Next, we discuss the forming of the firm's vision and mission—actions taken after the firm understands the realities of its external environment (Chapter 2) and internal organization (Chapter 3).

Vision and Mission

Core competencies are capabilities that serve as a source of competitive advantage for a firm over its rivals.

After studying the external environment and the internal organization, the firm has the information it needs to form its vision and a mission (see Figure 1.1). Stakeholders (those who affect or are affected by a firm's performance, as explained later in the chapter) learn a great deal about a firm by studying its vision and mission. Indeed, a key purpose of

Figure 1.3 The Resource-Based Model of Above-Average Returns

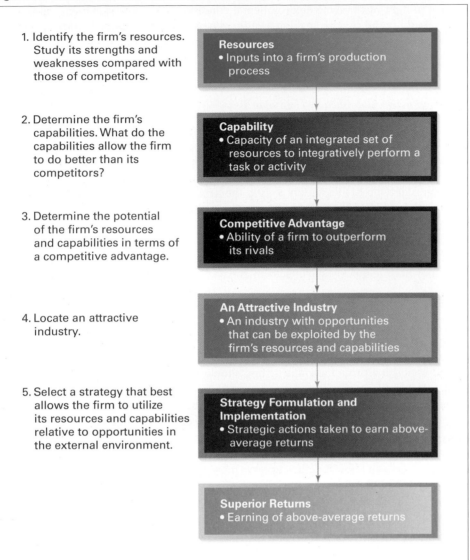

1. Identify the firm's resources. Study its strengths and weaknesses compared with those of competitors.

Resources
• Inputs into a firm's production process

2. Determine the firm's capabilities. What do the capabilities allow the firm to do better than its competitors?

Capability
• Capacity of an integrated set of resources to integratively perform a task or activity

3. Determine the potential of the firm's resources and capabilities in terms of a competitive advantage.

Competitive Advantage
• Ability of a firm to outperform its rivals

4. Locate an attractive industry.

An Attractive Industry
• An industry with opportunities that can be exploited by the firm's resources and capabilities

5. Select a strategy that best allows the firm to utilize its resources and capabilities relative to opportunities in the external environment.

Strategy Formulation and Implementation
• Strategic actions taken to earn above-average returns

Superior Returns
• Earning of above-average returns

vision and mission statements is to inform stakeholders of what the firm is, what it seeks to accomplish, and who it seeks to serve.

Vision

Vision is a picture of what the firm wants to be and, in broad terms, what it wants to ultimately achieve.[91] Thus, a vision statement articulates the ideal description of an organization and gives shape to its intended future. In other words, a vision statement points the firm in the direction of where it would eventually like to be in the years to come.[92] Vision is "big picture" thinking with passion that helps people *feel* what they are supposed to be doing in the organization.[93] People feel what they are to do when their firm's vision is simple, positive, and emotional. However, an effective vision stretches and challenges people as well.

It is also important to note that vision statements reflect a firm's values and aspirations and are intended to capture the heart and mind of each employee and, hopefully,

Vision is a picture of what the firm wants to be and, in broad terms, what it wants to ultimately achieve.

many of its other stakeholders. A firm's vision tends to be enduring while its mission can change in light of changing environmental conditions. A vision statement tends to be relatively short and concise, making it easily remembered. Examples of vision statements include the following:

> *Our vision is to be the world's best quick service restaurant. (McDonald's)*

> *To make the automobile accessible to every American. (Ford Motor Company's vision when established by Henry Ford)*

As a firm's most important and prominent strategic leader, the CEO is responsible for working with others to form the firm's vision. Experience shows that the most effective vision statement results when the CEO involves a host of stakeholders (e.g., other top-level managers, employees working in different parts of the organization, suppliers, and customers) to develop it. In addition, to help the firm reach its desired future state, a vision statement should be clearly tied to the conditions in the firm's external environment and internal organization. Moreover, the decisions and actions of those involved with developing the vision, especially the CEO and the other top-level managers, must be consistent with that vision. At McDonald's, for example, a failure to openly provide employees with what they need to quickly and effectively serve customers would be a recipe for disaster.

Mission

The vision is the foundation for the firm's mission. A **mission** specifies the business or businesses in which the firm intends to compete and the customers it intends to serve.[94] The firm's mission is more concrete than its vision. However, like the vision, a mission should establish a firm's individuality and should be inspiring and relevant to all stakeholders.[95] Together, vision and mission provide the foundation the firm needs to choose and implement one or more strategies. The probability of forming an effective mission increases when employees have a strong sense of the ethical standards that will guide their behaviors as they work to help the firm reach its vision.[96] Thus, business ethics are a vital part of the firm's discussions to decide what it wants to become (its vision) as well as who it intends to serve and how it desires to serve those individuals and groups (its mission).[97]

Even though the final responsibility for forming the firm's mission rests with the CEO, the CEO and other top-level managers tend to involve a larger number of people in forming the mission. The main reason is that the mission deals more directly with product markets and customers, and middle- and first-level managers and other employees have more direct contact with customers and the markets in which they are served. Examples of mission statements include the following:

> *Be the best employer for our people in each community around the world and deliver operational excellence to our customers in each of our restaurants. (McDonald's)*

> *Our mission is to be recognized by our customers as the leader in applications engineering. We always focus on the activities customers desire; we are highly motivated and strive to advance our technical knowledge in the areas of material, part design and fabrication technology. (LNP, a GE Plastics Company)*

Notice how the McDonald's mission statement flows from its vision of being the world's best quick-service restaurant. LNP's mission statement describes the business areas (material, part design, and fabrication technology) in which the firm intends to compete.

Some believe that vision and mission statements fail to create value for the firms forming them. One expert believes that "Most vision statements are either too vague, too broad in scope, or riddled with superlatives."[98] If this is the case, why do firms spend so much time developing these statements? As explained in the Strategic Focus, vision and mission statements that are poorly developed do not provide the direction the firm needs to take appropriate strategic actions. Still, as shown in Figure 1.1, the firm's vision and

STRATEGY RIGHT NOW

Explore how Juniper Networks, a leader in high-performance networking, established a vision for product innovation.

www.cengage.com/ management/hitt

A **mission** specifies the business or businesses in which the firm intends to compete and the customers it intends to serve.

EFFECTIVE VISION AND MISSION STATEMENTS: WHY FIRMS NEED THEM

Some clearly believe that working on vision and mission statements is a waste of time and energy. "We have more important things to accomplish"; "We are too busy fighting daily fires to spend time thinking about the future or dreaming about what we might want to be"; and "All vision and mission statements look alike across companies—there's just no difference among them, so why bother?" Almost everyone who has been involved with or worked for an organization either on or off campus has likely heard similar comments.

Thinking about the challenges facing firms today allows us to understand the reasons for the negative perspective some have about the benefits organizations gain by forming vision and mission statements. A difficult competitive environment and the realities of globalization are but two reasons that may cause some to react less-than-positively when asked to participate in efforts to form vision and mission statements for their organization. In addition, the difficulty and challenge associated with developing *effective* or *meaningful* vision and mission statements may be the key reasons some prefer not to bother trying to do so.

A vision is a picture of what the firm wants to be and, in broad terms, what it ultimately wants to achieve. Based on the vision, a firm's mission indicates the business or businesses in which the firm will compete and the customers it will serve. An important aspect of these statements is that deep, critical, and reflective thinking is required to form them. Moreover, forming these statements requires choices to be made—about what the firm wants to be, what it wants to achieve, and the businesses it will compete in, and the specific groups of customers it will serve. Simultaneously, the firm is deciding what it won't become, won't try to achieve, where it won't compete, and who it won't serve. These are hard choices that result only from intensive thinking and analysis. Having obtained information about the firm's external environment and its internal organization, those asked to form the firm's vision and mission statements must be willing to rigorously and thoroughly debate the realities and possibilities associated with the information that has been gathered.

There are benefits for organizations willing to accept the challenge of rigorously examining and interpreting this information. Internally, the benefits include (1) providing the direction required to select the firm's strategies, (2) prioritizing how the firm's resources will be allocated, (3) providing opportunities for people to work together to deal with significant issues, (4) gaining an appreciation for the necessity of making trade-offs, and (5) learning more about the firm's culture and character. Benefits for the firm's external environment include (1) showing how the organization differs from competitors, (2) reflecting the organization's priorities, and (3) signaling aspects of the firm's culture and values. In addition, strategic leaders should be aware of research evidence suggesting that there is a positive relationship between forming vision and mission statements that is consistent with the realities of their

CORBIS/Jupiter Images

external environment and internal organization and performance.[99] Thus, there are multiple reasons for firms to take the steps required to effectively develop a vision statement and a mission statement.

Sources: H. Ibarra & O. Obodaru, 2009, Women and the vision thing, *Harvard Business Review*, 87(1): 62–70; B. Bartkus & M. Glassman, 2008, Do firms practice what they preach? The relationship between mission statements and stakeholder management, *Journal of Business Ethics*, 83: 207–216; B. Perkins, 2008, State your purpose, *Computerworld*, May 12, 35; L. S. Williams, 2008, The mission statement, *Journal of Business Communication*, 45: 94–119; J. Davis, J. A. Ruhe, M. Lee, & U. Rajadhyaksha, 2007, Mission possible: Do school mission statements work? *Journal of Business Ethics*, 70: 99–110.

mission are critical aspects of the *strategic inputs* it requires to engage in *strategic actions* as the foundation for achieving strategic competitiveness and earning above-average returns. Therefore, as we discuss in the Strategic Focus, firms must accept the challenge of forming effective vision and mission statements.

Stakeholders

Every organization involves a system of primary stakeholder groups with whom it establishes and manages relationships.[100] **Stakeholders** are the individuals and groups who can affect the firm's vision and mission, are affected by the strategic outcomes achieved, and have enforceable claims on the firm's performance.[101] Claims on a firm's performance are enforced through the stakeholders' ability to withhold participation essential to the organization's survival, competitiveness, and profitability.[102] Stakeholders continue to support an organization when its performance meets or exceeds their expectations.[103] Also, research suggests that firms that effectively manage stakeholder relationships outperform those that do not. Stakeholder relationships can therefore be managed to be a source of competitive advantage.[104]

Although organizations have dependency relationships with their stakeholders, they are not equally dependent on all stakeholders at all times;[105] as a consequence, not every stakeholder has the same level of influence.[106] The more critical and valued a stakeholder's participation, the greater a firm's dependency on it. Greater dependence, in turn, gives the stakeholder more potential influence over a firm's commitments, decisions, and actions. Managers must find ways to either accommodate or insulate the organization from the demands of stakeholders controlling critical resources.[107]

Classifications of Stakeholders

The parties involved with a firm's operations can be separated into at least three groups.[108] As shown in Figure 1.4, these groups are the capital market stakeholders (shareholders and the major suppliers of a firm's capital), the product market stakeholders (the firm's primary customers, suppliers, host communities, and unions representing the workforce), and the organizational stakeholders (all of a firm's employees, including both nonmanagerial and managerial personnel).

Each stakeholder group expects those making strategic decisions in a firm to provide the leadership through which its valued objectives will be reached.[109] The objectives of the various stakeholder groups often differ from one another, sometimes placing those involved with a firm's strategic management process in situations where trade-offs have to be made. The most obvious stakeholders, at least in U.S. organizations, are *shareholders*—individuals and groups who have invested capital in a firm in the expectation of earning a positive return on their investments. These stakeholders' rights are grounded in laws governing private property and private enterprise.

Stakeholders are the individuals and groups who can affect the firm's vision and mission, are affected by the strategic outcomes achieved, and have enforceable claims on the firm's performance.

Figure 1.4 The Three Stakeholder Groups

In contrast to shareholders, another group of stakeholders—the firm's customers—prefers that investors receive a minimum return on their investments. Customers could have their interests maximized when the quality and reliability of a firm's products are improved, but without a price increase. High returns to customers might come at the expense of lower returns negotiated with capital market shareholders.

Because of potential conflicts, each firm is challenged to manage its stakeholders. First, a firm must carefully identify all important stakeholders. Second, it must prioritize them, in case it cannot satisfy all of them. Power is the most critical criterion in prioritizing stakeholders. Other criteria might include the urgency of satisfying each particular stakeholder group and the degree of importance of each to the firm.[110]

When the firm earns above-average returns, the challenge of effectively managing stakeholder relationships is lessened substantially. With the capability and flexibility provided by above-average returns, a firm can more easily satisfy multiple stakeholders simultaneously. When the firm earns only average returns, it is unable to maximize the interests of all stakeholders. The objective then becomes one of at least minimally satisfying each stakeholder. Trade-off decisions are made in light of how important the support of each stakeholder group is to the firm. For example, environmental groups may be very important to firms in the energy industry but less important to professional service firms.[111] A firm earning below-average returns does not have the capacity to minimally satisfy all stakeholders. The managerial challenge in this case is to make trade-offs that minimize the amount of support lost from stakeholders. Societal values also influence the general weightings allocated among the three stakeholder groups shown in Figure 1.4. Although all three groups are served by firms in the major industrialized nations, the priorities in their service vary because of cultural differences. Next, we present additional details about each of the three major stakeholder groups.

Capital Market Stakeholders

Shareholders and lenders both expect a firm to preserve and enhance the wealth they have entrusted to it. The returns they expect are commensurate with the degree of risk accepted with those investments (i.e., lower returns are expected with low-risk investments while higher returns are expected with high-risk investments). Dissatisfied lenders may impose stricter covenants on subsequent borrowing of capital. Dissatisfied shareholders may reflect their concerns through several means, including selling their stock.

When a firm is aware of potential or actual dissatisfactions among capital market stakeholders, it may respond to their concerns. The firm's response to stakeholders who are dissatisfied is affected by the nature of its dependency relationship with them (which, as noted earlier, is also influenced by a society's values). The greater and more significant the dependency relationship is, the more direct and significant the firm's response becomes. Before liquidating, Circuit City took several actions to try to satisfy its capital market stakeholders. In part, these actions were taken because of the significance of Circuit City's dependence on its capital market stakeholders. Closing stores, changing members of the firm's top management team, and seeking potential buyers are examples of the actions Circuit City took in the final few years before liquidating.[112] However, the reality is that none of these actions resulted in outcomes that allowed Circuit City to meet the expectations of its capital market stakeholders.

Product Market Stakeholders

Some might think that product market stakeholders (customers, suppliers, host communities, and unions) share few common interests. However, all four groups can benefit as firms engage in competitive battles. For example, depending on product and industry characteristics, marketplace competition may result in lower product prices being charged to a firm's customers and higher prices being paid to its suppliers (the firm might be willing to pay higher supplier prices to ensure delivery of the types of goods and services that are linked with its competitive success).[113]

Customers, as stakeholders, demand reliable products at the lowest possible prices. Suppliers seek loyal customers who are willing to pay the highest sustainable prices for the goods and services they receive. Host communities want companies willing to be long-term employers and providers of tax revenue without placing excessive demands on public support services. Union officials are interested in secure jobs, under highly desirable working conditions, for employees they represent. Thus, product market stakeholders are generally satisfied when a firm's profit margin reflects at least a balance between the returns to capital market stakeholders (i.e., the returns lenders and shareholders will accept and still retain their interests in the firm) and the returns in which they share.

Organizational Stakeholders

Employees—the firm's organizational stakeholders—expect the firm to provide a dynamic, stimulating, and rewarding work environment. As employees, we are usually satisfied working for a company that is growing and actively developing our skills, especially those skills required to be effective team members and to meet or exceed global work standards. Workers who learn how to use new knowledge productively are critical to organizational success. In a collective sense, the education and skills of a firm's workforce are competitive weapons affecting strategy implementation and firm performance.[114] As suggested by the following statement, strategic leaders are ultimately responsible for serving the needs of organizational stakeholders on a day-to-day basis: "[T]he job of [strategic] leadership is to fully utilize human potential, to create organizations in which people can grow and learn while still achieving a common objective, to nurture the human spirit."[115] Interestingly, research suggests that outside directors are more likely to propose layoffs compared to inside strategic leaders, while such insiders are likely to use preventative cost-cutting measures and seek to protect incumbent employees.[116]

Strategic Leaders

Strategic leaders are people located in different parts of the firm using the strategic management process to help the firm reach its vision and mission. Regardless of their location in the firm, successful strategic leaders are decisive, committed to nurturing those around them[117] and are committed to helping the firm create value for all stakeholder groups.[118] In this vein, research evidence suggests that employees who perceive that their CEO emphasizes the need for the firm to operate in ways that are consistent with the values of all stakeholder groups rather than focusing only on maximizing profits for shareholders identify that CEO as a visionary leader. In turn, visionary leadership is related to extra effort by employees, with employee effort leading to enhanced firm performance. These intriguing findings suggest that decision-making values "… that are oriented toward a range of stakeholders may yield more favorable outcomes for leaders than values that focus primarily on economic-based issues."[119] These findings are consistent with the argument that "To regain society's trust … business leaders must embrace a way of looking at their role that goes beyond their responsibility to the shareholder to include a civic and personal commitment to their duty as institutional custodians."[120]

When identifying strategic leaders, most of us tend to think of chief executive officers (CEOs) and other top-level managers. Clearly, these people are strategic leaders. And, in the final analysis, CEOs are responsible for making certain their firm effectively uses the strategic management process. Indeed, the pressure on CEOs to manage strategically is stronger than ever.[121] However, many other people in today's organizations help choose a firm's strategy and then determine the actions for successfully implementing it.[122] The main reason is that the realities of twenty-first–century competition that we discussed earlier in this chapter (e.g., the global economy, globalization, rapid technological change, and the increasing importance of knowledge and people as sources of competitive advantage) are creating a need for those "closest to the action" to be the ones making decisions and determining the actions to be taken.[123] In fact, the most effective CEOs and top-level managers understand how to delegate strategic responsibilities to people throughout the firm who influence the use of organizational resources.[124]

Organizational culture also affects strategic leaders and their work. In turn, strategic leaders' decisions and actions shape a firm's culture. **Organizational culture** refers to the complex set of ideologies, symbols, and core values that are shared throughout the firm and that influence how the firm conducts business. It is the social energy that drives—or fails to drive—the organization.[125] For example, Southwest Airlines is known for having a unique and valuable culture. Its culture encourages employees to work hard but also to have fun while doing so. Moreover, its culture entails respect for others—employees and customers alike. The firm also places a premium on service, as suggested by its commitment to provide POS (Positively Outrageous Service) to each customer.

Some organizational cultures are a source of disadvantage. It is important for strategic leaders to understand, however, that whether the firm's culture is functional or dysfunctional, their work takes place within the context of that culture. The relationship between organizational culture and strategic leaders' work is reciprocal in that the culture shapes how they work while their work helps shape an ever-evolving organizational culture.

The Work of Effective Strategic Leaders

Perhaps not surprisingly, hard work, thorough analyses, a willingness to be brutally honest, a penchant for wanting the firm and its people to accomplish more, and tenacity are prerequisites to an individual's success as a strategic leader.[126] In addition, strategic leaders must be able to "think seriously and deeply … about the purposes of the organizations they head or functions they perform, about the strategies, tactics, technologies, systems,

Strategic leaders are people located in different parts of the firm using the strategic management process to help the firm reach its vision and mission.

Organizational culture refers to the complex set of ideologies, symbols, and core values that are shared throughout the firm and that influence how the firm conducts business.

IBM's organizational culture holds that there is indeed a corporate responsibility to bettering society at large.

and people necessary to attain these purposes and about the important questions that always need to be asked."[127] In addition, effective strategic leaders work to set an ethical tone in their firms. For example, Kevin Thompson, IBM's Manager of Corporate Citizenship, suggests, "We don't think you can survive without integrating business and societal values."[128]

Strategic leaders, regardless of their location in the organization, often work long hours, and their work is filled with ambiguous decision situations.[129] However, the opportunities afforded by this work are appealing and offer exciting chances to dream and to act.[130] The following words, given as advice to the late Time Warner chair and co-CEO Steven J. Ross by his father, describe the opportunities in a strategic leader's work:

> There are three categories of people—the person who goes into the office, puts his feet up on his desk, and dreams for 12 hours; the person who arrives at 5 A.M. and works for 16 hours, never once stopping to dream; and the person who puts his feet up, dreams for one hour, then does something about those dreams.[131]

The organizational term used for a dream that challenges and energizes a company is vision. Strategic leaders have opportunities to dream and to act, and the most effective ones provide a vision as the foundation for the firm's mission and subsequent choice and use of one or more strategies.

Predicting Outcomes of Strategic Decisions: Profit Pools

Strategic leaders attempt to predict the outcomes of their decisions before taking efforts to implement them, which is difficult to do. Many decisions that are a part of the strategic management process are concerned with an uncertain future and the firm's place in that future.[132]

Mapping an industry's profit pool is something strategic leaders can do to anticipate the possible outcomes of different decisions and to focus on growth in profits rather than strictly growth in revenues. A **profit pool** entails the total profits earned in an industry at all points along the value chain.[133] (We explain the value chain in Chapter 3 and discuss it further in Chapter 4.) Analyzing the profit pool in the industry may help a firm see something others are unable to see by helping it understand the primary sources of profits in an industry. There are four steps to identifying profit pools: (1) define the pool's boundaries, (2) estimate the pool's overall size, (3) estimate the size of the value-chain activity in the pool, and (4) reconcile the calculations.[134]

Let's think about how McDonald's might map the quick-service restaurant industry's profit pools. First, McDonald's would need to define the industry's boundaries and, second, estimate its size. As discussed in the Opening Case, these boundaries would include markets across the globe. As noted, the size of the U.S. market is not currently expanding. The net result of this is that McDonald's is trying to increase its market share by taking market share away from competitors such as Burger King and Wendy's. Growth is more likely in international markets, which is why McDonald's is establishing more units internationally than it is domestically. Armed with information about its industry, McDonald's would then be prepared to estimate the amount of profit potential in each part of the value chain (step 3). In the quick-service restaurant industry, marketing campaigns and customer service are likely more important sources of potential profits than are inbound logistics' activities (see Chapter 3). With an understanding of where

A **profit pool** entails the total profits earned in an industry at all points along the value chain.

the greatest amount of profits are likely to be earned, McDonald's would then be ready to select the strategy to use to be successful where the largest profit pools are located in the value chain.[135] As this brief discussion shows, profit pools are a tool the firm's strategic leaders can use to help recognize the actions to take to increase the likelihood of increasing profits.

The Strategic Management Process

As suggested by Figure 1.1, the strategic management process is a rational approach firms use to achieve strategic competitiveness and earn above-average returns. Figure 1.1 also features the topics we examine in this book to present the strategic management process to you.

This book is divided into three parts. In Part 1, we describe what firms do to analyze their external environment (Chapter 2) and internal organization (Chapter 3). These analyses are completed to identify marketplace opportunities and threats in the external environment (Chapter 2) and to decide how to use the resources, capabilities, core competencies, and competitive advantages in the firm's internal organization to pursue opportunities and overcome threats (Chapter 3). With knowledge about its external environment and internal organization, the firm forms its vision and mission.

The firm's strategic inputs (see Figure 1.1) provide the foundation for choosing one or more strategies and deciding how to implement them. As suggested in Figure 1.1 by the horizontal arrow linking the two types of strategic actions, formulation and implementation must be simultaneously integrated if the firm is to successfully use the strategic management process. Integration happens as decision makers think about implementation issues when choosing strategies and as they think about possible changes to the firm's strategies while implementing a currently chosen strategy.

In Part 2 of this book, we discuss the different strategies firms may choose to use. First, we examine business-level strategies (Chapter 4). A business-level strategy describes the actions a firm decides to take in order to exploit its competitive advantage over rivals. A company competing in a single product market (e.g., a locally owned grocery store operating in only one location) has but one business-level strategy while a diversified firm competing in multiple product markets (e.g., General Electric) forms a business-level strategy for each of its businesses. In Chapter 5, we describe the actions and reactions that occur among firms while using their strategies in marketplace competitions. As we will see, competitors respond to and try to anticipate each other's actions. The dynamics of competition affect the strategies firms choose to use as well as how they try to implement the chosen strategies.[136]

For the diversified firm, corporate-level strategy (Chapter 6) is concerned with determining the businesses in which the company intends to compete as well as how to manage its different businesses. Other topics vital to strategy formulation, particularly in the diversified corporation, include acquiring other companies and, as appropriate, restructuring the firm's portfolio of businesses (Chapter 7) and selecting an international strategy (Chapter 8). With cooperative strategies (Chapter 9), firms form a partnership to share their resources and capabilities in order to develop a competitive advantage. Cooperative strategies are becoming increasingly important as firms seek ways to compete in the global economy's array of different markets.[137]

To examine actions taken to implement strategies, we consider several topics in Part 3 of the book. First, we examine the different mechanisms used to govern firms (Chapter 10). With demands for improved corporate governance being voiced today by many stakeholders, organizations are challenged to learn how to simultaneously satisfy their stakeholders' different interests.[138] Finally, the organizational structure and actions needed to control a firm's operations (Chapter 11), the patterns of strategic leadership appropriate for today's firms and competitive environments (Chapter 12), and strategic entrepreneurship (Chapter 13) as a path to continuous innovation are addressed.

Before closing this introductory chapter, it is important to emphasize that primarily because they are related to how a firm interacts with its stakeholders, almost all strategic management process decisions have ethical dimensions.[139] Organizational ethics are revealed by an organization's culture; that is to say, a firm's decisions are a product of the core values that are shared by most or all of a company's managers and employees. Especially in the turbulent and often ambiguous competitive landscape of the twenty-first century, those making decisions that are part of the strategic management process are challenged to recognize that their decisions affect capital market, product market, and organizational stakeholders differently and to evaluate the ethical implications of their decisions on a daily basis.[140] Decision makers failing to recognize these realities accept the risk of putting their firm at a competitive disadvantage when it comes to consistently engaging in ethical business practices.[141]

As you will discover, the strategic management process examined in this book calls for disciplined approaches to serve as the foundation for developing a competitive advantage. These approaches provide the pathway through which firms will be able to achieve strategic competitiveness and earn above-average returns. Mastery of this strategic management process will effectively serve you, our readers, and the organizations for which you will choose to work.

SUMMARY

- Firms use the strategic management process to achieve strategic competitiveness and earn above-average returns. Strategic competitiveness is achieved when a firm has developed and learned how to implement a value-creating strategy. Above-average returns (in excess of what investors expect to earn from other investments with similar levels of risk) provide the foundation a firm needs to simultaneously satisfy all of its stakeholders.

- The fundamental nature of competition is different in the current competitive landscape. As a result, those making strategic decisions must adopt a different mind-set, one that allows them to learn how to compete in highly turbulent and chaotic environments that are producing disorder and a great deal of uncertainty. The globalization of industries and their markets and rapid and significant technological changes are the two primary factors contributing to the turbulence of the competitive landscape.

- Firms use two major models to help them form their vision and mission and then choose one or more strategies to use in pursuit of strategic competitiveness and above-average returns. The core assumption of the I/O model is that the firm's external environment has more of an influence on the choice of strategies than do the firm's internal resources, capabilities, and core competencies. Thus, the I/O model is used to understand the effects an industry's characteristics can have on a firm when deciding what strategy or strategies to use to compete against rivals. The logic supporting the I/O model suggests that above-average returns are

earned when the firm locates an attractive industry or part of an industry and successfully implements the strategy dictated by that industry's characteristics. The core assumption of the resource-based model is that the firm's unique resources, capabilities, and core competencies have more of an influence on selecting and using strategies than does the firm's external environment. Above-average returns are earned when the firm uses its valuable, rare, costly-to-imitate, and nonsubstitutable resources and capabilities to compete against its rivals in one or more industries. Evidence indicates that both models yield insights that are linked to successfully selecting and using strategies. Thus, firms want to use their unique resources, capabilities, and core competencies as the foundation for one or more strategies that will allow them to compete in industries they understand.

- Vision and mission are formed in light of the information and insights gained from studying a firm's internal and external environments. Vision is a picture of what the firm wants to be and, in broad terms, what it wants to ultimately achieve. Flowing from the vision, the mission specifies the business or businesses in which the firm intends to compete and the customers it intends to serve. Vision and mission provide direction to the firm and signal important descriptive information to stakeholders.

- Stakeholders are those who can affect, and are affected by, a firm's strategic outcomes. Because a firm is dependent on the continuing support of stakeholders (shareholders, customers, suppliers, employees, host communities, etc.), they have enforceable claims on the company's performance. When earning above-average returns, a firm has the resources it needs to at minimum simultaneously satisfy the interests of all stakeholders. However, when earning only average returns, the firm must carefully manage its stakeholders in order to retain their support. A firm earning below-average returns must minimize the amount of support it loses from unsatisfied stakeholders.

- Strategic leaders are people located in different parts of the firm using the strategic management process to help the firm reach its vision and mission. In the final analysis, though, CEOs are responsible for making certain that their firms properly use the strategic management process. Today, the effectiveness of the strategic management process is increased when it is grounded in ethical intentions and behaviors. The strategic leader's work demands decision trade-offs, often among attractive alternatives. It is important for all strategic leaders and especially the CEO and other members of the top-management team to work hard, conduct thorough analyses of situations facing the firm, be brutally and consistently honest, and ask the right questions of the right people at the right time.

- Strategic leaders predict the potential outcomes of their strategic decisions. To do this, they must first calculate profit pools in their industry that are linked to value chain activities. Predicting the potential outcomes of their strategic decisions reduces the likelihood of the firm formulating and implementing ineffective strategies.

REVIEW QUESTIONS

1. What are strategic competitiveness, strategy, competitive advantage, above-average returns, and the strategic management process?

2. What are the characteristics of the current competitive landscape? What two factors are the primary drivers of this landscape?

3. According to the I/O model, what should a firm do to earn above-average returns?

4. What does the resource-based model suggest a firm should do to earn above-average returns?

5. What are vision and mission? What is their value for the strategic management process?

6. What are stakeholders? How do the three primary stakeholder groups influence organizations?

7. How would you describe the work of strategic leaders?

8. What are the elements of the strategic management process? How are they interrelated?

EXPERIENTIAL EXERCISES

EXERCISE 1: BUSINESS AND BLOGS

One element of industry structure analysis is the leverage that buyers can exert on firms. Is technology changing the balance of power between customers and companies? If so, how should business respond?

Blogs offer a mechanism for consumers to share their experiences—good or bad—regarding different companies. Bloggers first emerged in the late 1990s, and today the Technorati search engine currently monitors roughly 100 million blogs. With the wealth of this "citizen media" available, what are the implications for consumer power? One of the most famous cases of a blogger drawing attention to a company was Jeff Jarvis of the Web site http://www.buzzmachine.com. Jarvis, who writes on media topics, was having problems with his Dell computer and shared his experiences on the Web. Literally thousands of other people recounted similar experiences, and the phenomena became known as "Dell hell." Eventually, Dell created its own corporate blog in an effort to deflect this wave of consumer criticism. What are the implications of the rapid growth in blogs? Work in a group on the following exercise.

Part One

Visit a corporate blog. Only a small percentage of large firms maintain a blog presence on the Internet. *Hint:* Multiple wikis online provide lists of such companies. A Web search using the term *Fortune 500 blogs* will turn up several options. Review the content of the firm's blog. Was it updated regularly or not? Multiple contributors or just one? What was the writing style?

Did it read like a marketing brochure or something more informal? Did the blog allow viewer comments or post replies to consumer questions?

Part Two

Based on the information you collected in the blog review, answer the following questions:

- Have you ever used blogs to help make decisions about something that you are considering purchasing? If so, how did the blog material affect your decision? What factors would make you more (or less) likely to rely on a blog in making your decision?
- How did the content of corporate blogs affect your perception of that company and its good and services? Did it make you more or less likely to view the company favorably, or have no effect at all?
- Why do so few large companies maintain blogs?

EXERCISE 2: CREATING A SHARED VISION

Drawing on an analysis of internal and external conditions, firms create a mission and vision as a cornerstone of their strategy. This exercise examines some of the challenges associated with creating a firm's shared direction.

Part One

The instructor will break the class into a set of small teams. Half of the teams will be given an "A" designation, and the other half assigned as "B." Each individual team will need to plan a time outside class to complete Part 2; the exercise should take about half an hour.

Teams given the A designation will meet in a face-to-face setting. Each team member will need paper and a pen or pen-

cil. Your meeting location should be free from distraction. The location should have enough space so that no person can see another's notepad.

Teams given the B designation will meet electronically. You may choose to meet through text messaging or IM. Be sure to confirm everyone's contact information and meeting time beforehand.

Part Two

Each team member prepares a drawing of a real structure. It can be a famous building, a monument, museum, or even your dorm. Do not tell other team members what you drew.

Randomly select one team member. The goal is for everyone else to prepare a drawing as similar to the selected team member as possible. That person is not allowed to show his or her drawing to the rest of the team. The rest of the group can ask questions about the drawing, but only ones that can be answered "yes" or "no."

After 10 minutes, have everyone compare their drawings. If you are meeting electronically, describe your drawings, and save them for the next time your team meets face to face.

Next, select a second team member and repeat this process again.

Part Three

In class, discuss the following questions:

- How easy (or hard) was it for you to figure out the "vision" of your team members?
- Did you learn anything in the first iteration that made the second drawing more successful?
- What similarities might you find between this exercise and the challenge of sharing a vision among company employees?
- How did the communication structure affect your process and outcomes?

VIDEO | CASE

THE VALUE OF SETTING A LONG-TERM STRATEGY

Anders Dahlvig/Group President and CEO/IKEA Services

IKEA is a brand famous for its focus on innovative solutions to the business of selling high-quality, low-price home furnishings. Anders Dahlvig, IKEA's Group President and CEO, argues that long-term strategic planning is a key to their success. For the financial year ending August 2008, IKEA posted a 7 percent increase in sales over the prior annual period, recording €21.1 billion in revenue. The firm has more than 128,000 employees and operates in 24 countries.

Be prepared to discuss the following concepts and questions in class:

Concepts
- Vision and mission
- Long-term strategy
- Stakeholders
- Global economy
- Strategic leaders
- Organizational culture

Questions
1. What is this firm's vision?
2. What is the firm's mission or business idea?
3. Describe its competitive advantage. Why do you think competitors have found this concept difficult to imitate?
4. What is in the news about this company?
5. Describe Anders Dahlvig as a strategic leader.
6. Do you believe Anders Dahlvig is constrained in his strategic decision making because of the unique organizational culture at IKEA, or is he free to create and implement strategic decisions as he sees best for the firm?

CHAPTER 2

The External Environment: Opportunities, Threats, Competition, and Competitor Analysis

Studying this chapter should provide you with the strategic management knowledge needed to:

1. Explain the importance of analyzing and understanding the firm's external environment.

2. Define and describe the general environment and the industry environment.

3. Discuss the four activities of the external environmental analysis process.

4. Name and describe the general environment's seven segments.

5. Identify the five competitive forces and explain how they determine an industry's profit potential.

6. Define strategic groups and describe their influence on the firm.

7. Describe what firms need to know about their competitors and different methods (including ethical standards) used to collect intelligence about them.

PHILIP MORRIS INTERNATIONAL: THE EFFECTS OF ITS EXTERNAL ENVIRONMENT

Employing over 75,000 people, Philip Morris International (PMI) is the leading international tobacco company in terms of market share. The firm's product line features seven of the world's top 15 brands, including Marlboro, which is the top-selling cigarette brand on a worldwide basis. (In 2008, PMI sold 310.7 billion Marlboro cigarettes. Altria Group, Inc., which spun-off PMI from its operations in March 2008, sells the Marlboro brand in the United States.) PMI sells products in over 160 countries, holds about a 16 percent share of the total international cigarette market outside the United States, and has the largest market share in 11 of the top 30 cigarette markets, excluding the U.S. market. PMI continues to innovate across its brand portfolio to serve different needs of various customers and as a means of stimulating sales of its products.

As is true for all firms, the strategic actions (see Figure 1.1) PMI is taking today and will take in the future are influenced by conditions in its external environment. The challenge for a firm's strategic leaders (including those at PMI) is to understand what the external environment's effects are on the firm today and to predict (with as high a degree of accuracy as possible) what those effects will be on the firm's strategic actions in the future.

The regulations that are a part of the *political/legal segment* of PMI's general environment (the general environment and all of its segments are discussed in this chapter) affect how PMI conducts its business. In general, the regulations regarding the selling of tobacco products are less restrictive in global markets than in the U.S. market. Nonetheless, PMI

Catherine Karnow/CORBIS

Advertising such as this Marlboro Man billboard is more highly restricted in the United States than in many global markets.

must be aware of how the regulations might change in the markets it does serve as well as those it may desire to serve in the future and must prepare to deal with these changes. Aware of the possible effects of the political/legal environment on its operations in the future, PMI has made the following public pronouncement: "We are proactively working with governments and other stakeholders to advocate for a comprehensive, consistent and cohesive regulatory framework that applies to all to tobacco products and is based on the principle of harm reduction." (Encouraging all companies competing in the tobacco industry to develop products with the potential to reduce the risk of tobacco-related diseases is part of the harm reduction principle.)

The *global segment* of the general environment also affects PMI's strategic actions. To pursue what it believes are opportunities to sell additional quantities of its products, PMI recently acquired companies in Colombia, Indonesia, and Serbia to establish a stronger foothold in emerging markets. The facts that taxes on tobacco products are lower in many emerging markets compared to developed markets and that the consumption of tobacco products is increasing in these markets are conditions in the external environment influencing the choices PMI makes as it seeks growth. These conditions differ from those in the U.S. market where cigarette consumption is declining by approximately 3 to 4 percent annually and where in mid-2009, the U.S. Congress passed legislation (which President Obama then signed into law) that empowered the Food and Drug Administration to regulate "cigarettes and other forms of tobacco for the first time."

While cigarette consumption is increasing in some of its markets, PMI predicts that this will not always be the case. In this respect, PMI anticipates that changes will occur in the *sociocultural segment* of the general environment such that fewer people will be willing to risk disease by consuming tobacco products. Anticipating this possibility, PMI recently formed a joint venture with Swedish Match AB to market smokeless tobacco worldwide. This collaborative arrangement unites the world's largest seller of smokeless tobacco (Swedish Match) with a marketing powerhouse that has a strong global presence across multiple markets (PMI). Because it is less dangerous than cigarettes in terms of disease, smokeless tobacco is seen as a product with long-term growth potential. PMI will likely remain committed to the importance of its social performance as it pursues this joint venture. As a measure of the effects of the *physical environment segment* of the external environment, PMI says that it is strongly committed to the "promotion of sustainable tobacco farming, the efficient use of natural resources, the reduction of waste in (its) manufacturing processes, eliminating child labor and giving back to the communities in which (it) operates."

Sources: 2009, Altria Group Inc., *Standard & Poor's Stock Report*, http://standardandpoors.com, April 25; 2009, Philip Morris International home page, http://www.philipinternational.com, May 15; N. Byrnes & F. Balfour, Philip Morris' global race, *BusinessWeek Online*, http://www.businessweek.com, April 23; K. Helliker, 2009, Smokeless tobacco to get push by venture overseas, *Wall Street Journal Online*, http://www.wsj.com, February 4; A. Pressman, 2009, Philip Morris unbound, *BusinessWeek*, May 4, 66; D. Wilson, 2009, Senate votes to allow FDA to regulate tobacco, *Wall Street Journal Online*, http://www.wsj.com, June 12.

As described in the Opening Case and suggested by research, the external environment affects a firm's strategic actions.[1] For example, Philip Morris International (PMI) seeks to grow through a joint venture with Swedish Match AB to distribute smokeless tobacco in multiple global markets.[2] Because it is less dangerous than cigarettes in terms of contributing to disease, smokeless tobacco is thought to have growth potential in many markets.[3] In addition to this health-related influence that is a part of the sociocultural segment of PMI's external environment, the firm's strategic actions are affected by conditions in other segments of its general environment, such as the political/legal and the physical environment segments. As we explain in this chapter, a firm's external environment creates both opportunities (e.g., the opportunity for PMI to enter the smokeless tobacco market) and threats (e.g., the possibility that additional regulations in its markets will reduce consumption of PMI's tobacco products). Collectively, opportunities and threats affect a firm's strategic actions.[4]

Regardless of the industry in which they compete, the external environment influences firms as they seek strategic competitiveness and the earning of above-average returns. This chapter focuses on how firms analyze their external environment. The understanding about conditions in its external environment that the firm gains by analyzing that environment is matched with knowledge about its internal organization (discussed in the next chapter) as the foundation for forming the firm's vision, developing its mission, and identifying and implementing strategic actions (see Figure 1.1).

As noted in Chapter 1, the environmental conditions in the current global economy differ from historical conditions. For example, technological changes and the continuing growth of information gathering and processing capabilities increase the need for firms to develop effective competitive actions on a timely basis.[5] (In slightly different words, firms have little time to correct errors when implementing their competitive actions.) The rapid sociological changes occurring in many countries affect labor practices and the nature of products demanded by increasingly diverse consumers. Governmental policies and laws also affect where and how firms choose to compete.[6] In addition, changes to nations' financial regulatory systems that were enacted in 2009 and beyond are expected to increase the complexity of organizations' financial transactions.[7]

Viewed in their totality, the conditions that affect firms today indicate that for most organizations, their external environment is filled with uncertainty.[8] To successfully deal with this uncertainty and to achieve strategic competitiveness and thrive, firms must be aware of and fully understand the different segments of the external environment.

Firms understand the external environment by acquiring information about competitors, customers, and other stakeholders to build their own base of knowledge and capabilities.[9] On the basis of the new information, firms take actions, such as building new capabilities and core competencies, in hopes of buffering themselves from any negative environmental effects and to pursue opportunities as the basis for better serving their stakeholders' needs.[10] A firm's strategic actions are influenced by the conditions in the three parts (the general, industry, and competitor) of its external environment (see Figure 2.1).

The General, Industry, and Competitor Environments

The **general environment** is composed of dimensions in the broader society that influence an industry and the firms within it.[11] We group these dimensions into seven environmental *segments:* demographic, economic, political/legal, sociocultural, technological, global, and physical. Examples of *elements* analyzed in each of these segments are shown in Table 2.1.

Firms cannot directly control the general environment's segments. The recent bankruptcy filings by General Motors and Chrysler Corporation highlight this fact. These firms could not directly control various parts of their external environment, including the economic and political/legal segments; however, these segments are influencing the actions the firms are taking now including the forming of Chrysler's alliance with Fiat.[12] Because firms cannot directly control the segments of their external environment, successful ones learn how to gather the information needed to understand all segments and their implications for selecting and implementing the firm's strategies.

AP Photo/Seth Wenig

A woman bearing Chrysler paperwork waits to enter U.S. Bankruptcy Court for the Chrysler bankruptcy case in New York, Monday, May 4, 2009. Aspects of the external environment both contributed to Chrysler's bankruptcy filing as well as influenced the terms under which it quickly re-emerged.

Figure 2.1 The External Environment

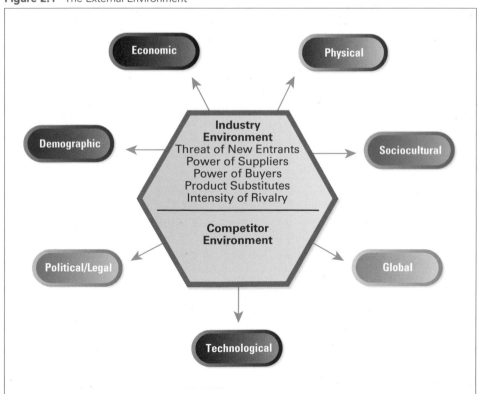

The **general environment** is composed of dimensions in the broader society that influence an industry and the firms within it.

Table 2.1 The General Environment: Segments and Elements

Demographic Segment	• Population size • Age structure • Geographic distribution	• Ethnic mix • Income distribution
Economic Segment	• Inflation rates • Interest rates • Trade deficits or surpluses • Budget deficits or surpluses	• Personal savings rate • Business savings rates • Gross domestic product
Political/Legal Segment	• Antitrust laws • Taxation laws • Deregulation philosophies	• Labor training laws • Educational philosophies and policies
Sociocultural Segment	• Women in the workforce • Workforce diversity • Attitudes about the quality of work life	• Shifts in work and career preferences • Shifts in preferences regarding product and service characteristics
Technological Segment	• Product innovations • Applications of knowledge	• Focus of private and government-supported R&D expenditures • New communication technologies
Global Segment	• Important political events • Critical global markets	• Newly industrialized countries • Different cultural and institutional attributes
Physical Environment Segment	• Energy consumption • Practices used to develop energy sources • Renewable energy efforts • Minimizing a firm's environmental footprint	• Availability of water as a resource • Producing environmentally friendly products

The **industry environment** is the set of factors that directly influences a firm and its competitive actions and responses:[13] the threat of new entrants, the power of suppliers, the power of buyers, the threat of product substitutes, and the intensity of rivalry among competitors. In total, the interactions among these five factors determine an industry's profit potential; in turn, the industry's profit potential influences the choices each firm makes about its strategic actions. The challenge for a firm is to locate a position within an industry where it can favorably influence the five factors or where it can successfully defend against their influence. The greater a firm's capacity to favorably influence its industry environment, the greater the likelihood that the firm will earn above-average returns.

How companies gather and interpret information about their competitors is called *competitor analysis.* Understanding the firm's competitor environment complements the insights provided by studying the general and industry environments.[14] This means, for example, that Philip Morris International wants to learn as much as it can about its two

The **industry environment** is the set of factors that directly influences a firm and its competitive actions and competitive responses: the threat of new entrants, the power of suppliers, the power of buyers, the threat of product substitutes, and the intensity of rivalry among competitors.

major competitors—British American Tobacco and Japan Tobacco International—while also learning about its general and industry environments.

Analysis of the general environment is focused on environmental trends while an analysis of the industry environment is focused on the factors and conditions influencing an industry's profitability potential and an analysis of competitors is focused on predicting competitors' actions, responses, and intentions. In combination, the results of these three analyses influence the firm's vision, mission, and strategic actions. Although we discuss each analysis separately, performance improves when the firm integrates the insights provided by analyses of the general environment, the industry environment, and the competitor environment.

External Environmental Analysis

Most firms face external environments that are highly turbulent, complex, and global— conditions that make interpreting those environments difficult.[15] To cope with often ambiguous and incomplete environmental data and to increase understanding of the general environment, firms engage in external environmental analysis. This analysis has four parts: scanning, monitoring, forecasting, and assessing (see Table 2.2). Analyzing the external environment is a difficult, yet significant, activity.[16]

Identifying opportunities and threats is an important objective of studying the general environment. An **opportunity** is a condition in the general environment that if exploited effectively, helps a company achieve strategic competitiveness. For example, recent market research results suggested to Procter & Gamble (P&G) that an increasing number of men across the globe are interested in fragrances and skin care products. To take advantage of this opportunity, P&G is reorienting "… its beauty business by gender, 'to better serve him and her' rather than its typical organization around product categories."[17]

A **threat** is a condition in the general environment that may hinder a company's efforts to achieve strategic competitiveness.[18] The once-revered firm Polaroid can attest to the seriousness of external threats. Polaroid was a leader in its industry and considered one of the top 50 firms in the United States. When its competitors developed photographic equipment using digital technology, Polaroid was unprepared and never responded effectively. It filed for bankruptcy in 2001. In 2002, the former Polaroid Corp. was sold to Bank One's OEP Imaging unit, which promptly changed its own name to Polaroid Corp. Jacques Nasser, a former CEO at Ford, took over as CEO at Polaroid and found that the brand had continued life. Nasser used the brand in a partnership with Petters Group to put the Polaroid name on "TVs and DVDs made in Asian factories and sell them through Wal-Mart and Target."[19] Polaroid went public again and was later

> An **opportunity** is a condition in the general environment that if exploited effectively, helps a company achieve strategic competitiveness.

> A **threat** is a condition in the general environment that may hinder a company's efforts to achieve strategic competitiveness.

Table 2.2 Components of the External Environmental Analysis

Scanning	• Identifying early signals of environmental changes and trends
Monitoring	• Detecting meaning through ongoing observations of environmental changes and trends
Forecasting	• Developing projections of anticipated outcomes based on monitored changes and trends
Assessing	• Determining the timing and importance of environmental changes and trends for firms' strategies and their management

sold to Petters Group in 2005. However, the firm then failed again, resulting in another bankruptcy filing in December 2008. On April 16, 2009, Polaroid was sold to a joint venture of Hilco Consumer Capital LP of Toronto and Gordon Brothers Brands LLC of Boston. At the time, the only assets remaining were the firm's name, its intellectual property, and its photography collection.[20] Thus, not responding to threats in its external environment resulted in the failure of the once highly successful Polaroid Corp.

Firms use several sources to analyze the general environment, including a wide variety of printed materials (such as trade publications, newspapers, business publications, and the results of academic research and public polls), trade shows and suppliers, customers, and employees of public-sector organizations. People in *boundary-spanning* positions can obtain a great deal of this type of information. Salespersons, purchasing managers, public relations directors, and customer service representatives, each of whom interacts with external constituents, are examples of boundary-spanning positions.

Scanning

Scanning entails the study of all segments in the general environment. Through scanning, firms identify early signals of potential changes in the general environment and detect changes that are already under way.[21] Scanning often reveals ambiguous, incomplete, or unconnected data and information. Thus, environmental scanning is challenging but critically important for firms, especially those competing in highly volatile environments.[22] In addition, scanning activities must be aligned with the organizational context; a scanning system designed for a volatile environment is inappropriate for a firm in a stable environment.[23]

Many firms use special software to help them identify events that are taking place in the environment and that are announced in public sources. For example, news event detection uses information-based systems to categorize text and reduce the trade-off between an important missed event and false alarm rates.[24] The Internet provides significant opportunities for scanning. Amazon.com, for example, records significant information about individuals visiting its Web site, particularly if a purchase is made. Amazon then welcomes these customers by name when they visit the Web site again. The firm sends messages to customers about specials and new products similar to those they purchased in previous visits. A number of other companies such as Netflix also collect demographic data about their customers in an attempt to identify their unique preferences (demographics is one of the segments in the general environment).

Philip Morris International continuously scans segments of its external environment to detect current conditions and to anticipate changes that might take place in different segments. For example, PMI always studies various nations' tax policies on cigarettes (these policies are part of the political/legal segment). The reason for this is that raising cigarette taxes might reduce sales while lowering these taxes might increase sales.

Monitoring

When *monitoring,* analysts observe environmental changes to see if an important trend is emerging from among those spotted through scanning.[25] Critical to successful monitoring is the firm's ability to detect meaning in different environmental events and trends. For example, the buying power of Hispanics is projected to increase to $1.3 trillion by 2013 (up from $984 billion in 2008). Particularly in the southwestern part of the United States, grocers believe that this growing population will increase its purchases of ethnic-oriented food products.[26] The recent financial crisis found companies carefully monitoring the emerging trend of customers deciding to "go back to basics" when purchasing products. A reduction in brand loyalty may be an outcome of this trend. Companies selling carefully branded products should monitor this trend to determine its meaning—both in the short and long term.[27]

Effective monitoring requires the firm to identify important stakeholders as the foundation for serving their unique needs.[28] (Stakeholders' unique needs are described in Chapter 1.) Scanning and monitoring are particularly important when a firm competes in an industry with high technological uncertainty.[29] Scanning and monitoring can provide the firm with information; they also serve as a means of importing knowledge about markets and about how to successfully commercialize new technologies the firm has developed.[30]

Forecasting

Scanning and monitoring are concerned with events and trends in the general environment at a point in time. When *forecasting*, analysts develop feasible projections of what might happen, and how quickly, as a result of the changes and trends detected through scanning and monitoring.[31] For example, analysts might forecast the time that will be required for a new technology to reach the marketplace, the length of time before different corporate training procedures are required to deal with anticipated changes in the composition of the workforce, or how much time will elapse before changes in governmental taxation policies affect consumers' purchasing patterns.

Forecasting events and outcomes accurately is challenging. Already in place, the trend of firms outsourcing call center work and logistics' activities to companies specializing in these activities appeared to accelerate as a result of the recent global crisis. Having noticed (through scanning) and monitoring these outsourcing trends for some time, logistics companies such as FedEx and United Parcel Service and call center provider Convergys are developing forecasts about possible increases in their business and how long the increasing trend of using their services might continue.[32] On the other hand, Procter & Gamble (P&G) and Colgate-Palmolive, two firms selling carefully branded consumer products, are now forecasting the effects of the trend for retailers to "… tout their lower-priced, private-label goods and pressure their suppliers for lower prices." Thus, P&G and Colgate are forecasting the effects of the twin issues of the decisions by the retailers to whom they sell products to manufacture and sell their own consumer products while simultaneously seeking lower prices on the products they do buy from them.[33]

Assessing

The objective of *assessing* is to determine the timing and significance of the effects of environmental changes and trends that have been identified.[34] Through scanning, monitoring, and forecasting, analysts are able to understand the general environment. Going a step further, the intent of assessment is to specify the implications of that understanding. Without assessment, the firm is left with data that may be interesting but are of unknown competitive relevance. Even if formal assessment is inadequate, the appropriate interpretation of that information is important: "Research found that how accurate senior executives are about their competitive environments is indeed less important for strategy and corresponding organizational changes than the way in which they interpret information about their environments."[35] Thus, although gathering and organizing information is important, appropriately interpreting that intelligence to determine if an identified trend in the external environment is an opportunity or threat is equally important.

As previously noted, through forecasting P&G and Colgate have identified a trend among many of the retailers to whom they sell their carefully branded products. Essentially, the trend is for these retailers to pressure firms such as P&G, Colgate, H. J. Heinz, and Kellogg's—to name a few—to reduce the prices at which they sell their products to the retailers. The ability of these retailers to produce and sell their own private-label merchandise supports their efforts to receive lower prices from branding giants such as those mentioned.

In addition, firms with well-known brands have detected a trend among consumers to receive more "value" when purchasing branded products. Having forecasted that this

CONSUMERS' DESIRE TO RECEIVE ADDITIONAL VALUE WHEN PURCHASING BRAND-NAME PRODUCTS

In Chapter 3, we note that *value* is measured by a product's performance characteristics and by its attributes for which customers are willing to pay. A number of companies producing brand-name products believe that the recent global crisis is producing a trend in which what customers *value* is changing. In slightly different words, through monitoring and scanning, companies are forecasting that the performance characteristics and product attributes for which today's customers are willing to pay are changing as a result of the recent global crisis. In addition, through assessment, companies producing name-brand products believe that changes in how customers define value are significant and may be long-lasting. In response, some firms are changing some of the performance characteristics and attributes of their products to create more value for customers. A comment from an analyst about this trend is: "… companies are having to consider their 'value' equation to try to serve the millions of consumers who either can't afford premium experiences, or just don't want them anymore."

Let's consider some examples of "different" value that companies are now providing to customers. The desire for smaller homes is a trend spotted by builders of premium-priced homes. The fact that the average size of a new home built in the United States declined in 2008 for the first time in 35 years is an indicator of this trend. Builders of premium homes are using better designs to improve space utilization and traffic flow and increases in energy efficiency to create more value for customers. Facilitating these builders' efforts are changes appliance manufacturers are making to the performance characteristics of their products, also in attempts to create more value for their customers. General Electric, for example, is offering a hybrid electric water heater that is estimated to save consumers $250 annually. The value created by this product is twofold—reduced cost to the consumer and a reduction to energy consumption as a benefit to society as a whole. Kohler is offering energy-efficient faucets, toilets, and showerheads at virtually the same price as its less energy-efficient products. Thus, these products also create customer value in the form of reduced cost while being environmentally friendly. Other appliance firms such as Whirlpool are producing products with similar performance characteristics to create customer value.

Elmund Sumner/Photolibrary

The attributes desired by buyers of premium homes are changing, and home builders are responding by delivering value in the form of greater energy efficiency and more modern designs. Would a smaller, more environmentally efficient home be of more value to you than a larger, less efficient one?

Other types of companies are also redefining the value their products provide to customers. Believing that "… value is not just cost; it's also taste, nutrition and quality," Del Monte Foods's advertising campaigns now emphasize that compared to some frozen and even fresh items, canned foods can offer better value when the customer combines cost with nutritional benefits. Frito-Lay (a division of PepsiCo) is increasing customer value by adding 20 percent more product to selected bags of Cheetos, Fritos, and Tostitos without increasing prices. Michaels, a large chain of craft outlets, now emphasizes that when customers purchase their goods as raw materials for making various items they are becoming more sustainable in that they are "making stuff" rather than simply "buying more stuff."

As these examples suggest, all types of companies (and especially those selling brand-name products) are trying to create a different type of value for customers in response to trends they are observing in their general environment. Regardless of the good or service a firm offers, it seems that the following words from an analyst capture the challenge facing today's companies: "So here's a call to all companies: evaluate everything you are offering consumers to see how you can infuse the value of good value into your brand."

Sources: A. Athavaley, 2009, Eco-friendly—and frugal, *Wall Street Journal Online*, http://www.wsj.com, February 11; S. Elliott, 2009, Food brands compete to stretch a dollar, *New York Times Online*, http://www.nytimes.com, May 10; D. Kaplan, 2009, Value-oriented chains thrive amid recession, *Houston Chronicle Online*, http://www.chron.com, April 24; M. Penn, 2009, Value is the new green, *Wall Street Journal Online*, http://www.wsj.com, March 13; C. C. Miller, 2008, For craft sales, the recession is a help, *New York Times Online*, http://www.nytimes.com, December 23.

trend toward "wanting more value" may last beyond the current global recession, many of these firms are taking actions in response to their assessment of the significance of what may be a long-lasting trend toward value purchases. In the Strategic Focus, we describe actions some firms with well-known brands are taking in response to an assessment that this trend may have significant effects on their operations, at least in the short run if not longer term as well.

Segments of the General Environment

The general environment is composed of segments that are external to the firm (see Table 2.1). Although the degree of impact varies, these environmental segments affect all industries and the firms competing in them. The challenge to each firm is to scan, monitor, forecast, and assess the elements in each segment to determine their effects on the firm. Effective scanning, monitoring, forecasting, and assessing are vital to the firm's efforts to recognize and evaluate opportunities and threats.

The Demographic Segment

The **demographic segment** is concerned with a population's size, age structure, geographic distribution, ethnic mix, and income distribution.[36] Demographic segments are commonly analyzed on a global basis because of their potential effects across countries' borders and because many firms compete in global markets.

Population Size

The world's population doubled (from 3 billion to 6 billion) in the roughly 40-year period between 1959 and 1999. Current projects suggest that population growth will continue in the twenty-first century, but at a slower pace. The U.S. Census Bureau projects that the world's population will be 9 billion by 2040.[37] By 2050, India is expected to be the most populous nation in the world (with over 1.8 billion people). China, the United States, Indonesia, and Pakistan are predicted to be the next four largest nations by population count in 2050. Firms seeking to find growing markets in which to sell their goods and services want to recognize the market potential that may exist for them in these five nations.

While observing the population of different nations and regions of the world, firms also want to study changes occurring within different populations to assess their strategic implications. For example, in 2006, 20 percent of Japan's citizens were 65 or older, while the United States and China will not reach this level until 2036.[38] Aging populations are a significant problem for countries because of the need for workers and the burden of

The **demographic segment** is concerned with a population's size, age structure, geographic distribution, ethnic mix, and income distribution.

funding retirement programs. In Japan and other countries, employees are urged to work longer to overcome these problems. Interestingly, the United States has a higher birthrate and significant immigration, placing it in a better position than Japan and other European nations.

Age Structure

As noted earlier, in Japan and other countries, the world's population is rapidly aging. In North America and Europe, millions of baby boomers are approaching retirement. However, even in developing countries with large numbers of people under the age of 35, birth rates have been declining sharply. In China, for example, by 2040 there will be more than 400 million people over the age of 60. The more than 90 million baby boomers in North America may postpone retirement given the recent financial crisis. In fact, data now suggest that baby boomers (those born between 1946 and 1965) are struggling to meet their retirement goals and are uncertain if they will actually be able to retire as originally expected. This is partly because of declines in the value of their homes as well as declines in their other retirement investments[39]—a number of baby boomers experienced at least a 20 percent decline in their retirement assets between 2007 and 2008. The possibility of future declines is creating uncertainty for baby boomers about how to invest and when they might be able to retire.[40] On the other hand, delayed retirements by baby boomers with value-creating skills may facilitate firms' efforts to successfully implement their strategies. Moreover, delayed retirements may allow companies to think of creative ways for skilled, long-time employees to impart their accumulated knowledge to younger employees as they work a bit longer than originally anticipated.

Geographic Distribution

For decades, the U.S. population has been shifting from the north and east to the west and south. Firms should consider the effects of this shift in demographics as well. For example, Florida is the U.S. state with the largest percentage of its population (17.6 percent) 65 years or older.[41] Thus, companies providing goods and services that are targeted to senior citizens might pay close attention to this group's geographic preference for states in the south (such as Florida) and the southwest (such as Texas). Similarly, the trend of relocating from metropolitan to nonmetropolitan areas continues in the United States. These trends are changing local and state governments' tax bases. In turn, business firms' decisions regarding location are influenced by the degree of support that different taxing agencies offer as well as the rates at which these agencies tax businesses.

Geographic distribution patterns are not identical throughout the world. For example, in China, 60 percent of the population lives in rural areas; however, the growth is in urban communities such as Shanghai (with a current population in excess of 13 million) and Beijing (over 12.2 million). These data suggest that firms seeking to sell their products in China should recognize the growth in metropolitan areas rather than in rural areas.[42]

Ethnic Mix

The ethnic mix of countries' populations continues to change. For example, with a population in excess of 40 million, Hispanics are now the largest ethnic minority in the United States. In fact, the U.S. Hispanic market is the third largest "Latin American" economy behind Brazil and Mexico. Spanish is now the dominant language in parts of U.S. states such as Texas, California, Florida, and New Mexico.[43] Given these facts, some firms might want to assess the degree to which their goods or services could be adapted to serve the unique needs of Hispanic consumers. This is particularly appropriate for companies competing in consumer sectors such as grocery stores, movie studios, financial services, and clothing stores.

Changes in the ethnic mix also affect a workforce's composition.[44] In the United States, for example, the population and labor force will continue to diversify, as immigration accounts for a sizable part of growth. Projections are that the combined Latino and Asian population shares will increase to more than 20 percent of the total U.S. population by 2014.[45] Interestingly, much of this immigrant workforce is bypassing high-cost coastal cities and settling in smaller rural towns. Many of these workers are in low-wage, labor-intensive industries such as construction, food service, lodging, and landscaping.[46] For this reason, if border security is tightened, these industries will likely face labor shortages.

Income Distribution

Understanding how income is distributed within and across populations informs firms of different groups' purchasing power and discretionary income. Studies of income distributions suggest that although living standards have improved over time, variations exist within and between nations.[47] Of interest to firms are the average incomes of households and individuals. For instance, the increase in dual-career couples has had a notable effect on average incomes. Although real income has been declining in general in some nations, the household income of dual-career couples has increased, especially in the United States. These figures yield strategically relevant information for firms. For instance, research indicates that whether an employee is part of a dual-career couple can strongly influence the willingness of the employee to accept an international assignment.[48]

The assessment by some that in 2005 about 55 percent of the world's population could be defined as "middle class" generates interesting possibilities for many firms. (For the purpose of this survey, middle class was defined as people with one third of their income left for discretionary spending after providing for basic food and shelter.) The size of this market may have "… immense implications for companies selling their products and services on a global scale."[49] Of course, the recent global financial crisis may affect the size of the world's "middle class."

The Economic Segment

The **economic environment** refers to the nature and direction of the economy in which a firm competes or may compete.[50] In general, firms seek to compete in relatively stable economies with strong growth potential. Because nations are interconnected as a result of the global economy, firms must scan, monitor, forecast, and assess the health of their host nation and the health of the economies outside their host nation.

As firms prepare to compete during the second decade of the twenty-first century, the world's economic environment is quite uncertain. Some businesspeople were even beginning to question the ability of economists to provide valid and reliable predictions about trends to anticipate in the world's economic environment.[51] The lack of confidence in predictions from those specializing in providing such predictions complicates firms' efforts to understand the conditions they might face during future competitive battles.

In terms of specific economic environments, companies competing in Japan or desiring to do so might carefully evaluate the meaning of the position recently taken by some that this nation's economy has ingrained flaws such as "… unwieldy corporate structures, dogged loyalty to increasingly commoditized business lines and a history of punting problems into the future."[52] Because of its acknowledged growth potential, a number of companies are evaluating the possibility of entering Russia to compete or, for those already competing in that nation, to expand the scope of their operations. However, statements by analysts in mid-2009 that "the banking crisis in Russia is in its very beginning"[53] warrant careful attention. If this prediction comes true, the Russian economy could become destabilized. In contrast, Vietnam's economy was expanding during late 2009 and being recognized as one in which opportunities might exist for companies from across the globe to pursue.[54]

The **economic environment** refers to the nature and direction of the economy in which a firm competes or may compete.

The Political/Legal Segment

The **political/legal segment** is the arena in which organizations and interest groups compete for attention, resources, and a voice in overseeing the body of laws and regulations guiding interactions among nations as well as between firms and various local governmental agencies.[55] Essentially, this segment represents how organizations try to influence governments and how they try to understand the influences (current and projected) of those governments on their strategic actions.

When regulations are formed in response to new laws that are legislated (e.g., the Sarbanes-Oxley Act dealing with corporate governance—see Chapter 10 for more information), they often influence a firm's strategic actions. For example, less-restrictive regulations on firms' actions are a product of the recent global trend toward privatization of government-owned or government-regulated firms. Some believe that the transformation from state-owned to private firms occurring in multiple nations has substantial implications for the competitive landscapes in a number of countries and across multiple industries.[56] In the United States, the 2009 allocation by the federal government of $13 billion to high-speed train travel is expected to provide a critical boost to the nation's efforts to reduce traffic congestion and cut pollution.[57] For global firms manufacturing high-speed rail equipment, this political support in the United States of systems requiring their products is a trend to forecast and assess.

Firms must carefully analyze a new political administration's business-related policies and philosophies. Antitrust laws, taxation laws, industries chosen for deregulation, labor training laws, and the degree of commitment to educational institutions are areas in which an administration's policies can affect the operations and profitability of industries and individual firms across the globe. For example, early signals from President Obama's administration that policies might be formed with the intention of reducing the amount of work U.S. companies outsource to firms in other nations seemingly could affect information technology outsourcing firms based in countries such as India.[58] The introduction of legislation in the U.S. Congress during the early tenure of the Obama administration suggested at least some support for these stated intentions.[59] Thus, these companies might want to carefully examine the newly elected U.S. administration's intentions to understand their potential effects.

To deal with issues such as those we are describing, firms develop a political strategy to influence governmental policies that might affect them. Some argue that developing an effective political strategy is essential to the newly formed General Motors' efforts to achieve strategic competitiveness.[60] In addition, the effects of global governmental policies (e.g., those related to firms in India that are engaging in IT outsourcing work) on a firm's competitive position increase the need for firms to form an effective political strategy.[61]

Firms competing in the global economy encounter an interesting array of political/legal questions and issues. For example, in mid-2009, leaders from South Korea and the European Union remained committed to developing a free trade agreement between the relevant parties. At the time, the two parties had worked for over two years to develop an agreement that many thought would benefit both by creating a host of opportunities for firms to sell their goods and services in what would be a new market for them. The key political challenge affecting the parties' efforts was the European Union's decision not to permit "… refunds South Korea pays to local companies who import parts from third countries before exporting finished goods."[62] Both South Korea and European Union firms are monitoring the progress of these talks in order to be able to forecast the effects of a possible trade agreement on their strategic actions.

The Sociocultural Segment

The **sociocultural segment** is concerned with a society's attitudes and cultural values. Because attitudes and values form the cornerstone of a society, they often drive demographic, economic, political/legal, and technological conditions and changes.

The **political/legal segment** is the arena in which organizations and interest groups compete for attention, resources, and a voice in overseeing the body of laws and regulations guiding interactions among nations as well as between firms and various local governmental agencies.

The **sociocultural segment** is concerned with a society's attitudes and cultural values.

Societies' attitudes and cultural values appear to be undergoing possible changes at the start of the second decade of the twenty-first century. This seems to be the case in the United States and other nations as well. Attitudes and values about health care in the United States is an area where sociocultural changes might occur. Statistics are a driving force for these potential changes. For example, while the United States "... has the highest overall health care expenditure as well as the highest expenditure per capital of any country in the world,"[63] millions of the nation's citizens lack health insurance. Some feel that effective health care reform in the United States requires securing coverage for all citizens and lowering the cost of services.[64] Changes to the nature of health care policies and their delivery would likely affect business firms, meaning that they must carefully monitor this possibility and future trends regarding health care in order to anticipate the effects on their operations.

As the U.S. labor force has increased, it has also become more diverse as significantly more women and minorities from a variety of cultures entered. In 1993, the total U.S. workforce was slightly less than 130 million; in 2005, it was slightly greater than 148 million. It is predicted to grow to more than 192 million by 2050. In the same year, 2050, the U.S. workforce is forecasted to be composed of 48 percent female workers, 11 percent Asian American workers, 14 percent African American workers and 24 percent Hispanic workers.[65] The growing gender, ethnic, and cultural diversity in this workforce creates challenges and opportunities, including combining the best of both men's and women's traditional leadership styles. Although diversity in the workforce has the potential to improve performance, research indicates that management of diversity initiatives is required in order to reap these organizational benefits. Human resource practitioners are trained to successfully manage diversity issues to enhance positive outcomes.[66]

Another manifestation of changing attitudes toward work is the continuing growth of contingency workers (part-time, temporary, and contract employees) throughout the global economy. This trend is significant in several parts of the world, including Canada, Japan, Latin America, Western Europe, and the United States. In the United States, the fastest growing group of contingency workers is those with 15 to 20 years of work experience. The layoffs resulting from the recent global crisis and the loss of retirement income of many "baby boomers"—many of whom feel they must work longer to recover losses to their retirement portfolios—are a key reason for this. Companies interested in hiring on a temporary basis may benefit by gaining access to the long-term work experiences of these newly available workers.[67]

Although the lifestyle and workforce changes referenced previously reflect the values of the U.S. population, each country and culture has unique values and trends. As suggested earlier, national cultural values affect behavior in organizations and thus also influence organizational outcomes.[68] For example, the importance of collectivism and social relations in Chinese and Russian cultures lead to the open sharing of information and knowledge among members of an organization.[69] Knowledge sharing is important for defusing new knowledge in organizations and increasing the speed in implementing innovations. Personal relationships are especially important in China as *guanxi* (personal connections) has become a way of doing business within the country and for individuals to advance their careers in what is becoming a more open market society.[70] Understanding the importance of guanxi is critical for foreign firms doing business in China.

The Technological Segment

Pervasive and diversified in scope, technological changes affect many parts of societies. These effects occur primarily through new products, processes, and materials. The **technological segment** includes the institutions and activities involved with creating new knowledge and translating that knowledge into new outputs, products, processes, and materials.

Given the rapid pace of technological change, it is vital for firms to thoroughly study the technological segment.[71] The importance of these efforts is suggested by the finding that early adopters of new technology often achieve higher market shares and earn

STRATEGY RIGHT NOW

Read what one leading marketing consultant says about changing consumer attitudes and how company's should be adapting.

www.cengage.com/ management/hitt

The **technological segment** includes the institutions and activities involved with creating new knowledge and translating that knowledge into new outputs, products, processes, and materials.

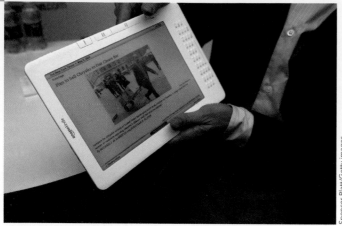

The Kindle DX, a new purpose-built reading device, features storage for up to 3,500 books. Amazon has also partnered with select major newspapers to offer readers discounts on the DX in return for long-term subscriptions.

higher returns. Thus, both large and small firms should continuously scan the external environment to identify potential substitutes for technologies that are in current use, as well as to identify newly emerging technologies from which their firm could derive competitive advantage.[72]

As a significant technological development, the Internet has become a remarkable capability to provide information easily, quickly, and effectively to an ever-increasing percentage of the world's population. Companies continue to study the Internet's capabilities to anticipate how it may allow them to create more value for customers in the future and to anticipate future trends.

In spite of the Internet's far-reaching effects, wireless communication technology is predicted to be the next significant technological opportunity for companies to apply when pursuing strategic competitiveness. Handheld devices and other wireless communications equipment are used to access a variety of network-based services. The use of handheld computers with wireless network connectivity, Web-enabled mobile phone handsets, and other emerging platforms (e.g., consumer Internet-access devices) is expected to increase substantially, soon becoming the dominant form of communication and commerce.[73]

Amazon.com's Kindle is an emerging wireless technology with capabilities firms should evaluate. In addition to books, customers can download an ever-increasing array of products to the Kindle. In mid-2009, over 275,000 of Amazon's books were available through the Kindle. Magazines and newspapers are available for purchase and use on the Kindle as well. The ease of reading daily newspapers on the Kindle without charge instead of waiting for hard copy to be delivered is threatening the very existence of a host of newspapers. The Kindle can also be used to surf the Web and send e-mail messages.[74]

Currently in its second generation, there is no doubt that Amazon will continue developing more advanced versions of the Kindle with each version having additional functionalities. As a service, the Kindle creates opportunities for those wanting to distribute knowledge electronically but is a threat to companies whose strategies call for the distribution of physical "hard copies" of written words. As such, many firms should study this technology to understand its competitive implications.

The Global Segment

The **global segment** includes relevant new global markets, existing markets that are changing, important international political events, and critical cultural and institutional characteristics of global markets.[75] There is little doubt that markets are becoming more global and that consumers as well as companies throughout the world accept this fact. Consider the automobile industry as an example of this. The global auto industry is one in which an increasing number of people believe that because "we live in a global community," consumers in multiple nations are willing to buy cars and trucks "from whatever area of the world."[76]

When studying the global segment, firms (including automobile manufacturers) should recognize that globalization of business markets may create *opportunities* to enter new markets as well as *threats* that new competitors from other economies may enter their market as well. This is both an opportunity and a threat for the world's automobile manufacturers—worldwide production capacity is now a potential threat to all of these global companies while entering another market to sell a company's products appears to be an opportunity. In terms of overcapacity, evidence indicated that in mid-2009, this global industry had "… the capacity to make an astounding 94 million vehicles each year (which is roughly) 34 million too many based on current sales."[77] This prediction of excess capacity suggests that most if not all automobile manufacturers may decide

The **global segment** includes relevant new global markets, existing markets that are changing, important international political events, and critical cultural and institutional characteristics of global markets.

to enter markets that are new to them in order to try to sell more of the units they are producing.

The markets from which firms generate sales and income are one indication of the degree to which they are participating in the global economy. For example, in 2008 53 percent of McDonald's operating income was accounted for by its international operations.[78] Food giant H. J. Heinz earns over 60 percent of its revenue outside the United States.[79] Consumer products giant Procter & Gamble, with operations in over 180 countries, recently generated over 56 percent of its sales revenue in markets outside the United States.[80] Thus, for these companies and so many others, understanding the conditions of today's global segment and being able to predict future conditions is critical to their success.

The global segment presents firms with both opportunities and threats or risks. Because of the threats and risks, some firms choose to take a more cautious approach to competing in international markets. These firms participate in what some refer to as *globalfocusing*. Globalfocusing often is used by firms with moderate levels of international operations who increase their internationalization by focusing on global niche markets.[81] In this way, they build on and use their special competencies and resources while limiting their risks with the niche market. Another way in which firms limit their risks in international markets is to focus their operations and sales in one region of the world.[82] In this way, they can build stronger relationships in and knowledge of their markets. As they build these strengths, rivals find it more difficult to enter their markets and compete successfully.

In all instances, firms competing in global markets should recognize the different sociocultural and institutional attributes of global markets. Earlier, we mentioned that South Korea and the European Union remain committed to developing a trade agreement that benefits both parties. If this happens, European Union companies (as well as those from other regions of the world as well) who choose to compete in South Korea must understand the value placed on hierarchical order, formality, and self-control, as well as on duty rather than rights. Furthermore, Korean ideology emphasizes communitarianism, a characteristic of many Asian countries. Korea's approach differs from those of Japan and China, however, in that it focuses on *inhwa*, or harmony. Inhwa is based on a respect of hierarchical relationships and obedience to authority. Alternatively, the approach in China stresses *guanxi*—personal relationships or good connections—while in Japan, the focus is on *wa*, or group harmony and social cohesion.[83] The institutional context of China suggests a major emphasis on centralized planning by the government. The Chinese government provides incentives to firms to develop alliances with foreign firms having sophisticated technology in hopes of building knowledge and introducing new technologies to the Chinese markets over time.[84]

The Physical Environment Segment

The **physical environment segment** refers to potential and actual changes in the physical environment and business practices that are intended to positively respond to and deal with those changes.[85] Concerned with trends oriented to sustaining the world's physical environment, firms recognize that ecological, social, and economic systems interactively influence what happens in this particular segment.[86]

There are many parts or attributes of the physical environment that firms should consider as they try to identify trends in this segment. Some argue that global warming is a trend firms and nations should carefully examine in efforts to predict any potential effects on the global society as well as on their business operations.[87] Energy consumption is another part of the physical environment that concerns both organizations and nations. Canada, for example, "… has formulated various strategic measures to accelerate the development of energy efficiency systems and renewable energy technologies and has made significant progress."[88]

Because of increasing concern about sustaining the quality of the physical environment, a number of companies are developing environmentally friendly policies.

The **physical environment segment** refers to potential and actual changes in the physical environment and business practices that are intended to positively respond to and deal with those changes.

Target Corporation operates in ways that will minimize the firm's environmental footprint. In the company's words, "Target strives to be a responsible steward of the environment. In addition to complying with all environmental legislation, we seek to understand our impact and continuously improve our business practices in many areas."[89] (Additional commentary about Target's actions toward the physical environment appears in a Strategic Focus in Chapter 4.) As noted in the Opening Case, Philip Morris International is committed to sustainable tobacco farming and the efficient use of resources in recognition of the effects of its operations on the physical environment.

We discuss other firms' efforts to "reduce their environmental footprint" and to be good stewards of the physical environment as a result of doing so in the following Strategic Focus. As we note, the number of "green" products companies are producing continues to increase.

As our discussion of the general environment shows, identifying anticipated changes and trends among external elements is a key objective of analyzing the firm's general environment. With a focus on the future, the analysis of the general environment allows firms to identify opportunities and threats. It is necessary to have a top management team with the experience, knowledge, and sensitivity required to effectively analyze this segment of the environment.[90] Also critical to a firm's choices of strategic actions to take is an understanding of its industry environment and its competitors; we consider these issues next.

Industry Environment Analysis

An **industry** is a group of firms producing products that are close substitutes. In the course of competition, these firms influence one another. Typically, industries include a rich mixture of competitive strategies that companies use in pursuing above-average returns. In part, these strategies are chosen because of the influence of an industry's characteristics.[91]

Compared with the general environment, the industry environment has a more direct effect on the firm's strategic competitiveness and ability to earn above-average returns.[92] An industry's profit potential is a function of five forces of competition: the threats posed by new entrants, the power of suppliers, the power of buyers, product substitutes, and the intensity of rivalry among competitors (see Figure 2.2, on page 52).

The five forces model of competition expands the arena for competitive analysis. Historically, when studying the competitive environment, firms concentrated on companies with which they competed directly. However, firms must search more broadly to recognize current and potential competitors by identifying potential customers as well as the firms serving them. For example, the communications industry is now broadly defined as encompassing media companies, telecoms, entertainment companies, and companies producing devices such as phones and iPods. In such an environment, firms must study many other industries to identify firms with capabilities (especially technology-based capabilities) that might be the foundation for producing a good or a service that can compete against what they are producing.[93] Using this perspective finds firms focusing on customers and their needs rather than on specific industry boundaries to define markets.

When studying the industry environment, firms must also recognize that suppliers can become a firm's competitors (by integrating forward) as can buyers (by integrating backward). For example, several firms have integrated forward in the pharmaceutical industry by acquiring distributors or wholesalers. In addition, firms choosing to enter a new market and those producing products that are adequate substitutes for existing products can become a company's competitors. Next, we examine the five forces the firm analyzes to understand the profitability potential within the industry (or a segment of an industry) in which it competes or may choose to compete.

An **industry** is a group of firms producing products that are close substitutes.

FIRMS' EFFORTS TO TAKE CARE OF THE PHYSICAL ENVIRONMENT IN WHICH THEY COMPETE

The number of companies throughout the world that recognize that they compete within the confines of the physical environment and that they are expected to reduce the negative effect of their operations on the physical environment while competing continues to increase. Those concerned about the physical environment value this trend.

Producing and selling additional "green" (i.e., environmentally friendly) products is one company response to this trend. By mid-2009, for example, firms had launched almost 460 new green products such as toilet paper, diapers, and household cleaning products in the United States alone. Analysts saw these launchings, which represented a threefold increase compared to launches in 2008, as more evidence that "green" is going mainstream.

In addition to products, companies across the globe are committing to or increasing their commitment to environmental sustainability. McDonald's, for example, "takes its responsibility to the environment seriously." Green restaurant design, sustainable packaging and waste management, and energy efficiency are areas where McDonald's acts to reduce its environmental footprint. Dell Inc. recently announced that its operations are now "carbon neutral." Dell envisions this as an important step in the firm's quest to become "the greenest technology company on the planet." Google and Yahoo! have also pledged to become carbon neutral.

Honest Tea produces "delicious, truly healthy, organic beverages." Since its founding in 1998, the firm has had a very strong commitment to environmentally friendly business practices, including the way its new corporate headquarters was designed. In the company's words, "When it came time for a new office, we did our best to walk our talk and create an office that is environmentally friendly to both the planet and our employees."

AP Photo/Wong Maye-E

Procter & Gamble's easily shipped PUR packets have helped provide over 1 billion liters of clean drinking water since the creation of the Children's Safe Drinking Water program in 2004.

Honest Tea used reclaimed bricks, flooring, and desks when building its new facility.

Procter & Gamble (P&G) recently announced increased targets for its 2012 sustainability goals. Among the goals are those to (1) "develop and market at least $50 billion in cumulative sales of sustainable innovation products, (2) deliver a 20 percent reduction (per unit of production) in carbon dioxide emissions, energy consumption, water usage and disposed waste from P&G plants, and (3) enable 300 million children to Live, Learn and Thrive and deliver three billion liters of clean water through P&G's Children's Safe Drinking Water program." Dutch consumer products giant Unilever also has an ongoing commitment to sustainability. The firm's sustainability actions include reducing water usage in its plants, working with its suppliers to encourage sustainability practices on their parts, and improving the eco-efficiency of their manufacturing facilities.

A number of other companies mirror the commitments of these firms in response to emerging trends in the physical environment segment. In addition to positively responding to the observed trends in this segment of the general environment, there is some evidence that firms engaging in these types of behaviors outperform those failing to do so. This emerging evidence suggests that these behaviors benefit companies, their stakeholders, and the physical environment in which they operate.

Sources: 2009, Eco-friendly growth, *BusinessWeek*, May 4,5–6; 2009, Honest Tea, http://www.honesttea.com; June 12; 2009, McDonald's Corporate Responsibility, http://www.mcdonalds.com, June 12; 2009, Procter & Gamble deepens corporate commitment to sustainability, http://www.pandg.com, April 29; 2009, Introduction to Unilever, http://www .unilever.com, June 12; 2008, Procter & Gamble, Sustainability Full Report, http://www.pandg.com, May 10; J. Ball, 2008, Green goal of "carbon neutrality" has limits, *Wall Street Journal Online*, http://www.wsj.com, December 28; T. B. Porter, 2008, Managerial applications of corporate social responsibility and systems thinking for achieving sustainability outcomes, *Systems Research and Behavioral Science*, 25: 397–411.

Threat of New Entrants

Identifying new entrants is important because they can threaten the market share of existing competitors.[94] One reason new entrants pose such a threat is that they bring additional production capacity. Unless the demand for a good or service is increasing, additional capacity holds consumers' costs down, resulting in less revenue and lower returns for competing firms. Often, new entrants have a keen interest in gaining a large market share. As a result, new competitors may force existing firms to be more efficient and to learn how to compete on new dimensions (e.g., using an Internet-based distribution channel).

The likelihood that firms will enter an industry is a function of two factors: barriers to entry and the retaliation expected from current industry participants. Entry barriers make it difficult for new firms to enter an industry and often place them at a competitive disadvantage even when they are able to enter. As such, high entry barriers tend to increase

Figure 2.2 The Five Forces of Competition Model

the returns for existing firms in the industry and may allow some firms to dominate the industry.[95] Thus, firms competing successfully in an industry want to maintain high entry barriers in order to discourage potential competitors from deciding to enter the industry.

Barriers to Entry

Firms competing in an industry (and especially those earning above-average returns) try to develop entry barriers to thwart potential competitors. For example, the server market is hypercompetitive and dominated by IBM, Hewlett-Packard, and Dell. Historically, the scale economies these firms have developed by operating efficiently and effectively have created significant entry barriers, causing potential competitors to think very carefully about entering the server market to compete against them. Recently though, Oracle paid $7.4 billion to acquire Sun Microsystems, which is primarily a computer hardware company. Early evidence suggests that Oracle intends to "… focus Sun's server business on a small but promising segment of the market: computer appliances preloaded with Oracle software."[96] The degree of success Oracle will achieve as a result of its decision to enter the server market via an acquisition remains uncertain.

Several kinds of potentially significant entry barriers may discourage competitors from entering a market.

Economies of Scale   *Economies of scale* are derived from incremental efficiency improvements through experience as a firm grows larger. Therefore, the cost of producing each unit declines as the quantity of a product produced during a given period increases. This is the case for IBM, Hewlett-Packard, and Dell in the server market, as previously described.

Economies of scale can be developed in most business functions, such as marketing, manufacturing, research and development, and purchasing.[97] Increasing economies of scale enhances a firm's flexibility. For example, a firm may choose to reduce its price and capture a greater share of the market. Alternatively, it may keep its price constant to increase profits. In so doing, it likely will increase its free cash flow, which is very helpful during financially challenging times.

New entrants face a dilemma when confronting current competitors' scale economies. Small-scale entry places them at a cost disadvantage. Given the size of Sun Microsystems relative to the three major competitors in the server market, Oracle may be at least initially be at a disadvantage in competing against them. Alternatively, large-scale entry, in which the new entrant manufactures large volumes of a product to gain economies of scale, risks strong competitive retaliation.

Some competitive conditions reduce the ability of economies of scale to create an entry barrier. Many companies now customize their products for large numbers of small customer groups. Customized products are not manufactured in the volumes necessary to achieve economies of scale. Customization is made possible by flexible manufacturing systems (this point is discussed further in Chapter 4). In fact, the new manufacturing technology facilitated by advanced information systems has allowed the development of mass customization in an increasing number of industries. Although it is not appropriate for all products and implementing it can be challenging, mass customization has become increasingly common in manufacturing products.[98] In fact, online ordering has enhanced the ability of customers to obtain customized products. They are often referred to as "markets of one."[99] Companies manufacturing customized products learn how to respond quickly to customers' needs in lieu of developing scale economies.

Product Differentiation   Over time, customers may come to believe that a firm's product is unique. This belief can result from the firm's service to the customer, effective advertising campaigns, or being the first to market a good or service. Currently, Ford Motor Company is seeking to differentiate its products from competitors on the basis that it is "... stronger, greener, and more technologically advanced than those other guys."[100] If successful with these efforts, Ford hopes those buying its cars today will generate the type of loyalty that results in repeat purchases.

Companies such as Procter & Gamble (P&G) and Colgate-Palmolive spend a great deal of money on advertising and product development to convince potential customers of their products' distinctiveness and of the value buying their brands provides.[101] Customers valuing a product's uniqueness tend to become loyal to both the product and the company producing it. In turn, customer loyalty is an entry barrier for firms thinking of an entering an industry and competing against the likes of P&G and Colgate. To compete against firms offering differentiated products to individuals who have become loyal customers, new entrants often allocate many resources to overcome existing customer loyalties. To combat the perception of uniqueness, new entrants frequently offer products at lower prices. This decision, however, may result in lower profits or even losses.

Capital Requirements   Competing in a new industry requires a firm to have resources to invest. In addition to physical facilities, capital is needed for inventories, marketing activities, and other critical business functions. Even when a new industry is attractive, the capital required for successful market entry may not be available to pursue the market opportunity. For example, defense industries are difficult to enter because of the substantial resource investments required to be competitive. In addition, because of the high knowledge requirements of the defense industry, a firm might acquire an existing company as a means of entering this industry. But it must have access to the capital necessary to do it. Obviously, Oracle had the capital required to acquire Sun Microsystems as a foundation for entering the server market.

Switching Costs   Switching costs are the one-time costs customers incur when they buy from a different supplier. The costs of buying new ancillary equipment and of retraining employees, and even the psychic costs of ending a relationship, may be incurred in switching to a new supplier. In some cases, switching costs are low, such as when the consumer switches to a different soft drink or when a smoker switches from a Philip Morris International cigarette to one produced by competitor Japan Tobacco International. Switching costs can vary as a function of time. For example, in terms of credit hours toward graduation, the cost to a student to transfer from one university to another as a freshman is much lower than it is when the student is entering the senior year. Occasionally, a decision made by manufacturers to produce a new, innovative product creates high switching costs for the final consumer. Customer loyalty programs, such as airlines' frequent flyer miles, are intended to increase the customer's switching costs.

If switching costs are high, a new entrant must offer either a substantially lower price or a much better product to attract buyers. Usually, the more established the relationships between parties, the greater are switching costs.

Access to Distribution Channels   Over time, industry participants typically develop effective means of distributing products. Once a relationship with its distributors has been built a firm will nurture it, thus creating switching costs for the distributors. Access to distribution channels can be a strong entry barrier for new entrants, particularly in consumer nondurable goods industries (e.g., in grocery stores where shelf space is limited) and in international markets. New entrants have to persuade distributors to carry their products, either in addition to or in place of those currently distributed. Price breaks and cooperative advertising allowances may be used for this purpose; however, those practices reduce the new entrant's profit potential.

Cost Disadvantages Independent of Scale   Sometimes, established competitors have cost advantages that new entrants cannot duplicate. Proprietary product technology, favorable access to raw materials, desirable locations, and government subsidies are examples.

Successful competition requires new entrants to reduce the strategic relevance of these factors. Delivering purchases directly to the buyer can counter the advantage of a desirable location; new food establishments in an undesirable location often follow this practice.

Government Policy   Through licensing and permit requirements, governments can also control entry into an industry. Liquor retailing, radio and TV broadcasting, banking, and trucking are examples of industries in which government decisions and actions affect entry possibilities. Also, governments often restrict entry into some industries because of the need to provide quality service or the need to protect jobs. Alternatively, deregulation of industries, exemplified by the airline industry and utilities in the United States, allows more firms to enter.[102] However, some of the most publicized government actions are those involving antitrust. In 2009, for example, the European Commission announced a fine of $1.4 billion—the largest the Commission had assessed—against Intel, the world's largest computer-chip maker. The fine was for "… breaking European antitrust rules."[103] The Commission's major conclusion was that Intel's competitive actions were blocking effective access by competitors to European markets. In response to the announcement, Intel indicated that it would appeal the fine as well as the ruling that the firm would have to change its business practices in the European Union.[104] These rulings caused other dominant firms such as Microsoft and Google to wonder about potential governmental rulings that the Commission might assess against them in the future.

Expected Retaliation

Companies seeking to enter an industry also anticipate the reactions of firms in the industry. An expectation of swift and vigorous competitive responses reduces the likelihood of entry. Vigorous retaliation can be expected when the existing firm has a major stake in the industry (e.g., it has fixed assets with few, if any, alternative uses), when it has substantial resources, and when industry growth is slow or constrained. For example, any firm attempting to enter the airline industry at the current time can expect significant retaliation from existing competitors due to overcapacity.

Locating market niches not being served by incumbents allows the new entrant to avoid entry barriers. Small entrepreneurial firms are generally best suited for identifying and serving neglected market segments. When Honda first entered the U.S. motorcycle market, it concentrated on small-engine motorcycles, a market that firms such as Harley-Davidson ignored. By targeting this neglected niche, Honda avoided competition. After consolidating its position, Honda used its strength to attack rivals by introducing larger motorcycles and competing in the broader market. Competitive actions and competitive responses between firms such as Honda and Harley-Davidson are discussed more fully in Chapter 5.

Bargaining Power of Suppliers

Increasing prices and reducing the quality of their products are potential means suppliers use to exert power over firms competing within an industry. If a firm is unable to recover cost increases by its suppliers through its own pricing structure, its profitability is reduced by its suppliers' actions. A supplier group is powerful when

- It is dominated by a few large companies and is more concentrated than the industry to which it sells.
- Satisfactory substitute products are not available to industry firms.
- Industry firms are not a significant customer for the supplier group.
- Suppliers' goods are critical to buyers' marketplace success.
- The effectiveness of suppliers' products has created high switching costs for industry firms.
- It poses a credible threat to integrate forward into the buyers' industry. Credibility is enhanced when suppliers have substantial resources and provide a highly differentiated product.

The airline industry is one in which suppliers' bargaining power is changing. Though the number of suppliers is low, the demand for major aircraft is also relatively low. Boeing and Airbus aggressively compete for orders of major aircraft, creating more power for buyers in the process. In mid-2009, United Airlines announced that it might place a "significant" order for wide-body airliners with either Airbus or Boeing in the fourth quarter of the year if the firm could earn an acceptable return on its investment. United's expectation that the winning bid from either Airbus or Boeing would include a financing arrangement that would strengthen its "… balance sheet over the long term and not impact (the firm's) cash flow position"[105] highlights the buyer's power in this proposed transaction.

Bargaining Power of Buyers

Firms seek to maximize the return on their invested capital. Alternatively, buyers (customers of an industry or a firm) want to buy products at the lowest possible price—the point at which the industry earns the lowest acceptable rate of return on its invested capital. To reduce their costs, buyers bargain for higher quality, greater levels of service, and lower prices. These outcomes are achieved by encouraging competitive battles among the industry's firms. Customers (buyer groups) are powerful when

■ They purchase a large portion of an industry's total output.
■ The sales of the product being purchased account for a significant portion of the seller's annual revenues.
■ They could switch to another product at little, if any, cost.
■ The industry's products are undifferentiated or standardized, and the buyers pose a credible threat if they were to integrate backward into the sellers' industry.

Armed with greater amounts of information about the manufacturer's costs and the power of the Internet as a shopping and distribution alternative have increased consumers' bargaining power in many industries. One reason for this shift is that individual buyers incur virtually zero switching costs when they decide to purchase from one manufacturer rather than another or from one dealer as opposed to a second or third one.

With consumer access to news at their fingertips via the iPhone and other wireless devices, newspapers and other traditional news sources face increasing competition for customers.

ICP-UK/Alamy

Threat of Substitute Products

Substitute products are goods or services from outside a given industry that perform similar or the same functions as a product that the industry produces. For example, as a sugar substitute, NutraSweet (and other sugar substitutes) places an upper limit on sugar manufacturers' prices—NutraSweet and sugar perform the same function, though with different characteristics. Other product substitutes include e-mail and fax machines instead of overnight deliveries, plastic containers rather than glass jars, and tea instead of coffee. Newspaper firms have experienced significant circulation declines over the past decade or more. The declines are due to substitute outlets for news including Internet sources, cable television news channels, and e-mail and cell phone alerts. These products are increasingly popular, especially among younger, and technologically savvy people, and as product substitutes they have significant potential to continue to reduce overall newspaper circulation sales.

In general, product substitutes present a strong threat to a firm when customers face few, if any, switching costs and when the substitute product's price is lower or its quality and performance capabilities are equal to or greater than those of the competing product. Differentiating a product along dimensions that customers value (such as quality, service after the sale, and location) reduces a substitute's attractiveness.

Intensity of Rivalry Among Competitors

Because an industry's firms are mutually dependent, actions taken by one company usually invite competitive responses. In many industries, firms actively compete against one another. Competitive rivalry intensifies when a firm is challenged by a competitor's actions or when a company recognizes an opportunity to improve its market position.

Firms within industries are rarely homogeneous; they differ in resources and capabilities and seek to differentiate themselves from competitors.[106] Typically, firms seek to differentiate their products from competitors' offerings in ways that customers value and in which the firms have a competitive advantage. Common dimensions on which rivalry is based include price, service after the sale, and innovation.

Next, we discuss the most prominent factors that experience shows to affect the intensity of firms' rivalries.

Numerous or Equally Balanced Competitors

Intense rivalries are common in industries with many companies. With multiple competitors, it is common for a few firms to believe they can act without eliciting a response. However, evidence suggests that other firms generally are aware of competitors' actions, often choosing to respond to them. At the other extreme, industries with only a few firms of equivalent size and power also tend to have strong rivalries. The large and often similar-sized resource bases of these firms permit vigorous actions and responses. The competitive battles between Airbus and Boeing exemplify intense rivalry between relatively equal competitors, and almost certainly will be so as the companies bid for the order to produce wide-body planes for United Airlines.

Slow Industry Growth

When a market is growing, firms try to effectively use resources to serve an expanding customer base. Growing markets reduce the pressure to take customers from competitors. However, rivalry in no-growth or slow-growth markets (slow change) becomes more intense as firms battle to increase their market shares by attracting competitors' customers.[107]

Typically, battles to protect market share are fierce. Certainly, this has been the case in the airline industry and in the fast-food industry as McDonald's, Wendy's, and Burger King try to win each other's customers. The instability in the market that results from these competitive engagements may reduce the profitability for all firms engaging in such competitive battles.

High Fixed Costs or High Storage Costs

When fixed costs account for a large part of total costs, companies try to maximize the use of their productive capacity. Doing so allows the firm to spread costs across a larger volume of output. However, when many firms attempt to maximize their productive capacity, excess capacity is created on an industry-wide basis. To then reduce inventories, individual companies typically cut the price of their product and offer rebates and other special discounts to customers. However, these practices, common in the automobile manufacturing industry in the recent past, often intensify competition. The pattern of excess capacity at the industry level followed by intense rivalry at the firm level is observed frequently in industries with high storage costs. Perishable products, for example, lose their value rapidly with the passage of time. As their inventories grow, producers of perishable goods often use pricing strategies to sell products quickly.

Lack of Differentiation or Low Switching Costs

When buyers find a differentiated product that satisfies their needs, they frequently purchase the product loyally over time. Industries with many companies that have successfully differentiated their products have less rivalry, resulting in lower competition for individual firms. Firms that develop and sustain a differentiated product that cannot be easily imitated by competitors often earn higher returns. However, when buyers view products as commodities (i.e., as products with few differentiated features or capabilities), rivalry intensifies. In these instances, buyers' purchasing decisions are based primarily on price and, to a lesser degree, service. Personal computers are a commodity product. Thus, the rivalry between Dell, Hewlett-Packard, and other computer manufacturers is strong and these companies are always trying to find ways to differentiate their offerings (Hewlett-Packard now pursues product design as a means of differentiation.)

High Strategic Stakes

Competitive rivalry is likely to be high when it is important for several of the competitors to perform well in the market. For example, although it is diversified and is a market leader in other businesses, Samsung has targeted market leadership in the consumer electronics market and is doing quite well. This market is quite important to Sony and other major competitors, such as Hitachi, Matsushita, NEC, and Mitsubishi, suggesting that rivalry among these competitors will remain strong.

High strategic stakes can also exist in terms of geographic locations. For example, Japanese automobile manufacturers are committed to a significant presence in the U.S. marketplace because it is the world's largest single market for automobiles and trucks. Because of the stakes involved in this country for Japanese and U.S. manufacturers, rivalry among firms in the U.S. and the global automobile industry is intense. With the excess capacity in this industry we mentioned earlier in this chapter, there is every reason to believe that the rivalry among global automobile manufacturers will become even more intense, certainly in the foreseeable future.

High Exit Barriers

Sometimes companies continue competing in an industry even though the returns on their invested capital are low or negative. Firms making this choice likely face high exit barriers, which include economic, strategic, and emotional factors causing them to remain in an industry when the profitability of doing so is questionable. Exit barriers are especially high in the airline industry. Although earning even average returns is difficult for these firms, they face substantial exit barriers, such as their ownership of specialized assets (e.g., large aircraft).[108] Common exit barriers include the following:

- Specialized assets (assets with values linked to a particular business or location)
- Fixed costs of exit (such as labor agreements)
- Strategic interrelationships (relationships of mutual dependence, such as those between one business and other parts of a company's operations, including shared facilities and access to financial markets)
- Emotional barriers (aversion to economically justified business decisions because of fear for one's own career, loyalty to employees, and so forth)
- Government and social restrictions (often based on government concerns for job losses and regional economic effects; more common outside the United States).

Interpreting Industry Analyses

Effective industry analyses are products of careful study and interpretation of data and information from multiple sources. A wealth of industry-specific data is available to be analyzed. Because of globalization, international markets and rivalries must be included in the firm's analyses. In fact, research shows that in some industries, international variables are more important than domestic ones as determinants of strategic competitiveness. Furthermore, because of the development of global markets, a country's borders no longer restrict industry structures. In fact, movement into international markets enhances the chances of success for new ventures as well as more established firms.[109]

Analysis of the five forces in the industry allows the firm to determine the industry's attractiveness in terms of the potential to earn adequate or superior returns. In general, the stronger competitive forces are, the lower the profit potential for an industry's firms. An unattractive industry has low entry barriers, suppliers and buyers with strong bargaining positions, strong competitive threats from product substitutes, and intense rivalry among competitors. These industry characteristics make it difficult for firms to achieve strategic competitiveness and earn above-average returns. Alternatively, an attractive industry has high entry barriers, suppliers and buyers with little bargaining power, few competitive threats from product substitutes, and relatively moderate rivalry.[110] Next, we explain strategic groups as an aspect of industry competition.

Strategic Groups

A set of firms that emphasize similar strategic dimensions and use a similar strategy is called a **strategic group**.[111] The competition between firms within a strategic group is greater than the competition between a member of a strategic group and companies outside that strategic group. Therefore, intrastrategic group competition is more intense than is interstrategic group competition. In fact, more heterogeneity is evident in the performance of firms within strategic groups than across the groups. The performance leaders within groups are able to follow strategies similar to those of other firms in the group and yet maintain strategic distinctiveness to gain and sustain a competitive advantage.[112]

The extent of technological leadership, product quality, pricing policies, distribution channels, and customer service are examples of strategic dimensions that firms in a strategic group may treat similarly. Thus, membership in a particular strategic group defines the essential characteristics of the firm's strategy.[113]

The notion of strategic groups can be useful for analyzing an industry's competitive structure. Such analyses can be helpful in diagnosing competition, positioning, and the profitability of firms within an industry.[114] High mobility barriers, high rivalry, and low resources among the firms within an industry limit the formation of strategic groups.[115] However, research suggests that after strategic groups are formed, their membership remains relatively stable over time, making analysis easier and more useful.[116] Using strategic groups to understand an industry's competitive structure requires the firm to plot companies' competitive actions and competitive responses along strategic dimensions such as pricing decisions, product quality, distribution channels, and so forth. This type of analysis shows the firm how certain companies are competing similarly in terms of how they use similar strategic dimensions.

Strategic groups have several implications. First, because firms within a group offer similar products to the same customers, the competitive rivalry among them can be intense. The more intense the rivalry, the greater the threat to each firm's profitability. Second, the strengths of the five industry forces differ across strategic groups. Third, the closer the strategic groups are in terms of their strategies, the greater is the likelihood of rivalry between the groups.

Competitor Analysis

The competitor environment is the final part of the external environment requiring study. Competitor analysis focuses on each company against which a firm directly competes. For example, Philip Morris International and Japan Tobacco International, Coca-Cola and PepsiCo, Home Depot and Lowe's, and Boeing and Airbus are keenly interested in understanding each other's objectives, strategies, assumptions, and capabilities. Indeed,

A **strategic group** is a set of firms emphasizing similar strategic dimensions to use a similar strategy.

intense rivalry creates a strong need to understand competitors.[117] In a competitor analysis, the firm seeks to understand the following:

- What drives the competitor, as shown by its *future objectives*
- What the competitor is doing and can do, as revealed by its *current strategy*
- What the competitor believes about the industry, as shown by its *assumptions*
- What the competitor's capabilities are, as shown by its *strengths* and *weaknesses*.[118]

Information about these four dimensions helps the firm prepare an anticipated response profile for each competitor (see Figure 2.3). The results of an effective competitor analysis help a firm understand, interpret, and predict its competitors' actions and responses. Understanding the actions of competitors clearly contributes to the firm's ability to compete successfully within the industry.[119] Interestingly, research suggests that executives often fail to analyze competitors' possible reactions to competitive actions their firm takes,[120] placing their firm at a potential competitive disadvantage as a result.

Critical to an effective competitor analysis is gathering data and information that can help the firm understand its competitors' intentions and the strategic implications resulting from them.[121] Useful data and information combine to form **competitor intelligence**: the set of data and information the firm gathers to better understand and better anticipate competitors' objectives, strategies, assumptions, and capabilities. In competitor analysis, the firm gathers intelligence not only about its competitors, but also regarding public policies in countries around the world. Such intelligence facilitates an understanding of the strategic posture of foreign competitors. Through effective competitive and public policy intelligence, the firm gains the insights needed to make effective strategic decisions about how to compete against its rivals.

Figure 2.3 Competitor Analysis Components

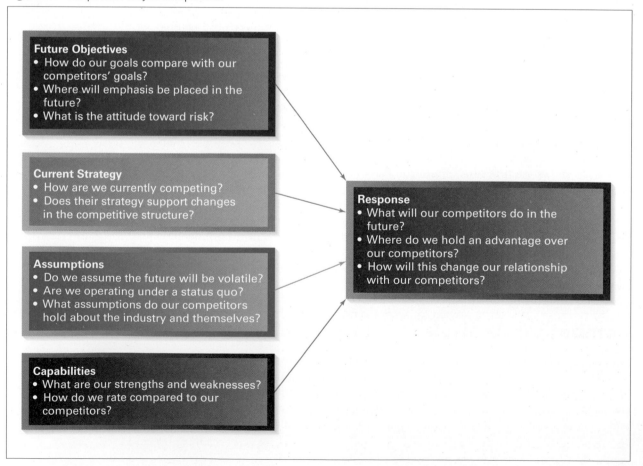

Future Objectives
- How do our goals compare with our competitors' goals?
- Where will emphasis be placed in the future?
- What is the attitude toward risk?

Current Strategy
- How are we currently competing?
- Does their strategy support changes in the competitive structure?

Assumptions
- Do we assume the future will be volatile?
- Are we operating under a status quo?
- What assumptions do our competitors hold about the industry and themselves?

Capabilities
- What are our strengths and weaknesses?
- How do we rate compared to our competitors?

Response
- What will our competitors do in the future?
- Where do we hold an advantage over our competitors?
- How will this change our relationship with our competitors?

When asked to describe competitive intelligence, it seems that a number of people respond with phrases such as "competitive spying" and "corporate espionage." These phrases denote the fact that competitive intelligence is an activity that appears to involve trade-offs.[122] According to some, the reason for this is that "what is ethical in one country is different from what is ethical in other countries." This position implies that the rules of engagement to follow when gathering competitive intelligence change in different contexts. However, firms avoid the possibility of legal entanglements and ethical quandaries only when their competitive intelligence gathering methods are governed by a strict set of legal and ethical guidelines.[123] This means that ethical behavior and actions as well as the mandates of relevant laws and regulations should be the foundation on which a firm's competitive intelligence-gathering process is formed. We address this matter in greater detail in the next section.

When gathering competitive intelligence, firms must also pay attention to the complementors of its products and strategy.[124] **Complementors** are companies or networks of companies that sell complementary goods or services that are compatible with the focal firm's good or service. When a complementor's good or service adds value to the sale of the focal firm's good or service it is likely to create value for the focal firm.

There are many examples of firms whose good or service complements other companies' offerings. For example, firms manufacturing affordable home photo printers complement other companies' efforts to sell digital cameras. Intel and Microsoft are perhaps the most widely recognized complementors. The Microsoft slogan "Intel Inside" demonstrates the relationship between two firms who do not directly buy from or sell to each other but whose products have a strong complementary relationship. Alliances among airline operations (e.g., the Star Alliance and the SkyTeam Alliance) find these companies sharing their route structures and customer loyalty programs as means of complementing each others' operations. (Each alliance is a network of complementors.) Recently, Continental Airlines announced that it was leaving the SkyTeam Alliance to join the Star Alliance. The primary reason for this change was to provide greater global coverage to Continental's customers by combining its routes with those of the other members of the Star Alliance.[125] In essence, Continental's conclusion was that the complementors of the Star Alliance created more value for its customers than did its complementors in the SkyTeam Alliance.

As our discussion shows, complementors expand the set of competitors firms must evaluate when completing a competitor analysis. For example, when Delta Airlines wants to study Continental Airlines, it must examine Continental's strategic actions as an independent company as well as its actions as a member of the Star Alliance. The same is true in reverse—Continental must study Delta's actions as an independent firm as well as its actions as a member of the SkyTeam Alliance. Similarly, Intel and Microsoft analyze each other's actions in that those actions might either help each firm gain a competitive advantage or damage each firm's ability to exploit a competitive advantage.

Ethical Considerations

Firms must follow relevant laws and regulations as well as carefully articulated ethical guidelines when gathering competitor intelligence. Industry associations often develop lists of these practices that firms can adopt. Practices considered both legal and ethical include (1) obtaining publicly available information (e.g., court records, competitors' help-wanted advertisements, annual reports, financial reports of publicly held corporations, and Uniform Commercial Code filings), and (2) attending trade fairs and shows to obtain competitors' brochures, view their exhibits, and listen to discussions about their products. In contrast, certain practices (including blackmail, trespassing, eavesdropping, and stealing drawings, samples, or documents) are widely viewed as unethical and often are illegal.

Some competitor intelligence practices may be legal, but a firm must decide whether they are also ethical, given the image it desires as a corporate citizen. Especially with electronic transmissions, the line between legal and ethical practices can be difficult to determine. For example, a firm may develop Web site addresses that are similar to those

Competitor intelligence is the set of data and information the firm gathers to better understand and better anticipate competitors' objectives, strategies, assumptions, and capabilities.

Complementors are companies or networks of companies that sell complementary goods or services that are compatible with the focal firm's good or service.

of its competitors and thus occasionally receive e-mail transmissions that were intended for those competitors. The practice is an example of the challenges companies face in deciding how to gather intelligence about competitors while simultaneously determining how to prevent competitors from learning too much about them. To deal with these challenges, firms should establish principles and take actions that are consistent with them. ING, a global financial company offering banking, investments, life insurance, and retirement services, expresses the principles guiding its actions as follows: "ING conducts business on the basis of clearly defined business principles. In all our activities, we carefully weigh the interests of our various stakeholders: customers, employees, communities and shareholders. ING strives to be a good corporate citizen."[126]

Open discussions of intelligence-gathering techniques can help a firm ensure that employees, customers, suppliers, and even potential competitors understand its convictions to follow ethical practices for gathering competitor intelligence. An appropriate guideline for competitor intelligence practices is to respect the principles of common morality and the right of competitors not to reveal certain information about their products, operations, and strategic intentions.[127]

SUMMARY

- The firm's external environment is challenging and complex. Because of the external environment's effect on performance, the firm must develop the skills required to identify opportunities and threats existing in that environment.

- The external environment has three major parts: (1) the general environment (elements in the broader society that affect industries and their firms), (2) the industry environment (factors that influence a firm, its competitive actions and responses, and the industry's profit potential), and (3) the competitor environment (in which the firm analyzes each major competitor's future objectives, current strategies, assumptions, and capabilities).

- The external environmental analysis process has four steps: scanning, monitoring, forecasting, and assessing. Through environmental analyses, the firm identifies opportunities and threats.

- The general environment has seven segments: demographic, economic, political/legal, sociocultural, technological, global, and physical. For each segment, the firm wants to determine the strategic relevance of environmental changes and trends.

- Compared with the general environment, the industry environment has a more direct effect on the firm's strategic actions. The five forces model of competition includes the threat of entry, the power of suppliers, the power of buyers, product

substitutes, and the intensity of rivalry among competitors. By studying these forces, the firm finds a position in an industry where it can influence the forces in its favor or where it can buffer itself from the power of the forces in order to achieve strategic competitiveness and earn above-average returns.

- Industries are populated with different strategic groups. A strategic group is a collection of firms following similar strategies along similar dimensions. Competitive rivalry is greater within a strategic group than between strategic groups.

- Competitor analysis informs the firm about the future objectives, current strategies, assumptions, and capabilities of the companies with which it competes directly. A thorough analysis examines complementors that sustain a competitor's strategy and major networks or alliances in which competitors participate. When analyzing competitors, the firm should also identify and carefully monitor major actions taken by firms with performance below the industry norm.

- Different techniques are used to create competitor intelligence: the set of data, information, and knowledge that allows the firm to better understand its competitors and thereby predict their likely strategic and tactical actions. Firms should use only legal and ethical practices to gather intelligence. The Internet enhances firms' capabilities to gather insights about competitors and their strategic intentions.

REVIEW QUESTIONS

1. Why is it important for a firm to study and understand the external environment?

2. What are the differences between the general environment and the industry environment? Why are these differences important?

3. What is the external environmental analysis process (four steps)? What does the firm want to learn when using this process?

4. What are the seven segments of the general environment? Explain the differences among them.

5. How do the five forces of competition in an industry affect its profit potential? Explain.

6. What is a strategic group? Of what value is knowledge of the firm's strategic group in formulating that firm's strategy?

7. What is the importance of collecting and interpreting data and information about competitors? What practices should a firm use to gather competitor intelligence and why?

EXPERIENTIAL EXERCISES

EXERCISE 1: AIRLINE COMPETITOR ANALYSIS

The International Air Transport Association (IATA) reports statistics on the number of passengers carried each year by major airlines. Passenger data for 2007 are reported for the top 10 carriers in three categories:

- International flights
- Domestic flights
- Combined traffic, domestic and international flights

The following table lists both passenger data and rankings for each category.

Airline	Intl Rank	Intl Passengers	Domestic Rank	Domestic Passengers	Combined Rank	Combined Passengers
Air France	3	31,549			8	50,465
All Nippon Airways			6	44,792		
American Airlines	7	21,479	2	76,687	2	98,166
British Airways	5	28,302				
Cathay Pacific	10	17,695				
China Southern Airlines			5	52,505	5	56,522
Continental Airlines			9	37,175	9	49,059
Delta Air Lines			3	61,651	3	73,086
Easyjet	4	30,173				
Emirates	8	20,448				
Japan Airlines International			10	35,583		
KLM	6	23,165				
Lufthansa	2	41,322			7	54,165
Northwest Airlines			7	44,337	6	54,696
Ryanair	1	49,030			10	49,030
Singapore Airlines	9	18,957				
Southwest Airlines			1	101,911	1	101,911
United Airlines			4	58,162	4	68,363
US Airways Inc.			8	37,560		

For this exercise, you will develop competitor profiles of selected air carriers.

Part One

Working in groups of five to seven people, each team member selects one airline from the table. The pool of selected airlines should contain a roughly even balance of three regions: North America, Europe/Middle East, and Asia. Answer the following questions:

1. What drives this competitor (i.e., what are its objectives)?
2. What is its current strategy?
3. What does this competitor believe about its industry?
4. What are its strengths and weaknesses?
5. Does this airline belong to an airline alliance (e.g., Oneworld, Star, SkyTeam)?

When researching your companies, you should use multiple resources. The company's Web site is a good starting point. Public firms headquartered in the United States will also have annual reports and 10-K reports filed with the Securities and Exchange Commission.

Part Two

As a group, summarize the results of each competitor profile into a single table with columns for objectives, current strategy, beliefs, strengths, weaknesses, and alliance partner(s). Then, discuss the following topics:

1. Which airlines had the most similar strategies? The most different? Would you consider any of the firms you studied to be in the same strategic group (i.e., a group of firms that follows similar strategies along similar dimensions)?
2. Create a composite five forces model based on the firms you reviewed. How might these elements of industry structure (e.g., substitutes, or bargaining power of buyers) differ from the perspective of individual airlines?
3. Which airlines appear best positioned to succeed in the future? Why?

EXERCISE 2: WHAT DOES THE FUTURE LOOK LIKE?

A critical ingredient to studying the general environment is identifying opportunities and threats. As discussed in this chapter, an opportunity is a condition in the environment that, if exploited, helps a company achieve strategic competitiveness. In order to identify opportunities, one must be aware of current and future trends affecting the world around us.

Thomas Fry, senior futurist at the DaVinci Institute, says that the chaotic nature of interconnecting trends and the vast array of possibilities that arise from them is somewhat akin to watching a spinning compass needle. From the way we use phones and e-mail, or recruit new workers to organizations, the climate for business is changing and shifting dramatically and at rapidly increasing rates. Sorting out these changes and making sense of them provides the basis for opportunity decision making. Which ones will dominate and which will fade? Understanding this is crucial for business success.

Your challenge (either individually or as a group) is to identify a trend, technology, entertainment, or design that is likely to alter the way in which business is conducted in the future. Once you have identified your topic, be prepared to discuss:

- Which of the seven segments of the general environment will this affect? (There may be more than one.)
- Describe the impact.
- List some business opportunities that will come from this.
- Identify some existing organizations that stand to benefit.
- What, if any, are the ethical implications?

You should consult a wide variety of sources. For example, the Gartner Group and McKinsey & Company produce market research and forecasts for business. There are also many Web forecasting tools and addresses such as TED (Technology, Entertainment, Design). TED hosts an annual conference for groundbreaking ideas, and you can find videos of their discussions on their Web site. Similarly the DaVinci Institute, Institute for Global Futures, and a host of others offer their own unique vision for tomorrow's environment.

VIDEO CASE

OUTWORK YOUR COMPETITION

Jerry Rice/Former Professional Football Player/NFL Hall of Famer

Jerry Rice (born October 13, 1962) is widely regarded as the greatest wide receiver ever and one of the greatest players in National Football League (NFL) history. He is the all-time leader in every major statistical category for wide receivers. In 20 NFL seasons, he was selected to the Pro Bowl 13 times (1986–1996, 1998, and 2002) and named All-Pro 10 times. He won three Super Bowl rings playing for the San Francisco 49ers and an AFC Championship with the Oakland Raiders.

Besides his exceptional ability as a receiver, Rice is remembered for his work ethic and dedication to the game. In his 20 NFL seasons, he missed only 10 regular season games. His 303 games are by far the most ever played by an NFL wide receiver. In addition to staying on the field, his work ethic showed in his dedication to conditioning and running precise routes.

Before you watch the video consider the following concepts and questions and be prepared to discuss them in class:

Concepts
- Competition
- Opportunity
- Threat
- Industry environment—five forces
- Competitor analysis

Questions

1. How competitive are you? How does this manifest itself in your everyday life?
2. What about goal setting in your life. Do you have objectives that you want to achieve five years after graduation?
3. How is your preparation and planning matched to your long-term objectives?
4. What, if any, difference is there between a company's objectives and those of its employees?

CHAPTER 3

The Internal Environment: Resources, Capabilities, Competencies, and Competitive Advantages

Studying this chapter should provide you with the strategic management knowledge needed to:

1. Explain why firms need to study and understand their internal organization.

2. Define value and discuss its importance.

3. Describe the differences between tangible and intangible resources.

4. Define capabilities and discuss their development.

5. Describe four criteria used to determine whether resources and capabilities are core competencies.

6. Explain how value chain analysis is used to identify and evaluate resources and capabilities.

7. Define outsourcing and discuss reasons for its use.

8. Discuss the importance of identifying internal strengths and weaknesses.

APPLE DEFIES GRAVITY WITH INNOVATIVE GENIUS

During a bad recession in 2008, Apple recorded record sales. The firm's strong performance in poor economic times is largely credited to its innovation capabilities. Apple has continued to upgrade its current products, such as its laptops, with enhancements (e.g., MacBook and MacBook Pro). Analysts believe that these innovative additions will keep Apple's "hot streak" alive and well. Furthermore, projections suggest that smartphone sales will surge over the next few years. These projections include a 200 percent increase in the sales of high-end mobile phones by 2013, to 300 million in annual sales. The growing popularity of Web 2.0 applications such as Facebook and Twitter are increasing the desire for these phones. Such demand is very positive for the future of BlackBerry and Apple's iPhone. By 2013, analysts believe that approximately 23 percent of all new mobile phone sales will be smartphones.

Apple has also continued to upgrade its innovative iPod with its second generation of iPod touch. One analyst gave it a perfect score for the significant enhancements made. And the iPod touch serves some similar functions as the iPhone such as providing an Internet connection, using the same touchscreen, and playing music and videos in the same way. An example of the continuous innovation is the 4-gigabyte iPod Shuffle introduced in 2009. It is less than two inches long (smaller than a double-A battery) and can store approximately 1,000 songs. This is the third-generation Shuffle—the first-generation Shuffle

Apple now offers more than 50,000 applications for the iPhone, enabling their customers to continually discover new uses for their smartphone.

launched in 2005 could store approximately 240 songs. In addition to increased storage, the new Shuffle can handle songs in 14 different languages. Apple has "set the standard" for design of personal computer since the mid-1990s. Since 1996, Apple product innovations include developing a tool that created a quantum increase in the sale of digital music, creating a mobile phone—a flexible computer—that is fun to use, and, in customer service, developing a chain of unique and popular retail stores. Thus, most external observers argue that Apple's innovative products have led to their becoming one of the fastest-growing companies in the United States.

Coupled with its innovation, Apple is an aggressive marketer. While most firms are paring back their costs and advertising during the recession, Apple has increased its marketing and advertising programs. It is the second most prolific technology advertiser, behind Microsoft.

While Apple is in a positive market position, it did experience potential problems in 2009. Its charismatic leader, Steve Jobs, had to take a medical leave of absence, causing uncertainty about the company's future. It also lost a few other top managers to key positions in other firms. Thus, investors became nervous and analysts questioned whether the firm could continue to be a market innovator, especially without Jobs.

Sources: C. Wildstrom, 2008, Apple laptops: The hits keep coming, *BusinessWeek*, http://businessweek.com, November 4; C. Edwards, 2008, Apple's superlative sequel: The latest iPod touch, *BusinessWeek*, http://businessweek.com, November 20; R. Waters & C. Nutialin, 2009, Apple moves to clear up uncertainty ahead of Jobs' absence, *Financial Times*, http://www.ft.com, January 16; B. Stone, 2009, Can Apple fill the void? *The New York Times*, http://www.nytimes.com, January 16; Apple bobbing, *Financial Times*,. http://www.ft.com, January 22; N. Lomas, 2009, Smartphones set to surge, *Business Week*, http://businessweek.com, February 3; B. Stone, 2009, In campaign wars, Apple still has Microsoft's number, *The New York Times*, http://www.nytimes.com, February 4; P. Elmer-Dewitt, 2009, Apple is 14th fastest-growing tech company, *Fortune*, http://www.fortune.com, February 6; Apple launches smaller, 4-gigabyte iPod shuffle, *Houston Chronicle*, http://www.chron.com, March 11.

As discussed in the first two chapters, several factors in the global economy, including the rapid development of the Internet's capabilities[1] and of globalization in general have made it increasingly difficult for firms to find ways to develop a competitive advantage that can be sustained for any period of time.[2] As is suggested by Apple's experiences, innovation may be a vital path to efforts to develop sustainable competitive advantages.[3] Sometimes, product innovation serves simultaneously as the foundation on which a firm is started as well as the source of its competitive advantages. This occurred with Apple. Steve Jobs was one of the cofounders of the company and helped to develop the personal computer that the company introduced to the market. Later, Jobs and the board of directors of Apple felt the need for more marketing expertise. So, a new CEO with a strong marketing background was brought in to the firm. Later Jobs was forced out and Apple lost its innovative approach. However, Jobs was brought back into the firm in 1997; he is commonly believed to be the savior of the company because he was able to revitalize the firm's innovation capabilities. Thus, his departure on medical leave, announced in December 2008 (see opening case), created uncertainty and concern on the part of investors.[4]

Competitive advantages and the differences they create in firm performance are often strongly related to the resources firms hold and how they are managed.[5] "Resources are the foundation for strategy, and unique bundles of resources generate competitive advantages that lead to wealth creation."[6] As Apple's experience shows, resources must be managed to simultaneously allow production efficiency and an ability to form competitive advantages such as the consistent development of innovative products.

To identify and successfully use resources over time, those leading firms need to think constantly about how to manage them to increase the value for customers who "are arbiters of value"[7] as they compare firms' goods and services against each other before making a purchase decision. As this chapter shows, firms achieve strategic competitiveness and earn above-average returns when their unique core competencies are effectively acquired, bundled, and leveraged to take advantage of opportunities in the external environment in ways that create value for customers.[8]

People are an especially critical resource for helping organizations learn how to continuously innovate as a means of achieving successful growth.[9] In other words, "smart growth" happens when the firm manages its need to grow with its ability to successfully manage growth.[10] People are a critical resource to efforts to grow successfully at 3M, where the director of global compensation says that harnessing the innovative powers of the firm's employees is the means for rekindling growth.[11] And, people at 3M as well as virtually all other firms who know how to effectively manage resources to help organizations learn how to continuously innovate are themselves a source of competitive advantage.[12] In fact, a global labor market now exists as firms seek talented individuals to add to their fold. As Richard Florida argues, "[W]herever talent goes, innovation, creativity, and economic growth are sure to follow."[13]

The fact that over time the benefits of any firm's value-creating strategy can be duplicated by its competitors is a key reason for having employees who know how to manage resources. These employees are critical to firms' efforts to perform well. Because all competitive advantages have a limited life,[14] the question of duplication is not if it will happen, but when. In general, the sustainability of a competitive advantage is a function of three factors: (1) the rate of core competence obsolescence because of environmental changes, (2) the availability of substitutes for the core competence, and (3) the imitability of the core competence.[15] The challenge for all firms, then, is to effectively manage current core competencies while simultaneously developing new ones.[16] Only when firms develop a continuous stream of capabilities that contribute to competitive advantages do they achieve strategic competitiveness, earn above-average returns, and remain ahead of competitors (see Chapter 5).

In Chapter 2, we examined general, industry, and competitor environments. Armed with this knowledge about the realities and conditions of their external environment, firms have a better understanding of marketplace opportunities and the characteristics of the competitive environment in which those opportunities exist. In this chapter, we focus on the firm itself. By analyzing its internal organization, a firm determines what it can do. Matching what a firm can do (a function of its resources, capabilities, core competencies, and competitive advantages) with what it might do (a function of opportunities and threats in the external environment) allows the firm to develop vision, pursue its mission, and select and implement its strategies.

We begin this chapter by briefly discussing conditions associated with analyzing the firm's internal organization. We then discuss the roles of resources and capabilities in developing core competencies, which are the sources of the firm's competitive advantages. Included in this discussion are the techniques firms use to identify and evaluate resources and capabilities and the criteria for selecting core competencies from among them. Resources and capabilities are not inherently valuable, but they create value when the firm can use them to perform certain activities that result in a competitive advantage. Accordingly, we also discuss the value chain concept and examine four criteria to evaluate core competencies that establish competitive advantage.[17] The chapter closes with cautionary comments about the need for firms to prevent their core competencies from becoming core rigidities. The existence of core rigidities indicates that the firm is too anchored to its past, which prevents it from continuously developing new competitive advantages.

Analyzing the Internal Organization

The Context of Internal Analysis

In the global economy, traditional factors such as labor costs, access to financial resources and raw materials, and protected or regulated markets remain sources of competitive advantage, but to a lesser degree.[18] One important reason is that competitors can apply their resources to successfully use an international strategy (discussed in Chapter 8) as a means of overcoming the advantages created by these more traditional sources. For example, Volkswagen began establishing production facilities in Slovakia "shortly after the Russians moved out" as part of its international strategy. Volkswagen is thought to have a competitive advantage over rivals such as France's Peugeot Citroen and South Korea's Kia Motors, firms that are now investing in Slovakia in an effort to duplicate the competitive advantage that has accrued to Volkswagen. In 2008, a total of 770,000 automobiles were manufactured in Slovakia[19]

Increasingly, those who analyze their firm's internal organization should use a **global mind-set** to do so. A global mind-set is the ability to analyze, understand, and manage (if in a managerial position) an internal organization in ways that are not dependent on the assumptions of a single country, culture, or context.[20] Because they are able to span artificial boundaries,[21] those with a global mind-set recognize that their firms must possess resources and capabilities that allow understanding of and appropriate responses to competitive situations that are influenced by country-specific factors and unique societal cultures. Firms populated with people having a global mind-set have a "key source of long-term competitive advantage in the global marketplace."[22]

Finally, analysis of the firm's internal organization requires that evaluators examine the firm's portfolio of resources and the *bundles* of heterogeneous resources and capabilities managers have created.[23] This perspective suggests that individual firms possess at least some resources and capabilities that other companies do not—at least not in the same combination. Resources are the source of capabilities, some of which

Using a global mind-set, Volkswagen's leaders decided that the firm should open facilities in Slovakia. Opening these facilities long before their competitors has led to a distinct competitive advantage for VW in Slovakia and surrounding countries.

© AP Photo/CTK, Jan Koller

A **global mind-set** is the ability to analyze, understand and manage an internal organization in ways that are not dependent on the assumptions of a single country, culture, or context.

lead to the development of a firm's core competencies or its competitive advantages.[24] Understanding how to *leverage* the firm's unique bundle of resources and capabilities is a key outcome decision makers seek when analyzing the internal organization.[25] Figure 3.1 illustrates the relationships among resources, capabilities, and core competencies and shows how firms use them to create strategic competitiveness. Before examining these topics in depth, we describe value and its creation.

Creating Value

By exploiting their core competencies to meet if not exceed the demanding standards of global competition, firms create value for customers.[26] **Value** is measured by a product's performance characteristics and by its attributes for which customers are willing to pay. Customers of Luby Cafeterias, for example, pay for meals that are value-priced, generally healthy, and served quickly in a casual setting.[27]

Firms with a competitive advantage offer value to customers that is superior to the value competitors provide.[28] Firms create value by innovatively bundling and leveraging their resources and capabilities.[29] Firms unable to creatively bundle and leverage their resources and capabilities in ways that create value for customers suffer performance declines. Sometimes, it seems that these declines may happen because firms fail to understand what customers value. For example, after learning that General Motors (GM) intended to focus on visual design to create value for buyers, one former GM customer said that in his view, people buying cars and trucks valued durability, reliability, good fuel economy, and a low cost of operation more than visual design.[30]

Ultimately, creating value for customers is the source of above-average returns for a firm. What the firm intends regarding value creation affects its choice of business-level strategy (see Chapter 4) and its organizational structure (see Chapter 11).[31] In Chapter 4's discussion of business-level strategies, we note that value is created by a product's low cost, by its highly differentiated features, or by a combination of low cost and high differentiation, compared with competitors' offerings. A business-level strategy

Value is measured by a product's performance characteristics and by its attributes for which customers are willing to pay.

Figure 3.1 Components of Internal Analysis Leading to Competitive Advantage and Strategic Competitiveness

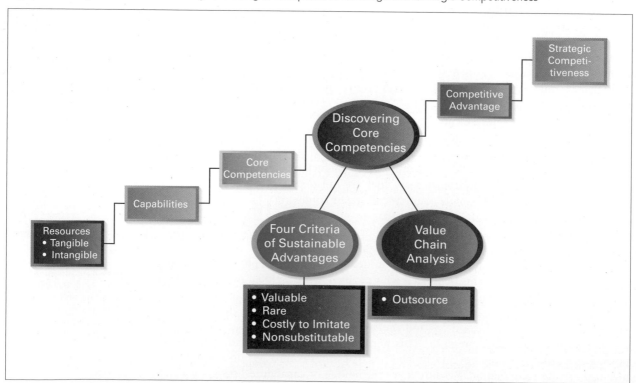

is effective only when it is grounded in exploiting the firm's core competencies and competitive advantages. Thus, successful firms continuously examine the effectiveness of current and future core competencies and advantages.[32]

At one time, the strategic management process was concerned largely with understanding the characteristics of the industry in which the firm competed and, in light of those characteristics, determining how the firm should be positioned relative to competitors. This emphasis on industry characteristics and competitive strategy underestimated the role of the firm's resources and capabilities in developing a competitive advantage. In fact, core competencies, in combination with product-market positions, are the firm's most important sources of competitive advantage.[33] The core competencies of a firm, in addition to results of analyses of its general, industry, and competitor environments, should drive its selection of strategies. The resources held by the firm and their context are important when formulating strategy.[34] As Clayton Christensen noted, "Successful strategists need to cultivate a deep understanding of the processes of competition and progress and of the factors that undergird each advantage. Only thus will they be able to see when old advantages are poised to disappear and how new advantages can be built in their stead."[35] By emphasizing core competencies when formulating strategies, companies learn to compete primarily on the basis of firm-specific differences, but they must be aware of how things are changing in the external environment as well.[36]

The Challenge of Analyzing the Internal Organization

The strategic decisions managers make about the components of their firm's internal organization are nonroutine,[37] have ethical implications,[38] and significantly influence the firm's ability to earn above-average returns.[39] These decisions involve choices about the assets the firm needs to collect and how to best use those assets. "Managers make choices precisely because they believe these contribute substantially to the performance and survival of their organizations."[40]

Making decisions involving the firm's assets—identifying, developing, deploying, and protecting resources, capabilities, and core competencies—may appear to be relatively easy. However, this task is as challenging and difficult as any other with which managers are involved; moreover, it is increasingly internationalized.[41] Some believe that the pressure on managers to pursue only decisions that help the firm meet the quarterly earnings expected by market analysts makes it difficult to accurately examine the firm's internal organization.[42]

The challenge and difficulty of making effective decisions are implied by preliminary evidence suggesting that one-half of organizational decisions fail.[43] Sometimes, mistakes are made as the firm analyzes conditions in its internal organization.[44] Managers might, for example, identify capabilities as core competencies that do not create a competitive advantage. This misidentification may have been the case at Polaroid Corporation as decision makers continued to believe that the skills it used to build its instant film cameras were highly relevant at the time its competitors were developing and using the skills required to introduce digital cameras.[45] When a mistake occurs, such as occurred at Polaroid, decision makers must have the confidence to admit it and take corrective actions.[46] A firm can still grow through well-intended errors; the learning generated by making and correcting mistakes can be important to the creation of new competitive advantages.[47] Moreover, firms and those managing them can learn from the failure resulting from a mistake—that is, what not to do when seeking competitive advantage.[48] Thus, difficult managerial decisions concerning resources, capabilities, and core competencies are characterized by three conditions: uncertainty, complexity, and intraorganizational conflicts (see Figure 3.2).[49]

Managers face *uncertainty* in terms of new proprietary technologies, rapidly changing economic and political trends, transformations in societal values, and shifts in customer demands.[50] Environmental uncertainty increases the *complexity* and range of issues to examine when studying the internal environment.[51] Consider the complexity associated with the decisions Gregory H. Boyce is encountering as CEO of Peabody Energy Corp.

Figure 3.2 Conditions Affecting Managerial Decisions about Resources, Capabilities, and Core Competencies

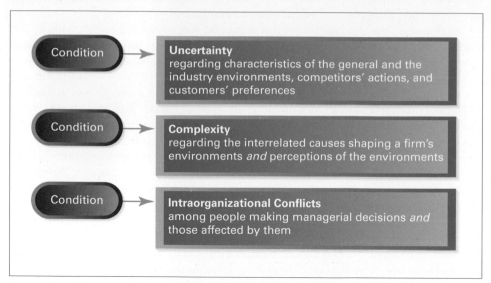

Source: Adapted from R. Amit & P. J. H. Schoemaker, 1993, Strategic assets and organizational rent, *Strategic Management Journal*, 14: 33.

Peabody is the world's largest coal company. But coal is thought of as a "dirty fuel," meaning that some think its future prospects are dim in light of global warming issues. Boyce is building a new "clean" coal-fired plant to produce energy and is a proponent of strong emissions standards. The firm argues for more use of "clean coal." Obviously, the complexity of these decisions is quite significant.[52] Biases about how to cope with uncertainty affect decisions about the resources and capabilities that will become the foundation of the firm's competitive advantage.[53] For example, Boyce strongly believes in coal's future, suggesting that automobiles capable of burning coal should be built. Finally, *intraorganizational conflict* surfaces when decisions are made about the core competencies to nurture as well as how to nurture them.

In making decisions affected by these three conditions, judgment is required. *Judgment* is the capability of making successful decisions when no obviously correct model or rule is available or when relevant data are unreliable or incomplete. In this type of situation, decision makers must be aware of possible cognitive biases. Overconfidence, for example, can often lower value when a correct decision is not obvious, such as making a judgment as to whether an internal resource is a strength or a weakness.[54]

When exercising judgment, decision makers often take intelligent risks. In the current competitive landscape, executive judgment can be a particularly important source of competitive advantage. One reason is that, over time, effective judgment allows a firm to build a strong reputation and retain the loyalty of stakeholders whose support is linked to above-average returns.[55]

As explained in the Strategic Focus, GE's managers build their capabilities in its executive leadership program. This program, which is recognized as one of the best in the world, helps GE's managers develop the capabilities to deal with uncertainty, complexity, and intraorganizational conflict. As such, they learn to use their judgment to make decisions that help GE navigate effectively in an uncertain and complex competitive landscape. The effectiveness of GE's managers and their ability to exercise good judgment in making strategic decisions is shown in the value GE has created for its shareholders and the number of former GE managers who are now CEOs of other major companies.

In the next section, we discuss how resources (such as young professionals and low-level managers) are developed and bundled to create capabilities.

GE BUILDS MANAGEMENT CAPABILITIES AND SHARES THEM WITH OTHERS

For many years, GE was considered one of the best organizations for management talent in the world. For the period, 1993–2002, GE was ranked first or second in market value added among the Stern Stewart 1,000 firms. In fact, GE was one of the top producers of shareholder value through the more than 20 years of Jack Welch's tenure as CEO. Most analysts attribute this phenomenal record to GE's exceptional leadership development program.

Approximately 9,000 managers participated in programs annually at GE's Leadership Center in Crotonville, New York. Managers received extensive leadership and team-based training in these programs. They even provided internal consulting by working on major GE projects, such as evaluating joint venture partners and analyzing opportunities for the use of artificial intelligence. Its world-class management development programs provided GE with an inventory of successors for almost any management position in the company. In fact, many analysts believe that the management development programs helped GE achieve a competitive advantage. Some argue that the management development process has the characteristics of a core competence; it is valuable, rare, difficult to imitate, and nonsubstitutable.

Jack Welch was often quoted as saying that people came first and strategy second. He actively participated in the management development program, sharing his expertise with other GE managers. Welch's successor, Jeff Immelt, does the same. Immelt believes that effective leaders learn constantly and also help others in the firm to learn as well. GE's leadership development program is so good that many companies look for talent among GE's management team because the program produces more leaders than it can usefully absorb. Thus, there are many company CEOs who are former GE managers. A study of these CEOs found they outperformed non-GE CEOs by a significant margin.

GE is experiencing problems in the economic malaise of 2008–2009. This is partly because of problems in its major financial services business (similar to the whole financial services industry). However, it is also partly due to the current CEO's emphasis on innovation for the future of the company. To innovate effectively requires that the firm invest now for returns several years later, which involves taking risks. As such, shorter-term returns are likely to suffer with high costs and lower returns awaiting the major longer-term payoffs of important innovations. Only time will tell if these investments to create innovations with long-term payoffs (as opposed to short-term returns) will work.

AP Photo/Mark Lennihan

GE CEO Jeff Immlet, like his predecessor Jack Welch, believes the development of leaders within the organization is an essential investment.

Sources: G. Spotts, 2006, GE's Immelt may have "ecomagination," but he needs project managers for jumbo-sized ideas, *FastCompany*, http://www.fastcompany.com, June 11; Things leaders do, *FastCompany*, http://www.fastcompany.com, December 19; S. Hamm, 2008, Tech innovations for tough times, ADNetAsia, http://www.zdnetasia.com, December 26; E. Smith, 2009, At GE, management development is a continuous process. Aprendia Corp, http://www.aprendiacorp.com, February 15; G. Rowe, R. E. White, D. Lehmbert, and J. R. Phillips, 2009, General Electric: An outlier in CEO talent development, *IVEY Business Journal*, http://www.iveybusinessjournal.com/article, January/February; P. Eavis & L. Denning, 2009, GE needs a circuit breaker, *Wall Street Journal*, http://www.wsj.com, March 5; P. Eaves, 2009, GE paper cut is greeted with relief, *Wall Street Journal*, http://www.wsj.com, March 13; D. Lehmberg, W. G. Rowe, R. E. White, and R. R. Phillips, 2009, The GE paradox: Competitive advantage through tangible non-firm-specific investment, *Journal of Management*, in press.

Resources, Capabilities, and Core Competencies

Resources, capabilities, and core competencies are the foundation of competitive advantage. Resources are bundled to create organizational capabilities. In turn, capabilities are the source of a firm's core competencies, which are the basis of competitive advantages.[56] Figure 3.1, on page 74, depicts these relationships. Here, we define and provide examples of these building blocks of competitive advantage.

Resources

Broad in scope, resources cover a spectrum of individual, social, and organizational phenomena.[57] Typically, resources alone do not yield a competitive advantage.[58] In fact, a competitive advantage is generally based on the unique bundling of several resources.[59] For example, Amazon.com combined service and distribution resources to develop its competitive advantages. The firm started as an online bookseller, directly shipping orders to customers. It quickly grew large and established a distribution network through which it could ship "millions of different items to millions of different customers." Lacking Amazon's combination of resources, traditional bricks-and-mortar companies, such as Borders, found it difficult to establish an effective online presence. These difficulties led some of them to develop partnerships with Amazon. Through these arrangements, Amazon now handles the online presence and the shipping of goods for several firms, including Borders—which now can focus on sales in its stores.[60] These types of arrangements are useful to the brick-and-mortar companies because they have little experience in shipping large amounts of diverse merchandise directly to individuals.

Some of a firm's resources (defined in Chapter 1 as inputs to the firm's production process) are tangible while others are intangible. **Tangible resources** are assets that can be observed and quantified. Production equipment, manufacturing facilities, distribution centers, and formal reporting structures are examples of tangible resources. Intangible resources are assets that are rooted deeply in the firm's history and have accumulated over time. Because they are embedded in unique patterns of routines, **intangible resources** are relatively difficult for competitors to analyze and imitate. Knowledge, trust between managers and employees, managerial capabilities, organizational routines (the unique ways people work together), scientific capabilities, the capacity for innovation, brand name, and the firm's reputation for its goods or services and how it interacts with people (such as employees, customers, and suppliers) are intangible resources.[61]

The four types of tangible resources are financial, organizational, physical, and technological (see Table 3.1). The three types of intangible resources are human, innovation, and reputational (see Table 3.2).

Tangible resources are assets that can be observed and quantified.

Intangible resources include assets that are rooted deeply in the firm's history, accumulate over time, and are relatively difficult for competitors to analyze and imitate.

Table 3.1 Tangible Resources

Financial Resources	• The firm's borrowing capacity • The firm's ability to generate internal funds
Organizational Resources	• The firm's formal reporting structure and its formal planning, controlling, and coordinating systems
Physical Resources	• Sophistication and location of a firm's plant and equipment • Access to raw materials
Technological Resources	• Stock of technology, such as patents, trademarks, copyrights, and trade secrets

Sources: Adapted from J. B. Barney, 1991, Firm resources and sustained competitive advantage, *Journal of Management*, 17: 101; R. M. Grant, 1991, *Contemporary Strategy Analysis*, Cambridge, U.K.: Blackwell Business, 100–102.

Table 3.2 Intangible Resources

Human Resources	• Knowledge
	• Trust
	• Managerial capabilities
	• Organizational routines
Innovation Resources	• Ideas
	• Scientific capabilities
	• Capacity to innovate
Reputational Resources	• Reputation with customers
	• Brand name
	• Perceptions of product quality, durability, and reliability
	• Reputation with suppliers
	• For efficient, effective, supportive, and mutually beneficial interactions and relationships

Sources: Adapted from R. Hall, 1992, The strategic analysis of intangible resources, *Strategic Management Journal*, 13: 136–139; R. M. Grant, 1991, *Contemporary Strategy Analysis*, Cambridge, U.K.: Blackwell Business, 101–104.

Tangible Resources

As tangible resources, a firm's borrowing capacity and the status of its physical facilities are visible. The value of many tangible resources can be established through financial statements, but these statements do not account for the value of all the firm's assets, because they disregard some intangible resources.[62] The value of tangible resources is also constrained because they are hard to leverage—it is difficult to derive additional business or value from a tangible resource. For example, an airplane is a tangible resource, but "You can't use the same airplane on five different routes at the same time. You can't put the same crew on five different routes at the same time. And the same goes for the financial investment you've made in the airplane."[63]

Although production assets are tangible, many of the processes necessary to use these assets are intangible. Thus, the learning and potential proprietary processes associated with a tangible resource, such as manufacturing facilities, can have unique intangible attributes, such as quality control processes, unique manufacturing processes, and technology that develop over time and create competitive advantage.[64]

Intangible Resources

Compared to tangible resources, intangible resources are a superior source of core competencies.[65] In fact, in the global economy, "the success of a corporation lies more in its intellectual and systems capabilities than in its physical assets. [Moreover], the capacity to manage human intellect—and to convert it into useful products and services—is fast becoming the critical executive skill of the age.[66]

Because intangible resources are less visible and more difficult for competitors to understand, purchase, imitate, or substitute for, firms prefer to rely on them rather than on tangible resources as the foundation for their capabilities and core competencies. In fact, the more unobservable (i.e., intangible) a resource is, the more sustainable will be the competitive advantage that is based on it.[67] Another benefit of intangible resources is that, unlike most tangible resources, their use can be leveraged. For instance, sharing knowledge among employees does not diminish its value for any one person. To the contrary, two people sharing their individualized knowledge sets often can be leveraged to create additional knowledge that, although new to each of them, contributes to performance improvements for the firm. This is especially true when members of the top management team share knowledge with each other to make more effective decisions. The new knowledge created is then often shared with managers and employees in each of the units managed by executives in the top management team.[68] With intangible resources, the larger the network of users, the greater the benefit to each party.

As shown in Table 3.2, the intangible resource of reputation is an important source of competitive advantage. Indeed, some argue that "a firm's reputation is widely considered to be a valuable resource associated with sustained competitive advantage."[69] Earned through the firm's actions as well as its words, a value-creating reputation is a product of years of superior marketplace competence as perceived by stakeholders.[70] A reputation indicates the level of awareness a firm has been able to develop among stakeholders and the degree to which they hold the firm in high esteem.[71]

A well-known and highly valued brand name is an application of reputation as a source of competitive advantage.[72] A continuing commitment to innovation and aggressive advertising facilitate firms' efforts to take advantage of the reputation associated with their brands.[73] Because of the desirability of its reputation, the Harley-Davidson brand name, for example, has such status that it adorns a limited edition Barbie doll, a popular restaurant in New York City, and a line of cologne. Additionally, the firm offers a broad range of clothing items, from black leather jackets to fashions for tots through Harley-Davidson MotorClothes.[74] Even established firms need to build their reputations in new markets that they enter. For example, Ford hired a well-respected Indian actor, Sunil Shetty, to serve as the brand ambassador for the Ford Endeavor launch in India. The Endeavor had the highest sales of SUVs in 2008.[75]

Harley Davidson's iconic reputation transcends motorcycles and for some represents an entire lifestyle.

Lon C. Diehl / PhotoEdit

Capabilities

Capabilities exist when resources have been purposely integrated to achieve a specific task or set of tasks. These tasks range from human resource selection to product marketing and research and development activities.[76] Critical to the building of competitive advantages, capabilities are often based on developing, carrying, and exchanging information and knowledge through the firm's human capital.[77] Client-specific capabilities often develop from repeated interactions with clients and the learning about their needs that occurs. As a result, capabilities often evolve and develop over time.[78] The foundation of many capabilities lies in the unique skills and knowledge of a firm's employees and, often, their functional expertise. Hence, the value of human capital in developing and using capabilities and, ultimately, core competencies cannot be overstated.[79]

While global business leaders increasingly support the view that the knowledge possessed by human capital is among the most significant of an organization's capabilities and may ultimately be at the root of all competitive advantages,[80] firms must also be able to utilize the knowledge they have and transfer it among their business units.[81] Given this reality, the firm's challenge is to create an environment that allows people to integrate their individual knowledge with that held by others in the firm so that, collectively, the firm has significant organizational knowledge.[82] As noted in the earlier Strategic Focus, GE has been effective in developing its human capital and in promoting the transfer of their knowledge throughout the company. Building important capabilities is critical to achieving high firm performance.[83]

As illustrated in Table 3.3, capabilities are often developed in specific functional areas (such as manufacturing, R&D, and marketing) or in a part of a functional area (e.g., advertising). Table 3.3 shows a grouping of organizational functions and the capabilities that some companies are thought to possess in terms of all or parts of those functions.

Core Competencies

Defined in Chapter 1, core competencies are capabilities that serve as a source of competitive advantage for a firm over its rivals. Core competencies distinguish a company competitively and reflect its personality. Core competencies emerge over time through an

Table 3.3 Examples of Firms' Capabilities

Functional Areas	Capabilities	Examples of Firms
Distribution	Effective use of logistics management techniques	Wal-Mart
Human Resources	Motivating, empowering, and retaining employees	Microsoft
Management Information Systems	Effective and efficient control of inventories through point-of-purchase data collection methods	Wal-Mart
Marketing	Effective promotion of brand-name products Effective customer service Innovative merchandising	Procter & Gamble Polo Ralph Lauren Corp. McKinsey & Co. Nordstrom Inc. Norrell Corporation Crate & Barrel
Management	Ability to envision the future of clothing Effective organizational structure	Hugo Boss PepsiCo
Manufacturing	Design and production skills yielding reliable products Product and design quality Miniaturization of components and products	Komatsu Witt Gas Technology Sony
Research & Development	Innovative technology Development of sophisticated elevator control solutions Rapid transformation of technology into new products and processes Digital technology	Caterpillar Otis Elevator Co. Chaparral Steel Thomson Consumer Electronics

organizational process of accumulating and learning how to deploy different resources and capabilities.[84] As the capacity to take action, core competencies are "crown jewels of a company," the activities the company performs especially well compared with competitors and through which the firm adds unique value to its goods or services over a long period of time.[85]

Innovation is thought to be a core competence at Xerox today. It is not surprising because this firm was built on a world-changing innovation—xerography. And even though Xerox was the first firm to integrate the mouse with the graphical user interface of a PC, it was Apple Computer that initially recognized the value of this innovation and derived value from it. In 2000, then-CEO Paul Allaire admitted that Xerox's business model no longer worked and that the firm had lost its innovative ability. Some nine-plus years later, things have changed for the better at Xerox. Using the capabilities of its scientists, engineers, and researchers, Xerox has reconstituted innovation as a core competence. For example, Xerox received more than 230 industry awards for the attributes of a range of products and services including image quality, performance, and technical innovation. One example of a recent focus of Xerox's research is on identifying products and services that help customers deal with the information explosion, according to Xerox's Chief Technology Officer, Sophie Vandebroek.[86]

How many core competencies are required for the firm to have a sustained competitive advantage? Responses to this question vary. McKinsey & Co. recommends that its clients identify no more than three or four competencies around which their strategic actions can be framed. Supporting and nurturing more than four core competencies may prevent a firm from developing the focus it needs to fully exploit its competencies in the marketplace. At Xerox, services expertise, employee talent, and technological skills are thought to be core competencies along with innovation.[87]

Building Core Competencies

Two tools help firms identify and build their core competencies. The first consists of four specific criteria of sustainable competitive advantage that firms can use to determine those capabilities that are core competencies. Because the capabilities shown in Table 3.3 have satisfied these four criteria, they are core competencies. The second tool is the value chain analysis. Firms use this tool to select the value-creating competencies that should be maintained, upgraded, or developed and those that should be outsourced.

Four Criteria of Sustainable Competitive Advantage

As shown in Table 3.4, capabilities that are valuable, rare, costly to imitate, and nonsubstitutable are core competencies. In turn, core competencies are sources of competitive advantage for the firm over its rivals. Capabilities failing to satisfy the four criteria of sustainable competitive advantage are not core competencies, meaning that although every core competence is a capability, not every capability is a core competence. In slightly different words, for a capability to be a core competence, it must be valuable and unique from a customer's point of view. For a competitive advantage to be sustainable, the core competence must be inimitable and nonsubstitutable by competitors.[88]

A sustained competitive advantage is achieved only when competitors cannot duplicate the benefits of a firm's strategy or when they lack the resources to attempt imitation. For some period of time, the firm may earn a competitive advantage by using capabilities that are, for example, valuable and rare, but imitable. For example, some firms are trying to gain an advantage by out-greening their competitors. Wal-Mart initiated a major sustainability program that helped to reduce the use of containers, saving approximately 1,000 barrels of oil and thousands of trees while simultaneously saving $2 million. GE's ecomanagement system, through which it has developed and introduced new, "greener" products to meet growing demand, is another example.[89] The length of time a firm can expect to retain its competitive advantage is a function of how quickly competitors can successfully imitate a good, service, or process. Sustainable competitive advantage results only when all four criteria are satisfied.

Valuable

Valuable capabilities allow the firm to exploit opportunities or neutralize threats in its external environment. By effectively using capabilities to exploit opportunities, a firm creates value for customers. Under former CEO Jack Welch's leadership, GE built a valuable competence in financial services. It built this powerful competence largely through acquisitions and its core competence in integrating newly acquired businesses. In addition, making such competencies as financial services highly successful required placing the right people in the right jobs. As noted in the opening case, Welch emphasized human capital because it is important in creating value for customers. That emphasis has continued in the company after Welch retired.

Table 3.4 The Four Criteria of Sustainable Competitive Advantage

Valuable Capabilities	• Help a firm neutralize threats or exploit opportunities
Rare Capabilities	• Are not possessed by many others
Costly-to-Imitate Capabilities	• Historical: A unique and a valuable organizational culture or brand name • Ambiguous cause: The causes and uses of a competence are unclear • Social complexity: Interpersonal relationships, trust, and friendship among managers, suppliers, and customers
Nonsubstitutable Capabilities	• No strategic equivalent

Valuable capabilities allow the firm to exploit opportunities or neutralize threats in its external environment.

Rare

Rare capabilities are capabilities that few, if any, competitors possess. A key question to be answered when evaluating this criterion is, "How many rival firms possess these valuable capabilities?" Capabilities possessed by many rivals are unlikely to be sources of competitive advantage for anyone of them. Instead, valuable but common (i.e., not rare) resources and capabilities are sources of competitive parity.[90] Competitive advantage results only when firms develop and exploit valuable capabilities that differ from those shared with competitors.

Costly to Imitate

Costly-to-imitate capabilities are capabilities that other firms cannot easily develop. Capabilities that are costly to imitate are created because of one reason or a combination of three reasons (see Table 3.4). First, a firm sometimes is able to develop capabilities because of *unique historical conditions*. As firms evolve, they often acquire or develop capabilities that are unique to them.[91]

A firm with a unique and valuable *organizational culture* that emerged in the early stages of the company's history "may have an imperfectly imitable advantage over firms founded in another historical period;"[92] one in which less valuable or less competitively useful values and beliefs strongly influenced the development of the firm's culture. Briefly discussed in Chapter 1, organizational culture is a set of values that are shared by members in the organization. This will be explained in more detail in Chapter 12. An organizational culture is a source of advantage when employees are held together tightly by their belief in it.[93]

For example, culture is a competitive advantage for Mustang Engineering (an engineering and project management firm based in Houston, Texas). Established as a place where people are expected to take care of people, Mustang offers "a company culture that we believe is unique in the industry. Mustang is a work place with a family feel. A client once described Mustang as a world-class company with a mom-and-pop culture."[94]

A second condition of being costly to imitate occurs when the link between the firm's capabilities and its competitive advantage is *causally ambiguous*.[95] In these instances, competitors can't clearly understand how a firm uses its capabilities as the foundation for competitive advantage. As a result, firms are uncertain about the capabilities they should develop to duplicate the benefits of a competitor's value-creating strategy. For years, firms tried to imitate Southwest Airlines' low-cost strategy but most have been unable to do so, primarily because they can't duplicate Southwest's unique culture. Of all Southwest imitators, Ryanair, an Irish airline headquartered in Dublin, is the most successful. However, Ryanair is also a controversial company, praised by some, criticized by others as described in the Strategic Focus. Ryanair's core competence is its capability to keep its costs excessively low and to generate alternative sources of revenue.

Social complexity is the third reason that capabilities can be costly to imitate. Social complexity means that at least some, and frequently many, of the firm's capabilities are the product of complex social phenomena. Interpersonal relationships, trust, friendships among managers and between managers and employees, and a firm's reputation with suppliers and customers are examples of socially complex capabilities. Southwest Airlines is careful to hire people who fit with its culture. This complex interrelationship between the culture and human capital adds value in ways that other airlines cannot, such as jokes on flights by the flight attendants or the cooperation between gate personnel and pilots.

Nonsubstitutable

Nonsubstitutable capabilities are capabilities that do not have strategic equivalents. This final criterion for a capability to be a source of competitive advantage "is that there must be no strategically equivalent valuable resources that are themselves either not rare or imitable. Two valuable firm resources (or two bundles of firm resources) are strategically equivalent when they each can be separately exploited to implement the same strategies."[96] In general, the strategic value of capabilities increases as they become more

Rare capabilities are capabilities that few, if any, competitors possess.

Costly-to-imitate capabilities are capabilities that other firms cannot easily develop.

Nonsubstitutable capabilities are capabilities that do not have strategic equivalents.

RYANAIR: THE PASSIONATE COST CUTTER THAT IS BOTH LOVED AND HATED

Ryanair is the leading low-cost airline in Europe. It has achieved a high market share by relentlessly holding down costs and thereby offering the lowest prices on its routes. To attract new customers, it once offered flights for one penny to selected destinations. It sold almost 500,000 tickets with the promotion. While Michael O'Leary, Ryanair CEO, is known to be cheap (he will not provide employees with pens; he recommends that they get them from hotels where they stay overnight), the primary reason for Ryanair's lowest cost status is that it has the fastest turnarounds in the industry (their speed resembles that of an auto racing pit crew). O'Leary is also constantly identifying new revenue streams such as charges for use of airport check-in facilities, charging for each piece of luggage, offering rental cars at the destination, charging to use the toilet on the plane, etc.

To obtain free publicity, O'Leary or other executives often make outrageous statements and roundly criticize their competitors to get Ryanair's name in the news. The firm uses multiple marketing gimmicks such as advertising that directly criticizes competitors and even some "off-color" advertising slogans. The firm's core competence is the capability to maintain the lowest costs in the industry and to generate alternative revenues. Because of its very low fares, its passenger load grew at an annual rate of approximately 25 percent until the economic crisis that began in 2008, but the company remained profitable in 2008.

Despite its success, Ryanair receives a significant amount of criticism. In 2006, for example, it was voted as the least favorite airline (despite its popularity evidenced in passenger numbers). Critics have also accused Ryanair of poor customer service, an unfriendly, uncaring staff, and hidden charges. Yet O'Leary believes that Ryanair may be one of the few airlines in Europe left standing after the latest severe economic recession. He is planning growth (although the airline announced some small reductions in service and staff in 2009) and is negotiating with Boeing and Airbus to buy as many as 400 new aircraft. With its decided strengths and acknowledged weaknesses, the future of Ryanair will be interesting to witness.

ULRICH PERREY/dpa /Landov

Michael O'Leary, CEO of low-cost airline Ryanair, poses with a model of an aircraft during a press conference in Hamburg, Germany. O'Leary's intense scrutiny of costs and monetizing of services may contribute to lower ticket prices but not necessarily customer satisfaction.

Sources: 2005, Ryanair exercises options on five Boeing 737s, Wikinews, http://en.wikinews.org, June 13; M. Scott, 2007, Ryanair flying high, *BusinessWeek*, http://www.businessweek.com, July 31; A. Davidson, 2008, Michael O'Leary: Ryanair's rebel with a cause, *The Sunday Times*, http://business.timesonline.co.uk, December 7; K. Done, 2009, Ryanair in talks to buy 400 aircraft, *Financial Times*, http://www.ft.com, February 2; K. Done, 2009, Virgin and Ryanair to cut jobs, *Financial Times*, http://www.ft.com, February 12; 2009, Ryanair Holdings PLC, http://www.answers.com, March 13; 2009, Ryanair, Wikipedia. http://www.wikipedia.org, March 13.

Table 3.5 Outcomes from Combinations of the Criteria for Sustainable Competitive Advantage

Is the Resource or Capability Valuable?	Is the Resource or Capability Rare?	Is the Resource or Capability Costly to Imitate?	Is the Resource or Capability Nonsubstitutable?	Competitive Consequences	Performance Implications
No	No	No	No	Competitive disadvantage	Below-average returns
Yes	No	No	Yes/no	Competitive parity	Average returns
Yes	Yes	No	Yes/no	Temporary competitive advantage	Average returns to above-average returns
Yes	Yes	Yes	Yes/no	Sustainable competitive advantage	Above-average returns

difficult to substitute. The more invisible capabilities are, the more difficult it is for firms to find substitutes and the greater the challenge is to competitors trying to imitate a firm's value-creating strategy. Firm-specific knowledge and trust-based working relationships between managers and nonmanagerial personnel, such as existed for years at Southwest Airlines, are examples of capabilities that are difficult to identify and for which finding a substitute is challenging. However, causal ambiguity may make it difficult for the firm to learn as well and may stifle progress, because the firm may not know how to improve processes that are not easily codified and thus are ambiguous.[97]

In summary, only using valuable, rare, costly-to-imitate, and nonsubstitutable capabilities creates sustainable competitive advantage. Table 3.5 shows the competitive consequences and performance implications resulting from combinations of the four criteria of sustainability. The analysis suggested by the table helps managers determine the strategic value of a firm's capabilities. The firm should not emphasize capabilities that fit the criteria described in the first row in the table (i.e., resources and capabilities that are neither valuable nor rare and that are imitable and for which strategic substitutes exist). Capabilities yielding competitive parity and either temporary or sustainable competitive advantage, however, will be supported. Some competitors such as Coca-Cola and PepsiCo may have capabilities that result in competitive parity. In such cases, the firms will nurture these capabilities while simultaneously trying to develop capabilities that can yield either a temporary or sustainable competitive advantage.

Value Chain Analysis

Value chain analysis allows the firm to understand the parts of its operations that create value and those that do not.[98] Understanding these issues is important because the firm earns above-average returns only when the value it creates is greater than the costs incurred to create that value.[99]

The value chain is a template that firms use to analyze their cost position and to identify the multiple means that can be used to facilitate implementation of a chosen business-level strategy.[100] Today's competitive landscape demands that firms examine their value chains in a global rather than a domestic-only context.[101] In particular, activities associated with supply chains should be studied within a global context.[102]

As shown in Figure 3.3, a firm's value chain is segmented into primary and support activities. **Primary activities** are involved with a product's physical creation, its sale and distribution to buyers, and its service after the sale. **Support activities** provide the assistance necessary for the primary activities to take place.

The value chain shows how a product moves from the raw-material stage to the final customer. For individual firms, the essential idea of the value chain is to create additional value without incurring significant costs while doing so and to capture the value that has

Primary activities are involved with a product's physical creation, its sale and distribution to buyers, and its service after the sale.

Support activities provide the assistance necessary for the primary activities to take place.

Figure 3.3 The Basic Value Chain

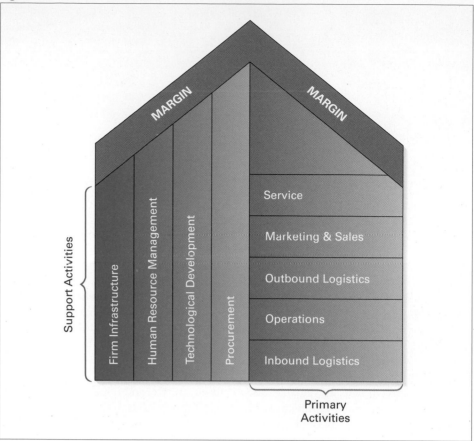

been created. In a globally competitive economy, the most valuable links on the chain are people who have knowledge about customers. This locus of value-creating possibilities applies just as strongly to retail and service firms as to manufacturers. Moreover, for organizations in all sectors, the effects of e-commerce make it increasingly necessary for companies to develop value-adding knowledge processes to compensate for the value and margin that the Internet strips from physical processes.[103]

Table 3.6 lists the items that can be evaluated to determine the value-creating potential of primary activities. In Table 3.7, the items for evaluating support activities are shown. All items in both tables should be evaluated relative to competitors' capabilities. To be a source of competitive advantage, a resource or capability must allow the firm (1) to perform an activity in a manner that provides value superior to that provided by competitors, or (2) to perform a value-creating activity that competitors cannot perform. Only under these conditions does a firm create value for customers and have opportunities to capture that value.

Creating value through value chain activities often requires building effective alliances with suppliers (and sometimes others to which the firm outsources activities, as discussed in the next section) and developing strong positive relationships with customers. When firms have such strong positive relationships with suppliers and customers, they are said to have "social capital."[104] The relationships themselves have value because they produce knowledge transfer and access to resources that a firm may not hold internally.[105] To build social capital whereby resources such as knowledge are transferred across organizations requires trust between the parties. The partners must trust each other in order to allow their resources to be used in such a way that both parties will benefit over time and neither party will take advantage of the other.[106] Trust and social capital usually evolve over time with repeated interactions but firms can also establish special means to jointly

Table 3.6 Examining the Value-Creating Potential of Primary Activities

Inbound Logistics

Activities, such as materials handling, warehousing, and inventory control, used to receive, store, and disseminate inputs to a product.

Operations

Activities necessary to convert the inputs provided by inbound logistics into final product form. Machining, packaging, assembly, and equipment maintenance are examples of operations activities.

Outbound Logistics

Activities involved with collecting, storing, and physically distributing the final product to customers. Examples of these activities include finished-goods warehousing, materials handling, and order processing.

Marketing and Sales

Activities completed to provide means through which customers can purchase products and to induce them to do so. To effectively market and sell products, firms develop advertising and promotional campaigns, select appropriate distribution channels, and select, develop, and support their sales force.

Service

Activities designed to enhance or maintain a product's value. Firms engage in a range of service-related activities, including installation, repair, training, and adjustment.

Each activity should be examined relative to competitors' abilities. Accordingly, firms rate each activity as *superior, equivalent,* or *inferior.*

Source: Adapted with the permission of The Free Press, an imprint of Simon & Schuster Adult Publishing Group, from *Competitive Advantage: Creating and Sustaining Superior Performance,* by Michael E. Porter, pp. 39–40, Copyright © 1985, 1998 by Michael E. Porter.

Table 3.7 Examining the Value-Creating Potential of Support Activities

Procurement

Activities completed to purchase the inputs needed to produce a firm's products. Purchased inputs include items fully consumed during the manufacture of products (e.g., raw materials and supplies, as well as fixed assets—machinery, laboratory equipment, office equipment, and buildings).

Technological Development

Activities completed to improve a firm's product and the processes used to manufacture it. Technological development takes many forms, such as process equipment, basic research and product design, and servicing procedures.

Human Resource Management

Activities involved with recruiting, hiring, training, developing, and compensating all personnel.

Firm Infrastructure

Firm infrastructure includes activities such as general management, planning, finance, accounting, legal support, and governmental relations that are required to support the work of the entire value chain. Through its infrastructure, the firm strives to effectively and consistently identify external opportunities and threats, identify resources and capabilities, and support core competencies.

Each activity should be examined relative to competitors' abilities. Accordingly, firms rate each activity as *superior, equivalent,* or *inferior.*

Source: Adapted with the permission of The Free Press, an imprint of Simon & Schuster Adult Publishing Group, from Competitive Advantage: Creating and Sustaining Superior Performance, by Michael E. Porter, pp. 40–43, Copyright © 1985, 1998 by Michael E. Porter.

manage alliances that promote greater trust with the outcome of enhanced benefits for both partners.[107]

Sometimes start-up firms create value by uniquely reconfiguring or recombining parts of the value chain. FedEx changed the nature of the delivery business by reconfiguring outbound logistics (a primary activity) and human resource management (a support activity) to provide overnight deliveries, creating value in the process. As shown in Figure 3.4, the Internet has changed many aspects of the value chain for a broad range of firms. A key reason is that the Internet affects how people communicate, locate information, and buy goods and services.

Evaluating a firm's capability to execute its primary and support activities is challenging. Earlier in the chapter, we noted that identifying and assessing the value of a firm's resources and capabilities requires judgment. Judgment is equally necessary when using value chain analysis, because no obviously correct model or rule is universally available to help in the process.

Figure 3.4 Prominent Applications of the Internet in the Value Chain

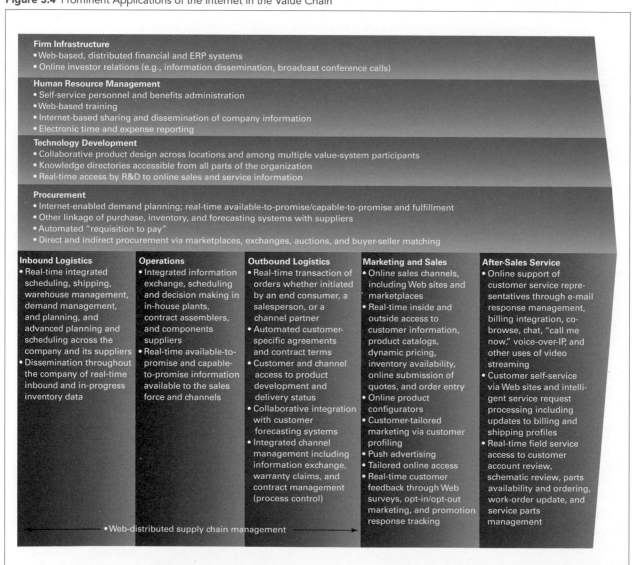

What should a firm do about primary and support activities in which its resources and capabilities are not a source of core competence and, hence, of competitive advantage? Outsourcing is one solution to consider.

Outsourcing

Concerned with how components, finished goods, or services will be obtained, **outsourcing** is the purchase of a value-creating activity from an external supplier.[108] Not-for-profit agencies as well as for-profit organizations actively engage in outsourcing.[109] Firms engaging in effective outsourcing increase their flexibility, mitigate risks, and reduce their capital investments.[110] In multiple global industries, the trend toward outsourcing continues at a rapid pace.[111] Moreover, in some industries virtually all firms seek the value that can be captured through effective outsourcing. As with other strategic management process decisions, careful analysis is required before the firm decides to engage in outsourcing.[112]

Outsourcing can be effective because few, if any, organizations possess the resources and capabilities required to achieve competitive superiority in all primary and support activities. For example, research suggests that few companies can afford to develop internally all the technologies that might lead to competitive advantage.[113] By nurturing a smaller number of capabilities, a firm increases the probability of developing a competitive advantage because it does not become overextended. In addition, by outsourcing activities in which it lacks competence, the firm can fully concentrate on those areas in which it can create value.

Firms must outsource only activities where they cannot create value or where they are at a substantial disadvantage compared to competitors.[114] To verify that the appropriate primary and support activities are outsourced, managers should have four skills: strategic thinking, deal making, partnership governance, and change management.[115] Managers need to understand whether and how outsourcing creates competitive advantage within their company—they need to think strategically. To complete effective outsourcing transactions, these managers must also be deal makers, able to secure rights from external providers that can be fully used by internal managers. They must be able to oversee[116] and govern appropriately the relationship with the company to which the services were outsourced. Because outsourcing can significantly change how an organization operates, managers administering these programs must also be able to manage that change, including resolving employee resistance that accompanies any significant change effort.[117]

The consequences of outsourcing cause additional concerns.[118] For the most part, these concerns revolve around the potential loss in firms' innovative ability and the loss of jobs within companies that decide to outsource some of their work activities to others. Thus, innovation and technological uncertainty are two important issues to consider in making outsourcing decisions. However, firms can also learn from outsource suppliers how to increase their own innovation capabilities.[119] Companies must be aware of these issues and be prepared to fully consider the concerns about opportunities from outsourcing suggested by different stakeholders (e.g., employees). The opportunities and concerns may be especially great when firms outsource activities or functions to a foreign supply source (often referred to as offshoring).[120] Bangalore and Belfast are the newest hotspots for technology outsourcing, competing with major operations in China and India.[121] Yet, IBM recently made the decision to keep outsourced activities in the United States instead of moving them to a foreign location.[122]

As is true with all strategic management tools and techniques, criteria should be established to guide outsourcing decisions. Outsourcing is big business, but not every outsourcing decision is successful. For example, amid delays and cost overruns, Electronic Data Systems abandoned a $1 billion opportunity to run Dow Chemical Co.'s phone and computer networks. These less-than-desirable outcomes indicate that firms should carefully study outsourcing opportunities to verify that they will indeed create value that exceeds the cost incurred.

STRATEGY RIGHT NOW

Read how Boeing's experience with the 787 Dreamliner highlights many of the benefits and concerns associated with outsourcing.

www.cengage.com/management/hitt

Outsourcing is the purchase of a value-creating activity from an external supplier.

Competencies, Strengths, Weaknesses, and Strategic Decisions

At the conclusion of the internal analysis, firms must identify their strengths and weaknesses in resources, capabilities, and core competencies. For example, if they have weak capabilities or do not have core competencies in areas required to achieve a competitive advantage, they must acquire those resources and build the capabilities and competencies needed. Alternatively, they could decide to outsource a function or activity where they are weak in order to improve the value that they provide to customers.[123]

Therefore, firms need to have the appropriate resources and capabilities to develop the desired strategy and create value for customers and other stakeholders such as shareholders.[124] Managers should understand that having a significant quantity of resources is not the same as having the "right" resources. Moreover, decision makers sometimes become more focused and productive when their organization's resources are constrained.[125] Managers must help the firm obtain and use resources, capabilities, and core competencies in ways that generate value-creating competitive advantages.

Tools such as outsourcing help the firm focus on its core competencies as the source of its competitive advantages. However, evidence shows that the value-creating ability of core competencies should never be taken for granted. Moreover, the ability of a core competence to be a permanent competitive advantage can't be assumed. The reason for these cautions is that all core competencies have the potential to become *core rigidities*. Thus, a core competence is usually a strength because it is a source of competitive advantage. If emphasized when it is no longer competitively relevant, it can become a weakness, a seed of organizational inertia.

The Ford Flex, which the company launched in fall 2008, was designed to turn heads and excite consumers interested in crossover vehicles. Could the Flex represent a shift toward more customer-centered product development?

Inertia embedded in the organizational culture may be a problem at Ford Motor Company, where some argue that the firm's culture has become a core rigidity that is constraining efforts to improve performance. In one writer's words: "One way or another, the company will have to figure out how to produce more vehicles that consumers actually want. And doing that will require addressing the most fundamental problem of all: Ford's dysfunctional, often defeatist culture."[126] In contrast, Toyota constantly reexamines product planning, customer service, sales and marketing, and employee training practices to prevent "being spoiled by success."[127]

Events occurring in the firm's external environment create conditions through which core competencies can become core rigidities, generate inertia, and stifle innovation. "Often the flip side, the dark side, of core capabilities is revealed due to external events when new competitors figure out a better way to serve the firm's customers, when new technologies emerge, or when political or social events shift the ground underneath."[128] However, in the final analysis, changes in the external environment do not cause core competencies to become core rigidities; rather, strategic myopia and inflexibility on the part of managers are the causes.

After studying its external environment to determine what it might choose to do (as explained in Chapter 2) and its internal organization to understand what it can do (as explained in this chapter), the firm has the information required to select a business-level strategy that will help it reach its vision and mission. We describe different business-level strategies in the next chapter.

SUMMARY

- In the global business environment, traditional factors (e.g., labor costs and superior access to financial resources and raw materials) can still create a competitive advantage. However, these factors are less often a source of competitive advantage in the current competitive landscape. In the current landscape, the resources, capabilities, and core competencies in the firm's internal organization likely have a stronger influence on its performance than do conditions in the external environment. The most effective organizations recognize that strategic competitiveness and above-average returns result only when core competencies (identified by studying the firm's internal organization) are matched with opportunities (determined by studying the firm's external environment).

- No competitive advantage lasts forever. Over time, rivals use their own unique resources, capabilities, and core competencies to form different value-creating propositions that duplicate the value-creating ability of the firm's competitive advantages. In general, the Internet's capabilities are reducing the sustainability of many competitive advantages. Because competitive advantages are not permanently sustainable, firms must exploit their current advantages while simultaneously using their resources and capabilities to form new advantages that can lead to future competitive success.

- Effectively managing core competencies requires careful analysis of the firm's resources (inputs to the production process) and capabilities (resources that have been purposely integrated to achieve a specific task or set of tasks). The knowledge possessed by human capital is among the most significant of an organization's capabilities and ultimately provides the base for most competitive advantages. The firm must create an environment that allows people to integrate their individual knowledge with that held by others so that, collectively, the firm has significant organizational knowledge.

- Individual resources are usually not a source of competitive advantage. Capabilities are a more likely source of competitive advantages, especially more sustainable ones. The firm's nurturing and support of core competencies that are based on capabilities are less visible to rivals and, as such, they are more difficult to understand and imitate.

- Only when a capability is valuable, rare, costly to imitate, and nonsubstitutable is it a core competence and a source of competitive advantage. Over time, core competencies must be supported, but they cannot be allowed to become core rigidities. Core competencies are a source of competitive advantage only when they allow the firm to create value by exploiting opportunities in its external environment. When it can no longer do so, the company shifts its attention to selecting or forming other capabilities that satisfy the four criteria of a sustainable competitive advantage.

- Value chain analysis is used to identify and evaluate the competitive potential of resources and capabilities. By studying their skills relative to those associated with primary and support activities, firms can understand their cost structure and identify the activities through which they can create value.

- When the firm cannot create value in either an internal primary or support activity, outsourcing is considered. Used commonly in the global economy, outsourcing is the purchase of a value-creating activity from an external supplier. The firm should outsource only to companies possessing a competitive advantage in terms of the particular primary or support activity under consideration. In addition, the firm must continuously verify that it is not outsourcing activities from which it could create value.

REVIEW | QUESTIONS

1. Why is it important for a firm to study and understand its internal organization?

2. What is value? Why is it critical for the firm to create value? How does it do so?

3. What are the differences between tangible and intangible resources? Why is it important for decision makers to understand these differences? Are tangible resources linked more closely to the creation of competitive advantages than are intangible resources, or is the reverse true? Why?

4. What are capabilities? How do firms create capabilities?

5. What are the four criteria used to determine which of a firm's capabilities are core competencies? Why is it important for firms to use these criteria in developing capabilities?

6. What is value chain analysis? What does the firm gain when it successfully uses this tool?

7. What is outsourcing? Why do firms outsource? Will outsourcing's importance grow as we progress in the twenty-first century? If so, why?

8. How do firms identify internal strengths and weaknesses? Why is it vital that managers have a clear understanding of their firm's strengths and weaknesses?

EXPERIENTIAL EXERCISES

EXERCISE 1: WHAT MAKES A GREAT OUTSOURCING FIRM?

The focus of this chapter is on understanding how firm resources and capabilities serve as the cornerstone for competencies, and, ultimately, a competitive advantage. However, when firms cannot create value in either a primary or support activity, outsourcing becomes a potential strategy. Yet with the recession that began in 2007 there seems to be a shift occurring. According to the International Association of Outsourcing Professionals (IAOP) at their 2008 annual conference, nearly 75 percent of organizations will do the same or more outsourcing in response to the financial crisis and that greater contract flexibility is their top need. However, 25 percent of organizations reported lower volumes and 19 percent said they have renegotiated lower prices on existing contracts. In addition, the IAOP reports more than 53 percent of respondents say they are doing more due diligence and also favor working with larger providers.

During that same 2008 conference, the IAOP announced their Global Outsourcing 100, a ranking of the world's best outsourcing service providers. The evaluation process mirrors that employed by many top customers and considers four key criteria: (1) size and growth in revenue, employees, centers, and countries served; (2) customer experience as demonstrated through the value being created for the company's top customers; (3) depth and breadth of competencies as demonstrated through industry recognition, relevant certifications, and investment in the development of people, processes, and technologies; and (4) management capabilities as reflected in the experience and accomplishments of the business's top leaders and investments in management systems that ensure outsourcing success. Below are the top 10 for 2008.

1. Accenture
2. IBM
3. Infosys Technologies
4. Sodexo
5. Capgemini
6. Tata Consultancy Services
7. Wipro Technologies
8. Hewlett-Packard
9. Genpact
10. Tech Mahindra

Split up into groups and pick one of the Global Outsourcing 100 to analyze. The complete list can be found on the IAOP website at http://www.outsourcingprofessional.org/. (A new list is published annually in *Fortune* magazine and updated on the IAOP website.) Prepare a brief presentation using your research and the contents of this chapter that addresses at a minimum the following questions:

- Why was this company chosen? What has been their history as regards outsourcing as a source of revenue?
- How does the firm describe, or imply, its value proposition?
- What unique competitive advantage does the firm exhibit?
- Do you consider this to be a sustainable competitive advantage? Utilize the four sources of sustainable competitive advantage as your guide.

EXERCISE 2: COMPETITIVE ADVANTAGE AND PRO SPORTS

What makes one team successful while another team struggles? At first glance, a National Football League franchise or Women's National Basketball Association team may not seem like a typical business. However, professional sports have been around for a long time: pro hockey in the United States emerged around World War I, and pro basketball shortly after World War II; both could be considered newcomers relative to the founding of baseball leagues. Pro sports are big business as well, as evidenced by the Boston Red Sox's 2009 opening day payroll of $121,745,999.

With this exercise, we will use tools and concepts from the chapter to analyze factors underlying the success or failure of different sports teams. Working as a group, pick two teams that play in the same league. For each team, address the following questions:

- How successful are the two teams you selected? How stable has their performance been over time?
- Make an inventory of the characteristics of the two teams. Characteristics you might choose to identify include reputation, coaching, fan base, playing style and tactics, individual players, and so on. For each characteristic you describe:
  - Decide if it is best characterized as tangible, intangible, or a capability.
  - Apply the concepts of value, rarity, imitation, and sustainability to analyze its value-creating ability.
- Is there evidence of bundling in this situation (i.e., the combination of different resources and capabilities)?
- What would it take for these two teams to substantially change their competitive position over time? For example, if a team is successful, what types of changes in resources and capabilities might affect it negatively? If a team is below average, what changes would you recommend to its portfolio of resources and capabilities?

VIDEO | CASE

BRIDGING THE KNOWING–DOING GAP

Professor Jeffrey Pfeffer/Graduate School of Business, Stanford University

Professor Jeffrey Pfeffer of Stanford Business School comments on a concept he coined the knowing–doing gap in which he discusses why conventional wisdom is often the correct path but quite often not the one taken. Why is this so?

Before you watch the video consider the following concepts and questions and be prepared to discuss them in class:

Concepts
- Human capital
- Value of intangible resources
- Sustainable competitive advantage
- Internal organization
- Capabilities
- Core competence

Questions

1. Do you think common sense today is a bit uncommon? If so, why do you think that is so? For example, at times are the things we know we need to do, not something we actually do?
2. What internal factors might inhibit organizations or individuals from doing the right thing

CHAPTER 4

Business-Level Strategy

Studying this chapter should provide you with the strategic management knowledge needed to:

1. Define business-level strategy.

2. Discuss the relationship between customers and business-level strategies in terms of *who*, *what*, and *how*.

3. Explain the differences among business-level strategies.

4. Use the five forces of competition model to explain how above-average returns can be earned through each business-level strategy.

5. Describe the risks of using each of the business-level strategies.

ACER GROUP: USING A "BARE BONES" COST STRUCTURE TO SUCCEED IN GLOBAL PC MARKETS

Established in 1976, Acer Group uses four PC brands—Acer, Gateway, Packard Bell, and eMachines—as the foundation for its multi-brand global strategy. Currently the third largest PC seller in the world (behind only Hewlett-Packard and Dell), Acer employs over 6,000 and had 2008 revenues of $16.65 billion. Impressively, Acer's operating profit rose 38 percent from 2007 to 2008, to roughly $415 million. These performance data suggest that Acer was competing very successfully during the global recession.

There is little question as to the business-level strategy Acer uses. Noting that running a business with lower costs is good when markets are growing but that doing so is even better when markets are not growing (which was the case during the global recession), Acer's CEO Gianfranco Lanci remains strongly committed to the cost leadership strategy (this strategy is discussed later in the chapter) as the path to strategic competitiveness and above-average returns for his firm.

According to Lanci, a focus on controlling costs is part of Acer's culture. In his words: "We have always operated on the assumption that costs need to be kept under control. It's a kind of overall culture we have in the company. If you are used to it, you can run low costs without running into trouble." A decision to sell only through retailers and other outlets and to outsource all manufacturing and assembly operations are other actions Acer takes to reduce its costs as it uses the cost leadership strategy. Combined, the distribution channels Acer uses and its outsourcing of operations help to cut overhead costs—research and development and marketing and general and administrative expenses—to 8 percent of sales, well below HP's 15 percent and Dell's 14 percent. Lanci describes the cost savings in the following manner: "We focus 100% on indirect sales, while today most of the people are running direct and indirect at the same time. If you run direct and indirect, you need different setups; by definition, you add costs. We also focus only on consumers and small and midsize businesses. We never said we wanted to address the enterprise segment. This is another big difference."

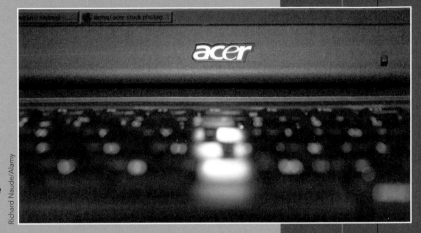

By diligently managing costs, Acer has offered consumers fully featured netbooks, such as their Aspire Timeline, at a price well below their major competitors.

Richard Naude/Alamy

Because of its lower overhead cost structure, Acer is able to price its products, such as netbooks, below those of competitors. Somewhat new to the PC market, netbooks are relatively small and inexpensive PCs with functionalities below those offered by laptops and desktops. However, their popularity continues to grow. Unlike Dell, HP, and Lenovo, Acer quickly entered the netbook market and sold 32 percent of all netbooks shipped worldwide at the end of 2008.

Acer uses its "bare bones" cost structure as the foundation for pricing its various products such as laptops very aggressively. The firm's new ultrathin laptop was expected to have a starting price of $650. For products with similar capabilities, the price for the HP product was around $1,800 and about $2,000 for the Dell product. After observing these prices, an analyst said that Acer was changing "… customers' perception of what you should pay for a computer."

Sources: 2009, Acer Group, http://www.acer.com, June 15; L. Chao, 2009, Acer expects low-cost laptops to lift shipments, *Wall Street Journal Online*, http://www.wsj.com, April 9; B. Einhorn, 2009, Acer closes in on Dell's No. 2 PC ranking, *BusinessWeek Online*, http://www.businessweek.com, January 15; B. Einhorn, 2009, How Acer is burning its PC rivals, *BusinessWeek Online*, http://www.businessweek.com, April 7; B. Einhorn, 2009, Acer boss Lanci takes aim at Dell and HP, *BusinessWeek Online*, http://www.businessweek.com, April 13; B. Einhorn, 2009, Acer's game-changing PC offensive, *BusinessWeek*, April 20, 65; S. Williams, 2009, Essentially cool: Acer's timeline notebooks, *New York Times Online*, http://www.nytimes.com, April 10.

Increasingly important to firm success,[1] strategy is concerned with making choices among two or more alternatives.[2] As we noted in Chapter 1, when choosing a strategy, the firm decides to pursue one course of action instead of others. The choices are influenced by opportunities and threats in the firm's external environment[3] (see Chapter 2) as well as the nature and quality of the resources, capabilities, and core competencies in its internal organization[4] (see Chapter 3). As we see in the Opening Case, Acer Group tries to drive its costs lower and lower as the foundation for how it competes in the global PC market. Recently, Acer's success has caused some of its competitors to renew their effort to reduce their costs. For example, Dell recently announced that it was committed to trimming $4 billion from its cost structure to improve its ability to compete against competitors such as Acer.[5]

The fundamental objective of using any type of strategy (see Figure 1.1) is to gain strategic competitiveness and earn above-average returns.[6] Strategies are purposeful, precede the taking of actions to which they apply, and demonstrate a shared understanding of the firm's vision and mission.[7] Acer's decisions to acquire Gateway and Packard Bell were quite purposeful. Acquiring Gateway helped the firm establish a better foothold in the U.S. market while acquiring Packard Bell helped it establish a stronger footprint in Europe.

An effectively formulated strategy marshals, integrates, and allocates the firm's resources, capabilities, and competencies so that it will be properly aligned with its external environment.[8] A properly developed strategy also rationalizes the firm's vision and mission along with the actions taken to achieve them.[9] Information about a host of variables including markets, customers, technology, worldwide finance, and the changing world economy must be collected and analyzed to properly form and use strategies. In the final analysis, sound strategic choices that reduce uncertainty regarding outcomes[10] are the foundation for building successful strategies.[11]

Business-level strategy, this chapter's focus, is an integrated and coordinated set of commitments and actions the firm uses to gain a competitive advantage by exploiting core competencies in specific product markets.[12] Business-level strategy indicates the choices the firm has made about how it intends to compete in individual product markets. The choices are important because long-term performance is linked to a firm's strategies.[13] Given the complexity of successfully competing in the global economy, the choices about how the firm will compete can be difficult.[14] For example, MySpace, a social networking site, recently reduced its workforce by almost one-third in order to "… rein in costs and contend with fast-growing rival Facebook Inc."[15] Competitive challenges in MySpace's U.S. and international operations contributed to the difficult decision to reduce the firm's workforce, partly with the purpose of operating more efficiently.[16] At the same time, competitor Facebook's recently announced strong move into additional international markets such as India challenged MySpace to further adjust or fine-tune its strategy as it engages its major competitor in various competitive battles.[17]

Every firm must form and use a business-level strategy. However, every firm may not use all the strategies—corporate-level, merger and acquisition, international, and cooperative—that we examine in Chapters 6 through 9. A firm competing in a single-product market area in a single geographic location does not need a corporate-level strategy to deal with product diversity or an international strategy to deal with geographic diversity. In contrast, a diversified firm will use one of the corporate-level strategies as well as a separate business-level strategy for each product market area in which it competes. Every firm—from the local dry cleaner to the multinational corporation—chooses at least one business-level strategy. Thus business-level strategy is the *core* strategy—the strategy that the firm forms to describe how it intends to compete in a product market.[18]

We discuss several topics to examine business-level strategies. Because customers are the foundation of successful business-level strategies and should never be taken for granted,[19] we present information about customers that is relevant to business-level strategies. In terms of customers, when selecting a business-level strategy the firm

A **business-level strategy** is an integrated and coordinated set of commitments and actions the firm uses to gain a competitive advantage by exploiting core competencies in specific product markets.

determines (1) *who* will be served, (2) *what* needs those target customers have that it will satisfy, and (3) *how* those needs will be satisfied. Selecting customers and deciding which of their needs the firm will try to satisfy, as well as how it will do so, are challenging tasks. Global competition has created many attractive options for customers, thus making it difficult to determine the strategy to best serve them. Effective global competitors have become adept at identifying the needs of customers in different cultures and geographic regions as well as learning how to quickly and successfully adapt the functionality of a firm's good or service to meet those needs.

Descriptions of the purpose of business-level strategies—and of the five business-level strategies—follow the discussion of customers. The five strategies we examine are called *generic* because they can be used in any organization competing in any industry.[20] Our analysis describes how effective use of each strategy allows the firm to favorably position itself relative to the five competitive forces in the industry (see Chapter 2). In addition, we use the value chain (see Chapter 3) to show examples of the primary and support activities necessary to implement specific business-level strategies. Because no strategy is risk-free,[21] we also describe the different risks the firm may encounter when using these strategies. In Chapter 11, we explain the organizational structures and controls linked with the successful use of each business-level strategy.

Customers: Their Relationship with Business-Level Strategies

Strategic competitiveness results only when the firm satisfies a group of customers by using its competitive advantages as the basis for competing in individual product markets.[22] A key reason firms must satisfy customers with their business-level strategy is that returns earned from relationships with customers are the lifeblood of all organizations.[23]

The most successful companies try to find new ways to satisfy current customers and/ or to meet the needs of new customers. Being able to do this can be even more difficult when firms and consumers face challenging economic conditions. During such times, firms may decide to reduce their workforce to control costs. As previously mentioned, MySpace has done this. This can lead to problems, however, when having fewer employees makes it harder for companies to meet individual customers' needs and expectations. In these instances, some suggest that firms should follow several courses of action, including "babying their best customers" by paying extra attention to them and developing a flexible workforce by cross-training employees so they can fill a variety of responsibilities on their jobs. Amazon.com, insurer USAA, and Lexus were recently identified as "customer service champs" because they devote extra care and attention to customer service during challenging economic times.[24]

Effectively Managing Relationships with Customers

The firm's relationships with its customers are strengthened when it delivers superior value to them. Strong interactive relationships with customers often provide the foundation for the firm's efforts to profitably serve customers' unique needs.

As the following statement shows, Harrah's Entertainment (the world's largest provider of branded casino entertainment) is committed to providing superior value to customers: "Harrah's Entertainment is focused on building loyalty and value with its customers through a unique combination of great service, excellent products, unsurpassed distribution, operational excellence and technology leadership."[25] Importantly, as Harrah's appears to anticipate, delivering superior value often results in increased customer loyalty. In turn, customer loyalty has a positive relationship with profitability. However, more choices and easily accessible information about the functionality of firms' products are creating increasingly sophisticated and knowledgeable customers, making it difficult to earn their loyalty.[26]

A number of companies have become skilled at the art of *managing* all aspects of their relationship with their customers.[27] For example, Amazon.com is widely recognized for the quality of information it maintains about its customers, the services it renders, and its ability to anticipate customers' needs. Using the information it has, Amazon tries to serve what it believes are the unique needs of each customer; and it has a strong reputation for being able to successfully do this.[28]

As we discuss next, firms' relationships with customers are characterized by three dimensions. Companies such as Acer and Amazon.com understand these dimensions and manage their relationships with customers in light of them.

Reach, Richness, and Affiliation

The *reach* dimension of relationships with customers is concerned with the firm's access and connection to customers. In general, firms seek to extend their reach, adding customers in the process of doing so.

Reach is an especially critical dimension for social networking sites such as Facebook and MySpace in that the value these firms create for users is to connect them with others. In mid-2009, traffic to MySpace was falling; at the same time, data showed that Facebook had matched MySpace in monthly U.S. visitors for the first time. Specifically, in May 2009, "MySpace attracted 70.2 million unique U.S. visitors … down 4.7% from a year ago while Facebook's U.S. audience nearly doubled to 70.3 million, according to comScore Media Metrix."[29] Reach is also important to Netflix. Fortunately for this firm, recent results indicate that its reach continues to expand: "Netflix ended the first quarter of 2009 with approximately 10,310,000 total subscribers, representing a 25 percent year-over-year growth from 8,234,000 total subscribers at the end of the first quarter of 2008 and a 10 percent sequential growth from 9,390,000 subscribers at the end of the fourth quarter of 2008."[30]

Facebook's reach continues to grow rapidly, with the company announcing that it had surpassed 250 million users in July 2009. Much of the company's recent growth has come largely from outside the United States.

AP Photo/Press Association

Richness, the second dimension of firms' relationships with customers, is concerned with the depth and detail of the two-way flow of information between the firm and the customer. The potential of the richness dimension to help the firm establish a competitive advantage in its relationship with customers leads many firms to offer online services in order to better manage information exchanges with their customers. Broader and deeper information-based exchanges allow firms to better understand their customers and their needs. Such exchanges also enable customers to become more knowledgeable about how the firm can satisfy them. Internet technology and e-commerce transactions have substantially reduced the costs of meaningful information exchanges with current and potential customers. As we have noted, Amazon is a leader in using the Internet to build relationships with customers. In fact, it bills itself as the most "customer-centric company" on earth. The firm's decision in June 2009 to launch "Your Amazon Ad Contest" demonstrates its belief in and focus on its customers. This contest asked Amazon customers to submit their vision of an Amazon television commercial to the firm. The winning entry was to receive $20,000 in Amazon.com gift cards.[31]

Affiliation, the third dimension, is concerned with facilitating useful interactions with customers. Viewing the world through the customer's eyes and constantly seeking ways to create more value for the customer have positive effects in terms of affiliation. Internet navigators such as Microsoft's MSN Autos helps online clients find and sort information. MSN Autos provides data and software to prospective car buyers that enable them to compare car models along multiple objective specifications. A prospective buyer who has selected a specific car based on comparisons of different models can then be linked to dealers that meet the customer's needs and purchasing requirements. Information about other relevant issues such as financing and insurance and even local traffic patterns is also available at the site. Because its revenues come not from the final customer or end user but from other sources (such as advertisements on its Web site, hyperlinks, and associated products and services), MSN Autos represents the customer's interests, a service that fosters affiliation.[32]

As we discuss next, effectively managing customer relationships (along the dimensions of reach, richness, and affiliation) helps the firm answer questions related to the issues of *who, what,* and *how.*

Who: Determining the Customers to Serve

Deciding *who* the target customer is that the firm intends to serve with its business-level strategy is an important decision.[33] Companies divide customers into groups based on differences in the customers' needs (needs are discussed further in the next section) to make this decision. Dividing customers into groups based on their needs is called **market segmentation**, which is a process that clusters people with similar needs into individual and identifiable groups.[34] In the animal food products business, for example, the food-product needs of owners of companion pets (e.g., dogs and cats) differ from the needs for food and health-related products of those owning production animals (e.g., livestock). A subsidiary of Colgate-Palmolive, Hill's Pet Nutrition sells food products for pets. In fact, the company's mission is "to help enrich and lengthen the special relationship between people and their pets."[35] Schering-Plough sells "more than 15 animal medicine products including antibiotics, fertility treatments and a number of vaccines for livestock."[36] Thus, Hill and Schering-Plough target the needs of different segments of customers with the food products they sell for animals.

Almost any identifiable human or organizational characteristic can be used to subdivide a market into segments that differ from one another on a given characteristic. Common characteristics on which customers' needs vary are illustrated in Table 4.1.

Table 4.1 Basis for Customer Segmentation

Consumer Markets
1. Demographic factors (age, income, sex, etc.)
2. Socioeconomic factors (social class, stage in the family life cycle)
3. Geographic factors (cultural, regional, and national differences)
4. Psychological factors (lifestyle, personality traits)
5. Consumption patterns (heavy, moderate, and light users)
6. Perceptual factors (benefit segmentation, perceptual mapping)
Industrial Markets
1. End-use segments (identified by SIC code)
2. Product segments (based on technological differences or production economics)
3. Geographic segments (defined by boundaries between countries or by regional differences within them)
4. Common buying factor segments (cut across product market and geographic segments)
5. Customer size segments

Source: Adapted from S. C. Jain, 2000, *Marketing Planning and Strategy,* Cincinnati: South-Western College Publishing, 120.

Market segmentation is a process used to cluster people with similar needs into individual and identifiable groups.

In light of what it learned about its customers, Gap Inc. used *shopping experience* as a characteristic to subdivide its customers into different segments as a basis for serving their unique needs. Specifically, Gap learned from market research that its female and male customers want different shopping experiences. In a company official's words, "Research showed that men want to come and go easily, while women want an exploration."[37] In light of these research results, women's sections in Gap stores are organized by occasion (e.g., work, entertainment) with accessories for those occasions scattered throughout the section to facilitate browsing. The men's sections of Gap stores are more straightforward, with signs directing male customers to clothing items that are commonly stacked by size.

What: Determining Which Customer Needs to Satisfy

After the firm decides *who* it will serve, it must identify the targeted customer group's needs that its goods or services can satisfy. In a general sense, *needs (what)* are related to a product's benefits and features.[38] Successful firms learn how to deliver to customers what they want and when they want it.[39] Having close and frequent interactions with both current and potential customers helps the firm identify those individuals' and groups' current and future needs.[40]

From a strategic perspective, a basic need of all customers is to buy products that create value for them. The generalized forms of value that goods or services provide are either low cost with acceptable features or highly differentiated features with acceptable cost. In the recent global financial crisis, companies across industries recognized their customers' need to feel as secure as possible when making purchases. Allowing customers to return their cars if they lose their job within 12 months of the purchase is how Hyundai Motors decided to address this consumer need, creating value in the form of security.[41]

The most effective firms continuously strive to anticipate changes in customers' needs. The firm that fails to anticipate and certainly to recognize changes in its customers' needs may lose its customers to competitors whose products can provide more value to the focal firm's customers. For example, Ford Motor Company concluded that customers' needs across the global automobile market were becoming more similar. In response, the firm decided to build the Fiesta as a world car. While the car will be tailored somewhat to the needs of different customers in different markets, analysts believe that the firm "… is betting that it has figured out what has bedeviled mass-market automakers for decades, which is hitting a home run in every market with the same car."[42] Ford believes that changes have occurred resulting in more similarity in customers' needs for automotive transportation across multiple markets. If this assessment is correct, the firm may take customers away from automobile manufacturers failing to see the trend toward similarity rather than differences in customers' needs within multiple market segments.

Though there are exceptions like the perceived market for Ford's Fiesta, consumers' needs within individual market segments often vary a great deal.[43] Jason's Deli tries to address consumers' desires for high-quality, fresh sandwiches. In contrast, many large fast-food companies satisfy customer needs for lower-cost food items with acceptable quality that are delivered quickly. Diversified food and soft-drink producer PepsiCo believes that "any one consumer has different needs at different times of the day." Through its soft drinks (Pepsi products), snacks (Frito-Lay), juices (Tropicana), and cereals (Quaker), PepsiCo is developing new products from breakfast bars to healthier potato chips "to make certain that it covers all those needs."[44]

How: Determining Core Competencies Necessary to Satisfy Customer Needs

After deciding *who* the firm will serve and the specific *needs* of those customers, the firm is prepared to determine how to use its capabilities and competencies to develop products that can satisfy the needs of its target customers. As explained in

Chapters 1 and 3, *core competencies* are resources and capabilities that serve as a source of competitive advantage for the firm over its rivals. Firms use core competencies (*how*) to implement value-creating strategies and thereby satisfy customers' needs. Only those firms with the capacity to continuously improve, innovate, and upgrade their competencies can expect to meet and hopefully exceed customers' expectations across time.[45]

Companies draw from a wide range of core competencies to produce goods or services that can satisfy customers' needs. ProEnergy Services is an integrated service company operating seven business units in the energy industry. Superior client satisfaction is a core competence the firm relies on in competition with its competitors.[46]

SAS Institute is the world's largest privately owned software company and is the leader in business intelligence and analytics. Customers use SAS's programs for data warehousing, data mining, and decision support purposes. Allocating approximately 22 percent of revenues to research and development (R&D), a percentage that exceeds percentages allocated by its competitors, SAS relies on its core competence in R&D to satisfy the data-related needs of such customers as the U.S. Census Bureau and a host of consumer goods firms (e.g., hotels, banks, and catalog companies).[47] Kraft Foods relies on the capabilities of its sales force to create value for its customers,[48] while Safeway Inc. uses its competence to understand customers' unique needs to create its successful private-label brands such as O Organics and Eating Right.[49]

Sometimes, firms may find it necessary to use their core competencies as the foundation for producing new goods or services for new customers. This may be the case for some small automobile parts suppliers in the United States. Given that U.S. auto production in recent years declined about a third from more typical levels, a number of these firms are seeking to diversify their operations, perhaps exiting the auto parts supplier industry as a result of doing so. Some analysts believe that the first rule for these small manufacturers is to determine how their current capabilities and competencies might be used to produce value-creating products for different customers. One analyst gave the following example of how this might work: "There may be no reason that a company making auto door handles couldn't make ball-and-socket joints for artificial shoulders."[50]

Our discussion about customers shows that all organizations must use their capabilities and core competencies (the *how*) to satisfy the needs (the *what*) of the target group of customers (the *who*) the firm has chosen to serve. Next, we describe the different business-level strategies that are available to firms to use to satisfy customers as the foundation for earning above-average returns.

Responding to the needs of customers concerned with food safety and quality, Safeway successfully launched the O Organics brand.

The Purpose of a Business-Level Strategy

The purpose of a business-level strategy is to create differences between the firm's position and those of its competitors.[51] To position itself differently from competitors, a firm must decide whether it intends to *perform activities differently* or to *perform different activities*. In fact, "choosing to perform activities differently or to perform different activities than rivals" is the essence of business-level strategy.[52] Thus, the firm's business-level strategy is a deliberate choice about how it will perform the value chain's primary and support activities to create unique value. Indeed, in the complex twenty-first–century competitive landscape, successful use of a business-level strategy results only when the firm learns how to integrate the activities it performs in ways that create superior value for customers.

Firms develop an activity map to show how they integrate the activities they perform. We show Southwest Airlines's activity map in Figure 4.1. The manner in which

Figure 4.1 Southwest Airlines Activity System

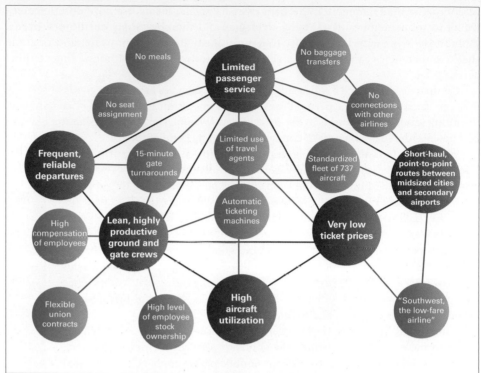

Southwest has integrated its activities is the foundation for the successful use of its cost leadership strategy (this strategy is discussed later in the chapter). The tight integration among Southwest's activities is a key source of the firm's ability to at least historically operate more profitably than its competitors.

As shown in Figure 4.1, Southwest Airlines has configured the activities it performs into six strategic themes—limited passenger service; frequent, reliable departures; lean, highly productive ground and gate crews; high aircraft utilization; very low ticket prices; and short-haul, point-to-point routes between mid-sized cities and secondary airports. Individual clusters of tightly linked activities make it possible for the outcome of a strategic theme to be achieved. For example, no meals, no seat assignments, and no baggage transfers form a cluster of individual activities that support the strategic theme of limited passenger service (see Figure 4.1).

Southwest's tightly integrated activities make it difficult for competitors to imitate the firm's cost leadership strategy. The firm's unique culture and customer service, both of which are sources of competitive advantages, are features that rivals have been unable to imitate, although some have tried. U.S. Airways's MetroJet subsidiary, United Airlines's United Shuttle, Delta's Song, and Continental Airlines's Continental Lite all failed in attempts to imitate Southwest's strategy. Hindsight shows that these competitors offered low prices to customers, but weren't able to operate at costs close to those of Southwest or to provide customers with any notable sources of differentiation, such as a unique experience while in the air. The key to Southwest's success has been its ability to continuously reduce its costs while providing customers with *acceptable* levels of differentiation such as an engaging culture. Firms using the cost leadership strategy must understand that in terms of sources of differentiation that accompany the cost leader's product, the customer defines *acceptable*.

Fit among activities is a key to the sustainability of competitive advantage for all firms, including Southwest Airlines. As Michael Porter comments, "Strategic fit among many activities is fundamental not only to competitive advantage but also to the sustainability of that advantage. It is harder for a rival to match an array of interlocked activities than it is merely to imitate a particular sales-force approach, match a process technology, or replicate a set of product features. Positions built on systems of activities are far more sustainable than those built on individual activities."[53]

Types of Business-Level Strategies

Firms choose from among five business-level strategies to establish and defend their desired strategic position against competitors: *cost leadership, differentiation, focused cost leadership, focused differentiation,* and *integrated cost leadership/differentiation* (see Figure 4.2). Each business-level strategy helps the firm to establish and exploit a particular *competitive advantage* within a particular *competitive scope.* How firms integrate the activities they perform within each different business-level strategy demonstrates how they differ from one another.[54] For example, firms have different activity maps, and thus, a Southwest Airlines activity map differs from those of competitors JetBlue, Continental, American Airlines, and so forth. Superior integration of activities increases the likelihood of being able to gain an advantage over competitors and to earn above-average returns.

When selecting a business-level strategy, firms evaluate two types of potential competitive advantages: "lower cost than rivals, or the ability to differentiate and command a premium price that exceeds the extra cost of doing so."[55] Having lower cost derives from the firm's ability to perform activities differently than rivals; being able to differentiate indicates the firm's capacity to perform different (and valuable) activities.[56] Thus, based on the nature and quality of its internal resources, capabilities, and core competencies,

Figure 4.2 Five Business-Level Strategies

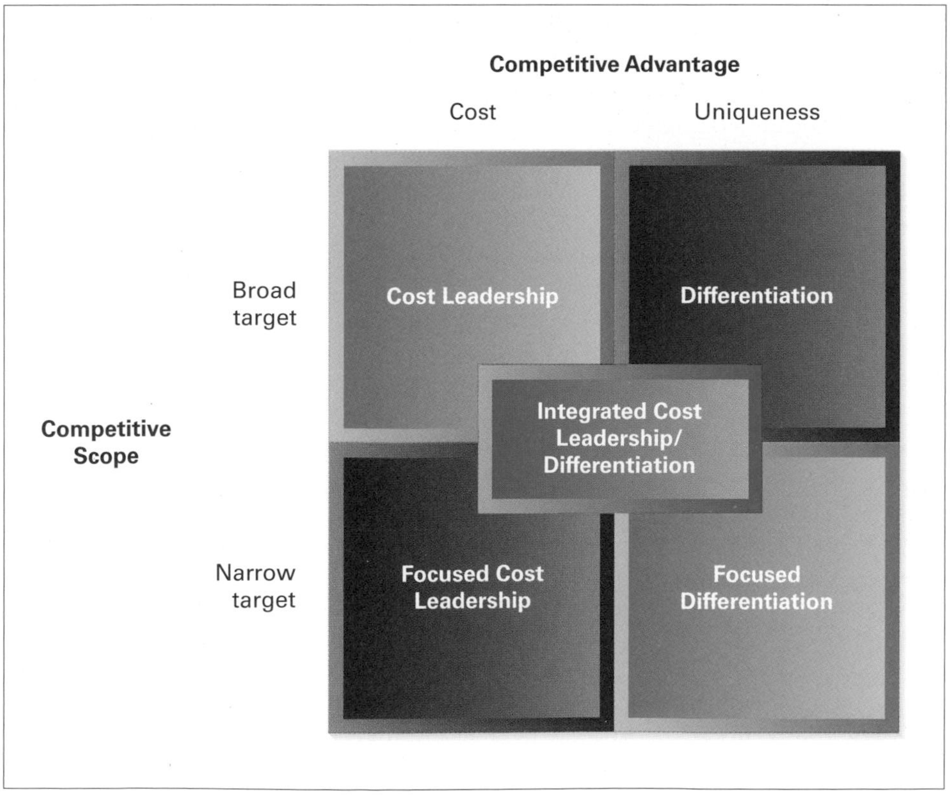

Source: Adapted with the permission of The Free Press, an imprint of Simon & Schuster Adult Publishing Group, from *Competitive Advantage: Creating and Sustaining Superior Performance,* by Michael E. Porter, 12. Copyright © 1985, 1998 by Michael E. Porter.

a firm seeks to form either a cost competitive advantage or a uniqueness competitive advantage as the basis for implementing its business-level strategy.

Two types of competitive scopes are broad target and narrow target (see Figure 4.2). Firms serving a broad target market seek to use their competitive advantage on an industry-wide basis. A narrow competitive scope means that the firm intends to serve the needs of a narrow target customer group. With focus strategies, the firm "selects a segment or group of segments in the industry and tailors its strategy to serving them to the exclusion of others."[57] Buyers with special needs and buyers located in specific geographic regions are examples of narrow target customer groups.[58] As shown in Figure 4.2, a firm could also strive to develop a combined cost/uniqueness competitive advantage as the foundation for serving a target customer group that is larger than a narrow segment but not as comprehensive as a broad (or industry-wide) customer group. In this instance, the firm uses the integrated cost leadership/differentiation strategy.

None of the five business-level strategies shown in Figure 4.2 is inherently or universally superior to the others.[59] The effectiveness of each strategy is contingent both on the opportunities and threats in a firm's external environment and on the strengths and weaknesses derived from the firm's resource portfolio. It is critical, therefore, for the firm to select a business-level strategy that is based on a match between the opportunities and threats in its external environment and the strengths of its internal organization as shown by its core competencies.[60] And, once the firm chooses its strategy, it should consistently emphasize actions that are required to successfully use it. Wal-Mart's continuous emphasis on driving its costs lower is thought to be a key to the firm's effective cost leadership strategy.[61]

Cost Leadership Strategy

The **cost leadership strategy** is an integrated set of actions taken to produce goods or services with features that are acceptable to customers at the lowest cost, relative to that of competitors.[62] Firms using the cost leadership strategy commonly sell standardized goods or services (but with competitive levels of differentiation) to the industry's most typical customers. Process innovations, which are newly designed production and distribution methods and techniques that allow the firm to operate more efficiently, are critical to successful use of the cost leadership strategy.[63]

As noted, cost leaders' goods and services must have competitive levels of differentiation that create value for customers. Recently, Kia Motors decided to emphasize the design of its cars in the U.S. market as a source of differentiation while implementing its cost leadership strategy. Called "cheap chic," some analysts had a positive view of this decision, saying that "When they're done, Kia's cars will still be low-end (in price), but they won't necessarily look like it."[64] It is important for firms using the cost leadership strategy, such as Kia, to do so in this way because concentrating only on reducing costs could result in the firm efficiently producing products that no customer wants to purchase. In fact, such extremes could lead to limited potential for all-important process innovations, employment of lower-skilled workers, poor conditions on the production line, accidents, and a poor quality of work life for employees.[65]

As shown in Figure 4.2, the firm using the cost leadership strategy targets a broad customer segment or group. Cost leaders concentrate on finding ways to lower their costs relative to competitors by constantly rethinking how to complete their primary and support activities to reduce costs still further while maintaining competitive levels of differentiation.[66]

For example, cost leader Greyhound Lines Inc. continuously seeks ways to reduce the costs it incurs to provide bus service while offering customers an acceptable level of differentiation. Greyhound is offering new services to customers as a way of improving the quality of the experience customers have when paying the firm's low prices for its services. Changes in the economic segment of the general environment (see Chapter 2) are creating an opportunity for Greyhound to do this. Specifically, the recent recession

The **cost leadership strategy** is an integrated set of actions taken to produce goods or services with features that are acceptable to customers at the lowest cost, relative to that of competitors.

found more people seeking to travel by bus instead of by planes and trains. However, these new customers "… insist on certain amenities they've grown accustomed to on planes and trains—such as Internet access and cushier seats, not to mention cleanliness." To maintain competitive levels of differentiation while using the cost leadership strategy, Greyhound recently starting using over 100 "motor coaches" that have leather seats, additional legroom, Wi-Fi access, and power outlets in every row.[67]

Greyhound enjoys economies of scale by serving more than 25 million passengers annually with about 2,300 destinations in the United States and operating approximately 1,250 buses. These scale economies allow the firm to keep its costs low while offering some of the differentiated services today's customers seek from the company. Demonstrating the firm's commitment to the physical environment segment of the general environment is the fact that "one Greyhound bus takes an average of 34 cars off the road."[68]

As primary activities, inbound logistics (e.g., materials handling, warehousing, and inventory control) and outbound logistics (e.g., collecting, storing, and distributing products to customers) often account for significant portions of the total cost to produce some goods and services. Research suggests that having a competitive advantage in terms of logistics creates more value when using the cost leadership strategy than when using the differentiation strategy.[69] Thus, cost leaders seeking competitively valuable ways to reduce costs may want to concentrate on the primary activities of inbound logistics and outbound logistics. In so doing many firms choose to outsource their manufacturing operations to low-cost firms with low-wage employees (e.g., China).[70]

Cost leaders also carefully examine all support activities to find additional sources of potential cost reductions. Developing new systems for finding the optimal combination of low cost and acceptable levels of differentiation in the raw materials required to produce the firm's goods or services is an example of how the procurement support activity can facilitate successful use of the cost leadership strategy.

Big Lots Inc. uses the cost leadership strategy. With its vision of being "The World's Best Bargain Place," Big Lots is the largest closeout retailer in the United States with annual sales of over $4.5 billion. For Big Lots, closeout goods "are the same first-quality, brand-name products found at other retailers, but at substantially lower prices."[71] The firm relies on a disciplined merchandise cost and inventory management system to continuously drive its costs lower.[72] The firm's stores sell name-brand products at prices that are 20 to 40 percent below those of discount retailers and roughly 70 percent below those of traditional retailers. Big Lots's buyers search for manufacturer overruns and discontinued styles to find goods priced well below wholesale prices. In addition, the firm buys from overseas suppliers. Big Lots satisfies the customers' need to access the differentiated features of brand-name products, but at a fraction of their initial cost. Tightly integrating its purchasing and inventory management activities across its stores is the main core competence Big Lots uses to satisfy its customers' needs.

As described in Chapter 3, firms use value-chain analysis to identify the parts of the company's operations that create value and those that do not. Figure 4.3 demonstrates the primary and support activities that allow a firm to create value through the cost leadership strategy. Companies unable to link the activities shown in this figure through the activity map they form typically lack the core competencies needed to successfully use the cost leadership strategy.

Effective use of the cost leadership strategy allows a firm to earn above-average returns in spite of the presence of strong competitive forces (see Chapter 2). The next sections (one for each of the five forces) explain how firms implement a cost leadership strategy.

Rivalry with Existing Competitors

Having the low-cost position is valuable to deal with rivals. Because of the cost leader's advantageous position, rivals hesitate to compete on the basis of price, especially before evaluating the potential outcomes of such competition.[73] Wal-Mart is known for its ability to continuously reduce its costs, creating value for customers in the process of doing so.

Figure 4.3 Examples of Value-Creating Activities Associated with the Cost Leadership Strategy

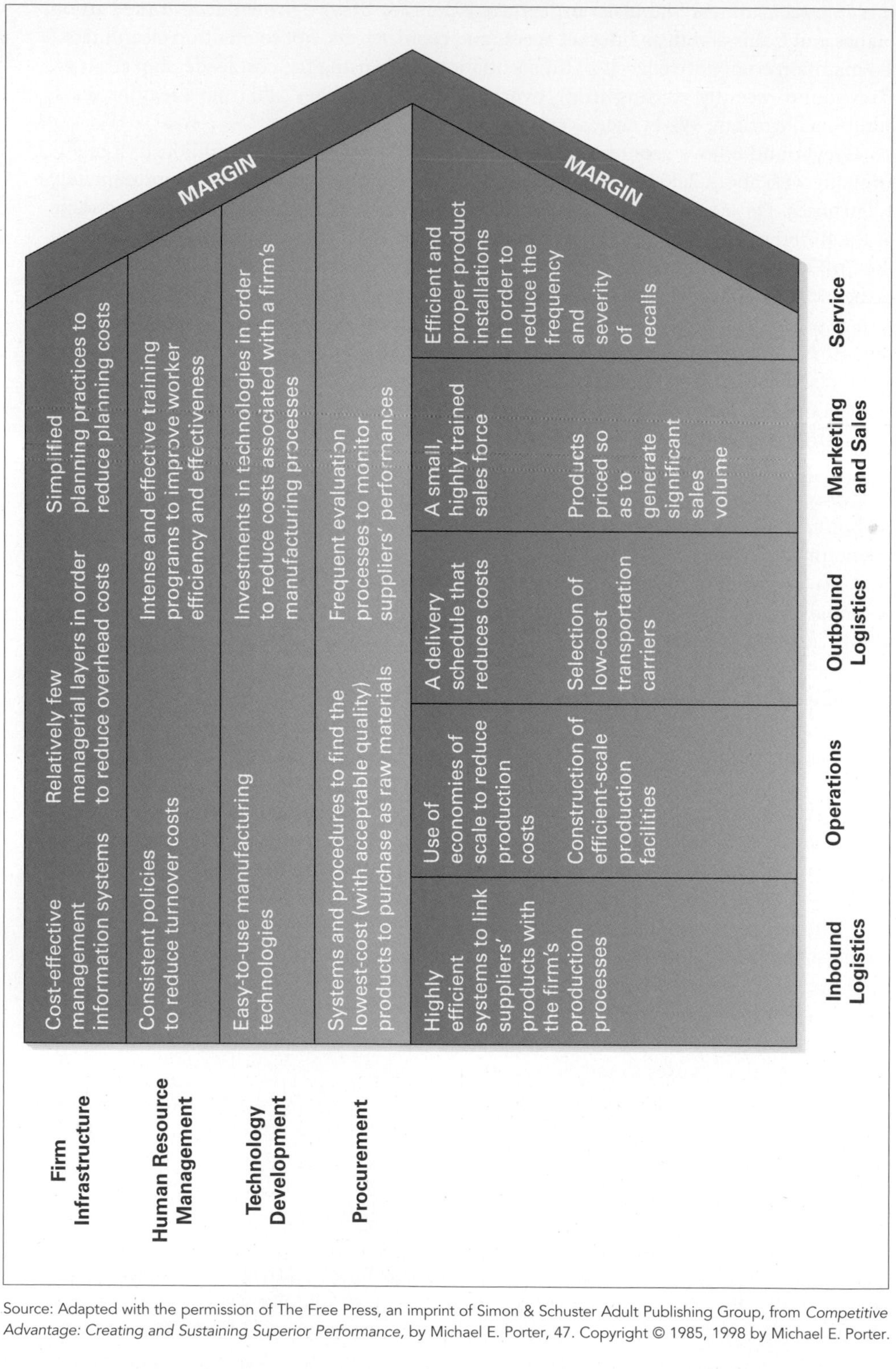

Source: Adapted with the permission of The Free Press, an imprint of Simon & Schuster Adult Publishing Group, from *Competitive Advantage: Creating and Sustaining Superior Performance*, by Michael E. Porter, 47. Copyright © 1985, 1998 by Michael E. Porter.

In light of this ability, rivals such as Costco and Target hesitate to compete against Wal-Mart strictly on the basis of costs and, subsequently, prices to consumers. Recently, Wal-Mart decided to expand "… its private-label line of food and household cleaners to take advantage of recession-pinched consumers' increasing desire to buy cheaper store brands rather than more expensive brand-name products." Because it controls the costs associated with producing its private-label products (Great Value is the name of Wal-Mart's private-label offerings), the firm is able to drive its costs lower when manufacturing and distributing its own products.

Bargaining Power of Buyers (Customers)

Powerful customers can force a cost leader to reduce its prices, but not below the level at which the cost leader's next-most-efficient industry competitor can earn average returns. Although powerful customers might be able to force the cost leader to reduce prices even below this level, they probably would not choose to do so. Prices that are low enough to prevent the next-most-efficient competitor from earning average returns would force that firm to exit the market, leaving the cost leader with less competition and in an even stronger position. Customers would thus lose their power and pay higher prices if they were forced to purchase from a single firm operating in an industry without rivals.

Bargaining Power of Suppliers

The cost leader operates with margins greater than those of competitors. Cost leaders want to constantly increase their margins by driving their costs lower. Big Lots's gross margin increased from 39.7 percent in 2008 to 40.4 percent in 2009,[74] an indication the firm was effectively using the cost leadership strategy. Among other benefits, higher gross margins relative to those of competitors make it possible for the cost leader to absorb its suppliers' price increases. When an industry faces substantial increases in the cost of its supplies, only the cost leader may be able to pay the higher prices and continue to earn either average or above-average returns. Alternatively, a powerful cost leader may be able to force its suppliers to hold down their prices, which would reduce the suppliers' margins in the process.

Wal-Mart uses its power with suppliers (gained because it buys such large quantities from many suppliers) to extract lower prices from them. These savings are then passed on to customers in the form of lower prices, which further strengthens Wal-Mart's position relative to competitors lacking the power to extract lower prices from suppliers. The fact that Wal-Mart is the largest retailer in North America is a key reason the firm has a great deal of power with its suppliers. Another indicator of this power is that with 25 percent of the total market, Wal-Mart is the largest supermarket operator in the United States; and its Sam's Club division is the second largest warehouse club in the United States. Collectively, this sales volume and the market penetration it suggests (over 100 million people visit a Wal-Mart store each week) create the ability for Wal-Mart to gain access to low prices from its suppliers.

Potential Entrants

Through continuous efforts to reduce costs to levels that are lower than competitors', a cost leader becomes highly efficient. Because ever-improving levels of efficiency (e.g., economies of scale) enhance profit margins, they serve as a significant entry barrier to potential competitors.[75] New entrants must be willing and able to accept no-better-than-average returns until they gain the experience required to approach the cost leader's efficiency. To earn even average returns, new entrants must have the competencies required to match the cost levels of competitors other than the cost leader. The low profit margins (relative to margins earned by firms implementing the differentiation strategy) make it necessary for the cost leader to sell large volumes of its product to earn above-average returns. However, firms striving to be the cost leader must avoid pricing their products so low that their ability to operate profitably is reduced, even though volume increases.

Product Substitutes

Compared with its industry rivals, the cost leader also holds an attractive position in terms of product substitutes. A product substitute becomes an issue for the cost leader when its features and characteristics, in terms of cost and differentiated features, are potentially attractive to the firm's customers. When faced with possible substitutes, the cost leader has more flexibility than its competitors. To retain customers, it can reduce the price of its good or service. With still lower prices and competitive levels of differentiation, the cost leader increases the probability that customers will prefer its product rather than a substitute.

Competitive Risks of the Cost Leadership Strategy

The cost leadership strategy is not risk free. One risk is that the processes used by the cost leader to produce and distribute its good or service could become obsolete because of competitors' innovations. These innovations may allow rivals to produce at costs lower than those of the original cost leader, or to provide additional differentiated features without increasing the product's price to customers.

A second risk is that too much focus by the cost leader on cost reductions may occur at the expense of trying to understand customers' perceptions of "competitive levels of differentiation." Wal-Mart, for example, has been criticized for having too few salespeople available to help customers and too few individuals at checkout registers. These complaints suggest that there might be a discrepancy between how Wal-Mart's customers define "minimal levels of service" and the firm's attempts to drive its costs lower and lower.

Imitation is a final risk of the cost leadership strategy. Using their own core competencies, competitors sometimes learn how to successfully imitate the cost leader's strategy. When this happens, the cost leader must increase the value its good or service provides to customers. Commonly, value is increased by selling the current product at an even lower price or by adding differentiated features that create value for customers while maintaining price.

Netflix may be encountering this risk from Redbox, which is the largest operator of DVD-rental kiosks in the United States. Using vending machines that Redbox has established in supermarkets and discount stores, customers pay $1 per day for DVDs. In contrast, Netflix's cheapest plan is $5 per month (the customer receives two DVDs by mail per month with this plan). An analyst using the following words to describe this situation: "Netflix CEO Reed Hastings has something to worry about: an even cheaper DVD rental service run by one of his former lieutenants."[76]

Differentiation Strategy

The **differentiation strategy** is an integrated set of actions taken to produce goods or services (at an acceptable cost) that customers perceive as being different in ways that are important to them.[77] While cost leaders serve a typical customer in an industry, differentiators target customers for whom value is created by the manner in which the firm's products differ from those produced and marketed by competitors. Product innovation, which is "the result of bringing to life a new way to solve the customer's problem— through a new product or service development—that benefits both the customer and the sponsoring company"[78] is critical to successful use of the differentiation strategy.[79]

Firms must be able to produce differentiated products at competitive costs to reduce upward pressure on the price that customers pay. When a product's differentiated features are produced at noncompetitive costs, the price for the product can exceed what the firm's target customers are willing to pay. When the firm has a thorough understanding of what its target customers value, the relative importance they attach to the satisfaction of different needs, and for what they are willing to pay a premium, the differentiation strategy can be effective in helping it earn above-average returns.

Through the differentiation strategy, the firm produces nonstandardized (that is, unique) products for customers who value differentiated features more than they value low cost. For example, superior product reliability and durability and high-performance sound systems are among the differentiated features of Toyota Motor Corporation's Lexus products. The Lexus promotional statement—"We pursue perfection, so you can

The **differentiation strategy** is an integrated set of actions taken to produce goods or services (at an acceptable cost) that customers perceive as being different in ways that are important to them.

pursue living"—suggests a strong commitment to overall product quality as a source of differentiation. However, Lexus offers its vehicles to customers at a competitive purchase price. As with Lexus products, a good's or service's unique attributes, rather than its purchase price, provide the value for which customers are willing to pay.

Continuous success with the differentiation strategy results when the firm consistently upgrades differentiated features that customers value and/or creates new valuable features (innovates) without significant cost increases.[80] This approach requires firms to constantly change their product lines.[81] These firms may also offer a portfolio of products that complement each other, thereby enriching the differentiation for the customer and perhaps satisfying a portfolio of consumer needs.[82] Because a differentiated product satisfies customers' unique needs, firms following the differentiation strategy are able to charge premium prices. Customers are willing to pay a premium price for a product only when a "firm (is) truly unique at something or be perceived as unique."[83] The ability to sell a good or service at a price that substantially exceeds the cost of creating its differentiated features allows the firm to outperform rivals and earn above-average returns. For example, shirt and neckwear manufacturer Robert Talbott follows stringent standards of craftsmanship and pays meticulous attention to every detail of production. The firm imports exclusive fabrics from the world's finest mills to make men's dress shirts and neckwear. Single-needle tailoring is used, and precise collar cuts are made to produce shirts. According to the company, customers purchasing one of its products can be assured that they are being provided with the finest fabrics available.[84] Thus, Robert Talbott's success rests on the firm's ability to produce and sell its differentiated products at a price exceeding the costs of imported fabrics and its unique manufacturing processes.

Rather than costs, a firm using the differentiation strategy always concentrates on investing in and developing features that differentiate a product in ways that create value for customers. Robert Talbott uses the finest silks from Europe and Asia to produce its "Best of Class" collection of ties. Overall, a firm using the differentiation strategy seeks to be different from its competitors on as many dimensions as possible. The less similarity between a firm's goods or services and those of competitors, the more buffered it is from rivals' actions. Commonly recognized differentiated goods include Toyota's Lexus, Ralph Lauren's wide array of product lines, and Caterpillar's heavy-duty earth-moving equipment. McKinsey & Co. is a well-known example of a firm that offers differentiated services.

A good or service can be differentiated in many ways. Unusual features, responsive customer service, rapid product innovations and technological leadership, perceived prestige and status, different tastes, and engineering design and performance are examples of approaches to differentiation.[85] While the number of ways to reduce costs may be finite, virtually anything a firm can do to create real or perceived value is a basis for differentiation. Consider product design as a case in point. Because it can create a positive experience for customers, design is becoming an increasingly important source of differentiation (even for cost leaders seeking to find ways to add functionalities to their low-cost products as a way of differentiating their products from competitors) and hopefully, for firms emphasizing it, of competitive advantage.[86] As we noted, design is a way Kia Motors is now trying to create some uniqueness for its products that are manufactured and sold as part of the firm's cost leadership strategy. Apple is often cited as the firm that sets the standard in design, with the iPod and the iPhone demonstrating Apple's product design capabilities.[87]

The value chain can be analyzed to determine if a firm is able to link the activities required to create value by using the differentiation strategy. Examples of primary and support activities that are commonly used to differentiate a good or service are shown in Figure 4.4. Companies without the skills needed to link these activities cannot expect to successfully use the differentiation strategy. Next, we explain how firms using the differentiation strategy can successfully position themselves in terms of the five forces of competition (see Chapter 2) to earn above-average returns.

Figure 4.4 Examples of Value-Creating Activities Associated with the Differentiation Strategy

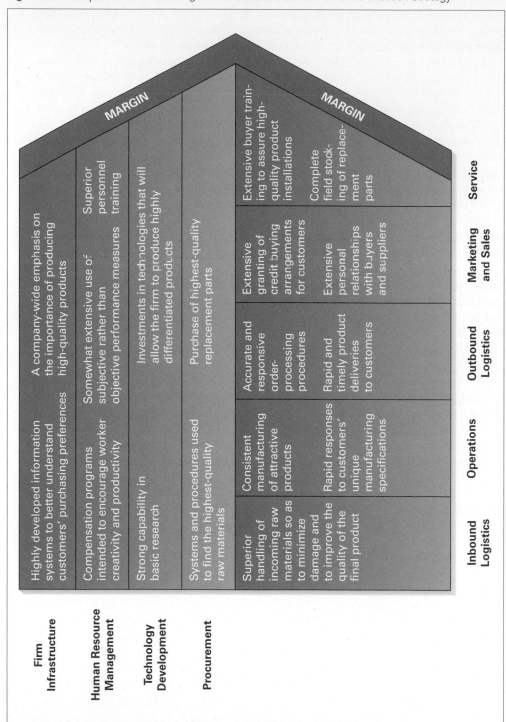

Source: Adapted with the permission of The Free Press, an imprint of Simon & Schuster Adult Publishing Group, from *Competitive Advantage: Creating and Sustaining Superior Performance,* by Michael E. Porter, 47. Copyright © 1985, 1998 by Michael E. Porter.

Rivalry with Existing Competitors

Customers tend to be loyal purchasers of products differentiated in ways that are meaningful to them. As their loyalty to a brand increases, customers' sensitivity to price increases is reduced. The relationship between brand loyalty and price sensitivity insulates a firm from competitive rivalry. Thus, Robert Talbott's "Best of Class" neckwear line is insulated from competition, even on the basis of price, as long as the company continues to satisfy the differentiated needs of its target customer group with the unique qualities of this line of ties. Likewise, Bose is insulated from intense rivalry as long as customers continue to perceive that its stereo equipment offers superior sound quality at a competitive purchase price. Both Robert Talbott and Bose have strong positive reputations for the high-quality and unique products that they provide. Thus, reputations can sustain the competitive advantage of firms following a differentiation strategy.[88]

Bargaining Power of Buyers (Customers)

The uniqueness of differentiated goods or services reduces customers' sensitivity to price increases. Customers are willing to accept a price increase when a product still satisfies their perceived unique needs better than does a competitor's offering. Thus, the golfer whose needs are uniquely satisfied by Callaway golf clubs will likely continue buying those products even if their cost increases. Similarly, the customer who has been highly satisfied with a Louis Vuitton wallet will probably replace that wallet with another one made by the same company even though the purchase price is higher than the original one. Purchasers of brand-name food items (e.g., Heinz ketchup and Kleenex tissues) will accept price increases in those products as long as they continue to perceive that the product satisfies their unique needs at an acceptable cost. In all of these instances, the customers are relatively insensitive to price increases because they do not think that an acceptable product alternative exists.

Bargaining Power of Suppliers

Because the firm using the differentiation strategy charges a premium price for its products, suppliers must provide high-quality components, driving up the firm's costs. However, the high margins the firm earns in these cases partially insulate it from the influence of suppliers in that higher supplier costs can be paid through these margins. Alternatively, because of buyers' relative insensitivity to price increases, the differentiated firm might choose to pass the additional cost of supplies on to the customer by increasing the price of its unique product.

Potential Entrants

Customer loyalty and the need to overcome the uniqueness of a differentiated product present substantial barriers to potential entrants. Entering an industry under these conditions typically demands significant investments of resources and patience while seeking customers' loyalty.

Product Substitutes

Firms selling brand-name goods and services to loyal customers are positioned effectively against product substitutes. In contrast, companies without brand loyalty face a higher probability of their customers switching either to products that offer differentiated features that serve the same function (particularly if the substitute has a lower price) or to products that offer more features and perform more attractive functions.

Competitive Risks of the Differentiation Strategy

One risk of the differentiation strategy is that customers might decide that the price differential between the differentiator's product and the cost leader's product is too large. In this instance, a firm may be offering differentiated features that exceed target customers' needs. The firm then becomes vulnerable to competitors that are able to offer customers a combination of features and price that is more consistent with their needs.

This risk is generalized across a number of companies producing different types of products during the recent global economic crisis—a time when forecasters suggested that "Sales of luxury goods, everything from apparel, to jewelry and leather goods, could plunge globally by 10% ... "[89] in 2009. The decline was expected to be more severe in the United States compared to Europe and Japan. A decision made during this time by

Coach Inc., a maker of high-quality, luxurious accessories and gifts for women and men, demonstrates one firm's reaction to the predicted decline in the sales of luxury goods. With an interest of providing products to increasingly cost-conscious customers without "cheapening" the firm's image, Coach chose to introduce a new line of its products called "Poppy"; the average price of items in this line is approximately 20 percent lower than the average price of Coach's typical products.[90]

Another risk of the differentiation strategy is that a firm's means of differentiation may cease to provide value for which customers are willing to pay. A differentiated product becomes less valuable if imitation by rivals causes customers to perceive that competitors offer essentially the same good or service, but at a lower price.[91] A third risk of the differentiation strategy is that experience can narrow customers' perceptions of the value of a product's differentiated features. For example, customers having positive experiences with generic tissues may decide that the differentiated features of the Kleenex product are not worth the extra cost. Similarly, while a customer may be impressed with the quality of a Robert Talbott "Best of Class" tie, positive experiences with less expensive ties may lead to a conclusion that the price of the "Best of Class" tie exceeds the benefit. To counter this risk, firms must continue to meaningfully differentiate their product for customers at a price they are willing to pay.

Counterfeiting is the differentiation strategy's fourth risk. "Counterfeits are those products bearing a trademark that is identical to or indistinguishable from a trademark registered to another party, thus infringing the rights of the older of the trademark."[92] We describe actions companies such as Hewlett-Packard take to deal with the problems counterfeit goods create for firms whose rights are infringed upon in the Strategic Focus.

Focus Strategies

The **focus strategy** is an integrated set of actions taken to produce goods or services that serve the needs of a particular competitive segment. Thus, firms use a focus strategy when they utilize their core competencies to serve the needs of a particular industry segment or niche to the exclusion of others. Examples of specific market segments that can be targeted by a focus strategy include (1) a particular buyer group (e.g., youths or senior citizens), (2) a different segment of a product line (e.g., products for professional painters or the do-it-yourself group), or (3) a different geographic market (e.g., northern or southern Italy).[93]

There are many specific customer needs firms can serve by using a focus strategy. For example, Los Angeles–based investment banking firm Greif & Company positions itself as "The Entrepreneur's Investment Bank." Greif & Company is a leader in providing merger and acquisition advice to medium-sized businesses located in the western United States.[94] Goya Foods is the largest U.S.-based Hispanic-owned food company in the United States. Segmenting the Hispanic market into unique groups, Goya offers more than 1,500 products to consumers. The firm seeks "to be the be-all for the Latin community."[95] Electronics retailer Conn's Inc., operating stores in Texas, Louisiana, and Oklahoma, uses a commissioned sales staff, which is "trained to explain increasingly complex televisions and washing machines," and its own financing business to help local citizens who dislike receiving what they perceive to be "impersonal" service from large national chains.[96] By successfully using a focus strategy, firms such as these gain a competitive advantage in specific market niches or segments, even though they do not possess an industry-wide competitive advantage.

Although the breadth of a target is clearly a matter of degree, the essence of the focus strategy "is the exploitation of a narrow target's differences from the balance of the industry."[97] Firms using the focus strategy intend to serve a particular segment of an industry more effectively than can industry-wide competitors. They succeed when they effectively serve a segment whose unique needs are so specialized that broad-based competitors choose not to serve that segment or when they satisfy the needs of a segment being served poorly by industry-wide competitors.[98]

The **focus strategy** is an integrated set of actions taken to produce goods or services that serve the needs of a particular competitive segment.

DECLARING WAR AGAINST COUNTERFEITERS TO PROTECT PRODUCT INTEGRITY AND PROFITABILITY

Many of us have seen them and some of us may own one or two of them—products that are intended to look like well-known branded items. Callaway golf clubs, Louis Vuitton purses and shoes, Coach handbags, and Rolex watches are but a few of the items that are counterfeited throughout the world. Counterfeiting is big business; regarded by some as "…one of the most significant threats to the free market." Supporting this assertion is the fact that according to the International Chamber of Commerce, counterfeit goods accounted for about $600 billion in sales in 2007, which is roughly 6 percent of global trade.

Producing and selling counterfeit products negatively affects societies and individual firms. Jobs are lost in companies making the "legitimate" versions of products that are sold by firms using the differentiation strategy. In turn, lost jobs mean lost tax revenues for local and national taxing agencies. While some work is created for those manufacturing the counterfeit goods, these jobs pay less and the companies and their employees typically pay few if any taxes on unreported sales at the firm level and unreported income at the individual employee level.

Adrian Brown/TCPI/The Canadian Press

The selling of counterfeit ink demonstrates the problems individual firms encounter. In 2008 alone, analysts estimate that Hewlett-Packard's (HP) imaging and printing group lost over $1 billion in revenue to counterfeit ink cartridges. In addition to losing sales revenue, HP is concerned that counterfeit cartridges lack product quality and integrity and may hurt the firm's reputation.

In light of the problems counterfeiting creates, HP has gone to war against counterfeiters. The firm employs teams of people to roam the globe looking for counterfeit versions of its products. Often, customers contact these teams if they suspect that a shipment of cartridges they purchased from a wholesaler is counterfeit. If HP's detectives discover that products are indeed counterfeit, "They take their findings to law enforcement to help nab big distributors of counterfeit ink supplies." HP views these actions as critical to the firm's efforts to earn revenues and profits from its products.

Sources: C. Edwards, 2009, HP declares war on counterfeiters, *BusinessWeek*, June 8, 44–45; P. E. Chaudhry, A. Zimmerman, J. R. Peters, & V. V. Cordell, 2009, Preserving intellectual property rights: Managerial insight into the escalating counterfeit market quandary, *Business Horizons*, 52: 57–66; I. Phau & M. Teah, 2009, Devil wears (counterfeit) Prada: A study of antecedents and outcomes of attitudes towards counterfeits of luxury brands, *Journal of Consumer Marketing*, 26: 15–27; J. Abelson, 2008, Grim competition with counterfeiters, *Boston Globe Online*, http://www.boston.com, August 21.

Firms can create value for customers in specific and unique market segments by using the focused cost leadership strategy or the focused differentiation strategy.

Focused Cost Leadership Strategy

Based in Sweden, IKEA, a global furniture retailer with locations in 24 countries and territories and sales revenue of 21.1 billion euros in 2008, uses the focused cost leadership strategy. Young buyers desiring style at a low cost are IKEA's target customers.[99] For these customers, the firm offers home furnishings that combine good design, function, and acceptable quality with low prices. According to the firm, "Low cost is always in focus. This applies to every phase of our activities."[100]

IKEA emphasizes several activities to keep its costs low. For example, instead of relying primarily on third-party manufacturers, the firm's engineers design low-cost, modular furniture ready for assembly by customers. To eliminate the need for sales associates or decorators, IKEA positions the products in its stores so that customers can view different living combinations (complete with sofas, chairs, tables, etc.) in a single room-like setting, which helps the customer imagine how a grouping of furniture will look in the home. A third practice that helps keep IKEA's costs low is requiring customers to transport their own purchases rather than providing delivery service.

Although it is a cost leader, IKEA also offers some differentiated features that appeal to its target customers, including its unique furniture designs, in-store playrooms for children, wheelchairs for customer use, and extended hours. IKEA believes that these services and products "are uniquely aligned with the needs of [its] customers, who are young, are not wealthy, are likely to have children (but no nanny), and, because they work, have a need to shop at odd hours."[101] Thus, IKEA's focused cost leadership strategy also includes some differentiated features with its low-cost products.

Focused Differentiation Strategy

Other firms implement the focused differentiation strategy. As noted earlier, there are many dimensions on which firms can differentiate their good or service. For example, New Look Laser Tattoo Removal, located in Houston, Texas, specializes in removing tattoos that customers no longer desire. According to the firm, some of its customers want to remove tattoos prior to interviewing for jobs while others believe that removing them can benefit their careers. As one of the firm's customers said, "Tattoos make you look a little rougher. I don't want to worry about what people are thinking about me."[102]

The new generation of lunch trucks populating cities such as New York, San Franciso, and Los Angeles also use the focused differentiation strategy. Serving "high-end fare such as grass-fed hamburgers, escargot and crème brulee," highly trained chefs and well-known restaurateurs own and operate many of these trucks. In fact, "the new breed of lunch truck is aggressively gourmet, tech-savvy and politically correct." Selling sustainably harvested fish tacos in a vehicle that is fueled by vegetable oil, the Green Truck, located in Los Angeles, demonstrates these characteristics. Moreover, the owners of these trucks often use Twitter and Facebook to inform customers of their locations as they move from point to point in their focal city.[103]

Denver-based Kazoo Toys uses the focused differentiation strategy to create value for parents and children interested in purchasing unique toys while simultaneously having access to unique services. As we explain in the Strategic Focus, continuously concentrating on ways to create unique value for its customers seems to be the foundation of the firm's continuing success.

With a focus strategy, firms such as Kazoo Toys must be able to complete various primary and support activities in a competitively superior manner to develop and sustain a competitive advantage and earn above-average returns. The activities required to use the focused cost leadership strategy are virtually identical to those of the industry-wide cost leadership strategy (Figure 4.3), and activities required to use the focused differentiation strategy are largely identical to those of the industry-wide differentiation strategy

KAZOO TOYS: CRISP DIFFERENTIATION AS A MEANS OF CREATING VALUE FOR A CERTAIN SET OF CUSTOMERS

Kazoo Toys is a full-service toy store in Denver, Colorado. Offering over 60,000 unique toys for kids of all ages in the brick and mortar location and an additional 6,000 products online at http://www.kazootoys.com, the firm is the world's largest seller of educational, non-violent toys. Children from birth to age 12 are the firm's target market. The essence of the differentiation Kazoo Toys provides its customers is described in the following words: "We know our toys, we know your kids, and we love good customer service. We remain dedicated to providing the best possible tools for your child's healthy play." With respect to toys specifically, the firm's slogan ("Toys That Play with Imagination!") captures the educational aspects of its products.

Kazoo Toys differs from competitors in a number of ways. For example, in terms of inventory, the firm does not stock well-known toy brands (e.g., Mattel and Fisher-Price) that are available from most large retailers. In contrast, Kazoo stocks harder-to-find products such as German-made, Gotz Dolls as well as a range of unique toys that are made in the United States, France, and many other countries. Stocking unique toys allows Kazoo to avoid competing on the price variable and to earn margins required to support the differentiated products and services the firm provides to its customers. Another source of differentiation is Kazoo's exclusive contract with the U.S. Army & Air Force Exchange Service (AAFES)—a contract in which Kazoo is the toy site of choice on military shopping sites.

The firm's open invitation to professionals is another way Kazoo differs from competitors. Speech therapists are welcomed to the store to try to locate toys that might help their patients. Although the store continues to expand to accommodate its success, the design remains unique in that it features smaller departments. For example, there is a "Thomas the Tank Engine" department and a Playmobil department. The inventory is freshened frequently to expose customers to the latest, most innovative, educational, and nonviolent toys. The company's online store (which now generates roughly 50 percent of the firm's revenue) is also known for its strong customer service. Here is how one customer described the online service she received: "Old-fashioned friendly service. When I called to check the delivery date of a little piano I had ordered for my grandson, I was actually speaking to a person that was friendly, polite, courteous, and just delightful. I will continue to buy from this company. They have a real interest in giving top-quality service. It has been a most enjoyable experience." As this comment suggests, excellent customer service is an important source of differentiation for Kazoo Toys.

Courtesy of Kazoo & Company Toys

Differentiating itself in terms of product lines and overall customer experience from its big box competitors has allowed CEO Diana Nelson to offer her customers at Kazoo Toys a unique toy shopping experience.

Sources: B. Ruggiero, 2009, Super staff and creative expansion keep toy store, Kazoo Toys blog, http://www.kazootoys. blogspot.com, March 11; E. Aguilera, 2008, Kazoo & Co. toys with growth, *Denver Post Online*, http://www.denverpost. com, July 3; B. R. Barringer & R. D. Ireland, 2008, *Entrepreneurship: Successfully launching new ventures*, 2nd ed., Prentice-Hall; T. Polanski, 2008, Diana Nelson, CEO of Kazoo Toys discusses business trials and triumphs with Tom Polanski, *eBizine.com*, http://www.ebizine.com, July 30.

(Figure 4.4). Similarly, the manner in which each of the two focus strategies allows a firm to deal successfully with the five competitive forces parallels those of the two broad strategies. The only difference is in the firm's competitive scope; the firm focuses on a narrow industry segment. Thus, Figures 4.3 and 4.4 and the text regarding the five competitive forces also describe the relationship between each of the two focus strategies and competitive advantage.

Competitive Risks of Focus Strategies

With either focus strategy, the firm faces the same general risks as does the company using the cost leadership or the differentiation strategy, respectively, on an industry-wide basis. However, focus strategies have three additional risks.

First, a competitor may be able to focus on a more narrowly defined competitive segment and "outfocus" the focuser. This would happen to IKEA if another firm found a way to offer IKEA's customers (young buyers interested in stylish furniture at a low cost) additional sources of differentiation while charging the same price or to provide the same service with the same sources of differentiation at a lower price. Second, a company competing on an industry-wide basis may decide that the market segment served by the firm using a focus strategy is attractive and worthy of competitive pursuit. For example, women's clothiers such as Chico's, Ann Taylor, and Liz Claiborne might conclude that the profit potential in the narrow segment being served by Anne Fontaine is attractive and to design and sell competitively similar clothing items. Initially, Anne Fontaine designed and sold only white shirts for women. Quite differentiated on the basis of their design, craftsmanship, and high quality of raw materials, one customer describes her reaction to wearing an Anne Fontaine shirt in this manner: "Once you put on a Fontaine design, you'll find that not one other white shirt can compare as far as design and quality craftsmanship are concerned."[104] The third risk involved with a focus strategy is that the needs of customers within a narrow competitive segment may become more similar to those of industry-wide customers as a whole over time. As a result, the advantages of a focus strategy are either reduced or eliminated. At some point, for example, the needs of Anne Fontaine's customers for high-quality, uniquely designed white shirts may dissipate. If this were to happen, Anne Fontaine's customers might choose to buy white shirts from chains such as Liz Claiborne that sell clothing items with some differentiation, but at a lower cost.

Integrated Cost Leadership/Differentiation Strategy

Most consumers have high expectations when purchasing a good or service. In general, it seems that most consumers want to pay a low price for products with somewhat highly differentiated features. Because of these customer expectations, a number of firms engage in primary and support activities that allow them to simultaneously pursue low cost and differentiation. Firm seeking to do this use the **integrated cost leadership/differentiation strategy**. The objective of using this strategy is to efficiently produce products with some differentiated features. Efficient production is the source of maintaining low costs while differentiation is the source of creating unique value. Firms that successfully use the integrated cost leadership/differentiation strategy usually adapt quickly to new technologies and rapid changes in their external environments. Simultaneously concentrating on developing two sources of competitive advantage (cost and differentiation) increases the number of primary and support activities in which the firm must become competent. Such firms often have strong networks with external parties that perform some of the primary and support activities.[105] In turn, having skills in a larger number of activities makes a firm more flexible.

Concentrating on the needs of its core customer group (higher-income, fashion-conscious discount shoppers), Target Stores uses an integrated cost leadership/differentiation strategy as shown by its "Expect More. Pay Less" brand promise. Target's annual report describes this strategy: "To ensure our guests understand our unique ability to meet their

The **integrated cost leadership/ differentiation strategy** involves engaging in primary and support activities that allow a firm to simultaneously pursue low cost and differentiation.

desire for everyday essentials and affordable indulgences, we elevated the prominence of the 'Pay Less' half of our brand promise in both our merchandising and marketing through in-store signing and presentation as well as new campaigns that emphasize our outstanding value. At the same time, we continued to deliver differentiation and new-ness on the 'Expect More' side of our brand promise with the introduction of Converse One Star in apparel and shoes, the launch of upscale beauty brands, an expanded owned brand presence and a continuous flow of designer collections at exceptional prices."[106] To implement this strategy, Target relies on its relationships with various companies to offer differentiated products at discounted prices. Collections from eco-conscious Rogan Gregory in apparel, Anya Hindmarch in handbags, Sigerson Morrison in shoes, and John Derian and Sami Hayek in home décor are some of the products available in Target's stores. While implementing its strategy, "Target strives to be a responsible steward of the environment."[107] To protect the physical environment, the firm takes several actions annually including recycling 47,600 broken shopping carts, 2.1 million pounds of plastic, and 153,000 pounds of metal from broken hangers.

European-based Zara, which pioneered "cheap chic" in clothing apparel, is another firm using the integrated cost leadership/differentiation strategy. Zara offers current and desirable fashion goods at relatively low prices. To implement this strategy effectively requires sophisticated designers and effective means of managing costs, which fits Zara's capabilities. Zara can design and begin manufacturing a new fashion in three weeks, which suggests a highly flexible orga-nization that can adapt easily to changes in the market or with competitors.[108]

Flexibility is required for firms to complete primary and support activities in ways that allow them to use the integrated cost leadership/differentiation strategy in order to produce somewhat differentiated products at relatively low costs. Flexible manufacturing systems, information networks, and total quality management systems are three sources of flexibility that are particularly useful for firms trying to balance the objectives of continuous cost reductions and contin-uous enhancements to sources of differentiation as called for by the integrated strategy.

FRANCIS DEAN/Alamy

Zara has been successful at offering its custom-ers the latest fashions at reasonable prices while also carefully managing their costs.

Flexible Manufacturing Systems

A flexible manufacturing system (FMS) increases the "flexibilities of human, physical, and information resources"[109] that the firm integrates to create relatively differentiated products at relatively low costs. A significant technological advance, FMS is a computer-controlled process used to produce a variety of products in moderate, flexible quanti-ties with a minimum of manual intervention.[110] Often the flexibility is derived from modularization of the manufacturing process (and sometimes other value chain activities as well).[111]

The goal of an FMS is to eliminate the "low cost versus product variety" trade-off that is inherent in traditional manufacturing technologies. Firms use an FMS to change quickly and easily from making one product to making another. Used properly, an FMS allows the firm to respond more effectively to changes in its customers' needs, while retaining low-cost advantages and consistent product quality.[112] Because an FMS also enables the firm to reduce the lot size needed to manufacture a product efficiently, the firm's capacity to serve the unique needs of a narrow competitive scope is higher. In industries of all types, effective mixes of the firm's tangible assets (e.g., machines) and intangible assets (e.g., people's skills) facilitate implementation of complex competitive strategies, especially the integrated cost leadership/differentiation strategy.[113]

Information Networks

By linking companies with their suppliers, distributors, and customers, information net-works provide another source of flexibility. These networks, when used effectively, help the firm satisfy customer expectations in terms of product quality and delivery speed.[114]

STRATEGY
RIGHT NOW

Following similar principles to the integrated cost leadership/differentiation strategy, read how companies are creating uncontested market space employing the Blue Ocean Strategy.

www.cengage.com/management/hitt

Earlier, we discussed the importance of managing the firm's relationships with its customers in order to understand their needs. Customer relationship management (CRM) is one form of an information-based network process that firms use for this purpose.[115] An effective CRM system provides a 360-degree view of the company's relationship with customers, encompassing all contact points, business processes, and communication media and sales channels.[116] The firm can then use this information to determine the trade-offs its customers are willing to make between differentiated features and low cost—an assessment that is vital for companies using the integrated cost leadership/differentiation strategy.

Thus, to make comprehensive strategic decisions with effective knowledge of the organization's context, good information flow is essential. Better quality managerial decisions require accurate information on the firm's environment.[117]

Total Quality Management Systems

Total quality management (TQM) is a "managerial innovation that emphasizes an organization's total commitment to the customer and to continuous improvement of every process through the use of data-driven, problem-solving approaches based on empowerment of employee groups and teams."[118] Firms develop and use TQM systems in order to (1) increase customer satisfaction, (2) cut costs, and (3) reduce the amount of time required to introduce innovative products to the marketplace.[119]

Firms able to simultaneously reduce costs while enhancing their ability to develop innovative products increase their flexibility, an outcome that is particularly helpful to firms implementing the integrated cost leadership/differentiation strategy. Exceeding customers' expectations regarding quality is a differentiating feature, and eliminating process inefficiencies to cut costs allows the firm to offer that quality to customers at a relatively low price. Thus, an effective TQM system helps the firm develop the flexibility needed to spot opportunities to simultaneously increase differentiation and reduce costs. Yet, TQM systems are available to all competitors. So they may help firms maintain competitive parity, but rarely alone will they lead to a competitive advantage.[120]

Competitive Risks of the Integrated Cost Leadership/Differentiation Strategy

The potential to earn above-average returns by successfully using the integrated cost leadership/differentiation strategy is appealing. However, it is a risky strategy, because firms find it difficult to perform primary and support activities in ways that allow them to produce relatively inexpensive products with levels of differentiation that create value for the target customer. Moreover, to properly use this strategy across time, firms must be able to simultaneously reduce costs incurred to produce products (as required by the cost leadership strategy) while increasing products' differentiation (as required by the differentiation strategy).

Firms that fail to perform the primary and support activities in an optimum manner become "stuck in the middle."[121] Being stuck in the middle means that the firm's cost structure is not low enough to allow it to attractively price its products and that its products are not sufficiently differentiated to create value for the target customer. These firms will not earn above-average returns and will earn average returns only when the structure of the industry in which it competes is highly favorable.[122] Thus, companies implementing the integrated cost leadership/differentiation strategy must be able to perform the primary and support activities in ways that allow them to produce products that offer the target customer some differentiated features at a relatively low cost/price.

Firms can also become stuck in the middle when they fail to successfully implement *either* the cost leadership *or* the differentiation strategy. In other words, industry-wide competitors too can become stuck in the middle. Trying to use the integrated strategy is costly in that firms must pursue both low costs and differentiation. Firms may need

Total quality management (TQM) is a managerial innovation that emphasizes an organization's total commitment to the customer and to continuous improvement of every process through the use of data-driven, problem-solving approaches based on empowerment of employee groups and teams.

to form alliances with other firms to achieve differentiation, yet alliance partners may extract prices for the use of their resources that make it difficult to meaningfully reduce costs.[123] Firms may be motivated to make acquisitions to maintain their differentiation through innovation or to add products to their portfolio not offered by competitors.[124] Recent research suggests that firms using "pure strategies," either cost leadership or differentiation, often outperform firms attempting to use a "hybrid strategy" (i.e., integrated cost leadership/differentiation strategy). This research suggests the risky nature of using an integrated strategy.[125] However, the integrated strategy is becoming more common and perhaps necessary in many industries because of technological advances and global competition.

SUMMARY

- A business-level strategy is an integrated and coordinated set of commitments and actions the firm uses to gain a competitive advantage by exploiting core competencies in specific product markets. Five business-level strategies (cost leadership, differentiation, focused cost leadership, focused differentiation, and integrated cost leadership/differentiation) are examined in the chapter.

- Customers are the foundation of successful business-level strategies. When considering customers, a firm simultaneously examines three issues: who, what, and how. These issues, respectively, refer to the customer groups to be served, the needs those customers have that the firm seeks to satisfy, and the core competencies the firm will use to satisfy customers' needs. Increasing segmentation of markets throughout the global economy creates opportunities for firms to identify more unique customer needs they can serve with one of the business-level strategies.

- Firms seeking competitive advantage through the cost leadership strategy produce no-frills, standardized products for an industry's typical customer. However, these low-cost products must be offered with competitive levels of differentiation. Above-average returns are earned when firms continuously emphasize efficiency such that their costs are lower than those of their competitors, while providing customers with products that have acceptable levels of differentiated features.

- Competitive risks associated with the cost leadership strategy include (1) a loss of competitive advantage to newer technologies, (2) a failure to detect changes in customers' needs, and (3) the ability of competitors to imitate the cost leader's competitive advantage through their own unique strategic actions.

- Through the differentiation strategy, firms provide customers with products that have different (and valued) features. Differentiated products must be sold at a cost that customers believe is competitive relative to the product's features as compared to the cost/feature combinations available from competitors' goods. Because of their uniqueness, differentiated goods or services are sold at a premium price. Products can be differentiated along any dimension that some customer group values.

Firms using this strategy seek to differentiate their products from competitors' goods or services along as many dimensions as possible. The less similarity to competitors' products, the more buffered a firm is from competition with its rivals.

- Risks associated with the differentiation strategy include (1) a customer group's decision that the differences between the differentiated product and the cost leader's goods or services are no longer worth a premium price, (2) the inability of a differentiated product to create the type of value for which customers are willing to pay a premium price, (3) the ability of competitors to provide customers with products that have features similar to those of the differentiated product, but at a lower cost, and (4) the threat of counterfeiting, whereby firms produce a cheap "knockoff" of a differentiated good or service.

- Through the cost leadership and the differentiated focus strategies, firms serve the needs of a narrow competitive segment (e.g., a buyer group, product segment, or geographic area). This strategy is successful when firms have the core competencies required to provide value to a specialized market segment that exceeds the value available from firms serving customers on an industry-wide basis.

- The competitive risks of focus strategies include (1) a competitor's ability to use its core competencies to "outfocus" the focuser by serving an even more narrowly defined market segment, (2) decisions by industry-wide competitors to focus on a customer group's specialized needs, and (3) a reduction in differences of the needs between customers in a narrow market segment and the industry-wide market.

- Firms using the integrated cost leadership/differentiation strategy strive to provide customers with relatively low-cost products that also have valued differentiated features. Flexibility is required for the firm to learn how to use primary and support activities in ways that allow them to produce differentiated products at relatively low costs. The primary risk of this strategy is that a firm might produce products that do not offer sufficient value in terms of either low cost or differentiation. In such cases, the company is "stuck in the middle." Firms stuck in the middle compete at a disadvantage and are unable to earn more than average returns.

REVIEW QUESTIONS

1. What is a business-level strategy?

2. What is the relationship between a firm's customers and its business-level strategy in terms of *who, what,* and *how*? Why is this relationship important?

3. What are the differences among the cost leadership, differentiation, focused cost leadership, focused differentiation, and integrated cost leadership/differentiation business-level strategies?

4. How can each one of the business-level strategies be used to position the firm relative to the five forces of competition in a way that helps the firm earn above-average returns?

5. What are the specific risks associated with using each business-level strategy?

EXPERIENTIAL EXERCISES

EXERCISE 1: CUSTOMER NEEDS AND STOCK TRADING

Nearly 100 million Americans have investments in the stock market through shares of individual companies or positions in mutual funds. At its peak volume, the New York Stock Exchange has traded more than 3.5 billion shares in a single day. Stock brokerage firms are the conduit to help individuals plan their portfolios and manage transactions. Given the scope of this industry, there is no single definition of what customers consider as "superior value" from a brokerage operation.

Part One

After forming small teams, the instructor will ask the teams to count off by threes. The teams will study three different brokerage firms, with team 1 examining TD Ameritrade (ticker: AMTD), team 2 E*TRADE (ticker: ETFC), and team 3, Charles Schwab (ticker: SCHW).

Part Two

Each team should research its target company to answer the following questions:

- Describe the "who, what, and how" for your firm. How stable is this focus? How much have these elements changed in the last five years?
- Describe your firm's strategy.
- How does your firm's strategy offer protection against each of the five forces?

Part Three

In class, the instructor will ask two teams for each firm to summarize their results. Next, the whole class will discuss which firm is most effective at meeting the needs of its customer base.

EXERCISE 2: CREATE A BUSINESS-LEVEL STRATEGY

This assignment brings together elements from the previous chapters. Accordingly, you and your team will create a business-level strategy for a firm of your own creation. The instructor will assign you an industry for which you will create an entry strategy using one of the five business-level strategies.

Each team is assigned one of the business-level strategies described in the chapter:

- Cost leadership
- Differentiation
- Focused cost leadership
- Focused differentiation
- Integrated cost leadership/differentiation

Part One

Research your industry and describe the general environment. Using the segments of the general environment, identify some factors for each segment that are influential for your industry. Next, describe the industry environment using Porter's five-forces model. Database services like Mint Global, Datamonitor, or IBISWorld can be helpful in this regard. If those are not available, consult your local librarian for assistance. After this, you should be able to clearly articulate the opportunities and the threats that exist.

Part Two

Create on a poster the business-level strategy assigned to your team. Be prepared to describe the following:

- Vision statement and mission statement
- Description of your target customer
- Picture of your business—for example, where is it located (downtown, suburb, rural, etc)?
- Describe trends that provide opportunities and threats for your intended strategy.
- List the resources, both tangible and intangible, required to compete successfully in this market.
- How will you go about creating a sustainable competitive advantage?

THE COUNTERINTUITIVE STRATEGY

William Johnson Chairman, president, and chief executive officer/H. J. Heinz Company

William Johnson discusses the rationalization of business segments that the company found itself holding in 2002.

Before you watch the video consider the following concepts and questions and be prepared to discuss them in class:

Concepts
- Customers
- Strategy
- Focusing on capabilities
- Portfolio of businesses
- Business-level strategy

Questions
1. Research H. J. Heinz Company and describe its portfolio of businesses and its business-level strategy.
2. Do you think the goal of any company should be to grow and get bigger—particularly a publicly-traded one like Heinz?
3. In any corporation, should underperforming business segments be sold?

CHAPTER 5

Competitive Rivalry and Dynamics

Studying this chapter should provide you with the strategic management knowledge needed to:

1. Define competitors, competitive rivalry, competitive behavior, and competitive dynamics.

2. Describe market commonality and resource similarity as the building blocks of a competitor analysis.

3. Explain awareness, motivation, and ability as drivers of competitive behaviors.

4. Discuss factors affecting the likelihood a competitor will take competitive actions.

5. Describe factors affecting the likelihood a competitor will respond to actions taken against it.

6. Explain the competitive dynamics in each of slow-cycle, fast-cycle, and standard-cycle markets.

COMPETITION IN RECESSIONS: LET THE BAD TIMES ROLL

Competitive rivalry often increases significantly during recessions, and some selected businesses in particular industries actually experience heightened demand. When economic times are bad, many people change their shopping behavior. In particular, people buy what they need in goods but also search for ways to escape their daily negative environment (e.g., through entertainment) and find ways to experience some form of enjoyment (e.g., eat sweets). For these reasons, staple goods manufacturers; retailers that sell consumer staple goods, health care products, and pharmaceuticals; movie studios and theaters; video game developers and distributors; candy manufacturers; and those making and distributing tobacco and alcohol tend to do well during recessionary times. For example, box-office receipts for movies increased by 20 percent in 2008 and sales were up over 17 percent in the first two months of 2009. Home viewing of movies increased as well. Netflix experienced an increase of 600,000 new subscribers in the first 1.5 months of 2009 alone. Parents can afford to take their children to the movies or rent them for viewing at home, substituting this form of entertainment for taking the children on major trips to Disneyland and similar more expensive adventures.

Bryan Bedder/Getty Images

While consumers frequently reduce spending on large ticket items during periods of economic strain, some businesses actually experience growth as people adjust their priorities.

People frequently will reduce major expenses where possible (e.g., increase carpooling to work, use coupons for purchases) but will also spend extra money for some enjoyment, such as candy. Consumers in the United States spend billions of dollars for candy each year, with an approximate increase of 3 percent in 2008. A Nielsen survey revealed that pasta, candy, and beer were relatively immune from the negative effects of a recession. Dylan Lauren, owner of Dylan's Candy Bar, noted that her company has experienced sales increases during bad times such as 9/11, war, and the falling stock market. In fact, she is currently expanding her business with plans to open new outlets in Los Angeles and Las Vegas and adding a candy cocktail bar to her headquarters in New York City. Of course, she has to compete with other specialty candy companies (e.g., Rocky Mountain Chocolate Factory) and even large candy manufacturers such as Hershey and Mars.

Water is a necessity, which draws increased attention even during bad economic times. While the bottled water industry suffered a little during the last recession (sales decreased by 2 percent in 2008), Coca-Cola, PepsiCo, and Nestle, three major bottled water distributors, are fighting to gain enhanced market shares by introducing lower-cost versions,

flavored-water varieties, and even vitamin-enhanced versions. In addition, they must deal with the environmental concerns about the plastic bottles in which their product is distributed. Interestingly, the economic decline has increased the number and type of competitors with which Coke, Pepsi, and Nestle must contend. For example, water filter manufacturers and distributors have experienced a growing demand for their products (replacing purchases of bottled water with filtered tap water). Clean drinking water is an increasing global concern, causing companies such as IBM to enter the market with new "water-management services." IBM projects the water-management services market to reach $20 billion by 2014. In addition, major firms such as GE, Siemens, and Veolia Environment (France) are developing significant plans to help provide clean water in different parts of the world.

Thus, we can conclude that competitive dynamics within industries vary considerably and not all are affected negatively by economic recessions. Yet, changes in the market can be quite challenging as markets are complex—new competitors enter and consumer tastes change, with some of the changes likely to be long term, continuing even after good economic times return.

Sources: 2008, Nielsen reveals consumer goods categories among those most immune, most vulnerable to recession, *Progressive Grocer*, http://www.progressivegrocer.com, June 5; J. Flanigan, 2008, Keeping the water pure is suddenly in demand, *The New York Times*, http://www.nytimes.com, June 19; M. Irvine, 2008, Candy a sweet spot in sour economy, *Newsvine*, http://www.newsvine.com, June 23; F. C. Gil, 2008, Industry insiders: Dylan Lauren, candy princess, *BlackBook*, http://www.blackbookmag.com, October 22; C. Palmer & N. Byrnes, 2009, Coke and Pepsi try reinventing water, *BusinessWeek*, http://www.businessweek.com, February 19; P. Huguenin, 2009. 10 industries going strong—despite the recession, *New York Daily News*, http://www.nydailynews.com, February 19; M. Cieply & B. Barnes, 2009, In downturn, Americans flock to the movies, *The New York Times*, http://www.nytimes.com, March 1; J. Robertson, 2009, IBM launches water-management services operation, *BusinessWeek*, http://www.businessweek.com, March 13.

Firms operating in the same market, offering similar products, and targeting similar customers are **competitors**.[1] Southwest Airlines, Delta, United, Continental, and JetBlue are competitors, as are PepsiCo and Coca-Cola Company. As described in the Opening Case, PepsiCo and Coca-Cola are currently engaging in a heated competitive battle in the market for bottled water with sales slipping and the two companies trying to maintain or even increase their market share. And, even though the candy market is growing in the recession, small candy retailers such as Dylan's Candy Bar must compete for the expanding market with other specialty candy retailers (e.g., Rocky Mountain Chocolate Factory) and large candy manufacturers (e.g., Hershey and Mars).

Firms interact with their competitors as part of the broad context within which they operate while attempting to earn above-average returns.[2] The decisions firms make about their interactions with their competitors significantly affect their ability to earn above-average returns.[3] Because 80 to 90 percent of new firms fail, learning how to select the markets in which to compete and how to best compete within them is highly important.[4]

Competitive rivalry is the ongoing set of competitive actions and competitive responses that occur among firms as they maneuver for an advantageous market position.[5] Especially in highly competitive industries, firms constantly jockey for advantage as they launch strategic actions and respond or react to rivals' moves.[6] It is important for those leading organizations to understand competitive rivalry, in that "the central, brute empirical fact in strategy is that some firms outperform others,"[7] meaning that competitive rivalry influences an individual firm's ability to gain and sustain competitive advantages.[8]

A sequence of firm-level moves, rivalry results from firms initiating their own competitive actions and then responding to actions taken by competitors.[9] **Competitive behavior** is the set of competitive actions and responses the firm takes to build or defend its competitive advantages and to improve its market position.[10] Through competitive behavior, the firm tries to successfully position itself relative to the five forces of competition (see Chapter 2) and to defend current competitive advantages while building advantages for the future (see Chapter 3). Increasingly, competitors engage in competitive actions and responses in more than one market.[11] Firms competing against each other in several product or geographic markets are engaged in **multimarket competition**.[12]

Competitors are firms operating in the same market, offering similar products, and targeting similar customers.

Competitive rivalry is the ongoing set of competitive actions and competitive responses that occur among firms as they maneuver for an advantageous market position.

Competitive behavior is the set of competitive actions and competitive responses the firm takes to build or defend its competitive advantages and to improve its market position.

Multimarket competition occurs when firms compete against each other in several product or geographic markets.

Figure 5.1 From Competitors to Competitive Dynamics

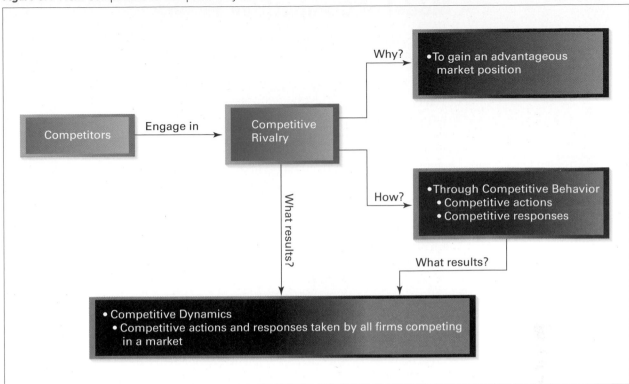

Source: Adapted from M. J. Chen, 1996, Competitor analysis and interfirm rivalry: Toward a theoretical integration, *Academy of Management Review*, 21: 100–134.

All competitive behavior—that is, the total set of actions and responses taken by all firms competing within a market—is called **competitive dynamics**. The relationships among these key concepts are shown in Figure 5.1.

This chapter focuses on competitive rivalry and competitive dynamics. A firm's strategies are dynamic in nature because actions taken by one firm elicit responses from competitors that, in turn, typically result in responses from the firm that took the initial action.[13] As explained in the Opening Case, Coca-Cola and PepsiCo are changing how they compete because of the recession, out of concern for the environment, and in response to each other and Nestle, another major competitor. Also, Dylan's Candy Bar is responding to increased demand by adding more outlets in additional cities. Yet, it must also be sensitive to how competitors such as the Rocky Mountain Chocolate Factory respond and actions taken by large, well-known candy manufacturers (e.g., Hershey).[14]

Competitive rivalry's effect on the firm's strategies is shown by the fact that a strategy's success is determined not only by the firm's initial competitive actions but also by how well it anticipates competitors' responses to them *and* by how well the firm anticipates and responds to its competitors' initial actions (also called attacks).[15] Although competitive rivalry affects all types of strategies (e.g., corporate-level, acquisition, and international), its dominant influence is on the firm's business-level strategy or strategies. Indeed, firms' actions and responses to those of their rivals are the basic building blocks of business-level strategies.[16] Recall from Chapter 4 that business-level strategy is concerned with what the firm does to successfully use its competitive advantages in specific product markets. In the global economy, competitive rivalry is intensifying,[17] meaning that the significance of its effect on firms' business-level strategies is increasing. However, firms that develop and use effective business-level strategies tend to outperform competitors in individual product markets, even when experiencing intense competitive rivalry that price cuts bring about.[18]

Competitive dynamics refer to all competitive behaviors—that is, the total set of actions and responses taken by all firms competing within a market.

A Model of Competitive Rivalry

Competitive rivalry evolves from the pattern of actions and responses as one firm's competitive actions have noticeable effects on competitors, eliciting competitive responses from them.[19] This pattern suggests that firms are mutually interdependent, that they are affected by each other's actions and responses, and that marketplace success is a function of both individual strategies and the consequences of their use.[20] Increasingly, too, executives recognize that competitive rivalry can have a major effect on the firm's financial performance[21] Research shows that intensified rivalry within an industry results in decreased average profitability for the competing firms.[22]

Figure 5.2 presents a straightforward model of competitive rivalry at the firm level; this type of rivalry is usually dynamic and complex.[23] The competitive actions and responses the firm takes are the foundation for successfully building and using its capabilities and core competencies to gain an advantageous market position.[24] The model in Figure 5.2 presents the sequence of activities commonly involved in competition between a particular firm and each of its competitors. Companies can use the model to understand how to be able to predict competitors' behavior (actions and responses) and reduce the uncertainty associated with competitors' actions.[25] Being able to predict competitors' actions and responses has a positive effect on the firm's market position and its subsequent financial performance.[26] The sum of all the individual rivalries modeled in Figure 5.2 that occur in a particular market reflects the competitive dynamics in that market.

The remainder of the chapter explains components of the model shown in Figure 5.2. We first describe market commonality and resource similarity as the building blocks of a competitor analysis. Next, we discuss the effects of three organizational characteristics— awareness, motivation, and ability—on the firm's competitive behavior. We then examine competitive rivalry between firms, or interfirm rivalry, in detail by describing the factors that affect the likelihood a firm will take a competitive action and the factors that affect the likelihood a firm will respond to a competitor's action. In the chapter's final section, we turn our attention to competitive dynamics to describe how market characteristics affect competitive rivalry in slow-cycle, fast-cycle, and standard-cycle markets.

Figure 5.2 A Model of Competitive Rivalry

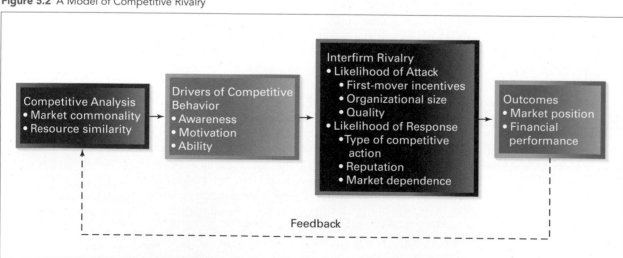

Source: Adapted from M. J. Chen, 1996, Competitor analysis and interfirm rivalry: Toward a theoretical integration, *Academy of Management Review*, 21: 100–134.

Competitor Analysis

As previously noted, a competitor analysis is the first step the firm takes to be able to predict the extent and nature of its rivalry with each competitor. The number of markets in which firms compete against each other (called market commonality, defined on the following pages) and the similarity in their resources (called resource similarity, also defined in the following section) determine the extent to which the firms are competitors. Firms with high market commonality and highly similar resources are "clearly direct and mutually acknowledged competitors."[27] The drivers of competitive behavior—as well as factors influencing the likelihood that a competitor will initiate competitive actions and will respond to its competitor's actions—influence the intensity of rivalry, even for direct competitors.[28]

In Chapter 2, we discussed competitor analysis as a technique firms use to understand their competitive environment. Together, the general, industry, and competitive environments comprise the firm's external environment. We also described how competitor analysis is used to help the firm *understand* its competitors. This understanding results from studying competitors' future objectives, current strategies, assumptions, and capabilities (see Figure 2.3 on page **60**). In this chapter, the discussion of competitor analysis is extended to describe what firms study to be able to *predict* competitors' behavior in the form of their competitive actions and responses. The discussions of competitor analysis in Chapter 2 and in this chapter are complementary in that firms must first *understand* competitors (Chapter 2) before their competitive actions and competitive responses can be *predicted* (this chapter). These analyses are highly important because they help managers to avoid "competitive blind spots," in which managers are unaware of specific competitors or their capabilities. If managers have competitive blind spots, they may be surprised by a competitor's actions, thereby allowing the competitor to increase its market share at the expense of the manager's firm.[29] Competitor analyses are especially important when a firm enters a foreign market. Managers need to understand the local competition and foreign competitors currently operating in the market.[30] Without such analyses, they are less likely to be successful.

Market Commonality

Each industry is composed of various markets. The financial services industry has markets for insurance, brokerage services, banks, and so forth. To concentrate on the needs of different, unique customer groups, markets can be further subdivided. The insurance market, for example, could be broken into market segments (such as commercial and consumer), product segments (such as health insurance and life insurance), and geographic markets (such as Western Europe and Southeast Asia). In general, the capabilities the Internet's technologies generate help to shape the nature of industries' markets along with the competition among firms operating in them.[31] For example, widely available electronic news sources affect how traditional print news distributors such as newspapers conduct their business.

Competitors tend to agree about the different characteristics of individual markets that form an industry.[32] For example, in the transportation industry, the commercial air travel market differs from the ground transportation market, which is served by such firms as YRC Worldwide (one of the largest transportation service providers in the world)[33] and major YRC competitors Arkansas Best, Con-way Inc., and FedEx Freight.[34] Although differences exist, many industries' markets are partially related in terms of technologies used or core competencies needed to develop a competitive advantage. For example, different types of transportation companies need to provide reliable and timely service. Commercial air carriers such as Southwest, Continental, and JetBlue must therefore develop service competencies to satisfy their passengers, while YRC and its major competitors must develop such competencies to serve the needs of those using their fleets to ship goods.

Firms sometimes compete against each other in several markets that are in different industries. As such these competitors interact with each other several times, a condition called market commonality. More formally, **market commonality** is concerned with the number of markets with which the firm and a competitor are jointly involved and the degree of importance of the individual markets to each.[35] When firms produce similar products and compete for the same customers, the competitive rivary is likely to be high.[36] Firms competing against one another in several or many markets engage in multimarket competition.[37] Coca-Cola and PepsiCo compete across a number of product (e.g., soft drinks, bottled water) and geographic markets (throughout the United States and in many foreign markets) as suggested in the Opening Case. Even smaller firms, such as Dylan's Candy Bar, are likely to compete with some competitors in several geographic markets as they enter new cities. Airlines, chemicals, pharmaceuticals, and consumer foods are examples of other industries in which firms often simultaneously compete against each other in multiple markets.

Firms competing in several markets have the potential to respond to a competitor's actions not only within the market in which the actions are taken, but also in other markets where they compete with the rival. This potential creates a complicated competitive mosaic in which "the moves an organization makes in one market are designed to achieve goals in another market in ways that aren't immediately apparent to its rivals."[38]

In order to grow, DHL Express is tasked with competing against UPS and FEDEX, much larger rivals with similar resources.

This potential complicates the rivalry between competitors. In fact, research suggests that "a firm with greater multimarket contact is less likely to initiate an attack, but more likely to move (respond) aggressively when attacked."[39] Thus, in general, multimarket competition reduces competitive rivalry, but some firms will still compete when the potential rewards (e.g., potential market share gain) are high.[40]

Resource Similarity

Resource similarity is the extent to which the firm's tangible and intangible resources are comparable to a competitor's in terms of both type and amount.[41] Firms with similar types and amounts of resources are likely to have similar strengths and weaknesses and use similar strategies.[42] The competition between FedEx and United Parcel Service (UPS) in using information technology to improve the efficiency of their operations and to reduce costs demonstrates these expectations. Pursuing similar strategies that are supported by similar resource profiles, personnel in these firms work at a feverish pace to receive, sort, and ship packages. At a UPS hub, for example, "workers have less than four hours (on a peak night) to process more than a million packages from at least 100 planes and probably 160 trucks."[43] FedEx and UPS are both spending more than $1 billion annually on research and development (R&D) to find ways to improve efficiency and reduce costs. Rival DHL Express is trying to compete with the two global giants supported by the privatized German postal service, Deutsche Post World Net, which acquired it in 2002. While DHL has made impressive gains in recent years (e.g., increasing its brand awareness and building impressive operations in the United States), it still must struggle to compete against its stronger rivals with similar resources. To survive, it has negotiated a partnership agreement with UPS in which UPS will handle DHL's air shipments. Such arrangements are often referred to as "coopetition" (cooperation between competitors).[44]

When performing a competitor analysis, a firm analyzes each of its competitors in terms of market commonality and resource similarity. The results of these analyses can be mapped for visual comparisons. In Figure 5.3, we show different hypothetical intersections

Market commonality is concerned with the number of markets with which the firm and a competitor are jointly involved and the degree of importance of the individual markets to each.

Resource similarity is the extent to which the firm's tangible and intangible resources are comparable to a competitor's in terms of both type and amount.

Figure 5.3 A Framework of Competitor Analysis

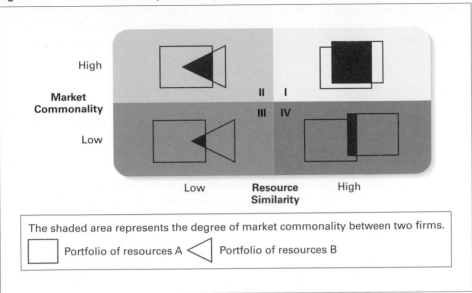

The shaded area represents the degree of market commonality between two firms.

☐ Portfolio of resources A ◁ Portfolio of resources B

Source: Adapted from M. J. Chen, 1996, Competitor analysis and interfirm rivalry: Toward a theoretical integration, *Academy of Management Review*, 21: 100–134.

between the firm and individual competitors in terms of market commonality and resource similarity. These intersections indicate the extent to which the firm and those with which it is compared are competitors. For example, the firm and its competitor displayed in quadrant I have similar types and amounts of resources (i.e., the two firms have a similar portfolio of resources). The firm and its competitor in quadrant I would use their similar resource portfolios to compete against each other in many markets that are important to each. These conditions lead to the conclusion that the firms modeled in quadrant I are direct and mutually acknowledged competitors (e.g., FedEx and UPS). In contrast, the firm and its competitor shown in quadrant III share few markets and have little similarity in their resources, indicating that they aren't direct and mutually acknowledged competitors. Thus, a small local, family-owned Italian restaurant does not compete directly against Olive Garden nor does it have resources that are similar to those of Darden Restaurants, Inc. (Olive Garden's owner). The firm's mapping of its competitive relationship with rivals is fluid as firms enter and exit markets and as companies' resources change in type and amount. Thus, the companies with which the firm is a direct competitor change across time.

Drivers of Competitive Actions and Responses

As shown in Figure 5.2 (on page **132**) market commonality and resource similarity influence the drivers (awareness, motivation, and ability) of competitive behavior. In turn, the drivers influence the firm's competitive behavior, as shown by the actions and responses it takes while engaged in competitive rivalry.[45]

Awareness, which is a prerequisite to any competitive action or response taken by a firm, refers to the extent to which competitors recognize the degree of their mutual interdependence that results from market commonality and resource similarity.[46] Awareness tends to be greatest when firms have highly similar resources (in terms of types and amounts) to use while competing against each other in multiple markets. Komatsu Ltd., Japan's top construction machinery maker and U.S.-based Caterpillar Inc. have similar resources and are certainly aware of each other's actions.[47] The same is true for Wal-Mart and France's Carrefour, the two largest supermarket groups in the world as noted in the Strategic Focus. The last two firms' joint awareness has increased as they use similar resources to compete against each other for dominant positions in multiple European and South American markets.[48] Awareness affects the extent to which the firm understands the consequences of its competitive actions and responses. A lack of awareness can lead to excessive competition, resulting in a negative effect on all competitors' performance.[49]

Motivation, which concerns the firm's incentive to take action or to respond to a competitor's attack, relates to perceived gains and losses. Thus, a firm may be aware of competitors but may not be motivated to engage in rivalry with them if it perceives that its position will not improve or that its market position won't be damaged if it doesn't respond.[50] In some cases, firms may locate near competitors in order to more easily access suppliers and customers. For example, Latin American banks have located operations in Miami, Florida, to reach customers from a similar culture and to access employees who understand this culture as well. In Miami, there are several Latin American banks that direct most of their competitive actions at U.S. financial institutions.[51]

Market commonality affects the firm's perceptions and resulting motivation. For example, the firm is generally more likely to attack the rival with whom it has low market commonality than the one with whom it competes in multiple markets. The primary reason is the high stakes involved in trying to gain a more advantageous position over a rival with whom the firm shares many markets. As mentioned earlier, multimarket competition can find a competitor responding to the firm's action in a market different from the one in which the initial action was taken. Actions and responses of this type can cause both firms to lose focus on core markets and to battle each other with resources that had been allocated for other purposes. Because of the high stakes of competition under the condition of market commonality, the probability is high that the attacked firm will respond to its competitor's action in an effort to protect its position in one or more markets.[52]

In some instances, the firm may be aware of the markets it shares with a competitor and be motivated to respond to an attack by that competitor, but lack the ability to do so. *Ability* relates to each firm's resources and the flexibility they provide. Without available resources (such as financial capital and people), the firm lacks the ability to attack a competitor or respond to its actions. For example, smaller and newer firms tend to be more innovative but generally have fewer resources to attack larger and established competitors. Likewise, foreign firms often are at a disadvantage against local firms because of the local firms' social capital (relationships) with consumers, suppliers, and government officials.[53] However, similar resources suggest similar abilities to attack and respond. When a firm faces a competitor with similar resources, careful study of a possible attack before initiating it is essential because the similarly resourced competitor is likely to respond to that action.[54]

Resource *dissimilarity* also influences competitive actions and responses between firms, in that "the greater is the resource imbalance between the acting firm and competitors or potential responders, the greater will be the delay in response"[55] by the firm with a resource disadvantage. For example, Wal-Mart initially used a focused cost leadership strategy to compete only in small communities (those with a population of 25,000 or less). Using sophisticated logistics systems and extremely efficient purchasing practices, among others, to gain competitive advantages, Wal-Mart created a new type of value (primarily in the form of wide selections of products at the lowest competitive prices) for customers in small retail markets. Local competitors lacked the ability to marshal needed resources at the pace required to respond quickly and effectively. However, even when facing competitors with greater resources (greater ability) or more attractive market positions, firms should eventually respond, no matter how daunting the task seems. Choosing not to respond can ultimately result in failure, as happened with at least some local retailers who didn't respond to Wal-Mart's competitive actions. Of course, the actions taken by Wal-Mart were only the beginning. Wal-Mart has become the largest retailer in the world and feared by all competitors, large and small as explained in the Strategic Focus.

**STRATEGY
RIGHT NOW**

In addition to delivering low prices, Wal-Mart is catering to their cash-strapped customers with financial services.

www.cengage.com/
management/hitt

THE COMPETITIVE BATTLE AMONG BIG BOX RETAILERS: WAL-MART VERSUS ALL THE OTHERS

When Wal-Mart enters a new market, the incumbent competitors commonly experience declines in their sales of 5 to 17 percent. Wal-Mart is the largest retailer in the world, with annual sales of more than $400 billion. As such, it buys in huge quantities and can command a very low price from all suppliers. Its low costs for goods and its highly efficient distribution system allow it to offer the lowest price on any goods it sells. If this is not enough, the severe global economic recession experienced in 2008 and 2009 attracted more customers to Wal-Mart and away from competitors such as Target and Carrefour. In fact, both Target and Carrefour experienced major reductions in their sales while Wal-Mart had small increases. For example, in December 2008, Target had a 4.1 percent decline in sales and Wal-Mart enjoyed a 2.5 percent increase. J. C. Penney's sales declined even more—8.8 percent. Wal-Mart's sales also increased in the first two months of 2009.

Target matches Wal-Mart's prices on approximately 25 percent of its products but cannot with more products because its cost structure is not as favorable. Carrefour tried to match Wal-Mart and other competitors by severely dropping its prices during the recession with the intent of keeping its customers, but it suffered from the lost margins. Through the worst stock market in many years, Wal-Mart's stock price only declined 2 percent while Carrefour's stock price decreased by 45 percent. Wal-Mart has a reputation for selling high-quality goods at the lowest possible prices. So, during the recession, many people shopped at Wal-Mart even when competitors matched Wal-Mart's prices. In fact, many families purposely "traded down" during the bad economic times. Even Sam's Club, Wal-Mart's warehouse retailer operations, performed well. Costco, its primary competitor, had outperformed Sam's for several years prior to the recession. However, during the recession Sam's passed Costco with sales increases of 5.9 percent in same-store sales compared to Costco's 4 percent increase.

James Leynse/CORBIS

Wal-Mart's consistently low prices and good quality have brought in new customers during the recession who might have otherwise shopped at a competitor.

The only way that competitors can usually survive in markets with Wal-Mart is to add differentiated products in niches where Wal-Mart is not strong. In fact, Target successfully positioned itself as an "upscale discounter" trying to avoid direct competition with Wal-Mart. However, during recessions, discounts on upscale goods are not as valuable. Thus, even Target tried to add more basic goods and add to its food lines. Interestingly, both Target and Wal-Mart planned to open a number of stores during 2009 even with the economic downturn. But, Target simultaneously downsized its headquarters' staff by 1,000 positions. The main concern of many Wal-Mart competitors now is how to regain the market share they lost in the recession when the economy recovers. The challenges ahead for Wal-Mart's competitors are substantial.

Sources: 2008, Wal-Mart, Wikipedia, http://www.wikipedia.org; S. Rosenbloom, 2008, For Wal-Mart, a Christmas that's made to order, *The New York Times,* http://www.nytimes.com, November 6; F. Forrest, 2009, What happens when Wal-Mart enters, *Insights,* Marketing Science Institute, Winter; J. Birchall, 2009, Target to cut 1,000 HQ positions, *Financial Times,* http://www.ft.com, January 27; M. Bustillo, 2009, New chief at Wal-Mart looks abroad for growth, *The Wall Street Journal,* http://www.wsj.com, February 2; J. Birchall, 2009, Wal-Mart's U.S. sales surge ahead, *Financial Times,* http://www.ft.com, March 5; A. Zimmerman, 2009, Wal-Mart tosses a PR "jump ball," *The Wall Street Journal,* http://www.wsj.com, March 12; M. Neal, 2009, Carrefour's no Wal-Mart, *The Wall Street Journal,* http://www.wsj.com, March 12; S. Gregory, 2009, Wal-Mart vs. Target: No contest in the recession, *Time,* http://www.time.com, March 14.

Competitive Rivalry

The ongoing competitive action/response sequence between a firm and a competitor affects the performance of both firms;[56] thus it is important for companies to carefully analyze and understand the competitive rivalry present in the markets they serve to select and implement successful strategies.[57] Understanding a competitor's awareness, motivation, and ability helps the firm to predict the likelihood of an attack by that competitor and the probability that a competitor will respond to actions taken against it.

As we described earlier, the predictions drawn from studying competitors in terms of awareness, motivation, and ability are grounded in market commonality and resource similarity. These predictions are fairly general. The value of the final set of predictions the firm develops about each of its competitors' competitive actions and responses is enhanced by studying the "Likelihood of Attack" factors (such as first-mover incentives and organizational size) and the "Likelihood of Response" factors (such as the actor's reputation) that are shown in Figure 5.2. Evaluating and understanding these factors allow the firm to refine the predictions it makes about its competitors' actions and responses.

In response to shrinking market share, executives at Guess, Inc. made the decision to take the brand upscale rather than cut prices and potentially see their brand equity decline.

Image courtesy of the Advertising Archives

Strategic and Tactical Actions

Firms use both strategic and tactical actions when forming their competitive actions and competitive responses in the course of engaging in competitive rivalry.[58] A **competitive action** is a strategic or tactical action the firm takes to build or defend its competitive advantages or improve its market position. A **competitive response** is a strategic or tactical action the firm takes to counter the effects of a competitor's competitive action. A **strategic action** or a **strategic response** is a market-based move that involve a significant commitment of organizational resources and is difficult to implement and reverse. A **tactical action** or a **tactical response** is a market-based move that is taken to fine-tune a strategy; it involves fewer resources and is relatively easy to implement and reverse.

The decision a few years ago by newly installed leaders at Guess Inc. to take their firm's brand of denims and related products upscale rather than dilute the brand more by lowering prices when Guess was losing market share is an example of a strategic response.[59] And Boeing's decision to commit the resources required to build the super-efficient 787 midsized jetliner with its first deliveries in 2007 and 2008[60] demonstrates a strategic action. Changes in airfares are somewhat frequently announced by airlines. As tactical actions that are easily reversed, pricing decisions are often taken by these firms to increase demand in certain markets during certain periods.

As discussed in the Strategic Focus, Wal-Mart prices aggressively as a means of increasing revenues and gaining market share at the expense of competitors. But discounted prices with high expenses (as implemented by Carrefour) weigh on margins and slow profit growth (or possibly even produce losses). Although pricing aggressively is at the core of what Wal-Mart is and how it competes, can the tactical action of aggressive pricing continue to lead to the competitive success the firm has enjoyed historically? Is Wal-Mart achieving the type of balance between strategic and tactical competitive actions and competitive responses that is a foundation for all firms' success in marketplace competitions?

When engaging rivals in competition, firms must recognize the differences between strategic and tactical actions and responses and should develop an effective balance between the two types of competitive actions and responses. Airbus, Boeing's major competitor in commercial airliners, is aware that Boeing is strongly committed to taking

A **competitive action** is a strategic or tactical action the firm takes to build or defend its competitive advantages or improve its market position.

A **competitive response** is a strategic or tactical action the firm takes to counter the effects of a competitor's competitive action.

A **strategic action** or a **strategic response** is a market-based move that involves a significant commitment of organizational resources and is difficult to implement and reverse.

A **tactical action** or a **tactical response** is a market-based move that is taken to fine-tune a strategy; it involves fewer resources and is relatively easy to implement and reverse.

actions it believes are necessary to successfully launch the 787 jetliner, because deciding to design, build, and launch the 787 is a major strategic action. In fact, many analysts believe that Boeing's development of the 787 airliner was a strategic response to Airbus's new A380 aircraft.

Likelihood of Attack

In addition to market commonality, resource similarity, and the drivers of awareness, motivation, and ability, other factors affect the likelihood a competitor will use strategic actions and tactical actions to attack its competitors. Three of these factors—first-mover incentives, organizational size, and quality—are discussed next.

First-Mover Incentives

A **first mover** is a firm that takes an initial competitive action in order to build or defend its competitive advantages or to improve its market position. The first-mover concept has been influenced by the work of the famous economist Joseph Schumpeter, who argued that firms achieve competitive advantage by taking innovative actions[61] (innovation is defined and described in detail in Chapter 13). In general, first movers "allocate funds for product innovation and development, aggressive advertising, and advanced research and development."[62]

The benefits of being a successful first mover can be substantial.[63] Especially in fast-cycle markets (discussed later in the chapter), where changes occur rapidly and where it is virtually impossible to sustain a competitive advantage for any length of time, a first mover can experience many times the valuation and revenue of a second mover.[64] This evidence suggests that although first-mover benefits are never absolute, they are often critical to a firm's success in industries experiencing rapid technological developments and relatively short product life cycles.[65] In addition to earning above-average returns until its competitors respond to its successful competitive action, the first mover can gain (1) the loyalty of customers who may become committed to the goods or services of the firm that first made them available, and (2) market share that can be difficult for competitors to take during future competitive rivalry.[66] The general evidence that first movers have greater survival rates than later market entrants[67] is perhaps the culmination of first-mover benefits.

The firm trying to predict its competitors' competitive actions might conclude that they will take aggressive strategic actions to gain first movers' benefits. However, even though a firm's competitors might be motivated to be first movers, they may lack the ability to do so. First movers tend to be aggressive and willing to experiment with innovation and take higher, yet reasonable, levels of risk.[68] To be a first mover, the firm must have readily available the resources to significantly invest in R&D as well as to rapidly and successfully produce and market a stream of innovative products.[69]

Organizational slack makes it possible for firms to have the ability (as measured by available resources) to be first movers. *Slack* is the buffer or cushion provided by actual or obtainable resources that aren't currently in use and are in excess of the minimum resources needed to produce a given level of organizational output.[70] As a liquid resource, slack can quickly be allocated to support competitive actions, such as R&D investments and aggressive marketing campaigns that lead to first-mover advantages. This relationship between slack and the ability to be a first mover allows the firm to predict that a first mover competitor likely has available slack and will probably take aggressive competitive actions to continuously introduce innovative products. Furthermore, the firm can predict that as a first mover, a competitor will try to rapidly gain market share and customer loyalty in order to earn above-average returns until its competitors are able to effectively respond to its first move.

Firms evaluating their competitors should realize that being a first mover carries risk. For example, it is difficult to accurately estimate the returns that will be earned from introducing product innovations to the marketplace.[71] Additionally, the first mover's

A **first mover** is a firm that takes an initial competitive action in order to build or defend its competitive advantages or to improve its market position.

cost to develop a product innovation can be substantial, reducing the slack available to support further innovation. Thus, the firm should carefully study the results a competitor achieves as a first mover. Continuous success by the competitor suggests additional product innovations, while lack of product acceptance over the course of the competitor's innovations may indicate less willingness in the future to accept the risks of being a first mover.[72]

A **second mover** is a firm that responds to the first mover's competitive action, typically through imitation. More cautious than the first mover, the second mover studies customers' reactions to product innovations. In the course of doing so, the second mover also tries to find any mistakes the first mover made so that it can avoid them and the problems they created. Often, successful imitation of the first mover's innovations allows the second mover to avoid the mistakes and the major investments required of the pioneers (first movers).[73]

Second movers also have the time to develop processes and technologies that are more efficient than those used by the first mover or that create additional value for consumers.[74] The most successful second movers rarely act too fast (so they can fully analyze the first mover's actions) nor too slow (so they do not give the first mover time to correct its mistakes and "lock in" customer loyalty).[75] Overall, the outcomes of the first mover's competitive actions may provide an effective blueprint for second and even late movers (discussed below) as they determine the nature and timing of their competitive responses.[76] Determining whether a competitor is an effective second mover (based on its past actions) allows a first-mover firm to predict that the competitor will respond quickly to successful, innovation-based market entries. The first mover can expect a successful second-mover competitor to study its market entries and to respond with a new entry into the market within a short time period. As a second mover, the competitor will try to respond with a product that provides greater customer value than does the first mover's product. The most successful second movers are able to rapidly and meaningfully interpret market feedback to respond quickly, yet successfully, to the first mover's successful innovations.

A **late mover** is a firm that responds to a competitive action a significant amount of time after the first mover's action and the second mover's response. Typically, a late response is better than no response at all, although any success achieved from the late competitive response tends to be considerably less than that achieved by first and second movers. However, on occasion, late movers can be successful if they develop a unique way to enter the market and compete.[77]

The firm competing against a late mover can predict that the competitor will likely enter a particular market only after both the first and second movers have achieved success in that market. Moreover, on a relative basis, the firm can predict that the late mover's competitive action will allow it to earn average returns only after the considerable time required for it to understand how to create at least as much customer value as that offered by the first and second movers' products.

Organizational Size

An organization's size affects the likelihood it will take competitive actions as well as the types and timing of those actions.[78] In general, small firms are more likely than large companies to launch competitive actions and tend to do it more quickly. Smaller firms are thus perceived as nimble and flexible competitors who rely on speed and surprise to defend their competitive advantages or develop new ones while engaged in competitive rivalry, especially with large companies, to gain an advantageous market position.[79] Small firms' flexibility and nimbleness allow them to develop variety in their competitive actions; large firms tend to limit the types of competitive actions used.[80]

Large firms, however, are likely to initiate more competitive actions along with more strategic actions during a given period.[81] Thus, when studying its competitors in terms of organizational size, the firm should use a measurement such as total sales revenue or

A **second mover** is a firm that responds to the first mover's competitive action, typically through imitation.

A **late mover** is a firm that responds to a competitive action a significant amount of time after the first mover's action and the second mover's response.

total number of employees. The competitive actions the firm likely will encounter from competitors larger than it is will be different from the competitive actions it will encounter from smaller competitors.

The organizational size factor adds another layer of complexity. When engaging in competitive rivalry, the firm often prefers a large number of unique competitive actions. Ideally, the organization has the amount of slack resources held by a large firm to launch a greater *number* of competitive actions and a small firm's flexibility to launch a greater *variety* of competitive actions. Herb Kelleher, cofounder and former CEO of Southwest Airlines, addressed this matter: "Think and act big and we'll get smaller. Think and act small and we'll get bigger."[82]

In the context of competitive rivalry, Kelleher's statement can be interpreted to mean that relying on a limited number or types of competitive actions (which is the large firm's tendency) can lead to reduced competitive success across time, partly because competitors learn how to effectively respond to the predictable. In contrast, remaining flexible and nimble (which is the small firm's tendency) in order to develop and use a wide variety of competitive actions contributes to success against rivals.

As explained in the Strategic Focus, Wal-Mart is a huge firm and generates annual sales revenue that makes it the world's largest company. Because of its size, scale, and resources, Wal-Mart has the flexibility required to take many types of competitive actions that few—if any—of its competitors can undertake. Demonstrating this type of flexibility in terms of competitive actions may prove critical to Wal-Mart's battles with competitors such as Costco and Target, among others.

Quality

Quality has many definitions, including well-established ones relating it to the production of goods or services with zero defects[83] and as a cycle of continuous improvement.[84] From a strategic perspective, we consider quality to be the outcome of how a firm completes primary and support activities (see Chapter 3). Thus, **quality** exists when the firm's goods or services meet or exceed customers' expectations. Some evidence suggests that quality may be the most critical component in satisfying the firm's customers.[85]

In the eyes of customers, quality is about doing the right things relative to performance measures that are important to them.[86] Customers may be interested in measuring the quality of a firm's goods and services against a broad range of dimensions. Sample quality dimensions in which customers commonly express an interest are shown in Table 5.1. Quality is possible only when top-level managers support it and when its importance is institutionalized throughout the entire organization and its value chain.[87] When quality is institutionalized and valued by all, employees and managers alike become vigilant about continuously finding ways to improve quality.[88]

Quality is a universal theme in the global economy and is a necessary but not sufficient condition for competitive success.[89] Without quality, a firm's products lack credibility, meaning that customers don't think of them as viable options. Indeed, customers won't consider buying a product until they believe that it can satisfy at least their base-level expectations in terms of quality dimensions that are important to them. Boeing's new 787 aircraft may have problems in the marketplace because of quality concerns. For example, Chi Zhou, Chairman of Shanghai Airlines, suggested that the 787 does not "fully meet the quality that Boeing touted earlier." As such Zhou stated that his airline may cancel or postpone delivery of its order for nine aircraft.[90]

Quality affects competitive rivalry. The firm evaluating a competitor whose products suffer from poor quality can predict declines in the competitor's sales revenue until the quality issues are resolved. In addition, the firm can predict that the competitor likely won't be aggressive in its competitive actions until the quality problems are corrected in order to gain credibility with customers. However, after the problems are corrected, that competitor is likely to take more aggressive competitive actions.

Quality exists when the firm's goods or services meet or exceed customers' expectations.

Table 5.1 Quality Dimensions of Goods and Services

Product Quality Dimensions
1. *Performance*—Operating characteristics
2. *Features*—Important special characteristics
3. *Flexibility*—Meeting operating specifications over some period of time
4. *Durability*—Amount of use before performance deteriorates
5. *Conformance*—Match with preestablished standards
6. *Serviceability*—Ease and speed of repair
7. *Aesthetics*—How a product looks and feels
8. *Perceived quality*—Subjective assessment of characteristics (Product image)
Service Quality Dimensions
1. *Timeliness*—Performed in the promised period of time
2. *Courtesy*—Performed cheerfully
3. *Consistency*—Giving all customers similar experiences each time
4. *Convenience*—Accessibility to customers
5. *Completeness*—Fully serviced, as required
6. *Accuracy*—Performed correctly each time

Source: Adapted from J. Evans, 2008, *Managing for Quality and Performance*, 7th ed., Mason, OH: Thomson Publishing.

Likelihood of Response

The success of a firm's competitive action is affected by the likelihood that a competitor will respond to it as well as by the type (strategic or tactical) and effectiveness of that response. As noted earlier, a competitive response is a strategic or tactical action the firm takes to counter the effects of a competitor's competitive action. In general, a firm is likely to respond to a competitor's action when (1) the action leads to better use of the competitor's capabilities to gain or produce stronger competitive advantages or an improvement in its market position, (2) the action damages the firm's ability to use its capabilities to create or maintain an advantage, or (3) the firm's market position becomes less defensible.[91]

In addition to market commonality and resource similarity and awareness, motivation, and ability, firms evaluate three other factors—type of competitive action, reputation, and market dependence—to predict how a competitor is likely to respond to competitive actions (see Figure 5.2 on page **133**).

Type of Competitive Action

Competitive responses to strategic actions differ from responses to tactical actions. These differences allow the firm to predict a competitor's likely response to a competitive action that has been launched against it. Strategic actions commonly receive strategic responses and tactical actions receive tactical responses. In general, strategic actions elicit fewer total competitive responses because strategic responses, such as market-based moves, involve a significant commitment of resources and are difficult to implement and reverse.[92]

Another reason that strategic actions elicit fewer responses than do tactical actions is that the time needed to implement a strategic action and to assess its effectiveness can delay the competitor's response to that action.[93] In contrast, a competitor likely will respond quickly to a tactical action, such as when an airline company almost immediately matches a competitor's tactical action of reducing prices in certain markets. Either strategic actions or tactical actions that target a large number of a rival's customers are likely to elicit strong responses.[94] In fact, if the effects of a competitor's strategic action on the focal firm are significant (e.g., loss of market share, loss of major resources such as critical employees), a response is likely to be swift and strong.[95]

Actor's Reputation

In the context of competitive rivalry, an *actor* is the firm taking an action or a response while *reputation* is "the positive or negative attribute ascribed by one rival to another based on past competitive behavior."[96] A positive reputation may be a source of above-average returns, especially for consumer goods producers.[97] Thus, a positive corporate reputation is of strategic value[98] and affects competitive rivalry. To predict the likelihood of a competitor's response to a current or planned action, firms evaluate the responses that the competitor has taken previously when attacked—past behavior is assumed to be a predictor of future behavior.

AP Photo/Ng Han Guan

While IBM's initial success in the PC market may have inspired a host of competitors, the competitive landscape has continued to shift with the acquisitions of Gateway by Acer, Compaq by HP, and IBM's PC division by Lenovo.

Competitors are more likely to respond to strategic or tactical actions when they are taken by a market leader.[99] In particular, evidence suggests that commonly successful actions, especially strategic actions, will be quickly imitated. For example, although a second mover, IBM committed significant resources to enter the PC market. When IBM was immediately successful in this endeavor, competitors such as Dell, Compaq, HP, and Gateway responded with strategic actions to enter the market. IBM's reputation as well as its successful strategic action strongly influenced entry by these competitors. However, the competitive landscape has changed dramatically over time. For example, Lenovo, a Chinese firm, paid $1.75 billion in 2005 to buy IBM's PC division.

In contrast to a firm with a strong reputation such as IBM, competitors are less likely to take responses against a company with a reputation for competitive behavior that is risky, complex, and unpredictable. The firm with a reputation as a price predator (an actor that frequently reduces prices to gain or maintain market share) generates few responses to its pricing tactical actions because price predators, which typically increase prices once their market share objective is reached, lack credibility with their competitors.[100] Occasionally, a firm with a minor reputation can sneak up on larger, more resourceful competitors and take market share from them. In recent years, for example, firms from emerging markets have taken market share from major competitors based in developed markets.[101]

Dependence on the Market

Market dependence denotes the extent to which a firm's revenues or profits are derived from a particular market.[102] In general, competitors with high market dependence are likely to respond strongly to attacks threatening their market position.[103] Interestingly, the threatened firm in these instances may not always respond quickly, even though an effective response to an attack on the firm's position in a critical market is important.

Sargento Foods is a family-owned company based in Wisconsin. The firm is a leading packager and marketer of "shredded, snack and specialty cheeses (that are) sold under the Sargento brand, cheese and non-cheese snack food items and ethnic sauces." With sales exceeding $600 million annually, Sargento's business is founded on a passion for cheese. Because Sargento's business operations revolve strictly around cheese products, it is totally dependent on the market for cheese. As such, any competitor that chooses to attack Sargento and its market positions can anticipate a strong response to its competitive actions.

Competitive Dynamics

Whereas competitive rivalry concerns the ongoing actions and responses between a firm and its direct competitors for an advantageous market position, competitive dynamics concern the ongoing actions and responses among *all* firms competing within a market for advantageous positions. Building and sustaining competitive advantages are at the core of competitive rivalry, in that advantages are the key to creating value for shareholders.[104]

To explain competitive dynamics, we explore the effects of varying rates of competitive speed in different markets (called slow-cycle, fast-cycle, and standard-cycle markets) on the behavior (actions and responses) of all competitors within a given market. Competitive behaviors as well as the reasons for taking them are similar within each market type, but differ across types of markets.[105] Thus, competitive dynamics differ in slow-cycle, fast-cycle, and standard-cycle markets. The sustainability of the firm's competitive advantages differs across the three market types.

As noted in Chapter 1, firms want to sustain their competitive advantages for as long as possible, although no advantage is permanently sustainable. The degree of sustainability is affected by how quickly competitive advantages can be imitated and how costly it is to do so.

Slow-Cycle Markets

Slow-cycle markets are those in which the firm's competitive advantages are shielded from imitation commonly for long periods of time and where imitation is costly.[106] Thus, competitive advantages are sustainable over longer periods of time in slow-cycle markets.

Building a unique and proprietary capability produces a competitive advantage and success in a slow-cycle market. This type of advantage is difficult for competitors to understand. As discussed in Chapter 3, a difficult-to-understand and costly-to-imitate resource or capability usually results from unique historical conditions, causal ambiguity, and/or social complexity. Copyrights, geography, patents, and ownership of an information resource are examples of resources.[107] After a proprietary advantage is developed, the firm's competitive behavior in a slow-cycle market is oriented to protecting, maintaining, and extending that advantage. Thus, the competitive dynamics in slow-cycle markets usually concentrate on competitive actions and responses that enable firms to protect, maintain, and extend their competitive advantage. Major strategic actions in these markets, such acquisitions, usually carry less risk than in faster-cycle markets.[108]

Walt Disney Co. continues to extend its proprietary characters, such as Mickey Mouse, Minnie Mouse, and Goofy. These characters have a unique historical development as a result of Walt and Roy Disney's creativity and vision for entertaining people. Products based on the characters seen in Disney's animated films are sold through Disney's theme park shops as well as freestanding retail outlets called Disney Stores. Because copyrights shield it, the proprietary nature of Disney's advantage in terms of animated character trademarks protects the firm from imitation by competitors.

Consistent with another attribute of competition in a slow-cycle market, Disney protects its exclusive rights to its characters and their use. As with all firms competing in slow-cycle markets, Disney's competitive actions (such as building theme parks in France, Japan, and China) and responses (such as lawsuits to protect its right to fully control use of its animated characters) maintain and extend its proprietary competitive advantage while protecting it.

Patent laws and regulatory requirements such as those in the United States requiring FDA (Food and Drug Administration) approval to launch new products shield pharmaceutical companies' positions. Competitors in this market try to extend patents on their

Slow-cycle markets are those in which the firm's competitive advantages are shielded from imitation commonly for long periods of time and where imitation is costly.

drugs to maintain advantageous positions that the patents provide. However, after a patent expires, the firm is no longer shielded from competition, allowing generic imitations and usually leading to a loss of sales.

The competitive dynamics generated by firms competing in slow-cycle markets are shown in Figure 5.4. In slow-cycle markets, firms launch a product (e.g., a new drug) that has been developed through a proprietary advantage (e.g., R&D) and then exploit it for as long as possible while the product is shielded from competition. Eventually, competitors respond to the action with a counterattack. In markets for drugs, this counterattack commonly occurs as patents expire or are broken through legal means, creating the need for another product launch by the firm seeking a protected market position.

Fast-Cycle Markets

Fast-cycle markets are markets in which the firm's capabilities that contribute to competitive advantages aren't shielded from imitation and where imitation is often rapid and inexpensive. Thus, competitive advantages aren't sustainable in fast-cycle markets. Firms competing in fast-cycle markets recognize the importance of speed; these companies appreciate that "time is as precious a business resource as money or head count—and that the costs of hesitation and delay are just as steep as going over budget or missing a financial forecast."[109] Such high-velocity environments place considerable pressures on top managers to quickly make strategic decisions that are also effective.[110] The often substantial competition and technology-based strategic focus make the strategic decision complex, increasing the need for a comprehensive approach integrated with decision speed, two often-conflicting characteristics of the strategic decision process.[111]

Reverse engineering and the rate of technology diffusion in fast-cycle markets facilitate rapid imitation. A competitor uses reverse engineering to quickly gain the knowledge required to imitate or improve the firm's products. Technology is diffused rapidly in fast-cycle markets, making it available to competitors in a short period. The technology often used by fast-cycle competitors isn't proprietary, nor is it protected by patents as is the technology used by firms competing in slow-cycle markets. For example, only a few hundred parts, which are readily available on the open market, are required to build a PC. Patents protect only a few of these parts, such as microprocessor chips.[112]

Figure 5.4 Gradual Erosion of a Sustained Competitive Advantage

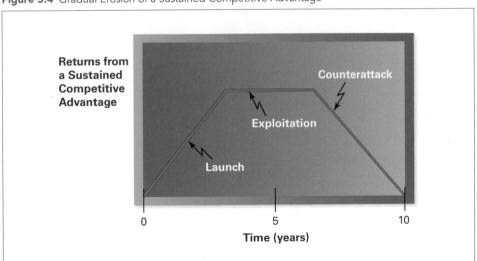

Source: Adapted from I. C. MacMillan, 1988, Controlling competitive dynamics by taking strategic initiative, *Academy of Management Executive*, II(2): 111–118.

Fast-cycle markets are markets in which the firm's capabilities that contribute to competitive advantages aren't shielded from imitation and where imitation is often rapid and inexpensive.

Fast-cycle markets are more volatile than slow-cycle and standard-cycle markets. Indeed, the pace of competition in fast-cycle markets is almost frenzied, as companies rely on innovations as the engines of their growth. Because prices often decline quickly in these markets, companies need to profit quickly from their product innovations. Imitation of many fast-cycle products is relatively easy, as demonstrated by Dell and HP, along with many other PC vendors that have partly or largely imitated the original PC design to create their products. Continuous reductions in the costs of parts, as well as the fact that the information required to assemble a PC isn't especially complicated and is readily available, make it possible for additional competitors to enter this market without significant difficulty.[113]

The fast-cycle market characteristics just described make it virtually impossible for companies in this type of market to develop sustainable competitive advantages. Recognizing this reality, firms avoid "loyalty" to any of their products, preferring to cannibalize their own before competitors learn how to do so through successful imitation. This emphasis creates competitive dynamics that differ substantially from those found in slow-cycle markets. Instead of concentrating on protecting, maintaining, and extending competitive advantages, as in slow-cycle markets, companies competing in fast-cycle markets focus on learning how to rapidly and continuously develop new competitive advantages that are superior to those they replace. They commonly search for fast and effective means of developing new products. For example, it is common in some industries for firms to use strategic alliances to gain access to new technologies and thereby develop and introduce more new products into the market.[114] In recent years, many of these alliances have been offshore (with partners in foreign countries) in order to access appropriate skills while maintaining lower costs to compete.[115]

The competitive behavior of firms competing in fast-cycle markets is shown in Figure 5.5. As suggested by the figure, competitive dynamics in this market type entail actions and responses that are oriented to rapid and continuous product introductions and the development of a stream of ever-changing competitive advantages. The firm launches a product to achieve a competitive advantage and then exploits the advantage for as long as possible. However, the firm also tries to develop another temporary competitive advantage before competitors can respond to the first one (see Figure 5.5). Thus, competitive dynamics in fast-cycle markets often result in rapid product upgrades as well as quick product innovations.[116]

Figure 5.5 Developing Temporary Advantages to Create Sustained Advantage

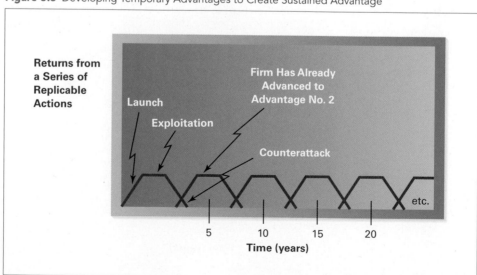

Source: Adapted from I. C. MacMillan, 1988, Controlling competitive dynamics by taking strategic initiative, *Academy of Management Executive*, II(2): 111–118.

SOOTHING THE SOUL WITH KISSES—CANDY KISSES THAT IS

As explained in the Opening Case, candy seems to be recession proof. For example, in the depression of the 1930s, candy companies actually performed well. In fact, several candy products that remain popular today were developed and introduced during the 1930s. For example, Snickers was introduced in 1930, Tootsie Roll Pops in 1931, and Mars Bars in 1932. During tough economic times, people spend more time at home and look for ways they can reduce their stress. Eating candy is an enjoyable way to relax and it is inexpensive compared to many other outlets one may seek. It is an affordable luxury. Eating candy makes people think of better times and may even remind them of enjoyable times as a child. One person who works in his father's candy store on the weekend says that he likes to do so because people are happy when they are buying candy.

For these reasons, the performance of candy manufacturers has been one of the few bright spots in the recession of 2008–2009. For example, the Hershey Company experienced a 3.8 percent sales increase in 2008 compared to 2007 as well as an increase in profits. Few companies in other industries had such a positive experience. In fact, Hershey announced plans to increase its advertising by almost 17 percent in 2009. Many of the best-selling candies during the recession are cheaper and old fashioned, which has also helped Hershey. However, even some of the more exclusive candy companies had performance gains during the recession. Godiva Chocolatier, Inc., expects continued growth, while Lindt & Sprungli AG, maker of premium candies, had a 5.8 percent increase in sales during 2008. Cadbury achieved a 30 percent increase in its annual profits. Nestle's profits were 10.9 percent higher in 2008 as well.

Hershey took several actions in recent years that have aided its performance gains. For example, it finally responded to its competitors' premium product lines (e.g., Godiva, Cadbury) with a premium line of its own, Bliss Chocolates. In addition, it developed a line of chocolates for Starbucks that are sold as premium candies. However, Hershey's best sales have come from its basic product lines such as Hershey Bars, Kisses, and Reese's Peanut Butter Cups. Thus, Hershey placed a renewed emphasis on these product lines. Hershey also experienced increased sales through discount retailers and at convenience stores (especially after the price of gasoline declined significantly).

Mark Savage/CORBIS

Not only have candy manufacturers seen sales increase during the recession, brands such as Hershey are investing more in marketing and launching new product lines to take on more upscale competitors.

Sources: S. Grimmett, 2008, Hershey (HSY): Kisses sweeten the recession, *Today's Financial News*, http://www.todaysfinancialnews.com, October 8; J. Gordon, 2008, Prospecting in the recession? Think chocolate, The Customer Collective, http://www.thecustomercollective.com, November 3; D. Hockens, 2009, Hershey's profits rise as economy slumps, *Pennlive Blog*, http://www.pennlive.com/blogs, January 27; J. Jargon & A. Cordeiro, 2009, Recession puts Hershey in sweet spot, *The Wall Street Journal*, http://www.wsj.com, January 28; 2009, Cadbury chocolate sales soar in recession, *YumSugar*, http://www.yumsugar.com, February 26; C. Haughney, 2009, When economy sours, tootsie rolls soothe souls, *The New York Times*, http://www.nytimes.com, March 24.

As our discussion suggests, innovation plays a critical role in the competitive dynamics in fast-cycle markets. For individual firms, then, innovation is a key source of competitive advantage. Through innovation, the firm can cannibalize its own products before competitors successfully imitate them.

Candy products represent a standard-cycle market. The firms in the industry take actions to build customer loyalty, seek high market shares and try to build positive brand names. We discuss standard-cycle markets such as this one in the next section.

Standard-Cycle Markets

Standard-cycle markets are markets in which the firm's competitive advantages are partially shielded from imitation and imitation is moderately costly. Competitive advantages are partially sustainable in standard-cycle markets, but only when the firm is able to continuously upgrade the quality of its capabilities to stay ahead of competitors. The competitive actions and responses in standard-cycle markets are designed to seek large market shares, to gain customer loyalty through brand names, and to carefully control a firm's operations in order to consistently provide the same positive experience for customers.[117]

Standard-cycle companies serve many customers in competitive markets. Because the capabilities and core competencies on which their competitive advantages are based are less specialized, imitation is faster and less costly for standard-cycle firms than for those competing in slow-cycle markets. However, imitation is slower and more expensive in these markets than in fast-cycle markets. Thus, competitive dynamics in standard-cycle markets rest midway between the characteristics of dynamics in slow-cycle and fast-cycle markets. Imitation comes less quickly and is more expensive for standard-cycle competitors when a firm is able to develop economies of scale by combining coordinated and integrated design and manufacturing processes with a large sales volume for its products.

Because of large volumes, the size of mass markets, and the need to develop scale economies, the competition for market share is intense in standard-cycle markets. This form of competition is readily evident in the battles among consumer foods' producers, such as the candy makers described in the Strategic Focus. Hershey competes in different market segments with Mars, Cadbury, Nestle, and Godiva. In addition, similar to other consumer food manufacturers, some candy makers have kept prices constant selling downsized packages (others, like Hershey, have increased their prices). Package design and ease of availability are the competitive dimensions on which these firms sometimes compete to outperform their rivals in this market.

Innovation can also drive competitive actions and responses in standard-cycle markets, especially when rivalry is intense. Some innovations in standard-cycle markets are incremental rather than radical in nature (incremental and radical innovations are discussed in Chapter 13). For example, consumer foods' producers are innovating in terms of healthy products. Overall, many firms are relying on innovation as a means of competing in standard-cycle markets and to earn above-average returns.

Overall, innovation has a substantial influence on competitive dynamics as it affects the actions and responses of all companies competing within a slow-cycle, fast-cycle, or standard-cycle market. We have emphasized the importance of innovation to the firm's strategic competitiveness in earlier chapters and do so again in Chapter 13. These discussions highlight the importance of innovation in most types of markets.

Standard-cycle markets are markets in which the firm's competitive advantages are moderately shielded from imitation and where imitation is moderately costly.

SUMMARY

- Competitors are firms competing in the same market, offering similar products, and targeting similar customers. Competitive rivalry is the ongoing set of competitive actions and competitive responses occurring between competitors as they compete against each other for an advantageous market position. The outcomes of competitive rivalry influence the firm's ability to sustain its competitive advantages as well as the level (average, below average, or above average) of its financial returns.

- The set of competitive actions and responses that an individual firm takes while engaged in competitive rivalry is called competitive behavior. Competitive dynamics is the set of actions and responses taken by all firms that are competitors within a particular market.

- Firms study competitive rivalry in order to predict the competitive actions and responses that each of their competitors likely will take. Competitive actions are either strategic or tactical in nature. The firm takes competitive actions to defend or build its competitive advantages or to improve its market position. Competitive responses are taken to counter the effects of a competitor's competitive action. A strategic action or a strategic response requires a significant commitment of organizational resources, is difficult to successfully implement, and is difficult to reverse. In contrast, a tactical action or a tactical response requires fewer organizational resources and is easier to implement and reverse. For example, for an airline company, entering major new markets is an example of a strategic action or a strategic response; changing its prices in a particular market is an example of a tactical action or a tactical response.

- A competitor analysis is the first step the firm takes to be able to predict its competitors' actions and responses. In Chapter 2, we discussed what firms do to *understand* competitors. This discussion was extended in this chapter to describe what the firm does to *predict* competitors' market-based actions. Thus, understanding precedes prediction. Market commonality (the number of markets with which competitors are jointly involved and their importance to each) and resource similarity (how comparable competitors' resources are in terms of type and amount) are studied to complete a competitor analysis. In general, the greater the market commonality and resource similarity, the more firms acknowledge that they are direct competitors.

- Market commonality and resource similarity shape the firm's awareness (the degree to which it and its competitors understand their mutual interdependence), motivation (the firm's incentive to attack or respond), and ability (the quality of the resources available to the firm to attack and respond). Having knowledge of these characteristics of a competitor increases the quality of the firm's predictions about that competitor's actions and responses.

- In addition to market commonality and resource similarity and awareness, motivation, and ability, three more specific factors affect the likelihood a competitor will take competitive actions. The first of these concerns first-mover incentives. First movers, those taking an initial competitive action, often gain loyal customers and earn above-average returns until competitors can successfully respond to their action. Not all firms can be first movers in that they may lack the awareness, motivation, or ability required to engage in this type of competitive behavior. Moreover, some firms prefer to be a second mover (the firm responding to the first mover's action). One reason for this is that second movers, especially those acting quickly, can successfully compete against the first mover. By evaluating the first mover's product, customers' reactions to it, and the responses of other competitors to the first mover, the second mover can avoid the early entrant's mistakes and find ways to improve upon the value created for customers by the first mover's good or service. Late movers (those that respond a long time after the original action was taken) commonly are lower performers and are much less competitive.

- Organizational size, the second factor, tends to reduce the variety of competitive actions that large firms launch while it increases the variety of actions undertaken by smaller competitors. Ideally, the firm would prefer to initiate a large number of diverse actions when engaged in competitive rivalry. The third factor, quality, is a base denominator to competing successfully in the global economy. It is a necessary prerequisite to achieve competitive parity. It is a necessary but insufficient condition for gaining an advantage.

- The type of action (strategic or tactical) the firm took, the competitor's reputation for the nature of its competitor behavior, and that competitor's dependence on the market in which the action was taken are studied to predict a competitor's response to the firm's action. In general, the number of tactical responses taken exceeds the number of strategic responses. Competitors respond more frequently to the actions taken by the firm with a reputation for predictable and understandable competitive behavior, especially if that firm is a market leader. In general, the firm can predict that when its competitor is highly dependent for its revenue and profitability in the market in which the firm took a competitive action, that competitor is likely to launch a strong response. However, firms that are more diversified across markets are less likely to respond to a particular action that affects only one of the markets in which they compete.

- In slow-cycle markets, where competitive advantages can be maintained for at least a period of time, the competitive dynamics often include firms taking actions and responses intended to protect, maintain, and extend their proprietary advantages. In fast-cycle markets, competition is substantial as firms concentrate on developing a series of temporary competitive advantages. This emphasis is necessary because firms' advantages in fast-cycle markets aren't proprietary and, as such, are subject to rapid and relatively inexpensive imitation. Standard-cycle markets have a level of competition between that in slow-cycle and fast-cycle markets; firms are moderately shielded from competition in these markets as they use capabilities that produce competitive advantages that are moderately sustainable. Competitors in standard-cycle markets serve mass markets and try to develop economies of scale to enhance their profitability. Innovation is vital to competitive success in each of the three types of markets. Companies should recognize that the set of competitive actions and responses taken by all firms differs by type of market.

REVIEW QUESTIONS

1. Who are competitors? How are competitive rivalry, competitive behavior, and competitive dynamics defined in the chapter?

2. What is market commonality? What is resource similarity? What does it mean to say that these concepts are the building blocks for a competitor analysis?

3. How do awareness, motivation, and ability affect the firm's competitive behavior?

4. What factors affect the likelihood a firm will take a competitive action?

5. What factors affect the likelihood a firm will initiate a competitive response to the action taken by a competitor?

6. What competitive dynamics can be expected among firms competing in slow-cycle markets? In fast-cycle markets? In standard-cycle markets?

EXPERIENTIAL EXERCISES

EXERCISE 1: WIN-WIN, WIN-LOSE, OR LOSE-LOSE?

A key aspect of company strategy concerns the interactions between two or more firms. When a new market segment emerges, should a firm strive for a first-mover advantage or wait to see how the market takes shape? Diversified firms compete against one another in multiple market segments and must often consider how actions in one market might be subject to retaliation by a competitor in another segment. Similarly, when a competitor initiates a price war, a firm must decide whether it should respond in kind or not.

Game theory is helpful for understanding the strategic interaction between firms. Game theory uses assumptions about the behavior of rivals to help a company choose a specific strategy that maximizes its return. In this exercise, you will use game theory to help analyze business decisions.

Individual

One of the classic illustrations of game theory can be found in the prisoner's dilemma. Two criminals have been apprehended by the police for suspicion of a robbery. The police separate the thieves and offer them the same deal: Inform on your peer and receive a lesser sentence. Let your peer inform on you, and receive a harsher sentence. What should you tell the police?

Visit http://www.gametheory.net where you can play the prisoner's dilemma against a computer. Play the dilemma using different parameters, and make notes of your experience.

Groups

There are many examples of game theory in popular culture, from the reality show *Survivor* to episodes of *The Simpsons*. Revisit http://www.gametheory.net and select either a television or movie illustration. Discuss the applications of game theory with your team.

As a group, prepare a one-page summary of how game theory can be applied to competitive interactions between firms.

EXERCISE 2: DOES THE FIRST MOVER TRULY HAVE AN ADVANTAGE?

Henry Ford is often credited with saying that he would rather be the first person to be second. This is strange coming from the innovator of the mass-produced automobile in the United States. So is the first-mover advantage a myth, or is it something that every firm should strive for?

First movers are considered to be the ones that initially introduce an innovative product or service into a market segment. The theory is that doing so creates an almost impenetrable competitive advantage that later entrants find difficult to overcome. However, history is replete with situations where second or later movers find success. If the best way to succeed in the future is to understand the past, then an understanding of why certain first movers succeeded and others failed should be instructive. This exercise requires you to investigate a first mover and identify specifically why, or why not, it was able to hold onto its first-mover advantage.

Part One

Pick an industry that you find of interest. This assignment can be done individually or in a team. Research that industry and identify one or two instances of a first mover—the introduction of new offering into new market segments. For example, you might pick consumer electronics and look for firms that initiated new products in new market segments. Your choice of industry must be approved in advance by your instructor as duplication of industry is to be avoided.

Part Two

Each individual or team is to present their findings with the discussion centering on the following:

- Provide a brief history and description of the industry chosen. Was this a fast-, standard-, or slow-cycle market at the time the first mover initiated its strategic action?

- How has innovation of new products been accomplished traditionally in this industry: through new firms entering the market or existing firms launching new offerings?
- Identify one or two first movers and provide a review of what happened when they entered that industry. Describe why the product or offering has been successful or why it failed.
- What did you learn as a result of this exercise? Do you consider the first mover a wise strategy; is your answer dependent on industry, timing, or luck?

VIDEO CASE

THE BIRTH OF NETJETS

Richard Santulli/Chairman and CEO/NetJets

In 1986, NetJets founder Richard Santulli created the fractional airline ownership business model. Today his airline flies over 390,000 flights annually to more than 173 different countries. With 800 planes under its management, NetJets is the second largest airline in the world.

Be prepared to discuss the following concepts and questions in class:

Concepts

- First mover

- Reputation
- Segmentation
- Industry competitive dynamics
- Standard-cycle markets

Questions

1. Think about the airline industry in terms of standard-cycle markets. What does being in this type of industry mean for most aviation transportation competitors?
2. Think through the benefits to being a first mover. Why is this many times not a sustainable advantage?
3. Why do you think Continental Airlines or American Airlines did not invent the concept of fractional ownership?

CHAPTER 6

Corporate-Level Strategy

Studying this chapter should provide you with the strategic management knowledge needed to:

1. Define corporate-level strategy and discuss its purpose.

2. Describe different levels of diversification with different corporate-level strategies.

3. Explain three primary reasons firms diversify.

4. Describe how firms can create value by using a related diversification strategy.

5. Explain the two ways value can be created with an unrelated diversification strategy.

6. Discuss the incentives and resources that encourage diversification.

7. Describe motives that can encourage managers to overdiversify a firm.

FOSTER'S GROUP DIVERSIFICATION INTO THE WINE BUSINESS

Foster's Group's slogan "Australian for beer" is fitting, given that it produces some of Australia's top beers, including Foster's Lager and Victoria beer. However, in 2008, wine contributed 76 percent of the company's sale earnings. Although Foster's was traditionally a brewer and distributor of beer products, it foresaw more growth prospects with the sales of wine than beer. It also perceived an opportunity to commingle the marketing and distribution of these two spirit products to create economies of scope (a concept defined later in the chapter).

In 2001, Foster's bought Beringer Wine Estates, a leading California winery with approximately $1.2 billion in sales. Then in 2005, Foster's acquired another premium winemaker, Southcorp; the acquisition of these companies made Foster's one of the world's biggest global wine companies.

In order to create synergy between the beer and wine assets, Foster's used one sales force to focus on the mass marketing of beer and cheap spirits, as well as selling high-priced wine to specialized restaurants and liquor stores selling to wine connoisseurs with more sophisticated tastes. The sharing of these activities between businesses that focus on low-cost mass marketing and focused differentiation (premium wines) turned out to be a significant mistake. Furthermore, the assets, especially Southcorp, were purchased at a distinct premium. Although the higher growth rate potential for wine sales seemed like the perfect strategic fit with the low growth rate of beer sales, the synergy between these two businesses was apparently not realized. Furthermore, currency problems contributed to the performance problem; the Southcorp assets were devalued as the U.S. dollar depreciated relative to the Australian dollar. One analyst said "they [Foster's] paid too much and they bought at the wrong time in the cycle."

Christian Heeb/laif/Redux

Despite perceived opportunities to leverage their existing brewery-focused marketing and distribution operations, Foster's encountered numerous problems in the integration of the Beringer and Southcorp wineries.

To correct the problem Foster's has recently been separating these businesses and creating a new marketing group for the wine business while maintaining its current expertise in the brewing and distribution of beer. Because the separation of these businesses is crucial for Foster's to remain profitable, it may be willing to divest one of these businesses, most likely the wine segment because its basic expertise among the key leaders and other personnel is in the beer business.

This is an example of related constrained diversification being poorly executed. Interestingly, a new CEO was appointed after the strategic mistakes occurred. Related constrained diversification, as defined later in the chapter, focuses on managing different businesses, which are potentially highly related in regard to the manufacturing, sales, and distribution activities among the firm's related business portfolio. Unfortunately, Foster's focused on the growth cycle differences and not the detailed implementation differences related to the sharing of actual activities between beer and premium wine, which were not as great a fit as earlier suspected.

Sources: C. Koons, 2009, Earnings: Foster's to retain, revamp struggling wine business, *Wall Street Journal*, February 18, B6; 2009, Foster's Company limited, 2009, *Hoovers Company Records*, http://www.hoovers.com, March 15, 42414; E. Ellis, 2008, What'll you have mate? *Barron's*, October 27, 34–36; S. Murdoch, 2008, Corporate news: Foster's Group names Johnston to be CEO, *Wall Street Journal*, September 27, D6; G. Charles, 2007, Foster's Group plans global wine brands relaunch, *Marketing*, November 29, 3.

Our discussions of business-level strategies (Chapter 4) and the competitive rivalry and competitive dynamics associated with them (Chapter 5) concentrate on firms competing in a single industry or product market.[1] In this chapter, we introduce you to corporate-level strategies, which are strategies firms use to *diversify* their operations from a single business competing in a single market into several product markets and, most commonly, into several businesses. Thus, a **corporate-level strategy** specifies actions a firm takes to gain a competitive advantage by selecting and managing a group of different businesses competing in different product markets. Corporate-level strategies help companies select new strategic positions—positions that are expected to increase the firm's value.[2] As explained in the Opening Case, Foster's Group Ltd., an Australian beverage company, competes in several different beverage segments dominated by beer and wine brands.

Another example is Interpublic Group, a marketing and advertising firm. It is taking advantage of the economic downturn to acquire companies at a decreased price and increase its portfolio of businesses. It is currently seeking to acquire firms in the digital and mobile sector to grow its Media Brands operations to help achieve its goal of being one of the top three players in its respective market by the year 2011.[3]

As is the case with Foster's, firms use corporate-level strategies as a means to grow revenues and profits. But there can be different strategic intents beside growth. Firms can pursue defensive or offensive strategies that realize growth but have different strategic intents. Firms can also pursue market development by moving into different geographic markets (this approach will be discussed in Chapter 8). Firms can acquire competitors (horizontal integration) or buy a supplier or customer (vertical integration). These strategies will be discussed in Chapter 7. The basic corporate strategy, the topic of this chapter, focuses on diversification.

The decision to take actions to pursue growth is never a risk-free choice for firms. Indeed, as the Opening Case illustrated, Foster's Group experienced difficulty in integrating the beer and wine marketing and sales operations to share these activities. Also, Luxottica Group, a leader in the fashion sunglasses industry, has faced risks associated with its acquisition of Oakley, a firm focused on producing sporty sunglasses. Can a luxury goods manufacturer successfully integrate a sporting goods manufacturing company?[4] Effective firms carefully evaluate their growth options (including the different corporate-level strategies) before committing firm resources to any of them.[5]

Because the diversified firm operates in several different and unique product markets and likely in several businesses, it forms two types of strategies: corporate-level (or company-wide) and business-level (or competitive).[6] Corporate-level strategy is concerned with two key issues: in what product markets and businesses the firm should compete and how corporate headquarters should manage those businesses.[7] For the diversified corporation, a business-level strategy (see Chapter 4) must be selected for each of the businesses in which the firm has decided to compete. In this regard, each of Foster's product divisions uses different business-level strategies; while both focus on differentiation, the beer business is focused more on differentiation by a mass market approach while the high-end of the wine business targets unique customers based on individual tastes desired by marketing "its pricey wines to chic restaurants and liquor stores catering to connoisseurs."[8]

As is the case with a business-level strategy, a corporate-level strategy is expected to help the firm earn above-average returns by creating value.[9] Some suggest that few corporate-level strategies actually create value.[10] As the Opening Case indicates, realizing value through a corporate strategy can be difficult to achieve. In fact, the degree to which corporate-level strategies create value beyond the sum of the value created by all of a firm's business units remains an important research question.[11]

Evidence suggests that a corporate-level strategy's value is ultimately determined by the degree to which "the businesses in the portfolio are worth more under the management of the company than they would be under any other ownership."[12] Thus, an effective

A **corporate-level strategy** specifies actions a firm takes to gain a competitive advantage by selecting and managing a group of different businesses competing in different product markets.

corporate-level strategy creates, across all of a firm's businesses, aggregate returns that exceed what those returns would be without the strategy[13] and contributes to the firm's strategic competitiveness and its ability to earn above-average returns.[14]

Product diversification, a primary form of corporate-level strategies, concerns the scope of the markets and industries in which the firm competes as well as "how managers buy, create and sell different businesses to match skills and strengths with opportunities presented to the firm."[15] Successful diversification is expected to reduce variability in the firm's profitability as earnings are generated from different businesses.[16] Because firms incur development and monitoring costs when diversifying, the ideal portfolio of businesses balances diversification's costs and benefits. CEOs and their top-management teams are responsible for determining the ideal portfolio for their company.[17]

We begin this chapter by examining different levels of diversification (from low to high). After describing the different reasons firms diversify their operations, we focus on two types of related diversification (related diversification signifies a moderate to high level of diversification for the firm). When properly used, these strategies help create value in the diversified firm, either through the sharing of resources (the related constrained strategy) or the transferring of core competencies across the firm's different businesses (the related linked strategy). We then discuss unrelated diversification, which is another corporate-level strategy that can create value. The chapter then shifts to the topic of incentives and resources that may stimulate diversification which is value neutral. However, managerial motives to diversify, the final topic in the chapter, can actually destroy some of the firm's value.

Levels of Diversification

Diversified firms vary according to their level of diversification and the connections between and among their businesses. Figure 6.1 lists and defines five categories of businesses according to increasing levels of diversification. The single- and dominant-business categories denote relatively low levels of diversification; more fully diversified firms are classified into related and unrelated categories. A firm is related through its diversification when its businesses share several links; for example, businesses may share products (goods or services), technologies, or distribution channels. The more links among businesses, the more "constrained" is the relatedness of diversification. Unrelatedness refers to the absence of direct links between businesses.

Low Levels of Diversification

A firm pursuing a low level of diversification uses either a single- or a dominant-business, corporate-level diversification strategy. A *single-business diversification strategy* is a corporate-level strategy wherein the firm generates 95 percent or more of its sales revenue from its core business area.[18] For example, Wm. Wrigley Jr. Company, the world's largest producer of chewing and bubble gums, historically used a single-business strategy while operating in relatively few product markets. Wrigley's trademark chewing gum brands include Spearmint, Doublemint, and Juicy Fruit, although the firm produces other products as well. Sugar-free Extra, which currently holds the largest share of the U.S. chewing gum market, was introduced in 1984.

In 2005, Wrigley shifted from its traditional focused strategy when it acquired the confectionary assets of Kraft Foods Inc., including the well-known brands Life Savers and Altoids. As Wrigley expanded, it may have intended to use the dominant-business strategy with the diversification of its product lines beyond gum; however, Wrigley was acquired in 2008 by Mars, a privately held global confection company (the maker of Snickers and M&Ms).[19]

Figure 6.1   Levels and Types of Diversification

Low Levels of Diversification

Single business: 95% or more of revenue comes from a single business.

Dominant business: Between 70% and 95% of revenue comes from a single business.

Moderate to High Levels of Diversification

Related constrained: Less than 70% of revenue comes from the dominant business, and all businesses share product, technological, and distribution linkages.

Related linked (mixed related and unrelated):   Less than 70% of revenue comes from the dominant business, and there are only limited links between businesses.

Very High Levels of Diversification

Unrelated: Less than 70% of revenue comes from the dominant business, and there are no common links between businesses.

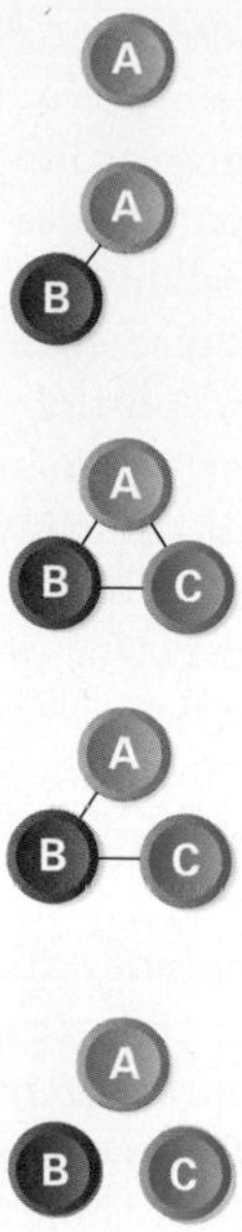

Source: Adapted from R. P. Rumelt, 1974, *Strategy, Structure and Economic Performance*, Boston: Harvard Business School.

With the *dominant-business diversification strategy,* the firm generates between 70 and 95 percent of its total revenue within a single business area. United Parcel Service (UPS) uses this strategy. Recently UPS generated 61 percent of its revenue from its U.S. package delivery business and 22 percent from its international package business, with the remaining 17 percent coming from the firm's non-package business.[20] Though the U.S. package delivery business currently generates the largest percentage of UPS's sales revenue, the firm anticipates that in the future its other two businesses will account for the majority of revenue growth. This expectation suggests that UPS may become more diversified, both in terms of its goods and services and in the number of countries in which those goods and services are offered.

Moderate and High Levels of Diversification

A firm generating more than 30 percent of its revenue outside a dominant business and whose businesses are related to each other in some manner uses a related diversification corporate-level strategy. When the links between the diversified firm's businesses are rather direct, a *related constrained diversification strategy* is being used. Campbell Soup, Procter & Gamble, and Merck & Company all use a related constrained strategy, as do some large cable companies. With a related constrained strategy, a firm shares resources and activities between its businesses.

The diversified company with a portfolio of businesses that have only a few links between them is called a mixed related and unrelated firm and is using the *related linked diversification strategy* (see Figure 6.1). General Electric (GE) uses this corporate-level diversification strategy. Compared with related constrained firms, related linked firms share fewer resources and assets between their businesses, concentrating instead on transferring knowledge and core competencies between the businesses. As with firms using each type of diversification strategy, companies implementing the related linked strategy constantly adjust the mix in their portfolio of businesses as well as make decisions about how to manage these businesses.

A highly diversified firm that has no relationships between its businesses follows an *unrelated diversification strategy*. United Technologies, Textron, Samsung, and Hutchison Whampoa Limited (HWL) are examples of firms using this type of corporate-level strategy. Commonly, firms using this strategy are called *conglomerates*.

HWL is a leading international corporation committed to innovation and technology with businesses spanning the globe.[21] Ports and related services, telecommunications, property and hotels, retail and manufacturing, and energy and infrastructure are HWL's five core businesses. These businesses are not related to each other, and the firm makes no efforts to share activities or to transfer core competencies between or among them. Each of these five businesses is quite large; for example, the retailing arm of the retail and manufacturing business has more than 6,200 stores in 31 countries. Groceries, cosmetics, electronics, wine, and airline tickets are some of the product categories featured in these stores. This firm's size and diversity suggest the challenge of successfully managing the unrelated diversification strategy. However, Hutchison's CEO Li Ka-shing has been successful at not only making smart acquisitions, but also at divesting businesses with good timing.[22]

MIKE CLARKE/AFP/Getty Images

Hutchison's CEO Li Ka-shing successfully manages a highly diverse organization with five core businesses, which operate with minimal interdependency.

Reasons for Diversification

A firm uses a corporate-level diversification strategy for a variety of reasons (see Table 6.1). Typically, a diversification strategy is used to increase the firm's value by improving its

Table 6.1 Reasons for Diversification

Value-Creating Diversification
- Economies of scope (related diversification)
  - Sharing activities
  - Transferring core competencies
- Market power (related diversification)
  - Blocking competitors through multipoint competition
  - Vertical integration
- Financial economies (unrelated diversification)
  - Efficient internal capital allocation
  - Business restructuring

Value-Neutral Diversification
- Antitrust regulation
- Tax laws
- Low performance
- Uncertain future cash flows
- Risk reduction for firm
- Tangible resources
- Intangible resources

Value-Reducing Diversification
- Diversifying managerial employment risk
- Increasing managerial compensation

overall performance. Value is created either through related diversification or through unrelated diversification when the strategy allows a company's businesses to increase revenues or reduce costs while implementing their business-level strategies.

Other reasons for using a diversification strategy may have nothing to do with increasing the firm's value; in fact, diversification can have neutral effects or even reduce a firm's value. Value-neutral reasons for diversification include a desire to match and thereby neutralize a competitor's market power (such as to neutralize another firm's advantage by acquiring a similar distribution outlet). Decisions to expand a firm's portfolio of businesses to reduce managerial risk can have a negative effect on the firm's value. Greater amounts of diversification reduce managerial risk in that if one of the businesses in a diversified firm fails, the top executive of that business does not risk total failure by the corporation. As such, this reduces the top executives' employment risk. In addition, because diversification can increase a firm's size and thus managerial compensation, managers have motives to diversify a firm to a level that reduces its value.[23] Diversification rationales that may have a neutral or negative effect on the firm's value are discussed later in the chapter.

Operational relatedness and corporate relatedness are two ways diversification strategies can create value (see Figure 6.2). Studies of these independent relatedness dimensions show the importance of resources and key competencies.[24] The figure's vertical dimension depicts opportunities to share operational activities between businesses (operational relatedness) while the horizontal dimension suggests opportunities for transferring corporate-level core competencies (corporate relatedness). The firm with a strong capability in managing operational synergy, especially in sharing assets between its businesses, falls in the upper left quadrant, which also represents vertical sharing of assets through vertical integration. The lower right quadrant represents a highly developed corporate capability for transferring one or more core competencies across businesses.

Figure 6.2 Value-Creating Diversification Strategies: Operational and Corporate Relatedness

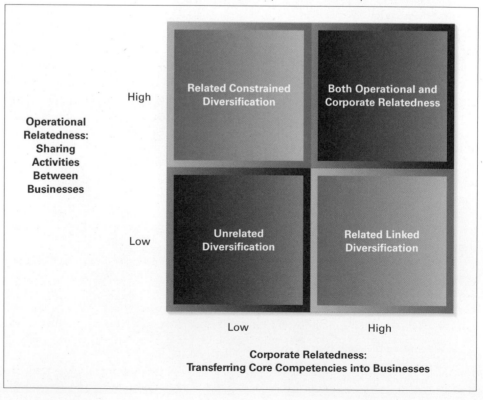

This capability is located primarily in the corporate headquarters office. Unrelated diversification is also illustrated in Figure 6.2 in the lower left quadrant. Financial economies (discussed later), rather than either operational or corporate relatedness, are the source of value creation for firms using the unrelated diversification strategy.

Value-Creating Diversification: Related Constrained and Related Linked Diversification

With the related diversification corporate-level strategy, the firm builds upon or extends its resources and capabilities to create value.[25] The company using the related diversification strategy wants to develop and exploit economies of scope between its businesses.[26] Available to companies operating in multiple product markets or industries,[27] **economies of scope** are cost savings that the firm creates by successfully sharing some of its resources and capabilities or transferring one or more corporate-level core competencies that were developed in one of its businesses to another of its businesses.

As illustrated in Figure 6.2, firms seek to create value from economies of scope through two basic kinds of operational economies: sharing activities (operational relatedness) and transferring corporate-level core competencies (corporate relatedness). The difference between sharing activities and transferring competencies is based on how separate resources are jointly used to create economies of scope. To create economies of scope tangible resources, such as plant and equipment or other business-unit physical assets, often must be shared. Less tangible resources, such as manufacturing know-how, can also be shared. However, know-how transferred between separate activities with no physical or tangible resource involved is a transfer of a corporate-level core competence, not an operational sharing of activities.[28]

Operational Relatedness: Sharing Activities

Firms can create operational relatedness by sharing either a primary activity (such as inventory delivery systems) or a support activity (such as purchasing practices)—see Chapter 3's discussion of the value chain. Firms using the related constrained diversification strategy share activities in order to create value. Procter & Gamble (P&G) uses this corporate-level strategy. P&G's paper towel business and baby diaper business both use paper products as a primary input to the manufacturing process. The firm's paper production plant produces inputs for both businesses and is an example of a shared activity. In addition, because they both produce consumer products, these two businesses are likely to share distribution channels and sales networks.

As noted in the Opening Case, Foster's Group sought to create operational relatedness between the beer and wine business. Firms expect activity sharing among units to result in increased strategic competitiveness and improved financial returns. Through its shared product approach, Foster's Group was unable to improve its market share position, especially in the wine business. As previously mentioned, pursuing operational relatedness is not easy, and often synergies are not realized as planned.

Activity sharing is also risky because ties among a firm's businesses create links between outcomes. For instance, if demand for one business's product is reduced, it may not generate sufficient revenues to cover the fixed costs required to operate the shared facilities. These types of organizational difficulties can reduce activity-sharing success. This problem occurred in the Foster's Group in the Opening Case because there were problems in the sharing of activities between the beer and wine businesses, especially in the marketing and distribution.

Although activity sharing across businesses is not risk-free, research shows that it can create value. For example, studies that acquisitions of firms in the same industry (horizontal

Economies of scope are cost savings that the firm creates by successfully sharing some of its resources and capabilities or transferring one or more corporate-level core competencies that were developed in one of its businesses to another of its businesses.

acquisitions), such as the banking industry and software (see the Oracle Strategic Focus), found that sharing resources and activities and thereby creating economies of scope contributed to postacquisition increases in performance and higher returns to shareholders.[29] Additionally, firms that sold off related units in which resource sharing was a possible source of economies of scope have been found to produce lower returns than those that sold off businesses unrelated to the firm's core business.[30] Still other research discovered that firms with closely related businesses have lower risk.[31] These results suggest that gaining economies of scope by sharing activities across a firm's businesses may be important in reducing risk and in creating value. Further, more attractive results are obtained through activity sharing when a strong corporate headquarters office facilitates it.[32]

The Strategic Focus on Oracle's acquisition strategy of other software firms represents an attempt to implement a related constrained strategy. However, as the example indicates it still remains to be seen how successful the strategy will be.

Corporate Relatedness: Transferring of Core Competencies

Over time, the firm's intangible resources, such as its know-how, become the foundation of core competencies. **Corporate-level core competencies** are complex sets of resources and capabilities that link different businesses, primarily through managerial and technological knowledge, experience, and expertise.[33] Firms seeking to create value through corporate relatedness use the related linked diversification strategy.

In at least two ways, the related linked diversification strategy helps firms to create value.[34] First, because the expense of developing a core competence has already been incurred in one of the firm's businesses, transferring this competence to a second business eliminates the need for that business to allocate resources to develop it. Such is the case at Hewlett-Packard (HP), where the firm transferred its competence in ink printers to high-end copiers. Rather than the standard laser printing technology in most high-end copiers, HP is using ink-based technology. One manager liked the product because, as he noted, "We are able to do a lot better quality at less price."[35] This capability will also give HP the opportunity to sell more ink products, which is how it has been able to create higher profit margins.

Resource intangibility is a second source of value creation through corporate relatedness. Intangible resources are difficult for competitors to understand and imitate. Because of this difficulty, the unit receiving a transferred corporate-level competence often gains an immediate competitive advantage over its rivals.[36]

A number of firms have successfully transferred one or more corporate-level core competencies across their businesses. Virgin Group Ltd. transfers its marketing core competence across airlines, cosmetics, music, drinks, mobile phones, health clubs, and a number of other businesses.[37] Honda has developed and transferred its competence in engine design and manufacturing among its businesses making products such as motorcycles, lawnmowers, and cars and trucks. Company officials indicate that "Honda is the world's largest manufacturer of engines and has earned its reputation for unsurpassed quality, performance and reliability."[38]

One way managers facilitate the transfer of corporate-level core competencies is by moving key people into new management positions.[39] However, the manager of an older business may be reluctant to transfer key people who have accumulated knowledge and experience critical to the business's success. Thus, managers with the ability to facilitate the transfer of a core competence may come at a premium, or the key people involved may not want to transfer. Additionally, the top-level managers from the transferring business may not want the competencies transferred to a new business to fulfill the firm's diversification objectives. Research also suggests too much dependence on outsourcing can lower the usefulness of core competencies and thereby reduce their useful transferability to other business units in the diversified firm.[40]

Corporate-level core competencies are complex sets of resources and capabilities that link different businesses, primarily through managerial and technological knowledge, experience, and expertise.

ORACLE'S RELATED CONSTRAINED DIVERSIFICATION STRATEGY

Oracle has been diversifying its software business in a related way through a significant acquisition program. In 2008 alone, it made 10 acquisitions of smaller software producers and companies that develop software production tools. Despite the economic downturn, by the end of 2008 Oracle had retained $13 billion, allowing it to pursue its acquisition strategy.

Historically, Oracle has been the largest player by market share in the "database" management software industry. Nonetheless, in 2003, it started buying large software makers including PeopleSoft (this was a hostile takeover bid, which did not close until January 2005). It also bought Siebel Systems, Hyperion Solutions, and in early 2008 acquired BEA Systems for approximately $8.5 billion. From 2004–2008 the company collectively spent approximately $25 billion on acquisitions. Oracle's positioning has also changed such that it derives more from enterprise resource planning (ERP) software (its largest acquisitions—for example, PeopleSoft, Siebel Systems, and BEA Systems) and less from database management as it seeks to combine the whole company and its different segments to position itself as a stronger competitor against SAP—the largest player in the ERP industry. Additionally, Oracle's maintenance contracts have helped offset some of its lower sales in basic software in the down cycle. However, over time customers might protest the large margins associated with these maintenance contracts and seek to cut back on them during the recession.

Stefan Obermeier/PhotoLibrary

In order to manage its strategy and to compete in a more focused way, Oracle has targeted specific industries to allow it to compete more effectively with competitors such as SAP. These industries include financial services, insurance, retail, and telecommunications. It set a goal to be the number one or number two software supplier in each of these industry segments.

However, the difficulty is to organize and coordinate these acquisitions into a cohesive set of businesses by which Oracle can create economies of scope through more efficient management techniques. This is somewhat hindered by the differences in cultures and structures of its acquisitions. The benefit has been that the assets have been purchased at lower prices because private equity investors' (i.e., venture capitalists) funding has decreased 80 percent, and thus Oracle has been the primary means for these firms to obtain funding. Corporate venture capital has been a mainstay for firms in the Silicon Valley, in which Oracle has done much acquisition activity.

In summary, the organizational integration aspects have prevented much of the possible sharing of activities that this strategy requires to be successful. Oracle's continued success will be determined by how far its stock price falls relative to its costs of acquisition of

AP Photo/Paul Sakuma

Oracle's acquisition of companies such as BEA Systems has positioned it to compete in the ERP industry with SAP; however, its performance will rely on how successfully it integrates these new businesses.

these new businesses and its ability to integrate these acquisitions into a cohesive structure that will allow the sharing of activities to take place more efficiently. It is important that central headquarters implement controls to foster the sharing of activities between related divisions for success to occur.

Sources: B. Worthen, 2009, Cash-rich Oracle scoops up bargains in recession spree, *Wall Street Journal*, February 17, A1, A12; J. Hodgson, 2009, Rethinking software support: Recession puts new focus on Oracle maintenance contracts, *Wall Street Journal*, March 12, B8; 2009, Oracle Corporation, *Hoovers Company Records*, March 15, 14337; M. V. Copeland, 2008, Big tech goes bargain hunting, *Fortune*, November 10, 43; B. Vara & B. Worthen, 2007, As software firms merge, synergy is elusive: Shareholders may prosper from trend, but customers see scant benefits so far, *Wall Street Journal*, November 20, B1.

Market Power

Firms using a related diversification strategy may gain market power when successfully using their related constrained or related linked strategy. **Market power** exists when a firm is able to sell its products above the existing competitive level or to reduce the costs of its primary and support activities below the competitive level, or both.[41] Mars' acquisition of the Wrigley assets was part of its related constrained diversification strategy and added market share to the Mars/Wrigley integrated firm, as it realized 14.4 percent of the market share. This catapulted Mars/Wrigley above Cadbury and Nestle, which have 10.1 and 7.7 percent of the market share, respectively, and left Hershey with only 5.5 percent of the market.[42]

In addition to efforts to gain scale as a means of increasing market power, as Mars did when it acquired Wrigley, firms can create market power through multipoint competition and vertical integration. **Multipoint competition** exists when two or more diversified firms simultaneously compete in the same product areas or geographic markets.[43] The actions taken by UPS and FedEx in two markets, overnight delivery and ground shipping, illustrate multipoint competition. UPS has moved into overnight delivery, FedEx's stronghold; FedEx has been buying trucking and ground shipping assets to move into ground shipping, UPS's stronghold. Moreover, geographic competition for markets increases. The strongest shipping company in Europe is DHL. All three competitors (UPS, FedEx, and DHL) are trying to move into large foreign markets to either gain a stake or to expand their existing share. For instance, because the area of China that is close to Hong Kong is becoming a top destination for shipping throughout Asia, competition is raging among these three international shippers.[44] If one of these firms successfully gains strong positions in several markets while competing against its rivals, its market power may increase. Interestingly, DHL had to exit the U.S. market because it was too difficult to compete against UPS and FedEx, which are dominant in the United States.

Some firms using a related diversification strategy engage in vertical integration to gain market power. **Vertical integration** exists when a company produces its own inputs (backward integration) or owns its own source of output distribution (forward integration). In some instances, firms partially integrate their operations, producing and selling their products by using company businesses as well as outside sources.[45]

Vertical integration is commonly used in the firm's core business to gain market power over rivals. Market power is gained as the firm develops the ability to save on its operations, avoid market costs, improve product quality, and, possibly, protect its technology from imitation by rivals.[46] Market power also is created when firms have strong ties between their assets for which no market prices exist. Establishing a market price would result in high search and transaction costs, so firms seek to vertically integrate rather than remain separate businesses.[47]

Vertical integration has its limitations. For example, an outside supplier may produce the product at a lower cost. As a result, internal transactions from vertical integration may be expensive and reduce profitability relative to competitors.[48] Also, bureaucratic costs may occur with vertical integration. And, because vertical integration can require substantial

Market power exists when a firm is able to sell its products above the existing competitive level or to reduce the costs of its primary and support activities below the competitive level, or both.

Multipoint competition exists when two or more diversified firms simultaneously compete in the same product areas or geographical markets.

Vertical integration exists when a company produces its own inputs (backward integration) or owns its own source of output distribution (forward integration).

investments in specific technologies, it may reduce the firm's flexibility, especially when technology changes quickly. Finally, changes in demand create capacity balance and coordination problems. If one business is building a part for another internal business but achieving economies of scale requires the first division to manufacture quantities that are beyond the capacity of the internal buyer to absorb, it would be necessary to sell the parts outside the firm as well as to the internal business. Thus, although vertical integration can create value, especially through market power over competitors, it is not without risks and costs.[49]

For example, CVS, a drugstore competitor to Walgreens, recently merged with Caremark, a large pharmaceutical benefits manager (PBM). For CVS this merger represents a forward vertical move broadening its business from retail into health care management. However, Medco, a competitor to Caremark, indicates that companies competing with CVS "are more comfortable with [their] neutral position than they are with the concept of a combination" between CVS and Caremark.[50] Thus, although CVS may gain some market power, it risks alienating rivals such as Walgreens, which may choose to collaborate with other benefit managers such as Medco or Express Scripts. Likewise, many health care insurance providers have vertically integrated into PBMs. However, as the larger PBMs such as Express Scripts, CVS/Caremark, and Medco Health Solutions increase in size, PBMs associated with particular insurance providers have not been able to compete successfully. This has led some large insurance providers to consider divestiture. For example, WellPoint announced recently that its in-house benefits management business, NextRx, is going to be sold.[51] In fact, Express Scripps was able to win the bidding for NextRx.[52] This could spur other insurance companies such as Aetna Inc. and Cigna Corp. to spin off their PBM businesses as well. The larger PBMs may be able to leverage their size and obtain cheaper drug prices from manufacturers and manage insurers' drug benefits at a lower cost.

Many manufacturing firms have been reducing vertical integration as a means of gaining market power.[53] In fact, deintegration is the focus of most manufacturing firms, such as Intel and Dell, and even some large auto companies, such as Ford and General Motors, as they develop independent supplier networks.[54] Flextronics, an electronics contract manufacturer, represents a new breed of large contract manufacturers that is helping to foster this revolution in supply-chain management.[55] Such firms often manage their customers' entire product lines and offer services ranging from inventory management to delivery and after-sales service. Conducting business through e-commerce also allows vertical integration to be changed into "virtual integration."[56] Thus, closer relationships are possible with suppliers and customers through virtual integration or electronic means of integration, allowing firms to reduce the costs of processing transactions while improving their supply-chain management skills and tightening the control of their inventories. This evidence suggests that *virtual integration* rather than *vertical integration* may be a more common source of market power gains for firms today.

Simultaneous Operational Relatedness and Corporate Relatedness

As Figure 6.2 suggests, some firms simultaneously seek operational and corporate relatedness to create economies of scope.[57] The ability to simultaneously create economies of scope by sharing activities (operational relatedness) and transferring core competencies (corporate relatedness) is difficult for competitors to understand and learn how to imitate. However, if the cost of realizing both types of relatedness is not offset by the benefits created, the result is diseconomies because the cost of organization and incentive structure is very expensive.[58]

As the Strategic Focus on Johnson & Johnson illustrates, this company uses a strategy that combines operational and corporate relatedness with some success. Likewise, Walt Disney Co. uses a related diversification strategy to simultaneously create economies of scope through operational and corporate relatedness. Within the firm's Studio Entertainment business, for example, Disney can gain economies of scope by sharing activities among its different movie distribution companies such as Touchstone Pictures, Hollywood Pictures, and Dimension Films. Broad and deep knowledge about its customers is a capability on which Disney relies to develop corporate-level core competencies in terms of advertising and marketing. With these competencies, Disney is able to create economies of scope through corporate relatedness as it cross-sells products that are highlighted in its movies through the distribution channels that are part of its Parks and Resorts and Consumer Products businesses. Thus, characters created in movies become figures that are marketed through Disney's retail stores (which are part of the Consumer Products business). In addition, themes established in movies become the source of new rides in the firm's theme parks, which are part of the Parks and Resorts business and provide themes for clothing and other retail business products.[59]

As we described, Johnson & Johnson and Walt Disney Co. have been able to successfully use related diversification as a corporate-level strategy through which they create economies of scope by sharing some activities and by transferring core competencies. However, it can be difficult for investors to actually observe the value created by a firm (such as Walt Disney Co.) as it shares activities and transfers core competencies. For this reason, the value of the assets of a firm using a diversification strategy to create economies of scope in this manner tends to be discounted by investors. For example, analysts have complained that both Citibank and UBS, two large multiplatform banks, have underperformed their more focused counterparts in regard to stock market appreciation. In fact, both banks have heard calls for breaking up their separate businesses in insurance, hedge funds, consumer lending, and investment banking.[60] One analyst speaking of Citigroup suggested that "creating real synergy between its divisions has been hard," implying that Citigroup's related diversification strategy suffered from some possible diseconomies of scale.[61] Due to its diseconomies and other losses related to the economic downturn, Citigroup has recently considered selling some of its foreign divisions, such as its Japanese investment bank and brokerage service.[62] USB is changing its strategy as well. The bank's three divisions—private banking, investment banking, and asset management—will be reorganized into a more centralized unit to reduce costs. Previously each segment was given more autonomy over its operations; this model proved too costly and the new CEO, Oswald Grubel, is seeking to reduce possible diseconomies of scale through the centralization, especially in regard to information technology.[63]

Unrelated Diversification

Firms do not seek either operational relatedness or corporate relatedness when using the unrelated diversification corporate-level strategy. An unrelated diversification strategy (see Figure 6.2) can create value through two types of financial economies. **Financial economies** are cost savings realized through improved allocations of financial resources based on investments inside or outside the firm.[64]

Efficient internal capital allocations can lead to financial economies. Efficient internal capital allocations reduce risk among the firm's businesses—for example, by leading to the development of a portfolio of businesses with different risk profiles. The second type of financial economy concerns the restructuring of acquired assets. Here, the diversified firm buys another company, restructures that company's assets in ways that allow it to operate more profitably, and then sells the company for a profit in the external market.[65] Next, we discuss the two types of financial economies in greater detail.

Efficient Internal Capital Market Allocation

In a market economy, capital markets are thought to efficiently allocate capital. Efficiency results as investors take equity positions (ownership) with high expected future cash-flow values. Capital is also allocated through debt as shareholders and debtholders try to improve the value of their investments by taking stakes in businesses with high growth and profitability prospects.

Financial economies are cost savings realized through improved allocations of financial resources based on investments inside or outside the firm.

JOHNSON & JOHNSON USES BOTH OPERATIONAL AND CORPORATE RELATEDNESS

Johnson & Johnson (J&J) is a widely diversified business. It is the world's seventh largest pharmaceutical company, fourth largest biologics company, the premier consumer health products company, and the largest medical devices and diagnostics company. These businesses are combined into three main groups: consumer health care, medical devices and diagnostics, and pharmaceuticals. The consumer health care business produces products for hair, skin, teeth, and babies. The medical devices and diagnostics business develops stents and many other products focused on cardiovascular care and equipment for surgical settings. The pharmaceutical business is focused on the central nervous system and internal medicines for helping with such disorders as schizophrenia, epilepsy, diabetes, and cardiovascular and infectious diseases. Within the pharmaceutical business, another unit focuses on biotechnology to treat autoimmune disorders such as rheumatoid arthritis, psoriasis, and Crohn's disease. Yet another unit, the neurology unit, focuses on developing drugs for HIV/AIDS, hepatitis C, and tuberculosis. Traditionally these businesses were managed with a mixed related and unrelated strategy. Associated with this strategy was a definite approach focused on decentralization.

More recently, J&J aspired to not only have relatedness within the major businesses, but also to have corporate relatedness across all of its business units. CEO William Bolden has sought to propel growth by getting autonomous divisions to work more closely together. "The move suggests the desire to increase interaction to squeeze more value from areas where they overlap." The integrated approach aims to harness expertise from various units to harness and use its diagnostics testing equipment in diagnosing disease earlier than other products on the market. It is also seeking to harness expertise to better assist its glucose monitoring segment to more effectively monitor diabetes.

Other drug companies have been focused on either pharmaceuticals or consumer products and have been reducing the overlap. J&J has taken advantage of both positions and as a result has been more profitable during the current economic downturn than the more focused pharmaceutical or principal products companies. One major innovation between the pharmaceuticals and the device business was the drug-coated stent, which was originally created by Cordis, a division of its medical equipment business. This spurred competition in this industry with other stent makers, including Boston Scientific and Abbott Laboratories. J&J also increased the competition with its new device, Nevo, "a totally redesigned product" in the stent business.

Johnson & Johnson's development of the drug-coated stent was made possible through the coordinated efforts of both their pharmaceutical and medical device businesses.

Besides innovation where the expertise of previously decentralized businesses is combined, J&J is seeking to pursue corporate relatedness in regard to marketing by completing a massive consolidation of its contracted media and advertising agencies. It has settled on a large involvement of several companies such as WPP and Interpublic Group. It is therefore pursuing a single brand according to market and channels and is forcing a consolidation of marketing across its businesses. The purpose for this strategic change is to create a more unified brand and decrease the high costs that are associated with each business unit handling its own media and advertising concepts.

In summary, J&J moved from a related linked strategy focused only on operational relatedness to a strategy that is focused more on pursuing both operational relatedness (with its separate businesses sharing operation activities) and corporate relatedness across its business units. It has strived to achieve greater innovation and management of the regulatory process as well as much better coordination across its businesses in marketing. There are other areas in which it is trying to develop more efficiencies, such as the production process. As such, it is pursuing both operational and corporate relatedness.

Sources: M. Arnold, 2009, J&J shows the way, *Medical Marketing and Media*, January, 39, 41, 43; 2008, J&J perks up, *Financial Times*, http://www.ft.com, December 1; J. Bennett, 2008, J&J: A balm for your portfolio, *Barron's*, October 27, 39; C. Bowe, 2008, Cautious chief with an impulse for innovation, *Financial Times*, http://www.ft.com, January 14, 14; P. Loftus & S. Wang, 2008, Earnings digest—pharmaceuticals: Diversified strategy buoys J&J's results, *Wall Street Journal*, July 16, B4; S. Wang, 2008, Corporate news: J&J acquires wellness firm, widening scope, *Wall Street Journal*, October 28, B3; A. Johnson, 2007, J&J realigns managers, revamps units; move calls for divisions to integrate their work, *Wall Street Journal*, November 16, A10.

In large diversified firms, the corporate headquarters office distributes capital to its businesses to create value for the overall corporation. The nature of these distributions may generate gains from internal capital market allocations that exceed the gains that would accrue to shareholders as a result of capital being allocated by the external capital market.[66] Because those in a firm's corporate headquarters generally have access to detailed and accurate information regarding the actual and prospective performance of the company's portfolio of businesses, they have the best information to make capital distribution decisions.

Compared with corporate office personnel, external investors have relatively limited access to internal information and can only estimate the performances of individual businesses as well as their future prospects. Moreover, although businesses seeking capital must provide information to potential suppliers (such as banks or insurance companies), firms with internal capital markets may have at least two informational advantages. First, information provided to capital markets through annual reports and other sources may not include negative information, instead emphasizing positive prospects and outcomes. External sources of capital have limited ability to understand the operational dynamics of large organizations. Even external shareholders who have access to information have no guarantee of full and complete disclosure.[67] Second, although a firm must disseminate information, that information also becomes simultaneously available to the firm's current and potential competitors. With insights gained by studying such information, competitors might attempt to duplicate a firm's value-creating strategy. Thus, an ability to efficiently allocate capital through an internal market may help the firm protect the competitive advantages it develops while using its corporate-level strategy as well as its various business-unit level strategies.

If intervention from outside the firm is required to make corrections to capital allocations, only significant changes are possible, such as forcing the firm into bankruptcy or changing the top management team. Alternatively, in an internal capital market, the corporate headquarters office can fine-tune its corrections, such as choosing to adjust managerial incentives or suggesting strategic changes in one of the firm's businesses. Thus, capital can be allocated according to more specific criteria than is possible with external market allocations. Because it has less accurate information, the external capital market may fail to allocate resources adequately to high-potential investments. The corporate headquarters office of a diversified company can more effectively perform such tasks as disciplining underperforming management teams through resource allocations.[68]

Large, highly diversified businesses often face what is known as the "conglomerate discount." This discount results from analysts not knowing how to value a vast

STRATEGY RIGHT NOW

Read more about the corporate-level strategies that guide decision-making at Johnson & Johnson.

www.cengage.com/management/hitt

array of large businesses with complex financial reports. For instance, one analyst suggested in regard to figuring out GE's financial results in its quarterly report, "A Rubik's cube may in fact be easier to figure out."[69] To overcome this discount, many unrelated diversified or industrial conglomerates have sought to establish a brand for the parent company. For instance, recent advertisements by GE "moved its focus from customer comfort and convenience ("We Bring Good Things to Life") to a more future-oriented mantra ("Imagination at Work") that promises creative and innovative products."[70] More recently, United Technologies initiated a brand development approach with the slogan "United Technologies. You can see everything from here." United Technologies suggested that its earnings multiple (PE ratio) compared to its stock price is only average even though its performance has been better than other conglomerates in its group. It is hoping that the "umbrella" brand advertisement will raise its PE to a level comparable to its competitors.[71]

In spite of the challenges associated with it, a number of corporations continue to use the unrelated diversification strategy, especially in Europe and in emerging markets. Siemens, for example, is a large German conglomerate with a highly diversified approach. Its former CEO argued that "When you are in an up-cycle and the capital markets have plenty of opportunities to invest in single-industry companies … investors savor those opportunities. But when things change pure plays go down faster than you can look."[72] In the current downturn, diversification is helping some companies improve future performance,[73] as the Oracle Strategic Focus illustrates.

The Achilles' heel for firms using the unrelated diversification strategy in a developed economy is that competitors can imitate financial economies more easily than they can replicate the value gained from the economies of scope developed through operational relatedness and corporate relatedness. This issue is less of a problem in emerging economies, where the absence of a "soft infrastructure" (including effective financial intermediaries, sound regulations, and contract laws) supports and encourages use of the unrelated diversification strategy.[74] In fact, in emerging economies such as those in Korea, India, and Chile, research has shown that diversification increases the performance of firms affiliated with large diversified business groups.[75]

Restructuring of Assets

Financial economies can also be created when firms learn how to create value by buying, restructuring, and then selling the restructured companies' assets in the external market.[76] As in the real estate business, buying assets at low prices, restructuring them, and selling them at a price that exceeds their cost generates a positive return on the firm's invested capital.

As the ensuing Strategic Focus on unrelated diversified companies that pursue this strategy suggests, creating financial economies by acquiring and restructuring other companies' assets involves significant trade-offs. For example, Danaher's success requires a focus on mature, manufacturing businesses because of the uncertainty of demand for high-technology products. In high-technology businesses, resource allocation decisions become too complex, creating information-processing overload on the small corporate headquarters offices that are common in unrelated diversified firms. High-technology businesses are often human-resource dependent; these people can leave or demand higher pay and thus appropriate or deplete the value of an acquired firm.[77]

Buying and then restructuring service-based assets so they can be profitably sold in the external market is also difficult. Sales in such instances are often a product of close personal relationships between a client and the representative of the firm being restructured. Thus, for both high-technology firms and service-based companies, relatively few tangible assets can be restructured to create value and sell profitably. It is difficult to restructure intangible assets such as human capital and effective relationships that have evolved over time between buyers (customers) and sellers (firm personnel). As the Strategic Focus Segment also indicates, care must be taken in a downturn to restructure

STRATEGIC FOCUS

DANAHER AND ITW: SERIAL ACQUIRERS OF DIVERSIFIED INDUSTRIAL MANUFACTURING BUSINESSES

Danaher has four broad industrial strategic business units, including professional instrumentation (test and measurement, and environmental instrumentation), medical technologies (dental equipment and consumables, life sciences and acute care, and diagnostics), industrial technologies (including motion and product identification, aerospace and defense, water quality, and censors and controls), and tools and components (Craftsman Hand Tools, Jacobs Chuck Manufacturing and Jacobs Vehicle Systems, Delta Consolidated Industries, and Hennessy Industries). Each set of businesses is quite broad and relatively diversified across the strategic business unit. Danaher's strategy is focused on acquisitions and restructuring of the acquired businesses.

Once a business is acquired, experts from the Danaher corporate headquarters visit the new subsidiary and seek to establish the firm's philosophy and value set and improve productivity through proven lean manufacturing techniques and processes. The processes are focused on improved quality, delivery of products, and cost improvement, as well as product and process innovation. Although its acquisition activity slowed down in 2008, Danaher generated $1.6 billion in free cash flow, which will allow it to pursue more acquisitions when opportunities arise. The company's largest deal occurred in 2007 when it purchased Tektronix, adding $1.2 billion in revenue to its overall $12.7 billion revenue in 2008.

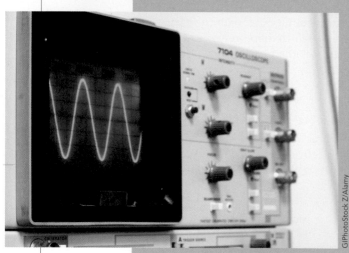

GIPhotoStock Z/Alamy

Interestingly, Danaher also sold off its power quality business to Thomas & Betts Corporation in 2007, illustrating that it also makes timely divestitures.

Illinois Tool Works (ITW), a similar serial acquirer, has bid against Danaher for deals in the past. It too slowed its M&A activity in 2008. ITW started out as a toolmaker and tripled its size in the past decade to 750 business units worldwide. Its acquisition and diversification strategy focuses on small, low-margin but mature industrial businesses. Examples of its products include screws, auto parts, deli-slicers, and the plastic rings that hold together soft drink cans. It seeks to restructure each business it acquires in order to increase the business unit's profit margins by focusing on a narrowly defined product range and targeting the most lucrative products and customers using the 80/20 concept, where 80 percent of the revenues are derived from 20 percent of the customers. Most of its acquisitions are under $100 million. These firms seek to buy low, restructure, and operate, as well as selectively divest after the restructuring.

Although no company is immune, Danaher has done better in the recession than other similar highly diversified industrial firms, such as General Electric, because it sells many of its products to universities and hospitals, which have not had drastic budget cuts as have other commercial businesses in the downturn.

Sources: B. Tita, 2009, Danaher defies skeptics, stands by 2009 forecast, *Wall Street Journal*, March 4, B7; 2008, Comparing the machinery companies, *Shareowner*, March 2008, 15–21; 2008, Danaher business system, http://www.danaher.com, March 21; D. K. Berman, 2007, Danaher is set to buy Tektronix: Purchase for $2.8 billion would be firm's largest: Big boost in test division, *Wall Street Journal*, October 15, A3; R. Brat, 2007, Turning managers into takeover artists: How conglomerate ITW mints new deal makers to fuel its expansion, *Wall Street Journal*, April 6, A1, A8.

and buy and sell at appropriate times. The downturn can also present opportunities as the Oracle Strategic Focus notes. Ideally, executives will follow a strategy of buying businesses when prices are lower, such as in the midst of a recession and selling them at late stages in an expansion.[78]

Value-Neutral Diversification: Incentives and Resources

The objectives firms seek when using related diversification and unrelated diversification strategies all have the potential to help the firm create value by using a corporate-level strategy. However, these strategies, as well as single- and dominant-business diversification strategies, are sometimes used with value-neutral rather than value-creating objectives in mind. As we discuss next, different incentives to diversify sometimes exist, and the quality of the firm's resources may permit only diversification that is value neutral rather than value creating.

Incentives to Diversify

Incentives to diversify come from both the external environment and a firm's internal environment. External incentives include antitrust regulations and tax laws. Internal incentives include low performance, uncertain future cash flows, and the pursuit of synergy and reduction of risk for the firm.

Antitrust Regulation and Tax Laws

Government antitrust policies and tax laws provided incentives for U.S. firms to diversify in the 1960s and 1970s.[79] Antitrust laws prohibiting mergers that created increased market power (via either vertical or horizontal integration) were stringently enforced during that period.[80] Merger activity that produced conglomerate diversification was encouraged primarily by the Celler-Kefauver Antimerger Act (1950), which discouraged horizontal and vertical mergers. As a result, many of the mergers during the 1960s and 1970s were "conglomerate" in character, involving companies pursuing different lines of business. Between 1973 and 1977, 79.1 percent of all mergers were conglomerate in nature.[81]

During the 1980s, antitrust enforcement lessened, resulting in more and larger horizontal mergers (acquisitions of target firms in the same line of business, such as a merger between two oil companies).[82] In addition, investment bankers became more open to the kinds of mergers facilitated by regulation changes; as a consequence, takeovers increased to unprecedented numbers.[83] The conglomerates, or highly diversified firms, of the 1960s and 1970s became more "focused" in the 1980s and early 1990s as merger constraints were relaxed and restructuring was implemented.[84]

In the late 1990s and early 2000s, antitrust concerns emerged again with the large volume of mergers and acquisitions (see Chapter 7).[85] Mergers are now receiving more scrutiny than they did in the 1980s and through the early 1990s.[86] For example, in the merger between P&G and Gillette, regulators required that each firm divest certain businesses before they were allowed to secure the deal.

The tax effects of diversification stem not only from corporate tax changes, but also from individual tax rates. Some companies (especially mature ones) generate more cash from their operations than they can reinvest profitably. Some argue that *free cash flows* (liquid financial assets for which investments in current businesses are no longer economically viable) should be redistributed to shareholders as dividends.[87] However, in the 1960s and 1970s, dividends were taxed more heavily than were capital gains. As a result, before 1980, shareholders preferred that firms use free cash flows to buy and build companies in high-performance industries. If the firm's stock value appreciated over the long term, shareholders might receive a better return on those funds than if the funds had been redistributed as dividends, because returns from stock sales would be taxed more lightly than would dividends.

Under the 1986 Tax Reform Act, however, the top individual ordinary income tax rate was reduced from 50 to 28 percent, and the special capital gains tax was changed to treat capital gains as ordinary income. These changes created an incentive for shareholders to stop encouraging firms to retain funds for purposes of diversification. These tax law changes also influenced an increase in divestitures of unrelated business units after 1984. Thus, while individual tax rates for capital gains and dividends created a shareholder incentive to increase diversification before 1986, they encouraged less diversification after 1986, unless it was funded by tax-deductible debt. The elimination of personal interest deductions, as well as the lower attractiveness of retained earnings to shareholders, might prompt the use of more leverage by firms (interest expenses are tax deductible).

Corporate tax laws also affect diversification. Acquisitions typically increase a firm's depreciable asset allowances. Increased depreciation (a non-cash-flow expense) produces lower taxable income, thereby providing an additional incentive for acquisitions. Before 1986, acquisitions may have been the most attractive means for securing tax benefits,[88] but the 1986 Tax Reform Act diminished some of the corporate tax advantages of diversification.[89] The recent changes recommended by the Financial Accounting Standards Board eliminated the "pooling of interests" method to account for the acquired firm's assets and it also eliminated the write-off for research and development in process, and thus reduced some of the incentives to make acquisitions, especially acquisitions in related high-technology industries (these changes are discussed further in Chapter 7).[90]

Although federal regulations were loosened somewhat in the 1980s and then retightened in the late 1990s, a number of industries experienced increased merger activity due to industry-specific deregulation activity, including banking, telecommunications, oil and gas, and electric utilities. For instance, in banking the Garns–St. Germain Deposit Institutions Act of 1982 (GDIA) and the Competitive Equality Banking Act of 1987 (CEBA) reshaped the acquisition frequency in banking by relaxing the regulations that limited interstate bank acquisitions.[91] Regulation changes have also affected convergence between media and telecommunications industries, which has allowed a number of mergers, such as the successive Time Warner and AOL mergers. The Federal Communications Commission (FCC) made a highly contested ruling "allowing broadcasters to own TV stations that reach 45 percent of U.S. households (up from 35 percent), own three stations in the largest markets (up from two), and own a TV station and newspaper in the same town."[92] Thus, regulatory changes such as the ones we have described create incentives or disincentives for diversification. Interestingly, European antitrust laws have historically been stricter regarding horizontal mergers than those in the United States, but more recently have become similar.[93]

Low Performance

Some research shows that low returns are related to greater levels of diversification.[94] If "high performance eliminates the need for greater diversification,"[95] then low performance may provide an incentive for diversification. In 2005, eBay acquired Skype for $3.1 billion in hopes that it would create synergies and improve communication between buyers and sellers. However, in 2008 eBay announced that it would sell Skype if the opportunity presents itself because it has failed to increase cash flow for its core e-commerce business and the synergies have not been realized. Some critics have even urged eBay to rid itself of PayPal in order to boost its share price.[96]

Research evidence and the experience of a number of firms suggest that an overall curvilinear relationship, as illustrated in Figure 6.3, may exist between diversification and performance.[97] Although low performance can be an incentive to diversify, firms that are more broadly diversified compared to their competitors may have overall lower performance. Further, broadly based banks, such as Citigroup and UBS as noted earlier, have been under pressure to "break up" because they seem to underperform compared to their peers. Additionally, before being acquired by Barclays in 2009, Lehman Brothers

Figure 6.3 The Curvilinear Relationship between Diversification and Performance

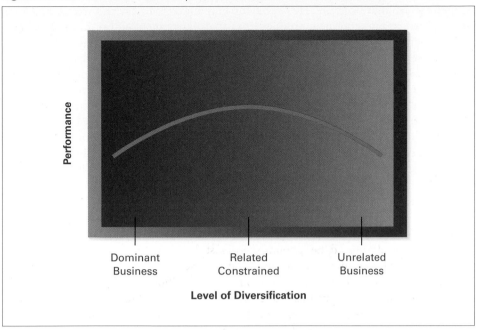

divested much of its asset management and commercial mortgage businesses to improve the company's cash flow.[98]

Uncertain Future Cash Flows

As a firm's product line matures or is threatened, diversification may be an important defensive strategy.[99] Small firms and companies in mature or maturing industries sometimes find it necessary to diversify for long-term survival.[100] For example, auto-industry suppliers have been slowly diversifying into other more promising businesses such as "green" businesses and medical supplies as the auto industry has declined. Dephi, for instance, once part of General Motors, has been expanding its electric car battery expertise into residential energy systems. Abbott Workholding Products, Inc. has been expanding its industrial tools business into tools for making artificial knee and bone replacements.[101]

Diversifying into other product markets or into other businesses can reduce the uncertainty about a firm's future cash flows. Merck looked to expand into the biosimilars business (production of drugs which are similar to approved drugs) in hopes of stimulating its prescription drug business due to lower expected results as many of its drug patents expire.[102] For example, in 2009 it purchased Insmed's portfolio of follow-on biologics for $130 million. It will carry out the development of biologics that prevent infections in cancer patients receiving chemotherapy. Such drugs include, INS-19 is in late-stage trials while INS-20 is in early-stage development.[103]

Synergy and Firm Risk Reduction

Diversified firms pursuing economies of scope often have investments that are too inflexible to realize synergy between business units. As a result, a number of problems may arise. **Synergy** exists when the value created by business units working together exceeds the value that those same units create working independently. But as a firm increases its relatedness between business units, it also increases its risk of corporate failure, because synergy produces joint interdependence between businesses that constrains the firm's flexibility to respond. This threat may force two basic decisions.

Synergy exists when the value created by business units working together exceeds the value that those same units create working independently.

First, the firm may reduce its level of technological change by operating in environments that are more certain. This behavior may make the firm risk averse and thus uninterested in pursuing new product lines that have potential, but are not proven. Alternatively, the firm may constrain its level of activity sharing and forgo synergy's potential benefits. Either or both decisions may lead to further diversification.[104] The former would lead to related diversification into industries in which more certainty exists. The latter may produce additional, but unrelated, diversification.[105] Research suggests that a firm using a related diversification strategy is more careful in bidding for new businesses, whereas a firm pursuing an unrelated diversification strategy may be more likely to overprice its bid, because an unrelated bidder may not have full information about the acquired firm.[106] However, firms using either a related or an unrelated diversification strategy must understand the consequences of paying large premiums.[107] In the situation with eBay, former CEO Meg Whitman received heavy criticism for paying such a high price for Skype, especially when the firm did not realize the synergies it was seeking.

Resources and Diversification

As already discussed, firms may have several value-neutral incentives as well as value-creating incentives (such as the ability to create economies of scope) to diversify. However, even when incentives to diversify exist, a firm must have the types and levels of resources and capabilities needed to successfully use a corporate-level diversification strategy.[108] Although both tangible and intangible resources facilitate diversification, they vary in their ability to create value. Indeed, the degree to which resources are valuable, rare, difficult to imitate, and nonsubstitutable (see Chapter 3) influences a firm's ability to create value through diversification. For instance, free cash flows are a tangible financial resource that may be used to diversify the firm. However, compared with diversification that is grounded in intangible resources, diversification based on financial resources only is more visible to competitors and thus more imitable and less likely to create value on a long-term basis.[109]

Tangible resources usually include the plant and equipment necessary to produce a product and tend to be less-flexible assets. Any excess capacity often can be used only for closely related products, especially those requiring highly similar manufacturing technologies. For example, Acer Inc. hopes to benefit during the current economic downturn and build market share through a related diversification move. Acer believes that the large computer makers such as Dell and Hewlett-Packard have underestimated the demand for mini-notebook or "netbook" computers. Acer diversified into these compact machines and now has about 30 percent of the market share. These smaller and less expensive machines are expected to become 15 to 20 percent of the overall PC market. It has also expanded into "smart phones" and at the same time has created seamless integration between such phones and PCs for data transfer. There are obvious manufacturing and sales integration opportunities between its basic tangible assets and these related diversification moves.[110]

Excess capacity of other tangible resources, such as a sales force, can be used to diversify more easily. Again, excess capacity in a sales force is more effective with related diversification, because it may be utilized to sell similar products. The sales force would be more knowledgeable about related-product characteristics, customers, and distribution channels.[111] Tangible resources may create resource interrelationships in production, marketing, procurement, and technology, defined earlier as activity sharing. Intangible resources are more flexible than tangible physical assets in facilitating diversification. Although the sharing of tangible resources may induce diversification, intangible resources such as tacit knowledge could encourage even more diversification.[112]

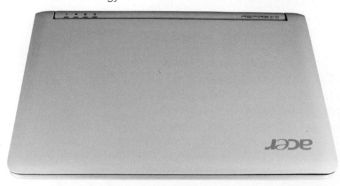

The small "EEE" Acer notebook computer (shown here in white) facilitates Acer's related diversification strategy.

Sometimes, however, the benefits expected from using resources to diversify the firm for either value-creating or value-neutral reasons are not gained.[113] For example, as noted in the Opening Case, implementing operational relatedness has been difficult for the Foster's Group in integrating the wine and beer businesses; the joint marketing operation was a failure. Also, Sara Lee executives found that they could not realize synergy between elements of its diversified portfolio, and subsequently shed businesses accounting for 40 percent of is revenue to focus on food and food-related products to more readily achieve synergy. The downturn has caused Sara Lee to continue this process in order to more sharply focus possible synergies between businesses.[114]

Value-Reducing Diversification: Managerial Motives to Diversify

Managerial motives to diversify can exist independent of value-neutral reasons (i.e., incentives and resources) and value-creating reasons (e.g., economies of scope). The desire for increased compensation and reduced managerial risk are two motives for top-level executives to diversify their firm beyond value-creating and value-neutral levels.[115] In slightly different words, top-level executives may diversify a firm in order to diversify their own employment risk, as long as profitability does not suffer excessively.[116]

Diversification provides additional benefits to top-level managers that shareholders do not enjoy. Research evidence shows that diversification and firm size are highly correlated, and as firm size increases, so does executive compensation.[117] Because large firms are complex, difficult-to-manage organizations, top-level managers commonly receive substantial levels of compensation to lead them.[118] Greater levels of diversification can increase a firm's complexity, resulting in still more compensation for executives to lead an increasingly diversified organization. Governance mechanisms, such as the board of directors, monitoring by owners, executive compensation practices, and the market for corporate control, may limit managerial tendencies to overdiversify. These mechanisms are discussed in more detail in Chapter 10.

In some instances, though, a firm's governance mechanisms may not be strong, resulting in a situation in which executives may diversify the firm to the point that it fails to earn even average returns.[119] The loss of adequate internal governance may result in poor relative performance, thereby triggering a threat of takeover. Although takeovers may improve efficiency by replacing ineffective managerial teams, managers may avoid takeovers through defensive tactics, such as "poison pills," or may reduce their own exposure with "golden parachute" agreements.[120] Therefore, an external governance threat, although restraining managers, does not flawlessly control managerial motives for diversification.[121]

Most large publicly held firms are profitable because the managers leading them are positive stewards of firm resources, and many of their strategic actions, including those related to selecting a corporate-level diversification strategy, contribute to the firm's success.[122] As mentioned, governance mechanisms should be designed to deal with exceptions to the managerial norms of making decisions and taking actions that will increase the firm's ability to earn above-average returns. Thus, it is overly pessimistic to assume that managers usually act in their own self-interest as opposed to their firm's interest.[123]

Top-level executives' diversification decisions may also be held in check by concerns for their reputation. If a positive reputation facilitates development and use of managerial power, a poor reputation may reduce it. Likewise, a strong external market for managerial talent may deter managers from pursuing inappropriate diversification.[124] In addition, a diversified firm may police other firms by acquiring those that are poorly managed in order to restructure its own asset base. Knowing that their firms could be acquired if they are not managed successfully encourages executives to use value-creating, diversification strategies.

As shown in Figure 6.4, the level of diversification that can be expected to have the greatest positive effect on performance is based partly on how the interaction of resources, managerial motives, and incentives affects the adoption of particular diversification strategies. As indicated earlier, the greater the incentives and the more flexible the resources, the higher the level of expected diversification. Financial resources (the most flexible) should have a stronger relationship to the extent of diversification than either tangible or intangible resources. Tangible resources (the most inflexible) are useful primarily for related diversification.

As discussed in this chapter, firms can create more value by effectively using diversification strategies. However, diversification must be kept in check by corporate governance (see Chapter 10). Appropriate strategy implementation tools, such as organizational structures, are also important (see Chapter 11).

We have described corporate-level strategies in this chapter. In the next chapter, we discuss mergers and acquisitions as prominent means for firms to diversify and to grow profitably. These trends toward more diversification through acquisitions, which have been partially reversed due to restructuring (see Chapter 7), indicate that learning has taken place regarding corporate-level diversification strategies.[125] Accordingly, firms that diversify should do so cautiously, choosing to focus on relatively few, rather than many, businesses. In fact, research suggests that although unrelated diversification has

Figure 6.4 Summary Model of the Relationship between Diversification and Firm Performance

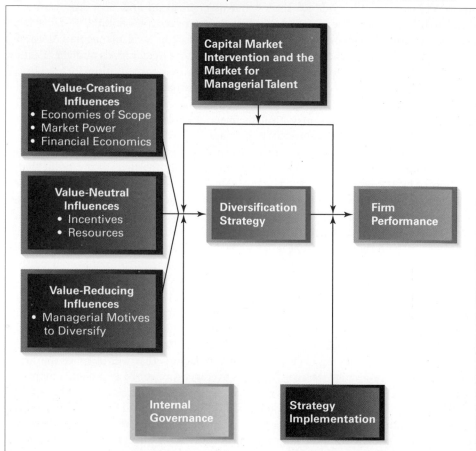

Source: Adapted from R. E. Hoskisson & M. A. Hitt, 1990, Antecedents and performance outcomes of diversification: A review and critique of theoretical perspectives, *Journal of Management*, 16: 498.

decreased, related diversification has increased, possibly due to the restructuring that continued into the 1990s and early twenty-first century. This sequence of diversification followed by restructuring is now taking place in Europe and other places such as Korea, mirroring actions of firms in the United States and the United Kingdom.[126] Firms can improve their strategic competitiveness when they pursue a level of diversification that is appropriate for their resources (especially financial resources) and core competencies and the opportunities and threats in their country's institutional and competitive environments.[127]

SUMMARY

- The primary reason a firm uses a corporate-level strategy to become more diversified is to create additional value. Using a single- or dominant-business corporate-level strategy may be preferable to seeking a more diversified strategy, unless a corporation can develop economies of scope or financial economies between businesses, or unless it can obtain market power through additional levels of diversification. Economies of scope and market power are the main sources of value creation when the firm diversifies by using a corporate-level strategy with moderate to high levels of diversification.

- The related diversification corporate-level strategy helps the firm create value by sharing activities or transferring competencies between different businesses in the company's portfolio.

- Sharing activities usually involves sharing tangible resources between businesses. Transferring core competencies involves transferring core competencies developed in one business to another business. It also may involve transferring competencies between the corporate headquarters office and a business unit.

- Sharing activities is usually associated with the related constrained diversification corporate-level strategy. Activity sharing is costly to implement and coordinate, may create unequal benefits for the divisions involved in the sharing, and may lead to fewer managerial risk-taking behaviors.

- Transferring core competencies is often associated with related linked (or mixed related and unrelated) diversification,

although firms pursuing both sharing activities and transferring core competencies can also use the related linked strategy.

- Efficiently allocating resources or restructuring a target firm's assets and placing them under rigorous financial controls are two ways to accomplish successful unrelated diversification. Firms using the unrelated diversification strategy focus on creating financial economies to generate value.

- Diversification is sometimes pursued for value-neutral reasons. Incentives from tax and antitrust government policies, performance disappointments, or uncertainties about future cash flow are examples of value-neutral reasons that firms may choose to become more diversified.

- Managerial motives to diversify (including to increase compensation) can lead to overdiversification and a subsequent reduction in a firm's ability to create value. Evidence suggests, however, that the majority of top-level executives seek to be good stewards of the firm's assets and avoid diversifying the firm in ways and amounts that destroy value.

- Managers need to pay attention to their firm's internal organization and its external environment when making decisions about the optimum level of diversification for their company. Of course, internal resources are important determinants of the direction that diversification should take. However, conditions in the firm's external environment may facilitate additional levels of diversification, as might unexpected threats from competitors.

REVIEW QUESTIONS

1. What is corporate-level strategy and why is it important?

2. What are the different levels of diversification firms can pursue by using different corporate-level strategies?

3. What are three reasons firms choose to diversify their operations?

4. How do firms create value when using a related diversification strategy?

5. What are the two ways to obtain financial economies when using an unrelated diversification strategy?

6. What incentives and resources encourage diversification?

7. What motives might encourage managers to overdiversify their firm?

EXPERIENTIAL EXERCISES

EXERCISE 1: COMPARISON OF DIVERSIFICATION STRATEGIES

The use of diversification varies both across and within industries. In some industries, most firms may follow a single- or dominant-product approach. Other industries are characterized by a mix of both single-product and heavily diversified firms. The purpose of this exercise is to learn how the use of diversification varies across firms in an industry, and the implications of such use.

Part One

Working in small teams of four to seven people, choose an industry to research. You will then select two firms in that industry for further analysis. Many resources can aid you in identifying specific firms in an industry for analysis. One option is to visit the Web site of the New York Stock Exchange (http://www.nyse.com), which has an option to screen firms by industry group. A second option is http://www.hoovers.com, which offers similar listings. Identify two public firms based in the United States. (Note that Hoovers includes some private firms, and the NYSE includes some foreign firms. Data for the exercise are often unavailable for foreign or private companies.)

Once a target firm is identified, you will need to collect business segment data for each company. Segment data break down the company's revenues and net income by major lines of business. These data are reported in the firm's SEC 10-K filing and may also be reported in the annual report. Both the annual report and 10-K are usually found on the company's Web site; both the Hoovers and NYSE listings include company homepage information. For the most recent three-year period available, calculate the following:

- Percentage growth in segment sales
- Net profit margin by segment

- Bonus item: compare profitability to industry averages (*Industry Norms and Key Business Ratios* publishes profit norms by major industry segment)

Next, based on your reading of the company filings and these statistics, determine whether the firm is best classified as:

- Single product
- Dominant product
- Related diversified
- Unrelated diversified

Part Two

Prepare a brief PowerPoint presentation for use in class discussion. Address the following in the presentation:

- Describe the extent and nature of diversification used at each firm.
- Can you provide a motive for the firm's diversification strategy, given the rationales for diversification put forth in the chapter?
- Which firm's diversification strategy appears to be more effective? Try to justify your answer by explaining why you think one firm's strategy is more effective than the other.

EXERCISE 2: HOW DOES THE FIRM'S PORTFOLIO STACK UP?

The BCG (Boston Consulting Group) product portfolio matrix has been around for decades and was introduced by the BCG as a way for firms to understand the priorities that should be given to the various segments within their mix of businesses. It is based on a matrix with two vertices: firm market share and projected market growth rate, as shown below:

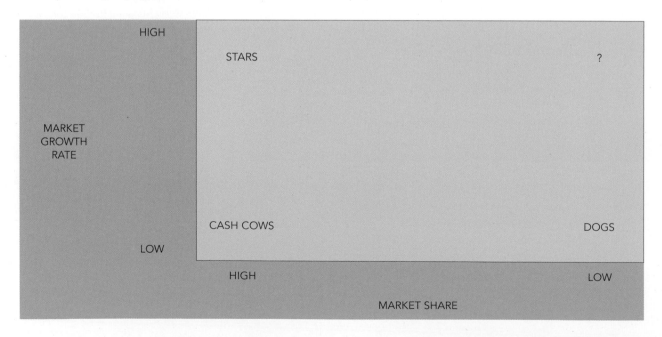

Each firm therefore can categorize its business units as follows:

- Stars: High growth and high market share. These business units generate large amounts of cash but also use large amounts of cash. These are often the focus of the firm's priorities as these segments have a potentially bright future.
- Cash Cows: Low market growth coupled with high market share. Profits and cash generated are high; the need for new cash is low. Provides a foundation for the firm from which it can launch new initiatives.
- Dogs: Low market growth and low market share. This is usually a situation firms seek to avoid. This is quite often the target of a turnaround plan or liquidation effort.
- Question Marks: High market growth but low market share. Creates a need to move strategically because of high demands on cash due to market needs yet low cash returns because of the low firm market share.

This way to analyze a firm's corporate level strategy or the way in which it rewards and prioritizes its business units has come under some criticism. For one, market share is not the only way in which a firm should view success or potential success; second, market growth is not the only indicator for the attractiveness of a market; and third, sometimes "dogs" can earn as much cash as "cows."

Part One

Pick a publicly traded firm that has a diversified corporate-level strategy. The more unrelated the segments the better.

Part Two

Analyze the firm using the BCG matrix. In order to do this you will need to develop market share ratings for each operating unit and assess the overall market attractiveness for that segment.

VIDEO CASE

THE RISKS OF DIVERSIFICATION

Sir Mark Weinberg President/St. James's Place Capital

Sir Mark Weinberg discusses the wisdom, or lack thereof, in firms that diversify their portfolio of businesses. Having been a director of a firm (British American Tobacco) that implemented an unrelated diversification strategy to reduce risk in the company's core business units, Sir Weinberg has keen insights into the wisdom of this strategy.

Before you watch the video consider the following concepts and questions and be prepared to discuss them in class:

Concepts

- Executive hubris
- Diversification
- Risk
- Unrelated acquisition
- Core competency

Questions

1. Think about firms that implement an unrelated diversification strategy. Why are some firms able to implement this corporate level strategy effectively while others struggle?
2. Read the history of British American Tobacco since 1969 from the company's Web site. What impressions do you take away from this?
3. British American Tobacco utilized the concept of risk minimization as a reason for diversification away from its core business. Do you consider this to be a valid rationale for implementing an unrelated diversification strategy?
4. How do public equity markets value unrelated diversification strategies and why do you think they do so?

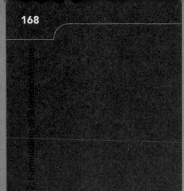

and all other companies must carefully evaluate the "deal" (either a merger or an acquisition) they are contemplating to verify that completing the transaction will facilitate the firm's efforts to achieve strategic competitiveness and create value for stakeholders as a result of doing so.

Sources: P. Hannon, 2009, Foreign investing decreased by half earlier this year, *Wall Street Journal Online*, http://www.wsj.com, June 25; S. Jung-a, 2009, Mergers & acquisitions: Ambitious companies with war-chests look for value, *Financial Times Online*, http://www.ft.com, May 20; Z. Kouwe, 2009, Deals on ice in first half, with 40% drop in M.&A., *New York Times Online*, http://www.nytimes.com, July 1; J. Silver-Greenberg, 2009, Dealmakers test the waters, *BusinessWeek*, March 2, 18–20; 2008, Global M&A falls in 2008, *New York Times Online*, http://www.nytimes.com, December 22; L. Saigol, 2008, Record number of M&A deals cancelled in 2008, *Financial Times Online*, http://www.ft.com, December 22.

We examined corporate-level strategy in Chapter 6, focusing on types and levels of product diversification strategies that firms derive from their core competencies to create competitive advantages and value for stakeholders. As noted in that chapter, diversification allows a firm to create value by productively using excess resources.[1] In this chapter, we explore merger and acquisition strategies. Firms throughout the world use these strategies, often in concert with diversification strategies, to become more diversified. As noted in the Opening Case, even though the amount of merger and acquisition activity completed in 2008 and through mid-2009 fell short of such activity in previous years, merger and acquisition strategies remain popular as a source of firm growth and hopefully, of above-average returns.

Most corporations are very familiar with merger and acquisition strategies. For example, the latter half of the twentieth century found major companies using these strategies to grow and to deal with the competitive challenges in their domestic markets as well as those emerging from global competitors. Today, smaller firms also use merger and acquisition strategies to grow in their existing markets and to enter new markets.[2]

Not unexpectedly, some mergers and acquisitions fail to reach their promise.[3] Accordingly, explaining how firms can successfully use merger and acquisition strategies to create stakeholder value[4] is a key purpose of this chapter. To do this we first explain the continuing popularity of merger and acquisition strategies as a choice firms evaluate when seeking growth and strategic competitiveness. As part of this explanation, we describe the differences between mergers, acquisitions, and takeovers. We next discuss specific reasons firms choose to use acquisition strategies and some of the problems organizations may encounter when implementing them. We then describe the characteristics associated with effective acquisitions before closing the chapter with a discussion of different types of restructuring strategies. Restructuring strategies are commonly used to correct or deal with the results of ineffective mergers and acquisitions.

The Popularity of Merger and Acquisition Strategies

Merger and acquisition strategies have been popular among U.S. firms for many years. Some believe that these strategies played a central role in the restructuring of U.S. businesses during the 1980s and 1990s and that they continue generating these types of benefits in the twenty-first century.[5]

Although popular and appropriately so as a means of growth with the potential to lead to strategic competitiveness, it is important to emphasize that changing conditions in the external environment influence the type of M&A activity firms pursue. During the recent financial crisis for example, tightening credit markets made it more difficult for firms to complete "megadeals" (those costing $10 billion or more). As a result, "... many acquirers are focusing on smaller targets with a niche focus that complements their existing business."[6] Additionally, the relatively weak U.S. dollar increased the interest of firms from other nations to acquire U.S. companies. For example, speculation surfaced in mid-2009 that Singapore's sovereign wealth fund, Temasek Holdings, was considering acquiring the aircraft-leasing unit of insurer AIG.

In the final analysis, firms use merger and acquisition strategies to improve their ability to create more value for all stakeholders including shareholders. As suggested by Figure 1.1, this reasoning applies equally to all of the other strategies (e.g., business-level, corporate-level, international and cooperative) a firm may formulate and then implement.

However, evidence suggests that using merger and acquisition strategies in ways that consistently create value is challenging. This is particularly true for acquiring firms in that some research results indicate that shareholders of acquired firms often earn above-average returns from acquisitions while shareholders of acquiring firms typically earn returns that are close to zero.[7] Moreover, in approximately two-thirds of all acquisitions, the acquiring firm's stock price falls immediately after the intended transaction is announced. This negative response reflects investors' skepticism about the likelihood that the acquirer will be able to achieve the synergies required to justify the premium.[8] Premiums can sometimes be excessive, as appears to be the case with NetApp's proposed acquisition of Data Domain in mid-2009: "On straightforward valuation measures, the (acquisition) price already looks in the stratosphere. At $33.50, the offer is 419 times Data Domain's consensus 2009 earnings, including the enormous cost of employee stock options."[9] Obviously, creating the amount of value required to account for this type of premium would be extremely difficult. Overall then, those leading firms that are using merger and acquisition strategies must recognize that creating more value for their stakeholders by doing so is indeed difficult.[10]

Mergers, Acquisitions, and Takeovers: What Are the Differences?

A **merger** is a strategy through which two firms agree to integrate their operations on a relatively coequal basis. Recently, Towers Perrin Forster & Crosby Inc. and Watson Wyatt Worldwide Inc., two large human-resources consulting firms, agreed to merge. Shareholders of each firm will own 50 percent of the newly formed company, which will be "…the world's biggest employee-benefits consultancy…."[11]

Even though the transaction between Towers Perrin and Watson Wyatt appears to be a merger, the reality is that few true mergers actually take place. The main reason for this is that one party to the transaction is usually dominant in regard to various characteristics such as market share, size, or value of assets. The transaction proposed between Xstrata and Anglo American appears to be an example of this.

In 2009, Swiss-based Xstrata (a global diversified mining group) proposed a friendly merger with London-based Anglo American (a diversified mining and natural resource group). While some analysts thought the proposed merger of equals "should create some value," they also concluded that the "…friendly merger with Anglo American (was) a pretty aggressive bear hug" given the terms Xstrata was seeking and its potential inability to pay the premium Anglo's shareholders expected. In this case too some felt that Anglo's assets were of higher quality, reducing the likelihood that the transaction was actually one of "equals."[12]

An **acquisition** is a strategy through which one firm buys a controlling, or 100 percent, interest in another firm with the intent of making the acquired firm a subsidiary business within its portfolio. After completing the transaction, the management of the acquired firm reports to the management of the acquiring firm.

In spite of the situation we described dealing with Xstrata and Anglo American, most of the mergers that are completed are friendly in nature. However, acquisitions can be friendly or unfriendly. A **takeover** is a special type of acquisition wherein the target firm does not solicit the acquiring firm's bid; thus, takeovers are unfriendly acquisitions. Research evidence showing "…that hostile acquirers deliver significantly higher shareholder value than friendly acquirers" for the acquiring firm[13] is a reason

A **merger** is a strategy through which two firms agree to integrate their operations on a relatively coequal basis.

An **acquisition** is a strategy through which one firm buys a controlling, or 100 percent, interest in another firm with the intent of making the acquired firm a subsidiary business within its portfolio.

A **takeover** is a special type of acquisition wherein the target firm does not solicit the acquiring firm's bid; thus, takeovers are unfriendly acquisitions.

some firms are willing to pursue buying another company even when that firm is not interested in being bought. Often, determining the price the acquiring firm is willing to pay to "take over" the target firm is the core issue in these transactions. In July 2009, for example, Exelon "…raised its hostile bid for rival power producer NRG Energy to nearly $7.5 billion in stock, marking the latest twist in the months-long takeover feud." At issue was NRG's position that Exelon's bids were inadequate. At the same time however, NRG "…said that it remained open to a deal at a fair price."[14]

On a comparative basis, acquisitions are more common than mergers and takeovers. Accordingly, we focus the remainder of this chapter's discussion on acquisitions.

Reasons for Acquisitions

In this section, we discuss reasons firms decide to acquire another company. Although each reason can provide a legitimate rationale, acquisitions are not always as successful as the involved parties want to be the case. Later in the chapter, we examine problems firms may encounter when seeking growth and strategic competitiveness through acquisitions.

Increased Market Power

Achieving greater market power is a primary reason for acquisitions.[15] Defined in Chapter 6, *market power* exists when a firm is able to sell its goods or services above competitive levels or when the costs of its primary or support activities are lower than those of its competitors. Market power usually is derived from the size of the firm and its resources and capabilities to compete in the marketplace;[16] it is also affected by the firm's share of the market. Therefore, most acquisitions that are designed to achieve greater market power entail buying a competitor, a supplier, a distributor, or a business in a highly related industry to allow the exercise of a core competence and to gain competitive advantage in the acquiring firm's primary market.

If a firm achieves enough market power, it can become a market leader, which is the goal of many firms. For example, having already acquired Gateway and Packard Bell (see the Strategic Focus in Chapter 4), Acer is contemplating acquiring other firms (perhaps Asustek of Taiwan or Lenovo of China) as a means of getting closer to its goal of being the leading maker and seller of personal computers.[17] Vertu, already the ninth-largest motor retailer in the United Kingdom, recently acquired some of the businesses and assets of Brooklyn Motor, a Ford and Mazda dealership. The transaction provided Vertu with its first Mazda franchise and facilitated the firm's intention of increasing its share of its core market in the Worcestershire area.[18]

Next, we discuss how firms use horizontal, vertical, and related types of acquisitions to increase their market power.

Horizontal Acquisitions

The acquisition of a company competing in the same industry as the acquiring firm is a *horizontal acquisition*. Horizontal acquisitions increase a firm's market power by exploiting cost-based and revenue-based synergies.[19] For example, National Australia Bank Ltd. recently acquired the wealth-management assets from Aviva PLC's Australian business. A company spokesman said that the acquisition would enhance National Australia's "…offering in key wealth-management segments including insurance and investment platforms, adding scale, efficiency and new capabilities to our operations."[20] Toys "R" Us Inc.'s acquisition of specialty toy retailer FAO Schwarz is another example of a horizontal acquisition. Toys "R" Us officials indicated that they intended to use their firm's "…buying clout to offer a slightly broader appeal to FAO's toy offerings…"[21] and to reduce the price FAO was paying to buy products for its stores.

Research suggests that horizontal acquisitions result in higher performance when the firms have similar characteristics,[22] such as strategy, managerial styles, and resource allocation patterns. Similarities in these characteristics support efforts to integrate the acquiring and the acquired firm. The similarity in the strategies they use should facilitate the integration of National Australia's and Aviva's wealth-management assets. Toys "R" Us and FAO Schwarz share similar product lines and allocate their resources similarly to buy and sell their products. Horizontal acquisitions are often most effective when the acquiring firm integrates the acquired firm's assets with its own assets, but only after evaluating and divesting excess capacity and assets that do not complement the newly combined firm's core competencies.[23]

Martin Sasse/laif/Redux Pictures

Toys "R" Us pursued an aggressive horizontal acquisitions strategy in 2009, with the acquisition of several small online toy retailers in early spring, FAO Schwarz in May, and the bankrupt KB Toys in the Fall.

Vertical Acquisitions

A *vertical acquisition* refers to a firm acquiring a supplier or distributor of one or more of its goods or services.[24] Through a vertical acquisition, the newly formed firm controls additional parts of the value chain (see Chapters 3 and 6),[25] which is how vertical acquisitions lead to increased market power.

CVS/Caremark, a firm that was formed as a result of a transaction completed in 2007, is a product of a vertical acquisition. In 2007, CVS Corporation (a retail pharmacy) acquired Caremark Rx, Inc. (a PBM or pharmacy benefits manager) to create CVS/Caremark, which is the largest integrated pharmacy services provider in the United States. In the firm's words: "Payers and patients count on CVS/Caremark for a broad range of services, from managing pharmacy benefits to filling prescriptions by mail or offering clinical expertise."[26] CVS/Caremark controls multiple parts of the value chain allowing it to use the size of its purchases to gain price concessions from those selling medicines and related products to it.

Related Acquisitions

Acquiring a firm in a highly related industry is called a *related acquisition*. Through a related acquisition, firms seek to create value through the synergy that can be generated by integrating some of their resources and capabilities. For example, Boeing recently acquired eXMeritus Inc., a company providing hardware and software to federal government and law enforcement agencies. eXMeritus's products are intended to help agencies securely share information across classified and unclassified networks and systems. eXMeritus is operating as part of Boeing's Integrated Defense Systems Network and Space Systems business unit. This related acquisition facilitates Boeing's intention of expanding its presence in the cyber and intelligence markets—markets that are related to other aspects of the firm's Integrated Defense Systems operations.[27]

Sometimes, firms fail to create value through a related acquisition. This is the case for FAO Schwarz's recent acquisition of Best Co., a fashion-oriented children's clothing company. The economic downturn that started around 2007 made it extremely difficult for FAO Schwarz to generate the type of operational synergies it expected to accrue through this related acquisition. Indeed, acquiring Best Co. weakened FAO, making it a target for Toys "R" Us as a horizontal acquisition.

Horizontal, vertical, and related acquisitions that firms complete to increase their market power are subject to regulatory review as well as to analysis by financial markets.[28] For example, Procter & Gamble (P&G) completed a horizontal acquisition of Gillette Co. in 2006. In announcing the transaction, P&G noted that integrating Gillette into P&G's operations would result in between $1 and $1.2 billion in annual cost synergies and a 1 percent incremental annual sales growth from revenue synergies for the first three years following the acquisition. However, before being finalized, this acquisition was subjected to a significant amount of government scrutiny as well as close examination by financial analysts. Ultimately, P&G had to sell off several businesses to gain the Federal Trade Commission's approval to acquire Gillette.[29] Thus, firms seeking growth and market power through acquisitions must understand the political/legal segment of the general environment (see Chapter 2) in order to successfully use an acquisition strategy.

Overcoming Entry Barriers

Barriers to entry (introduced in Chapter 2) are factors associated with a market or with the firms currently operating in it that increase the expense and difficulty new firms encounter when trying to enter that particular market. For example, well-established competitors may have economies of scale in the manufacture or service of their products. In addition, enduring relationships with customers often create product loyalties that are difficult for new entrants to overcome. When facing differentiated products, new entrants typically must spend considerable resources to advertise their products and may find it necessary to sell at prices below competitors' to entice new customers.

Facing the entry barriers that economies of scale and differentiated products create, a new entrant may find acquiring an established company to be more effective than entering the market as a competitor offering a product that is unfamiliar to current buyers. In fact, the higher the barriers to market entry, the greater the probability that a firm will acquire an existing firm to overcome them.

As this discussion suggests, a key advantage of using an acquisition strategy to overcome entry barriers is that the acquiring firm gains immediate access to a market. This advantage can be particularly attractive for firms seeking to overcome entry barriers associated with entering international markets.[30] Large multinational corporations from developed economies seek to enter emerging economies such as Brazil, Russia, India, and China (BRIC) because they are among the fastest-growing economies in the world.[31] As discussed next, completing a cross-border acquisition of a local target allows a firm to quickly enter fast-growing economies such as these.

Cross-Border Acquisitions

Acquisitions made between companies with headquarters in different countries are called *cross-border acquisitions*.[32] The purchase of U.K. carmakers Jaguar and Land Rover by India's Tata Motors is an example of a cross-border acquisition. We discuss this acquisition further later in this chapter.

We noted in the Opening Case that global M&A activity declined in the recent global financial crisis. The declines continued throughout the first half of 2009 largely because "… shrinking economies, volatile markets and scarce debt hammered corporate confidence."[33] This decline was in stark contrast to the significant increase in cross-border M&A activity during the 1990s. Nonetheless, as explained in the Opening Case, cross-border acquisitions remain popular as a viable path to firm growth and strategic competitiveness.

There are other interesting changes taking place in terms of cross-border acquisition activity. Historically, North American and European companies were the most active acquirers of companies outside their domestic markets. However, the current global competitive landscape is one in which firms from other nations may use an acquisition strategy more frequently than do their counterparts in North America and Europe. In this regard, some believe that "…the next wave of cross-border M&A may be led out of Asia. Chinese companies, in particular, are well positioned for cross-border acquisitions. Relative to their overseas peers, Chinese corporates are well capitalized with strong balance sheets and cash reserves."[34] In the Strategic Focus, we describe recent cross-border acquisitions some Chinese companies have completed or are evaluating. As you will see, the acquisitions we discuss involve natural resource companies and many are horizontal acquisitions through which the acquiring companies seek to increase their market power.

Firms headquartered in India are also completing more cross-border acquisitions than in the past. The weakening U.S. dollar and more favorable government policies toward cross-border acquisitions are supporting Indian companies' desire to rapidly become "global powerhouses."[35] In addition to rapid market entry, Indian companies typically seek access to product innovation capabilities and new brands and distribution channels when acquiring firms outside their domestic market.

Firms using an acquisition strategy to complete cross-border acquisitions should understand that these transactions are not risk free. For example, firms seeking to acquire companies in China must recognize that "…China remains a challenging environment for foreign investors. Cultural, regulatory, due diligence, and legal obstacles make acquisitions in China risky and difficult."[36] Thus, firms must carefully study the risks as well as the potential benefits when contemplating cross-border acquisitions.

STRATEGY RIGHT NOW

Learn more about how the recent global economic crisis changed the cross-border acquisition environment.

www.cengage.com/management/hitt

Cost of New Product Development and Increased Speed to Market

Developing new products internally and successfully introducing them into the marketplace often requires significant investment of a firm's resources, including time, making it difficult to quickly earn a profitable return.[37] Because an estimated 88 percent of innovations fail to achieve adequate returns, firm managers are also concerned with achieving adequate returns from the capital invested to develop and commercialize new products. Potentially contributing to these less-than-desirable rates of return is the successful imitation of approximately 60 percent of innovations within four years after the patents are obtained. These types of outcomes may lead managers to perceive internal product development as a high-risk activity.[38]

Acquisitions are another means a firm can use to gain access to new products and to current products that are new to the firm. Compared with internal product development processes, acquisitions provide more predictable returns as well as faster market entry. Returns are more predictable because the performance of the acquired firm's products can be assessed prior to completing the acquisition.[39]

Recently, America Online (AOL) acquired two online media companies, Patch Media Corp. and Going Inc. AOL acquired these firms to move more rapidly into the relatively fast-growing local online and advertising market. Patch operates Web sites to help local communities publish news and information while Going makes it possible for users to share information about local events. Access to these new products and services supports AOL's other products in the local online and advertising market space such as MapQuest and social networking site Bebo.[40]

STRATEGIC FOCUS

THE INCREASING USE OF ACQUISITION STRATEGIES BY CHINESE FIRMS AS A MEANS OF GAINING MARKET POWER IN A PARTICULAR INDUSTRY

Taking advantage of depressed prices for oil and gas assets and through the access to credit in their home country, Chinese state-owned companies have begun to use acquisitions as the path to securing "the resources needed to power China's growing economy" and to secure access to energy in future years. The belief that the recent global financial crisis has created an "unmatched buying opportunity" is also driving Chinese firms to acquire companies to gain access to their assets and to increase their market power.

The pace of Chinese firms' cross-border acquisitions quickened in 2009. By mid-2009, Chinese companies had completed 10 transactions in the oil and gas space. In contrast, these firms completed only 14 transactions in this space in all of 2008. Moreover, if outstanding bids were accepted by target companies, the amount Chinese firms will have spent on acquisitions would be 80 percent greater than the amount spent previously on a year-to-year basis.

Completed in mid-2009, state-owned Sinopec Group's acquisition of oil exploration company Addax Petroleum Corp. for $8.27 billion Canadian dollars was at the time the largest cross-border acquisition by a Chinese company. Calling the acquisition a "transformational transaction" that would accelerate its international growth, Sinopec paid a 16 percent premium for Addax. Based in Switzerland and listed in London and Toronto, Addax is one of the world's largest independent oil producers in West Africa and the Middle East on the basis of volume. Around the same time, CNOCC, China's top offshore oil and gas producer, hired Goldman Sachs to advise it on bidding to acquire a stake in Kosmos Energy, an Africa-focused oil and gas exploration company. CNOCC hired an investment advisory firm in anticipation of a bidding war breaking out for Kosmos, largely because of the attractiveness of the firm's assets.

AP Photo/Imaginechina

The 2009 acquisition of Addax Petroleum Corp. with its holdings in Africa and the Middle East by the state-owned Sinopec Group represented at the time the largest Chinese cross-border oil and gas acquisition in history.

Analysts studying these acquisitions and others that likely will be completed conclude that Chinese energy companies are becoming more confident in their ability to create value and gain market power through acquisitions. Business writers describe this confidence as follows: "...deals like the Addax acquisition show (that) they are gradually growing into international oil companies, capable of striking high-profile, cross-border deals. They are even expanding into countries, such as Syria, deemed too risky by Western oil companies."

But not all of the cross-border acquisitions attempted by Chinese companies have been successful. For example, Anglo-American mining giant Rio Tinto Ltd. rejected Aluminum Corp. of China's (Chinalco) $19.5 billion bid to buy 18 percent of the company. Rio was attractive to Chinalco in that at the time, it was the world's third-largest miner and owned rich iron-ore and copper mines in locations throughout the world, including major facilities in

Australia. This acquisition would have given Chinalco a direct stake in mining assets—assets that were important to China's growth. In particular, iron ore is a crucial ingredient in China's steelmaking operations. Although disappointing, the rejection by Rio Tinto was not expected to slow China's commitment to allow its state-owned companies to pursue cross-border acquisitions as a means of improving their competitiveness in the global economy and as a means of gaining ownership of natural resources the nation believes are vital to its long-term growth.

Sources: 2009, Is China Inc. overpaying in its merger deals? *Wall Street Journal Online*, http://www.wsj.com, June 25; R. Carew, 2009, Chinalco acts to preserve its stake in Rio Tinto, *Wall Street Journal Online*, http://www.wsj.com, July 1; G. Chazan & S. Oster, 2009, Sinopec pact for Addax boosts China's buying binge, *Wall Street Journal Online*, http://www.wsj.com, June 25; E. Fry, 2009, Chinalco buys $1.5 bn Rio Tinto shares, Financial Times Online, http://www.ft.com, July 2; K. Maxwell, 2009, Shinsei and Aozora still talking, *Wall Street Journal Online*, http://www.wsj.com, June 26; S. Tucker, 2009, CNOCC considers Kosmos stake bid, Financial Times Online, http://www.ft.com, June 20.

A number of pharmaceutical firms use an acquisition strategy because of the cost of new product development. Acquisitions can enable firms to enter markets quickly and to increase the predictability of returns on their investments. To expand on these points, we discuss Pfizer's recently announced horizontal acquisition of Wyeth in the Strategic Focus.

Lower Risk Compared to Developing New Products

Because the outcomes of an acquisition can be estimated more easily and accurately than the outcomes of an internal product development process, managers may view acquisitions as being less risky.[41] However, firms should exercise caution when using acquisitions to reduce their risks relative to the risks the firm incurs when developing new products internally. Indeed, even though research suggests acquisition strategies are a common means of avoiding risky internal ventures (and therefore risky R&D investments), acquisitions may also become a substitute for innovation. Accordingly, acquisitions should always be strategic rather than defensive in nature. Thus, Pfizer's acquisition of Wyeth should be driven by strategic factors (e.g., cost and revenue synergies) instead of by defensive reasons (e.g., to gain sales revenue in the short term that will compensate for the revenue that will be lost when Lipitor goes off patent). Moreover, Pfizer should not reduce its emphasis on increasing the productivity from its R&D expenditures as a result of acquiring Wyeth.

Increased Diversification

Acquisitions are also used to diversify firms. Based on experience and the insights resulting from it, firms typically find it easier to develop and introduce new products in markets they are currently serving. In contrast, it is difficult for companies to develop products that differ from their current lines for markets in which they lack experience.[42] Thus, it is relatively uncommon for a firm to develop new products internally to diversify its product lines.[43]

Cisco Systems is an example of a firm that uses acquisitions to become more diversified. Historically, these acquisitions have helped the firm build its network components business that is focused on producing hardware. Recently, however, Cisco purchased IronPort Systems Inc., a company focused on producing security software for networks. This acquisition will help Cisco diversify its operations beyond its original expertise in network hardware and basic software. Cisco previously acquired technology in the security area through its purchase of Riverhead Networks Inc., Protego Networks Inc., and Perfigo Inc. However, the IronPort deal provides software service in networks that can help guard against spam and viruses that travel through e-mail and Web-based traffic.[44] In 2009, Cisco IronPort announced its "…new managed, hosted and hybrid hosted e-mail security systems that provide the industry's most versatile set of e-mail protection offerings."[45] Thus, the IronPort acquisition seems to be successful in terms of helping Cisco diversify its operations in ways that create value.

PFIZER'S PROPOSED ACQUISITION OF WYETH: WILL THIS ACQUISITION BE SUCCESSFUL?

Pharmaceutical companies allocate significant amounts of money to research and development (R&D) in efforts to successfully develop new drugs. Pfizer Inc., for example, spends 15 percent of its sales revenue on R&D. As is the case for most if not all of its major competitors, Pfizer is committed to upholding the highest ethical standards when engaging in R&D. According to Pfizer, the firm is "… committed to the safety of patients who take part in our trials and upholds the highest ethical standards in all of (its) research initiatives."

In the words of a scholar who studies innovation: "R&D dollars by definition lead to uncertain outcomes." Because of the high levels of uncertainty associated with efforts to develop products internally, a number of pharmaceutical companies use acquisitions to gain access to new products and to a target firm's capabilities. At this time, some believe that the acquisitions taking place among these firms are "… reconfiguring the entire pharmaceutical sector."

Announced in early 2009, Pfizer's horizontal acquisition of Wyeth for roughly $68 billion was the largest transaction in the pharmaceutical industry in almost a decade. The purchase price meant that Pfizer would pay a premium of approximately 29 percent to acquire Wyeth. As a horizontal acquisition, this price suggested that Pfizer felt that the transaction would result in cost and revenue synergies that at least equaled the amount of the premium it was willing to pay.

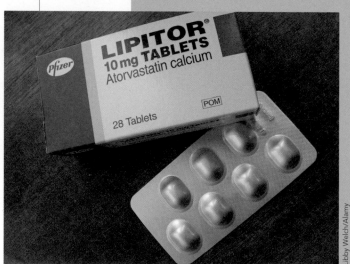

Libby Welch/Alamy

With the patent on Lipitor due to expire in 2011 and generic competitors lining up, Pfizer's acquisition of Wyeth and its pipeline of new products could help replace anticipated lost revenue.

Why did Pfizer conclude that this acquisition was in the best interests of its stakeholders—including its shareholders? A key reason was that Wyeth had been investing heavily in biotechnology and vaccines for about three decades. In fact, Wyeth had become the third-largest biotechnology company behind Amgen Inc. and Genentech Inc. Pfizer wanted to gain access to the new products that might flow from Wyeth's biotechnology-oriented R&D investments. Equally important is the contribution Wyeth would make to Pfizer's sales revenue—revenue that was expected to decline significantly after November 2011 when its hugely successful Lipitor drug (a drug for patients to control their high cholesterol) is scheduled to come off patent. The impact of generic drugs being produced to compete against Lipitor was potentially huge for Pfizer in that this drug alone generates about 25 percent of the firm's total revenue.

Analysts' reactions to this acquisition were mixed to negative. Some said that the core problem is that although Wyeth's sales revenue would help Pfizer replace the revenue it will lose after Lipitor goes off patent, it does not deal with the fact that Pfizer is struggling to develop new products in-house. One analyst said that "Pfizer is spending $7.5 billion a year in research and producing almost nothing and now it has to buy Wyeth. If its pipeline were producing it wouldn't need to buy Wyeth."

Evidence suggests that acquisitions in the pharmaceutical industry do tend to generate cost savings through operational synergies. Accordingly, Pfizer's intended acquisition of Wyeth may achieve one of the benefits of a horizontal acquisition. Simultaneously though, Pfizer seeks to rely on Wyeth's capabilities in the biotechnology space to develop new products that the newly formed firm can quickly introduce to the market.

Sources: 2009, Pfizer's acquisition of Wyeth brings scale but will fail to deliver sustainable sales growth, *Trading Markets. com*, http://www.tradingmarkets.com, January 28; C. Arnst, 2009, The drug mergers' harsh side effects, *BusinessWeek Online*, http://www.businessweek.com, March 12; R. Jana, 2009, Do ideas cost too much? *BusinessWeek*, April 20, 46–58; J. Jannarone, 2009, Pfizer treatment is no cure, *Wall Street Journal Online*, http://www.wsj.com, January 24; S. Pettyprice, T. Randall, & Z. Mider, 2009, Pfizer's $68 billion Wyeth deal eases Lipitor loss, *Bloomberg.com*, http://www.bloomberg.com, January 26.

Acquisition strategies can be used to support use of both unrelated and related diversification strategies (see Chapter 6).[46] For example, United Technologies Corp. (UTC) uses acquisitions as the foundation for implementing its unrelated diversification strategy. Since the mid-1970s it has been building a portfolio of stable and noncyclical businesses including Otis Elevator Co. (elevators, escalators, and moving walkways) and Carrier Corporation (heating and air conditioning systems) in order to reduce its dependence on the volatile aerospace industry. Pratt & Whitney (aircraft engines), Hamilton Sundstrand (aerospace and industrial systems), Sikorsky (helicopters), UTC Fire & Security (fire safety and security products and services), and UTC Power (fuel cells and power systems) are the other businesses in which UTC competes as a result of using its acquisition strategy. While each business UTC acquires manufactures industrial and/or commercial products, many have a relatively low focus on technology (e.g., elevators, air conditioners, and security systems).[47] In contrast to UTC, Procter & Gamble (P&G) uses acquisitions to implement its related diversification strategy. Beauty, Health & Well-Being, and Household Care are P&G's core business segments. Gillette's products are included in the Beauty segment, where they are related to other products in this segment such as cosmetics, hair care, and skin care. As noted earlier in the chapter, P&G completed a horizontal acquisition of Gillette in 2006.

Firms using acquisition strategies should be aware that in general, the more related the acquired firm is to the acquiring firm, the greater is the probability the acquisition will be successful.[48] Thus, horizontal acquisitions and related acquisitions tend to contribute more to the firm's strategic competitiveness than do acquisitions of companies operating in product markets that are quite different from those in which the acquiring firm competes.[49]

Reshaping the Firm's Competitive Scope

As discussed in Chapter 2, the intensity of competitive rivalry is an industry characteristic that affects the firm's profitability.[50] To reduce the negative effect of an intense rivalry on their financial performance, firms may use acquisitions to lessen their dependence on one or more products or markets. Reducing a company's dependence on specific markets shapes the firm's competitive scope.

Each time UTC enters a new business (such as UTC Power, the firm's latest business segment), the corporation reshapes its competitive scope. In a more subtle manner, P&G's acquisition of Gillette reshaped its competitive scope by giving P&G a stronger presence in some products for whom men are the target market. By merging their operations, Towers Perrin and Watson Wyatt reshaped the scope of their formerly independent firms' operations in that Towers was stronger in health care consulting while Watson Wyatt was stronger in pension consulting. Thus, using an acquisition strategy reshaped the competitive scope of each of these firms.

Learning and Developing New Capabilities

Firms sometimes complete acquisitions to gain access to capabilities they lack. For example, acquisitions may be used to acquire a special technological capability. Research shows that firms can broaden their knowledge base and reduce inertia through acquisitions.[51]

For example, research suggests that firms increase the potential of their capabilities when they acquire diverse talent through cross-border acquisitions.[52] Of course, firms are better able to learn these capabilities if they share some similar properties with the firm's current capabilities. Thus, firms should seek to acquire companies with different but related and complementary capabilities in order to build their own knowledge base.[53]

A number of large pharmaceutical firms are acquiring the ability to create "large molecule" drugs, also known as biological drugs, by buying bio-technology firms. Thus, these firms are seeking access to both the pipeline of possible drugs and the capabilities that these firms have to produce them. Such capabilities are important for large pharmaceutical firms because these biological drugs are more difficult to duplicate by chemistry alone (the historical basis on which most pharmaceutical firms have expertise). These capabilities will allow generic drug makers to be more successful after chemistry-based drug patents expire. To illustrate the difference between these types of drugs, David Brennen, CEO of British drug maker AstraZeneca, suggested, "Some of these [biological-based drugs] have demonstrated that they're not just symptomatic treatments but that they actually alter the course of the disease."[54] Furthermore, biological drugs must clear more regulatory barriers or hurdles which, when accomplished, add more to the advantage the acquiring firm develops through successful acquisitions.

Problems in Achieving Acquisition Success

Acquisition strategies based on reasons described in this chapter can increase strategic competitiveness and help firms earn above-average returns. However, even when pursued for value-creating reasons, acquisition strategies are not problem-free. Reasons for the use of acquisition strategies and potential problems with such strategies are shown in Figure 7.1.

Research suggests that perhaps 20 percent of all mergers and acquisitions are successful, approximately 60 percent produce disappointing results, and the remaining 20 percent are clear failures.[55] In general, though, companies appear to be increasing their ability to effectively use acquisition strategies. An investment banker representing acquisition clients describes this improvement in the following manner: "I've been doing this work for 20-odd years, and I can tell you that the sophistication of companies going through transactions has increased exponentially."[56] Greater acquisition success accrues to firms able to (1) select the "right" target, (2) avoid paying too high a premium (doing appropriate due diligence), and (3) effectively integrate the operations of the acquiring and target firms.[57] In addition, retaining the target firm's human capital is foundational to efforts by employees of the acquiring firm to fully understand the target firm's operations and the capabilities on which those operations are based.[58] As shown in Figure 7.1, several problems may prevent successful acquisitions.

Integration Difficulties

The importance of a successful integration should not be underestimated.[59] As suggested by a researcher studying the process, "Managerial practice and academic writings show that the post-acquisition integration phase is probably the single most important determinant of shareholder value creation (and equally of value destruction) in mergers and acquisitions."[60]

Although critical to acquisition success, firms should recognize that integrating two companies following an acquisition can be quite difficult. Melding two corporate cultures, linking different financial and control systems, building effective working relationships (particularly when management styles differ), and resolving problems regarding the status of the newly acquired firm's executives are examples of integration challenges firms often face.[61]

Integration is complex and involves a large number of activities, which if overlooked can lead to significant difficulties. For example, when United Parcel Service (UPS) acquired Mail Boxes Etc., a large retail shipping chain, it appeared to be a merger that would generate benefits for both firms. The problem is that most of the Mail Boxes Etc.

Figure 7.1 Reasons for Acquisitions and Problems in Achieving Success

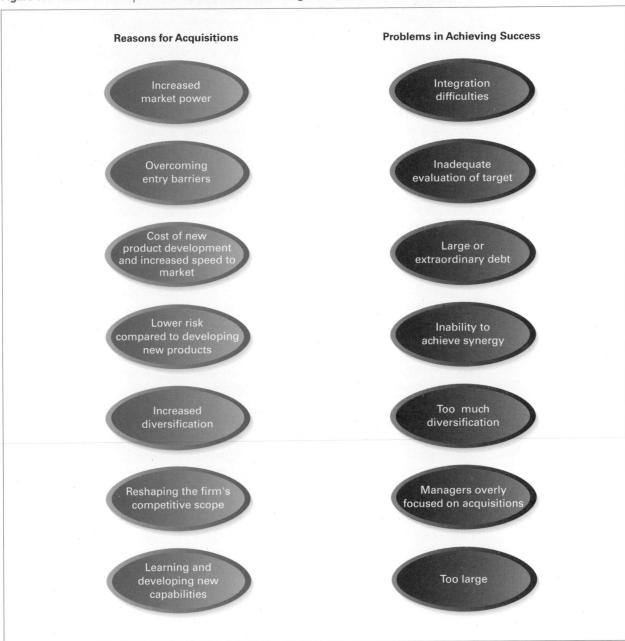

Reasons for Acquisitions

- Increased market power
- Overcoming entry barriers
- Cost of new product development and increased speed to market
- Lower risk compared to developing new products
- Increased diversification
- Reshaping the firm's competitive scope
- Learning and developing new capabilities

Problems in Achieving Success

- Integration difficulties
- Inadequate evaluation of target
- Large or extraordinary debt
- Inability to achieve synergy
- Too much diversification
- Managers overly focused on acquisitions
- Too large

outlets were owned by franchisees. Following the merger, the franchisees lost the ability to deal with other shipping companies such as FedEx, which reduced their competitiveness. Furthermore, franchisees complained that UPS often built company-owned shipping stores close by franchisee outlets of Mail Boxes Etc. Additionally, a culture clash evolved between the free-wheeling entrepreneurs who owned the franchises of Mail Boxes Etc. and the efficiency-oriented corporate approach of the UPS operation, which focused on managing a large fleet of trucks and an information system to efficiently pick up and deliver packages. Also, Mail Boxes Etc. was focused on retail traffic, whereas UPS was focused more on the logistics of wholesale pickup and delivery. Although 87 percent of Mail Boxes Etc. franchisees decided to rebrand under the UPS name, many formed an owner's group and even filed suit against UPS in regard to the unfavorable nature of the franchisee contract.[62]

Inadequate Evaluation of Target

Due diligence is a process through which a potential acquirer evaluates a target firm for acquisition. In an effective due-diligence process, hundreds of items are examined in areas as diverse as the financing for the intended transaction, differences in cultures between the acquiring and target firm, tax consequences of the transaction, and actions that would be necessary to successfully meld the two workforces. Due diligence is commonly performed by investment bankers such as Deutsche Bank, Goldman Sachs, and Morgan Stanley, as well as accountants, lawyers, and management consultants specializing in that activity, although firms actively pursuing acquisitions may form their own internal due-diligence team.[63]

The failure to complete an effective due-diligence process may easily result in the acquiring firm paying an excessive premium for the target company. Interestingly, research shows that in times of high or increasing stock prices due diligence is relaxed; firms often overpay during these periods and long-run performance of the newly formed firm suffers.[64] Research also shows that without due diligence, "the purchase price is driven by the pricing of other 'comparable' acquisitions rather than by a rigorous assessment of where, when, and how management can drive real performance gains. [In these cases], the price paid may have little to do with achievable value."[65]

In addition, firms sometimes allow themselves to enter a "bidding war" for a target, even though they realize that their current bids exceed the parameters identified through due diligence. Earlier, we mentioned NetApp's bid for Data Domain that represents a 419 percent premium. Commenting about this, an analyst said that "…NetApp wouldn't be the first company to stay in a bidding war even when discretion was the better part of valor."[66] Rather than enter a bidding war, firms should only extend bids that are consistent with the results of their due diligence process.

Large or Extraordinary Debt

To finance a number of acquisitions completed during the 1980s and 1990s, some companies significantly increased their levels of debt. A financial innovation called junk bonds helped make this possible. *Junk bonds* are a financing option through which risky acquisitions are financed with money (debt) that provides a large potential return to lenders (bondholders). Because junk bonds are unsecured obligations that are not tied to specific assets for collateral, interest rates for these high-risk debt instruments sometimes reached between 18 and 20 percent during the 1980s.[67] Some prominent financial economists viewed debt as a means to discipline managers, causing them to act in the shareholders' best interests.[68] Managers holding this view are less concerned about the amount of debt their firm assumes when acquiring other companies.

Junk bonds are now used less frequently to finance acquisitions, and the conviction that debt disciplines managers is less strong. Nonetheless, firms sometimes still take on what turns out to be too much debt when acquiring companies. This may be the case for Tata Motors. Some analysts describe Tata's problems with debt this way: "Tata Motors' troubles began last year when it paid $2.3bn for Jaguar and Land Rover and borrowed $3bn to finance the transaction and provide additional working capital."[69] Because of this, some felt that the firm was less capable of providing the capital its various units required to remain competitive.

High debt can have several negative effects on the firm. For example, because high debt increases the likelihood of bankruptcy, it can lead to a downgrade in the firm's credit rating by agencies such as Moody's and Standard & Poor's.[70] In other instances, a firm may have to divest some assets to relieve its debt burden. South Korea's Kimho Asiana Group's decision to divest its Daewoo Engineering & Construction Co. may be an example of this in that the firm's liquidity was being questioned after acquiring both Daewoo and Korea Express within a short time period.[71] Thus, firms using an acquisition strategy must be certain that their purchases do not create a debt load that overpowers the company's ability to remain solvent.

Inability to Achieve Synergy

Derived from *synergos,* a Greek word that means "working together," *synergy* exists when the value created by units working together exceeds the value those units could create working independently (see Chapter 6). That is, synergy exists when assets are worth more when used in conjunction with each other than when they are used separately. For shareholders, synergy generates gains in their wealth that they could not duplicate or exceed through their own portfolio diversification decisions.[72] Synergy is created by the efficiencies derived from economies of scale and economies of scope and by sharing resources (e.g., human capital and knowledge) across the businesses in the merged firm.[73]

A firm develops a competitive advantage through an acquisition strategy only when a transaction generates private synergy. *Private synergy* is created when combining and integrating the acquiring and acquired firms' assets yield capabilities and core competencies that could not be developed by combining and integrating either firm's assets with another company. Private synergy is possible when firms' assets are complementary in unique ways; that is, the unique type of asset complementarity is not possible by combining either company's assets with another firm's assets.[74] Because of its uniqueness, private synergy is difficult for competitors to understand and imitate. However, private synergy is difficult to create.

A firm's ability to account for costs that are necessary to create anticipated revenue- and cost-based synergies affects its efforts to create private synergy. Firms experience several expenses when trying to create private synergy through acquisitions. Called transaction costs, these expenses are incurred when firms use acquisition strategies to create synergy.[75] Transaction costs may be direct or indirect. Direct costs include legal fees and charges from investment bankers who complete due diligence for the acquiring firm. Indirect costs include managerial time to evaluate target firms and then to complete negotiations, as well as the loss of key managers and employees following an acquisition.[76] Firms tend to underestimate the sum of indirect costs when the value of the synergy that may be created by combining and integrating the acquired firm's assets with the acquiring firm's assets is calculated.

Too Much Diversification

As explained in Chapter 6, diversification strategies can lead to strategic competitiveness and above-average returns. In general, firms using related diversification strategies outperform those employing unrelated diversification strategies. However, conglomerates formed by using an unrelated diversification strategy also can be successful, as demonstrated by United Technologies Corp.

At some point, however, firms can become overdiversified. The level at which overdiversification occurs varies across companies because each firm has different capabilities to manage diversification. Recall from Chapter 6 that related diversification requires more information processing than does unrelated diversification. Because of this additional information processing, related diversified firms become overdiversified with a smaller number of business units than do firms using an unrelated diversification strategy.[77] Regardless of the type of diversification strategy implemented, however, overdiversification leads to a decline in performance, after which business units are often divested.[78] Commonly, such divestments, which tend to reshape a firm's competitive scope, are part of a firm's restructuring strategy. (We discuss the strategy in greater detail later in the chapter.)

Even when a firm is not overdiversified, a high level of diversification can have a negative effect on its long-term performance. For example, the scope created by additional amounts of diversification often causes managers to rely on financial rather than strategic controls to evaluate business units' performance (we define and explain financial and strategic controls in Chapters 11 and 12). Top-level executives often rely on financial controls to assess the performance of business units when they do not have a rich understanding of business units' objectives and strategies. Using financial controls, such as return on investment (ROI), causes individual business-unit managers to focus on short-term outcomes at the expense of long-term investments. When long-term investments are reduced to increase short-term profits, a firm's overall strategic competitiveness may be harmed.[79]

Another problem resulting from too much diversification is the tendency for acquisitions to become substitutes for innovation. As we noted earlier, pharmaceutical firms such as Pfizer must be aware of this tendency as they acquire other firms to gain access to their products and capabilities. Typically, managers have no interest in acquisitions substituting for internal R&D efforts and the innovative outcomes that they can produce. However, a reinforcing cycle evolves. Costs associated with acquisitions may result in fewer allocations to activities, such as R&D, that are linked to innovation. Without adequate support, a firm's innovation skills begin to atrophy. Without internal innovation skills, the only option available to a firm to gain access to innovation is to complete still more acquisitions. Evidence suggests that a firm using acquisitions as a substitute for internal innovations eventually encounters performance problems.[80]

Managers Overly Focused on Acquisitions

Typically, a considerable amount of managerial time and energy is required for acquisition strategies to be used successfully. Activities with which managers become involved include (1) searching for viable acquisition candidates, (2) completing effective due-diligence processes, (3) preparing for negotiations, and (4) managing the integration process after completing the acquisition.

Top-level managers do not personally gather all of the data and information required to make acquisitions. However, these executives do make critical decisions on the firms to be targeted, the nature of the negotiations, and so forth. Company experiences show that participating in and overseeing the activities required for making acquisitions can divert managerial attention from other matters that are necessary for long-term competitive success, such as identifying and taking advantage of other opportunities and interacting with important external stakeholders.[81]

Both theory and research suggest that managers can become overly involved in the process of making acquisitions.[82] One observer suggested, "Some executives can become preoccupied with making deals—and the thrill of selecting, chasing and seizing a target."[83] The overinvolvement can be surmounted by learning from mistakes and by not having too much agreement in the boardroom. Dissent is helpful to make sure that all sides of a question are considered (see Chapter 10).[84] When failure does occur, leaders may be tempted to blame the failure on others and on unforeseen circumstances rather than on their excessive involvement in the acquisition process.

Actions taken at Liz Claiborne Inc. demonstrate the problem of being overly focused on acquisitions. Over time, Claiborne acquired a number of firms in sportswear apparel, growing from 16 to 36 brands in the process of doing so. However, while its managers were focused on making acquisitions, changes were taking place in the firm's external environment, including industry consolidation. Specifically, while most Claiborne sales were focused on traditional department stores, consolidation through acquisitions in this sector left less room for as many brands, given the purchasing practices of the large department stores. Additionally, competitors were gaining favor with customers, leaving fewer sales for Claiborne's

In response to a changing external environment, Liz Claiborne CEO William McComb made the decision to slow acquisitions and refocus on key brands and driving cost-efficiencies.

Brendan McDermid/Reuters/Landov

products. In response to these problems, CEO William McComb announced in July 2007 a "…framework of a new organizational structure that was a crucial step in making Liz Claiborne Inc. into a more brand-focused and cost-effective business that (could) successfully navigate a rapidly changing retail environment." As a result of these actions, Claiborne is less diversified in terms of brands and less focused on acquisitions. Today, the firm has three distinct brand segments—domestic-based direct brands, international-based direct brands, and partnered brands.[85]

Too Large

Most acquisitions create a larger firm, which should help increase its economies of scale. These economies can then lead to more efficient operations—for example, two sales organizations can be integrated using fewer sales representatives because such sales personnel can sell the products of both firms (particularly if the products of the acquiring and target firms are highly related).[86]

Many firms seek increases in size because of the potential economies of scale and enhanced market power (discussed earlier). At some level, the additional costs required to manage the larger firm will exceed the benefits of the economies of scale and additional market power. The complexities generated by the larger size often lead managers to implement more bureaucratic controls to manage the combined firm's operations. *Bureaucratic controls* are formalized supervisory and behavioral rules and policies designed to ensure consistency of decisions and actions across different units of a firm. However, through time, formalized controls often lead to relatively rigid and standardized managerial behavior. Certainly, in the long run, the diminished flexibility that accompanies rigid and standardized managerial behavior may produce less innovation. Because of innovation's importance to competitive success, the bureaucratic controls resulting from a large organization (i.e., built by acquisitions) can have a detrimental effect on performance. As one analyst noted, "Striving for size per se is not necessarily going to make a company more successful. In fact, a strategy in which acquisitions are undertaken as a substitute for organic growth has a bad track record in terms of adding value."[87]

Effective Acquisitions

Earlier in the chapter, we noted that acquisition strategies do not always lead to above-average returns for the acquiring firm's shareholders.[88] Nonetheless, some companies are able to create value when using an acquisition strategy.[89] The probability of success increases when the firm's actions are consistent with the "attributes of successful acquisitions" shown in Table 7.1.

Cisco Systems is an example of a firm that appears to pay close attention to Table 7.1's attributes when using its acquisition strategy. In fact, Cisco is admired for its ability to complete successful acquisitions. A number of other network companies pursued acquisitions to build up their ability to sell into the network equipment binge, but only Cisco retained much of its value in the post-bubble era. Many firms, such as Lucent, Nortel, and Ericsson, teetered on the edge of bankruptcy after the dot-com bubble burst. When it makes an acquisition, "Cisco has gone much further in its thinking about integration. Not only is retention important, but Cisco also works to minimize the distractions caused by an acquisition. This is important, because the speed of change is so great, that even if the target firm's product development teams are distracted, they will be slowed, contributing to acquisition failure. So, integration must be rapid and reassuring."[90] For example, Cisco facilitates acquired employees' transitions to their new organization through a link on its Web site called "Connection for Acquired Employees." This Web site has been specifically designed for newly acquired employees and provides up-to-date materials tailored to their new jobs.[91]

Table 7.1 Attributes of Successful Acquisitions

Attributes	Results
1. Acquired firm has assets or resources that are complementary to the acquiring firm's core business	1. High probability of synergy and competitive advantage by maintaining strengths
2. Acquisition is friendly	2. Faster and more effective integration and possibly lower premiums
3. Acquiring firm conducts effective due diligence to select target firms and evaluate the target firm's health (financial, cultural, and human resources)	3. Firms with strongest complementarities are acquired and overpayment is avoided
4. Acquiring firm has financial slack (cash or a favorable debt position)	4. Financing (debt or equity) is easier and less costly to obtain
5. Merged firm maintains low to moderate debt position	5. Lower financing cost, lower risk (e.g., of bankruptcy), and avoidance of trade-offs that are associated with high debt
6. Acquiring firm has sustained and consistent emphasis on R&D and innovation	6. Maintain long-term competitive advantage in markets
7. Acquiring firm manages change well and is flexible and adaptable	7. Faster and more effective integration facilitates achievement of synergy

Results from a research study shed light on the differences between unsuccessful and successful acquisition strategies and suggest that a pattern of actions improves the probability of acquisition success.[92] The study shows that when the target firm's assets are complementary to the acquired firm's assets, an acquisition is more successful. With complementary assets, the integration of two firms' operations has a higher probability of creating synergy. In fact, integrating two firms with complementary assets frequently produces unique capabilities and core competencies. With complementary assets, the acquiring firm can maintain its focus on core businesses and leverage the complementary assets and capabilities from the acquired firm. In effective acquisitions, targets are often selected and "groomed" by establishing a working relationship prior to the acquisition.[93] As discussed in Chapter 9, strategic alliances are sometimes used to test the feasibility of a future merger or acquisition between the involved firms.[94]

The study's results also show that friendly acquisitions facilitate integration of the firms involved in an acquisition. Through friendly acquisitions, firms work together to find ways to integrate their operations to create synergy.[95] In hostile takeovers, animosity often results between the two top-management teams, a condition that in turn affects working relationships in the newly created firm. As a result, more key personnel in the acquired firm may be lost, and those who remain may resist the changes necessary to integrate the two firms.[96] With effort, cultural clashes can be overcome, and fewer key managers and employees will become discouraged and leave.[97]

Additionally, effective due-diligence processes involving the deliberate and careful selection of target firms and an evaluation of the relative health of those firms (financial health, cultural fit, and the value of human resources) contribute to successful acquisitions.[98] Financial slack in the form of debt equity or cash, in both the acquiring and acquired firms, also frequently contributes to acquisition success. Even though financial slack provides access to financing for the acquisition, it is still important to maintain a low or moderate level of debt after the acquisition to keep debt costs low. When substantial debt was used to finance the acquisition, companies with successful acquisitions reduced the debt quickly, partly by selling off assets from the acquired firm, especially noncomplementary or poorly performing assets. For these firms, debt costs do not prevent long-term investments such as R&D, and managerial discretion in the use of cash flow is relatively flexible.

Another attribute of successful acquisition strategies is an emphasis on innovation, as demonstrated by continuing investments in R&D activities. Significant R&D investments show a strong managerial commitment to innovation, a characteristic that is increasingly important to overall competitiveness in the global economy as well as to acquisition success.

Flexibility and adaptability are the final two attributes of successful acquisitions. When executives of both the acquiring and the target firms have experience in managing change and learning from acquisitions, they will be more skilled at adapting their capabilities to new environments.[99] As a result, they will be more adept at integrating the two organizations, which is particularly important when firms have different organizational cultures.

As we have learned, firms use an acquisition strategy to grow and achieve strategic competitiveness. Sometimes, though, the actual results of an acquisition strategy fall short of the projected results. When this happens, firms consider using restructuring strategies.

Restructuring

Restructuring is a strategy through which a firm changes its set of businesses or its financial structure.[100] Restructuring is a global phenomenon.[101] From the 1970s into the 2000s, divesting businesses from company portfolios and downsizing accounted for a large percentage of firms' restructuring strategies. Commonly, firms focus on a fewer number of products and markets following restructuring. The words of an executive describe this typical outcome: "Focus on your core business, but don't be distracted, let other people buy assets that aren't right for you."[102]

Although restructuring strategies are generally used to deal with acquisitions that are not reaching expectations, firms sometimes use these strategies because of changes they have detected in their external environment. For example, opportunities sometimes surface in a firm's external environment that a diversified firm can pursue because of the capabilities it has formed by integrating firms' operations. In such cases, restructuring may be appropriate to position the firm to create more value for stakeholders, given the environmental changes.[103]

As discussed next, firms use three types of restructuring strategies: downsizing, downscoping, and leveraged buyouts.

Downsizing

Downsizing is a reduction in the number of a firm's employees and, sometimes, in the number of its operating units, but it may or may not change the composition of businesses in the company's portfolio. Thus, downsizing is an intentional proactive management strategy whereas "decline is an environmental or organizational phenomenon that occurs involuntarily and results in erosion of an organization's resource base."[104] Downsizing is often a part of acquisitions that fail to create the value anticipated when the transaction was completed. Downsizing is often used when the acquiring firm paid too high of a premium to acquire the target firm.[105] Once thought to be an indicator of organizational decline, downsizing is now recognized as a legitimate restructuring strategy.

Reducing the number of employees and/or the firm's scope in terms of products produced and markets served occurs in firms to enhance the value being created as a result of

Restructuring is a strategy through which a firm changes its set of businesses or its financial structure.

completing an acquisition. When integrating the operations of the acquired firm and the acquiring firm, managers may not at first appropriately downsize. This is understandable in that "no one likes to lay people off or close facilities."[106] However, downsizing may be necessary because acquisitions often create a situation in which the newly formed firm has duplicate organizational functions such as sales, manufacturing, distribution, human resource management, and so forth. Failing to downsize appropriately may lead to too many employees doing the same work and prevent the new firm from realizing the cost synergies it anticipated. Managers should remember that as a strategy, downsizing will be far more effective when they consistently use human resource practices that ensure procedural justice and fairness in downsizing decisions.[107]

Downscoping

Downscoping refers to divestiture, spin-off, or some other means of eliminating businesses that are unrelated to a firm's core businesses. Downscoping has a more positive effect on firm performance than does downsizing[108] because firms commonly find that downscoping causes them to refocus on their core business.[109] Managerial effectiveness increases because the firm has become less diversified, allowing the top management team to better understand and manage the remaining businesses.[110]

Motorola Inc. is a firm that has struggled recently. With an interest of refocusing on "technologies that can grow its business" as one path to reversing the firm's fortunes, Motorola is divesting assets that are not related to its core businesses. The recent sale of its fiber-to-the-node product line to Communications Test Design Inc., an engineering, repair, and logistics company, is an example of Motorola's use of a downscoping strategy.[111] In mid-2009, the McGraw-Hill Companies indicated that it was seeking a buyer for *BusinessWeek* magazine. This magazine was one of the products in McGraw's Information and Media business unit (the firm has two other business units). As was the case with many other magazines during the global financial crisis, *BusinessWeek* was being hurt "... by defections of readers and advertisers to the Internet" as well as by the oversupply of business magazine titles.[112] Divesting *BusinessWeek* would allow those leading McGraw's Information & Media unit to refocus on its other businesses, such as J.D. Power and Associates and the Aviation Week Group. Previous to the announcement, McGraw had already divested most of its periodicals.[113]

Firms often use the downscoping and the downsizing strategies simultaneously. However, when doing this, firms avoid layoffs of key employees, in that such layoffs might lead to a loss of one or more core competencies. Instead, a firm that is simultaneously downscoping and downsizing becomes smaller by reducing the diversity of businesses in its portfolio.[114]

In general, U.S. firms use downscoping as a restructuring strategy more frequently than do European companies—in fact, the trend in Europe, Latin America, and Asia has been to build conglomerates. In Latin America, these conglomerates are called *grupos*. Many Asian and Latin American conglomerates have begun to adopt Western corporate strategies in recent years and have been refocusing on their core businesses. This downscoping has occurred simultaneously with increasing globalization and with more open markets that have greatly enhanced competition. By downscoping, these firms have been able to focus on their core businesses and improve their competitiveness.[115]

In response to increasingly negative sales trends in print periodicals and to allow for more internal focus on growth-oriented services, McGraw-Hill is selling BusinessWeek which has been in publication since 1929.

Colin Young-Wolff/PhotoEdit

Leveraged Buyouts

A *leveraged buyout* (LBO) is a restructuring strategy whereby a party (typically a private equity firm) buys all of a firm's assets in order to take the firm private. Once the transaction is completed, the company's stock is no longer traded publicly. Traditionally, leveraged buyouts were used as a restructuring strategy to correct for managerial mistakes or because the firm's managers were making decisions that primarily served their own interests rather than those of shareholders.[116] However, some firms use buyouts to build firm resources and expand rather than simply restructure distressed assets.[117]

Significant amounts of debt are commonly incurred to finance a buyout; hence, the term *leveraged* buyout. To support debt payments and to downscope the company to concentrate on the firm's core businesses, the new owners may immediately sell a number of assets.[118] It is not uncommon for those buying a firm through an LBO to restructure the firm to the point that it can be sold at a profit within a five- to eight-year period.

Management buyouts (MBOs), employee buyouts (EBOs), and whole-firm buyouts, in which one company or partnership purchases an entire company instead of a part of it, are the three types of LBOs. In part because of managerial incentives, MBOs, more so than EBOs and whole-firm buyouts, have been found to lead to downscoping, increased strategic focus, and improved performance.[119] Research shows that management buyouts can lead to greater entrepreneurial activity and growth.[120] As such, buyouts can represent a form of firm rebirth to facilitate entrepreneurial efforts and stimulate strategic growth.[121]

Restructuring Outcomes

The short- and long-term outcomes associated with the three restructuring strategies are shown in Figure 7.2. As indicated, downsizing typically does not lead to higher firm performance.[122] In fact, some research results show that downsizing contributes to lower returns for both U.S. and Japanese firms. The stock markets in the firms' respective

Figure 7.2 Restructuring and Outcomes

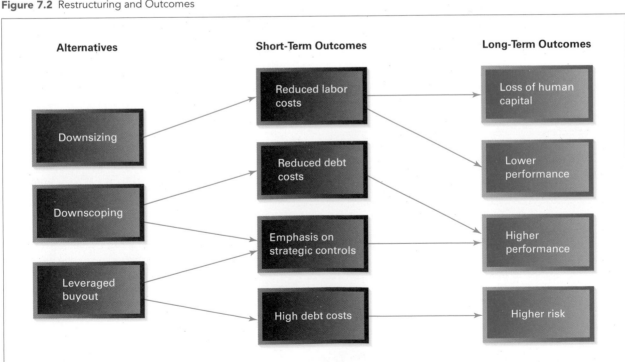

nations evaluated downsizing negatively, believing that it would have long-term negative effects on the firm's efforts to achieve strategic competitiveness. Investors also seem to conclude that downsizing occurs as a consequence of other problems in a company.[123] This assumption may be caused by a firm's diminished corporate reputation when a major downsizing is announced.[124]

The loss of human capital is another potential problem of downsizing (see Figure 7.2). Losing employees with many years of experience with the firm represents a major loss of knowledge. As noted in Chapter 3, knowledge is vital to competitive success in the global economy. Thus, in general, research evidence and corporate experience suggest that downsizing may be of more tactical (or short-term) value than strategic (or long-term) value,[125] meaning that firms should exercise caution when restructuring through downsizing.

Downscoping generally leads to more positive outcomes in both the short and long term than does downsizing or a leveraged buyout. Downscoping's desirable long-term outcome of higher performance is a product of reduced debt costs and the emphasis on strategic controls derived from concentrating on the firm's core businesses. In so doing, the refocused firm should be able to increase its ability to compete.[126]

Although whole-firm LBOs have been hailed as a significant innovation in the financial restructuring of firms, they can involve negative trade-offs.[127] First, the resulting large debt increases the firm's financial risk, as is evidenced by the number of companies that filed for bankruptcy in the 1990s after executing a whole-firm LBO. Sometimes, the intent of the owners to increase the efficiency of the bought-out firm and then sell it within five to eight years creates a short-term and risk-averse managerial focus.[128] As a result, these firms may fail to invest adequately in R&D or take other major actions designed to maintain or improve the company's core competence.[129] Research also suggests that in firms with an entrepreneurial mind-set, buyouts can lead to greater innovation, especially if the debt load is not too great.[130] However, because buyouts more often result in significant debt, most LBOs have been completed in mature industries where stable cash flows are possible.

SUMMARY

- Although the number of mergers and acquisitions completed declined in 2008 and early 2009, largely because of the global financial crisis, merger and acquisition strategies remain popular as a path to firm growth and earning of strategic competitiveness. Globalization and deregulation of multiple industries in many economies are two of the factors making mergers and acquisitions attractive to large corporations and small firms.

- Firms use acquisition strategies to (1) increase market power, (2) overcome entry barriers to new markets or regions, (3) avoid the costs of developing new products and increase the speed of new market entries, (4) reduce the risk of entering a new business, (5) become more diversified, (6) reshape their competitive scope by developing a different portfolio of businesses, and (7) enhance their learning as the foundation for developing new capabilities.

- Among the problems associated with using an acquisition strategy are (1) the difficulty of effectively integrating the firms involved, (2) incorrectly evaluating the target firm's value, (3) creating debt loads that preclude adequate long-term investments (e.g., R&D), (4) overestimating the potential for synergy, (5) creating a firm that is too diversified, (6) creating an internal environment in which managers devote increasing amounts of their time and energy to analyzing and completing the acquisition, and (7) developing a combined firm that is too large, necessitating extensive use of bureaucratic, rather than strategic, controls.

- Effective acquisitions have the following characteristics: (1) the acquiring and target firms have complementary resources that are the foundation for developing new capabilities; (2) the acquisition is friendly, thereby facilitating integration of the firms' resources; (3) the target firm is selected and purchased based on thorough due diligence; (4) the acquiring and target firms have considerable slack in the form of cash or debt capacity; (5) the newly formed firm maintains a low or moderate level of debt by selling off portions of the acquired firm or some of the acquiring firm's poorly performing units; (6) the acquiring and acquired firms have experience in terms of adapting to change; and (7) R&D and innovation are emphasized in the new firm.

- Restructuring is used to improve a firm's performance by correcting for problems created by ineffective management. Restructuring by downsizing involves reducing the number of employees and hierarchical levels in the firm. Although it can lead to short-term cost reductions, they may be realized at the expense of long-term success, because of the loss of valuable human resources (and knowledge) and overall corporate reputation.

- The goal of restructuring through downscoping is to reduce the firm's level of diversification. Often, the firm divests unrelated businesses to achieve this goal. Eliminating unrelated businesses makes it easier for the firm and its top-level managers to refocus on the core businesses.

- Through an LBO, a firm is purchased so that it can become a private entity. LBOs usually are financed largely through debt. Management buyouts (MBOs), employee buyouts (EBOs), and whole-firm LBOs are the three types of LBOs. Because they provide clear managerial incentives, MBOs have been the most successful of the three. Often, the intent of a buyout is to improve efficiency and performance to the point where the firm can be sold successfully within five to eight years.

- Commonly, restructuring's primary goal is gaining or reestablishing effective strategic control of the firm. Of the three restructuring strategies, downscoping is aligned most closely with establishing and using strategic controls and usually improves performance more on a comparative basis.

REVIEW QUESTIONS

1. Why are merger and acquisition strategies popular in many firms competing in the global economy?

2. What reasons account for firms' decisions to use acquisition strategies as a means to achieving strategic competitiveness?

3. What are the seven primary problems that affect a firm's efforts to successfully use an acquisition strategy?

4. What are the attributes associated with a successful acquisition strategy?

5. What is the restructuring strategy, and what are its common forms?

6. What are the short- and long-term outcomes associated with the different restructuring strategies?

EXPERIENTIAL EXERCISES

EXERCISE 1: HOW DID THE DEAL WORK OUT?

The text argues that mergers and acquisitions are a popular strategy for businesses both in the United States and abroad. However, returns for acquiring firms do not always live up to expectations. This exercise seeks to address this notion by analyzing, pre and post hoc, the results of actual acquisitions. By looking at the notifications of a deal beforehand, categorizing that deal, and then following it for a year, you will be able to learn about actual deals and their implications for strategic leaders and their firms.

Working in teams, identify a merger or acquisition that was completed in the last few years. This may be a cross-border acquisition or one centered in the United States. A couple of possible sources for this information are Reuters's Online M&A section or Yahoo! Finance's U.S. Mergers and Acquisitions Calendar. Each team must have its M&A choice approved in advance so as to avoid duplicates.

To complete this assignment you should be prepared to answer the following questions:

1. Describe the environment for the merger or acquisition you identified at the time it was completed. Using concepts discussed in the text, focus on management's representation to shareholders, industry environment, and the overall rationale for the transaction.

2. Did the acquirer pay a premium for the target firm? If so, how much? In addition, search for investor comments regarding the

wisdom of the transaction. Attempt to identify how the market reacted at the announcement of the transaction (LexisNexis often provides an article that will address this issue).

3. Describe the transaction going forward. Use concepts from the text such as, but not limited to:

   - The reason for the transaction (i.e., market power, overcoming entry barriers, etc.)
   - Any problems in achieving acquisition success
   - Whether the transaction has been a success or not and why.

   Prepare a 10- to 15-minute presentation for the class describing your findings. Organize the presentation as if you were updating the shareholders of the newly formed firm.

EXERCISE 2: CADBURY SCHWEPPES

Cadbury and Schweppes are two prominent and long-established companies. Cadbury was founded in 1824 and is the world's largest confectionary company. The bulk of Cadbury's sales are generated in Europe, with a substantially smaller presence in the Americas. Schweppes was founded in 1783, when its founder Jacob Schweppes invented a system to carbonate mineral water. Its brands include 7-Up, Dr Pepper, Sunkist, Snapple, Schweppes, and Mott's. Cadbury and Schweppes merged in 1969. In 2008, the combined firm posted approximately $32 billion in revenue and an $8.8 billion loss. The firm employed 160,000 people at this time. In what is termed a "demerger," the firm in 2008 spun off its North American beverage unit (Dr Pepper Snapple Group) and changed its name from Cadbury Schweppes to just Cadbury. Working in teams, prepare a brief PowerPoint presentation to address the following questions. You will need to consult the company's now separate Web sites http://www.drpeppersnapplegroup.com/ and http://www.cadbury.com, as well as news articles published about this event. Lexis Nexis is a good resource for news on topics such as this.

1. Why did Cadbury decide to divest itself of the beverage business?
2. What does it mean that Cadbury listed the separation as a demerger?
3. What factors hindered the success of a combined Cadbury Schweppes?
4. Do you feel that both the beverage and confectionary businesses are better or worse off being separated?

VIDEO CASE

FOCUS ON WHY A DEAL IS DONE, NOT HOW

Stuart Grief/Vice President of Strategy and Development/Textron

Stuart Grief, Vice President of Strategy and Development at Textron, talks about the art of the deal and how the company he represents goes through deal-making analysis. As you prepare for the video, consider the concepts of negotiation and deal-making; important ingredients of any M&A activity.

Before you watch the video consider the following concepts and questions and be prepared to discuss them in class:

Concepts
- M&A strategies
- Reasons for acquisition
- Problems in achieving success

Questions

1. Think through a deal or transaction you have recently made or considered making (i.e., purchased a car, bought a new computer, leased an apartment, took out a loan). Describe the deal-making process and why you ultimately decided to either make the deal or walk away from it.
2. How would you characterize Textron's corporate-level strategy? Visit the firm's Web site to see the various business units it manages. Describe what you think are the criteria the firm uses when evaluating targets for acquisition. Does it appear that Textron is willing to acquire any type of firm in any industry?
3. Overall, how should a company plan and undertake its merger and acquisition strategic initiatives?

CHAPTER 8

Global Strategy

Studying this chapter should provide you with the strategic management knowledge needed to:

1. Explain traditional and emerging motives for firms to pursue international diversification.

2. Identify the four major benefits of an international strategy.

3. Explore the four factors that provide a basis for international business-level strategies.

4. Describe the three international corporate-level strategies: multidomestic, global, and transnational.

5. Discuss the environmental trends affecting international strategy, especially liability of foreignness and regionalization.

6. Name and describe the five alternative modes for entering international markets.

7. Explain the effects of international diversification on firm returns and innovation.

8. Name and describe two major risks of international diversification.

ENTRY INTO CHINA BY FOREIGN FIRMS AND CHINESE FIRMS REACHING FOR GLOBAL MARKETS

Many foreign firms choose to operate in the Chinese market because it is so large and important. This is certainly the case for automobile firms that have used China as a base to both produce cars more cheaply and expand their market by selling in China. In particular General Motors (GM), through its partnership with Shanghai Automotive Industry Corporation (SAIC), has created successful joint ventures. Because this venture continues to be successful, Fritz Henderson, GM's CEO since its bankruptcy filing, has indicated that none of GM's operations in China are for sale. In fact, GM is seeking to extend its operations in China, possibly with new ventures. Volkswagen also has a joint venture with SAIC. Recently SAIC has sought to introduce its own automobiles domestically and plans to participate in global markets when possible. Similarly, another GM partner in China, Liuzhou Wuling Motors Co., is planning to develop its own vehicles rather than through a GM brand such as Chevrolet.

Because the U.S. auto market and other auto markets elsewhere in the world are experiencing substantially lower sales, the Chinese market is becoming more important. Porsche AG now owns 50.76 percent of Volkswagen and is launching the first exposure of its new model, the Panamera, in a Shanghai auto show in April 2009. Although the U.S. market still counts as the most important sale zone for Porsche, China is expected to have the largest auto market by sales volume in 2009.

The Chinese market is not only important for manufacturing such as the automobile industry, but also for service industries. For example, Google recently launched a music service supported by

Peter Parks/AFP/Getty Images

Models pose next to a Porsche Panamera, a new four-door sports car making its international debut at Auto Shanghai, China's largest auto show.

the world's four largest music labels: Warner Music Group Corp., Vivendi SA's Universal Music, EMI Group Ltd., and Sony Corp.'s Music Entertainment. Google and its partners hope to draw users away from Google's main Chinese competitors, especially Baidu Inc. Baidu is the dominant market share holder, with approximately 62 percent of the search market for Web downloads in China. Google increased its search engine market in China to 28 percent in 2008, up from 23 percent in 2007, but Baidu retained its dominance with a 62 percent market share, up from 59 percent in 2007.

Interestingly, some Chinese firms are more successful abroad than they are in their home market. Huawei Technologies Co. Ltd. is making inroads in the U.S. market. Huawei, a Chinese telecom equipment supplier, recently won a contract with Cox Communications, a U.S. TV cable provider. Huawei is also in the running for a potentially bigger contract with Clearwire Corporation. Clearwire is in the process of helping to build a wireless broadband network that would serve 120 million people in the United States by 2010. Other finalists for the contract include Motorola Inc., Samsung Electronics Co., and Nokia Siemens Networks. More generally, other competitors include Alcatel-Lucent and Telefon AB L.M. Ericsson. Another Chinese company, ZTE, competes with these firms as well. Although Huwaei and ZTE have had more success in developing regions of the world, Huawei has become a major vendor in Europe, where it has won numerous contracts with significant telecom providers such as Vodaphone Group PLC and France Telecom SA's Orange. Huawei also has a foothold in Canada, where it is building a third-generation (3G) network for BCE Inc.'s partners Bell Canada and Telus Corp.

Additionally, Huawei and ZTE were laggards in selling telephone equipment in their home market against Telefon AB L.M. Ericsson, Alcatel-Lucent, and Nokia Siemens

Networks (a joint venture of Nokia Corp. and Siemens AG), mainly because they were an unknown company when the first wireless networks were developed in China. However, thanks to government support for new wireless technology and an aggressive strategy of deeply undercutting competitors' prices, these two firms are beating out their rivals for an estimated $59 billion of spending over the next three years for new 3G wireless networks. China has approximately 659 million mobile subscribers, and the rollout of 3G is making sales growth for these markets even more important. It is expected that Huawei and ZTE will double their combined market share for 3G revenue with current wireless network growth. Although Ericsson's market share is remaining stable, market shares for Alcatel-Lucent and Nokia Siemens are expected to decline in China. Historically, Ericsson won the lion's share because Huawei and ZTE, as noted, were small when the existing network was built in the 1990s. Both companies have access to large credit lines from China's state-owned banks and other perks such as low cost land. This has allowed them to have more flexibility in pricing and to operate with lower margins without shareholder pressure. It will be interesting to see what happens when the fourth-generation (4G) networks are rolled out in a few years.

Sources: A. Back & L. Chao, 2009, Google begins China music service; Partnership with record labels gives users free access to licensed tracks, *Wall Street Journal*, March 30, B3; L. Chao, 2009, China's telecom-gear makers, once laggards at home, pass foreign rivals, *Wall Street Journal*, April 10, B1; K. Hille & A. Parker, 2009, Upwardly mobile Huawei, *Financial Times*, http://www.ft.com, March 20; K. Li, 2009, Google launches China service, *Financial Times*, March 31, 20; C. Rauwald, 2009, Porsche chooses the China road; four-door Panamera's Shanghai debut signals focus on emerging markets, *Wall Street Journal*, April 20, B2; A. Sharma & S. Silver, 2009, Huawei tries to crack U.S. market; Chinese telecom supplier wins Cox contract, is finalist for Clearwire deal, *Wall Street Journal*, March 26, B2; N. Shirouzu, P. J. Ho, & K. Rapoza, 2009, Corporate news: GM plans to retain China, Brazil units. *Wall Street Journal* June 3, B2; J. D. Stoll, 2009, Corporate news: GM pushes the throttle in China—affiliate's plan to expand into cars is seen as a key to growth in Asia, *Wall Street Journal*, April 27, B3; M. B. Teagarden & D. H. Cai, 2009, Learning from dragons who are learning from us; developmental lessons from China's global companies, *Organizational Dynamics*, 38(1): 73; C.-C. Tschang, 2009, Search engine squeeze? *BusinessWeek*, January 12, 21; E. Woyke, 2009, ZTE's smart phone ambitions, *Forbes*, http://www.forbes.com, March 16; B. Einhorn, 2008, Huawei, *BusinessWeek*, December 22, 51; S. Tucker, 2008, Case study: Huawei of China takes stock after frustrating year, *Financial Times*, http://www.ft.com, November 25.

As the Opening Case indicates, firms are entering China because of its large market, but China's firms are building their competitive capabilities and also seeking to enter foreign markets. China's entrance into the World Trade Organization (WTO) brought change not only to China and its trading partners but also to industries and firms throughout the world. Despite its developing market and institutional environment, Chinese firms such as Huawei Technologies Co. are taking advantage of the growing size of the Chinese market; they had previously learned new technologies and managerial capabilities from foreign partners and are now competing more strongly in domestic as well as foreign markets.[1]

Many firms choose direct investment in assets in foreign countries (e.g., establishing new subsidiaries, making acquisitions, or building joint ventures) over indirect investment because it provides better protection for their assets.[2] As indicated in the Opening Case, Chinese firms are developing their manufacturing capabilities and building their own branded products (e.g., Huawei and ZTE Corporation). As such, the potential global market power of Chinese firms is astounding.[3]

As foreign firms enter China and as Chinese firms enter into other foreign markets, both opportunities and threats for firms competing in global markets are exemplified. This chapter examines opportunities facing firms as they seek to develop and exploit core competencies by diversifying into global markets. In addition, we discuss different problems, complexities, and threats that might accompany a firm's international strategy.[4] Although national boundaries, cultural differences, and geographic distances all pose barriers to entry into many markets, significant opportunities motivate businesses to enter international markets. A business that plans to operate globally must formulate a successful strategy to take advantage of these global opportunities.[5] Furthermore, to mold their firms into truly global companies, managers must develop global mind-sets.[6] As firms move into international markets, they develop relationships with suppliers, customers, and partners and learning from these relationships. For example, as the Opening Case illustrates, SAIC learned new capabilities from its partnerships with GM and Volkswagen.

As illustrated in Figure 1.1, we discuss the importance of international strategy as a source of strategic competitiveness and above-average returns. This chapter focuses on the incentives to internationalize. After a firm decides to compete internationally, it must select its strategy and choose a mode of entry into international markets. It may enter international markets by exporting from domestic-based operations, licensing some of its products or services, forming joint ventures with international partners, acquiring a foreign-based firm, or establishing a new subsidiary. Such international diversification can extend product life cycles, provide incentives for more innovation, and produce above-average returns. These benefits are tempered by political and economic risks and the problems of managing a complex international firm with operations in multiple countries.

Figure 8.1 provides an overview of the various choices and outcomes of strategic competitiveness. The relationships among international opportunities, the resources and capabilities that result from such strategies, and the modes of entry that are based on core competencies are explored in this chapter.

Identifying International Opportunities: Incentives to Use an International Strategy

An **international strategy** is a strategy through which the firm sells its goods or services outside its domestic market.[7] One of the primary reasons for implementing an international strategy (as opposed to a strategy focused on the domestic market) is that international markets yield potential new opportunities.[8]

Raymond Vernon captured the classic rationale for international diversification.[9] He suggested that typically a firm discovers an innovation in its home-country market, especially in an advanced economy such as that of the United States. Often demand for

An **international strategy** is a strategy through which the firm sells its goods or services outside its domestic market.

Figure 8.1 Opportunities and Outcomes of International Strategy

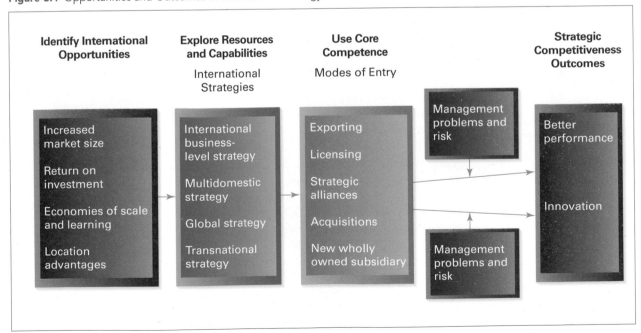

the product then develops in other countries, and exports are provided by domestic operations. Increased demand in foreign countries justifies making investments in foreign operations, especially to fend off foreign competitors. Vernon, therefore, observed that one reason why firms pursue international diversification is to extend a product's life cycle.

Another traditional motive for firms to become multinational is to secure needed resources. Key supplies of raw material—especially minerals and energy—are important in some industries. Other industries, such as clothing, electronics, and watchmaking, have moved portions of their operations to foreign locations in pursuit of lower production costs. Clearly one of the reasons for Chinese firms to expand internationally is to gain access to important resources.[10]

Although these traditional motives persist, other emerging motivations also drive international expansion (see Chapter 1). For instance, pressure has increased for a global integration of operations, mostly driven by more universal product demand. As nations industrialize, the demand for some products and commodities appears to become more similar. This borderless demand for globally branded products may be due to similarities in lifestyle in developed nations. Increases in global communication media also facilitate the ability of people in different countries to visualize and model lifestyles in different cultures.[11] IKEA, for example, has become a global brand by selling furniture in 44 countries through more than 300 stores that it owns and operates through franchisees. All of its furniture is sold in components that can be packaged in flat packs and assembled by the consumer after purchase. This arrangement has allowed for easier shipping and handling than fully assembled units and has facilitated the development of the global brand. Because of its low-cost approach, sales are increasing even during the economic downturn.[12]

In some industries, technology drives globalization because the economies of scale necessary to reduce costs to the lowest level often require an investment greater than that needed to meet domestic market demand. Companies also experience pressure for cost reductions, achieved by purchasing from the lowest-cost global suppliers. For instance, research and development expertise for an emerging business startup may not exist in the domestic market, but as foreign firms locate in the domestic market learning spillovers occur for domestic firms.[13]

New large-scale, emerging markets, such as China and India, provide a strong internationalization incentive based on their high potential demand for consumer products and services.[14] Because of currency fluctuations, firms may also choose to distribute their operations across many countries, including emerging ones, in order to reduce the risk of devaluation in one country.[15] However, the uniqueness of emerging markets presents both opportunities and challenges.[16] Even though India, for example, differs from Western countries in many respects, including culture, politics, and the precepts of its economic system, it also offers a huge potential market and its government is becoming more supportive of foreign direct investment.[17] However, the differences between China, India, and Western countries pose serious challenges to Western competitive paradigms that emphasize the skills needed to manage financial, economic, and political risks.[18]

Employment contracts and labor forces differ significantly in international markets. For example, it is more difficult to lay off employees in Europe than in the United States because of employment contract differences. In many cases, host governments demand joint ownership with a local company in order to invest in local operations; this allows the foreign firm to avoid tariffs. Also, host governments frequently require a high percentage of procurements, manufacturing, and R&D to use local sources.[19] These issues increase the need for local investment and responsiveness as opposed to seeking global economies of scale.

We've discussed incentives that influence firms to use international strategies. When these strategies are successful, firms can derive four basic benefits: (1) increased market size; (2) greater returns on major capital investments or on investments in new products and processes; (3) greater economies of scale, scope, or learning; and (4) a competitive advantage through location (e.g., access to low-cost labor, critical resources, or customers). We examine these benefits in terms of both their costs (such as higher coordination expenses and limited access to knowledge about host country political influences)[20] and their managerial challenges.

Increased Market Size

Firms can expand the size of their potential market—sometimes dramatically—by moving into international markets. Pharmaceutical firms have been doing significant foreign direct investment into both developed and emerging markets in an attempt to increase the market potential for new drugs. For example, when Japanese pharmaceutical firms made acquisitions of international rivals in 2008, one analyst noted: "One factor [driving the trend for outbound M&A] is that there are limited domestic growth opportunities… [These Japanese] companies are cash-rich and are in a good position to conduct acquisitions."[21] Indeed, Japan's large pharmaceutical firms collectively paid more than $20 billion during 2008 to buy overseas firms.

Although seeking to manage different consumer tastes and practices linked to cultural values or traditions is not simple, following an international strategy is a particularly attractive option to firms competing in domestic markets that have limited growth opportunities. For example, firms in the domestic soft drink industry have been searching for growth in foreign markets for some time now. Major competitors Pepsi and Coca-Cola have had relatively stable market shares in the United States for several years. Most of their sales growth has come from foreign markets. Coke, for instance, has used a strategy of buying overseas bottlers or expanding into other beverages such as fruit juice. However, a recent acquisition attempt of China's largest fruit-juice producer, China Huiyuan Juice Group Ltd., was turned down by Beijing regulators claiming that it would crowd out smaller players and increase consumer prices. China is Coke's fourth largest market by volume after the United States, Mexico, and Brazil. As with other emerging markets, it is growing faster than the U.S. market.[22]

The size of an international market also affects a firm's willingness to invest in R&D to build competitive advantages in that market. Larger markets usually offer higher potential returns and thus pose less risk for a firm's investments. The strength of the science base of the country in question also can affect a firm's foreign R&D investments.[23] Most firms prefer to invest more heavily in those countries with the scientific knowledge and talent to produce value-creating products and processes from their R&D activities.[24]

Return on Investment

Large markets may be crucial for earning a return on significant investments, such as plant and capital equipment or R&D. Therefore, most R&D-intensive industries such as electronics are international. In addition to the need for a large market to recoup heavy investment in R&D, the development pace for new technology is increasing. New products become obsolete more rapidly, and therefore investments need to be recouped more quickly. Moreover, firms' abilities to develop new technologies are expanding, and because of different patent laws across country borders, imitation by competitors is more likely. Through reverse engineering, competitors are able to disassemble a product, learn the new technology, and develop a similar product. Because competitors can imitate new technologies relatively quickly, firms need to recoup new product development costs even more rapidly. Consequently, the larger markets provided by international expansion are particularly attractive in many industries such as pharmaceutical firms, because they expand the opportunity for the firm to recoup significant capital investments and large-scale R&D expenditures.[25]

Regardless of other motives however, the primary reason for investing in international markets is to generate above-average returns on investments. Still, firms from different countries have different expectations and use different criteria to decide whether to invest in international markets, such as industry conditions and the potential for knowledge transfer.[26]

Economies of Scale and Learning

By expanding their markets, firms may be able to enjoy economies of scale, particularly in their manufacturing operations. To the extent that a firm can standardize its products across country borders and use the same or similar production facilities, thereby coordinating critical resource functions, it is more likely to achieve optimal economies of scale.[27]

Economies of scale are critical in the global auto industry. China's decision to join the World Trade Organization has allowed carmakers from other countries to enter their market and for lower tariffs to be charged (in the past, Chinese carmakers have had an advantage over foreign carmakers due to tariffs). Ford, Honda, General Motors, and Volkswagen are each producing an economy car to compete with the existing cars in China. Because of global economies of scale (allowing them to price their products competitively) and local investments in China, all of these companies are likely to obtain significant market share in China. Alternatively, SAIC is developing its branded vehicles to compete with the foreign automakers. SAIC's joint ventures with both GM and Volkswagen have been highly successful (as explained in the Opening Case). However, as also explained in the Opening Case, Porsche is seeking to market its vehicles in China to extend its scale economies, while Chinese firms are seeking to begin exporting vehicles overseas and perhaps enter foreign markets in other ways, such as through acquisitions.[28]

Firms may also be able to exploit core competencies in international markets through resource and knowledge sharing between units and network partners across country borders.[29] This sharing generates synergy, which helps the firm produce higher-quality goods or services at lower cost. In addition, working across international markets provides the firm with new learning opportunities.[30] Multinational firms have substantial occasions to learn from the different practices they encounter in separate international markets. However, research finds that to take advantage of international R&D investments, firms need to already have a strong R&D system in place to absorb the knowledge.[31]

Location Advantages

Firms may locate facilities in other countries to lower the basic costs of the goods or services they provide. These facilities may provide easier access to lower-cost labor, energy, and other natural resources. Other location advantages include access to critical supplies and to customers. Once positioned favorably with an attractive location, firms must manage their facilities effectively to gain the full benefit of a location advantage.[32]

Such location advantages can be influenced by costs of production and transportation requirements as well as by the needs of the intended customers.[33] Cultural influences may also affect location advantages and disadvantages. If there is a strong match between the cultures in which international transactions are carried out, the liability of foreignness is lower than if there is high cultural distance.[34] Research also suggests that regulation distances influence the ownership positions of multinational firms as well as their strategies for managing local and expatriate human resources.[35]

As suggested in the Opening Case, General Motors (GM) entered international markets to expand its market size. While GM has lost its position as the world's largest automaker after 76 years, even in bankruptcy it has expansion plans for its China ventures.[36] Still, GM faces a number of challenges from domestic Chinese competitors, such as its partners, SAIC and Liuzhou Wuling Motors Co., and from foreign competitors, such as Toyota and Volkswagen. It will have to formulate and implement a successful strategy for the Chinese market to maintain a competitive advantage there. Interestingly, given the downturn in sales, China may overtake the United States in domestic sales. An article in the *Wall Street Journal* noted: "China is expected to become the world's number one vehicle producer this year [2009], surpassing Japan. Mr. Young [chief financial officer of GM] said he is starting to think China could outmuscle the United States this year as the number one market for vehicle sales. GM had been predicting China would surpass the United States in 2015, but Chinese sales leapfrogged those in the United States in the first quarter [2009]."[37]

International Strategies

Firms choose to use one or both of two basic types of international strategies: business-level international strategy and corporate-level international strategy. At the business level, firms follow generic strategies: cost leadership, differentiation, focused cost leadership, focused differentiation, or integrated cost leadership/differentiation. The three corporate-level international strategies are multidomestic, global, or transnational (a combination of multidomestic and global). To create competitive advantage, each strategy must utilize a core competence based on difficult-to-imitate resources and capabilities.[38] As discussed in Chapters 4 and 6, firms expect to create value through the implementation of a business-level strategy and a corporate-level strategy.

International Business-Level Strategy

Each business must develop a competitive strategy focused on its own domestic market. We discussed business-level strategies in Chapter 4 and competitive rivalry and competitive dynamics in Chapter 5. International business-level strategies have some unique features. In an international business-level strategy, the home country of operation is often the most important source of competitive advantage.[39] The resources and capabilities established in the home country frequently allow the firm to pursue the strategy into markets located in other countries.[40] However, research indicates that as a firm continues its growth into multiple international locations, the country of origin is less important for competitive advantage.[41]

Michael Porter's model, illustrated in Figure 8.2, describes the factors contributing to the advantage of firms in a dominant global industry and associated with a specific home country or regional environment.[42] The first dimension in Porter's model is the factors of production. This dimension refers to the inputs necessary to compete in any industry—labor, land, natural resources, capital, and infrastructure (such as transportation, postal, and communication systems). There are basic factors (for example, natural and labor resources) and advanced factors (such as digital communication systems and a highly educated workforce). Other production factors are generalized (highway systems and the supply of debt capital) and specialized (skilled personnel in a specific industry, such as the workers in a port that specialize in handling bulk chemicals). If a country has both advanced and specialized production factors, it is likely to serve an industry well by spawning strong home-country competitors that also can be successful global competitors.

Ironically, countries often develop advanced and specialized factors because they lack critical basic resources. For example, some Asian countries, such as South Korea, lack abundant natural resources but offer a strong work ethic, a large number of engineers, and systems of large firms to create an expertise in manufacturing. Similarly, Germany developed a strong chemical industry, partially because Hoechst and BASF spent years creating a synthetic indigo dye to reduce their dependence on imports, unlike Britain, whose colonies provided large supplies of natural indigo.[43]

The second dimension in Porter's model, demand conditions, is characterized by the nature and size of buyers' needs in the home market for the industry's goods or services. A large market segment can produce the demand necessary to create scale-efficient facilities.

Figure 8.2 Determinants of National Advantage

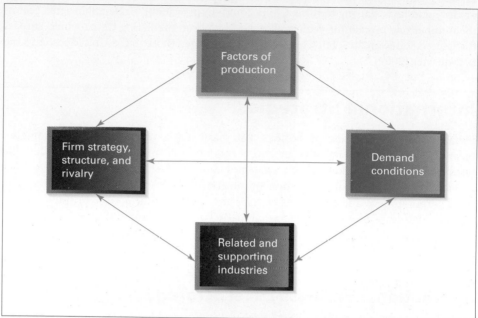

Chinese manufacturing companies have spent years focused on building their businesses in China, but are now beginning to look at markets beyond their borders, as described in the Opening Case about SAIC. As mentioned, SAIC (along with other Chinese firms) has begun the challenging process of building its brand equity in China but especially in other countries. In doing so, most Chinese firms begin in the Far East with the intention to move into Western markets when ready. Companies such as SAIC have been helped by China's entry to the World Trade Organization. Of course, companies such as SAIC are interested in entering international markets to increase their market share and profits.

Related and supporting industries are the third dimension in Porter's model. Italy has become the leader in the shoe industry because of related and supporting industries; a well-established leather-processing industry provides the leather needed to construct shoes and related products. Also, many people travel to Italy to purchase leather goods, providing support in distribution. Supporting industries in leather-working machinery and design services also contribute to the success of the shoe industry. In fact, the design services industry supports its own related industries, such as ski boots, fashion apparel, and furniture. In Japan, cameras and copiers are related industries. Similarly, it is argued that the creative resources associated with "popular cartoons such as Manga and the animation sector along with technological knowledge from the consumer electronics industry facilitated the emergence of a successful video game industry in Japan."[44]

Firm strategy, structure, and rivalry make up the final country dimension and also foster the growth of certain industries. The types of strategy, structure, and rivalry among firms vary greatly from nation to nation. The excellent technical training system in Germany fosters a strong emphasis on continuous product and process improvements. In Japan, unusual cooperative and competitive systems have facilitated the cross-functional management of complex assembly operations. In Italy, the national pride of the country's designers has spawned strong industries in sports cars, fashion apparel, and furniture. In the United States, competition among computer manufacturers and software producers has contributed to the development of these industries.

The four basic dimensions of the "diamond" model in Figure 8.2 emphasize the environmental or structural attributes of a national economy that contribute to national advantage. Government policy also clearly contributes to the success and failure of many firms and industries. For example, as illustrated in the Strategic Focus, the Chinese government has provided incentives for SunTech, a Chinese firm focused on creating solar power for utilities around the world, particularly in Europe.[45] SunTech is a "born global" firm that went directly into international markets that were emerging within the solar power industry. It has been successful so far because of the low-cost manufacturing and the high levels of engineering talent available in China. Likewise, Yandex in Russia (see the Strategic Focus) was successful because it found a way to meet the complexities of developing a search tool for the complex Russian language, which turned out to be an advantage in global competition.[46] Also, Yandex had strong demand conditions in Russia for Internet service and has been able to maintain its market share against strong competition from Google. Yandex is now entering the U.S. market and establishing a research base near Google's headquarters.

Although each firm must create its own success, not all firms will survive to become global competitors—not even those operating with the same country factors that spawned other successful firms. The actual strategic choices managers make

AP Photo/Ric Francis

NCsoft, a Korean game developer, has launched several successful online games featuring manga-inspired graphics.

may be the most compelling reasons for success or failure. Accordingly, the factors illustrated in Figure 8.2 are likely to produce competitive advantages only when the firm develops and implements an appropriate strategy that takes advantage of distinct country factors. Thus, these distinct country factors must be given thorough consideration when making a decision regarding the business-level strategy to use (i.e., cost leadership, differentiation, focused cost leadership, focused differentiation, and integrated cost leadership/differentiation, discussed in Chapter 4) in an international context. However, pursuing an international strategy leads to more adjustment and learning as the firm adjusts to competition in the host country. Such adjustments are continuous as illustrated by SunTech's operations, given the steep decline in demand for solar facilities in the economic downturn. It must adapt to the increasing competition from other startups and its major competitors in global markets.

International Corporate-Level Strategy

The international business-level strategies are based at least partially on the type of international corporate-level strategy the firm has chosen. Some corporate strategies give individual country units the authority to develop their own business-level strategies; other corporate strategies dictate the business-level strategies in order to standardize the firm's products and sharing of resources across countries.[47] International corporate-level strategy focuses on the scope of a firm's operations through both product and geographic diversification.[48] International corporate-level strategy is required when the firm operates in multiple industries and multiple countries or regions.[49] The headquarters unit guides the strategy, although business- or country-level managers can have substantial strategic

STRATEGIC FOCUS

COUNTRY CONDITIONS SPAWN SUCCESSFUL HIGH TECH FIRMS IN EMERGING MARKETS

Few firms from large emerging economies have been more successful than SunTech Power Holdings, which manufactures solar panels in China for the global electric utilities industry. It was a "born global" firm founded in China and quickly began competing with large firms that dominated the industry such as Sharpe, Siemens, and BP Solar. It was initiated by Shi Zhengrong and he is still the CEO. He was allocated $6 million startup money from the government of Wuxi in China's Jiangsu province. Shi was trained in Australia at the University of New South Wales in Sydney, where he earned his Ph.D.

SunTech's biggest markets for solar panels and modules are in Europe, with German companies providing its largest amount of revenue. It is listed on the U.S. stock exchange with an all-time stock price high of $85 in 2007. There was overcapacity in the industry in 2009, partly because SunTech spawned lots of imitators; however, iSuppli, a research company that provides analytical data for the solar industry, suggests that there will be 11.1 gigawatts of panels produced in 2009, which is up 62 percent from 7.7 gigawatts in 2008. SunTech itself produces one gigawatt and hoped to produce 1.4 gigawatts by the end of 2009 and two gigawatts by 2010. However, SunTech's expansion plans are currently on hold until the financial crisis is over and the markets improve; in fact, SunTech had to lay off 800 employees in 2008.

Fomichev Mikhail/ITAR-TASS/Landov

The big advantage that SunTech has is its low-cost production system in China. It hopes to have "grid parity," which means that the cost of producing solar energy is at the point where there is no difference between competing fossil fuels such as coal and natural gas relative to that produced by solar panels. Currently SunTech is producing at a cost of $.35 per kilowatt hour whereas the grid parity cost is near $.14. Although this suggests that the firm has a long way to go to realize grid parity, Shi believes it can be realized in several years given its low cost of production and improvements in technological efficiency. The company has improved the collective power of its solar panels primarily through advancements in silicon technology. Shi predicts that with the new Obama administration the subsidies will improve and stimulate demand, and that striving to reach grid parity will also help the company as it moves toward a "post carbon" future.

Russia's largest online search company, Yandex, is equivalent to Google in the United States. Interestingly, Yandex started in the 1980s, long before Google's founders Sergey Brin and Larry Page had envisioned their company. Yandex arguably has superior search technology because of the peculiarities of the Russian language. Russian words often have 20 different endings that indicate their relationship to one another and make the language much more precise, but at the same time it makes searching for Russian words much more difficult than searching for English words. However, Yandex found a way to catch all of this phraseology and as such it controls 56 percent of the search engine market share in Russia compared to Google's 23 percent. More impressively, it has two thirds of all of the revenue from the search ads and draws three billion hits a month. Because of this FireFox has dropped Google as its default search engine in Russia in favor of Yandex.

Nonetheless, Yandex realizes that it must continue to innovate. For instance, it has an image search engine that eliminates repeated images and filters out faces, thus it provides better search capabilities for imaging. In addition, as mentioned in the chapter, Yandex has opened labs not far from Google's headquarters in Mountain View, California, with a staff of 20 or more engineers who index pages for a Russian audience but also keep abreast of technology developments that surface near Silicone Valley. According to Arkady Volozh, CEO of Yandex, Yahoo!, Microsoft, and Google have made repeated buyout offers for Yandex. Such offers suggest that Google and other companies would be interested in increasing their market share in Russia. One reason for this interest is that Russia has the fastest-growing Internet population in Europe. Google has increased its market share from 6 percent in 2001 to 23 percent in 2009; most likely because it hired engineers who understand the Russian language. One analyst indicated that due to the high demand for Internet service "Russia is a pivotal country for Google."

Yandex is one of the few high tech companies that was home-grown in Russia and is successful. The Russians are proud of this fact. The company hopes to continue to be successful and possibly even compete for market share in the United States. Yandex has been given the opportunity to list on the Nasdaq Exchange; however, it has put off doing an IPO because of the financial crisis.

Sources: J. Ioffe, 2009, The Russians are coming, *Fortune*, February 16, 36–38; B. Powell, 2009, China's new king of solar, *Fortune*, February 16, 94–97; G. L. White, 2009, Russia Web firm negotiates autonomy, *Wall Street Journal*, April 22, A10; 2008, China-based SunTech plans to triple U.S. sales through acquisitions, residential sales, *FinancialWire*, http://www.financialwire.net, October 2; J. Bush, 2008, Where Google isn't Goliath: Russia's Yandex—set to go public on Nasdaq—is innovating in a hurry to hold off the U.S. giant, *BusinessWeek*, http://www.businessweek.com, June 26; P. Ghemawat & T. Hout, 2008, Tomorrow's global giants: Not the usual suspects, *Harvard Business Review*, 86(11): 80–88.

input, depending on the type of international corporate-level strategy followed. The three international corporate-level strategies are multidomestic, global, and transnational, as shown in Figure 8.3.

Multidomestic Strategy

A **multidomestic strategy** is an international strategy in which strategic and operating decisions are decentralized to the strategic business unit in each country so as to allow that unit to tailor products to the local market.[50] A multidomestic strategy focuses on competition within each country. It assumes that the markets differ and therefore are segmented by country boundaries. The multidomestic strategy uses a highly decentralized approach, allowing each division to focus on a geographic area, region, or country.[51] In other words, consumer needs and desires, industry conditions (e.g., the number and type of competitors), political and legal structures, and social norms vary by country. With multidomestic strategies, the country managers have the autonomy to customize the firm's products as necessary to meet the specific needs and preferences of local customers. Therefore, these strategies should maximize a firm's competitive response to the idiosyncratic requirements of each market.[52]

The use of multidomestic strategies usually expands the firm's local market share because the firm can pay attention to the needs of the local clientele.[53] However, the use of these strategies results in less knowledge sharing for the corporation as a whole because of the differences across markets, decentralization, and the different strategies employed by local country units.[54] Moreover, multidomestic strategies do not allow the development of economies of scale and thus can be more costly. As a result, firms employing a multidomestic strategy decentralize their strategic and operating decisions

A **multidomestic strategy** is an international strategy in which strategic and operating decisions are decentralized to the strategic business unit in each country so as to allow that unit to tailor products to the local market.

Figure 8.3 International Corporate-Level Strategies

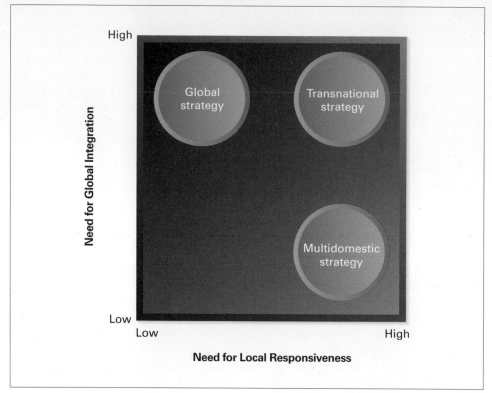

to the business units operating in each country. Historically, Unilever, a large European consumer products firm, has had a highly decentralized approach to managing its international operations. This approach allows regional managers considerable autonomy to adapt the product offerings to fit the market needs. However, more recently it has sought to have better coordination between its independent country subsidiaries and develop a strong global brand presence.[55]

Global Strategy

In contrast to a multidomestic strategy, a global strategy assumes more standardization of products across country markets.[56] As a result, a global strategy is centralized and controlled by the home office. The strategic business units operating in each country are assumed to be interdependent, and the home office attempts to achieve integration across these businesses.[57] The firm uses a **global strategy** to offer standardized products across country markets, with competitive strategy being dictated by the home office. Thus, a global strategy emphasizes economies of scale and offers greater opportunities to take innovations developed at the corporate level or in one country and utilize them in other markets.[58] Improvements in global accounting and financial reporting standards are facilitating this strategy.[59]

Although a global strategy produces lower risk, it may cause the firm to forgo growth opportunities in local markets, either because those markets are less likely to be identified as opportunities or because the opportunities require that products be adapted to the local market.[60] The global strategy is not as responsive to local markets and is difficult to manage because of the need to coordinate strategies and operating decisions across country borders. Yahoo! and eBay experienced these challenges when they moved into specific Asian markets. For example, eBay was unsuccessful in both the Japanese and Chinese markets when attempting to export its business model and approach from

A **global strategy** is an international strategy through which the firm offers standardized products across country markets, with competitive strategy being dictated by the home office.

North America to these two countries. It has reentered China but Meg Whitman, former CEO of eBay, suggested that she had no plans to reenter the Japanese market. Yahoo! has had rough times in China, going through several CEOs and trying to find the right formula to compete effectively in the Chinese market.[61] Also, as the Opening Case indicates, Google has had difficulty penetrating foreign markets such as China and competing against local competitors such as Baidu.

Achieving efficient operations with a global strategy requires sharing resources and facilitating coordination and cooperation across country boundaries, which in turn require centralization and headquarters control. Furthermore, research suggests that the performance of the global strategy is enhanced if it deploys in areas where regional integration among countries is occurring, such as the European Union.[62] Many Japanese firms have successfully used the global strategy.[63]

CEMEX is the third largest cement company in the world, behind France's Lafarge and Switzerland's Holcim, and is the largest producer of ready mix, a prepackaged product that contains all the ingredients needed to make localized cement products.

CEMEX has strong market power in the Americas as well as in Europe. CEMEX serves customers in more than 50 countries with more than 50,000 employees globally. Because CEMEX pursues a global strategy effectively, its centralization process has facilitated the integration of several businesses it acquired in the United States, Europe, and Asia. To integrate its businesses globally, CEMEX uses the Internet to improve logistics and manage an extensive supply network, thereby increasing revenue and reducing costs. Connectivity between the operations in different countries and universal standards dominates its approach. However, because of its recent acquisition of Ringer, a large Australian cement producer, it took on too much debt during the downturn and has had a very difficult time meeting its debt obligations.[64] Because of increasing global competition and the need to be cost efficient while simultaneously providing high-quality differentiated products, a number of firms have begun to pursue the transnational strategy, which is described next.

Transnational Strategy

A **transnational strategy** is an international strategy through which the firm seeks to achieve both global efficiency and local responsiveness. Realizing these goals is difficult: One requires close global coordination while the other requires local flexibility. "Flexible coordination"—building a shared vision and individual commitment through an integrated network—is required to implement the transnational strategy. Such integrated networks allow a firm to manage its connections with customers, suppliers, partners, and other parties more efficiently rather than using arm's-length transactions.[65] The transnational strategy is difficult to use because of its conflicting goals (see Chapter 11 for more on the implementation of this and other corporate-level international strategies). On the positive side, the effective implementation of a transnational strategy often produces higher performance than does the implementation of either the multidomestic or global international corporate-level strategies, although it is difficult to accomplish.[66]

Transnational strategies are challenging to implement but are becoming increasingly necessary to compete in international markets. The growing number of global competitors heightens the requirement to hold costs down. However, the increasing sophistication of markets with greater information flow (e.g., based on the diffusion of the Internet) and the desire for specialized products to meet consumers' needs pressures firms to differentiate and even customize their products in local markets. Differences in culture and institutional environments also require firms to adapt their products and approaches to local environments. However, some argue that most multinationals pursue more regional strategies and as such transnational strategies and structures may not be as necessary as once thought.[67]

A **transnational strategy** is an international strategy through which the firm seeks to achieve both global efficiency and local responsiveness.

Environmental Trends

Although the transnational strategy is difficult to implement, emphasis on global efficiency is increasing as more industries begin to experience global competition. To add to the problem, an increased emphasis on local requirements means that global goods and services often demand some customization to meet government regulations within particular countries or to fit customer tastes and preferences. In addition, most multinational firms desire coordination and sharing of resources across country markets to hold down costs, as illustrated by the CEMEX example.[68] Furthermore, some products and industries may be more suited than others for standardization across country borders.

As a result, some large multinational firms with diverse products employ a multidomestic strategy with certain product lines and a global strategy with others. Many multinational firms may require this type of flexibility if they are to be strategically competitive, in part due to trends that change over time. Two important trends are the liability of foreignness, which has increased since the terrorist attacks and the war in Iraq, and regionalization.

Liability of Foreignness

The dramatic success of Japanese firms such as Toyota and Sony in the United States and other international markets in the 1980s was a powerful jolt to U.S. managers and awakened them to the importance of international competition in markets that were rapidly becoming global markets. In the twenty-first century, China, India, Brazil, and Russia represent major international market opportunities for firms from many countries, including the United States, Japan, Korea, and the European Union.[69] However, there are legitimate concerns about the relative attractiveness of global strategies, due to the extra costs incurred to pursue internationalization, or the liability of foreignness relative to domestic competitors in a host country.[70] This is illustrated by the experience of Walt Disney Company in opening theme parks in foreign countries. For example, Disney suffered "lawsuits in France, at Disneyland Paris, because of the lack of fit between its transferred personnel policies and the French employees charged to enact them."[71] Disney executives learned from this experience in building the firm's newest theme park in Hong Kong.

Research shows that global strategies are not as prevalent as they once were and are still difficult to implement, even when using Internet-based strategies.[72] In addition, the amount of competition vying for a limited amount of resources and customers can limit firms' focus to regional rather than global markets. A regional focus allows firms to marshal their resources to compete effectively in regional markets rather than spreading their limited resources across many international markets.[73]

As such, firms may focus less on truly global markets and more on regional adaptation. Although parallel developments in the Internet and mobile telecommunication facilitate communications across the globe, as noted earlier, the implementation of Web-based strategies also requires local adaptation. The globalization of businesses with local strategies is demonstrated by the strategy that Google is using (see the Opening Case) by developing an online music download business in China.

Regionalization

Regionalization is a second trend that has become more common in global markets. Because a firm's location can affect its strategic competitiveness,[74] it must decide whether to compete in all or many global markets, or to focus on a particular region or regions. Competing in all markets provides economies that can be achieved because of the combined market size. Research suggests that firms that compete in risky emerging markets can also have higher performance.[75]

However, a firm that competes in industries where the international markets differ greatly (in which it must employ a multidomestic strategy) may wish to narrow its focus to a particular region of the world. In so doing, it can better understand the cultures, legal and social norms, and other factors that are important for effective competition in those markets. For example, a firm may focus on Far East markets only rather than competing simultaneously in the Middle East, Europe, and the Far East. Or the firm may choose a region of the world where the markets are more similar and some coordination and sharing of resources would be possible. In this way, the firm may be able not only to better understand the markets in which it competes, but also to achieve some economies, even though it may have to employ a multidomestic strategy. For instance, research suggests that most large retailers are better at focusing on a particular region rather than being truly global.[76] Firms commonly focus much of their international market entries into countries adjacent to their home country, which might be referred to as their home region.[77]

Countries that develop trade agreements to increase the economic power of their regions may promote regional strategies. The European Union (EU) and South America's Organization of American States (OAS) are country associations that developed trade agreements to promote the flow of trade across country boundaries within their respective regions.[78] Many European firms acquire and integrate their businesses in Europe to better coordinate pan-European brands as the EU creates more unity in European markets. With this process likely to continue as new countries are added to the agreement, some international firms may prefer to pursue regional strategies versus global strategies because the size of the market is increasing.[79]

The North American Free Trade Agreement (NAFTA), signed by the United States, Canada, and Mexico, facilitates free trade across country borders in North America. NAFTA loosens restrictions on international strategies within this region and provides greater opportunity for regional international strategies.[80] NAFTA does not exist for the sole purpose of U.S. businesses moving across its borders. In fact, Mexico is the number two trading partner of the United States, and NAFTA greatly increased Mexico's exports to the United States. Research suggests that managers of small- and medium-sized firms are influenced by the strategy they implement (those with a differentiation strategy are more positively disposed to the agreement than are those pursuing a cost leadership strategy) and by their experience and rivalry with exporting firms.[81]

Orlando Sierra/AFP/Getty Images

US Secretary of State Hillary Clinton and Hondoran President Manuel Zelaya meet with reporters following the 2009 general assembly meeting of the OAS in Hondoras.

Most firms enter regional markets sequentially, beginning in markets with which they are more familiar. They also introduce their largest and strongest lines of business into these markets first, followed by their other lines of business once the first lines achieve success. They also usually invest in the same area as their original investment location.[82] However, research also suggests that the size of the market and industry characteristics can influence this decision.[83]

After the firm selects its international strategies and decides whether to employ them in regional or world markets, it must choose a market entry mode.[84]

Choice of International Entry Mode

International expansion is accomplished by exporting products, participating in licensing arrangements, forming strategic alliances, making acquisitions, and establishing new wholly owned subsidiaries. These means of entering international markets and their characteristics are shown in Table 8.1. Each means of market entry has its advantages and disadvantages. Thus, choosing the appropriate mode or path to enter international markets affects the firm's performance in those markets.

Exporting

Many industrial firms begin their international expansion by exporting goods or services to other countries.[85] Exporting does not require the expense of establishing operations in the host countries, but exporters must establish some means of marketing and distributing their products. Usually, exporting firms develop contractual arrangements with host-country firms.

The disadvantages of exporting include the often-high costs of transportation and tariffs placed on some incoming goods. Furthermore, the exporter has less control over the marketing and distribution of its products in the host country and must either pay the distributor or allow the distributor to add to the price to recoup its costs and earn a profit.

As a result, it may be difficult to market a competitive product through exporting or to provide a product that is customized to each international market.[86] However, evidence suggests that cost leadership strategies enhance the performance of exports in developed countries, whereas differentiation strategies with larger scale are more successful in emerging economies.[87]

Firms export mostly to countries that are closest to their facilities because of the lower transportation costs and the usually greater similarity between geographic neighbors. For example, United States' NAFTA partners Mexico and Canada account for more than half of the goods exported from Texas. The Internet has also made exporting easier. Even small firms can access critical information about foreign markets, examine a target market, research the competition, and find lists of potential customers.[88] Governments also use the Internet to facilitate applications for export and import licenses. Although terrorist threat is likely to slow its progress, high-speed technology is still the wave of the future.[89]

Small businesses are most likely to use the exporting mode of international entry; up to 50 percent of small U.S. firms will be involved in international trade by 2018, most of them through export.[90] Currency exchange rates are one of the most significant problems faced by small businesses. The United States in recent years has supported a weak dollar against the euro, which makes imports to the United States more expensive to U.S. consumers and U.S. goods less costly to foreign buyers, thus providing some economic relief for U.S. exporters.[91]

Licensing

Licensing is an increasingly common form of organizational network, particularly among smaller firms.[92] A licensing arrangement allows a foreign company to purchase the right

Table 8.1 Global Market Entry: Choice of Entry

Type of Entry	Characteristics
Exporting	High cost, low control
Licensing	Low cost, low risk, little control, low returns
Strategic alliances	Shared costs, shared resources, shared risks, problems of integration (e.g., two corporate cultures)
Acquisition	Quick access to new market, high cost, complex negotiations, problems of merging with domestic operations
New wholly owned subsidiary	Complex, often costly, time consuming, high risk, maximum control, potential above-average returns

to manufacture and sell the firm's products within a host country or set of countries.[93] The licensor is normally paid a royalty on each unit produced and sold. The licensee takes the risks and makes the monetary investments in facilities for manufacturing, marketing, and distributing the goods or services. As a result, licensing is possibly the least costly form of international expansion.

China is a large and growing market for cigarettes, while the U.S. market is shrinking due to health concerns. But U.S. cigarette firms have had trouble entering the Chinese market because state-owned tobacco firms have lobbied against such entry. As such, cigarette company Philip Morris International (PMI), which was separated from its former parent company Altria, had an incentive to form a deal with these state-owned firms. Such an agreement provides the state-owned firms access to the most famous brand in the world, Marlboro. Accordingly, both the Chinese firms and PMI have formed a licensing agreement to take advantage of the opportunity as China opens its markets more fully.[94] Because it is a licensing agreement rather than a foreign direct investment by PMI, China maintains control of the distribution. However, the Chinese state-owned tobacco monopoly, as part of the agreement, also gets to have PMI's help to distribute its own brands in select foreign markets. "The question is whether it can pluck three cigarette brands—RGD, Harmony and Dubliss—from relative obscurity and elevate them to an international, or at least regional, presence."[95]

Licensing is also a way to expand returns based on prior innovations.[96] Even if product life cycles are short, licensing may be a useful tool. For instance, because the toy industry faces relentless change and unpredictable buying patterns, licensing is used and contracts are often completed in foreign markets where labor may be less expensive.[97] Google, as the Opening Case illustrates, facilitated license agreements with the top four music producers in support of its strategy to gain more market share from Baidu in China.

Licensing also has disadvantages. For example, it gives the firm little control over the manufacture and marketing of its products in other countries. Thus, license deals must be structured properly.[98] In addition, licensing provides the least potential returns, because returns must be shared between the licensor and the licensee. Additionally, the international firm may learn the technology and produce and sell a similar competitive product after the license expires. Komatsu, for example, first licensed much of its technology from International Harvester, Bucyrus-Erie, and Cummins Engine to compete against Caterpillar in the earthmoving equipment business. Komatsu then dropped these licenses and developed its own products using the technology it had gained from the U.S. companies.[99] Like most global hotel chains, Starwood Hotels & Resorts Worldwide Inc. uses a franchise licensing arrangement and does not own most of its hotels. While focusing on other brands, it has let its Sheraton brand slip in quality. Given the current economic downturn, it is going to be difficult to get the owners to invest in needed design improvements and upgrades, especially given the owner differences in varying geographic markets.[100] Thus licensing can also lead to inflexibilities, and as such it is important that a firm think ahead and consider the consequences of each entry, especially in international markets.[101]

Strategic Alliances

In recent years, strategic alliances have become a popular means of international expansion.[102] Strategic alliances allow firms to share the risks and the resources required to enter international markets.[103] Moreover, strategic alliances can facilitate the development of new core competencies that contribute to the firm's future strategic competitiveness.[104]

As explained in the Opening Case, GM formed a joint venture with SAIC. This venture produced Buick and Cadillac automobiles for the Chinese market. The alliance has been highly successful for both firms. Similar to this example, most international strategic alliances are formed with a host-country firm that knows and understands the competitive conditions, legal and social norms, and cultural idiosyncrasies of the country, which helps the expanding firm manufacture and market a competitive product.

Often, firms in emerging economies want to form international alliances and ventures to gain access to sophisticated technologies that are new to them. Gaining access to new technologies and markets is one of ZTE's goals in seeking alliances with the mobile phone systems of Sprint, AT&T, and Verizon. ZTE, as introduced in the Opening Case, is a telecommunications network gear producer; it also produces mobile phones. It now is working on agreements with these three phone companies to produce "smartphones" for 3G and 4G systems to advance its product portfolio.[105] This type of arrangement can also benefit the non-emerging economy firm, in that it gains access to a new market and does not have to pay tariffs to do so (because it is partnering with a local company). In return, the host-country firm may find its new access to the expanding firm's technology and innovative products attractive.

Each partner in an alliance brings knowledge or resources to the partnership. Indeed, partners often enter an alliance with the purpose of learning new capabilities.[106] Common among those desired capabilities are technological skills. However, for technological knowledge to be transferred in an alliance usually requires trust between the partners.[107] Managing these expectations can facilitate improved performance.

The alliance between GM and SAIC has been successful over the years because of the way it is managed. In fact, both firms are pleased with the outcomes. Research suggests that company executives need to know their own firm well, understand factors that determine the norms in different countries, know how the firm is seen by other partners in the venture, and learn to adapt while remaining consistent with their own company cultural values. Such a multifaceted and versatile approach has helped the GM and SAIC alliance succeed.

ZTE Corporation, one of the largest Chinese telecommunication equipment manufacturers, has set the goal of becoming the third largest global provider of handsets by 2014 based on sales of its newly unveiled portfolio of smartphones and other wireless devices.

Xinhua /Landov

Not all alliances are successful; in fact, many fail.[108] The primary reasons for failure include incompatible partners and conflict between the partners. International strategic alliances are especially difficult to manage. Several factors may cause a relationship to sour. Trust between the partners is critical and is affected by at least four fundamental issues: the initial condition of the relationship, the negotiation process to arrive at an agreement, partner interactions, and external events.[109] Trust is also influenced by the country cultures involved in the alliance or joint venture.[110]

Research has shown that equity-based alliances, over which a firm has more control, tend to produce more positive returns.[111] (Strategic alliances are discussed in greater depth in Chapter 9.) However, if trust is required to develop new capabilities in a research collaboration, equity can serve as a barrier to the necessary relationship building. If conflict in a strategic alliance or joint venture is not manageable, an acquisition may be a better option.[112] Alliances can also lead to an acquisition, which is discussed next.

Acquisitions

As free trade has continued to expand in global markets, cross-border acquisitions have also been increasing significantly. In 2008, cross-border acquisitions comprised about 40 percent of all acquisitions completed worldwide, down from 45 percent in previous years.[113] As explained in Chapter 7, acquisitions can provide quick access to a new market. In fact, acquisitions often provide the fastest and the largest initial international expansion of any of the alternatives.[114] Thus, entry is much quicker than by other modes. For example, Wal-Mart entered Germany and the United Kingdom by acquiring local firms. Later, Wal-Mart withdrew from Germany.[115]

Although acquisitions have become a popular mode of entering international markets, they are not without costs. International acquisitions carry some of the disadvantages of domestic acquisitions (see Chapter 7). In addition, they can be expensive and also often require debt financing, which carries an extra cost. International negotiations for acquisitions can be exceedingly complex and are generally more complicated than domestic acquisitions. For example, acquisitions are being used by firms in emerging economies to enter developed economies. China has been buying firms in foreign countries that have assets in natural resources. For instance, China Minmetals, a state-owned mining firm, tried to acquire Oz Minerals, the world's second largest zinc miner based in Australia. However, this acquisition, like many others, has been opposed by the government because of the potential for a sovereign power to take control of important natural resources.[116]

Interestingly, acquirers make fewer acquisitions in countries with significant corruption. They choose to use international joint ventures instead. However, these ventures fail more often, although this is moderated by the acquiring firms' past experience with such deals. When acquisitions are made in such countries, acquirers commonly pay smaller premiums to buy the target firms.[117]

Dealing with the legal and regulatory requirements in the target firm's country and obtaining appropriate information to negotiate an agreement are frequent problems. Finally, the merging of the new firm into the acquiring firm is often more complex than in domestic acquisitions. The acquiring firm must deal not only with different corporate cultures, but also with potentially different social cultures and practices.[118] These differences make the integration of the two firms after the acquisition more challenging; it is difficult to capture the potential synergy when integration is slowed or stymied because of cultural differences.[119] Therefore, while international acquisitions have been popular because of the rapid access to new markets they provide, they also carry with them important costs and multiple risks.

SAIC acquired assets of the MG Rover Group, the British auto producer, which was insolvent at the time. This acquisition gave the Chinese firm an entry point into Europe and an opportunity to establish its own brand through the MG Rover label. SAIC previously considered a joint venture but decided to make the acquisition bid, worth $104 million. However, SAIC experienced formidable government opposition in the United Kingdom and had to clear extra regulatory hurdles to receive approval. By 2008 it had not produced one of the MG roadsters that it had intended because of "quality issues."[120]

New Wholly Owned Subsidiary

The establishment of a new wholly owned subsidiary is referred to as a **greenfield venture.** The process of creating such ventures is often complex and potentially costly, but it affords maximum control to the firm and has the most potential to provide above-average returns. This potential is especially true of firms with strong intangible capabilities that might be leveraged through a greenfield venture.[121] A firm maintains full control of its operations with a greenfield venture. More control is especially advantageous if the firm has proprietary technology. Research also suggests that "wholly owned subsidiaries and expatriate staff are preferred" in service industries where "close contacts with end customers" and "high levels of professional skills, specialized know-how, and customization" are required.[122] Other research suggests that greenfield investments are more prominent where physical capital-intensive plants are planned and that acquisitions are more likely preferred when a firm is human capital intensive—that is, where a strong local degree of unionization and high cultural distance would cause difficulty in transferring knowledge to a host nation through a greenfield approach.[123]

The risks are also high, however, because of the costs of establishing a new business operation in a new country. The firm may have to acquire the knowledge and expertise of the existing market by hiring either host-country nationals, possibly from competitors, or through consultants, which can be costly. Still, the firm maintains control over the technology, marketing, and distribution of its products. Furthermore, the company must build new manufacturing facilities, establish distribution networks, and learn and

The establishment of a new wholly owned subsidiary is referred to as a **greenfield venture.**

implement appropriate marketing strategies to compete in the new market.[124] Research also suggests that when the country risk is high, firms prefer to enter with joint ventures instead of greenfield investments in order to manage the risk. However, if they have previous experience in a country, they prefer to use a wholly owned greenfield venture rather than a joint venture.[125]

The globalization of the air cargo industry has implications for companies such as UPS and FedEx. The impact of this globalization is especially pertinent to China and the Asia Pacific region. China's air cargo market is expected to grow 11 percent per year through 2023. Accordingly, in 2008, both UPS and FedEx opened new hub operations in Shanghai and Gangzhou, respectively; each firm has about 6,000 employees in China. These hubs facilitated their distribution and logistics business during the Olympics in Beijing. These investments are wholly owned because these firms need to maintain the integrity of their IT and logistics systems in order to maximize efficiency. Greenfield ventures also help the firms to maintain the proprietary nature of their systems.[126]

Dynamics of Mode of Entry

A firm's mode of entry into international markets is affected by a number of factors.[127] Initially, market entry is often achieved through export, which requires no foreign manufacturing expertise and investment only in distribution. Licensing can facilitate the product improvements necessary to enter foreign markets, as in the Komatsu example. Strategic alliances have been popular because they allow a firm to connect with an experienced partner already in the targeted market. Strategic alliances also reduce risk through the sharing of costs. Therefore, all three modes—export, licensing, and strategic alliance—are good tactics for early market development. Also, the strategic alliance is often used in more uncertain situations, such as an emerging economy where there is significant risk, such as Venezuela or Colombia.[128] However, if intellectual property rights in the emerging economy are not well protected, the number of firms in the industry is growing fast, and the need for global integration is high, a joint venture or wholly owned subsidiary entry mode is preferred.[129]

To secure a stronger presence in international markets, acquisitions or greenfield ventures may be required. Aerospace firms Airbus and Boeing have used joint ventures, especially in large markets, to facilitate entry, while military equipment firms such as Thales SA have used acquisitions to build a global presence. Japanese auto manufacturers, such as Toyota, have gained a presence in the United States through both greenfield ventures and joint ventures. Because of Toyota's highly efficient manufacturing process, it wants to maintain control over its auto manufacturing when possible. It has engaged in a joint venture in the United States with General Motors,[130] but most of its manufacturing facilities are greenfield investments. It opened a new plant in Canada in 2008 and plans on opening a new plant in Mississippi in 2010, although this project may be delayed or postponed given the economic downturn.[131] Therefore, Toyota uses some form of foreign direct investment (e.g., greenfield ventures and joint ventures) rather than another mode of entry (although it may use exporting in new markets as it did in China). Both acquisitions and greenfield ventures are likely to come at later stages in the development of an international strategy.

Large diversified business groups, often found in emerging economies, not only gain resources through diversification but also have specialized abilities in managing differences in inward and outward flows of foreign direct investment.[132] For instance, in India such groups have facilitated the development of a thriving pharmaceutical industry.[133]

Thus, to enter a global market, a firm selects the entry mode that is best suited to the situation at hand. In some instances, the various options will be followed sequentially, beginning with exporting and ending with greenfield ventures. In other cases, the firm may use several, but not all, of the different entry modes, each in different markets. The decision regarding which entry mode to use is primarily a result of the industry's competitive conditions, the country's situation and government policies, and the firm's unique set of resources, capabilities, and core competencies.

Strategic Competitive Outcomes

After its international strategy and mode of entry have been selected, the firm turns its attention to implementation issues (see Chapter 11). Implementation is highly important, because international expansion is risky, making it difficult to achieve a competitive advantage (see Figure 8.1). The probability the firm will be successful with an international strategy increases when it is effectively implemented.

International Diversification and Returns

Firms have numerous reasons to diversify internationally.[134] **International diversification** is a strategy through which a firm expands the sales of its goods or services across the borders of global regions and countries into different geographic locations or markets. Because of its potential advantages, international diversification should be related positively to firms' returns. Research has shown that, as international diversification increases, firms' returns decrease initially but then increase quickly as firms learn to manage international expansion.[135] In fact, the stock market is particularly sensitive to investments in international markets. Firms that are broadly diversified into multiple international markets usually achieve the most positive stock returns, especially when they diversify geographically into core business areas.[136] Many factors contribute to the positive effects of international diversification, such as private versus government ownership, potential economies of scale and experience, location advantages, increased market size, and the opportunity to stabilize returns. The stabilization of returns helps reduce a firm's overall risk.[137] All of these outcomes can be achieved by smaller and newer ventures, as well as by larger and established firms.

Toyota has found that international diversification allows it to better exploit its core competencies, because sharing knowledge resources across subsidiaries can produce synergy. Also, a firm's returns may affect its decision to diversify internationally. For example, poor returns in a domestic market may encourage a firm to expand internationally in order to enhance its profit potential. In addition, internationally diversified firms may have access to more flexible labor markets, as the Japanese do in the United States, and may thereby benefit from scanning international markets for competition and market opportunities. Also, through global networks with assets in many countries, firms can develop more flexible structures to adjust to changes that might occur. "Offshore outsourcing" has created significant value-creation opportunities for firms engaged in it, especially as firms move into markets with more flexible labor markets. Furthermore, offshoring increases exports to firms that receive the offshoring contract.[138]

International Diversification and Innovation

In Chapter 1, we indicated that the development of new technology is at the heart of strategic competitiveness. As noted in Porter's model (see Figure 8.2), a nation's competitiveness depends, in part, on the capacity of its industry to innovate. Eventually and inevitably, competitors outperform firms that fail to innovate and improve their operations and products. Therefore, the only way to sustain a competitive advantage is to upgrade it continually.[139]

International diversification provides the potential for firms to achieve greater returns on their innovations (through larger or more numerous markets) and reduces the often substantial risks of R&D investments. Therefore, international diversification provides incentives for firms to innovate. Additionally, the firm uses its primary resources and capabilities to diversify internationally and thus earn further returns on these capabilities (e.g., capability to innovate).[140]

In addition, international diversification may be necessary to generate the resources required to sustain a large-scale R&D operation. An environment of rapid technological obsolescence makes it difficult to invest in new technology and the capital-intensive operations necessary to compete in this environment. Firms operating solely in domestic markets may find such investments difficult because of the length of time required to

International diversification is a strategy through which a firm expands the sales of its goods or services across the borders of global regions and countries into different geographic locations or markets.

recoup the original investment. If the time is extended, it may not be possible to recover the investment before the technology becomes obsolete. However, international diversification improves a firm's ability to appropriate additional returns from innovation before competitors can overcome the initial competitive advantage created by the innovation. In addition, firms moving into international markets are exposed to new products and processes. If they learn about those products and processes and integrate this knowledge into their operations, further innovation can be developed. To incorporate the learning into their own R&D processes, firms must manage those processes effectively in order to absorb and use the new knowledge to create further innovations.[141]

The relationship among international diversification, innovation, and returns is complex. Some level of performance is necessary to provide the resources to generate international diversification, which in turn provides incentives and resources to invest in research and development. The latter, if done appropriately, should enhance the returns of the firm, which then provides more resources for continued international diversification and investment in R&D. Of course, these relationships have to be managed well by a firm's top level managers. Evidence suggests that more culturally diverse top management teams often have a greater knowledge of international markets and their idiosyncrasies, but their orientation to expand internationally can be affected by the nature of their compensation.[142] (Top management teams are discussed further in Chapter 12.) Moreover, managing the diverse business units of a multinational firm requires skill, not only in managing a decentralized set of businesses, but also coordinating diverse points of view derived from regionalized businesses without descending into chaos. Firms that are able to do this will challenge the best global industry incumbents.[143] This topic will be addressed next.

Complexity of Managing Multinational Firms

Although firms can realize many benefits by implementing an international strategy, doing so is complex and can produce greater uncertainty.[144] For example, multiple risks are involved when a firm operates in several different countries. Firms can grow only so large and diverse before becoming unmanageable, or before the costs of managing them exceed their benefits. Managers are constrained by the complexity and sometimes by the culture and institutional systems within which they must operate.[145] The complexities involved in managing diverse international operations are shown in the problems experienced by even high-performing firms such as Toyota. Toyota became overly focused on sales in the North American market and began to experience quality problems (i.e., increased number of recalls) and reduced customer satisfaction. It also was late in entering the Chinese market with manufacturing and as a result, it was behind the market leaders, Volkswagen and GM. However, by 2008 it had recovered and actually was outselling both firms in China, but only in passenger cars.[146] Other complexities include the highly competitive nature of global markets, multiple cultural environments, potentially rapid shifts in the value of different currencies, and the instability of some national governments.

Risks in an International Environment

International diversification carries multiple risks. Because of these risks, international expansion is difficult to implement and manage. The chief risks are political and economic. Specific examples of political and economic risks are shown in Figure 8.4.

Political Risks

Political risks are risks related to instability in national governments and to war, both civil and international. Instability in a national government creates numerous problems, including economic risks and uncertainty created by government regulation; the existence of many, possibly conflicting, legal authorities or corruption; and the potential nationalization of private assets.[147] Foreign firms that invest in another country may have

Figure 8.4 Risk in the International Environment

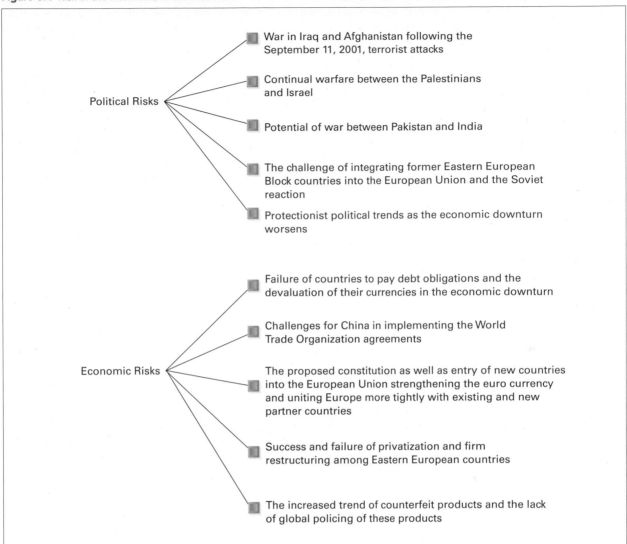

Sources: 2009, Euro-Zone PPI posts biggest annual drop in 22 years, *Wall Street Journal*, http://www.online.wsj.com, May 5; 2009, The nuts and bolts come apart: As global demand contracts, trade is slumping and protectionism rising, *Economist*, http://www.economist.com, March 26; 2009, New fund, old fundamentals: Has the IMF changed or has the world? *Economist*, http://www.economist.com, April 30; 2009, Competitive devaluations, *Financial Times*, http://www .ft.com, March 14; D. Bilefsky, 2009, A crisis is separating Eastern Europe's strong from its weak, *New York Times*, http://www.nytimes.com, February 23; I. Dreyer, 2009, Mending EU-China trade ties, *Wall Street Journal*, http://www.online.wsj.com, May 6; J. Garten, 2009, The dangers of turning inward, *Wall Street Journal*, http://www.online.wsj.com, March 5; S. Levine, 2009, Emergency loans for European banks: Three international development banks pledged nearly $30 billion to shore up the troubled Eastern European banking system, *BusinessWeek*, http://www.businessweek.com, February 28; M. Singh, 2009, India launches a toy trade war with China, *Time*, http://www.time.com, February 6; 2008, The best way to do business with Russia, *Financial Times*, http:// www.ft.com, August 21; 2008, Strong dollar, weak dollar, *Russia Today*, http://www.russiatoday.com, October 28; J. Barnham, 2008, China's pirates move up value chain, *Security Management*, June 44; L. Burkitt, 2008, Fighting fakes, *Forbes*, August 11, 44; B. Szlanko, 2008, Will the crisis spur Hungary to reform? *BusinessWeek*, http://www.businessweek.com, November, 13; B. Szlanko, Europe: Tougher than it looks on Russia, *BusinessWeek*, http://www.businessweek .com, September 4; C.-C. Tschang, 2008, Currency stalemate at U.S.-China meeting, *BusinessWeek*, http://www.businessweek.com, December 5.

concerns about the stability of the national government and the effects of unrest and government instability on their investments or assets.[148]

Russia has experienced a relatively high level of institutional instability in the years following its revolutionary transition to a more democratic government. Decentralized political control and frequent changes in policies created chaos for many, but especially for those in the business landscape. In an effort to regain more central control and reduce the chaos, Russian leaders took actions such as prosecuting powerful private firm executives, seeking to gain state control of firm assets, and not approving some foreign acquisitions of Russian businesses. The initial institutional instability, followed by the actions of the central government, caused some firms to have delayed or negated significant foreign direct investment in Russia. Although leaders in Russia have tried to reassure potential investors about their property rights, prior actions, the fact that other laws (e.g., environmental and employee laws) are weak, and the fact that government corruption is common makes firms leery of investing in Russia.[149]

Economic Risks

As illustrated in the example of Russian institutional instability and property rights, economic risks are interdependent with political risks. If firms cannot protect their intellectual property, they are highly unlikely to make foreign direct investments. Countries therefore need to create and sustain strong intellectual property rights and enforce them in order to attract desired foreign direct investment. As noted in the Strategic Focus, there is a growing problem with the continuing trend of counterfeit or fake products, especially as the market for these products becomes globalized. Firms like eBay get caught up in the struggle when authentic producers desire to punish the counterfeit producers for selling products on the Internet.

Another economic risk is the perceived security risk of a foreign firm acquiring firms that have key natural resources or firms that may be considered strategic in regard to intellectual property. For instance, many Chinese firms have been buying natural resource firms in Australia and Latin America as well as manufacturing assets in the United States. This has made the governments of the key resource firms nervous about such strategic assets falling under the control of state-owned Chinese firms.[150] Terrorism has also been of concern. Indonesia has difficulty competing for investment against China and India, countries that are viewed to have fewer security risks.

As noted earlier, foremost among the economic risks of international diversification are the differences and fluctuations in the value of different currencies.[151] The value of the dollar relative to other currencies determines the value of the international assets and earnings of U.S. firms; for example, an increase in the value of the U.S. dollar can reduce the value of U.S. multinational firms' international assets and earnings in other countries. Furthermore, the value of different currencies can also, at times, dramatically affect a firm's competitiveness in global markets because of its effect on the prices of goods manufactured in different countries.[152] An increase in the value of the dollar can harm U.S. firms' exports to international markets because of the price differential of the products. Thus, government oversight and control of economic and financial capital in the country affect not only local economic activity, but also foreign investments in the country. Certainly, the political and policy changes in Eastern Europe have stimulated much more FDI due to the significant changes there since the early 1990s.[153]

Google is the market leader in the Internet search markets in the United States and Europe. However, its expansion into Russia and Asian countries has experienced difficulties. As noted earlier, in the Strategic Focus, it has dominant competitors in Russia (Yandex) and China (Baidu). It learned from its previous difficulties and is managing with a persistent strategy, but these competitors are dominating, especially given the additional support that they receive from their local governments, formally and informally.

Limits to International Expansion: Management Problems

After learning how to operate effectively in international markets, firms tend to earn positive returns on international diversification. But, the returns often level off and become negative as the diversification increases past a certain point.[154] Several reasons explain the limits to the positive effects of international diversification. First, greater geographic dispersion across country borders increases the costs of coordination between units and the distribution of products. Second, trade barriers, logistical costs, cultural diversity, and other differences by country (e.g., access to raw materials and different employee skill levels) greatly complicate the implementation of an international diversification strategy.

Institutional and cultural factors can present strong barriers to the transfer of a firm's competitive advantages from one country to another. Marketing programs often have to be

THE CONTINUING THREAT TO LEGITIMATE COMPANIES FROM COUNTERFEIT OR FAKE PRODUCTS

The International Anti-Counterfeiting Coalition has estimated that counterfeit or fake products make up 7 percent of the world's goods. This is an issue of growing importance, especially for firms competing on a more global basis and for firms that have significant profit margins associated with intellectual property rights, such as software makers, entertainment content businesses (i.e., music producers), and branded products. As businesses or governments implement solutions to overcome counterfeit products, the "pirates" often move up the value chain to copy more high-tech, high-margin products. China's rock bottom production costs have turned it into the "world's workshop and [have] empowered an economic boom;" however, China's environment, because of lax legal enforcement, creates an incentive for counterfeit product makers to create fake products and software and also to supply "nonstandard" electronic components, which are less traceable.

For example, Philip Morris has filed a compliant with the International Trade Commission (ITC) to stop illegal import of "gray market" cigarettes from China and other regions bearing Philip Morris USA's trademarks, including Marlboro. Charlie Whitaker, the vice president of compliance and brand integrity for Philip Morris USA, suggests that "our brands are among our company's most valuable assets and we take many steps to protect them." The firm complains that Internet-based cigarette vendors are selling Philip Morris–labeled products in violation of U.S. intellectual property laws and the Lanham Act.

Many of the counterfeit products are sold on the Internet, similar to the cigarette example. French perfume producer L'Oréal has mounted a legal challenge to eBay for sales of fake products using its brand. L'Oréal argues that by failing to police fake products, eBay is in fact acting in concert with the sellers of those goods. Of course, eBay denies the claim saying that it is simply providing a trading platform and that the responsibility for looking after L'Oréal's trademarks should rest with L'Oréal. Interestingly, luxury good manufacturers LVMH and Hermes have won rulings in French courts on similar issues against eBay, but eBay has triumphed in other cases, such as one in a Belgium court.

Some counterfeit products are more than just a nuisance—they are dangerous. One firm identified bogus pesticides used to treat crops that could create health risks and reduce farmers' livelihoods. Additionally, the U.S. military is facing a growing threat from fatal equipment failures and even foreign espionage through computer components that might be embedded in war planes, ships, and communication networks. For instance, BEA Systems experienced field failures of some military equipment with bogus parts, and

Mario Tama/Getty Images

Brooklyn district attorney displays seized counterfeit goods as evidence for court proceedings.

some defense contractors have traced Chinese producers to fake microchips as well as tiny electronic circuits found in computer equipment and other electric gear. Because of these threats, the Pentagon has established more secure buying procedures to prevent the spread of counterfeit military-grade chips as aging equipment needs updating.

These and other problems illustrate the importance of protecting intellectual property and the risks associated with pursuing global trade and production. Firms might pursue legal challenges, but this is often difficult in emerging economies such as China and Russia, where there is weak legal protection. Some products such as fashion and clothing items can be protected with more sophisticated labels that guard against counterfeiters. As firms pursue international strategies by using strategies based on intellectual property and which require significant R&D investments, the loss of such intellectual property to counterfeiting increases and proactive strategies must be taken to protect against significant losses.

Sources: M. Murphy & N. Tait, 2009, L'Oréal mounts legal challenges over eBay sales, *Financial Times*, March 10, 4; J. Barnham, 2008, China's pirates move up value chain, *Security Management*, June 44; L. Burkitt, 2008, Fighting fakes, *Forbes*, August 11, 44; M. Fairley, 2008, Brand protection: Label makers become vital security link in anti-counterfeiting, *Converting Magazine*, August, 20; B. Grow, C.-C. Tschang, B. Burnsed, & K. Epstein, 2008, Dangerous fakes, *BusinessWeek*, October 13, 34–37; J. Slota & M. Humphreys, 2008, Connect the dots, *Pharmaceutical Executive*, July 67–70; 2008, Alarm at flood of bogus pesticides, *Financial Times*, May 20, 12.

STRATEGY RIGHT NOW

Learn how leading companies such as Unilever are using information technologies to help manage international diversification.

www.cengage.com/management/hitt

redesigned and new distribution networks established when firms expand into new countries. In addition, firms may encounter different labor costs and capital charges. In general, it is difficult to effectively implement, manage, and control a firm's international operations.

The amount of international diversification that can be managed varies from firm to firm and according to the abilities of each firm's managers. The problems of central coordination and integration are mitigated if the firm diversifies into more friendly countries that are geographically close and have cultures similar to its own country's culture. In that case, the firm is likely to encounter fewer trade barriers, the laws and customs are better understood, and the product is easier to adapt to local markets.[155] For example, U.S. firms may find it less difficult to expand their operations into Mexico, Canada, and Western European countries than into Asian countries.

Management must also be concerned with the relationship between the host government and the multinational corporation.[156] Although government policy and regulations are often barriers, many firms, such as Toyota and General Motors, have turned to strategic alliances, as they did in China, to overcome those barriers. By forming interorganizational networks, such as strategic alliances (see Chapter 9), firms can share resources and risks but also build flexibility. However, large networks can be difficult to manage.[157]

SUMMARY

- The use of international strategies is increasing. Traditional motives include extending the product life cycle, securing key resources, and having access to low-cost labor. Emerging motives include the integration of the Internet and mobile telecommunications, which facilitates global transactions. Also, firms experience increased pressure for global integration as the demand for commodities becomes borderless, and yet they feel simultaneous pressure for local country responsiveness.

- An international strategy is commonly designed primarily to capitalize on four benefits: increased market size; earning a

return on large investments; economies of scale and learning; and advantages of location.

- International business-level strategies are usually grounded in one or more home-country advantages, as Porter's model suggests. Porter's model emphasizes four determinants: factors of production; demand conditions; related and supporting industries; and patterns of firm strategy, structure, and rivalry.

- There are three types of international corporate-level strategies. A multidomestic strategy focuses on competition within each country in which the firm competes. Firms using a multidomestic strategy decentralize strategic and operating decisions to the business units operating in each country, so that each unit can tailor its goods and services to the local market. A global strategy assumes more standardization of products across country boundaries; therefore, a competitive strategy is centralized and controlled by the home office. A transnational strategy seeks to integrate characteristics of both multidomestic and global strategies to emphasize both local responsiveness and global integration and coordination. This strategy is difficult to implement, requiring an integrated network and a culture of individual commitment.

- Although the transnational strategy's implementation is a challenge, environmental trends are causing many multinational firms to consider the need for both global efficiency and local responsiveness. Many large multinational firms, particularly those with many diverse products, use a multidomestic strategy with some product lines and a global strategy with others.

- The threat of wars and terrorist attacks increases the risks and costs of international strategies. Furthermore, research suggests that the liability of foreignness is more difficult to overcome than once thought.

- Some firms decide to compete only in certain regions of the world, as opposed to viewing all markets in the world as potential opportunities. Competing in regional markets allows firms and managers to focus their learning on specific markets, cultures, locations, resources, and other factors.

- Firms may enter international markets in one of several ways, including exporting, licensing, forming strategic alliances, making acquisitions, and establishing new wholly owned subsidiaries,

often referred to as greenfield ventures. Most firms begin with exporting or licensing, because of their lower costs and risks, but later they might use strategic alliances and acquisitions to expand internationally. The most expensive and risky means of entering a new international market is through the establishment of a new wholly owned subsidiary. On the other hand, such subsidiaries provide the advantages of maximum control by the firm and, if it is successful, the greatest returns.

- International diversification facilitates innovation in a firm, because it provides a larger market to gain more and faster returns from investments in innovation. In addition, international diversification may generate the resources necessary to sustain a large-scale R&D program.

- In general, international diversification is related to above-average returns, but this assumes that the diversification is effectively implemented and that the firm's international operations are well managed. International diversification provides greater economies of scope and learning which, along with greater innovation, help produce above-average returns.

- Several risks are involved with managing multinational operations. Among these are political risks (e.g., instability of national governments) and economic risks (e.g., fluctuations in the value of a country's currency).

- Some limits also constrain the ability to manage international expansion effectively. International diversification increases coordination and distribution costs, and management problems are exacerbated by trade barriers, logistical costs, and cultural diversity, among other factors.

REVIEW QUESTIONS

1. What are the traditional and emerging motives that cause firms to expand internationally?

2. What are the four primary benefits of an international strategy?

3. What four factors provide a basis for international business-level strategies?

4. What are the three international corporate-level strategies? How do they differ from each other? What factors lead to their development?

5. What environmental trends are affecting international strategy?

6. What five modes of international expansion are available, and what is the normal sequence of their use?

7. What is the relationship between international diversification and innovation? How does international diversification affect innovation? What is the effect of international diversification on a firm's returns?

8. What are the risks of international diversification? What are the challenges of managing multinational firms?

EXPERIENTIAL EXERCISES

EXERCISE 1: MCDONALD'S: GLOBAL, MULTICOUNTRY, OR TRANSNATIONAL STRATEGY?

McDonald's is one of the world's best-known brands: the company has approximately 31,000 restaurants located in more than 118 countries and serves 58 million customers *every day*. McDonald's opened its first international restaurant in Japan in 1971. Its Golden Arches are featured prominently in two former

bastions of communism: Puskin Square in Moscow and Tiananmen Square in Beijing, China.

What strategy has McDonald's used to achieve such visibility? For this exercise, each group will be asked to conduct some background research on the firm and then make a brief presentation to identify the international strategy (i.e., global, multidomestic, or transnational) McDonald's is implementing.

Individual

Use the Internet to find examples of menu variations in different countries. How much do menu items differ for a McDonald's in the United States from other locations outside the United States?

Groups

Review the characteristics of global, multidomestic, and transnational strategies. Conduct additional research to assess what strategy best describes the one McDonald's is using. Prepare a flip chart with a single page of bullet points to explain your reasoning.

Whole Class

Each group should have five to seven minutes to explain its reasoning. Following Q&A for each group, ask class members to vote for the respective strategy choices.

EXERCISE 2: DOES THE WORLD NEED MORE BURRITOS?

Chipotle Mexican Grill (CMG) is a public company listed on the NYSE, founded in 1993. The highly recognizable brand is prolific in the United States with 837 company-operated units as of the end of 2008. There is one operating store in Toronto as of this time, which represents the only non–U.S. concern. There are plans to open about 120 new stores in 2009. Even though there are quite a few U.S. states in which the firm has no locations, the management team has been seriously considering an international expansion program.

For purposes of this exercise, assume you have been retained by the top management team of Chipotle to evaluate its international expansion options. Management has concluded that the following options are the most promising:

1. Continue expansion throughout the United States.
2. Expand into Mexico.
3. Increase expansion throughout Canada.
4. Expand to the United Kingdom.

Part One

Working in teams, select one of the four options above as approved by the instructor. Next, with Porter's determinates of national advantage as a foundation, identify the factors that work either in favor of or against your strategy.

To begin this assignment, each team must prepare a strategy for expansion. Using information gleaned from the 2008 annual report; identify Chipotle's main strategies for growth. For instance, what is their position on franchise vs. company-owned stores (this helps determine cash needs)? What are their most significant needs for expansion regarding resources? (Hint: Think through their "Food with Integrity" program.)

Conduct research on your team's selected area for expansion on the following criteria:

- Economic characteristics: Gross national product, wages, unemployment, inflation, and so on. Trend analysis of these data (e.g., are wages rising or falling, rate of change in wages, etc.) is preferable to single point-in-time snapshots.
- Social characteristics: Life expectancy, education norms, income distributions, literacy, and so on.
- Risk factors: Economic and political risk assessment.

The following Internet resources may be useful in your research:

- The Library of Congress has a collection of country studies.
- BBC News offers country profiles online.
- *The Economist Intelligence Unit* (http://www.eiu.com) offers country profiles.
- Both the United Nations and International Monetary Fund provide statistics and research reports.
- The *CIA World Factbook* has profiles of different regions.
- *The Global Entrepreneurship Monitor* provides reports with detailed information about economic conditions and social aspects for a number of countries.
- Links can be found at http://www.countryrisk.com to a number of resources that assess both political and economic risk for individual countries.
- For U.S. data, see http://www.census.gov.

Part Two

Based on your research, each team is to prepare a presentation (10 to 15 minutes) highlighting the strategic advantages and disadvantages of their assigned country's opportunities and threats as regards expansion potential. Each team must also decide which corporate level strategy should be utilized if their country expansion were chosen and why.

Next, as a class, be prepared to discuss what the overall consensus would be if you were making the decision at Chipotle.

VIDEO CASE

UNDERSTAND THE DIFFERENCES WHEN DOING BUSINESS ABROAD

Andrew Sherman/Co-Founder/Grow Fast Grow Right

Andrew Sherman, cofounder of Grow Fast Grow Right, suggests that global business strategy is like the pizza business. There are four key elements: crust; cheese; sauce; and toppings. Further, he argues that only one of those four should vary by international location, the toppings.

Before you watch the video consider the following concepts and questions and be prepared to discuss them in class:

Concepts

- International expansion
- Cultural differences
- Risks
- Organizational size
- Transnational strategy

Questions

1. Given the international experience you have had or observed, do you also feel that Mr. Sherman's pizza analogy is appropriately applied to international strategy?

2. What do you consider some of the mistakes that might occur when companies go international?

3. How can a company better understand the cultures and methods of business when entering a new location?

4. Is it harder or easier for a small entrepreneurial firm to go international than a large firm?

CHAPTER 9

Cooperative Implications for Strategy

Studying this chapter should provide you with the strategic management knowledge needed to:

1. Define cooperative strategies and explain why firms use them.

2. Define and discuss three types of strategic alliances.

3. Name the business-level cooperative strategies and describe their use.

4. Discuss the use of corporate-level cooperative strategies in diversified firms.

5. Understand the importance of cross-border strategic alliances as an international cooperative strategy.

6. Explain cooperative strategies' risks.

7. Describe two approaches used to manage cooperative strategies.

USING COOPERATIVE STRATEGIES AT IBM

A company widely known throughout the world, IBM, has over 350,000 employees working in design, manufacturing, sales, and service advanced information technologies such as computer systems, storage systems, software, and microelectronics. The firm's extensive lineup of products and services is grouped into three core business units—Systems and Financing, Software, and Services.

As is true for all companies, IBM uses three means to grow—internal developments (primarily through innovation), mergers and acquisitions (such as the recent purchase of France-based ILOG, which produces software tools to automate and speed up a firm's decision-making process), and cooperative strategies. Interestingly, IBM had a ten-year partnership with ILOG before making the acquisition. By cooperating with other companies, IBM is able to leverage its core competencies to grow and improve its performance.

Through cooperative strategies (e.g., strategic alliances and joint ventures, both of which are defined and discussed in this chapter), IBM finds itself working with a variety of firms in order to deliver products and services. However, IBM has specific performance-related objectives it wants to accomplish as it engages in an array of cooperative arrangements. For example, with regard to its systems business, IBM works to develop leading-edge chip technology. In order to do this it has formed five separate alliances to develop the most advanced semiconductor research and expand its facilities by purchasing the latest chip-making equipment. These allies provide brainpower, including more than 250 scientists and engineers that work along with IBM's engineers and scientists to foster innovation. Some of these innovations come through new advances in materials and chemistry. For instance, IBM signed an agreement with Japan's JSR, a Japanese firm engaged in materials science, to develop materials and processes for circuitry necessary to advance futuristic semiconductors.

Alessandro Della Bella/Keystone/Landor

IBM works in collaboration with several companies in Europe such as CEA, a French public research and technology organization focused on semiconductor and nano-electronics technology.

Even during the economic downturn, IBM's business analytics business is growing. The ILOG acquisition, noted previously, is an example of IBM's thrust into this area. IBM has created a new unit called IBM Business Analytics and Optimization Services. This business provides software solutions to help a firm better analyze data and make smarter decisions. It has 4,000 consultants who examine IBM's research and software divisions for algorithms, applications, and other innovations to help provide solutions to companies. This is just one aspect of the services business that IBM pursues with its consulting services. Of course it needs software to produce the solutions. Many of these solutions come through partnerships with small providers that IBM manages through cooperative agreements and often these cooperative agreements lead to an acquisition (see for instance the ILOG acquisition noted earlier).

However, other firms are entering into this space through their own acquisitions or alliances. For instance, Sun Microsystems had an alliance with IBM to produce software in competition with Hewlett-Packard. IBM bid for Sun in an acquisition attempt but was bested by Oracle, which won with a $7.3 billion bid. Thus the competition for the solutions service and network business has heated up through acquisitions and especially through partnerships, which IBM has used to facilitate its change from solely producing hardware to adding solution services and software. One study concluded that IBM was able to make this significant shift by managing its alliance of networks according to three principles. First, that company alliance networks may be used not just for individual projects but to facilitate strategic change inside a company; second, that two principal mechanisms can bring about this change: (1) increasing speed of change through partners and (2) finding partners in areas outside existing competencies; and finally, that companies can shape their alliance networks by conscious actions. Other firms are observing IBM's actions and learning and seeking to catch up fast through their own partnerships, as illustrated by a recent partnership between Cisco and the Japanese firm Fujitsu. These two firms are traditionally hardware firms that build networks, such as for phone companies, but are moving to increase their service options, especially among mobile telephone providers.

As one might anticipate, a firm as large and diverse as IBM is involved with a number of cooperative relationships. Given the challenges associated with achieving and maintaining superior performance, and in light of its general success with cooperative relationships, IBM will likely continue to use cooperative strategies as a path toward growth and enhanced performance.

Sources: R. Agarwal & C. E. Helfat, 2009, Strategic renewal of organizations, *Organization Science*, 20(2): 281–293; W. M. Bulkeley, 2009, Corporate news: IBM buoyed by its balance of business, *Wall Street Journal*, April 20, B3; W. M. Bulkeley, 2009, IBM results are clouded by Oracle's deal for Sun, *Wall Street Journal*, April 21, B1; S. Hamm, 2009, Big blue goes into analysis, *BusinessWeek*, April 27, 16; J. Menn, 2009, IBM focuses on software and services to meet targets, *Financial Times*, April 21, 19; J. M. O'Brien, 2009, IBM's grand plan to save the planet, *Fortune*, May 4, 84–91; 2009, IBM completes acquisition of ILOG, *2009 Journal OR-MS Today*, 36(1): 60; W. M. Bulkeley, 2008, Business technology, A service rival looms for IBM; H-P deal for EDS to pose challenge for big blue unit, *Wall Street Journal*, May 20, B6; K. Dittrich, G. Duysters, & A.-P. de Man, 2007, Strategic repositioning by means of alliance networks: The case of IBM, *Research Policy*, 36: 1496–1511; S. Hamm, 2007, Radical collaboration: Lessons from IBM's innovation factory, *BusinessWeek*, September 10, 16.

As noted in the Opening Case, firms use three means to grow and improve their performance—internal development, mergers and acquisitions, and cooperation. In each of these cases, the firm seeks to use its resources in ways that will create the greatest amount of value for stakeholders.[1]

Recognized as a viable engine of firm growth,[2] a **cooperative strategy** is a means by which firms work together to achieve a shared objective.[3] Thus, cooperating with other firms is another strategy firms use to create value for a customer at a lower cost than it would to do it by the firm itself and thereby establish a favorable position relative to competition.[4]

As explained in the Opening Case, IBM is involved with a number of cooperative arrangements. The intention of serving customers better than its competitors serve them and of gaining an advantageous position relative to competitors drive this firm's use of cooperative strategies. IBM's corporate-level cooperative strategy in services and software finds it seeking to deliver server technologies in ways that maximize customer value while improving the firm's position relative to competitors. For example, Hewlett-Packard recently bought EDS to battle IBM for the leadership position in the global services market.[5] IBM has many business-level alliances with partner firms focusing on what they believe are better ways to improve services for customer firms, such as the cooperative agreements that IBM has through its new division in business analytics.[6] The objectives IBM and its various partners seek by working together highlight the reality that in the twenty-first century landscape, firms must develop the skills required to successfully use cooperative strategies as a complement to their abilities to grow and improve performance through internally developed strategies and mergers and acquisitions.[7]

A **cooperative strategy** is a strategy in which firms work together to achieve a shared objective.

We examine several topics in this chapter. First, we define and offer examples of different strategic alliances as primary types of cooperative strategies. Next, we discuss the extensive use of cooperative strategies in the global economy and reasons for them. In succession, we describe business-level (including collusive strategies), corporate-level, international, and network cooperative strategies. The chapter closes with discussion of the risks of using cooperative strategies as well as how effective management of them can reduce those risks.

As you will see, we focus on strategic alliances in this chapter because firms use them more frequently than other types of cooperative relationships. Although not frequently used, collusive strategies are another type of cooperative strategy discussed in this chapter. In a *collusive strategy,* two or more firms cooperate to increase prices above the fully competitive level.[8]

Strategic Alliances as a Primary Type of Cooperative Strategy

A **strategic alliance** is a cooperative strategy in which firms combine some of their resources and capabilities to create a competitive advantage.[9] Thus, strategic alliances involve firms with some degree of exchange and sharing of resources and capabilities to co-develop, sell, and service goods or services.[10] Strategic alliances allow firms to leverage their existing resources and capabilities while working with partners to develop additional resources and capabilities as the foundation for new competitive advantages.[11] To be certain, the reality today is that "strategic alliances have become a cornerstone of many firms' competitive strategy."[12]

Consider the case of Kodak. CEO Antonio Perez stated, "Kodak today is involved with partnerships that would have been unthinkable a few short years ago."[13] His comment suggests the breadth and depth of cooperative relationships with which the firm is involved. Each of the cooperative relationships is intended to lead to a new competitive advantage as a source of growth and performance improvement. Kodak has changed from a firm rooted in film and imaging into a digital technology–oriented company.[14]

A competitive advantage developed through a cooperative strategy often is called a *collaborative* or *relational* advantage.[15] As previously discussed, particularly in Chapter 4, competitive advantages enhance the firm's marketplace success. Rapid technological changes and the global economy are examples of factors challenging firms to constantly upgrade current competitive advantages while they develop new ones to maintain strategic competitiveness.[16]

Many firms, especially large global competitors, establish multiple strategic alliances. Although we discussed only a few of them in the Opening Case, the reality is that IBM has formed hundreds of partnerships through cooperative strategies. IBM is not alone in its decision to frequently use cooperative strategies as a means of competition. Focusing on developing advanced technologies, Lockheed Martin has formed more than 250 alliances with firms in more than 30 countries as it concentrates on its primary business of defense modernization and serving the needs of the air transportation industry. For instance, Lockheed Martin recently entered into an alliance with Northrop Grumman Corp. and Alliant Techsystems Inc. These three firms are contracted to develop multirole missiles which have both air-to-air and air-to-ground capabilities. This missile would give aircraft much more flexibility in pursuing either air or ground targets and thus boost the target efficiency of each flight sortie.[17] For all cooperative arrangements, including those we are describing here, success is more likely when partners behave cooperatively. Actively solving problems, being trustworthy, and consistently pursuing ways to combine partners' resources and capabilities to create value are examples of cooperative behavior known to contribute to alliance success.[18]

STRATEGY RIGHT NOW

Read about the cooperative strategy formed between Kodak and the PGA and its benefits and costs.

www.cengage.com/ management/hitt

A **strategic alliance** is a cooperative strategy in which firms combine some of their resources and capabilities to create a competitive advantage.

Three Types of Strategic Alliances

The three major types of strategic alliances include joint venture, equity strategic alliance, and nonequity strategic alliance. These alliance types are classified by their ownership arrangements; later, we classify alliances by strategic categorizations.

A **joint venture** is a strategic alliance in which two or more firms create a legally independent company to share some of their resources and capabilities to develop a competitive advantage. Joint ventures, which are often formed to improve firms' abilities to compete in uncertain competitive environments,[19] are effective in establishing long-term relationships and in transferring tacit knowledge. Because it can't be codified, tacit knowledge is learned through experiences such as those taking place when people from partner firms work together in a joint venture.[20] As discussed in Chapter 3, tacit knowledge is an important source of competitive advantage for many firms.[21]

Typically, partners in a joint venture own equal percentages and contribute equally to the venture's operations. Germany's Siemens AG and Japan's Fujitsu Ltd. equally own the joint venture Fujitsu Siemens Computers. Although the joint venture has been losing money, Fujitsu has decided that it wants to increase its market share from 4 to 10 percent, so it is taking over the joint venture. The new entity will be called Fujitsu Technology Solutions.[22] Overall, evidence suggests that a joint venture may be the optimal type of cooperative arrangement when firms need to combine their resources and capabilities to create a competitive advantage that is substantially different from any they possess individually and when the partners intend to enter highly uncertain markets.[23] These conditions influenced the two independent companies' decision to form Fujitsu Siemens Computers.

An **equity strategic alliance** is an alliance in which two or more firms own different percentages of the company they have formed by combining some of their resources and capabilities to create a competitive advantage. Many foreign direct investments, such as those made by Japanese and U.S. companies in China, are completed through equity strategic alliances.[24]

Interestingly, as many banks have suffered poor results in the United States, foreign banks have been creating equity alliances to provide U.S. banks with the necessary capital to survive and expand. For instance, 21 percent of Morgan Stanley's ownership was sold to Mitsubishi UFJ Financial Group in 2008. As a result, Nobuyuki Hirano, a senior executive for Mitsubishi, took a seat on the board of directors of Morgan Stanley. This will enhance Mitsubishi's understanding of Morgan Stanley's U.S. strategy. The relationship may move towards combining Mitsubishi's and Morgan Stanley Japan's Securities Corporation into a single entity in Japan.[25]

A **nonequity strategic alliance** is an alliance in which two or more firms develop a contractual relationship to share some of their unique resources and capabilities to create a competitive advantage.[26] In this type of alliance, firms do not establish a separate independent company and therefore do not take equity positions. For this reason, nonequity strategic alliances are less formal and demand fewer partner commitments than do joint ventures and equity strategic alliances, though research evidence indicates that they create value for the firms involved.[27] The relative informality and lower commitment levels characterizing nonequity strategic alliances make them unsuitable for complex projects where success requires effective transfers of tacit knowledge between partners.[28]

Forms of nonequity strategic alliances include licensing agreements, distribution agreements, and supply contracts. Hewlett-Packard (HP), which actively "partners to create new markets … and new business models," licenses some of its intellectual property through strategic alliances.[29] Typically, outsourcing commitments are specified in the form of a nonequity strategic alliance. (Discussed in Chapter 3, *outsourcing* is the purchase of a value-creating primary or support activity from another firm.) Dell Inc. and

A **joint venture** is a strategic alliance in which two or more firms create a legally independent company to share some of their resources and capabilities to develop a competitive advantage.

An **equity strategic alliance** is an alliance in which two or more firms own different percentages of the company they have formed by combining some of their resources and capabilities to create a competitive advantage.

A **nonequity strategic alliance** is an alliance in which two or more firms develop a contractual relationship to share some of their unique resources and capabilities to create a competitive advantage.

most other computer firms outsource most or all of their production of laptop computers and often form nonequity strategic alliances to detail the nature of the relationship with firms to whom they outsource. Interestingly, many of these firms that outsource introduce modularity that prevents the contracting partner or outsourcee from gaining too much knowledge or from sharing certain aspects of the business the outsourcing firm does not want revealed.[30]

Reasons Firms Develop Strategic Alliances

As our discussion to this point implies, cooperative strategies are an integral part of the competitive landscape and are quite important to many companies and even to educational institutions. In fact, many firms are cooperating with educational institutions to help commercialize ideas coming from basic research at universities.[31] In for-profit organizations, many executives believe that strategic alliances are central to their firm's success.[32] One executive's position that "you have to partner today or you will miss the next wave ... and that ... you cannot possibly acquire the technology fast enough, so partnering is essential"[33] highlights this belief.

Among other benefits, strategic alliances allow partners to create value that they couldn't develop by acting independently and to enter markets more quickly and with greater market penetration possibilities.[34] Moreover, most (if not all) firms lack the full set of resources and capabilities needed to reach their objectives, which indicates that partnering with others will increase the probability of reaching firm-specific performance objectives.[35] Dow Jones & Co., the publisher of *Wall Street Journal* and owned by News Corp., is forming a joint venture with SBI Holdings Inc. to create a Japanese edition of the *Wall Street Journal*'s Web site. It will primarily feature Japanese translations of news articles, videos, multimedia print, and other features of online editions of the *Wall Street Journal*. In particular this venture will develop mobile products and services in conjunction with the Web site. This is the second news Web site launched by Dow Jones in Asia; the first was launched in China in 2002.[36]

The effects of the greater use of cooperative strategies—particularly in the form of strategic alliances—are noticeable. In large firms, for example, alliances can account for 25 percent or more of sales revenue. Many executives believe that alliances are a prime vehicle for firm growth.[37] In some industries, alliance versus alliance is becoming more prominent than firm versus firm as a point of competition. In the global airline industry, for example, competition is increasingly between large alliances rather than between airlines.[38]

In summary, we can note that firms form strategic alliances to reduce competition, enhance their competitive capabilities, gain access to resources, take advantage of opportunities, build strategic flexibility, and innovate. To achieve these objectives, they must select the right partners and develop trust.[39] Thus, firms attempt to develop a network portfolio of alliances in which they create social capital that affords them flexibility.[40] Because of the social capital, they can call on their partners for help when needed. Of course, social capital means reciprocity exists: Partners can ask them for help as well (and they are expected to provide it).[41]

The individually unique competitive conditions of slow-cycle, fast-cycle, and standard-cycle markets[42] find firms using cooperative strategies to achieve slightly different objectives (see Table 9.1). We discussed these three market types in Chapter 5 while examining competitive rivalry and competitive dynamics. *Slow-cycle markets* are markets where the firm's competitive advantages are shielded from imitation for relatively long periods of time and where imitation is costly. These markets are close to monopolistic conditions. Railroads and, historically, telecommunications, utilities, and financial services are examples of industries characterized as slow-cycle markets. In *fast-cycle markets,* the firm's competitive advantages are not shielded from imitation, preventing their long-term sustainability. Competitive advantages are moderately shielded from imitation in *standard-cycle markets,* typically allowing them to be sustained for a longer

Table 9.1 Reasons for Strategic Alliances by Market Type

Market	Reason
Slow-Cycle	• Gain access to a restricted market • Establish a franchise in a new market • Maintain market stability (e.g., establishing standards)
Fast-Cycle	• Speed up development of new goods or services • Speed up new market entry • Maintain market leadership • Form an industry technology standard • Share risky R&D expenses • Overcome uncertainty
Standard-Cycle	• Gain market power (reduce industry overcapacity) • Gain access to complementary resources • Establish better economies of scale • Overcome trade barriers • Meet competitive challenges from other competitors • Pool resources for very large capital projects • Learn new business techniques

period of time than in fast-cycle market situations, but for a shorter period of time than in slow-cycle markets.

Slow-Cycle Markets

Firms in slow-cycle markets often use strategic alliances to enter restricted markets or to establish franchises in new markets. For example, because of consolidating acquisitions that have occurred over the last dozen or so years, the American steel industry has only two remaining major players: U.S. Steel and Nucor. To improve their ability to compete successfully in the global steel market, these companies are forming cooperative relationships. They have formed strategic alliances in Europe and Asia and are invested in ventures in South America and Australia. Most recently Nucor has established a 50/50 joint venture with Duferco Group's subsidiary Duferdofin to produce steel joists and beams in Italy and then to distribute these products in Europe and North Africa. Duferco has been seeking alliances with major players in order to continue operating on a global basis.[43] Simultaneously however, companies around the world, especially in China, are forming or expanding alliances in order to establish supply sources that are important for steel-making, in particular coal and iron ore. In 2008 Sinosteel Corp., a Chinese state-owned steelmaker, boosted its ownership in Midwest Corp. to 44 percent. Midwest Corp. is an Australian iron ore producer. The reason for this is that the raw materials account for 50 percent of the selling price where as a decade ago iron ore accounted for about 15 percent of the selling price.[44] Although 2009 commodity prices were depressed due to the economic downturn, it is expected that commodity prices will go higher as the economy improves and the partnering and joint venturing pace will increase.

The truth of the matter is that slow-cycle markets are becoming rare in the twenty-first century competitive landscape for several reasons, including the privatization of industries and economies, the rapid expansion of the Internet's capabilities for the quick dissemination of information, and the speed with which advancing technologies make quickly imitating even complex products possible.[45] Firms competing in slow-cycle markets, including steel manufacturers, should recognize the future likelihood that they'll encounter situations in which their competitive advantages become partially sustainable (in the instance of a standard-cycle market) or unsustainable (in the case of a fast-cycle market). Cooperative strategies can be helpful to firms transitioning from relatively sheltered markets to more competitive ones.[46]

Fast-Cycle Markets

Fast-cycle markets are unstable, unpredictable, and complex; in a word, "hypercompetitive" (a concept that was discussed in Chapter 5).[47] Combined, these conditions virtually preclude establishing long-lasting competitive advantages, forcing firms to constantly seek sources of new competitive advantages while creating value by using current ones. "You are looking at the future, when U.S. companies will be competing not only with European, Japanese, South Korean and Chinese companies but also with highly competitive companies from every corner of the world: Argentina, Brazil, Chile, Egypt, Hungary, India, Indonesia, Malaysia, Mexico, Poland,

Mike Margol/PhotoEdit

The rapidly evolving media landscape lead competitors ABC, FOX, and NBC Universal to be cooperative in the development and launch of Hulu.com where many of their top rated shows can be watched online.

Russia, Thailand, Turkey, Vietnam and places you'd never expect."[48] Alliances between firms with current excess resources and capabilities and those with promising capabilities help companies compete in fast-cycle markets to effectively transition from the present to the future and to gain rapid entry into new markets. As such a "collaboration mindset" is paramount.[49]

The entertainment business is fast becoming a new digital marketplace as television content is now available on the Web. This has led the entertainment business into a fast-cycle market where collaboration is important not only to succeed but to survive. Many of the firms that have digital video content have also sought to make a profit through digital music and have had difficulties in extracting profits from their earlier ventures. In 2007 GE's NBC Universal and News Corp.'s FOX formed a new website named http://www.Hulu.com. Walt Disney Corporation in 2009 became a third partner contributing content and capital in this joint venture along with an investment stake held by private equity firm Providence Equity Partners. Thus this Web site will be co-owned by direct competitors. ABC (owned by Disney) will shift much of its content to the Hulu site and viewers will be able to stream ABC TV shows such as *Lost* and *Grey's Anatomy*. CBS will be the only major network not participating in the Hulu venture with NBC Universal, FOX, and ABC. As digital video content moves onto the Web, it will be interesting to see how the competition and cooperation between all of these firms evolve.[50]

Standard-Cycle Markets

In standard-cycle markets, alliances are more likely to be made by partners with complementary resources and capabilities. Even though airline alliances were originally set up to increase revenue,[51] airlines have realized that they can also be used to reduce costs. SkyTeam (chaired by Delta and Air France) developed an internal Web site to speed up joint purchasing and to swap tips on pricing. Managers at Oneworld (American Airlines and British Airways) say the alliance's members have already saved more than $200 million through joint purchasing, and Star Alliance (United and Lufthansa) estimates that its member airlines save up to 25 percent on joint orders.

Given the geographic areas where markets are growing, these global alliances are adding partners from Asia. In recent years, China Southern Airlines joined the SkyTeam alliance, Air China and Shanghai Airlines were added to the Star Alliance, and Dragonair joined as an affiliate of Oneworld. One of the competitive difficulties with the airline alliances is that major partners often switch between airlines. For instance, Continental

Airlines, which was part of SkyTeam, recently switched to the Star Alliance with United Airlines, Air Canada, and Lufthansa. Although this move has been approved by the U.S. Department of Transportation, it still lacks approval from the European Union regulators.[52] The fact that Oneworld, SkyTeam, and Star Alliance account for more than 60 percent of the world's airline capacity suggests that firms participating in these alliances have gained scale economies.

Business-Level Cooperative Strategy

A firm uses a **business-level cooperative strategy** to grow and improve its performance in individual product markets. As discussed in Chapter 4, business-level strategy details what the firm intends to do to gain a competitive advantage in specific product markets. Thus, the firm forms a business-level cooperative strategy when it believes that combining its resources and capabilities with those of one or more partners will create competitive advantages that it can't create by itself and will lead to success in a specific product market. The four business-level cooperative strategies are listed in Figure 9.1.

Complementary Strategic Alliances

Complementary strategic alliances are business-level alliances in which firms share some of their resources and capabilities in complementary ways to develop competitive advantages.[53] Vertical and horizontal are the two types of complementary strategic alliances (see Figure 9.1).

Vertical Complementary Strategic Alliance

In a *vertical complementary strategic alliance,* firms share their resources and capabilities from different stages of the value chain to create a competitive advantage (see Figure 9.2).[54] Oftentimes, vertical complementary alliances are formed to adapt to environmental changes;[55] sometimes the changes represent an opportunity for partnering firms to innovate while adapting.[56]

The Strategic Focus on complementary alliances discusses what is happening with vertical alliances given the downturn in the world economy. In particular, it points out that economic pressures are creating stress in the vertical alliance relationships between buyers and suppliers in the grocery and apparel retail industry supply chains. However, in other industries it is leading to new partnerships where complementary strategic alliances are more likely to increase, such as in the steelmaking industry.

Another example of a vertical complementary alliance is Nintendo and its need for additional software and games for its Wii game console. To fulfill this need Nintendo has developed a partnership with Electronic Arts. Through this partnership, it will release two sports games prior to the release of its brand new hardware: *Tiger Woods PGA Tour 10*

Figure 9.1 Business-Level Cooperative Strategies

- Complementary strategic alliances
  - Vertical
  - Horizontal
- Competition response strategy
- Uncertainty-reducing strategy
- Competition-reducing strategy

A firm uses a **business-level cooperative strategy** to grow and improve its performance in individual product markets.

Complementary strategic alliances are business-level alliances in which firms share some of their resources and capabilities in complementary ways to develop competitive advantages.

Figure 9.2 Vertical and Horizontal Complementary Strategic Alliances

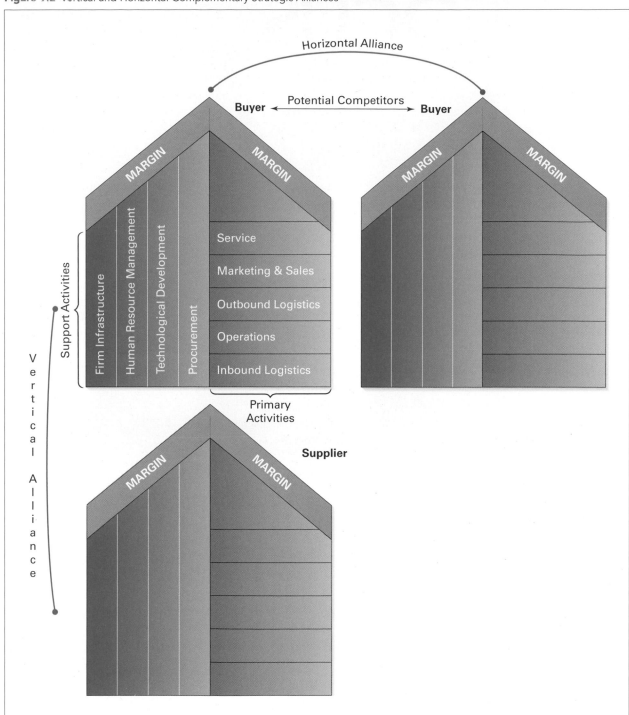

and *Grand Slam Tennis*. Nintendo is allowing these games to be sold even before it releases more of its own games. Previously, Nintendo trailed other game platforms in its production of new releases because it stressed its own games over those of other game software producers and would not release its hardware details to them in advance. It has changed its policy to encourage more vertical relationships with game software producing firms such as Electronic Arts and Activision Blizzard, Inc.[57]

STRATEGIC FOCUS

HOW COMPLEMENTARY ALLIANCES ARE AFFECTED BY THE GLOBAL ECONOMIC DOWNTURN

Supply chain management principles have changed over the last decade as suppliers have sought to work more closely with buyers. Traditionally a company's purchasing office dealt with a relatively small group of suppliers and had the overall goal of obtaining as many price cuts as possible. This changed, however, because as globalization and outsourcing increased the supply chain decision-making process involved a greater network of partners around the world. This drove companies to collaborate with suppliers and develop stronger relationships to reduce waste and develop products more quickly. As such, supply chain managers have had to shoulder a lot more responsibility, which has required much more emphasis on collaborative skills.

In the economic downturn, however, many of these collaborative relationships and partnerships—which are complementary by nature, especially in the vertical supply chain—have been strained. Large retailers have been squeezing their vendors in order to survive the requirement for heavy sales promotions and lower prices to sell their apparel products. This strategy has affected firms like Liz Claiborne, Phillips-Van Heusen, and Jones Apparel Group. Because large stores such as Macy's have many vendors to choose from, they have power to force price cuts from their suppliers. Macy's has power over Liz Claiborne because it buys in large volume. However, this has strained their relationship because both companies "require long-term, healthy partners to operate efficiently." Hartmarx Corp., a men's clothing producer whose main customers are Dillard's, Nordstrom, and Bloomingdale's (owned by Macy's), has been forced to file for Chapter 11 bankruptcy court protection due to the pressure. On the other hand, JCPenney has had long-term relationships with its vendors and its spokesperson noted, "We don't view 'squeezing' of vendors to protect our bottom line as a viable long-term strategy."

Similar events are happening in the grocery industry. For example, Unilever has been trying to stop its price margins from shrinking by forcing price increases on retailers such as the Belgian supermarket chain Delhaize Group SA. Delhaize operates the Food Lion chain and other grocery stores in the United States. In 2008, Unilever pushed worldwide price increases of more than 9 percent. Because of the price increases forced on Delhaize, it banished products by Unilever such as Dove soap and Axe deodorant from its U.S. stores. At the same time, commodity prices dropped and British retailer Tesco PLC urged suppliers to pass onto stores the recent drops in prices for commodities and oil that are used to produce food products. In response, firms like Wal-Mart (Great Value) have started to freshen up their in-house brands. As such, when large food producers such as Unilever do not respond appropriately, Wal-Mart can cut back on stocking national brands.

AP Photo/Shoun Hill

Shoppers at Food Lion found Axe and other Unilever products off the shelves as Delhaize, operator of the supermarket, responded to price increases passed on from the manufacturer.

While the downturn has put stress on some vertical alliances as previously noted, it has also created opportunities for new partnerships in other areas. For example, many private equity firms have experienced a significant decrease in the amount of funds invested in the

United States. Blackstone Group has formed global joint ventures to increase its fund supply. It has formed a joint venture with Bank Larrain Vial in Latin America and Och-Ziff Capital Management. In Latin America in particular there is a large opportunity in Chile, where private pension funds hold $82 billion in assets due to a pioneering program that places 12.3 percent of all payroll into private pension accounts. This complementary alliance would most likely not have occurred if the economy did not turn for the worse. Blackstone Group will also help diversify pension funds by investing in private equity and hedge funds. South and Central America have almost $200 billion in assets under management, which is comparable to the California Public Employees Retirement System (CalPERS). This is a significant opportunity for private equity funds such as the Blackstone Group to increase their supply of capital.

Sources: M. Arnold, 2009, Private equity boost for Latin America, *Financial Times*, May 12, 6; L. C. Gunipero, R. V. Handfield, & D. L. Johansen, 2008, Beyond buying: Supply chain managers used to have one main job: Purchasing stuff cheaply, *Wall Street Journal*, March 10, R8; P. Lattman, 2009, Schwarzman's Latin sojourn, *Wall Street Journal*, May 22, C2; S. Pignal, 2009, Delhaize shrugs off Unilever clash, *Financial Times*, March 13, 18; C. Rohwedder, A. O. Patrick, & T. W. Martin, 2009, Big grocers pulls Unilever items over pricing, *Wall Street Journal*, February 11, D1, B5l; K. Talley, 2009, Retailers, apparel firms tussle over tough deals, *Wall Street Journal*, February 11, B6.

Horizontal Complementary Strategic Alliance

A *horizontal complementary strategic alliance* is an alliance in which firms share some of their resources and capabilities from the same stage (or stages) of the value chain to create a competitive advantage (see Figure 9.2). Commonly, firms use complementary strategic alliances to focus on joint long-term product development and distribution opportunities.[58] As previously noted in the example regarding www.Hulu.com, GE's Universal Pictures, Disney's ABC, and News Corp's FOX Video Production have formed a joint Web site to distribute video content. Recently, pharmaceutical companies have been pursuing horizontal alliances as well. As healthcare reform takes place in the United States, large pharmaceutical firms are seeking relationships with generic drug producers. For example, Pfizer has reached marketing agreements with two Indian makers of generic drugs: Aurobindo Pharma Ltd. and Claris Lifesciences Ltd. These two firms produce and sell 60 and 15 off-patent drugs and injectables, respectively. Similarly, Novartis AG is acquiring Ebewe Pharma, an Austrian drugmaker, which will partner with the Novartis generic drug subsidiary, Sandoz. These moves are targeted to tap into the growing generic drug market, which was $3.5 billion in 2008 and is expected to be $9 billion by 2015.[59]

The automotive manufacturing industry is one in which many horizontal complementary strategic alliances are formed. In fact, virtually all global automobile manufacturers use cooperative strategies to form scores of cooperative relationships. The Renault-Nissan alliance, signed in March 1999, is a prominent example of a horizontal complementary strategic alliance. Thought to be successful, the challenge is to integrate the partners' operations to create value while maintaining their unique cultures.

Competition Response Strategy

As discussed in Chapter 5, competitors initiate competitive actions to attack rivals and launch competitive responses to their competitors' actions. Strategic alliances can be used at the business level to respond to competitors' attacks. Because they can be difficult to reverse and expensive to operate, strategic alliances are primarily formed to take strategic rather than tactical actions and to respond to competitors' actions in a like manner.

Many complementary horizontal alliances are created in response to heavy competition. For instance, digital music producers have been trying to extract more value from their products beyond what they can collect through middle-men such as Apple's iTunes distribution outlet. Many music producers have sought to develop their own distribution outlets through joint partnership, in response to Apple's success, such as Blue Matter Press, Jimmy and Doug's Farmclub, and eMusic, but most have failed. Now many of them are seeking online advertisements through Web sites that distribute music and video. For instance, Warner Music has invested in LaLa Media and a startup company called imeem, Inc. because MySpace Music, a joint venture among four major labels and News Corp., was not generating enough advertising revenue. In response to the focus on advertising, Universal Music, a division of Vivendi SA, through a joint venture with Google has created a new online site for music videos called VEVO. Most of these actions are attempts to bolster revenue because digital music downloads are increasing, but not quickly enough to offset the steep decline in CD sales.[60]

Uncertainty-Reducing Strategy

Some firms use business-level strategic alliances to hedge against risk and uncertainty, especially in fast-cycle markets.[61] These strategies are also used where uncertainty exists, such as in entering new product markets or emerging economies.

As large global auto firms manufacture more hybrid vehicles, there is insufficient capacity in the battery industry to meet future demand. Volkswagen AG is partnering with China's BYD Co. to produce hybrid and electric vehicles powered by lithium batteries. BYD is the one of the world's largest cell phone battery producers and is also a fledgling auto producer as it moves to launch a plug-in car before more established rival firms. Volkswagen has also made agreements with Samuel Electric and Toshiba Corp. of Japan to reduce the uncertainty about the insufficient capacity for lithium-ion batteries used in hybrid vehicles.[62]

Competition-Reducing Strategy

Used to reduce competition, collusive strategies differ from strategic alliances in that collusive strategies are often an illegal type of cooperative strategy. Two types of collusive strategies are explicit collusion and tacit collusion.

When two or more firms negotiate directly with the intention of jointly agreeing about the amount to produce and the price of the products that are produced, *explicit collusion* exists.[63] Explicit collusion strategies are illegal in the United States and most developed economies (except in regulated industries).

Firms that use explicit collusion strategies may find others challenging their competitive actions. In early 2009, for example, the U.S. Department of Justice joined forces with European officials to investigate alleged "price coordination" among three air cargo carriers. Luxembourg's Cargolux, Japan's Nippon Cargo Airlines, and Korea's Asiana Airlines plead guilty and paid criminal fines of $214 million for their role in a global conspiracy to fix prices on air freight. This investigation began in 2001 and prosecution began in 2006. Throughout the history of the investigation more than 15 air cargo airlines have been prosecuted and fined over $1.6 billion. The investigation continues in the air freight industry and is one of the world's biggest cartel probes by competition officials around the world.[64] As this example suggests, any firm that may use explicit collusion as a strategy should recognize that competitors and regulatory bodies might challenge the acceptability of their competitive actions.

Tacit collusion exists when several firms in an industry indirectly coordinate their production and pricing decisions by observing each other's competitive actions and responses.[65] Tacit collusion results in production output that is below fully competitive levels and above fully competitive prices. Unlike explicit collusion, firms engaging in tacit collusion do not directly negotiate output and pricing decisions. However, research suggests that joint ventures or cooperation between two firms can lead to less competition in other markets in which both firms operate.[66]

Tacit collusion tends to be used as a business-level, competition-reducing strategy in highly concentrated industries, such as airlines and breakfast cereals. Research in the airline industry suggests that tacit collusion reduces service quality and on-time performance.[67] Firms in these industries recognize that they are interdependent and that their competitive actions and responses significantly affect competitors' behavior toward them. Understanding this interdependence and carefully observing competitors can lead to tacit collusion.

Four firms (Kellogg's, General Mills, Post, and Quaker) have accounted for as much as 80 percent of sales volume in the ready-to-eat segment of the U.S. cereal market.[68] Some believe that this high degree of concentration results in "prices for branded cereals that are well above [the] costs of production."[69] The *Wall Street Journal* reported in 2008 that prices for breakfast cereals were among the easiest to inflate when there are commodity shortages.[70] Prices above the competitive level in this industry suggest the possibility that the dominant firms use a tacit collusion cooperative strategy.

Discussed in Chapter 6, *mutual forbearance* is a form of tacit collusion in which firms do not take competitive actions against rivals they meet in multiple markets. Rivals learn a great deal about each other when engaging in multimarket competition, including how to deter the effects of their rival's competitive attacks and responses. Given what they know about each other as a competitor, firms choose not to engage in what could be destructive competitions in multiple product markets.[71]

In general, governments in free-market economies need to determine how rivals can collaborate to increase their competitiveness without violating established regulations.[72] However, this task is challenging when evaluating collusive strategies, particularly tacit ones. For example, regulation of pharmaceutical and biotech firms who collaborate to meet global competition might lead to too much price fixing and, therefore, regulation is required to make sure that the balance is right, although sometimes the regulation gets in the way of efficient markets.[73] Individual companies must analyze the effect of a competition-reducing strategy on their performance and competitiveness.

Assessment of Business-Level Cooperative Strategies

Firms use business-level strategies to develop competitive advantages that can contribute to successful positions and performance in individual product markets. To develop a competitive advantage using an alliance, the resources and capabilities that are integrated through the alliance must be valuable, rare, imperfectly imitable, and nonsubstitutable (see Chapter 3).

Evidence suggests that complementary business-level strategic alliances, especially vertical ones, have the greatest probability of creating a sustainable competitive advantage.[74] Horizontal complementary alliances are sometimes difficult to maintain because they are often between rivalrous competitors. In this instance, firms may feel a "push" toward and a "pull" from alliances. Airline firms, for example, want to compete aggressively against others serving their markets and target customers. However, the need to develop scale economies and to share resources and capabilities (such as scheduling systems) dictates that alliances be formed so the firms can compete by using cooperative actions and responses while they simultaneously compete against one another through competitive actions and responses. As noted previously, this has led to many changes in the large airline alliances—for instance, with Continental recently aligning with United and Lufthansa rather than Delta and AirFrance-KLM.[75] The challenge in these instances is for each firm to find ways to create the greatest amount of value from both their competitive and cooperative actions. It seems that Nissan and Renault have learned how to achieve this balance.

Although strategic alliances designed to respond to competition and to reduce uncertainty can also create competitive advantages, these advantages often are more temporary than those developed through complementary (both vertical and horizontal) strategic alliances. The primary reason is that complementary alliances have a stronger focus on creating value than do competition-reducing and uncertainty-reducing alliances, which are formed to respond to competitors' actions or reduce uncertainty rather than to attack competitors.

Of the four business-level cooperative strategies, the competition-reducing strategy has the lowest probability of creating a sustainable competitive advantage. For example, research suggests that firms following a foreign direct investment strategy using alliances as a follow-the-leader imitation approach may not have strong strategic or learning goals. Thus, such investment could be attributable to tacit collusion among the participating firms rather than to forming a competitive advantage (which should be the core objective).

Corporate-Level Cooperative Strategy

A firm uses a **corporate-level cooperative strategy** to help it diversify in terms of products offered or markets served, or both. Diversifying alliances, synergistic alliances, and franchising are the most commonly used corporate-level cooperative strategies (see Figure 9.3).

Firms use diversifying alliances and synergistic alliances to grow and improve performance by diversifying their operations through a means other than a merger or an acquisition.[76] When a firm seeks to diversify into markets in which the host nation's government prevents mergers and acquisitions, alliances become an especially appropriate option. Corporate-level strategic alliances are also attractive compared with mergers and particularly acquisitions, because they require fewer resource commitments[77] and permit greater flexibility in terms of efforts to diversify partners' operations.[78] An alliance can be used as a way to determine whether the partners might benefit from a future merger or acquisition between them. This "testing" process often characterizes alliances formed to combine firms' unique technological resources and capabilities.[79]

Diversifying Strategic Alliance

A **diversifying strategic alliance** is a corporate-level cooperative strategy in which firms share some of their resources and capabilities to diversify into new product or market areas. The spread of high-speed wireless networks and devices with global positioning chips and the popularity of Web site applications running on Apple's iPhone and Research in Motion's BlackBerry (and other smartphones) shows that consumers are increasingly accessing mobile information. Equipped with this knowledge, Alcatel-Lucent is entering the market through mobile advertising, which will allow a cell phone carrier to alert customers about the location of a favorite store or the closest ATM. It is pursuing this diversification alliance with 1020 Placecast, a California-based developer of cell phone online ads associated with user locations. Hyatt, FedEx, and Avis are especially interested in using the service. The ads will also include a link to coupons or other promotions. Other mobile phone producers have started to sell mobile phone display ads in other metropolitan areas through Nokia Phones. These networks are trying to gain a share of the profits that would normally be out of their reach through revenue-sharing models with companies that are advertising as well as the ad-producing service companies.[80]

A firm uses a **corporate-level cooperative strategy** to help it diversify in terms of products offered or markets served, or both.

A **diversifying strategic alliance** is a corporate-level cooperative strategy in which firms share some of their resources and capabilities to diversify into new product or market areas.

Figure 9.3 Corporate-Level Cooperative Strategies

- Diversifying alliances
- Synergistic alliances
- Franchising

It should be noted that highly diverse networks of alliances can lead to poorer performance by partner firms.[81] However, cooperative ventures are also used to reduce diversification in firms that have overdiversified.[82] Japanese chipmakers Fujitsu, Mitsubishi Electric, Hitachi, NEC, and Toshiba have been using joint ventures to consolidate and then spin off diversified businesses that were performing poorly. For example, Fujitsu, realizing that memory chips were becoming a financial burden, dumped its flash memory business into a joint venture company controlled by Advanced Micro Devices. This alliance helped Fujitsu refocus on its core businesses.[83]

Synergistic Strategic Alliance

A **synergistic strategic alliance** is a corporate-level cooperative strategy in which firms share some of their resources and capabilities to create economies of scope. Similar to the business-level horizontal complementary strategic alliance, synergistic strategic alliances create synergy across multiple functions or multiple businesses between partner firms. The most recent development for Disney's media segment, and ABC in particular, is a partnership with Google's YouTube that will allow it to advertise its movies and products by showing short clips and selling ads.[84] This is an example of a synergistic diversification alliance.

In recent years, there has been much more competitive interaction between hardware and software firms. Cisco, traditionally a network telecommunications equipment manufacturer, is moving into computers—in particular, servers. After HP moved into selling network equipment, Cisco decided to move more fully into developing its server business. To drive its computer business Cisco needs to develop a service segment, although it is not trying to upset its historical partners, HP and IBM, which have large service businesses. Both IBM and HP have large service businesses. As such, Cisco developed partnership agreements with Accenture Ltd. and India-based Tata Consulting Services Ltd. to help market Cisco's products to businesses around the world. These were synergistic alliances to foster this diversification move by Cisco into services.[85]

AP Photo/M. Spencer Green

With apps like the Slacker personalized radio and hundreds of others available for the BlackBerry and iPhone, companies are already looking at these devices as a means of conveying personalized advertising as well.

Franchising

Franchising is a corporate-level cooperative strategy in which a firm (the franchisor) uses a franchise as a contractual relationship to describe and control the sharing of its resources and capabilities with partners (the franchisees).[86] A *franchise* is a "contractual agreement between two legally independent companies whereby the franchisor grants the right to the franchisee to sell the franchisor's product or do business under its trademarks in a given location for a specified period of time."[87] Success is often determined in these strategic alliances by how well the franchisor can replicate its success across multiple partners in a cost-effective way.[88] Research suggests that too much innovation results in difficulties for replicating this success.[89]

Franchising is a popular strategy. In the United States alone, more than 2,500 franchise systems are located in more than 75 industries; and those operating franchising outlets generate roughly one-third of all U.S. retail sales.[90] Already frequently used in developed nations, franchising is also expected to account for significant portions of growth in emerging economies in the twenty-first century.[91] As with diversifying and synergistic strategic alliances, franchising is an alternative to pursuing growth through mergers and acquisitions. McDonald's, Hilton International, Marriott International,

A **synergistic strategic alliance** is a corporate-level cooperative strategy in which firms share some of their resources and capabilities to create economies of scope.

Franchising is a corporate-level cooperative strategy in which a firm (the franchisor) uses a franchise as a contractual relationship to describe and control the sharing of its resources and capabilities with partners (the franchisees).

Mrs. Fields Cookies, Subway, and Ace Hardware are well-known examples of firms using the franchising corporate-level cooperative strategy.

Franchising is a particularly attractive strategy to use in fragmented industries, such as retailing, hotels and motels, and commercial printing. In fragmented industries, a large number of small and medium-sized firms compete as rivals; however, no firm or small set of firms has a dominant share, making it possible for a company to gain a large market share by consolidating independent companies through contractual relationships.

In the most successful franchising strategy, the partners (the franchisor and the franchisees) work closely together.[92] A primary responsibility of the franchisor is to develop programs to transfer to the franchisees the knowledge and skills that are needed to successfully compete at the local level.[93] In return, franchisees should provide feedback to the franchisor regarding how their units could become more effective and efficient.[94] Working cooperatively, the franchisor and its franchisees find ways to strengthen the core company's brand name, which is often the most important competitive advantage for franchisees operating in their local markets.[95]

Assessment of Corporate-Level Cooperative Strategies

Costs are incurred with each type of cooperative strategy.[96] Compared with those at the business level, corporate-level cooperative strategies commonly are broader in scope and more complex, making them relatively more costly. Those forming and using cooperative strategies, especially corporate-level ones, should be aware of alliance costs and carefully monitor them.

In spite of these costs, firms can create competitive advantages and value when they effectively form and use corporate-level cooperative strategies.[97] When successful alliance experiences are internalized, it is more likely that the strategy will attain the desired advantages. In other words, those involved with forming and using corporate-level cooperative strategies can also use them to develop useful knowledge about how to succeed in the future. To gain maximum value from this knowledge, firms should organize it and verify that it is always properly distributed to those involved with forming and using alliances.[98]

We explain in Chapter 6 that firms answer two questions to form a corporate-level strategy—in which businesses will the diversified firm compete and how will those businesses be managed? These questions are also answered as firms form corporate-level cooperative strategies. Thus, firms able to develop corporate-level cooperative strategies and manage them in ways that are valuable, rare, imperfectly imitable, and nonsubstitutable (see Chapter 3) develop a competitive advantage that is in addition to advantages gained through the activities of individual cooperative strategies. (Later in the chapter, we further describe alliance management as another potential competitive advantage.)

International Cooperative Strategy

A **cross-border strategic alliance** is an international cooperative strategy in which firms with headquarters in different nations decide to combine some of their resources and capabilities to create a competitive advantage. Taking place in virtually all industries, the number of cross-border alliances continues to increase.[99] These alliances too are sometimes formed instead of mergers and acquisitions (which can be riskier).[100] Even though cross-border alliances can themselves be complex and hard to manage,[101] they have the potential to help firms use their resources and capabilities to create value in locations outside their home market.

A **cross-border strategic alliance** is an international cooperative strategy in which firms with headquarters in different nations decide to combine some of their resources and capabilities to create a competitive advantage.

IMG Worldwide, Inc. is one of the largest producers and distributors of sports entertainment in the world. It pursues its strategy through international joint ventures with other broadcasting firms. The events that it currently broadcasts include two tennis "Grand Slam" events, Wimbledon and the Australian Open. In an effort to expand into emerging economies, IMG recently signed a 20-year sporting event partnership with China Central Television, the main Chinese broadcasting organization. A national broadcast of this size could have an audience of 740 million viewers daily. The first two events that will be broadcast through this venture are the China Open Tennis Tournament in Beijing and the Chengdu Open Tennis Tournament in 2009. The top 50 women players in the world are expected to play in the China Open tournament. Through this strategic alliance, IMG will substantially broaden its international reach.[102]

Several reasons explain the increasing use of cross-border strategic alliances, including the fact that in general, multinational corporations outperform domestic-only firms.[103] What takes place with a cross-border alliance is that a firm leverages core competencies that are the foundation of its domestic success in international markets.[104] Nike provides an example as it leverages its core competence with celebrity marketing to expand globally with its diverse line of athletic goods and apparel. With a $2 billion celebrity endorsement budget, Nike has formed relationships with athletes who have global appeal. Tiger Woods, Michael Phelps, and LeBron James are recent endorsers, while seven-time Tour de France winner Lance Armstrong, Michael Jordan, and Magic Johnson are historic examples of these types of individuals. In addition, Nike has endorsement relationships with star athletes and organizations outside the United States, such as Brazilian soccer star Ronaldo and Manchester United, the world's most popular soccer team.[105] Coupling these alliances with Nike's powerful global brand name helps the firm apply its marketing competencies in foreign markets. However, the downturn in the economy is causing problems such that even these relationships are not protecting sales declines.[106]

Limited domestic growth opportunities and foreign government economic policies are additional reasons firms use cross-border alliances. As discussed in Chapter 8, local ownership is an important national policy objective in some nations. In India and China, for example, governmental policies reflect a strong preference to license local companies. Thus, in some countries, the full range of entry mode choices that we described in Chapter 8 may not be available to firms seeking to diversify internationally. Indeed, investment by foreign firms in these instances may be allowed only through a partnership with a local firm, such as in a cross-border alliance. Especially important, strategic alliances with local partners can help firms overcome certain liabilities of moving into a foreign country, such as lack of knowledge of the local culture or institutional norms.[107] A cross-border strategic alliance can also be helpful to foreign partners from an operational perspective, because the local partner has significantly more information about factors contributing to competitive success such as local markets, sources of capital, legal procedures, and politics.[108] Interestingly, recent research suggests that firms with foreign operations have longer survival rates than domestic-only firms, although this is reduced if there are competition problems between foreign subsidiaries.[109]

In general, cross-border alliances are more complex and risky than domestic strategic alliances, especially in emerging economies.[110] However, the fact that firms competing internationally tend to outperform domestic-only competitors suggests the importance of learning how to diversify into international markets. Compared with mergers and acquisitions, cross-border alliances may be a better way to learn this process, especially in the early stages of the firms' geographic diversification efforts. Starbucks is a case in point.

When Starbucks sought overseas expansion, it wanted to do so quickly as a means of supporting its strong orientation to continuous growth. Thus, it agreed to a complex series of joint ventures in many countries in the interest of speed. While the company receives a percentage of the revenues and profits as well as licensing fees for supplying its coffee, controlling costs abroad is more difficult than in the United States. Starbucks is learning from the results achieved from the collaborative relationships it initially established. In light of what it has learned, the firm continues to collaborate with others in different countries including China. At Starbuck's 10-year anniversary mark in China, one analyst noted that "China, conventionally a coffee exporter, may become a net importer in 2009 with demand outpacing supply, as Starbucks Coffee Co. and other coffee chains mushroom around the country."[111] Among other actions, Starbucks is taking larger equity positions in some of the joint ventures with which it is now involved in different countries (such as China).

Network Cooperative Strategy

In addition to forming their own alliances with individual companies, a growing number of firms are joining forces in multiple networks.[112] A **network cooperative strategy** is a cooperative strategy wherein several firms agree to form multiple partnerships to achieve shared objectives. As noted, Cisco has multiple cooperative arrangements with IBM and HP, and with service providers Accenture Ltd. and Tata Consulting Services Ltd. Demonstrating the complexity of network cooperative strategies is the fact that Cisco has a set of unique collaborations with both IBM and HP, but is also competing with them as they move into servers. The fact is that the number of network cooperative strategies being formed today continues to increase as firms seek to find the best ways to create value by offering multiple goods and services in multiple geographic (domestic and international) locations.

A network cooperative strategy is particularly effective when it is formed by geographically clustered firms,[113] as in California's Silicon Valley (where "the culture of Silicon Valley encourages collaborative webs"[114]) and Singapore's Biopolis (in the bio-medical sciences) and the new fusionopolis (collaborations in "physical sciences and engineering to tackle global science and technology challenges").[115] Effective social relationships and interactions among partners while sharing their resources and capabilities make it more likely that a network cooperative strategy will be successful,[116] as does having a productive *strategic center firm* (we discuss strategic center firms in detail in Chapter 11). Firms involved in networks gain information and knowledge from multiple sources. They can use these heterogeneous knowledge sets to produce more and better innovation. As a result, firms involved in networks of alliances tend to be more innovative.[117] However, there are disadvantages to participating in networks as a firm can be locked into its partnerships, precluding the development of alliances with others. In certain types of networks, such as Japanese *keiretsus*, firms in the network are expected to help other firms in the network whenever they need aid. Such expectations can become a burden and reduce the focal firm's performance over time.[118]

Alliance Network Types

An important advantage of a network cooperative strategy is that firms gain access to their partners' other partners. Having access to multiple collaborations increases the likelihood that additional competitive advantages will be formed as the set of shared resources and capabilities expands.[119] In turn, being able to develop new capabilities further stimulates product innovations that are critical to strategic competitiveness in the global economy.[120]

A network cooperative strategy is a cooperative strategy wherein several firms agree to form multiple partnerships to achieve shared objectives.

The set of strategic alliance partnerships resulting from the use of a network cooperative strategy is commonly called an *alliance network.* The alliance networks that companies develop vary by industry conditions. A *stable alliance network* is formed in mature industries where demand is relatively constant and predictable. Through a stable alliance network, firms try to extend their competitive advantages to other settings while continuing to profit from operations in their core, relatively mature industry. Thus, stable networks are built primarily to *exploit* the economies (scale and/or scope) that exist between the partners such as in the airline industry.[121] *Dynamic alliance networks* are used in industries characterized by frequent product innovations and short product life cycles.[122] For instance, the pace of innovation in the information technology (IT) industry (as well as other industries that are characterized by fast-cycle markets) is too fast for any one company to be successful across time if it only competes independently. Another example is the movie industry, which has a lot of collaborative ventures and networked firms to produce and distribute movies.[123] In dynamic alliance networks, partners typically *explore* new ideas and possibilities with the potential to lead to product innovations, entries to new markets, and the development of new markets.[124] Often, large firms in such industries as software and pharmaceuticals create networks of relationships with smaller entrepreneurial startup firms in their search for innovation-based outcomes.[125] An important outcome for small firms successfully partnering with larger firms in an alliance network is the credibility they build by being associated with their larger collaborators.[126]

Competitive Risks with Cooperative Strategies

Stated simply, many cooperative strategies fail. In fact, evidence shows that two-thirds of cooperative strategies have serious problems in their first two years and that as many as 50 percent of them fail. This failure rate suggests that even when the partnership has potential complementarities and synergies, alliance success is elusive.[127] Although failure is undesirable, it can be a valuable learning experience, meaning that firms should carefully study a cooperative strategy's failure to gain insights with respect to how to form and manage future cooperative arrangements.[128] We show prominent cooperative strategy risks in Figure 9.4.

Figure 9.4 Managing Competitive Risks in Cooperative Strategies

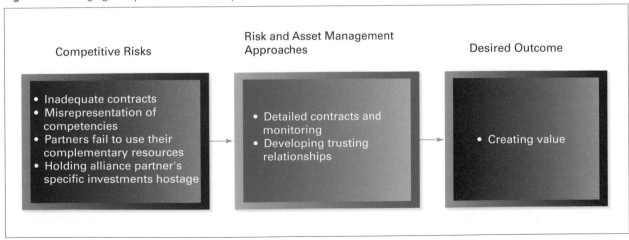

One cooperative strategy risk is that a partner may act opportunistically. Opportunistic behaviors surface either when formal contracts fail to prevent them or when an alliance is based on a false perception of partner trustworthiness. Not infrequently, the opportunistic firm wants to acquire as much of its partner's tacit knowledge as it can.[129] Full awareness of what a partner wants in a cooperative strategy reduces the likelihood that a firm will suffer from another's opportunistic actions.[130] The Strategic Focus on TNK-BP, a 50/50 joint venture between three Russian oil tycoons and British Petroleum, demonstrates potential opportunistic actions by parties involved and some of the potential risks of joint ventures, especially in an emerging economy like Russia.

Some cooperative strategies fail when it is discovered that a firm has misrepresented the competencies it can bring to the partnership. The risk of competence misrepresentation is more common when the partner's contribution is grounded in some of its intangible assets. Superior knowledge of local conditions is an example of an intangible asset that partners often fail to deliver. An effective way to deal with this risk may be to ask the partner to provide evidence that it does possess the resources and capabilities (even when they are largely intangible) it will share in the cooperative strategy.[131]

Another risk is a firm failing to make available to its partners the resources and capabilities (such as the most sophisticated technologies) that it committed to the cooperative strategy. For example, in the Strategic Focus, TNK-BP did not meet agreed-upon targets and this put them in a situation of weakness relative to both its powerful partners and the Russian government. This risk surfaces most commonly when firms form an international cooperative strategy, especially in emerging economies.[132] In these instances, different cultures and languages can cause misinterpretations of contractual terms or trust-based expectations.

A final risk is that one firm may make investments that are specific to the alliance while its partner does not. For example, the firm might commit resources and capabilities to develop manufacturing equipment that can be used only to produce items coming from the alliance. If the partner isn't also making alliance-specific investments, the firm is at a relative disadvantage in terms of returns earned from the alliance compared with investments made to earn the returns. This is certainly an issue in the TNK-BP alliance in which BP is continuing to make investments, although it is losing control in managing those investments.

Managing Cooperative Strategies

Although cooperative strategies are an important means of firm growth and enhanced performance, managing these strategies is challenging. However, learning how to effectively manage cooperative strategies is important such that it can be a source of competitive advantage.[133] Because the ability to effectively manage cooperative strategies is unevenly distributed across organizations in general, assigning managerial responsibility for a firm's cooperative strategies to a high-level executive or to a team improves the likelihood that the strategies will be well managed.

Those responsible for managing the firm's set of cooperative strategies should take the actions necessary to coordinate activities, categorize knowledge learned from previous experiences, and make certain that what the firm knows about how to effectively form and use cooperative strategies is in the hands of the right people at the right time. Firms must also learn how to manage both the tangible and intangible assets (such as knowledge) that are involved with a cooperative arrangement. Too often, partners concentrate on managing tangible assets at the expense of taking action to also manage a cooperative relationship's intangible assets.[134]

TROUBLES IN THE RUSSIAN OIL JOINT VENTURE, TNK-BP

The situation in 2009 with the joint venture that British Petroleum (BP) formed in 2003 with three Russian oil tycoons, Mikhail Fridman, Viktor Vekselberg, and Leonard Blavatnik, demonstrates opportunistic behavior as well as political risks. These three oil oligarchs own 50 percent of the venture labeled TNK-BP, and BP owns the remaining 50 percent. The venture gave a Western company unprecedented access to vital Russian oil and gas resources. However, the Kremlin is becoming increasingly involved in the nation's energy production activities and it has claimed that TNK-BP failed to fulfill all terms of its license regarding a particular oil field (the Kovykta field). This claim threatens the joint venture's viability. Part of the problem is that members of the Kremlin feel uncomfortable with the Russian tycoons having control of the state-owned assets and are even more uncomfortable with the fact that BP officials head the joint venture. It has been speculated that Gazprom, the state-run gas giant, may join the venture as a partner to improve the production deficit in the main oil field. If Gazprom does indeed become part owner, it is questionable what it will compensate BP for its ownership position. Over the years, BP has tried to develop a good relationship with the Russian government and demonstrate its commitment by investing billions of dollars. BP has also invested in other Russian ventures to drill in other oil fields, for instance, as a minority stakeholder with Rosneft.

This situation culminated with a battle over who would run TNK-BP, the third largest oil operation in Russia with 17 percent of Russia's reserves. The Russian shareholders charged that BP was running TNK-BP as a BP subsidiary and thereby depressing its values. BP officials considered the conflict as an attempt at "corporate raiding," accusing the rich Russian partners of hardball tactics. For example, Robert Dudley, the nominated chief executive of TNK-BP, was unable to get a visa and subsequently was banned by Russian courts from serving as CEO. BP officials suspected that this "paper-work problem" was orchestrated by Russian shareholders.

Fridman, one of the Russian owners, was appointed as the interim CEO, and all officials agreed to hire a new CEO that must be fluent in Russian and have business experience in Russia. New members were appointed to help keep the peace on the board, including former German Chancellor Gerhard Schroder. Not only did Dudley leave from the BP side, but the chief financial officer also felt pressure and resigned and left Russia. Thus, the bottom line appears to be that BP is conceding overall control to the Russians, but it is at least maintaining its 50 percent ownership position.

Sergei Kappukhin/Reuters/Landov

The fate of the second biggest foreign investment company in Russia and one of the world's biggest oil companies, TNK-BP, hangs in the balance amid signs of a shifting mood in the Kremlin.

Although BP has realized a positive return on its investment, it faces continued risk because of the organization's power structure and it will likely be under the control of the Russian tycoons, who are also subject to influence by government policy. As this example shows, firms that are pursuing international joint ventures need to be concerned about the opportunistic behavior of their partners as well as the political risks involved. Interestingly, other firms have had less control than BP in Russian joint ventures and in fact have lost their ownership positions through pressure by the Russian partners. In this light BP has done better than others, but risks obviously remain.

Sources: Associated Press, 2009, TNK-BP names tycoon Mikhail Fridman interim CEO, *Forbes*, http://www
.forbes.com, May 27; C. Belton & E. Krooks, 2009, Schroder a vital link with Russian TNK-BP, *Financial Times*,
January 16, 19; B. Gimbel, 2009, Russia's king of crude, *Fortune*, February 2, 88; I. Gorst, 2009, BP moves to
settle TNK clash, *Financial Times*, May 26, 15; J. Herron, 2009, Corporate news: Schroder to join TNK-BP board;
Venture makes room for ex-German leader, two other independent directors, *Wall Street Journal*, January 16,
B2; S. Reed & M. Elder, 2008, BP's dream deal hits a rough patch, *BusinessWeek*, August 11, 50; G. L. White &
G. Chazan, 2008, International business: BP retains its stake in TNK-BP; Russians gain clout, oust CEO Dudley;
IPO in 2010 likely, *Wall Street Journal*, September 5, B2; 2008, BP pays price for staying in Russia: Company
must take account of increased political risk, *Financial Times*, September 5, 8.

Two primary approaches are used to manage cooperative strategies—cost minimization and opportunity maximization[135] (see Figure 9.4). In the *cost minimization* management approach, the firm develops formal contracts with its partners. These contracts specify how the cooperative strategy is to be monitored and how partner behavior is to be controlled. The TNK-BP joint venture discussed previously is managed through contractual agreements. The goal of the cost-minimization approach is to minimize the cooperative strategy's cost and to prevent opportunistic behavior by a partner. The focus of the second managerial approach—*opportunity maximization*—is on maximizing a partnership's value-creation opportunities. In this case, partners are prepared to take advantage of unexpected opportunities to learn from each other and to explore additional marketplace possibilities. Less formal contracts, with fewer constraints on partners' behaviors, make it possible for partners to explore how their resources and capabilities can be shared in multiple value-creating ways.

Firms can successfully use both approaches to manage cooperative strategies. However, the costs to monitor the cooperative strategy are greater with cost minimization, in that writing detailed contracts and using extensive monitoring mechanisms is expensive, even though the approach is intended to reduce alliance costs. Although monitoring systems may prevent partners from acting in their own best interests, they also often preclude positive responses to new opportunities that surface to use the alliance's competitive advantages. Thus, formal contracts and extensive monitoring systems tend to stifle partners' efforts to gain maximum value from their participation in a cooperative strategy and require significant resources to be put into place and used.[136]

The relative lack of detail and formality that is a part of the contract developed by firms using the second management approach of opportunity maximization means that firms need to trust each other to act in the partnership's best interests. The psychological state of *trust* in the context of cooperative arrangements is "the expectation held by one firm that another will not exploit its vulnerabilities when faced with the opportunity to do so."[137] When partners trust each other, there is less need to write detailed formal contracts to specify each firm's alliance behaviors,[138] and the cooperative relationship tends to be more stable.[139] On a relative basis, trust tends to be more difficult to establish in international cooperative strategies compared with domestic ones. Differences in trade policies, cultures, laws, and politics that are part of cross-border alliances account for the increased difficulty. When trust exists, monitoring costs are reduced and opportunities to create value are maximized. Essentially, in these cases, the firms have built social capital.[140] According to company officials, the alliance between Renault and Nissan is built on "mutual trust between the two partners … together with operating and confidentiality rules."[141]

Research showing that trust between partners increases the likelihood of alliance success seems to highlight the benefits of the opportunity-maximization approach to managing cooperative strategies. Trust may also be the most efficient way to influence and control alliance partners' behaviors. Research indicates that trust can be a capability that is valuable, rare, imperfectly imitable, and often nonsubstitutable.[142] Thus, firms known to be trustworthy can have a competitive advantage in terms of how they develop and use cooperative strategies.[143] One reason is that it is impossible to specify all operational details of a cooperative strategy in a formal contract. Confidence that its partner can be trusted reduces the firm's concern about the inability to contractually control all alliance details.

SUMMARY

- A cooperative strategy is one such that firms work together to achieve a shared objective. Strategic alliances, where firms combine some of their resources and capabilities to create a competitive advantage, are the primary form of cooperative strategies. Joint ventures (where firms create and own equal shares of a new venture that is intended to develop competitive advantages), equity strategic alliances (where firms own different shares of a newly created venture), and nonequity strategic alliances (where firms cooperate through a contractual relationship) are the three basic types of strategic alliances. Outsourcing, discussed in Chapter 3, commonly occurs as firms form nonequity strategic alliances.

- Collusive strategies are the second type of cooperative strategies (with strategic alliances being the other). In many economies, explicit collusive strategies are illegal unless sanctioned by government policies. Increasing globalization has led to fewer government-sanctioned situations of explicit collusion. Tacit collusion, also called mutual forbearance, is a cooperative strategy through which firms tacitly cooperate to reduce industry output below the potential competitive output level, thereby raising prices above the competitive level.

- The reasons firms use cooperative strategies vary by slow-cycle, fast-cycle, and standard-cycle market conditions. To enter restricted markets (slow cycle), to move quickly from one competitive advantage to another (fast cycle), and to gain market power (standard cycle) are among the reasons why firms choose to use cooperative strategies.

- Four business-level cooperative strategies are used to help the firm improve its performance in individual product markets. (1) Through vertical and horizontal complementary alliances, companies combine their resources and capabilities to create value in different parts (vertical) or the same parts (horizontal) of the value chain. (2) Competition-responding strategies are formed to respond to competitors' actions, especially strategic ones. (3) Competition-reducing strategies are used to avoid excessive competition while the firm marshals its resources and capabilities to improve its competitiveness. (4) Uncertainty-reducing strategies are used to hedge against the risks created by the conditions of uncertain competitive environments (such as new product markets). Complementary alliances have the highest probability of yielding a sustainable competitive advantage; competition-reducing alliances have the lowest probability.

- Firms use corporate-level cooperative strategies to engage in product and/or geographic diversification. Through diversifying strategic alliances, firms agree to share some of their resources and capabilities to enter new markets or produce new products. Synergistic alliances are ones where firms share resources and capabilities to develop economies of scope. This alliance is similar to the business-level horizontal complementary alliance where firms try to develop operational synergy, except that synergistic alliances are used to develop synergy at the corporate level. Franchising is a corporate-level cooperative strategy where the franchisor uses a franchise as a contractual relationship to specify how resources and capabilities will be shared with franchisees.

- As an international cooperative strategy, a cross-border alliance is used for several reasons, including the performance superiority of firms competing in markets outside their domestic market and governmental restrictions on growth through mergers and acquisitions. Commonly, cross-border alliances are riskier than their domestic counterparts, particularly when partners aren't fully aware of each other's purpose for participating in the partnership.

- In a network cooperative strategy, several firms agree to form multiple partnerships to achieve shared objectives. A primary benefit of a network cooperative strategy is the firm's opportunity to gain access "to its partner's other partnerships." When this happens, the probability greatly increases that partners will find unique ways to share their resources and capabilities to form competitive advantages. Network cooperative strategies are used to form either a stable alliance network or a dynamic alliance network. Used in mature industries, partners use stable networks to extend competitive advantages into new areas. In rapidly changing environments where frequent product innovations occur, dynamic networks are primarily used as a tool of innovation.

- Cooperative strategies aren't risk free. If a contract is not developed appropriately, or if a partner misrepresents its competencies or fails to make them available, failure is likely. Furthermore, a firm may be held hostage through asset-specific investments made in conjunction with a partner, which may be exploited.

- Trust is an increasingly important aspect of successful cooperative strategies. Firms recognize the value of partnering with companies known for their trustworthiness. When trust exists, a cooperative strategy is managed to maximize the pursuit of opportunities between partners. Without trust, formal contracts and extensive monitoring systems are used to manage cooperative strategies. In this case, the interest is to minimize costs rather than to maximize opportunities by participating in a cooperative strategy.

1. What is the definition of cooperative strategy, and why is this strategy important to firms competing in the twenty-first century competitive landscape?

2. What is a strategic alliance? What are the three types of strategic alliances firms use to develop a competitive advantage?

3. What are the four business-level cooperative strategies, and what are the differences among them?

4. What are the three corporate-level cooperative strategies?

How do firms use each one to create a competitive advantage?

5. Why do firms use cross-border strategic alliances?

6. What risks are firms likely to experience as they use cooperative strategies?

7. What are the differences between the cost-minimization approach and the opportunity-maximization approach to managing cooperative strategies?

EXPERIENTIAL EXERCISES

EXERCISE 1: WHAT IS IT: TV, INTERNET, OR BOTH?

Hulu (http://www.hulu.com) is a Web site and a cooperative alliance that offers commercially supported content of TV (video on demand) shows through the Internet. The name is derived from a Chinese word which translated means "holder of precious things." The alliance has many different partners related in interesting ways. In addition, the alliance includes firms and partners from very different market types.

Working in groups, answer the following questions:

1. How would you describe the alliance partners? Characterize the market type for each (slow cycle, fast cycle, standard cycle).
2. What type of strategic alliance has Hulu become?
3. In what type of market is Hulu competing?
4. Why did this alliance form? List some competitive pressures that made this alliance a necessity for its partners.
5. What does the future hold for this alliance?

EXERCISE 2: THE SWATCHMOBILE

Swatch is well known for its line of stylish, affordable wristwatches. In the early 1990s, Swatch CEO Nicholas Hayek had a novel idea

to diversify his company's product offerings: a stylish, affordable automobile. His vision was to create a two-seat car with minimal storage space. Hayek expected these fuel-efficient cars would be highly attractive to younger European car buyers. Drawing on the company's watch designs, the Swatch car was intended to have removable body panels so that owners could change the car's look on a whim.

Swatch initially partnered with Volkswagen, but the alliance never reached production. In 1994, Swatch partnered with Mercedes-Benz. The vehicle was named SMART, which stood for "Swatch Mercedes Art."

Using Internet resources, answer the following questions:

1. What resources did each partner bring to the partnership?
2. How successful has the partnership been for each company?
3. Which company seems to be deriving the greatest benefit from the partnership and why?

COOPERATION VS. COMPETITION

Lynda Gratton/Professor of Management Practice/London Business School

Lynda Gratton, Professor of Management Practice at the London Business School, talks about the role of cooperation coming from a profession that is really quite competitive. As you prepare for this video consider the concepts of cooperation and competition in dynamic environments. Are they complementary or contradictory?

Before you watch the video consider the following concepts and questions and be prepared to discuss them in class:

Concepts
- Trust
- Networking
- Cooperation

Questions
1. Cooperation vs. competition: Which drives performance the most? Can we have one without the other?
2. Think about what you consider to be the firm of the future. What will it look like and how will employee roles shift?
3. Is cooperation necessary in today's environment, or is it merely a nicety?

CHAPTER 10

Corporate Governance and Ethics

Studying this chapter should provide you with the strategic management knowledge needed to:

1. Define corporate governance and explain why it is used to monitor and control managers' strategic decisions.

2. Explain why ownership has been largely separated from managerial control in the corporation.

3. Define an agency relationship and managerial opportunism and describe their strategic implications.

4. Explain how three internal governance mechanisms—ownership concentration, the board of directors, and executive compensation—are used to monitor and control managerial decisions.

5. Discuss the types of compensation executives receive and their effects on strategic decisions.

6. Describe how the external corporate governance mechanism—the market for corporate control—acts as a restraint on top-level managers' strategic decisions.

7. Discuss the use of corporate governance in international settings, especially in Germany, Japan, and China.

8. Describe how corporate governance fosters ethical strategic decisions and the importance of such behaviors on the part of top level managers.

IS CEO PAY OUTRAGEOUS, IRRESPONSIBILE, OR GREEDY?

In 2008, the ten most highly paid CEOs earned a total of $472.2 million. Furthermore, seven of these CEOs who worked at the same companies in 2007 received an increase in pay of approximately 26 percent over the previous year. Placing this in perspective, an average of $47.22 million was paid to these CEOs in a year when most large firms—including theirs—lost significant market value, and many experienced net losses. In 2008, we learned that the U.S. economy and, indeed, much of the rest of the world, was in a deep recession. In fact, it is perhaps the worst since the Great Depression in the 1930s. Many believe that this recession was largely caused by irresponsible and greedy strategies followed by top-level managers in the financial services and real estate industries. In addition, the corporate governance system failed to rein in these managers, who took extreme risks causing billions of dollars in losses. Real estate values plummeted in many parts of the country, there were a substantial number of mortgage foreclosures, unemployment increased substantially, and the stock market took a nosedive.

In this context, top executive pay came under intense criticism. In recent years, supposedly knowledgeable people argued that top-level managers were being paid for performance. If so, how could they earn such high compensation when their companies were performing poorly? Many CEOs earn more than 100 times the amount received by their firm's lowest-paid employee. Despite the average increases for the highest-paid CEOs, the median salary and bonuses for CEOs of the largest 200 U.S. firms decreased by 8.5 percent in 2008, but their total direct compensation only fell by 3.4 percent. The decline in the financial services industry was much greater, as could be expected. Still, the median value of perks provided to CEOs in 2008 increased by about 7 percent. "Perks"

Julia Hiebaum/Alamy

include many possible benefits, such as club memberships, free personal travel in company jets, bodyguards, and chauffeured cars. In fact, the CEO of Occidental Petroleum received $400,000 worth of financial planning. This was a part of his compensation in 2008, which totaled $30 million. While this benefit for financial planning is only 1.33 percent of his total pay for the year, $400,000 is greater than the total annual household income for most U.S. citizens.

In a survey conducted by the *Financial Times*, respondents from France, Germany, Italy, Spain, the United Kingdom, and the United States stated that they believed that business leaders were paid too much. The lowest percentage believing that top-level managers were overpaid was about 75 percent in France, while almost 90 percent in Germany felt they were overpaid. When the feelings of the general public are combined with the poor performance of companies in a weak economy, pundits often blame an inadequate system of corporate governance. This concern is amplified by reports of bad strategic decisions of business leaders blamed for creating the economic crisis. Thus, governments and others have begun to explore the governance mechanisms including compensation systems, boards of directors, ownership, and disciplining from the markets. It is likely that new regulations will be proposed and adopted to control what the public perceives to be irresponsibility and greed on the part of business leaders.

Sources: V. Tong, 2009, As pay falls, CEOs get more perks, YAHOO! News, http://news.yahoo.com, May 1; 2009, The pay at the top, *The New York Times*, http://www.nytimes.com, April 16; R. Milne, 2009, Sharp divide on executive pay, *Financial Times*, http://www.ft.com, April 13; J. S. Lublin, 2009, CEO pay sinks along with profits, *Wall Street Journal*, http://www.wsj.com, April 6; T. Carr, 2008, An ethical analysis of CEO compensation, *Fast Company*, http://www.fastcompany.com, November 28; A. Cohen, 2008, CEO pay; outrageous—and bad for MBA programs, *Fast Company*, http://www.fastcompany.com, April 6.

As the Opening Case illustrates, governance mechanisms designed to ensure effective leadership of firms to develop and implement strategies that create value for stakeholders is challenging. However, corporate governance is critical to firms' success and thus has become an increasingly important part of the strategic management process.[1] If the board makes the wrong decisions in selecting, governing, and compensating the firm's strategic leader (e.g., CEO), the shareholders and the firm suffer. When CEOs are motivated to act in the best interests of the firm—in particular, the shareholders—the firm's value should increase.

As suggested in the Opening Case, many people now believe that CEOs in the United States are paid too much; the hefty increases in their incentive compensation in recent years ostensibly come from trying to link pay to their firms' performance. However, research also suggests that firms with a smaller pay gap between the CEO and other top level managers perform better, especially when collaboration among top management team members is more important.[2] The performance improvement in these cases is due to better cooperation among the top management team members. Other research suggests that CEOs receive excessive compensation when corporate governance is the weakest.[3]

Corporate governance is the set of mechanisms used to manage the relationship among stakeholders and to determine and control the strategic direction and performance of organizations.[4] At its core, corporate governance is concerned with identifying ways to ensure that strategic decisions are made effectively.[5] Governance can also be thought of as a means to establish harmony between parties (the firm's owners and its top-level managers) whose interests may conflict. In modern corporations—especially those in the United States and the United Kingdom—a primary objective of corporate governance is to ensure that the interests of top-level managers are aligned with the interests of the shareholders. Corporate governance involves oversight in areas where owners, managers, and members of boards of directors may have conflicts of interest. These areas include the election of directors, the general supervision of CEO pay and more focused supervision of director pay, and the corporation's overall structure and strategic direction.[6]

Recent emphasis on corporate governance stems mainly from the failure of corporate governance mechanisms to adequately monitor and control top-level managers' decisions. This situation results in changes in governance mechanisms in corporations throughout the world, especially with respect to efforts intended to improve the performance of boards of directors. A second and more positive reason for this interest comes from evidence that a well-functioning corporate governance and control system can create a competitive advantage for an individual firm.[7] Thus, in this chapter, we describe actions designed to implement strategies that focus on monitoring and controlling mechanisms that are designed to ensure that top-level managerial actions contribute to the firm's strategic competitiveness and its ability to earn above-average returns.

Effective corporate governance is also of interest to nations.[8] Although corporate governance reflects company standards, it also collectively reflects country societal standards.[9] As with these firms and their boards, nations that effectively govern their corporations may gain a competitive advantage over rival countries. In a range of countries, but especially in the United States and the United Kingdom, the fundamental goal of business organizations is to maximize shareholder value.[10] Traditionally, shareholders are treated as the firm's key stakeholders, because they are the company's legal owners. The firm's owners expect top-level managers and others influencing the corporation's actions (e.g., the board of directors) to make decisions that will maximize the company's value and, hence, the owners' wealth.[11] Research shows that national models of corporate governance influence firms' decisions to invest and operate in different countries.[12]

In the first section of this chapter, we describe the relationship that is the foundation on which the modern corporation is built: the relationship between owners and managers. The majority of this chapter is used to explain various mechanisms owners use to govern managers and to ensure that they comply with their responsibility to maximize shareholder value.

Corporate governance is the set of mechanisms used to manage the relationship among stakeholders and to determine and control the strategic direction and performance of organizations.

Three internal governance mechanisms and a single external one are used in the modern corporation. The three internal governance mechanisms we describe in this chapter are (1) ownership concentration, represented by types of shareholders and their different incentives to monitor managers; (2) the board of directors; and (3) executive compensation. We then consider the market for corporate control, an external corporate governance mechanism. Essentially, this market is a set of potential owners seeking to acquire undervalued firms and earn above-average returns on their investments by replacing ineffective top-level management teams.[13] The chapter's focus then shifts to the issue of international corporate governance. We briefly describe governance approaches used in German, Japanese, and Chinese firms whose traditional governance structures are being affected by the realities of global competition. In part, this discussion suggests that the structures used to govern global companies in many different countries, including Germany, Japan, the United Kingdom, and the United States, as well as emerging economies such as China and India, are becoming more, rather than less, similar. Closing our analysis of corporate governance is a consideration of the need for these control mechanisms to encourage and support ethical behavior in organizations.

Importantly, the mechanisms discussed in this chapter can positively influence the governance of the modern corporation, which has placed significant responsibility and authority in the hands of top-level managers. With multiple governance mechanisms operating simultaneously, however, it is also possible for some of the governance mechanisms to be in conflict.[14] Later, we review how these conflicts can occur.

Separation of Ownership and Managerial Control

Historically, U.S. firms were managed by the founder-owners and their descendants. In these cases, corporate ownership and control resided in the same persons. As firms grew larger, "the managerial revolution led to a separation of ownership and control in most large corporations, where control of the firm shifted from entrepreneurs to professional managers while ownership became dispersed among thousands of unorganized stockholders who were removed from the day-to-day management of the firm."[15] These changes created the modern public corporation, which is based on the efficient separation of ownership and managerial control. Supporting the separation is a basic legal premise suggesting that the primary objective of a firm's activities is to increase the corporation's profit and, thereby, the financial gains of the owners (the shareholders).[16]

The separation of ownership and managerial control allows shareholders to purchase stock, which entitles them to income (residual returns) from the firm's operations after paying expenses. This right, however, requires that they also take a risk that the firm's expenses may exceed its revenues. In order to manage this investment risk, shareholders maintain a diversified portfolio by investing in several companies to reduce their overall risk.[17] The poor performance or failure of any one firm in which they invest has less overall effect on the value of the entire portfolio of investments. Thus, shareholders specialize in managing their investment risk.

In small firms, managers often are high percentage owners, which means less separation between ownership and managerial control. In fact, in a large number of family-owned firms, ownership and managerial control are not separated. In the United States, at least one-third of the S&P 500 firms have substantial family ownership, holding on average about 18 percent of the outstanding equity. And family-owned firms perform better when a member of the family is the CEO than when the CEO is an outsider.[18] In many countries outside the United States, such as in Latin America, Asia, and some European countries, family-owned firms represent the dominant form.[19] The primary purpose of most of these firms is to increase the family's wealth, which explains why a family CEO often is better than an outside CEO.

Family-controlled firms face at least two critical issues. First, as they grow, they may not have access to all of the skills needed to effectively manage the firm and maximize its returns for the family. Thus, they may need outsiders. Also, as they grow, they may need to seek outside capital and thus give up some of the ownership. In these cases, protection of the minority owners' rights becomes important.[20] To avoid these potential problems, when these firms grow and become more complex, their owner-managers may contract with managerial specialists. These managers make major decisions in the owners' firm and are compensated on the basis of their decision-making skills. As such, recent research suggests that firms in which families own enough equity to have influence without major control tend to make the best strategic decisions.[21]

Without owner (shareholder) specialization in risk bearing and management specialization in decision making, a firm may be limited by the abilities of its owners to manage and make effective strategic decisions. Thus, the separation and specialization of ownership (risk bearing) and managerial control (decision making) should produce the highest returns for the firm's owners.

Shareholder value is reflected by the price of the firm's stock. As stated earlier, corporate governance mechanisms, such as the board of directors, or compensation based on the performance of a firm is the reason that CEOs show general concern about the firm's stock price.

Agency Relationships

The separation between owners and managers creates an agency relationship. An **agency relationship** exists when one or more persons (the principal or principals) hire another person or persons (the agent or agents) as decision-making specialists to perform a service.[22] Thus, an agency relationship exists when one party delegates decision-making responsibility to a second party for compensation (see Figure 10.1).[23] In addition to shareholders and top-level managers, other examples of agency relationships are consultants and clients and insured and insurer. Moreover, within organizations, an agency relationship exists between managers and their employees, as well as between top level managers and the firm's owners.[24] However, in this chapter we focus on the agency relationship between the firm's owners (the principals) and top-level managers (the principals' agents) because these managers formulate and implement the firm's strategies, which have major effects on firm performance.[25]

The separation between ownership and managerial control can be problematic. Research evidence documents a variety of agency problems in the modern corporation.[26] Problems can surface because the principal and the agent have different interests and goals, or because shareholders lack direct control of large publicly traded corporations. Problems also arise when an agent makes decisions that result in the pursuit of goals that conflict with those of the principals. Thus, the separation of ownership and control potentially allows divergent interests (between principals and agents) to surface, which can lead to managerial opportunism.

Managerial opportunism is the seeking of self-interest with guile (i.e., cunning or deceit).[27] Opportunism is both an attitude (e.g., an inclination) and a set of behaviors (i.e., specific acts of self-interest).[28] It is not possible for principals to know beforehand which agents will or will not act opportunistically. The reputations of top level managers are an imperfect predictor, and opportunistic behavior cannot be observed until it has occurred. Thus, principals establish governance and control mechanisms to prevent agents from acting opportunistically, even though only a few are likely to do so. Interestingly, research suggests that when CEOs feel constrained by governance mechanisms, they are more likely to seek external advice that in turn helps them to make better strategic decisions.[29] Any time that principals delegate decision-making responsibilities to agents, the opportunity for conflicts of interest exists. Top-level managers, for example, may make strategic decisions that maximize their personal welfare and minimize

An **agency relationship** exists when one or more persons (the principal or principals) hire another person or persons (the agent or agents) as decision-making specialists to perform a service.

Managerial opportunism is the seeking of self-interest with guile (i.e., cunning or deceit).

Figure 10.1 An Agency Relationship

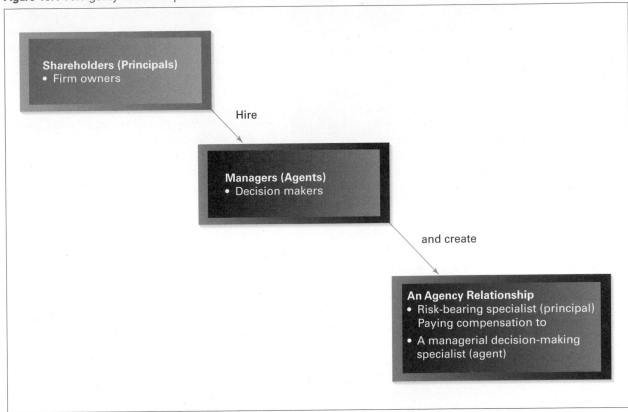

their personal risk.[30] Decisions such as these prevent the maximization of shareholder wealth. Decisions regarding product diversification demonstrate this alternative.

Product Diversification as an Example of an Agency Problem

As explained in Chapter 6, a corporate-level strategy to diversify the firm's product lines can enhance a firm's strategic competitiveness and increase its returns, both of which serve the interests of shareholders and the top-level managers. However, product diversification can result in two benefits to managers that shareholders do not enjoy, so top level managers may prefer product diversification more than shareholders do.[31]

First, diversification usually increases the size of a firm, and size is positively related to executive compensation. Also, diversification increases the complexity of managing a firm and its network of businesses, possibly requiring more pay because of this complexity.[32] Thus, increased product diversification provides an opportunity for top-level managers to increase their compensation.[33]

Second, product diversification and the resulting diversification of the firm's portfolio of businesses can reduce top-level managers' employment risk. Managerial employment risk is the risk of job loss, loss of compensation, and loss of managerial reputation.[34] These risks are reduced with increased diversification, because a firm and its upper-level managers are less vulnerable to the reduction in demand associated with a single or limited number of product lines or businesses. For example, Kellogg Co. was almost entirely focused on breakfast cereal in 2001 when it suffered its first-ever market share leadership loss to perennial number two, General Mills, Inc. Upon appointing Carlos Gutierrez, a longtime manager at Kellogg, to the CEO position, the

AP Photo/M. Spencer Green

The Kashi acquisition, one of many by Kellogg, helped drive the company's net earnings up during a recessionary economy.

company embarked on a new strategy to overcome its poor performance. A *BusinessWeek* article outlined his strategy results as follows: "To drive sales, Gutierrez unveiled such novel products as Special K snack bars, bought cookie maker Keebler Co., and ramped up Kellogg's health-foods presence by snapping up Worthington Foods Inc., a maker of soy and vegetarian products, and cereal maker Kashi. He pushed net earnings up 77 percent, to $890.6 million, from 1998 to 2004, as sales rose 42 percent, to $9.6 billion."[35] Kellogg's revenues continued to increase to approximately $13 billion a year in 2008, which was almost 8 percent higher than 2007.[36] This is a remarkable accomplishment during a recessionary economy. Kellogg's diversified scope increased, yet it was accomplished in highly related businesses that provided synergy. Through this strategy, the CEO's risk of job loss was substantially reduced. Recent research shows that this type of diversification can be profitable.[37]

Another potential agency problem is a firm's free cash flows over which top-level managers have control. Free cash flows are resources remaining after the firm has invested in all projects that have positive net present value within its current businesses.[38] In anticipation of positive returns, managers may decide to invest these funds in products that are not associated with the firm's current lines of business to increase the firm's level of diversification. The managerial decision to use free cash flows to overdiversify the firm is an example of self-serving and opportunistic managerial behavior. In contrast to managers, shareholders may prefer that free cash flows be distributed to them as dividends, so they can control how the cash is invested.[39]

Figure 10.2 Manager and Shareholder Risk and Diversification

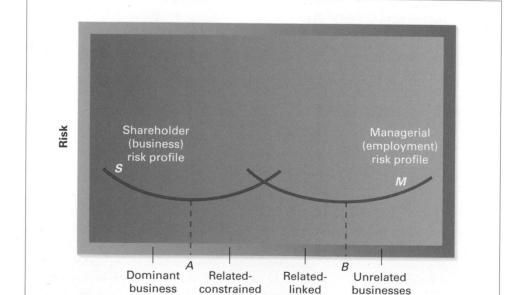

Curve S in Figure 10.2 depicts the shareholders' optimal level of diversification. Owners seek the level of diversification that reduces the risk of the firm's total failure while simultaneously increasing the company's value through the development of economies of scale and scope (see Chapter 6). Of the four corporate-level diversification strategies shown in Figure 10.2, shareholders likely prefer the diversified position noted by point A on curve S—a position that is located between the dominant business and related-constrained diversification strategies. Of course, the optimum level of diversification owners seek varies from firm to firm.[40] Factors that affect shareholders' preferences include the firm's primary industry, the intensity of rivalry among competitors in that industry, and the top management team's experience with implementing diversification strategies and its effects on other firm strategies, such as its entry into international markets (see Chapter 8).[41]

As do principals, top level managers—as agents—also seek an optimal level of diversification. Declining performance resulting from too much product diversification increases the probability that corporate control of the firm will be acquired in the market. After a firm is acquired, the employment risk for the firm's top-level managers increases substantially. Furthermore, a manager's employment opportunities in the external managerial labor market (discussed in Chapter 12) are affected negatively by a firm's poor performance. Therefore, top level managers prefer diversification, but not to a point that it increases their employment risk and reduces their employment opportunities.[42] Curve M in Figure 10.2 shows that top level managers prefer higher levels of product diversification than do shareholders. Top-level managers might prefer the level of diversification shown by point B on curve M.

In general, shareholders prefer riskier strategies and more focused diversification. They reduce their risk through holding a diversified portfolio of equity investments. Alternatively, managers cannot balance their employment risk by working for a diverse portfolio of firms, and therefore, may prefer a level of diversification that maximizes firm size and their compensation while also reducing their employment risk. Product diversification, therefore, is a potential agency problem that could result in principals incurring costs to control their agents' behaviors.

Agency Costs and Governance Mechanisms

The potential conflict illustrated by Figure 10.2, coupled with the fact that principals cannot easily predict which managers might act opportunistically, demonstrates why principals establish governance mechanisms. However, the firm incurs costs when it uses one or more governance mechanisms. **Agency costs** are the sum of incentive costs, monitoring costs, enforcement costs, and individual financial losses incurred by principals because governance mechanisms cannot guarantee total compliance by the agent. If a firm is diversified, governance costs increase because it is more difficult to monitor what is going on inside the firm.[43]

In general, managerial interests may prevail when governance mechanisms are weak; this is exemplified in situations where managers have a significant amount of autonomy to make strategic decisions. If, however, the board of directors controls managerial autonomy, or if other strong governance mechanisms are used, the firm's strategies should better reflect the interests of the shareholders. More recently, governance observers have been concerned about more egregious behavior beyond inefficient corporate strategy.

Due to fraudulent behavior such as that found at Enron and WorldCom, concerns regarding corporate governance continue to grow. In 2002, the U.S. Congress enacted the Sarbanes-Oxley (SOX) Act, which increased the intensity of corporate governance mechanisms.[44] Furthermore, the serious problems experienced in the financial services industry are likely the result of poor governance and top-level managers making very bad strategic decisions. In fact, the bonuses paid to Merrill Lynch executives after extremely poor performance (described in the Opening Case) likely reflect managerial opportunism.

Agency costs are the sum of incentive costs, monitoring costs, enforcement costs, and individual financial losses incurred by principals because governance mechanisms cannot guarantee total compliance by the agent.

While the implementation of the Sarbanes-Oxley Act in 2002 has been controversial to some, most believe that the results of it have been generally positive. Section 404 of SOX, which prescribes significant transparency improvement on internal controls associated with accounting and auditing, has arguably improved the internal auditing scrutiny and thereby trust in such financial reporting. A recent study indicated that internal controls associated with Section 404 increased shareholder value.[45] However, some argue that the Act, especially Section 404, creates excessive costs for firms. In addition, a decrease in foreign firms listing on U.S. stock exchanges occurred at the same time as listing on foreign exchanges increased. In part, this shift may be due to the costs associated with listing on U.S. exchanges associated with requirements of SOX.

More intensive application of governance mechanisms may produce significant changes in strategies. For example, because of more intense governance, firms may take on fewer risky projects and thus decrease potential shareholder wealth. Next, we explain the effects of different governance mechanisms on the decisions managers make about the choice and the use of the firm's strategies.

Ownership Concentration

Both the number of large-block shareholders and the total percentage of shares they own define **ownership concentration. Large-block shareholders** typically own at least 5 percent of a corporation's issued shares. Ownership concentration as a governance mechanism has received considerable interest because large-block shareholders are increasingly active in their demands that corporations adopt effective governance mechanisms to control managerial decisions.[46]

In general, diffuse ownership (a large number of shareholders with small holdings and few, if any, large-block shareholders) produces weak monitoring of managers' decisions. For example, diffuse ownership makes it difficult for owners to effectively coordinate their actions. Diversification of the firm's product lines beyond the shareholders' optimum level can result from ineffective monitoring of managers' decisions. Higher levels of monitoring could encourage managers to avoid strategic decisions that harm shareholder value. In fact, research evidence shows that ownership concentration is associated with lower levels of firm product diversification.[47] Thus, with high degrees of ownership concentration, the probability is greater that managers' strategic decisions will be designed to maximize shareholder value.[48]

As noted, such concentration of ownership has an influence on strategies and firm value, mostly positive but perhaps not in all cases. For example, when large shareholders have a high degree of wealth, they have power relative to minority shareholders in extracting wealth from the firm, especially when they are in managerial positions. The importance of boards of directors in mitigating expropriation of minority shareholder value has been found in firms with strong family ownership wherein family members have incentive to appropriate shareholder wealth, especially in the second generation after the founder has departed.[49] Such expropriation is often found in countries such as Korea where minority shareholder rights are not as protected as they are in the United States.[50] However, in the United States much of the ownership concentration has come from increasing equity ownership by institutional investors.

The Growing Influence of Institutional Owners

A classic work published in the 1930s argued that the "modern" corporation was characterized by a separation of ownership and control.[51] The change occurred primarily because growth prevented founders-owners from maintaining their dual positions in their increasingly complex companies. More recently, another shift has occurred: Ownership of many modern corporations is now concentrated in the hands of institutional investors rather than individual shareholders.[52]

Both the number of large-block shareholders and the total percentage of shares they own define **ownership concentration.**

Large-block shareholders typically own at least 5 percent of a corporation's issued shares.

Institutional owners are financial institutions such as stock mutual funds and pension funds that control large-block shareholder positions. Because of their prominent ownership positions, institutional owners, as large-block shareholders, are a powerful governance mechanism. Institutions of these types now own more than 60 percent of the stock in large U.S. corporations. Pension funds alone control at least one-half of corporate equity.[53]

These ownership percentages suggest that as investors, institutional owners have both the size and the incentive to discipline ineffective top-level managers and can significantly influence a firm's choice of strategies and overall strategic decisions.[54] Research evidence indicates that institutional and other large-block shareholders are becoming more active in their efforts to influence a corporation's strategic decisions, unless they have a business relationship with the firm. Initially, these shareholder activists and institutional investors concentrated on the performance and accountability of CEOs and contributed to the dismissal of a number of them. They often target the actions of boards more directly via proxy vote proposals that are intended to give shareholders more decision rights because they believe board processes have been ineffective.[55] In fact, a new rule recently proposed and approved by the U.S. Securities and Exchange Commission allows large shareholders (owning 1 to 5 percent of a company's stock) to nominate up to 25 percent of a company's board of directors.[56]

For example, CalPERS provides retirement and health coverage to more than 1.3 million current and retired public employees. At the end of 2008, it was the largest public employee pension fund in the United States, but the economic crisis caused its total assets to decrease by approximately 30 percent.[57] Still, CalPERS is respected and even feared in some companies' boardrooms. It is generally thought to act aggressively to promote governance decisions and actions that it believes will enhance shareholder value in companies in which it invests. For instance, CalPERS places five or so companies on its "Focus List" each year. This type of public acknowledgement may influence the board of directors and top level managers to take action, which in turn often increases the firm's shareholder value. For example, the CalPERS focus list for 2009 had four firms on it led by Eli Lilly.[58] The largest institutional investor, TIAA-CREF, has taken actions similar to those of CalPERS, but with a less publicly aggressive stance. To date, research suggests that institutional activism may not have a strong effect on firm performance, but that its influence may be indirect through its effects on important strategic decisions, such as those concerned with international diversification and innovation.[59] With the increased intensity of governance associated with the passage of the SOX Act and the latest economic crisis largely created by poor strategic decisions in the financial services industry, institutional investors and other groups have been emboldened in their activism.

Board of Directors

Typically, shareholders monitor the managerial decisions and actions of a firm through the board of directors. Shareholders elect members to their firm's board. Those who are elected are expected to oversee managers and to ensure that the corporation is operated in ways that will maximize its shareholders' wealth. Even with large institutional investors having major equity ownership in U.S. firms, diffuse ownership continues to exist in most firms, which means that in large corporations, monitoring and control of managers by individual shareholders is limited. Furthermore, large financial institutions, such as banks, are prevented from directly owning stock in firms and from having representatives on companies' boards of directors, although this restriction is not the case in Europe and elsewhere.[60] These conditions highlight the importance of the board of directors for corporate governance. Unfortunately, over time, boards of directors have not been highly effective in monitoring and controlling top management's actions.[61]

Institutional owners are financial institutions such as stock mutual funds and pension funds that control large-block shareholder positions.

Given the recent problems with top-level managers making less than ethical decisions, boards are experiencing increasing pressure from shareholders, lawmakers, and regulators to become more forceful in their oversight role to prevent inappropriate actions by top-level managers. Furthermore, boards not only serve a monitoring role, but they also provide resources to firms. These resources include their personal knowledge and expertise as well as their access to resources of other firms through their external contacts and relationships.[62]

The **board of directors** is a group of elected individuals whose primary responsibility is to act in the owners' best interests by formally monitoring and controlling the corporation's top-level managers.[63] Boards have the power to direct the affairs of the organization, punish and reward managers, and protect shareholders' rights and interests. Thus, an appropriately structured and effective board of directors protects owners from managerial opportunism such as that found at Enron and WorldCom and at financial services firms including AIG and Merrill Lynch, where shareholders and employees encountered significant losses. Board members are seen as stewards of their company's resources, and the way they carry out these responsibilities affects the society in which their firm operates. For instance, research suggests that better governance produces more effective strategic decisions, which lead to higher firm performance.[64]

Generally, board members (often called directors) are classified into one of three groups (see Table 10.1). *Insiders* are active top-level managers in the corporation who are elected to the board because they are a source of information about the firm's day-to-day operations.[65] *Related outsiders* have some relationship with the firm, contractual or otherwise, that may create questions about their independence, but these individuals are not involved with the corporation's day-to-day activities. *Outsiders* provide independent counsel to the firm and may hold top-level managerial positions in other companies or may have been elected to the board prior to the beginning of the current CEO's tenure.[66]

Historically, boards of directors were primarily dominated by inside managers. A widely accepted view is that a board with a significant percentage of its membership from the firm's top-level managers provides relatively weak monitoring and control of managerial decisions.[67] Managers have sometimes used their power to select and compensate directors and exploit their personal ties with them. In response to the SEC's proposal to require audit committees to be composed of outside directors, in 1984, the New York Stock Exchange implemented a rule requiring outside directors to head the audit committee. Subsequently, other rules required important committees such as the compensation committee and the nomination committee to be headed by independent outside directors.[68] These other requirements were instituted after the Sarbanes-Oxley Act was passed, and policies of the New York Stock Exchange now require companies to maintain boards of directors that are composed of a majority of outside independent directors and to maintain full independent audit committees. Thus, corporate governance is becoming more intense especially with the oversight of the board of directors.

Table 10.1 Classifications of Board of Director Members

Insiders
• The firm's CEO and other top-level managers

Related outsiders
• Individuals not involved with the firm's day-to-day operations, but who have a relationship with the company

Outsiders
• Individuals who are independent of the firm in terms of day-to-day operations and other relationships

The **board of directors** is a group of elected individuals whose primary responsibility is to act in the owners' interests by formally monitoring and controlling the corporation's top-level managers.

Critics advocate reforms to ensure that independent outside directors represent a significant majority of the total membership of a board, which research suggests has been accomplished.[69] On the other hand, others argue that having outside directors is not enough to resolve the problems; it depends on the power of the CEO. One proposal to reduce the power of the CEO is to separate the chairperson's role and the CEO's role on the board so that the same person does not hold both positions.[70] Yet, having a board that actively monitors top executive decisions and actions does not ensure high performance. The value that the directors bring to the company also influences the outcomes. For example, boards with members having significant relevant experience and knowledge are the most likely to help the firm formulate effective strategies and to implement them successfully.[71]

Alternatively, having a large number of outside board members can also create some problems. Outsiders do not have contact with the firm's day-to-day operations and typically do not have easy access to the level of information about managers and their skills that is required to effectively evaluate managerial decisions and initiatives.[72] Outsiders can, however, obtain valuable information through frequent interactions with inside board members, during board meetings, and otherwise. Insiders possess such information by virtue of their organizational positions. Thus, boards with a critical mass of insiders typically are better informed about intended strategic initiatives, the reasons for the initiatives, and the outcomes expected from them.[73] Without this type of information, outsider-dominated boards may emphasize the use of financial, as opposed to strategic, controls to gather performance information to evaluate managers' and business units' performances. A virtually exclusive reliance on financial evaluations shifts risk to top-level managers, who, in turn, may make decisions to maximize their interests and reduce their employment risk. Reductions in R&D investments, additional diversification of the firm, and the pursuit of greater levels of compensation are some of the results of managers' actions to achieve financial goals set by outsider-dominated boards.[74] Additionally, boards can make mistakes in CEO succession decisions because of the lack of important information about candidates as well as specific needs of the firm. As you would expect, knowledgeable and balanced boards are likely to be the most effective over time.[75]

Enhancing the Effectiveness of the Board of Directors

As explained in the Strategic Focus, because of the importance of boards of directors in corporate governance and as a result of increased scrutiny from shareholders—in particular, large institutional investors—the performances of individual board members and of entire boards are being evaluated more formally and with greater intensity.[76] Given the demand for greater accountability and improved performance, many boards have initiated voluntary changes (e.g., those described at Borders and EasyJet). Among these changes are (1) increases in the diversity of the backgrounds of board members (e.g., a greater number of directors from public service, academic, and scientific settings; a greater percentage of ethnic minorities and women; and members from different countries on boards of U.S. firms), (2) the strengthening of internal management and accounting control systems, and (3) the establishment and consistent use of formal processes to evaluate the board's performance.[77] Additional changes include (4) the creation of a "lead director" role that has strong powers with regard to the board agenda and oversight of non-management board member activities, and (5) modification of the compensation of directors, especially reducing or eliminating stock options as a part of the package.

Boards are increasingly involved in the strategic decision-making process, so they must work collaboratively. Some argue that improving the processes used by boards to make decisions and monitor managers and firm outcomes is important for board effectiveness.[78] Moreover, because of the increased pressure from owners and the potential

WHERE HAVE ALL THE GOOD DIRECTORS GONE?

The global economic crisis, largely the result of extremely poor strategic decisions made by top-level managers in the financial services industry, laid bare the holes in the U.S. corporate governance system. In particular, the crisis showed that many boards of directors were very weak. In the early 2000s, boards of directors suffered significant criticism for the failures in monitoring executive actions at Enron, Tyco, WorldCom, and other companies. With more recent failures, boards are now experiencing substantial public animosity. Many people do not understand how top-level managers were allowed to take the extreme risks that have melted away corporate value when the debt became too heavy for most of the firms.

The weakness of corporate boards is exemplified by the fact that the President of the United States had to fire a highly ineffective CEO because the board of General Motors had failed to act in recent years.

As a result of the economic meltdown, the obviously poor strategic decisions leading to it, and the inability of previous boards to prevent the problems, many boards are now changing. Old board members are resigning or being replaced and many new members are joining boards. For example, in 2009, Citigroup, one of the major contributors to the problems in the financial services industry, nominated four new independent directors. Boardroom shakeups are also occurring outside of the financial services industry. For example, EasyJet announced that it had appointed a new chairman of its board to replace the current chairman, Colin Chandler. The new chairman, Michael Rake, formerly headed the BT Group.

In an industry challenged by technology developments and the recession, Borders has suffered the most. Its poor financial results are the outcome of its inability to keep pace. Thus, in 2009, Borders made major changes in the top management team and announced that seven of its ten directors were departing. Only five of them will be replaced, thereby shrinking the number of members on the board to eight. The former executive team and board tried unsuccessfully to sell the firm. The new team will focus on restructuring the firm.

Interestingly, research suggests that smaller boards are more effective in governing companies than are larger boards. Thus, Borders' decision to downsize its board may be a good one. Changes are being made in the processes used by many boards in order to improve their monitoring function. These changes extend to the balance of independent and inside members, renewed emphasis on audit and compensation committees, and ensuring that outside board members spend an adequate amount of time on board business so that they can make informed decisions. Furthermore, there are other moves afoot to change the governance practices in firms. These include new rules and a renewed scrutiny by the U.S. Securities and Exchange Commission and other governmental agencies. In addition, the chairman of the Financial Reporting Council in the United Kingdom announced a complete review of the Combined Code, a template of corporate governance used by investors and

Rick Wagoner is the former CEO of GM, who was asked to resign by President Obama.

conflict among board members, procedures are necessary to help boards function effectively in facilitating the strategic decision-making process.

Increasingly, outside directors are being required to own significant equity stakes as a prerequisite to holding a board seat. In fact, some research suggests that firms perform better if outside directors have such a stake; the trend is toward higher pay for directors with more stock ownership, but with fewer stock options.[79] However, other research suggests that too much ownership can lead to lower independence for board members.[80] In addition, other research suggests that diverse boards help firms make more effective strategic decisions and perform better over time.[81] Although questions remain about whether more independent and diverse boards enhance board effectiveness, the trends for greater independence and increasing diversity among board members are likely to continue. Clearly, the corporate failures in the first decade of the 21st century suggest the need for more effective boards.

Executive Compensation

As the Opening Case illustrates, the compensation of top-level managers, and especially of CEOs, generates a great deal of interest and strongly held opinions. One reason for this widespread interest can be traced to a natural curiosity about extremes and excesses. For example, the *Los Angeles Times* reported that "CEO compensation tripled from 1990 to 2004, rising at more than three times the rate of corporate earnings. CEOs at 11 of the largest U.S. companies received $865 million in a five-year period while presiding over losses in shareholder value."[82] As stated in the Opening Case, the ten highest-paid executives in 2008, during a strong recession, earned an average of $47.22 million. Some consider this excessive pay, especially for those whose firms suffered net losses during this year, because most firms lost market value in 2008. Another stems from a more substantive view that CEO pay is tied in an indirect but tangible way to the fundamental governance processes in large corporations. Some believe that while highly paid, CEOs are not overpaid.[83] Others argue that not only are they highly paid, they are overpaid. These critics are especially concerned that compensation is not as strongly related to performance as some believe.[84]

Executive compensation is a governance mechanism that seeks to align the interests of managers and owners through salaries, bonuses, and long-term incentive compensation, such as stock awards and options.[85] Long-term incentive plans have become a critical part of compensation packages in U.S. firms. The use of longer-term pay theoretically helps firms cope with or avoid potential agency problems by linking managerial wealth to the wealth of common shareholders.[86]

Sometimes the use of a long-term incentive plan prevents major stockholders (e.g., institutional investors) from pressing for changes in the composition of the board of directors, because they assume the long-term incentives will ensure that top executives will act in shareholders' best interests. Alternatively, stockholders largely assume that top-executive pay and the performance of a firm are more closely aligned when firms have boards that are dominated by outside members. However, research shows that fraudulent behavior can be associated with stock option incentives, such as earnings manipulation.[87]

STRATEGY
RIGHT NOW

Read further about the GM bankruptcy and what it means for its board of directors moving forward.

www.cengage.com/
management/hitt

Executive compensation is a governance mechanism that seeks to align the interests of managers and owners through salaries, bonuses, and long-term incentive compensation, such as stock awards and options.

Effectively using executive compensation as a governance mechanism is particularly challenging to firms implementing international strategies. For example, the interests of owners of multinational corporations may be best served by less uniformity among the firm's foreign subsidiaries' compensation plans.[88] Developing an array of unique compensation plans requires additional monitoring and increases the firm's potential agency costs. Importantly, levels of pay vary by regions of the world. For example, managerial pay is highest in the United States and much lower in Asia. Compensation is lower in India partly because many of the largest firms have strong family ownership and control.[89] As corporations acquire firms in other countries, the managerial compensation puzzle for boards becomes more complex and may cause additional governance problems.[90]

The Effectiveness of Executive Compensation

Executive compensation—especially long-term incentive compensation—is complicated for several reasons. First, the strategic decisions made by top-level managers are typically complex and nonroutine, so direct supervision of executives is inappropriate for judging the quality of their decisions. The result is a tendency to link the compensation of top-level managers to measurable outcomes, such as the firm's financial performance. Second, an executive's decision often affects a firm's financial outcomes over an extended period, making it difficult to assess the effect of current decisions on the corporation's performance. In fact, strategic decisions are more likely to have long-term, rather than short-term, effects on a company's strategic outcomes. Third, a number of other factors affect a firm's performance besides top-level managerial decisions and behavior. Unpredictable economic, social, or legal changes (see Chapter 2) make it difficult to identify the effects of strategic decisions. Thus, although performance-based compensation may provide incentives to top management teams to make decisions that best serve shareholders' interests, such compensation plans alone cannot fully control managers. Still, incentive compensation represents a significant portion of many executives' total pay.

Although incentive compensation plans may increase the value of a firm in line with shareholder expectations, such plans are subject to managerial manipulation.[91] Additionally, annual bonuses may provide incentives to pursue short-run objectives at the expense of the firm's long-term interests. Although long-term, performance-based incentives may reduce the temptation to under-invest in the short run, they increase executive exposure to risks associated with uncontrollable events, such as market fluctuations and industry decline. The longer term the focus of incentive compensation, the greater are the long-term risks borne by top-level managers. Also, because long-term incentives tie a manager's overall wealth to the firm in a way that is inflexible, such incentives and ownership may not be valued as highly by a manager as by outside investors who have the opportunity to diversify their wealth in a number of other financial investments.[92] Thus, firms may have to overcompensate for managers using long-term incentives.

Even though some stock option–based compensation plans are well designed with option strike prices substantially higher than current stock prices, some have been designed with the primary purpose of giving executives more compensation. Research of stock option repricing where the strike price value of the option has been lowered from its original position suggests that action is taken more frequently in high-risk situations.[93] However, repricing also happens when firm performance is poor, to restore the incentive effect for the option. Evidence also suggests that politics are often involved, which has resulted in "option backdating."[94] While this evidence shows that no internal governance mechanism is perfect, some compensation plans accomplish their purpose. For example, recent research suggests that long-term pay designed to encourage managers to be environmentally friendly has been linked to higher success in preventing pollution.[95]

Stock options became highly popular as a means of compensating top executives and linking pay with performance, but they also have become controversial of late as indicated in the Opening Case. Because all internal governance mechanisms are imperfect, external mechanisms are also needed. One such governance device is the market for corporate control.

Market for Corporate Control

The **market for corporate control** is an external governance mechanism that becomes active when a firm's internal controls fail.[96] The market for corporate control is composed of individuals and firms that buy ownership positions in or take over potentially undervalued corporations so they can form new divisions in established diversified companies or merge two previously separate firms. Because the undervalued firm's top-level managers are assumed to be responsible for formulating and implementing the strategy that led to poor performance, they are usually replaced. Thus, when the market for corporate control operates effectively, it ensures that managers who are ineffective or act opportunistically are disciplined.[97]

The takeover market as a source of external discipline is used only when internal governance mechanisms are relatively weak and have proven to be ineffective. Alternatively, other research suggests that the rationale for takeovers as a corporate governance strategy is not as strong as the rationale for takeovers as an ownership investment in target candidates where the firm is performing well and does not need discipline.[98] A study of active corporate raiders in the 1980s showed that takeover attempts often were focused on above-average performance firms in an industry.[99] Taken together, this research suggests that takeover targets are not always low performers with weak governance. As such, the market for corporate control may not be as efficient as a governance device as theory suggests.[100] At the very least, internal governance controls are much more precise relative to this external control mechanism.

Hedge funds have become a source of activist investors as noted in Chapter 7. An enormous amount of money has been invested in hedge funds, and because it is significantly more difficult to gain high returns in the market, hedge funds turned to activism. Likewise in a competitive environment characterized by a greater willingness on part of investors to hold underperforming managers accountable, hedge funds have been given license for increased activity.[101] Traditionally, hedge funds are a portfolio of stocks or bonds, or both, managed by an individual or a team on behalf of a large number of investors. Activism allows them to influence the market by taking a large position in seeking to drive the stock price up in a short period of time and then sell. Most hedge funds have been unregulated relative to the Securities and Exchange Commission because they represent a set of private investors. However, the recent economic crisis has increased the scrutiny of hedge funds' actions by government regulatory bodies.

Although the market for corporate control may be a blunt instrument for corporate governance, the takeover market continues to be active even in the economic crisis. In fact, the more intense governance environment has fostered an increasingly active takeover market. Certainly, the government has played a highly active role in the acquisitions of major U.S. financial institutions (e.g., Merrill Lynch's acquisition by Bank of America). Target firms earn a substantial premium over the acquiring firm.[102] At the same time, managers who have ownership positions or stock options are likely to gain in making a transaction with an acquiring firm. Even more evidence indicates that this type of gain may be the case, given the increasing number of firms that have golden parachutes that allow up to three years of additional compensation plus other incentives if a firm is taken over. These compensation contracts reduce the risk for managers if a firm is taken over. Private equity firms often seek to obtain a lower price in the market through initiating friendly takeover deals. The target firm's top-level managers may be amenable to such

The **market for corporate control** is an external governance mechanism that becomes active when a firm's internal controls fail.

"friendly" deals because not only do they get the payout through a golden parachute, but at their next firm they may get a "golden hello" as a signing bonus to work for the new firm.[103] Golden parachutes help them leave, but "golden hellos are increasingly needed to get them in the door" of the next firm.[104] Although the 1980s had more defenses put up against hostile takeovers, the more recent environment has been much friendlier. However, the recent economic crisis has led to significant criticism of golden parachutes, especially for executives of poorly performing firms. For example, there was significant criticism of the large bonuses paid to Merrill Lynch managers after the acquisition by Bank of America. This is because of the huge loss suffered by Merrill Lynch because of poor strategic decisions executed by these managers. Furthermore, there were issues with AIG, which received billions of dollars in government support to stay afloat yet paid huge managerial bonuses. As a result of the criticism, the firm cancelled its $10 million golden parachute for its departing CFO, Steven Bensinger.[105]

The market for corporate control governance mechanisms should be triggered by a firm's poor performance relative to industry competitors. A firm's poor performance, often demonstrated by the firm's below-average returns, is an indicator that internal governance mechanisms have failed; that is, their use did not result in managerial decisions that maximized shareholder value. Yet, although these acquisitions often involve highly underperforming firms and the changes needed may appear obvious, there are no guarantees of success. The acquired firm's assets still must be integrated effectively into the acquiring firm's operation to earn positive returns from the takeover. Also, integration is an exceedingly complex challenge.[106] Even active acquirers often fail to earn positive returns from some of their acquisitions, but some acquirers are successful and earn significant returns from the assets they acquire.[107]

Target firm managers and members of the boards of directors are commonly sensitive about hostile takeover bids. It frequently means that they have not done an effective job in managing the company. If they accept the offer, they are likely to lose their jobs; the acquiring firm will insert its own management. If they reject the offer and fend off the takeover attempt, they must improve the performance of the firm or risk losing their jobs as well.[108]

Managerial Defense Tactics

Hostile takeovers are the major activity in the market for corporate control governance mechanism. Not all hostile takeovers are prompted by poorly performing targets, and firms targeted for hostile takeovers may use multiple defense tactics to fend off the takeover attempt. Historically, the increased use of the market for corporate control has enhanced the sophistication and variety of managerial defense tactics that are used in takeovers. The market for corporate control tends to increase risk for managers. As a result, managerial pay is often augmented indirectly through golden parachutes (wherein, a CEO can receive up to three years' salary if his or her firm is taken over). Golden parachutes, similar to most other defense tactics, are controversial.

Among other outcomes, takeover defenses increase the costs of mounting a takeover, causing the incumbent management to become entrenched while reducing the chances of introducing a new management team.[109] One takeover defense is traditionally known as a "poison pill." This defense mechanism usually allows shareholders (other than the acquirer) to convert "shareholders' rights" into a large number of common shares if anyone acquires

Merrill Lynch's acquisition by Bank of America has not been without controversy, including the awarding of large bonuses to Merrill Lynch managers after the acquisition despite enormous losses.

James Leynse/Documentary Value/CORBIS

more than a set amount of the target's stock (typically 10 to 20 percent). This move dilutes the percentage of shares that the acquiring firm must purchase at a premium and in effect raises the cost of the deal for the acquiring firm.

Table 10.2 lists a number of additional takeover defense strategies. Some defense tactics necessitate only changes in the financial structure of the firm, such as repurchasing shares of the firm's outstanding stock.[110] Some tactics (e.g., reincorporation of the firm in another state) require shareholder approval, but the greenmail tactic, wherein money is used to repurchase stock from a corporate raider to avoid the takeover of the firm, does not. Some firms use rotating board member elections as a defense tactic where only one third of members are up for reelection each year. Research shows that this results in managerial entrenchment and reduced vulnerability to hostile takeovers.[111]

Most institutional investors oppose the use of defense tactics. TIAA-CREF and CalPERS have taken actions to have several firms' poison pills eliminated. Many institutional investors also oppose severance packages (golden parachutes), and the opposition is growing significantly in Europe as well.[112] However, as previously noted, an advantage to severance packages is that they may encourage top level managers to accept takeover bids that are attractive to shareholders.[113] Alternatively, recent research has shown that the use of takeover defenses reduces pressure experienced by managers for short-term performance gains. As such, managers engage in longer-term strategies and pay more

Table 10.2 Hostile Takeover Defense Strategies

Defense strategy	Category	Popularity among firms	Effectiveness as a defense	Stockholder wealth effects
Poison pill Preferred stock in the merged firm offered to shareholders at a highly attractive rate of exchange.	Preventive	High	High	Positive
Corporate charter amendment An amendment to stagger the elections of members to the board of directors of the attacked firm so that all are not elected during the same year, which prevents a bidder from installing a completely new board in the same year.	Preventive	Medium	Very low	Negative
Golden parachute Lump-sum payments of cash that are distributed to a select group of senior executives when the firm is acquired in a takeover bid.	Preventive	Medium	Low	Negligible
Litigation Lawsuits that help a target company stall hostile attacks; areas may include antitrust, fraud, inadequate disclosure.	Reactive	Medium	Low	Positive
Greenmail The repurchase of shares of stock that have been acquired by the aggressor at a premium in exchange for an agreement that the aggressor will no longer target the company for takeover.	Reactive	Very low	Medium	Negative
Standstill agreement Contract between the parties in which the pursuer agrees not to acquire any more stock of the target firm for a specified period of time in exchange for the firm paying the pursuer a fee.	Reactive	Low	Low	Negative
Capital structure change Dilution of stock, making it more costly for a bidder to acquire; may include employee stock option plans (ESOPs), recapitalization, new debt, stock selling, share buybacks.	Reactive	Medium	Medium	Inconclusive

Source: J. A. Pearce II & R. B. Robinson, Jr., 2004, Hostile takeover defenses that maximize shareholder wealth, *Business Horizons*, 47(5): 15–24.

attention to the firm's stakeholders. When they do this, the firm's market value increases, which rewards the shareholders.[114]

A potential problem with the market for corporate control is that it may not be totally efficient. A study of several of the most active corporate raiders in the 1980s showed that approximately 50 percent of their takeover attempts targeted firms with above-average performance in their industry—corporations that were neither under-valued nor poorly managed.[115] The targeting of high-performance businesses may lead to acquisitions at premium prices and to decisions by managers of the targeted firm to establish what may prove to be costly takeover defense tactics to protect their corporate positions.[116]

Although the market for corporate control lacks the precision of internal governance mechanisms, the fear of acquisition and influence by corporate raiders is an effective constraint on the managerial-growth motive. The market for corporate control has been responsible for significant changes in many firms' strategies and, when used appropri-ately, has served shareholders' interests. But this market and other means of corporate governance vary by region of the world and by country. Accordingly, we next address the topic of international corporate governance.

International Corporate Governance

Understanding the corporate governance structure of the United Kingdom and the United States is inadequate for a multinational firm in the current global economy.[117] The stability associated with German and Japanese governance structures has historically been viewed as an asset, but the governance systems in these countries are changing, similar to other parts of the world. The importance of these changes has been heightened by the global economic crisis.[118] These changes are partly the result of multinational firms operating in many different countries and attempting to develop a more global governance system.[119] Although the similarity among national governance systems is increasing, significant differences remain evident, and firms employing an international strategy must understand these differences in order to operate effectively in different international markets.[120]

Corporate Governance in Germany and Japan

In many private German firms, the owner and manager may still be the same indi-vidual. In these instances, agency problems are not present.[121] Even in publicly traded German corporations, a single shareholder is often dominant. Thus, the concentration of ownership is an important means of corporate governance in Germany, as it is in the United States.[122]

Historically, banks occupied the center of the German corporate governance struc-ture, as is also the case in many other European countries, such as Italy and France. As lenders, banks become major shareholders when companies they financed earlier seek funding on the stock market or default on loans. Although the stakes are usually less than 10 percent, banks can hold a single ownership position up to but not exceeding 15 percent of the bank's capital. Shareholders can tell the banks how to vote their own-ership position, they generally do not do so. The banks monitor and control managers, both as lenders and as shareholders, by electing representatives to supervisory boards.

German firms with more than 2,000 employees are required to have a two-tiered board structure that places the responsibility for monitoring and controlling managerial (or supervisory) decisions and actions in the hands of a separate group.[123] All the functions of strategy and management are the responsibility of the management board (the Vorstand), but appointment to the Vorstand is the responsibility of the supervisory tier (the Aufsichtsrat). Employees, union members, and shareholders appoint members to the Aufsichtsrat. Proponents of the German structure suggest that it helps prevent corporate wrongdoing and rash decisions by "dictatorial CEOs." However, critics maintain that it slows decision making and often ties a CEO's hands. The corporate governance framework in Germany has made it difficult to restructure companies as quickly as can be done in the United States when performance suffers. Because of the role of local government (through the board structure) and the power of banks in Germany's corporate governance structure, private shareholders rarely have major ownership positions in German firms. Large institutional investors, such as pension funds and insurance companies, are also relatively insignificant owners of corporate stock. Thus, at least historically, German executives generally have not been dedicated to the maximization of shareholder value that occurs in many countries.[124]

However, corporate governance in Germany is changing, at least partially, because of the increasing globalization of business. Many German firms are beginning to gravitate toward the U.S. system. Recent research suggests that the traditional system produced some agency costs because of a lack of external ownership power. Interestingly, German firms with listings on the U.S. stock exchange have increasingly adopted executive stock option compensation as a long-term incentive pay policy.[125]

Attitudes toward corporate governance in Japan are affected by the concepts of obligation, family, and consensus.[126] In Japan, an obligation "may be to return a service for one rendered or it may derive from a more general relationship, for example, to one's family or old alumni, or one's company (or Ministry), or the country. This sense of particular obligation is common elsewhere but it feels stronger in Japan."[127] As part of a company family, individuals are members of a unit that envelops their lives; families command the attention and allegiance of parties throughout corporations. Moreover, a *keiretsu* (a group of firms tied together by cross-shareholdings) is more than an economic concept; it, too, is a family. Consensus, an important influence in Japanese corporate governance, calls for the expenditure of significant amounts of energy to win the hearts and minds of people whenever possible, as opposed to top executives issuing edicts.[128] Consensus is highly valued, even when it results in a slow and cumbersome decision-making process.

As in Germany, banks in Japan play an important role in financing and monitoring large public firms.[129] The bank owning the largest share of stocks and the largest amount of debt—the main bank—has the closest relationship with the company's top executives. The main bank provides financial advice to the firm and also closely monitors managers. Thus, Japan has a bank-based financial and corporate governance structure, whereas the United States has a market-based financial and governance structure.[130]

Aside from lending money, a Japanese bank can hold up to 5 percent of a firm's total stock; a group of related financial institutions can hold up to 40 percent. In many cases, main-bank relationships are part of a horizontal keiretsu. A keiretsu firm usually owns less than 2 percent of any other member firm; however, each company typically has a stake of that size in every firm in the keiretsu. As a result, somewhere between 30 and 90 percent of a firm is owned by other members of the keiretsu. Thus, a keiretsu is a system of relationship investments.

As is the case in Germany, Japan's structure of corporate governance is changing. For example, because of Japanese banks' continuing development as economic organizations, their role in the monitoring and control of managerial behavior and firm outcomes is less significant than in the past.[131] Also, deregulation in the financial sector reduced the cost of mounting hostile takeovers.[132] As such, deregulation facilitated more activity in Japan's market for corporate control, which was nonexistent in past years.[133] Interestingly, however, recent research shows that CEOs of both public and private companies in Japan receive similar levels of compensation and their compensation is tied closely to observable performance goals.[134]

Corporate Governance in China

Corporate governance in China has changed dramatically in the past decade, as has the privatization of business and the development of the equity market. The stock markets in China are young. In their early years, these markets were weak because of significant insider trading. However, research has shown that they have improved with stronger governance in recent years.[135] The Chinese institutional environment is unique. While there has been a gradual decline in the equity held in state-owned enterprises and the number and percentage of private firms have grown, the state still dominates the strategies employed by most firms through direct or indirect controls.

Recent research shows that firms with higher state ownership tend to have lower market value and more volatility in those values over time. This is because of agency conflicts in the firms and because the executives do not seek to maximize shareholder returns. They also have social goals they must meet placed on them by the government.[136] This suggests a potential conflict between the principals, particularly the state owner and the private equity owners of the state-owned enterprises.[137]

The Chinese governance system has been moving toward the Western model in recent years. For example, China YCT International recently announced that it was strengthening its corporate governance, with the establishment of an audit committee within its board of directors, and appointing three new independent directors.[138] In addition, recent research shows that the compensation of top executives of Chinese companies is closely related to prior and current financial performance of the firm.[139] While state ownership and indirect controls complicate governance in Chinese companies, research in other countries suggests that some state ownership in recently privatized firms provides some benefits. It signals support and temporarily buoys stock prices, but over time continued state ownership and involvement tend to have negative effects on the stock price.[140] Thus, the corporate governance system in China and the heavy oversight of the Chinese government will need to be observed to determine the long-term effects.

Global Corporate Governance

As noted in the Strategic Focus, corporate governance is becoming an increasingly important issue in economies around the world, even in emerging economies. The problems with Satyam in India could be repeated in other parts of the world if diligence in governance is not exercised. This concern is stronger because of the globalization in trade, investments, and equity markets. Countries and major companies based in them want to attract foreign investment. To do so, the foreign investors must be confident of adequate corporate governance. Effective corporate governance is also required to attract domestic investors. Although many times domestic shareholders will vote with management, as activist foreign investors enter a country it gives domestic institutional investors the courage to become more active in shareholder proposals, which will increase shareholder welfare.

For example, Steel Partners, LLC, focused its attention on Korean cigarette maker KT&G. Warren Lichtenstein of Steel Partners and Carl Icahn pressured KT&G to increase its market value. Lichtenstein and Icahn began their activism in February 2006, by nominating a slate of board directors as well as pushing KT&G to sell off its lucrative Ginseng unit, which manufactures popular herbal products in Korea. They also demanded that the company sell off its real estate assets, raise its dividends, and buy back common shares. Lichtenstein and Icahn threatened a hostile tender offer if their demands were not met. Shareholders showed support for Steel Partners' activism such that they elected Lichtenstein to KT&G's board. In 2008, Lichtenstein resigned from the board with the election of four new independent directors. During his service on the board, KT&G's market value increased and its corporate governance improved.[141] Steel Partners recently targeted Aderans Holdings Company Limited in Japan for major changes. Steel Partners is Aderans's largest shareholder with about 27 percent of the outstanding stock. Steel Partners is unhappy with Aderans's efforts to turnaround its performance and has proposed replacing most of its board members and undergoing

THE SATYAM TRUTH: CEO FRAUD AND CORPORATE GOVERNANCE FAILURE

In 2008, Satyam was India's fourth largest IT company with clients around the world. The firm provided IT services to more than one third of the *Fortune 500* companies. The company and its founder and CEO, Ramalinga Raju, were well known and respected. In September 2008, Raju was named the Ernst & Young Entrepreneur of the Year. On December 16, 2008, he was given the Golden Peacock Award for Corporate Governance and Compliance. But then his term as CEO started to unravel.

On December 17, 2008, Raju announced plans to acquire two companies, Maytas Infra and Maytas Properties, both owned by members of his family. The rationale was to diversify Satyam's business portfolio to avoid being so tied to the IT services market. However, the stockholders strongly protested these acquisitions. They believed that only Raju and his family would benefit from the acquisition but Satyam would not.

On December 23, 2008, the World Bank announced that Satyam was barred from doing business with the bank because of alleged malpractices in securing previous contracts (e.g., paying bribes). In turn, Satyam requested an apology from the World Bank. Shortly thereafter, the price of Satyam's stock declined to a four-year low. Then, on December 26 three major outside directors resigned from Satyam's board of directors.

Worst of all, on January 7, 2009, Raju sent a letter to the Satyam board of directors and India's Securities and Exchange Commission. In this letter, he admitted his involvement in overstating the amount of cash held by Satyam on its balance sheet. The overstatement was approximately $1 billion. Furthermore, Satyam had a liability for $253 million arranged for his personal use, and he overstated Satyam's September 2008 quarterly revenues by 76% and its quarterly profits by 97%. This announcement sent shockwaves through corporate India and through India's stock market. Not only did Satyam's stock price suffer greatly (78% decline) but the overall market decreased by 7.3% on the day of the announcement.

Sadly, Satyam means "truth" in Sanskrit. While the CEO has been arrested and charged, others are working hard to save the company—and it appears that Satyam will be saved. Tech Malindra outbid two other firms to acquire an eventual 51% of Satyam and thus will have controlling interest in the company. The sale was due partly to swift government intervention to arrange a sale and save the company. Even though Satyam has been saved, corporate governance in India has taken a big hit and its reputation has been tarnished.

AP Photo/Mahesh Kumar A

Ramalinga Raju, Satyam's chairman quit after admitting the company's profits had been doctored for several years, shaking faith in the country's corporate giants as shares of the software services provider plunged nearly 80 percent.

Sources: P. G. Thakurta, 2009, Satyam scam questions corporate governance, IPS Inter Press Service, http://www.ipsnews.net. April 21; G. Anand, 2009, How Satyam was saved, *Wall Street Journal*, http://www.wsj.com, April 14; 2009, Satyam-chronology, Trading Markets, http://www.tradingmarkets.com, April 7; H. Timmons & B. Wassener, 2009, Satyam chief admits huge fraud, *New York Times*, http://nytimes.com, January 8; H. Arakali, 2009, Satyam chairman resigns after falsifying accounts, Bloomberg, http://bloomberg.com, January 7; M. Kripalani, 2009, India's Madoff? Satyam scandal rocks outsourcing industry, *BusinessWeek*, http://www.businessweek.com, January 7; J. Riberiro, 2008, Satyam demands apology from World Bank, Network World, http://www.networkworld.com, December 26.

a major restructuring.[142] Research suggests that foreign investors are likely to focus on critical strategic decisions and their input tends to increase a firm's movement into international markets.[143] Thus, foreign investors are playing major roles in the governance of firms in many countries.

Not only has the legislation that produced the Sarbanes-Oxley Act in 2002 increased the intensity of corporate governance in the United States,[144] but other governments around the world are seeking to increase the transparency and intensity of corporate governance to prevent the types of scandals found in the United States and other places around the world. For example, the British government in 2003 implemented the findings of the Derek Higgs report, which increased governance intensity mandated by the United Kingdom's Combined Code on Corporate Governance, a template of corporate governance used by investors and listed companies. Also, as reported in the earlier Strategic Focus, in 2009 the chairman of the Financial Reporting Council in the United Kingdom announced a complete review of the Combined Code. In addition, the European Union enacted what is known as the "Transparency Directive," which is aimed at enhancing reporting and the disclosure of financial reports by firms within the European capital markets. Another European Union initiative labeled "Modernizing Company Law and Enhancing Corporate Governance" is designed to improve the responsibility and liability of executive officers, board members, and others to important stakeholders such as shareholders, creditors, and members of the public at large.[145] Thus, governance is becoming more intense around the world.

Governance Mechanisms and Ethical Behavior

The governance mechanisms described in this chapter are designed to ensure that the agents of the firm's owners—the corporation's top-level managers—make strategic decisions that best serve the interests of the entire group of stakeholders, as described in Chapter 1. In the United States, shareholders are recognized as the company's most significant stakeholders. Thus, governance mechanisms focus on the control of managerial decisions to ensure that shareholders' interests will be served, but product market stakeholders (e.g., customers, suppliers, and host communities) and organizational stakeholders (e.g., managerial and nonmanagerial employees) are important as well.[146] Therefore, at least the minimal interests or needs of all stakeholders must be satisfied through the firm's actions. Otherwise, dissatisfied stakeholders will withdraw their support from one firm and provide it to another (e.g., customers will purchase products from a supplier offering an acceptable substitute).

The firm's strategic competitiveness is enhanced when its governance mechanisms take into consideration the interests of all stakeholders. Although the idea is subject to debate, some believe that ethically responsible companies design and use governance mechanisms that serve all stakeholders' interests. The more critical relationship, however, is found between ethical behavior and corporate governance mechanisms. The Enron disaster and the sad affair at Satyam (described in the Strategic Focus) illustrate the devastating effect of poor ethical behavior not only on a firm's stakeholders, but also on other firms. This issue is being taken seriously in other countries. The trend toward increased governance scrutiny continues to spread around the world.[147]

In addition to Enron, scandals at WorldCom, HealthSouth, Tyco, and Satyam along with the questionable behavior of top-level managers in several of the major U.S. financial services firms (Merrill Lynch, AIG) show that all corporate owners are vulnerable to unethical behavior and very poor judgments exercised by their employees, including top-level managers—the agents who have been hired to make decisions that are in shareholders' best interests. The decisions and actions of a corporation's board of directors can be an effective deterrent to these behaviors. In fact, some believe that the most effective boards participate actively to set boundaries for their firms' business ethics and values.[148] Once formulated, the board's expectations related to ethical decisions and actions of all of the firm's stakeholders must be clearly communicated to its top-level managers. Moreover, as shareholders' agents, these managers must understand that the board will hold them fully accountable for the development and support of an organizational culture that allows unethical decisions and behaviors. As will be explained in Chapter 12, CEOs can be positive role models for improved ethical behavior.

Only when the proper corporate governance is exercised can strategies be formulated and implemented that will help the firm achieve strategic competitiveness and earn above-average returns. While there are many examples of poor governance, Cummins Inc. is a positive example. In 2009 it was given the highest possible rating for its corporate governance by GovernanceMetrics International. The rating is based on careful evaluation of board accountability and financial disclosure, executive compensation, shareholder rights, ownership base, takeover provisions, corporate behavior, and overall responsibility exhibited by the company.[149] As the discussion in this chapter suggests, corporate governance mechanisms are a vital, yet imperfect, part of firms' efforts to select and successfully use strategies.

SUMMARY

- Corporate governance is a relationship among stakeholders that is used to determine a firm's direction and control its performance. How firms monitor and control top-level managers' decisions and actions affects the implementation of strategies. Effective governance that aligns managers' decisions with shareholders' interests can help produce a competitive advantage.

- Three internal governance mechanisms in the modern corporation include (1) ownership concentration, (2) the board of directors, and (3) executive compensation. The market for corporate control is the single external governance mechanism influencing managers' decisions and the outcomes resulting from them.

- Ownership is separated from control in the modern corporation. Owners (principals) hire managers (agents) to make decisions that maximize the firm's value. As risk-bearing specialists, owners diversify their risk by investing in multiple corporations with different risk profiles. As decision-making specialists, owners expect their agents (the firm's top-level managers) to make decisions that will help to maximize the value of their firm. Thus, modern corporations are characterized by an agency relationship that is created when one party (the firm's owners) hires and pays another party (top-level managers) to use its decision-making skills.

- Separation of ownership and control creates an agency problem when an agent pursues goals that conflict with principals' goals. Principals establish and use governance mechanisms to control this problem.

- Ownership concentration is based on the number of large-block shareholders and the percentage of shares they own. With significant ownership percentages, such as those held by large mutual funds and pension funds, institutional investors often are able to influence top-level managers' strategic decisions and actions. Thus, unlike diffuse ownership, which tends to result in relatively weak monitoring and control of managerial decisions, concentrated ownership produces more active and effective monitoring. Institutional investors are a powerful force in corporate America and actively use their positions of concentrated ownership to force managers and boards of directors to make decisions that maximize a firm's value.

- In the United States and the United Kingdom, a firm's board of directors, composed of insiders, related outsiders, and outsiders, is a governance mechanism expected to represent shareholders' collective interests. The percentage of outside directors on many boards now exceeds the percentage of inside directors. Through the implementation of the SOX Act, outsiders are expected to be more independent of a firm's top-level managers compared with directors selected from inside the firm. New rules imposed by the U.S. Securities and Exchange Commission to allow owners with large stakes to propose new directors are likely to change the balance even more in favor of outside and independent directors.

- Executive compensation is a highly visible and often criticized governance mechanism. Salary, bonuses, and long-term incentives are used to strengthen the alignment between managers' and shareholders' interests. A firm's board of directors is responsible for determining the effectiveness of the firm's executive compensation system. An effective system elicits managerial decisions that are in shareholders' best interests.

- In general, evidence suggests that shareholders and boards of directors have become more vigilant in their control of managerial decisions. Nonetheless, these mechanisms are insufficient to govern managerial behavior in many large companies as shown in the latest economic crisis brought on by poor strategic decisions made by top-level managers in financial services firms. Therefore, the market for corporate control is an important governance mechanism. Although it, too, is imperfect, the market for corporate control has been effective in causing corporations to combat inefficient diversification and to implement more effective strategic decisions.

- Corporate governance structures used in Germany, Japan, and China differ from each other and from the structure used in the United States. Historically, the U.S. governance structure focused on maximizing shareholder value. In Germany,

employees, as a stakeholder group, take a more prominent role in governance. By contrast, until recently, Japanese shareholders played virtually no role in the monitoring and control of top-level managers. However, now Japanese firms are being challenged by "activist" shareholders. China's governance system is the youngest and has a number of characteristics that mirror those in the United States. However, the central government still plays a major role in governance in China as well. Internationally, all these systems are becoming increasingly similar, as are many governance systems both in developed countries, such as France and Spain, and in transitional economies, such as Russia and India.

- Effective governance mechanisms ensure that the interests of all stakeholders are served. Thus, long-term strategic success results when firms are governed in ways that permit at least minimal satisfaction of capital market stakeholders (e.g., shareholders), product market stakeholders (e.g., customers and suppliers), and organizational stakeholders (managerial and nonmanagerial employees; see Chapter 2). Moreover, effective governance produces ethical behavior in the formulation and implementation of strategies.

REVIEW QUESTIONS

1. What is corporate governance? What factors account for the considerable amount of attention corporate governance receives from several parties, including shareholder activists, business press writers, and academic scholars? Why is governance necessary to control managers' decisions?

2. What is meant by the statement that ownership is separated from managerial control in the corporation? Why does this separation exist?

3. What is an agency relationship? What is managerial opportunism? What assumptions do owners of corporations make about managers as agents?

4. How is each of the three internal governance mechanisms—ownership concentration, boards of directors, and executive

compensation—used to align the interests of managerial agents with those of the firm's owners?

5. What trends exist regarding executive compensation? What is the effect of the increased use of long-term incentives on executives' strategic decisions?

6. What is the market for corporate control? What conditions generally cause this external governance mechanism to become active? How does the mechanism constrain top-level managers' decisions and actions?

7. What is the nature of corporate governance in Germany, Japan, and China?

8. How can corporate governance foster ethical strategic decisions and behaviors on the part of managers as agents?

EXPERIENTIAL EXERCISES

EXERCISE 1: INTERNATIONAL GOVERNANCE CODES

As described in the chapter, passage of the Sarbanes-Oxley Act in 2002 has drawn attention to the importance of corporate governance. Similar legislation is pending in other nations as well. However, interest in improved governance predated SOX by a decade in the form of governance codes or guidelines. These codes established sets of "best practices" for both board composition and processes. The first such code was developed by the Cadbury Committee for the London Stock Exchange

in 1992. The Australian Stock Exchange developed its guidelines in the Hilmer Report, released in 1993. The Toronto Stock Exchange developed its guidelines the following year in the Dey Report. Today, most major stock exchanges have governance codes.

Working in small groups, find the governance codes of two stock exchanges. Prepare a short (two to three pages, single-spaced) bullet-point comparison of the similarities and differences between the two codes. Be sure to include the following topics in your analysis:

- How are the guidelines structured? Do they consist of rules (i.e., required) or recommendations (i.e., suggestions)? What mechanism is included to monitor or enforce the guidelines?
- What board roles are addressed in the guidelines? For example, some codes may place most or all of their emphasis on functions derived from the importance of the agency relationship illustrated in Figure 10.1 on page 289, such as monitoring, oversight, and reporting. Codes might also mention the board's role in supporting strategy, or their contribution to firm performance and shareholder wealth.
- What aspects of board composition and structure are covered in the guidelines? For instance, items included in different codes include the balance of insiders and outsiders, committees, whether the CEO also serves as board chair, director education and/or evaluation, compensation of officers and directors, and ownership by board members.

EXERCISE 2: GOVERNANCE: DOES IT MATTER COMPETITIVELY?

Governance mechanisms are considered to be effective if they meet the needs of all stakeholders, including shareholders. Governance mechanisms are also an important way to ensure that strategic decisions are made effectively. As a potential employee, how would you go about investigating a firm's governance structure and would that investigation weigh in your decision to become an employee or not? Identify a firm that you would like to join or one that you just find interesting. Working individually, complete the following research on your target firm:

- Find a copy of the company's most recent proxy statement and 10-K. Proxy statements are mailed to shareholders prior to each year's annual meeting and contain detailed information about the company's governance and present issues on which a shareholder vote might be held. Proxy statements are typically available from a firm's Web site (look for an "Investors" submenu). You can also access proxy statements and other government filings such as the 10-K from the SEC's EDGAR database (http://www.sec.gov/edgar.shtml). Alongside the proxy you should also be able to access the firm's annual 10-K. Here you will find information on performance, governance, and the firm's outlook, among other things.
- Identify one of the company's main competitors for comparison purposes. You can find this information using company analysis tools such as Datamonitor.

Some of the topics that you should examine include:

- Compensation plans (for both the CEO and board members; be sure to look for any difference between fixed and incentive compensation)
- Board composition (e.g., board size, insiders and outsiders, interlocking directorates, functional experience, how many active CEOs, how many retired CEOs, what is the demographic makeup, age diversity, etc.)
- Committees (how many, composition, compensation)
- Stock ownership by officers and directors—identify beneficial ownership from stock owned (you will need to look through the notes sections of the ownership tables to comprehend this)
- Ownership concentration. How much of the firm's outstanding stock is owned by institutions, individuals, and insiders? How many large-block shareholders are there (owners of 5 percent or more of stock)?
- Does the firm utilize a duality structure for the CEO?
- Is there a lead director who is not an officer of the company?
- Activities by activist shareholders regarding corporate governance issues of concern
- Are there any managerial defense tactics employed by the firm? For example, what does it take for a shareholder proposal to come to a vote and be adopted?
- List the firm's code of conduct.

Prepare a double-spaced memo summarizing the results of your findings with a side-by-side comparison of your target and its competitor. Your memo should include the following topics:

- Summarize what you consider to be the key aspects of the firm's governance mechanisms.
- Attach to your memo a single graph covering the last 10-year historical stock performance for both companies. If applicable, find a representative index to compare both with, such as the S&P, NASDAQ, or other applicable industry index.
- Highlight key differences between your target firm and its competitor.
- Based on your review of the firm's governance, did you change your opinion of the firm's desirability as an employer? How does the competitor stack up, governance wise? Why or why not?

VIDEO | CASE

EFFECTIVE CORPORATE GOVERNANCE

Paul Skinner/Former Chairman/Rio Tinto

Paul Skinner, former chairman of Rio Tinto Corporation, discusses how the firm went through some significant governance changes. Spend some time with the Rio Tinto Web site and familiarize yourself with its governance structure and philosophy.

Before you watch the video consider the following concepts and questions and be prepared to discuss them in class:

Concepts
- CEO duality
- Board of directors
- Director demographics
- Corporate governance

Questions

1. What do you think is meant by the term *good governance*?
2. Do you think separation of the chairman and CEO positions should be mandatory for every company?
3. In designing a firm for "good governance," what do you consider important structural arrangements? For example, how should the board be organized, what roles should nonexecutive members have, how many committees should there be, what types of board members, etc.?
4. What do you think of the way that Rio Tinto views governance?

CHAPTER 11

Structure and Controls with Organizations

Studying this chapter should provide you with the strategic management knowledge needed to:

1. Define organizational structure and controls and discuss the difference between strategic and financial controls.

2. Describe the relationship between strategy and structure.

3. Discuss the functional structures used to implement business-level strategies.

4. Explain the use of three versions of the multidivisional (M-form) structure to implement different diversification strategies.

5. Discuss the organizational structures used to implement three international strategies.

6. Define strategic networks and discuss how strategic center firms implement such networks at the business, corporate, and international levels.

CISCO'S EVOLUTION OF STRATEGY AND STRUCTURE

Cisco's focus traditionally has been on producing network equipment that enables voice, video, and data to travel across computer networks. Accordingly, its products are at the heart of allowing the Internet and intranets to function across most corporate, public, and educational institutions around the world. Because Cisco's rapid growth was influenced by the Internet, it focused on three semiautonomous lines of business with distinct customers: Internet service providers, large enterprises, and small and medium-sized businesses. Within each of these three lines of business was a self-contained organization with separate marketing and operational groups. This allowed the firm to grow rapidly by focusing on the idiosyncratic needs of different customer segments.

This structure worked because the market was expanding quickly. However, in 2001, the explosive growth ceased when the Internet bubble burst. Thus, on August 23, 2001, Cisco announced a reorganization. The restructuring created 11 technology groups or divisions, all of which had previously been in the three separate business organizations. The sales groups, however, maintained their focus on the three particular customer segments. The integration across technologies allowed for more efficient cost reduction, which was necessary given the external environment change. Despite the many changes, Cisco emphasized its constant focus on customers because of the informal organization and previous personal interconnections between people in the reorganized engineering groups and the marketing segments.

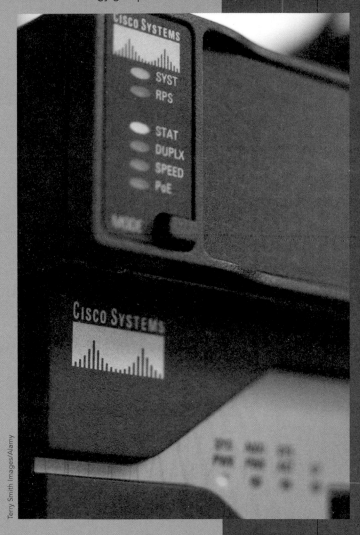

Terry Smith Images/Alamy

Over time, Cisco has also evolved its approach with the external environment. As networks matured, Cisco focused more on large-firm data centers. Therefore, Cisco has changed from a pure networking player focused on routers and switches to an overall information technology (IT) supplier. Thus it needed to build new software businesses as well as service collaborations. Furthermore it has expanded through acquisitions of software and hardware firms to create the necessary capabilities to develop a more integrated support system necessary to serve large corporate data centers. It also developed a consumer strategy by acquiring Linksys for home network systems and Scientific-Atlanta for television network boxes to facilitate cable systems. Likewise, it purchased software firms such as WebEx and IronPort to facilitate its corporate communication business and network security business, respectively. In addition, it has been collaborating with Accenture and Tata Consulting Services to provide an overall solutions business (as discussed in Chapter 9). Accordingly, not only is Cisco changing its focus on large and small customers, but it is offering software and consulting solution services.

The current downturn in the economy is forcing Cisco and other major firms to reposition and expand into nontraditional businesses in order to gain revenues lost in other areas. Most recently, it moved into "servers, which have been the traditional business of its former partners Hewlett-Packard and IBM. To manage this expansion and the integration process, Cisco needs to change its structure again. It is more likely that a corporate M-form will be necessary (this structure will be defined later in the chapter) because Cisco will need to not only have a large group of separate businesses, but it will need to integrate these businesses in a cooperative way such that all of the services are bundled and sold together to large IT centers. It will probably develop different structural approaches to manage its consumer businesses. It remains to be seen whether Cisco can make these changes effectively. Cisco does have one thing going for it—its strong culture focused on customer satisfaction. As stated earlier, customer focus is even embedded in its engineering divisions. But it will need more than a strategy—it will need a finely tuned organization to make it all work. Only time will tell whether Cisco is successful with this new strategy and the necessary structural adaptation.

Sources: R. Gulati & P. Puranam, 2009, Renewal through reorganization: The value of inconsistencies between formal and informal organization, *Organizational Science*, 20(2): 422–440; S. Lohr, 2009, In Sun, Oracle sees a software gem, *The New York Times*, http://www.nytimes.com, April 20; S. H. Wildstrom, 2009, Meet Cisco, the consumer company, *BusinessWeek*, May 4, 73; B. Worthen & J. Scheck, 2009, As growth slows, ex-allies square off in a turf war, *Wall Street Journal*, March 16, A1; J. Duffy, 2008, Cisco accelerates shift to software, data center, *Network World*, January 7, 12; J. Duffy, 2008, Cisco plans data center product overhaul, *Network World*, December 15, 1–2; B. Novak, 2008, Cisco connects the dots; aligning leaders with new organizational structure, *Global Business and Organizational Excellence*, 27(5): 22–32.

As we explain in Chapter 4, all firms use one or more business-level strategies. In Chapters 6–9, we discuss other strategies firms may choose to use (corporate-level, international, and cooperative). Once selected, strategies are not implemented in a vacuum. Organizational structure and controls, this chapter's topic, provide the framework within which strategies are used in both for-profit organizations and not-for-profit agencies.[1] However, as we explain, separate structures and controls are required to successfully implement different strategies. In all organizations, top-level managers have the final responsibility for ensuring that the firm has matched each of its strategies with the appropriate organizational structure and that both change when necessary. Thus, John Chambers, the CEO of Cisco, is responsible for changing its organizational structure if the firm decides to use a different business or corporate-level strategy. The match or degree of fit between strategy and structure influences the firm's attempts to earn above-average returns.[2] Thus, the ability to select an appropriate strategy and match it with the appropriate structure is an important characteristic of effective strategic leadership.[3]

This chapter opens with an introduction to organizational structure and controls. We then provide more details about the need for the firm's strategy and structure to be properly matched. Affecting firms' efforts to match strategy and structure is their influence on each other.[4] As we discuss, strategy has a more important influence on structure, although once in place, structure influences strategy.[5] Next, we describe the relationship between growth and structural change successful firms experience. We then discuss the different organizational structures firms use to implement the separate business-level, corporate-level, international, and cooperative strategies. A series of figures highlights the different structures firms match with strategies. Across time and based on their experiences, organizations, especially large and complex ones, customize these general structures to meet their unique needs.[6] Typically, the firm tries to form a structure that is complex enough to facilitate use of its strategies but simple enough for all parties to understand and implement.[7] When strategies become more diversified as with Cisco's in the Opening Case, a firm must adjust its structure to deal with the increased complexity.[8]

Organizational Structure and Controls

Research shows that organizational structure and the controls that are a part of the structure affect firm performance.[9] In particular, evidence suggests that performance declines when the firm's strategy is not matched with the most appropriate structure and controls.[10] Even though mismatches between strategy and structure do occur, research indicates that managers try to act rationally when forming or changing their firm's structure.[11] His record of success at General Electric (GE) suggests that CEO Jeffrey

Immelt pays close attention to the need to make certain that strategy and structure remain matched, as evidenced by restructuring alignments in GE Capital, GE's financial service group, during the economic downturn.[12]

Organizational Structure

Organizational structure specifies the firm's formal reporting relationships, procedures, controls, and authority and decision-making processes.[13] Developing an organizational structure that effectively supports the firm's strategy is difficult, especially because of the uncertainty (or unpredictable variation[14]) about cause-effect relationships in the global economy's rapidly changing and dynamic competitive environments.[15] When a structure's elements (e.g., reporting relationships, procedures, etc.) are properly aligned with one another, the structure facilitates effective use of the firm's strategies.[16] Thus, organizational structure is a critical component of effective strategy implementation processes.[17]

A firm's structure specifies the work to be done and how to do it, given the firm's strategy or strategies.[18] Thus, organizational structure influences how managers work and the decisions resulting from that work.[19] Supporting the implementation of strategies, structure is concerned with processes used to complete organizational tasks.[20] Having the right structure and process is important. For example, many product-oriented firms have been moving to develop service businesses associated with those products. This has been a strategy used by many of GE's businesses, such as medical equipment. However, research suggests that developing a separate division for such services in product-oriented companies, rather than managing the service business within the product divisions, leads to additional growth and profitability in the service business.[21]

Effective structures provide the stability a firm needs to successfully implement its strategies and maintain its current competitive advantages while simultaneously providing the flexibility to develop advantages it will need in the future.[22] *Structural stability* provides the capacity the firm requires to consistently and predictably manage its daily work routines[23] while *structural flexibility* provides the opportunity to explore competitive possibilities and then allocate resources to activities that will shape the competitive advantages the firm will need to be successful in the future.[24] An effectively flexible organizational structure allows the firm to *exploit* current competitive advantages while *developing* new ones that can potentially be used in the future.[25] For example, the management system at Cisco is said to provide "speed, skill, and flexibility."[26] Cisco is able to accomplish this by using team-based processes as an overlay to its basic structure, allowing it to exploit its current advantages while exploring for new ones.

Modifications to the firm's current strategy or selection of a new strategy call for changes to its organizational structure. However, research shows that once in place, organizational inertia often inhibits efforts to change structure, even when the firm's performance suggests that it is time to do so.[27] In his pioneering work, Alfred Chandler found that organizations change their structures when inefficiencies force them to.[28] Chandler's contributions to our understanding of organizational structure and its relationship to strategies and performance are quite significant. Indeed, some believe that Chandler's emphasis on "organizational structure so transformed the field of business history that some call the period before Dr. Chandler's publications 'B.C.,' meaning 'before Chandler.'"[29]

Firms seem to prefer the structural status quo and its familiar working relationships until the firm's performance declines to the point where change is absolutely necessary.[30] For example, necessity is obviously the case for General Motors given that it went into bankruptcy to force the required restructuring.[31]

In addition to the issues we already mentioned, it is important to note that top-level managers hesitate to conclude that the firm's structure (or its strategy, for that matter) are the problem, in that doing so suggests that their previous choices were not the best ones. Because of these inertial tendencies, structural change is often induced instead by actions

Organizational structure specifies the firm's formal reporting relationships, procedures, controls, and authority and decision-making processes.

from stakeholders (e.g., those from the capital market and customers—see Chapter 2) who are no longer willing to tolerate the firm's performance. Evidence shows that appropriate timing of structural change happens when top-level managers recognize that a current organizational structure no longer provides the coordination and direction needed for the firm to successfully implement its strategies.[32] Interestingly, many organizational changes are taking place in the current economic downturn, apparently because poor performance reveals organizational weaknesses. As we discuss next, effective organizational controls help managers recognize when it is time to adjust the firm's structure.

Organizational Controls

Organizational controls are an important aspect of structure.[33] **Organizational controls** guide the use of strategy, indicate how to compare actual results with expected results, and suggest corrective actions to take when the difference is unacceptable. When fewer differences separate actual from expected outcomes, the organization's controls are more effective.[34] It is difficult for the company to successfully exploit its competitive advantages without effective organizational controls.[35] Properly designed organizational controls provide clear insights regarding behaviors that enhance firm performance.[36] Firms use both strategic controls and financial controls to support using their strategies.

Strategic controls are largely subjective criteria intended to verify that the firm is using appropriate strategies for the conditions in the external environment and the company's competitive advantages. Thus, strategic controls are concerned with examining the fit between what the firm *might do* (as suggested by opportunities in its external environment) and what it *can do* (as indicated by its competitive advantages). Effective strategic controls help the firm understand what it takes to be successful.[37] Strategic controls demand rich communications between managers responsible for using them to judge the firm's performance and those with primary responsibility for implementing the firm's strategies (such as middle and first-level managers). These frequent exchanges are both formal and informal in nature.[38]

Strategic controls are also used to evaluate the degree to which the firm focuses on the requirements to implement its strategies. For a business-level strategy, for example, the strategic controls are used to study primary and support activities (see Tables 3.6 and 3.7, on page 87) to verify that the critical activities are being emphasized and properly executed.[39] With related corporate-level strategies, strategic controls are used by corporate strategic leaders to verify the sharing of appropriate strategic factors such as knowledge, markets, and technologies across businesses. To effectively use strategic controls when evaluating related diversification strategies, headquarter executives must have a deep understanding of each unit's business-level strategy.[40]

As we described in the Opening Case, Cisco's executives allocate a great deal of time and energy to issues related to strategic control. Constantly challenged to meet the demands of an ever-changing market, John Chambers, Cisco's CEO, was able to implement a revised strategic controls system where he "was able to surrender his role as a command-and-control CEO and institute a collaborative decision-making model that allows the company to respond speedily to emerging transitions."[41] Using this system on strategic control allowed Cisco to move to open source software development before competitors such as Microsoft. They also were one of the first companies to move to Web-based customer service centers from call centers having foreseen this change through their strategic control system.

Financial controls are largely objective criteria used to measure the firm's performance against previously established quantitative standards. Accounting-based measures such as return on investment (ROI) and return on assets (ROA) as well as market-based measures such as economic value added are examples of financial controls. Partly because strategic controls are difficult to use with extensive diversification,[42] financial controls are emphasized to evaluate the performance of the firm using the unrelated diversification strategy. The unrelated diversification strategy's focus on financial outcomes (see Chapter 6)

Organizational controls guide the use of strategy, indicate how to compare actual results with expected results, and suggest corrective actions to take when the difference is unacceptable.

Strategic controls are largely subjective criteria intended to verify that the firm is using appropriate strategies for the conditions in the external environment and the company's competitive advantages.

Financial controls are largely objective criteria used to measure the firm's performance against previously established quantitative standards.

requires using standardized financial controls to compare performances between business units and associated managers.[43]

When using financial controls, firms evaluate their current performance against previous outcomes as well as against competitors' performance and industry averages. In the global economy, technological advances are being used to develop highly sophisticated financial controls, making it possible for firms to more thoroughly analyze their performance results and to assure compliance with regulations. Companies such as Oracle and SAP sell software tools that automate processes firms use to meet the financial reporting requirements specified by the Sarbanes-Oxley Act. (As noted in Chapter 10, this act requires a firm's principal executive and financial officers to certify corporate financial and related information in quarterly and annual reports submitted to the Securities and Exchange Commission.)

Image99/Image100/Jupiter Images

Both strategic and financial controls are important aspects of each organizational structure, and as we noted previously, any structure's effectiveness is determined by using a combination of strategic and financial controls. However, the relative use of controls varies by type of strategy. For example, companies and business units of large diversified firms using the cost leadership strategy emphasize financial controls (such as quantitative cost goals), while companies and business units using the differentiation strategy emphasize strategic controls (such as subjective measures of the effectiveness of product development teams).[44] As previously explained, a corporate-wide emphasis on sharing among business units (as called for by related diversification strategies) results in an emphasis on strategic controls, while financial controls are emphasized for strategies in which activities or capabilities are not shared (e.g., in an unrelated diversification strategy).

As firms consider controls, the important point is to properly balance the use of strategic and financial controls. Indeed, overemphasizing one at the expense of the other can lead to performance declines. According to Michael Dell, an overemphasis on financial controls to produce attractive short-term results contributed to performance difficulties at Dell Inc. In addressing this issue, Dell said the following: "The company was too focused on the short term, and the balance of priorities was way too leaning toward things that deliver short-term results."[45] Executives at Dell have now achieved a more appropriate emphasis on the long term as well as the short term due a reemphasis on strategic controls, although Dell is still playing catch up to Hewlett-Packard.[46]

The complexities of managing global companies are driving the development and implementation of sophisticated financial control applications.

STRATEGY RIGHT NOW

For another example of how organizations use both strategic and financial controls, read about the FDIC's (Federal Deposit Insurance Corporation) recent passage of new rules governing deposit rates and credit reporting.

www.cengage.com/management/hitt

Relationships between Strategy and Structure

Strategy and structure have a reciprocal relationship.[47] This relationship highlights the interconnectedness between strategy formulation (Chapters 4, 6–9) and strategy implementation (Chapters 10–13). In general, this reciprocal relationship finds structure flowing from or following selection of the firm's strategy. Once in place though, structure can influence current strategic actions as well as choices about future strategies. Consider, for example, the possible influences of the Cisco's structure and control system in influencing its strategy as illustrated in the Opening Case.

The general nature of the strategy/structure relationship means that changes to the firm's strategy create the need to change how the organization completes its work. In the "structure influences strategy" direction, firms must be vigilant in their efforts to verify that how their structure calls for work to be completed remains consistent with the implementation requirements of chosen strategies. Research shows, however, that "strategy has a much more important influence on structure than the reverse."[48]

Regardless of the strength of the reciprocal relationships between strategy and structure, those choosing the firm's strategy and structure should be committed to matching each strategy with a structure that provides the stability needed to use current competitive advantages as well as the flexibility required to develop future advantages. Therefore, when changing strategies, the firm should simultaneously consider the structure that will be needed to support use of the new strategy; properly matching strategy and structure can create a competitive advantage.[49]

Evolutionary Patterns of Strategy and Organizational Structure

Research suggests that most firms experience a certain pattern of relationships between strategy and structure. Chandler[50] found that firms tend to grow in somewhat predictable

Figure 11.1 Strategy and Structure Growth Pattern

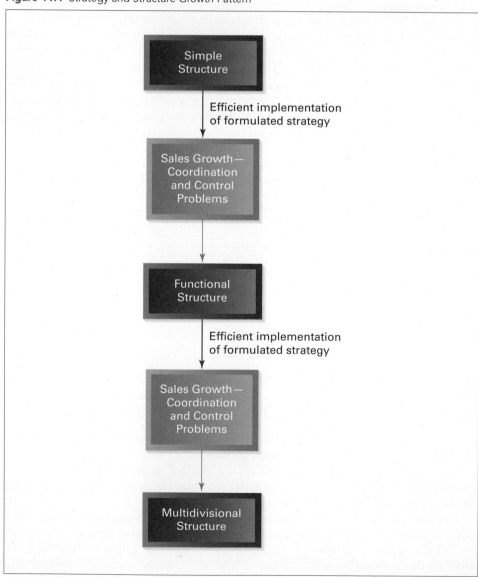

patterns: "first by volume, then by geography, then integration (vertical, horizontal), and finally through product/business diversification"[51] (see Figure 11.1). Chandler interpreted his findings as an indication that firms' growth patterns determine their structural form.

As shown in Figure 11.1, sales growth creates coordination and control problems the existing organizational structure cannot efficiently handle. Organizational growth creates the opportunity for the firm to change its strategy to try to become even more successful. However, the existing structure's formal reporting relationships, procedures, controls, and authority and decision-making processes lack the sophistication required to support using the new strategy.[52] A new structure is needed to help decision makers gain access to the knowledge and understanding required to effectively integrate and coordinate actions to implement the new strategy.[53]

Firms choose from among three major types of organizational structures—simple, functional, and multidivisional—to implement strategies. Across time, successful firms move from the simple to the functional to the multidivisional structure to support changes in their growth strategies.[54]

Simple Structure

The **simple structure** is a structure in which the owner-manager makes all major decisions and monitors all activities while the staff serves as an extension of the manager's supervisory authority.[55] Typically, the owner-manager actively works in the business on a daily basis. Informal relationships, few rules, limited task specialization, and unsophisticated information systems characterize this structure. Frequent and informal communications between the owner-manager and employees make coordinating the work to be done relatively easy. The simple structure is matched with focus strategies and business-level strategies, as firms implementing these strategies commonly compete by offering a single product line in a single geographic market. Local restaurants, repair businesses, and other specialized enterprises are examples of firms using the simple structure.

As the small firm grows larger and becomes more complex, managerial and structural challenges emerge. For example, the amount of competitively relevant information requiring analysis substantially increases, placing significant pressure on the owner-manager. Additional growth and success may cause the firm to change its strategy. Even if the strategy remains the same, the firm's larger size dictates the need for more sophisticated workflows and integrating mechanisms. At this evolutionary point, firms tend to move from the simple structure to a functional organizational structure.[56]

Functional Structure

The **functional structure** consists of a chief executive officer and a limited corporate staff, with functional line managers in dominant organizational areas such as production, accounting, marketing, R&D, engineering, and human resources.[57] This structure allows for functional specialization,[58] thereby facilitating active sharing of knowledge within each functional area. Knowledge sharing facilitates career paths as well as professional development of functional specialists. However, a functional orientation can negatively affect communication and coordination among those representing different organizational functions. For this reason, the CEO must work hard to verify that the decisions and actions of individual business functions promote the entire firm rather than a single function. The functional structure supports implementing business-level strategies and some corporate-level strategies (e.g., single or dominant business) with low levels of diversification. When changing from a simple to a functional structure, firms want to avoid introducing value-destroying bureaucratic procedures such as failing to promote innovation and creativity.[59]

Multidivisional Structure

With continuing growth and success, firms often consider greater levels of diversification. Successfully using a diversification strategy requires analyzing substantially greater

The **simple structure** is a structure in which the owner-manager makes all major decisions and monitors all activities while the staff serves as an extension of the manager's supervisory authority.

The **functional structure** consists of a chief executive officer and a limited corporate staff, with functional line managers in dominant organizational areas such as production, accounting, marketing, R&D, engineering, and human resources.

amounts of data and information when the firm offers the same products in different markets (market or geographic diversification) or offers different products in several markets (product diversification). In addition, trying to manage high levels of diversification through functional structures creates serious coordination and control problems,[60] a fact that commonly leads to a new structural form.[61]

The **multidivisional (M-form) structure** consists of a corporate office and operating divisions, each operating division representing a separate business or profit center in which the top corporate officer delegates responsibilities for day-to-day operations and business-unit strategy to division managers. Each division represents a distinct, self-contained business with its own functional hierarchy.[62] As initially designed, the M-form was thought to have three major benefits: "(1) it enabled corporate officers to more accurately monitor the performance of each business, which simplified the problem of control; (2) it facilitated comparisons between divisions, which improved the resource allocation process; and (3) it stimulated managers of poorly performing divisions to look for ways of improving performance."[63] Active monitoring of performance through the M-form increases the likelihood that decisions made by managers heading individual units will be in stakeholders' best interests. Because diversification is a dominant corporate-level strategy used in the global economy, the M-form is a widely adopted organizational structure.[64]

Used to support implementation of related and unrelated diversification strategies, the M-form helps firms successfully manage diversification's many demands.[65] Chandler viewed the M-form as an innovative response to coordination and control problems that surfaced during the 1920s in the functional structures then used by large firms such as DuPont and General Motors.[66] Research shows that the M-form is appropriate when the firm grows through diversification.[67] Partly because of its value to diversified corporations, some consider the multidivisional structure to be one of the twentieth century's most significant organizational innovations.[68]

No one organizational structure (simple, functional, or multidivisional) is inherently superior to the others.[69] Peter Drucker says the following about this matter: "There is no one right organization. … Rather the task … is to select the organization for the particular task and mission at hand."[70] In our context, Drucker is saying that the firm must select a structure that is "right" for successfully using the chosen strategy. Because no single structure is optimal in all instances, managers concentrate on developing proper matches between strategies and organizational structures rather than searching for an "optimal" structure. This matching of structure and strategy is taking place at Cisco. As noted in the Opening Case, John Chambers is increasing the firm's level of diversification and as such is adjusting its structure to match.

We now describe the strategy/structure matches that evidence shows positively contribute to firm performance.

Matches between Business-Level Strategies and the Functional Structure

Firms use different forms of the functional organizational structure to support implementing the cost leadership, differentiation, and integrated cost leadership/differentiation strategies. The differences in these forms are accounted for primarily by different uses of three important structural characteristics: *specialization* (concerned with the type and number of jobs required to complete work[71]), *centralization* (the degree to which decision-making authority is retained at higher managerial levels[72]), and *formalization* (the degree to which formal rules and procedures govern work[73]).

Using the Functional Structure to Implement the Cost Leadership Strategy

Firms using the cost leadership strategy sell large quantities of standardized products to an industry's typical customer. Simple reporting relationships, few layers in the decision-making and authority structure, a centralized corporate staff, and a strong focus on

The **multidivisional (M-form) structure** consists of a corporate office and operating divisions, each operating division representing a separate business or profit center in which the top corporate officer delegates responsibilities for day-to-day operations and business-unit strategy to division managers.

process improvements through the manufacturing function rather than the development of new products by emphasizing product R&D characterize the cost leadership form of the functional structure[74] (see Figure 11.2). This structure contributes to the emergence of a low-cost culture—a culture in which employees constantly try to find ways to reduce the costs incurred to complete their work.[75]

In terms of centralization, decision-making authority is centralized in a staff function to maintain a cost-reducing emphasis within each organizational function (engineering, marketing, etc.). While encouraging continuous cost reductions, the centralized staff also verifies that further cuts in costs in one function won't adversely affect the productivity levels in other functions.[76]

Jobs are highly specialized in the cost leadership functional structure; work is divided into homogeneous subgroups. Organizational functions are the most common subgroup, although work is sometimes batched on the basis of products produced or clients served. Specializing in their work allows employees to increase their efficiency, resulting in reduced costs. Guiding individuals' work in this structure are highly formalized rules and procedures, which often emanate from the centralized staff.

Wal-Mart Stores Inc. uses the functional structure to implement cost leadership strategies in each of its three segments (Wal-Mart Stores, Sam's Clubs, and International). In the Wal-Mart Stores segment (which generates the largest share of the firm's total sales), the cost leadership strategy is used in the firm's Supercenter, Discount, and Neighborhood Market retailing formats.[77] Long known for its "Always Low Prices" slogan (which was used for 19 years), Wal-Mart recently changed to a new slogan— "Save Money, Live Better."[78] Although the slogan is new, Wal-Mart continues using the functional organizational structure in its divisions to drive costs lower. As discussed in Chapter 4, competitors' efforts to duplicate the success of Wal-Mart's cost leadership

Figure 11.2 Functional Structure for Implementing a Cost Leadership Strategy

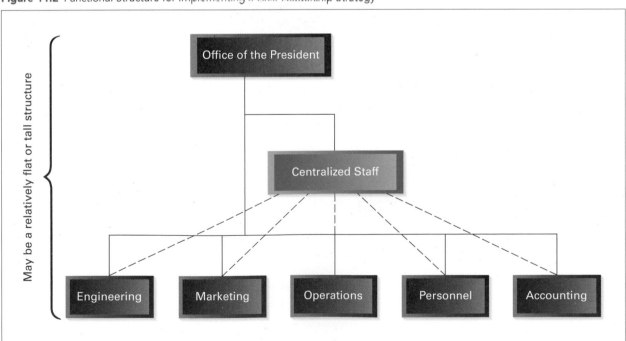

Notes:
- Operations is the main function
- Process engineering is emphasized rather than new product R&D
- Relatively large centralized staff coordinates functions
- Formalized procedures allow for emergence of a low-cost culture
- Overall structure is mechanistic; job roles are highly structured

strategies have generally failed, partly because of the effective strategy/structure matches in each of the firm's segments.

Using the Functional Structure to Implement the Differentiation Strategy

Firms using the differentiation strategy produce products customers perceive as being different in ways that create value for them. With this strategy, the firm wants to sell non-standardized products to customers with unique needs. Relatively complex and flexible reporting relationships, frequent use of cross-functional product development teams, and a strong focus on marketing and product R&D rather than manufacturing and process R&D (as with the cost leadership form of the functional structure) characterize the differentiation form of the functional structure (see Figure 11.3). From this structure emerges a development-oriented culture in which employees try to find ways to further differentiate current products and to develop new, highly differentiated products.[79]

Continuous product innovation demands that people throughout the firm interpret and take action based on information that is often ambiguous, incomplete, and uncertain. Following a strong focus on the external environment to identify new opportunities, employees often gather this information from people outside the firm (e.g., customers and suppliers). Commonly, rapid responses to the possibilities indicated by the collected information are necessary, suggesting the need for decentralized decision-making responsibility and authority. To support creativity and the continuous pursuit of new sources of differentiation and new products, jobs in this structure are not highly specialized. This lack of specialization means that workers have a relatively large number of tasks in their job descriptions. Few formal rules and procedures also characterize this structure. Low formalization, decentralization of decision-making authority and responsibility, and low specialization of work tasks combine to create a structure in which people interact frequently to exchange ideas about how to further differentiate current products while developing ideas for new products that can be crisply differentiated.

Figure 11.3 Functional Structure for Implementing a Differentiation Strategy

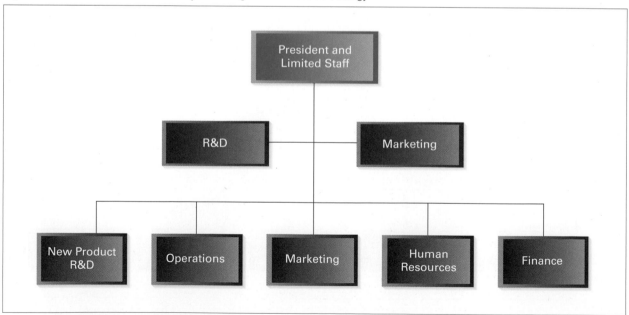

Notes:
- Marketing is the main function for keeping track of new product ideas
- New product R&D is emphasized
- Most functions are decentralized, but R&D and marketing may have centralized staffs that work closely with each other
- Formalization is limited so that new product ideas can emerge easily and change is more readily accomplished
- Overall structure is organic; job roles are less structured

Under Armour has used a differentiation strategy and matching structure to create success in the sports apparel market. Under Armour's objective was to create improved athletic performance through innovative design, testing, and marketing, especially to professional athletes and teams, and translate that perception to the broader market. With a strong match between strategy and structure, it has successfully created innovative sports performance products and challenged Nike and other sports apparel competitors.[80]

Using the Functional Structure to Implement the Integrated Cost Leadership/Differentiation Strategy

Firms using the integrated cost leadership/differentiation strategy sell products that create value because of their relatively low cost and reasonable sources of differentiation. The cost of these products is low "relative" to the cost leader's prices while their differentiation is "reasonable" when compared with the clearly unique features of the differentiator's products.

Although challenging to implement, the integrated cost leadership/differentiation strategy is used frequently in the global economy. The challenge of using this structure is due largely to the fact that different primary and support activities (see Chapter 3) are emphasized when using the cost leadership and differentiation strategies. To achieve the cost leadership position, production and process engineering are emphasized, with infrequent product changes. To achieve a differentiated position, marketing and new product R&D are emphasized while production and process engineering are not. Thus, effective use of the integrated strategy depends on the firm's successful combination of activities intended to reduce costs with activities intended to create additional differentiation features. As a result, the integrated form of the functional structure must have decision-making patterns that are partially centralized and partially decentralized. Additionally, jobs are semispecialized, and rules and procedures call for some formal and some informal job behavior.

Matches between Corporate-Level Strategies and the Multidivisional Structure

As explained earlier, Chandler's research shows that the firm's continuing success leads to product or market diversification or both.[81] The firm's level of diversification is a function of decisions about the number and type of businesses in which it will compete as well as how it will manage the businesses (see Chapter 6). Geared to managing individual organizational functions, increasing diversification eventually creates information processing, coordination, and control problems that the functional structure cannot handle. Thus, using a diversification strategy requires the firm to change from the functional structure to the multidivisional structure to develop an appropriate strategy/structure match.

As defined in Figure 6.1, corporate-level strategies have different degrees of product and market diversification. The demands created by different levels of diversification highlight the need for a unique organizational structure to effectively implement each strategy (see Figure 11.4).

Using the Cooperative Form of the Multidivisional Structure to Implement the Related Constrained Strategy

The **cooperative form** is an M-form structure in which horizontal integration is used to bring about interdivisional cooperation. Divisions in a firm using the related constrained diversification strategy commonly are formed around products, markets, or both. In Figure 11.5, we use product divisions as part of the representation of the cooperative form of the multidivisional structure, although market divisions could be used instead of or in addition to product divisions to develop the figure.

Using this structure, Hewlett-Packard (HP) has implemented the related constrained strategy as described in the Strategic Focus. HP's intent is to sell integrated solutions to corporate data centers, so it has placed an emphasis on creating more relationships

The **cooperative form** is an M-form structure in which horizontal integration is used to bring about interdivisional cooperation.

Figure 11.4 Three Variations of the Multidivisional Structure

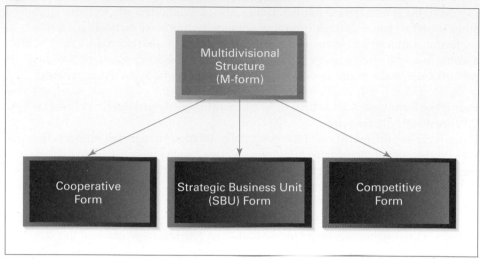

Figure 11.5 Cooperative Form of the Multidivisional Structure for Implementing a Related Constrained Strategy

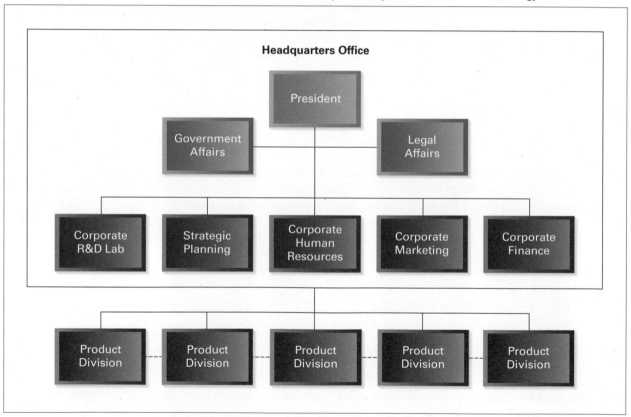

Notes:
- Structural integration devices create tight links among all divisions
- Corporate office emphasizes centralized strategic planning, human resources, and marketing to foster cooperation between divisions
- R&D is likely to be centralized
- Rewards are subjective and tend to emphasize overall corporate performance in addition to divisional performance
- Culture emphasizes cooperative sharing

HEWLETT-PACKARD IMPLEMENTS THE RELATED CONSTRAINED STRATEGY THROUGH THE COOPERATIVE M-FORM STRUCTURE

Hewlett-Packard (HP) has three main related businesses through which it pursues industry leadership and technology development. First, it has the Personal Systems Group, including business and consumer PCs, mobile computing, and workstation devices. Second, it has a complementary business with a very large market share in Imaging and Printing, which includes inkjet and laserjet printers, commercial printing, printing supplies, digital photography, and entertainment products and support. Finally, it has a Technology Service Solutions Group, which includes business products focused on servers and storage, managed services and software, and services solutions. This group has been augmented through its recent acquisition of Electronic Data Systems (EDS). HP is number nine in the 2009 *Fortune* 500 Ranking with more than $118 billion in total revenue for fiscal year 2008.

Its main focus for customers is on corporate data centers that allow connected mobile computing, printing, and imaging delivery. HP pursues a related constrained strategy (as discussed in Chapter 6) by using the cooperative M-form structure. As firms pursue diversified growth and the economy becomes more Internet based, corporate data centers are increasingly important to help firms pursue improved top-line and bottom-line growth. HP's three main businesses allow the related strategy to work well by focusing on the growing importance of corporate data centers. Firms that seek to deliver the products and services necessary to the centers are required to have interrelated services and businesses to sell integrated solutions.

This is driving firms that have a dominant focus on one product category to move into the other categories. For instance, Cisco, as noted in the Opening Case, is moving toward a corporate data center approach but coming at it from a traditional focus on network equipment. For this reason it is now moving into servers, which has been one of HP's dominant businesses (Cisco previously partnered with HP in this area). Like Cisco, HP has moved away from its formerly decentralized structure toward a related constrained strategy by seeking to implement the cooperative M-form organization structure. The cooperative M-form requires more centralization to make it function appropriately and to foster cooperation between the separate divisions within and across business unit divisions. This requires distinctive leadership and focus on improved execution to function properly.

Mark Hurd, the current CEO who succeeded Carly Fiorina in 2005, has been able to fine-tune HP's structural approach through his "get things done" mentality. One security analyst describes Hurd as someone who is, "… all about execution and has an uncanny ability to get things done." Furthermore, this same analyst suggests, "He is the most adept at taking costs out of the system than any executive I know." His no-nonsense style has led to increasing operational efficiency by realizing a strong implementation of the cooperative M-form structure. For instance, through the $13 billion acquisition of the consulting services firm

David Paul Morris/Getty Images News/Getty Images

Mark Hurd, President and CEO of Hewlett-Packard, has increased efficiency and reduced costs at HP through the implementation of the cooperative M-form structure.

EDS in 2008, Hurd cut 15,000 jobs or 10 percent of the workforce to create the synergistic effect needed across all businesses. In 2009, this led HP to project a decline of 5 percent in revenues, but to still be able to project a 6 percent growth in profits, all despite the economic downturn.

Although the cooperative structure implementation has created wealth and efficiency, there are those who speculate that Hurd's approach has an Achilles heel because it lacks an emphasis on breakthrough innovation such as Apple's iPod and iPhone. Robert Burgelman, a Stanford professor who has studied Hurd, says, "He will not tell them we should do this project or that project. He helps them think more clearly about the space in which they are operating." While these actions have made HP's R&D operations more efficient, Hurd may need to give employees more creative license if he wants breakthrough innovations that would allow HP to compete more effectively with IBM and Apple.

Sources: J. Brodkin, 2009, HP BladeSystem, Matrix takes aim at Cisco, *Network World*, April 20, 34; A. Lashinsky, 2009, Mark Hurd's moment, *Fortune*, March 16, 90–100; J. Scheck, 2009, Corporate news: HP chief sees more pain ahead, trims more jobs, *Wall Street Journal*, May 20, B3; B. Worthen & J. Scheck, 2009, H-P to step up fight in market for servers, *Wall Street Journal*, April 16, B5; C. Edwards, 2008, How HP got the wow! back, *BusinessWeek*, December 20, 60; J. Fortt, 2008, Mark Hurd, superstar, *Fortune*, June 29, 35; J. Jain, 2008, Decision sciences: A story of excellence at Hewlett-Packard, *OR-MS Today*, 35(2): 20; L. Lee, 2008, HP's Hurd is about to be tested: After a sterling three-year run, the company's CEO faces a weaker PC market and a stronger Dell, *BusinessWeek*, February 14, 59–60; 2008, Business: Now services; Hewlett-Packard, *Economist*, May, 78; D. M. Zell, A. M. Glassman, & S. A. Duron, 2007, Strategic management in turbulent times: The short and glorious history of accelerated decision making at Hewlett-Packard, *Organizational Dynamics*, 36(1): 93–104.

among its products (servers, storage, mobile computing, and high-speed printers) and coordinating these products through value-added services. This has required the implementation of the cooperative M-form and more centralization among the various business units to foster cooperation and synergy.

Sharing divisional competencies facilitates the corporation's efforts to develop economies of scope. As explained in Chapter 6, economies of scope (cost savings resulting from the sharing of competencies developed in one division with another division) are linked with successful use of the related constrained strategy. Interdivisional sharing of competencies depends on cooperation, suggesting the use of the cooperative form of the multidivisional structure.[82] HP seems to have developed the structure and processes well to accomplish this.

The cooperative structure uses different characteristics of structure (centralization, standardization, and formalization) as integrating mechanisms to facilitate interdivisional cooperation. Frequent, direct contact between division managers, another integrating mechanism, encourages and supports cooperation and the sharing of competencies or resources that could be used to create new advantages. Sometimes, liaison roles are established in each division to reduce the time division managers spend integrating and coordinating their unit's work with the work occurring in other divisions. Temporary teams or task forces may be formed around projects whose success depends on sharing competencies that are embedded within several divisions. Cisco has used these devices to develop new cooperative strategies, as illustrated in the Opening Case. Formal integration departments might be established in firms frequently using temporary teams or task forces.

Ultimately, a matrix organization may evolve in firms implementing the related constrained strategy. A *matrix organization* is an organizational structure in which there is a dual structure combining both functional specialization and business product or project specialization.[83] Although complicated, an effective matrix structure can lead to improved coordination among a firm's divisions.[84]

The success of the cooperative multidivisional structure is significantly affected by how well divisions process information. However, because cooperation among divisions implies a loss of managerial autonomy, division managers may not readily commit themselves to the type of integrative information-processing activities that this structure demands. Moreover, coordination among divisions sometimes results in an unequal flow of positive outcomes to divisional managers. In other words, when managerial rewards are based at least in part on the performance of individual divisions, the manager of the division that is able to benefit the most by the sharing of corporate competencies might be viewed as receiving relative gains at others' expense. Strategic controls are important in these instances, as divisional managers' performance can be evaluated at least partly on the basis of how well they have facilitated interdivisional cooperative efforts. In addition, using reward systems that emphasize overall company performance, besides outcomes achieved by individual divisions, helps overcome problems associated with the cooperative form.

Using the Strategic Business Unit Form of the Multidivisional Structure to Implement the Related Linked Strategy

Firms with fewer links or less constrained links among their divisions use the related linked diversification strategy. The strategic business unit form of the multidivisional structure supports implementation of this strategy. The **strategic business unit (SBU) form** is an M-form structure consisting of three levels: corporate headquarters, strategic business units (SBUs), and SBU divisions (see Figure 11.6). The SBU structure is used by large firms and can be complex, given associated organization size and product and market diversity.

The **strategic business unit (SBU) form** is an M-form consisting of three levels: corporate headquarters, strategic business units (SBUs), and SBU divisions.

Figure 11.6 SBU Form of the Multidivisional Structure for Implementing a Related Linked Strategy

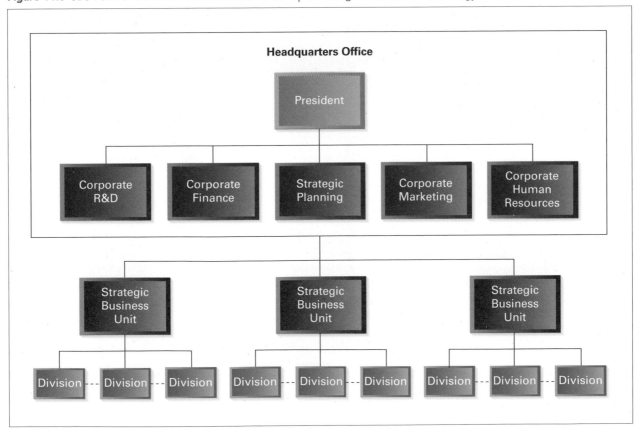

Notes:
- Structural integration among divisions within SBUs, but independence across SBUs
- Strategic planning may be the most prominent function in headquarters for managing the strategic planning approval process of SBUs for the president
- Each SBU may have its own budget for staff to foster integration
- Corporate headquarters staff members serve as consultants to SBUs and divisions, rather than having direct input to product strategy, as in the cooperative form

The divisions within each SBU are related in terms of shared products or markets or both, but the divisions of one SBU have little in common with the divisions of the other SBUs. Divisions within each SBU share product or market competencies to develop economies of scope and possibly economies of scale. The integrating mechanisms used by the divisions in this structure can be equally well used by the divisions within the individual strategic business units that are part of the SBU form of the multidivisional structure. In this structure, each SBU is a profit center that is controlled and evaluated by the headquarters office. Although both financial and strategic controls are important, on a relative basis financial controls are vital to headquarters' evaluation of each SBU; strategic controls are critical when the heads of SBUs evaluate their divisions' performances. Strategic controls are also critical to the headquarters' efforts to determine whether the company has formed an effective portfolio of businesses and whether those businesses are being successfully managed.

Sears Holdings changed to the SBU form in 2008 by dividing into five strategic business units (with multiple divisions as parts of each SBU): brands, real estate, support, online, and store operations.[85] This allowed for related businesses to work together (such as Sears and K-Mart) to focus on their distinct customer sets, but also provided for better control for headquarters in order to evaluate performance of each strategic business unit and division within the SBU.

Sharing competencies among units within an SBU is an important characteristic of the SBU form of the multidivisional structure (see the notes to Figure 11.6). A drawback to the SBU structure is that multifaceted businesses often have difficulties in communicating this complex business model to stockholders.[86] Furthermore, if coordination between SBUs is needed, problems can arise because the SBU structure, similar to the competitive form discussed next, does not readily foster cooperation across SBUs.

Using the Competitive Form of the Multidivisional Structure to Implement the Unrelated Diversification Strategy

Firms using the unrelated diversification strategy want to create value through efficient internal capital allocations or by restructuring, buying, and selling businesses.[87] The competitive form of the multidivisional structure supports implementation of this strategy.

The **competitive form** is an M-form structure characterized by complete independence among the firm's divisions which compete for corporate resources (see Figure 11.7). Unlike the divisions included in the cooperative structure, divisions that are part of the competitive structure do not share common corporate strengths. Because strengths are not shared, integrating devices are not developed for use by the divisions included in the competitive structure.

The efficient internal capital market that is the foundation for using the unrelated diversification strategy requires organizational arrangements emphasizing divisional competition rather than cooperation.[88] Three benefits are expected from the internal competition. First, internal competition creates flexibility (e.g., corporate headquarters can have divisions working on different technologies and projects to identify those with the greatest potential). Resources can then be allocated to the division appearing to have the most potential to fuel the entire firm's success. Second, internal competition challenges the status quo and inertia, because division heads know that future resource allocations are a product of excellent current performance as well as superior positioning in terms of future performance. Last, internal competition motivates effort in that the challenge of competing against internal peers can be as great as the challenge of competing against external rivals.[89] In this structure, organizational controls (primarily financial controls) are used to emphasize and support internal competition among separate divisions and as the basis for allocating corporate capital based on divisions' performances.

Textron Inc., a large "multi-industry" company seeks "to identify, research, select, acquire and integrate companies, and has developed a set of rigorous criteria to guide

The **competitive form** is an M-form structure characterized by complete independence among the firm's divisions which compete for corporate resources.

Figure 11.7 Competitive Form of the Multidivisional Structure for Implementing an Unrelated Strategy

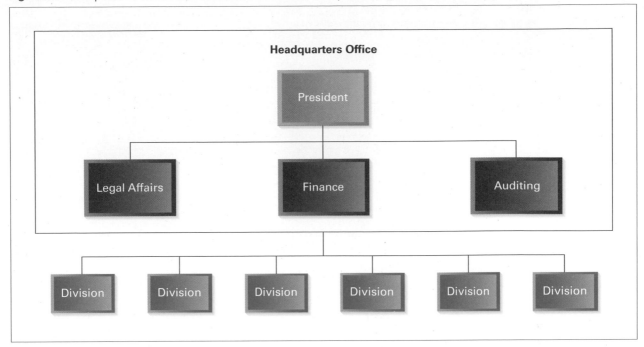

Notes:
- Corporate headquarters has a small staff
- Finance and auditing are the most prominent functions in the headquarters office to manage cash flow and assure the accuracy of performance data coming from divisions
- The legal affairs function becomes important when the firm acquires or divests assets
- Divisions are independent and separate for financial evaluation purposes
- Divisions retain strategic control, but cash is managed by the corporate office
- Divisions compete for corporate resources

decision making." Textron continuously looks "to enhance and reshape its portfolio by divesting non-core assets and acquiring branded businesses in attractive industries with substantial long-term growth potential." Textron operates four independent businesses—Bell Helicopter (20 percent of revenue), Cessna Aircraft (40 percent), Textron Systems (15 percent), Finance (5 percent), and Industrial (20 percent). The firm uses return on invested capital (ROIC) as a way to evaluate the contribution of its diversified set of businesses as they compete internally for resources.[90]

To emphasize competitiveness among divisions, the headquarters office maintains an arm's-length relationship with them, intervening in divisional affairs only to audit operations and discipline managers whose divisions perform poorly. In emphasizing competition between divisions, the headquarters office relies on strategic controls to set rate-of-return targets and financial controls to monitor divisional performance relative to those targets. The headquarters office then allocates cash flow on a competitive basis, rather than automatically returning cash to the division that produced it. Thus, the focus of the headquarters' work is on performance appraisal, resource allocation, and long-range planning to verify that the firm's portfolio of businesses will lead to financial success.[91]

Transtock/Terra/CORBIS

Made of up four independent businesses, including Cessna Aircraft, Textron relies on an analysis of return on invested capital to determine the allocation of internal resources.

Table 11.1 Characteristics of the Structures Necessary to Implement the Related Constrained, Related Linked, and Unrelated Diversification Strategies

Structural Characteristics	Overall Structural Form		
	Cooperative M-Form (Related Constrained Strategy)[a]	SBU M-Form (Related Linked Strategy)[a]	Competitive M-Form (Unrelated Diversification Strategy)[a]
Centralization of operations	Centralized at corporate office	Partially centralized (in SBUs)	Decentralized to divisions
Use of integration mechanisms	Extensive	Moderate	Nonexistent
Divisional performance appraisals	Emphasize subjective (strategic) criteria	Use a mixture of subjective (strategic) and objective (financial) criteria	Emphasize objective (financial) criteria
Divisional incentive compensation	Linked to overall corporate performance	Mixed linkage to corporate, SBU, and divisional performance	Linked to divisional performance

[a]Strategy implemented with structural form.

The three major forms of the multidivisional structure should each be paired with a particular corporate-level strategy. Table 11.1 shows these structures' characteristics. Differences exist in the degree of centralization, the focus of the performance appraisal, the horizontal structures (integrating mechanisms), and the incentive compensation schemes. The most centralized and most costly structural form is the cooperative structure. The least centralized, with the lowest bureaucratic costs, is the competitive structure. The SBU structure requires partial centralization and involves some of the mechanisms necessary to implement the relatedness between divisions. Also, the divisional incentive compensation awards are allocated according to both SBUs and corporate performance.

Matches between International Strategies and Worldwide Structure

As explained in Chapter 8, international strategies are becoming increasingly important for long-term competitive success[92] in what continues to become an increasingly border-less global economy.[93] Among other benefits, international strategies allow the firm to search for new markets, resources, core competencies, and technologies as part of its efforts to outperform competitors.[94]

As with business-level and corporate-level strategies, unique organizational structures are necessary to successfully implement the different international strategies.[95] Forming proper matches between international strategies and organizational structures facilitates the firm's efforts to effectively coordinate and control its global operations. More importantly, research findings confirm the validity of the international strategy/structure matches we discuss here.[96]

Using the Worldwide Geographic Area Structure to Implement the Multidomestic Strategy

The *multidomestic strategy* decentralizes the firm's strategic and operating decisions to business units in each country so that product characteristics can be tailored to local preferences. Firms using this strategy try to isolate themselves from global competitive forces by establishing protected market positions or by competing in industry segments that are most affected by differences among local countries. The worldwide geographic area structure is used to implement this strategy. The **worldwide geographic area structure** emphasizes national interests and facilitates the firm's efforts to satisfy local differences (see Figure 11.8).

The **worldwide geographic area structure** emphasizes national interests and facilitates the firm's efforts to satisfy local differences.

Figure 11.8 Worldwide Geographic Area Structure for Implementing a Multidomestic Strategy

Notes:
- The perimeter circles indicate decentralization of operations
- Emphasis is on differentiation by local demand to fit an area or country culture
- Corporate headquarters coordinates financial resources among independent subsidiaries
- The organization is like a decentralized federation

Although the automobile industry is doing poorly in global markets, on a relative basis Ford of Europe is doing better than other auto firms in Europe within the same middle market segment strategy. This is due to the fact that Ford implemented the worldwide geographic area structure more than a decade ago to give local European managers more autonomy to manage their operations. One analysis called Ford "the most efficient volume carmaker in Europe."[97] Furthermore, they have an efficient set of designs matched responsively to the European market. They have kept costs down by partnering with European automakers such as Fiat and France's PSA Peugeot Citroen on chassis and engines. The timing of the release of their new models was also good to take advantage of the European "cash for clunkers" program, although the underlying market is still weak.

Using the multidomestic strategy requires little coordination between different country markets, meaning that integrating mechanisms among divisions around the world are not needed. Coordination among units in a firm's worldwide geographic area structure is often informal.

The multidomestic strategy/worldwide geographic area structure match evolved as a natural outgrowth of the multicultural European marketplace. Friends and family members of the main business who were sent as expatriates into foreign countries to develop the independent country subsidiary often used this structure for the main business. The relationship to corporate headquarters by divisions took place through informal communication among "family members."[98]

A key disadvantage of the multidomestic strategy/worldwide geographic area structure match is the inability to create strong global efficiency. With an increasing emphasis on lower-cost products in international markets, the need to pursue worldwide economies of scale has also increased. These changes foster use of the global strategy and its structural match, the worldwide product divisional structure.

Using the Worldwide Product Divisional Structure to Implement the Global Strategy

With the corporation's home office dictating competitive strategy, the *global strategy* is one through which the firm offers standardized products across country markets. The firm's success depends on its ability to develop economies of scope and economies of scale on a global level. Decisions to outsource or maintain integrated subsidiaries may in part depend on the country risk and institutional environment in which the firm is entering.[99]

The worldwide product divisional structure supports use of the global strategy. In the **worldwide product divisional structure**, decision-making authority is centralized in the worldwide division headquarters to coordinate and integrate decisions and actions among divisional business units (see Figure 11.9). This structure is often used in rapidly growing firms seeking to manage their diversified product lines effectively. Avon Products, Inc. is an example of a firm using the worldwide product divisional structure.

Avon is a global brand leader in products for women such as lipsticks, fragrances, and anti-aging skin care. Committed to "empowering women all over the world since 1886," Avon relies on product innovation to be a first-mover in its markets. For years, Avon used the multidomestic strategy. However, the firm's growth came to a screeching halt in 2006. Contributing to this decline were simultaneous stumbles in sales revenues in emerging markets (e.g., Russia and Central Europe), the United States, and Mexico. To cope with its problems, the firm changed to a global strategy and to the worldwide product divisional structure to support its use. Commenting on this change, CEO Andrea Jung noted that, "Previously, Avon managers from Poland to Mexico ran their own plants, developed new products, and created their own ads, often relying as much

Figure 11.9 Worldwide Product Divisional Structure for Implementing a Global Strategy

Notes:
• The headquarters' circle indicates centralization to coordinate information flow among worldwide products
• Corporate headquarters uses many intercoordination devices to facilitate global economies of scale and scope
• Corporate headquarters also allocates financial resources in a cooperative way
• The organization is like a centralized federation

In the **worldwide product divisional structure**, decision-making authority is centralized in the worldwide division headquarters to coordinate and integrate decisions and actions among divisional business units.

on gut as numbers."[100] Today, Avon is organized around product divisions including Avon Color, the firm's "flagship global color cosmetics brand, which offers a variety of color cosmetics products, including foundations, powders, lip, eye, and nail products," Skincare, Bath & Body, Hair Care, Wellness, and Fragrance. The analysis of these product divisions' performances is conducted by individuals in the firm's New York headquarters. One of the purposes of changing strategy and structure is for Avon to control its costs and gain additional scale economies as paths to performance improvements. Avon has announced the success of this restructuring program and vowed to cut costs even further; the original program is "expected to result in annual savings of about $430 million by 2011–12," while the new changes will result in "another $450 million expected to be saved beginning in 2010."[101]

Integrating mechanisms are important in the effective use of the worldwide product divisional structure. Direct contact between managers, liaison roles between departments, and temporary task forces as well as permanent teams are examples of these mechanisms. One researcher describes the use of these mechanisms in the worldwide structure: "There is extensive and formal use of task forces and operating committees to supplement communication and coordination of worldwide operations."[102] The disadvantages of the global strategy/worldwide structure combination are the difficulty involved with coordinating decisions and actions across country borders and the inability to quickly respond to local needs and preferences.

To deal with these types of disadvantages, Avon has a vast set of local salespeople who are committed to the organization and who help the company to become locally responsive. Another solution is to develop a regional approach in addition to the product focus, which might be similar to the combination structure discussed next.[103]

Using the Combination Structure to Implement the Transnational Strategy

The *transnational strategy* calls for the firm to combine the multidomestic strategy's local responsiveness with the global strategy's efficiency. Firms using this strategy are trying to gain the advantages of both local responsiveness and global efficiency. The combination structure is used to implement the transnational strategy. The **combination structure** is a structure drawing characteristics and mechanisms from both the worldwide geographic area structure and the worldwide product divisional structure. The transnational strategy is often implemented through two possible combination structures: a global matrix structure and a hybrid global design.[104]

The global matrix design brings together both local market and product expertise into teams that develop and respond to the global marketplace. The global matrix design (the basic matrix structure was defined earlier) promotes flexibility in designing products and responding to customer needs. However, it has severe limitations in that it places employees in a position of being accountable to more than one manager. At any given time, an employee may be a member of several functional or product group teams. Relationships that evolve from multiple memberships can make it difficult for employees to be simultaneously loyal to all of them. Although the matrix places authority in the hands of managers who are most able to use it, it creates problems in regard to corporate reporting relationships that are so complex and vague that it is difficult and time-consuming to receive approval for major decisions.

We illustrate the hybrid structure in Figure 11.10. In this design, some divisions are oriented toward products while others are oriented toward market areas. Thus, in some cases when the geographic area is more important, the division managers are area-oriented. In other divisions where worldwide product coordination and efficiencies are more important, the division manager is more product-oriented. The Strategic Focus on PepsiCo illustrates the hybrid design. Although PepsiCo is generally focused on geographic areas like most consumer product companies, as it has diversified into snacks and other foods, it also has product divisions to build better worldwide efficiencies.

The **combination structure** is a structure drawing characteristics and mechanisms from both the worldwide geographic area structure and the worldwide product divisional structure.

Figure 11.10 Hybrid Form of the Combination Structure for Implementing a Transnational Strategy

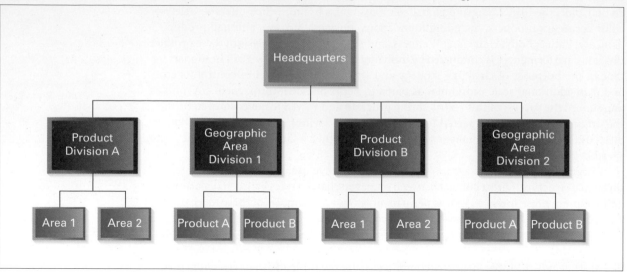

The fits between the multidomestic strategy and the worldwide geographic area structure and between the global strategy and the worldwide product divisional structure are apparent. However, when a firm wants to implement the multidomestic and global strategies simultaneously through a combination structure, the appropriate integrating mechanisms are less obvious. The structure used to implement the transnational strategy must be simultaneously centralized and decentralized; integrated and nonintegrated; formalized and nonformalized.

IKEA has done a good job of balancing these organization aspects in implementing the transnational strategy.[105] IKEA is a global furniture retailer with outlets in more than 35 countries. IKEA focuses on lowering its costs and also understanding its customers' needs, especially younger customers. It has been able to manage these seemingly opposite characteristics through its structure and management process. It has also been able to encourage its employees to understand the effects of cultural and geographic diversity on firm operations. IKEA's system also has internal network attributes, which will be discussed next in regard to external interorganizational networks.

Matches between Cooperative Strategies and Network Structures

As discussed in Chapter 9, a network strategy exists when partners form several alliances in order to improve the performance of the alliance network itself through cooperative endeavors.[106] The greater levels of environmental complexity and uncertainty facing companies in today's competitive environment are causing more firms to use cooperative strategies such as strategic alliances and joint ventures.[107]

The breadth and scope of firms' operations in the global economy create many opportunities for firms to cooperate.[108] In fact, a firm can develop cooperative relationships with many of its stakeholders, including customers, suppliers, and competitors. When a firm becomes involved with combinations of cooperative relationships, it is part of a strategic network, or what others call an alliance constellation or portfolio.[109]

A *strategic network* is a group of firms that has been formed to create value by participating in multiple cooperative arrangements. An effective strategic network facilitates discovering opportunities beyond those identified by individual network participants.[110] A strategic network can be a source of competitive advantage for its members when its operations create value that is difficult for competitors to duplicate and that network members can't create by themselves.[111] Strategic networks are used to implement business-level, corporate-level, and international cooperative strategies.

PEPSICO: MOVING FROM THE GEOGRAPHIC AREA STRUCTURE TOWARD THE COMBINED STRUCTURE IMPLEMENTING THE TRANSNATIONAL STRATEGY

PepsiCo has organized its businesses into three groups: PepsiCo North American Beverages (PNAB), PepsiCo Americas Foods (PAF), and PepsiCo International (PI). PNAB focuses on the Pepsi brand that includes carbonated soft drinks, juices and juice drinks, ready-to-drink teas and coffees, and isotonic sports drinks (Gatorade). It also has Aquafina water, Sierra Mist, Mug root beer, Tropicana juice drinks, Propel, SoBe, Slice, Dole, Tropicana Twister, and Tropicana Season's Best. Some of these drinks are through joint ventures such as with the Thomas J. Lipton Company (tea) and Starbucks coffee (Frappuccino). Gatorade became part of PepsiCo through a 2001 acquisition of Quaker Oats Company.

PAF is focused on food and snacks in North and South America including the products of Frito-Lay, Quaker Oats, Sabritas (Mexican snacks and fun food), and Gamesa (one of Mexico's top brands for cookies, pastries, oats, and cereals).

PepsiCo International includes the PepsiCo businesses in Europe, Asia, Africa, and Australia. Originally, this segment focused on distribution of beverages, but in 2003 it combined food and beverages to form PepsiCo International.

As you can see from these descriptions of its business segments, PepsiCo is primarily organized geographically—beverages in North America, food in North America, and food and beverages internationally by region. Accordingly, like most consumer product firms, it has traditionally implemented the multidomestic strategy with a regional focus, using the worldwide geographic area structure to better create a marketing approach that is adaptable to various languages, cultures, and lifestyles. However, as it has diversified into a variety of beverages and snack foods, it has consequently organized into product divisions as well to gain greater efficiencies in managing these products worldwide. Although it is still predominately area focused through the management structure, it has additional structures that allow the product divisions to be managed more efficiently. Accordingly, PepsiCo is moving toward implementing the transnational strategy through the combination structure.

Neville Elder/CORBIS

PepsiCo's geographic organization and move toward the implementation of a transnational strategy are supported by a highly diverse leadership team, headed by CEO and chairman of the board, Indra Nooyi, who is originally from India.

Interestingly, PepsiCo has one of the most diverse leadership teams. Its CEO and chairman of the board, Indra Nooyi, is originally from India. A large number of board members possess significant international experience, including the ability to speak several languages. These board members allow a broad understanding of cultures and buying habits within geographic regions outside of the United States. The diversity on the board supports the geographic focus maintained by the company and has added to the success of marketing the PepsiCo brands and products throughout the world.

Sources: 2009, The PepsiCo family, http://www.pepsico.com, June 25; H. Ehein, 2009, Internal relations, *Brand Week*, February 16, 8–9; D. Morris, 2008, The Pepsi challenge, *Fortune*, March 3, 54; M. Useem, 2008, America's best leaders: Indra Nooyi, PepsiCo CEO, *US News & World Report*, http://www.usnews.com, November 19; 2008, Global companies with global boards, *Directorship*, 34(5): 28–30; 2008, Pepsi versus Coke: An unhealthy obsession: They are global, but are they relevant? *Strategic Direction*, 24(1): 6–8.

Commonly, a strategic network is a loose federation of partners participating in the network's operations on a flexible basis. At the core or center of the strategic network, the *strategic center firm* is the one around which the network's cooperative relationships revolve (see Figure 11.11).

Because of its central position, the strategic center firm is the foundation for the strategic network's structure. Concerned with various aspects of organizational structure, such as formal reporting relationships and procedures, the strategic center firm manages what are often complex, cooperative interactions among network partners. To perform the tasks discussed next, the strategic center firm must make sure that incentives for participating in the network are aligned so that network firms continue to have a reason to remain connected.[112] The strategic center firm is engaged in four primary tasks as it manages the strategic network and controls its operations:[113]

Strategic outsourcing. The strategic center firm outsources and partners with more firms than other network members. At the same time, the strategic center firm requires network partners to be more than contractors. Members are expected to find opportunities for the network to create value through its cooperative work.

Competencies. To increase network effectiveness, the strategic center firm seeks ways to support each member's efforts to develop core competencies with the potential of benefiting the network.

Technology. The strategic center firm is responsible for managing the development and sharing of technology-based ideas among network members. The structural requirement that members submit formal reports detailing the technology-oriented outcomes of their efforts to the strategic center firm facilitates this activity.[114]

Race to learn. The strategic center firm emphasizes that the principal dimensions of competition are between value chains and between networks of value chains. Because of this interconnection, the strategic network is only as strong as its weakest value-chain link.

Figure 11.11 A Strategic Network

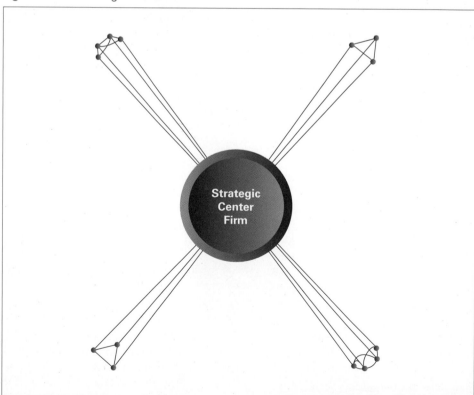

With its centralized decision-making authority and responsibility, the strategic center firm guides participants in efforts to form network-specific competitive advantages. The need for each participant to have capabilities that can be the foundation for the network's competitive advantages encourages friendly rivalry among participants seeking to develop the skills needed to quickly form new capabilities that create value for the network.[115]

Interestingly, strategic networks are being used more frequently, partly because of the ability of a strategic center firm to execute a strategy that effectively and efficiently links partner firms. Improved information systems and communication capabilities (e.g., the Internet) make such networks possible.[116]

Implementing Business-Level Cooperative Strategies

As noted in Chapter 9, the two types of business-level complementary alliances are vertical and horizontal. Firms with competencies in different stages of the value chain form a vertical alliance to cooperatively integrate their different, but complementary, skills. Firms combining their competencies to create value in the same stage of the value chain are using a horizontal alliance. Vertical complementary strategic alliances such as those developed by Toyota Motor Company are formed more frequently than horizontal alliances.[117]

A strategic network of vertical relationships such as the network in Japan between Toyota and its suppliers often involves a number of implementation issues.[118] First, the strategic center firm encourages subcontractors to modernize their facilities and provides them with technical and financial assistance to do so, if necessary. Second, the strategic center firm reduces its transaction costs by promoting longer-term contracts with subcontractors, so that supplier-partners increase their long-term productivity. This approach is diametrically opposed to that of continually negotiating short-term contracts based on unit pricing. Third, the strategic center firm enables engineers in upstream companies (suppliers) to have better communication with those companies with whom it has contracts for services. As a result, suppliers and the strategic center firm become more interdependent and less independent.[119]

The lean production system (a vertical complementary strategic alliance) pioneered by Toyota and others has been diffused throughout the global auto industry.[120] However, no auto company has learned how to duplicate the manufacturing effectiveness and efficiency Toyota derives from the cooperative arrangements in its strategic network.[121] A key factor accounting for Toyota's manufacturing-based competitive advantage is the cost other firms would incur to imitate the structural form used to support Toyota's application. In part, then, the structure of Toyota's strategic network that it created as the strategic center firm facilitates cooperative actions among network participants that competitors can't fully understand or duplicate.

In vertical complementary strategic alliances, such as the one between Toyota and its suppliers, the strategic center firm is obvious, as is the structure that firm establishes. However, the same is not always true with horizontal complementary strategic alliances where firms try to create value in the same part of the value chain, as with airline alliances that are commonly formed to create value in the marketing and sales primary activity segment of the value chain (see Table 3.6). Because air carriers commonly participate in multiple horizontal complementary alliances such as the Star Alliance between Lufthansa, United, Continental, US Airways, Thai, Air Canada, SAS, and others, it is difficult to determine the strategic center firm. Moreover, participating in several alliances can cause firms to question partners' true loyalties and intentions. Also, if rivals band together in too many collaborative activities, one or more governments may suspect the possibility of illegal collusive activities. For these reasons, horizontal complementary alliances are used less often and less successfully than their vertical counterpart, although there are examples of success, for instance, among auto and aircraft manufacturers.[122]

Implementing Corporate-Level Cooperative Strategies

Corporate-level cooperative strategies (such as franchising) are used to facilitate product and market diversification. As a cooperative strategy, franchising allows the firm to use its competencies to extend or diversify its product or market reach, but without completing a merger or an acquisition.[123] Research suggests that knowledge embedded in corporate-level cooperative strategies facilitates synergy.[124] For example, McDonald's Corporation pursues a franchising strategy, emphasizing a limited value-priced menu in more than 100 countries. The McDonald's franchising system is a strategic network. McDonald's headquarters serves as the strategic center firm for the network's franchisees. The headquarters office uses strategic and financial controls to verify that the franchisees' operations create the greatest value for the entire network.

An important strategic control issue for McDonald's is the location of its franchisee units. Because it believes that its greatest expansion opportunities are outside the United States, the firm has decided to continue expanding in countries such as China and India, where it might need to adjust its menu according to the local culture. For example, "McDonald's adapts its restaurants in India to local tastes; in a nation that is predominantly Hindu and reveres the cow, beef isn't on the menu, for instance, replaced by chicken burgers and vegetable patties."[125] It plans on expanding the number of restaurants in India by 40 in 2009 bringing the total to 200; it expanded by 25 restaurants in 2008. Accordingly, as the strategic center firm around the globe for its restaurants, McDonald's is devoting the majority of its capital expenditures to develop units in non–U.S. markets.

Implementing International Cooperative Strategies

Strategic networks formed to implement international cooperative strategies result in firms competing in several countries.[126] Differences among countries' regulatory environments increase the challenge of managing international networks and verifying that at a minimum, the network's operations comply with all legal requirements.[127]

Distributed strategic networks are the organizational structure used to manage international cooperative strategies. As shown in Figure 11.12, several regional strategic center firms are included in the distributed network to manage partner firms' multiple cooperative arrangements.[128]

Hewlett-Packard recently acquired EDS, a large information technology consulting firm. One of EDS's assets is the EDS Agility Alliance, its distributed strategic network. "The Agility Alliance is EDS' premiere partner program bringing together industry-leading technology providers to build and deliver end to end IT solutions."[129] EDS is the main strategic center firm in this alliance and has two dedicated centers that are the hubs for jointly developing initiatives with its partners. Cisco, SAP, Sun, Xerox, Oracle, EMC, and Microsoft are members of this distributed strategic network. Symantec, an Internet antivirus and security firm, was recently added as a partner to respond to clients' needs "for more innovative security products and solutions that help them better secure their mission-critical business data and address specific enterprise security issues."[130] EDS's partners each work with their own networks to complete projects that are a part of the Agility Alliance. As this example demonstrates, the structure used to implement the international cooperative strategy is complex and demands careful attention to be used successfully.

Figure 11.12 A Distributed Strategic Network

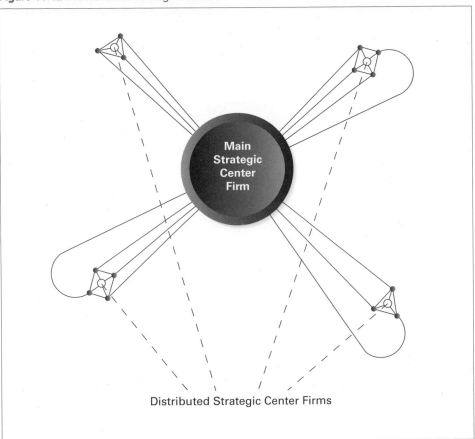

Distributed Strategic Center Firms

SUMMARY

- Organizational structure specifies the firm's formal reporting relationships, procedures, controls, and authority and decision-making processes. Essentially, organizational structure details the work to be done in a firm and how that work is to be accomplished. Organizational controls guide the use of strategy, indicate how to compare actual and expected results, and suggest actions to take to improve performance when it falls below expectations. A proper match between strategy and structure can lead to a competitive advantage.

- Strategic controls (largely subjective criteria) and financial controls (largely objective criteria) are the two types of organizational controls used to implement a strategy. Both controls are critical, although their degree of emphasis varies based on individual matches between strategy and structure.

- Strategy and structure influence each other; overall though, strategy has a stronger influence on structure. Research indicates that firms tend to change structure when declining performance forces them to do so. Effective managers anticipate the need for structural change and quickly modify structure to better accommodate the firm's strategy when evidence calls for that action.

- The functional structure is used to implement business-level strategies. The cost leadership strategy requires a centralized functional structure—one in which manufacturing efficiency and process engineering are emphasized. The differentiation strategy's functional structure decentralizes implementation-related decisions, especially those concerned with marketing, to those involved with individual organizational functions. Focus strategies, often used in small firms, require a simple structure until such time that the firm diversifies in terms of products and/or markets.

- Unique combinations of different forms of the multidivisional structure are matched with different corporate-level diversification strategies to properly implement these strategies. The cooperative M-form, used to implement the related constrained corporate-level strategy, has a centralized corporate office and extensive integrating mechanisms. Divisional incentives are linked to overall corporate performance to foster cooperation among divisions. The related linked SBU M-form structure establishes separate profit centers within the diversified firm. Each profit center or SBU may have divisions offering similar products, but the SBUs are often unrelated to each other. The competitive M-form structure, used to implement the unrelated diversification strategy, is highly decentralized, lacks integrating mechanisms, and utilizes objective financial criteria to evaluate each unit's performance.

- The multidomestic strategy, implemented through the worldwide geographic area structure, emphasizes decentralization and locates all functional activities in the host country or geographic area. The worldwide product divisional structure is used to implement the global strategy. This structure is centralized in order to coordinate and integrate different functions' activities so as to gain global economies of scope and economies of scale. Decision-making authority is centralized in the firm's worldwide division headquarters.

- The transnational strategy—a strategy through which the firm seeks the local responsiveness of the multidomestic strategy and the global efficiency of the global strategy—is

implemented through the combination structure. Because it must be simultaneously centralized and decentralized, integrated and nonintegrated, and formalized and nonformalized, the combination structure is difficult to organize and successfully manage. However, two structural designs are suggested: the matrix and the hybrid structure with both geographic and product-oriented divisions.

- Increasingly important to competitive success, cooperative strategies are implemented through organizational structures framed around strategic networks. Strategic center firms play a critical role in managing strategic networks. Business-level strategies are often employed in vertical and horizontal alliance networks. Corporate-level cooperative strategies are used to pursue product and market diversification. Franchising is one type of corporate strategy that uses a strategic network to implement this strategy. This is also true for international cooperative strategies, where distributed networks are often used.

REVIEW QUESTIONS

1. What is organizational structure and what are organizational controls? What are the differences between strategic controls and financial controls? What is the importance of these differences?

2. What does it mean to say that strategy and structure have a reciprocal relationship?

3. What are the characteristics of the functional structures used to implement the cost leadership, differentiation, integrated cost leadership/differentiation, and focused business-level strategies?

4. What are the differences among the three versions of the multidivisional (M-form) organizational structures that are used to implement the related constrained, the related linked, and the unrelated corporate-level diversification strategies?

5. What organizational structures are used to implement the multidomestic, global, and transnational international strategies?

6. What is a strategic network? What is a strategic center firm? How is a strategic center used in business-level, corporate-level, and international cooperative strategies?

EXPERIENTIAL EXERCISES

EXERCISE 1: ORGANIZATIONAL STRUCTURE AND BUSINESS-LEVEL STRATEGY

The purpose of this exercise is to apply the concepts introduced in this chapter to live examples of business-level strategies and how various firms actually structure their organizations to compete. In teams, your instructor will assign a business-level strategy such as differentiation or cost leader. You are to identify a firm that exemplifies this strategy and pictorially draw out its corporate structure. You will need to present the results of your investigation by comparing your firm's organizational chart with that in your text identified for your particular business-level strategy. (See text for figures labeled "Functional Structure for Implementing a Differentiation [or Cost Leadership] Strategy.") Be prepared to address the following issues:

1. Describe your firm's business-level strategy. Why do you consider it to be a cost leader or a differentiator?
2. What is the mission statement and/or vision statement of this firm? Is this firm targeting specific strategic goals?

3. Using the text examples for a functional structure, how does your firm match those structures or differ, if it does?
4. Summarize your conclusions. Does your team believe that this firm is structured appropriately considering its current and future strategic goals?

EXERCISE 2: BURGER BUDDY AND MA MAISON

Assume that it is a few months before your college graduation. You and some classmates have decided to become entrepreneurs. The group has agreed on the restaurant industry, but your discussions thus far have gone back and forth between two different dining concepts: Burger Buddy and Ma Maison.

Burger Buddy would operate near campus in order to serve the student market. Burger Buddy would be a 1950s-themed hamburger joint, emphasizing large portions and affordable prices.

Ma Maison is the alternate concept. One of your partners has attended cooking school and has proposed the idea of a small, upscale French restaurant. The menu would have no set items, but would vary on a daily basis instead. Ma Maison would position itself as a boutique restaurant providing superb customer service and unique offerings.

Working in small groups, answer the following questions:

1. What is the underlying strategy for each restaurant concept?
2. How would the organizational structure of the two restaurant concepts differ?

3. How would the nature of work vary between the two restaurants?
4. If the business concept is successful, how might you expect the organizational structure and nature of work at each restaurant to change in the next five to seven years?

VIDEO CASE

ORGANIZATIONAL STRUCTURE AND ACCOUNTABILITY

Roger Parry/Former Chairman and CEO/Clear Channel International

Roger Parry, former chairman and CEO of Clear Channel International, discusses structure and control inside of an organization. Before you view the video, think through your concept of an organizational chart and its role in the modern corporation.

Before you watch the video consider the following concepts and questions and be prepared to discuss them in class:

Concepts

- Organizational structure
- Organizational control
- Strategy and structure
- Performance due to proper strategy and structure alignment

Questions

1. Do you think it is important for an organization to have an organizational chart?
2. How can organizations use structure to allow business units to meet their goals as well as corporate goals?
3. How important is it for everyone in the organization to know precisely their responsibility and that proper control is in place to ensure that these responsibilities are being met?

CHAPTER 12

Leadership Implications for Strategy

Studying this chapter should provide you with the strategic management knowledge needed to:

1. Define strategic leadership and describe top-level managers' importance.

2. Explain what top management teams are and how they affect firm performance.

3. Describe the managerial succession process using internal and external managerial labor markets.

4. Discuss the value of strategic leadership in determining the firm's strategic direction.

5. Describe the importance of strategic leaders in managing the firm's resources.

6. Define organizational culture and explain what must be done to sustain an effective culture.

7. Explain what strategic leaders can do to establish and emphasize ethical practices.

8. Discuss the importance and use of organizational controls.

SELECTING A NEW CEO: THE IMPORTANCE OF STRATEGIC LEADERS

Evidence shows that the shelf life of a CEO is not long, and it continues to get shorter. In 2005, the average CEO tenure was 7.3 years and is becoming even shorter today (about 6 years).

The brevity of CEOs and top-level managers' tenure means that planning for and selecting new leaders should be continuous processes. Furthermore, the importance of strategic leaders to a firm's overall health and success makes selecting effective leaders critical. For example, in 2008 almost 1,500 CEOs of U.S.–based firms left their jobs. Despite this high number of strategic leader departures, boards of directors are rarely effective in planning for and completing the succession. A survey of boards found that over 40 percent of the firms had no succession plan. In another survey, more than 50 percent of directors rated the boards at their firms as ineffective in succession planning. Changes in the CEO often occur without warning. For example, in 2009 the CEOs at Toyota, Lenovo, and Ranbaxy unexpectedly resigned or were replaced. In the cases of Toyota and Lenovo, poor firm performance was the reason for change. Both suffered net losses in 2008 and Lenovo's market share declined from third to fourth place in the PC industry.

The importance of CEOs and planning for succession is clearly evident with Steve Jobs at Apple. Jobs took time off from the CEO role in 2009 due to illness. Analysts expressed major concerns about his ability to continue because of his importance to the success of the firm. He is believed to be especially important to Apple's innovation capability. While he does not design new products, he reviews each new project and serves as an internal champion for those he feels are worthy. For example, Jobs supported the work on the iPod in its early stages despite the skepticism of several others in the company. Furthermore, Jobs will not accept compromises; he pushes project teams to do everything possible to make the product right.

AP Photo/Bradley C. Bower

The leadership transition at DuPont was highly successful due to the early identification of Ellen Kullman as the likely successor to CEO, Charles Holliday and his ability to then serve as her mentor.

Jobs is a co-founder of Apple but left the company for 12 years. During that time, the company foundered. He returned in 1997 and Apple has had a number of market successes since that time. This is why many wonder if Jobs can be replaced. One analyst referred to Apple without Jobs as similar to a John Wayne movie without John Wayne. Another stated that Apple without Jobs is Sony. While Jobs has trained and delegated authority over innovation at Apple, few believe that he can be adequately replaced. Thus, the selection of a new CEO for Apple whenever Jobs departs will be critical for the company.

Companies can develop effective succession plans. Usually such plans call for selecting one or more potential successors and helping them to build the capabilities necessary to be effective CEOs. For example, they may be given challenging assignments where they can build valuable knowledge of critical markets and/or establish relationships with important stakeholders. They can receive mentoring and 360-degree feedback to identify positive traits and work on negative ones. For example, Ellen Kullman was identified as a potential CEO several years before she assumed the position at DuPont. The CEO whom she replaced, Charles Holliday, mentored Kullman and gave her challenging assignments. He was especially impressed with her willingness to learn. As a result, the transition from Holliday to Kullman was seamless and successful.

Identifying potential CEOs is a difficult assignment because of the many and varied capabilities needed for the job. Recent efforts to identify potential successors for CEOs focused on people who were innovative and championed innovation, had vision and could gain others commitment to that vision, nurtured important human capital, and built relationships with critical constituencies such as customers and suppliers.

Sources: S. Tobak, 2009, What happens when Steve Jobs leaves Apple? BNET, http://www.blogs.bnet.com, May 26; L. Whipp, 2009, Ranbaxy chief to step down, *Financial Times*, http://www.ft.com, May 24; J. Soble, 2009, Toyota plans top-level overhaul, *Financial Times*, http://www.ft.com, May 14; M. Boyle, 2009, The art of succession, *BusinessWeek*, May 11, 30–37; M. Boyle, 2009, The art of CEO succession, *BusinessWeek*, http://www.businessweek.com, April 30; F. Balfour and B. Einhorn, 2009, Lenovo CEO is out; Chinese execs return, *BusinessWeek*, http://www.businessweek.com, February 5; J. Scheck & N. Wingfield, 2008, How Apple could survive without Steve Jobs, *Wall Street Journal*, http://www.wsj.com, December 19; B. Behan, 2008, Shareholder proposals on CEO succession planning, *BusinessWeek*, http://www.businessweek.com, January 24.

As the Opening Case implies, strategic leaders' work is demanding, challenging, and may last for a long period of time. Regardless of how long they remain in their positions, strategic leaders (and most prominently CEOs) can make a major difference in how a firm performs.[1] If a strategic leader can create a strategic vision for the firm using forward thinking, she may be able to energize the firm's human capital and achieve positive outcomes. However, the challenge of strategic leadership is significant. For example, replacing Steve Jobs at Apple will be difficult because of his special skills in identifying and nurturing creative new products that have significant market potential. On the other hand, the transition at DuPont was smooth because a person was identified early and groomed to take over the CEO role when change was necessary.

A major message in this chapter is that effective strategic leadership is the foundation for successfully using the strategic management process. As is implied in Figure 1.1 (on page 5), strategic leaders guide the firm in ways that result in forming a vision and mission (see Chapter 1). Often, this guidance finds leaders thinking of ways to create goals that stretch everyone in the organization to improve performance.[2] Moreover, strategic leaders facilitate the development of appropriate strategic actions and determine how to implement them. As we show in Figure 12.1, these actions are the path to strategic competitiveness and above-average returns.[3]

We begin this chapter with a definition of strategic leadership; we then discuss its importance as a potential source of competitive advantage as well as effective strategic leadership styles. Next, we examine top management teams and their effects on innovation, strategic change, and firm performance. Following this discussion, we analyze the internal and external managerial labor markets from which strategic leaders are selected. Closing the chapter are descriptions of the five key components of effective strategic leadership: determining a strategic direction, effectively managing the firm's resource portfolio (which includes exploiting and maintaining core competencies along with developing human capital and social capital), sustaining an effective organizational culture, emphasizing ethical practices, and establishing balanced organizational controls.

Strategic Leadership and Style

Strategic leadership is the ability to anticipate, envision, maintain flexibility, and empower others to create strategic change as necessary. Multifunctional in nature, strategic leadership involves managing through others, managing an entire enterprise rather than a functional subunit, and coping with change that continues to increase in the global economy. Because of the global economy's complexity, strategic leaders must learn how to effectively influence human behavior, often in uncertain environments. By word or by personal example, and through their ability to envision the future, effective strategic leaders meaningfully influence the behaviors, thoughts, and feelings of those with whom they work.[4]

Strategic leadership is the ability to anticipate, envision, maintain flexibility, and empower others to create strategic change as necessary.

Figure 12.1 Strategic Leadership and the Strategic Management Process

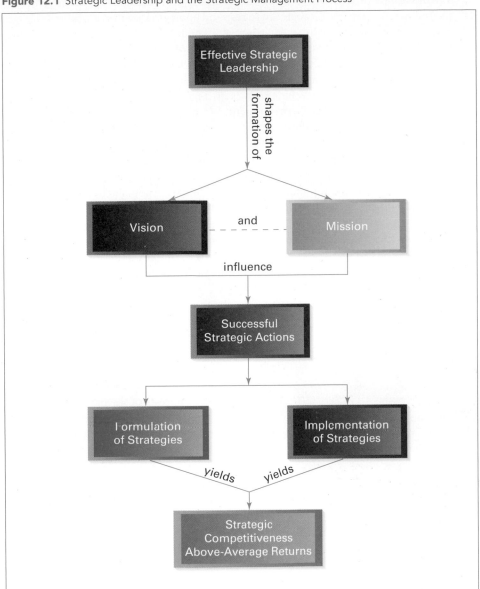

The ability to attract and then manage human capital may be the most critical of the strategic leader's skills,[5] especially because the lack of talented human capital constrains firm growth.[6] Increasingly, leaders throughout the global economy possess or are developing this skill. Some believe, for example, that leaders now surfacing in Chinese companies understand the rules of competition in market-based economies and are leading in ways that will develop their firm's human capital.[7]

In the twenty-first century, intellectual capital that the firm's human capital possesses, including the ability to manage knowledge and create and commercialize innovation, affects a strategic leader's success.[8] Effective strategic leaders also establish the context through which stakeholders (such as employees, customers, and suppliers) can perform at peak efficiency.[9] Being able to demonstrate these skills is important, given that the crux of strategic leadership is the ability to manage the firm's operations effectively and sustain high performance over time.[10]

A firm's ability to achieve a competitive advantage and earn above-average returns is compromised when strategic leaders fail to respond appropriately and quickly to changes in the complex global competitive environment. The inability to respond or to identify the need for change in the competitive environment is one of the reasons some CEOs fail, as shown by the replacement of CEOs in Toyota and Lenovo described in the Opening Case. Therefore, strategic leaders must learn how to deal with diverse and complex environmental situations. Individual judgment is an important part of learning about and analyzing the firm's competitive environment.[11] In particular, effective strategic leaders build strong ties with external stakeholders to gain access to information and advice on the events in the external environment.[12]

The primary responsibility for effective strategic leadership rests at the top, in particular with the CEO. Other commonly recognized strategic leaders include members of the board of directors, the top management team, and divisional general managers. In truth, any individual with responsibility for the performance of human capital and/or a part of the firm (e.g., a production unit) is a strategic leader. Regardless of their title and organizational function, strategic leaders have substantial decision-making responsibilities that cannot be delegated.[13] Strategic leadership is a complex but critical form of leadership. Strategies cannot be formulated and implemented for the purpose of achieving above-average returns without effective strategic leaders.[14]

Top-level management decisions influence the culture of firms as well as how organizations are structured and how goals are set and achieved.

The styles used to provide leadership often affect the productivity of those being led. Transformational leadership is the most effective strategic leadership style. This style entails motivating followers to exceed the expectations others have of them, to continuously enrich their capabilities, and to place the interests of the organization above their own.[15] Transformational leaders develop and communicate a vision for the organization and formulate a strategy to achieve the vision. They make followers aware of the need to achieve valued organizational outcomes and encourage them to continuously strive for higher levels of achievement. These types of leaders have a high degree of integrity (Roy Kroc, founder of McDonald's, was a strategic leader valued for his high degree of integrity)[16] and character. Speaking about character, one CEO said the following: "Leaders are shaped and defined by character. Leaders inspire and enable others to do excellent work and realize their potential. As a result, they build successful, enduring organizations."[17] Additionally, transformational leaders have emotional intelligence. Emotionally intelligent leaders understand themselves well, have strong motivation, are empathetic with others, and have effective interpersonal skills.[18] As a result of these characteristics, transformational leaders are especially effective in promoting and nurturing innovation in firms.[19]

The Role of Top-Level Managers

Top-level managers play a critical role in that they are charged to make certain their firm is able to effectively formulate and implement strategies.[20] Top-level managers' strategic decisions influence how the firm is designed and goals will be achieved. Thus, a critical element of organizational success is having a top management team with superior managerial skills.[21]

Managers often use their discretion (or latitude for action) when making strategic decisions, including those concerned with effectively implementing strategies.[22] Managerial discretion differs significantly across industries. The primary factors that determine the amount of decision-making discretion held by a manager (especially a top-level manager) are (1) external environmental sources such as the industry structure, the rate of market growth in the firm's primary industry, and the degree to which products can be differentiated; (2) characteristics of the organization, including its size, age, resources, and culture; and (3) characteristics of the manager, including commitment to the firm and its strategic outcomes, tolerance for ambiguity, skills in working with different people, and aspiration levels (see Figure 12.2). Because strategic leaders' decisions are intended to help the firm gain a competitive advantage, how managers exercise discretion when determining appropriate strategic actions is critical to the firm's success.[23]

In addition to determining new strategic initiatives, top-level managers develop a firm's organizational structure and reward systems. Top executives also have a major effect on a firm's culture. Evidence suggests that managers' values are critical in shaping a firm's cultural values.[24] Accordingly, top-level managers have an important effect on organizational activities and performance.[25] Because of the challenges top executives face, they often are more effective when they operate as top management teams.

Top Management Teams

In most firms, the complexity of challenges and the need for substantial amounts of information and knowledge require strategic leadership by a team of executives. Using

Figure 12.2 Factors Affecting Managerial Discretion

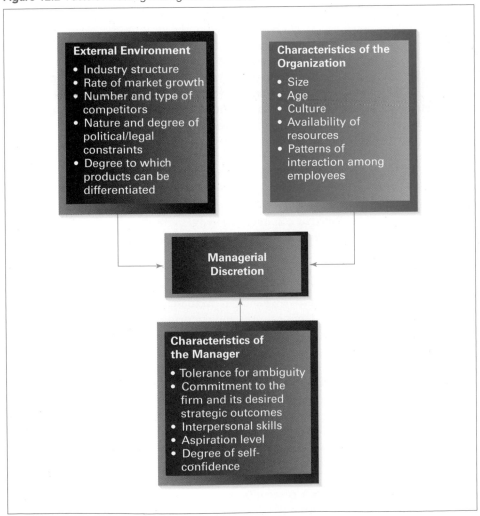

Source: Adapted from S. Finkelstein & D. C. Hambrick, 1996, *Strategic Leadership: Top Executives and Their Effects on Organizations*, St. Paul, MN: West Publishing Company.

a team to make strategic decisions also helps to avoid another potential problem when these decisions are made by the CEO alone: managerial hubris. Research evidence shows that when CEOs begin to believe glowing press accounts and to feel that they are unlikely to make errors, they are more likely to make poor strategic decisions.[26] Top executives need to have self-confidence but must guard against allowing it to become arrogance and a false belief in their own invincibility.[27] To guard against CEO overconfidence and poor strategic decisions, firms often use the top management team to consider strategic opportunities and problems and to make strategic decisions. The **top management team** is composed of the key individuals who are responsible for selecting and implementing the firm's strategies. Typically, the top management team includes the officers of the corporation, defined by the title of vice president and above or by service as a member of the board of directors.[28] The quality of the strategic decisions made by a top management team affects the firm's ability to innovate and engage in effective strategic change.[29]

Top Management Team, Firm Performance, and Strategic Change

The job of top-level executives is complex and requires a broad knowledge of the firm's operations, as well as the three key parts of the firm's external environment—the general, industry, and competitor environments, as discussed in Chapter 2. Therefore, firms try to form a top management team with knowledge and expertise needed to operate the internal organization, yet that also can deal with all the firm's stakeholders as well as its competitors.[30] To have these characteristics normally requires a heterogeneous top management team. A **heterogeneous top management team** is composed of individuals with different functional backgrounds, experience, and education.

Members of a heterogeneous top management team benefit from discussing the different perspectives advanced by team members.[31] In many cases, these discussions increase the quality of the team's decisions, especially when a synthesis emerges within the team after evaluating the diverse perspectives.[32] The net benefit of such actions by heterogeneous teams has been positive in terms of market share and above-average returns. Research shows that more heterogeneity among top management team members promotes debate, which often leads to better strategic decisions. In turn, better strategic decisions produce higher firm performance.[33]

It is also important for top management team members to function cohesively. In general, the more heterogeneous and larger the top management team is, the more difficult it is for the team to effectively implement strategies.[34] Comprehensive and long-term strategic plans can be inhibited by communication difficulties among top executives who have different backgrounds and different cognitive skills.[35] Alternatively, communication among diverse top management team members can be facilitated through electronic communications, sometimes reducing the barriers before face-to-face meetings.[36] However, a group of top executives with diverse backgrounds may inhibit the process of decision making if it is not effectively managed. In these cases, top management teams may fail to comprehensively examine threats and opportunities, leading to a suboptimal strategic decision. Thus, the CEO must attempt to achieve behavioral integration among the team members.[37]

Having members with substantive expertise in the firm's core functions and businesses is also important to a top management team's effectiveness.[38] In a high-technology industry, it may be critical for a firm's top management team members to have R&D expertise, particularly when growth strategies are being implemented. Yet their eventual effect on strategic decisions depends not only on their expertise and the way the team is managed but also on the context in which they make the decisions (the governance structure, incentive compensation, etc.).[39]

The characteristics of top management teams are related to innovation and strategic change.[40] For example, more heterogeneous top management teams are positively associated with innovation and strategic change. The heterogeneity may force the team or some of its members to "think outside of the box" and thus be more creative in making decisions.[41]

The **top management team** is composed of the key individuals who are responsible for selecting and implementing the firm's strategies.

A **heterogeneous top management team** is composed of individuals with different functional backgrounds, experience, and education.

Therefore, firms that need to change their strategies are more likely to do so if they have top management teams with diverse backgrounds and expertise. When a new CEO is hired from outside the industry, the probability of strategic change is greater than if the new CEO is from inside the firm or inside the industry.[42] Although hiring a new CEO from outside the industry adds diversity to the team, the top management team must be managed effectively to use the diversity in a positive way. Thus, to successfully create strategic change, the CEO should exercise transformational leadership.[43] A top management team with various areas of expertise is more likely to identify environmental changes (opportunities and threats) or changes within the firm, suggesting the need for a different strategic direction.

In the current competitive environment, an understanding of international markets is vital. However, recent research suggests that only about 15 percent of the top executives in *Fortune* 500 firms have global leadership expertise.[44] Executives generally gain this knowledge by working in one of the firm's international subsidiaries but can also gain some knowledge by working with international alliance partners.[45]

The CEO and Top Management Team Power

As noted in Chapter 10, the board of directors is an important governance mechanism for monitoring a firm's strategic direction and for representing stakeholders' interests, especially those of shareholders.[46] In fact, higher performance normally is achieved when the board of directors is more directly involved in shaping a firm's strategic direction.[47]

Boards of directors, however, may find it difficult to direct the strategic actions of powerful CEOs and top management teams.[48] Often, a powerful CEO appoints a number of sympathetic outside members to the board or may have inside board members who are also on the top management team and report to her or him.[49] In either case, the CEO may significantly influence the board's actions. Thus, the amount of discretion a CEO has in making strategic decisions is related to the board of directors and how it chooses to oversee the actions of the CEO and the top management team.[50]

CEOs and top management team members can achieve power in other ways. A CEO who also holds the position of chairperson of the board usually has more power than the CEO who does not.[51] Some analysts and corporate "watchdogs" criticize the practice of CEO duality (when the CEO and the chairperson of the board are the same) because it can lead to poor performance and slow response to change.[52]

Although it varies across industries, CEO duality occurs most commonly in larger firms. Increased shareholder activism, however, has brought CEO duality under scrutiny and attack in both U.S. and European firms. As reported in Chapter 10, an independent board leadership structure in which the same person did not hold the positions of CEO and chair is commonly believed to enhance a board's ability to monitor top-level managers' decisions and actions, particularly with respect to financial performance.[53] On the other hand, if a CEO acts as a steward, holding the dual roles facilitates effective decisions and actions. In these instances, the increased effectiveness gained through CEO duality accrues from the individual who wants to perform effectively and desires to be the best possible steward of the firm's assets. Because of this person's positive orientation and actions, extra governance and the coordination costs resulting from an independent board leadership structure would be unnecessary.[54]

Top management team members and CEOs who have long tenure—on the team and in the organization—have a greater influence on board decisions. CEOs with greater influence may take actions in their own best interests, the outcomes of which increase their compensation from the company.[55] As reported in Chapter 10, many people are angry about excessive top executive compensation, especially during poor economic times when others are losing their jobs because ineffective strategic decisions made by the same managers.

In general, long tenure is thought to constrain the breadth of an executive's knowledge base. Some evidence suggests that with the limited perspectives associated with a

STRATEGY
RIGHT NOW

Read more about the role of the board of directors in a firm's top management dynamic.

www.cengage.com/management/hitt

restricted knowledge base, long-tenured top executives typically develop fewer alternatives to evaluate in making strategic decisions.[56] However, long-tenured managers also may be able to exercise more effective strategic control, thereby obviating the need for board members' involvement because effective strategic control generally produces higher performance.[57] Intriguingly, recent findings suggest that "the liabilities of short tenure … appear to exceed the advantages, while the advantages of long tenure—firm-specific human and social capital, knowledge, and power—seem to outweigh the disadvantages of rigidity and maintaining the status quo."[58] Overall then the relationship between CEO tenure and firm performance is complex, indicating that to strengthen the firm, boards of directors should develop an effective relationship with the top management team.

In summary, the relative degrees of power held by the board and top management team members should be examined in light of an individual firm's situation. For example, the abundance of resources in a firm's external environment and the volatility of that environment may affect the ideal balance of power between the board and the top management teams. Moreover, a volatile and uncertain environment may create a situation where a powerful CEO is needed to move quickly, but a diverse top management team may create less cohesion among team members and prevent or stall necessary strategic actions. With effective working relationships, boards, CEOs, and other top management team members have the foundation required to select arrangements with the highest probability of best serving stakeholders' interests.[59]

Managerial Succession

The choice of top executives—especially CEOs—is a critical decision with important implications for the firm's performance.[60] Many companies use leadership screening systems to identify individuals with managerial and strategic leadership potential as well as to determine the criteria individuals should satisfy to be candidates for the CEO position.[61]

The most effective of these systems assesses people within the firm and gains valuable information about the capabilities of other companies' managers, particularly their strategic leaders.[62] Based on the results of these assessments, training and development programs are provided for current individuals in an attempt to preselect and shape the skills of people who may become tomorrow's leaders. Because of the quality of its programs, General Electric "is famous for developing leaders who are dedicated to turning imaginative ideas into leading products and services."[63]

Organizations select managers and strategic leaders from two types of managerial labor markets—internal and external.[64] An **internal managerial labor market** consists of a firm's opportunities for managerial positions and the qualified employees within that firm. An **external managerial labor market** is the collection of managerial career opportunities and the qualified people who are external to the organization in which the opportunities exist.

Several benefits are thought to accrue to a firm when the internal labor market is used to select an insider as the new CEO. Because of their experience with the firm and the industry environment in which it competes, insiders are familiar with company products, markets, technologies, and operating procedures. Also, internal hiring produces lower turnover among existing personnel, many of whom possess valuable firm-specific knowledge. When the firm is performing well, internal succession is favored to sustain high performance. It is assumed that hiring from inside keeps the important knowledge necessary to sustain performance.

Results of work completed by management consultant Jim Collins support the value of using the internal labor market when selecting a CEO. Collins found that high-performing firms almost always appoint an insider to be the new CEO. He argues that bringing in a

An **internal managerial labor market** consists of a firm's opportunities for managerial positions and the qualified employees within that firm.

An **external managerial labor market** is the collection of managerial career opportunities and the qualified people who are external to the organization in which the opportunities exist.

well-known outsider, to whom he refers as a "white knight," is a recipe for mediocrity.[65] For example, given the phenomenal success of General Electric (GE) during Jack Welch's tenure as CEO and the firm's highly effective management and leadership development programs, insider Jeffrey Immelt was chosen to succeed Welch. However, shareholders have become disgruntled because GE's stock values have decreased in recent years; GE has suffered along with many other firms in the global economic crisis experienced in 2008 and 2009. Thus, GE under Immelt's leadership is not experiencing the returns achieved by his predecessor.

Employees commonly prefer the internal managerial labor market when selecting top management team members and a new CEO. In the past, companies have also had a preference for insiders to fill top-level management positions because of a desire for continuity and a continuing commitment to the firm's current vision, mission, and chosen strategies.[66] However, because of a changing competitive landscape and varying levels of performance, an increasing number of boards of directors are turning to outsiders to succeed CEOs. Although the circumstances are rather unique, Ed Whitacre, former CEO of AT&T was chosen to be the new chairman for GM. Of course, he will have to help GM come out of bankruptcy.[67] A firm often has valid reasons to select an outsider as its new CEO. In some situations, long tenure with a firm may reduce strategic leaders' level of commitment to pursue innovation. Given innovation's importance to firm success (see Chapter 13), this hesitation could be a liability for a strategic leader.

In Figure 12.3, we show how the composition of the top management team and the CEO succession (managerial labor market) interact to affect strategy. For example, when the top management team is homogeneous (its members have similar functional experiences and educational backgrounds) and a new CEO is selected from inside the firm, the firm's current strategy is unlikely to change. Alternatively, when a new CEO is selected from outside the firm and the top management team is heterogeneous, the probability is high that strategy will change. When the new CEO is from inside the firm and a heterogeneous top management team is in place, the strategy may not change, but innovation is likely to continue. An external CEO succession with a homogeneous team creates a more ambiguous situation. The selection of Sir Howard Stringer as CEO of Sony signaled major changes in that firm's future. He is not only an outsider but also a foreigner. He is making major changes in the hopes of turning around Sony's poor performance. His intent is to have Sony regain its traditional excellence in innovative products.[68]

Figure 12.3 Effects of CEO Succession and Top Management Team Composition on Strategy

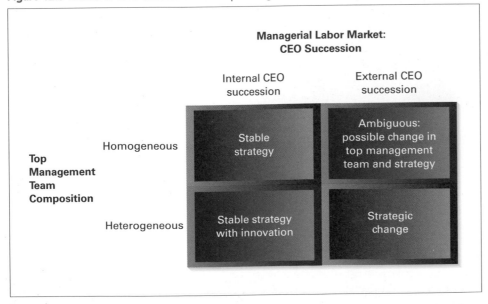

THE MODEL SUCCESSION AT XEROX

Anne Mulcahy became CEO of Xerox in 2001 and is credited with restoring the company's profitability and market leadership during her tenure. She championed innovation and built a strong relationship with customers. In fact, the firm was close to bankruptcy when she became the CEO. She told Xerox shareholders that the company's business model at the time was not sustainable. She was advised to declare bankruptcy but refused to do so. To gain the support needed for changes, she had personal meetings with the top 100 managers at Xerox. She refused to cut R&D or sales but did reduce costs significantly in other areas. The lead independent director, N. J. Nicholas, believes she created a major turnaround that built Xerox into an innovative technology and services company. Her work as CEO has earned her recognition as one of America's best leaders.

The succession process she has used reinforces that recognition. Ursula Burns was selected as heir apparent and given the job as president to "learn the ropes" for a couple of years before Mulcahy decided to take early retirement (Mulcahy was only 56 years old in 2009). Actually, Burns played a major role in Xerox's turnaround. She served as Mulcahy's lieutenant and managed most of the day-to-day operations. She also helped to identify gaps in Xerox's product portfolio and found products to fill those gaps. With the largest product portfolio in Xerox's history, it became a major competitor in marketing products to small and medium-sized businesses. Interestingly, Burns is the first African-American woman to head a major U.S. corporation. Burns (CEO) and Mulcahy (Chairman) are planning to work as a team for a couple of years. This is probably good because Xerox faces multiple challenges given the negative economic environment. Burns receives praise from insiders and external analysts for her deep knowledge of the industry and business and her technological expertise. She is also known for her willingness to take risks. One observer called the selection of Burns and model transition between Mulcahy and Burns as a "bases-loaded home run." Xerox is a unique technology-based company because approximately one third of its almost 4,000 executives are women. Observers expect the transition from Mulcahy to Burns to be a major success.

Anne Mulcahy, Chairman of Xerox

Jeff Weiner/Courtesy of Xerox Corporation

Sources: N. Byrnes and R. O. Crockett, 2009, An historic succession at Xerox, *BusinessWeek*, June 8, 18–22; W. M. Bulkeley, 2009, Xerox names Burns chief as Mulcahy retires early, *Wall Street Journal*, http://www.wsj.com, May 22; 2009, Chief executive is retiring at Xerox, *New York Times*, http://www.nytimes.com, May 22; 2009, Anne Mulcahy to retire as Xerox CEO; Ursula Burns named successor, FreshNews, http://www.freshnews.com, May 21; E. White, 2009, Xerox succession a 'model' case, *Wall Street Journal*, http://www.wsj.com, May 21; D. Gelles, 2009, Burns to replace Mulcahy at Xerox, *Financial Times*, http://www.ft.com, May 21; 2008, Women CEOs, Xerox, *Financial Times*, http://www.ft.com, December 31; B. George, 2008, America's best leaders: Anne Mulcahy, Xerox CEO, *US News*, http://www.usnews.com, November 19.

Ursula Burns, CEO of Xerox

Nik Rocklin/Courtesy of Xerox Corporation

Including talent from all parts of both the internal and external labor markets increases the likelihood that the firm will be able to form an effective top-management team. Evidence suggests that women are a qualified source of talent as strategic leaders that have been somewhat overlooked. In light of the success of a growing number of female executives, the foundation for change may be established. Trailblazers such as Catherine Elizabeth Hughes (the first African-American woman to head a firm that was publicly traded on a U.S. stock exchange), Muriel Siebert (the first woman to purchase a seat on the New York Stock Exchange), and publisher Judith Regan have made important contributions as strategic leaders. Recent years have produced several prominent female CEOs, such as Anne Mulcahy (Xerox Corporation), Meg Whitman (eBay), and Andrea Jung (Avon Products). As noted in the Strategic Focus, Anne Mulcahy stepped out of the role of CEO and became chairman of the board for Xerox in 2009. Ursula Burns succeeded her as the CEO.

Managerial talent is critical to a firm's success as noted earlier. And, one area in which managerial talent is crucial is in the integration of an acquired firm into the acquiring business. In fact, the top management team of an acquired firm is vital to a successful integration process because they play a critical role in helping the change be implemented and accepted by the acquired firm's employees.[69] However, it is common for there to be major turnover among the top management team of acquired firms. Sometimes it occurs because the acquiring firm unwisely replaces them. In other cases, the managers depart voluntarily to seek other top management positions. Research shows that high turnover among the acquired firm's top managers often produces poor performance and perhaps even leads to a failed acquisition.[70] Therefore, acquiring firms should work hard to avoid successions during the integration process and thereafter.

Key Strategic Leadership Actions

Certain actions characterize effective strategic leadership; we present the most important ones in Figure 12.4. Many of the actions interact with each other. For example, managing the firm's resources effectively includes developing human capital and contributes to establishing a strategic direction, fostering an effective culture, exploiting core competencies, using effective organizational control systems, and establishing ethical practices. The most effective strategic leaders create viable options in making decisions regarding each of the key strategic leadership actions.[71]

Determining Strategic Direction

Determining strategic direction involves specifying the image and character the firm seeks to develop over time.[72] The strategic direction is framed within the context of the conditions (i.e., opportunities and threats) strategic leaders expect their firm to face in roughly the next three to five years.

The ideal long-term strategic direction has two parts: a core ideology and an envisioned future. The core ideology motivates employees through the company's heritage, but the envisioned future encourages employees to stretch beyond their expectations of accomplishment and requires significant change and progress to be realized.[73] The envisioned future serves as a guide to many aspects of a firm's strategy implementation process, including motivation, leadership, employee empowerment, and organizational design. The strategic direction could include such actions as entering new international markets and developing a set of new suppliers to add to the firm's value chain.[74]

Most changes in strategic direction are difficult to design and implement; however, CEO Jeffrey Immelt has an even greater challenge at GE. GE performed exceptionally well under Jack Welch's leadership. Although change is necessary because the competitive landscape has shifted significantly, stakeholders accustomed to Jack Welch and high performance are experiencing problems in accepting Immelt's changes (e.g., changes to

Determining strategic direction involves specifying the image and character the firm seeks to develop over time.

Figure 12.4 Exercise of Effective Strategic Leadership

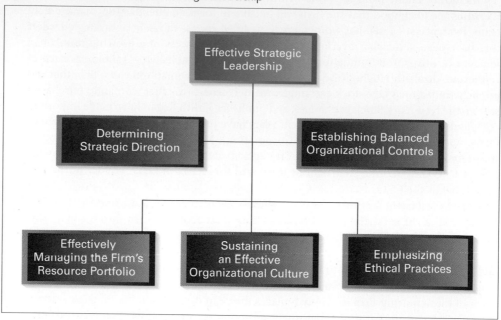

the firm's corporate-level strategy and structure). His challenges are made even more difficult because GE is experiencing performance problems partly the result of the difficult economic climate.[75] Additionally, information regarding the firm's strategic direction must be consistently and clearly communicated to all affected parties.[76]

A charismatic CEO may foster stakeholders' commitment to a new vision and strategic direction. Nonetheless, it is important not to lose sight of the organization's strengths when making changes required by a new strategic direction. Immelt, for example, needs to use GE's strengths to ensure continued positive performance. The goal is to pursue the firm's short-term need to adjust to a new vision and strategic direction while maintaining its long-term survivability by effectively managing its portfolio of resources.

Effectively Managing the Firm's Resource Portfolio

Effectively managing the firm's portfolio of resources may be the most important strategic leadership task. The firm's resources are categorized as financial capital, human capital, social capital, and organizational capital (including organizational culture).[77]

Clearly, financial capital is critical to organizational success; strategic leaders understand this reality.[78] However, the most effective strategic leaders recognize the equivalent importance of managing each remaining type of resource as well as managing the integration of resources (e.g., using financial capital to provide training opportunities through which human capital is able to learn and maximize its performance). Most importantly, effective strategic leaders manage the firm's resource portfolio by organizing them into capabilities, structuring the firm to facilitate using those capabilities, and choosing strategies through which the capabilities are successfully leveraged to create value for customers.[79] Exploiting and maintaining core competencies and developing and retaining the firm's human and social capital are actions taken to reach these important objectives.

Exploiting and Maintaining Core Competencies

Examined in Chapters 1 and 3, *core competencies* are capabilities that serve as a source of competitive advantage for a firm over its rivals. Typically, core competencies relate to an organization's functional skills, such as manufacturing, finance, marketing, and research and development. Strategic leaders must verify that the firm's competencies are emphasized when implementing strategies. Intel, for example, has core competencies of *competitive agility* (an ability to act in a variety of competitively relevant ways) and *competitive speed* (an ability to act quickly when facing environmental and competitive pressures).[80] Capabilities are developed over time as firms learn from their actions and enhance their knowledge about specific actions needed. For example, through repeated interactions, some firms have formed a capability allowing them to fully understand customers' needs as they change.[81] Firms with capabilities in R&D that develop into core competencies are rewarded by the market because of the critical nature of innovation in many industries.[82]

In many large firms, and certainly in related diversified ones, core competencies are effectively exploited when they are developed and applied across different organizational units (see Chapter 6). For example, PepsiCo purchased Quaker Oats (now called Quaker Foods), which makes the sports drink Gatorade. PepsiCo uses its competence in distribution systems to exploit the Quaker assets. In this instance, Pepsi soft drinks (e.g., Pepsi Cola and Mountain Dew) and Gatorade share the logistics activity. Similarly, PepsiCo uses this competence to distribute Quaker's healthy snacks and Frito-Lay salty snacks through the same channels. Today, PepsiCo seeks "to be the world's premiere consumer products company focused on convenient foods and beverages."[83]

Firms must continuously develop and, when appropriate, change their core competencies to outperform rivals. If they have a competence that provides an advantage but does not change it, competitors will eventually imitate that competence and reduce or eliminate the firm's competitive advantage. Additionally, firms must guard against the competence becoming a liability, thereby preventing change.

As we discuss next, human capital is critical to a firm's success. One reason it's so critical is that human capital is the resource through which core competencies are developed and used.

Dave & Les Jacobs/Cultura/Getty Images

Training and development programs can provide the means by which new strategic leaders are cultivated within an organization.

Developing Human Capital and Social Capital

Human capital refers to the knowledge and skills of a firm's entire workforce. From the perspective of human capital, employees are viewed as a capital resource requiring continuous investment.[84] At PepsiCo, people are identified as the key to the firm's continuing success. Given the need to "sustain its talent," PepsiCo invests in its human capital in the form of a host of programs and development-oriented experiences.[85]

Investments such as those being made at PepsiCo are productive, in that much of the development of U.S. industry can be attributed to the effectiveness of its human capital. This fact suggests that "as the dynamics of competition accelerate, people are perhaps the only truly sustainable source of competitive advantage."[86] In all types of organizations—large and small, new and established, and so forth—human capital's increasing importance suggests a significant role for the firm's human resource management activities.[87] As a support activity (see Chapter 3), human resource management practices facilitate people's efforts to successfully select and especially to use the firm's strategies.[88]

Effective training and development programs increase the probability of individuals becoming successful strategic leaders.[89] These programs are increasingly linked to firm

Human capital refers to the knowledge and skills of a firm's entire workforce.

success as knowledge becomes more integral to gaining and sustaining a competitive advantage.[90] Additionally, such programs build knowledge and skills, inculcate a common set of core values, and offer a systematic view of the organization, thus promoting the firm's vision and organizational cohesion. For example, PepsiCo's development programs emphasize its "performance with purpose," which focuses on building shareholder value while simultaneously ensuring human, environmental, and talent sustainability.[91]

Effective training and development programs also contribute positively to the firm's efforts to form core competencies.[92] Furthermore, they help strategic leaders improve skills that are critical to completing other tasks associated with effective strategic leadership, such as determining the firm's strategic direction, exploiting and maintaining the firm's core competencies, and developing an organizational culture that supports ethical practices. Thus, building human capital is vital to the effective execution of strategic leadership. Indeed, some argue that the world's "best companies are realizing that no matter what business they're in, their real business is building leaders."[93]

Strategic leaders must acquire the skills necessary to help develop human capital in their areas of responsibility.[94] When human capital investments are successful, the result is a workforce capable of learning continuously. Continuous learning and leveraging the firm's expanding knowledge base are linked with strategic success.[95]

Learning also can preclude making errors. Strategic leaders tend to learn more from their failures than their successes because they sometimes make the wrong attributions for the successes.[96] For example, the effectiveness of certain approaches and knowledge can be context specific.[97] Thus, some "best practices" may not work well in all situations. We know that using teams to make decisions can be effective, but sometimes it is better for leaders to make decisions alone, especially when the decisions must be made and implemented quickly (e.g., in crisis situations).[98] Thus, effective strategic leaders recognize the importance of learning from success *and* from failure.

Learning and building knowledge are important for creating innovation in firms.[99] Innovation leads to competitive advantage. Overall, firms that create and maintain greater knowledge usually achieve and maintain competitive advantages. However, as noted with core competencies, strategic leaders must guard against allowing high levels of knowledge in one area to lead to myopia and overlooking knowledge development opportunities in other important areas of the business.[100]

When facing challenging conditions, firms sometimes decide to lay off some of their human capital. Strategic leaders must recognize though that layoffs can result in a significant loss of the knowledge possessed by the firm's human capital. Research evidence shows that moderate-sized layoffs may improve firm performance, but large layoffs produce stronger performance downturns in firms because of the loss of human capital.[101] Although it is also not uncommon for restructuring firms to reduce their expenditures on or investments in training and development programs, restructuring may actually be an important time to increase investments in these programs. The reason for increased focus on training and development is that restructuring firms have less slack and cannot absorb as many errors; moreover, the employees who remain after layoffs may find themselves in positions without all the skills or knowledge they need to perform the required tasks effectively.

Viewing employees as a resource to be maximized rather than as a cost to be minimized facilitates successful implementation of a firm's strategies as does the strategic leader's ability to approach layoffs in a manner that employees believe is fair and equitable.[102] A critical issue for employees is the fairness in the layoffs and in treatment in their jobs.[103]

Social capital involves relationships inside and outside the firm that help the firm accomplish tasks and create value for customers and shareholders.[104] Social capital is a critical asset for a firm. Inside the firm, employees and units must cooperate to get the work done. In multinational organizations, employees often must cooperate

Social capital involves relationships inside and outside the firm that help the firm accomplish tasks and create value for customers and shareholders.

across country boundaries on activities such as R&D to achieve performance objectives (e.g., developing new products).[105]

External social capital is increasingly critical to firm success. The reason for this is that few if any companies have all of the resources they need to successfully compete against their rivals. Firms can use cooperative strategies such as strategic alliances (see Chapter 9) to develop social capital. Social capital can develop in strategic alliances as firms share complementary resources. Resource sharing must be effectively managed, though, to ensure that the partner trusts the firm and is willing to share the desired resources.[106]

Research evidence suggests that the success of many types of firms may partially depend on social capital. Large multinational firms often must establish alliances in order to enter new foreign markets. Likewise, entrepreneurial firms often must establish alliances to gain access to resources, venture capital, or other types of resources (e.g., special expertise that the entrepreneurial firm cannot afford to maintain in-house).[107] Retaining quality human capital and maintaining strong internal social capital can be affected strongly by the firm's culture.

Sustaining an Effective Organizational Culture

In Chapter 1, we define **organizational culture** as a complex set of ideologies, symbols, and core values that are shared throughout the firm and influence the way business is conducted. Evidence suggests that a firm can develop core competencies in terms of both the capabilities it possesses and the way the capabilities are leveraged when implementing strategies to produce desired outcomes. In other words, because the organizational culture influences how the firm conducts its business and helps regulate and control employees' behavior, it can be a source of competitive advantage[108] and is a "critical factor in promoting innovation."[109] Given its importance, it may be that a vibrant organizational culture is the most valuable competitive differentiator for business organizations. Thus, shaping the context within which the firm formulates and implements its strategies—that is, shaping the organizational culture—is an essential strategic leadership action.[110]

Entrepreneurial Mind-Set

Especially in large organizations, an organizational culture often encourages (or discourages) strategic leaders from pursuing (or not pursuing) entrepreneurial opportunities.[111] This issue is important because entrepreneurial opportunities are a vital source of growth and innovation.[112] Therefore, a key role of strategic leaders is to encourage and promote innovation by pursuing entrepreneurial opportunities.[113]

One way to encourage innovation is to invest in opportunities as real options—that is, invest in an opportunity in order to provide the potential option of taking advantage of the opportunity at some point in the future.[114] For example, a firm might buy a piece of land to have the option to build on it at some time in the future should the company need more space and should that location increase in value to the company. Firms might enter strategic alliances for similar reasons. In this instance, a firm might form an alliance to have the option of acquiring the partner later or of building a stronger relationship with it (e.g., developing a joint new venture).[115]

In Chapter 13, we describe how large firms use strategic entrepreneurship to pursue entrepreneurial opportunities and to gain first-mover advantages. Small and medium-sized firms also rely on strategic entrepreneurship when trying to develop innovations as the foundation for profitable growth. In firms of all sizes, strategic entrepreneurship is more likely to be successful when employees have an entrepreneurial mind-set.[116]

Five dimensions characterize a firm's entrepreneurial mind-set: autonomy, innovativeness, risk taking, proactiveness, and competitive aggressiveness.[117] In combination, these dimensions influence the actions a firm takes to be innovative and launch new ventures. In sum, strategic leaders with an entrepreneurial mind-set are committed to pursuing profitable growth.[118]

An **organizational culture** consists of a complex set of ideologies, symbols, and core values that are shared throughout the firm and influence the way business is conducted.

Autonomy, the first of an entrepreneurial orientation's five dimensions, allows employees to take actions that are free of organizational constraints and permits individuals and groups to be self-directed. The second dimension, *innovativeness,* "reflects a firm's tendency to engage in and support new ideas, novelty, experimentation, and creative processes that may result in new products, services, or technological processes."[119] Cultures with a tendency toward innovativeness encourage employees to think beyond existing knowledge, technologies, and parameters to find creative ways to add value. *Risk taking* reflects a willingness by employees and their firm to accept risks when pursuing entrepreneurial opportunities. Assuming significant levels of debt and allocating large amounts of other resources (e.g., people) to projects that may not be completed are examples of these risks. The fourth dimension of an entrepreneurial orientation, *proactiveness,* describes a firm's ability to be a market leader rather than a follower. Proactive organizational cultures constantly use processes to anticipate future market needs and to satisfy them before competitors learn how to do so. Finally, *competitive aggressiveness* is a firm's propensity to take actions that allow it to consistently and substantially outperform its rivals.[120]

Changing the Organizational Culture and Restructuring

Changing a firm's organizational culture is more difficult than maintaining it; however, effective strategic leaders recognize when change is needed. Incremental changes to the firm's culture typically are used to implement strategies.[121] More significant and sometimes even radical changes to organizational culture support selecting strategies that differ from those the firm has implemented historically. Regardless of the reasons for change, shaping and reinforcing a new culture require effective communication and problem solving, along with selecting the right people (those who have the values desired for the organization), engaging in effective performance appraisals (establishing goals and measuring individual performance toward goals that fit in with the new core values), and using appropriate reward systems (rewarding the desired behaviors that reflect the new core values).[122]

Evidence suggests that cultural changes succeed only when the firm's CEO, other key top management team members, and middle-level managers actively support them.[123] To effect change, middle-level managers in particular need to be highly disciplined to energize the culture and foster alignment with the strategic vision.[124] In addition, managers must be sensitive to the effects of other major strategic changes on organizational culture. For example, major downsizings can have negative effects on an organization's culture, especially if it is not implemented in accordance with the dominant organizational values.[125]

Emphasizing Ethical Practices

The effectiveness of processes used to implement the firm's strategies increases when they are based on ethical practices. Ethical companies encourage and enable people at all organizational levels to act ethically when doing what is necessary to implement strategies. In turn, ethical practices and the judgment on which they are based create "social capital" in the organization, increasing the "goodwill available to individuals and groups" in the organization.[126] Alternatively, when unethical practices evolve in an organization, they may become acceptable to many managers and employees.[127] One study found that in these circumstances, managers were particularly likely to engage in unethical practices to meet their goals when current efforts to meet them were insufficient.[128]

To properly influence employees' judgment and behavior, ethical practices must shape the firm's decision-making process and must be an integral part of organizational culture. In fact, research evidence suggests that a value-based culture is the most effective means of ensuring that employees comply with the firm's ethical requirements.[129] As we explained in Chapter 10, managers may act opportunistically, making decisions that are in their own best interests but not in the firm's best interests when facing lax expectations regarding ethical behavior. In other words, managers acting opportunistically take advantage of their positions, making decisions that benefit themselves to the detriment of the firm's stakeholders.[130] But strategic leaders are most likely to integrate ethical values into their decisions when the company has explicit ethics codes, the code is integrated into the business through extensive ethics training, and shareholders expect ethical behavior.[131]

Firms should employ ethical strategic leaders—leaders who include ethical practices as part of their strategic direction for the firm, who desire to do the right thing, and for whom honesty, trust, and integrity are important.[132] Strategic leaders who consistently display these qualities inspire employees as they work with others to develop and support an organizational culture in which ethical practices are the expected behavioral norms.[133]

Strategic leaders can take several actions to develop an ethical organizational culture. Examples of these actions include (1) establishing and communicating specific goals to describe the firm's ethical standards (e.g., developing and disseminating a code of conduct); (2) continuously revising and updating the code of conduct, based on inputs from people throughout the firm and from other stakeholders (e.g., customers and suppliers); (3) disseminating the code of conduct to all stakeholders to inform them of the firm's ethical standards and practices; (4) developing and implementing methods and procedures to use in achieving the firm's ethical standards (e.g., using internal auditing practices that are consistent with the standards); (5) creating and using explicit reward systems that recognize acts of courage (e.g., rewarding those who use proper channels and procedures to report observed wrongdoings); and (6) creating a work environment in which all people are treated with dignity.[134] The effectiveness of these actions increases when they are taken simultaneously and thereby are mutually supportive. When strategic leaders and others throughout the firm fail to take actions such as these—perhaps because an ethical culture has not been created—problems are likely to occur. As we discuss next, formal organizational controls can help prevent further problems and reinforce better ethical practices.[135]

Establishing Balanced Organizational Controls

Organizational controls are basic to a capitalistic system and have long been viewed as an important part of strategy implementation processes.[136] Controls are necessary to help ensure that firms achieve their desired outcomes.[137] Defined as the "formal, information-based … procedures used by managers to maintain or alter patterns in organizational activities," controls help strategic leaders build credibility, demonstrate the value of strategies to the firm's stakeholders, and promote and support strategic change.[138] Most critically, controls provide the parameters for implementing strategies as well as the corrective actions to be taken when implementation-related adjustments are required.

In this chapter, we focus on two organizational controls—strategic and financial—that were introduced in Chapter 11. Our discussion of organizational controls here emphasizes strategic and financial controls because strategic leaders, especially those at the top of the organization, are responsible for their development and effective use.

As we explained in Chapter 11, financial control focuses on short-term financial outcomes. In contrast, strategic control focuses on the *content* of strategic actions rather than their *outcomes*. Some strategic actions can be correct but still result in poor financial outcomes because of external conditions such as a recession in the economy, unexpected domestic or foreign government actions, or natural disasters. Therefore, emphasizing financial controls often produces more short-term and risk-averse managerial decisions, because financial outcomes may be caused by events beyond managers' direct control. Alternatively, strategic control encourages lower-level managers to make decisions that incorporate moderate and acceptable levels of risk because outcomes are shared between the business-level executives making strategic proposals and the corporate-level executives evaluating them.

The challenge strategic leaders face is to verify that their firm is emphasizing financial and strategic controls so that firm performance improves. The Balanced Scorecard is a tool that helps strategic leaders assess the effectiveness of the controls.

The Balanced Scorecard

The **balanced scorecard** is a framework firms can use to verify that they have established both strategic and financial controls to assess their performance.[139] This technique is most appropriate for use when dealing with business-level strategies; however, it can also be used with the other strategies firms may choose to implement (e.g., corporate level, international, and cooperative).

The underlying premise of the balanced scorecard is that firms jeopardize their future performance possibilities when financial controls are emphasized at the expense of strategic controls,[140] in that financial controls provide feedback about outcomes achieved from past actions, but do not communicate the drivers of future performance.[141] Thus, an overemphasis on financial controls has the potential to promote managerial behavior that sacrifices the firm's long-term, value-creating potential for short-term performance gains.[142] An appropriate balance of strategic controls and financial controls, rather than an overemphasis on either, allows firms to effectively monitor their performance.

Four perspectives are integrated to form the balanced scorecard framework: *financial* (concerned with growth, profitability, and risk from the shareholders' perspective), *customer* (concerned with the amount of value customers perceive was created by the firm's products), *internal business processes* (with a focus on the priorities for various business processes that create customer and shareholder satisfaction), and *learning and growth* (concerned with the firm's effort to create a climate that supports change, innovation, and growth). Thus, using the balanced scorecard framework allows the firm to understand how it looks to shareholders (financial perspective), how customers view it (customer perspective), the processes it must emphasize to successfully use its competitive advantage (internal perspective), and what it can do to improve its performance in order to grow (learning and growth perspective).[143] Generally speaking, strategic controls tend to be emphasized when the firm assesses its performance relative to the learning and growth perspective, whereas financial controls are emphasized when assessing performance in terms of the financial perspective.

Firms use different criteria to measure their standing relative to the scorecard's four perspectives. We show sample criteria in Figure 12.5. The firm should select the number of criteria that will allow it to have both a strategic understanding and a financial understanding of its performance without becoming immersed in too many details.[144] For example, we know from research that a firm's innovation, quality of its goods and services, growth of its sales, and its profitability are all interrelated.[145]

Strategic leaders play an important role in determining a proper balance between strategic controls and financial controls, whether they are in single-business firms or large diversified firms. A proper balance between controls is important, in that "wealth creation for organizations where strategic leadership is exercised is possible because these leaders make appropriate investments for future viability [through strategic control], while maintaining an appropriate level of financial stability in the present [through financial control]."[146] In fact, most corporate restructuring is designed to refocus the firm on its core businesses, thereby allowing top executives to reestablish strategic control of their separate business units.[147]

Successfully using strategic control frequently is integrated with appropriate autonomy for the various subunits so that they can gain a competitive advantage in their respective markets.[148] Strategic control can be used to promote the sharing of both tangible and intangible resources among interdependent businesses within a firm's portfolio. In addition, the autonomy provided allows the flexibility necessary to take advantage of

The **balanced scorecard** is a framework firms can use to verify that they have established both strategic and financial controls to assess their performance.

Figure 12.5 Strategic Controls and Financial Controls in a Balanced Scorecard Framework

Perspectives	Criteria
Financial	• Cash flow • Return on equity • Return on assets
Customer	• Assessment of ability to anticipate customers' needs • Effectiveness of customer service practices • Percentage of repeat business • Quality of communications with customers
Internal Business Processes	• Asset utilization improvements • Improvements in employee morale • Changes in turnover rates
Learning and Growth	• Improvements in innovation ability • Number of new products compared to competitors • Increases in employees' skills

specific marketplace opportunities. As a result, strategic leadership promotes simultaneous use of strategic control and autonomy.[149]

The balanced scorecard is being used by car manufacturer Porsche. After this manufacturer of sought-after sports cars regained its market-leading position, it implemented a balanced scorecard approach in an effort to maintain this position. In particular, Porsche used the balanced scorecard to promote learning and continuously improve the business. For example, knowledge was collected from all Porsche dealerships throughout the world. The instrument used to collect the information was referred to as "Porsche Key Performance Indicators." The fact that Porsche is now the world's most profitable automaker suggests the value the firm gained and is gaining by using the balanced scorecard as a foundation for simultaneously emphasizing strategic and financial controls.[150]

As we have explained, strategic leaders are critical to a firm's ability to successfully use all parts of the strategic management process. As described in the Strategic Focus, the new CEO for Wal-Mart, Mike Duke, has the strategic leadership skills to position him and his company for future success. Certainly, the future for strategic leaders similar to Duke is likely to be challenging; but he is leading a highly successful company that is increasing its market share and is likely to grow in international markets, where he has significant experience and knowledge. He appears to emphasize balanced organizational controls and uses many of the principles of the Balanced Scorecard. With people like Mike Duke in these roles, the work of strategic leaders will remain exciting and has a strong possibility of creating positive outcomes for all of a firm's stakeholders.

STRATEGIC FOCUS

THE "GLOBAL DUKE OF RETAIL": THE NEW STRATEGIC LEADER OF WAL-MART

On February 1, 2009, Mike Duke was named the CEO of Wal-Mart. Duke had been chief of the international division and vice chairman of the board of directors prior to his new appointment. The prior CEO, Lee Scott, was in the job for almost 10 years. During his time as CEO, many changes were made in the Wal-Mart strategy. In particular, it went back to its roots with a primary focus on providing value at the lowest possible price. He also started a major public relations program to answer Wal-Mart critics and placed a major emphasis on environment and sustainability. His changes started to pay off for Wal-Mart as its stock price increased 18 percent in 2008, the best performer in the Dow Jones industrial average. Wal-Mart's profits increased during 2008, a year when most companies—especially retailers—experienced declines because of the severe economic climate.

Duke began his tenure at Wal-Mart in 1995 as vice president of logistics after 23 years with Federated Department Stores. Duke eventually ascended to the leadership of the international division and presided over its unprecedented growth. That division is larger than most multinational companies with more than 3,500 stores, 680,000 employees (or "associates" in Wal-Mart terms), and approximately $100 billion in annual sales. Duke was known for building a strong international leadership team. In fact, he is likely to emphasize global business even more for Wal-Mart as a strategy to enhance growth.

Duke is also known for emphasizing high standards of excellence for the company's resources and people. This includes the redesign of the logistics and merchandise distribution system, known as the best in the world, and in recruiting strong talent and building excellent leadership teams. He has already announced that he will increase the speed of and enlarge Wal-Mart's commitment to sustainability as a major part of the firm's organizational culture. Duke is considered to be a strategic thinker and a risk taker. He believes Wal-Mart should try to be the market share leader in every foreign market it enters. Wal-Mart pulled out of Germany and Korea for this reason. Duke is also known to have excellent interpersonal skills.

Wal-Mart is the leading retailer in the world and one of the largest corporations with more than $400 billion in sales. It has been positioned for much future growth and success and Mike Duke has the strategic leadership skills to achieve these goals.

Sources: 2009, Michael T. Duke, Wal-Mart, http://www.walmartstores.com, accessed on May 26; 2009, Wal-Mart reports first quarter financial results, New YorkTtimes, http://markets.on.nytimes.com, May 14; S. Kapner, 2009, Changing of the guard at Wal-Mart, Fortune, March 2. 68–74; S. Rosenbloom, 2009, Wal-Mart hopes to hold onto customers it gained from recession, New York Times, http://wwww.nytimes.com, February 18; 2008, Wal-Mart picks Mike Duke as new CEO, MSNBC.com, http://www.msnbc.msn.com, November 21; S. Rosenbloom, 2008, Wal-Mart taps new chief executive, New York Times, http://www.nytimes.com, October 21.

AP Photo/April L. Brown

Wal-Mart Stores Inc. President and Chief Financial Officer Mike Duke speaks during the annual Wal-Mart shareholder's meeting in Fayetteville, Arkansas. Duke has pledged to shareholders that the world's largest retailer will build on its success by keeping its customers even when the economy improves.

SUMMARY

- Effective strategic leadership is a prerequisite to successfully using the strategic management process. Strategic leadership entails the ability to anticipate events, envision possibilities, maintain flexibility, and empower others to create strategic change.

- Top-level managers are an important resource for firms to develop and exploit competitive advantages. In addition, when they and their work are valuable, rare, imperfectly imitable, and nonsubstitutable, strategic leaders are also a source of competitive advantage.

- The top management team is composed of key managers who play a critical role in selecting and implementing the firm's strategies. Generally, they are officers of the corporation and/or members of the board of directors.

- The top management team's characteristics, a firm's strategies, and its performance are all interrelated. For example, a top management team with significant marketing and R&D knowledge positively contributes to the firm's use of a growth strategy. Overall, having diverse skills increases most top management teams' effectiveness.

- Typically, performance improves when the board of directors is involved in shaping a firm's strategic direction. However, when the CEO has a great deal of power, the board may be less involved in decisions about strategy formulation and implementation. By appointing people to the board and simultaneously serving as CEO and chair of the board, CEOs increase their power.

- In managerial succession, strategic leaders are selected from either the internal or the external managerial labor market. Because of their effect on firm performance, selection of strategic leaders has implications for a firm's effectiveness. Companies use a variety of reasons for selecting the firm's strategic leaders either internally or externally. In most instances, the internal market is used to select the CEO; but the number of outsiders chosen is increasing. Outsiders often are selected to initiate major changes in strategy.

- Effective strategic leadership has five major components: determining the firm's strategic direction, effectively managing the firm's resource portfolio (including exploiting and maintaining core competencies and managing human capital and social capital), sustaining an effective organizational culture, emphasizing ethical practices, and establishing balanced organizational controls.

- Strategic leaders must develop the firm's strategic direction. The strategic direction specifies the image and character the firm wants to develop over time. To form the strategic direction, strategic leaders evaluate the conditions (e.g., opportunities and threats in the external environment) they expect their firm to face over the next three to five years.

- Strategic leaders must ensure that their firm exploits its core competencies, which are used to produce and deliver products that create value for customers, when implementing its strategies. In related diversified and large firms in particular, core competencies are exploited by sharing them across units and products.

- The ability to manage the firm's resource portfolio and manage the processes used to effectively implement the firm's strategy are critical elements of strategic leadership. Managing the resource portfolio includes integrating resources to create capabilities and leveraging those capabilities through strategies to build competitive advantages. Human capital and social capital are perhaps the most important resources.

- As a part of managing the firm's resources, strategic leaders must develop a firm's human capital. Effective strategic leaders view human capital as a resource to be maximized—not as a cost to be minimized. Such leaders develop and use programs designed to train current and future strategic leaders to build the skills needed to nurture the rest of the firm's human capital.

- Effective strategic leaders also build and maintain internal and external social capital. Internal social capital promotes cooperation and coordination within and across units in the firm. External social capital provides access to resources the firm needs to compete effectively.

- Shaping the firm's culture is a central task of effective strategic leadership. An appropriate organizational culture encourages the development of an entrepreneurial orientation among employees and an ability to change the culture as necessary.

- In ethical organizations, employees are encouraged to exercise ethical judgment and to always act ethically. Improved ethical practices foster social capital. Setting specific goals to meet the firm's ethical standards, using a code of conduct, rewarding ethical behaviors, and creating a work environment where all people are treated with dignity are actions that facilitate and support ethical behavior.

- Developing and using balanced organizational controls are the final components of effective strategic leadership. The balanced scorecard is a tool that measures the effectiveness of the firm's strategic and financial controls. An effective balance between strategic and financial controls allows for flexible use of core competencies, but within the parameters of the firm's financial position.

1. What is strategic leadership? In what ways are top executives considered important resources for an organization?

2. What is a top management team, and how does it affect a firm's performance and its abilities to innovate and design and implement effective strategic changes?

3. How do the internal and external managerial labor markets affect the managerial succession process?

4. What is the effect of strategic leadership on determining the firm's strategic direction?

5. How do strategic leaders effectively manage their firm's resource portfolio to exploit its core competencies and

leverage the human capital and social capital to achieve a competitive advantage?

6. What is organizational culture? What must strategic leaders do to develop and sustain an effective organizational culture?

7. As a strategic leader, what actions could you take to establish and emphasize ethical practices in your firm?

8. What are organizational controls? Why are strategic controls and financial controls important aspects of the strategic management process?

EXPERIENTIAL EXERCISES

EXERCISE 1: EXECUTIVE SUCCESSION

For this exercise, you will identify and analyze a case of CEO succession. Working in small groups, find a publicly held firm that has changed CEOs. The turnover event must have happened at least twelve months ago, but no more than twenty four months ago. Use a combination of company documents and news articles to answer the following questions:

1. Why did the CEO leave? Common reasons for CEO turnover include death or illness, retirement, accepting a new position, change in ownership or control, or termination. In cases of termination, there is often no official statement as to why the CEO departed. Consequently, you may have to rely on news articles that speculate why a CEO was fired, or forced to resign.

2. Did the replacement CEO come from inside the organization, or outside?

3. What are the similarities and differences between the new CEO and the CEO who was replaced? Possible comparison items could include functional experience, industry experience, etc. If your library has a subscription to *Hoover's Online*, you can find information on top managers through this resource.

4. At the time of the succession event, how did the firm's financial performance compare to industry norms? Has the firm's

standing relative to the industry changed since the new CEO took over?

5. Has the firm made major strategic changes since the succession event? Has the firm made major acquisitions or divestitures? Launched or closed down product lines?

Create a PowerPoint presentation that presents answers to each of the above questions. Your presentation should be brief, consisting of no more than five to seven slides.

EXERCISE 2: STRATEGIC LEADERSHIP IS TOUGH!

Your textbook defines strategic leadership as "The ability to anticipate, envision, maintain flexibility, and empower others...." Accordingly, this exercise combines the practical elements of leadership in an experiential exercise. You are asked to replicate leaders and followers in the attainment of a defined goal.

First, the class is divided into teams of three to five individuals. Next, each team chooses a leader, which also dictates who the followers will be. It is important to choose your leader wisely. The classroom instructor will then assign the task to be completed.

Students should be prepared to debrief the assignment when completed. Your instructor will guide this discussion.

VIDEO CASE

LEADERS ARE MADE, NOT BORN

Sanjiv Ahuja/Chairman/Orange, UK

Sanjiv Ahuja, Chairman of Orange, UK talks about leadership. In particular, those who believe they have the desire and capability to be leaders and whether people are born with these traits or if they can acquire them. Much of what he talks about is having the right attitude.

Before you watch the video consider the following concepts and questions and be prepared to discuss them in class:

Concepts

- Leadership traits
- Effectively managing your personal resource portfolio
- Entrepreneurial mind-set

Questions

1. Do you believe that one's propensity to become a leader is an acquired skill or that the ability to be a leader is something that individuals are born with?

2. How well do you know yourself? Think through a top 5 list of your personal strengths and weaknesses.

3. Once you have identified personal strengths and weaknesses, think through an action plan to either leverage your strengths or work on weaknesses.

CHAPTER 13

Entrepreneurial Implications for Strategy

Studying this chapter should provide you with the strategic management knowledge needed to:

1. Define strategic entrepreneurship and corporate entrepreneurship.

2. Define entrepreneurship and entrepreneurial opportunities and explain their importance.

3. Define invention, innovation, and imitation, and describe the relationship among them.

4. Describe entrepreneurs and the entrepreneurial mind-set.

5. Explain international entrepreneurship and its importance.

6. Describe how firms internally develop innovations.

7. Explain how firms use cooperative strategies to innovate.

8. Describe how firms use acquisitions as a means of innovation.

9. Explain how strategic entrepreneurship helps firms create value.

THE CONTINUING INNOVATION REVOLUTION AT AMAZON: THE KINDLE AND E-BOOKS

Jeff Bezos led the Internet retailing revolution with his entry into the book retail market in 1995. Since that time, Amazon.com has significantly expanded its product lines and implemented several innovations, especially in processes and approaches to marketing their products. Recently, Bezos and Amazon are leading a potential revolution in the book market with the Kindle, which provides easy access to store and read many e-books. Let's be clear—Amazon did not create the digital book. E-books have been available for several years, but access to and use of e-books has not been necessarily easy. But, with the development of the Kindle e-reader, access to and ease of reading e-books has been simplified and it is predicted to revolutionize the book publishing business within the next five years.

The Kindle was first introduced in 2007, and two newer and improved versions were introduced in 2009. The Kindle 2 was introduced in February 2009 and according to market analysts, it literally "flew off the shelves" at a time when consumers were curtailing purchases of most other products. Then in May 2009, Amazon introduced a large-screen version of the Kindle 2, the Kindle DX, which has a 9.7-inch screen. While the DX appears to be a little cumbersome, it provides larger screen access to graphics-heavy publications common in college textbooks. The Kindle currently can be used to download any of the 285,000 e-books available in Amazon's inventory. Amazon's new Kindles are thinner than a pencil and offer a feature allowing text to be translated into voice. This means that

AP Photo/Mark Lennihan

The new Kindle 2 electronic reader "flew off the shelves" at a time when consumers were curtailing purchases of most other products.

it can read to you! Bezos demonstrated this feature at the introduction by having the computer-generated voice read the Gettysburg Address.

Amazon's success in the first quarter of 2009 (e.g., a 24 percent increase in earnings from the first quarter 2008) was largely attributed to the Kindle. It is predicted to be wildly successful. Barclays Capital has predicted that it will reach annual sales of $3.7 billion in 2012 with a profit of $840 million. This amount would account for approximately 20 percent of Amazon's predicted sales that year. Amazon also earns a return by selling content for use on the Kindle in the form of e-books and other electronic content. For example, Amazon sells subscriptions to 37 different newspapers for the Kindle at $10 per month. This set includes such respected newspapers as the *New York Times, Boston Globe,* and *Washington Post.* It also has an agreement for a pilot program at five major universities, hoping that students will soon be carrying all of their textbooks on the Kindle in their backpacks.

Clearly, Amazon's biggest potential challenge may come from competitors. The Kindle technology is likely imitable and Sony already has a competitor e-reader on the market. Thus, Amazon must entrench the Kindle quickly and continue to enrich its features (the Kindle currently only provides "black-and-white" content even though it is said to provide better resolution than can be obtained in print copies). While the Kindle may help Amazon become the Apple of the e-reader market, the Kindle is likely to revolutionize all publishing industries (e.g., book publishers, newspapers).

Sources: S. Stein, 2009, Old, real book vs. Kindle alternative: Which will win? CNET.com, http://www.cnet.com, June 12; J. M. O'Brien, 2009, Amazon's next revolution, *Fortune*, June 8, 68–76; B. Stone & M. Rich, 2009, Amazon introduces big-screen Kindle, *New York Times*, http://www.nytimes.com, May 7; D. MacMillan, 2009, Amazon's widescreen Kindle DX: Winners and losers, *BusinessWeek*, http://businessweek.com, May 7; C. Dannen, 2009, Amazon CEO Jeff Bezos unveils Kindle DX in New York, *Fast Company*, http://www.fastcompany.com, May 6; D. Darlin, 2009, First impressions of the new Kindle DX, *New York Times*, http://www.gadgetwise.blogs.nytimes.com, May 6; C. Gallo, 2009, How Amazon's Bezos sparked demand for Kindle 2, *BusinessWeek*, http://businessweek.com, February, 24.

In Chapter 1, we indicated that *organizational culture* refers to the complex set of ideologies, symbols, and core values that are shared throughout the firm and that influence how the firm conducts business. Thus, culture is the social energy that drives—or fails to drive—the organization. The Opening Case explains Amazon's new innovation, the Kindle, that is expected to revolutionize the publishing industries (any businesses which provide products printed with ink on paper). Increasingly, a firm's ability to engage in innovation makes the difference in gaining and maintaining a competitive advantage and achieving performance targets.[1]

Amazon is clearly an entrepreneurial and innovative company. Amazon is the leading Internet retailer in the world and also consistently produces innovations. Not all of them are successful, but the Kindle appears to be on the verge of being highly successful. From reading this chapter, you will understand that Amazon's ability to innovate shows that it successfully practices strategic entrepreneurship.

Strategic entrepreneurship is taking entrepreneurial actions using a strategic perspective. In this process, the firm tries to find opportunities in its external environment that it can try to exploit through innovations. Identifying opportunities to exploit through innovations is the *entrepreneurship* dimension of strategic entrepreneurship, while determining the best way to manage the firm's innovation efforts is the *strategic* dimension. Thus, firms engaging in strategic entrepreneurship integrate their actions to find opportunities and to successfully innovate in order to pursue them.[2] In the twenty-first–century competitive landscape, firm survival and success depend on a firm's ability to continuously find new opportunities and quickly produce innovations to pursue them.[3]

To examine strategic entrepreneurship, we consider several topics in this chapter. First, we examine entrepreneurship and innovation in a strategic context. Definitions of entrepreneurship, entrepreneurial opportunities, and entrepreneurs as those who engage in entrepreneurship to pursue entrepreneurial opportunities are presented. We then describe international entrepreneurship, a phenomenon reflecting the increased use of entrepreneurship in economies throughout the world. After this discussion, the chapter shifts to descriptions of the three ways firms innovate. Internally, firms innovate through either autonomous or induced strategic behavior. We then describe actions firms take to implement the innovations resulting from those two types of strategic behaviors.

In addition to innovating within the firm, firms can develop innovations by using cooperative strategies, such as strategic alliances, and by acquiring other companies to gain access to their innovations and innovative capabilities.[4] Most large, complex firms use all three methods to innovate. The chapter closes with summary comments about how firms use strategic entrepreneurship to create value and earn above-average returns.

As emphasized in this chapter, innovation and entrepreneurship are vital for young and old and for large and small firms, for service companies as well as manufacturing firms, and for high-technology ventures.[5] In the global competitive landscape, the long-term success of new ventures and established firms is a function of their ability to meld entrepreneurship with strategic management.[6]

A major portion of the material in this chapter is on innovation and entrepreneurship within established organizations. This phenomenon is called **corporate entrepreneurship**, which is the use or application of entrepreneurship within an established firm.[7] Corporate entrepreneurship has become critical to the survival and success of established organizations.[8] Indeed, established firms use entrepreneurship to strengthen their performance and to enhance growth opportunities.[9] Of course, innovation and entrepreneurship play a critical role in the degree of success achieved by startup entrepreneurial ventures as well. Much of the content examined in this chapter is equally important in entrepreneurial ventures (sometimes called "startups") and established organizations.[10]

Strategic entrepreneurship is taking entrepreneurial actions using a strategic perspective.

Corporate entrepreneurship is the use or application of entrepreneurship within an established firm.

Entrepreneurship and Entrepreneurial Opportunities

Entrepreneurship is the process by which individuals, teams, or organizations identify and pursue entrepreneurial opportunities without being immediately constrained by the resources they currently control.[11] **Entrepreneurial opportunities** are conditions in which new goods or services can satisfy a need in the market. These opportunities exist because of competitive imperfections in markets and among the factors of production used to produce them or because they were independently developed by entrepreneurs.[12] Entrepreneurial opportunities come in many forms such as the chance to develop and sell a new product and the chance to sell an existing product in a new market.[13] Firms should be receptive to pursuing entrepreneurial opportunities whenever and wherever they may surface.[14]

As these two definitions suggest, the essence of entrepreneurship is to identify and exploit entrepreneurial opportunities—that is, opportunities others do not see or for which they do not recognize the commercial potential.[15] As a process, entrepreneurship results in the "creative destruction" of existing products (goods or services) or methods of producing them and replaces them with new products and production methods.[16] Thus, firms engaging in entrepreneurship place high value on individual innovations as well as the ability to continuously innovate across time.[17]

We study entrepreneurship at the level of the individual firm. However, evidence suggests that entrepreneurship is the economic engine driving many nations' economies in the global competitive landscape.[18] Thus, entrepreneurship, and the innovation it spawns, is important for companies competing in the global economy and for countries seeking to stimulate economic climates with the potential to enhance the living standard of their citizens.[19] A recent study conducted by the Boston Consulting Group and the Small Business Division of Intuit found that 10 million people in the United States were considering starting a new business. About one-third of those who do will expand into international markets. The study suggested that by 2017 the number of entrepreneurs will increase, and the entrepreneurs will be younger and include more women and immigrants. Thus, even though the importance of entrepreneurship continues to grow, the "face" of those who start new ventures is also changing.[20]

Innovation

Peter Drucker argued that "innovation is the specific function of entrepreneurship, whether in an existing business, a public service institution, or a new venture started by a lone individual."[21] Moreover, Drucker suggested that innovation is "the means by which the entrepreneur either creates new wealth-producing resources or endows existing resources with enhanced potential for creating wealth."[22] Thus, entrepreneurship and the innovation resulting from it are critically important for all firms. The realities of competition in the competitive landscape of the twenty-first century suggest that to be market leaders, companies must regularly develop innovative products desired by customers. This means that innovation should be an intrinsic part of virtually all of a firm's activities.[23]

Innovation is a key outcome firms seek through entrepreneurship and is often the source of competitive success, especially in turbulent, highly competitive environments.[24] For example, research results show that firms competing in global industries that invest more in innovation also achieve the highest returns.[25] In fact, investors often react positively to the introduction of a new product, thereby increasing the price of a firm's stock. Furthermore, "innovation may be required to maintain or achieve competitive parity,

Entrepreneurship is the process by which individuals, teams, or organizations identify and pursue entrepreneurial opportunities without being immediately constrained by the resources they currently control.

Entrepreneurial opportunities are conditions in which new goods or services can satisfy a need in the market.

much less a competitive advantage in many global markets."[26] Investing in the development of new technologies can increase the performance of firms that operate in different but related product markets (refer to the discussion of related diversification in Chapter 6). In this way, the innovations can be used in multiple markets, and return on the investments is earned more quickly.[27]

In his classic work, Schumpeter argued that firms engage in three types of innovative activities.[28] **Invention** is the act of creating or developing a new product or process. **Innovation** is the process of creating a commercial product from an invention. Innovation begins after an invention is chosen for development.[29] Thus, an invention brings something new into being, while an innovation brings something new into use. Accordingly, technical criteria are used to determine the success of an invention, whereas commercial criteria are used to determine the success of an innovation.[30] Finally, **imitation** is the adoption of a similar innovation by different firms. Imitation usually leads to product or process standardization, and products based on imitation often are offered at lower prices, but without as many features. Entrepreneurship is critical to innovative activity in that it acts as the linchpin between invention and innovation.[31]

In the United States in particular, innovation is the most critical of the three types of innovative activities. Many companies are able to create ideas that lead to inventions, but commercializing those inventions has, at times, proved difficult.[32] This difficulty is suggested by the fact that approximately 80 percent of R&D occurs in large firms, but these same firms produce fewer than 50 percent of the patents.[33] Patents are a strategic asset and the ability to regularly produce them can be an important source of competitive advantage, especially for firms competing in knowledge-intensive industries (e.g., pharmaceuticals).[34]

Entrepreneurs

Entrepreneurs are individuals, acting independently or as part of an organization, who perceive an entrepreneurial opportunity and then take risks to develop an innovation to pursue it. Entrepreneurs can be found throughout an organization—from top-level managers to those working to produce a firm's goods or services. Entrepreneurs are found throughout Amazon, for example. Many Amazon employees must devote at least a portion of their time to develop innovations. Entrepreneurs tend to demonstrate several characteristics: They are highly motivated, willing to take responsibility for their projects, self-confident, and often optimistic.[35] In addition, entrepreneurs tend to be passionate and emotional about the value and importance of their innovation-based ideas.[36] They are able to deal with uncertainty and are more alert to opportunities than others.[37] Interestingly, recent research found that genetic factors partly influence people to engage in entrepreneurship.[38] To be successful, entrepreneurs often need to have good social skills and to plan exceptionally well (e.g., to obtain venture capital).[39] Entrepreneurship entails much hard work to be successful but it can also be highly satisfying. As noted by Mary Kay Ash, founder of Mary Kay Cosmetics, "It is far better to be exhausted from success than to be rested from failure."[40]

Evidence suggests that successful entrepreneurs have an entrepreneurial mind-set. The person with an **entrepreneurial mind-set** values uncertainty in the marketplace and seeks to continuously identify opportunities with the potential to lead to important innovations.[41] Because it has the potential to lead to continuous innovations, an individual's entrepreneurial mind-set can be a source of competitive advantage for a firm.[42] Entrepreneurial mind-sets are fostered and supported when knowledge is readily available throughout a firm. Indeed, research has shown that units within firms are more innovative when they have access to new knowledge.[43] Transferring knowledge, however, can be difficult, often because the receiving party must have adequate absorptive capacity (or the ability) to learn the knowledge.[44] Learning requires that the new knowledge be

Invention is the act of creating or developing a new product or process.

Innovation is the process of creating a commercial product from an invention.

Imitation is the adoption of a similar innovation by different firms.

Entrepreneurs are individuals, acting independently or as part of an organization, who perceive an entrepreneurial opportunity and then take risks to develop an innovation to exploit it.

The person with an **entrepreneurial mind-set** values uncertainty in the marketplace and seeks to continuously identify opportunities with the potential to lead to important innovations.

linked to the existing knowledge. Thus, managers need to develop the capabilities of their human capital to build on their current knowledge base while incrementally expanding that knowledge.[45]

Some companies are known for their entrepreneurial culture. For example, in 2008 Apple was ranked as the most innovative company for the fourth year in a row. The rest of the top 10 most innovative companies were Google, Toyota, General Electric, Microsoft, Tata Group, Nintendo, Procter & Gamble, Sony, and Nokia. Yet, there are other companies known as the antithesis of innovative. For example, GM was known for sacrificing innovation for profits. Of course, this approach eventually led to GM's demise.[46]

International Entrepreneurship

International entrepreneurship is a process in which firms creatively discover and exploit opportunities that are outside their domestic markets in order to develop a competitive advantage.[47] As the practices suggested by this definition show, entrepreneurship is a global phenomenon.[48] As noted earlier, approximately one-third of new ventures move into international markets early in their life cycle. Most large established companies have significant foreign operations and often start new ventures in domestic and international markets. Large multinational companies, for example, generate approximately 54 percent of their sales outside their domestic market, and more than 50 percent of their employees work outside of the company's home country.[49]

A key reason that entrepreneurship has become a global phenomenon is that in general, internationalization leads to improved firm performance.[50] Nonetheless, decision makers should recognize that the decision to internationalize exposes their firms to various risks, including those of unstable foreign currencies, problems with market efficiencies, insufficient infrastructures to support businesses, and limitations on market size.[51] Thus, the decision to engage in international entrepreneurship should be a product of careful analysis.

Because of its positive benefits, entrepreneurship is at the top of public policy agendas in many of the world's countries, including Finland, Ireland, Israel, and the United States. Entrepreneurship has become a particularly important public agenda item with the global economic crisis, which began in late 2007. For example, the U.S. government and the Michigan state government are emphasizing entrepreneurial activity to revitalize the Detroit area hurt seriously by the loss of jobs due to the U.S. auto companies' decline.[52]

Even though entrepreneurship is a global phenomenon, the rate of entrepreneurship differs across countries. A study of 43 countries found that the percentage of adults involved in entrepreneurial activity ranged from a high of more than 45 percent in Bolivia to a low of approximately 4.4 percent in Russia. The United States had a rate of almost 19 percent. Importantly, this study also found a strong positive relationship between the rate of entrepreneurial activity and economic development in a country.[53]

Culture is one of the reasons for the differences in rates of entrepreneurship among different countries. The research suggests that a balance between individual initiative and a spirit of cooperation and group ownership of innovation is needed to encourage entrepreneurial behavior. For firms to be entrepreneurial, they must provide appropriate autonomy and incentives for individual initiative to surface, but also promote cooperation and group ownership of an innovation if it is to be implemented successfully. Thus, international entrepreneurship often requires teams of people with unique skills and resources, especially in cultures that highly value individualism or collectivism. In addition to a balance of values for individual initiative and cooperative behaviors, firms must build the capabilities to be innovative and acquire the resources needed to support innovative activities.[54]

International entrepreneurship is a process in which firms creatively discover and exploit opportunities that are outside their domestic markets in order to develop a competitive advantage.

The level of investment outside of the home country made by young ventures is also an important dimension of international entrepreneurship. In fact, with increasing globalization, a greater number of new ventures have been "born global."[55] Research has shown that new ventures that enter international markets increase their learning of new technological knowledge and thereby enhance their performance.[56]

The probability of entering international markets increases when the firm has top executives with international experience, which increases the likelihood of the firm successfully competing in those markets.[57] Because of the learning and economies of scale and scope afforded by operating in international markets, both young and established internationally diversified firms often are stronger competitors in their domestic market as well. Additionally, as research has shown, internationally diversified firms are generally more innovative.[58]

As explained in the Strategic Focus, innovation has become highly important in the global competitive landscape. Thus, the ability of firms to gain and sustain a competitive advantage may be based partly or largely on the capability to produce innovations. Thus, we next discuss different types of innovations.

Internal Innovation

In established organizations, most innovation comes from efforts in research and development (R&D). Effective R&D often leads to firms' filing for patents to protect their innovative work. Increasingly, successful R&D results from integrating the skills available in the global workforce. Thus, the ability to have a competitive advantage based on innovation is more likely to accrue to firms capable of integrating the talent of human capital from countries around the world.[59]

Both Intel and Nokia have been innovative firms and market leaders. In 2009, they announced an agreement to jointly develop new mobile computing products that provide functions beyond the current smartphones and netbooks. The new products likely will integrate features of both phones and computers. Thus, the two companies can combine and integrate their current knowledge and capabilities of both types of products and the markets for them. While Intel has not yet "cracked" the smartphone market with its memory chips, Nokia has been successful with smartphones but was caught off guard when Apple introduced its now highly popular iPhone. Therefore, the marriage between the two should help each to overcome its weaknesses by integrating their strengths. In addition to the development of new products from their joint R&D efforts, they also plan to develop software for devices using the Linux operating system.[60]

Increasingly, it seems possible that in the twenty-first century competitive landscape, R&D may be the most critical factor in gaining and sustaining a competitive advantage in some industries, such as pharmaceuticals. Larger, established firms, certainly those competing globally, often try to use their R&D labs to create competence-destroying new technologies and products. Being able to innovate in this manner can create a competitive advantage for firms in many industries.[61] Although critical to long-term corporate success, the outcomes of R&D investments are uncertain and often not achieved in the short term, meaning that patience is required as firms evaluate the outcomes of their R&D efforts.[62]

Incremental and Radical Innovation

Firms produce two types of internal innovations—incremental and radical innovations—when using their R&D activities. Most innovations are *incremental*—that is, they build on existing knowledge bases and provide small improvements in the current product lines. Incremental innovations are evolutionary and linear in nature.[63] "The markets for incremental innovations are well-defined, product characteristics are well understood, profit margins tend to be lower, production technologies are efficient, and competition

COMPETITIVENESS AND INNOVATION: ARE WE EXPERIENCING A PARADIGM SHIFT?

In 2009, the United States continued to be ranked as the most competitive nation. This top ranking and those of some other developed countries are based on the quality of infrastructures, educational systems, and laws regarding business operations. It is also due to their advanced levels of innovation over the years. Yet, the major economic crisis beginning in late 2007 and early 2008 has shown some "cracks" in the economic leadership of these countries. In the twenty-first century, economic power has begun to shift to major emerging economies such as China and India.

However, the shift may be even more fundamental, as many believe that innovation is the most critical factor in a nation's competitiveness over time. In fact, the United States competitiveness is likely based on the significant innovative capabilities and innovative output of its businesses. While certain business leaders in the United States understand the importance of innovation (e.g., members of the U.S. Council on Competitiveness), the country is no longer ranked as the most innovative nation. In fact, the United States ranked eighth in the 2009 International Innovation Index (among the 110 countries ranked). Singapore was ranked first. In a report issued by the Information Technology and Innovation Foundation, the United States was ranked sixth among 40 countries and regions around the world. Singapore was also ranked first in this report. Singapore developed a strategy to promote specific programs by investing heavily in attracting major technologies and recruiting top scientists to develop more innovation. That strategy is now paying substantial dividends. Firms based in the United States have focused too much on producing short-term returns, leading to an overemphasis on incremental innovations. As a result, the country is now in danger of losing its lead in science and technology. Perhaps one of the most prominent examples is Exxon-Mobil, which receives approximately $756,000 in revenue per minute. Rather than focus on developing new sources of energy, it seeks to enhance its ability to gain access to and extract with greater efficiency black gold or oil.

According to a 2009 report in *BusinessWeek*, technological breakthroughs in a number of fields have been few in number since 1998 (e.g., medical science, drugs, information technology, etc.). The leadership in these fields is largely represented by firms based in the United States. However, future technological breakthroughs in these fields are likely to be produced by firms based in other countries. Regaining this lead will require a major change in mind-set, investments, and promotion of entrepreneurial endeavors. Efforts have been implemented to encourage and develop more entrepreneurial activities in a number of industries and geographic regions to stop the economic decline and facilitate economic growth in the United States. It is unclear if these efforts will be successful in the short or long term.

With forward-thinking investments in the recruitment of top scientists and attraction of key technologies, Singapore is the world leader in innovation.

Sources: M. Mandel, 2009, Innovation interrupted, *BusinessWeek*, June 15, 034–040; 2009, International innovation index, Wikipedia, http://www.answers.com, June 13; B. Ott, 2009, Top companies can tame bear markets, Yahoo News, http://www.yahoo.com, June 11; A. S. Choi, 2009, Can entrepreneurs save this town? *BusinessWeek*, http://www.businessweek.com, June 5; M. Scott, 2009, Competitiveness: The U.S. and Europe are tops, *BusinessWeek*, http://www.businessweek.com, May 19; M. Richtel & J. Wortham, 2009, Weary of looking for work, some create their own, *New York Times*, http://www.nytimes.com, March 14; S. Lohr, 2009, In innovation, U.S. said to be losing competitive edge, *New York Times*, http://www.nytimes.com, February 25; J. Rae-Dupree, 2009, Innovation should mean more jobs, not less, *New York Times*, http://www.nytimes.com, January 4; R. Empson, 2008, Encouraging innovation: How can we do it better? *Fast Company*, http://www.fastcompany.com, August 1.

is primarily on the basis of price."[64] Adding a different kind of whitening agent to a soap detergent is an example of an incremental innovation, as are improvements in televisions over the last few decades. Companies launch far more incremental innovations than radical innovations because they are cheaper, easier and faster to produce, and involve less risk.[65]

In contrast to incremental innovations, *radical innovations* usually provide significant technological breakthroughs and create new knowledge.[66] Radical innovations, which are revolutionary and nonlinear in nature, typically use new technologies to serve newly created markets. The development of the original personal computer (PC) was a radical innovation at the time. Reinventing the computer by developing a "radically new computer-brain chip" (e.g., with the capability to process a trillion calculations per second) is an example of a radical innovation. Obviously, such a radical innovation would seem to have the capacity to revolutionize the tasks computers could perform. Perhaps some of the new products to be produced by the joint venture between Intel and Nokia integrating smartphones and computers will be considered to be radical innovations.

Because they establish new functionalities for users, radical innovations have strong potential to lead to significant growth in revenue and profits.[67] Developing new processes is a critical part of producing radical innovations. Both types of innovations can create value, meaning that firms should determine when it is appropriate to emphasize either incremental or radical innovation. However, radical innovations have the potential to contribute more significantly to a firm's efforts to earn above-average returns.

Radical innovations are rare because of the difficulty and risk involved in developing them. The value of the technology and the market opportunities are highly uncertain.[68] Because radical innovation creates new knowledge and uses only some or little of a firm's current product or technological knowledge, creativity is required. However, creativity does not produce something from nothing. Rather, creativity discovers, combines, or synthesizes current knowledge, often from diverse areas.[69] This knowledge is then used to develop new products that can be used in an entrepreneurial manner to move into new markets, capture new customers, and gain access to new resources.[70] Such innovations are often developed in separate business units that start internal ventures.[71]

Internally developed incremental and radical innovations result from deliberate efforts. These deliberate efforts are called *internal corporate venturing,* which is the set of activities firms use to develop internal inventions and especially innovations.[72] As shown in Figure 13.1, autonomous and induced strategic behaviors are the two types of internal corporate venturing. Each venturing type facilitates incremental and radical innovations. However, a larger number of radical innovations spring from autonomous strategic behavior while the greatest percentage of incremental innovations come from induced strategic behavior.

Autonomous Strategic Behavior

Autonomous strategic behavior is a bottom-up process in which product champions pursue new ideas, often through a political process, by means of which they develop and coordinate the commercialization of a new good or service until it achieves success in the marketplace. A *product champion* is an organizational member with an entrepreneurial vision of a new good or service who seeks to create support for its commercialization. Product champions play critical roles in moving innovations forward. Indeed, in many corporations, "Champions are widely acknowledged as pivotal to innovation speed and success."[73] Champions are vital to sell the ideas to others in the organization so that the innovations will be commercialized. Commonly, product champions use their social capital to develop informal networks within the firm. As progress is made, these networks become more formal as a means of pushing an innovation to the point of successful commercialization.[74] Internal innovations springing from autonomous strategic behavior frequently differ from the firm's current strategy, taking it into new markets and perhaps new ways of creating value for customers and other stakeholders.

Figure 13.1 Model of Internal Corporate Venturing

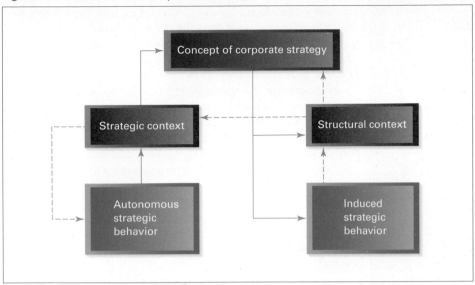

Source: Adapted from R. A. Burgelman, 1983, A model of the interactions of strategic behavior, corporate context, and the concept of strategy, *Academy of Management Review*, 8: 65.

Autonomous strategic behavior is based on a firm's wellspring of knowledge and resources that are the sources of the firm's innovation. Thus, a firm's technological capabilities and competencies are the basis for new products and processes.[75] As described in the Strategic Focus, Exxon-Mobil does not appear to use autonomous strategic behavior to identify new technologies and products that can better serve its customers. Alternatively, the iPod likely resulted from autonomous strategic behavior in Apple, though the development of the iPhone was more the result of induced strategic behavior discussed in the next section.

Changing the concept of corporate-level strategy through autonomous strategic behavior results when a product is championed within strategic and structural contexts (see Figure 13.1). Such a transformation occurred with the development of the iPod and introduction of iTunes at Apple. The strategic context is the process used to arrive at strategic decisions (often requiring political processes to gain acceptance). The best firms keep changing their strategic context and strategies because of the continuous changes in the current competitive landscape. Thus, some believe that the most competitively successful firms reinvent their industry or develop a completely new one across time as they compete with current and future rivals.[76]

To be effective, an autonomous process for developing new products requires that new knowledge be continuously diffused throughout the firm. In particular, the diffusion of tacit knowledge is important for development of more effective new products.[77] Interestingly, some of the processes important for the promotion of autonomous new product development behavior vary by the environment and country in which a firm operates. For example, the Japanese culture is high on uncertainty avoidance. As such, research has found that Japanese firms are more likely to engage in autonomous behaviors under conditions of low uncertainty.[78]

Induced Strategic Behavior

The second of the two forms of internal corporate venturing, *induced strategic behavior,* is a top-down process whereby the firm's current strategy and structure foster innovations that are closely associated with that strategy and structure.[79] In this form of venturing, the strategy in place is filtered through a matching structural hierarchy. In essence, induced strategic behavior results in internal innovations that are highly consistent with the firm's

Vivek Prakash/Reuters/Landov

Nokia is trying to overcome the iPhone's lead in the smartphone market through a joint venture with Intel.

current strategy. Thus, the top management team plays a key role in induced strategic behavior, suggesting that the composition and the effectiveness of the team are important.[80]

Nokia's joint venture with Intel is an example of induced innovation. The two firms have specific goals in the development of new products to support their strategies. Intel has had a strategic interest in the smartphone market, and Nokia is trying to overcome Apple's lead in this market with the iPhone. The strategic intent of these firms is to develop a market leading product in the smartphone market that incorporates more features of the personal computer and sophisticated software to enrich the functionality of the product. These actions and approaches are intended to ensure that both firms are number one in the global market.

Implementing Internal Innovations

An entrepreneurial mind-set is required to be innovative and to develop successful internal corporate ventures. Because of environmental and market uncertainty, individuals and firms must be willing to take risks to commercialize innovations. Although they must continuously attempt to identify opportunities, they must also select and pursue the best opportunities and do so with discipline. Employing an entrepreneurial mind-set entails not only developing new products and markets but also execution in order to do these things effectively. Often, firms provide incentives to managers to be entrepreneurial and to commercialize innovations.[81]

Having processes and structures in place through which a firm can successfully implement the outcomes of internal corporate ventures and commercialize the innovations is critical. Indeed, the successful introduction of innovations into the marketplace reflects implementation effectiveness.[82] In the context of internal corporate ventures, managers must allocate resources, coordinate activities, communicate with many different parties in the organization, and make a series of decisions to convert the innovations resulting from either autonomous or induced strategic behaviors into successful market entries.[83] As we describe in Chapter 11, organizational structures are the sets of formal relationships that support processes managers use to commercialize innovations.

Effective integration of the various functions involved in innovation processes—from engineering to manufacturing and, ultimately, market distribution—is required to implement the incremental and radical innovations resulting from internal corporate ventures.[84] Increasingly, product development teams are being used to integrate the activities associated with different organizational functions. Such integration involves coordinating and applying the knowledge and skills of different functional areas in order to maximize innovation.[85] Teams must help to make decisions as to which projects should be commercialized and which ones should end. Although ending a project is difficult, sometimes because of emotional commitments to innovation-based projects, effective teams recognize when conditions change such that the innovation cannot create value as originally anticipated.

Cross-Functional Product Development Teams

Cross-functional teams facilitate efforts to integrate activities associated with different organizational functions, such as design, manufacturing, and marketing. These teams may also include representatives from major suppliers because they can facilitate the firm's innovation processes.[86] In addition, new product development processes can be completed more quickly and the products more easily commercialized when cross-functional teams work effectively.[87] Using cross-functional teams, product development stages are grouped into parallel or overlapping processes to allow the firm to tailor its product development efforts to its unique core competencies and to the needs of the market.

Horizontal organizational structures support the use of cross-functional teams in their efforts to integrate innovation-based activities across organizational functions.[88] Therefore, instead of being designed around vertical hierarchical functions or departments, the organization is built around core horizontal processes that are used to produce and manage innovations. Some of the core horizontal processes that are critical to innovation efforts are formal; they may be defined and documented as procedures and practices. More commonly, however, these processes are informal: "They are routines or ways of working that evolve over time."[89] Often invisible, informal processes are critical to successful innovations and are supported properly through horizontal organizational structures more so than through vertical organizational structures.

Two primary barriers that may prevent the successful use of cross-functional teams as a means of integrating organizational functions are independent frames of reference of team members and organizational politics.[90] Team members working within a distinct specialization (e.g., a particular organizational function) may have an independent frame of reference typically based on common backgrounds and experiences. They are likely to use the same decision criteria to evaluate issues such as product development efforts as they do within their functional units. Research suggests that functional departments vary along four dimensions: time orientation, interpersonal orientation, goal orientation, and formality of structure.[91] Thus, individuals from different functional departments having different orientations on these dimensions can be expected to perceive product development activities in different ways. For example, a design engineer may consider the characteristics that make a product functional and workable to be the most important of the product's characteristics. Alternatively, a person from the marketing function may hold characteristics that satisfy customer needs most important. These different orientations can create barriers to effective communication across functions and even produce conflict in the team at times.[92]

Organizational politics is the second potential barrier to effective integration in cross-functional teams. In some organizations, considerable political activity may center on allocating resources to different functions. Interunit conflict may result from aggressive competition for resources among those representing different organizational functions. This dysfunctional conflict between functions creates a barrier to their integration.[93] Methods must be found to achieve cross-functional integration without excessive political conflict and without changing the basic structural characteristics necessary for task specialization and efficiency.

Facilitating Integration and Innovation

Shared values and effective leadership are important for achieving cross-functional integration and implementing innovation.[94] Highly effective shared values are framed around the firm's vision and mission and become the glue that promotes integration between functional units. Thus, the firm's culture promotes unity and internal innovation.[95]

Strategic leadership is also highly important for achieving cross-functional integration and promoting innovation. Leaders set the goals and allocate resources. The goals include integrated development and commercialization of new goods and services. Effective strategic leaders also ensure a high-quality communication system to facilitate cross-functional integration. A critical benefit of effective communication is the sharing of knowledge among team members. Effective communication thus helps create synergy and gains team members' commitment to an innovation throughout the organization. Shared values and leadership practices shape the communication systems that are formed to support the development and commercialization of new products.[96]

Creating Value from Internal Innovation

The model in Figure 13.2 shows how firms can create value from the internal corporate venturing processes they use to develop and commercialize new goods and services. An entrepreneurial mind-set is necessary so that managers and employees will consistently try to identify entrepreneurial opportunities the firm can pursue by developing new goods and services and new markets. Cross-functional teams are important for promoting integrated new product design ideas and commitment to their subsequent implementation. Effective leadership and shared values promote integration and vision for innovation and commitment to it. The end result for the firm is the creation of value for the customers and shareholders by developing and commercializing new products.[97] We should acknowledge that not all entrepreneurial efforts succeed, even with effective management. Sometimes managers must exit the market as well to avoid value decline.[98]

In the next two sections, we discuss the other ways firms innovate—by using cooperative strategies and by acquiring companies.

Innovation through Cooperative Strategies

Virtually all firms lack the breadth and depth of resources (e.g., human capital and social capital) in their R&D activities needed to internally develop a sufficient number of innovations to meet the needs of the market and remain competitive. As such, firms must be open to using external resources to help produce innovations.[99] Alliances with other firms can contribute to innovations in several ways. First, they provide information on new business opportunities and how to exploit them.[100] In other instances, firms use cooperative strategies to align what they believe are complementary assets with the potential to lead to future innovations.[101]

Figure 13.2 Creating Value through Internal Innovation Processes

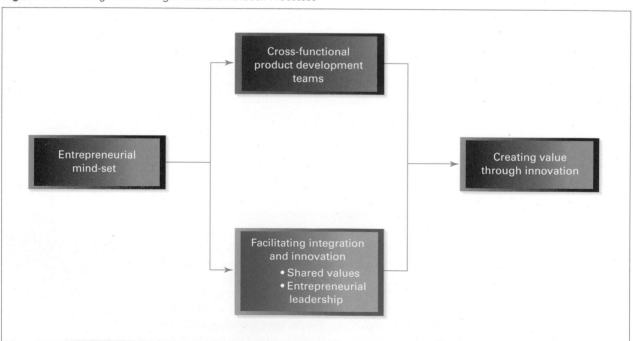

The rapidly changing technologies of the twenty-first–century competitive landscape, globalization, and the need to innovate at world-class levels are primary influences on firms' decisions to innovate by cooperating with other companies. Evidence shows that the skills and knowledge contributed by firms forming a cooperative strategy to innovate tend to be technology-based, a fact suggesting how technologies and their applications continue to influence the choices firms make while competing in the twenty-first century competitive landscape.[102] Indeed, some believe that because of these conditions, firms are becoming increasingly dependent on cooperative strategies as a path to successful competition in the global economy.[103] Even venerable old firms such as Intel and Nokia have learned that they need help to create innovations necessary to be competitive in a twenty-first–century environment. Their agreement to jointly develop products that integrate functions of the smartphones and personal computers is based on their realization that they need great capabilities to develop market-leading products in the dynamic and highly competitive markets in which they participate.

Both entrepreneurial firms and established firms use cooperative strategies (e.g., strategic alliances and joint ventures) to innovate. An entrepreneurial firm, for example, may seek investment capital as well as established firms' distribution capabilities to successfully introduce one of its innovative products to the market.[104] Alternatively, more-established companies may need new technological knowledge and can gain access to it by forming a cooperative strategy with entrepreneurial ventures.[105] Alliances between large pharmaceutical firms and biotechnology companies increasingly have been formed to integrate the knowledge and resources of both to develop new products and bring them to market.[106]

Because of the importance of strategic alliances, particularly in the development of new technology and in commercializing innovations, firms are beginning to build networks of alliances that represent a form of social capital to them.[107] Building social capital in the form of relationships with other firms provides access to the knowledge and other resources necessary to develop innovations.[108] Knowledge from these alliances helps firms develop new capabilities.[109] Some firms now even allow other companies to participate in their internal new product development processes. It is not uncommon, for example, for firms to have supplier representatives on their cross-functional innovation teams because of the importance of the suppliers' input to ensure quality materials for any new product developed.[110]

However, alliances formed for the purpose of innovation are not without risks. In addition to conflict that is natural when firms try to work together to reach a mutual goal,[111] cooperative strategy participants also take a risk that a partner will appropriate a firm's technology or knowledge and use it to enhance its own competitive abilities.[112] To prevent or at least minimize this risk, firms, particularly new ventures, need to select their partners carefully. The ideal partnership is one in which the firms have complementary skills as well as compatible strategic goals.[113] However, because companies are operating in a network of firms and thus may be participating in multiple alliances simultaneously, they encounter challenges in managing the alliances.[114] Research has shown that firms can become involved in too many alliances, which can harm rather than facilitate their innovation capabilities.[115] Thus, effectively managing a cooperative strategy to produce innovation is critical.

As explained in the Strategic Focus, the social networking Internet sites have become highly popular with the general public and with professionals as well. Furthermore, entrepreneurs have begun to use them in ways to facilitate their businesses. These sites provide many opportunities for businesses and especially for gaining access to ideas and information. Therefore, they can facilitate innovation. Firms can use them to identify unique product ideas, to do market research, and to access new markets and new customers. As a result the social networking sites are highly valuable business mechanisms.

STRATEGIC FOCUS

ALL IN A TWITTER ABOUT MY SPACE IN ORDER TO BE LINKED IN TO THE BOOK OF FACES: THE SOCIAL NETWORKING PHENOMENON

Social networks are one of the major innovations in the first decade of the twenty-first century. Perhaps the most popular and important social networking Internet sites are Facebook, MySpace, Twitter, and LinkedIn. In 2009, Facebook reached a level of approximately 1.2 million visits per month. MySpace was second with slightly more than 800,000 monthly visits, followed by Twitter in third place. LinkedIn was fifth but growing rapidly among professionals. While these are all largely used for personal social networking, their potential uses are much greater. For example, Facebook is used by approximately 150 million people globally with more than 50 million unique visitors monthly. Facebook is used in 170 different countries and territories and appears in 35 different languages. The access to people for many different reasons is substantial—perhaps larger than through any other single means other than television. In addition MySpace has 76 million members with the average user spending about 4.4 hours per month on the site, about 1.7 hours longer than users on the site of its nearest competitor. The "rage" most recently has been Twitter, which is a microblogging Web site. Its use grew by 752 percent in 2008 alone. It has attracted a more educated young adult audience.

Smart entrepreneurs are identifying ways to use these social networking sites for business purposes. For example, they may be useful to access markets. Gary Vaynerchuk used Twitter to grow his wine distribution business from $5 million (when he took over the business from his father) to $50 million within three years. He performed an experiment using a direct mail advertisement, a billboard, and a Twitter announcement to determine which would bring in more new customers (at the lowest cost). The direct mail ad brought in 200 new customers (at a cost of $75 each); the billboard brought in 300 new customers (at a cost of $25 each) and the Twitter announcement brought in 1,800 new customers (at no additional cost). He now produces short videos on wine for use on Twitter.

Social networking sites are also being used to identify potential new employees and to make all types of professional and business contacts. They provide access to new ideas and information that can be useful for solving problems and even for making strategic decisions. The access to information and ideas makes these sites excellent sources in the innovation process. For example, the use of cross-functional teams and an occasional outsider to develop new products has been valuable because of the integration of diverse ideas incorporating multiple and important perspectives. Yet, social networking sites provide access to many more and diverse perspectives and ideas. In addition, the opportunity to perform virtual market tests with a large sample from the market exists with these sites. Finally, they provide the opportunity to identify new and different markets for existing and new product ideas. Therefore, if managed properly, they could be highly valuable in the innovation process, from the identification of new product ideas, through market research to market reach (many, many potential customers).

davidbleekerphotography.com/Alamy

The demographics of social media usage are shifting quickly, with adults rapidly coming online and driving the growth of newer services such as Twitter.

Sources: L. Safko, 2009, The twitter about Twitter, *Fast Company*, http://fastcompany.com, June 13; M. Conlin & D. MacMillan, 2009, Managing the tweets, *BusinessWeek*, June 1, 20–21; A. Yee, 2009, Social network rankings: Who's hot and who's not, *ebiz*, http://www.ebizq.net, April 13; J. F. Rayport, 2009, Social networks are the new web portals, *BusinessWeek*, http://www.businessweek.com, January 21; J. Owyang, 2009, A collection of social network stats for 2009, *Web Strategist*, http://www.web-strategist.com, January 11; K. E. Klein, 2008, Are social networking sites useful for business? *BusinessWeek*, http://www.businessweek.com, August 6.

Innovation through Acquisitions

Firms sometimes acquire companies to gain access to their innovations and to their innovative capabilities. One reason companies make these acquisitions is that the capital market values growth; acquisitions provide a means to rapidly extend one or more product lines and increase the firm's revenues.[116] Acquisitions pursued for this reason should, nonetheless, have a strategic rationale. For example, several large pharmaceutical firms have made acquisitions in recent years for several reasons, such as enhancing growth. However, a primary reason for acquisitions in this industry has been to acquire innovation—new drugs that can be commercialized. In this way they strengthen their new product pipeline.[117]

Similar to internal corporate venturing and strategic alliances, acquisitions are not a risk-free approach to innovating. A key risk of acquisitions is that a firm may substitute an ability to buy innovations for an ability to produce innovations internally. In support of this contention, research shows that firms engaging in acquisitions introduce fewer new products into the market.[118] This substitution may take place because firms lose strategic control and focus instead on financial control of their original and, especially, of their acquired business units. Yet, careful selection of companies to acquire—ones with complimentary science and technology knowledge—can enhance innovation if the knowledge acquired is used effectively.[119]

We note in Chapter 7 that companies can also learn new capabilities from firms they acquire. Thus, firms may gain capabilities to produce innovation from an acquired company. Additionally, firms that emphasize innovation and carefully select companies for acquisition that also emphasize innovation are likely to remain innovative.[120] Likewise, firms must manage well the integration of the acquired firms' technical capabilities so that they remain productive and continue to produce innovation after the acquired firm is merged into the acquiring firm.[121] Cisco has been highly successful with the integration of acquired technology firms. Cisco managers take great care not to lose key personnel in the acquired firm, realizing they are the source of many innovations.

This chapter closes with an assessment of how strategic entrepreneurship helps firms create value for stakeholders through its operations.

STRATEGY RIGHT NOW

Learn more about emerging Twitter business applications, including best practices and potential pitfalls.

www.cengage.com/management/hitt

Creating Value through Strategic Entrepreneurship

Newer entrepreneurial firms often are more effective than larger established firms in the identification of entrepreneurial opportunities.[122] As a consequence, entrepreneurial ventures often produce more radical innovations than do their larger, more established counterparts. Entrepreneurial ventures' strategic flexibility and willingness to take risks at least partially account for their ability to identify opportunities and then develop radical innovations to exploit them.

Alternatively, larger and well-established firms often have more resources and capabilities to exploit identified opportunities.[123] Younger, entrepreneurial firms generally excel in the opportunity-seeking dimension of strategic entrepreneurship while more

Spencer Platt/Getty Images

Established companies such as Williams-Sonoma are seeking to identify and capitalize on entrepreneurial opportunities by devoting top managers to the development of emerging brands.

established firms generally excel in the advantage-seeking dimension. However, to compete effectively in the twenty-first century competitive landscape, firms must not only identify and exploit opportunities but do so while achieving and sustaining a competitive advantage.[124] Thus, on a relative basis, newer entrepreneurial firms must learn how to gain a competitive advantage (advantage-seeking behaviors), and older, more established firms must relearn how to identify entrepreneurial opportunities (opportunity-seeking skills).

In some large organizations, action is being taken to deal with these matters. For example, an increasing number of widely known, large firms, including Williams-Sonoma, Inc., Wendy's International, AstraZeneca, and Choice Hotels, have created a new, top-level managerial position commonly called president or executive vice president of emerging brands. The essential responsibility for people holding these positions is to find entrepreneurial opportunities for their firms. If a decision is made to pursue one or more of the identified opportunities, this person also leads the analysis to determine whether the innovations should be internally developed, pursued through a cooperative venture, or acquired. The objective is to help firms develop successful incremental and radical innovations.

To be entrepreneurial, firms must develop an entrepreneurial mind-set among their managers and employees. Managers must emphasize the management of their resources, particularly human capital and social capital.[125] The importance of knowledge to identify and exploit opportunities as well as to gain and sustain a competitive advantage suggests that firms must have strong human capital.[126] Social capital is critical for access to complementary resources from partners in order to compete effectively in domestic and international markets.[127]

Many entrepreneurial opportunities continue to surface in international markets, a reality that is contributing to firms' willingness to engage in international entrepreneurship. By entering global markets that are new to them, firms can learn new technologies and management practices and diffuse this knowledge throughout the entire enterprise. Furthermore, the knowledge firms gain can contribute to their innovations. Research has shown that firms operating in international markets tend to be more innovative.[128] Entrepreneurial ventures and large firms now regularly enter international markets. Both types of firms must also be innovative to compete effectively. Thus, by developing resources (human and social capital), taking advantage of opportunities in domestic and international markets, and using the resources and knowledge gained in these markets to be innovative, firms achieve competitive advantages.[129] In so doing, they create value for their customers and shareholders.

Firms practicing strategic entrepreneurship contribute to a country's economic development. In fact, some countries have made dramatic economic progress by changing the institutional rules for businesses operating in the country. This approach could be construed as a form of institutional entrepreneurship. Likewise, firms that seek to establish their technology as a standard, also representing institutional entrepreneurship, are engaging in strategic entrepreneurship because creating a standard produces a competitive advantage for the firm.[130]

Research shows that because of its economic importance and individual motives, entrepreneurial activity is increasing around the globe. Furthermore, more women are becoming entrepreneurs because of the economic opportunity entrepreneurship provides and the individual independence it affords. Recent research showed that about one-third of all entrepreneurs are now women.[131] In the United States, for example, women are the nation's fastest-growing group of entrepreneurs.[132] In future years, entrepreneurial activity may increase the wealth of less-affluent countries and continue to contribute to the economic development of the more-affluent countries. Regardless, the entrepreneurial ventures and large, established firms that choose to practice strategic entrepreneurship are likely to be the winners in the twenty-first century.[133]

After identifying opportunities, entrepreneurs must develop capabilities that will become the basis of their firm's core competencies and competitive advantages. The process of identifying opportunities is entrepreneurial, but this activity alone is not sufficient to create maximum wealth or even to survive over time.[134] As we learned in Chapter 3, to successfully exploit opportunities, a firm must develop capabilities that are valuable, rare, difficult to imitate, and nonsubstitutable. When capabilities satisfy these four criteria, the firm has one or more competitive advantages to exploit the identified opportunities (as described in Chapter 3). Without a competitive advantage, the firm's success will be only temporary (as explained in Chapter 1). An innovation may be valuable and rare early in its life, if a market perspective is used in its development. However, competitive actions must be taken to introduce the new product to the market and protect its position in the market against competitors to gain a competitive advantage. [135] These actions combined represent strategic entrepreneurship.

SUMMARY

- Strategic entrepreneurship is taking entrepreneurial actions using a strategic perspective. Firms engaging in strategic entrepreneurship simultaneously engage in opportunity-seeking and advantage-seeking behaviors. The purpose is to continuously find new opportunities and quickly develop innovations to exploit them.

- Entrepreneurship is a process used by individuals, teams, and organizations to identify entrepreneurial opportunities without being immediately constrained by the resources they control. Corporate entrepreneurship is the application of entrepreneurship (including the identification of entrepreneurial opportunities) within ongoing, established organizations. Entrepreneurial opportunities are conditions in which new goods or services can satisfy a need in the market. Increasingly, entrepreneurship positively contributes to individual firms' performance and stimulates growth in countries' economies.

- Firms engage in three types of innovative activities: (1) invention, which is the act of creating a new good or process, (2) innovation, or the process of creating a commercial product from an invention, and (3) imitation, which is the adoption of similar innovations by different firms. Invention brings something new into being while innovation brings something new into use.

- Entrepreneurs see or envision entrepreneurial opportunities and then take actions to develop innovations to exploit them. The most successful entrepreneurs (whether they are establishing their own venture or are working in an ongoing organization) have an entrepreneurial mind-set, which is an orientation that values the potential opportunities available because of marketplace uncertainties.

- International entrepreneurship, or the process of identifying and exploiting entrepreneurial opportunities outside the firm's domestic markets, is important to firms around the globe. Evidence suggests that firms capable of effectively engaging in international entrepreneurship outperform those competing only in their domestic markets.

- Three basic approaches are used to produce innovation: (1) internal innovation, which involves R&D and forming internal corporate ventures, (2) cooperative strategies such as strategic alliances, and (3) acquisitions. Autonomous strategic behavior and induced strategic behavior are the two forms of internal corporate venturing. Autonomous strategic behavior is a bottom-up process through which a product champion facilitates the commercialization of an innovative good or service. Induced strategic behavior is a top-down process in which a firm's current strategy and structure facilitate the development and implementation of product or process innovations. Thus, induced strategic behavior is driven by the organization's current corporate strategy and structure while autonomous strategic behavior can result in a change to the firm's current strategy and structure arrangements.

- Firms create two types of innovations—incremental and radical—through internal innovation that takes place in the form of autonomous strategic behavior or induced strategic behavior. Overall, firms produce more incremental innovations but radical innovations have a higher probability of significantly increasing sales revenue and profits. Cross-functional integration is often vital to a firm's efforts to develop and implement internal corporate venturing activities and to commercialize the resulting innovation. The cross-functional teams now commonly include representatives from external organizations such as suppliers. Additionally, integration and innovation can be facilitated by developing shared values and effectively using strategic leadership.

- To gain access to the specialized knowledge commonly required to innovate in the complex global economy, firms may form a cooperative relationship such as a strategic alliance with other companies, some of which may be competitors.

- Acquisitions are another means firms use to obtain innovation. Innovation can be acquired through direct acquisition, or firms can learn new capabilities from an acquisition, thereby enriching their internal innovation abilities.

- The practice of strategic entrepreneurship by all types of firms, large and small, new and more established, creates value for all stakeholders, especially for shareholders and customers. Strategic entrepreneurship also contributes to the economic development of countries.

REVIEW QUESTIONS

1. What is strategic entrepreneurship? What is corporate entrepreneurship?

2. What is entrepreneurship, and what are entrepreneurial opportunities? Why are they important for firms competing in the twenty-first–century competitive landscape?

3. What are invention, innovation, and imitation? How are these concepts interrelated?

4. What is an entrepreneur, and what is an entrepreneurial mind-set?

5. What is international entrepreneurship? Why is it important?

6. How do firms develop innovations internally?

7. How do firms use cooperative strategies to innovate and to have access to innovative capabilities?

8. How does a firm acquire other companies to increase the number of innovations it produces and improve its capability to produce innovations?

9. How does strategic entrepreneurship help firms to create value?

EXPERIENTIAL EXERCISES

EXERCISE 1: DO YOU WANT TO BE AN ENTREPRENEUR?

Would you make a good entrepreneur? In this exercise, we will explore how individual attributes and characteristics contribute to entrepreneurial success. If you believe that you have the traits of a successful entrepreneur, would you be more effective working within a large firm or starting your own business? Complete the first stage of the exercise individually, then meet in small groups to discuss your answers.

Individual

Brainstorm a list of personal attributes or characteristics that could help (or hinder) a person's success as an entrepreneur. Next, evaluate the importance of each item on your list. Finally, compare your prioritized list against your personal characteristics. Do you think that you are a good candidate to be an entrepreneur? Why or why not?

Group

First, compare each person's list of attributes and characteristics. Combine similar items and create a composite list. Second, as a group, evaluate the importance of each item on the list. It is not important to rank order the characteristics. Rather, sort them into the categories "very important," "somewhat important," and "minimally important." Then, discuss within your group which team member seems to be the best suited to be an entrepreneur. Create a brief profile of how to describe that person if he or she were applying for a job at an innovative company such as Google, Intel, or Motorola.

Whole Class

The instructor will ask for student volunteers to present their interview profiles.

EXERCISE 2: THE SOCIAL NATURE OF ENTREPRENEURSHIP

Entrepreneurship is said to be as much about social connections and networks as it is about the fundamentals of running a new venture. The relationships that an entrepreneur can count upon are also a key resource for financial capital, human capital, mentoring, and legal advice.

A popular blog covering social media and Web 2.0, http://mashable.com, recently identified what it considered to be the top 10 social networks for entrepreneurs (http://mashable.com, March 12, 2009):

1. Entrepreneur Connect
2. PartnerUp
3. StartupNation
4. LinkedIn

5. Biznik
6. Perfect Business
7. Go Big Network
8. Cofoundr
9. The Funded
10. Young Entrepreneur

In teams, choose one of the sites from the list; each team must select a different site. Then, spend some time reading the posts on that site to get a feel for the types of information that is presented. After your review, prepare a 10-minute presentation to the class on your network site, paying attention to address the following, at a minimum:

1. Provide an overview of the site—what it is used for, how popular is it, features, types of conversations, etc.
2. What is unique about this site? Why does it attract followers? What technologies are enabled here—RSS, Twitter, etc.?
3. Describe the target audience for this site. Who would use it and what types of information are available to entrepreneurs?
4. How do you think this site maintains it presence? Does it support itself with ad revenue, corporate sponsor, a not-for-profit sponsor, etc.?
5. Would this site be useful for corporate entrepreneurs as well as startup entrepreneurs? If so, how?

VIDEO CASE

THE DNA OF THE ENTREPRENEUR

Dame Anita Roddick/Founder/The Body Shop International

Dame Anita Roddick, founder of The Body Shop International, talks about the skill set required for an entrepreneur to grow a business. Roddick founded her firm in 1976 with no experience or training, but due to life experiences and economic necessity created a very successful firm dedicated to the pursuit of social and environmental causes.

Before you watch the video consider the following concepts and questions and be prepared to discuss them in class:

Concepts

- Entrepreneur
- Entrepreneurial mind-set
- Entrepreneurial opportunities

Questions

1. Research Dame Anita Roddick and describe her as an entrepreneur.
2. What do you think about entrepreneurs who are interested in personal wealth creation vs. those with aspirations about building a business that may not lead to personal wealth creation?
3. Can large organizations encourage entrepreneurship within their existing structures?
4. Are you a future entrepreneur? Why or why not?

Chapter 1

1. J. McGregor, 2009, Smart management for tough times, *BusinessWeek*, http://www.businessweek.com, March 12.

2. McDonald's Corp., 2009, Standard & Poor's Stock Reports, http://www.standardandpoors.com, April 23.

3. The secret sauce at In-N-Out Burger, 2009, *BusinessWeek*, April 20, 68–69.

4. D. Kiley, 2009, Ford heats out on a road of its own, *BusinessWeek*, January 19, 47–49.

5. H. R. Greve, 2009, Bigger and safer: The diffusion of competitive advantage, *Strategic Management Journal*, 30: 1–23; D. G. Sirmon, M. A. Hitt, & R. D. Ireland, 2007, Managing firm resources in dynamic environments to create value: Looking inside the black box, *Academy of Management Review*, 32: 273–292.

6. R. D. Ireland & J. W. Webb, 2009, Crossing the great divide of strategic entrepreneurship: Transitioning between exploration and exploitation, *Business Horizons*, in press; D. Lei & J. W. Slocum, 2005, Strategic and organizational requirements for competitive advantage, *Academy of Management Executive*, 19(1): 31–45.

7. J. A. Lamberg, H. Tikkanen, T. Nokelainen, & H. Suur-Inkeroinen, 2009, Competitive dynamics, strategic consistency, and organizational survival, *Strategic Management Journal*, 30: 45–60; G. Pacheco-de-Almeida & P. Zemsky, 2007, The timing of resource development and sustainable competitive advantage, *Management Science*, 53: 651–666.

8. K. D. Miller, 2007, Risk and rationality in entrepreneurial processes, *Strategic Entrepreneurship Journal*, 1: 57–74.

9. R. M. Stulz, 2009, 6 ways companies mismanage risk, *Harvard Business Review*, 87(3): 86–94.

10. P. Steffens, P. Davidsson, & J. Fitzsimmons, 2009, Performance configurations over time: Implications for growth- and profit-oriented strategies, *Entrepreneurship Theory and Practice*, 33: 125–148.

11. J. C. Short, A. McKelvie, D. J. Ketchen, Jr., & G. N. Chandler, 2009, Firm and industry effects on firm performance: A generalization and extension for new ventures, *Strategic Entrepreneurship Journal*, 3: 47–65; T. Bates, 2005, Analysis of young, small firms that have closed: Delineating successful from unsuccessful closures, *Journal of Business Venturing*, 20: 343–358.

12. K. D. Miller, F. Fabian, & S.-J. Lin, 2009, Strategies for online communities, *Strategic Management Journal*, 30: 305–322; A. M. McGahan & M. E. Porter, 2003, The emergence and sustainability of abnormal profits, *Strategic Organization*, 1: 79–108.

13. J. Kell, 2009, Circuit City to liquidate, meaning 30,000 job losses, *Wall Street Journal*, http://www.wsj.com, January 16.

14. P. B. Kavilanz, 2009, Circuit City to shut down, *CNN Money*, http://www.cnn.money.com, January 16.

15. Ibid.

16. D. Marginson & L. McAulay, 2008, Exploring the debate on short-termism: A theoretical and empirical analysis, *Strategic Management Journal*, 29: 273–292.

17. M. Bustillo, 2009, Best Buy confronts newer nemesis, *Wall Street Journal*, http://www.wsj.com, March 16.

18. M. Bustillo & C. Lawton, 2009, Best Buy expands private-label brands, *Wall Street Journal*, http://www.wsj.com, April 27.

19. 2009, Best Buy vs. Wal-Mart: Is there room for both, and others? *Knowledge@Wharton*, http://knowledge.wharton.upenn.com, April 1.

20. T. R. Crook, D. J. Ketchen, Jr., J. G. Combs, & S. Y. Todd, 2008, Strategic resources and performance: A meta-analysis, *Strategic Management Journal*, 29: 1141–1154; J. T. Mahoney & A. M. McGahan, 2007, The field of strategic management within the evolving science of strategic organization, *Strategic Organization*, 5: 79–99.

21. J. Barthelemy, 2008, Opportunism, knowledge, and the performance of franchise chains, *Strategic Management Journal*, 29: 1451–1463.

22. J. Li, 2008, Asymmetric interactions between foreign and domestic banks: Effects on market entry, *Strategic Management Journal*, 29: 873–893.

23. P. Ghemawat & T. Hout, 2008, Tomorrow's global giants, *Harvard Business Review*, 86(11): 80–88.

24. M. A. Delmas & M. W. Toffel, 2008, Organizational responses to environmental demands: Opening the black box, *Strategic Management Journal*, 29: 1027–1055; A. M. McGahan & M. E. Porter, 1997, How much does industry matter, really? *Strategic Management Journal*, 18 (Special Issue): 15–30.

25. T. R. Holcomb, R. M. Holmes, Jr., & B. L. Connelly, 2009, Making the most of what you have: Managerial ability as a source of resource value creation, *Strategic Management Journal*, 30: 457–485; J. Acedo, C. Barroso, & J. L. Galan, 2006, The resource-based theory: Dissemination and main trends, *Strategic Management Journal*, 27: 621–636.

26. E. Thornton, 2009, The new rules, *BusinessWeek*, January 19, 30–34; T. Friedman, 2005, *The World Is Flat: A Brief History of the 21s Century*, New York: Farrar, Strauss and Giroux.

27. D. Searcey, 2006, Beyond cable. Beyond DSL. *Wall Street Journal*, July 24, R9.

28. 2009, NBC Universal company overview, http://www.nbcuniversal.com, April 23.

29. P. Taylor, 2007, Tools to bridge the divide: Raketu aims to outperform Skype in Internet telephony while throwing in a range of information and entertainment services, *Financial Times*, May 11, 16.

30. 2009, Be entertained, http://www.raketu.com, April 22.

31. 2009, Social networking websites review, http://www.social-networking-websites-review.toptenreivews.com, April 22.

32. D. F. Kuratko & D. B. Audretsch, 2009, Strategic entrepreneurship: Exploring different perspectives of an emerging concept, *Entrepreneurship Theory and Practice*, 33: 1–17.

33. J. Hagel, III, J. S. Brown, & L. Davison, 2008, Shaping strategy in a world of constant disruption, *Harvard Business Review*, 86(10): 81–89; G. Probst & S. Raisch, 2005, Organizational crisis: The logic of failure, *Academy of Management Executive*, 19(1): 90–105.

34. J. W. Selsky, J. Goes, & O. N. Babüroglu, 2007, Contrasting perspectives of strategy making: Applications in "Hyper" environments, *Organization*

Studies, 28(1): 71–94; G. McNamara, P. M. Vaaler, & C. Devers, 2003, Same as it ever was: The search for evidence of increasing hypercompetition, *Strategic Management Journal*, 24: 261–278.

35. A. V. Izosimov, 2008, Managing hypergrowth, *Harvard Business Review*, 86(4): 121–127.

36. R. A. D'Aveni, 1995, Coping with hypercompetition: Utilizing the new 7S's framework, *Academy of Management Executive*, 9(3): 46.

37. D. J. Bryce & J. H. Dyer, 2007, Strategies to crack well-guarded markets, *Harvard Business Review* 85(5): 84–92; R. A. D'Aveni, 2004, Corporate spheres of influence, *MIT Sloan Management Review*, 45(4): 38–46; W. J. Ferrier, 2001, Navigating the competitive landscape: The drivers and consequences of competitive aggressiveness, *Academy of Management Journal*, 44: 858–877.

38. S. H. Lee & M. Makhija, 2009, Flexibility in internationalization: Is it valuable during an economic crisis? *Strategic Management Journal*, 30: 537–555; S. J. Chang & S. Park, 2005, Types of firms generating network externalities and MNCs' co-location decisions, *Strategic Management Journal*, 26: 595–615.

39. S. E. Feinberg & A. K. Gupta, 2009, MNC subsidiaries and country risk: Internalization as a safeguard against weak external institutions, *Academy of Management Journal*, 52: 381–399; R. Belderbos & L. Sleuwaegen, 2005, Competitive drivers and international plant configuration strategies: A product-level test, *Strategic Management Journal*, 26: 577–593.

40. 2005, Organisation for Economic Cooperation and Development, OCED Statistical Profile of the United States—2005, http://www.oced.org; S. Koudsi & L. A. Costa, 1998, America vs. the new Europe: By the numbers, *Fortune*, December 21, 149–156.

41. Y. Luo, 2007, From foreign investors to strategic insiders: Shifting parameters, prescriptions and paradigms for MNCs in China, *Journal of World Business*, 42(1): 14–34.

42. M. A. Hitt & X. He, 2008, Firm strategies in a changing global competitive landscape, *Business Horizons*, 51:363–369; A. Ratanpal, 2008, Indian economy and Indian private equity, *Thunderbird International Business Review*, 50: 353–358.

43. Y. Gorodnichenko, J. Svejnar, & K. Terrell, 2008, Globalization and innovation in emerging markets, NBER Working Paper No. w14481. Available at SSRN: http://ssrn.com/abstract=1301929.

44. K. Kranhold, 2005, GE pins hopes on emerging markets, *Wall Street Journal*, http://www.wsj.com, March 2.

45. C. H. Oh, 2009, The international scale and scope of European multinationals, *European Management Journal*, in press; G. D. Bruton, G. G. Dess & J. J. Janney, 2007, Knowledge management in technology-focused

firms in emerging economies: Caveats on capabilities, networks, and real options, *Asia Pacific Journal of Management*, 24(2): 115–130;

46. A. Ciarione, P. Piselli, & G. Trebeschi, 2009, Emerging markets' spreads and global financial conditions, *Journal of International Financial Markets, Institutions and Money*, 19: 222–239.

47. 2009, Wal-Mart Stores Inc., *Standard & Poor's Stock Reports*, http://www.standardandpoors.com, April 18.

48. M. A. Prospero, 2005, The march of war, *Fast Company*, May, 14.

49. B. Elango, 2009, Minimizing effects of "liability of foreignness": Response strategies of foreign firms in the United States, *Journal of World Business*, 44: 51–62.

50. D. J. McCarthy & S. M. Puffer, 2008, Interpreting the ethicality of corporate governance decisions in Russia: Utilizing integrative social contracts theory to evaluate the relevance of agency theory norms, *Academy of Management Review*, 33: 11–31.

51. M. A. Hitt, R. E. Hoskisson, & H. Kim, 1997, International diversification: Effects on innovation and firm performance in product-diversified firms, *Academy of Management Journal*, 40: 767–798.

52. R. D. Ireland & J. W. Webb, 2007, Strategic entrepreneurship: Creating competitive advantage through streams of innovation, *Business Horizons*, 50(1): 49–59; G. Hamel, 2001, Revolution vs. evolution: You need both, *Harvard Business Review*, 79(5): 150–156.

53. K. H. Hammonds, 2001, What is the state of the new economy? *Fast Company*, September, 101–104.

54. B. Peters, 2009, Persistence of innovation: Stylised facts and panel data evidence, *The Journal of Technology Transfer*, 34: 226–243.

55. J. L. Boyd & R. K. F. Bresser, 2008, Performance implications of delayed competitive responses: Evidence from the U.S. retail industry, *Strategic Management Journal*, 29: 1077–1096; T. Talaulicar, J. Grundei, & A. V. Werder, 2005, Strategic decision making in startups: The effect of top management team organization and processes on speed and comprehensiveness, *Journal of Business Venturing*, 20: 519–541.

56. J. Kao, 2009, Tapping the world's innovation hot spots, *Harvard Business Review*, 87(3): 109–117.

57. C. W. L. Hill, 1997, Establishing a standard: Competitive strategy and technological standards in winner-take-all industries, *Academy of Management Executive*, 11(2): 7–25.

58. J. L. Funk, 2008, Components, systems and technological discontinuities: Lessons from the IT sector, *Long Range Planning*, 41: 555–573; C. M. Christensen, 1997, *The Innovator's Dilemma*, Boston: Harvard Business School Press.

59. C. M. Christensen, 2006, The ongoing process of building a theory of disruption,

Journal of Product Innovation Management, 23(1): 39–55; R. Adner, 2002, When are technologies disruptive? A demand-based view of the emergence of competition, *Strategic Management Journal*, 23: 667–688; G. Ahuja & C. M. Lampert, 2001, Entrepreneurship in the large corporation: A longitudinal study of how established firms create breakthrough inventions, *Strategic Management Journal*, 22 (Special Issue): 521–543.

60. C. L. Nichols-Nixon & C. Y. Woo, 2003, Technology sourcing and output of established firms in a regime of encompassing technological change, *Strategic Management Journal*, 24: 651–666; C. W. L. Hill & F. T. Rothaermel, 2003, The performance of incumbent firms in the face of radical technological innovation, *Academy of Management Review*, 28: 257–274.

61. K. Celuch, G. B. Murphy, & S. K. Callaway, 2007, More bang for your buck: Small firms and the importance of aligned information technology capabilities and strategic flexibility, *Journal of High Technology Management Research*, 17: 187–197.

62. V. Godinez, 2009, Broadband ISPs test download caps, face resistance from more data-heavy users, *The Dallas Morning News*, http://www.dallasnews.com, April 26.

63. C. F. Fey & P. Furu, 2008, Top management incentive compensation and knowledge sharing in multinational corporations, *Strategic Management Journal*, 29: 1301–1323.

64. M. Gottfredson, R. Puryear, & S. Phillips, 2005, Strategic sourcing: From periphery to the core, *Harvard Business Review*, 83(2): 132–139.

65. L. F. Mesquita, J. Anand, & T. H. Brush 2008, Comparing the resource-based and relational views: Knowledge transfer and spillover in vertical alliances, *Strategic Management Journal*, 29: 913–941; K. G. Smith, C. J. Collins, & K. D. Clark, 2005, Existing knowledge, knowledge creation capability, and the rate of new product introduction in high-technology firms, *Academy of Management Journal*, 48: 346–357.

66. A. Capaldo, 2007, Network structure and innovation: The leveraging of a dual network as a distinctive relational capability, *Strategic Management Journal*, 28: 585–608; S. K. Ethirau, P. Kale, M. S. Krishnan, & J. V. Singh, 2005, Where do capabilities come from and how do they matter? *Strategic Management Journal*, 26: 25–45.

67. Sirmon, Hitt, & Ireland, Managing firm resources.

68. A. C. Inkpen, 2008, Knowledge transfer and international joint ventures: The case of NUMMI and General Motors, *Strategic Management Journal*, 29: 447–453; P. L. Robertson & P. R. Patel, 2007, New wine in old bottles: Technological diffusion in developed economies, *Research Policy*, 36(5): 708–721; K. Asakawa & M. Lehrer,

2003, Managing local knowledge assets globally: The role of regional innovation relays, *Journal of World Business*, 38: 31–42.

69. R. E. Hoskisson, M. A. Hitt, & R. D. Ireland, 2008, *Competing for Advantage*, 2nd ed., Cincinnati: Thomson South-Western; K. R. Harrigan, 2001, Strategic flexibility in old and new economies, in M. A. Hitt, R. E. Freeman, & J. S. Harrison (eds.), *Handbook of Strategic Management*, Oxford, UK: Blackwell Publishers, 97–123.

70. S. Nadkarni & V. K. Narayanan, 2007, Strategic schemas, strategic flexibility, and firm performance: The moderating role of industry clockspeed, *Strategic Management Journal*, 28: 243–270.

71. L. Gratton & S. Ghoshal, 2005, Beyond best practice, *MIT Sloan Management Review*, 46(3): 49–55.

72. A. C. Edmondson, 2008, The competitive imperative of learning, *Harvard Business Review*, 86(7/8): 60–67; K. Shimizu & M. A. Hitt, 2004, Strategic flexibility: Organizational preparedness to reverse ineffective strategic decisions, *Academy of Management Executive*, 18(4): 44–59; K. Uhlenbruck, K. E. Meyer, & M. A. Hitt, 2003, Organizational transformation in transition economies: Resource-based and organizational learning perspectives, *Journal of Management Studies*, 40: 257–282.

73. R. E. Hoskisson, M. A. Hitt, W. P. Wan, & D. Yiu, 1999, Swings of a pendulum: Theory and research in strategic management, *Journal of Management*, 25: 417–456.

74. E. H. Bowman & C. E. Helfat, 2001, Does corporate strategy matter? *Strategic Management Journal*, 22: 1–23.

75. M. A. Delmas & M. W. Toffel, 2008, Organizational responses to environmental demands: Opening the black box, *Strategic Management Journal*, 29: 1027–1055; J. Shamsie, 2003, The context of dominance: An industry-driven framework for exploiting reputation, *Strategic Management Journal*, 24: 199–215.

76. J. Galbreath & P. Galvin, 2008, Firm factors, industry structure and performance variation: New empirical evidence to a classic debate, *Journal of Business Research*, 61: 109–117.

77. M. B. Lieberman & S. Asaba, 2006, Why do firms imitate each other? *Academy of Management Journal*, 31: 366–385; L. F. Feldman, C. G. Brush, & T. Manolova, 2005, Co-alignment in the resource-performance relationship: Strategy as mediator, *Journal of Business Venturing*, 20: 359–383.

78. M. E. Porter, 1985, *Competitive Advantage*, New York: Free Press; M. E. Porter, 1980, *Competitive Strategy*, New York: Free Press.

79. J. C. Short, D. J. Ketchen, Jr., T. B. Palmer, & G. T. M. Hult, 2007, Firm, strategic group, and industry influences on performance, *Strategic Management Journal*, 28: 147–167.

80. P. Ziobro, 2009, McDonald's pounds out good quarter, *Wall Street Journal*, http://www.wsj.com, April 23.

81. A. M. McGahan, 1999, Competition, strategy and business performance, *California Management Review*, 41(3): 74–101; McGahan & Porter, How much does industry matter, really?

82. S. L. Newbert, 2008, Value, rareness, competitive advantage, and performance: A conceptual-level empirical investigation of the resource-based view of the firm, *Strategic Management Journal*, 29: 745–768; F. J. Acedo, C. Barroso, & J. L. Galan, 2006, The resource-based theory: Dissemination and main trends, *Strategic Management Journal*, 27: 621–636.

83. E. Verwall, H. Commandeur, & W. Verbeke, 2009, Value creation and value claiming in strategic outsourcing decisions: A resource contingency perspective, *Journal of Management*, 35: 420–444; B.-S. Teng & J. L. Cummings, 2002, Trade-offs in managing resources and capabilities, *Academy of Management Executive*, 16(2): 81–91.

84. S. Kaplan, 2008, Cognition, capabilities, and incentives: Assessing firm response to the fiber-optic revolution, *Academy of Management Journal*, 51: 672–694; S. A. Zahra, H. Sapienza, & P. Davidsson, 2006, Entrepreneurship and dynamic capabilities: A review, model and research agenda, *Journal of Management Studies*, 43(4): 927–955; M. Blyler & R. W. Coff, 2003, Dynamic capabilities, social capital, and rent appropriation: Ties that split pies, *Strategic Management Journal*, 24: 677–686.

85. S. L. Newbert, 2007, Empirical research on the resource-based view of the firm: An assessment and suggestions for future research, *Strategic Management Journal*, 28: 121–146; P. Bansal, 2005, Evolving sustainability: A longitudinal study of corporate sustainable development, *Strategic Management Journal*, 26: 197–218.

86. P. J. H. Schoemaker & R. Amit, 1994, Investment in strategic assets: Industry and firm-level perspectives, in P. Shrivastava, A. Huff, & J. Dutton (eds.), *Advances in Strategic Management*, Greenwich, CT: JAI Press, 9.

87. A. A. Lado, N. G. Boyd, P. Wright, & M. Kroll, 2006, Paradox and theorizing within the resource-based view, *Academy of Management Review*, 31: 115–131; D. M. DeCarolis, 2003, Competencies and imitability in the pharmaceutical industry: An analysis of their relationship with firm performance, *Journal of Management*, 29: 27–50.

88. C. Zott, 2003, Dynamic capabilities and the emergence of intraindustry differential firm performance: Insights from a simulation study, *Strategic Management Journal*, 24: 97–125.

89. E. Levitas & H. A. Ndofor, 2006, What to do with the resource-based view: A few suggestions for what ails the RBV that

supporters and opponents might accept, *Journal of Management Inquiry*, 15(2): 135–144; G. Hawawini, V. Subramanian, & P. Verdin, 2003, Is performance driven by industry- or firm-specific factors? A new look at the evidence, *Strategic Management Journal*, 24: 1–16.

90. M. Makhija, 2003, Comparing the resource-based and market-based views of the firm: Empirical evidence from Czech privatization, *Strategic Management Journal*, 24: 433–451; T. J. Douglas & J. A. Ryman, 2003, Understanding competitive advantage in the general hospital industry: Evaluating strategic competencies, *Strategic Management Journal*, 24: 333–347.

91. R. D. Ireland, R. E. Hoskisson, & M. A. Hitt. 2009, *Understanding Business Strategy*, 2nd Edition, Cincinnati: South-Western Cengage Learning, 6.

92. S. Ward, 2009, Vision statement, *About.com*, http://www.sbinfocanada.about.com, April 22; R. Zolli, 2006, Recognizing tomorrow's hot ideas today, *BusinessWeek*, September 25: 12.

93. 2005, The CEO's secret handbook, *Business 2.0*, July, 69–76.

94. S. Kemp & L. Dwyer, 2003, Mission statements of international airlines: A content analysis, *Tourism Management*, 24: 635–653; R. D. Ireland & M. A. Hitt, 1992, Mission statements: Importance, challenge, and recommendations for development, *Business Horizons*, 35(3): 34–42.

95. J. I. Siciliano, 2008, A comparison of CEO and director perceptions of board involvement in strategy, *Nonprofit and Voluntary Sector Quarterly*, 27: 152–162; W. J. Duncan, 1999, *Management: Ideas and Actions*, New York: Oxford University Press, 122–125.

96. J. H. Davis, J. A. Ruhe, M. Lee, & U. Rajadhyaksha, 2007, Mission possible: Do school mission statements work? *Journal of Business Ethics*, 70: 99–110.

97. L. W. Fry & J. W. Slocum, Jr., 2008, Maximizing the triple bottom line through spiritual leadership, *Organizational Dynamics*, 37: 86–96; A. J. Ward, M. J. Lankau, A. C. Amason, J. A. Sonnenfeld, & B. A. Agle, 2007, Improving the performance of top management teams, *MIT Sloan Management Review*, 48(3): 85–90.

98. M. Rahman, 2009, Why strategic vision statements *won't* measure up, *Strategic Direction*, 25: 3–4.

99. R. Kaufman, 2006, *Change, Choices, and Consequences: A Guide to Mega Thinking and Planning*, Amherst, MA: HRD Press; J. Humphreys, 2004, The vision thing, *MIT Sloan Management Review*, 45(4): 96.

100. K. Basu & G. Palazzo, 2008, Corporate social responsibility: A process model of sensemaking, *Academy of Management Review*, 33: 122–136.

101. D. A. Bosse, R. A. Phillips, & J. S. Harrison, 2009, Stakeholders, reciprocity, and firm performance, *Strategic Management Journal*, 30: 447–456; J. P. Walsh &

W. R. Nord, 2005, Taking stock of stakeholder management, *Academy of Management Review*, 30: 426–438; T. M. Jones & A. C. Wicks, 1999, Convergent stakeholder theory, *Academy of Management Review*, 24: 206–221.

102. G. Donaldson & J. W. Lorsch, 1983, *Decision Making at the Top: The Shaping of Strategic Direction*, New York: Basic Books, 37–40.

103. S. Sharma & I. Henriques, 2005, Stakeholder influences on sustainability practices in the Canadian Forest products industry, *Strategic Management Journal*, 26: 159–180.

104. A. Mackey, T. B. Mackey, & J. B. Barney, 2007, Corporate social responsibility and firm performance: Investor preferences and corporate strategies, *Academy of Management Review*, 32: 817–835; A. J. Hillman & G. D. Keim, 2001, Shareholder value, stakeholder management, and social issues: What's the bottom line? *Strategic Management Journal*, 22: 125–139.

105. G. Van der Laan, H. Van Ees, & A. Van Witteloostuijn, 2008, Corporate social and financial performance: An extended stakeholder theory, and empirical test with accounting measures, *Journal of Business Ethics*, 79: 299–310; J. M. Stevens, H. K. Steensma, D. A. Harrison, & P. L. Cochran, 2005, Symbolic or substantive document? The influence of ethics codes on financial executives' decisions, *Strategic Management Journal*, 26: 181–195.

106. M. L. Barnett & R. M. Salomon, 2006, Beyond dichotomy: The curvilinear relationship between social responsibility and financial performance, *Strategic Management Journal*, 27: 1101–1122.

107. T. Kuhn, 2008, A communicative theory of the firm: Developing an alternative perspective on intra-organizational power and stakeholder relationships, *Organization Studies*, 29: 1227–1254; L. Vilanova, 2007, Neither shareholder nor stakeholder management: What happens when firms are run for their short-term salient stakeholder? *European Management Journal*, 25(2): 146–162.

108. J. L. Murrillo-Luna, C. Garces-Ayerbe, & P. Rivera-Torres, 2008, Why do patterns of environmental response differ? A stakeholders' pressure approach, *Strategic Management Journal*, 29: 1225–1240; R. E. Freeman & J. McVea, 2001, A stakeholder approach to strategic management, in M. A. Hitt, R. E. Freeman, & J. S. Harrison (eds.), *Handbook of Strategic Management*, Oxford, UK: Blackwell Publishers, 189–207.

109. R. Boutilier, 2009, *Stakeholder Politics: Social Capital, Sustainable Development, and the Corporation*, Sheffield, United Kingdom, Greenleaf Publishing; C. Caldwell & R. Karri, 2005, Organizational governance and ethical systems: A conventional approach to building trust, *Journal of Business Ethics*, 58: 249–267.

110. F. G. A. de Bakker & F. den Hond, 2008, Introducing the politics of stakeholder influence, *Business & Society*, 47: 8–20; C. Hardy, T. B. Lawrence, & D. Grant, 2005, Discourse and collaboration: The role of conversations and collective identity, *Academy of Management Review*, 30: 58–77.

111. P. Berrone & L. R. Gomez-Meija, 2009, Environmental performance and executive compensation: An integrated agency-institutional perspective, *Academy of Management Journal*, 52: 103-126; S. Maitlis, 2005, The social process of organizational sensemaking, *Academy of Management Journal*, 48: 21–49.

112. 2009, Circuit City to liquidate U.S. stores, *MSNBC*, http://www.msnbc.com, January 16.

113. L. Pierce, 2009, Big losses in ecosystems niches: How core firm decisions drive complementary product shakeouts, *Strategic Management Journal*, 30: 323-347; B. A. Neville & B. Menguc, 2006, Stakeholder multiplicity: Toward an understanding of the interactions between stakeholders, *Journal of Business Ethics*, 66: 377–391.

114. D. A. Ready, L. A. Hill, & J. A. Conger, 2008, Winning the race for talent in emerging markets, *Harvard Business Review*, 86(11): 62–70; A. M. Grant, J. E. Dutton, & B. D. Rosso, 2008, Giving commitment: Employee support programs and the prosocial sensemaking process, *Academy of Management Journal*, 51: 898–918; T. M. Gardner, 2005, Interfirm competition for human resources: Evidence from the software industry, *Academy of Management Journal*, 48: 237–256.

115. J. A. Byrne, 2005, Working for the boss from hell, *Fast Company*, July, 14.

116. N. Abe & S. Shimizutani, 2007, Employment policy and corporate governance—An empirical comparison of the stakeholder and the profit-maximization model, *Journal of Comparative Economics*, 35: 346–368.

117. J. Welch & S. Welch, 2009, An employee bill of rights, *BusinessWeek*, March 16, 72.

118. J. P. Jansen, D. Vera, & M. Crossan, 2008, Strategic leadership for exploration and exploitation: The moderating role of environmental dynamism, *The Leadership Quarterly*, 20: 5–18; E. T. Prince, 2005, The fiscal behavior of CEOs, *MIT Sloan Management Review*, 46(3): 23–26.

119. M. S. de Luque, N. T. Washburn, D. A. Waldman, & R. J. House, 2008, Unrequited profit: How stakeholder and economic values related to subordinates' perceptions of leadership and firm performance, *Administrative Science Quarterly*, 53: 626–654.

120. R. Khurana & N. Nohria, 2008, It's time to make management a true profession, *Harvard Business Review*, 86(10): 70–77.

121. N. Byrnes, 2009, Executives on a tightrope, *BusinessWeek*, January 19, 43; D. C. Hambrick, 2007, Upper

echelons theory: An update, *Academy of Management Review*, 32: 334–339.

122. J. C. Camillus, 2008, Strategy as a wicked problem, *Harvard Business Review* 86(5): 99–106; A. Priestland & T. R. Hanig, 2005, Developing first-level managers, *Harvard Business Review*, 83(6): 113–120.

123. R. J. Harrington & A. K. Tjan, 2008, Transforming strategy one customer at a time, *Harvard Business Review*, 86(3): 62–72; R. T. Pascale & J. Sternin, 2005, Your company's secret change agent, *Harvard Business Review*, 83(5): 72–81.

124. Y. L. Doz & M. Kosonen, 2007, The new deal at the top, *Harvard Business Review*, 85(6): 98–104.

125. B. Stevens, 2008, Corporate ethical codes: Effective instruments for influencing behavior, *Journal of Business Ethics*, 78: 601–609; D. Lavie, 2006, The competitive advantage of interconnected firms: An extension of the resource-based view, *Academy of Management Review*, 31: 638–658.

126. H. Ibarra & O. Obodru, 2009, Women and the vision thing, *Harvard Business Review*, 87(1): 62–70; M. Crossan, D. Vera, & L. Nanjad, 2008, Transcendent leadership: Strategic leadership in dynamic environments, *The Leadership Quarterly*, 19: 569–581.

127. T. Leavitt, 1991, *Thinking about Management*, New York: Free Press, 9.

128. 2007, 100 best corporate citizens for 2007, *CRO Magazine*, http://www.thecro com, June 19.

129. C. A. Montgomery, 2008, Putting leadership back into strategy, *Harvard Business Review*, 86(1): 54–60; D. C. Hambrick, S. Finkelstein, & A. C. Mooney, 2005, Executive job demands: New insights for explaining strategic decisions and leader behaviors, *Academy of Management Review*, 30: 472–491; J. Brett & L. K. Stroh, 2003, Working 61 plus hours a week: Why do managers do it? *Journal of Applied Psychology*, 88: 67–78.

130. J. A. Byrne, 2005, Great work if you can get it, *Fast Company*, April, 14.

131. M. Loeb, 1993, Steven J. Ross, 1927–1992, *Fortune*, January 25, 4.

132. K. M. Green, J. G. Covin, & D. P. Slevin, 2008, Exploring the relationship between strategic reactiveness and entrepreneurial orientation: The role of structure-style fit, *Journal of Business Venturing*, 23: 356–383.

133. O. Gadiesh & J. L. Gilbert, 1998, Profit pools: A fresh look at strategy, *Harvard Business Review*, 76(3): 139–147.

134. O. Gadiesh & J. L. Gilbert, 1998, How to map your industry's profit pool, *Harvard Business Review*, 76(3): 149–162.

135. C. Zook, 2007, Finding your next CORE business, *Harvard Business Review*, 85(4): 66–75; M. J. Epstein & R. A. Westbrook, 2001, Linking actions to profits in strategic decision making, *Sloan Management Review*, 42(3): 39–49.

136. T. Yu, M. Subramaniam, & A. A. Cannella, Jr., 2009, Rivalry deterrence

in international markets: Contingencies governing the mutual forbearance hypothesis, *Academy of Management Journal*, 52: 127–147; D. J. Ketchen, C. C. Snow, & V. L. Street, 2004, Improving firm performance by matching strategic decision-making processes to competitive dynamics, *Academy of Management Executive*, 18(4): 29–43.

137. P. Ozcan & K. M. Eisenhardt, 2009, Origin of alliance portfolios: Entrepreneurs, network strategies, and firm performance, *Academy of Management Journal*, 52: 246–279.

138. S. D. Julian, J. C. Ofori-Dankwa, & R. T. Justis, 2008, Understanding strategic responses to interest group pressures, *Strategic Management Journal*, 29: 963–984; C. Eesley & M. J. Lenox, 2006, Firm responses to secondary stakeholder action, *Strategic Management Journal*, 27: 765–781.

139. Y. Luo, 2008, Procedural fairness and interfirm cooperation in strategic alliances, *Strategic Management Journal*, 29: 27–46; S. J. Reynolds, F. C. Schultz, & D. R. Hekman, 2006, Stakeholder theory and managerial decision-making: Constraints

and implications of balancing stakeholder interests, *Journal of Business Ethics*, 64: 285–301; L. K. Trevino & G. R. Weaver, 2003, *Managing Ethics in Business Organizations*, Stanford, CA: Stanford University Press.

140. D. Pastoriza, M. A. Arino, & J. E. Ricart, 2008, Ethical managerial behavior as an antecedent of organizational social capital, *Journal of Business Ethics*, 78: 329–341.

141. B. W. Heineman Jr., 2007, Avoiding integrity land mines, *Harvard Business Review*, 85(4): 100–108.

Chapter 2

1. D. A. Bosse, R. A. Phillips, & J. S. Harrison, 2009, Stakeholders, reciprocity, and firm performance, *Strategic Management Journal*, 30: 447–456.

2. K. Helliker, 2009, Smokeless tobacco to get push by venture overseas, *Wall Street Journal Online*, http://www.wsj.com, February 4.

3. K. Helliker, 2009, Smokeless tobacco to get push by venture overseas, *Wall Street Journal Online*, http://www.wsj.com, February 4.

4. P. Berrone & L. R. Gomez-Mejia, 2009, Environmental performance and executive compensation: An integrated agency-institutional perspective, *Academy of Management Journal*, 52: 103–126; P. Chattopadhyay, W. H. Glick, & G. P. Huber, 2001, Organizational actions in response to threats and opportunities, *Academy of Management Journal*, 44: 937–955.

5. C. Weigelt & M. B. Sarkar, 2009, Learning from supply-side agents: The impact of technology solution providers' experiential diversity on clients' innovation adoption, *Academy of Management Journal*, 52: 37–60; D. G. Sirmon, S. Gove, & M. A. Hitt, 2008, Resource management in dyadic competitive rivalry: The effects of resource bundling and deployment, *Academy of Management Journal*, 51: 919–935.

6. J. P. Bonardi, G. I. F. Holburn, & R. G. Vanden Bergh, 2006, Nonmarket strategy performance: Evidence from U.S. electric utilities, *Academy of Management Journal*, 49: 1209–1228.

7. S. Labaton, 2009, Obama plans fast action to tighten financial rules, *New York Times Online*, http://www.nytimes.com, January 25.

8. J. Welch & S. Welch, 2009, The economy: A little clarity, *BusinessWeek*, May 4, 80.

9. J. Uotila, M. Maula, T. Keil, & S. A. Zahra, 2009, Exploration, exploitation, and financial performance: Analysis of S&P 500 corporations, *Strategic Management Journal*, 30: 221–231; J. L. Murillo-Luna, C. Garces-Ayerbe, & P. Rivera-Torres, 2008, Why do patterns of environmental

response differ? A stakeholder's pressure approach, *Strategic Management Journal*, 29: 1225–1240.

10. A. Kacperczyk, 2009, With greater power comes greater responsibility? Takeover protection and corporate attention to stakeholders, *Strategic Management Journal*, 30: 261–285; C. Eesley & M. J. Lenox, 2006, Firm responses to secondary stakeholder action, *Strategic Management Journal*, 27: 765–781.

11. L. Fahey, 1999, *Competitors*, New York: John Wiley & Sons; B. A. Walters & R. L. Priem, 1999, Business strategy and CEO intelligence acquisition, *Competitive Intelligence Review*, 10(2): 15–22.

12. A. P. Kellogg & J. Bennett, 2009, Chrysler' bankruptcy deals blow to affiliates, *Wall Street Journal Online*, http://www.wsj.com, May 2.

13. J. C. Short, D. J. Ketchen, Jr., T. B. Palmer, & G. T. Hult, 2007, Firm, strategic group, and industry influences on performance, *Strategic Management Journal*, 28: 147–167.

14. K. P. Coyne & J. Horn, 2009, Predicting your competitor's reaction, *Harvard Business Review*, 87(4): 90–97.

15. D. Sull, 2009, How to thrive in turbulent markets, *Harvard Business Review*, 87(2): 78–88; J. Hagel, III, J. S. Brown, & L. Davison, 2008, Shaping strategy in a world of constant disruption, *Harvard Business Review* 86(10): 80–89.

16. J. A. Lamberg, H. Tikkanen, T. Nokelainen, & H. Suur-Inkeroinen, 2009, Competitive dynamics, strategic consistency, and organizational survival, *Strategic Management Journal*, 30: 45–60.

17. E. Byron, 2009, P&G makes a bigger play for men, *Wall Street Journal Online*, http://www.wsj.com, April 29.

18. W. B. Gartner, K. G. Shaver, & J. Liao, 2008, Opportunities as attributions: Categorizing strategic issues from an attributional perspective, *Strategic Entrepreneurship Journal*, 2: 301–315.

19. P. Lattman, 2005, Rebound, *Forbes*, March 28, 58.

20. P. Lattman & J. McCracken, 2009, Vultures vie in auction for the remains of Polaroid,

Wall Street Journal, http://www.wsj.com, April 17.

21. W. H. Stewart, R. C. May, & A. Kalla, 2008, Environmental perceptions and scanning in the United States and India: Convergence in entrepreneurial information seeking? *Entrepreneurship Theory and Practice*, 32: 83–106; K. M. Patton & T. M. McKenna, 2005, Scanning for competitive intelligence, *Competitive Intelligence Magazine*, 8(2): 24–26.

22. J. O. Schwarz, 2008, Assessing the future of futures studies in management, *Futures*, 40: 237–246; K. M. Eisenhardt, 2002, Has strategy changed? *MIT Sloan Management Review*, 43(2): 88–91.

23. J. R. Hough & M. A. White, 2004, Scanning actions and environmental dynamism: Gathering information for strategic decision making, *Management Decision*, 42: 781–793; V. K. Garg, B. A. Walters, & R. L. Priem, 2003, Chief executive scanning emphases, environmental dynamism, and manufacturing firm performance, *Strategic Management Journal*, 24: 725–744.

24. C.-P. Wei & Y.-H. Lee, 2004, Event detection from online news documents for supporting environmental scanning, *Decision Support Systems*, 36: 385–401.

25. Fahey, *Competitors*, 71–73.

26. J. Moreno, 2009, Wal-Mart gives its Supermercado concept a tryout, *Houston Chronicle Online*, http://www.chron.com, April 30.

27. S. M. Kalita, 2009, Companies world-wide rethink strategies, *Wall Street Journal Online*, http://www.wsj.com, April 29.

28. T. M. Jones, W. Felps, & G. A. Bigley, 2007, Ethical theory and stakeholder-related decisions: The role of stakeholder culture, *Academy of Management Review*, 32: 137–155.

29. M. J. Leiblein & T. L. Madsen, 2009, Unbundling competitive heterogeneity: Incentive structures and capability influences on technological innovation, *Strategic Management Journal*, 30: 711–735.

30. D. Matten & J. Moon, 2008, Implicit and explicit CSR: A conceptual framework for a comparative understanding of

corporate social responsibility, *Academy of Management Review*, 33: 404–424; F. Sanna-Randaccio & R. Veugelers, 2007, Multinational knowledge spillovers with decentralized R&D: A game theoretic approach, *Journal of International Business Studies*, 38: 47–63.

31. Fahey, *Competitors*.

32. S. Lohr, 2009, How crisis shapes the corporate model, *Wall Street Journal Online*, http://www.wsj.com, March 29.

33. E. Byron, 2009, P&G investors need a little pampering, *Wall Street Journal Online*, http://www.wsj.com, April 30.

34. P. E. Bierly, III, F. Damanpour, & M. D. Santoro, 2009, The application of external knowledge: Organizational conditions for exploration and exploitation, *Journal of Management Studies*, 46: 481–509; Fahey, *Competitors*, 75–77.

35. K. M. Sutcliffe & K. Weber, 2003, The high cost of accurate knowledge, *Harvard Business Review*, 81(5): 74–82.

36. E. K. Foedermayr & A. Diamantopoulos, 2008, Market segmentation in practice: Review of empirical studies, methodological assessment, and agenda for future research, *Journal of Strategic Marketing*, 16: 223–265; L. Fahey & V. K. Narayanan, 1986, *Macroenvironmental Analysis for Strategic Management*, St. Paul, MN: West Publishing Company, 58.

37. U.S. Census Bureau, 2009, International data base, http://www.census.gov/pic/www/idb/worldpopgraph.html, May 24.

38. S. Moffett, 2005, Fast-aging Japan keeps its elders on the job longer, *Wall Street Journal*, June 15, A1, A8.

39. S. Armour, 2009, Mortgage crisis robbing seniors of golden years, *USA Today*, June 5–7, A1 & A2.

40. J. M. Nittoli, 2009, Now is no time to skimp on retirement plans, *Wall Street Journal*, http://www.wsj.com, June 5.

41. 2009, Migration and geographic distribution, http://www.medicine.jrank.org, June 5.

42. 2009, CultureGrams world edition, http://www.culturegrams.com, June 5.

43. 2009, StrictlySpanish, The growing Hispanic market in the United States, http://www.strictlyspanish.com, June 5.

44. J. A. Chatman & S. E. Spataro, 2005, Using self-categorization theory to understand relational demography-based variations in people's responsiveness to organizational culture, *Academy of Management Journal*, 48: 321–331.

45. 2006, Characteristics of the civilian labor force, 2004 and 2014, U.S. Department of Labor, Bureau of Labor Statistics data, http://www.bls.gov, May.

46. J. Millman, 2005, Low-wage U.S. jobs get "Mexicanized," but there's a price, *Wall Street Journal*, May 2, A2.

47. A. K. Fosu, 2008, Inequality and the growth-poverty nexus: Specification empirics using African data, *Applied Economics Letters*, 15: 563–566; A. McKeown, 2007, Periodizing globalization, *History Workshop Journal*, 63(1): 218–230.

48. O. Sullivan, 2008, Busyness, status distinction and consumption strategies of the income rich, time poor, *Time & Society*, 17: 5–26.

49. 2009, Half the world is middle class???, http:///www.edwardsglobal.com, May 10.

50. D. Vrontis & P. Pavlou, 2008, *Journal for International Business and Entrepreneurship Development*, 3: 289–307; A. Jones & N. Ennis, 2007, Bringing the environment into economic development, *Local Economy*, 22(1): 1–5; Fahey & Narayanan, *Macroenvironmental Analysis*, 105.

51. P. Coy, 2009, What good are economists anyway? *BusinessWeek*, April 27, 26–31.

52. J. Simms, 2009, Losses at Japan's electronics companies are no shock, *Wall Street Journal Online*, http://www.wsj.com, February 4.

53. J. Bush, 2009, The worries facing Russia's banks, *Wall Street Journal Online*, http://www.wsj.com, April 13.

54. A. Peaple & N. P. Muoi, 2009, Vietnam's market—the fizz is deliberate, *Wall Street Journal Online*, http://www.wsj.com, June 11.

55. R. H. Lester, A. Hillman, A. Zardkoohi, & A. A. Cannella, Jr., 2008, Former government officials as outside directors: The role of human and social capital, *Academy of Management Journal*, 51; 999–1013; C. Oliver & I. Holzinger, 2008, The effectiveness of strategic political management: A dynamic capabilities framework, *Academy of Management Review*, 33: 496–520.

56. J. W. Spencer, 2008, The impact of multinational enterprise strategy on indigenous enterprises: Horizontal spillovers and crowding out in developing countries, *Academy of Management Review*, 33: 341–361; W. Chen, 2007, Does the colour of the cat matter? The red hat strategy in China's private enterprises, *Management and Organizational Review*, 3: 55–80.

57. P. Engardio, 2009, Clearing the track for high-speed rail, *BusinessWeek*, May 4, 29.

58. M. Srivastava, 2009, The sudden chill at an Indian hot spot, *BusinessWeek*, May 4, 59.

59. 2009, Taking aim at outsources on U.S. soil, *BusinessWeek*, June 15, 10.

60. H. W. Jenkins, Jr., 2009, GM needs a political strategy, *Wall Street Journal Online*, http://www.wsj.com, June 10.

61. G. L. F. Holburn & R. G. Vanden Bergh, 2008, The effectiveness of strategic political management: A dynamic capabilities framework, *Academy of Management Review*, 33: 521–540; M. A. Hitt, L. Bierman, K. Uhlenbruck, & K. Shimizu, 2006, The importance of resources in the internationalization of professional service firms: The good, the bad, and the ugly, *Academy of Management Journal*, 49: 1137–1157.

62. K. Olsen, 2009, S. Korea, EU call for early conclusion of trade pact, *Houston Chronicle Online*, http://www.chron.com, May 23.

63. L. Manchikanti, 2008, Health care reform in the United States: Radical surgery needed now more than ever, *Pain Physician*, 11: 13–42.

64. S. A. Burd, 2009, How Safeway is cutting health-care costs, *Wall Street Journal Online*, http://www.wsj.com, June 12.

65. 2009, Characteristics of the civilian labor force, U.S. Department of Labor, Bureau of Labor Statistics data, http://www.bls.gov, June.

66. E. S. W. Ng, 2008, Why organizations choose to manage diversity: Toward a leadership-based theoretical framework, *Human Resource Development Review*, 7: 58–78.

67. A. McConnon, 2009, For a temp giant, a boom in boomers, *BusinessWeek*, June 1, 54.

68. F. Moore & C. Rees, 2008, Culture against cohesion: Global corporate strategy and employee diversity in the UK plant of a German MNC, *Employee Relations*, 30: 176–189; B. L. Kirkman, K. B. Lowe, & C. B. Gibson, 2006, A quarter of a century of culture's consequences: A review of old empirical research incorporating Hofstede's cultural values framework, *Journal of International Business Studies*, 37: 285–320.

69. S. Michailova & K. Hutchings, 2006, National cultural influences on knowledge sharing: A comparison of China and Russia, *Journal of Management Studies*, 43: 384–405.

70. J. B. Knight & L. Yueh, 2008, The role of social capital in the labour market in China, *Economics of Transition*, 16: 389–414; P. J. Buckley, J. Clegg, & H. Tan, 2006, Cultural awareness in knowledge transfer to China—The role of guanxi and mianzi, *Journal of World Business*, 41: 275–288.

71. R. K. Sinha & C. H. Noble, 2008, The adoption of radical manufacturing technologies and firm survival, *Strategic Management Journal*, 29: 943–962.

72. K. H. Tsai & J.-C. Wang, 2008, External technology acquisition and firm performance: A longitudinal study, *Journal of Business Venturing*, 23: 91–112; D. Lavie, 2006, Capability reconfiguration: An analysis of incumbent responses to technological change, *Academy of Management Review*, 31: 153–174.

73. S. A. Brown, 2008, Household technology adoption, use, and impacts: Past, present, and future, *Information Systems Frontiers*, 10: 397–402.

74. W. S. Mossberg, 2009, The latest Kindle: Bigger, not better, than its sibling, *Wall Street Journal Online*, http://www.wsj.com, June 11.

75. L. F. Mesquita & S. G. Lazzarini, 2008, Horizontal and vertical relationships in developing economies: Implications for SMEs' access to global markets, *Academy of Management Journal*, 51: 359–380; W. P. Wan, 2005, Country resource environments, firm capabilities, and corporate diversification strategies,

Journal of Management Studies, 42: 161–182.

76. J. R. Healey, 2009, Penske-Saturn deal could change how cars are sold, *USA Today*, June 8, B2.

77. D. Welch, 2009, A hundred factories too many, *BusinessWeek*, January 12, 42–43.

78. 2009, McDonald's Corp, *Standard & Poor's Stock Report*, http://www .standardandpoors.com, May 16.

79. G. Marcial, 2009, Heinz: The time may be ripe, *BusinessWeek*, May 11, 67.

80. 2009, Procter & Gamble Co, *Standard & Poor's Stock Report*, http://www .standardandpoors.com, May 16.

81. K. E. Meyer, 2009, Uncommon common sense, *Business Strategy Review*, 20: 38–43; K. E. Meyer, 2006, Globalfocusing: From domestic conglomerates to global specialists, *Journal of Management Studies*, 43: 1110–1144.

82. C. H. Oh & A. M. Rugman, 2007, Regional multinationals and the Korean cosmetics industry, *Asia Pacific Journal of Management*, 24: 27–42.

83. P. K. Ong & Y. Kathawala, 2009, Competitive advantage through good Guanxi in the marine industry, *International Journal of Chinese Culture and Management*, 2: 28–55; X.-P. Chen & S. Peng, 2008, Guanxi dynamics: Shifts in the closeness of ties between Chinese coworkers, *Management and Organizational Review*, 4: 63–80; M. A. Hitt, M. T. Dacin, B. B. Tyler, & D. Park, 1997, Understanding the differences in Korean and U.S. executives' strategic orientations, *Strategic Management Journal*, 18: 159–167.

84. M. A. Hitt, D. Ahlstrom, M. T. Dacin, E. Levitas, & L. Svobodina, 2004, The institutional effects on strategic alliance partner selection: China versus Russia, *Organization Science*, 15: 173–185.

85. L. Berchicci & A. King, 2008, Postcards from the edge: A review of the business and environment literature, in J. P. Walsh & A. P. Brief (eds.) *Academy of Management Annals*, New York: Lawrence Erlbaum Associates, 513–547.

86. M. J. Hutchins & J. W. Sutherland, 2008, An exploration of measures of social sustainability and their application to supply chain decisions, *Journal of Cleaner Production*, 16: 1688–1698.

87. P. K. Dutta & R. Radner, 2009, A strategic analysis of global warming: Theory and some numbers, *Journal of Economic Behavior & Organization*, in press.

88. H. Liming, E. Haque, & S. Barg, 2008, Public policy discourse, planning and measure toward sustainable energy strategies in Canada, *Renewable and Sustainable Energy Reviews*, 12: 91–115.

89. 2009, Target Corporation, Environment, http://www.target.com, June 12.

90. C. A. Bartlett & S. Ghoshal, 2003, What is a global manager? *Harvard Business Review*, 81(8): 101–108; M. A. Carpenter & J. W. Fredrickson, 2001, Top management teams, global strategic posture and the moderating role of uncertainty, *Academy of Management Journal*, 44: 533–545.

91. J. Galbreath & P. Galvin, 2008, Firm factors, industry structure and performance variation: New empirical evidence to a classic debate, *Journal of Business Research*, 61: 109–117; B. R. Koka & J. E. Prescott, 2008, Designing alliance networks: The influence of network position, environmental change, and strategy on firm performance, *Strategic Management Journal*, 29: 639–661.

92. V. F. Misangyi, H. Elms, T. Greckhamer, & J. A. Lepine, 2006, A new perspective on a fundamental debate: A multilevel approach to industry, corporate, and business unit effects, *Strategic Management Journal*, 27: 571–590; G. Hawawini, V. Subramanian, & P. Verdin, 2003, Is performance driven by industry or firm-specific factors? A new look at the evidence, *Strategic Management Journal*, 24: 1–16.

93. D. Bonnet & G. S. Yip, 2009, Strategy convergence, *Business Strategy Review*, 20: 50–55; E. Nelson, R. van den Dam, & H. Kline, 2008, A future in content(ion): Can telecom providers win a share of the digital content market? *Journal of Telecommunications Management*, 1: 125–138.

94. K. E. Kushida & J. Zysman, 2009, The services transformation and network policy: The new logic of value creation, *Review of Policy Research*, 26: 173–194; E. D. Jaffe, I. D. Nebenzahl, & I. Schorr, 2005, Strategic options of home country firms faced with MNC entry, *Long Range Planning*, 38: 183–196.

95. M. R. Peneder, 2008, Firm entry and turnover: The nexus with profitability and growth, *Small Business Economics*, 30: 327–344; A. V. Mainkar, M. Lubatkin, & W. S. Schulze, 2006, Toward a product-proliferation theory of entry barriers, *Academy of Management Review*, 31: 1062–1075; J. Shamsie, 2003, The context of dominance: An industry-driven framework for exploiting reputation, *Strategic Management Journal*, 24: 199–215.

96. S. Hamm, 2009, Oracle faces its toughest deal yet, *BusinessWeek*, May 4, 24.

97. S. K. Ethiraj & D. H. Zhu, 2008, Performance effects of imitative entry, *Strategic Management Journal*, 29: 797–817; R. Makadok, 1999, Interfirm differences in scale economies and the evolution of market shares, *Strategic Management Journal*, 20: 935–952.

98. M. J. Rungtusanatham & F. Salvador, 2008, From mass production to mass customization: Hindrance factors, structural inertia, and transition hazard, *Production and Operations Management*, 17: 385–396; F. Salvador & C. Forza, 2007, Principles for efficient and effective sales configuration design, *International Journal of Mass Customisation*, 2(1,2): 114–127.

99. F. Keenan, S. Holmes, J. Greene, & R. O. Crockett, 2002, A mass market of one, *BusinessWeek*, December 2, 68–72.

100. D. Kiley, 2009, Ford heads out on a road of its own, *BusinessWeek*, January 19, 47–49.

101. E. Byron, 2009, P&G, Colgate hit by consumer thrift, *Wall Street Journal Online*, http://www.wsj.com, May 1.

102. M. A. Hitt, R. M. Holmes, T. Miller, & M. P. Salmador, 2006, Modeling country institutional profiles: The dimensions and dynamics of institutional environments, presented at the Strategic Management Society Conference, October.

103. P. Kiviniem, 2009, Intel to get EU antitrust fine, *Wall Street Journal Online*, http://www.wsj.com, May 14.

104. C. Forelle & D. Clark, 2009, Intel fine jolts tech sector, *Wall Street Journal Online*, http://www.wsj.com, May 14.

105. L. Ranson, 2009, United confirms aircraft order talks with Airbus and Boeing, *FlightGlobal*, http://www.flightglobal.com, April 6.

106. D. G. Sirmon, S. Gove, & M. H. Hitt, 2008, Resource management in dyadic competitive rivalry: The effects of resource bundling and deployment, *Academy of Management Journal*, 51: 919–935.

107. S. Nadkarni & V. K. Narayanan, 2007, Strategic schemas, strategic flexibility, and firm performance: The moderating role of industry clockspeed, *Strategic Management Journal*, 28: 243–270.

108. P. Prada & M. Esterl, 2009, Airlines predict more trouble, broaden cuts, *Wall Street Journal Online*, http://www.wsj.com, June 12.

109. S. E. Feinberg & A. K. Gupta, 2009, MNC subsidiaries and country risk: Internalization as a safeguard against weak external institutions, *Academy of Management Journal*, 52: 381–399.

110. M. E. Porter, 1980, *Competitive Strategy*, New York: Free Press.

111. B. Kabanoff & S. Brown, 2008, Knowledge structures of prospectors, analyzers, and defenders: Content, structure, stability, and performance, *Strategic Management Journal*, 29: 149–171; M. S. Hunt, 1972, Competition in the major home appliance industry, 1960–1970 (doctoral dissertation, Harvard University); Porter, *Competitive Strategy*, 129.

112. G. McNamara, D. L. Deephouse, & R. A. Luce, 2003, Competitive positioning within and across a strategic group structure: The performance of core, secondary, and solitary firms, *Strategic Management Journal*, 24: 161–181.

113. F. Zen & C. Baldan, 2008, The strategic paths and performance of Italian mutual banks: A nonparametric analysis, *International Journal of Banking, Accounting and Finance*, 1: 189–214; M. W. Peng, J. Tan, & T. W. Tong, 2004, Ownership types and strategic groups in an emerging economy, *Journal of Management Studies*, 41: 1105–1129.

114. W. S. DeSarbo & R. Grewal, 2008. Hybrid strategic groups, *Strategic Management Journal*, 29: 293–317; M. Peteraf & M. Shanley, 1997, Getting to know you:

A theory of strategic group identity, *Strategic Management Journal*, 18(Special Issue): 165–186.

115. J. Lee, K. Lee, & S. Rho, 2002, An evolutionary perspective on strategic group emergence: A genetic algorithm-based model, *Strategic Management Journal*, 23: 727–746.

116. J. A. Zuniga-Vicente, J. M. de la Fuente Sabate, & I. S. Gonzalez, 2004, Dynamics of the strategic group membership-performance linkage in rapidly changing environments, *Journal of Business Research*, 57: 1378–1390.

117. T. Yu, M. Subramaniam, & A. A. Cannella, Jr., 2009, Rivalry deterrence in international markets: Contingencies governing the mutual forbearance hypothesis, *Academy of Management Journal*, 52: 127–147.

118. Porter, *Competitive Strategy*, 49.

119. L. Capron & O. Chatain, 2008, Competitors' resource-oriented strategies: Acting on competitors' resources through interventions in factor markets and political markets, *Academy of Management Review*, 33: 97–121; M. B. Lieberman & S. Asaba, 2006, Why do firms imitate each other? *Academy of Management Journal*, 31: 366–385.

120. D. B. Montgomery, M. C. Moore, & J. E. Urbany, 2005, Reasoning about competitive reactions: Evidence from executives, *Marketing Science*, 24: 138–149.

121. S. Jain, 2008, Digital piracy: A competitive analysis, *Marketing Science*, 27: 610–626.

122. J. G. York, 2009, Pragmatic sustainability: Translating environmental ethics into competitive advantage, *Journal of Business Ethics*, 85: 97–109.

123. K. A. Sawka, 2008, The ethics of competitive intelligence, *Kiplinger Business Resource Center Online*, http://www.kiplinger.com, March.

124. T. Mazzarol & S. Reboud, 2008, The role of complementary actors in the development of innovation in small firms, *International Journal of Innovation Management*, 12: 223–253; A. Brandenburger & B. Nalebuff, 1996, *Co-opetition*, New York: Currency Doubleday.

125. 2009, Continental to join Star alliance, *Continental Airlines Homepage*, http://www.continental.com, June 12.

126. 2009, ING Profile and fast facts, http://www.ing.com, June 12.

127. C. S. Fleisher & S. Wright, 2009, Examining differences in competitive intelligence practice: China, Japan, and the West, *Thunderbird International Business Review*, 51: 249–261; A. Crane, 2005, In the company of spies: When competitive intelligence gathering becomes industrial espionage, Business Horizons, 48(3): 233–240.

Chapter 3

1. M. E. Mangelsdorf, 2007, Beyond enterprise 2.0, *MIT Sloan Management Review*, 48(3): 50–55.

2. J. G. Covin & M. P. Miles, 2007, Strategic use of corporate venturing, *Entrepreneurship Theory and Practice*, 31: 183–207; R. R. Wiggins & T. W. Ruefli, 2002, Sustained competitive advantage: Temporal dynamics and the incidence of persistence of superior economic performance, *Organization Science*, 13: 82–105.

3. W. M. Becker & V. M. Freeman, 2006, Going from global trends to corporate strategy, *McKinsey Quarterly*, Number 3:17–27; S. K. McEvily, K. M. Eisenhardt, & J. E. Prescott, 2004, The global acquisition, leverage, and protection of technological competencies, *Strategic Management Journal*, 25: 713–722.

4. J. Schenck & N. Wingfield, 2008, How Apple could survive without Steve Jobs, *Wall Street Journal*, http://www.wsj.com, December 8.

5. R. T. Crook, D. J. Ketchen, J. G. Combs, & S. Y. Todd, 2008, Strategic resources and performance: A meta-analysis, *Strategic Management Journal*, 29: 1141–1154; N. T. Sheehan & N. J. Foss, 2007, Enhancing the prescriptiveness of the resource-based view through Porterian activity analysis, *Management Decision*, 45: 450-461; S. Dutta, M. J. Zbaracki, & M. Bergen, 2003, Pricing process as a capability: A resource-based perspective, *Strategic Management Journal*, 24: 615–630.

6. C. G. Brush, P. G. Greene, & M. M. Hart, 2001, From initial idea to unique advantage: The entrepreneurial challenge of constructing a resource base, *Academy of Management Executive*, 15(1): 64–78.

7. L. Priem, 2007, A consumer perspective on value creation, *Academy of Management Review*, 32: 219–235.

8. D. G. Sirmon, M. A. Hitt, & R. D. Ireland, 2007, Managing firm resources in dynamic markets to create value: Looking inside the black box, *Academy of Management Review*, 32: 273–292.

9. A. Leiponen, 2008, Control of intellectual assets in client relationships: Implications for innovation, *Strategic Management Journal*, 29: 1371–1394; S. C. Kang, S. S. Morris, & S. A. Snell, 2007, Relational archetypes, organizational learning, and value creation: Extending the human resource architecture, *Academy of Management Review*, 32: 236–256.

10. S. Raisch & G. von Krog, 2007, Navigating a path to smart growth, MIT *Sloan Management Review*, 48(3): 65–72.

11. D. DePass, 2006, Cuts in incentives upset 3M supervisors, *Star Tribune*, December 16.

12. C. D. Zatzick & R. D. Iverson, 2007, High-involvement management and work force reduction: Competitive advantage or disadvantage? *Academy of Management Journal*, 49: 999–1015.

13. R. Florida, 2005, *The Flight of the Creative Class*, New York: HarperBusiness.

14. A. W. King, 2007, Disentangling interfirm and intrafirm causal ambiguity: A conceptual model of causal ambiguity and sustainable competitive advantage, *Academy of Management Review*, 32: 156–178; J. Shamsie, 2003, The context of dominance: An industry-driven framework for exploiting reputation, *Strategic Management Journal*, 24: 199–215.

15. U. Ljungquist, 2007, Core competency beyond identification: Presentation of a model, *Management Decision*, 45: 393–402; M. Makhija, 2003, Comparing the resource-based and market-based view of the firm: Empirical evidence from Czech privatization, *Strategic Management Journal*, 24: 433–451.

16. R. D. Ireland & J. W. Webb, 2007, Strategic entrepreneurship: Creating competitive advantage through streams of innovation, *Business Horizons*, 50: 49–59.

17. M. A. Peteraf & J. B. Barney, 2003, Unraveling the resource-based tangle, *Managerial and Decision Economics*, 24: 309–323; J. B. Barney, 2001, Is the resource-based "view" a useful perspective for strategic management research? Yes, *Academy of Management Review*, 26: 41–56.

18. D. P. Lepak, K. G. Smith, & M. Susan Taylor, 2007, Value creation and value capture: A multilevel perspective, *Academy of Management Review*, 32: 180–194.

19. T. Papot, 2009, Slovakia's headache as car sales fall, Radio Netherlands Worldwide, http://www.radionetherlands.nl, March 5; Z. Vilikovska, 2008, Slovak factories manufactured around 770,000 cars in 2008, Flash News, http://www.spector.sk; G. Katz. 2007, Assembling a future, *Houston Chronicle*, July 5, D1, D4.

20. M. Javidan, R. M. Steers, & M. A. Hitt (eds.), 2007, *The Global Mindset*, Amsterdam: Elsevier Ltd; T. M. Begley & D. P. Boyd, 2003, The need for a corporate global mindset, MIT *Sloan Management Review*, 44(2): 25–32.

21. L. Gratton, 2007, Handling hot spots, *Business Strategy Review*, 18(2): 9–14.

22. O. Levy, S. Beechler, S. Taylor, & N. A. Boyacigiller, 2007, What we talk about when we talk about "global

mindset": Managerial cognition in multinational corporations, *Journal of International Business Studies*, 38: 231–258.

23. Sirmon, Hitt, & Ireland, Managing resources in a dynamic environment.

24. E. Danneels, 2008, Organizational antecedents of second-order competences, *Strategic Management Journal*, 29: 519–543; Barney, Is the resource-based "view" a useful perspective for strategic management research? Yes.

25. S. Kaplan, 2008, Cognition, capabilities, and incentives: Assessing firm response to the fiber-optic revolution, *Academy of Management Journal*, 51: 672–695; K. J. Mayer & R. M. Salomon, 2006, Capabilities, contractual hazards, and governance: Integrating resource-based and transaction cost perspectives, *Academy of Management Journal*, 49: 942–959.

26. S. K. McEvily & B. Chakravarthy, 2002, The persistence of knowledge-based advantage: An empirical test for product performance and technological knowledge, *Strategic Management Journal*, 23: 285–305.

27. D. Kaplan, 2007, A new look for Luby's, *Houston Chronicle*, July 4, D1, D5.

28. J. Barthelemy, 2008, Opportunism, knowledge, and the performance of franchise chains, *Strategic Management Journal*, 29: 1451–1463; J. L. Morrow, Jr., D. G. Sirmon, M. A. Hitt, & T. R. Holcomb, 2007, Creating value in the face of declining performance: Firm strategies and organizational recovery, *Strategic Management Journal*, 28: 271–283.

29. D. G. Sirmon, S. Gove, & M. A. Hitt, 2008, Resource management in dyadic competitive rivalry: The effects of resource bundling and deployment, *Academy of Management Journal*, 51: 919–935; E. Danneels, 2007, The process of technological competence leveraging, *Strategic Management Journal*, 28: 511–533.

30. Putting co-creation to work for you: Build more value by co-creating with your customers, 2009, Internetviz, http://www.internetviz-newsletters.com. J. J. Neff, 2007, What drives consumers not to buy cars, *BusinessWeek*, July 9, 16.

31. K. Chaharbaghi, 2007, The problematic of strategy: A way of seeing is also a way of not seeing, *Management Decision*, 45: 327–339.

32. V. Shankar & B. L. Bayus, 2003, Network effects and competition: An empirical analysis of the home video game industry, *Strategic Management Journal*, 24: 375–384.

33. Morrow, Sirmon, Hitt, & Holcomb, Creating value in the face of declining performance; G. Hawawini, V. Subramanian, & P. Verdin, 2003, Is performance driven by industry- or firm-specific factors? A new look at the evidence, *Strategic Management Journal*, 24: 1–16.

34. J. Woiceshyn & L. Falkenberg, 2008, Value creation in knowledge-based firms: Aligning problems and resources, *Academy of Management Perspectives*, 22 (2): 85–99; M. R. Haas & M. T. Hansen, 2005, When using knowledge can hurt performance: The value of organizational capabilities in a management consulting company, *Strategic Management Journal*, 26: 1–24.

35. C. M. Christensen, 2001, The past and future of competitive advantage, *Sloan Management Review*, 42(2): 105–109.

36. O. Gottschalg & M. Zollo, 2007, Interest alignment and competitive advantage, *Academy of Management Review*. 32: 418–437.

37. D. P. Forbes, 2007, Reconsidering the strategic implications of decision comprehensiveness, *Academy of Management Review*, 32: 361–376; J. R. Hough & M. A. White, 2003, Environmental dynamism and strategic decision-making rationality: An examination at the decision level, *Strategic Management Journal*, 24: 481–489.

38. T. M. Jones, W. Felps, & G. A. Bigley, 2007, Ethical theory and stakeholder-related decisions: The role of stakeholder culture, *Academy of Management Review*, 32: 137–155; D. C. Kayes, D. Stirling, & T. M. Nielsen, 2007, Building organizational integrity, *Business Horizons*, 50: 61–70.

39. Y. Deutsch, T. Keil, & T. Laamanen, 2007, Decision making in acquisitions: The effect of outside directors' compensation on acquisition patterns, *Journal of Management*. 33: 30–56.

40. M. De Rond & R. A. Thietart, 2007, Choice, chance, and inevitability in strategy, *Strategic Management Journal*, 28: 535–551.

41. A. Phene & P. Almieda, 2008, Innovation in multinational subsidiaries: The role of knowledge assimilation and subsidiary capabilities, *Journal of International Business Studies*, 39: 901–919; C. C. Miller & R. D. Ireland, 2005, Intuition in strategic decision making: Friend or foe in the fast-paced 21st century? *Academy of Management Executive*, 19(1): 19–30.

42. L. M. Lodish & C. F. Mela, 2007, If brands are built over years, why are they managed over quarters? *Harvard Business Review*, 85(7/8): 104–112; H. J. Smith, 2003, The shareholders vs. stakeholders debate, MIT *Sloan Management Review*, 44(4): 85–90.

43. P. C. Nutt, 2002. *Why Decisions Fail*, San Francisco: Berrett-Koehler Publishers.

44. R. Martin, 2007. How successful leaders think, *Harvard Business Review*, 85(6): 61–67.

45. Polaroid Corporation, 2007, Wikipedia, http://en.wikipedia.org/wiki/Polaroid_Corporation, July 5.

46. 46. J. M. Mezias & W. H. Starbuck, 2003, What do managers know, anyway? *Harvard Business Review*, 81 (5): 16–17.

47. I. Mitroff, 2008, Knowing: How we know is as important as what we know, *Journal of Business Strategy*, 29 (3): 13–22;

P. G. Audia, E. Locke, & K. G. Smith, 2000, The paradox of success: An archival and a laboratory study of strategic persistence following radical environmental change, *Academy of Management Journal*, 43: 837–853.

48. C. O. Longenecker, M. J. Neubert, & L. S. Fink, 2007, Causes and consequences of managerial failure in rapidly changing organizations, *Business Horizons*, 50:145–155; G. P. West III & J. DeCastro, 2001, The Achilles' heel of firm strategy: Resource weaknesses and distinctive inadequacies, *Journal of Management Studies*, 38: 417–442; G. Gavetti & D. Levinthal, 2000, Looking forward and looking backward: Cognitive and experimental search, *Administrative Science Quarterly*, 45: 113–137.

49. R. Amit & P. J. H. Schoemaker, 1993, Strategic assets and organizational rent, *Strategic Management Journal*, 14: 33–46.

50. S. J. Carson, A. Madhok, & T. Wu, 2006, Uncertainty, opportunism, and governance: The effects of volatility and ambiguity on formal and relational contracting, *Academy of Management Journal*. 49: 1058–1077; R. E. Hoskisson & L. W. Busenitz, 2001, Market uncertainty and learning distance in corporate entrepreneurship entry mode choice, in M. A. Hitt, R. D. Ireland, S. M. Camp, & D. L. Sexton (eds.), *Strategic Entrepreneurship: Creating a New Integrated Mindset*, Oxford, UK: Blackwell Publishers, 151–172.

51. C. M. Fiol & E. J. O'Connor, 2003, Waking up! Mindfulness in the face of bandwagons, *Academy of Management Review*. 28: 54–70.

52. P. Davidson, Coal king Peabody cleans up, *USA Today*, http://www.usatoday.com, August 18; J. Pasternak, 2008, Global warming has a new battleground: Coal plants, *Chicago Tribune*, http://www.chicagotribune.com, April 14.

53. G. P. West, III, 2007, Collective cognition: When entrepreneurial teams, not individuals, make decisions, *Entrepreneurship Theory and Practice*, 31: 77–102.

54. N. J. Hiller & D. C. Hambrick, 2005, Conceptualizing executive hubris: The role of (hyper-) core self-evaluations in strategic decision making, *Strategic Management Journal*, 26: 297–319.

55. C. Stadler, 2007, The four principles of enduring success, *Harvard Business Review*, 85(7/8): 62–72.

56. Mayer & Salomon, Capabilities, contractual hazards, and governance; D. M. De Carolis, 2003, Competencies and imitability in the pharmaceutical industry: An analysis of their relationship with firm performance, *Journal of Management*, 29: 27–50.

57. R. H. Lester, A. Hillman, A. Zardkoohi, & A. A. Cannella, 2008, Former government officials as outside directors: The role of human and social capital, *Academy of Management Journal*, 51: 999–1013; G. Ahuja & R. Katila, 2004, Where do resources come from? The role

of idiosyncratic situations, *Strategic Management Journal*, 25: 887–907.

58. K. Meyer, S. Estrin, S. K. Bhaumik, & M. W. Peng, 2009, Institutions, resources, and entry strategies in emerging economies, *Strategic Management Journal*, 30: 61–80; J. McGee & H. Thomas, 2007, Knowledge as a lens on the jigsaw puzzle of strategy, *Management Decision*, 45: 539–563.

59. Sirmon, Hitt, & Ireland, Managing firm resources in dynamic environments; S. Berman, J. Down, & C. Hill, 2002, Tacit knowledge as a source of competitive advantage in the National Basketball Association, *Academy of Management Journal*, 45: 13–31.

60. 2007, Borders teamed with Amazon.com, http://www.amazon.com, July 7.

61. K. G. Smith, C. J. Collins, & K. D. Clark, 2005, Existing knowledge, knowledge creation capability, and the rate of new product introduction in high-technology firms, *Academy of Management Journal*, 48: 346–357; S. G, Winter, 2005, Developing evolutionary theory for economics and management, in K. G. Smith and M. A. Hitt (eds.), *Great Minds in Management: The Process of Theory Development*, Oxford, UK: Oxford University Press, 509–546.

62. J. A. Dubin, 2007, Valuing intangible assets with a nested logit market share model, *Journal of Econometrics*, 139: 285–302.

63. A. M. Webber, 2000, New math for a new economy, *Fast Company*, January/February, 214–224.

64. F. T. Rothaermel & W. Boeker, 2008, Old technology meets new technology: Complementarities, similarities, and alliance formation, *Strategic Management Journal*, 29: 47–77; M. Song, C. Droge, S. Hanvanich, & R. Calantone, 2005, Marketing and technology resource complementarity: An analysis of their interaction effect in two environmental contexts, *Strategic Management Journal*, 26: 259–276.

65. M. A. Hitt & R. D. Ireland, 2002, The essence of strategic leadership: Managing human and social capital, *Journal of Leadership and Organization Studies*, 9(1): 3–14.

66. J. B. Quinn, P. Anderson, & S. Finkelstein, 1996, Making the most of the best, *Harvard Business Review*, 74(2): 71–80.

67. N. Stieglitz & K. Heine, 2007, Innovations and the role of complementarities in a strategic theory of the firm, *Strategic Management Journal*, 28: 1–15.

68. S. A. Fernhaber, B. A. Gilbert, & P. P. McDougal, 2008, International entrepreneurship and geographic location: An empirical examination of new venture internationalization, *Journal of International Business Studies*, 39: 267–290; R. D. Ireland, M. A. Hitt, & D. Vaidyanath, 2002, Managing strategic alliances to achieve a competitive advantage, *Journal of Management*, 28: 416–446.

69. E. Fischer & R. Reuber, 2007, The good, the bad, and the unfamiliar: The challenges of reputation formation facing new firms, *Entrepreneurship Theory and Practice*, 31: 53–75.

70. D. L. Deephouse, 2000. Media reputation as a strategic resource: An integration of mass communication and resource-based theories, *Journal of Management*, 26: 1091–1112.

71. P. Engardio & M. Arndt, 2007, What price reputation? *BusinessWeek*, July 9, 70–79.

72. P. Berthon, M. B. Holbrook, & J. M. Hulbert, 2003, Understanding and managing the brand space, *MIT Sloan Management Review*, 44(2): 49–54; D. B. Holt, 2003, What becomes an icon most? *Harvard Business Review*, 81(3): 43–49.

73. J. Song & J. Shin, 2008, The paradox of technological capabilities: A study of knowledge sourcing from host countries of overseas R&D operations, *Journal of International Business Studies*, 39: 291–303; J. Blasberg & V. Vishwanath, 2003, Making cool brands hot, *Harvard Business Review*, 81(6): 20–22.

74. 2007, Harley-Davidson Motor Clothes Merchandise, July 7, http://www.harley-davidson.com.

75. S. Kalepu, 2009, Ford names Sunil Shetty as its brand ambassador, *CaretradeIndia*, http://www.cartradeindia.com, January 22.

76. T. Isobe, S. Makino, & D. B. Montgomery, 2008, Technological capabilities and firm performance: The case of small manufacturing firms in Japan, *Asia Pacific Journal of Management*, 25: 413–425; S. Dutta, O. Narasimhan, & S. Rajiv, 2005, Conceptualizing and measuring capabilities: Methodology and empirical application, *Strategic Management Journal*, 26: 277–285.

77. M. Kroll, B. A. Walters, & P. Wright, 2008, Board vigilance, director experience and corporate outcomes, *Strategic Management Journal*, 29: 363–282; J. Bitar & T. Hafsi, 2007, Strategizing through the capability lens: Sources and outcomes of integration, *Management Decision*, 45: 403–419.

78. S. K. Ethiraj, P. Kale, M. S. Krishnan, & J. V. Singh, 2005, Where do capabilities come from and do they matter? A study in the software services industry, *Strategic Management Journal*, 26: 25–45; M. G. Jacobides & S. G. Winter, 2005, The co-evolution of capabilities and transaction costs: Explaining the institutional structure of production, *Strategic Management Journal*, 26: 395–413.

79. T. A. Stewart & A. P. Raman, 2007, Lessons from Toyota's long drive, *Harvard Business Review*, 85(7/8): 74–83.

80. Y. Uu, J. G. Combs, D. J. Ketchen, Jr., & R. D. Ireland, 2007, The value of human resource management for organizational performance, *Business Horizons*, 50: 503–511.

81. B. Connelly, M. A. Hitt, A. S. DeNisi, & R. D. Ireland, 2007, Expatriates and corporate-level international strategy: Governing with the knowledge contract, *Management Decision*, 45: 564–581.

82. M. J. Tippins & R. S. Sohi, 2003, IT competency and firm performance: Is organizational learning a missing link? *Strategic Management Journal*, 24: 745–761.

83. M. B. Neeley & R. Jacobson, 2008, The recency of technological inputs and financial performance, *Strategic Management Journal*, 29: 723–744.

84. 84. Meyer, Estrin, Bhaumik, & Peng, Institutions, resources, and entry strategies in emerging markets; C. Zott, 2003, Dynamic capabilities and the emergence of intraindustry differential firm performance: Insights from a simulation study, *Strategic Management Journal*, 24:97–125.

85. H. R. Greve, 2009, Bigger and safer: The diffusion of competitive advantage, *Strategic Management Journal*, 30: 1–23; C. K. Prahalad & G. Hamel, 1990, The core competence of the corporation, *Harvard Business Review*, 68(3): 79–93.

86. D. Bidleman, 2009, Xerox innovation shines through industry recognition, *YAHOO!Finance*, http://finance.yahoo.com, January 26.

87. D. K. Taft, 2009, Microsoft, Xerox invest in innovation, *eWeek*, http://www.eweek.com, March 5; 2006, Xerox Annual Report, December, http://www.xerox.com.

88. S. Newbert, 2008, Value, rareness, competitive advantage, and performance: A conceptual-level empirical investigation of the resource-based view of the firm, *Strategic Management Journal*, 29: 745–768.

89. D. Seidman, 2008, Out-greening delivers sustainable competitive advantage, *BusinessWeek*, http://www.businessweek.com, December 5.

90. S. A. Zahra, 2008, The virtuous cycle of discovery and creation of entrepreneurial opportunities, *Strategic Entrepreneurship Journal*, 2: 243–257; J. B. Barney, 1995, Looking inside for competitive advantage, *Academy of Management Executive*, 9(4): 49–60.

91. G. Pacheco-de-Almeida, J. E. Henderson, & K. O. Cool, 2008, Resolving the commitment versus flexibility trade-off: The role of resource accumulation lags, *Academy of Management Journal*, 51: 517–536.

92. J. B. Barney, 1991, Firm resources and sustained competitive advantage, *Journal of Management*, 17: 99–120.

93. L. E. Tetrick & N. Da Silva, 2003, Assessing the culture and climate for organizational learning, in S. E. Jackson, M. A. Hitt, & A. S. DeNisi (eds.), *Managing Knowledge for Sustained Competitive Advantage*, San Francisco: Jossey-Bass, 333–359.

94. K. Stinebaker, 2007, Global company puts focus on people, *Houston Chronicle Online*, http://www.chron.com, February 18.

95. A. W. King & C. P. Zeithaml, 2001, Competencies and firm performance: Examining the causal ambiguity paradox, *Strategic Management Journal*, 22: 75–99.

96. Barney, Firm resources, 111.

97. A. K. Chatterjee, 2009, Spawned with a silver spoon? Entrepreneurial performance and innovation in the medical device

industry, *Strategic Management Journal*, 30: 185–206; S. K. McEvily, S. Das, & K. McCabe, 2000, Avoiding competence substitution through knowledge sharing, *Academy of Management Review*, 25: 294–311.

98. D. J. Ketchen, Jr., & G. T. M. Hult, 2007, Bridging organization theory and supply chain management: The case of best value supply chains, *Journal of Operations Management*, 25: 573–580.

99. M. E. Porter, 1985, *Competitive Advantage*, New York: Free Press, 33–61.

100. J. Alcacer, 2006, Location choices across the value chain: How activity and capability influence co-location, *Management Science*, 52: 1457–1471.

101. H. U. Lee & J.-H. Park, 2008, The influence of top management team international exposure on international alliance formation, *Journal of Management Studies*, 45: 961–981; 2007, Riding the global value chain, *Chief Executive Online*, January/February, http://www.chiefexecutive.net.

102. R. Locke & M. Romis, 2007, Global supply chain, MIT *Sloan Management Review*, 48(2): 54–62.

103. R. Amit & C. Zott, 2001, Value creation in e-business, *Strategic Management Journal*, 22 (Special Issue): 493–520; M. E. Porter, 2001, Strategy and the Internet, *Harvard Business Review*, 79(3): 62–78.

104. C. L. Luk, O. H. M. Yau, L. Y. M. Sin, A. C. B. Tse, R. P. M. Chow, & J. S. Y. Lee, 2008, The effects of social capital and organizational innovativeness in different institutional contexts, *Journal of International Business Studies*, 39: 589–612.

105. L .F. Mesquita, J. Anand, & T. H. Brush, 2008, Comparing the resource-based and relational views: Knowledge transfer and spillover in vertical alliances, *Strategic Management Journal*, 29: 913–941; A. Azadegan, K. J. Dooley, P. L. Carter, & J .R. Carter, 2008, Supplier innovativeness and the role of interorganizational learning in enhancing manufacturer capabilities, *Journal of Supply Chain Management*, 44(4): 14–35.

106. A. A. Lado, R. R. Dant, & A. G. Tekleab, 2008, Trust-opportunism paradox, relationalism, and performance in interfirm relationships: Evidence from the retail industry, *Strategic Management Journal*, 29: 401–423; S. N. Wasti & S. A. Wasti, 2008, Trust in buyer-supplier relations: The case of the Turkish automotive industry, *Journal of International Business Studies*, 39:118–131.

107. D. Faems, M. Janssens, A. Madhok, & B. Van Looy, 2008, Toward an integrative perspective on alliance governance: Connecting contract design, trust dynamics and contract application, *Academy of Management Review*, 51:1053–1078.

108. M. J. Power, K. C. DeSouze, & C. Bonifazi, 2006, *The Outsourcing Handbook: How to Implement a Successful Outsourcing Process*, Philadelphia: Kogan Page.

109. P. W. Tam, 2007, Business technology: Outsourcing finds new niche, *Wall Street Journal*, April 17, B5.

110. S. Nambisan & M. Sawhney, 2007, A buyer's guide to the innovation bazaar, *Harvard Business Review*, 85(6): 109–118.

111. Y. Shi, 2007, Today's solution and tomorrow's problem: The business process outsourcing risk management puzzle, *California Management Review*, 49(3): 27–44.

112. C. C. De Fontenay & J. S. Gans, 2008, A bargaining perspective on strategic outsourcing and supply competition, *Strategic Management Journal*, 29: 819–839; A. Tiwana & M. Keil, 2007, Does peripheral knowledge complement control? An empirical test in technology outsourcing alliances, *Strategic Management Journal*, 28: 623–634.

113. A. Tiwana, 2008, Does interfirm modularity complement ignorance? A field study of software outsourcing alliances, *Strategic Management Journal*, 29: 1241–1252; J. C. Linder, S. Jarvenpaa, & T. H. Davenport, 2003, Toward an innovation sourcing strategy, MIT *Sloan Management Review*, 44(41): 43–49.

114. S. Lohr, 2007, At IBM, a smarter way to outsource, *New York Times Online*, July 5, http://nytimes.com.

115. C. Horng & W. Chen, 2008, From contract manufacturing to own brand management: The role of learning and cultural heritage identity, *Management and Organization Review*, 4: 109–133; M. Useem & J. Harder, 2000, Leading laterally in company outsourcing, *Sloan Management Review*, 41(2): 25–36.

116. R. C. Insinga & M. J. Werle, 2000, Linking outsourcing to business strategy, *Academy of Management Executive*, 14(41): 58–70.

117. B. Arrunada & X. H. Vazquez, 2006, When your contract manufacturer becomes your competitor, *Harvard Business Review*, 84(9): 135–144.

118. C. S. Katsikeas, D. Skarmeas, & D. C. Bello, 2009, Developing successful trust-based international exchange relationships, *Journal of International Business Studies*, 40: 132–155; E. Perez &

J. Karp, 2007, U.S. to probe outsourcing after ITT case, *Wall Street Journal* (Eastern Edition), March 28, A3, A6.

119. C. Weigelt & M. B. Sarkar, 2009, Learning from supply-side agents: The impact of technology solution providers' experiential diversity on clients' innovation adoption, 52: 37–60; M. J. Mol, P. Pauwels, P. Matthyssens, & L. Quintens, 2004, A technological contingency perspective on the depth and scope of international outsourcing, *Journal of International Management*, 10: 287–305.

120. K. Couke & L. Sleuwaegen, 2008, Offshoring as a survival strategy: Evidence from manufacturing firms in Belgium, *Journal of International Business Studies*, 39: 1261–1277.

121. N. Heath, 2009, Outsourcing: The new hot spots, *BusinessWeek*, http://www.businessweek.com, February 20.

122. S. Hamm, 2009, IBM: Outsourcing at home, *BusinessWeek*, http://www.businessweek.com, January 16.

123. M. H. Safizadeh, J. M. Field, & L. P. Ritzman, 2008, Sourcing practices and boundaries of the firm in the financial services industry, *Strategic Management Journal*, 29: 79–91; M. A. Hitt, D. Ahlstrom, M. T. Dacin, E. Levitas, & L. Svobodina, 2004, The institutional effects on strategic alliance partner selection in transition economies: China versus Russia, *Organization Science*, 15: 173–185.

124. T. Felin & W. S. Hesterly, 2007, The knowledge-based view, nested heterogeneity, and new value creation: Philosophical considerations on the locus of knowledge, *Academy of Management Review*, 32: 195–218; Y. Mishina, T. G. Pollock, & J. F. Porac, 2004, Are more resources always better for growth? Resource stickiness in market and product expansion, *Strategic Management Journal*, 25: 1179–1197.

125. M. Gibbert, M. Hoegl, & L. Valikangas, 2007, In praise of resource constraints, *MIT Sloan Management Review*, 48(3): 15–17. 126; D. S. Elenkov & I. M. Manev, 2005, Top management leadership and influence in innovation: The role of sociocultural context, *Journal of Management*, 31: 381–402.

126. D. Kiley, 2007, The new heat on Ford, *BusinessWeek*, June 4, 32–37.

127. D. Welch, 2007, Staying paranoid at Toyota, *BusinessWeek*, July 2, 80–82.

128. L. Barton, Wellsprings of knowledge, 30–31.

Chapter 4

1. D. J. Collis & M. G. Rukstad, 2008, Can you say what your strategy is? *Harvard Business Review*, 86(4): 82–90.

2. H. Greve, 2009, Bigger and safer: The diffusion of competitive advantage, *Strategic Management Journal*, 30: 1–23.

3. M. A. Delmas & M. W. Toffel, 2008, Organizational responses to environmental demands: Opening the black box, *Strategic Management Journal*, 29: 1027–1055; S. Elbanna & J. Child, 2007, The influence of decision,

environmental and firm characteristics on the rationality of strategic decision-making, *Journal of Management Studies*, 44: 561–591; T. Yu & A. A. Cannella, Jr., 2007, Rivalry between multinational enterprises: An event history approach,

Notes

Academy of Management Journal, 50: 665–686.

4. S. L. Newbert, 2008, Value, rareness, competitive advantage, and performance: A conceptual-level empirical investigation of the resource-based view of the firm, *Strategic Management Journal*, 29: 745–768.

5. M. V. Copeland, 2009, Dell's bread-and-butter puts it in a jam, *CNNMoney.com*, http://www.cnnmoney.com, February 27.

6. N. A. Morgan & L. L. Rego, 2009, Brand portfolio strategy and firm performance, *Journal of Marketing*, 73: 59–74; C. Zott & R. Amit, 2008, The fit between product market strategy and business model: Implications for firm performance, *Strategic Management Journal*, 29: 1–26.

7. S. Kaplan, 2008, Framing contests: Strategy making under uncertainty, *Organization Science*, 19: 729–752.

8. S. Maxfield, 2008, Reconciling corporate citizenship and competitive strategy: Insights from economic theory, *Journal of Business Ethics*, 80: 367–377; K. Shimizu & M. A. Hitt, 2004, Strategic flexibility: Organizational preparedness to reverse ineffective strategic decisions, *Academy of Management Executive*, 18(4): 44–59.

9. B. Chakravarthy & P. Lorange, 2008, Driving renewal: The entrepreneur-manager, *Journal of Business Strategy*, 29: 14–21.

10. R. Oriani & M. Sobrero, 2008, Uncertainty and the market valuation of R&D within a real options logic, *Strategic Management Journal*, 29: 343–361.

11. J. A. Lamberg, H. Tikkanen, T. Nokelainen, & H. Suur-Inkeroinen, 2009, Competitive dynamics, strategic consistency, and organizational survival, *Strategic Management Journal*, 30: 45–60; R. D. Ireland & C. C. Miller, 2005, Decision-making and firm success, *Academy of Management Executive*, 18(4): 8–12.

12. I. Goll, N. B. Johnson, & A. A. Rasheed, 2008, Top management team demographic characteristics, business strategy, and firm performance in the US airline industry: The role of managerial discretion, *Management Decision*, 46: 201–222; J. R. Hough, 2006, Business segment performance redux: A multilevel approach, *Strategic Management Journal*, 27: 45–61.

13. P. Ozcan & K. M. Eisenhardt, 2009, Origin of alliance portfolios: Entrepreneurs, network strategies, and firm performance, *Academy of Management Journal*, 52: 246–279; B. Choi, S. K. Poon, & J. G. Davis, 2008, Effects of knowledge management strategy on organizational performance: A complementarity theory-based approach, *Omega*, 36: 235–251.

14. J. W. Spencer, 2008, The impact of multinational enterprise strategy on indigenous enterprises: Horizontal spill-overs and crowding out in developing countries, *Academy of Management Review*, 33: 341–361.

15. E. Steel, 2009, MySpace slashes jobs as growth slows down, *Wall Street Journal Online*, http://www.wsj.com, June 17.

16. R. Grover, 2009, Van Natta cuts jobs at MySpace, *Wall Street Journal Online*, http://www.wsj.com, June 16.

17. B. Einhorn & M. Srivastava, 2009, Social networking: Facebook looks to India, *Wall Street Journal Online*, http://www.wsj.com, June 15.

18. D. Lei & J. W. Slocum, 2009, The tipping points of business strategy: The rise and decline of competitiveness, *Organizational Dynamics*, 38: 131–147.

19. R. J. Harrington & A. K. Tjan, 2008, Transforming strategy one customer at a time, *Harvard Business Review*, 86(3): 62–72; R. Priem, 2007, A consumer perspective on value creation, *Academy of Management Review*, 32: 219–235.

20. M. E. Porter, 1980, *Competitive Strategy*, New York: Free Press.

21. M. Baghai, S. Smit, & P. Viguerie, 2009, Is your growth strategy flying blind? *Harvard Business Review*, 87(5): 86–96.

22. D. G. Sirmon, S. Gove, & M. A. Hitt, 2008, Resource management in dyadic competitive rivalry: The effects of resource bundling and deployment, *Academy of Management Journal*, 51: 919–935; D. G. Sirmon, M. A. Hitt, & R. D. Ireland, 2007, Managing firm resources in dynamic environments to create value: Inside the black box, *Academy of Management Review*, 32: 273–292.

23. A. Wetergins & R. Boschma, 2009, Does spatial proximity to customers matter for innovative performance? Evidence from the Dutch software sector, *Research Policy*, 38: 746–755.

24. J. McGregor, 2009, When service means survival, *BusinessWeek*, March 2: 26–33.

25. 2009, Company information, http://www.harrahs.com, June 17.

26. Y. Liu & R. Yang, 2009, Competing loyalty programs: Impact of market saturation, market share, and category expandability, *Journal of Marketing*, 73: 93–108; P. R. Berthon, L. F. Pitt, I. McCarthy, & S. M. Kates, 2007, When customers get clever: Managerial approaches to dealing with creative customers, *Business Horizons*, 50(1): 39–47.

27. P. E. Frown & A. F. Payne, 2009, Customer relationship management: A strategic perspective, *Journal of Business Market Management*, 3: 7–27.

28. H. Green, 2009, How Amazon aims to keep you clicking, *BusinessWeek*, March 2: 34–35.

29. E. Steel, 2009, MySpace slashes jobs as growth slows down, *Wall Street Journal Online*, http://www.wsj.com, June 17.

30. 2009, Netflix announces Q1 2009 financial results, http://www.netflix.com, April 23.

31. 2009, Amazon turns to customers for new TV advertising campaign, http://www.amazon.com, June 8.

32. 2009, http://www.autos.msn.com, June 17.

33. I. C. MacMillan & L. Selden, 2008, The incumbent's advantage, *Harvard Business Review*, 86(10): 111–121; G. Dowell, 2006, Product-line strategies of new entrants in an established industry: Evidence from the U. S. bicycle industry, *Strategic Management Journal*, 27: 959–979.

34. J. Zhang & M. Wedel, 2009, The effectiveness of customized promotions in online and offline stores, *Journal of Marketing Research*, 46: 190–206; C. W. Lamb Jr., J. F. Hair Jr., & C. McDaniel, 2006, *Marketing*, 8th ed., Mason, OH: Thomson South-Western, 224.

35. 2009, About Hill's pet nutrition, http://www.hillspet.com, June 17.

36. 2009, Merck mulls selling off veterinary products, its own or Schering-Plough's before $41 merger, http://www.blog.taragana.com, June 3.

37. S. Hamner, 2005, Filling the gap, *Business 2.0*, July, 30.

38. S. French, 2009, Re-framing strategic thinking: The research-aims and outcomes, *Journal of Management Development*, 28: 205–224.

39. R. J. Brodie, J. R. M. Whittome, & G. J. Brush, 2009, Investigating the service brand: A customer value perspective, *Journal of Business Research*, 62: 345–355; P. D. Ellis, 2006, Market orientation and performance: A meta-analysis and cross-national comparisons, *Journal of Management Studies*, 43: 1089–1107.

40. L. A. Bettencourt & A. W. Ulwick, 2008, The customer-centered innovation map, *Harvard Business Review*, 86(5): 109–114.

41. A. Feldman, 2009, Wooing the worried, *BusinessWeek*, April 27, 24.

42. D. Kiley, 2009, One Ford for the whole wide world, *BusinessWeek*, June 15, 58–59.

43. E. A. Borg, 2009, The marketing of innovations in high-technology companies: A network approach, *European Journal of Marketing*, 43: 364–70.

44. D. Foust, F. F. Jespersen, F. Katzenberg, A. Barrett, & R. O. Crockett, 2003, The best performers, *BusinessWeek Online*, http://www.businessweek.com, March 24.

45. T. Y. Eng & J. G. Spickett-Jones, 2009, An investigation of marketing capabilities and upgrading performance of manufacturers in Mainland China and Hong Kong, *Journal of World Business*, in press; M. B. Heeley & R. Jacobson, 2008, The recency of technological inputs and financial performance, *Strategic Management Journal*, 29: 723–744.

46. 2009, Experience our energy, http://www.proenergyservices.com, June 17.

47. 2009, SAS honored with 2009 Asia Pacific Forst & Sullivan ICT aware for business intelligence, http://www.sas.com, June 9.

48. 2009, Strategies, http://www.kraft.com, June 17.

49. T. W. Martin, 2009, Safeway cultivates its private labels as brands to be sold by other chains, *Wall Street Journal Online*, http://www.wsj.com, May 7.

50. K. E. Klein, 2009, Survival advice for auto parts suppliers, *Wall Street Journal Online*, http://www.wsj.com, June 16.

51. M. E. Porter, 1985, *Competitive Advantage,* New York: Free Press, 26.

52. M. E. Porter, 1996, What is strategy? *Harvard Business Review,* 74(6): 61–78.

53. Porter, What is strategy?

54. M. Reitzig & P. Puranam, 2009, Value appropriation as an organizational capability: The case of IP protection through patents, *Strategic Management Journal,* 30: 765–789; C. Zott, 2003, Dynamic capabilities and the emergence of intraindustry differential firm performance: Insights from a simulation study, *Strategic Management Journal,* 24: 97–125.

55. M. E. Porter, 1994, Toward a dynamic theory of strategy, in R. P. Rumelt, D. E. Schendel, & D. J. Teece (eds.), *Fundamental Issues in Strategy,* Boston: Harvard Business School Press: 423–461.

56. Porter, What is strategy? 62.

57. Porter, *Competitive Advantage,* 15.

58. S. Sun, 2009, An analysis on the conditions and methods of market segmentation, *International Journal of Business and Management,* 4: 63–70.

59. J. Gonzales-Benito & I. Suarez-Gonzalez, 2009, A study of the role played by manufacturing strategic objectives and capabilities in understanding the relationship between Porter's generic strategies and business performance, *British Journal of Management,* in press.

60. G. B. Voss, D. Sirdeshmukh, & Z. G. Voss, 2008, The effects of slack resources and environmental threat on product exploration and exploitation, *Academy of Management Journal,* 51: 147–158.

61. S. McKee, 2009, Customers your company doesn't want, *Wall Street Journal Online,* http://www.wsj.com, June 12.

62. Porter, *Competitive Strategy,* 35–40.

63. M. J. Gehlhar, A. Regmi, S. E. Stefanou, & B. L. Zoumas, 2009, Brand leadership and product innovation as firm strategies in global food markets, *Journal of Product & Brand Management,* 18: 115–126.

64. M. Ihlwan, 2009, Kia Motors: Still cheap, now chic, *BusinessWeek,* June 1, 58.

65. D. Mehri, 2006, The dark side of lean: An insider's perspective on the realities of the Toyota production system, *Academy of Management Perspectives,* 20(2): 21–42.

66. N. T. Sheehan & G. Vaidyanathan, 2009, using a value creation compass to discover "Blue Oceans," *Strategy & Leadership,* 37: 13-20; D. F. Spulber, 2004, *Management Strategy,* New York: McGraw Hill/Irwin, 175.

67. A. M. Chaker, 2009, Planes, trains … and buses? *Wall Street Journal Online,* http://www.wsj.com, June 18.

68. 2009, About Greyhound, http://www.greyhound.com, June 17.

69. M. Kotabe & R. Mudambi, 2009, Global sourcing and value creation: Opportunities and challenges, *Journal of International Management,* 15: 121–125; D. F. Lynch, S. B. Keller, & J. Ozment, 2000, The effects of logistics capabilities and strategy on firm performance, *Journal of Business Logistics,* 21(2): 47–68.

70. J. Hatonen & T. Erikson, 2009, 30+ years of research and practice of outsourcing—Exploring the past and anticipating the future, *Journal of International Management,* 15: 142–155; P. Edwards & M. Ram, 2006, Surviving on the margins of the economy: Working relationships in small, low-wage firms, *Journal of Management Studies,* 43: 895–916.

71. 2009, What is a closeout? http://www.biglots.com, June 18.

72. 2009, Big Lots, *Standard & Poor's Stock Reports,* http://www.standardandpoors.com, June 13.

73. J. Morehouse, B. O'Mera, C. Hagen, & T. Huseby, 2008, Hitting back: Strategic responses to low-cost rivals, *Strategy & Leadership,* 36: 4–13; L. K. Johnson, 2003, Dueling pricing strategies, *The McKinsey Quarterly,* 44(3): 10–11.

74. K. E. Grace, 2009, Big Lots net falls 14%, expects 2009 earnings above views, *Wall Street Journal Online,* http://www.wsj.com, March 4.

75. O. Ormanidhi & O. Stringa, 2008, Porter's model of generic competitive strategies, *Business Economics,* 43: 55–64; J. Bercovitz & W. Mitchell, 2007, When is more better? The impact of business scale and scope on long-term business survival, while controlling for profitability, *Strategic Management Journal,* 28: 61–79.

76. J. Mintz, 2009, Redbox's kiosks take on Netflix's red envelopes, *The Eagle,* June 21, A14.

77. Porter, *Competitive Strategy,* 35–40.

78. 2009, Product innovation, http://www.1000ventures.com, June 19.

79. R. Cowan & N. Jonard, 2009, Knowledge portfolios and the organization of innovation networks, *Academy of Management Review,* 34: 320–342.

80. D. Ashmos Plowman, L. T. Baker, T. E. Beck, M. Kulkarni, S. Thomas-Solansky, & D. V. Travis, 2007, Radical change accidentally: The emergence and amplification of small change, *Academy of Management Journal,* 50: 515–543; A. Wadhwa & S. Kotha, 2006, Knowledge creation through external venturing: Evidence from the telecommunications equipment manufacturing industry, *Academy of Management Journal,* 49: 819–835.

81. D. W. Baack & D. J. Boggs, 2008, The difficulties in using a cost leadership strategy in emerging markets, *International Journal of Emerging Markets,* 3: 125–139; M. J. Benner, 2007, The incumbent discount: Stock market categories and response to radical technological change, *Academy of Management Review,* 32: 703–720.

82. F. T. Rothaermel, M. A. Hitt, & L. A. Jobe, 2006, Balancing vertical integration and strategic outsourcing: Effects on product portfolio, product success and firm performance, *Strategic Management Journal,* 27: 1033–1056; A. V. Mainkar, M. Lubatkin, & W. S. Schulze, 2006, Toward a product-proliferation

theory of entry barriers, *Academy of Management Review,* 31: 1062–1075.

83. Porter, *Competitive Advantage,* 14.

84. 2009, History, http://www.roberttalbott.com, June 19.

85. L. A. Bettencourt & A. W. Ulwick, 2008, The customer-centered innovation map, *Harvard Business Review,* 86(5): 109–114; W. C. Bogner & P. Bansal, 2007, Knowledge management as a basis for sustained high performance, *Journal of Management Studies,* 44:165–188; M. Semadeni, 2006, Minding your distance: How management consulting firms use service marks to position competitively, *Strategic Management Journal,* 27: 169–187.

86. M. Abbott, R. Holland, J. Giacomin, & J. Shackleton, 2009, Changing affective content in brand and product attributes, *Journal of Product & Brand Management,* 18: 17–26; P. Best, Using design to drive innovation, *BusinessWeek Online,* http://www.businessweek.com, June 29.

87. B. Charny & J. A. Dicolo, 2009, Apple debuts new iPhones to long lines, *Wall Street Journal Online,* http://www.wsj.com, June 19.

88. M. Jensen & A. Roy, 2008, Staging exchange partner choices: When do status and reputation matter? *Academy of Management Journal,* 51: 495–516; V. P. Rindova, T. G. Pollock, & M. A. Hayward, 2006, Celebrity firms: The social construction of market popularity, *Academy of Management Review,* 31: 50–71.

89. V. O'Connell, 2009, Sales of luxury goods seen falling by 10%, *Wall Street Journal Online,* http://www.wsj.com, April 11.

90. S. Berfield, 2009, Coach's new bag, *BusinessWeek,* June 29: 41-43; S. Berfield, 2009, Coach's Poppy line is luxury for recessionary times, *BusinessWeek Online,* http://www.wsj.com, June 18.

91. D. G. Sirmon, J.-L. Arregle, M. A. Hitt, & J. W. Webb, 2008, The role of family influence in firms' strategic responses to threat of imitation, *Entrepreneurship Theory and Practice,* 32: 979–998; F. K. Pil & S. K. Cohen, 2006, Modularity: Implications for imitation, innovation, and sustained advantage, *Academy of Management Review,* 31: 995–1011.

92. X. Bian & L. Moutinho, 2009, An investigation of determinants of counterfeit purchase consideration, *Journal of Business Research,* 62: 368–378.

93. Porter, *Competitive Strategy,* 98.

94. 2009, Greif & Co., http://www.greifco.com, June 19.

95. 2009, About Goya foods, http://www.goyafoods.com, June 20.

96. M. Bustillo, 2009, Small electronics chains thrive in downturn, *Wall Street Journal Online,* http://www.wsj.com, May 27.

97. Porter, *Competitive Advantage,* 15.

98. Ibid., 15–16.

99. K. Kling & I. Goteman, 2003, IKEA CEO Andres Dahlvig on international growth and IKEA's unique corporate culture and

brand identity, *Academy of Management Executive*, 17(1): 31–37.

100. 2009, About IKEA, http://www.ikea.com, June 21.

101. G. Evans, 2003, Why some stores strike me as special, *Furniture Today*, 27(24): 91; Porter, What is strategy?, 65.

102. J. Latson, 2009, Tattoo removal makes mark in slow economy, *Houston Chronicle Online*, http://www.chron.com, April 25.

103. K. McLaughlin, 2009, Food truck nation, *Wall Street Journal Online*, http://www.wsj.com, June 5.

104. 2009, Woman of style: CEO Anne Fontaine, http://www.factio-magazine.com, June 20.

105. O. Furrer, D. Sudharshan, H. Thomas, & M. T. Zlexandre, 2008, Resource configurations, generic strategies, and firm performance: Exploring the parallels between resource based and competitive strategy theories in a new industry, *Journal of Strategy and Management*, 1: 15–40; J. H. Dyer & N. W. Hatch, 2006, Relation-specific capabilities and barriers to knowledge transfers: Creating advantage through network relationships, *Strategic Management Journal*, 27: 701–719.

106. 2008, Letter to our shareholders, http://www.target.com, June 20.

107. 2009, Environment, http://www.target.com, June 21.

108. K. Capell, 2008, Zara thrives by breaking all the rules, *BusinessWeek*, October 20, 66.

109. R. Sanchez, 1995, Strategic flexibility in product competition, *Strategic Management Journal*, 16 (Special Issue): 140.

110. M. I. M. Wahab, D. Wu, and C.-G. Lee, 2008, A generic approach to measuring the machine flexibility of manufacturing

systems, *European Journal of Operational Research*, 186: 137–149.

111. M. Kotabe, R. Parente, & J. Y. Murray, 2007, Antecedents and outcomes of modular production in the Brazilian automobile industry: A grounded theory approach, *Journal of International Business Studies*, 38: 84–106.

112. T. Raj, R. Shankar, & M. Sunhaib, 2009, An ISM approach to analyse interaction between barriers of transition to Flexible Manufacturing Systems, *International Journal of Manufacturing Technology and Management*, 16: 417–438. E. K. Bish, A. Muriel, & S. Biller, 2005, Managing flexible capacity in a make-to-order environment, *Management Science*, 51: 167–180.

113. S. M. Iravani, M. P. van Oyen, & K. T. Sims, 2005, Structural flexibility: A new perspective on the design of manufacturing and service operations, *Management Science*, 51: 151–166.

114. P. Theodorou & G. Florou, 2008, Manufacturing strategies and financial performance—the effect of advanced information Technology: CAD/CAM systems, *Omega*, 36: 107–121.

115. N. A. Morgan & L. L. Rego, 2009, Brand portfolio strategy and firm performance, *Journal of Marketing*, 73: 59–74.

116. D. Elmuti, H. Jia, & D. Gray, 2009, Customer relationship management strategic application and organizational effectiveness: An empirical investigation, *Journal of Strategic Marketing*, 17: 75–96.

117. D. P. Forbes, 2007, Reconsidering the strategic implications of decision comprehensiveness, *Academy of Management Review*, 32: 361–376.

118. J. D. Westphal, R. Gulati, & S. M. Shortell, 1997, Customization or conformity: An institutional and network perspective on the content and consequences of TQM adoption, *Administrative Science Quarterly*, 42: 366–394.

119. S. Modell, 2009, Bundling management control innovations: A field study of organisational experimenting with total quality management and the balanced scorecard, *Accounting, Auditing & Accountability Journal*, 22: 59–90.

120. A. Keramati & A. Albadvi, 2009, Exploring the relationship between use of information technology in total quality management and SMEs performance using canonical correlation analysis: A survey on Swedish car part supplier sector, *International Journal of Information Technology and Management*, 8: 442–462; R. J. David & S. Strang, 2006, When fashion is fleeting: Transitory collective beliefs and the dynamics of TQM consulting, *Academy of Management Journal*, 49: 215–233.

121. Porter, *Competitive Advantage*, 16.

122. Ibid., 17.

123. M. A. Hitt, L. Bierman, K. Uhlenbruck, & K. Shimizu, 2006, The importance of resources in the internationalization of professional service firms: The good, the bad, and the ugly, *Academy of Management Journal*, 49: 1137–1157.

124. P. Puranam, H. Singh, & M. Zollo, 2006, Organizing for innovation: Managing the coordination-autonomy dilemma in technology acquisitions, *Academy of Management Journal*, 49: 263–280.

125. S. Thornhill & R. E. White, 2007, Strategic purity: A multi-industry evaluation of pure vs. hybrid business strategies, *Strategic Management Journal*, 28: 553–561.

Chapter 5

1. D. F. Spulber, 2004, *Management Strategy*, Boston: McGraw-Hill/Irwin, 87–88; M.-J. Chen, 1996, Competitor analysis and interfirm rivalry: Toward a theoretical integration, *Academy of Management Review*, 21: 100–134.

2. M. Schrage, 2007, The myth of commoditization, *MIT Sloan Management Review*, 48(2): 10–14; T. Galvin, 2002, Examining institutional change: Evidence from the founding dynamics of U.S. health care interest associations, *Academy of Management Journal*, 45: 673–696.

3. R. D. Ireland & J. W. Webb, 2007, Strategic entrepreneurship: Creating competitive advantage through streams of innovation, *Business Horizons*, 50: 49–59.

4. B. R. Barringer & R. D. Ireland, 2008, *Entrepreneurship: Successfully Launching New Ventures*, 2nd ed., Upper Saddle River, NJ: Prentice Hall; A. M. Knott & H. E. Posen, 2005, Is failure good? *Strategic Management Journal*, 26: 617–641.

5. P. J. Derfus, P. G. Maggitti, C. M. Grimm, & K. G. Smith, 2008, The red queen effect:

Competitive actions and firm performance, *Academy of Management Journal*, 51; 61–80; C. M. Grimm, H. Lee, & K. G. Smith, 2006, *Strategy as Action: Competitive Dynamics and Competitive Advantage*, New York: Oxford University Press.

6. J. W. Selsky, J. Goes, & O. N. Baburoglu, 2007, Contrasting perspectives of strategy making: Applications in "hyper" environments, *Organization Studies*, 28(1): 71–94; A. Nair & L. Filer, 2003, Cointegration of firm strategies within groups: A long-run analysis of firm behavior in the Japanese steel industry, *Strategic Management Journal*, 24: 145–159.

7. T. C. Powell, 2003, Varieties of competitive parity, *Strategic Management Journal*, 24: 61–86.

8. D. G. Sirmon, S. Gove, & M. A. Hitt, 2008, Resource management in dyadic competitive rivalry: The effects of resource bundling and deployment, *Academy of Management Journal*, 51: 919–935; J. Rodriguez-Pinto, J. Gutierrez-Cillan, & A. I. Rodriguez-Escudero, 2007, Order and scale market entry, firm resources,

and performance, *European Journal of Marketing*, 41: 590–607.

9. S. K. Ethitaj & D. H. Zhu, 2008, Performance effects of imitative entry, *Strategic Management Journal*, 29: 797–817.

10. Grimm, Lee, & Smith, *Strategy as Action*; G. Young, K. G. Smith, C. M. Grimm, & D. Simon, 2000, Multimarket contact and resource dissimilarity: A competitive dynamics perspective, *Journal of Management*, 26: 1217–1236.

11. E. I. Rose & K. Ito, 2008, Competitive interactions: The international investment patterns of Japanese automobile manufacturers, *Journal of International Business Studies*, 39: 864–879; T. L. Sorenson, 2007, Credible collusion in multimarket oligopoly, *Managerial and Decision Economics*, 28(2): 115–128.

12. T. Yu, M. Subramaniam, & A. A. Cannella, 2009, Rivalry deterrence in international markets: Contingencies governing the mutual forbearance hypothesis, *Academy of Management Journal*, 52: 127–147; K. G. Smith, W. J. Ferrier, & H. Ndofor,

2001, Competitive dynamics research: Critique and future directions, in M. A. Hitt, R. E. Freeman, & J. S. Harrison (eds.), *Handbook of Strategic Management*, Oxford, UK: Blackwell Publishers, 326.

13. G. Young, K. G. Smith, & C. M. Grimm, 1996, "Austrian" and industrial organization perspectives on firm-level competitive activity and performance, *Organization Science*, 73: 243–254.

14. 2007, Dell to sell PCs at Wal-Mart in retail drive, http://www.reuters.com, May 24.

15. H. D. Hopkins, 2003, The response strategies of dominant U.S. firms to Japanese challengers, *Journal of Management*, 29: 5–25; G. S. Day & D. J. Reibstein, 1997, The dynamic challenges for theory and practice, in G. S. Day & D. J. Reibstein (eds.), *Wharton on Competitive Strategy*, New York: John Wiley & Sons, 2.

16. J. J. Li, K. Z. Zhou, & A. T. Shao, 2009, Competitive position, managerial ties & profitability of foreign firms in China: An interactive perspective, *Journal of International Business Studies*, 40: 339–352; M.-J. Chen & D. C. Hambrick, 1995, Speed, stealth, and selective attack: How small firms differ from large firms in competitive behavior, *Academy of Management Journal*, 38: 453–482.

17. T. Dewett & S. David, 2007, Innovators and imitators in novelty-intensive markets: A research agenda, *Creativity and Innovation Management*, 16(1): 80–92.

18. A. Sahay, 2007, How to reap higher profits with dynamic pricing, *MIT Sloan Management Review*, 48(4): 53–60; T. J. Douglas & J. A. Ryman, 2003, Understanding competitive advantage in the general hospital industry: Evaluating strategic competencies, *Strategic Management Journal*, 24: 333–347.

19. T. Yu & A. A. Cannella, Jr., 2007, Rivalry between multinational enterprises: An event history approach, *Academy of Management Journal*, 50: 665–686; W. J. Ferrier, 2001, Navigating the competitive landscape: The drivers and consequences of competitive aggressiveness, *Academy of Management Journal*, 44: 858–877.

20. Smith, Ferrier, & Ndofor, Competitive dynamics research, 319.

21. E. G. Olson & D. Sharma, 2008, Beating the commoditization trend: A framework from the electronics industry, *Journal of Business Strategy*, 29(4): 22–28; J. Shamsie, 2003, The context of dominance: An industry-driven framework for exploiting reputation, *Strategic Management Journal*, 24: 199–215.

22. J. Li, 2008, Asymmetric interactions between foreign and domestic banks: Effects on market entry, *Strategic Management Journal*, 29: 873–893; K. Cool, L. H. Roller, & B. Leleux, 1999, The relative impact of actual and potential rivalry on firm profitability in the pharmaceutical industry, *Strategic Management Journal*, 20: 1–14.

23. G. Leask & D. Parker, 2007, Strategic groups, competitive groups and performance within the U.K. pharmaceutical industry: Improving our understanding of the competitive process, *Strategic Management Journal*, 28: 723–745; D. R. Gnyawali & R. Madhavan, 2001, Cooperative networks and competitive dynamics: A structural embeddedness perspective, *Academy of Management Review*, 26: 431–445.

24. V. La, P. Patterson & C. Styls, 2009, Client-perceived performance and value in professional B2B services: An international perspective, *Journal of International Business Studies*, 40: 274–300; Y. Y. Kor & J. T. Mahoney, 2005, How dynamics, management, and governance of resource deployments influence firm-level performance, *Strategic Management Journal*, 26: 489–496.

25. R. L. Priem, L. G. Love, & M. A. Shaffer, 2002, Executives' perceptions of uncertainty scores: A numerical taxonomy and underlying dimensions, *Journal of Management*, 28: 725–746.

26. J. C. Bou & A. Satorra, 2007, The persistence of abnormal returns at industry and firm levels: Evidence from Spain, *Strategic Management Journal*, 28: 707–722.

27. Chen, Competitor analysis, 108.

28. Chen, Competitor analysis, 109.

29. D. Ng, R. Westgren, & S. Sonka, 2009, Competitive blind spots in an institutional field, *Strategic Management Journal*, 30: 349–369.

30. S. J. Chang & D. Xu, 2008, Spillovers and competition among foreign and local firms in China, *Strategic Management Journal*, 29: 495–518.

31. K. Uhlenbruck, M. A. Hitt, & M. Semadeni, 2005, Market value effects of acquisitions of Internet firms: A resource-based analysis, working paper, University of Montana; A. Afuah, 2003, Redefining firm boundaries in the face of the Internet: Are firms really shrinking? *Academy of Management Review*, 28: 34–53.

32. H. Gebauer, 2007, Entering low-end markets: A new strategy for Swiss companies, *Journal of Business Strategy*, 27(5): 23–31.

33. 2007, YRC Worldwide, http://www.yrcw.com, July 30.

34. 2007, YRC Worldwide, *Hoovers*, http://www.hoovers.com/yrc-worldwide, July 30.

35. Chen, Competitor analysis, 106.

36. A. Kachra & R. E. White, 2008, Know-how transfer: The role of social, economic/competitive, and firm boundary factors, *Strategic Management Journal*, 29: 425–445.

37. M. J. Chen, K.-H. Su, & W. Tsai, 2007, Competitive tension: The awareness-motivation-capability perspective, *Academy of Management Journal*, 50: 101–118; J. Gimeno & C. Y. Woo, 1999, Multimarket contact, economies of scope, and firm performance, *Academy of Management Journal*, 42: 239–259.

38. I. C. MacMillan, A. B. van Putten, & R. S. McGrath, 2003, Global gamesmanship, *Harvard Business Review*, 81(5): 62–71.

39. Young, Smith, Grimm, & Simon, Multimarket contact, 1230.

40. H. R. Greve, 2008, Multimarket contact and sales growth: Evidence from insurance, *Strategic Management Journal*, 29: 229–249; J. Gimeno, 1999, Reciprocal threats in multimarket rivalry: Staking out "spheres of influence" in the U.S. airline industry, *Strategic Management Journal*, 20: 101–128.

41. S. Jayachandran, J. Gimeno, & P. R. Varadarajan, 1999, Theory of multimarket competition: A synthesis and implications for marketing strategy, *Journal of Marketing*, 63: 49–66; Chen, Competitor analysis, 107.

42. H. Schiele, 2008, Location, location: The geography of industry clusters, *Journal of Business Strategy*, 29(3): 29–36; J. Gimeno & C. Y. Woo, 1996, Hypercompetition in a multimarket environment: The role of strategic similarity and multimarket contact on competitive de-escalation, *Organization Science*, 7: 322–341.

43. C. H. Deutsch, 2007, UPS embraces high-tech delivery methods, *New York Times Online*, http://www.nytimes.com, July 12.

44. S. MacMillan, 2008, The issue: DHL turns to rival UPS, *BusinessWeek*, http//:www.businessweek.com, June.

45. Chen, Su, & Tsai, Competitive tension; Chen, Competitor analysis, 110.

46. Ibid.; W. Ocasio, 1997, Towards an attention-based view of the firm, *Strategic Management Journal*, 18 (Special Issue): 187–206; Smith, Ferrier, & Ndofor, Competitive dynamics research, 320.

47. 2007, Komatsu lifts outlook, outdoes rival Caterpillar, *New York Times Online*, http://www.nytimes.com, July 30.

48. M. Neal, 2009, Carrefour's no Wal-Mart, *Wall StreetJjournal*, //:www.wsj.com, March 12; 2007, Carrefour battles Wal-Mart in South America, Elsevier Food International, http://www.foodinternational.net, July 31.

49. S. Tallman, M. Jenkins, N. Henry, & S. Pinch, 2004, Knowledge, clusters and competitive advantage, *Academy of Management Review*, 29: 258–271; J. F. Porac & H. Thomas, 1994, Cognitive categorization and subjective rivalry among retailers in a small city, *Journal of Applied Psychology*, 79: 54–66.

50. S. H. Park & D. Zhou, 2005, Firm heterogeneity and competitive dynamics in alliance formation, *Academy of Management Review*, 30: 531–554.

51. S. R. Miller, D. E. Thomas, L. Eden & M. A. Hitt, 2008, Knee deep in the big muddy: The survival of emerging market firms in developed markets, *Management International Review*, 48: 645–666.

52. Chen, Competitor analysis, 113.

53. M. Leiblein & T. Madsen, 2009, Unbundling competitive heterogeneity: Incentive structures and capability influences

on technological innovation, *Strategic Management Journal*, 30: in press; J. J. Li, L. Poppo, & K. Z. Zhou, 2008, Do managerial ties in China always produce value? Competition, uncertainty and domestic vs. foreign competition, *Strategic Management Journal*, 29: 383–400.

54. R. Belderbos & L. Sleuwaegen, 2005, Competitive drivers and international plant configuration strategies: A product-level test, *Strategic Management Journal*, 26: 577–593.

55. C. M. Grimm & K. G. Smith, 1997, *Strategy as Action: Industry Rivalry and Coordination*, Cincinnati: South-Western Publishing Co., 125.

56. B. Webber, 2007, Volatile markets, *Business Strategy Review*, 18(2): 60–67; K. G. Smith, W. J. Ferrier, & C. M. Grimm, 2001, King of the hill: Dethroning the industry leader, *Academy of Management Executive*, 15(2): 59–70.

57. S. E. Jackson, 2008, Grow your business without leaving your competitive stronghold, *Journal of Business Strategy*, 29(4): 60–62.

58. W. J. Ferrier & H. Lee, 2003, Strategic aggressiveness, variation, and surprise: How the sequential pattern of competitive rivalry influences stock market returns, *Journal of Managerial Issues*, 14: 162–180.

59. C. Palmeri, 2007, How Guess got its groove back, *BusinessWeek*, July 23, 126.

60. S. Holmes, 2007, Better living at 30,000 feet, *BusinessWeek*, August 6, 76–77.

61. J. Schumpeter, 1934, *The Theory of Economic Development*, Cambridge, MA: Harvard University Press.

62. J. L. C. Cheng & I. F. Kesner, 1997, Organizational slack and response to environmental shifts: The impact of resource allocation patterns, *Journal of Management*, 23: 1–18.

63. F. F. Suarez & G. Lanzolla, 2007, The role of environmental dynamics in building a first mover advantage theory, *Academy of Management Review*, 32: 377–392.

64. G. M. McNamara, J. Haleblian, & B. J. Dykes, 2008, The performance implications of participating in an acquisition wave: Early mover advantages, bandwagon effects, and the moderating influence of industry characteristics and acquirer tactics, *Academy of Management Journal*, 51, 113–130; F. Wang, 2000, Too appealing to overlook, *America's Network*, December, 10–12.

65. R. K. Sinha & C. H. Noble, 2008, The adoption of radical manufacturing technologies and firm survival, *Strategic Management Journal*, 29: 943–962; D. P. Forbes, 2005, Managerial determinants of decision speed in new ventures, *Strategic Management Journal*, 26: 355–366.

66. H. R. Greve, 2009, Bigger and safer: The diffusion of competitive advantage, *Strategic Management Journal*, 30: 1–23; W. T. Robinson & S. Min, 2002, Is the first to market the first to fail? Empirical evidence for industrial goods businesses, *Journal of Marketing Research*, 39: 120–128.

67. T. Cottrell & B. R. Nault, 2004, *Strategic Management Journal*, 25: 1005–1025; R. Agarwal, M. B. Sarkar, & R. Echambadi, 2002, The conditioning effect of time on firm survival: An industry life cycle approach, *Academy of Management Journal*, 45: 971–994.

68. A. Srivastava & H. Lee, 2005, Predicting order and timing of new product moves: The role of top management in corporate entrepreneurship, *Journal of Business Venturing*, 20: 459–481.

69. M. S. Giarratana & A. Fosfuri, 2007, Product strategies and survival in Schumpeterian environments: Evidence from the U.S. security software industry, *Organization Studies*, 28(6): 909–929; J. W. Spencer & T. P. Murtha, 2005, How do governments matter to new industry creation? *Academy of Management Review*, 30: 321–337.

70. Z. Simsek, J. F. Veiga, & M. H. Lubatkin, 2007, The impact of managerial environmental perceptions on corporate entrepreneurship: Toward understanding discretionary slack's pivotal role, *Journal of Management Studies*, 44:1398–1424; S. W. Geiger & L. H. Cashen, 2002, A multidimensional examination of slack and its impact on innovation, *Journal of Managerial Issues*, 14: 68–84.

71. B. S. Teng, 2007, Corporate entrepreneurship activities through strategic alliances: A resource-based approach toward competitive advantage, *Journal of Management Studies*, 44: 119–142; M. B. Lieberman & D. B. Montgomery, 1988, First-mover advantages, *Strategic Management Journal*, 9: 41–58.

72. D. Lange, S. Boivie, & A. D. Henderson, 2009, The parenting paradox: How multibusiness diversifiers endorse disruptive technologies while their corporate children struggle, *Academy of Management Journal*, 52: 179–198.

73. S. Jonsson & P. Regner, 2009, Normative barriers to imitation: Social complexity of core competences in a mutual fund industry, *Strategic Management Journal*, 30: 517–536; 2001, Older, wiser, webbier, *The Economist*, June 30, 10.

74. M. Shank, 2002, Executive strategy report, IBM business strategy consulting, http://www.ibm.com, March 14; W. Boulding & M. Christen, 2001, First-mover disadvantage, *Harvard Business Review*, 79(9): 20–21.

75. J. L. Boyd & R. K. F. Bresser, 2008, Performance implications of delayed competitive responses: Evidence from the U.S. retail industry, *Strategic Management Journal*, 29: 1077–1096.

76. J. Gimeno, R. E. Hoskisson, B. B. Beal, & W. P. Wan, 2005, Explaining the clustering of international expansion moves: A critical test in the U.S. telecommunications industry, *Academy of Management Journal*, 48: 297–319; K. G. Smith, C. M. Grimm, & M. J. Gannon, 1992, *Dynamics of Competitive Strategy*, Newberry Park, CA.: Sage Publications.

77. J. Li & R. K. Koxhikode, 2008, Knowledge management and innovation strategy: The challenge for latecomers in emerging economies, *Asia Pacific Journal of Management*, 25: 429–450.

78. S. D. Dobrev & G. R. Carroll, 2003, Size (and competition) among organizations: Modeling scale-based selection among automobile producers in four major countries, 1885–1981, *Strategic Management Journal*, 24: 541–558.

79. L. F. Mesquita & S. G. Lazzarini, 2008, Horizontal and vertical relationships in developing economies: Implications for SMEs access to global markets, *Academy of Management Journal*, 51: 359–380; F. K. Pil & M. Hoiweg, 2003, Exploring scale: The advantage of thinking small, *The McKinsey Quarterly*, 44(2): 33–39.

80. M. A. Hitt, L. Bierman, & J. D. Collins, 2007, The strategic evolution of U.S. law firms, *Business Horizons*, 50: 17–28; D. Miller & M. J. Chen, 1996, The simplicity of competitive repertoires: An empirical analysis, *Strategic Management Journal*, 17: 419–440.

81. Young, Smith, & Grimm, "Austrian" and industrial organization perspectives.

82. B. A. Melcher, 1993, How Goliaths can act like Davids, *BusinessWeek*, Special Issue, 193.

83. P. B. Crosby, 1980, *Quality Is Free*, New York: Penguin.

84. W. E. Deming, 1986, *Out of the Crisis*, Cambridge, MA: MIT Press.

85. D. A. Mollenkopf, E. Rabinovich, T. M. Laseter, & K. K. Boyer, 2007, Managing Internet product returns: A focus on effective service operations, *Decision Sciences*, 38: 215–250; L. B. Crosby, R. DeVito, & J. M. Pearson, 2003, Manage your customers' perception of quality, *Review of Business*, 24(1): 18–24.

86. K. Watanabe, 2007, Lessons from Toyota's long drive, *Harvard Business Review*, 85(7/8): 74–83; R. S. Kaplan & D. P. Norton, 2001, *The Strategy-Focused Organization*, Boston: Harvard Business School Press.

87. A. Azadegan, K. J. Dooley, P. I. Carter, & J. R. Carter, 2008, Supplier innovativeness and the role of interorganizational learning in enhancing manufacturing capabilities, *Journal of Supply Chain Management*, 44(4): 14—5; O. Bayazit & B. Karpak, 2007, An analytical network process-based framework for successful total quality management (TQM): An assessment of Turkish manufacturing industry readiness, *International Journal of Production Economics*, 105(1) 79–96.

88. K. E. Weick & K. M. Sutcliffe, 2001, *Managing the Unexpected*, San Francisco: Jossey-Bass, 81–82.

89. G. Macintosh, 2007, Customer orientation, relationship quality, and relational benefits to the firm, *Journal of Services Marketing*, 21(3): 150–159; G. Yeung & V. Mok, 2005, What are the impacts of implementing ISOs on the competitiveness of manufacturing industry in China, *Journal of World Business*, 40: 139–157.

90. J Wallace, 2009, Boeing at risk of losing more 787 orders, *Seattle-Post-Intelligencer*, http//:www.seattlepi.nwsource.com, March 13.

91. T. R. Cook, D. J. Ketchen, J. G. Combs, & S. Y. Todd, 2008, Strategic resources and performance: A meta-analysis, *Strategic Management Journal*, 29: 1141–1154; Smith, Ferrier, & Ndofor, Competitive dynamics research, 323.

92. M. J. Chen & I. C. MacMillan, 1992, Nonresponse and delayed response to competitive moves, *Academy of Management Journal*, 35: 539–570; Smith, Ferrier, & Ndofor, Competitive dynamics research, 335.

93. M. J. Chen, K. G. Smith, & C. M. Grimm, 1992, Action characteristics as predictors of competitive responses, *Management Science*, 38: 439–455.

94. M. J. Chen & D. Miller, 1994, Competitive attack, retaliation and performance: An expectancy-valence framework, *Strategic Management Journal*, 15: 85–102.

95. T. Gardner, 2005, Interfirm competition for human resources: Evidence from the software industry, *Academy of Management Journal*, 48: 237–258; N. Huyghebaert & L. M. van de Gucht, 2004, Incumbent strategic behavior in financial markets and the exit of entrepreneurial start-ups, *Strategic Management Journal*, 25: 669–688.

96. Smith, Ferrier, & Ndofor, Competitive dynamics research, 333.

97. V. P. Rindova, A. P. Petkova, & S. Kotha, 2007, Standing out: How firms in emerging markets build reputation, *Strategic Organization*, 5: 31–70; J. Shamsie, 2003, The context of dominance: An industry-driven framework for exploiting reputation, *Strategic Management Journal*, 24: 199–215.

98. A. D. Smith, 2007, Making the case for the competitive advantage of corporate social responsibility, *Business Strategy Series*, 8(3): 186–195; P. W. Roberts & G. R. Dowling, 2003, Corporate reputation and sustained superior financial performance, *Strategic Management Journal*, 24: 1077–1093.

99. W. J. Ferrier, K. G. Smith, & C. M. Grimm, 1999, The role of competitive actions in market share erosion and industry dethronement: A study of industry leaders and challengers, *Academy of Management Journal*, 42: 372–388.

100. Smith, Grimm, & Gannon, *Dynamics of Competitive Strategy*.

101. L. Li, L. Zhang, & B. Arys, 2008, The turtle–hare story revisited: Social capital and resource accumulation for firms from emerging economies, *Asia Pacific Journal of Management*, 25: 251–275.

102. A. Karnani & B. Wernerfelt, 1985, Multiple point competition, *Strategic Management Journal*, 6: 87–97.

103. Smith, Ferrier, & Ndofor, Competitive dynamics research, 330.

104. S. L. Newbert, 2007, Empirical research on the resource-based view of the firm: An assessment and suggestions for future research, *Strategic Management Journal*, 28: 121–146; G. McNamara, P. M. Vaaler, & C. Devers, 2003, Same as it ever was: The search for evidence of increasing hypercompetition, *Strategic Management Journal*, 24: 261–278.

105. M. F. Wiersema & H. P. Bowen, 2008, Corporate diversification: The impact of foreign competition, industry globalization and product diversification, *Strategic Management Journal*, 29: 115–132; A. Kalnins & W. Chung, 2004, Resource-seeking agglomeration: A study of market entry in the lodging industry, *Strategic Management Journal*, 25: 689–699.

106. J. R. Williams, 1992, How sustainable is your competitive advantage? *California Management Review*, 34(3): 29–51.

107. J. A. Lamberg, H. Tikkanen, & T. Nokelainen, 2009, Competitive dynamics, strategic consistency and organizational survival, *Strategic Management Journal*, 30: 45–60; D. A. Chmielewski & A. Paladino, 2007, Driving a resource orientation: Reviewing the role of resources and capability characteristics, *Management Decision*, 45: 462–483.

108. N. Pangarkar & J. R. Lie, 2004, The impact of market cycle on the performance of Singapore acquirers, *Strategic Management Journal*, 25: 1209–1216.

109. 2003, How fast is your company? *Fast Company*, June, 18.

110. D. P. Forbes, 2007, Reconsidering the strategic implications of decision comprehensiveness, *Academy of Management Review*, 32: 361–376; T. Talaulicar, J. Grundei, & A. V. Werder, 2005, Strategic decision making in startups: The effect of top management team organization and processes on speed and comprehensiveness, *Journal of Business Venturing*, 20: 519–541.

111. A. H. Ang, 2008, Competitive intensity and collaboration: Impact on firm growth across technological environments, *Strategic Management Journal*, 29: 1057–1075; M. Song, C. Droge, S. Hanvanich, & R. Calantone, 2005, Marketing and technology resource complementarity: An analysis of their interaction effect in two environmental contexts, *Strategic Management Journal*, 26: 259–276.

112. R. Williams, 1999, Renewable advantage: Crafting strategy through economic time, New York: Free Press, 8.

113. Ibid.

114. D. Li, L. E. Eden, M. A. Hitt, & R. D. Ireland, 2008, Friends, acquaintances or strangers? Partner selection in R&D alliances, *Academy of Management Journal*, 51: 315–334; D. Gerwin, 2004, Coordinating new product development in strategic alliances, *Academy of Management Review*, 29: 241–257.

115. K. Coucke & L. Sleuwaegen, 2008, Offshoring as a survival strategy: Evidence from manufacturing firms in Belgium, *Journal of international Business Studies*, 39: 1261–1277.

116. P. Carbonell & A. I. Rodriguez, 2006, The impact of market characteristics and innovation speed on perceptions of positional advantage and new product performance, *International Journal of Research in Marketing*, 23(1): 1–12; R. Sanchez, 1995, Strategic flexibility in production competition, *Strategic Management Journal*, 16 (Special Issue): 9–26.

117. R. Adner & D. Levinthal, 2008, Doing versus seeing: Acts of exploitation and perceptions of exploration, *Strategic Entrepreneurship Journal*, 2: 43–52; Williams, *Renewable Advantage*, 7.

Chapter 6

1. M. E. Porter, 1980, *Competitive Strategy*, New York: The Free Press, xvi.

2. M. D. R. Chari, S. Devaraj, & P. David, 2008, The impact of information technology investments and diversification strategies on firm performance, *Management Science*, 54: 224–234; A. Pehrsson, 2006, Business relatedness and performance: A study of managerial perceptions, *Strategic Management Journal*, 27: 265–282.

3. A. Hargrave-Silk, 2008, Media Brands moves to diversify, Media 3, November.

4. S. Walters & R. Stone, 2007, The trouble with rose-colored glasses, *Barron's*, June 25, M10.

5. A. O'Connell, 2009, Lego CEO Jørgen Vig Knudstorp on leading through survival and growth, *Harvard Business Review*, 87(1): 1–2.

6. M. E. Porter, 1987, From competitive advantage to corporate strategy, *Harvard Business Review*, 65(3): 43–59.

7. Ibid.; M. E. Raynor, 2007, What is corporate strategy, really? *Ivey Business Journal*, 71(8): 1–3.

8. E. Ellis, 2008, What'll you have, mate? *Barron's*, October 27, 34–36.

9. A. A. Calart & J. E. Ricart, 2007, Corporate strategy: An agent-based approach, *European Management Review*, 4: 107–120; M. Kwak, 2002, Maximizing value through diversification, *MIT Sloan Management Review*, 43(2): 10.

10. K. Lee, M. W. Peng, & K. Lee, 2008, From diversification premium to diversification discount during institutional transitions, *Journal of World Business*, 43(1): 47–65; M. Ammann & M. Verhofen,

2006, The conglomerate discount: A new explanation based on credit risk, *International Journal of Theoretical & Applied Finance,* 9(8): 1201–1214; S. A. Mansi & D. M. Reeb, 2002, Corporate diversification: What gets discounted? *Journal of Finance,* 57: 2167–2183.

11. N. M. Schmid & I. Walter, 2009, Do financial conglomerates create or destroy economic value? *Journal of Financial Intermediation,* 18(2): 193–216; C. E. Helfat & K. M. Eisenhardt, 2004, Intertemporal economies of scope organizational modularity, and the dynamics of diversification, *Strategic Management Journal,* 25: 1217–1232.

12. A. Campbell, M. Goold, & M. Alexander, 1995, Corporate strategy: The question for parenting advantage, *Harvard Business Review,* 73(2): 120–132.

13. D. Collis, D. Young, & M. Goold, 2007, The size, structure, and performance of corporate headquarters, *Strategic Management Journal,* 28: 283–405; M. Goold & A. Campbell, 2002, Parenting in complex structures, *Long Range Planning,* 35(3): 219–243; T. H. Brush, P. Bromiley, & M. Hendrickx, 1999, The relative influence of industry and corporation on business segment performance: An alternative estimate, *Strategic Management Journal,* 20: 519–547.

14. H. Chesbrough, 2007, The market for innovation: Implications for corporate strategy, *California Management Review,* 49(3): 45–66; D. Miller, 2006, Technological diversity, related diversification, and firm performance, *Strategic Management Journal,* 27: 601–619; D. J. Miller, 2004, Firms' technological resources and the performance effects of diversification: A longitudinal study, *Strategic Management Journal,* 25: 1097–1119.

15. D. D. Bergh, 2001, Diversification strategy research at a crossroads: Established, emerging and anticipated paths, in M. A. Hitt, R. E. Freeman, & J. S. Harrison (eds.), *Handbook of Strategic Management,* Oxford, UK: Blackwell Publishers, 363–383.

16. H. C. Wang & J. B. Barney, 2006, Employee incentives to make firm-specific investments: Implications for resource-based theories of corporate diversification, *Academy of Management Journal,* 31: 466–476.

17. J. J. Marcel, 2009, Why top management team characteristics matter when employing a chief operating officer: A strategic contingency perspective, *Strategic Management Journal,* 30(6): 647–658; A. J. Ward, M. J. Lankau, A. C. Amason, J. A. Sonnenfeld, & B. R. Agle, 2007, Improving the performance of top management teams, *MIT Sloan Management Review,* 48(3): 85–90.

18. R. P. Rumelt, *Strategy, Structure, and Economic Performance,* Boston: Harvard Business School, 1974; L. Wrigley, 1970, *Divisional Autonomy and Diversification*

(Ph.D. dissertation), Harvard Business School.

19. P. Gogoi, N. Arndt, & J. Crown, 2008, A bittersweet deal for Wrigley: Selling the family business wasn't William Wrigley Jr.'s plan, but the Mars offer was too good to refuse, *BusinessWeek,* May 12, 34.

20. 2009, United Parcel Service 2008 Annual Report, http://www.ups.com, June 14.

21. 2009, Hutchison Whampoa Limited, http://www.hoovers.com, March 15; J. Spencer, 2007, Hutchison's Li looks to make well-timed exit; Indian wireless assets may yield a windfall; a bigger risk to buyers, *Wall Street Journal,* January 29, B4.

22. M. Lee, 2008, Hutch Telecom to pay special dividend; shares surge (update2), http://www.bloomberg.com, November 12; 2007, What has Superman got up his sleeve? *Euroweek,* February 23, 1.

23. M. A. Williams, T. B. Michael, & E. R. Waller, 2008, Managerial incentives and acquisitions: A survey of the literature. *Managerial Finance,* 34(5): 328–341; S. W. Geiger & L. H. Cashen, 2007, Organizational size and CEO compensation: The moderating effect of diversification in downscoping organizations, *Journal of Managerial Issues,* 9(2): 233–252; R. K. Aggarwal & A. A. Samwick, 2003, Why do managers diversify their firms? Agency reconsidered, *Journal of Finance,* 58: 71–118.

24. D. J. Miller, M. J. Fern, & L. B. Cardinal, 2007, The use of knowledge for technological innovation within diversified firms, *Academy of Management Journal,* 50: 308–326.

25. H. Tanriverdi & C. -H. Lee, 2008, Within-industry diversification and firm performance in the presence of network externalities: Evidence from the software industry, *Academy of Management Journal,* 51(2): 381–397; H. Tanriverdi & N. Venkatraman, 2005, Knowledge relatedness and the performance of multibusiness firms, *Strategic Management Journal,* 26: 97–119.

26. M. D. R. Chari, S. Devaraj, & P. David, 2008, The impact of information technology investments and diversification strategies on firm performance, *Management Science,* 54(1): 224–234; H. Tanriverdi, 2006, Performance effects of information technology synergies in multibusiness firms, *MIS Quarterly,* 30(1): 57–78.

27. M. E. Porter, 1985, *Competitive Advantage,* New York: Free Press, 328.

28. N. Shin, 2009, Information technology and diversification: How their relationship affects firm performance. *International Journal of E-Collaboration,* 5(1): 69–83; D. Miller, 2006, Technological diversity, related diversification, and firm performance, *Strategic Management Journal,* 27: 601–619.

29. Tanriverdi & Lee, Within-industry diversification and firm performance in the presence of network externalities: Evidence from the software industry; P. Puranam & K. Srikanth, 2007, What they

know vs. what they do: How acquirers leverage technology acquisitions, *Strategic Management Journal,* 28: 805–825; C. Park, 2003, Prior performance characteristics of related and unrelated acquirers, *Strategic Management Journal,* 24: 471–480; G. Delong, 2001, Stockholder gains from focusing versus diversifying bank mergers, *Journal of Financial Economics,* 2: 221–252; T. H. Brush, 1996, Predicted change in operational synergy and post-acquisition performance of acquired businesses, *Strategic Management Journal,* 17.

30. D. D. Bergh, 1995, Size and relatedness of units sold: An agency theory and resource-based perspective, *Strategic Management Journal,* 16: 221–239.

31. M. Lubatkin & S. Chatterjee, 1994, Extending modern portfolio theory into the domain of corporate diversification: Does it apply? *Academy of Management Journal,* 37: 109–136.

32. E. Dooms & A. A. Van Oijen, 2008, The balance between tailoring and standardizing control, *European Management Review,* 5(4): 245–252; T. Kono, 1999, A strong head office makes a strong company, *Long Range Planning,* 32(2): 225.

33. I. -C. Hsu & Y.-S. Wang, 2008, A model of intraorganizational knowledge sharing: Development and initial test. *Journal of Global Information Management,* 16(3): 45–73; Puranam & Srikanth, What they know vs. what they do; F. T. Rothaermel, M. A. Hitt, & L. A. Jobe, 2006, Balancing vertical integration and strategic outsourcing: Effects on product portfolio, product success, and firm performance, *Strategic Management Journal,* 27: 1033–1056; S. Chatterjee & B. Wernerfelt, 1991, The link between resources and type of diversification: Theory and evidence, *Strategic Management Journal,* 12: 33–48.

34. A. Rodríguez-Duarte, F. D. Sandulli, B. Minguela-Rata, & J. I. López-Sánchez, 2007, The endogenous relationship between innovation and diversification, and the impact of technological resources on the form of diversification, *Research Policy,* 36: 652–664; L. Capron & N. Pistre, 2002, When do acquirers earn abnormal returns? *Strategic Management Journal,* 23: 781–794.

35. C. Lawton, 2007, H-P begins push into high-end copiers, *Wall Street Journal,* April 24, B3.

36. Miller, Fern, & Cardinal, The use of knowledge for technological innovation within diversified firms; J. W. Spencer, 2003, Firms' knowledge-sharing strategies in the global innovation system: Empirical evidence from the flat panel display industry, *Strategic Management Journal,* 24: 217–233.

37. J. Thottam, 2008, Branson's flight plan, *Time,* April 28, 40.

38. 2009, Honda engines, Honda motor company, http://www.honda.com, March 30.

39. L. C. Thang, C. Rowley, T. Quang, & M. Warner, 2007, To what extent can

management practices be transferred between countries?: The case of human resource management in Vietnam, *Journal of World Business*, 42(1): 113–127; G. Stalk Jr., 2005, Rotate the core, *Harvard Business Review*, 83(3): 18–19.

40. S. Gupta, A. Woodside, C. Dubelaar, & D. Bradmore, 2009, Diffusing knowledge-based core competencies for leveraging innovation strategies: Modeling outsourcing to knowledge process organizations (KPOs) in pharmaceutical networks, *Industrial Marketing Management*, 38(2): 219–227.

41. S. Chatterjee & J. Singh, 1999, Are trade-offs inherent in diversification moves? A simultaneous model for type of diversification and mode of expansion decisions, *Management Science*, 45: 25–41.

42. J. Wiggins, 2008, Mars' move for Wrigley leaves rivals trailing, *Financial Times*, April 29, 24.

43. L. Fuentelsaz & J. Gomez, 2006, Multi-point competition, strategic similarity and entry into geographic markets, *Strategic Management Journal*, 27: 477–499; J. Gimeno & C. Y. Woo, 1999, Multimarket contact, economies of scope, and firm performance, *Academy of Management Journal*, 42: 239–259.

44. B. P. Biederman, 2008, Preparing for take-off, *Journal of Commerce*, July 28; R. Kwong, 2007, Big four hope expansion will deliver the goods, *Financial Times*, May 23, 15.

45. T. A. Shervani, G. Frazier, & G. Challagalla, 2007, The moderating influence of firm market power on the transaction cost economics model: An empirical test in a forward channel integration context, *Strategic Management Journal*, 28: 635–652; R. Gulati, P. R. Lawrence, & P. Puranam, 2005, Adaptation in vertical relationships: Beyond incentive conflict, *Strategic Management Journal*, 26: 415–440.

46. P. Broedner, S. Kinkel, & G. Lay, 2009, Productivity effects of outsourcing: New evidence on the strategic importance of vertical integration decisions, *International Journal of Operations & Production Management*, 29(2): 127–150; D. A. Griffin, A. Chandra, & T. Fealey, 2005, Strategically employing natural channels in an emerging market, *Thunderbird International Business Review*, 47(3): 287–311.

47. R. Carter & G. M. Hodgson, 2006, The impact of empirical tests of transaction cost economics on the debate on the nature of the firm, *Strategic Management Journal*, 27: 461–476; O. E. Williamson, 1996, Economics and organization: A primer, *California Management Review*, 38(2): 131–146.

48. S. Novak & S. Stern, 2008, How does outsourcing affect performance dynamics? Evidence from the automobile industry, *Management Science*, 54(12): 1963–1979.

49. C. Wolter & F. M. Veloso, 2008, The effects of innovation on vertical structure: Perspectives on transaction costs and competences, *Academy of Management Review*, 33(3): 586–605; M. G. Jacobides, 2005, Industry change through vertical disintegration: How and why markets emerged in mortgage banking, *Academy of Management Journal*, 48: 465–498.

50. W. D. Brin, 2007, Earnings digest—Health care: As rivals tussle, Medco sees gains; drug-benefit manager cites competitive edge due to business model, *Wall Street Journal*, February 22, C6.

51. V. Fuhmans & M. Karnitschnig, 2009, Corporate news: WellPoint puts NextRx on the auction block, *Wall Street Journal*, March 6, B3.

52. A. R. Sorkin & M. J. de le Merced, 2009, Express Scripts is said to be near a deal for WellPoint's pharmacy unit, *New York Times*, http://www.nytimes.com, April 13.

53. L. R. Kopczak & M. E. Johnson, 2003, The supply-chain management effect, *MIT Sloan Management Review*, 3: 27–34; K.R. Harrigan, 2001, Strategic flexibility in the old and new economies, in M. A. Hitt, R. E. Freeman, & J. S. Harrison (eds.), *Handbook of Strategic Management*, Oxford, UK: Blackwell Publishers, 97–123.

54. T. Hutzschenreuter & F. Gröne, 2009, Changing vertical integration strategies under pressure from foreign competition: The case of U.S. and German multinationals, *Journal of Management Studies*, 46(2): 269–307.

55. 2009, Flextronics International Ltd., http://www.hoovers.com, March 15.

56. P. Kothandaraman & D. T. Wilson, 2001, The future of competition: Value-creating networks, *Industrial Marketing Management*, 30: 379–389.

57. K. M. Eisenhardt & D. C. Galunic, 2000, Coevolving: At last, a way to make synergies work, *Harvard Business Review*, 78(1): 91–111.

58. J. A. Nickerson & T. R. Zenger, 2008, Envy, comparison costs, and the economic theory of the firm, *Strategic Management Journal*, 13: 1429–1449.

59. L Greene, 2009, Adult nostalgia for childhood brands, *Financial Times*. http://www.ft.com, February 14; M. Marr, 2007, The magic kingdom looks to hit the road, *Wall Street Journal*, http://www.wsj.com, February 8.

60. E. Taylor & J. Singer, 2007, New UBS chief keeps strategy intact, *Wall Street Journal*, July 7, A3.

61. 2009, Breaking up the Citi, *Wall Street Journal*, January 14, A12; 2007, http://www.breakingviews.com: Citi to world: Drop "group," *Wall Street Journal*, January 17, C16.

62. 2009, Citigroup may sell Japanese units to raise cash, *Business 24-7*, http://www.business24-7.ae, February 26.

63. K. Bart, 2009, International finance: He cut costs at Credit Suisse; now he'll do it at UBS, *Wall Street Journal*, April 2, C2.

64. D. W. Ng, 2007, A modern resource based approach to unrelated diversification. *Journal of Management Studies*, 44(8): 1481–1502; D. D. Bergh, 1997, Predicting divestiture of unrelated acquisitions: An integrative model of ex ante conditions, *Strategic Management Journal*, 18: 715–731; C. W. L. Hill, 1994, Diversification and economic performance: Bringing structure and corporate management back into the picture, in R. P. Rumelt, D. E. Schendel, & D. J. Teece (eds.), *Fundamental Issues in Strategy*, Boston: Harvard Business School Press, 297–321.

65. Porter, *Competitive Advantage*.

66. S. Lee, K. Park, H. H. Shin, 2009, Disappearing internal capital markets: Evidence from diversified business groups in Korea. *Journal of Banking & Finance*, 33(2): 326–334; D. Collis, D. Young, & M. Goold, 2007, The size, structure, and performance of corporate headquarters, *Strategic Management Journal*, 28: 283–405; O. E. Williamson, 1975, *Markets and Hierarchies: Analysis and Antitrust Implications*, New York: Macmillan Free Press.

67. R. Aggarwal & N. A. Kyaw, 2009, International variations in transparency and capital structure: Evidence from european firms. *Journal of International Financial Management & Accounting*, 20(1): 1–34; R. J. Indjejikian, 2007, Discussion of accounting information, disclosure, and the cost of capital, *Journal of Accounting Research*, 45(2): 421–426.

68. A. Mackey, 2008, The effect of CEOs on firm performance, *Strategic Management Journal*, 29(12): 1357–1367; Dooms & Van Oijen, The balance between tailoring and standardizing control; D. Miller, R. Eisenstat, & N. Foote, 2002, Strategy from the inside out: Building capability-creating organizations, *California Management Review*, 44(3): 37–54; M. E. Raynor & J. L. Bower, 2001, Lead from the center: How to manage divisions dynamically, *Harvard Business Review*, 79(5): 92–100.

69. K. Kranhold, 2007, GE report raises doubts, *Wall Street Journal*, January 20–21, A3.

70. R. Ettenson & J. Knowles, 2008, Don't confuse reputation with brand. *MIT Sloan Management Review*, 49(2): 21.

71. P. Engardio & M. Arndt, 2007, What price reputation: Many savvy companies are starting to realize that a good name can be their most important asset—and actually boost the stock price. *Business Week*, July 8, 70–79; J. Lunsford & B. Steinberg, 2006, Conglomerates' conundrum, *Wall Street Journal*, B1, B7.

72. F. Guerrera, 2007, Siemens chief makes the case for conglomerates, *Financial Times*, http://www.ft.com, February 5.

73. B. Quint, 2009, Companies deal with tough times through diversification. *Information Today*, 26(3): 7–8.

74. A. Delios, D. Xu, & P. W. Beamish, 2008, Within-country product diversification and foreign subsidiary performance, *Journal of International Business Studies*, 39(4): 706–724; M. W. Peng & A. Delios, 2006, What determines the scope of the firm over time and around the world? An Asia Pacific perspective, *Asia Pacific Journal*

of Management, 23: 385–405; T. Khanna, K. G. Palepu, & J. Sinha, 2005, Strategies that fit emerging markets, Harvard Business Review, 83(6): 63–76.

75. Lee, Park, Shin, Disappearing internal capital markets: Evidence from diversified business groups in Korea; A. Chakrabarti, K. Singh, & I. Mahmood, 2006, Diversification and performance: Evidence from East Asian firms, Strategic Management Journal, 28: 101–120; T. Khanna & K. Palepu, 2000, Is group affiliation profitable in emerging markets? An analysis of diversified Indian business groups, Journal of Finance, 55: 867–892; T. Khanna & K. Palepu, 2000, The future of business groups in emerging markets: Long-run evidence from Chile, Academy of Management Journal, 43: 268–285.

76. D. D. Bergh, R. A. Johnson, & R. L. Dewitt, 2008, Restructuring through spin-off or sell-off: Transforming information asymmetries into financial gain, Strategic Management Journal, 29(2): 133–148; C. Decker & M. Mellewigt, 2007, Thirty years after Michael E. Porter: What do we know about business exit? Academy of Management Perspectives, 2: 41–55; S. J. Chang & H. Singh, 1999, The impact of entry and resource fit on modes of exit by multibusiness firms, Strategic Management Journal, 20: 1019–1035.

77. R. Coff, 2003, Bidding wars over R&D-intensive firms: Knowledge, opportunism, and the market for corporate control, Academy of Management Journal, 46: 74–85.

78. P. Navarro, 2009, Recession-proofing your organization, MIT Sloan Management Review, 50(3): 45–51.

79. M. Lubatkin, H. Merchant, & M. Srinivasan, 1997, Merger strategies and shareholder value during times of relaxed antitrust enforcement: The case of large mergers during the 1980s, Journal of Management, 23: 61–81.

80. D. P. Champlin & J. T. Knoedler, 1999, Restructuring by design? Government's complicity in corporate restructuring, Journal of Economic Issues, 33(1): 41–57.

81. R. M. Scherer & D. Ross, 1990, Industrial Market Structure and Economic Performance, Boston: Houghton Mifflin.

82. A. Shleifer & R. W. Vishny, 1994, Takeovers in the 1960s and 1980s: Evidence and implications, in R. P. Rumelt, D. E. Schendel, & D. J. Teece (eds.), Fundamental Issues in Strategy, Boston: Harvard Business School Press, 403–422.

83. S. Chatterjee, J. S. Harrison, & D. D. Bergh, 2003, Failed takeover attempts, corporate governance and refocusing, Strategic Management Journal, 24: 87–96; Lubatkin, Merchant, & Srinivasan, Merger strategies and shareholder value; D. J. Ravenscraft & R. M. Scherer, 1987, Mergers, Sell-Offs and Economic Efficiency, Washington, DC: Brookings Institution, 22.

84. D. A. Zalewski, 2001, Corporate takeovers, fairness, and public policy, Journal of Economic Issues, 35: 431–437; P. L. Zweig, J. P. Kline, S. A. Forest, & K. Gudridge, 1995, The case against mergers, BusinessWeek, October 30, 122–130; J. R. Williams, B. L. Paez, & L. Sanders, 1988, Conglomerates revisited, Strategic Management Journal, 9: 403–414.

85. E. J. Lopez, 2001, New anti-merger theories: A critique, Cato Journal, 20: 359–378; 1998, The trustbusters' new tools, The Economist, May 2, 62–64.

86. R. Croyle & P. Kager, 2002, Giving mergers a head start, Harvard Business Review, 80(10): 20–21.

87. M. C. Jensen, 1986, Agency costs of free cash flow, corporate finance, and takeovers, American Economic Review, 76: 323–329.

88. R. Gilson, M. Scholes, & M. Wolfson, 1988, Taxation and the dynamics of corporate control: The uncertain case for tax motivated acquisitions, in J. C. Coffee, L. Lowenstein, & S. Rose-Ackerman (eds.), Knights, Raiders, and Targets: The Impact of the Hostile Takeover, New York: Oxford University Press, 271–299.

89. C. Steindel, 1986, Tax reform and the merger and acquisition market: The repeal of the general utilities, Federal Reserve Bank of New York Quarterly Review, 11(3): 31–35.

90. M. A. Hitt, J. S. Harrison, & R. D. Ireland, 2001, Mergers and Acquisitions: A Guide to Creating Value for Stakeholders, New York: Oxford University Press.

91. J. Haleblian; J.-Y. Kim, & N. Rajagopalan, 2006, The influence of acquisition experience and performance on acquisition behavior: Evidence from the U.S. commercial banking industry, Academy of Management Journal, 49: 357–370.

92. D. B. Wilkerson & R. Britt, 2003, It's showtime for media deals: Radio lessons fuel debate over control of TV, newspapers, MarketWatch, http://www.marketwatch.com, May 30.

93. M. T. Brouwer, 2008, Horizontal mergers and efficiencies; theory and antitrust practice, European Journal of Law and Economics, 26(1): 11–26.

94. T. Afza, C. Slahudin, & M. S. Nazir, 2008, Diversification and corporate performance: An evaluation of Pakistani firms, South Asian Journal of Management, 15(3): 7–18; J. M. Shaver, 2006, A paradox of synergy: Contagion and capacity effects in mergers and acquisitions, Academy of Management Journal, 31: 962–976; C. Park, 2002, The effects of prior performance on the choice between related and unrelated acquisitions: Implications for the performance consequences of diversification strategy, Journal of Management Studies, 39: 1003–1019.

95. Rumelt, Strategy, Structure and Economic Performance, 125.

96. R. Waters, 2008, eBay ready to sell Skype if strong synergies prove elusive, Financial Times, April 18, 17; A. Lashinsky, 2008, Is Skype on sale at eBay? Fortune, October 27, 158(8): 48.

97. L. E. Palich, L. B. Cardinal, & C. C. Miller, 2000, Curvilinearity in the diversification-performance linkage: An examination of over three decades of research, Strategic Management Journal, 21: 155–174.

98. P. Eavis, 2008, Lehman faces dilemma; signs of weakness abound with talk of Neuberger sale, Wall Street Journal, August 19, C14.

99. D. G. Sirmon, M. A. Hitt, & R. D. Ireland, 2007, Managing firm resources in dynamic environments to create value: Looking inside the black box, Academy of Management Review, 32: 273–292; A. E. Bernardo & B. Chowdhry, 2002, Resources, real options, and corporate strategy, Journal of Financial Economics, 63: 211–234.

100. W. H. Tsai, Y. C. Kuo, J.-H. Hung, 2009, Corporate diversification and CEO turnover in family businesses: Self-entrenchment or risk reduction? Small Business Economics, 32(1): 57–76; N. W. C. Harper & S. P. Viguerie, 2002, Are you too focused? McKinsey Quarterly, Mid-Summer, 29–38; J. C. Sandvig & L. Coakley, 1998, Best practices in small firm diversification, Business Horizons, 41(3): 33–40.

101. T. Aeppel, 2009, Auto suppliers attempt reinvention, Wall Street Journal, June 15, B1-B2.

102. L. Jarvis, 2008, Pharma strategies: Merck launches into the biosimilars business, Chemical & Engineering News, December, 86(50): 7.

103. J. Carroll, 2009, Merck acquires bio-similars in $130M pact, Fierce Biotech, http://www.fiercebiotech.com, February 12.

104. T. B. Folta & J. P. O'Brien, 2008, Determinants of firm-specific thresholds in acquisition decisions, Managerial and Decision Economics, 29(2/3): 209–225.

105. N. M. Kay & A. Diamantopoulos, 1987, Uncertainty and synergy: Towards a formal model of corporate strategy, Managerial and Decision Economics, 8: 121–130.

106. R. W. Coff, 1999, How buyers cope with uncertainty when acquiring firms in knowledge-intensive industries: Caveat emptor, Organization Science, 10: 144–161.

107. P. B. Carroll & C. Muim 2008, 7 ways to fail big, Harvard Business Review, 86(9): 82–91.

108. D. G. Sirmon, S. Gove, & M. A. Hitt, 2008, Resource management in dyadic competitive rivalry: The effects of resource bundling and deployment, Academy of Management Journal, 51(5): 919–935; S. J. Chatterjee & B. Wernerfelt, 1991, The link between resources and type of diversification: Theory and evidence, Strategic Management Journal, 12: 33–48.

109. E. N. K. Lim, S. S. Das, & A. Das, 2009, Diversification strategy, capital structure, and the Asian financial crisis (1997–1998): Evidence from Singapore firms, Strategic Management Journal, 30(6): 577–594;

W. Keuslein, 2003, The Ebitda folly, *Forbes*, March 17, 165–167.

110. T.-I.Tsai & I. Johnson, 2009, Acer hopes to thrive in downturn, *Wall Street Journal*, February 17, B7.

111. L. Capron & J. Hulland, 1999, Redeployment of brands, sales forces, and general marketing management expertise following horizontal acquisitions: A resource-based view, *Journal of Marketing*, 63(2): 41–54.

112. M. V. S. Kumar, 2009, The relationship between product and international diversification: The effects of short-run constraints and endogeneity. *Strategic Management Journal*, 30(1): 99–116; C. B. Malone & L. C. Rose, 2006. Intangible assets and firm diversification, *International Journal of Managerial Finance*, 2(2): 136–153; A. M. Knott, D. J. Bryce, & H. E. Posen, 2003, On the strategic accumulation of intangible assets, *Organization Science*, 14: 192–207.

113. Bergh, Johnson, & Dewitt, Restructuring through spin-off or sell-off: Transforming information asymmetries into financial gain; K. Shimizu & M. A. Hitt, 2005, What constrains or facilitates divestitures of formerly acquired firms? The effects of organizational inertia, *Journal of Management*, 31: 50–72.

114. D. Cimilluca & J. Jargon, 2009, Corporate news: Sara Lee weighs sale of European business, *Wall Street Journal*, March 13, B3; J. Jargon & J. Vuocolo, 2007, Sara Lee CEO challenged on antitakeover defenses, *Wall Street Journal*, May 11, B4.

115. M. A. Williams, T. B. Michael, & E. R. Waller, 2008, Managerial incentives and acquisitions: a survey of the literature. *Managerial Finance*, 34(5): 328–341; J. G. Combs & M. S. Skill, 2003, Managerialist and human capital explanation for key executive pay premiums: A contingency perspective, *Academy of Management Journal*, 46: 63–73; M. A. Geletkanycz, B. K. Boyd, & S. Finkelstein, 2001, The strategic value of CEO external directorate networks: Implications for CEO compensation, *Strategic Management Journal*, 9: 889–898; W. Grossman & R. E. Hoskisson, 1998, CEO pay at the crossroads of Wall Street and Main: Toward the strategic design of executive compensation, *Academy of Management Executive*, 12(1): 43–57.

116. R. E. Hoskisson, M. W. Castleton, & M. C. Withers, 2009, Complementarity in monitoring and bonding: More intense monitoring leads to higher

executive compensation, *Academy of Management Perspectives*, 23(2): 57–74; Kaplan, S. N. 2008a. Are CEOs overpaid? *Academy of Management Perspectives*, 22(2): 5–20.

117. Geiger & Cashen, Organizational size and CEO compensation; J. J. Cordeiro & R. Veliyath, 2003, Beyond pay for performance: A panel study of the determinants of CEO compensation, *American Business Review*, 21(1): 56–66; Wright, Kroll, & Elenkov, Acquisition returns, increase in firm size, and chief executive officer compensation; S. R. Gray & A. A. Cannella Jr., 1997, The role of risk in executive compensation, *Journal of Management*, 23: 517–540.

118. Kaplan, Are CEOs overpaid?; R. Bliss & R. Rosen, 2001, CEO compensation and bank mergers, *Journal of Financial Economics*, 1: 107–138; W. G. Sanders & M. A. Carpenter, 1998, Internationalization and firm governance: The roles of CEO compensation, top team composition, and board structure, *Academy of Management Journal*, 41: 158–178.

119. J. Bogle, 2008, Reflections on CEO compensation, *Academy of Management Perspectives*, 22(2): 21–25; J. J. Janney, 2002, Eat or get eaten? How equity ownership and diversification shape CEO risk-taking, *Academy of Management Executive*, 14(4): 157–158; J. W. Lorsch, A. S. Zelleke, & K. Pick, 2001, Unbalanced boards, *Harvard Business Review*, 79(2): 28–30; R. E. Hoskisson & T. Turk, 1990, Corporate restructuring: Governance and control limits of the internal market, *Academy of Management Review*, 15: 459–477.

120. M. Kahan & E. B. Rock, 2002, How I learned to stop worrying and love the pill: Adaptive responses to takeover law, *University of Chicago Law Review*, 69(3): 871–915.

121. R. C. Anderson, T. W. Bates, J. M. Bizjak, & M. L. Lemmon, 2000, Corporate governance and firm diversification, *Financial Management*, 29(1): 5–22; J. D. Westphal, 1998, Board games: How CEOs adapt to increases in structural board independence from management, *Administrative Science Quarterly*, 43: 511–537; J. K. Seward & J. P. Walsh, 1996, The governance and control of voluntary corporate spin offs, *Strategic Management Journal*, 17: 25–39; J. P. Walsh & J. K. Seward, 1990, On the efficiency of internal and external corporate control mechanisms, *Academy of Management Review*, 15: 421–458.

122. S. M. Campbell, A. J. Ward, J. A. Sonnenfeld, & B. R. Agle, 2008, Relational ties that bind: Leader-follower relationship dimensions and charismatic attribution. *Leadership Quarterly*, 19(5): 556–568; M. Wiersema, 2002, Holes at the top: Why CEO firings backfire, *Harvard Business Review*, 80(12): 70–77.

123. J. M. Bizjak, M. L. Lemmon, & L. Naveen, 2008, Does the use of peer groups contribute to higher pay and less efficient compensation? *Journal of Financial Economics*, 90(2): 152–168; N. Wasserman, 2006, Stewards, agents, and the founder discount: Executive compensation in new ventures, *Academy of Management Journal*, 49: 960–976; V. Kisfalvi & P. Pitcher, 2003, Doing what feels right: The influence of CEO character and emotions on top management team dynamics, *Journal of Management Inquiry*, 12(10): 42–66; W. G. Rowe, 2001, Creating wealth in organizations: The role of strategic leadership, *Academy of Management Executive*, 15(1): 81–94.

124. E. F. Fama, 1980, Agency problems and the theory of the firm, *Journal of Political Economy*, 88: 288–307.

125. M. Y. Brannen & M. F. Peterson, 2009, Merging without alienating: Interventions promoting cross-cultural organizational integration and their limitations, *Journal of International Business Studies*, 40(3): 468–489; M. L. A. Hayward, 2002, When do firms learn from their acquisition experience? Evidence from 1990–1995, *Strategic Management Journal*, 23: 21–39; L. Capron, W. Mitchell, & A. Swaminathan, 2001, Asset divestiture following horizontal acquisitions: A dynamic view, *Strategic Management Journal*, 22: 817–844.

126. R. E. Hoskisson, R. A. Johnson, L. Tihanyi, & R. E. White, 2005, Diversified business groups and corporate refocusing in emerging economies, *Journal of Management*, 31: 941–965.

127. C. N. Chung & X. Luo, 2008, Institutional logics or agency costs: The influence of corporate governance models on business group restructuring in emerging economies, *Organization Science*, 19(5): 766–784; Chakrabarti, Singh, & Mahmood, Diversification and performance: Evidence from East Asian firms; W. P. Wan & R. E. Hoskisson, 2003, Home country environments, corporate diversification strategies, and firm performance, *Academy of Management Journal*, 46: 27–45.

Chapter 7

1. M. L. McDonald, J. D. Westphal, & M. E. Graebner, 2008, What do they know? The effects of outside director acquisition experience on firm acquisition performance, *Strategic Management Journal*, 29: 1155–1177; K. Uhlenbruck,

M. A. Hitt, & M. Semadeni, 2006, Market value effects of acquisitions involving Internet firms: A resource-based analysis, *Strategic Management Journal*, 27: 899–913.

2. J. Wiklund & D. A. Shepherd, 2009, The effectiveness of alliances and acquisitions:

The role of resource combination activities, *Entrepreneurship Theory and Practice*, 33: 193–212; C.-C. Lu, 2006, Growth strategies and merger patterns among small and medium sized enterprises: An empirical study,

International Journal of Management, 23: 529–547.

3. M. A. Hitt, D. King, H. Krishnan, M. Makri, M. Schijven, K. Shimizu, & H. Zhu, 2009, Mergers and acquisitions: Overcoming pitfalls, building synergy and creating value, *Business Horizons,* in press.

4. G. M. McNamara, J. Haleblian, & B. J. Dykes, 2008, The performance implications of participating in an acquisition wave: Early mover advantages, bandwagon effects, and the moderating influence of industry characteristics and acquirer tactics, *Academy of Management Journal,* 51: 113–130; J. Haleblian; J. Y. Kim, & N. Rajagopalan, 2006, The influence of acquisition experience and performance on acquisition behavior: Evidence from the U.S. commercial banking industry, *Academy of Management Journal,* 49: 357–370; M. A. Hitt, J. S. Harrison, & R. D. Ireland, 2001, *Mergers and Acquisitions: A Guide to Creating Value for Stakeholders,* New York: Oxford University Press.

5. R. Dobbs & V. Tortorici, 2007, Cool heads will bring in the best deals; Boardroom discipline is vital if the M&A boom is to benefit shareholders, *Financial Times,* February 28, 6.

6. J. Silver-Greenberg, 2009, Dealmakers test the waters, *BusinessWeek,* March 2, 18–20.

7. J. Y. Kim & S. Finkelstein, 2009, The effects of strategic and market complementarity on acquisition performance: Evidence from the U.S. commercial banking industry, 1989–2001; *Strategic Management Review,* 30: 617–646; J. J. Reuer, 2005, Avoiding lemons in M&A deals, *MIT Sloan Management Review,* 46(3).

8. M. Baker, X. Pan, & J. Wurgler, 2009, The psychology of pricing in mergers and acquisitions, Working Paper: http://www.papers.ssrn.com/so13/papers.cfm?abstract_id=1364152; K. Cool & M. Van de Laar, 2006, The performance of acquisitive companies in the U.S. In L. Renneboog (ed.), *Advances in Corporate Finance and Asset Pricing,* Amsterdam, Netherlands: Elsevier Science, 77–105.

9. M. Peers, 2009, NetApp should end Data Domain chase, *Wall Street Journal Online,* http://www.wsj.com, July 6.

10. K. J. Martijn Cremers, V. B. Nair, & K. John, 2009, Takeovers and the cross-section of returns, *Review of Financial Studies,* 22: 1409–1445; C. Tuch & N. O'Sullivan, 2007, The impact of acquisitions on firm performance: A review of the evidence, *International Journal of Management Review,* 9(2): 141–170.

11. J. McCracken & J. S. Lublin, 2009, Towers Perrin and Watson Wyatt to merge, *Wall Street Journal Online,* http://www.wsj.com, June 29.

12. M. Curtin, 2009, Xstrata's well-timed bear hug, *Wall Street Journal Online,* http://www.wsj.com, June 22.

13. S. Sudarsanam & A. A. Mahate, 2006, Are friendly acquisitions too bad for shareholders and managers? Long-term value creation and top management turnover in hostile and friendly acquirers, *British Journal of Management: Supplement,* 17(1): S7–S30.

14. A. R. Sorkin, 2009, Exelon raises hostile bid for NRG, *New York Times Online,* http://www.nytimes.com, July 2.

15. E. Akdogu, 2009, Gaining a competitive edge through acquisitions: Evidence from the telecommunications industry, *Journal of Corporate Finance,* 15: 99–112; E. Devos, P.-R. Kadapakkam, & S. Krishnamurthy, 2009, How do mergers create value? A comparison of taxes, market power, and efficiency improvements as explanations for synergies, *Review of Financial Studies,* 22: 1179–1211.

16. J. Haleblian, C. E. Devers, G. McNamara, M. A. Carpenter, & R. B. Davison, 2009, Taking stock of what we know about mergers and acquisitions: A review and research agenda, *Journal of Management,* 35: 469–502; P. Wright, M. Kroll, & D. Elenkov, 2002, Acquisition returns, increase in firm size and chief executive officer compensation: The moderating role of monitoring, *Academy of Management Journal,* 45: 599–608.

17. A. Vance, 2009, Acer's chief urges more consolidation of the PC industry, *New York Times Online,* http://www.nytimes.com, July 7.

18. C. Tighe, 2009, Vertu buys up Brooklyn assets, *Financial Times Online,* http://www.ft.com, June 27;

19. K. E. Meyer, S. Estrin, S. K. Bhaumik, & M. W. Peng, 2009, Institutions, resources, and entry strategies in emerging economies, *Strategic Management Journal,* 30: 61–80; D. K. Oler, J. S. Harrison, & M. R. Allen, 2008, The danger of misinterpreting short-window event study findings in strategic management research: An empirical illustration using horizontal acquisitions, *Strategic Organization,* 6: 151–184.

20. A. Harrison, 2009, NAB buys Aviva assets, *Wall Street Journal Online,* http://www.wsj.com, June 23.

21. N. Casey, 2009, Toys "R" Us is purchasing retailer FAO Schwarz, *Wall Street Journal Online,* http://www.wsj.com, May 28.

22. C. E. Fee & S. Thomas, 2004, Sources of gains in horizontal mergers: Evidence from customer, supplier, and rival firms, *Journal of Financial Economics,* 74: 423–460.

23. T. Ushijima, 2009, R&D intensity and acquisition and divestiture of corporate assets: Evidence from Japan, *Journal of Economics and Business,* 61(5): 415–433; L. Capron, W. Mitchell, & A. Swaminathan, 2001, Asset divestiture following horizontal acquisitions: A dynamic view, *Strategic Management Journal,* 22: 817–844.

24. B. Gulbrandsen, K. Sandvik, & S. A. Haugland, 2009, Antecedents of vertical integration: Transaction cost economics and resource-based explanations, *Journal of Purchasing and Supply Management,* 15: 89–102; F. T. Rothaermel, M. A. Hitt, & L. A. Jobe, 2006, Balancing vertical integration and strategic outsourcing: Effects on product portfolio, product success, and firm performance, *Strategic Management Journal,* 27: 1033–1056.

25. A. Parmigiani, 2007, Why do firms both make and buy? An investigation of concurrent sourcing, *Strategic Management Journal,* 28: 285–311.

26. 2009, Our businesses, http://www.info.cvscaremark.com, July 7.

27. 2009, Boeing completes acquisition of eXMeritus Inc., http://www.boeing.mediaroom.com, June 22.

28. J. W. Brock & N. P. Obst, 2009, Market concentration, economic welfare, and antitrust policy, *Journal of Industry, Competition and Trade,* 9: 65–75; M. T. Brouwer, 2008, Horizontal mergers and efficiencies: Theory and antitrust practice, *European Journal of Law and Economics,* 26: 11–26.

29. 2008, Procter & Gamble Annual Report, http://www.pg.com, July.

30. K. E. Meyer, M. Wright, & S. Pruthi, 2009, Managing knowledge in foreign entry strategies: A resource-based analysis, *Strategic Management Journal,* 30: 557–574; S.-F. S. Chen & M. Zeng, 2004, Japanese investors' choice of acquisitions vs. startups in the U.S.: The role of reputation barriers and advertising outlays, *International Journal of Research in Marketing,* 21(2): 123–136.

31. C. Y. Tseng, 2009, Technological innovation in the BRIC economies, *Research-Technology Management,* 52: 29–35; S. McGee, 2007, Seeking value in BRICs, *Barron's,* July 9, L10–L11.

32. R. Chakrabarti, N. Jayaraman, & S. Mukherjee, 2009, Mars-Venus marriages: Culture and cross-border M&A, *Journal of International Business Studies,* 40: 216–237.

33. S. Jessop, 2009, "Brave" post-Lehman M&A rewarded by market—Study, *New York Times Online,* http://www.nytimes.com, July 5.

34. E. Zabinski, D. Freeman, & X. Jian, 2009, Navigating the challenges of cross-border M&A, *The Deal Magazine,* http://www.thedeal.com, May 29.

35. N. Kumar, 2009, *The Economic Times,* http://www.economictimes.indiatimes.com, March 27.

36. J. Chapman & W. Xu, 2008, Ten strategies for successful cross-border acquisitions in China, Nixon Peabody LLP Special Report, Mergers & Acquisitions, September, 30–35.

37. M. Makri, M. A. Hitt, & P. J. Lane, 2009, Complementary technologies, knowledge relatedness, and invention outcomes in high technology M&As, *Strategic Management Journal,* in press; C. Homburg & M. Bucerius, 2006, Is speed of integration really a success

factor of mergers and acquisitions? An analysis of the role of internal and external relatedness, *Strategic Management Journal*, 27: 347–367.

38. H. K. Ellonen, P. Wilstrom, & A. Jantunen, 2009, Linking dynamic-capability portfolios and innovation outcomes, *Technovation*, in press; M. Song & C. A. De Benedetto, 2008, Supplier's involvement and success of radical new product development in new ventures, *Journal of Operations Management*, 26: 1–22; S. Karim, 2006, Modularity in organizational structure: The reconfiguration of internally developed and acquired business units, *Strategic Management Journal*, 27: 799–823.

39. R. E. Hoskisson & L. W. Busenitz, 2002, Market uncertainty and learning distance in corporate entrepreneurship entry mode choice, in M. A. Hitt, R. D. Ireland, S. M. Camp, & D. L. Sexton (eds.), *Strategic Entrepreneurship: Creating a New Mindset*, Oxford, U.K.: Blackwell Publishers, 151–172; M. A. Hitt, R. E. Hoskisson, R. A. Johnson, & D. D. Moesel, 1996, The market for corporate control and firm innovation, *Academy of Management Journal*, 39: 1084–1119.

40. E. Steel, 2009, AOL buys two companies specializing in local online media, *Wall Street Journal Online*, http://www.wsj.com, June 11.

41. W. P. Wan & D. W Yiu, 2009, From crisis to opportunity: Environmental jolt, corporate acquisitions, and firm performance, *Strategic Management Journal*, 30: 791–801; L. F. Hsieh & Y.-T. Tsai, 2005, Technology investment mode of innovative technological corporations: M&A strategy intended to facilitate innovation, *Journal of American Academy of Business*, 6(1): 185–194; G. Ahuja & R. Katila, 2001, Technological acquisitions and the innovation performance of acquiring firms: A longitudinal study, *Strategic Management Journal*, 22: 197–220.

42. F. Damanpour, R. M. Walker, & C. N. Avellaneda, 2009, Combinative effects of innovation types and organizational performance: A longitudinal study of service organizations, *Journal of Management Studies*, 46: 650–675.

43. F. Vermeulen, 2005, How acquisitions can revitalize companies, *MIT Sloan Management Review*, 46(4): 45–51; M. A. Hitt, R. E. Hoskisson, R. D. Ireland, & J. S. Harrison, 1991, Effects of acquisitions on R&D inputs and outputs, *Academy of Management Journal*, 34: 693–706.

44. B. White, 2007, Cisco to buy IronPort, a network-security firm, *Wall Street Journal*, January 4, A10.

45. 2009, Cisco breaks new ground in e-mail security, http://www.cisco.com, March 3.

46. H. Prechel, T. Morris, T. Woods, & R. Walden, 2008, Corporate diversification revisited: The political-legal environment, the multilayer-subsidiary form, and mergers and acquisitions, *The Sociological Quarterly*, 49: 849–878; C. E. Helfat & K. M. Eisenhardt, 2004, Inter-temporal economies of scope, organizational modularity, and the dynamics of diversification, *Strategic Management Journal*, 25: 1217–1232.

47. J. L. Lunsford, 2007, Boss talk: Transformer in transition; He turned UTC into giant; now, CEO George David carefully prepares successor, *Wall Street Journal*, May 17, B1.

48. T. Laamanen & T. Keil, 2008, Performance of serial acquirers: Toward an acquisition program perspective, *Strategic Management Journal*, 29: 663–672; D. J. Miller, M. J. Fern, & L. B. Cardinal, 2007, The use of knowledge for technological innovation within diversified firms, *Academy of Management Journal*, 50: 308–326.

49. J. Anand & H. Singh, 1997, Asset redeployment, acquisitions and corporate strategy in declining industries, *Strategic Management Journal*, 18 (Special Issue): 99–118.

50. T. Yu, M. Subramaniam, & A. A. Cannella, Jr., 2009, Rivalry deterrence in international markets: Contingencies governing the mutual forbearance hypothesis, *Academy of Management Journal*, 52: 127–147; D. G. Sirmon, S. Gove, & M. A. Hitt, 2008, Resource management in dyadic competitive rivalry: The effects of resource bundling and deployment, *Academy of Management Journal*, 51: 919–933.

51. H. Rui & G. S. Yip, 2008, Foreign acquisitions by Chinese firms: A strategic intent perspective, *Journal of World Business*, 43: 213–226; P. Puranam & K. Srikanth, 2007, What they know vs. what they do: How acquirers leverage technology acquisitions, *Strategic Management Journal*, 28: 805–825.

52. S. A. Zahra & J. C. Hayton, 2008, The effect of international venturing on firm performance: The moderating influence of absorptive capacity, *Journal of Business Venturing*, 23: 195–220.

53. J. S. Harrison, M. A. Hitt, R. E. Hoskisson, & R. D. Ireland, 2001, Resource complementarity in business combinations: Extending the logic to organizational alliances, *Journal of Management*, 27: 679–690.

54. J. Whalen, 2007, AstraZeneca thinks bigger; new chief increases commitment to 'large molecule' biological drugs, *Wall Street Journal*, May 22, A7.

55. J. A. Schmidt, 2002, Business perspective on mergers and acquisitions, in J. A. Schmidt (ed.), *Making Mergers Work*, Alexandria, VA: Society for Human Resource Management, 23–46.

56. Jessop, "Brave" post-Lehman M&A rewarded by market.

57. M. Cording, P. Christmann, & D. R. King, 2008, Reducing causal ambiguity in acquisition integration: Intermediate goals as mediators of integration decisions and acquisition performance, *Academy of Management Journal*, 51: 744–767; M. Zollo & H. Singh, 2004, Deliberate learning in corporate acquisitions: Post-acquisition strategies and integration capability in U.S. bank mergers, *Strategic Management Journal*, 25: 1233–1256.

58. N. Kumar, 2009, How emerging giants are rewriting the rules of M&A, *Harvard Business Review*, 87(5): 115–121; M. C. Sturman, 2008, The value of human capital specificity versus transferability, *Journal of Management*, 34: 290–316.

59. K. M. Ellis, T. H. Reus, & B. T. Lamont, 2009, The effects of procedural and informational justice in the integration of related acquisitions, *Strategic Management Journal*, 30: 137–161; F. Vermeulen, 2007, Business insight (a special report); bad deals: Eight warning signs that an acquisition may not pay off, *Wall Street Journal*, April 28, R10.

60. M. Zollo, 1999, M&A—The challenge of learning to integrate: Mastering strategy (part eleven), *Financial Times*, December 6, 14–15.

61. H. G. Barkema & M. Schijven, 2008, Toward unlocking the full potential of acquisitions: The role of organizational restructuring, *Academy of Management Journal*, 51: 696–722; J. Harrison, 2007, Why integration success eludes many buyers, *Mergers and Acquisitions*, 42(3): 18–20.

62. R. Gibson, 2006, Package deal; UPS's purchase of Mail Boxes Etc. looked great on paper. Then came the culture clash, *Wall Street Journal*, May 8, R13.

63. Z. Kouwe, 2009, Deals on ice in first half, with 40% drop in M&A, *New York Times Online*, http://www.nytimes.com, July 1.

64. T. B. Folta & J. P. O'Brien, 2008, Determinants of firm-specific thresholds in acquisition decisions, *Managerial and Decision Economics*, 29: 209–225; R. J. Rosen, 2006, Merger momentum and investor sentiment: The stock market reaction to merger announcements, *Journal of Business*, 79: 987–1017.

65. A. Rappaport & Sirower, Stock or cash? *Harvard Business Review*, 77(6): 149.

66. Peers, NetApp should end Data Domain chase.

67. G. Yago, 1991, *Junk Bonds: How High Yield Securities Restructured Corporate America*, New York: Oxford University Press, 146–148.

68. M. C. Jensen, 1986, Agency costs of free cash flow, corporate finance, and takeovers, *American Economic Review*, 76: 323–329.

69. J. Leahy & J. Reed, 2009, Tata strained by UK acquisitions, *Financial Times Online*, http://www.ft.com, May 21.

70. T. H. Noe & M. J. Rebello, 2006, The role of debt purchases in takeovers: A tale of two retailers, *Journal of Economics & Management Strategy*, 15 (3): 609–648; M. A. Hitt & D. L. Smart, 1994, Debt: A disciplining force for managers or a debilitating force for organizations?

Journal of Management Inquiry, 3: 144–152.

71. C. Jong-Woo, 2009, Kumho Asiana to sell Daewoo Engineering, *Fidelity.com,* http://www.fidelity.com, June 28.

72. S. W. Bauguess, S. B. Moeller, F. P. Schlingemann, & C. J. Zutter, 2009, Ownership structure and target returns, *Journal of Corporate Finance,* 15: 48–65; H. Donker & S. Zahir, 2008, Takeovers, corporate control, and return to target shareholders, *International Journal of Corporate Governance,* 1: 106–134.

73. A. B. Sorescu, R. K. Chandy, & J. C. Prabhu, 2007, Why some acquisitions do better than others: Product capital as a driver of long-term stock returns, *Journal of Marketing Research,* 44(1): 57–72; T. Saxton & M. Dollinger, 2004, Target reputation and appropriability: Picking and deploying resources in acquisitions, *Journal of Management,* 30: 123–147.

74. J. B. Barney, 1988, Returns to bidding firms in mergers and acquisitions: Reconsidering the relatedness hypothesis, *Strategic Management Journal,* 9 (Special Issue): 71–78.

75. O. E. Williamson, 1999, Strategy research: Governance and competence perspectives, *Strategic Management Journal,* 20: 1087–1108.

76. S. Chatterjee, 2007, Why is synergy so difficult in mergers of related businesses? *Strategy & Leadership,* 35(2): 46–52.

77. J. Santalo & M. Becerra, 2009, Competition from specialized firms and the diversification-performance linkage, *Journal of Finance,* 63: 851–883; C. W. L. Hill & R. E. Hoskisson, 1987, Strategy and structure in the multiproduct firm, *Academy of Management Review,* 12: 331–341.

78. M. L. A. Hayward & K. Shimizu, 2006, De-commitment to losing strategic action: Evidence from the divestiture of poorly performing acquisitions, *Strategic Management Journal,* 27: 541–557; R. A. Johnson, R. E. Hoskisson, & M. A. Hitt, 1993, Board of director involvement in restructuring: The effects of board versus managerial controls and characteristics, *Strategic Management Journal,* 14 (Special Issue): 33–50; C. C. Markides, 1992, Consequences of corporate refocusing: Ex ante evidence, *Academy of Management Journal,* 35: 398–412.

79. D. Marginso & L. McAulay, 2008, Exploring the debate on short-termism: A theoretical and empirical analysis, *Strategic Management Journal,* 29: 273–292; R. E. Hoskisson & R. A. Johnson, 1992, Corporate restructuring and strategic change: The effect on diversification strategy and R&D intensity, *Strategic Management Journal,* 13: 625–634.

80. T. Keil, M. V. J. Maula, H. Schildt, & S. A. Zahra, 2008, The effect of governance modes and relatedness of external business development activities on innovative performance, *Strategic Management Journal,* 29: 895–907; K. H. Tsai & J. C. Wang, 2008, External technology acquisition and firm performance: A longitudinal study, *Journal of Business Venturing,* 23: 91–112.

81. A. Kacperczyk, 2009, With greater power comes greater responsibility? Takeover protection and corporate attention to stakeholders, *Strategic Management Journal,* 30: 261–285; L. H. Lin, 2009, Mergers and acquisitions, alliances and technology development: An empirical study of the global auto industry, *International Journal of Technology Management,* 48: 295–307; M. L. Barnett, 2008, An attention-based view of real options reasoning, *Academy of Management Review,* 33: 606–628.

82. M. L. A. Hayward & D. C. Hambrick, 1997, Explaining the premiums paid for large acquisitions: Evidence of CEO hubris, *Administrative Science Quarterly* 42: 103–127; R. Roll, 1986, The hubris hypothesis of corporate takeovers, *Journal of Business,* 59: 197–216.

83. Vermeulen, Business insight (a special report); bad deals: Eight warning signs that an acquisition may not pay off.

84. L. A. Nemanich & D. Vera, 2009, Transformational leadership and ambidexterity in the context of an acquisition, *The Leadership Quarterly,* 20: 19–33.

85. 2009, Our company, http://www.lizclaiborne.com, July 12; R. Dobbs, 2007, Claiborne seeks to shed 16 apparel brands, *Wall Street Journal,* July 11, B1, B2.

86. V. Swaminathan, F. Murshed, & J. Hulland, 2008, Value creation following merger and acquisition announcements: The role of strategic emphasis alignment, *Journal of Marketing Research,* 45: 33–47.

87. Vermeulen, Business insight (a special report); bad deals: Eight warning signs that an acquisition may not pay off.

88. H. G. Barkema & M. Schijven, 2008, How do firms learn to make acquisitions? A review of past research and an agenda for the future, *Journal of Management,* 34: 594–634.

89. S. Chatterjee, 2009, The keys to successful acquisition programmes, *Long Range Planning,* 42: 137–163; C. M. Sanchez & S. R. Goldberg, 2009, Strategic M&As: Stronger in tough times? *Journal of Corporate Accounting & Finance,* 20: 3–7; C. Duncan & M. Mtar, 2006, Determinants of international acquisition success: Lessons from FirstGroup in North America, *European Management Journal,* 24: 396–410.

90. D. Mayer & M. Kenney, 2004, Economic action does not take place in a vacuum: Understanding Cisco's acquisition and development strategy, *Industry and Innovation,* 11(4): 299–325.

91. 2009, Connection for acquired employees, http://www.cisco.com, July 12.

92. M. A. Hitt, R. D. Ireland, J. S. Harrison, & A. Best, 1998, Attributes of successful and unsuccessful acquisitions of U.S. firms, *British Journal of Management,* 9: 91–114.

93. Uhlenbruck, Hitt, & Semadeni, Market value effects of acquisitions involving Internet firms: A resource-based analysis; J. Hagedoorn & G. Dysters, 2002, External sources of innovative capabilities: The preference for strategic alliances or mergers and acquisitions, *Journal of Management Studies,* 39: 167–188.

94. J. J. Reuer & R. Ragozzino, 2006, Agency hazards and alliance portfolios, *Strategic Management Journal,* 27: 27–43; P. Porrini, 2004, Can a previous alliance between an acquirer and a target affect acquisition performance? *Journal of Management,* 30: 545–562.

95. D. J. Kisgen, J. Qian, & W. Song, 2009, Are fairness opinions fair? The case of mergers and acquisitions, *Journal of Financial Economics,* 91: 179–207; R. J. Aiello & M. D. Watkins, 2000, The fine art of friendly acquisition, *Harvard Business Review,* 78(6): 100–107.

96. S. Chatterjee, 2009, Does increased equity ownership lead to more strategically involved boards? *Journal of Business Ethics,* 87: 267–277; D. D. Bergh, 2001, Executive retention and acquisition outcomes: A test of opposing views on the influence of organizational tenure, *Journal of Management,* 27: 603–622; J. P. Walsh, 1989, Doing a deal: Merger and acquisition negotiations and their impact upon target company top management turnover, *Strategic Management Journal,* 10: 307–322.

97. D. A. Waldman & M. Javidan, 2009, Alternative forms of charismatic leadership in the integration of mergers and acquisitions, *The Leadership Quarterly,* 20: 130–142; F. J. Froese, Y. S. Pak, & L. C. Chong, 2008, Managing the human side of cross-border acquisitions in South Korea, *Journal of World Business,* 43: 97–108.

98. M. E. Graebner, 2009, Caveat Venditor: Trust asymmetries in acquisitions of entrepreneurial firms, *Academy of Management Journal,* 52: 435–472; N. J. Morrison, G. Kinley, & K. L. Ficery, 2008, Merger deal breakers: When operational due diligence exposes risk, *Journal of Business Strategy,* 29: 23–28.

99. J. M. Shaver & J. M. Mezias, 2009, Diseconomies of managing in acquisitions: Evidence from civil lawsuits, *Organization Science,* 20: 206–222; M. L. McDonald, J. D. Westphal, & M. E. Graebner, What do they know? The effects of outside director acquisition experience on firm acquisition performance, *Strategic Management Journal,* 29: 1155–1177.

100. D. D. Bergh & E. N.-K. Lim, 2008, Learning how to restructure: Absorptive capacity and improvisational views of restructuring actions and performance, *Strategic Management Journal,* 29: 593–616; J. K. Kang, J. M. Kim, W. L. Liu, & S. Yi, 2006, Post-takeover restructuring and the sources of gains in foreign takeovers: Evidence from U.S. targets. *Journal of Business,* 79(5): 2503–2537.

101. Y. G. Suh & E. Howard, 2009, Restructuring retailing in Korea: The case of Samsung-Tesco, *Asia Pacific Business Review,* 15: 29–40; Z. Wu & A. Delios, 2009, The emergence of portfolio

restructuring in Japan, *Management International Review*, 49: 313–335; R. E. Hoskisson, A. A. Cannella, L. Tihanyi, & R. Faraci, 2004. Asset restructuring and business group affiliation in French civil law countries, *Strategic Management Journal*, 25: 525–539.

102. S. Thurm, 2008, Who are the best CEOs of 2008, *Wall Street Journal Online*, http://www.wsj.com, December 15.

103. J. L. Morrow Jr., D. G. Sirmon, M. A. Hitt, & T. R. Holcomb, 2007, Creating value in the face of declining performance: Firm strategies and organizational recovery, *Strategic Management Journal*, 28: 271–283; J. L. Morrow Jr., R. A. Johnson, & L. W. Busenitz, 2004, The effects of cost and asset retrenchment on firm performance: The overlooked role of a firm's competitive environment, *Journal of Management*, 30: 189–208.

104. G. J. Castrogiovanni & G. D. Bruton, 2000, Business turnaround processes following acquisitions: Reconsidering the role of retrenchment, *Journal of Business Research*, 48: 25–34; W. McKinley, J. Zhao, & K. G. Rust, 2000, A sociocognitive interpretation of organizational downsizing, *Academy of Management Review*, 25: 227–243.

105. J. D. Evans & F. Hefner, 2009, Business ethics and the decision to adopt golden parachute contracts: Empirical evidence of concern for all stakeholders, *Journal of Business Ethics*, 86: 65–79; H. A. Krishnan, M. A. Hitt, & D. Park, 2007, Acquisition premiums, subsequent workforce reductions and post-acquisition performance, *Journal of Management*, 44: 709–732.

106. K. McFarland, 2008, Four mistakes leaders make when downsizing, *BusinessWeek Online*, http://www.businessweek.com, October 24.

107. C. O. Trevor & A. J. Nyberg, 2008, Keeping your headcount when all about you are losing theirs: Downsizing, voluntary turnover rates, and the moderating role of HR practices, *Academy of Management Journal*, 51: 259–276.

108. Berg & Lim, Learning how to restructure; R. E. Hoskisson & M. A. Hitt, 1994, *Downscoping: How to Tame the Diversified Firm*, New York: Oxford University Press.

109. Ushijima, R&D intensity and acquisition and divestiture of corporate assets; G. Benou, J. Madura, & T. Ngo, 2008, Wealth creation from high-tech divestitures, *The Quarterly Review of Economics and Finance*, 48: 505–519; L. Dranikoff, T. Koller, & A. Schneider, 2002, Divestiture: Strategy's missing link, *Harvard Business Review*, 80(5): 74–83.

110. R. E. Hoskisson & M. A. Hitt, 1990, Antecedents and performance outcomes of diversification: A review and critique of theoretical perspectives, *Journal of Management*, 16: 461–509.

111. 2009, Motorola sells fiber-to-the-node product line, *New York Times Online*, http://www.nytimes.com, July 7.

112. M. Peers, 2009, Magazine business suffers shakeout, *Wall Street Journal Online*, http://www.wsj.com, July 13.

113. R. Perez-Pena, 2009, McGraw-Hill is said to be seeking a buyer for *BusinessWeek*, *New York Times Online*, http://www.nytimes.com, July 14.

114. A. Kambil, 2008, What is your recession playbook? *Journal of Business Strategy*, 29: 50–52; M. Rajand & M. Forsyth, 2002, Hostile bidders, long-term performance, and restructuring methods: Evidence from the UK, *American Business Review*, 20: 71–81.

115. D. Hillier, P. McColgan, & S. Werema, 2008, Asset sales and firm strategy: An analysis of divestitures by UK companies, *The European Journal of Finance*, 15: 71–87; R. E. Hoskisson, R. A. Johnson, L. Tihanyi, & R. E. White, 2005, Diversified business groups and corporate refocusing in emerging economies, *Journal of Management*, 31: 941–965.

116. S. N. Kaplan & P. Stromberg, 2009, Leveraged buyouts and private equity, *Journal of Economic Perspectives*, 23: 121–146; C. Moschieri & J. Mair, 2008, Research on corporate divestures: A synthesis, *Journal of Management & Organization*, 14: 399–422.

117. J. Mair & C. Moschieri, 2006, Unbundling frees business for take off, *Financial Times*, October 19, 2.

118. K. H. Wruck, 2009, Private equity, corporate governance, and the reinvention of the market for corporate control, *Journal of Applied Corporate Finance*, 20: 8–21; M. F. Wiersema & J. P. Liebeskind, 1995, The effects of leveraged buyouts on corporate growth and diversification in large firms, *Strategic Management Journal*, 16: 447–460.

119. R. Harris, D. S. Siegel, & M. Wright, 2005, Assessing the impact of management buyouts on economic efficiency: Plant-level evidence from the United Kingdom, *Review of Economics and Statistics*, 87: 148–153; A. Seth & J. Easterwood, 1995, Strategic redirection in large management buyouts: The evidence from post-buyout restructuring activity, *Strategic Management Journal*, 14: 251–274; P. H. Phan & C. W. L. Hill, 1995, Organizational restructuring and economic performance in leveraged buyouts: An ex-post study, *Academy of Management Journal*, 38: 704–739.

120. M. Meuleman, K. Amess, M. Wright, & L. Scholes, 2009, Agency, strategic entrepreneurship, and the performance of private equity-backed buyouts, *Entrepreneurship Theory and Practice*, 33: 213–239; C. M. Daily, P. P. McDougall, J. G. Covin, & D. R. Dalton, 2002, Governance and strategic leadership in entrepreneurial firms, *Journal of Management*, 3: 387–412.

121. W. Kiechel III, 2007, Private equity's long view, *Harvard Business Review*, 85(8): 18–20; M. Wright, R. E. Hoskisson, & L. W. Busenitz, 2001, Firm rebirth: Buyouts as facilitators of strategic growth and entrepreneurship, *Academy of Management Executive*, 15(1): 111–125.

122. E. G. Love & M. Kraatz, 2009, Character, conformity, or the bottom line? How

and why downsizing affected corporate reputation, *Academy of Management Journal*, 52: 314–335; J. P. Guthrie & D. K. Datta, 2008, Dumb and dumber: The impact of downsizing on firm performance as moderated by industry conditions, *Organization Science*, 19: 108–123.

123. H. A. Krishnan & D. Park, 2002, The impact of work force reduction on subsequent performance in major mergers and acquisitions: An exploratory study, *Journal of Business Research*, 55(4): 285–292; P. M. Lee, 1997, A comparative analysis of layoff announcements and stock price reactions in the United States and Japan, *Strategic Management Journal*, 18: 879–894.

124. D. J. Flanagan & K. C. O'Shaughnessy, 2005, The effect of layoffs on firm reputation, *Journal of Management*, 31: 445–463.

125. D. S. DeRue, J. R. Hollenbeck, M. D. Johnson, D. R. Ilgen, & D. K. Jundt, 2008, How different team downsizing approaches influence team-level adaptation and performance, *Academy of Management Journal*, 51: 182–196; C. D. Zatzick & R. D. Iverson, 2006, High-involvement management and workforce reduction: Competitive advantage or disadvantage? *Academy of Management Journal*, 49: 999–1015; N. Mirabal & R. DeYoung, 2005, Downsizing as a strategic intervention, *Journal of American Academy of Business*, 6(1): 39–45.

126. K. Shimizu & M. A. Hitt, 2005, What constrains or facilitates divestitures of formerly acquired firms? The effects of organizational inertia, *Journal of Management*, 31: 50–72.

127. D. T. Brown, C. E. Fee, & S. E. Thomas, 2009, Financial leverage and bargaining power with suppliers: Evidence from leveraged buyouts, *Journal of Corporate Finance*, 15: 196–211; S. Toms & M. Wright, 2005, Divergence and convergence within Anglo-American corporate governance systems: Evidence from the US and UK, 1950–2000, *Business History*, 47(2): 267–295.

128. G. Wood & M. Wright, 2009, Private equity: A review and synthesis, *International Journal of Management Reviews*, in press; A.-L. Le Nadant & F. Perdreau, 2006, Financial profile of leveraged buy-out targets: Some French evidence, *Review of Accounting and Finance*, (4): 370–392.

129. G. D. Bruton, J. K. Keels, & E. L. Scifres, 2002, Corporate restructuring and performance: An agency perspective on the complete buyout cycle, *Journal of Business Research*, 55: 709–724; W. F. Long & D. J. Ravenscraft, 1993, LBOs, debt, and R&D intensity, *Strategic Management Journal*, 14 (Special Issue): 119–135.

130. S. A. Zahra, 1995, Corporate entrepreneurship and financial performance: The case of management leveraged buyouts, *Journal of Business Venturing*, 10: 225–248.

Chapter 8

1. W. He & M. A. Lyles, 2009, China's outward foreign direct investment, *Business Horizons*, 51(6): 485–491.

2. B.C. Kho, R. M. Stulz, & F. E. Warnock, 2009, Financial globalization, governance, and the evolution of the home bias. *Journal of Accounting Research*, 47(2): 597–635; S. Li, 2005, Why a poor governance environment does not deter foreign direct investment: The case of China and its implications for investment protection, *Business Horizons*, 48(4): 297–302.

3. G. L. Ge & D. Z. Ding, 2009, A strategic analysis of surging Chinese manufacturers: The case of Galanz. *Asia Pacific Journal of Management*, 25(4): 667–683; A. K. Gupta & H. Wang, 2007, How to get China and India right: Western companies need to become smarter—and they need to do it quickly, *Wall Street Journal*, April 28, R4.

4. D. Kronborg & S. Thomsen, 2009, Foreign ownership and long-term survival, *Strategic Management Journal*, 30(2): 207–220; H. J. Sapienza, E. Autio, G. George, & S. A. Zahra, 2006, A capabilities perspective on the effects of early internationalization on firm survival and growth, *Academy of Management Review*, 31: 914–933; W. P. Wan, 2005, Country resource environments, firm capabilities, and corporate diversification strategies. *Journal of Management Studies*, 42: 161–182.

5. P. Enderwick, 2009, Large emerging markets (LEMs) and international strategy. *International Marketing Review*, 26(1): 7–16; F. T. Rothaermel, S. Kotha, & H. K. Steensma, 2006, International market entry by U.S. Internet firms: An empirical analysis of country risk, national culture and market size, *Journal of Management*, 32: 56–82; R. E. Hoskisson, H. Kim, R. E. White, & L. Tihanyi, 2004, A framework for understanding international diversification by business groups from emerging economies, in M. A. Hitt & J. L. C. Cheng (eds.), *Theories of the Multinational Enterprise: Diversity, Complexity, and Relevance. Advances in International Management*, Oxford, UK: Elsevier/JAI Press, 137–163.

6. M. Javidan, R. Steers, & M. A. Hitt (eds.), 2007, *The Global Mindset*. Oxford, UK: Elsevier Publishing; T. M. Begley & D. P. Boyd, 2003, The need for a corporate global mind-set, *MIT Sloan Management Review*, 44(2): 25–32.

7. M. W. Peng & E. G. Pleggenkuhle-Miles, 2009, Current debates in global strategy, *International Journal of Management Reviews*, 11(1): 51–68; M. A. Hitt, L. Tihanyi, T. Miller, & B. Connelly, 2006, International diversification: Antecedents, outcomes and moderators, *Journal of Management*, 32: 831–867.

8. Y. Luo & R. L. Tung, 2007, International expansion of emerging market enterprises: A springboard perspective, *Journal of International Business Studies* 38: 481–498; J. E. Ricart, M. J. Enright, P. Ghemawat, S. L. Hart, & T. Khanna, 2004, New frontiers in international strategy, *Journal of International Business Studies*, 35: 175–200.

9. R. Vernon, 1996, International investment and international trade in the product cycle, *Quarterly Journal of Economics*, 80: 190–207.

10. He & Lyles, China's outward foreign direct investment; P. J. Buckley, L. J. Clegg, A. R. Cross, X. Liu, H. Voss, & P. Zheng, 2006, The determinants of Chinese outward foreign direct investment, *Journal of International Business Studies*, 38: 499–518.

11. L. Yu, 2003, The global-brand advantage, *MIT Sloan Management Review*, 44(3): 13.

12. M. E. Lloyd, 2009, IKEA sees opportunity during hard times—as expansion in U.S. continues, Swedish retailer expects its value furnishings to appeal to shoppers amid economic slump, *Wall Street Journal*, February 18, B5A.

13. X. Liu & H. Zou, 2008, The impact of greenfield FDI and mergers and acquisitions on innovation in Chinese high-tech industries, *Journal of World Business*, 43(3): 352–364.

14. F. Fortanier & R. Van Tulder, 2009, Internationalization trajectories—a cross-country comparison: Are large Chinese and Indian companies different? *Industrial and Corporate Change*, 18(2 Special Issue): 223–247.

15. K. Addae-Dapaah & W. T. Y. Hwee, 2009, The unsung impact of currency risk on the performance of international real property investment, *Review of Financial Economics*, 18(1): 56–65; C. C. Y. Kwok & D. M. Reeb, 2000, Internationalization and firm risk: An upstream-downstream hypothesis, *Journal of International Business Studies*, 31: 611–629.

16. M. Wright, I. Filatotchev, R. E. Hoskisson, & M. W. Peng, 2005, Strategy research in emerging economies: Challenging the conventional wisdom, *Journal of Management Studies*, 42: 1–30; T. London & S. Hart, 2004, Reinventing strategies for emerging markets: Beyond the transnational model, *Journal of International Business Studies*, 35: 350–370; R. E. Hoskisson, L. Eden, C. M. Lau, & M. Wright, 2000, Strategy in emerging economies, *Academy of Management Journal*, 43: 249–267.

17. P. Zheng, 2009, A comparison of FDI determinants in China and India, *Thunderbird International Business Review*, 51(3): 263–279; H. Sender, 2005, The economy; the outlook: India comes of age, as focus on returns lures foreign capital, *Wall Street Journal*, June 6, A2.

18. S. Athreye & S. Kapur, 2009, Introduction: The internationalization of Chinese and Indian firms—trends, motivations and strategy. *Industrial and Corporate Change*,18(2 Special Issue): 209–221; M. A. Witt & A. Y. Lewin, 2007, Outward foreign direct investment as escape to home country institutional constraints, *Journal of International Business Studies*, 38: 579–594; M. W. Peng, S.-H. Lee, & D. Y. L. Wang, 2005, What determines the scope of the firm over time? A focus on institutional relatedness, *Academy of Management Review*, 30: 622–633.

19. J. W. Spencer, T. P. Murtha, & S. A. Lenway, 2005, How governments matter to new industry creation, *Academy of Management Review*, 30: 321–337; I. P. Mahmood & C. Rufin, 2005, Government's dilemma: The role of government in imitation and innovation, *Academy of Management Review*, 30: 338–360.

20. B. Elango, 2009, Minimizing effects of "liability of foreignness": Response strategies of foreign firms in the United States, *Journal of World Business*, 44(1), 51–62; L. Eden & S. Miller, 2004, Distance matters: Liability of foreignness, institutional distance and ownership strategy, in M. A. Hitt & J. L. Cheng (eds.), *Advances in International Management*, Oxford, UK: Elsevier/JAI Press, 187–221.

21. S. Anand, 2008, Japan M&A, Prescription for Growth, *BusinessWeek*, http://www.businessweek.com, November 17.

22. V. Bauerlein and G. Fairclough, 2009, Beijing thwarts Coke's takeover bid, *Wall Street Journal*, http://www.wsj.com, March 19.

23. H. Barnard, 2008, Uneven domestic knowledge bases and the success of foreign firms in the USA, *Research Policy*, 37(10): 1674–1683.

24. S. Shimizutani & Y. Todo, 2008, What determines overseas R&D activities? The case of Japanese multinational firms, *Research Policy*, 37(3): 530–544; J. Cantwell, J. Dunning, & O. Janne, 2004, Towards a technology-seeking explanation of U.S. direct investment in the United Kingdom, *Journal of International Management*, 10: 5–20; W. Chung & J. Alcacer, 2002, Knowledge seeking and location choice of foreign direct investment in the United States, *Management Science*, 48(12): 1534–1554.

25. F. Jiang, 2005, Driving forces of inter-national pharmaceutical firms' FDI into China, *Journal of Business Research*, 22(1): 21–39.

26. M. D. R. Chari, S. Devaraj, & P. David, 2007, International diversification and firm performance: Role of information technology investments, *Journal of World Business*, 42: 184–197; W. Chung, 2001, Identifying technology transfer in foreign direct investment: Influence of industry

conditions and investing firm motives, *Journal of International Business Studies*, 32: 211–229.

27. M. V. S. Kumar, 2009, The relationship between product and international diversification: The effects of short-run constraints and endogeneity. *Strategic Management Journal*, 30(1): 99–116; K. J. Petersen, R. B. Handfield, & G. L. Ragatz, 2005, Supplier integration into new product development: Co-ordinating product process and supply chain design, *Journal of Operations Management*, 23: 371–388.

28. C. Rauwald, 2009, Porsche chooses the China road; four-door Panamera's Shanghai debut signals focus on emerging markets, *Wall Street Journal*, April 20, B2; A. Webb, 2007, China needs strong automakers—not more. *Automotive News*, http://www.autonews.com, July 20; China's SAIC says first half sales up 23 percent. 2007, *Reuters*, http://www.reuters.com, July 12; A. Taylor, 2004, Shanghai Auto wants to be the world's next great car company, *Fortune*, October 4, 103–109.

29. K. D. Brouthers, L. E., Brouthers, & S. Werner, 2008, Resource-based advantages in an international context, *Journal of Management*, 34: 189–217; N. Karra, N. Phillips, & P. Tracey, 2008, Building the born global firm developing entrepreneurial capabilities for international new venture success, *Long Range Planning*, 41(4): 440–458; L. Zhou, W.-P. Wu, & X. Luo, 2007, Internationalization and the performance of born-global SMEs: The mediating role of social networks, *Journal of International Business Studies*, 38: 673–690.

30. H. Zou & P. N. Ghauri, 2009, Learning through international acquisitions: The process of knowledge acquisition in China, *Management International Review*, 48(2), 207–226; H. Berry, 2006, Leaders, laggards, and the pursuit of foreign knowledge, *Strategic Management Journal*, 27: 151–168.

31. J. Song & J. Shin, 2008, The paradox of technological capabilities: A study of knowledge sourcing from host countries of overseas R&D operations, *Journal of International Business Studies*, 39: 291–303; J. Penner-Hahn & J. M. Shaver, 2005, Does international research increase patent output? An analysis of Japanese pharmaceutical firms, *Strategic Management Journal*, 26: 121–140.

32. D. Strutton, 2009, Horseshoes, global supply chains, and an emerging Chinese threat: Creating remedies one idea at a time, *Business Horizons*, 52(1): 31–43.

33. A. M. Rugman & A. Verbeke, 2009, A new perspective on the regional and global strategies of multinational services firms, *Management International Review*, 48(4): 397–411; R. Tahir & J. Larimo, 2004, Understanding the location strategies of the European firms in Asian countries, *Journal of American Academy of Business*, 5: 102–110.

34. R. Chakrabarti, S. Gupta-Mukherjee, & N. Jayaraman, 2009, Mars-Venus marriages: Culture and cross-border M&A, *Journal of International Business Studies*, 40(2): 216–236; D. Xu & O. Shenkar, 2004, Institutional distance and the multinational enterprise, *Academy of Management Review*, 27: 608–618.

35. C. C. J. M. Millar & C. J. Choi, 2009, Worker identity, the liability of foreignness, the exclusion of local managers and unionism: A conceptual analysis, *Journal of Organizational Change Management*, 21(4): 460–470; D. Xu, Y. Pan, & P. W. Beamish, 2004, The effect of regulative and normative distances on MNE ownership and expatriate strategies, *Management International Review*, 44(3): 285–307.

36. N. Shirouzu, P. J. Ho, & K. Rapoza, 2009, Corporate news: GM plans to retain China, Brazil units, June 3, B2.

37. J. D. Stoll, 2009, Corporate news: GM pushes the throttle in China—affiliate's plan to expand into cars is seen as a key to growth in Asia, *Wall Street Journal*, April 27, B3.

38. J. Li & D. R. Yue, 2009, Market size, legal institutions, and international diversification strategies: Implications for the performance of multinational firms, *Management International Review*, 48(6): 667–688; T. D. A. Griffith & M. G. Harvey, 2001, A resource perspective of global dynamic capabilities, *Journal of International Business Studies*, 32: 597–606; Y. Luo, 2000, Dynamic capabilities in international expansion, *Journal of World Business*, 35(4): 355–378.

39. R. Morck, B. Yeung, & M. Zhao, 2008, Perspectives on China's outward foreign direct investment, *Journal of International Business Studies*, 39: 337–350; J. Gimeno, R. E. Hoskisson, B.D. Beal, & W. P. Wan, 2005, Explaining the clustering of international expansion moves: A critical test in the U.S. telecommunications industry, *Academy of Management Journal*, 48: 297–319.

40. A. Cuervo-Cazurra & M. Gene, 2008, Transforming disadvantages into advantages: Developing-country MNEs in the least developed countries, *Journal of International Business Studies*, 39: 957–979; M. A. Hitt, L. Bierman, K. Uhlenbruck, & K. Shimizu, 2006, The importance of resources in the internationalization of professional service firms: The good, the bad and the ugly, *Academy of Management Journal*, 49: 1137–1157.

41. P. Dastidar, 2009, International corporate diversification and performance: Does firm self-selection matter?, *Journal of International Business Studies*, 40: 71–85; L. Nachum, 2001, The impact of home countries on the competitiveness of advertising TNCs, *Management International Review*, 41(1): 77–98.

42. M. E. Porter, 1990, *The Competitive Advantage of Nations*, New York: The Free Press.

43. Ibid, 84.

44. C. Storz, 2008, Dynamics in innovation systems: Evidence from Japan's game software industry. *Research Policy*, 37(9): 1480–1491; Y. Aoyama & H. Izushi, 2003, Hardware gimmick or cultural innovation? Technological, cultural, and social foundations of the Japanese video game industry, *Research Policy*, 32: 423–443.

45. B. Powell, 2009, China's new king of solar, *Fortune*, February 16, 94–97.

46. J. Ioffe, 2009, Search wars; the Russians are coming, *Fortune*, February 16, 36–38.

47. A. Tempel & P. Walgenbach, 2007, Global standardization of organizational forms and management practices? What new institutionalism and business systems approach can learn from each other, *Journal of Management Studies*, 44: 1–24.

48. Kumar, The relationship between product and international diversification; W. P. Wan & R. E. Hoskisson, 2003, Home country environments, corporate diversification strategies and firm performance, *Academy of Management Journal*, 46: 27–45; J. M. Geringer, S. Tallman, & D. M. Olsen, 2000, Product and international diversification among Japanese multinational firms, *Strategic Management Journal*, 21: 51–80.

49. Kumar, The relationship between product and international diversification; M. A. Hitt, R. E. Hoskisson, & R. D. Ireland, 1994, A mid-range theory of the interactive effects of international and product diversification on innovation and performance, *Journal of Management*, 20: 297–326.

50. D. A. Ralston, D. H. Holt, R. H. Terpstra, & Y. Kai-Cheng, 2008, The impact of national culture and economic ideology on managerial work values: A study of the United States, Russia, Japan, and China, *Journal of International Business Studies*, 39(1): 8–26; B. B. Alred & K. S. Swan, 2004, Global versus multidomestic: Culture's consequences on innovation, *Management International Review*, 44: 81–105.

51. D. Grewal, G. R. Iyer, W. A. Kamakura, A. Mehrotra, & A. Sharma, 2009, Evaluation of subsidiary marketing performance: Combining process and outcome performance metrics, *Academy of Marketing Science Journal*, 37(2): 117–120; A. Ferner, P. Almond, I. Clark, T. Colling, & T. Edwards, 2004, The dynamics of central control and subsidiary anatomy in the management of human resources: Case study evidence from U.S. MNCs in the U.K., *Organization Studies*, 25: 363–392.

52. N. Guimarães-Costa & M. P. E. Cunha, 2009, Foreign locals: A liminal perspective of international managers, *Organizational Dynamics*, 38(2): 158–166; B. Connelly, M. A. Hitt, A. S. DeNisi, & R. D. Ireland, 2007, Expatriates and corporate-level international strategy: Governing with the knowledge contract, *Management Decision*, 45: 564–581; L. Nachum, 2003, Does nationality of ownership make any difference and if so, under

what circumstances? Professional service MNEs in global competition, *Journal of International Management*, 9: 1–32.

53. M. W. Hansen, T. Pedersen, & B. Petersen, 2009, MNC strategies and linkage effects in developing countries, *Journal of World Business*, 44(2): 121–139; Y. Luo, 2001, Determinants of local responsiveness: Perspectives from foreign subsidiaries in an emerging market, *Journal of Management*, 27: 451–477.

54. H. Kasper, M. Lehrer, J. Mühlbacher, & B. Müller, 2009, Integration-responsiveness and knowledge-management perspectives on the MNC: A typology and field study of cross-site knowledge-sharing practices, *Journal of Leadership & Organizational Studies*, 15(3): 287–303.

55. J. Neff, 2008, Unilever's CMO finally gets down to business, *Advertising Age*, July, 11; G. Jones, 2002, Control, performance, and knowledge transfers in large multinationals: Unilever in the United States, 1945–1980, *Business History Review*, 76(3): 435–478.

56. P. J. Buckley, 2009, The impact of the global factory on economic development, *Journal of World Business*, 44(2): 131–143; Tempel & Walgenbach, Global standardization of organizational forms and management practices; Li, Is regional strategy more effective than global strategy in the U.S. service industries?

57. H.C. Moon & M.-Y. Kim, 2009, A new framework for global expansion: A dynamic diversification-coordination (DDC) model, *Management Decision*, 46(1): 131–151.

58. Connelly, Hitt, DeNisi, & Ireland, Expatriates and corporate-level international strategy; J. F. L. Hong, M. Easterby-Smith, & R. S. Snell, 2006, Transferring organizational learning systems to Japanese subsidiaries in China, *Journal of Management Studies*, 43: 1027–1058.

59. Kho, Stulz, & Warnock, Financial globalization, governance, and the evolution of the home bias; R. G. Barker, 2003, Trend: Global accounting is coming, *Harvard Business Review*, 81 (4): 24–25.

60. A. Yaprak, 2002, Globalization: Strategies to build a great global firm in the new economy, *Thunderbird International Business Review*, 44(2): 297–302; D. G. McKendrick, 2001, Global strategy and population level learning: The case of hard disk drives, *Strategic Management Journal*, 22: 307–334.

61. P. Komiak, S. Y. X. Komiak, & M. Imhof, 2008, Conducting international business at eBay: The determinants of success of e-stores, *Electronic Markets*, 18(2): 187–204; V. Shannon, 2007, eBay is preparing to re-enter the China auction business, *New York Times*, http://www.nytimes .com, June 22; B Einhorn, 2007, A break in Yahoo's China clouds? *BusinessWeek*, http://www.businessweek.com, June 20.

62. M. Demirbag & E. Tatoglu, 2009, Competitive strategy choices of Turkish manufacturing firms in European

Union, *The Journal of Management Development*, 27(7): 727–743; K. E. Meyer, 2006, Globalfocusing: From domestic conglomerates to global specialists, *Journal of Management Studies*, 43: 1109–1144; A. Delios & P. W. Beamish, 2005, Regional and global strategies of Japanese firms, *Management International Review*, 45: 19–36.

63. A. Delios, D. Xu & P. W. Beamish, 2008, Within-country product diversification and foreign subsidiary performance, *Journal of International Business Studies*, 39(4): 706–724; S. Massini, A. Y. Lewin, T. Numagami, & A. Pettigrew, 2002, The evolution of organizational routines among large Western and Japanese firms, *Research Policy*, 31(8,9): 1333–1348.

64. J. Millman, 2008, The fallen: Lorenzo Zambrano: Hard times for cement man, *Wall Street Journal*, December 11, A1; K. A. Garrett, 2005, Cemex, *Business Mexico*, April 23.

65. B. Elango & C. Pattnaik, 2007, Building capabilities for international operations through networks: A study of Indian firms, *Journal of International Business Studies*, 38: 541–555; T. B. Lawrence, E. A. Morse, & S. W. Fowler, 2005, Managing your portfolio of connections, *MIT Sloan Management Review*, 46(2): 59–65; C. A. Bartlett & S. Ghoshal, 1989, *Managing across Borders: The Transnational Solution*, Boston: Harvard Business School Press.

66. A. M. Rugman & A. Verbeke, 2008, A regional solution to the strategy and structure of multinationals, *European Management Journal*, 26(5): 305–313. A. Abbott & K. Banerji, 2003, Strategic flexibility and firm performance: The case of U.S. based transnational corporations, *Global Journal of Flexible Systems Management*, 4(1/2): 1–7; J. Child & Y. Van, 2001, National and transnational effects in international business: Indications from Sino-foreign joint ventures, *Management International Review*, 41(1): 53–75.

67. Rugman & Verbeke, A regional solution to the strategy and structure of multinationals.

68. A. M. Rugman & A. Verbeke, 2003, Extending the theory of the multinational enterprise: Internalization and strategic management perspectives, *Journal of International Business Studies*, 34: 125–137.

69. H. F. Cheng, M. Gutierrez, A. Mahajan, Y. Shachmurove, & M. Shahrokhi, 2007, A future global economy to be built by BRICs, *Global Finance Journal*, 18(2): 143–156; Wright, Filatotchev, Hoskisson, & Peng, Strategy research in emerging economies: Challenging the conventional wisdom.

70. Elango, Minimizing effects of "liability of foreignness": Response strategies of foreign firms in the United States.

71. N. Y. Brannen, 2004, When Mickey loses face: Recontextualization, semantic fit

and semiotics of foreignness, *Academy of Management Review*, 29: 593–616.

72. A. M. Rugman & A. Verbeke, 2007, Liabilities of foreignness and the use of firm-level versus country-level data: A response to Dunning et al. (2007), *Journal of International Business Studies*, 38: 200–205; S. Zaheer & A. Zaheer, 2001, Market microstructure in a global B2B network, *Strategic Management Journal*, 22: 859–873.

73. Rugman & Verbeke, A new perspective on the regional and global strategies of multinational services firms; S. R. Miller & L. Eden, 2006, Local density and foreign subsidiary performance, *Academy of Management Journal*, 49: 341–355.

74. Rugman & Verbeke, A new perspective on the regional and global strategies of multinational services firms; C. H. Oh & A. M. Rugman, 2007, Regional multi-nationals and the Korean cosmetics industry, *Asia Pacific Journal of Management*, 24: 27–42; A. Rugman & A. Verbeke, 2004, A perspective on regional and global strategies of multinational enterprises, *Journal of International Business Studies*, 35: 3–18.

75. A. K. Bhattacharya & D. C. Michael, 2008, How local companies keep multinationals at bay, *Harvard Business Review*, 86(3): 84–95; C. Pantzalis, 2001, Does location matter? An empirical analysis of geographic scope and MNC market valuation, *Journal of International Business Studies*, 32: 133–155.

76. A. Rugman & S. Girod, 2003, Retail multinationals and globalization: The evidence is regional, *European Management Journal*, 21(1): 24–37.

77. D. E. Westney, 2006. Review of the regional multinationals: MNEs and global strategic management (book review), *Journal of International Business Studies*, 37: 445–449.

78. R. D. Ludema, 2002, Increasing returns, multinationals and geography of preferential trade agreements, *Journal of International Economics*, 56: 329–358.

79. Meyer, Globalfocusing: From domestic conglomerates to global specialists; Delios & Beamish, Regional and global strategies of Japanese firms.

80. M. Aspinwall, 2009, NAFTA-ization: Regionalization and domestic political adjustment in the North American economic area. *Journal of Common Market Studies*, 47(1): 1–24.

81. T. L. Pett & J. A. Wolff, 2003, Firm characteristic and managerial perceptions of NAFTA: An assessment of export implications for U.S. SMEs, *Journal of Small Business Management*, 41(2): 117–132.

82. Morck, Yeung, & Zhao, Perspectives on China's outward foreign direct investment; W. Chung & J. Song, 2004, Sequential investment, firm motives, and agglomeration of Japanese electronics firms in the United States, *Journal of Economics and Management Strategy*, 13: 539–560; D. Xu & O. Shenkar, 2002,

Institutional distance and the multinational enterprise, *Academy of Management Review*, 27(4): 608–618.

83. A. Ojala, 2008, Entry in a psychically distant market: Finnish small and medium-sized software firms in Japan, *European Management Journal*, 26(2): 135–144.

84. K. D. Brouthers, L. E. Brouthers, & S. Werner, 2008, Real options, international entry mode choice and performance. *Journal of Management Studies*, 45(5): 936–960.

85. C. A. Cinquetti, 2009, Multinationals and exports in a large and protected developing country, *Review of International Economics*, 16(5): 904–918.

86. Luo, Determinants of local responsiveness.

87. S. Shankar, C. Ormiston, N. Bloch, & R. Schaus, 2008, How to win in emerging markets, *MIT Sloan Management Review*, 49(3): 19–23; M. A. Raymond, J. Kim, & A. T. Shao, 2001, Export strategy and performance: A comparison of exporters in a developed market and an emerging market, *Journal of Global Marketing*, 15(2): 5–29.

88. A. Haahti, V. Madupu, U. Yavas, & E. Babakus, 2005, Cooperative strategy, knowledge intensity and export performance of small and medium-sized enterprises, *Journal of World Business*, 40(2): 124–138.

89. G. R. G. Clarke, 2008, Has the internet increased exports for firms from low and middle-income countries, *Information Economics and Policy*, 20(1): 16–37; K. A. Houghton & H. Winklhofer, 2004, The effect of Web site and ecommerce adoption on the relationship between SMEs and their export intermediaries, *International Small Business Journal*, 22: 369–385.

90. M. Bandyk, 2008, Now even small firms can go global, *U.S. News & World Report*, March 10, 52.

91. J. Slater, 2008, Weak dollar hits Europe, helps emerging markets, *Wall Street Journal (Europe)*, December 29, 1.

92. U. Lichtenthaler, 2008, Externally commercializing technology assets: An examination of different process stages, *Journal of Business Venturing*, 23(4): 445–664; D. Kline, 2003, Sharing the corporate crown jewels, *MIT Sloan Management Review*, 44(3): 83–88.

93. R. Bird & D. R. Cahoy, 2008, The impact of compulsory licensing on foreign direct investment: A collective bargaining approach, *American Business Law Journal*, 45(2): 283–330; A. Arora & A. Fosfuri, 2000, Wholly owned subsidiary versus technology licensing in the worldwide chemical industry, *Journal of International Business Studies*, 31: 555–572.

94. N. Byrnes & F. Balfour, 2009, Philip Morris unbound, *BusinessWeek*, May 4, 38–42; N. Zamiska, J. Ye, & V. O'Connell, 2008, Chinese cigarettes to go global, *Wall Street Journal*, January 30, B4; N. Zamiska & V. O'Connell, 2005, Philip Morris is in talks to make Marlboros in China, *Wall Street Journal*, April 21, B1, B2.

95. Zamiska, Ye, & O'Connell, Chinese cigarettes to go global, B4.

96. S. Nagaoka, 2009, Does strong patent protection facilitate international technology transfer? Some evidence from licensing contracts of Japanese firms, *Journal of Technology Transfer*, 34(2): 128–144.

97. M. Johnson, 2001, Learning from toys: Lessons in managing supply chain risk from the toy industry, *California Management Review*, 43(3): 106–124.

98. U. Lichtenthaler & H. Ernst, 2007, Business insight (a special report); Think strategically about technology licensing, *Wall Street Journal*, R4

99. C. A. Bartlett & S. Rangan, 1992, Komatsu limited, in C. A. Bartlett & S. Ghoshal (eds.), *Transnational Management: Text, Cases and Readings in Cross-Border Management*, Homewood, IL: Irwin, 311–326.

100. T. Audi, 2008, Last resort: Ailing Sheraton shoots for a room upgrade; Starwood to tackle biggest hotel brand; the "ugly stepchild," *Wall Street Journal*, March 25, A1.

101. T. W. Tong, J. J. Reuer, & M. W. Peng, 2008. International joint ventures and the value of growth options, *Academy of Management Journal*, 51: 1014–1029; A. A. Ziedonis, 2007, Real options in technology licensing, *Management Science*, 53(10): 1618–1633.

102. H. K. Steensma, J. Q. Barden, C. Dhanaraj, M. Lyles, & L. Tihanyi, 2008, The evolution and internalization of international joint ventures in a transitioning economy, *Journal of International Business Studies*, 39(3): 491–507; M. Nippa, S. Beechler, & A. Klossek, 2007, Success factors for managing international joint ventures: A review and an integrative framework, *Management and Organization Review*, 3: 277–310.

103. N. Rahman, 2008, Resource and risk trade-offs in Guanxi-based IJVs in China, *Asia Pacific Business Review*, 14(2): 233–251; J. S. Harrison, M. A. Hitt, R. E. Hoskisson, & R. D. Ireland, 2001, Resource complementarity in business combinations: Extending the logic to organization alliances, *Journal of Management*, 27: 679–690.

104. W. Zhan, R. Chen, M. K. Erramilli, & D. T, Nguyen, 2009, Acquisition of organizational capabilities and competitive advantage of IJVs in transition economies: The case of Vietnam. *Asia Pacific Journal of Management*, 26(2): 285–308; M. A. Hitt, D. Ahlstrom, M. T. Dacin, E. Levitas, & L. Svobodina, 2004, The institutional effects on strategic alliance partner selection in transition economies: China versus Russia, *Organization Science*, 15: 173–185.

105. E. Woyke, 2009, ZTE's smart phone ambitions; The company is betting on advanced phones to crack the U.S. market, *Forbes*, http://www.forbes.com, March 16.

106. T. Chi & A. Seth, 2009, A dynamic model of the choice of mode for exploiting complementary capabilities, *Journal of International Business Studies*, 40(3): 365–387; M. A. Lyles & J. E. Salk, 2007, Knowledge acquisition from foreign parents in international joint ventures: An empirical examination in the Hungarian context, *Journal of International Business Studies*, 38: 3–18; E. W. K. Tsang, 2002, Acquiring knowledge by foreign partners for international joint ventures in a transition economy: Learning-by-doing and learning myopia, *Strategic Management Journal*, 23(9): 835–854.

107. M. J. Robson, C. S. Katsikeas, & D. C. Bello, 2008, Drivers and performance outcomes of trust in international strategic alliances: The role of organizational complexity, *Organization Science*, 19(4): 647–668; S. Zaheer & A. Zaheer, 2007, Trust across borders, *Journal of International Business Studies*, 38: 21–29.

108. M. H. Ogasavara & Y. Hoshino, 2009, The effects of entry strategy and inter-firm trust on the survival of Japanese manufacturing subsidiaries in Brazil, *Asian Business & Management*, 7(3): 353–380; M. W. Peng & O. Shenkar, 2002, Joint venture dissolution as corporate divorce, *Academy of Management Executive*, 16(2): 92–105.

109. Y. Luo, O. Shenkar, & H. Gurnani, 2008, Control-cooperation interfaces in global strategic alliances: A situational typology and strategic responses, *Journal of International Business Studies*, 9(3): 428–453; A. Madhok, 2006, Revisiting multinational firms' tolerance for joint ventures: A trust-based approach, *Journal of International Business Studies*, 37: 30–43; J. Child & Y. Van, 2003, Predicting the performance of international joint ventures: An investigation in China, *Journal of Management Studies*, 40(2): 283–320; J. P. Johnson, M. A. Korsgaard, & H. J. Sapienza, 2002, Perceived fairness, decision control, and commitment in international joint venture management teams, *Strategic Management Journal*, 23(12): 1141–1160.

110. X. Lin & C. L. Wang, 2008, Enforcement and performance: The role of ownership, legalism and trust in international joint ventures, *Journal of World Business*, 43(3): 340–351; L. Huff & L. Kelley, 2003, Levels of organizational trust in individualist versus collectivist societies: A seven-nation study, *Organization Science*, 14(1): 81–90.

111. D. Li, L. Eden, M. A. Hitt, & R. D. Ireland, 2008, Friends, acquaintances and strangers? Partner selection in R&D alliances, *Academy of Management Journal*, 51: 315–334; Y. Pan & D. K. Tse, 2000, The hierarchical model of market entry modes, *Journal of International Business Studies*, 31: 535–554.

112. J. Wiklund & D. A. Shepherd, 2009, The effectiveness of alliances and acquisitions: The role of resource combination activities, *Entrepreneurship Theory and Practice*, 33(1): 193–212; P. Porrini, 2004, Can a previous alliance between an acquirer and a target affect acquisition

performance? *Journal of Management*, 30: 545–562.

113. C. M. Sanchez & S. R. Goldberg, 2009, Strategic M&As: Stronger in tough times, *Journal of Corporate Accounting & Finance*, 20(2): 3–7; K. Shimizu, M. A. Hitt, D. Vaidyanath, & V. Pisano, 2004, Theoretical foundations of cross-border mergers and acquisitions: A review of current research and recommendations for the future, *Journal of International Management*, 10: 307–353; M. A. Hitt, J. S. Harrison, & R. D. Ireland, 2001, *Mergers and Acquisitions: A Guide to Creating Value for Stakeholders*, New York: Oxford University Press.

114. A. Boateng, W. Qian, & Y. Tianle, 2008, Cross-border M&As by Chinese firms: An analysis of strategic motives and performance, *Thunderbird International Business Review*, 50(4): 259–270; M. A. Hitt & V. Pisano, 2003, The cross-border merger and acquisition strategy, *Management Research*, 1: 133–144.

115. International operational fact sheet, 2007, http://www.walmartfacts.com, July; J. Levine, 2004, Europe: Gold mines and quicksand, *Forbes*, April 12, 76.

116. B. Powell, 2009, Buying binge, *Time*, April 20, GB1.

117. P. X. Meschi, 2009, Government corruption and foreign stakes in international joint ventures in emerging economies, *Asia Pacific Journal of Management*, 26(2): 241–261; U. Weitzel & S. Berns, 2006, Cross-border takeovers, corruption, and related aspects of governance, *Journal of International Business Studies*, 37: 786–806.

118. Chakrabarti, Gupta-Mukherjee, & Jayaraman, Mars-Venus marriages: Culture and cross-border M&A; A. H. L. Slangen, 2006, National cultural distance and initial foreign acquisition performance: The moderating effect of integration, *Journal of World Business*, 41: 161–170.

119. S. F. S. Chen, 2008, The motives for international acquisitions: Capability procurements, strategic considerations, and the role of ownership structures, *Journal of International Business Studies*, 39(3): 454–471; I. Bjorkman, G. K. Stahl, & E. Vaara, 2007, Cultural differences and capability transfer in cross-border acquisitions: The mediating roles of capability complementarity, absorptive capacity, and social integration, *Journal of International Business Studies*, 38: 658–672.

120. J. Reed, 2008, SAIC plans U.K. comeback for MG TF roadster, *Financial Times*, April 21, 25; C. Buckley, 2005, SAIC to fund MG Rover bid, *The Times of London*, http://www.timesonline.co.uk, July 18.

121. H. Raff, M. Ryan, F. Stähler, 2009, The choice of market entry mode: Greenfield investment, M&A and joint venture, *International Review of Economics & Finance*, 18(1): 3–10; A.-W. Harzing, 2002, Acquisitions versus greenfield investments: International strategy and management of entry modes, *Strategic Management Journal*, 23: 211–227.

122. C. Bouquet, L. Hebert, & A. Delios, 2004, Foreign expansion in service industries: Separability and human capital intensity, *Journal of Business Research*, 57: 35–46.

123. K. F. Meyer, S. Estrin, S. K. Bhaumik, & M. W. Peng, 2009, Institutions, resources, and entry strategies in emerging economies, *Strategic Management Journal*, 30(1): 61–80.

124. K. F. Meyer, M. Wright, & S. Pruthi, 2009, Managing knowledge in foreign entry strategies: a resource-based analysis, *Strategic Management Journal*, 30(5): 557–574.

125. Y. Park & B. Sternquist, 2008, The global retailer's strategic proposition and choice of entry mode, *International Journal of Retail & Distribution Management*, 36(4): 281–299; S. Mani, K. D. Antia, & A. Rindfleisch, 2007, Entry mode and equity level: A multilevel examination of foreign direct investment ownership structure, *Strategic Management Journal*, 28: 857–866.

126. A. Roth, 2008, Beijing Olympics 2008: UPS markets its delivery for China only; Company transports gear for the Games; face-off with FedEx, *Wall Street Journal* (Europe), August 11, 29.

127. D. L. Paul & R. B. Wooster, 2008, Strategic investments by U.S. firms in transition economies, *Journal of International Business Studies*, 39(2): 249–266; V. Gaba, Y. Pan, & G. R. Ungson, 2002, Timing of entry in international market: An empirical study of U.S. Fortune 500 firms in China, *Journal of International Business Studies*, 33(1): 39–55; S.-J. Chang & P. Rosenzweig, 2001, The choice of entry mode in sequential foreign direct investment, *Strategic Management Journal*, 22: 747–776.

128. Meschi, Government corruption and foreign stakes in international joint ventures in emerging economies; R. Farzad, 2007, Extreme investing: Inside Colombia, *BusinessWeek*, May 28, 50–58; K. E. Myer, 2001, Institutions, transaction costs, and entry mode choice in Eastern Europe, *Journal of International Business Studies*, 32: 357–367.

129. J. Che & G. Facchini, 2009, Cultural differences, insecure property rights and the mode of entry decision, *Economic Theory*, 38(3): 465–484; S. Li, 2004, Why are property rights protections lacking in China? An institutional explanation, *California Management Review*, 46(3): 100–115.

130. A. C. Inkpen, 2008, Knowledge transfer and international joint ventures: The case of NUMMI and General Motors, *Strategic Management Journal*, 29(4): 447–453.

131. D. Hannon, 2008, Shorter is better for Toyota's supply chain, *Purchasing*, August, 46–47; M. Zimmerman, 2007, Toyota ends GM's reign as car sales leader, *Los Angeles Times*, April 25, 2007, C1; L. J. Howell & J. C. Hsu, 2002, Globalization within the auto industry, *Research Technology Management*, 45(4): 43–49.

132. J. W. Lu & X. Ma, 2008, The contingent value of local partners' business group affiliations, *Academy of Management Journal*, 51(2): 295–314; A. Chacar & B. Vissa, 2005, Are emerging economies less efficient? Performance persistence and the impact of business group affiliation, *Strategic Management Journal*, 26: 933–946; Hoskisson, Kim, Tihanyi, & White, A framework for understanding international diversification by business groups from emerging economies.

133. R. Chittoor, M. B. Sarkar, S. Ray, & P. S. Aulakh, 2009, Third-world copycats to emerging multinationals: Institutional changes and organizational transformation in the Indian pharmaceutical industry, *Organization Science*, 20(1): 187–205.

134. M. F. Wiersma & H. P. Bowen, 2008, Corporate international diversification: The impact of foreign competition, industry globalization and product diversification, *Strategic Management Journal*, 29: 115–132.

135. Dastidar, International corporate diversification and performance; L. Li, 2007, Multinationality and performance: A synthetic review and research agenda, *International Journal of Management Reviews*, 9: 117–139; J. A. Doukas & O. B. Kan, 2006, Does global diversification destroy firm value, *Journal of International Business Studies*, 37: 352–371; J. W. Lu & P. W. Beamish, 2004, International diversification and firm performance: The S-curve hypothesis, *Academy of Management Journal*, 47: 598–609.

136. S. E. Christophe & H. Lee, 2005, What matters about internationalization: A market-based assessment, *Journal of Business Research*. 58: 536–643; J. A. Doukas & L. H. P. Lang, 2003, Foreign direct investment, diversification and firm performance, *Journal of International Business Studies*, 34: 153–172.

137. H. Zou & M. B. Adams, 2009, Corporate ownership, equity risk and returns in the People's Republic of China, *Journal of International Business Studies*, 39(7): 1149–1168; Hitt, Tihanyi, Miller, & Connelly, International diversification; Kwok & Reeb, Internationalization and firm risk.

138. A. Birnik & R. Moat, 2009, Mapping multinational operations, *Business Strategy Review*, 20(1): 30–33; T. R. Holcomb & M. A. Hitt, 2007, Toward a model of strategic outsourcing, *Journal of Operations Management*, 25: 464–481; J. P. Doh, 2005, Offshore outsourcing: Implications for international business and strategic management theory and practice, *Journal of Management Studies*, 42: 695–704.

139. Song & Shin, The paradox of technological capabilities: A study of knowledge sourcing from host countries of overseas R&D operations; J. Penner-Hahn & J. M. Shaver, 2005, Does international research and development increase patent output? An analysis of

Japanese pharmaceutical firms, *Strategic Management Journal*, 26: 121–140.

140. Shimizutani & Todo, What determines overseas R&D activities? The case of Japanese multinational firms; Hitt, Bierman, Uhlenbruck, & Shimizu, The importance of resources in the internationalization of professional service firms; L. Tihanyi, R. A. Johnson, R. E. Hoskisson, & M. A. Hitt, 2003, Institutional ownership differences and international diversification: The effects of board of directors and technological opportunity, *Academy of Management Journal*, 46:195–211.

141. Zou & Ghauri, Learning through international acquisitions; B. Ambos & B. B. Schlegelmilch, 2007, Innovation and control in the multinational firm: A comparison of political and contingency approaches, *Strategic Management Journal*, 28: 473–486.

142. E. Matta & P. W. Beamish, 2008, The accentuated CEO career horizon problem: Evidence from international acquisitions, *Strategic Management Journal*, 29(7): 683; D. S. Elenkov, W. Judge, & P. Wright, 2005, Strategic leadership and executive innovation influence: An international multi-cluster comparative study, *Strategic Management Journal*, 26: 665–682; P. Herrmann, 2002, The influence of CEO characteristics on the international diversification of manufacturing firms: An empirical study in the United States, *International Journal of Management*, 19(2): 279–289.

143. H. L. Sirkin, J. W. Hemerling, & A. K. Bhattacharya, 2009, Globality: Challenger companies are radically redefining the competitive landscape, *Strategy & Leadership*, 36(6): 36–41; M. A. Hitt, R. E. Hoskisson, & H. Kim, 1997, International diversification: Effects on innovation and firm performance in product-diversified firms, *Academy of Management Journal*, 40: 767–798.

144. E. García-Canal & M. F. Guillén, 2009, Risk and the strategy of foreign location choice in regulated industries, *Strategic Management Journal*, 29(10): 1097–1115; J. Child, L. Chung, & H. Davies, 2003, The performance of cross-border units in China: A test of natural selection, strategic choice and contingency theories, *Journal of International Business Studies*, 34: 242–254.

145. C. Crossland & D. C. Hambrick, 2007, How national systems differ in their constraints on corporate executives: A study of CEO effects in three countries, *Strategic Management Journal*, 28: 767–789; M. Javidan, P. W. Dorfman, M. S. de Luque, & R. J. House, 2006, In the eye of the beholder: Cross-cultural lessons in leadership from Project GLOBE, *Academy of Management Perspectives*, 20 (1): 67–90.

146. N. Shirouzu, 2008, Corporate news: GM's car sales slide in China; Toyota, Honda zoom ahead as buyers concentrate on fuel economy, quality, *Wall Street Journal*, September 26, B1.

147. I. Alon & T. T. Herbert, 2009, A stranger in a strange land: Micro political risk and the multinational firm, *Business Horizons*, 52(2): 127–137; P. Rodriguez, K. Uhlenbruck, & L. Eden, 2005, Government corruption and the entry strategies of multinationals, *Academy of Management Review*, 30: 383–396; J. H. Zhao, S. H. Kim, & J. Du, 2003, The impact of corruption and transparency on foreign direct investment: An empirical analysis, *Management International Review*, 43(1): 41–62.

148. F. Wu, 2009, Singapore's sovereign wealth funds: The political risk of overseas investments. *World Economics*, 9(3): 97–122; P. S. Ring, G. A. Bigley, T. D'aunno, & T. Khanna, 2005, Perspectives on how governments matter, *Academy of Management Review*, 30: 308–320; A. Delios & W. J. Henisz, 2003, Policy uncertainty and the sequence of entry by Japanese firms, 1980–1998, *Journal of International Business Studies*, 34: 227–241.

149. A. Kouznetsov, 2009, Entry modes employed by multinational manufacturing enterprises and review of factors that affect entry mode choices in Russia, *The Business Review*, Cambridge, 10(2): 316–323.

150. S. Globerman & D. Shapiro, 2009, Economic and strategic considerations surrounding Chinese FDI in the United States, *Asia Pacific Journal of Management*, 26(1): 163–183.

151. I. G. Kawaller, 2009, Hedging currency exposures by multinationals: Things to consider, *Journal of Applied Finance*, 18(1): 92–98; Addae-Dapaah & Hwee, The unsung impact of currency risk on the performance of international real property investment; T. Vestring, T. Rouse, & U. Reinert, 2005, Hedging your offshoring bets, *MIT Sloan Management Review*, 46(3): 26–29.

152. T. G. Andrews & N. Chompusri, 2005, Temporal dynamics of crossvergence: Institutionalizing MNC integration strategies in post-crisis ASEAN, *Asia Pacific Journal of Management*, 22(1): 5–22; S. Mudd, R. Grosse, & J. Mathis, 2002, Dealing with financial crises in emerging markets, *Thunderbird International Business Review*, 44(3): 399–430.

153. N. Bandelj, 2009, The global economy as instituted process: The case of Central and Eastern Europe, *American Sociological Review*, 74(1): 128–149; L. Tihanyi & W. H. Hegarty, 2007, Political interests and the emergence of commercial banking in transition economies, *Journal of Management Studies*, 44: 789–813.

154. Lu & Beamish, International diversification and firm performance: The s-curve hypothesis; Wan & Hoskisson, Home country environments, corporate diversification strategies and firm performance; Hitt, Hoskisson, & Kim, International diversification.

155. A. Ojala, 2008, Entry in a psychically distant market: Finnish small and medium-sized software firms in Japan, *European Management Journal*, 26(2): 135–144; D. W. Yiu, C. M. Lau, & G. D. Bruton, 2007, International venturing by emerging economy firms: The effects of firm capabilities, home country networks, and corporate entrepreneurship, *Journal of International Business Studies*, 38: 519–540; P. S. Barr & M. A. Glynn, 2004, Cultural variations in strategic issue interpretation: Relating cultural uncertainty avoidance to controllability in discriminating threat and opportunity, *Strategic Management Journal*, 25: 59–67.

156. M. L. L. Lam, 2009, Beyond credibility of doing business in China: Strategies for improving corporate citizenship of foreign multinational enterprises in China, *Journal of Business Ethics*: Supplement, 87: 137–146; W. P. J. Henisz & B. A. Zeiner, 2005, Legitimacy, interest group pressures and change in emergent institutions, the case of foreign investors and host country governments, *Academy of Management Review*, 30: 361–382; T. P. Blumentritt & D. Nigh, 2002, The integration of subsidiary political activities in multinational corporations, *Journal of International Business Studies*, 33: 57–77.

157. D. Lavie & S. Miller, 2009, Alliance portfolio internationalization and firm performance, Organization Science, 19(4): 623–646.

Chapter 9

1. D. Lavie, 2009, Capturing value from alliance portfolios, *Organizational Dynamics*, 38(1): 26–36; J. L. Morrow, Jr., D. G. Sirmon, M. A. Hitt, & T. R. Holcomb, 2007, Creating value in the face of declining performance: Firm strategies and organizational recovery, *Strategic Management Journal*, 28: 271–283.

2. T. W. Tong, J. J. Reuer, & M. W. Peng, 2008, International joint ventures and the value of growth options, *Academy of Management Journal*, 51: 1014–1029.

3. H. Ness, 2009, Governance, negotiations, and alliance dynamics: Explaining the evolution of relational practice, *Journal of Management Studies*, 46(3): 451–480;

R. C. Fink, L. F. Edelman, & K. J. Hatten, 2007, Supplier performance improvements in relational exchanges, *Journal of Business & Industrial Marketing*, 22: 29–40.

4. M. J. Chen, 2008, Reconceptualizing the competition cooperation relationship: A transparadox perspective, *Journal of Management Inquiry*, 17(4): 288–304;

P. E. Bierly III & S. Gallagher, 2007, Explaining alliance partner selection: Fit, trust and strategic expediency, *Long Range Planning*, 40: 134–153; K. Singh & W. Mitchell, 2005, Growth dynamics: The bidirectional relationship between interfirm collaboration and business sales in entrant and incumbent alliances, *Strategic Management Journal*, 26: 497–521.

5. W. M. Bulkeley, 2008, Business technology, A service rival looms for IBM: H-P deal for EDS to pose challenges for big blue unit, *Wall Street Journal*, May 20, B6.

6. S. Hamm, 2009, Big blue goes into analysis, *BusinessWeek*, April 27, 16.

7. R. Agarwal & C. E. Helfat, 2009, Strategic renewal of organizations, *Organization Science*, 20(2): 281–293; P. M. Senge, B. B. Lichtenstein, K. Kaeufer, H. Bradbury, & J. Carroll, 2007, Collaborating for systemic change, *MIT Sloan Management Review*, 48(2): 44–53; R. Vassolo, J. Anand, & T. B. Folta, 2004, Non-additivity in portfolios of exploration activities: A real options-based analysis of equity alliances in biotechnology, *Strategic Management Journal*, 25: 1045–1061.

8. R. C. Marshall, L. M. Marx, & M. E. Raiff, 2008, Cartel price announcement: The vitamins industry, *International Journal of Industrial Organization*, 26(3): 762–802; T. L. Sorenson, 2007, Credible collusion in multimarket oligopoly, *Managerial and Decision Economics*, 28: 115–128.

9. C. E. Ybarra & T. A. Turk, 2009, The evolution of trust in information technology alliances, *Journal of High Technology Management Research*, 20(1): 62–74; R. D. Ireland, M. A. Hitt, & D. Vaidyanath, 2002, Alliance management as a source of competitive advantage, *Journal of Management*, 28: 413–446; J. G. Coombs & D. J. Ketchen, 1999, Exploring interfirm cooperation and performance: Toward a reconciliation of predictions from the resource-based view and organizational economics, *Strategic Management Journal*, 20: 867–888.

10. M. A. Schilling, 2009, Understanding the alliance data, *Strategic Management Journal*, 30(3): 233–260; J. J. Reuer & A. Arino, 2007, Strategic alliance contracts: Dimensions and determinants of contractual complexity, *Strategic Management Journal*, 28: 313–330; M. R. Subramani & N. Venkatraman, 2003, Safeguarding investments in asymmetric interorganizational relationships: Theory and evidence, *Academy of Management Journal*, 46(1): 46–62.

11. S. Lahiri & B. L. Kedia, 2009, The effects of internal resources and partnership quality on firm performance: An examination of Indian BPO providers, *Journal of International Management*, 15(2): 209–22; R. Krishnan, X. Martin, & N. G. Noorderhaven, 2007, When does trust matter to alliance performance? *Academy of Management Journal*, 49: 894–917; P. Kale, J. H. Dyer, & H. Singh, 2002, Alliance capability, stock market response, and long-term alliance success: The role of the alliance function, *Strategic Management Journal*, 23: 747–767.

12. K. H. Heimeriks & G. Duysters, 2007, Alliance capability as a mediator between experience and alliance performance: An empirical investigation into the alliance capability development process, *Journal of Management Studies*, 44: 25–49.

13. R. E. Hoskisson, M. A. Hitt, R. D. Ireland, & J. S. Harrison, 2008, *Competing for Advantage*, 2nd ed., Thomson/Southwestern, 184.

14. B. S. Bulik, 2009, Kodak develops as modern brand with digital shift, *Advertising Age*, April 27, 26.

15. R. Lunnan & S. A. Haugland, 2008, Predicting and measuring alliance performance: A multi-dimensional analysis, *Strategic Management Journal*, 29(5): 545–556; R. Seppanen, K. Blomqvist, & S. Sundqvist, 2007, Measuring interorganizational trust—A critical review of the empirical research in 1990–2003, *Industrial Marketing Management*, 36: 249–265; T. K. Das & B.-S. Teng, 2001, A risk perception model of alliance structuring, *Journal of International Management*, 7: 1–29.

16. L. F. Mesquita, J. Anand, & T. H. Brush, 2008, Comparing the resource-based and relational views: Knowledge transfer and spillover in vertical alliances, *Strategic Management Journal*, 29: 913–941; F. F. Suarez & G. Lanzolla, 2007, The role of environmental dynamics in building a first mover advantage theory, *Academy of Management Review*, 32: 377–392; M. A. Geletkanycz & S. S. Black, 2001, Bound by the past? Experience-based effects on commitment to the strategic status quo, *Journal of Management*, 27: 3–21.

17. A. Pasztor & A. Cole, 2008, New multirole missile is planned, *Wall Street Journal*, July 16, A13.

18. K. H. Heimeriks, E. Klijn, & J. J. Reuer, 2009, Building capabilities for alliance portfolios, *Long Range Planning*, 42(1): 96–114; D. Gerwin, 2004, Coordinating new product development in strategic alliances, *Academy of Management Review*, 29: 241–257; Ireland, Hitt, & Vaidyanath, Alliance management as a source of competitive advantage.

19. X. Lin & C. L. Wang, 2008, Enforcement and performance: The role of ownership, legalism and trust in international joint ventures, *Journal of World Business*, 43(3): 340–351; Y. Luo, 2007, Are joint venture partners more opportunistic in a more volatile environment? *Strategic Management Journal*, 28: 39–60.

20. F. Evangelista & L. N. Hau, 2008, Organizational context and knowledge acquisition in IJVs: An empirical study, *Journal of World Business*, 44(1): 63–73; S. L. Berman, J. Down, & C. W. L. Hill, 2002, Tacit knowledge as a source of competitive advantage in the National Basketball Association, *Academy of Management Journal*, 45: 13–31.

21. M. Becerra, R. Lunnan, & L. Huemer, 2008, Trustworthiness, risk, and the transfer of tacit and explicit knowledge between alliance partners, *Journal of Management Studies*, 45(4): 691–713.

22. Y. Yamaguchi, 2009, Leading the news: Fujitsu targets 10% share of markets for servers, *Asian Wall Street Journal*, March 31, 3.

23. A. Tiwana, 2008, Do bridging ties complement strong ties? An empirical examination of alliance ambidexterity, *Strategic Management Journal*, 29(3): 251–272; R. E. Hoskisson & L. W. Busenitz, 2002, Market uncertainty and learning distance in corporate entrepreneurship entry mode choice, in M. A. Hitt, R. D. Ireland, S. M. Camp, & D. L. Sexton (eds.), *Strategic Entrepreneurship: Creating a New Mindset*, Oxford, UK: Blackwell Publishers, 151–172.

24. J. Xia, J. Tan, & D. Tan, 2008, Mimetic entry and bandwagon affect: The rise and decline of international equity joint venture in China, *Strategic Management Journal*, 29(2): 195–217.

25. A. Tudor & A. Lucchetti, 2009, MUFG's Hirano takes Morgan Stanley role, *Wall Street Journal*, March 12, C5.

26. Y. Wang & S. Nicholas, 2007, The formation and evolution of nonequity strategic alliances in China, *Asia Pacific Journal of Management*, 24: 131–150.

27. N. Garcia-Casarejos, N. Alcalde-Fradejas, & M. Espitia-Escuer, 2009, Staying close to the core: Lessons of studying the cost of unrelated alliances in Spanish banking, *Long Range Planning*, 42(2): 194–215; S. C. Chang, S.-S. Chen, & J. H. Lai, 2008, The wealth effect of Japanese-U.S. strategic alliances, *Financial Management*, 37(2): 271–301.

28. C. Weigelt, 2009, The impact of outsourcing new technologies on integrative capabilities and performance, *Strategic Management Journal*, 30(6): 595–616; S. Comino, P. Mariel, & J. Sandonis, 2007, Joint ventures versus contractual agreements: An empirical investigation, *Spanish Economic Journal*, 9: 159–175.

29. 2007, Intellectual property licensing, http://www.hp.com, August 30.

30. A. Tiwana, 2008, Does interfirm modularity complement ignorance? A field study of software outsourcing alliances, *Strategic Management Journal*, 29(11): 1241–1252.

31. A. L. Sherwood & J. G. Covin, 2008, Knowledge acquisition in university–industry alliances: An empirical investigation from a learning theory perspective, *Journal of Product Innovation Management*, 25: 162–179.

32. P. Beamish & N. Lupton, 2009, Managing joint ventures, *Academy of Management Perspectives*, 23(2): 75–94.

33. A. C. Inkpen & J. Ross, 2001, Why do some strategic alliances persist beyond their useful life? *California Management Review*, 44(1): 132–148.

34. A. Al-Laham, T. L. Amburgey, & K. Bates, 2008, The dynamics of research alliances: Examining the effect of alliance

experience and partner characteristics on the speed of alliance entry in the biotech industry, *British Journal of Management*, 19(4): 343–364; F. Rothaermel & D. L. Deeds, 2006, Alliance type, alliance experience and alliance management capability in high-technology ventures, *Journal of Business Venturing*, 21: 429–460; L. Fuentelsaz, J. Gomez, & Y. Polo, 2002, Followers' entry timing: Evidence from the Spanish banking sector after deregulation, *Strategic Management Journal*, 23: 245–264.

35. Mesquita, Anand, Brush, Comparing the resource-based and relational views: Knowledge transfer and spillover in vertical alliances; B. L. Bourdeau, J. J. Cronink, Jr., & C. M. Voorhees, 2007, Modeling service alliances: An exploratory investigation of spillover effects in service partnerships, *Strategic Management Journal*, 28: 609–622.

36. J. Murphy, 2009, Dow Jones: Venture to launch site for newspaper in Japanese, *Wall Street Journal*, May 8, B3.

37. J. J. Reuer, P. Olk & A. Arino, 2010, *Entrepreneurial Alliances*, Prentice Hall, forthcoming.

38. R. Fores-Fillol, 2009, Allied alliances: Parallel or complementary? *Applied Economic Letters*, 16(6): 585–590; S. G. Lazzarini, 2007, The impact of membership in competing alliance constellations: Evidence on the operational performance of global airlines, *Strategic Management Journal*, 28: 345–367.

39. S. R. Holmberg & J. L. Cummings, 2009, Building successful strategic alliance: Strategic process and analytical tools for selecting partner industries and firms, *Long Range Planning*, 42(2): 164–193; M. A. Hitt, D. Ahlstrom, M. T. Dacin, E. Levitas, & L. Svobodina, 2004, The institutional effects of strategic alliance partner selection in transition economies: China versus Russia, *Organization Science*, 15: 173–185; P. A. Saparito, C. C. Chen, & H. J. Sapienza, 2004, The role of relational trust in bank-small firm relationships, *Academy of Management Journal*, 47: 400–410.

40. G. Padula, 2008, Enhancing the innovation performance of firms by balancing cohesiveness and bridging ties, *Long Range Planning*, 41(4): 395–419; A. C. Inkpen & E. W. K. Tsang, 2005, Social capital, networks and knowledge transfer, *Academy of Management Review*, 30: 146–165.

41. W. P. Wan, D. Yiu, R. E. Hoskisson, & H. Kim, 2008, The performance implications of relationship banking during macroeconomic expansion and contraction: A study of Japanese banks' social relationships and overseas expansion, *Journal of International Business Studies*, 39: 406–447; M. Hughes, R. D. Ireland, & R. E. Morgan, 2007, Stimulating dynamic value: Social capital and business incubation as a pathway to competitive success, *Long Range Planning*, 40(2): 154–177; T. G. Pollock, J. F. Porac, & J. B. Wade,

2004, Constructing deal networks: Brokers as network "architects" in the U.S. IPO market and other examples, *Academy of Management Review*, 29: 50–72.

42. J. R. Williams, 1998, *Renewable Advantage: Crafting Strategy Through Economic Time*, New York: Free Press.

43. 2008, Nucor, Duferco team up in foreign beam venture, *Metal Center News*, February, 84.

44. R. G. Matthews, 2008, World steel makers go prospecting; Industry plows profits into buying coal or mines to reduce vulnerability to rising commodity prices, *Wall Street Journal*, June 20, B1.

45. S. A. Zahra, R. D. Ireland, I. Gutierrez, & M. A. Hitt, 2000, Privatization and entrepreneurial transformation: Emerging issues and a future research agenda, *Academy of Management Review*, 25: 509–524.

46. H. K. Steensma, J. Q. Barden, C. Dhanaraj, M. Lyles, & L. Tihanyi, 2008, The evolution and internalization of international joint ventures in a transitioning economy, *Journal of International Business Studies*, 39(3): 491–507; I. Filatotchev, M. Wright, K. Uhlenbruck, L. Tihanyi, & R. E. Hoskisson, 2003, Governance, organizational capabilities, and restructuring in transition economies, *Journal of World Business*, 38(4): 331–347.

47. H. L. Sirkin, 2008, New world disorder, *Time*, October 27, GB1; J. Lash & F. Wellington, 2007, Competitive advantage on a warming planet, *Harvard Business Review*, 85(3): 94–102; K. M. Eisenhardt, 2002, Has strategy changed? *MIT Sloan Management Review*, 43(2): 88–91.

48. Ibid., GB1.

49. S. Lahiri, L. Perez-Nordtvedt, & R. W. Renn, 2008, Will the new competitive landscape cause your firm's decline? It depends on your mindset, *Business Horizons*, 51(4): 311–320.

50. S. Schechner & E. Holmes, 2009, Disney teams up with other networks online, buying stake in Hulu site, *Wall Street Journal*, May 1, B1.

51. C. Czipura & D. R. Jolly, 2007, Global airline alliances: Sparking profitability for a troubled industry, *Journal of Business Strategy*, 28(2): 57–64.

52. C. Conkey & P. Prada, 2009, Corporate news: Continental wins nod to join Star Alliance, *Wall Street Journal*, April 8, B4.

53. S. G. Lazzarini, D. P. Claro, & L. F. Mesquita, 2008, Buyer-supplier and supplier-supplier alliances: Do they reinforce or undermine one another? *Journal of Management Studies*, 45(3): 561–584; D. R. King, J. G. Covin, & H. Hegarty, 2003, Complementary resources and the exploitation of technological innovations, *Journal of Management*, 29: 589–606; J. S. Harrison, M. A. Hitt, R. E. Hoskisson, & R. D. Ireland, 2001, Resource complementarity in business combinations: Extending the logic to organizational alliances, *Journal of Management*, 27: 679–699.

54. T. E. Stuart, S. Z. Ozdemir, & W. W. Ding, 2007, Vertical alliance networks: The case of university-biotechnology-pharmaceutical alliance chains. *Research Policy*, 36(4): 477–498; F. T. Rothaermel, M. A. Hitt, & L. A. Jobe, 2006, Balancing vertical integration and strategic outsourcing: Effects on product portfolio, product success, and firm performance, *Strategic Management Journal*, 27: 1033–1056.

55. Y. Yan, D. Ding, & S. Mak, 2009, The impact of business investment on capability exploitation and organizational control in international strategic alliances, *Journal of Change Management*, 9(1): 49–65; R. Gulati, P. R. Lawrence, & P. Puranam, 2005, Adaptation in vertical relationships beyond incentive conflict, *Strategic Management Journal*, 26: 415–440.

56. J. Wiklund & D. A. Shepherd, 2009, The effectiveness of alliances and acquisitions: The role of resource combination activities, *Theory and Practice*, 31(1): 193–212; B.-S. Teng, 2007, Corporate entrepreneurship activities through strategic alliances: A resource-based approach toward competitive advantage, *Journal of Management Studies*, 44: 119–142.

57. Y. I. Kane & D. Wakabayashi, 2009, Nintendo looks outside the box, *Wall Street Journal*, May 27, B5.

58. F. A. Ghisi, J. A.G. da Silveira, T. Kristensen, M. Hingley, & A. Lindgreen, 2008, Horizontal alliances amongst small retailers in Brazil, *British Food Journal*, 110(4/5): 514–538; Tiwana, Do bridging ties complement strong ties? An empirical examination of alliance ambidexterity; F. T. Rothaermel & M. Thursby, 2007, The nanotech versus the biotech revolution: Sources of productivity in incumbent firm research, *Research Policy*, 36: 832–849; T. H. Oum, J. H.Park, K. Kim & C. Yu, 2004, The effect of horizontal alliances on firm productivity and profitability: Evidence from the global airline industry, *Journal of Business Research*, 57: 844–853.

59. A. Johnson & A. Greil, 2009, Pfizer, Novartis disclose separate deals in generic drugs, *Wall Street Journal*, May 21, B3.

60. E. Smith, 2009, Universal takes another stab online, *Wall Street Journal*, May 15, B8.

61. Tong, Reuer, & Peng, International joint ventures and the value of growth options; J. J. Reuer & T. W. Tong, 2005, Real options in international joint ventures, *Journal of Management*, 31: 403–423; S. Chatterjee, R. M. Wiseman, A. Fiegenbaum, & C. E. Devers, 2003, Integrating behavioral and economic concepts of risk into strategic management: The twain shall meet, *Long Range Planning*, 36(1): 61–80.

62. C. Rauwald & N. Shirouzu, 2009, Volkswagen eyes China venture, *Wall Street Journal*, May 27, B4.

63. L. Tesfatsion, 2007, Agents come to bits: Toward a constructive comprehensive

taxonomy of economic entities, *Journal of Economic Behavior & Organization*, 63: 333–346.

64. K. Done, 2009, Cargo airlines fined $214 for price fixing, *Financial Times*, http://www.ft.com, April 12.

65. C. d'Aspremont, R. D. S. Ferreira & L. A.Gerard-Varet, 2007, Competition for market share or for market size: Oligopolistic equilibria with varying competitive toughness, *International Economic Review*, 48: 761–784.

66. R. W. Cooper & T. W. Ross, 2009, Sustaining cooperation with joint ventures, *Journal of Law Economics and Organization*, 25(1): 31–54.

67. J. T. Prince & D. H. Simon, 2009, Multi-market contact and service quality: Evidence from on-time performance in the U.S. airline industry, *Academy of Management Journal*, 52(2): 336–354.

68. G. K. Price & J. M. Connor, 2003, Modeling coupon values for ready-to-eat breakfast cereals, *Agribusiness*, 19(2): 223–244.

69. G. K. Price, 2000, Cereal sales soggy despite price cuts and reduced couponing, *Food Review*, 23(2): 21–28.

70. S. Kilman, 2008, Food giants race to pass rising costs to shoppers, *Wall Street Journal*, August 8, A1.

71. Kilman, Food giants race to pass rising costs to shoppers; J. Hagedoorn & G. Hesen, 2007, Contract law and the governance of interfirm technology partnerships—An analysis of different modes of partnering and their contractual implications, *Journal of Management Studies*, 44: 342–366; B. R. Golden & H. Ma, 2003, Mutual forbearance: The role of intrafirm integration and rewards, *Academy of Management Review*, 28: 479–493.

72. J. Apesteguia, M. Dufwenberg, & R. Selton, 2007, Blowing the whistle, *Economic Theory*, 31: 127–142.

73. J. D. Rockoff, 2009, Drug CEOs switch tactics on reform; Pharmaceutical companies join health-care overhaul hoping to influence where costs are cut, *Wall Street Journal*, May 27, B1, B2; J. H. Johnson & G. K. Leonard, 2007, Economics and the rigorous analysis of class certification in antitrust cases, *Journal of Competition Law and Economics*, http://jcle.oxfordjournals.org, June 26.

74. Lazzarini, Claro, & Mesquita, Buyer-supplier and supplier-supplier alliances: Do they reinforce or undermine one another?; P. Dussauge, B. Garrette, & W. Mitchell, 2004, Asymmetric performances: The market share impact of scale ad link alliances in global auto industry, *Strategic Management Journal*, 25: 701–711.

75. Conkey & Prada, Corporate news: Continental wins nod to join Star Alliance.

76. Harrison, Hitt, Hoskisson, & Ireland, Resource complementarity, 684–685.

77. L. H.Lin, 2009, Mergers and acquisitions, alliances and technology development: An empirical study of the global auto industry, *International Journal of Technology Management*, 48(3): 295–307; Wiklund & Shepherd, The effectiveness of alliances and acquisitions: The role of resource combination activities; A. E. Bernardo & B. Chowdhry, 2002, Resources, real options, and corporate strategy, *Journal of Financial Economics*, 63: 211–234.

78. J. Li, C. Dhanaraj, & R. L. Shockley, 2008, Joint venture evolution: Extending the real options approach, *Managerial and Decision Economics*, 29(4): 317–336.

79. V. Moatti, 2009, Learning to expand or expanding to learn? The role of imitation and experience in the choice among several expansion modes, *European Management Journal*, 27(1): 36–46; C. C. Pegels & Y. I. Song, 2007, Market competition and cooperation: Identifying competitive/cooperative interaction groups, *International Journal of Services Technology and Management*, 2/3: 139–154

80. S. Silver & E. Steel, 2009, Alcatel gets into mobile ads; Service will target cell phone users based on location, *Wall Street Journal*, May 21, B9.

81. A. Goerzen & P. W. Beamish, 2005, The effect of alliance network diversity on multinational enterprise performance, *Strategic Management Journal*, 333–354.

82. M. V. Shyam Kumar, 2005, The value from acquiring and divesting a joint venture: A real options approach, *Strategic Management Journal*, 26: 321–331.

83. J. Yang, 2003, One step forward for Japan's chipmakers, *BusinessWeek Online*, http://www.businessweek.com, July 7.

84. J. E. Vascellaro & E. Holmes, 2009, YouTube seals deal on ABC, ESPN clips, Wall Street Journal online, http:// www.wsj.com, March 31.

85. B. Worthen & J. Scheck, 2009, As growth slows, ex-allies square off in a turf war, *Wall Street Journal*, March 16, A1.

86. A. M. Doherty, 2009, Market and partner selection processes in international retail franchising, *Journal of Business Research*, 62(5): 528–534; M. Tuunanen & F. Hoy, 2007, Franchising—multifaceted form of entrepreneurship, *International Journal of Entrepreneurship and Small Business*, 4: 52–67; J. G. Combs & D. J. Ketchen Jr., 2003, Why do firms use franchising as an entrepreneurial strategy? A meta-analysis, *Journal of Management*, 29: 427–443.

87. F. Lafontaine, 1999, Myths and strengths of franchising, "Mastering Strategy" (Part Nine), *Financial Times*, November 22, 8–10.

88. A. M. Hayashi, 2008, How to replicate success, *MIT Sloan Management Review*, 49(3): 6–7.

89. G. Szulanski & R. J. Jensen, 2008, Growing through copying: The negative consequences of innovation on franchise network growth, *Research Policy*, 37(10): 1732–1741.

90. B. Barringer & R. D. Ireland, 2008, *Entrepreneurship: Successfully Launching New Ventures*, 2nd ed., Prentice Hall, 440.

91. L. Sanders, 2009, International expansion: Proven strategy during economic uncertainty, *Franchising World*, March, 16–17; B. Duckett, 2008, Business format franchising: A strategic option for business growth—at home and abroad, *Strategic Direction*, 4(2): 3–4.

92. Doherty, Market and partner selection processes in international retail franchising; R. B. DiPietro, D. H. B. Welsh, P. V. Raven, & D. Severt, 2007, A message of hope in franchises systems: Assessing franchisee, top executives, and franchisors, *Journal of Leadership & Organizational Studies*, 13(3): 59–66; S. C. Michael, 2002, Can a franchise chain coordinate? *Journal of Business Venturing*, 17: 325–342.

93. A. K. Paswan & C. M. Wittmann, 2009, Knowledge management and franchise systems, *Industrial Marketing Management*, 38(2): 173–180.

94. J. Torikka, 2007, Franchisees can be made: Empirical evidence from a follow-up study, *International Journal of Entrepreneurship and Small Business*, 4: 68–96; P. J. Kaufmann & S. Eroglu, 1999, Standardization and adaptation in business format franchising, *Journal of Business Venturing*, 14: 69–85.

95. B. Arruñada, L. Vázquez, & G. Zanarone, 2009, Institutional constraints on organizations: The case of Spanish car dealerships, *Managerial and Decision Economics*, 30(1): 15–26; J. Barthélemy, 2008, Opportunism, knowledge, and the performance of franchise chains, *Strategic Management Journal*, 29(13): 1451–1463.

96. A. Tiwana, 2008, Does technological modularity substitute for control? A study of alliance performance in software outsourcing, *Strategic Management Journal*, 29(7): 769–780; M. Zollo, J. J. Reuer, & H. Singh, 2002, Interorganizational routines and performance in strategic alliances, *Organization Science*, 13: 701–714.

97. E. Levitas & M. A. McFadyen, 2009, Managing liquidity in research-intensive firms: Signaling and cash flow effects of patents and alliance activities, *Strategic Management Journal*, 30(6): 659–678; Ireland, Hitt, & Vaidyanath, Alliance management.

98. R. Durand, O. Bruyaka, & V. Mangematin, 2008, Do science and money go together? The case of the French biotech industry, *Strategic Management Journal*, 29(12): 1281–1299; A. V. Shipilov, 2007, Network strategies and performance of Canadian investment banks, *Academy of Management Journal*, 49: 590–604; P. Almeida, G. Dokko, & L. Rosenkopf, 2003, Startup size and the mechanisms of external learning: Increasing opportunity and decreasing ability? *Research Policy*, 32(2): 301–316.

99. H. Ren, B. Gray, & K. Kim, 2009, Performance of international joint ventures: What factors really make a difference and how? *Journal of Management*, 35(3): 805–832; R. Narula &

G. Duysters, 2004, Globalization and trends in international R&D alliances, *Journal of International Management*, 10: 199–218; M. A. Hitt, M. T. Dacin, E. Levitas, J.-L. Arregle, & A. Borza, 2000, Partner selection in emerging and developed market contexts: Resource-based and organizational learning perspectives, *Academy of Management Journal*, 43: 449–467.

100. W. Zhan, R. Chen, M. K. Erramilli, & D. T. Nguyen, 2009, Acquisition of organizational capabilities and competitive advantage of IJVs in transition economies: The case of Vietnam, *Asia Pacific Journal of Management*, 26(2): 285–308; Tong, Reuer, & Peng, International joint ventures and the value of growth option; J. H. Dyer, P. Kale, & H. Singh, 2004, When to ally & when to acquire, *Harvard Business Review*, 81(7/8): 109–115.

101. 1Y. Yan, D. Ding, & S. Mak, 2009, The impact of business investment on capability exploitation and organizational control in international strategic alliances, *Journal of Change Management*, 9(1): 49–65; P. Ghemawat, 2007, Managing differences: The central challenge of global strategy, *Harvard Business Review*, 85(3): 59–68.

102. L. Chao, 2009, IMG China venture opens with tennis, *Wall Street Journal*, May 26, B10.

103. Ren, Gray, & Kim, Performance of international joint ventures: What factors really make a difference and how; L. Dong & K.W. Glaister, 2007, National and corporate culture differences in international strategic alliances: Perceptions of Chinese partners, *Asia Pacific Journal of Management*, 24: 191–205; I. M. Manev, 2003, The managerial network in a multinational enterprise and the resource profiles of subsidiaries, *Journal of International Management*, 9: 133–152.

104. P. H. Dickson, K. M. Weaver, & F. Hoy, 2006, Opportunism in the R&D alliances of SMEs: The roles of the institutional environment and SME size, *Journal of Business Venturing*, 21: 487–513; H. K. Steensma, L. Tihanyi, M. A. Lyles, & C. Dhanaraj, 2005, The evolving value of foreign partnerships in transitioning economies, *Academy of Management Journal*, 48: 213–235.

105. 2007, Branding and celebrity endorsements, *VentureRepublic*, http://venturerepublic.com, August 31.

106. 2009, Nike winded, *Financial Times*, March 20, 14.

107. B. Elango, 2009, Minimizing effects of "liability of foreignness": Response strategies of foreign firms in the United States, *Journal of World Business*, 44(1): 51–62; Y. Luo, O. Shenkar, & M.-K. Nyaw, 2002, Mitigating the liabilities of foreignness: Defensive versus offensive approaches, *Journal of International Management*, 8: 283–300.

108. T. J. Wilkinson, A. R. Thomas, & J. M. Hawes, 2009, Managing relationships with Chinese joint venture partners, *Journal of Global Marketing*, 22(2): 109–210; S. R. Miller & A. Parkhe, 2002, Is there a liability of foreignness in global banking? An empirical test of banks' x-efficiency, *Strategic Management Journal*, 23: 55–75; Y. Luo, 2001, Determinants of local responsiveness: Perspectives from foreign subsidiaries in an emerging market, *Journal of Management*, 27: 451–477.

109. D. Kronborg & S. Thomsen, 2009, Foreign ownership and long-term survival, *Strategic Management Journal*, 30(2): 207–220.

110. E. Rodríguez, 2008, Cooperative ventures in emerging economies, *Journal of Business Research*, 61(6): 640–647; D. Li, L. E. Eden, M. A. Hitt, & R. D. Ireland, 2008, Friends, acquaintances or strangers? Partner selection in R&D alliances, *Academy of Management Journal*, 51: 315–334; J. E. Oxley & R. C. Sampson, 2004, The scope and governance of international R&D alliances, *Strategic Management Journal*, 25: 723–749.

111. H. Sun, 2009, China poised to be net importer of coffee, *Wall Street Journal*, January 20, C10; 2006, Starbucks acquires control of China joint venture, *Apostille US*, http://apostille.us/, October 25.

112. D. Lavie, 2009, Capturing value from alliance portfolios, *Organizational Dynamics*, 38(1): 26–36; D. Lavie, C. Lechner, & H. Singh, 2007, The performance implications of timing of entry and involvement in multipartner alliances, *Academy of Management Journal*, 49: 569–604.

113. K. Atkins, J. Chen, V. S. A. Kumar, M. Macauley, & A. Marathe, 2009, Locational market power in network constrained markets, *Journal of Economic Behavior & Organization*, 70(1/2): 416–430; A. Nosella & G. Petroni, 2007, Multiple network leadership as a strategic asset: The Carlo Gavazzi space case, *Long Range Planning*, 40: 178–201.

114. K. Sawyer, 2007, Strength in webs, *The Conference Board*, July/August, 9–11.

115. C. Yarbrough, 2008, Singapore to open fusionopolis, *Research Technology Management*, 51(5): 4–5; A. H. Van de Ven, H. J. Sapienza, & J. Villanueva, 2007, Entrepreneurial pursuits of self- and collective interests, *Strategic Entrepreneurship Journal*, 1(3/4): 353–370.

116. Lavie, Capturing value from alliance portfolios; D. Lavie, 2007, Alliance portfolios and firm performance: A study of value creation and appropriation in the U.S. software industry, *Strategic Management Journal*, 28(12): 1187–1212; G. K. Lee, 2007, The significance of network resources in the race to enter emerging product markets: The convergence of telephony communications and computer networking, 1989–2001, *Strategic Management Journal*, 28: 17–37.

117. R. Cowan & N. Jonard, 2009, Knowledge portfolios and the organization of innovation networks, *Academy of Management Review*, 34(2): 320–342; G. G. Bell, 2005, Clusters, networks, and firm innovativeness, *Strategic Management Journal*, 26: 287–295.

118. H. Kim, R. E. Hoskisson, & W. P. Wan, 2004, Power, dependence, diversification strategy and performance in keiretsu member firms, *Strategic Management Journal*, 25: 613–636.

119. A. V. Shipilov, 2009, Firm scope experience, historic multimarket contact with partners, centrality, and the relationship between structural holes and performance, *Organization Science*, 20(1): 85–106; M. Rudberg & J. Olhager, 2003, Manufacturing networks and supply chains: An operations strategy perspective, *Omega*, 31(1): 29–39.

120. Cowan & Jonard, Knowledge portfolios and the organization of innovation networks; E. J. Kleinschmidt, U. de Brentani, & S. Salomo, 2007, Programs: A resource-based view, *Journal of Product Innovation Management*, 24: 419–441; G. J. Young, M. P. Charns, & S. M. Shortell, 2001, Top manager and network effects on the adoption of innovative management practices: A study of TQM in a public hospital system, *Strategic Management Journal*, 22: 935–951.

121. Prince & Simon, Multi-market contact and service quality: Evidence from on-time performance in the U.S. airline industry; E. Garcia-Canal, C. L. Duarte, J. R. Criado, & A. V. Llaneza, 2002, Accelerating international expansion through global alliances: A typology of cooperative strategies, *Journal of World Business*, 37(2): 91–107; F. T. Rothaermel, 2001, Complementary assets, strategic alliances, and the incumbent's advantage: An empirical study of industry and firm effects in the biopharmaceutical industry, *Research Policy*, 30: 1235–1251.

122. T. Kiessling & M. Harvey, 2008, Globalisation of internal venture capital opportunities in developing small and medium enterprises' relationships, *International Journal of Entrepreneurship and Innovation Management*, 8(3): 233–253; V. Shankar & B. L. Bayus, 2003, Network effects and competition: An empirical analysis of the home video game industry, *Strategic Management Journal*, 24: 375–384.

123. A. Schwab & A. S. Miner, 2008, Learning in hybrid-project systems: The effects of project performance on repeated collaboration, *Academy of Management Journal*, 51(6): 1117–1149.

124. A. E. Leiponen, 2008, Competing through cooperation: The organization of standard setting in wireless telecommunications, *Management Science*, 54(11): 1904–1919; Z. Simsek, M. H. Lubatkin, & D. Kandemir, 2003, Inter-firm networks and entrepreneurial behavior: A structural embeddedness perspective, *Journal of Management*, 29: 401–426.

125. H. W. Gottinger & C. L. Umali, 2008, The evolution of the pharmaceutical-biotechnology industry, *Business History*,

50(5): 583–601; F. T. Rothaermel & W. Boeker, 2008, Old technology meets new technology: Complementarities, similarities, and alliance formation, *Strategic Management Journal*, 29(1): 47–77; P. Puranam & K. Srikanth, 2007, What they know vs. what they do: How acquirers leverage technology acquisitions, *Strategic Management Journal*, 28: 805–825; M. Moensted, 2007, Strategic networking in small high-tech firms, *The International Entrepreneurship and Management Journal*, 3: 15–27.

126. P. Ozcan & K. M. Eisenhardt, 2009, Origin of alliance portfolios: Entrepreneurs, network strategies, and firm performance, *Academy of Management Journal*, 52(2): 246–279; C. T. Street & A.-F. Cameron, 2007, External relationships and the small business: A review of small business alliance and network research, *Journal of Small Business Management*, 45: 239–266.

127. M. Rod, 2009, A model for the effective management of joint ventures: A case study approach, *International Journal of Management*, 26(1): 3–17; T. K. Das & R. Kumar, 2007, Learning dynamics in the alliance development process, *Management Decision*, 45: 684–707.

128. A. Carmeli & Z. Sheaffer, 2008, How learning leadership and organizational learning from failures enhance perceived organizational capacity to adapt to the task environment, *Journal of Applied Behavioral Science*, 44(4): 468–489; J.-Y. Kim & A. S. Miner, 2007, Vicarious learning from the failures and near-failures of others: Evidence from the U.S. commercial banking industry, *Academy of Management Journal*, 49: 687–714.

129. Y. Li, Y. Liu, M. Li, & H. Wu, 2008, Transformational offshore outsourcing: Empirical evidence from alliances in China, *Journal of Operations Management*, 26(2): 257–274; P. M. Norman, 2002, Protecting knowledge in strategic alliances—Resource and relational characteristics, *Journal of High Technology Management Research*, 13(2): 177–202; P. M. Norman, 2001, Are your secrets safe? Knowledge protection in strategic alliances, *Business Horizons*, November–December, 51–60.

130. Heimeriks, Klijn, & Reuer, Building capabilities for alliance portfolios; Al-Laham, Amburgey, & Bates, The dynamics of research alliances: Examining the effect of alliance experience and partner characteristics on the speed of alliance entry in the biotech industry; J. Connell & R. Voola, 2007, Strategic alliances and knowledge sharing: Synergies or silos? *Journal of Knowledge Management*, 11: 52–66.

131. M. B. Sarkar, P. S. Aulakh, & A. Madhok, 2009, Process capabilities and value generation in alliance portfolios, *Organization Science*, 20(3): 583–600.

132. P.-X. Meschi, 2009, Government corruption and foreign stakes in international joint ventures in emerging economies, *Asia Pacific Journal of Management*, 26(2): 241–261.

133. M. H. Hansen, R. E. Hoskisson, & J. B. Barney, 2008, Competitive advantage in alliance governance: Resolving the opportunism minimization-gain maximization paradox, *Managerial and Decision Economics*, 29: 191–208; J. H. Dyer, P. Kale, & H. Singh, 2001, How to make strategic alliances work, *MIT Sloan Management Review*, 42(4): 37–43.

134. Connell & Voola, Strategic alliances and knowledge sharing.

135. Levitas & McFadyen, Managing liquidity in research-intensive firms: Signaling and cash flow effects of patents and alliance activities; Hansen, Hoskisson, & Barney, Competitive advantage in alliance governance: Resolving the opportunism minimization-gain maximization paradox; J. H. Dyer, 1997, Effective interfirm collaboration: How firms minimize transaction costs and maximize transaction value, *Strategic Management Journal*, 18: 535–556.

136. L. Poppo, K. Z. Zhou, & S. Ryu, 2008, Alternative origins to interorganizational trust: An interdependence perspective on the shadow of the past and the shadow of the future, *Organization Science*, 19(1): 39–56; J. H. Dyer & C. Wujin, 2003, The role of trustworthiness in reducing transaction costs and improving performance: Empirical evidence from the United States, Japan, and Korea, *Organization Science*, 14: 57–69.

137. Krishnan, Martin, & Noorderhaven, When does trust matter to alliance performance?

138. K. Langfield-Smith, 2008, The relations between transactional characteristics, trust and risk in the start-up phase of a collaborative alliance, *Management Accounting Research*, 19(4): 344–364; M. Lundin, 2007, Explaining cooperation: How resource interdependence, goal congruence, and trust affect joint actions in policy implementation, *Journal of Public Administration Research and Theory*, 17(4): 651–672.

139. T. K. Das & R. Kumar, 2009, Interpartner harmony in strategic alliances: Managing commitment and forbearance, *International Journal of Strategic Business Alliances*, 1(1): 24–52; V. Perrone, A. Zaheer, & B. McEvily, 2003, Free to be trusted? Boundary constraints on trust in boundary spanners, *Organization Science*, 14: 422–439.

140. J. W. Rottman, 2008, Successful knowledge transfer within offshore supplier networks: A case study exploring social capital in strategic alliances, *Journal of Information Technology*: Special Issue: Global Sourcing, 23(1): 31–43; R. D. Ireland & J. W. Webb, 2007, A multi-theoretic perspective on trust and power in strategic supply chains, *Journal of Operations Management*, 25: 482–497.

141. 2007, The principles of the alliance, http://www.renault.com, August 26.

142. C. E. Ybarra & T. A. Turk, 2009, The evolution of trust in information technology alliances, *Journal of High Technology Management Research*, 20(1): 62–74; F. D. Schoorman, R. C. Mayer, & J. H. Davis, 2007, An integrative model of organizational trust: Past, present, and future, *Academy of Management Review*, 344–354; J. H. Davis, F. D. Schoorman, R. C. Mayer, & H. H. Tan, 2000, The trusted general manager and business unit performance: Empirical evidence of a competitive advantage, *Strategic Management Journal*, 21: 563–576.

143. Y. Luo, 2008, Procedural fairness and interfirm cooperation in strategic alliances, *Strategic Management Journal*, 29(1): 27–46; B. Hillebrand & W. G. Biemans, 2003, The relationship between internal and external cooperation: Literature review and propositions, *Journal of Business Research*, 56: 735–744.

Chapter 10

1. B. W. Heineman, Jr., 2009, Redefining the CEO role. *BusinessWeek*, http://www.businessweek.com, April 16; C. Thomas, D. Kidd, & C. Fernández-Aráoz, 2007, Are you underutilizing your board? *MIT Sloan Management Review*, 48(2): 71–76; D. C. Carey &, M. Patsalos-Fox, 2006, Shaping strategy from the boardroom. *McKinsey Quarterly*, 3: 90–94.

2. J. B. Wade, C. A. O'Reilly, & T. G. Pollock, 2006, Overpaid CEOs and underpaid managers: Fairness and executive compensation, *Organization Science*, 17: 527–544; A. Henderson & J. Fredrickson, 2001, Top management team coordination needs and the CEO pay gap: A competitive test of economic and behavioral views, *Academy of Management Journal*, 44: 96–117.

3. A. D. F. Penalva, 2006, Governance structure and the weighting of performance measures in CEO compensation, *Review of Accounting Studies*, 11: 463–493; S. Werner, H. L. Tosi, & L. Gomez-Mejia, 2005, Organizational governance and employee pay: How ownership structure affects the firm's compensation strategy, *Strategic Management Journal*, 26: 377–384.

4. C. Crossland & D. C. Hambrick, 2007, How national systems differ in their constraints on corporate executives: A study of CEO effects in three countries,

Strategic Management Journal, 28: 767–789; M. D. Lynall, B. R. Golden, & A. J. Hillman, 2003, Board composition from adolescence to maturity: A multitheoretic view, *Academy of Management Review*, 28: 416–431.

5. M. A. Rutherford, A. K. Buchholtz, & J. A. Brown, 2007, Examining the relationships between monitoring and incentives in corporate governance, *Journal of Management Studies* 44: 414–430; C. M. Daily, D. R. Dalton, & A. A. Cannella, 2003, Corporate governance: Decades of dialogue and data, *Academy of Management Review*, 28: 371–382; P. Stiles, 2001, The impact of the board on strategy: An empirical examination, *Journal of Management Studies*, 38: 627–650.

6. D. R. Dalton, M. A. Hitt, S. T. Certo, & C. M. Dalton, 2008, The fundamental agency problem and its mitigation: Independence, equity and the market for corporate control, in J. P. Walsh and A. P. Brief (eds.), *The Academy of Management Annals*, New York: Lawrence Erlbaum Associates, 1–64; E. F. Fama & M. C. Jensen, 1983, Separation of ownership and control, *Journal of Law and Economics*, 26: 301–325.

7. I. Le Breton-Miller & D. Miller, 2006, Why do some family businesses out-compete? Governance, long-term orientations, and sustainable capability, *Entrepreneurship Theory and Practice*, 30: 731–746; M. Carney, 2005, Corporate governance and competitive advantage in family-controlled firms, *Entrepreneurship Theory and Practice*, 29: 249–265; R. Charan, 1998, *How Corporate Boards Create Competitive Advantage*, San Francisco: Jossey-Bass.

8. X. Wu, 2005, Corporate governance and corruption: A cross-country analysis, *Governance*, 18(2): 151–170; J. McGuire & S. Dow, 2002, The Japanese keiretsu system: An empirical analysis, *Journal of Business Research*, 55: 33–40.

9. R. E. Hoskisson, D. Yiu, & H. Kim, 2004, Corporate governance systems: Effects of capital and labor market congruency on corporate innovation and global competitiveness, *Journal of High Technology Management*, 15: 293–315.

10. Crossland & Hambrick, How national systems differ in their constraints on corporate executives; R. Aguilera & G. Jackson, 2003, The cross-national diversity of corporate governance: Dimensions and determinants, *Academy of Management Review*, 28: 447–465.

11. R. P. Wright, 2004, Top managers' strategic cognitions of the strategy making process: Differences between high and low performing firms, *Journal of General Management*, 30(1): 61–78.

12. X. Luo, C. N. Chung, & M. Sobczak, 2009, How do corporate governance model differences affect foreign direct investment in emerging economies? *Journal of International Business Studies*, 40: 444–467; A. Bris & C. Cabous, 2006,

In a merger, two companies come together and integrate their distribution lines, brands, work forces, management teams, strategies and cultures, *Financial Times*, October 6, 1.

13. S. Sudarsanam & A. A. Mahate, 2006, Are friendly acquisitions too bad for shareholders and managers? Long-term value creation and top management turnover in hostile and friendly acquirers, *British Journal of Management: Supplement*, 17(1): S7–S30; T. Moeller, 2005, Let's make a deal! How shareholder control impacts merger payoffs, *Journal of Financial Economics*, 76(1): 167–190; M. A. Hitt, R. E. Hoskisson, R. A. Johnson, & D. D. Moesel, 1996, The market for corporate control and firm innovation, *Academy of Management Journal*, 39: 1084–1119.

14. R. E. Hoskisson, M. A. Hitt, R. A. Johnson, & W. Grossman, 2002, Conflicting voices: The effects of ownership heterogeneity and internal governance on corporate strategy, *Academy of Management Journal*, 45: 697–716.

15. G. E. Davis & T. A. Thompson, 1994, A social movement perspective on corporate control, *Administrative Science Quarterly*, 39: 141–173.

16. R. Bricker & N. Chandar, 2000, Where Berle and Means went wrong: A reassessment of capital market agency and financial reporting, *Accounting, Organizations, and Society*, 25: 529–554; M. A. Eisenberg, 1989, The structure of corporation law, *Columbia Law Review*, 89(7): 1461, as cited in R. A. G. Monks & N. Minow, 1995, *Corporate Governance*, Cambridge, MA: Blackwell Business, 7.

17. R. M. Wiseman & L. R. Gomez-Mejia, 1999, A behavioral agency model of managerial risk taking, *Academy of Management Review*, 23: 133–153.

18. T. Zellweger, 2007, Time horizon, costs of equity capital, and generic investment strategies of firms, *Family Business Review*, 20(1): 1–15; R. C. Anderson & D. M. Reeb, 2004, Board composition: Balancing family influence in S&P 500 firms, *Administrative Science Quarterly*, 49: 209–237.

19. Carney, Corporate governance and competitive advantage in family-controlled firms; N. Anthanassiou, W. F. Crittenden, L. M. Kelly, & P. Marquez, 2002, Founder centrality effects on the Mexican family firm's top management group: Firm culture, strategic vision and goals and firm performance, *Journal of World Business*, 37: 139–150.

20. M. Santiago-Castro & C. J. Brown, 2007, Ownership structure and minority rights: A Latin American view, *Journal of Economics and Business*, 59: 430–442; M. Carney & E. Gedajlovic, 2003, Strategic innovation and the administrative heritage of East Asian family business groups, *Asia Pacific Journal of Management*, 20: 5–26; D. Miller & I. Le Breton-Miller, 2003, Challenge versus advantage in family business, *Strategic Organization*, 1: 127–134.

21. D. G. Sirmon, J.-L. Arregle, M. A. Hitt, & J. Webb, 2008, Strategic responses to the threat of imitation, *Entrepreneurship Theory and Practice*, 32: 979–998.

22. Rutherford, Buchholtz, & Brown, Examining the relationships between monitoring and incentives in corporate governance; D. Dalton, C. Daily, T. Certo, & R. Roengpitya, 2003, Meta-analyses of financial performance and equity: Fusion or confusion? *Academy of Management Journal*, 46: 13–26; M. Jensen & W. Meckling, 1976, Theory of the firm: Managerial behavior, agency costs, and ownership structure, *Journal of Financial Economics*, 11: 305–360.

23. G. C. Rodríguez, C. A.-D. Espejo, & R. Valle Cabrera, 2007, Incentives management during privatization: An agency perspective, *Journal of Management Studies*, 44: 536–560; D. C. Hambrick, S. Finkelstein, & A. C. Mooney, 2005, Executive job demands: New insights for explaining strategic decisions and leader behaviors, *Academy of Management Review*, 30: 472–491.

24. T. G. Habbershon, 2006, Commentary: A framework for managing the familiness and agency advantages in family firms, *Entrepreneurship Theory and Practice*, 30: 879–886; M. G. Jacobides & D. C. Croson, 2001, Information policy: Shaping the value of agency relationships, *Academy of Management Review*, 26: 202–223.

25. A. Mackey, 2008, The effects of CEOs on firm performance, *Strategic Management Journal*, 29: 1357–1367; Y. Y. Kor, 2006, Direct and interaction effects of top management team and board compositions on R&D investment strategy, *Strategic Management Journal*, 27: 1081–1099.

26. Dalton, Hitt, Certo, & Dalton, 2008, The fundamental agency problem and its mitigation: Independence, equity and the market for corporate control; A. Ghosh, D. Moon, & K. Tandon, 2007, CEO ownership and discretionary investments, *Journal of Business Finance & Accounting*, 34: 819–839.

27. S. Ghoshal & P. Moran, 1996, Bad for practice: A critique of the transaction cost theory, *Academy of Management Review*, 21: 13–47; O. E. Williamson, 1996, *The Mechanisms of Governance*, New York: Oxford University Press, 6.

28. B. E. Ashforth, D. A. Gioia, S. L. Robinson, & L. K. Trevino, 2008, Reviewing organizational corruption, *Academy of Management Review*, 33: 670–684; E. Kang, 2006, Investors' perceptions of managerial opportunism in corporate acquisitions: The moderating role of environmental condition, *Corporate Governance*, 14: 377–387; R. W. Coff & P. M. Lee, 2003, Insider trading as a vehicle to appropriate rent from R&D. *Strategic Management Journal*, 24: 183–190.

29. M. L. McDonald, P. Khanna, & J. D. Westphal, 2008, Getting them to think outside the circle: Corporate

governance, CEOs' external advice networks, and firm performance, *Academy of Management Journal*, 51: 453–475.

30. Fama, Agency problems and the theory of the firm.

31. P. Jiraporn, Y. Sang Kim, W. N. Davidson, & M. Singh, 2006, Corporate governance, shareholder rights and firm diversification: An empirical analysis, *Journal of Banking & Finance*, 30: 947–963; R. C. Anderson, T. W. Bates, J. M. Bizjak, & M. L. Lemmon, 2000, Corporate governance and firm diversification, *Financial Management*, 29(1): 5–22; R. E. Hoskisson & T. A. Turk, 1990, Corporate restructuring: Governance and control limits of the internal market, *Academy of Management Review*, 15: 459–477.

32. G. P. Baker & B. J. Hall, 2004, CEO incentives and firm size, *Journal of Labor Economics*, 22: 767–798; R. Bushman, Q. Chen, E. Engel, & A. Smith, 2004, Financial accounting information, organizational complexity and corporate governance systems, *Journal of Accounting & Economics*, 7: 167–201; M. A. Geletkanycz, B. K. Boyd, & S. Finkelstein, 2001, The strategic value of CEO external directorate networks: Implications for CEO compensation, *Strategic Management Journal*, 9: 889–898.

33. S. W. Geiger & L. H. Cashen, 2007, Organizational size and CEO compensation: The moderating effect of diversification in downscoping organizations, *Journal of Managerial Issues*, 9(2): 233–252; Y. Grinstein & P. Hribar, 2004, CEO compensation and incentives: Evidence from M&A bonuses, *Journal of Financial Economics*, 73: 119–143;

34. S. Rajgopal, T. Shevlin, & V. Zamora, 2006, CEOs' outside employment opportunities and the lack of relative performance evaluation in compensation contracts, *Journal of Finance*, 61: 1813–1844.

35. J. Weber, 2007, The accidental CEO (well, not really); Kellogg needed a new boss, fast. Here's how it groomed insider David Mackay, *BusinessWeek*, April 23, 65.

36. Kellogg's Annual Report, 2008. Kellogg, Michigan.

37. M. Ganco & R. Agarwal, 2009, Performance differentials between diversifying entrants and entrepreneurial start-ups: A complexity approach, *Academy of Management Review*, 34: 228–252.

38. M. S. Jensen, 1986, Agency costs of free cash flow, corporate finance, and takeovers, *American Economic Review*, 76: 323–329.

39. A. V. Douglas, 2007, Managerial opportunism and proportional corporate payout policies, *Managerial Finance*, 33(1): 26–42; M. Jensen & E. Zajac, 2004, Corporate elites and corporate strategy: How demographic preferences and structural position shape the scope of the firm, *Strategic Management Journal*, 25: 507–524; T. H. Brush, P. Bromiley, & M. Hendrickx, 2000, The free cash flow hypothesis for sales growth and firm

40. J. Lunsford & B. Steinberg, 2006, Conglomerates' conundrum, *Wall Street Journal*, September 14, B1, B7; K. Ramaswamy, M. Li, & B. S. P. Petitt, 2004, Who drives unrelated diversification? A study of Indian manufacturing firms, *Asia Pacific Journal of Management*, 21: 403–423.

41. M. V. S. Kumar, 2009, The relationship between product and international diversification: The effects of short-run constraints and endogeneity, *Strategic Management Journal*, 30: 99–116; M. F. Wiersema & H. P. Bowen, 2008, Corporate diversification: The impact of foreign competition, industry globalization and product diversification, *Strategic Management Journal*, 29: 115–132.

42. D. D. Bergh, R. A. Johnson, & R.-L. Dewitt, 2008, Restructuring through spin-off or sell-off: Transforming information asymmetries into financial gain, *Strategic Management Journal*, 29: 133–148; K. B. Lee, M. W. Peng, & K. Lee, 2008, From diversification premium to diversification discount during institutional transitions, *Journal of World Business*, 43: 47–65.

43. T. K. Berry, J. M. Bizjak, M. L. Lemmon, & L. Naveen, 2006, Organizational complexity and CEO labor markets: Evidence from diversified firms, *Journal of Corporate Finance*, 12: 797–817; R. Rajan, H. Servaes, & L. Zingales, 2001, The cost of diversity: The diversification discount and inefficient investment, *Journal of Finance*, 55: 35–79; A. Sharma, 1997, Professional as agent: Knowledge asymmetry in agency exchange, *Academy of Management Review*, 22: 758–798.

44. V. Chhaochharia & Y. Grinstein, 2007, Corporate governance and firm value: The impact of the 2002 governance rules, *Journal of Finance*, 62: 1789–1825; A. Borrus, L. Lavelle, D. Brady, M. Arndt, & J. Weber, 2005, Death, taxes and Sarbanes-Oxley? Executives may be frustrated with the law's burdens, but corporate performance is here to stay, *BusinessWeek*, January 17, 28–31.

45. D. Reilly, 2006, Checks on internal controls pay off, *Wall Street Journal*, August 10, C3.

46. F. Navissi & V. Naiker, 2006, Institutional ownership and corporate value, *Managerial Finance*, 32: 247–256; A. de Miguel, J. Pindado, & C. de la Torre, 2004, Ownership structure and firm value: New evidence from Spain, *Strategic Management Journal*, 25: 1199–1207; J. Coles, N. Sen, & V. McWilliams, 2001, An examination of the relationship of governance mechanisms to performance, *Journal of Management*, 27: 23–50.

47. Jiraporn, Kim, Davidson, & Singh, Corporate governance, shareholder rights and firm diversification; M. Singh, I. Mathur, & K. C. Gleason, 2004, Governance and performance implications

of diversification strategies: Evidence from large U.S. firms, *Financial Review*, 39: 489–526; R. E. Hoskisson, R. A. Johnson, & D. D. Moesel, 1994, Corporate divestiture intensity in restructuring firms: Effects of governance, strategy, and performance, *Academy of Management Journal*, 37: 1207–1251.

48. G. Iannotta, G. Nocera, & A. Sironi, 2007, Ownership structure, risk and performance in the European banking industry, *Journal of Banking & Finance*, 31: 2127–2149.

49. B. Villalonga & R. Amit, 2006, How do family ownership, control and management affect firm value? *Journal of Financial Economics*, 80: 385–417; R. C. Anderson & D. M. Reeb, 2004, Board composition: Balancing family influence in S&P 500 firms, *Administrative Science Quarterly*, 49: 209–237.

50. M. Fackler, 2008, South Korea faces question of corporate control, *New York Times*, http://www.nytimes.com, April 24; S. J. Chang, 2003, Ownership structure, expropriation and performance of group-affiliated companies in Korea, *Academy of Management Journal*, 46: 238–253.

51. A. Berle & G. Means, 1932, *The Modern Corporation and Private Property*, New York: Macmillan.

52. M. Gietzmann, 2006, Disclosure of timely and forward-looking statements and strategic management of major institutional ownership, *Long Range Planning*, 39(4): 409–427; B. Ajinkya, S. Bhojraj, & P. Sengupta, 2005, The association between outside directors, institutional investors and the properties of management earnings forecasts, *Journal of Accounting Research*, 43: 343–376; M. P. Smith, 1996, Shareholder activism by institutional investors: Evidence from CalPERS, *Journal of Finance*, 51: 227–252.

53. K. Schnatterly, K. W. Shaw, & W. W. Jennings, 2008, Information advantages of large institutional owners, *Strategic Management Journal*, 29: 219–227; Hoskisson, Hitt, Johnson, & Grossman, Conflicting voices.

54. S. D. Chowdhury & E. Z. Wang, 2009, Institutional activism types and CEO compensation: A time-series analysis of large Canadian corporations, *Journal of Management*, 35: 5–36; M. Musteen, D. K. Datta, & P. Herrmann, 2009, Ownership structure and CEO compensation: Implications for the choice of foreign market entry modes, *Journal of International Business Studies*, 40: 321–338.

55. T. W. Briggs, 2007, Corporate governance and the new hedge fund activism: An empirical analysis. *Journal of Corporation Law*, 32(4): 681–723, 725–738; K. Rebeiz, 2001, Corporate governance effectiveness in American corporations: A survey, *International Management Journal*, 18(1): 74–80.

56. D. Brewster, 2009, U.S. investors get to nominate boards, *Financial Times*, http://www.ft.com, May 20.

57. CalPERS, 2009, *Wikipedia*, http://en.wikipedia.org/wiki/CalPERS, May 13.

58. M. Anderson, 2009, Eli Lilly heads CalPERS' "underperforming" list, *Sacramento Business Journal*, http://www.bizjournals.com, March 19.

59. S. Thurm, When investor activism doesn't pay, *Wall Street Journal*, September 12, A2; S. M. Jacoby, 2007, Principles and agents: CalPERS and corporate governance in Japan, *Corporate Governance*, 15(1): 5–15; L. Tihanyi, R. A. Johnson, R. E. Hoskisson, & M. A. Hitt, 2003, Institutional ownership differences and international diversification: The effects of boards of directors and technological opportunity, *Academy of Management Journal*, 46: 195–211; Hoskisson, Hitt, Johnson, & Grossman, Conflicting voices; P. David, M. A. Hitt, & J. Gimeno, 2001, The role of institutional investors in influencing R&D, *Academy of Management Journal*, 44: 144–157.

60. V. Krivogorsky, 2006, Ownership, board structure, and performance in continental Europe, *International Journal of Accounting*, 41(2): 176–197; S. Thomsen & T. Pedersen, 2000, Ownership structure and economic performance in the largest European companies, *Strategic Management Journal*, 21: 689–705.

61. Dalton, Hitt, Certo, & Dalton, The fundamental agency problem and its mitigation: Independence, equity and the market for corporate control; C. M. Dalton & D. R. Dalton, 2006, Corporate governance best practices: The proof is in the process, *Journal of Business Strategy*, 27(4), 5–7; R. V. Aguilera, 2005, Corporate governance and director accountability: An institutional comparative perspective, *British Journal of Management*, 16(S1), S39–S53.

62. R. H. Lester, A. Hillman, A. Zardkoohi, & A. A. Cannella, 2008, Former government officials as outside directors: The role of human and social capital, *Academy of Management Journal*, 51: 999–1013; M. L. McDonald, J. D. Westphal, & M. E. Graebner, 2008, What do they know? The effects of outside director acquisition experience on firm acquisition performance, *Strategic Management Journal*, 29: 1155–1177; Hillman & Dalziel, Boards of directors and firm performance.

63. L. Bonazzi & S. M. N. Islam, 2007, Agency theory and corporate governance: A study of the effectiveness of board in their monitoring of the CEO, *Journal of Modeling in Management*, 2(1): 7–23; Rebeiz, Corporate governance effectiveness in American corporations.

64. E. Kang, 2008, Director interlocks and spillover effects of reputational penalties from financial reporting fraud, *Academy of Management Journal*, 51: 537–555; N. Chipalkatti, Q. V. Le, & M. Rishi, 2007, Portfolio flows to emerging capital markets: Do corporate transparency and public governance matter? *Business and Society Review*, 112(2): 227–249.

65. Krivogorsky, Ownership, board structure, and performance in continental Europe; Hoskisson, Hitt, Johnson, & Grossman, Conflicting voices; B. D. Baysinger & R. E. Hoskisson, 1990, The composition of boards of directors and strategic control: Effects on corporate strategy, *Academy of Management Review*, 15: 72–87.

66. Y. Y. Kor & V. F. Misangyi, 2008, Outside directors' industry-specific experience and firms' liability of newness, *Strategic Management Journal*, 29: 1345–1355; E. E. Lawler III & D. Finegold, 2006, Who's in the boardroom and does it matter: The impact of having non-director executives attend board meetings, *Organizational Dynamics*, 35(1): 106–115.

67. E. M. Fich & A. Shivdasani, 2006, Are busy boards effective monitors? *Journal of Finance*, 61: 689–724; J. Westphal & L. Milton, 2000, How experience and network ties affect the influence of demographic minorities on corporate boards, *Administrative Science Quarterly*, 45(2): 366–398.

68. Fich & Shivdasani, Are busy boards effective monitors; S. T. Petra, 2005, Do outside independent directors strengthen corporate boards? *Corporate Governance*, 5(1): 55–65.

69. S. K. Lee & L. R. Carlson, 2007, The changing board of directors: Board independence in S & P 500 firms, *Journal of Organizational Culture, Communication and Conflict*, 11(1): 31–41.

70. R. C. Pozen, 2006, Before you split that CEO/chair, *Harvard Business Review*, 84(4): 26–28; J. W. Lorsch & A. Zelleke, 2005, Should the CEO be the chairman, *MIT Sloan Management Review*, 46(2): 71–74.

71. M. Kroll, B. A. Walters, & P. Wright, 2008, Board vigilance, director experience and corporate outcomes, *Strategic Management Journal*, 29: 363–382.

72. Fich & Shivdasani, Are busy boards effective monitors; J. Roberts, T. McNulty, &, P. Stiles, 2005, Beyond agency conceptions of the work of the non-executive director: Creating accountability in the boardroom, *British Journal of Management*, 16(S1): S5–S26.

73. Fich & Shivdasani, Are busy boards effective monitors; S. Zahra, 1996, Governance, ownership and corporate entrepreneurship among the *Fortune* 500: The moderating impact of industry technological opportunity, *Academy of Management Journal*, 39: 1713–1735.

74. Baysinger, & Hoskisson, Board composition and strategic control: The effect on corporate strategy.

75. Y. Zhang, 2008, Information asymmetry and the dismissal of newly appointed CEOs: An empirical investigation, *Strategic Management Journal*, 29: 859–872.

76. Lawler & Finegold, Who's in the boardroom and does it matter?; E. E. Lawler III & D. L. Finegold, 2005, The changing face of corporate boards, *MIT Sloan Management Review*, 46(2): 67–70; A. Conger, E. E. Lawler, & D. L. Finegold, 2001, *Corporate Boards: New Strategies for Adding Value at the Top*, San Francisco: Jossey-Bass; J. A. Conger, D. Finegold, & E. E. Lawler III, 1998, Appraising boardroom performance, *Harvard Business Review*, 76(1): 136–148.

77. A. L. Boone, L. C. Field, J. M. Karpoff, & C. G. Raheja, 2007, The determinants of corporate board size and composition: An empirical analysis, *Journal of Financial Economics*, 85(1): 66–101; J. Marshall, 2001, As boards shrink, responsibilities grow, *Financial Executive*, 17(4): 36–39.

78. T. Long, 2007, The evolution of FTSE 250 boards of directors: Key factors influencing board performance and effectiveness, *Journal of General Management*, 32(3): 45–60; S. Finkelstein & A. C. Mooney, 2003, Not the usual suspects: How to use board process to make boards better, *Academy of Management Executive*, 17: 101–113.

79. J. L. Koors, 2006 Director pay: A work in progress, *The Corporate Governance Advisor*, 14(5): 25–31; W. Shen, 2005, Improve board effectiveness: The need for incentives, *British Journal of Management*, 16(S1): S81–S89; M. Gerety, C. Hoi, & A. Robin, 2001, Do shareholders benefit from the adoption of incentive pay for directors? *Financial Management*, 30: 45–61; D. C. Hambrick & E. M. Jackson, 2000, Outside directors with a stake: The linchpin in improving governance, *California Management Review*, 42(4): 108–127.

80. Y. Deutsch, T. Keil, & T. Laamanen, 2007, Decision making in acquisitions: the effect of outside directors' compensation on acquisition patterns, *Journal of Management*, 33(1): 30–56.

81. A. J. Hillman, C. Shropshire, & A. A. Cannella, Jr. 2007, Organizational predictors of women on corporate boards, *Academy of Management Journal*, 50: 941–952; I. Filatotchev & S. Toms, 2003, Corporate governance, strategy and survival in a declining industry: A study of UK cotton textile companies, *Journal of Management Studies*, 40: 895–920.

82. 2007, Wall St. roundup; pay increases for CEOs fall below 10% in 2006, *Los Angeles Times*, April 3, C4.

83. S. N. Kaplan, 2008, Are U.S. CEOs overpaid? *Academy of Management Perspectives*, 22(2): 5–20.

84. J. P. Walsh, 2009, Are U.S. CEOs overpaid? A partial response to Kaplan, *Academy of Management Perspectives*, 23(1): 73–75; J. P. Walsh, 2008, CEO compensation and the responsibilities of the business scholar to society, *Academy of Management Perspectives*, 22(3): 26–33.

85. K. Rehbein, 2007, Explaining CEO compensation: How do talent, governance, and markets fit in? *Academy of Management Perspectives*, 21(1): 75–77; J. S. Miller, R. M. Wiseman, & L. R. Gomez-Mejia, 2002, The fit between CEO compensation design and firm risk, *Academy of Management Journal*, 45: 745–756.

86. M. Larraza-Kintana, R. M. Wiseman, L. R. Gomez-Mejia, & T. M. Welbourne, 2007, Disentangling compensation and employment risks using the behavioral agency model, *Strategic Management Journal*, 28: 1001–1019; J. McGuire & E. Matta, 2003, CEO stock options: The silent dimension of ownership, *Academy of Management Journal*, 46: 255–265.

87. X. Zhang, K. M. Bartol, K. G. Smith, M. D. Pfarrer, & D. M. Khanin, 2008, CEOs on the edge: Earnings manipulations and stock-based incentive misalignment, *Academy of Management Journal*, 51: 241–258; J. P. O'Connor, R. L. Priem, J. E. Coombs, & K. M. Gilley, 2006, Do CEO stock options prevent or promote fraudulent financial reporting? *Academy of Management Journal*, 49: 483–500.

88. S. O'Donnell, 2000, Managing foreign subsidiaries: Agents of headquarters, or an interdependent network? *Strategic Management Journal*, 21: 521–548; K. Roth & S. O'Donnell, 1996, Foreign subsidiary compensation: An agency theory perspective, *Academy of Management Journal*, 39: 678–703.

89. A. Ghosh, 2006, Determination of executive compensation in an emerging economy: Evidence from India, *Emerging Markets, Finance & Trade*, 42(3): 66–90; K. Ramaswamy, R. Veliyath, & L. Gomes, 2000, A study of the determinants of CEO compensation in India, *Management International Review*, 40(2): 167–191.

90. C. L. Staples, 2007, Board globalization in the world's largest TNCs 1993–2005, *Corporate Governance*, 15(2): 311–32.

91. P. Kalyta, 2009, Compensation transparency and managerial opportunism: A study of supplemental retirement plans, *Strategic Management Journal*, 30: 405–423.

92. L. K. Meulbroek, 2001, The efficiency of equity-linked compensation: Understanding the full cost of awarding executive stock options, *Financial Management*, 30(2): 5–44.

93. C. E. Devers, R. M. Wiseman, & R. M. Holmes Jr., 2007, The effects of endowment and loss aversion in managerial stock option valuation, *Academy of Management Journal*, 50: 191–208; J. C. Bettis, J. M. Biziak, & M. L. Lemmon, 2005, Exercise behavior, valuation and the incentive effects of employee stock options, *Journal of Financial Economics*, 76: 445–470.

94. M. Klausner, 2007, Reducing directors' legal risk, *Harvard Business Review*, 85(4), 28; T. G. Pollock, H. M. Fischer, & J. B. Wade, 2002, The role of politics in repricing executive options, *Academy of Management Journal*, 45: 1172–1182; M. E. Carter & L. J. Lynch, 2001, An examination of executive stock option repricing, *Journal of Financial Economics*, 59: 207–225; D. Chance, R. Kumar, & R. Todd, 2001, The "repricing" of

executive stock options, *Journal of Financial Economics*, 59: 129–154.

95. P. Berrone & L. R. Gomez-Mejia, 2009, Environmental performance and executive compensation: An integrated agency-institutional perspective, *Academy of Management Journal*, 52: 103–126.

96. R. Sinha, 2006, Regulation: The market for corporate control and corporate governance, *Global Finance Journal*, 16(3): 264–282; R. Coff, 2002, Bidding wars over R&D intensive firms: Knowledge, opportunism and the market for corporate control, *Academy of Management Journal*, 46: 74–85; Hitt, Hoskisson, Johnson, & Moesel, The market for corporate control and firm innovation.

97. D. N. Iyer & K. D. Miller, 2008, Performance feedback, slack, and the timing of acquisitions, *Academy of Management Journal*, 51: 808–822; R. W. Masulis, C. Wang, & F. Xie, 2007, Corporate governance and acquirer returns, *Journal of Finance*, 62(4): 1851–1889; R. Sinha, 2004, The role of hostile takeovers in corporate governance, *Applied Financial Economics*, 14: 1291–1305.

98. K. Ruckman, 2009, Technology sourcing acquisitions: What they mean for innovation potential, *Journal of Strategy and Management*, 2: 56–75.

99. J. P. Walsh & R. Kosnik, 1993, Corporate raiders and their disciplinary role in the market for corporate control, *Academy of Management Journal*, 36: 671–700.

100. J. Haleblian, C. E. Devers, G. McNamara, M. A. Carpenter, & R. B. Davison, 2009, Taking stock of what we know about mergers and acquisitions: A review and research agenda, *Journal of Management*, 35: 469–502; B. Kalpic, 2008, Why bigger is not always better: The strategic logic of value creation through M&As, *Journal of Business Strategy*, 29(6): 4–13.

101. T. W. Briggs, 2007, Corporate governance and a new hedge fund activism: *Empirical Analysis*, 32(4): 681–723.

102. Thurm, When investor activism doesn't pay.

103. N. Goodway, 2009, Credit Suisse pays 25 million pounds in golden hellos, *Evening Standard*, http://www.standard.co.uk, March 24; R. B. Adams & D. Ferreira, 2007, A theory of friendly boards, *Journal of Finance*, 62: 217–250.

104. J Cresswell, 2006, Gilded paychecks: Pay packages allow executives to jump ship with less risk, *New York Times*, http://www.nyt.com, December 29.

105. C. Icahn, 2009, We're not the boss of AIG, *New York Times*, http://www.nytimes.com, March 29; G. Blain & C. Siemaszko, 2008, AIG agrees to cut golden parachute for CEO, trim spending, *New York Daily News*, http://www.nydailynews.com, October 16.

106. H. G. Barkema & M. Schijven, 2008, Toward unlocking the full potential of

acquisition: The role of organizational restructuring, *Academy of Management Journal*, 51: 696–722; M. Cording, P. Chritmann, & D. R. King, 2008, Reducing causal ambiguity in acquisition integration: Intermediate goals as mediators of integration decisions and acquisition performance, *Academy of Management Journal*, 51: 744–767.

107. T. Laamanen & T. Keil, 2008, Performance of serial acquirers: Toward an acquisition program perspective, *Strategic Management Journal*, 29: 663–672; G. M. McNamara, J. Haleblian, & B. J. Dykes, 2008, The performance implications of participating in an acquisition wave: Early mover advantages, bandwagon effects, and the moderating influence of industry characteristics and acquirer tactics, *Academy of Management Journal*, 51: 113–130.

108. J. A. Krug & W. Shill, 2008, The big exit: Executive churn in the wake of M&As, *Journal of Business Strategy*, 29(4): 15–21; J. Harford, 2003, Takeover bids and target directors' incentives: The impact of a bid on directors' wealth and board seats, *Journal of Financial Economics*, 69: 51–83; S. Chatterjee, J. S. Harrison, & D. D. Bergh, 2003, Failed takeover attempts, corporate governance, and refocusing, *Strategic Management Journal*, 24: 87–96.

109. E. Webb, 2006, Relationships between board structure and takeover defenses, *Corporate Governance*, 6(3): 268–280; C. Sundaramurthy, J. M. Mahoney, & J. T. Mahoney, 1997, Board structure, antitakeover provisions, and stockholder wealth, *Strategic Management Journal*, 18: 231–246.

110. W. G. Sanders & M. A. Carpenter, 2003, Strategic satisficing? A behavioral-agency theory perspective on stock repurchase program announcements, *Academy of Management Journal*, 46: 160–178; J. Westphal & E. Zajac, 2001, Decoupling policy from practice: The case of stock repurchase programs, *Administrative Science Quarterly*, 46: 202–228.

111. O. Faleye, 2007, Classified boards, firm value, and managerial entrenchment, *Journal of Financial Economics*, 83: 501–529.

112. 2007, Leaders: Pay slips; management in Europe, *Economist*, June 23, 14: A. Cala, 2005, Carrying golden parachutes; France joins EU trend to reign in executive severance deals, *Wall Street Journal*, June 8, A13.

113. J. A. Pearce II & R. B. Robinson Jr., 2004, Hostile takeover defenses that maximize shareholder wealth, *Business Horizons*, 47(5): 15–24.

114. A. Kacperzyk, 2009, With greater power comes greater responsibility? Takeover protection and corporate attention to stakeholders, *Strategic Management Journal*, 30: 261–285.

115. Walsh & Kosnik, Corporate raiders.

116. A. Chakraborty & R. Arnott, 2001, Takeover defenses and dilution: A welfare analysis, *Journal of Financial and Quantitative Analysis*, 36: 311–334.

117. M. Wolf, 2007, The new capitalism: How unfettered finance is fast reshaping the global economy, *Financial Times*, June 19, 13: C. Millar, T. I. Eldomiaty, C. J. Choi, & B. Hilton, 2005, Corporate governance and institutional transparency in emerging markets, *Journal of Business Ethics*, 59: 163–174; D. Norburn, B. K. Boyd, M. Fox, & M. Muth, 2000, International corporate governance reform, *European Business Journal*, 12(3): 116–133.

118. China YCT International strengthens corporate governance with establishment of audit committee and appointments of three new independent directors, 2009, *Quamnet.com Stock News*, http://www.quamnet.com, April 13; P. Aldrick, 2009, RBS investors threaten to vote down pay report, *Telegraph.co.uk*, http://www.telegraph.co.uk, March 24.

119. P. Witt, 2004, The competition of international corporate governance systems—A German perspective, *Management International Review*, 44: 309–333; L. Nachum, 2003, Does nationality of ownership make any difference and if so, under what circumstances? Professional service MNEs in global competition, *Journal of International Management*, 9: 1–32.

120. Crossland & Hambrick, How national systems differ in their constraints on corporate executives; Aguilera & Jackson, The cross-national diversity of corporate governance: Dimensions and determinants.

121. Carney, Corporate governance and competitive advantage in family-controlled firms; S. Klein, 2000, Family businesses in Germany: Significance and structure, *Family Business Review*, 13: 157–181.

122. A. Tuschke & W. G. Sanders, 2003, Antecedents and consequences of corporate governance reform: The case of Germany, *Strategic Management Journal*, 24: 631–649; J. Edwards & M. Nibler, 2000, Corporate governance in Germany: The role of banks and ownership concentration, *Economic Policy*, 31: 237–268; E. R. Gedajlovic & D. M. Shapiro, 1998, Management and ownership effects: Evidence from five countries, *Strategic Management Journal*, 19: 533–553.

123. P. C. Fiss, 2006, Social influence effects and managerial compensation evidence from Germany, *Strategic Management Journal*, 27: 1013–1031; S. Douma, 1997, The two-tier system of corporate governance, *Long Range Planning*, 30(4): 612–615.

124. P. C. Fiss & E. J. Zajac, 2004, The diffusion of ideas over contested terrain: The (non) adoption of a shareholder value orientation among German firms, *Administrative Science Quarterly*, 49: 501–534.

125. W. G. Sanders & A. C. Tuschke, 2007, The adoption of the institutionally contested organizational practices: The emergence of stock option pay in Germany, *Academy of Management Journal*, 57: 33–56.

126. T. Hoshi, A. K. Kashyap, & S. Fischer, 2001, *Corporate Financing and Governance in Japan*, Boston: MIT Press.

127. J. P. Charkham, 1994. *Keeping Good Companies: A Study of Corporate Governance in Five Countries*. New York: Oxford University Press, 70.

128. M. A. Hitt, H. Lee, & E. Yucel, 2002, The importance of social capital to the management of multinational enterprises: Relational networks among Asian and Western firms, *Asia Pacific Journal of Management*, 19: 353–372.

129. W. P. Wan, D. W. Yiu, R. E. Hoskisson, & H. Kim, 2008, The performance implications of relationship banking during macroeconomic expansion and contraction: A study of Japanese banks' social relationships and overseas expansion, *Journal of International Business Studies*, 39: 406–427.

130. P. M. Lee & H. M. O'Neill, 2003, Ownership structures and R&D investments of U.S. and Japanese firms: Agency and stewardship perspectives, *Academy of Management Journal*, 46: 212–225.

131. I. S. Dinc, 2006, Monitoring the monitors: The corporate governance in Japanese banks and their real estate lending in the 1980s, *Journal of Business*, 79(6): 3057–3081; A. Kawaura, 2004, Deregulation and governance: Plight of Japanese banks in the 1990s, *Applied Economics*, 36: 479–484; B. Bremner, 2001, Cleaning up the banks—finally, *BusinessWeek*, December 17, 86; 2000, Business: Japan's corporate-governance U-turn, *The Economist*, November 18, 73.

132. N. Isagawa, 2007, A theory of unwinding of cross-shareholding under managerial entrenchment, *Journal of Financial Research*, 30: 163–179.

133. C. L. Ahmadjian & G. E. Robbins, 2005, A clash of capitalisms: Foreign shareholders and corporate restructuring in 1990s Japan, *American Sociological Review*, 70: 451–471.

134. J. M. Ramseyer, M. Nakazato, & E. B. Rasmusen, 2009, Public and private firm compensation: Evidence from Japanese tax returns, Harvard Law and Economics Discussion Paper, February 1.

135. S. R. Miller, D. Li, L. Eden, & M. A. Hitt, 2008, Insider trading and the valuation of international strategic alliances in emerging stock markets. *Journal of International Business Studies*, 39: 102–117.

136. H. Zou & M. B. Adams, 2008, Corporate ownership, equity risk and returns in the People's Republic of China, *Journal of International Business Studies*, 39: 1149–1168.

137. Y. Su, D. Xu, & P. H. Phan, 2008, Principal-principal conflict in the governance of the Chinese public corporation, *Management and Organization Review*, 4: 17–38.

138. China YCT International strengthens corporate governance with establishment of audit committee and appointments of three new independent directors, 2009.

139. T. Buck, X. Lui, & R. Skovoroda, 2008, Top executives pay and firm performance in China, *Journal of International Business Studies*, 39: 833–850.

140. P. M. Vaaler & B. N. Schrage, 2009, Residual state ownership, policy stability and financial performance following strategic decisions by privatizing telecoms, *Journal of International Business Studies*, 40: 621–641.

141. Steel Partners issues statement on changes to KT&G's board of directors, 2008, *Reuters*, http://www.reuters.com, March 13; L. Santini, 2007, Rematch: KT&G vs. Steel Partners: Korean cigarette maker again angers an activist fund, *Wall Street Journal*, June 22, C5.

142. Steel Partners LLC, 2009, *BusinessWeek*, http://investing.businessweek.com, April 16.

143. I. Filatotchev, J. Stephan, & B. Jindra, 2008, Ownership structure, strategic controls and export intensity of foreign-invested firms in transition economies, *Journal of International Business Studies*, 39: 1133–1148.

144. T. J. Healey, 2007, Sarbox was the right medicine, *Wall Street Journal*, August 9, A13.

145. J. D. Hughes & J. H. Lee, 2007, The changing landscape of D & O liability, *Risk Management Journal*, January, 18–22.

146. C. Shropshire & A. J. Hillman, 2007, A longitudinal study of significant change in stakeholder management, *Business and Society*, 46(1): 63–87; S. Sharma & I. Henriques, 2005, Stakeholder influences on sustainability practices in the Canadian Forest products industry, *Strategic Management Journal*, 26: 159–180; A. J. Hillman, G. D. Keim, & R. A. Luce, 2001, Board composition and stakeholder performance: Do stakeholder directors make a difference? *Business and Society*, 40: 295–314.

147. D. L. Gold & J. W. Dienhart, 2007, Business ethics in the corporate governance era: Domestic and international trends in transparency, regulation, and corporate governance, *Business and Society Review*, 112(2): 163–170; N. Demise, 2005, Business ethics and corporate governance in Japan, *Business and Society*, 44: 211–217.

148. R. V. Aguilera, D. E. Rupp, C. A. Williams, & J. Ganapathi, 2007, Putting the S back in corporate social responsibility: A multilevel theory of social change in organizations, *Academy of Management Review*, 32(3): 836–863; Caldwell & Karri, Organizational governance and ethical systems: A covenantal approach to building trust; A. Felo, 2001, Ethics programs, board involvement, and potential conflicts of interest in corporate governance, *Journal of Business Ethics*, 32: 205–218.

149. Cummins achieves top ranking for corporate governance, 2009, *AEDNews*, http://www.aednet.org, March 16.

Chapter 11

1. P. Jarzabkowski, 2008, Shaping strategy as a structuration process, *Academy of Management Journal*, 51(4): 621–650; B. Ambos & B. B. Schlegelmilch, 2007, Innovation and control in the multinational firm: A comparison of political and contingency approaches, *Strategic Management Journal*, 28: 473–486; S. Kumar, S. Kant, & T. L. Amburgey, 2007, Public agencies and collaborative management approaches, *Administration & Society*, 39: 569–610.

2. R. Gulati & P. Puranam, 2009, Renewal through reorganization: The value of inconsistencies between formal and informal organization, *Organization Science*, 20(2): 422–440; R. E. Miles & C. C. Snow, 1978, *Organizational Strategy, Structure and Process*, New York: McGraw-Hill.

3. S. T. Hannah & P. B. Lester, 2009, A multilevel approach to building and leading learning organizations, *Leadership Quarterly*, 20(1): 34–48; E. M. Olson, S. F. Slater, & G. T. M. Hult, 2007, The importance of structure and process to strategy implementation, *Business Horizons*, 48(1): 47–54; D. N. Sull & C. Spinosa, 2007, Promise-based management, *Harvard Business Review*, 85(4):79–86.

4. R. Ireland, J. Covin, & D. Kuratko, 2009, Conceptualizing corporate entrepreneurship strategy, *Entrepreneurship Theory and Practice*, 33(1): 19–46; T. Amburgey & T. Dacin, 1994, As the left foot follows the right? The dynamics of strategic and structural change, *Academy of Management Journal*, 37: 1427–1452.

5. L. F. Monteiro, N. Arvidsson, & J. Birkinshaw, 2008, Knowledge flows within multinational corporations: Explaining subsidiary isolation and its performance implications, *Organization Science*, 19(1): 90–107; P. Ghemawat, 2007, Managing differences: The central challenge of global strategy, *Harvard Business Review*, 85(3): 59–68; B. Keats & H. O'Neill, 2001, Organizational structure: Looking through a strategy lens, in M. A. Hitt, R. E. Freeman, & J. S. Harrison (eds.), *Handbook of Strategic Management*, Oxford, UK: Blackwell Publishers, 520–542.

6. R. E. Hoskisson, C. W. L. Hill, & H. Kim, 1993, The multidivisional structure: Organizational fossil or source of value? *Journal of Management*, 19: 269–298.

7. Jarzabkowski, Shaping strategy as a structuration process; E. M. Olson, S. F. Slater, G. Tomas, & G. T. M. Hult, 2005, The performance implications of fit among business strategy, marketing organization structure, and strategic behavior, *Journal of Marketing*, 69(3): 49–65.

8. B. Novak, 2008, Cisco connects the dots: Aligning leaders with a new organizational structure, *Global Business and Organizational Excellence*: 27(5): 22–32.

9. T. Burns & G. M. Stalker, 1961, *The Management of Innovation*, London: Tavistok; P. R. Lawrence & J. W. Lorsch, 1967, *Organization and Environment*, Homewood, IL: Richard D. Irwin; J. Woodward, 1965, *Industrial Organization: Theory and Practice*, London: Oxford University Press.

10. A. M. Rugman & A. Verbeke, 2008, A regional solution to the strategy and structure of multinationals, *European Management Journal*, 26(5): 305–313; H. Kim, R. E. Hoskisson, L. Tihanyi, & J. Hong, 2004, Evolution and restructuring of diversified business groups in emerging markets: The lessons from chaebols in Korea, *Asia Pacific Journal of Management*, 21: 25–48.

11. R. Kathuria, M. P. Joshi, & S. J. Porth, 2007, Organizational alignment and performance: Past, present and future, *Management Decision*, 45: 503–517.

12. B. Sechler, 2008, Corporate news: General Electric's reorganization resurrects GE Capital, *Wall Street Journal*, August 1, B3.

13. A. Tempel & P. Walgenbach, 2007, Global standardization of organizational forms and management practices: What new institutionalism and the business-systems approach can learn from each other, *Journal of Management Studies*, 44: 1–24; Keats & O'Neill, Organizational structure, 533.

14. Tieying Yu, M. S. Insead, & R. H. Lester, 2008, Misery loves company: The spread of negative impacts resulting from an organizational crisis, *Academy of Management Review*, 33(2): 452–472; R. L. Priem, L. G. Love, & M. A. Shaffer, 2002, Executives' perceptions of uncertainty sources: A numerical taxonomy and underlying dimensions, *Journal of Management*, 28: 725–746.

15. A. N. Shub & P. W. Stonebraker, 2009, The human impact on supply chains: Evaluating the importance of "soft" areas on integration and performance, *Supply Chain Management*, 14(1): 31–40; S. K. Ethiraj & D. Levinthal, 2004, Bounded rationality and the search for organizational architecture: An evolutionary perspective on the design of organizations and their evolvability, *Administrative Science Quarterly*, 49: 404–437.

16. R. Khadem, 2008, Alignment and follow-up: Steps to strategy execution, *Journal of Business Strategy*, 29(6): 29–35; J. G. Covin, D. P. Slevin, & M. B. Heeley, 2001, Strategic decision making in an intuitive vs. technocratic mode: Structural and environmental consideration, *Journal of Business Research*, 52: 51–67.

17. J. R. Maxwell, 2008, Work system design to improve the economic performance of the firm, *Business Process Management Journal*, 14(3): 432–446; E. M. Olson, S. F. Slater, & G. T. M. Hult, 2005, The importance of structure and process to strategy implementation, *Business Horizons*, 48(1): 47–54.

18. L. Donaldson, 2001, *The contingency theory of organizations*, Thousand Oaks, CA: Sage; Jenster & Hussey, *Company Analysis*, 169.

19. M. A. Schilling & H. K. Steensma, 2001, The use of modular organizational forms: An industry-level analysis, *Academy of Management Journal*, 44: 1149–1168.

20. P. Legerer, T. Pfeiffer, G. Schneider, & J. Wagner, 2009, Organizational structure and managerial decisions, *International Journal of the Economics of Business*, 16(2): 147–159; C. B. Dobni & G. Luffman, 2003, Determining the scope and impact of market orientation profiles on strategy implementation and performance, *Strategic Management Journal*, 24: 577–585.

21. H. Gebauer & F. Putz, 2009, Organizational structures for the service business in product-oriented companies, *International Journal of Services Technology and Management*, 11(1): 64–81; M. Hammer, 2007, The process audit, *Harvard Business Review*, 85(4): 111–123.

22. R. D. Ireland & J. W. Webb, 2007, Strategic entrepreneurship: Creating competitive advantage through streams of innovation, *Business Horizons*, 50: 49–59; T. J. Andersen, 2004, Integrating decentralized strategy making and strategic planning processes in dynamic environments, *Journal of Management Studies*, 41: 1271–1299.

23. J. Rivkin & N. Siggelkow, 2003, Balancing search and stability: Interdependencies among elements of organizational design, *Management Science*, 49: 290–321; G. A. Bigley & K. H. Roberts, 2001, The incident command system: High-reliability organizing for complex and volatile task environments, *Academy of Management Journal*, 44: 1281–1299.

24. Monteiro, Arvidsson, & Birkinshaw, Knowledge flows within multinational corporations; S. Nadkarni & V. K. Narayanan, 2007, Strategic schemas, strategic flexibility, and firm performance: The moderating role of industry clockspeed, *Strategic Management Journal*, 28: 243–270; K. D. Miller & A. T. Arikan, 2004, Technology search investments: Evolutionary, option reasoning, and option pricing approaches, *Strategic Management Journal*, 25: 473–485.

25. S. Raisch & J. Birkinshaw, 2008, Organizational ambidexterity: Antecedents, outcomes, and moderators, *Journal of Management* 34: 375–409; C. Zook, 2007, Finding your next core business, *Harvard Business Review*, 85(4): 66–75.

26. M. Kimes, 2008, World's most admired companies: Cisco Systems layers it on, *Fortune*, December 8, 24.

27. S. K. Maheshwari & D. Ahlstrom, 2004, Turning around a state owned enterprise: The case of Scooters India Limited, *Asia Pacific Journal of Management*, 21(1–2): 75–101; B. W. Keats & M. A. Hitt, 1988, A causal model of linkages among environmental dimensions, macroorgani-zational characteristics, and performance, *Academy of Management Journal*, 31: 570–598.

28. A. Chandler, 1962, *Strategy and Structure*, Cambridge, MA: MIT Press.

29. D. Martin, 2007, Alfred D. Chandler, Jr., a business historian, dies at 88, *New York Times Online*, http://www.nytimes.com, May 12.

30. R. E. Hoskisson, R. A. Johnson, L. Tihanyi, & R. E. White, 2005, Diversified business groups and corporate refocusing in emerging economies, *Journal of Management*, 31: 941–965; J. D. Day, E. Lawson, & K. Leslie, 2003, When reorganization works, *The McKinsey Quarterly*, (2), 20–29.

31. B. Simon, 2009, Restructuring chief sees benefits in GM's maligned culture, *Financial Times*, July 4, 16.

32. S. K. Ethiraj, 2007, Allocation of inventive effort in complex product systems, *Strategic Management Journal*, 28: 563–584.

33. A. M. Kleinbaum & M. L. Tushman, 2008, Managing corporate social networks, *Harvard Business Review*, 86(7): 26–27; A. Weibel, 2007, Formal control and trustworthiness, *Group & Organization Management*, 32: 500–517; P. K. Mills & G. R. Ungson, 2003, Reassessing the limits of structural empowerment: Organizational constitution and trust as controls, *Academy of Management Review*, 28: 143–153.

34. C. Rowe, J. G. Birnberg, & M. D. Shields, 2008, Effects of organizational process change on responsibility accounting and managers' revelations of private knowledge, *Accounting, Organizations and Society*, 33(2/3): 164–198; M. Santala & P. Parvinen, 2007, From strategic fit to customer fit, *Management Decision*, 45: 582–601; R. Reed, W. J. Donoher, & S. F. Barnes, 2004, Predicting misleading disclosures: The effects of control, pressure, and compensation, *Journal of Managerial Issues*, 16: 322–336.

35. P. Greve, S. Nielsen, & W. Ruigrok, 2009, Transcending borders with international top management teams: A study of European financial multinational corporations, *European Management Journal*, 27(3): 213–224; T. Galpin, R. Hilpirt, & B. Evans, 2007, The connected enterprise: Beyond division of labor, *Journal of Business Strategy*, 28(2): 38–47; C. Sundaramurthy & M. Lewis, 2003, Control and collaboration: Paradoxes of governance, *Academy of Management Review*, 28: 397–415.

36. M. A. Desai, 2008, The finance function in a global corporation, *Harvard Business Review*, 86(7): 108–112; Y. Li, L. Li, Y. Liu, & L. Wang, 2005, Linking management control system with product development and process decisions to cope with environment complexity, *International Journal of Production Research*, 43: 2577–2591.

37. I. Filatotchev, J. Stephan, & B. Jindra, 2008, Ownership structure, strategic controls and export intensity of foreign-invested firms in transition economies, *Journal of International Business Studies*, 39(7): 1133–1148; G. J. M. Braam & E. J. Nijssen, 2004, Performance effects of using the Balanced Scorecard: A note on the Dutch experience, *Long Range Planning*, 37: 335–349; S. D. Julian & E. Scifres, 2002, An interpretive perspective on the role of strategic control in triggering strategic change, *Journal of Business Strategies*, 19: 141–159.

38. J. Kratzer, H. G. Gemünden, C. Lettl, 2008, Balancing creativity and time efficiency in multi-team R&D projects: the alignment of formal and informal networks, *R & D Management*, 38(5): 538–549; D. F. Kuratko, R. D. Ireland, & J. S. Hornsby, 2004, Corporate entrepreneurship behavior among managers: A review of theory, research, and practice, in J. A. Katz & D. A. Shepherd (eds.), *Advances in Entrepreneurship: Firm Emergence and Growth: Corporate Entrepreneurship*, Oxford, UK: Elsevier Publishing, 7–45.

39. Y. Doz & M. Kosonen, 2008, The dynamics of strategic agility: Nokia's rollercoaster experience, *California Management Review*, 50(3): 95–118.

40. Y. Liu & T. Ravichandran, 2008, A comprehensive investigation on the relationship between information technology investments and firm diversification, *Information Technology and Management*, 9(3): 169–180; K. L. Turner & M. V. Makhija, 2006, The role of organizational controls in managing knowledge, *Academy of Management Review*, 31: 197–217; M. A. Hitt, R. E. Hoskisson, R. A. Johnson, & D. D. Moesel, 1996, The market for corporate control and firm innovation, *Academy of Management Journal*, 39: 1084–1119.

41. B. Fryer & T. A. Stewart, 2008, Cisco sees the future, *Harvard Business Review*, 86(11): 72–79.

42. Desai, The finance function in a global corporation; M. A. Hitt, L. Tihanyi, T. Miller, & B. Connelly, 2006, International diversification: Antecedents, outcomes, and moderators, *Journal of Management*, 32: 831–867; R. E. Hoskisson & M. A. Hitt, 1988, Strategic control and relative R&D investment in multiproduct firms, *Strategic Management Journal*, 9: 605–621.

43. S. Lee, K. Park, H. H. Shin, 2009, Disappearing internal capital markets: Evidence from diversified business groups in Korea, *Journal of Banking & Finance*, 33(2): 326–334; D. Collis, D. Young, & M. Goold, 2007, The size, structure, and performance of corporate headquarters, *Strategic Management Journal*, 28: 383–405.

44. X. S. Y. Spencer, T. A. Joiner, & S. Salmon, 2009, Differentiation strategy, performance measurement systems and organizational performance: Evidence from Australia, *International Journal of Business*, 14(1): 83–103; K. Chaharbaghi, 2007, The problematic of strategy: A way of seeing is also a way of not seeing, *Management Decision*, 45: 327–339; J. B. Barney, 2002, *Gaining and Sustaining Competitive Advantage*, 2nd ed., Upper Saddle River, NJ: Prentice Hall.

45. S. Lohr, 2007, Can Michael Dell refocus his namesake? *New York Times Online*, http://www.nytimes.com, September 9.

46. L. Lee, 2008, HP's Hurd is about to be tested: After a sterling three-year run, the company's CEO faces a weaker PC market and a stronger Dell, *BusinessWeek*, February 14, 59–60.

47. Gebauer & Putz, 2009, Organizational structures for the service business in product-oriented companies; X. Yin & E. J. Zajac, 2004, The strategy/governance structure fit relationship: Theory and evidence in franchising arrangements, *Strategic Management Journal*, 25: 365–383.

48. Keats & O'Neill, Organizational structure, 531.

49. K. Wakabayashi, 2008, Relationship between business definition and corporate growth: The effect of functional alignment, *Pacific Economic Review*, 13(5): 663–679; K. M. Green, J. G. Covin, D. P. Slevin, 2008, Exploring the relationship between strategic reactiveness and entrepreneurial orientation: The role of structure-style fit. *Journal of Business Venturing*, 23(3): 356; Olson, Slater, & Hult, The importance of structure and process to strategy implementation; D. Miller & J. O. Whitney, 1999, Beyond strategy: Configuration as a pillar of competitive advantage, *Business Horizons*, 42(3): 5–17.

50. Chandler, *Strategy and Structure*.

51. Keats & O'Neill, Organizational structure, 524.

52. E. Rawley, 2009, Diversification, coordination costs and organizational rigidity: Evidence from microdata, *Strategic Management Journal*; forthcoming; M. E. Sosa, S. D. Eppinger, & C. M. Rowles, 2004, The misalignment of product architecture and organizational structure in complex product development, *Management Science*, 50: 1674–1689.

53. J. W. Yoo, R. Reed, S. J. Shin, & D. J. Lemak, 2009, Strategic choice and performance in late movers: Influence of the top management team's external ties, *Journal of Management Studies*, 46(2): 308–335; S. Karim & W. Mitchell, 2004, Innovating through acquisition and internal development: A quarter-century of boundary evolution at Johnson & Johnson, *Long Range Planning*, 37: 525–547.

54. I. Daizadeh, 2006, Using intellectual property to map the organizational

evolution of firms: Tracing a biotechnology company from startup to bureaucracy to a multidivisional firm, *Journal of Commercial Biotechnology*, 13: 28–36.

55. C. Levicki, 1999, *The Interactive Strategy Workout*, 2nd ed., London: Prentice Hall.

56. E. E. Entin, F. J. Diedrich, & B. Rubineau, 2003, Adaptive communication patterns in different organizational structures, *Human Factors and Ergonomics Society Annual Meeting Proceedings*, 405–409; H. M. O'Neill, R. W. Pouder, & A. K. Buchholtz, 1998, Patterns in the diffusion of strategies across organizations: Insights from the innovation diffusion literature, *Academy of Management Review*, 23: 98–114.

57. Spencer, Joiner, & Salmon, Differentiation strategy, performance measurement systems and organizational performance; 2007, Organizational structure, *Wikipedia*, http://en.wikipedia.org; Gallbraith, *Designing Organizations*, 25.

58. Keats & O'Neill, Organizational structure, 539.

59. C. M. Christensen, S. P. Kaufman, & W. C. Shih, 2008, Innovation killers, *Harvard Business Review*: Special HBS Centennial Issue, 86(1): 98–105; J. Welch & S. Welch, 2006, Growing up but staying young, *BusinessWeek*, December 11, 112.

60. O. E. Williamson, 1975, *Markets and Hierarchies: Analysis and Anti-Trust Implications*, New York: The Free Press.

61. S. H. Mialon, 2008, Efficient horizontal mergers: The effects of internal capital reallocation and organizational form, *International Journal of Industrial Organization*, 26(4): 861–877; Chandler, *Strategy and Structure*.

62. R. Inderst, H. M. Muller, & K. Warneryd, 2007, Distributional conflict in organizations, *European Economic Review*, 51: 385–402; J. Greco, 1999, Alfred P. Sloan Jr. (1875–1966): The original organizational man, *Journal of Business Strategy*, 20(5): 30–31.

63. Hoskisson, Hill, & Kim, The multidivisional structure, 269–298.

64. Mialon, Efficient horizontal mergers: The effects of internal capital reallocation and organizational form; H. Zhou, 2005, Market structure and organizational form, *Southern Economic Journal*, 71: 705–719; W. G. Rowe & P. M. Wright, 1997, Related and unrelated diversification and their effect on human resource management controls, *Strategic Management Journal*, 18: 329–338.

65. C. E. Helfat & K. M. Eisenhardt, 2004, Inter-temporal economies of scope, organizational modularity, and the dynamics of diversification, *Strategic Management Journal*, 25: 1217–1232; A. D. Chandler, 1994, The functions of the HQ unit in the multibusiness firm, in R. P. Rumelt, D. E. Schendel, & D. J. Teece (eds.), *Fundamental Issues in Strategy*, Cambridge, MA: Harvard Business School Press, 327.

66. O. E. Williamson, 1994, Strategizing, economizing, and economic organization, in R. P. Rumelt, D. E. Schendel, & D. J. Teece (eds.), *Fundamental Issues in Strategy*, Cambridge, MA: Harvard Business School Press, 361–401.

67. Hoskisson, Hill, & Kim, The multidivisional structure: Organizational fossil or source of value?; R. M. Burton & B. Obel, 1980, A computer simulation test of the M-form hypothesis, *Administrative Science Quarterly*, 25: 457–476.

68. O. E. Williamson, 1985, *The Economic Institutions of Capitalism: Firms, Markets, and Relational Contracting*, New York: Macmillan.

69. Keats & O'Neill, Organizational structure, 532.

70. M. F. Wolff, 1999, In the organization of the future, competitive advantage will be inspired, *Research Technology Management*, 42(4): 2–4.

71. R. H. Hall, 1996, *Organizations: Structures, Processes, and Outcomes*, 6th ed., Englewood Cliffs, NJ: Prentice Hall, 13; S. Baiman, D. F. Larcker, & M. V. Rajan, 1995, Organizational design for business units, *Journal of Accounting Research*, 33: 205–229.

72. L. G. Love, R. L. Priem, & G. T. Lumpkin, 2002, Explicitly articulated strategy and firm performance under alternative levels of centralization, *Journal of Management*, 28: 611–627.

73. Hall, *Organizations*, 64–75.

74. Barney, *Gaining and Sustaining Competitive Advantage*, 257.

75. H. Karandikar & S. Nidamarthi, 2007, Implementing a platform strategy for a systems business via standardization, *Journal of Manufacturing Technology Management*, 18: 267–280.

76. Olson, Slater, Tomas, & Hult, The performance implications of fit.

77. 2007, Wal-Mart Stores, Inc, *New York Times Online*, http://www.nytimes.com, July 21.

78. 2007, Wal-Mart rolling out new company slogan, *New York Times Online*, http://www.nytimes.com, July 12.

79. Olson, Slater, Tomas, & Hult, The performance implications of fit.

80. T. Heath, 2008, In pursuit of innovation at Under Armour: Founder Kevin Plank says Super Bowl commercial has generated "buzz," *Washington Post*, February 25, D03.

81. Chandler, *Strategy and Structure*.

82. C. C. Markides & P. J. Williamson, 1996, Corporate diversification and organizational structure: A resource-based view, *Academy of Management Journal*, 39: 340–367; C. W. L. Hill, M. A. Hitt, & R. E. Hoskisson, 1992, Cooperative versus competitive structures in related and unrelated diversified firms, *Organization Science*, 3: 501–521.

83. S. H. Appelbaum, D. Nadeau, & M. Cyr, 2008, Performance evaluation in a matrix organization: A case study (part two), *Industrial and Commercial Training*, 40(6): 295–299.

84. S. H. Appelbaum, D. Nadeau, & M. Cyr, 2009, Performance evaluation in a matrix organization: A case study (part three), *Industrial and Commercial Training*, 41(1): 9–14; M. Goold & A. Campbell, 2003, Structured networks: Towards the well designed matrix, *Long Range Planning*, 36(5): 427–439.

85. P. Eavis, 2008, The pain at Sears grows, *The Wall Street Journal Online*, www.wsj.com, May 30.

86. N. M. Schmid & I. Walter, 2009, Do financial conglomerates create or destroy economic value? *Journal of Financial Intermediation*, 18(2): 193–216; P. A. Argenti, R. A. Howell, & K. A. Beck, 2005, The strategic communication imperative, *MIT Sloan Management Review*, 46(3): 84–89.

87. M. F. Wiersema & H. P. Bowen, 2008, Corporate diversification: The impact of foreign competition, industry globalization, and product diversification, *Strategic Management Journal*, 29: 115–132; R. E. Hoskisson & M. A. Hitt, 1990, Antecedents and performance outcomes of diversification: A review and critique of theoretical perspectives, *Journal of Management*, 16: 461–509.

88. Hill, Hitt, & Hoskisson, Cooperative versus competitive structures, 512.

89. Lee, Park, & Shin, Disappearing internal capital markets: Evidence from diversified business groups in Korea; J. Birkinshaw, 2001, Strategies for managing internal competition, *California Management Review*, 44(1): 21–38.

90. 2009, Vision and strategy, http://www.textron.com, July 16.

91. M. Maremont, 2004, Leadership; more can be more: Is the conglomerate a dinosaur from a bygone era? The answer is no—with a caveat, *Wall Street Journal*, October 24, R4; T. R. Eisenmann & J. L. Bower, 2000, The entrepreneurial M-form: Strategic integration in global media firms, *Organization Science*, 11: 348–355.

92. T. Yu & A. A. Cannella, Jr., 2007, Rivalry between multinational enterprises: An event history approach, *Academy of Management Journal*, 50: 665–686; S. E. Christophe & H. Lee, 2005, What matters about internationalization: A market-based assessment, *Journal of Business Research*, 58: 636–643; Y. Luo, 2002, Product diversification in international joint ventures: Performance implications in an emerging market, *Strategic Management Journal*, 23: 1–20.

93. M. Mandel, 2007, Globalization vs. immigration reform, *BusinessWeek*, June 4, 40.

94. T. M. Begley & D. P. Boyd, 2003, The need for a corporate global mind-set, *MIT Sloan Management Review*, 44(2): 25–32; Tallman, Global strategic management, 467.

95. T. Kostova & K. Roth, 2003, Social capital in multinational corporations and a micro-macro model of its formation, *Academy of Management Review*, 28: 297–317.

96. J. Jermias & L. Gani, 2005, Ownership structure, contingent-fit, and business-

unit performance: A research model and evidence, *The International Journal of Accounting*, 40: 65–85; J. Wolf & W. G. Egelhoff, 2002, A reexamination and extension of international strategy-structure theory, *Strategic Management Journal*, 23: 181–189.

97. J. Ewing, 2009, A magic moment for Ford of Europe, *BusinessWeek*, July 6, 48–49.

98. C. A. Bartlett & S. Ghoshal, 1989, *Managing Across Borders: The Transnational Solution*, Boston: Harvard Business School Press.

99. S. Feinberg, & A. Gupta, 2009, MNC subsidiaries and country risk: Internalization as a safeguard against weak external institutions, *Academy of Management Journal* 52(2): 381–399; S. T. Cavusgil, S. Yeniyurt, & J. D. Townsend, 2004, The framework of a global company: A conceptualization and preliminary validation, *Industrial Marketing Management*, 33: 711–716.

100. N. Byrnes, 2007, Avon: More than cosmetic changes, *BusinessWeek*, March 12, 62–63.

101. K. Nolan, 2009, Corporate news: Avon unveils new cost cuts, *Wall Street Journal*, February 20, B2.

102. Malnight, Emerging structural patterns, 1197.

103. Rugman & Verbeke, A regional solution to the strategy and structure of multinationals.

104. B. Connelly, M. A. Hitt, A. DeNisi, & R. D. Ireland, 2007, Expatriates and corporate-level international strategy: Governing with the knowledge contract, *Management Decision*, 45: 564–581.

105. M. E. Lloyd, 2009, IKEA sees opportunity in slump, Wall Street Journal Online, http://online.wsj.com, February 17; E. Baraldi, 2008, Strategy in industrial Networks: Experiences from IKEA, *California Management Review*, 50(4): 99–126.

106. D. Lavie, 2009, Capturing value from alliance portfolios, *Organizational Dynamics*, 38(1): 26–36; S. G. Lazzarini, 2007, The impact of membership in competing alliance constellations: Evidence on the operational performance of global airlines, *Strategic Management Journal*, 28: 345–367; Y. L. Doz & G. Hamel, 1998, *Alliance Advantage: The Art of Creating Value through Partnering*, Boston: Harvard Business School Press, 222.

107. J. Li, C. Zhou, & E. J. Zajac, 2009, Control, collaboration, and productivity in international joint ventures: Theory and evidence, *Strategic Management Journal*, 30: 865–884; Y. Luo, 2007, Are joint venture partners more opportunistic in a more volatile environment? *Strategic Management Journal*, 28: 39–60; K. Moller, A. Rajala, & S. Svahn, 2005, Strategic business nets—their type and management, *Journal of Business Research*, 58: 1274–1284.

108. D. Li, L. E. Eden, M. A. Hitt, & R. D. Ireland, 2008, Friends, acquaintances, or strangers? Partner selection in R&D alliances, *Academy of Management Journal*, 51(2): 315–334.

109. Lavie, Capturing value from alliance portfolios; B. Comes-Casseres, 2003, Competitive advantage in alliance constellations, *Strategic Organization*, 1: 327–335; T. K. Das & B. S. Teng, 2002, Alliance constellations: A social exchange perspective, *Academy of Management Review*, 27: 445–456.

110. T. Vapola, P. Tossavainen, & M. Gabrielsson, 2008, The battleship strategy: The complementing role of born globals in MNC's new opportunity creation, *Journal of International Entrepreneurship*: 6(1): 1–21; S. Tallman, M. Jenkins, N. Henry, & S. Pinch, 2004, Knowledge, clusters, and competitive advantage, *Academy of Management Review*, 29: 258–271.

111. V. Moatti, 2009, Learning to expand or expanding to learn? The role of imitation and experience in the choice among several expansion modes, *European Management Journal*, 27(1): 36–46; A. Capaldo, 2007, Network structure and innovation: The leveraging of a dual network as a distinctive relational capability, *Strategic Management Journal*, 28: 585–608; A. Zaheer & G. G. Bell, 2005, Benefiting from network position: Firm capabilities, structural holes, and performance, *Strategic Management Journal*, 26: 809–825.

112. J. Wiklund & D. A. Shepherd, 2009, The effectiveness of alliances and acquisitions: The role of resource combination activities, *Theory and Practice*, 31(1): 193–212; R. D. Ireland & J. W. Webb, 2007, A multi-theoretic perspective on trust and power in strategic supply chains, *Journal of Operations Management*, 25: 482–497; V. G. Narayanan & A. Raman, 2004, Aligning incentives in supply chains, *Harvard Business Review*, 82(11): 94–102.

113. S. Harrison, 1998, *Japanese Technology and Innovation Management*, Northampton, MA: Edward Elgar.

114. M. H. Hansen, R. E. Hoskisson, & J. B. Barney, 2008, Competitive advantage in alliance governance: Resolving the opportunism minimization-gain maximization paradox, *Managerial and Decision Economics*, 29: 191–208; T. Keil, 2004, Building external corporate venturing capability, *Journal of Management Studies*, 41: 799–825.

115. Vapola, Tossavainen, & Gabrielsson, The battleship strategy: The complementing role of born globals in MNC's new opportunity creation; P. Dussauge, B. Garrette, & W. Mitchell, 2004, Learning from competing partners: Outcomes and duration of scale and link alliances in Europe, North America and Asia, *Strategic Management Journal*, 21: 99–126; G. Lorenzoni & C. Baden-Fuller, 1995, Creating a strategic center to manage a web of partners, *California Management Review*, 37(3): 146–163.

116. S. R. Holmberg & J. L. Cummings, 2009, Building successful strategic alliances: Strategic process and analytical tools for selecting partner industries and firms, *Long Range Planning*, 42(2): 164–193; B. J. Bergiel, E. B. Bergiel, & P. W. Balsmeier, 2008, Nature of virtual teams: A summary of their advantages and disadvantages, *Management Research News*, 31(2): 99–110.

117. A. C. Inkpen, 2008, Knowledge transfer and international joint ventures: The case of NUMMI and General Motors, *Strategic Management Journal*, 29(4): 447–453; T. A. Stewart & A. P. Raman, 2007, Lessons from Toyota's long drive, *Harvard Business Review*, 85(7/8): 74–83; J. H. Dyer & K. Nobeoka, 2000, Creating and managing a high-performance knowledge-sharing network: The Toyota case, *Strategic Management Journal*, 21: 345–367.

118. L. F. Mesquita, J. Anand, & J. H. Brush, 2008, Comparing the resource-based and relational views: Knowledge transfer and spillover in vertical alliances, *Strategic Management Journal*, 29: 913–941; M. Kotabe, X. Martin, & H. Domoto, 2003, Gaining from vertical partnerships: Knowledge transfer, relationship duration and supplier performance improvement in the U.S. and Japanese automotive industries, *Strategic Management Journal*, 24: 293–316.

119. T. Nishiguchi, 1994, *Strategic Industrial Sourcing: The Japanese Advantage*, New York: Oxford University Press.

120. S. G. Lazzarini, D. P. Claro, & L. F. Mesquita, 2008, Buyer-supplier and supplier-supplier alliances: Do they reinforce or undermine one another? *Journal of Management Studies*, 45(3): 561–584; P. Dussauge, B. Garrette, & W. Mitchell, 2004, Asymmetric performance: The market share impact of scale and link alliances in the global auto industry, *Strategic Management Journal*, 25: 701–711.

121. J. Shook, 2009, Toyota's secret: The A3 report, *MIT Sloan Management Review*, 50(4): 30–33; C. Dawson & K. N. Anhalt, 2005, A "China price" for Toyota, *BusinessWeek*, February 21, 50–51; W. M. Fruin, 1992, *The Japanese Enterprise System*, New York: Oxford University Press.

122. B. Garrette, X. Castañer, & P. Dussauge, 2009, Horizontal alliances as an alternative to autonomous production: Product expansion mode choice in the worldwide aircraft industry 1945–2000, *Strategic Management Journal*, 30(8): 885–894.

123. A. M. Hayashi, 2008, How to replicate success. *MIT Sloan Management Review*, 49(3): 6–7; M. Tuunanen & F. Hoy, 2007, Franchising: Multifaceted form of entrepreneurship, *International Journal of Entrepreneurship and Small Business*, 4: 52–67.

124. J. Li, C. Dhanaraj, & R. L. Shockley, 2008, Joint venture evolution: Extending the real options approach, *Managerial and Decision Economics*, 29(4): 317–336; B. B. Nielsen, 2005, The role of knowledge embeddedness in the creation of synergies in strategic alliances, *Journal of Business Research*, 58: 1194–1204.

125. E. Bellman, 2009, Corporate news: McDonald's plans expansion in India, *Wall Street Journal*, June 30, B4.

126. T. W. Tong, J. J. Reuer, & M. W. Peng, 2008. International joint ventures and the value of growth options, *Academy of Management Journal*, 51: 1014–1029; P. H. Andersen & P. R. Christensen, 2005, Bridges over troubled water: Suppliers as connective nodes in global supply networks, *Journal of Business Research*, 58: 1261–1273; C. Jones, W. S. Hesterly, & S. P. Borgatti, 1997, A general theory of network governance: Exchange conditions and social mechanisms, *Academy of Management Review*, 22: 911–945.

127. M. W. Hansen, T. Pedersen, & B. Petersen, 2009, MNC strategies and linkage effects in developing countries, *Journal of World Business*, 44(2): 121–139; A. Goerzen, 2005, Managing alliance networks: Emerging practices of multinational corporations, *Academy of Management Executive*, 19(2): 94–107.

128. L. H. Lin, 2009, Mergers and acquisitions, alliances and technology development: An empirical study of the global auto industry, *International Journal of Technology Management*, 48(3): 295–307; R. E. Miles, C. C. Snow, J. A. Mathews, G. Miles, & J. J. Coleman Jr., 1997, Organizing in the knowledge age: Anticipating the cellular form, *Academy of Management Executive*, 11(4): 7–20.

129. 2009, EDS Agility Alliance: Collaboration for better business outcomes, http://www.eds.com, July 16.

130. 2009, EDS Agility Alliance reaches milestone, *Wireless News*, June 3.

Chapter 12

1. A. Mackey, 2008, The effect of CEOs on firm performance, *Strategic Management Journal*, 29: 1357–1367.

2. E. F. Goldman, 2007, Strategic thinking at the top, *MIT Sloan Management Review*, 48(4): 75–81.

3. L. Bassi & D. McMurrer, 2007, Maximizing your return on people, *Harvard Business Review*, 85(3): 115–123; R. D. Ireland & M. A. Hitt, 2005, Achieving and maintaining strategic competitiveness in the 21st century: The role of strategic leadership, *Academy of Management Executive*, 19: 63–77.

4. J. P. Kotter, 2007, Leading change: Why transformation efforts fail, *Harvard Business Review*, 85(1): 96–103.

5. M. A. Hitt, C. Miller, & A. Collella, 2009, *Organizational Behavior: A Strategic Approach*, 2nd ed., New York: John Wiley & Sons; M. A. Hitt & R. D. Ireland, 2002, The essence of strategic leadership: Managing human and social capital, *Journal of Leadership and Organizational Studies*, 9: 3–14.

6. D. A. Ready & J. A. Conger, 2007, Make your company a talent factory, *Harvard Business Review*, 85(6): 69–77.

7. D. Roberts & C.-C. Tschang, 2007, China's rising leaders, *BusinessWeek*, October 1, 33–35.

8. P. A. Gloor & S. M. Cooper, 2007, The new principles of a swarm business, *MIT Sloan Management Review*, 48(3): 81–85; A. S. DeNisi, M. A. Hitt, & S. E. Jackson, 2003, The knowledge-based approach to sustainable competitive advantage, in S. E. Jackson, M. A. Hitt, & A. S. DeNisi (eds.), *Managing Knowledge for Sustained Competitive Advantage*, San Francisco: Jossey-Bass, 3–33.

9. L. Bossidy, 2007, What your leader expects of you: And what you should expect in return, *Harvard Business Review*, 85(4): 58–65; J. E. Post, L. E. Preston, & S. Sachs, 2002, Managing the extended enterprise: The new stakeholder view, *California Management Review*, 45(1): 6–28.

10. A. McKee & D. Massimilian, 2007, Resonant leadership: A new kind of leadership for the digital age, *Journal of Business Strategy*, 27(5): 45–49.

11. E. Baraldi, R. Brennan, D. Harrison, A. Tunisini, & J. Zolkiewski, 2007, Strategic thinking and the IMP approach: A comparative analysis, *Industrial Marketing Management*, 36: 879–894; C. L. Shook, R. L. Priem, & J. E. McGee, 2003, Venture creation and the enterprising individual: A review and synthesis, *Journal of Management*, 29: 379–399.

12. M. L. McDonald, P. Khanna, & J. D. Westphal, 2008, Getting them to think outside the circle: Corporate governace, CEOs' external advice networks and firm performance, *Academy of Management Journal*, 51: 453–475.

13. R. A. Burgleman & A. S. Grove, 2007, Let chaos reign, then rein in chaos— repeatedly: Managing strategic dynamics for corporate longevity, *Strategic Management Journal*, 28: 965–979.

14. T. R. Holcomb, R. M. Holmes, & B. L. Connelly, 2009, Making the most of what you have: Managerial ability as a source of resource value creation, *Strategic Management Journal*, 30: 457–485.

15. A. E. Colbert, A. L. Kristof-Brown, B. H. Bradley, & M. R. Barrick, 2008, CEO transformational leadership: The role of goal importance congruence in top management teams, *Academy of Management Journal*, 51: 81–96; S. Borener, S. A. Eisenbeiss, & D. Griesser, 2007, Follower behavior and organizational performance: The impact of transformational leaders, *Journal of Leadership & Organizational Studies*, 13(3): 15–26.

16. T. G. Buchholz, 2007, The Kroc legacy at McDonald's, *The Conference Review Board*, July/August, 14–15.

17. H. S. Givray, 2007, When CEOs aren't leaders, *BusinessWeek*, September 3, 102.

18. D. Goleman, 2004, What makes a leader? *Harvard Business Review*, 82(1): 82–91.

19. Y. Ling, Z. Simsek, M. H. Lubatkin, & J. F. Veiga, Transformational leadership's role in promoting corporate entrepreneurship: Examining the CEO-TMT interface, *Academy of Management Journal*, 51: 557–576.

20. J. L. Morrow, Jr., D. G. Sirmon, M. A. Hitt, & T. R. Holcomb, 2007, Creating value in the face of declining performance: Firm strategies and organizational recovery, *Strategic Management Journal*, 28: 271–283; R. Castanias & C. Helfat, 2001, The managerial rents model: Theory and empirical analysis, *Journal of Management*, 27: 661–678.

21. H. G. Barkema & O. Shvyrkov, 2007, Does top management team diversity promote or hamper foreign expansion? *Strategic Management Journal*, 28: 663–680; M. Beer & R. Eisenstat, 2000, The silent killers of strategy implementation and learning, *Sloan Management Review*, 41(4): 29–40.

22. V. Santos & T. Garcia, 2007, The complexity of the organizational renewal decision: The management role, *Leadership & Organization Development Journal*, 28: 336–355; M. Wright, R. E. Hoskisson, L. W. Busenitz, & J. Dial, 2000, Entrepreneurial growth through privatization: The upside of management buyouts, *Academy of Management Review*, 25: 591–601.

23. D. G. Sirmon, J.-L. Arregle, M. A. Hitt, & J. W. Webb, 2008, The role of family influence in firms' strategic responses to threat of imitation, *Entrepreneurship Theory and Practice*, 32: 979–998; Y. L. Doz & M. Kosonen, 2007, The new deal at the top, *Harvard Business Review*, 85(6): 98–104.

24. A. S. Tsui, Z.-X. Zhang, H. Wang, K. R. Xin, & J. B. Wu, 2006, Unpacking the relationship between CEO leadership behavior and organizational culture, *The Leadership Quarterly*, 17: 113–137; J. A. Petrick & J. F. Quinn, 2001, The challenge of leadership accountability for integrity capacity as a strategic asset, *Journal of Business Ethics*, 34: 331–343.

25. D. G. Sirmon, S. Gove, & M. A. Hitt, 2008, Resource management in dyadic competitive rivalry: The effects of resource bundling and deployment, *Academy of Management Journal*, 51: 918–935; R. Martin, 2007, How successful leaders think, *Harvard Business Review*, 85(6): 60–67.

26. M. L. A. Hayward, V. P. Rindova, & T. G. Pollock, 2004, Believing one's own

press: The causes and consequences of CEO celebrity, *Strategic Management Journal*, 25: 637–653.

27. K. M. Hmieleski & R. A. Baron, 2008, When does entrepreneurial self-efficacy enhance versus reduce firm performance? *Strategic Entrepreneurship Journal*, 2: 57–72; N. J. Hiller & D. C. Hambrick, 2005, Conceptualizing executive hubris: The role of (hyper-) core self-evaluations in strategic decision making, *Strategic Management Journal*, 26: 297–319.

28. A. M. L. Raes, U. Glunk, M. G. Heijitjes, & R. A. Roe, 2007, Top management team and middle managers, *Small Group Research*, 38: 360–386; I. Goll, R. Sambharya, & L. Tucci, 2001, Top management team composition, corporate ideology, and firm performance, *Management International Review*, 41(2): 109–129.

29. J. Bunderson, 2003, Team member functional background and involvement in management teams: Direct effects and the moderating role of power and centralization, *Academy of Management Journal*, 46: 458–474; L. Markoczy, 2001, Consensus formation during strategic change, *Strategic Management Journal*, 22: 1013–1031.

30. C. Pegels, Y. Song, & B. Yang, 2000, Management heterogeneity, competitive interaction groups, and firm performance, *Strategic Management Journal*, 21: 911–923.

31. R. Rico, E. Molleman, M. Sanchez-Manzanares, & G. S. Van der Vegt, 2007, The effects of diversity faultlines and team task autonomy on decision quality and social integration, *Journal of Management*, 33: 111–132.

32. A. Srivastava, K. M. Bartol, & E. A. Locke, 2006, Empowering leadership in management teams: Effects on knowledge sharing, efficacy, and performance, *Academy of Management Journal*, 49: 1239–1251; D. Knight, C. L. Pearce, K. G. Smith, J. D. Olian, H. P. Sims, K. A. Smith, & P. Flood, 1999, Top management team diversity, group process, and strategic consensus, *Strategic Management Journal*, 20: 446–465.

33. B. J. Olson, S. Parayitam, & Y. Bao, 2007, Strategic decision making: The effects of cognitive diversity, conflict, and trust on decision outcomes, *Journal of Management*, 33: 196–222; T. Simons, L. H. Pelled, & K. A. Smith, 1999, Making use of difference, diversity, debate, and decision comprehensiveness in top management teams, *Academy of Management Journal*, 42: 662–673.

34. S. Finkelstein, D. C. Hambrick, & A. A. Cannella, Jr., 2008, *Strategic Leadership: Top Executives and Their Effects on Organizations*, New York: Oxford University Press.

35. J. J. Marcel, 2009, Why top management team characteristics matter when employing a chief operating officer: A strategic contingency perspective, *Strategic Management Journal*, 30: 647–658; S. Barsade, A. Ward, J. Turner, & J. Sonnenfeld, 2000, To your heart's content: A model of affective diversity in top management teams, *Administrative Science Quarterly*, 45: 802–836.

36. B. J. Avolio & S. S. Kahai, 2002, Adding the "e" to e-leadership: How it may impact your leadership, *Organizational Dynamics*, 31: 325–338.

37. Z. Simsek, J. F. Veiga, M. L. Lubatkin, & R. H. Dino, 2005, Modeling the multilevel determinants of top management team behavioral integration, *Academy of Management Journal*, 48: 69–84.

38. A. A. Cannella, J. H. Park, & H. U. Lee, 2008, Top management team functional background diversity and firm performance: Examining the roles of team member collocation and environmental uncertainty, *Academy of Management Journal*, 51: 768–784.

39. M. Jensen & E. J. Zajac, 2004, Corporate elites and corporate strategy: How demographic preferences and structural position shape the scope of the firm, *Strategic Management Journal*, 25: 507–524.

40. R. Yokota & H. Mitsuhashi, Attributive change in top management teams as a driver of strategic change, *Asia Pacific Journal of Management*, 25: 297–315; W. B. Werther, 2003, Strategic change and leader-follower alignment, *Organizational Dynamics*, 32: 32–45.

41. H. Li & J. Li, 2009, Top management team conflict and entrepreneurial strategy making in China, *Asia Pacific Journal of Management*, 26: 263–283; S. C. Parker, 2009, Can cognitive biases explain venture team homophily? *Strategic Entrepreneurship Journal*, 3: 67–83.

42. Y. Zhang & N. Rajagopalan, 2003, Explaining the new CEO origin: Firm versus industry antecedents, *Academy of Management Journal*, 46: 327–338.

43. T. Dvir, D. Eden, B. J. Avolio, & B. Shamir, 2002, Impact of transformational leadership on follower development and performance: A field experiment, *Academy of Management Journal*, 45: 735–744.

44. J. P. Muczyk & D. T. Holt, 2008, Toward a cultural contingency model of leadership, *Journal of Leadership and Organizational Studies*, 14: 277–286.

45. C. Bouquet, A. Morrison, & J. Birkinshaw, 2009, International attention and multinational enterprise performance, *Journal of International Business Studies*, 40: 108–131; H. U. Lee & J. H. Park, 2008, The influence of top management team international exposure on international alliance formation, *Journal of Management Studies*, 45: 961–981.

46. C. Thomas, D. Kidd, & C. Fernandez-Araoz, 2007, Are you underutilizing your board? *MIT Sloan Management Review*, 48(2): 71–76.

47. F. Adjaoud, D. Zeghal & S. Andaleeb, 2007, The effect of board's quality on performance: A study of Canadian firms, *Corporate Governance: An International Review*, 15: 623–635; L. Tihanyi, R. A. Johnson, R. E. Hoskisson, & M. A. Hitt, 2003, Institutional ownership and international diversification: The effects of boards of directors and technological opportunity, *Academy of Management Journal*, 46: 195–211.

48. B. R. Golden & E. J. Zajac, 2001, When will boards influence strategy? Inclination times power equals strategic change, *Strategic Management Journal*, 22: 1087–1111.

49. M. Carpenter & J. Westphal, 2001, Strategic context of external network ties: Examining the impact of director appointments on board involvement in strategic decision making, *Academy of Management Journal*, 44: 639–660.

50. M. A. Rutherford & A. K. Buchholtz, 2007, Investigating the relationship between board characteristics and board information, *Corporate Governance: An International Review*, 15: 576–584.

51. X. Huafang & Y. Jianguo, 2007, Ownership structure, board composition and corporate voluntary disclosure: Evidence from listed companies in China, *Managerial Auditing Journal*, 22: 604–619.

52. J. Coles, N. Sen, & V. McWilliams, 2001, An examination of the relationship of governance mechanisms to performance, *Journal of Management*, 27: 23–50; J. Coles & W. Hesterly, 2000, Independence of the chairman and board composition: Firm choices and shareholder value, *Journal of Management*, 26: 195–214.

53. C. M. Daily & D. R. Dalton, 1995, CEO and director turnover in failing firms: An illusion of change? *Strategic Management Journal*, 16: 393–400.

54. D. Miller, I. LeBreton-Miller, & B. Scholnick, 2008, Stewardship vs. stagnation: An empirical comparison of small family and non-family businesses, *Journal of Management Studies*, 51: 51–78; J. H. Davis, F. D. Schoorman, & L. Donaldson, 1997, Toward a stewardship theory of management, *Academy of Management Review*, 22: 20–47.

55. P. Kalyta, 2009, Compensation transparency and managerial opportunism: A study of supplemental retirement plans, *Strategic Management Journal*, 30: 405–423; J. G. Combs & M. S. Skill, 2003, Managerialist and human capital explanations for key executive pay premiums: A contingency perspective, *Academy of Management Journal*, 46: 63–73.

56. E. Matta & P. W. Beamish, 2008, The accentuated CEO career horizon problem: Evidence from international acquisitions, *Strategic Management Journal*, 29: 683–700; N. Rajagopalan & D. Datta, 1996, CEO characteristics: Does industry matter? *Academy of Management Journal*, 39: 197–215.

57. R. A. Johnson, R. E. Hoskisson, & M. A. Hitt, 1993, Board involvement in restructuring: The effect of board versus

managerial controls and characteristics, *Strategic Management Journal*, 14 (Special Issue): 33–50.

58. Z. Simsek, 2007, CEO tenure and organizational performance: An intervening model, *Strategic Management Journal*, 28: 653–662.

59. M. Schneider, 2002, A stakeholder model of organizational leadership, *Organization Science*, 13: 209–220.

60. M. Sorcher & J. Brant, 2002, Are you picking the right leaders? *Harvard Business Review*, 80(2): 78–85; D. A. Waldman, G. G. Ramirez, R. J. House, & P. Puranam, 2001, Does leadership matter? CEO leadership attributes and profitability under conditions of perceived environmental uncertainty, *Academy of Management Journal*, 44: 134–143.

61. J. Werdigier, 2007, UBS not willing to talk about departure of chief, *New York Times Online*, http://www.nytimes.com, July /.

62. W. Shen & A. A. Cannella, 2002, Revisiting the performance consequences of CEO succession: The impacts of successor type, postsuccession senior executive turnover, and departing CEO tenure, *Academy of Management Journal*, 45: 717–734.

63. D. Ulrich & N. Smallwood, 2007, Building a leadership brand, *Harvard Business Review*, 85(7/8): 93–100.

64. G. A. Ballinger & F. D. Schoorman, 2007, Individual reactions to leadership succession in workgroups, *Academy of Management Review*, 32: 116–136; R. E. Hoskisson, D. Yiu, & H. Kim, 2000, Capital and labor market congruence and corporate governance: Effects on corporate innovation and global competitiveness, in S. S. Cohen & G. Boyd (eds.), *Corporate Governance and Globalization*, Northampton, MA: Edward Elgar, 129–154.

65. M. Hurlbert, 2005, Lo! A white knight! So why isn't the market cheering? *New York Times Online*, http://www.nytimes.com, March 27.

66. W. Shen & A. A. Cannella, 2003, Will succession planning increase shareholder wealth? Evidence from investor reactions to relay CEO successions, *Strategic Management Journal*, 24: 191–198.

67. S. Carty and L. Cauley, 2009, AT&T's former CEO Ed Whitacre joins GM as chairman, *USA Today*, http://www.usatoday.com, June 10.

68. Y. Tanokura, 2009, Special interview: Sony chairman, CEO Howard Stringer, *Nikkei Electronics Asia*, http://www.techon.nikkeibp.co.jp, May 26.

69. T. Kiessling, M. Harvey & J. T. Heames, 2008, Operational changes to the acquired firm's top management team and subsequent organizational performance, *Journal of Leadership and Organizational Studies*, 14: 287–302.

70. J. A. Krug & W. Shill, 2008, The big exit: Executive churn in the wake of M&As, *Journal of Business Strategy*, 29(4): 15–21.

71. J. O'Toole & E. E. Lawler, Jr., 2006, The choices managers make—or don't make, *The Conference Board*, September/October, 24–29.

72. S. Nadkarni & P. S. Barr, 2008, Environmental context, managerial cognition, and strategic action: An integrated view, *Strategic Management Journal*, 29: 1395–1427; M. A. Hitt, B. W. Keats, & E. Yucel, 2003, Strategic leadership in global business organizations, in W. H. Mobley & P. W. Dorfman (eds.), *Advances in Global Leadership*, Oxford, UK: Elsevier Science, Ltd., 9–35.

73. I. M. Levin, 2000, Vision revisited, *Journal of Applied Behavioral Science*, 36: 91–107.

74. E. Verwaal, H. Commandeur, & W. Verbeke, 2009, Value creation and value claiming in strategic outsourcing decisions: A resource contingency perspective, *Journal of Management*, 35: 420–444; S. R. Miller, D. E. Thomas, L. Eden, & M. Hitt, 2008, Knee deep in the big muddy: The survival of emerging market firms in developed markets, *Management International Review*, 48: 645–666.

75. G. Hall, 2009, Today's outrage: GE's Immelt flip flops, *TheStreet.com*, http://www.thestreet.com, May 26.

76. J. Welch & S. Welch, 2007, When to talk, when to balk, *BusinessWeek*, April 30, 102.

77. J. Barney & A. M. Arikan, 2001, The resource-based view: Origins and implications, in M. A. Hitt, R. E. Freeman, & J. S. Harrison (eds.), *Handbook of Strategic Management*, Oxford, UK: Blackwell Publishers, 124–188.

78. E. T. Prince, 2005, The fiscal behavior of CEOs, *Managerial Economics*, 46(3): 23–26.

79. Holcomb, Holmes, & Connelly, Making the most of what you have; Sirmon, Gove, & Hitt, Resource management in dyadic competitive rivalry.

80. R. A. Burgelman, 2001, *Strategy Is Destiny: How Strategy-Making Shapes a Company's Future*, New York: The Free Press.

81. D. J. Ketchen, Jr., G. T. M. Hult, & S. F. Slater, 2007, Toward greater understanding of market orientation and the resource-based view, *Strategic Management Journal*, 28: 961–964; S. K. Ethiraj, P. Kale, M. S. Krishnan, & J. V. Singh, 2005, Where do capabilities come from and how do they matter? A study in the software services industry, *Strategic Management Journal*, 26: 25–45.

82. S. K. Ethiraj, 2007, Allocation of inventive effort in complex product systems, *Strategic Management Journal*, 28: 563–584; S. Dutta, O. Narasimhan, & S. Rajiv, 2005, Conceptualizing and measuring capabilities: Methodology and empirical application, *Strategic Management Journal*, 26: 277–285.

83. 2009, PepsiCo Mission and Vision, http://www.pepsico.com/Company/Our-Mission-and-Vision.aspx, June.

84. M. Larson & F. Luthans, 2006, Potential added value of psychological capital in predicting work attitudes, *Journal of Leadership & Organizational Studies*, 13: 45–62; N. W. Hatch & J. H. Dyer, 2004, Human capital and learning as a source of sustainable competitive advantage, *Strategic Management Journal*, 25: 1155–1178.

85. 2009, PepsiCo Careers: Taste the success, http://www.pepsico.com/Carers/Taste-the-Success.aspx, June.

86. M. A. Hitt, L. Bierman, K. Uhlenbruck, & K. Shimizu, 2006, The importance of resources in the internationalization of professional service firms: The good, the bad and the ugly, *Academy of Management Journal*, 49: 1137–1157; M. A. Hitt, L. Bierman, K. Shimizu, & R. Kochhar, 2001, Direct and moderating effects of human capital on strategy and performance in professional service firms: A resource-based perspective, *Academy of Management Journal*, 44: 13–28.

87. S. E. Jackson, M. A. Hitt, & A. S. DeNisi (eds.), 2003, *Managing Knowledge for Sustained Competitive Advantage: Designing Strategies for Effective Human Resource Management*, Oxford, UK: Elsevier Science, Ltd.

88. B. E. Becker & M. A. Huselid, 2007, Strategic human resources management: Where do we go from here? *Journal of Management*, 32: 898–925.

89. R. E. Ployhart, 2007, Staffing in the 21st century: New challenges and strategic opportunities, *Journal of Management*, 32: 868–897.

90. R. A. Noe, J. A. Colquitt, M. J. Simmering, & S. A. Alvarez, 2003, Knowledge management: Developing intellectual and social capital, in S. E. Jackson, M. A. Hitt, & A. S. DeNisi (eds.), 2003, *Managing Knowledge for Sustained Competitive Advantage: Designing Strategies for Effective Human Resource Management*, Oxford, UK: Elsevier Science, Ltd., 209–242.

91. PepsiCo mission and vision, http://www.pepsico.com/Company/Our-Mission-and-Vision.aspx

92. G. P. Hollenbeck & M. W. McCall Jr., 2003, Competence, not competencies: Making a global executive development work, in W. H. Mobley & P. W. Dorfman (eds.), *Advances in Global Leadership*, Oxford, UK: Elsevier Science, Ltd., 101–119; J. Sandberg, 2000, Understanding human competence at work: An interpretative approach, *Academy of Management Journal*, 43: 9–25.

93. G. Colvin, 2007, Leader machines, *Fortune*, October 1, 100–106.

94. Y. Liu, J. G. Combs, D. A. Ketchen, Jr., & R. D. Ireland, 2007, The value of human resource management for organizational performance, *Business Horizons*, 6: 503–511.

95. T. R. Holcomb, R. D. Ireland, R. M. Holmes, & M. A. Hitt, 2009, Architecture of entrepreneurial learning: Exploring the link among heuristics, Knowledge, and action, *Entrepreneurship, Theory & Practice*, 33: 173–198; J. S. Bunderson & K. M. Sutcliffe, 2003, Management

team learning orientation and business unit performance, *Journal of Applied Psychology*, 88: 552–560.

96. R. J. Thomas, 2009, The leadership lessons of crucible experiences, *Journal of Business Strategy*, 30(1): 21–26; J. D. Bragger, D. A. Hantula, D. Bragger, J. Kirnan, & E. Kutcher, 2003, When success breeds failure: History, hysteresis, and delayed exit decisions, *Journal of Applied Psychology*, 88: 6–14.

97. M. R. Haas & M. T. Hansen, 2005, When using knowledge can hurt performance: The value of organizational capabilities in a management consulting company, *Strategic Management Journal*, 26: 1–24; G. Ahuja & R. Katila, 2004, Where do resources come from? The role of idiosyncratic situations, *Strategic Management Journal*, 25: 887–907.

98. Hitt, Miller, & Colella, *Organizational Behavior*.

99. A. Carmeli & B. Azeroual, 2009, How relational capital and knowledge combination capability enhance the performance of work units in a high technology industry, *Strategic Entrepreneurship Journal*, 3: 85–103; J. W. Spencer, 2003, Firms' knowledge-sharing strategies in the global innovation system: Empirical evidence from the flat-panel display industry, *Strategic Management Journal*, 24: 217–233.

100. K. D. Miller, 2002, Knowledge inventories and managerial myopia, *Strategic Management Journal*, 23: 689–706.

101. R. D. Nixon, M. A. Hitt, H. Lee, & E. Jeong, 2004, Market reactions to corporate announcements of downsizing actions and implementation strategies, *Strategic Management Journal*, 25: 1121–1129.

102. Nixon, Hitt, Lee, & Jeong, Market reactions to corporate announcements of downsizing actions.

103. T. Simons & Q. Roberson, 2003, Why managers should care about fairness: The effects of aggregate justice perceptions on organizational outcomes, *Journal of Applied Psychology*, 88: 432–443; M. L. Ambrose & R. Cropanzano, 2003, A longitudinal analysis of organizational fairness: An examination of reactions to tenure and promotion decisions, *Journal of Applied Psychology*, 88: 266–275.

104. C.-L. Luk, O. H. M. Yau, L. Y. M. Sin, A. C. B. Tse, R. P .M. Chow, & J. S. Y. Lee, 2008, The effects of social capital and organizational innovativeness in different institutional contexts, *Journal of International Business Studies*, 39: 589–612; P. S. Adler & S. W. Kwon, 2002, Social capital: Prospects for a new concept, *Academy of Management Review*, 27: 17–40.

105. J. J. Li, L. Poppo, & K. Z. Zhou, 2008, Do managerial ties in China always produce value? Competition, uncertainty, and domestic vs. foreign firms, *Strategic Management Journal*, 29: 383–400; S. Gao, K. Xu, & J. Yang, 2008, Managerial ties, Absorptive capacity & innovation,

Asia Pacific Journal of Management, 25: 395–412.

106. P. Ozcan & K. M. Eisenhardt, 2009, Origin of alliance portfolios: Entrepreneurs, network strategies, and firm performance, *Academy of Management Journal*, 52: 246–279; W. H. Hoffmann, 2007, Strategies for managing a portfolio of alliances, *Strategic Management Journal*, 28: 827–856.

107. H. E. Aldrich & P. H. Kim 2007, Small worlds, infinite possibilities? How social networks affect entrepreneurial team formation and search, *Strategic Entrepreneurship Journal*, 1: 147–165; P. Davidsson & B. Honig, 2003, The role of social and human capital among nascent entrepreneurs, *Journal of Business Venturing*, 18: 301–331.

108. C. M. Fiol, 1991, Managing culture as a competitive resource: An identity-based view of sustainable competitive advantage, *Journal of Management*, 17: 191–211; J. B. Barney, 1986, Organizational culture: Can it be a source of sustained competitive advantage? *Academy of Management Review*, 11: 656–665.

109. 2006, Connecting the dots between innovation and leadership, *Knowledge@Wharton*, http://www.knowledge.wharton.upenn.edu, October 4.

110. V. Govindarajan & A. K. Gupta, 2001, Building an effective global business team, *Sloan Management Review*, 42(4): 63–71; S. Ghoshal & C. A. Bartlett, 1994, Linking organizational context and managerial action: The dimensions of quality of management, *Strategic Management Journal*, 15: 91–112.

111. R. D. Ireland, J. G. Covin, & D. F. Kuratko, 2009, Conceptualizing corporate entrepreneurship strategy, *Entrepreneurship Theory and Practice*, 33(1): 19–46; D. F. Kuratko, R. D. Ireland, & J. S. Hornsby, 2001, Improving firm performance through entrepreneurial actions: Acordia's corporate entrepreneurship strategy, *Academy of Management Executive*, 15(4): 60–71.

112. J. H. Dyer, H. B. Gregersen, & C. Christensen, 2008, Entrepreneur behaviors, opportunity recognition and the origins of innovative ventures, *Strategic Entrepreneurship Journal*, 2: 317–338; R. D. Ireland & J. W. Webb, 2007, Strategic entrepreneurship: Creating competitive advantage through streams of innovation, *Business Horizons*, 50: 49–49.

113. S. A. Alvarez & J. B. Barney, 2008, Opportunities, organizations and entrepreneurship, *Strategic Entrepreneurship Journal*, 2: 171–174; D. S. Elenkov, W. Judge, & P. Wright, 2005, Strategic leadership and executive innovation influence: An international multi-cluster comparative study, *Strategic Management Journal*, 26: 665–682.

114. R. E. Hoskisson, M. A. Hitt, R. D. Ireland, & J. S. Harrison, 2008, *Competing for Advantage*, 2nd ed., Thomson Publishing; R. G. McGrath, W. J. Ferrier, & A. L. Mendelow, 2004, Real options as engines of choice and heterogeneity, *Academy of Management Review*, 29: 86–101.

115. Y. Luo, 2008, Structuring interorganizational cooperation: The role of economic integration in strategic alliances, *Strategic Management Journal*, 29: 617–637; R. S. Vassolo, J. Anand, & T. B. Folta, 2004, Non-additivity in portfolios of exploration activities: A real options analysis of equity alliances in biotechnology, *Strategic Management Journal*, 25: 1045–1061.

116. P. G. Kein, 2008, Opportunity discovery, entrepreneurial action and economic organization, *Strategic Entrepreneurship Journal*, 2: 175–190; R. D. Ireland, M. A. Hitt, & D. Sirmon, 2003, A model of strategic entrepreneurship: The construct and its dimensions, *Journal of Management*, 29: 963–989.

117. G. T. Lumpkin & G. G. Dess, 1996, Clarifying the entrepreneurial orientation construct and linking it to performance, *Academy of Management Review*, 21: 135–172; R. G. McGrath & I. MacMillan, 2000, *The Entrepreneurial Mindset*, Boston: Harvard Business School Press.

118. C. Heath & D. Heath, 2007, Leadership is a muscle, *Fast Company*, July/August, 62–63.

119. Lumpkin & Dess, Clarifying the entrepreneurial orientation construct, 142.

120. Ibid., 137.

121. D. D. Bergh, R. A. Johnson, & R. Dewitt, 2008, Restructuring through spinoff or sell-off: Transforming information asymmetries into financial gain, *Strategic Management Journal*, 29: 133–148; P. Pyoria, 2007, Informal organizational culture: The foundation of knowledge workers' performance, *Journal of Knowledge Management*, 11(3): 16–30.

122. M. Kuenzi & M. Schminke, 2009, Assembling fragments into a lens: A review, critique, and proposed research agenda for the organizational work climate literature, *Journal of Management*, 35: 634–717; C. M. Christensen & S. D. Anthony, 2007, Put investors in their place, *BusinessWeek*, May 28, 10.

123. D. D. Bergh & E. N.-K. Lim, 2008, Learning how to restructure: Absorptive capacity and improvisational views of restructuring actions and performance, *Strategic Management Journal*, 29: 593–616; J. S. Hornsby, D. F. Kuratko, & S. A. Zahra, 2002, Middle managers' perception of the internal environment for corporate entrepreneurship: Assessing a measurement scale, *Journal of Business Venturing*, 17: 253–273.

124. D. F. Kuratko, R. D. Ireland, J. G. Covin, & J. S. Hornsby, 2005, A model of middle-level managers' entrepreneurial behavior, *Entrepreneurship Theory and Practice*, 29: 699–716.

125. E. G. Love & M. Kraatz, 2009, Character, conformity, or the bottom line? How and why downsizing affected corporate reputation, *Academy of Management Journal*, 52: 314–335.

126. Adler & Kwon, Social capital.

127. J. Pinto, C. R. Leana, & F. K. Pil, 2008, Corrupt organizations or organizations of corrupt individuals? Two types of

organization-level corruption, *Academy of Management Review*, 33: 685–709.

128. M. E. Scheitzer, L. Ordonez, & M. Hoegl, 2004, Goal setting as a motivator of unethical behavior, *Academy of Management Journal*, 47: 422–432.

129. D. C. Kayes, D. Stirling, & T. M. Nielsen, 2007, Building organizational integrity, *Business Horizons*, 50: 61–70; L. K. Trevino, G. R. Weaver, D. G. Toffler, & B. Ley, 1999, Managing ethics and legal compliance: What works and what hurts, *California Management Review*, 41(2): 131–151.

130. X. Zhang, K. M. Bartol, K. G. Smith, M. D. Pfaffer, & D. M. Khanin, 2008, CEOs on the edge: Earnings manipulation and stock-based incentive misalignment, *Academy of Management Journal*, 51: 241–258; M. A. Hitt & J. D. Collins, 2007, Business ethics, strategic decision making, and firm performance, *Business Horizons*, 50: 353–357.

131. J. M. Stevens, H. K. Steensma, D. A. Harrison, & P. L. Cochran, 2005, Symbolic or substantive document? Influence of ethics codes on financial executives' decisions, *Strategic Management Journal*, 26: 181–195.

132. Y. Zhang & M. F. Wiersema, 2009, Stock market reaction to CEO certification: The signaling role of CEO background, *Strategic Management Journal*, 30: 693–710; C. Driscoll & M. McKee, 2007, Restorying a culture of ethical and spiritual values: A role for leader storytelling, *Journal of Business Ethics*, 73: 205–217.

133. C. Caldwell & L. A. Hayes, 2007, Leadership, trustworthiness, and the mediating lens, *Journal of Management Development*, 26: 261–281.

134. B. E. Ashforth, D. A. Gioia, S. L. Robinson, & L. K. Trevino, 2008, Re-viewing organizational corruption, *Academy of Management Review*, 33: 670–684; M. Schminke, A. Arnaud, & M. Kuenzi, 2007,

The power of ethical work climates, *Organizational Dynamics*, 36: 171–186; L. B. Ncube & M. H. Wasburn, 2006, Strategic collaboration for ethical leadership: A mentoring framework for business and organizational decision making, *Journal of Leadership & Organizational Studies*, 13: 77–92.

135. J. Welch & S. Welch, 2007, Flying solo: A reality check, *BusinessWeek*, June 4, 116.

136. A. Weibel, 2007, Formal control and trustworthiness, *Group & Organization Management*, 32: 500–517; G. Redding, 2002, The capitalist business system of China and its rationale, *Asia Pacific Journal of Management*, 19: 221–249.

137. B. D. Rostker, R. S. Leonard, O. Younassi, M. V. Arena, & J. Riposo, 2009, Cost controls: How the government can get more bag for its buck, *Rand Review*, http://www.rand.org/publications/randreview/issues/spring2009; A. C. Costa, 2007, Trust and control interrelations, *Group & Organization Management*, 32: 392–406;

138. M. D. Shields, F. J. Deng, & Y. Kato, 2000, The design and effects of control systems: Tests of direct- and indirect-effects models, *Accounting, Organizations and Society*, 25: 185–202.

139. R. S. Kaplan & D. P. Norton, 2009, The balanced scorecard: Measures that drive performance (HBR OnPoint Enhanced Edition), *Harvard Business Review*, Boston, MA, March; R. S. Kaplan & D. P. Norton, 2001, The strategy-focused organization, *Strategy & Leadership*, 29(3): 41–42; R. S. Kaplan & D. P. Norton, 2000, *The Strategy-Focused Organization: How Balanced Scorecard Companies Thrive in the New Business Environment*, Boston: Harvard Business School Press.

140. B. E. Becker, M. A. Huselid, & D. Ulrich, 2001, *The HR Scorecard: Linking People,*

Strategy, and Performance, Boston: Harvard Business School Press, 21.

141. Kaplan & Norton, The strategy-focused organization.

142. R. S. Kaplan & D. P. Norton, 2001, Transforming the balanced scorecard from performance measurement to strategic management: Part I, *Accounting Horizons*, 15(1): 87–104.

143. R. S. Kaplan & D. P. Norton, 1992, The balanced scorecard—measures that drive performance, *Harvard Business Review*, 70(1): 71–79.

144. M. A. Mische, 2001, *Strategic Renewal: Becoming a High-Performance Organization*, Upper Saddle River, NJ: Prentice Hall, 181.

145. H. J. Cho & V. Pucik, 2005, Relationship between innovativeness, quality, growth, profitability and market value, *Strategic Management Journal*, 26: 555–575.

146. G. Rowe, 2001, Creating wealth in organizations: The role of strategic leadership, *Academy of Management Executive*, 15(1): 81–94.

147. R. E. Hoskisson, R. A. Johnson, D. Yiu, & W. P. Wan, 2001, Restructuring strategies of diversified business groups: Differences associated with country institutional environments, in M. A. Hitt, R. E. Freeman, & J. S. Harrison (eds.), *Handbook of Strategic Management*, Oxford, UK: Blackwell Publishers, 433–463.

148. J. Birkinshaw & N. Hood, 2001, Unleash innovation in foreign subsidiaries, *Harvard Business Review*, 79(3): 131–137.

149. Ireland & Hitt, Achieving and maintaining strategic competitiveness.

150. G. Edmondson, 2007, Pedal to the metal at Porsche, *BusinessWeek*, September 3, 68; J. D. Gunkel & G. Probst, 2003, Implementation of the balanced scorecard as a means of corporate learning: The Porsche case, European Case Clearing House, Cranfield, UK.

Chapter 13

1. S. Sato, 2009, Beyond good: Great innovations through design, *Journal of Business Strategy*, 30(2/3): 40–49; D. J. Miller, M. J. Fern, & L. B. Cardinal, 2007, The use of knowledge for technological innovation within diversified firms, *Academy of Management Journal*, 50: 308–326.

2. R. D. Ireland & J. W. Webb, 2007, Strategic entrepreneurship: Creating competitive advantage through streams of innovation, *Business Horizons*, 50(4): 49–59; M. A. Hitt, R. D. Ireland, S. M. Camp, & D. L. Sexton, 2002, Strategic entrepreneurship: Integrating entrepreneurial and strategic management perspectives, in M. A. Hitt, R. D. Ireland, S. M. Camp, & D. L. Sexton (eds.), *Strategic Entrepreneurship: Creating a New Mindset*, Oxford, UK: Blackwell

Publishers, 1–16; M. A. Hitt, R. D. Ireland, S. M. Camp, & D. L. Sexton, 2001, Strategic entrepreneurship: Entrepreneurial strategies for wealth creation, *Strategic Management Journal*, 22 (Special Issue): 479–491.

3. R. Durand, O. Bruyaka & V. Mangematin, 2008, Do science and money go together? The case of the French biotech industry, *Strategic Management Journal*, 29: 1281–1299; R. K. Sinha & C. H. Noble, 2008, The adoption of radical manufacturing technologies and firm survival, *Strategic Management Journal*, 29: 943–962.

4. E. Levitas & M. A. McFadyen, 2009, Managing liquidity in research-intensive firms: Signalling and cash flow effects of patents and alliance activities, *Strategic Management Journal*, 30: 659–678.

5. J. L. Morrow, D. G. Sirmon, M. A. Hitt, & T. R. Holcomb, 2007, Creating value in

the face of declining performance: Firm strategies and organizational recovery, *Strategic Management Journal*, 28: 271–283; K. G. Smith, C. J. Collins, & K. D. Clark, 2005, Existing knowledge, knowledge creation capability, and the rate of new product introduction in high-technology firms, *Academy of Management Journal*, 48: 346–357.

6. D. F. Kuratko, 2007, Entrepreneurial leadership in the 21st century, *Journal of Leadership and Organizational Studies*, 13(4): 1–11; R. D. Ireland, M. A. Hitt, & D. G. Sirmon, 2003, A model of strategic entrepreneurship: The construct and its dimensions, *Journal of Management*, 29: 963–989.

7. B. R. Barringer & R. D. Ireland, 2008, *Entrepreneurship: Successfully Launching New Ventures*, Upper Saddle River, NJ: Pearson Prentice Hall, 5; D. T. Holt,

M. W. Rutherford, & G. R. Clohessy, 2007, Corporate entrepreneurship: An empirical look at individual characteristics, context and process, *Journal of Leadership and Organizational Studies*, 13(4): 40–54.

8. M. H. Morris, S. Coombes, & M. Schindehutte, 2007, Antecedents and outcomes of entrepreneurial and market orientations in a non-profit context: Theoretical and empirical insights, *Journal of Leadership and Organizational Studies*, 13(4): 12–39; H. A. Schildt, M. V. J. Maula, & T. Keil, 2005, Explorative and exploitative learning from external corporate ventures, *Entrepreneurship Theory and Practice*, 29: 493–515.

9. J. Uotila, M. Maula, T. Keil, & S. A. Zahra, 2009, Exploration, exploitation and financial performance: Analysis of S&P 500 corporations, *Strategic Management Journal*, 30: 221–231; G. T. Lumpkin & B. B. Lichtenstein, 2005, The role of organizational learning in the opportunity-recognition process, *Entrepreneurship Theory and Practice*, 29: 451–472.

10. B. A. Gilbert, P. P. McDougall, & D. B. Audretsch, 2006, New venture growth: A review and extension, *Journal of Management*, 32: 926–950.

11. Barringer & Ireland, *Entrepreneurship*; S. A. Zahra, H. J. Sapienza, & P. Davidsson, 2006, Entrepreneurship and dynamic capabilities: A review, model and research agenda, *Journal of Management Studies*, 43: 917–955.

12. S. A. Alvarez & J. B. Barney, 2008, Opportunities, organizations and entrepreneurship, *Strategic Entrepreneurship Journal*, 2: 265–267; S. A. Alvarez & J. B. Barney, 2005, Organizing rent generation and appropriation: Toward a theory of the entrepreneurial firm, *Journal of Business Venturing*, 19: 621–635.

13. P. G. Klein, 2008, Opportunity discovery, entrepreneurial action and economic organization, *Strategic Entrepreneurship Journal*, 2: 175–190; W. Kuemmerle, 2005, The entrepreneur's path to global expansion, *MIT Sloan Management Review*, 46(2): 42–49.

14. R. K. Mitchell, J. R. Mitchell, & J. B. Smith, 2008, Inside opportunity formation: Enterprise failure, cognition and the creation of opportunities, *Strategic Entrepreneurship Journal*, 2: 225–242; C. Marquis & M. Lounsbury, 2007, Vive la resistance: Competing logics and the consolidation of U.S. community banking, *Academy of Management Journal*, 50: 799–820.

15. S. A. Zahra, 2008, The virtuous cycle of discovery and creation of entrepreneurial opportunities, *Strategic Entrepreneurship Journal*, 2: 243–257; N. Wasserman, 2006, Stewards, agents, and the founder discount: Executive compensation in new ventures, *Academy of Management Journal*, 49: 960–976.

16. J. Schumpeter, 1934, *The Theory of Economic Development*, Cambridge, MA: Harvard University Press.

17. J. H. Dyer, H. B. Gregersen, & C. Christensen, 2008, Entrepreneur behaviors and the origins of innovative ventures, *Strategic Entrepreneurship Journal*, 2: 317–338; R. Greenwood & R. Suddaby, 2006, Institutional entrepreneurship in mature fields: The big five accounting firms, *Academy of Management Journal*, 49: 27–48.

18. W. J. Baumol, R. E. Litan, & C. J. Schramm, 2007, *Good capitalism, bad capitalism, and the economics of growth and prosperity*, New Haven: Yale University Press; R. G. Holcombe, 2003, The origins of entrepreneurial opportunities, *Review of Austrian Economics*, 16: 25–54.

19. R. D. Ireland, J. W. Webb, & J. E. Coombs, 2005, Theory and methodology in entrepre-neurship research, in D. J. Ketchen Jr. & D. D. Bergh (eds.), *Research Methodology in Strategy and Management* (Vol. 2), San Diego: Elsevier Publishers, 111–141.

20. K. E. Klein, 2007, The face of entrepre-neurship in 2017, *BusinessWeek*, http://www.businessweek.com, January 31.

21. P. F. Drucker, 1998, The discipline of innovation, *Harvard Business Review*, 76(6): 149–157.

22. Ibid.

23. A. Leiponen, 2008, Control of intellectual assets in client relationships: Implications for innovation, *Strategic Management Journal*, 29: 1371–1394; M. Subramaniam & M. A. Youndt, 2005, The influence of intellectual capital on the types of innovative capabilities, *Academy of Management Journal*, 48: 450–463.

24. F. F. Suarez & G. Lanzolla, 2007, The role of environmental dynamics in building a first mover advantage theory, *Academy of Management Review*, 32: 377–392.

25. M. J. Leiblein & T. L. Madsen, 2009, Unbundling competitive heterogeneity: Incentive structures and capability influences on technological innovation, *Strategic Management Journal*, 30: 711–735; R. Price, 1996, Technology and strategic advantage, *California Management Review*, 38(3): 38–56.

26. M. A. Hitt, R. D. Nixon, R. E. Hoskisson, & R. Kochhar, 1999, Corporate entrepreneurship and cross-functional fertilization: Activation, process and disintegration of a new product design team, *Entrepreneurship: Theory and Practice*, 23(3): 145–167.

27. R. Oriani & M. Sobero, 2008, Uncertainty and the market valuation of R&D within a real options logic, *Strategic Management Journal*, 29: 343–361; D. J. Miller, 2006, Technological diversity, related diversification, and firm performance, *Strategic Management Journal*, 27: 601–619.

28. Schumpeter, *The Theory of Economic Development*.

29. R. Katila & S. Shane, 2005, When does lack of resources make new firms innovative? *Academy of Management Journal*, 48: 814–829.

30. P. Sharma & J. L. Chrisman, 1999, Toward a reconciliation of the definitional issues in the field of corporate entrepreneurship, *Entrepreneurship: Theory and Practice*, 23(3): 11–27; R. A. Burgelman & L. R. Sayles, 1986, *Inside Corporate Innovation: Strategy, Structure, and Managerial Skills*, New York: Free Press.

31. D. G. Sirmon, J.-L. Arregle, M. A. Hitt, & J. W. Webb, 2008, The role of family influence in firms' strategic responses to the threat of imitation, *Entrepreneurship Theory and Practice*, 32: 979–998; D. K. Dutta & M. M. Crossan, 2005, The nature of entrepreneurial opportunities: Understanding the process using the 4I organizational learning framework, *Entrepreneurship Theory and Practice* 29: 425–449.

32. S. F. Latham & M. Braun, 2009, Managerial risk, innovation and organizational decline, *Journal of Management*, 35: 258–281.

33. R. E. Hoskisson & L. W. Busenitz, 2002, Market uncertainty and learning distance in corporate entrepreneurship entry mode choice, in M. A. Hitt, R. D. Ireland, S. M. Camp, & D. L. Sexton (eds.), *Strategic Entrepreneurship: Creating a New Mindset*, Oxford, UK: Blackwell Publishers, 151–172.

34. S. Thornhill, 2006, Knowledge, innovation, and firm performance in high- and low-technology regimes, *Journal of Business Venturing*, 21: 687–703; D. Somaya, 2003, Strategic determinants of decisions not to settle patent litigation, *Strategic Management Journal*, 24: 17–38.

35. K. M. Hmielski & R. A. Baron, 2009, Entrepreneurs' optimism and new venture performance: A social cognitive perspective, *Academy of Management Journal*, 52: 473–488; K. M. Hmielski & R. A. Baron, 2008, When does entrepre-neurial self-efficacy enhance versus reduce firm performance? *Strategic Entrepreneurship Journal*, 2: 57–72; D. Duffy, 2004, Corporate entrepreneurship: Entrepreneurial skills for personal and corporate success, *Center for Excellence*, http://www.centerforexcellence.net, June 14.

36. M. S. Cardon, J. Wincent, J. Singh, & M. Drovsek, 2009, The nature and experience of entrepreneurial passion, *Academy of Management Review*, 34, 511–532.

37. J. O. Fiet, 2007, A prescriptive analysis of search and discovery, *Journal of Management Studies*, 44: 592–611; J. S. McMullen & D. A. Shepherd, 2006, Entrepreneurial action and the role of uncertainty in the theory of the entrepreneur, *Academy of Management Review*, 31: 132–152.

38. N. Nicolaou, S. Shane, L. Cherkas, & T. D. Spector, 2008, The influence of sensation seeking in the heritability of entrepreneurship, *Strategic Entrepreneurship Journal*, 2: 7–21.

39. X. P. Chen, X. Yao, & S. Kowtha, 2009, Entrepreneur passion and preparedness in

business plan presentations: A persuasion analysis of venture capitalists' funding decisions, *Academy of Management Journal*, 52: 199–214; S. F. Matusik, J. M. George, & M. B. Heeley, 2008, Values and judgment under uncertainty: Evidence from venture capitalist assessments of founders, *Strategic Entrepreneurship Journal*, 2: 95–115.

40. S. Allen, 2009, Entrepreneurs: Quotations from famous entrepreneurs on entrepreneurship, *About.com*, http://entrepreneurs.about.com, June 13.

41. W. Stam & T. Elfring, 2008, Entrepreneurial orientation and new venture performance: The moderating role of intra- and extraindustry social capital, *Academy of Management Journal*, 51: 97–111; R. A. Baron, 2006, Opportunity recognition as pattern recognition: How entrepreneurs "connect the dots" to identify new business opportunities, *Academy of Management Perspectives*, 20(1): 104–119; R. G. McGrath & I. MacMillan, 2000, *The Entrepreneurial Mindset*, Boston, MA: Harvard Business School Press.

42. R. D. Ireland, M. A. Hitt, & J. W. Webb, 2005, Entrepreneurial alliances and networks, in O. Shenkar and J. J. Reuer (eds.), *Handbook of Strategic Alliances*, Thousand Oaks, CA: Sage Publications, 333–352; T. M. Begley & D. P. Boyd, 2003, The need for a corporate global mind-set, *MIT Sloan Management Review*, 44(2): 25–32.

43. W. Tsai, 2001, Knowledge transfer in intraorganizational networks: Effects of network position and absorptive capacity on business unit innovation and performance, *Academy of Management Journal*, 44: 996–1004.

44. S. A. Zahra & G. George, 2002, Absorptive capacity: A review, reconceptualization, and extension, *Academy of Management Review*, 27: 185–203.

45. M. A. Hitt, L. Bierman, K. Uhlenbruck, & K. Shimizu, 2006, The importance of resources in the internationalization of professional service firms: The good, the bad and the ugly, *Academy of Management Journal*, 49: 1137–1157; M. A. Hitt, L. Bierman, K. Shimizu, & R. Kochhar, 2001, Direct and moderating effects of human capital on strategy and performance in professional service firms, *Academy of Management Journal*, 44: 13–28.

46. M. Maynard, 2008, At G.M., innovation sacrificed to profits, *New York Times*, http://www.nytimes.com, December 6; 2008, Creativity and innovation driving business— Innovation index, *BusinessWeek/Boston Consulting Group*, http://www.creativityandinnovationblogspot.com, April 22.

47. M. M. Keupp & O. Gassman, 2009, The past and future of international entrepreneurship: A review and suggestions for developing the field, *Journal of Management*, 35: 600–633.

48. H. J. Sapienza, E. Autio, G. George, & S. A. Zahra, 2006, A capabilities perspective on the effects of early internationalization on firm survival and growth, *Academy of Management Review*, 31: 914–933; T. M. Begley, W.-L. Tan, & H. Schoch, 2005, Politico-economic factors associated with interest in starting a business: A multi-country study, *Entrepreneurship Theory and Practice*, 29: 35–52.

49. M. Javidan, R. M. Steers, & M. A. Hitt, 2007, *The Global Mindset*, Amsterdam: Elsevier Ltd.

50. S. A. Fernhaber, B. A. Gilbert, & P. P. McDougal, 2008, International entrepreneurship and geographic location: An empirical examination of new venture internationalization, *Journal of International Business Studies*, 39: 267–290; Hitt, Bierman, Uhlenbruck, & Shimizu, The importance of resources in the internationalization of professional service firm.

51. H. Ren, B. Gray, & K. Kim, 2009, Performance of international joint ventures: What factors really make a difference and how? *Journal of Management*, 35: 805–832; Q. Yang & C. X. Jiang, 2007, Location advantages and subsidiaries' R&D activities in emerging economies: Exploring the effect of employee mobility, *Asia Pacific Journal of Management*, 24: 341–358.

52. 2009, Revitalizing Detroit one business at a time, Kauffman Foundation, http://www.kauffman.org, June.

53. N. Bosma, Z. J. Acs, E. Autio, A. Conduras, & J. Levie, 2009, *Global Entrepreneurship Monitor: 2008 Executive Report*, Global Entrepreneurship Research Consortium, http://www.gemconsortium.org, June 23.

54. R. A. Baron & J. Tang, 2009, Entrepreneurs' social skills and new venture performance: Mediating mechanisms and cultural generality, *Journal of Management*, 35: 282–306; D. W. Yiu, C. M. Lau, & G. D. Bruton, 2007, International venturing by emerging economy firms: The effects of firm capabilities, home country networks, and corporate entrepreneurship, *Journal of International Business Studies*, 38: 519–540.

55. N. Nummeia, S. Saarenketo, & K. Puumalainen, 2005, Rapidly with a rifle or more slowly with a shotgun? Stretching the company boundaries of internationalizing ICT firms, *Journal of International Entrepreneurship*, 2: 275–288; S. A. Zahra & G. George, 2002, International entrepreneurship: The state of the field and future research agenda, in M. A. Hitt, R. D. Ireland, S. M. Camp, & D. L. Sexton (eds.), *Strategic Entrepreneurship: Creating a New Mindset*, Oxford, UK: Blackwell Publishers, 255–288.

56. S. A. Zahra, R. D. Ireland, & M. A. Hitt, 2000, International expansion by new venture firms: International diversity, mode of market entry, technological

learning and performance, *Academy of Management Journal*, 43: 925–950.

57. H. U. Lee & J.H. Park, 2008, The influence of top management team international exposure on international alliance formation, *Journal of Management Studies*, 45: 961–981; Barkema & O. Chvyrkov, 2007, Does top management team diversity promote or hamper foreign expansion? *Strategic Management Journal*, 28: 663–680.

58. T. S. Frost, 2001, The geographic sources of foreign subsidiaries' innovations, *Strategic Management Journal*, 22: 101–122.

59. J. Song & J. Shin, 2008, The paradox of technological capabilities: A study of knowledge sourcing from host countries of overseas R&D operations, *Journal of International Business Studies*, 39: 291–303.

60. A. Vance, 2009, Nokia and Intel to pair up on mobile devices, *New York Times*, http://www.nytimes.com, June 24; M. Palmer & C. Nuttall, 2009, Nokia and Intel strike research deal, *Financial Times*, http://www.ft.com, June 23.

61. W. Chung & S. Yeaple, 2008, International knowledge sourcing: Evidence from U.S. firms expanding abroad, *Strategic Management Journal*, 29: 1207–1224; J. Santos, Y. Doz, & P. Williamson, 2004, Is your innovation process global? *MIT Sloan Management Review*, 45(4): 31–37.

62. Y.-S. Su, E. W. K. Tsang, & M. W. Peng, 2009, How do internal capabilities and external partnerships affect innovativeness? *Asia Pacific Journal of Management*, 26: 309–331; J. A. Fraser, 2004, A return to basics at Kellogg, *MIT Sloan Management Review*, 45(4): 27–30.

63. F. K. Pil & S. K. Cohen, 2006, Modularity: Implications for imitation, innovation, and sustained advantage, *Academy of Management Review*, 31: 995–1011; S. Kola-Nystrom, 2003, Theory of conceptualizing the challenge of corporate renewal, Lappeenranta University of Technology, working paper.

64. 2005, Radical and incremental innovation styles, *Strategies 2 innovate*, http://www.strategies2innovate.com, July 12.

65. E. Xu & H. Zhang, 2008. The impact of state shares on corporate innovation strategy and performance in China, *Asia Pacific Journal of Management*, 25: 473–487; W. C. Kim & R. Mauborgne, 2005, Navigating toward blue oceans, *Optimize*, February, 44–52.

66. A. Phene & P. Almieda, 2008, Innovation in multinational subsidiaries: The role of knowledge assimilation and subsidiary capabilities, *Journal of International Business Studies*, 39: 901–919; G. Ahuja & M. Lampert, 2001, Entrepreneurship in the large corporation: A longitudinal study of how established firms create breakthrough inventions, *Strategic Management Journal*, 22 (Special Issue): 521–543.

67. 2005, Getting an edge on innovation, *BusinessWeek*, March 21, 124.

68. A. J. Chatterji, 2009, Spawned with a silver spoon? Entrepreneurial performance and innovation in the medical device industry, *Strategic Management Journal*, 30: 185–206; J. Goldenberg, R. Horowitz, A. Levav, & D. Mazursky, 2003, Finding your innovation sweet spot, *Harvard Business Review*, 81(3): 120–129.

69. C. E. Shalley & J. E. Perry-Smith, 2008, The emergence of team creative cognition: The role of diverse outside ties, socio-cognitive network centrality, and team evolution, *Strategic Entrepreneurship Journal*, 2: 1, 23–41; R. I. Sutton, 2002, Weird ideas that spark innovation, *MIT Sloan Management Review*, 43(2): 83–87.

70. K. G. Smith & D. Di Gregorio, 2002, Bisociation, discovery, and the role of entrepreneurial action, in M. A. Hitt, R. D. Ireland, S. M. Camp, & D. L. Sexton (eds.), *Strategic Entrepreneurship: Creating a New Mindset*, Oxford, UK: Blackwell Publishers, 129–150.

71. S. A. Hill, M. V. J. Maula, J. M. Birkinshaw & G. C. Murray, 2009, Transferability of the venture capital model to the corporate context: Implications for the performance of corporate venture units, *Strategic Entrepreneurship Journal*, 3: 3–27; Hoskisson & Busenitz, Market uncertainty and learning distance.

72. Hill, Maula, Birkinshaw, & Murray, Transferability of the venture capital model to the corporate context; R. A. Burgelman, 1995, *Strategic Management of Technology and Innovation*, Boston: Irwin.

73. J. M. Howell, 2005, The right stuff: Identifying and developing effective champions of innovation, *Academy of Management Executive*, 19(2): 108–119.

74. M. D. Hutt & T. W. Seph, 2009, *Business Marketing Management: B@B*, 10th ed., Mason, OH: Cengage South-Western.

75. S. K. Ethiraj, 2007, Allocation of inventive effort in complex product systems, *Strategic Management Journal*, 28: 563–584; M. A. Hitt, R. D. Ireland, & H. Lee, 2000, Technological learning, knowledge management, firm growth and performance, *Journal of Engineering and Technology Management*, 17: 231–246.

76. V. Gaba & A. D. Meyer, 2008, Crossing the organizational species barrier: How venture capital practices infiltrated the information technology sector, *Academy of Management Journal*, 51: 976–998; H. W. Chesbrough, 2002, Making sense of corporate venture capital, *Harvard Business Review*, 80(3): 90–99.

77. M. Subramaniam & N. Venkatraman, 2001, Determinants of transnational new product development capability: Testing the influence of transferring and deploying tacit overseas knowledge, *Strategic Management Journal*, 22: 359–378.

78. M. Song & M. M. Montoya-Weiss, 2001, The effect of perceived technological uncertainty on Japanese new product development, *Academy of Management Journal*, 44: 61–80.

79. B. Ambos & B. B. Schegelmilch, 2007, Innovation and control in the multinational firm: A comparison of political and contingency approaches, *Strategic Management Journal*, 28: 473–486.

80. H. Li & J. Li, 2009, Top management team conflict and entrepreneurial strategy in China, *Asia Pacific Journal of Management*, 26: 263–283; S.C. Parker, 2009, Can cognitive biases explain venture team homophily, *Strategic Entrepreneurship Journal*, 3: 67–83.

81. M. Makri, P. J. Lane, & L. R. Gomez-Mejia, 2006, CEO incentives, innovation and performance in technology-intensive firms: A reconciliation of outcome and behavior-based incentive schemes, *Strategic Management Journal*, 27: 1057–1080.

82. A. Tiwana, 2008, Does technological modularity substitute for control? A study of alliance performance in software outsourcing, *Strategic Management Journal*, 29: 769–780.

83. C. Zhou & J. Li, 2008, Product innovation in emerging market-based international joint ventures: An organizational ecology perspective, *Journal of International Business Studies*, 39: 1114–1132; E. Danneels, 2007, The process of technological competence leveraging, *Strategic Management Journal*, 28: 511–533.

84. F. T. Rothaermel & W. Boeker, 2008, Old technology meets new technology: Complementarities, similarities and alliance formation, *Strategic Management Journal*, 29: 47–77; L. Yu, 2002, Marketers and engineers: Why can't we just get along? *MIT Sloan Management Review*, 43(1): 13.

85. R. Cowan & N. Jonard, 2009, Knowledge portfolios and the organization of innovation networks, *Academy of Management Review*, 34: 320–342; A. Somech, 2006, The effects of leadership style and team process on performance and innovation in functionally hetergeneous teams, *Journal of Management*, 32: 132–157.

86. A. Azadegan, K. J. Dooley, P. L. Carter & J. R. Carter, 2008, Supplier innovativeness and the role of interorganizational learning in enhancing manufacturer capabilities, *Journal of Supply Chain Management*, 44(4): 14–34; P. Evans & B. Wolf, 2005, Collaboration rules, *Harvard Business Review*, 83(7): 96–104.

87. B. Fischer & A. Boynton, 2005, Virtuoso teams, *Harvard Business Review*, 83(7): 116–123.

88. Hitt, Nixon, Hoskisson, & Kochhar, Corporate entrepreneurship.

89. Christensen & Overdorf, Meeting the challenge of disruptive change.

90. Hitt, Nixon, Hoskisson, & Kochhar, Corporate entrepreneurship.

91. A. C. Amason, 1996, Distinguishing the effects of functional and dysfunctional conflict on strategic decision making: Resolving a paradox for top management teams, *Academy of Management Journal*, 39: 123–148; P. R. Lawrence &

J. W. Lorsch, 1969, *Organization and Environment*, Homewood, IL: Richard D. Irwin.

92. M. A. Cronin & L. R. Weingart, 2007, Representational gaps, information processing, and conflict in functionally heterogeneous teams, *Academy of Management Review*, 32: 761–773; D. Dougherty, L. Borrelli, K. Muncir, & A. O'Sullivan, 2000, Systems of organizational sensemaking for sustained product innovation, *Journal of Engineering and Technology Management*, 17: 321–355.

93. Hitt, Nixon, Hoskisson, & Kochhar, Corporate entrepreneurship.

94. V. Ambrosini, N. Collier, & M. Jenkins, 2009, A configurational approach to the dynamics of firm level knowledge, *Journal of Strategy and Management*, 2: 4–30; E. C. Wenger & W. M. Snyder, 2000, Communities of practice: The organizational frontier, *Harvard Business Review*, 78(1): 139–144.

95. Gary Hamel, 2000, *Leading the Revolution*, Boston: Harvard Business School Press.

96. P. H. Kim, K. T. Dirks & C. D. Cooper, 2009, The repair of trust: A dynamic bilateral perspective and multilevel conceptualization, *Academy of Management Review*, 34: 401–422; Q. M. Roberson & J. A. Colquitt, 2005, Shared and configural justice: A social network model of justice in teams, *Academy of Management Review*, 30: 595–607.

97. N. Stieglitz & L. Heine, 2007, Innovations and the role of complementarities in a strategic theory of the firm, *Strategic Management Journal*, 28: 1–15; S. W. Fowler, A. W. King, S. J. Marsh, & B. Victor, 2000, Beyond products: New strategic imperatives for developing competencies in dynamic environments, *Journal of Engineering and Technology Management*, 17: 357–377.

98. J. C. Short, A. McKelvie, D. J. Ketchen & G. N. Chandler, 2009, Firm and industry effects on firm performance: A generalization and extension for new ventures, *Strategic Entrepreneurship Journal*, 3: 47–65; M. B. Sarkar, R. Echamabadi, R. Agarwal, & B. Sen, 2006, The effect of the innovative environment on exit of entrepreneurial firms, *Strategic Management Journal*, 27: 519–539.

99. T. Keil, M. Maula, H. Schildt, & S.A. Zahra, 2008, The effect of governance modes and relatedness of external business development activities on innovative performance, *Strategic Management Journal*, 29: 895–907; K. Larsen & A. Salter, 2006, Open for innovation: The role of openness in explaining innovation performance among U.K. manufacturing firms, *Strategic Management Journal*, 27: 131–150.

100. P. Ozcan & K. M. Eisenhardt, 2009, Origin of alliance portfolios: Entrepreneurs, network strategies, and firm performance, *Academy of*

Notes

Management Journal, 52: 246–279;
A. Tiwana & M. Keil, 2007, Does
peripheral knowledge complement
control? An empirical test in technology
outsourcing alliances, *Strategic
Management Journal*, 28: 623–634.

101. K. B. Whittington, J. Owen-Smith, &
W. W. Powell, 2009, Networks,
propinquity, and innovation in knowledge-
intensive industries, *Administrative
Science Quarterly*, 54: 90–122; C.
Dhanaraj & A. Parkhe, 2006, Orchestrating
innovation networks, *Academy of
Management Review*, 31: 659–669.

102. K. Ruckman, 2009, Technology
sourcing acquisitions: What they mean
for innovation potential, *Journal of
Strategy and Management*, 2: 56–75;
F. T. Rothaermel & D. L. Deeds, 2004,
Exploration and exploitation alliances in
biotechnology: A system of new product
development, *Strategic Management
Journal*, 25: 201–221.

103. D. Li, L. Eden, M. A. Hitt, & R. D. Ireland,
2008, Friends, acquaintances, or strangers?
Partner selection in R&D alliances,
Academy of Management Journal, 51:
315–334; F. T. Rothaermel, M. A. Hitt,
& L. A. Jobe, 2006, Balancing vertical
integration and strategic outsourcing:
Effects on product portfolio, product
success and firm performance, *Strategic
Management Journal*, 27: 1033–1056.

104. A. C. Cooper, 2002, Networks, alliances
and entrepreneurship, in M. A. Hitt,
R. D. Ireland, S. M. Camp, & D. L. Sexton
(eds.), *Strategic Entrepreneurship:
Creating a New Mindset*, Oxford, UK:
Blackwell Publishers, 204–222.

105. B. S. Teng, 2007, Corporate entrepreneurship activities through strategic
alliances: A resource-based approach
toward competitive advantage, *Journal
of Management Studies*, 44: 119–142;
S. A. Alvarez & J. B. Barney, 2001, How
entrepreneurial firms can benefit from
alliances with large partners, *Academy
of Management Executive*, 15(1): 139–
148.

106. F. T. Rothaermel, 2001, Incumbent's
advantage through exploiting
complementary assets via interfirm
cooperation, *Strategic Management
Journal*, 22 (Special Issue): 687–699.

107. B. R. Koka & J. E. Prescott, 2008,
Designing alliance networks: The influence
of network position, environmental
change and strategy on firm performance,
Strategic Management Journal, 29: 639–
661; A. Capaldo, 2007, Network structure
and innovation: The leveraging of a dual
network as a distinctive capability,
Strategic Management Journal, 28:
585–608.

108. C. L. Luk, O. H. M. Yau, L. Y. M. Sin,
A. C. B. Tse, R. P. M. Chow, & J. S. Y.
Lee, 2008, The effects of social capital
and organizational innovativeness in
different institutional contexts, *Journal

of International Business Studies*, 39:
89–612; H. Yli-Renko, E. Autio, & H. J.
Sapienza, 2001, Social capital, knowledge
acquisition and knowledge exploitation in
young technology-based firms, *Strategic
Management Journal*, 22 (Special Issue):
587–613.

109. A. Tiwana, 2008, Do bridging ties
complement strong ties? An empirical
examination of alliance ambidexterity,
Strategic Management Journal, 29:
251–272; C. Lee, K. Lee, & J. M. Pennings,
2001, Internal capabilities, external
networks and performance: A study of
technology-based ventures, *Strategic
Management Journal*, 22 (Special Issue):
615–640.

110. Azadegan, Dooley, Carter, & Carter,
Supplier innovativeness and the role of
interorganizational learning in enhancing
manufacturer capabilities; A. Takeishi,
2001, Bridging inter- and intra-firm
boundaries: Management of supplier
involvement in automobile product
development, *Strategic Management
Journal*, 22: 403–433.

111. R. C. Sampson, 2007, R&D alliances
and firm performance: The impact of
technological diversity and alliance
organization on innovation, *Academy
of Management Journal*, 50: 364–386;
J. Weiss & J. Hughes, 2005, Want
collaboration? Accept—and actively
manage—conflict, *Harvard Business
Review*, 83(3): 92–101.

112. R. H. Shah & V. Swaminathan, 2008,
Factors influencing partner selection
in strategic alliances: The moderating
role of alliance context, *Strategic
Management Journal*, 29: 471–494;
Li, Eden, Hitt, & Ireland, Friends,
acquaintances, or strangers?; R. D.
Ireland, M. A. Hitt, & D. Vaidyanath,
2002, Strategic alliances as a pathway
to competitive success, *Journal of
Management*, 28: 413–446.

113. M. A. Hitt, M. T. Dacin, E. Levitas, J.
L. Arregle, & A. Borza, 2000, Partner
selection in emerging and developed
market contexts: Resource-based and
organizational learning perspectives,
Academy of Management Journal, 43:
449–467.

114. J. D. Westphal & M. B. Crant, 2008,
Sociopolitical dynamics in relations
between top managers and security
analysts: Favor rendering, reciprocity, and
analyst stock recommendations, *Academy
of Management Journal*, 51: 873–897.

115. J. J. Reuer, M. Zollo, & H. Singh, 2002,
Post-formation dynamics in strategic
alliances, *Strategic Management Journal*,
23: 135–151.

116. M. A. Hitt, D. King, H. Krishnan, M. Makri,
M. Schijven, K. Shimizu, & H. Zhu, 2009,
Mergers and Acquisitions: Overcoming
pitfalls, building synergy and creating value,
Business Horizons, in press; H. G. Barkema
& M. Schijven, 2008, Toward unlocking the

full potential of acquisitions: The role of
organizational restructuring, *Academy of
Management Journal*, 51: 696–722.

117. 2005, Novartis announces completion
of Hexal AG acquisition, http:// www
.novartis.com, June 6; 2005, Pfizer sees
sustained long-term growth, http://www
.pfizer.com, April 5.

118. M. A. Hitt, R. E. Hoskisson, R. A. Johnson,
& D. D. Moesel, 1996, The market for
corporate control and firm innovation,
Academy of Management Journal, 39:
1084–1119.

119. M. Makri, M. A. Hitt, & P. J. Lane, 2009,
Complementary technologies, knowledge
relatedness, and invention outcomes
in high technology M&As, *Strategic
Management Journal*, in press.

120. Ruckman, 2009, Technology sourcing
acquisitions; P. Puranam & K. Srikanth,
2007, What they know vs. what they
do: How acquirers leverage technology
acquisitions, *Strategic Management
Journal*, 28: 805–825; M. A. Hitt,
J. S. Harrison, & R. D. Ireland, 2001,
*Mergers and Acquisitions: A Guide to
Creating Value for Stakeholders*, New
York: Oxford University Press.

121. M. Cording, P. Christman, & D. King,
2008. Reducing causal ambiguity in
acquisition integration: Intermediate
goals as mediators of integration
decisions and acquisition performance,
Academy of Management Journal, 51:
744–767; P. Puranam, H. Singh, & M.
Zollo, 2006, Organizing for innovation:
Managing the coordination-autonomy
dilemma in technology, *Academy
of Management Journal*, 49: 263–280.

122. Ireland, Hitt, & Sirmon, A model of
strategic entrepreneurship.

123. A. Afuah, 2009, *Strategic Innovation:
New game strategies for competitive
advantage*, New York: Routledge.

124. Hitt, Ireland, Camp, & Sexton, Strategic
entrepreneurship.

125. D. G. Sirmon, M. A. Hitt, & R. D. Ireland,
2007, Managing firm resources in
dynamic environment to create value:
Looking inside the black box, *Academy of
Management Review*, 32: 273–292.

126. D. G. Sirmon, S. Gove, & M. A. Hitt,
2008, Resource management in dyadic
competitive rivalry: The effects of
resource bundling and deployment,
Academy of Management Journal,
51:918–935; Hitt, Bierman, Shimizu, &
Kochhar, Direct and moderating effects
of human capital.

127. Tiwana, Do bridging ties complement
strong ties? Hitt, Bierman, Uhlenbruck, &
Shimizu, The importance of resources in
the internationalization of professional
service firms.

128. K. Asakawa & A. Som, 2008, Internationalization of R&D in China and India:
Conventional wisdom versus reality, *Asia
Pacific Journal of Management*, 25:
375–394; M. A. Hitt, R. E. Hoskisson, &

H. Kim, 1997, International diversification: Effects on innovation and firm performance in product diversified firms, *Academy of Management Journal*, 40: 767–798.

129. M. A. Hitt & R. D. Ireland, 2002, The essence of strategic leadership: Managing human and social capital, *Journal of Leadership and Organization Studies*, 9(1): 3–14.

130. Baumol, Litan, & Schramm, *Good capitalism, bad capitalism*; R. Garud, S. Jain, & A. Kumaraswamy, 2002, Institutional entrepreneurship in the sponsorship of common technological standards: The case of Sun Microsystems and JAVA, *Academy of Management Journal*, 45: 196–214.

131. B. Batjargal, A. Tsui, M. A. Hitt, J. L. Arregle, T. Miller, & J. Webb, 2009, How relationships matter: Women and men entrepreneurs' social networks and new venture success across cultures, paper presented at the Academy of Management Conference, Chicago, August; I. E. Allen, N. Langowitz, & M. Minniti, 2007, Global entrepreneurship monitor: 2006 report on women in entrepreneurship, Babson College, http://www3.babson.edu/ESHIP/research-publications/gem.cfm, March 1.

132. J. D. Jardins, 2005, I am woman (I think), *Fast Company*, May, 25–26.

133. Hitt, Ireland, Camp, & Sexton, Strategic entrepreneurship.

134. C. W. L. Hill & F. T. Rothaermel, 2003, The performance of incumbent firms in the face of radical technological innovation, *Academy of Management Review*, 28: 257–274.

135. D. G. Sirmon & M. A. Hitt, 2009, Contingencies within dynamic managerial capabilities: Interdependent effects of resource investment and deployment on firm performance, *Strategic Management Journal*, in press.

Case Studies

What to Expect From In-Class Case Discussions

As you will learn, classroom discussions of cases differ significantly from lectures. The case method calls for your instructor to guide the discussion and to solicit alternative views as a way of encouraging your active participation when analyzing a case. When alternative views are not forthcoming, your instructor might take a position just to challenge you and your peers to respond thoughtfully as a way of generating still additional alternatives. Often, instructors will evaluate your work in terms of both the quantity and the quality of your contributions to in-class case discussions. The in-class discussions are important in that you can derive significant benefit by having your ideas and recommendations examined against those of your peers and by responding to thoughtful challenges by other class members and/or the instructor.

During case discussions, your instructor will likely listen, question, and probe to extend the analysis of case issues. In the course of these actions, your peers and/or your instructor may challenge an individual's views and the validity of alternative perspectives that have been expressed. These challenges are offered in a constructive manner; their intent is to help all parties involved with analyzing a case develop their analytical and communication skills. Developing these skills is important in that they will serve you well when working for all types of organizations. Commonly, instructors will encourage you and your peers to be innovative and original when developing and presenting ideas. Over the course of an individual discussion, you are likely to form a more complex view of the case as a result of listening to and thinking about the diverse inputs offered by your peers and instructor. Among other benefits, experience with multiple case discussions will increase your knowledge of the advantages and disadvantages of group decision-making processes.

Both your peers and instructor will value comments that contribute to identifying problems as well as solutions to them. To offer relevant contributions, you are encouraged to think independently and, through discussions with your peers outside of class, to refine your thinking. We also encourage you to avoid using "I think," "I believe," and "I feel" to discuss your inputs to a case analysis process. Instead, consider using a less emotion laden phrase, such as "My analysis shows . . . ." This highlights the logical nature of the approach you have taken to analyze a case. When preparing for an in-class case discussion, you should plan to use the case data to explain your assessment of the situation. Assume that your peers and instructor are familiar with the basic facts included in the case. In addition, it is good practice to prepare notes regarding your analysis of case facts before class discussions and use them when explaining your perspectives. Effective notes signal to classmates and the instructor that you are prepared to engage in a thorough discussion of a case. Moreover, comprehensive and detailed notes eliminate the need for you to memorize the facts and figures needed to successfully discuss a case.

The case analysis process described above will help prepare you effectively to discuss a case during class meetings. Using this process results in consideration of the issues required to identify a focal firm's problems and to propose strategic actions through which the firm can increase the probability it will outperform its rivals. In some instances, your instructor may ask you to prepare either an oral or a written analysis of a particular case. Typically, such an assignment demands even more thorough study and analysis of the case contents. At your instructor's discretion, oral and written analyses may be completed by individuals or by groups of three or more people. The information and insights gained by completing the six steps shown in Table 1 often are of value when developing an oral or a written analysis. However, when preparing an oral or written presentation, you must consider the overall framework in which your information and inputs will be presented. Such a framework is the focus of the next section.

Preparing an Oral/Written Case Presentation

Experience shows that two types of thinking (analysis and synthesis) are necessary to develop an effective oral or written presentation (see Exhibit 1). In the analysis stage, you should first analyze the general external environmental issues affecting the firm. Next, your environmental analysis should focus on the particular industry (or industries, in the case of a diversified company) in which a firm operates. Finally, you should examine companies against which the focal firm competes. By studying the three levels of the external environment (general, industry, and competitor), you will be able to identify a firm's opportunities and threats. Following the external environmental analysis is the analysis of the firm's internal organization. This analysis provides the insights needed to identify the firm's strengths and weaknesses.

As noted in Exhibit 1, you must then change the focus from analysis to synthesis. Specifically, you must synthesize information gained from your analysis of the firm's external environment and internal organization. Synthesizing information allows you to generate alternatives that can resolve the significant problems or challenges facing the focal firm. Once you identify a best alternative, from an evaluation based on predetermined criteria and goals, you must explore implementation actions.

In Table 2, we outline the sections that should be included in either an oral or a written presentation: strategic profile and case analysis purpose, situation analysis, statements of strengths/weaknesses and opportunities/threats, strategy formulation, and strategy implementation. These sections are described in the following discussion. Familiarity with the contents of your book's thirteen chapters is helpful because the general outline for an oral or a written presentation shown in Table 2 is based on an understanding of the strategic management process detailed in those chapters. We follow the discussions of the parts of Table 2 with a few comments about the "process" to use to present the results of your case analysis in either a written or oral format.

Table 1 An Effective Case Analysis Process

Step 1: Gaining Familiarity	a. In general—determine who, what, how, where, and when (the critical facts of the case). b. In detail—identify the places, persons, activities, and contexts of the situation. c. Recognize the degree of certainty/uncertainty of acquired information.
Step 2: Recognizing Symptoms	a. List all indicators (including stated "problems") that something is not as expected or as desired. b. Ensure that symptoms are not assumed to be the problem (symptoms should lead to identification of the problem).
Step 3: Identifying Goals	a. Identify critical statements by major parties (for example, people, groups, the work unit, and so on). b. List all goals of the major parties that exist or can be reasonably inferred.
Step 4: Conducting the Analysis	a. Decide which ideas, models, and theories seem useful. b. Apply these conceptual tools to the situation. c. As new information is revealed, cycle back to substeps a and b.
Step 5: Making the Diagnosis	a. Identify predicaments (goal inconsistencies). b. Identify problems (discrepancies between goals and performance). c. Prioritize predicaments/problems regarding timing, importance, and so on.
Step 6: Doing the Action Planning	a. Specify and prioritize the criteria used to choose action alternatives. b. Discover or invent feasible action alternatives. c. Examine the probable consequences of action alternatives. d. Select a course of action. e. Design an implementation plan/schedule. f. Create a plan for assessing the action to be implemented.

Source: C. C. Lundberg and C. Enz, 1993, A framework for student case preparation, Case Research Journal, 13 (Summer): 144. Reprinted by permission of NACRA, North American Case Research Association.

Exhibit 1 Types of Thinking in Case Preparation: Analysis and Synthesis

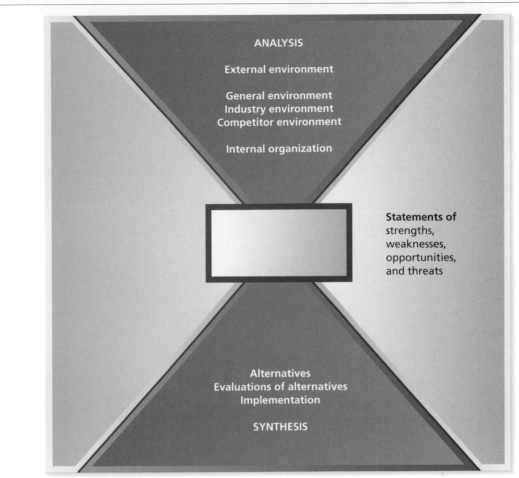

Strategic Profile and Case Analysis Purpose

You will use the strategic profile to briefly present the critical facts from the case that have affected the focal firm's historical strategic direction and performance. The case facts should not be restated in the profile; rather, these comments should show how the critical facts lead to a particular focus for your analysis. This primary focus should be emphasized in this section's conclusion. In addition, this section should state important assumptions about case facts on which your analyses are based.

Situation Analysis

As shown in Table 2, a general starting place for completing a situation analysis is the general environment.

General Environmental Analysis. Your analysis of the general environment should focus on trends in the six segments of the general environment (see Table 3). Many of the segment issues shown in Table 3 for the six segments are explained more fully in Chapter 2 of your book. The objective you should have in evaluating these trends is to be able to *predict* the segments that you expect

Table 2 General Outline for an Oral or Written Presentation

I. Strategic Profile and Case Analysis Purpose

II. Situation Analysis
 A. General environmental analysis
 B. Industry analysis
 C. Competitor analysis
 D. Internal analysis

III. Identification of Environmental Opportunities and Threats and Firm Strengths and Weaknesses (SWOT Analysis)

IV. Strategy Formulation
 A. Strategic alternatives
 B. Alternative evaluation
 C. Alternative choice

V. Strategic Alternative Implementation
 A. Action items
 B. Action plan

to have the most significant influence on your focal firm over the next several years (say three to five years) and to explain your reasoning for your predictions.

Industry Analysis. Porter's five force model is a useful tool for analyzing the industry (or industries) in which

Table 3 Sample General Environmental Categories

Technological Trends
- Information technology continues to become cheaper with more practical applications
- Database technology enables organization of complex data and distribution of information
- Telecommunications technology and networks increasingly provide fast transmission of all sources of data, including voice, written communications, and video information
- Computerized design and manufacturing technologies continue to facilitate quality and flexibility

Demographic Trends
- Regional changes in population due to migration
- Changing ethnic composition of the population
- Aging of the population
- Aging of the "baby boom" generation

Economic Trends
- Interest rates
- Inflation rates
- Savings rates
- Exchange rates
- Trade deficits
- Budget deficits

Political/Legal Trends
- Antitrust enforcement
- Tax policy changes
- Environmental protection laws
- Extent of regulation/deregulation
- Privatizing state monopolies
- State-owned industries

Sociocultural Trends
- Women in the workforce
- Awareness of health and fitness issues
- Concern for the environment
- Concern for customers

Global Trends
- Currency exchange rates
- Free-trade agreements
- Trade deficits

your firm competes. We explain how to use this tool in Chapter 2. In this part of your analysis, you want to determine the attractiveness of an industry (or a segment of an industry) in which your firm is competing. As attractiveness increases, so does the possibility your firm will be able to earn profits by using its chosen strategies. After evaluating the power of the five forces relative to your firm, you should make a judgment as to *how* attractive the industry is in which your firm is competing.

Competitor Analysis. Firms also need to analyze each of their primary competitors. This analysis should identify competitors' current strategies, strategic intent, strategic mission, capabilities, core competencies, and a competitive response profile (see Chapter 2). This information is useful to the focal firm in formulating an appropriate strategy and in predicting competitors' probable responses. Sources that can be used to gather information about an industry and companies with whom the focal firm competes are listed in Appendix I. Included in this list is a wide range of

publications, such as periodicals, newspapers, bibliographies, directories of companies, industry ratios, forecasts, rankings/ratings, and other valuable statistics.

Internal Analysis. Assessing a firm's strengths and weaknesses through a value chain analysis facilitates moving from the external environment to the internal organization. Analysis of the primary and support activities of the value chain provides opportunities to understand how external environmental trends affect the specific activities of a firm. Such analysis helps highlight strengths and weaknesses (see Chapter 3 for an explanation and use of the value chain).

For purposes of preparing an oral or a written presentation, it is important to note that strengths are internal resources and capabilities that have the potential to be core competencies. Weaknesses, on the other hand, are internal resources and capabilities that have the potential to place a firm at a competitive disadvantage relative to its rivals. Thus, some of a firm's resources and capabilities are strengths; others are weaknesses.

When evaluating the internal characteristics of the firm, your analysis of the functional activities emphasized is critical. For instance, if the strategy of the firm is primarily technology driven, it is important to evaluate the firm's R&D activities. If the strategy is market driven, marketing functional activities are of paramount importance. If a firm has financial difficulties, critical financial ratios would require careful evaluation. In fact, because of the importance of financial health, most cases require financial analyses. Appendix II lists and operationally defines several common financial ratios. Included are tables describing profitability, liquidity, leverage, activity, and shareholders' return ratios. Leadership, organizational culture, structure, and control systems are other characteristics of firms you should examine to fully understand the "internal" part of your firm.

Identification of Environmental Opportunities and Threats and Firm Strengths and Weaknesses (SWOT Analysis).

The outcome of the situation analysis is the identification of a firm's strengths and weaknesses and its environmental threats and opportunities. The next step requires that you analyze the strengths and weaknesses and the opportunities and threats for configurations that benefit or do not benefit your firm's efforts to perform well. Case analysts and organizational strategists as well seek to match a firm's strengths with its opportunities. In addition, strengths are chosen to prevent any serious environmental threat from negatively affecting the firm's performance. The key objective of conducting a SWOT analysis is to determine how to position the firm so it can take advantage of opportunities, while simultaneously avoiding or minimizing environmental threats. Results from a SWOT analysis yield valuable insights into the selection of a firm's strategies. The analysis of a case should not be overemphasized relative to the synthesis of results gained from your analytical efforts. There may be a temptation to spend most of your oral or written case analysis on results from the analysis. It is important, however, that you make an equal effort to develop and evaluate alternatives and to design implementation of the chosen strategy.

Strategy Formulation—Strategic Alternatives, Alternative Evaluation, and Alternative Choice.

Developing alternatives is often one of the most difficult steps in preparing an oral or a written presentation. Developing three to four alternative strategies is common (see Chapter 4 for business-level strategy alternatives and Chapter 6 for corporate-level strategy alternatives). Each alternative should be feasible (i.e., it should match the firm's strengths, capabilities, and especially core competencies), and feasibility should be demonstrated. In addition, you should show how each alternative takes advantage of the environmental opportunity or avoids/buffers against environmental threats.

Developing carefully thought out alternatives requires synthesis of your analyses' results and creates greater credibility in oral and written case presentations.

Once you develop strong alternatives, you must evaluate the set to choose the best one. Your choice should be defensible and provide benefits over the other alternatives. Thus, it is important that both alternative development and evaluation of alternatives be thorough. The choice of the best alternative should be explained and defended.

Strategic Alternative Implementation–Action Items and Action Plan.

After selecting the most appropriate strategy (that is, the strategy with the highest probability of helping your firm in its efforts to earn profits), implementation issues require attention. Effective synthesis is important to ensure that you have considered and evaluated all critical implementation issues. Issues you might consider include the structural changes necessary to implement the new strategy. In addition, leadership changes and new controls or incentives may be necessary to implement strategic actions. The implementation actions you recommend should be explicit and thoroughly explained. Occasionally, careful evaluation of implementation actions may show the strategy to be less favorable than you thought originally. A strategy is only as good as the firm's ability to implement it.

Process Issues.

You should ensure that your presentation (either oral or written) has logical consistency throughout. For example, if your presentation identifies one purpose, but your analysis focuses on issues that differ from the stated purpose, the logical inconsistency will be apparent. Likewise, your alternatives should flow from the configuration of strengths, weaknesses, opportunities, and threats you identified by analyzing your firm's external environment and internal organization.

Thoroughness and clarity also are critical to an effective presentation. Thoroughness is represented by the comprehensiveness of the analysis and alternative generation. Furthermore, clarity in the results of the analyses, selection of the best alternative strategy, and design of implementation actions are important. For example, your statement of the strengths and weaknesses should flow clearly and logically from your analysis of your firm's internal organization.

Presentations (oral or written) that show logical consistency, thoroughness, and clarity of purpose, effective analyses, and feasible recommendations (strategy and implementation) are more effective and are likely to be more positively received by your instructor and peers. Furthermore, developing the skills necessary to make such presentations will enhance your future job performance and career success.

Appendix I Sources for Industry and Competitor Analyses

Abstracts and Indexes	
Periodicals	ABI/*Inform* *Business Periodicals Index* *InfoTrac* Custom Journals *InfoTrac* Custom Newspapers *InfoTrac* OneFile EBSCO Business Source Premiere Lexis/Nexis Academic *Public Affairs Information Service Bulletin* (PAIS) *Reader's Guide to Periodical Literature*
Newspapers	*NewsBank—Foreign Broadcast Information* *NewsBank-Global NewsBank* *New York Times Index* *Wall Street Journal Index* *Wall Street Journal/Barron's Index* *Washington Post Index*
Bibliographies	*Encyclopedia of Business Information Sources*
Directories	
Companies—General	*America's Corporate Families and International Affiliates* *Hoover's Online: The Business Network* www.hoovers.com/free D&B Million Dollar Directory (databases: http://www.dnbmdd.com) *Standard & Poor's Corporation Records* *Standard & Poor's Register of Corporations, Directors, and Executives* (http://www.netadvantage.standardandpoors.com for all of *Standard & Poor's*) *Ward's Business Directory of Largest U.S. Companies*
Companies—International	*America's Corporate Families and International Affiliates* *Business Asia* *Business China* *Business Eastern Europe* *Business Europe* *Business International* *Business International Money Report* *Business Latin America* *Directory of American Firms Operating in Foreign Countries* *Directory of Foreign Firms Operating in the United States* *Hoover's Handbook of World Business* *International Directory of Company Histories* *Mergent's International Manual* Mergent Online (http://www.fisonline.com—for "Business and Financial Information Connection to the World") *Who Owns Whom*
Companies—Manufacturers	*Thomas Register of American Manufacturers* U.S. Office of Management and Budget, Executive Office of the President, *Standard Industrial Classification Manual* *U.S. Manufacturer's Directory, Manufacturing & Distribution, USA*
Companies—Private	*D&B Million Dollar Directory* *Ward's Business Directory of Largest U.S. Companies*

Appendix I Sources for Industry and Competitor Analyses (*Continued*)

Companies—Public	Annual Reports and 10-K Reports *Disclosure* (corporate reports) Q-File Security and Exchange Commision Filings & Forms (EDGAR) http://www.sec.gov/edgar.shtml *Mergent's Manuals:* • *Mergent's Bank and Finance Manual* • *Mergent's Industrial Manual* • *Mergent's International Manual* • *Mergent's Municipal and Government Manual* • *Mergent's OTC Industrial Manual* • *Mergent's OTC Unlisted Manual* • *Mergent's Public Utility Manual* • *Mergent's Transportation Manual* Standard & Poor's Corporation, *Standard Corporation Descriptions:* http://www.netadvantage.standardandpoors.com • *Standard & Poor's Analyst Handbook* • *Standard & Poor's Industry Surveys* • *Standard & Poor's Statistical Service*
Companies—Subsidiaries and Affiliates	*America's Corporate Families and International Affiliates* *Ward's Directory* *Who Owns Whom* *Mergent's Industry Review* *Standard & Poor's Analyst's Handbook* *Standard & Poor's Industry Surveys* (2 volumes) U.S. Department of Commerce, *U.S. Industrial Outlook*
Industry Ratios	Dun & Bradstreet, *Industry Norms and Key Business Ratios* *RMA's Annual Statement Studies* *Troy Almanac of Business and Industrial Financial Ratios*
Industry Forecasts	International Trade Administration, *U.S. Industry & Trade Outlook*
Rankings & Ratings	Annual Report on American Industry in *Forbes* *Business Rankings Annual* *Mergent's Industry Review* http://www.worldcatlibraries.org *Standard & Poor's Industry Report Service* http://www.netadvantage.standardandpoors.com *Value Line Investment Survey* *Ward's Business Directory of Largest U.S. Companies*
Statistics	*American Statistics Index (ASI)* Bureau of the Census, U.S. Department of Commerce, *Economic Census Publications* Bureau of the Census, U.S. Department of Commerce, *Statistical Abstract of the United States* Bureau of Economic Analysis, U.S. Department of Commerce, *Survey of Current Business* Internal Revenue Service, U.S. Treasury Department, *Statistics of Income: Corporation Income Tax Returns* *Statistical Reference Index (SRI)*

Appendix II Financial Analysis in Case Studies

Table A-1 Profitability Ratios

Ratio	Formula	What It Shows
1. Return on total assets	$$\frac{\text{Profits after taxes}}{\text{Total assets}}$$ or $$\frac{\text{Profits after taxes + Interest}}{\text{Total assets}}$$	The net return on total investments of the firm or The return on both creditors' and shareholders' investments
2. Return on stockholder's equity (or return on net worth)	$$\frac{\text{Profits after taxes}}{\text{Total stockholder's equity}}$$	How profitably the company is utilizing shareholders' funds
3. Return on common equity	$$\frac{\text{Profits after taxes} - \text{Preferred stock dividends}}{\text{Total stockholder's equity} - \text{Par value of preferred stock}}$$	The net return to common stockholders
4. Operating profit margin (or return on sales)	$$\frac{\text{Profits before taxes and before interest}}{\text{Sales}}$$	The firm's profitability from regular operations
5. Net profit margin (or net return on sales)	$$\frac{\text{Profits after taxes}}{\text{Sales}}$$	The firm's net profit as a percentage of total sales

Table A-2 Liquidity Ratios

Ratio	Formula	What It Shows
1. Current ratio	$$\frac{\text{Current assets}}{\text{Current liabilities}}$$	The firm's ability to meet its current financial liabilities
2. Quick ratio (or acid-test ratio)	$$\frac{\text{Current assets} - \text{Inventory}}{\text{Current liabilities}}$$	The firm's ability to pay off short-term obligations without relying on sales of inventory
3. Inventory to net working capital	$$\frac{\text{Inventory}}{\text{Current assets} - \text{Current liabilities}}$$	The extent to which the firm's working capital is tied up in inventory

Table A-3 Leverage Ratios

Ratio	Formula	What It Shows
1. Debt-to-assets	$$\frac{\text{Total debt}}{\text{Total assets}}$$	Total borrowed funds as a percentage of total assets
2. Debt-to-equity	$$\frac{\text{Total debt}}{\text{Total shareholders' equity}}$$	Borrowed funds versus the funds provided by shareholders
3. Long-term debt-to-equity	$$\frac{\text{Long-term debt}}{\text{Total shareholders' equity}}$$	Leverage used by the firm
4. Times-interest-earned (or coverage ratio)	$$\frac{\text{Profits before interest and taxes}}{\text{Total interest charges}}$$	The firm's ability to meet all interest payments
5. Fixed charge coverage	$$\frac{\text{Profits before taxes and interest} + \text{Lease obligations}}{\text{Total interest charges} + \text{Lease obligations}}$$	The firm's ability to meet all fixed-charge obligations including lease payments

Table A-4 Activity Ratios

Ratio	Formula	What It Shows
1. Inventory turnover	$\dfrac{\text{Sales}}{\text{Inventory of finished goods}}$	The effectiveness of the firm in employing inventory
2. Fixed-assets turnover	$\dfrac{\text{Sales}}{\text{Fixed assets}}$	The effectiveness of the firm in utilizing plant and equipment
3. Total assets turnover	$\dfrac{\text{Sales}}{\text{Total assets}}$	The effectiveness of the firm in utilizing total assets
4. Accounts receivable turnover	$\dfrac{\text{Annual credit sales}}{\text{Accounts receivable}}$	How many times the total receivables have been collected during the accounting period
5. Average collecting period	$\dfrac{\text{Accounts receivable}}{\text{Average daily sales}}$	The average length of time the firm waits to collect payment after sales

Table A-5 Shareholders' Return Ratios

Ratio	Formula	What It Shows
1. Dividend yield on common stock	$\dfrac{\text{Annual dividend per share}}{\text{Current market price per share}}$	A measure of return to common stockholders in the form of dividends
2. Price-earnings ratio	$\dfrac{\text{Current market price per share}}{\text{After-tax earnings per share}}$	An indication of market perception of the firm; usually, the faster-growing or less risky firms tend to have higher PE ratios than the slower-growing or more risky firms
3. Dividend payout ratio	$\dfrac{\text{Annual dividends per share}}{\text{After-tax earnings per share}}$	An indication of dividends paid out as a percentage of profits
4. Cash flow per share	$\dfrac{\text{After-tax profits} + \text{Depression}}{\text{Number of common shares outstanding}}$	A measure of total cash per share available for use by the firm

IVEY

Richard Ivey School of Business
The University of Western Ontario

John G. McIntyre leaned back from his computer and considered the just-released Statements of Allegations of the Staff of the Ontario Securities Commission and the U.S. Securities and Exchange Commission against Biovail Corporation and four of its current and former executives. His firm, McIntyre and Associates, was a boutique accounting firm that specialized in providing analysis and recommendations to legal firms representing various classes of shareholders in class action lawsuits. McIntyre had the pending Biovail allegations on his radar since late 2003, when Banc of America issued a "sell rating" on Biovail stock, citing the company's aggressive accounting practices. In light of these new charges, McIntyre was convinced that his firm would be engaged by one of his law firm clients to provide the forensic accounting analysis to them as the legal representatives of shareholders in a suit. McIntyre needed to review the multitude of information accumulated in the Biovail files and determine which of the many issues should be investigated more fully to support any case.

The Pharmaceutical Industry

The pharmaceutical industry was one of the largest and fastest growing manufacturing industries in Canada, contributing approximately $6 billion to Canadian GDP in 2005 and boasting an annual industry growth rate of 7.7 percent.[2] The industry was highly competitive and included brand-name corporations, generic drug manufacturers, smaller biopharmaceutical companies, and well-known research and clinical trial organizations. Exhibit 1 provides summary information from some of the largest, multinational players in the industry.

Most large pharmaceutical companies with locations in Canada were clustered in metropolitan areas such as Montreal and Toronto. The pharmaceutical industry was research and development (R&D) intensive. In 2007, the pharmaceutical industry was responsible for $1.96 billion, or 19 percent of total Canadian R&D spending.[3] The highly skilled Canadian workforce and the Canadian government's commitment to funding pharmaceutical research, either directly or via research and development tax credits, made Canada an attractive investment location for multinational pharmaceutical companies.[4] Furthermore, the North American Free Trade Agreement provided these multinational companies with tariff-free access to the large North American market, enhancing this industry's competitiveness.

Each new drug required a great deal of R&D before it could be approved. The approval process started with preclinical testing. This stage consisted of laboratory tests to show the efficacy and safety of the drug. Following successful preclinical testing, a company filed an Investigational New Drug application (IND) with the Food and Drug Administration (FDA) before it could begin to test the drug on humans. After approval was granted, three phases of clinical trials were conducted. These experimental phases studied the dosage, efficacy and side effects associated with the drug. The clinical trials included up to 3,000 human volunteers. Lastly, a company had to file a New Drug Application (NDA) with the FDA. In the United States, only five in 5,000 compounds that entered preclinical testing made it to human testing. Moreover, only one of those five tested on people was approved.[5] A company's bottom line could suffer drastically if the FDA did not grant approval.

Biovail Company Background

Eugene Melnyk started his first company in 1982 when he was just 23 years old. As the son of a Toronto doctor, he recognized the need of physicians to have a more time-efficient way to read the lengthy medical literature available to them. On this idea, Melnyk founded a publishing company called Trimel, which focused on creating crib notes for physicians who did not have time to read the extensive medical literature available to them.

In October 1990, Melnyk sold Trimel for Cdn$ 6.5 million and shifted focus toward the drug technologies of the pharmaceutical field. With a particular interest in the area of controlled-release drug delivery,[6] Melnyk acquired the proprietary technology. Melnyk then purchased a half-interest in Biovail SA, a financially troubled but well-respected Swiss pharmaceutical company.[7] The new company's operations were consolidated under the name Biovail.

Initially, Biovail licensed its products early in the development cycle to pharmaceutical companies that conducted clinical trials, regulatory processes, and the manufacturing and sale of their products. However, by the mid-1990s, Biovail had become an international, full-service pharmaceutical company based in Mississauga, Ontario.

In December 2001, Melnyk assumed the position of chief executive officer (CEO) of Biovail. The period during Melnyk's tenure as CEO was the focus of numerous civil, criminal, and regulatory investigations that severely increased expenses and legal fees and distracted the Biovail board and management. Melnyk stepped down from his role of CEO in October 2004.

Melnyk was also chairman of the board of directors during his tenure as CEO, and he remained as chairman until his resignation from the board in June 2007. As the reason for his resignation, however, Melnyk told shareholders at the company's annual meeting that he "can point to a dozen successful business deals in the last dozen years, but [he has] a hard time remembering a dozen quality days at home in the last six months."[8]

As of 2008, Biovail invested over 12 percent of its product sales back into research and development of drug technologies. The company's current commercial portfolio included Zovirax® Cream, Zovirax® Ointment, Wellbutrin XL®, Ultram® ER, Cardizem® LA, and a variety of generic[9] medications for therapeutic categories, including cardiology, depression and the central nervous system.[10]

In 2007, Melnyk, who was by this time a 48-year-old multi-millionaire and owner of the Ottawa Senators, was named the 70th wealthiest person in Canada with a net worth of $759 million.[11] In that year, Biovail reported revenues of US$801 million and net income of US$195.5 million.[12] Exhibit 2 includes condensed financial statements for the years 2006 and 2007.

The Truck Accident

On October 1, 2003, a fatal traffic accident occurred involving one of Biovail's delivery trucks. Before long, Biovail would blame this accident for its weak third-quarter revenues. Eight people were killed and 16 people were injured when an 18-wheeler truck crashed into a tour bus. The tour bus, in turn, crashed into Biovail's contract carrier. Though no one was hurt in Biovail's tractor-trailer, the vehicle (which had left the plant on September 30, 2003, F.O.B. destination) was loaded with finished goods that management claimed were severely damaged and, therefore, not salable.

Shortly after the accident, Biovail issued a press release[13] warning that the company's revenues for the third quarter of 2003 would be lower than previously expected. According to management, Biovail's ill-fated shipment contained $15 million to $20 million of one of the company's main revenue drivers, Wellbutrin XL®, an anti-depression medication.

The latest appearance of Biovail in the news, including pictures of the damaged truck, was fueling the fire for skeptical analysts who questioned the timing of the truck accident as well as the quantity of inventory involved. One analyst was quoted as saying "it is a curious thing when a company's financials are so dependent on one truckload of products that it just happens to be shipping on the last day of the quarter."[14]

Regardless of the most recent events, by 2003, Biovail had earned a questionable reputation. With a number of class action lawsuits outstanding and a chief executive officer whose conduct was constantly challenged by analysts, Biovail received widespread scrutiny from the media. Furthermore, Biovail's accounting methods were being questioned, leading investors to wonder whether the company had actually achieved the level of success that was previously reported in their statements.

The Banc of America Research Report

On October 8, 2003, seven days after the accident, Biovail's stock dropped 33 percent on the TSX to $25.20 per share. The plummet in stock value was assumed to be due to the aftermath of the inability for Biovail to meet its earnings forecast and to the October 2003 Banc of America research report that labelled Biovail's stock with a "sell rating." A TSX stock chart and historical prices for Biovail are presented in Exhibit 3.

The Banc of America report sought out the opinions of three forensic accounting experts who studied Biovail's press releases, transcripts, and most recent public filings. In the final report, one expert noted that Biovail's practices may be "aggressive but legal"; another noted that while Biovail's practices did not show that there was any widespread accounting impropriety, there was "perhaps aggressiveness beyond what we have observed at peer companies."[15]

The forensic accountants went on to criticize the company in many areas. The experts questioned the truck accident, noting that after they undertook further investigation, the situation seemed even more surprising. Having studied the photographs and video of the accident scene, they noted that, contrary to Biovail's high damage estimates, one-third to one-half of the truck interior appeared to be empty.

In addition to the peculiar traffic accident, the Banc of America report referenced many other reasons for the sell rating. For example, the experts noted that Biovail's product sales growth had become negative in 2003. Product sales growth, normally the company's primary growth driver, had significantly slowed for Biovail. In the company's statements, overall sales appeared solid but had been helped by royalties and licensing revenue gains. The experts questioned the sustainability of these two types of revenue streams.

Other areas of criticism included Biovail's declining R&D spending, its highly leveraged balance sheet and the company's low tax rate. The experts reported that Biovail's research and development spending had dropped substantially in the past few years. In addition, the report noted that in 2003, each of Biovail's top 10 selling products was purchased rather than developed in-house. The company's balance sheet contained an extremely high level of debt relative to its peer companies. Additionally, Biovail's tax rate was 6.9 percent, as compared to the next lowest tax rate in its peer group at 19.8 percent, and the report questioned whether or not this lower rate was sustainable.[16]

Finally, the area of analysis that was most troubling to the experts concerned Biovail's quality of earnings. The forensic accountants wrote about Biovail's long history of reporting operating earnings results that differed substantially from its GAAP earnings results. The accounting team was particularly concerned with the company's reliance on pro forma earnings.[17] While regulatory filings, including quarterly and annual reports, are prepared using Generally Accepted Accounting Principles (GAAP), press releases and conference calls provide management with other opportunities to communicate with investors about a company's performance using information that was generally not audited prior to its release.

As noted by Biovail management:

Management utilizes a measure of net income and earnings per share on a basis that excludes certain charges to better assess operating performance. Each of the items excluded is considered to be of a non-operational nature in the applicable period. Management has consistently applied this measure when discussing earnings or earnings guidance and will continue to do so going forward. Management believes that most of the Company's shareholders prefer to analyze the Company's results based on this measure, as it is consistent with industry practice. Earnings excluding charges are also disclosed to give investors the ability to further analyze the Company's results.[18]

Banc of America contended that the gap between Biovail's pro forma earnings and its GAAP earnings was among the largest in its peer group. Skepticism surrounded the non-GAAP earnings which portrayed a company that was growing faster than its underlying organic growth.[19] Exhibit 4 provides actual and pro forma financial statements for Biovail for the years 2001 and 2002 and the second quarter of 2003. Exhibit 5 provides select information from the Banc of America research report for Biovail and two of its competitors, Abbott Laboratories and Cephalon, Inc. Exhibits 6 and 7 provide earnings releases for the same two competitors.

Pointing Fingers

"As it has been throughout his career, Melnyk's entrepreneurial drive could be inspiring and effective in his organization. It could also be annoying and frustrating even to his own shareholders because Melnyk would not let even the slightest criticism from regulators and analysts pass."[20]

In March 2006, while he was executive chairman to the Biovail board of directors, Melnyk brought action against 22 defendants, alleging a market manipulation scheme was the reason for the drastic decline in Biovail's stock market price in recent years.[21] Specific allegations were released against Banc of America Securities in response to their October 2003 report. Melnyk accused reporters of influencing independent analysts to broadcast materially false and misleading information about Biovail.[22]

In early April 2006, weeks after Melnyk's market manipulation allegations, Melnyk found himself at the center of media attention as the OSC and SEC acknowledged probable suspicious trading activity.[23] Melnyk was accused of failing to file insider trading reports and acting contrary to public interest by failing to disclose his holdings to the public and understating his ownership stake in the company. The investigation encompassed a large number of trades in Cayman Island trust accounts where Melnyk was believed to be a beneficiary.[24] These trades occurred throughout Melnyk's tenure as chief executive officer from December 2001 through to October 2004.

On May 14, 2007, Eugene Melnyk and other Biovail executives received Wells Notices[25] from the U.S. Securities and Exchange Commission. The Wells Notices encompassed alleged violations of federal securities laws in accounting and disclosure practices.[26] Specific enforcement action against Melnyk was expected regarding his trading and reporting ownership positions of Biovail securities.

On May 18, 2007, Melnyk settled allegations from the Ontario Securities Commission concerning his failure to disclose US$1.3 billion in trades of Biovail shares. To settle this dispute, Melnyk paid the OSC Cdn$1 million and agreed to step down as executive chairman of the board, Biovail Corporation, and from all other director and officer roles relating to Biovail subsidiaries.[27]

On June 30, 2007, Melnyk retired from the board of Biovail Corporation. Since then, the role of executive chairman was assumed by Dr. Douglas Squires.[28] Squires had served Biovail as a director since 2005 and as lead director since 2007. Other new appointments included William Wells as the chief executive officer. Appointments were decided and announced by the Compensation, Nominating, and Corporate Governance Committee of the board of directors.[29] This committee was designed to insure independence and strategic appointments for Biovail leadership.

On February 25, 2008, Melnyk resigned as director and officer of BLS, another Biovail subsidiary. As of February 25, 2008, Melnyk was no longer employed by or a director of Biovail Corporation or any of its subsidiaries.

OSC and SEC Charges Laid

On March 24, 2008, not unexpectedly, both the Ontario Securities Commission and the U.S. Securities and Exchange Commission released a Statement of Allegations targeting Biovail Corporation and four former and current executives[30] and the company's financial reports for 2001, 2002 and Q1 and Q2, 2003. See Exhibit 8 for a summary of the key allegations.

The SEC's statement was particularly scathing, accusing the company and its management team of chronic fraudulent conduct, including financial reporting fraud and other intentional public misrepresentations as a result of their obsession with meeting quarterly and annual earnings targets. The SEC continued by alleging that when it "ultimately became impossible to continue to conceal the company's poor performance, Biovail actively misled investors and analysts as to its cause"[31] referring to the October 1, 2003, truck accident.

The alleged financial reporting fraud involved three accounting schemes that affected reporting periods from 2001 to 2003, including the improper use of a special purpose entity, revenue manipulation, and an intentional misstatement of foreign exchange losses.

Biovail created a special purpose entity, Pharmaceutical Technologies Corp. (Pharmatech), a development-stage company, to undertake an estimated $125 million[32] in research and development activities on behalf of Biovail in return for royalties in mid-2001. Pharmatech's sole shareholder, a past consultant for Biovail, invested US$1 million of which $350,000 was immediately refunded as a fee. The remainder was fully secured by Biovail.[33] As well, the company entered into a share option agreement with the sole shareholder of Pharmatech permitting Biovail to purchase all of the stockholder's Pharmatech shares at any time until December 31, 2006, in exchange for a fixed purchase price. On December 27, 2002, as a result of Pharmatech's banker's refusal to extend financing directly to Pharmatech, Biovail exercised its purchase option and repaid the bank (which also happened to be the company's principal bank) in full. As a result of these transactions, the SEC concluded that Biovail's financial reports were materially false and misleading, causing net income to be overstated by approximately 50 percent in the third quarter of 2001, 32 percent in the 2001 annual financial statements, 15 percent in the first quarter 2002, 18 percent in the second quarter 2002, and 16 percent in the third quarter 2002, and understated by approximately 17 percent in the 2002 annual financial statements.[34]

In October 2001, Biovail entered into an agreement with a distributor whereby Biovail would produce Wellbutrin XL (WXL), which had not yet received FDA approval, and then sell it to the distributor. Biovail was to produce sample products (sold at cost), which the distributor could distribute to physicians as a promotional tour as well as trade products (sold at normal markups) packaged and labeled for commercial sale. By June 2003, the FDA had indicated that WXL was "approvable" subject to some labeling changes. Final approval was not received until August 29, 2003. On June 19, 2003, Biovail contacted its distributor and requested that, prior to June 30, 2003, the distributor place an order for trade WXL. Biovail committed to segregating the specific inventory related to the purchase order in a separate location in its Manitoba warehouse.[35] Biovail further indicated that if the distributor failed to place such an order, the company would not fully commit its manufacturing facilities to producing WXL tablets in advance of the product launch. The distributor sent Biovail a purchase order, and Biovail invoiced the distributor for approximately US$8 million, resulting in an increased second quarter operating income of US$4.4 million.[36] Subsequent to the receipt of the purchase order, management became concerned about the expiry date on the segregated inventory. The segregated inventory was then used to fill orders from the distributor for sample products (at sample- or cost-based prices).

In December 2002, Biovail acquired the rights to certain drugs and assumed a liability denominated in Canadian dollars. Since Biovail reported its results in U.S. dollars, it was required to account for this liability in its financial statements in U.S. dollars by converting the liability at the current rate at each balance sheet date. On March 31, 2003, the Canadian dollar had strengthened against the U.S. dollar compared to its December 31, 2002, rate. Though the company correctly accounted for the liability on its 2002 year-end balance sheet, it continued to use the exchange rate from December 2002 on its March 31, 2003, and June 30, 2003, balance sheets. As a result, the quarterly financial statements for first two quarters of 2003 did not reflect the resultant exchange loss or an accurate statement of the liability. Biovail overstated its net income by approximately US$5 million and US$4 million in the first and second quarters of 2003, respectively. According to the OSC and the SEC, the chief financial officer (CFO) at the time became aware of the error in early July 2003, but took no steps to correct the error or to disclose the error until the company's March 3, 2004, press release.

As McIntyre pondered the two Statements of Allegations in front of him, he found it particularly interesting that Biovail's claim that the truck accident had caused the company to miss its third quarter earnings target appeared to have precipitated the OSC and SEC's investigation. Much of both documents focused on the allegations that the statements made in the company's October 3, 2003, press release were materially misleading or untrue.

Class Action Law Suit

McIntyre and Associates had significant experience in providing forensic accounting analysis to law firms involved in class action lawsuits against corporations accused of breaching securities laws by making false and misleading statements about the state of their business. A class action lawsuit organized the claims of numerous people, in this case shareholders, with a common interest to engage corporate entities in legal action to rectify any immoral actions committed by these entities.[37]

The typical process for a class action lawsuit involved the hiring of legal representation and soliciting the court for "class action" case certification. The certification of "class action" was contingent on the number of shareholders involved in the suit, the extent of commonality in damages experienced by these shareholders and whether the legal representation was aligned with and representative of the shareholder interests.[38] A time period was established for the start and end of the claims period, and only holders of shares during that period were eligible to participate in the class action lawsuit. Once class-action certification was granted, all eligible shareholders were informed and prompted to contribute input into the case. Eligible shareholders then became entitled to a pro-rated portion of any awards received, net of legal expenses.

Class action claims could be settled through negotiation agreements with the corporation, or they could be brought to trial where a judge would render a decision. In order to gain negotiating leverage, the plaintiff had to prove that management intentionally misled shareholders through their actions or through the information that they distributed and that those actions lead to a destruction of shareholder value.[39]

McIntyre's Task

As he sifted through the Biovail files, McIntyre knew there were several issues to consider when preparing the supporting arguments for a law firm to take the lead in a possible class action suit on behalf of Biovail shareholders. Much of what he had read about the actions of Biovail executives might be construed as just poor management judgment; on the other hand, as noted by the OSC and SEC, perhaps this was a case of fraudulent conduct. McIntyre would also have to identify a period of time for which the issues would have impacted shareholders and new purchasers of Biovail shares. The chosen time period would determine the eligible members of the class action suit and the market value destruction that had occurred to their investments in Biovail. McIntyre took a sip of his cappuccino and began to investigate the issues that he believed warranted further examination.

Exhibit 1 Forbes 2000 Largest Companies Drug & Biotechnology Industry (in US$ billions)

Global Rank	Company	Country	Sales	Profits	Assets
57	Pfizer	United States	48.42	8.14	115.27
58	Johnson & Johnson	United States	61.10	10.58	80.95
67	Sanofi-aventis	France	40.95	7.68	104.98
72	Novartis	Switzerland	40.22	12.62	71.89
74	Roche Holding	Switzerland	40.65	8.60	67.72
79	GlaxoSmithKline	United Kingdom	45.07	10.35	57.16
148	AstraZeneca	United Kingdom	29.21	5.53	46.91
162	Merck & Co.	United States	24.20	3.28	48.35
167	Abbott Laboratories	United States	25.91	3.61	39.71
171	Wyeth	United States	22.40	4.62	42.72
228	Amgen	United States	14.77	3.17	34.64
229	Eli Lilly & Co.	United States	18.63	2.95	26.79
257	Bristol-Myers Squibb	United States	19.35	2.17	26.17

Source: http://www.forbes.com/lists, accessed September 27, 2008.

Exhibit 2 Biovail Corporation Consolidated Statements of Income in accordance with United Stated Generally Accepted Accounting Principles (All dollar amounts expressed in thousands of U.S. dollars)

	2007	2006
REVENUE		
Product sales	$801,046	$1,021,278
Research and development	23,828	21,593
Royalty and other	17,944	24,851
	842,818	1,067,722
EXPENSES		
Cost of goods sold	223,680	211,152
Research and development	118,117	95,479
Selling, general and administrative	161,001	238,441
Amortization	48,049	56,457
Legal settlements, net of insurance recoveries	95,114	14,400
Asset impairments, net of gain on disposal	9,910	143,000
Restructuring costs	668	15,126
Contract costs (recovery)	(1,735)	54,800
	654,804	828,855
Operating income	188,014	238,867
Interest income	24,563	29,199
Interest expense	(9,745)	(35,203)

(Continued)

Exhibit 2 Biovail Corporation Consolidated Statements of Income in accordance with United Stated Generally Accepted Accounting Principles (All dollar amounts expressed in thousands of U.S. dollars)

	2007	2006
Foreign exchange gain	5,491	(2,360)
Equity loss	(2,528)	(529)
Other income (expense)	2,944	—
Income from continuing operations before provision for income taxes	208,739	229,974
Provision for income taxes	13,200	14,500
Income from continuing operations	195,539	215,474
Loss from discontinued operation	0	−3,848
Net income	$ 195,539	$ 211,626

Sources: http://www.biovail.com.

Exhibit 2 (*Continued*) Biovail Corporation Consolidated Balance Sheets in accordance with United Stated Generally Accepted Accounting Principles (All dollar amounts expressed in Thousands of U.S. dollars)

	2007	2006
ASSETS		
Current	2007	2006
Cash and cash equivalents	$ 433,641	$ 834,540
Marketable securities	3,895	—
Accounts receivable	111,114	129,247
Insurance recoveries receivable	62,942	—
Inventories	80,745	78,871
Prepaid expenses and other current assets	14,680	15,056
	707,017	1,057,624
Marketable securities	24,417	5,677
Long-term investments	24,834	56,442
Property, plant and equipment, net	238,457	211,979
Intangible assets, net	630,514	697,645
Good will	100,294	100,294
Deferred tax assets, net of valuation allowance	20,700	—
Other long-term assets, net	35,882	62,781
	$ 1,782,115	$ 2,192,442
LIABILITIES		
Current		
Accounts payable	50,415	44,988
Dividends payable	—	80,222

(Continued)

Exhibit 2 (*Continued*) Biovail Corporation Consolidated Balance Sheets in accordance with United Stated Generally Accepted Accounting Principles (All dollar amounts expressed in thousands of U.S. dollars)

	2007	2006
Accrued liabilities	74,363	101,219
Accrued legal settlements	148,000	14,400
Accrued contract costs	45,065	54,800
Income taxes payable	647	41,596
Deferrend revenue	49,088	61,916
Current portion of long-term liabilities	—	11,146
	$ 367,578	$ 410,287
Deferred revenue	55,653	73,621
Income taxes payable	54,100	—
Long-term obligations	—	399,379
Other long-term liabilities	6,965	6,898
	484,296	890,185
SHAREHOLDER'S EQUITY		
Common shares, no par value, unlimited shares authorized,161,023,729, and 160,444,070 issues and outstanding at December 31, 2007 and 2006, respectively	1,489,807	1,476,930
Additional paid in capital	23,925	14,952
Deficit	(278,495)	(232,733)
Accumulated other comprehensive income	62,582	43,108
	$ 1,782,115	$ 2,192,442

Sources: http://www.biovail.com.

Exhibit 2 (*Continued*) Biovail Corporation Consolidated Statements of Cash Flows in accordance with United Stated Generally Accepted Accounting Principles (All dollar amounts expressed in thousands of U.S. dollars)

	2007	2006
CASH FLOWS FROM OPERATING ACTIVITIES		
Net income	$195,539	$211,626
Adjustments to reconcile net income to net cash provided by continuing operating activities		
Depreciation and amortization	94,985	92,150
Amortization and write-down of deferred financing costs	4,821	2,300
Amortization and write-down of discounts on long-term obligations	962	1,291
Accrued legal settlements, net of insurance recoveries	78,652	14,400
Gains on disposal of investments and intangible assets	24,356	4,000
Impairment charges and asset write-offs	21,268	151,140

(Continued)

Exhibit 2 (*Continued***)** Biovail Corporation Consolidated Statements of Cash Flows in accordance with United Stated Generally Accepted Accounting Principles (All dollar amounts expressed in thousands of U.S. dollars)

	2007	2006
Stock-based compensation	10,633	14,794
Accrued contract costs	9,735	54,800
Premium paid on early extinguishment of debt	7,854	—
Equity loss	2,528	529
Loss from discontinued operations	—	3,848
Other	5,578	2,083
Changes in operating assets and liabilities		
Accounts receivable	18,052	4,688
Insurance recoveries receivable	7,994	—
Inventories	3,023	10,906
Prepaid expenses and other current assets	376	311
Accounts payable	3,273	12,999
Accrued liabilities	26,496	13,694
Income taxes payable	7,514	3,897
Deferred revenue	30,796	42,319
Net cash provided by continuing operating activities	340,853	522,517
CASH FLOWS FROM INVESTING ACTIVITIES		
Proceeds on disposals of investments, net of costs	52,669	—
Additions to property, plant, and equipment, net	35,086	44,802
Additions to marketable securities	34,534	3,196
Proceeds from sales and maturities of marketable securities	3,282	4,854
Additions to long-term investments	1,376	1,303
Proceeds on disposals of intangible assets	—	4,000
Acquisitions of intangible assets	—	—
Net cash provided by (used in) continuing investing activities	15,045	40,447
CASH FLOWS FROM FINANCING ACTIVITIES		
Redemption of Senior Subordinated Notes	406,756	1,098
Dividends paid	321,523	80,062
Repayments of other long-term obligations	11,250	25,280
Issuance of common shares	11,217	15,634
Repayment of deferred compensation obligation, net	338	175
Financing costs paid	—	1,275
Payment on termination of interest rate swap	—	—

(Continued)

Exhibit 2 (*Continued***)** Biovail Corporation Consolidated Statements of Cash Flows in accordance with United Stated Generally Accepted Accounting Principles (All dollar amounts expressed in thousands of U.S. dollars)

	2007	2006
Net cash used in continuing financing activities	728,650	92,256
CASH FLOWS FROM DISCONTINUED OPERATION		
Net cash used in operating activities	—	558
Net cash used in investing activities	—	—
Net cash used in discontinued operation	—	558
Effect of exchange rate changes on cash and cash equivalents	1,943	5
Net increase (decrease) in cash and cash equivalents	400,899	389,251
Cash and cash equivalents, beginning of year	834,540	445,289
Cash and cash equivalents, end of year	$ 433,641	$ 834,540

Sources: http://www.biovail.com.

Exhibit 3 Biovail Stock Price History

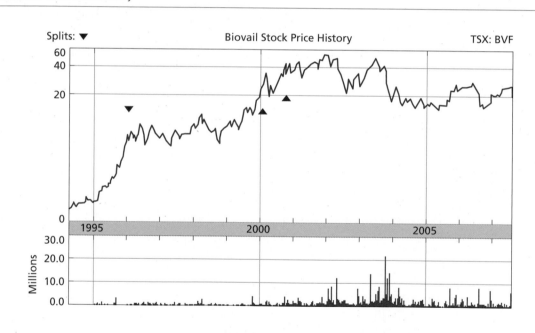

BVF.TO		
Date	Open	Close
29-Sep-03	$ 36.80	$ 38.14
30-Sep-03	$ 38.10	$ 37.15
01-Oct-03	$ 37.50	$ 37.24
02-Oct-03	$ 36.80	$ 37.77
03-Oct-03	$ 31.94	$ 31.10
06-Oct-03	$ 30.82	$ 28.70
07-Oct-03	$ 28.85	$ 29.05
08-Oct-03	$ 27.65	$ 25.20

Source: http://ca.finance.yahoo.com/q/bc?s. Copyright 2008 Yahoo! Inc., http://finance.yahoo.com.

Exhibit 4 Biovail Corporation Earnings Release Income Statement (US$ millions)

	2001	2002	2003 2Q cum
Revenue			
Product sales	$521.2	$646.0	$284.6
Research and development	14.6	28.4	6.3
Co-promotion, royalty and licensing	47.5	113.6	117.8
	583.3	788.0	408.7
Expenses			
Cost of goods sold	126.0	164.7	48.7
Research and development	51.0	52.2	39.8
Seling, general and administrative	110.1	165.7	103.1
Amortization	44.5	71.5	86.4
Write-down of assets	80.5	31.9	—
Acquired research and development	—	167.7	84.2
Settlements	—	—	(34.1)
	412.1	653.7	328.1
Operating income (loss)	171.2	134.3	80.6
Interest income	2.7	3.6	4.7
Interest expense	(36.2)	(32.0)	(19.5)
Other income	—	3.4	6.7
Debt conversion premiums	(34.9)	—	—
Income (loss) before provision for income taxes	102.8	109.3	72.5
Provision for income taxes	15.3	21.5	10.4
Net income (loss)	$87.5	$87.8	$62.1
Diluted earning per share	$0.58	$0.55	$0.39
Net income (loss)	$ 87.5	$87.8	$62.1
Add (deduct) certain items			
Write-down of assets	80.5	31.9	—
Acquired research and development	—	167.7	84.2
Other income	—	(3.4)	—
Debt conversion premiums	34.9	—	—
Net income excluding certain items	$202.9	$284.0	$146.3
Diluted earnings per share excluding certain items	$1.35	$1.77	$0.91

Source: www.sedar.com, Biovail press release.

Exhibit 5 Excerpts from Banc of America Research Report Earnings Quality Analysis

Aggregate ProForma Earnings versus Aggregate GAAP Earnings from 1998 to 2002

Company	ProForma EPS	GAAP EPS	Absolute Difference	Relative Earnings Ratio*
Median**	$4.07	$3.05	$0.53	12%
Abbott Labs	$8.90	$7.63	$1.27	14%
Cephalon	$(3.83)	$(5.60)	$1.77	46%
Biovail	$4.75	$(0.59)	$5.34	112%

*Calculated as (ProForma earnings – GAAP earnings)/ProForma Earnings.
**Median represents the median return on invested capital for 16 companies in Biovail's peer group.

Return on Invested Capital*—GAAP Earnings versus ProForma Earnings

ROIC – GAAP Earnings

Company	2000	2001	2002	2003 2Q
Median**	13.20%	11.40%	14.10%	14.40%
Abbott	29.70%	13.50%	19.90%	15.70%
Cephalon	N/A	−2.80%	13.80%	9.20%
Biovail	−18.90%	10.40%	8.00%	4.20%

ROIC – ProForma Earnings

Company	2000	2001	2002	2003 2Q
Median**	14.90%	13.70%	16.30%	17.90%
Abbott	29.70%	24.10%	22.90%	20.90%
Cephalon	N/A	2.40%	7.40%	4.40%
Biovail	14.80%	20.90%	21.40%	17.70%

*Return on Invested Capital is calculated using the formula: (Net Income – Dividends)/Total Capital.
**Median represents the median return on invested capital for 16 companies in Biovail's peer group.
Source: Banc of America Research Report, October 10, 2003.

Exhibit 6 Abbott Laboratories Earnings Release Income Statement (US$ millions)

	2001	2002
Net sales	$16,285.2	$17,684.7
Cost of products sold	7,748.4	8,506.3
Research & development (R&D)	1,577.5	1,561.8
Acquired in-process R&D	1,330.4	107.7
Selling, general & administrative	3,734.9	3,978.8
Total operating cost and expenses	14,391.2	14,154.6
Operating earnings	1,894.0	3,530.1
Net interest expense	234.8	205.2
Net foreign exchange loss	31.4	74.6

(Continued)

Exhibit 6 Abbott Laboratories Income Statement (US$ millions)

	2001	2002
(Income) from TAP Pharm. Products Inc. joint venture	(333.8)	(666.8)
Other (income)/expense, net	78.5	243.7
Earnings before taxes	1,883.1	3,673.4
Taxes on earnings	332.8	879.7
Net earnings	$1,550.3	$2,793.7
Net earnings excluding acquired in-process R&D and other one-time charges	$2,942.8	$3,242.5
(Note 1)		
Diluted earnings per common share (US GAAP)	$0.99	$1.78
Diluted earnings per common share excluding acquired in-process R&D and other one-time charges	$1.88	$2.06
Average no. of common shares outstanding plus dilutive common stock options	$1,566.0	$1,573.3

Note 1: Year 2002 excludes a non-cash charge of $0.05 for acquired in-process research and development related to the acquisition of Biocompatibles' stent business and the Medtronic alliance, $0.06 for one-time charges related to the consent decree with the FDA, $0.09 non-cash charge related to the decline in the value of certain equity investments, and $0.08 related to previously announced restructuring expenses. Year 2001 excludes non-cash charge of $0.56 for acquired in-process research and development, $0.17 for a one-time adjustment to income from TAP joint venture and $0.16 for other one-time charges related to the acquisition of the pharmaceutical business of BASF.

Source: http://www.abbott.com.

Exhibit 7 Cephalon Inc. Earnings Release Income Statement (US$ millions)

	2001	2002
Revenues		
Product sales	$226.1	$465.9
Other revenues	35.9	41.0
	262.0	506.9
Cost and Expenses		
Cost of product sales	44.9	74.2
Research and development	83.0	128.3
Selling, general and administrative	96.2	172.8
Merger and integration costs	0.1	—
Acquired in-process research and development	20.0	—
	244.2	375.3
EBITDA (a)	17.9	131.6
Depreciation and amortization	(14.4)	(35.5)
Debt exchange expense	(52.4)	—
Gain (charge) on early extinguishment of debt	3.0	(7.1)
Other income (expense), net	(9.4)	(26.6)

(Continued)

Exhibit 7 Cephalon Inc. Earnings Release Income Statement (US$ millions)

	2001	2002
Income (loss) before income taxes	(55.4)	62.4
Income tax benefit (expense), net	—	112.6
Income before cumulative effect of changing inventory costing method	(55.4)	175.0
Cumulative effect of changing inventory costing method from FIFO to LIFO	—	(3.5)
Net income (loss)	(55.4)	171.5
Dividends on convertible exchangeable preferred stock	(5.7)	—
Income (loss) applicable to common shares	$(61.1)	$ 171.5
Basic income (loss) per common share		
Income (loss) per common share excluding cumulative effect of changing inventory method	$(1.27)	$3.17
Cumulative effect of changing inventory costing method	$ —	$(0.06)
	$ (1.27)	$ 3.11
Diluted income (loss) per common share		
Income (loss) per common share excluding the effect of changing the inventory method	$ (1.27)	$ 3.07
Cumulative effect of changing inventory costing method	$ —	$ (0.06)
	$ (1.27)	$ 3.01
Weighted average number of common shares outstanding	48.3	55.1
Weighted average number of common shares outstanding - assuming dilution	48.3	57.0
Reconciliation of Income (loss) applicable to common shares to adjusted net income:		
Income (loss) applicable to common shares	$ (61.1)	$ 171.5
Certain charges:		
Deferred tax valuation adjustment	—	(116.7)
CNS joint venture (b)	—	6.5
Short-term bridge financing and other merger related expenses	1.6	—
Acquired in-process research and development	20.0	—
Debt exchange expense	52.4	—
(Gain) charge on early extinguishment of debt	(3.0)	7.1
Cumulative effect of changing inventory costing method	—	3.5
Adjusted net income	$ 9.9	$ 71.9
Basic adjusted net income per common share	$ 0.20	$ 1.31
Diluted adjusted net income per common share	$ 0.19	$ 1.26

(a) Earnings (loss) before net interest, depreciation, amortization, debt exchange expense, foreign currency exchange, dividends on convertible exchangeable preferred stock and cumulative effect of changing inventory costing method.
(b) Includes $3,508,000 from selling, general and administrative expense and $2,973,000 from other expense.

Source: Cephalon, Inc.

Exhibit 8 Summary of Key Allegations in the OSC and SEC Reports

Biovail Corporation engaged in chronic fraudulent conduct including financial reporting fraud and other intentional public misrepresentations. Obsessed with meeting quarterly and annual earnings guidance, Biovail executives repeatedly overstated earnings and hid losses in order to deceive investors and create the appearance of achieving that goal. When it became impossible to conceal the company's poor performance, Biovail actively misled investors to create the appearance of meeting their goals.

The financial reporting fraud involves three accounting schemes that affected reporting periods from 2001 to 2003. They are:

1. A transaction through which Biovail, over a period of several reporting periods in 2001 and 2002, improperly moved off its financial statements to the statements of a special purpose entity known as Parmatech. Revenent transactions included the movement of expenses incurred in the R&D of Biovail products that totaled $47 million through September 30, 2002 and liabilities that exceeded $51 million through that date.
2. A fictitious bill and hold transaction that Biovail created to record approximately $8 million in revenue in the second quarter.
3. An intentional misstatement of foreign exchange losses that caused Biovail's second quarter 2003 loss to be understated by about $3.9 million.

In October 2003, Biovail intentionally and falsely attributed nearly half of its failure to meet its third quarter 2003 earnings guidance to a truck accident involving a shipment of Wellbutrin XL®. Biovail intentionally misstated in press releases and public statements both the effect of the accident on Biovail's third quarter earnings as well as grossly overstating the value of the product involved in the truck accident. The accident, in fact, had no effect on third quarter earnings.

Each of the fraudulent accounting schemes had a material effect on Biovail's financial statements from the relevant quarter and years and was engineered by Biovail's senior management in order to manage Biovail's earnings. In effecting these schemes, Biovail management also intentionally deceived its auditors as to the true nature of the transactions. The truck accident misstatements were intended to and did mislead analysts and the investing public concerning the significance of Biovail's failure to meet its own guidance.

Biovail's then-chairman and chief executive, Eugene Melnyk, also violated share ownership disclosure provisions by failing to identify his beneficial ownership held by several trusts in which he continued to exercise both investment and trading authority.

Source: Statement of Allegations of Staff of the Ontario Securities Commission in the Matter of Biovail Corporation, Eugene N. Melnyk, Brian H. Crombie, John R. Miszuk, and Kenneth G. Howling at March 24, 2008; Securities and Exchange Commission against Biovail Corporation, Eugene N. Melnyk, Brian Crombie, John Miszuk, and Kenneth G. Howling at March 24, 2008.

NOTES

1. This case has been written on the basis of published sources only. Consequently, the interpretation and perspectives presented in this case are not necessarily those of Biovail Corporation or of any of its employees.
2. http://www.ic.gc.ca/epic/site/lsi-isv.nsf/en/li00256e.html, accessed October 20, 2008.
3. http://www.newswire.ca/en/releases/archive/October2008/23/c8768.html, accessed November 17, 2008.
4. Ibid.
5. http://www.allp.com/drug_dev.htm, accessed June 23, 2003.
6. Rather than an individual taking several doses of the same pill in one day, controlled-release technology allows people to take only one dosage of medication, and the technology releases the drug at a controlled pace.
7. Report on business, *The Globe and Mail*, October 2008.
8. http://www.cbc.ca/money/story/2007/05/16/biovailmelynk.html, accessed October 2, 2008.
9. A generic drug is the proven bioequivalent to its branded counterpart. Generic drugs are offered at a lower price.
10. http://www.biovail.com, accessed October 23, 2008.
11. http://www.canadianbusiness.com/after_hours/article.jsp?content=20071128_210746_3160&page=2, October 23, 2008.
12. *Triangle Business Journal*, April 21, 2003.

13. Known as the "October 3, 2003" press release.
14. Ibid.
15. Banc of America report, October 10, 2003.
16. Ibid.
17. Pro forma reporting had long been used by companies to paint a "what if" picture, where pro forma numbers were used to show the comparability of financial information in a year when a company acquired or divested of another company to how the financial statements would have looked had the merger taken place at an earlier time or not at all. In recent years companies, including Biovail, have been using unregulated pro forma earnings as a means of showing shareholders a more sustainable view of company profits. Pro forma earnings were often higher than GAAP earnings since companies often excluded a number of expenses they considered to be non-recurring, such as asset write-downs, litigation settlements, merger/acquisition-related expenses, restructuring charges, amortization expenses, research and development charges and stock-related compensation expenses.
18. Biovail press release, March 4, 2003.
19. Ibid.
20. Report on Business, *The Globe and Mail*, October 2008.

21. http://www.sedar.com, Notice of Annual Meeting of Shareholders & Management Proxy Circular, June 25, 2008.

22. http://www.globeandmail.com, March 28, 2006.

23. http://www.globeandmail.com, April 4, 2006.

24. http://www.globeandmail.com, July 31, 2006.

25. A Wells Notice is a letter that the U.S. Securities and Exchange Commission sends to people or firms when it is planning to bring an enforcement action against them.

26. http://www.reportonbusiness.com, May 14, 2007.

27. http://www.globeandmail.com, March 24, 2008.

28. http://www.sedar.com, Management Discussion and Analysis, November 2007.

29. http://www.sedar.com, Biovail Press Release, June 28, 2007.

30. Executives included Eugene Melnyk, Brian Crombie (former CFO), John Miszuk (VP, Controller and Assistant Secretary), and Kenneth Howling (Senior VP and CFO).

31. Securities and Exchange Commission, Statement of Allegations, March 24, 2008.

32. Ontario Securities Commission, Statement of Allegations, March 24, 2008.

33. Ibid.

34. Securities and Exchange Commission, Statement of Allegations, March 24, 2008.

35. Hence the designation of this transaction as a "bill and hold" transaction.

36. Ontario Securities Commission, Statement of Allegations, March 24, 2008.

37. http://www.classaction.ca, accessed November 17, 2008.

38. http://classactiondefense.jmbm.com/2006/05/defending_against_class_action_4.html, accessed November 17, 2008.

39. http://www.web-access.net/~aclark/frames45.htm, accessed November 17, 2008.

CASE 2
Wal-Mart Stores, Inc. (WMT)

Francine Barley, David Bragg, Misty Dawson, Hammad Shah, Brian Sillanpaa, Nathan Sleeper
Dominik Steinkuler, Prof. Lutz Kaufmann, Daniel Schmidt

Arizona State University

Lee Scott ignored his fear of public speaking as he prepared to step in front of 20,000 people at the Bud Walton Arena in Fayetteville, Arkansas, on June 1, 2007.[1] For his seventh year as Wal-Mart CEO, Scott addressed his company's shareholders at its annual meeting.

Outside the building, the local "Against the Wal" protesters were back for the fourth year in a row, clutching a list of seven demands: "living wage," "affordable health care," "end discrimination," "zero tolerance on child labor," "respect communities," "respect the environment," and "stop union busting."[2]

Inside the arena, shareholders had their own concerns, with declining share prices and 11 shareholder proposals—all opposed by the company.[3] Since Scott became CEO in 2000, Wal-Mart's stock price has dipped about 27 percent, from $64.50 to the $47 range.[4]

In the same timeframe, competitor Costco's stock price has appreciated roughly 20 percent, and Target's has climbed more than 70 percent[5] (see Exhibit 1). Analysts are saying Wal-Mart's "glory days are over" and its stock is "dead money."[6] Some observers are speculating that Scott's days as CEO may be numbered if he is unable to get the company back on track soon.

It is a big company to change. From its humble origins 45 years ago as a single shop in the Ozarks, Wal-Mart has grown to 1.8 million employees supporting more than 6,700 stores in 14 countries, serving 175 million customers per week and pulling in an average of $6.6 billion in weekly sales.[7] Over the past decade, Wal-Mart doubled its store count, tripled its revenue, and nearly quadrupled its net income[8] (see Exhibits 2 and 3). Wal-Mart earned more in its first quarter of fiscal 2007

-Mart, Target, and Costco, January 3, 2000, through May 14, 2007

ıhoo.com/charts#chart6:symbol=wmt;range=20000103,20070518;compare=cost+tgt;indicator=volume;charttype=
ed, May 17.

Exhibit 2 Wal-Mart Retail Units and Sales, 1997–2007

	2007	2006	2005	2004	2003	2002	2001	2000	1999	1998	1997
Number of retail units											
Wal-Mart Stores	1,074	1,209	1,353	1,478	1,568	1,647	1,736	1,801	1,869	1,921	1,960
Supercenters	2,257	1,980	1,713	1,471	1,258	1,066	888	721	564	441	344
Neighborhood Markets	112	100	85	64	49	31	19	7	4	0	0
SAM'S Clubs	579	567	551	538	525	500	475	463	451	443	436
US Stores Total	4,022	3,856	3,702	3,551	3,400	3,244	3,118	2,992	2,888	2,805	2,740
International Stores	2,760	2,181	1,480	1,248	1,163	1,050	955	892	605	568	314
Total Stores	**6,782**	**6,037**	**5,182**	**4,799**	**4,563**	**4,294**	**4,073**	**3,884**	**3,493**	**3,373**	**3,054**
Percentage of total retail units											
Wal-Mart Stores	26.7%	31.4%	36.5%	41.6%	46.1%	50.8%	55.7%	60.2%	64.7%	68.5%	71.5%
Supercenters	56.1%	51.3%	46.3%	41.4%	37.0%	32.9%	28.5%	24.1%	19.5%	15.7%	12.6%
Neighborhood Markets	2.8%	2.6%	2.3%	1.8%	1.4%	1.0%	0.6%	0.2%	0.1%	0.0%	0.0%
SAM'S Clubs	14.4%	14.7%	14.9%	15.2%	15.4%	15.4%	15.2%	15.5%	15.6%	15.8%	15.9%
International	40.7%	36.1%	28.6%	26.0%	25.5%	24.5%	23.4%	23.0%	17.3%	16.8%	10.3%
Sales by segment											
Wal-Mart	$226,294	$209,910	$191,826	$174,220	$157,120	$139,131	$121,889	$108,721	$95,395	$83,820	$74,840
SAM'S Clubs	$41,582	$39,798	$37,119	$34,537	$31,702	$29,395	$26,798	$24,801	$22,881	$20,668	$19,785
International	$77,116	$59,237	$52,543	$47,572	$40,794	$35,485	$32,100	$22,728	$12,247	$7,517	$5,002
Total	**$344,992**	**$308,945**	**$281,488**	**$256,329**	**$229,616**	**$204,011**	**$180,787**	**$156,250**	**$130,523**	**$112,005**	**$99,627**
Percentage of sales by segment											
Wal-Mart	65.6%	67.9%	68.1%	68.0%	68.4%	68.2%	67.4%	69.6%	73.1%	74.8%	75.1%
SAM'S Clubs	12.1%	12.9%	13.2%	13.5%	13.8%	14.4%	14.8%	15.9%	17.5%	18.5%	19.9%
International	22.4%	19.2%	18.7%	18.6%	17.8%	17.4%	17.8%	14.5%	9.4%	6.7%	5.0%
Percentage of sales											
Domestic	77.6%	80.8%	81.3%	81.4%	82.2%	82.6%	82.2%	85.5%	90.6%	93.3%	95.0%
International	22.4%	19.2%	18.7%	18.6%	17.8%	17.4%	17.8%	14.5%	9.4%	6.7%	5.0%
Percentage change in sales											
Domestic	7.3%	9.1%	9.7%	10.6%	12.0%	13.3%	11.4%	12.9%	13.2%	10.4%	2.0%
International	30.2%	12.7%	10.4%	16.6%	15.0%	10.5%	41.2%	85.6%	62.9%	50.3%	25.9%
Percentage sales change											
Domestic	50.4%	75.6%	80.2%	74.6%	79.3%	85.4%	61.8%	59.3%	74.5%	79.7%	
International	49.6%	24.4%	19.8%	25.4%	20.7%	14.6%	33.2%	40.7%	25.5%	20.3%	

Source: 2007, 2002, Wal-Mart Annual Reports.

Exhibit 3 Wal-Mart Income, 1997–2007

Income Statement
(figures in $ millions; fiscal year ends 1/31)

	2007	2006	2005	2004	2003	2002	2001	2000	1999	1998	1997
Total Operating Revenue	$348,650	$312,101	$284,310	$252,791	$226,479	$201,166	$178,028	$153,345	$129,161	$112,005	$99,627
Cost of Sales	$264,152	$237,649	$216,832	$195,922	$175,769	$156,807	$138,438	$119,526	$101,456	$88,163	$78,897
Gross Operating Profit	**$ 84,498**	**$ 74,452**	**$ 67,478**	**$ 56,869**	**$ 50,710**	**$ 44,359**	**$ 39,590**	**$ 33,819**	**$ 27,705**	**$ 23,842**	**$20,730**
Gross Margins	24.2%	23.9%	23.7%	22.5%	22.4%	22.1%	22.2%	22.1%	21.4%	21.3%	20.8%
Operating, Selling, G&A Exp.	$ 64,001	$ 55,739	$ 50,178	$ 43,877	$ 39,178	$ 34,275	$ 29,942	$ 25,182	$ 21,469	$ 18,831	$ 16,437
Operating Income	**$ 20,497**	**$ 18,713**	**$ 17,300**	**$ 12,992**	**$ 11,532**	**$ 10,084**	**$ 9,648**	**$ 8,637**	**$ 6,236**	**$ 5,011**	**$ 4,293**
Net Interest Expense	$ 1,529	$ 1,178	$ 980	$ 825	$ 930	$ 1,183	$ 1,194	$ 837	$ 595	$ 716	$ 807
Income Before Taxes	$ 18,968	$ 17,535	$ 16,320	$ 12,167	$ 10,602	$ 8,901	$ 8,454	$ 7,800	$ 5,641	$ 4,295	$ 3,486
Taxes	$ 6,365	$ 5,803	$ 5,589	$ 3,071	$ 2,662	$ 2,183	$ 2,008	$ 2,218	$ 1,432	$ 871	$ 508
Effective Tax Rate	33.6%	33.1%	34.2%	25.2%	25.1%	24.5%	23.8%	28.4%	25.4%	20.3%	14.6%
Net Income from Operations	$ 12,603	$ 11,732	$ 10,731	$ 9,096	$ 7,940	$ 6,718	$ 6,446	$ 5,582	$ 4,209	$ 3,424	$ 2,978
Other Items	$ (894)	$ (177)	$ (215)	$ (42)	$ 15	$ (126)	$ (211)	$ (258)	$ 188	$ 80	$ 64
Net Income	$ 11,709	$ 11,555	$ 10,516	$ 9,054	$ 7,955	$ 6,592	$ 6,235	$ 5,324	$ 4,397	$ 3,504	$ 3,042
Shareholder Income											
EPS (diluted) ($dollars)	$ 2.71	$ 2.68	$ 2.41	$ 2.07	$ 1.79	$ 1.50	$ 1.44	$ 1.25	$ 0.94	$ 0.76	$ 0.65
Dividend ($dollars)	$ 0.67	$ 0.60	$ 0.52	$ 0.36	$ 0.30	$ 0.28	$ 0.24	$ 0.20	$ 0.16	$ 0.14	$ 0.11

Source: 2007, 2002, Wal-Mart Annual Reports.

($78.8 billion) than Target made all year ($59.5 billion).[9] Wal-Mart's revenue gave it the No. 1 spot on *Fortune's* April 2007 list of America's largest corporations.[10] By contrast, its profit as a percentage of revenue came in at 3.2 percent, and its total return to investors was 0.1 percent, earning Wal-Mart sub-par ranks by those measures (no. 354 and no. 355, respectively).[11]

Over the past several years, Wal-Mart has stumbled upon a variety of compounding difficulties. Opposition has been mounting against not only Wal-Mart's practices, but also its very presence, due to multiple relationship issues with employees, communities, and governments.[12] It is increasingly challenging for the company to expand at its current rate, both in the United States and abroad. Meanwhile, key competitors have been "growing two to five times faster than Wal-Mart" in same-store sales.[13]

As a result, the company has gradually been losing some of its luster, even in the eyes of its former admirers. In 2004, Wal-Mart had been number one on *Fortune* magazine's list of "America's Most Admired Companies" for the second year running, notwithstanding "a year of bad press and lagging stock price."[14] In 2007, by contrast, Wal-Mart was tied for number 19, behind Costco (no. 18) and Target (no. 13).[15]

What had worked in the past was no longer sustainable in the current competitive environment. Scott wondered whether the change efforts he had started over the past few years would begin to have a positive effect or whether he should somehow adjust Wal-Mart's course.

Company History

Origins

Before founding Wal-Mart, Sam Walton accumulated experience in variety store retailing as a JCPenney management trainee and a franchisee of Ben Franklin stores.[16] Anticipating discount market growth, Walton opened his first Wal-Mart store in Rogers, Arkansas, in 1962, the same year Kmart and Target were founded.[17] Wal-Mart opened 24 more stores by 1967.[18] This start was slow compared with Kmart, which had already opened 162 stores by 1966.[19] Wal-Mart went public in 1970, giving it access to the financial resources needed to begin a decades-long expansion campaign that led to the opening of 3,800 stores by 2005.[20] Wal-Mart opened its first Sam's Club warehouse in 1983 and its first international store in 1991, and the company's national and international multiplatform expansion continues[21] (see Exhibit 4).

Recent History

Wal-Mart's growth soared in recent years, with the company adding nearly one new store every day (since 2006).[22] The company's rapid expansion brought its total retail store presence to 6,782 units worldwide as of February 8, 2007.[23] Wal-Mart spread with a missionary zeal, to "save people money so they can live better."[24] As Wal-Mart's presence continued to grow, so did its sales, to a record $345 billion in the fiscal year ended January 31, 2007 (hereafter referred to as 2007).

The company's massive growth brought with it massive controversies, however. Wal-Mart faced multiple accusations, charges, and lawsuits, many resulting in fines, including environmental violations, child labor law violations, use of illegal immigrants by subcontractors, and allegedly poor working conditions for associates.[25] Side effects of these issues include communities rejecting expansion of Wal-Mart stores into their neighborhoods.[26] Anti-Wal-Mart press is also on the rise, with books such as *How Wal-Mart Is Destroying America and the World: And What You Can Do About It* by Bill Quinn, and Robert Greenwald's film, *Wal-Mart: The High Cost of Low Price.* By one estimate, Wal-Mart's reputation issues have cost it $16 billion in market capitalization and an unknown amount of lost business in each store category or business segment.[27]

Business Segments

Wal-Mart's three business segments are Wal-Mart Stores, Sam's Club, and Wal-Mart International.[28] The Wal-Mart Stores segment includes walmart.com and three retail store formats in all 50 of the United States, including 2,257 Supercenters, 1,074 Discount Stores, and 112 Neighborhood Markets.[29] The Neighborhood Markets have the smallest format, with an average size of 42,000 square feet, and a primary focus on grocery products.[30] Wal-Mart's Discount Stores "offer a wide assortment of general merchandise and a limited variety of food products" within 107,000 square feet of selling space.[31] Supercenters average 187,000 square feet and add a full line of food products to Discount Stores' typical selection.[32] Wal-Mart converted 147 Discount Stores into Supercenters in 2007.[33] Overall, Wal-Mart Stores opened 303 new units in 2007 (276 Supercenters, 15 Discount Stores, and 12 Neighborhood Markets).[34]

Membership-based Sam's Club operates in a retail warehouse format, as well as online at samsclub.com. The segment's 579 clubs average 132,000 square feet, and provide "exceptional value on brand-name merchandise at 'members only' prices for both business and personal use."[35] Sam's Club opened 15 new units in 2007.[36]

Wal-Mart International added 576 (net) new stores in 2006—on its way to doubling its total retail unit count over the past few years.[37] Wal-Mart now operates 2,760 stores outside the United States in various formats, under diverse brand names, in 13 foreign countries and territories.[38] Wal-Mart International includes "wholly owned operations in Argentina, Brazil, Canada, Puerto Rico,

Exhibit 4 Wal-Mart Key Events, 1962–2004

1960s
1962: Company founded with opening of first Wal-Mart in Rogers, Arkansas.
1967: Wal-Mart's 24 stores total $12.6 million in sales.
1968: Wal-Mart moves outside Arkansas with stores in Missouri and Oklahoma.
1969: Company incorporated as Wal-Mart Stores, Inc., on October 31.

1970s
1970: Wal-Mart opens first distribution center and home office in Bentonville, Arkansas. Wal-Mart stock first traded over the counter as a publicly held company. 38 stores now in operation with sales at $44.2 million. Total number of associates is 1,500.
1971: Wal-Mart is now in five states: Arkansas, Kansas, Louisiana, Missouri, and Oklahoma.
1972: Wal-Mart approved and listed on the New York Stock Exchange.
1973: Wal-Mart enters Tennessee.
1974: Wal-Mart stores now in Kentucky and Mississippi.
1975: 125 stores in operation with sales of $340.3 million and 7,500 associates. Wal-Mart enters ninth state: Texas.
1977: Wal-Mart enters its 10th state: Illinois.
1979: Wal-Mart is the first company to reach $1 billion in sales in such a short period of time: $1.248 billion. Wal-Mart now has 276 stores, 21,000 associates and is in its 11th state: Alabama.

1980s
1981: Wal-Mart enters Georgia and South Carolina.
1982: Wal-Mart enters Florida and Nebraska.
1983: First Sam's Club opened in April in Midwest City, Oklahoma. Wal-Mart enters Indiana, Iowa, New Mexico, and North Carolina. For eighth year straight Forbes magazine ranks Wal-Mart No. 1 among general retailers.
1984: Wal-Mart enters Virginia.
1985: Wal-Mart has 882 stores with sales of $8.4 billion and 104,000 associates. Company adds stores in Wisconsin and Colorado.
1986: Wal-Mart enters Minnesota.
1987: Wal-Mart's 25th anniversary: 1,198 stores with sales of $15.9 billion and 200,000 associates.
1988: First Supercenter opened in Washington, Missouri.
1989: Wal-Mart is now in 26 states with the addition of Michigan, West Virginia, and Wyoming.

1990s
1990: Wal-Mart enters California, Nevada, North Dakota, Pennsylvania, South Dakota, and Utah.
1991: Wal-Mart enters Connecticut, Delaware, Maine, Maryland, Massachusetts, New Hampshire, New Jersey, and New York. International market entered for first time with the opening of two units in Mexico City. Wal-Mart has entered 45 states with the addition of Idaho, Montana, and Oregon. Wal-Mart enters Puerto Rico.
1993: Wal-Mart enters Alaska, Hawaii, Rhode Island, and Washington.
1994: Three value clubs open in Hong Kong. Canada has 123 stores and Mexico has 96.
1995: Wal-Mart Stores, Inc., has 1,995 Wal-Mart stores, 239 Supercenters, 433 Sam's Clubs, and 276 International stores with sales at $93.6 billion and 675,000 associates. Wal-Mart enters its 50th state, Vermont, and builds three units in Argentina and five in Brazil.
1996: Wal-Mart enters China through a joint-venture agreement.
1997: Wal-Mart replaces Woolworth on the Dow Jones Industrial Average.
1998: Wal-Mart enters Korea through a joint venture agreement.
1999: Wal-Mart has 1,140,000 associates, making the company the largest private employer in the world.

2000s
2000: Wal-Mart ranked 5th by Fortune magazine in its Global Most Admired All-Stars list.
2001: Wal-Mart named by Fortune magazine as the third most admired company in America.
2002: Wal-Mart ranked #1 on the Fortune 500 listing.
2002: Wal-Mart has the biggest single day sales in history: $1.43 billion on the day after Thanksgiving.
2003: Wal-Mart named by Fortune magazine as the most admired company in America.
2004: Fortune magazine placed Wal-Mart in the top spot on its "Most Admired Companies" list for the second year in a row.

Source: 2007, The Wal-Mart Timeline, Wal-Mart Facts, http://www.walmartfacts.com/content/default.aspx?id=3, April 1.

and the United Kingdom; the operation of joint ventures in China; and the operations of majority-owned subsidiaries in Central America, Japan, and Mexico."[39] In 2006, Wal-Mart divested its operations in Germany and Korea.[40] Mike Duke, vice chairperson of Wal-Mart Stores and head of the International Division, commented that it had "'become increasingly clear that in Germany's [and South Korea's] business environment it would be difficult to obtain the scale and results we desire.' Wal-Mart seeks markets where it feels that there is potential for it to become a top three retailer, an opportunity that did not exist for it in Germany [or South Korea]."[41] Wal-Mart International's U.K.-based Asda subsidiary brings in the largest share of the company's international revenue, at

Exhibit 5 International Wal-Mart Retail Units and Banners, 2007

2,760 total units

Country	Retail Units	Date of Entry
Mexico	889	November 1991
Puerto Rico	54	August 1992
Canada	289	November 1994
Argentina	13	November 1995
Brazil	302	May 1995
China	73	August 1996
United Kingdom	335	July 1999
Japan	392	March 2002
Costa Rica	137	September 2005
El Salvador	63	September 2005
Guatemala	132	September 2005
Honduras	41	September 2005
Nicaragua	40	September 2005

Wal-Mart Stores, Inc. These are our banners worldwide. We are united in saving our customers money so they can live better.

Sources: 2007, International Data Sheet, Wal-Mart Stores, http://walmartstores.com/Files/Intl_operations.pdf, February 8; 2007, Wal-Mart Annual Report, 24.

37.4 percent.[42] Wal-Mart de Mexico provides the next largest share, at 23.6 percent of Wal-Mart International sales[43] (see Exhibit 5).

One of the challenges for each of Wal-Mart's segments is determining the appropriate product offerings for each location.

Product/Service Diversification

Wal-Mart continues to build on the discount general-store concept that reflects founder Sam Walton's ideals: "a wide assortment of good quality merchandise;

the lowest possible prices; guaranteed satisfaction with what you buy; friendly, knowledgeable service; convenient hours; free parking; [and] a pleasant shopping experience."[44] The company's Neighborhood Market locations provide an average of 29,000 items per store; its Discount Stores offer 120,000 items in each store; and its Supercenters stock more than 142,000 different items. Walmart.com offers customers 1 million SKUs (stock keeping units or items in stock), multiple times the number offered in Wal-Mart's retail stores.[45] Sam's Club features appliances, electronics, furniture, jewelry, and office products, plus healthcare, business, personal and financial services.[46] Interestingly, Wal-Mart "caters heavily to customers with little or no access to banking services, often described as the 'unbanked.'"[47] This category fits 20 percent of Wal-Mart's customer base and, as such, Wal-Mart provides substantial financial services for this customer segment by providing services such as check cashing. It has 170 money centers in its approximately 4,000 U.S. stores.

Product and service offerings are just one of the many complex decisions that Wal-Mart's strategic leaders have to make.

Strategic Leaders

Ultimate leadership control has remained in the Walton family, with chairmanship changing hands only once, from father to son. Successors to the highest executive positions at Wal-Mart have always come from within the company. After eight years as CFO and executive vice president, David Glass succeeded Sam Walton as president and later as CEO.[48] H. Lee Scott joined Wal-Mart in 1979 and was named CEO by David Glass in 2000[49] (see Exhibit 6).

Decision Makers

Twenty-five senior Wal-Mart officers meet via weekly videoconferences "to review the Company's ongoing performance, focus on initiatives to drive sales and customer service, and address broader issues"[50] (see Exhibit 7). Eight of these senior officers currently have the most critical roles.

The most powerful among them is S. Robson (Rob) Walton, first son of Sam Walton and chair of the board of directors since 1992.[51] Rob Walton was initiated into the fledgling family business one night in the early 1960s after he earned his driver's license when Sam recruited him to truck goods from a garage in Bentonville to a Wal-Mart store.[52] Rob officially joined the company in 1969, shortly after graduating from law school, worked his way up to the vice chair position, and became board chair in 1992 after his father died.[53] "We lead when we embrace my dad's vision," according to Rob, "to improve the lives of everyday people by making everyday things more affordable."[54] Rob now lives in Colorado, where he races bicycles and sports cars in his spare time, and flies the company jet to his Bentonville office.[55] He continues to serve as the primary conduit for Walton family input related to company proceedings.[56]

CEO Lee Scott "rose through the ranks by excelling at the mechanical aspects of retailing, playing an indispensable part in Wal-Mart's technology-induced rebound in the latter half of the 1990s."[57] The son of a gas station owner and a music teacher in small-town Kansas, Scott worked factory night shifts to pay for college, while he, his wife, and their baby lived in a mobile home.[58] He put his business degree to use in logistics, first as a dispatcher for Yellow Freight, then as a "headstrong," "aggressive, even abrasive" Wal-Mart transportation manager.[59] His skill in reducing costs helped him ascend to senior logistics jobs, then into the top merchandising post, where he cut billions in excess inventory in the late 1990s.[60] Next Scott ran the 2,300-unit Wal-Mart Stores Division for a year before becoming Wal-Mart's chief operating officer and vice chairperson in 1999.[61] He became CEO in January 2000.[62]

Mike Duke, an industrial engineer who had 23 years of experience with Federated and May Department Stores, followed Scott's path, climbing the distribution and logistics ladder to the leadership of Wal-Mart Stores Division.[63] Now he oversees international operations as vice chairperson.[64]

John Menzer, who joined Wal-Mart in 1995 after 10 years with Ben Franklin Retail Stores, served as Wal-Mart's chief financial officer before becoming CEO of Wal-Mart International in 1999.[65] He led the acquisitions of Seiyu (a majority-owned subsidiary in Japan) and Asda.[66] Now as vice chairperson, Menzer is responsible for Wal-Mart Stores and various corporate functions, including strategic planning.[67]

A native of Ecuador, Eduardo Castro-Wright leads the Wal-Mart Stores Division in the United States after leading Wal-Mart de Mexico from 2001 to 2005, following a distinguished career with Nabisco in the Latin America and Asia-Pacific regions.[68]

Doug McMillon became president and CEO of Sam's Club after a 15-year career with Wal-Mart, first as a buyer, then as a merchandising manager and leader.[69]

Nineteen-year Target veteran John Fleming ascended through Walmart.com in the early 2000s to become Wal-Mart Stores' chief marketing officer, prior to his January 2007 induction as chief merchandising officer for Wal-Mart Stores.[70]

Exhibit 6 History of Leadership Succession at Wal-Mart

History of Leadership Succession at Wal-Mart			
Year	President	CEO	Chairman
1962	Sam Walton	Sam Walton	Sam Walton
1984	David Glass	Sam Walton	Sam Walton
1988	David Glass	David Glass	Sam Walton
1992	David Glass	David Glass	Rob Walton
2000	H. Lee Scott	H. Lee Scott	Rob Walton

Sources: 2007, The Wal-Mart Timeline, Wal-Mart Facts, http://www.walmartfacts.com/content/default.aspx?id=3, April 1; D. Longo, 1998, Wal-Mart hands CEO crown to David Glass, *Discount Store News*, February 15.

Exhibit 7 Wal-Mart Senior Officers, May 2007

Eduardo Castro-Wright
Executive Vice President and President and Chief Executive Officer, Wal-Mart Stores Division

M. Susan Chambers
Executive Vice President of People Division

Patricia A. Curran
Executive Vice President, Store Operations, Wal-Mart Stores Division

Leslie A. Dach
Executive Vice President, Corporate Affairs and Government Relations

Linda M. Dillman
Executive Vice President, Risk Management and Benefits Administration

Michael T. Duke
Vice Chairman, Responsible for International

Johnnie C. Dobbs
Executive Vice President, Logistics and Supply Chain

John E. Fleming
Executive Vice President and Chief Merchandising Officer, Wal-Mart Stores Division

Rollin L. Ford
Executive Vice President, Chief Information Officer

Craig R. Herkert
Executive Vice President and President and Chief Executive Officer, The Americas, International

Charles M. Holley, Jr.
Executive Vice President, Finance and Treasurer

Thomas D. Hyde
Executive Vice President and Corporate Secretary

Gregory L. Johnston
Executive Vice President, Club Operations, SAM'S CLUB

Thomas A. Mars
Executive Vice President and General Counsel

C. Douglas McMillon
Executive Vice President and President and Chief Executive Officer, SAM'S CLUB

John B. Menzer
Vice Chairman, Responsible for U.S.

Stephen Quinn
Executive Vice President and Chief Marketing Officer, Wal-Mart Stores, Inc.

Thomas M. Schoewe
Executive Vice President and Chief Financial Officer

H. Lee Scott, Jr.
President and Chief Executive Officer

William S. Simon
Executive Vice President and Chief Operating Officer, Professional Services and New Business Development

Gregory E. Spragg
Executive Vice President, Merchandising and Replenishment, SAM'S CLUB

S. Robson Walton
Chairman of the Board of Directors of Wal-Mart Stores, Inc.

Claire A. Watts
Executive Vice President, Merchandising, Wal-Mart Stores Division-US

Steven P. Whaley
Senior Vice President, Controller, Wal-Mart Stores Inc.

Eric S. Zorn
Executive Vice President and President, Wal-Mart Realty

Source: 2007, Senior Officers, WalMartStores.com, http://walmartstores.com/GlobalWMStoresWeb/navigate.do?catg=540, May 25.

After 13 years in marketing roles with PepsiCo, Stephen Quinn joined Wal-Mart as senior vice president of marketing in 2005, and then in January 2007 took over Fleming's former position as chief marketing officer for Wal-Mart Stores.[71]

These eight leaders are supported and monitored by the board of directors.

Board of Directors

Wal-Mart has an active, high-caliber, 14-member board of directors that may soon get even more powerful. "The Board has been instrumental in encouraging the company to more quickly address critical issues, and I am extremely pleased that they are not reticent about sharing their opinions," Rob Walton recently wrote, adding: "Today's Board is the furthest thing from a rubber stamp."[72] Two out of three board members have held

CEO positions and/or chaired the boards of various companies. Retail turnaround guru Allen Questrom, who overhauled JCPenney, joined the board in June 2007.[73] Questrom recently told *Women's Wear Daily*: "[Wal-Mart is] never going to be a leader in fashion apparel. That's not their calling. But can they improve on that, sure they can."[74] The most famous former board member is New York Senator and Democratic presidential candidate Hillary Rodham Clinton, who served on the Wal-Mart board from 1986 to 1992 as a "loyalist reformer"[75] (see Exhibit 8).

Several board members are among the largest shareholders in the company.

Shareholders

Of the 4.1 billion Wal-Mart shares outstanding, insiders and beneficial owners hold 42 percent, while institutional investors and mutual funds hold 37 percent.[76]

Exhibit 8 Wal-Mart Board of Directors, May 2007

Aida M. Alvarez, 57
Former Administrator of the U.S. Small Business Administration; joined board in 2006

James W. Breyer, 45
Managing Partner of Accel Partners; joined board in 2001

M. Michele Burns, 49
Chairman and CEO of Mercer Human Resources Consulting; joined board in 2003

James Cash, Jr., Ph.D., 59
Retired Professor of Business Administration at Harvard Business School; joined board in 2006

Roger C. Corbett, 64
Retired CEO and Group Managing Director of Woolworths Limited; joined board in 2006

Douglas N. Daft, 64
Retired Chairman of the Board and CEO of The Coca-Cola Company; joined board in 2005

David D. Glass, 71
Former President and CEO of Wal-Mart Stores, Inc.; joined board in 1977

Roland A. Hernandez, 49
Retired Chairman and CEO of Telemundo Group, Inc.; joined board in 1998

Allen I. Questrom, 67
Former Chairman and CEO of JCPenney Company; Barneys New York, Inc.; The Neiman Marcus Group, Inc.; and Federated Department Stores, Inc.; standing for election in June 2007

H. Lee Scott, Jr., 58
President and Chief Executive Officer of Wal-Mart Stores, Inc.; joined board in 1999

Jack C. Shewmaker, 69
Retired Vice Chairman of Wal-Mart Stores, Inc.; joined board in 1977

Jim C. Walton, 58
Chairman of the Board and CEO of Arvest Bank Group, Inc.; joined board in 2005

S. Robson Walton, 62
Chairman of the Board of Directors of Wal-Mart Stores, Inc.; joined board in 1978

Christopher J. Williams, 49
Chairman and CEO of The Williams Capital Group, L.P.; joined board in 2004

Linda S. Wolf, 59
Former Chairman of the Board and CEO of Leo Burnett Worldwide, Inc.; joined board in 2005

Sources: 2007, Board of Directors, WalMartStores.com, http://walmartstores.com/GlobalWMStoresWeb/navigate.do?catg=502, May 25; 2007, Wal-Mart Stores, Inc., Form DEF 14A, Proxy Statement, Notice of 2007 Annual Shareholders' Meeting, U.S. SEC, April 19.

The Walton family owns almost 1.7 billion shares through its holding company, Walton Enterprises, LLC, whose directors were five of America's ten wealthiest individuals in 2005: Sam's three sons, Rob Walton, director Jim C. Walton, and John T. Walton (d. 2005); daughter Alice L. Walton; and widow Helen R. Walton (d. 2007).[77]

Top non-Walton inside shareholders include CEO Lee Scott (1.2 million shares), director David D. Glass (1.2 million shares), director Jack C. Shewmaker (557,674 shares), Mike Duke (413,213 shares), and John Menzer (401,883 shares).[78]

Some 1,127 institutions own Wal-Mart stock.[79] Nearly 536 million Wal-Mart shares are owned by 785 mutual funds.[80]

In total, as many as 312,423 shareholders held common stock in Wal-Mart on March 16, 2007, when the company finalized its annual report for fiscal 2007.[81]

Financial Results

Fiscal 2007 and Recent Years[82]

Over the past 10 years, Wal-Mart's net income has nearly quadrupled, from $3 billion in 1997 to $11.7 billion in 2007. Revenues have more than tripled, from $100 billion to $345 billion. Meanwhile, operating, selling, and general administration expenses have quadrupled, outstripping the increase in revenue and net income, averaging 14.6 percent of sales. Despite the increase in expenses, steadily higher gross margins have boosted operating income (refer to Exhibit 3).

Wal-Mart had assets totaling $151 billion in 2007, up from $39 billion in 1997. Concurrent with the increase in assets, liabilities have grown 319 percent over the same period, from $21.4 billion to $89.6 billion. Shareholder return on equity measured 22 percent in 2007, close to its 10-year average. Total shareholder equity rose from $17.2 billion in 1997 to $61.8 billion in 2007 (see Exhibit 9).

Wal-Mart has improved its profitability over the last several years. Compared with an average operating profit margin of 5.1 percent in the prior three-year period, Wal-Mart has averaged 6.0 percent in the past three years. In 1997, Wal-Mart's operating profit margin was 4.3 percent. From a debt perspective, Wal-Mart has fluctuated up and down, with a debt ratio between 55.1 percent and 61.5 percent over the last 10 years. As of 2007, it measured 59.3 percent, 150 basis points over its 10-year median (see Exhibit 10).

Comparative Revenue[83]

Sales by Region. Of nearly $345 billion in total sales in 2007 (not including Sam's Club fees), domestic U.S. revenues totaled nearly $268 billion, or 77.6 percent of sales, while international revenues were $77 billion, or 22.4 percent of sales. International operations are becoming increasingly important to the company. Driving

Exhibit 9 Wal-Mart Balance Sheet, 1997–2007

Balance Sheet
(all figures in $millions; fiscal year ends 1/31)

	2007	2006	2005	2004	2003	2002	2001	2000	1999	1998	1997
Assets											
Inventories	$ 33,685	$ 31,910	29,419	26,263	24,098	21,793	20,710	18,961	16,058	16,005	15,556
Other Current Assets	$ 12,903	$ 11,915	$ 8,494	$ 7,285	$ 4,769	$ 4,122	$ 4,086	$ 4,021	$ 3,445	$ 2,584	$ 1,829
Total Current Assets	$ 46,588	$ 43,825	$ 37,913	$ 33,548	$ 28,867	$ 25,915	$ 24,796	$ 22,982	$ 19,503	$ 18,589	$ 17,385
Net Property, Equipment & Leases	$ 88,440	$ 77,865	$ 66,549	$ 57,591	$ 50,053	$ 44,172	$ 39,439	$ 34,570	$ 24,824	$ 23,237	$ 19,935
Goodwill & Other Long-term Assets	$ 16,165	$ 13,934	$ 12,677	$ 11,316	$ 11,309	$ 9,214	$ 10,082	$ 9,738	$ 2,739	$ 2,395	$ 1,251
Total Assets	$151,193	$135,624	$117,139	$102,455	$90,229	$79,301	$74,317	$67,290	$47,066	$44,221	$38,571
Return on Assets	8.8%	9.3%	9.8%	9.7%	9.6%	9.0%	9.3%	10.1%	9.6%	8.5%	8.0%
Liabilities & Shareholder Equity											
Current Liabilities	$ 51,754	$ 48,348	$ 42,609	$ 37,308	$ 31,752	$ 26,309	$ 28,096	$ 25,058	$ 15,848	$ 13,930	$ 10,432
Long-Term Debt	$ 27,222	$ 26,429	$ 20,087	$ 17,088	$ 16,545	$ 15,632	$ 12,453	$ 13,650	$ 6,875	$ 7,169	$ 7,685
Long-Term Leases	$ 3,513	$ 3,667	$ 3,073	$ 2,888	$ 2,903	$ 2,956	$ 3,054	$ 2,852	$ 2,697	$ 2,480	$ 2,304
Other Liabilities (minority interest, discontinued ops, deferred taxes)	$ 7,131	$ 4,009	$ 1,974	$ 1,548	$ (432)	$ (788)	$ (693)	$ (148)	$ 505	$ 2,123	$ 999
Total Liabilities	$ 89,620	$ 82,453	$ 67,743	$ 58,832	$50,768	$44,109	$42,910	$41,412	$25,925	$25,702	$21,420
Shareholder Equity	$ 61,573	$ 53,171	$ 49,396	$ 43,623	$39,461	$35,192	$31,407	$25,878	$21,141	$18,519	$17,151
Return on Equity	22.0%	22.9%	23.1%	22.4%	21.8%	20.7%	23.0%	24.5%	22.0%	19.6%	18.8%

Source: 2007, 2002, Wal-Mart Annual Reports.

Exhibit 10 Wal-Mart Financial Ratios, 1997–2007

	2007	2006	2005	2004	2003	2002	2001	2000	1999	1998	1997
Stability											
Debt Ratio	59.3%	60.8%	57.8%	57.4%	56.3%	55.6%	57.7%	61.5%	55.1%	58.1%	55.5%
Stockholders Equity to Assets	40.7%	39.2%	42.2%	42.6%	43.7%	44.4%	42.3%	38.5%	44.9%	41.9%	44.5%
Leverage	2.50	2.46	2.36	2.32	2.27	2.31	2.47	2.43	2.30	2.32	n/a
Debt to Equity Ratio	1.46	1.55	1.37	1.35	1.29	1.25	1.37	1.60	1.23	1.39	1.25
Debt to Capitization Ratio	0.38	0.39	0.34	0.33	0.33	0.34	0.32	0.39	0.32	0.39	0.39
Liquidity											
Current Ratio	0.90	0.91	0.89	0.90	0.91	0.99	0.88	0.92	1.23	1.33	1.67
Quick Ratio	0.25	0.25	0.20	0.20	0.15	0.16	0.15	0.16	0.22	0.19	0.18
Profitability											
Operating Profit Margin	5.9%	6.0%	6.1%	5.1%	5.1%	5.0%	5.4%	5.6%	4.8%	4.5%	4.3%
Operating Ratio	18.4%	17.9%	17.6%	17.4%	17.3%	17.0%	16.8%	16.4%	16.6%	16.8%	16.5%
Net Profit Margin	3.3%	3.6%	3.6%	3.6%	3.5%	3.3%	3.5%	3.5%	3.4%	3.1%	3.1%
Total Asset Turnover	2.4	2.5	2.6	2.6	2.7	2.6	2.5	2.7	2.8	2.7	n/a

Source: 2007, 2002, Wal-Mart Annual Reports.

Wal-Mart's overall growth, international sales growth has averaged 33.6 percent over the past 10 years, whereas domestic sales have grown an average of only 11.0 percent in the same period. In the last three years, domestic sales growth has averaged 8.7 percent versus average international growth of 17.8 percent (refer to Exhibit 2).

Wal-Mart has experienced varying rates of growth in international markets. Nonetheless, international revenue has been a constant source of sales growth for Wal-Mart, outpacing the revenue contribution from the Sam's Club segment since 2001.

Sales by Segment. Wal-Mart Stores brought in 65.6 percent of all sales in 2007, down from 75.1 percent of sales in 1997. Wal-Mart International was responsible for 22.4 percent of sales, up from 5.0 percent a decade earlier, while Sam's Club accounted for 12.1 percent of sales in 2007, down from 19.9 percent in 1997 (refer to Exhibit 2).

Sam's Club has suffered against rival Costco for years, losing the battle for comparable-store sales in "64 of the past 73 months," according to one researcher, as well as the battle for membership renewals.[84] Average annual sales per warehouse were $73 million for Sam's Club versus $135 million for Costco in fiscal 2006.[85]

Wal-Mart's online business has not been a significant source of revenue, bringing in an estimated $135 million in sales in 2002, the same year JCPenney.com had sales of $324 million and Amazon.com reached sales greater than $3 billion.[86]

Wal-Mart Supercenters drove 56.1 percent of the company's sales, reflecting the company's competitive strength in traditional nonmembership discount formats.

Results Relative to Competitors

Market Leadership. Wal-Mart is the number one retailer in 77 of the 100 largest general merchandise markets in America, squaring up against Target or Costco in all but 11 of these markets.[87] Either Wal-Mart, Costco, or Target holds the top position in 91 of the top 100 largest general merchandise markets in the United States.[88] Geographically, Wal-Mart is the dominant retailer in the South and throughout midsized and small-town markets, while Costco is the leader in California and Washington.[89] According to ACNielsen, (the world's leading marketing information company), in the United States, Wal-Mart "controls 20 percent of dry grocery, 29 percent of non-food grocery, 30 percent of health and beauty aids, and 45 percent of general merchandise sales."[90] It also controls 45 percent of the retail toy segment.[91] However, Target, Kroger, and Family Dollar Stores are all growing revenue faster than Wal-Mart, threatening its dominance (see Exhibit 11).

Financial Ratios. From a competitive profitability perspective, Wal-Mart's 5.87 percent operating margin and 3.23 percent net margin put it in the middle of the pack relative to its key competitors (refer to Exhibit 11). Target enjoys higher margins, closer to those of JCPenney, while Costco has lower margins, closer to those of Dollar General and Kroger. Wal-Mart's

Exhibit 11 Comparison of Financial Ratios

	Quarterly Growth (yoy)		Profitability (ttm)		Management Effectiveness (ttm)	
Financial Ratios of Select Retailers (sorted by revenue growth, as of May 26, 2007)	Revenue Growth	Earnings Growth	Net Profit Margin	Operating Margin	Return on Assets	Return on Equity
Amazon.com, Inc.	32.30%	117.60%	2.18%	3.74%	10.37%	73.86%
Target Corporation	16.30%	19.20%	4.69%	8.52%	8.93%	18.68%
Kroger Co.	14.50%	36.50%	1.69%	3.47%	7.10%	23.95%
Family Dollar Stores, Inc.	12.20%	66.00%	3.49%	5.70%	9.44%	17.68%
Wal-Mart Stores, Inc.	9.60%	8.10%	3.23%	5.87%	8.81%	21.80%
Costco Wholesale Corp.	7.50%	−15.80%	1.73%	2.55%	6.25%	12.07%
J.C. Penney Corporation	3.10%	13.30%	5.90%	9.73%	9.57%	26.43%
Dollar General Corp.	3.00%	−65.50%	1.50%	2.67%	5.24%	7.96%
Sears Holdings Corporation	1.30%	26.50%	2.81%	4.59%	5.06%	12.25%

Sources: 2007, Key Statistics, Capital IQ, A Division of Standard & Poor's, Yahoo! Finance, http://finance.yahoo.com/q/ks?s=WMT, http://finance.yahoo.com/q/ks?s=TGT, http://finance.yahoo.com/q/ks?s=COST, http://finance.yahoo.com/q/ks?s=KR, http://finance.yahoo.com/q/ks?s=DG, http://finance.yahoo.com/q/ks?s=FDO, http://finance.yahoo.com/q/ks?s=SHLD, http://finance.yahoo.com/q/ks?s=JCP, http://finance.yahoo.com/q/ks?s=AMZN, May 26.

margins are nearest those of Family Dollar Stores and Sears Holdings (Kmart and Sears). Wal-Mart's profit margin may be held down somewhat by its presence in the lower margin grocery business, especially in its Neighborhood Markets format.[92] In Supercenters, groceries serve a larger role of driving store traffic and drawing customers toward higher margin products. From a management effectiveness standpoint, Wal-Mart is creating a return on equity that is higher than Target's and much higher than Costco's and a return on assets that is nearly identical to Target's and higher than Costco's.

First Quarter, Fiscal 2008 (Quarter Ending April 30, 2007)

Wal-Mart had a difficult first quarter. Revenue and earnings "were not where we would have expected [them] to be, nor where we believe they should be," according to CEO Scott.[93] "Quite honestly, we're not satisfied with our overall performance."[94] Wal-Mart increased company sales (not including Sam's Club fees) by 8.3 percent in the first quarter to $85.3 billion.[95] Overall operating income increased 7.9 percent year-over-year, with nearly 53.1 percent of the change coming from Wal-Mart's international operations[96] (see Exhibit 12).

Closing out the first quarter on a down note, Wal-Mart's April same-store sales decrease was the worst ever recorded in 28 years of tracking: an overall U.S. comparable-store sales slide of 3.5 percent for the month, with a 4.6 percent drop at Wal-Mart Stores offset by a 2.5 percent increase at Sam's Clubs.[97] Much of the April decline was blamed on the apparel business, which constitutes 10 percent of Wal-Mart's sales.[98] Recent failed forays into fashion appear to have dragged down overall same-stores sales.[99] Wal-Mart wasn't the only retailer to have a bad April. The International Council of Shopping Centers reported an average 2.3 percent drop in same-store sales across 51 chains.[100] Against the trend, Costco posted a 6 percent same-store sales gain in April (see Exhibit 13).

The financial situation might be better considered with an understanding of the competitive situation in Wal-Mart's industry.

Competitive Situation

We face strong sales competition from other discount, department, drug, variety and specialty stores and super-markets, many of which are national, regional or international chains, as well as internet-based retailers and catalog businesses. Additionally, we compete with a number of companies for prime retail site locations, as well as in attracting and retaining quality employees ("associates"). We, along with other retail companies, are influenced by a number of factors . . . cost of goods, consumer debt levels and buying patterns, economic conditions, interest rates, customer preferences, unemployment, labor costs, inflation, currency exchange fluctuations, fuel prices, weather patterns, catastrophic events, competitive pressures and insurance costs. Our Sam's Club segment faces strong sales competition from other wholesale club operators, catalogs businesses, internet-based and other retailers."

—2007 WAL-MART ANNUAL REPORT, 28–29

Exhibit 12 Wal-Mart Fiscal 2008 First Quarter Results versus Target

Wall-Mart Stores, Inc. Fiscal 2008 First Quarter Results Quarters Ending 4/30, all figures in $millions			
Income	Q1 2008	Q1 2007	YoY% Chng
Total Operating Revenue	$86,410	$79,676	8.5%
Cost of Sales	$65,311	$60,237	8.4%
Gross Operating Profit	**$21,099**	**$19,439**	8.5%
Gross Margins	24.4%	24.4%	
Operating, Selling, G&A Exp.	$16,249	$14,944	8.7%
Operating Income	**$ 4,850**	**$ 4,495**	7.9%
Net Interest Expense	$ 392	$ 368	6.5%
Income Before Taxes	$ 4,458	$ 4,127	8.0%
Provision for Taxes	$ 1,532	$ 1,388	10.4%
Effective Tax Rate	34.4%	33.6%	2.2%
Net Income from Operations	$ 2,926	$ 2,739	6.8%
Other Items	$ (100)	$ (124)	
Net Income	**$ 2,826**	**$ 2,615**	8.1%
Shareholder Income ($dollars)			
EPS (diluted)	$ 0.68	$ 0.63	7.9%
Dividend	$ 0.67	$ 0.60	
Comparable-Store Sales Growth	**0.6%**	**3.8%**	
Wal-Mart Stores	–0.1%	3.8%	
Sam's Club (excl. fuel)	4.7%	4.3%	
Segment Breakdown			
Revenue by Segment			
Wal-Mart Stores	$55,437	$52,499	5.6%
Sam's Club	$10,323	$ 9,775	5.6%
International	$19,627	$16,561	18.5%
Total (excludes other income)	$85,387	$78,835	8.3%
Operating Income by Segment			
Wal-Mart Stores	$ 3,927	$ 3,858	1.8%
Sam's Club	$ 363	$ 303	19.8%
International	$ 903	$ 757	19.3%
Total (excludes other income)	$ 5,193	$ 4,918	5.6%
Operating Margins by Segment			
Wal-Mart Stores	7.1%	7.3%	–3.6%
Sam's Club	3.5%	3.1%	13.4%
International	4.6%	4.6%	0.7%
Total (excludes other income)	6.1%	6.2%	–2.5%
Cash Flows			
Net Income	$ 2,826	$ 2,615	
Change in Inventories	$ (1,280)	$ 259	
Accounts Payable	$ (1,115)	$ (442)	
Accounts Receivable	$ 62	$ 219	
Cash Flows from Operating Activities	**$ 493**	**$ 2,651**	

Target Corporation Fiscal 2008 First Quarter Results Quarters Ending 5/5/07 and 4/29/06, all figures in $millions			
Income	Q1 2008	Q1 2007	YoY%Chng
Total Operating Revenue*	$14,041	$12,863	9.2%
Cost of Sales	$ 9,186	$ 8,473	8.4%
Gross Operating Profit	**$ 4,855**	**$ 4,390**	10.6%
Gross Margins	34.6%	34.1%	
Operating, Selling, G&A Exp.**	$ 3,655	$ 3,373	8.4%
Operating Income	**$ 1,200**	**$ 1,017**	18.0%
Net Interest Expense	$ 136	$ 131	3.6%
Income Before Taxes	$ 1,064	$ 886	20.2%
Provision for Taxes	$ 413	$ 332	24.5%
Effective Tax Rate	38.8%	37.5%	3.6%
Net Income from Operations	$ 651	$ 554	17.6%
Other Items	$ –	$ –	
Net Income	**$ 651**	**$ 554**	17.5%
Shareholder Income ($dollars)			
EPS (diluted)	$ 0.75	$ 0.63	19.6%

*includes sales and net credit card revenues
**includes SG&A, credit card expenses, depreciation and amortization

Comparable-Store Sales Growth	4.3%	5.1%	

Sources: 2007, Wal-Mart Stores, Inc., Form 8-K, U.S. SEC, May 15; and 2007, Target Corporation, Form 8-K, U.S. SEC, May 23.

Exhibit 13 April 2007 Same-Store Sales Growth

April 2007 Same-Store Sales Growth	
Discounters	
Wal-Mart	−3.5%
Costco	+6.0%
Target	−6.1%
Dollar General	−2.4%
Department Stores	
Federated	−2.2%
JCPenney	−4.7%
Nordstrom	+3.1%
Dillard's	−14.0%
Neiman Marcus	+1.0%
Saks	+11.7%
Apparel	
TJX	−1.0%
Kohl's	−10.5%
Gap	−16.0%
Limited	−1.0%
AnnTaylor	−12.8%
Teen Apparel	
Abercrombie & Fitch	−15.0%
American Eagle Outfitters	−10.0%

Source: J. Covert, 2007, Retail-sales slide fuels concern: Decline of 2.3% in April among worst on record; even Wal-Mart slipped, *Wall Street Journal*, May 11, A3.

Competitors

Target. Target Corporation operates 1,318 general merchandise stores and 182 SuperTarget stores in 47 states, in addition to its online business, target.com.[101] Target describes itself as "an upscale discounter that provides high-quality, on-trend merchandise at attractive prices in clean, spacious and guest-friendly stores."[102] Target has

grown revenue from $33 billion in 2001 to more than $59 billion in 2006, a compound annual growth rate of 12.5 percent.[103] Profits have risen as well, as earnings from continuing operations averaged an annual growth rate of 20.4 percent over the same period[104] (see Exhibit 14).

Costco. Costco Wholesale Corporation runs 510 warehouses, averaging 140,000 square feet, in 38 states, six foreign countries (Canada, Mexico, the United Kingdom, Taiwan, Korea, and Japan), and Puerto Rico.[105] Costco offers three kinds of membership and roughly 4,000 products, 10 to 15 times fewer than many competitors, according to the company.[106] Costco benefits from a limited number of products sold in high volumes, high inventory turnover, low costs via purchasing discounts and a no-frills approach, and favorable real estate locations. Gross margins have averaged about 10.6 percent over the past five years, and operating income has increased an average of 10.5 percent over the same period[107] (see Exhibit 15).

Kroger. The Kroger Co. is "one of the nation's largest retailers, operating 2,468 supermarket and multidepartment stores under two dozen banners including Kroger, Ralphs, Fred Meyer, Food 4 Less, King Soopers, Smith's, Fry's, Fry's Marketplace, Dillons, QFC, and City Market."[108] Kroger's operating income fell 13.1 percent between 2002 and 2006, from $2.8 billion to $2.2 billion, despite an increase in revenue of 27.7 percent.[109] Operating margins have averaged 24.8 percent over the last three years, up from 15.7 percent in the three years prior[110] (see Exhibit 16).

Other General Discount Competitors. Sears Holdings (Kmart and Sears) offer some additional U.S. competition in general merchandise, while Tesco of Britain and Carrefour of France compete with Wal-Mart internationally. Carrefour is the second-largest retailer in the world

Exhibit 14 Target Performance, 2001–2006

Target	2001	2002	2003	2004	2005	2006
Revenue	$33,021	$ 37,410	$42,025	$46,839	$52,620	$59,940
COGS	$23,030	$25,948	$28,389	$31,445	$34,927	$39,399
Gross Margin	$ 9,991	$11,462	$13,636	$15,394	$ 17,693	$20,541
Gross Margin %	30.3%	30.6%	32.4%	32.9%	33.6%	34.3%
Operating Income/EBIT	$ 2,246	2,811	3,159	3,601	4,323	5,069
		25.2%	12.4%	14.0%	20.0%	17.3%
Net Income	$ 1,101	$ 1,376	$ 1,619	$ 1,885	$ 2,408	$ 2,787
Net Income % chg		25.0%	17.7%	16.4%	27.7%	15.7%

Note: $ in millions

Source: 2006, Target Corporation Annual Report.

Exhibit 15 Costco Performance, 2001–2006

Costco	2001	2002	2003	2004	2005	2006
Revenue	$ 34,137,021	$37,994,608	$41,694,561	$ 47,148,627	$51,879,070	$58,963,180
COGS	$30,598,140	$33,983,121	$ 37,235,383	$42,092,016	$46,346,961	$52,745,497
Gross Margin	$ 3,538,881	$ 4,011,487	$ 4,459,178	$ 5,056,611	$ 5,532,109	$ 6,217,683
Gross Margin %	10.4%	10.6%	10.7%	10.7%	10.7%	10.5%
Operating Income/ EBIT	$ 992,267	1,131,535	1,156,628	1,385,648	1,474,303	1,625,632
		14.0%	2.2%	19.8%	6.4%	10.3%
Net Income	$ 602,089	$ 699,983	$ 721,000	$ 882,393	$ 1,063,092	$ 1,103,215
Net Income % chg		16.3%	3.0%	22.4%	20.5%	3.8%

Note: $ in thousands

Source: 2006, Costco Wholesale Corp. Annual Report.

Exhibit 16 Kroger Performance, 2001–2006

Kroger	2001	2002	2003	2004	2005	2006
Revenue	$49,000	$ 51,760	$53,791	$56,434	$60,553	$ 66,111
COGS	$36,398	$ 37,810	$39,637	$42,140	$45,565	$ 50,115
Gross Margin	$12,602	$13,950	$14,154	$14,294	$14,988	$ 15,996
Gross Margin %	25.7%	10.6%	10.7%	25.3%	24.8%	24.2%
Operating Income/ EBIT	$ 2,359	$ 2,573	$ 1,374	$ 843	$ 2,035	$ 2,236
		9.1%	−46.6%	−38.6%	141.4%	9.9%
Net Income	$ 877	$ 1,202	$ 285	$ (104)	$ 958	$ 1,115
Net Income % chg		37.1%	−76.3%	−136.5%	$ 1021.2%	$ 16.4%

Note: $ in millions

Source: 2006 The Kroger Co. Annual Report.

(after Wal-Mart) and is probably its closest international competitor from a strategy perspective, as it focuses on hypermarkets (similar to Supercenters), in addition to a variety of other formats.[111] Tesco emphasizes convenience and competes primarily in groceries, but also in general merchandise against Wal-Mart's U.K. subsidiary Asda.[112] Tesco is looking to expand to the West Coast of the United States in 2007.[113] Amazon.com adds another level of global competition for Wal-Mart due to its high number of SKUs and its convenience.

Niche Competitors. Other retailers compete with Wal-Mart at the department level, including Safeway, Best Buy, Circuit City, Home Depot, Ace Hardware, Lowe's, Kohl's, Mervyn's California, Barnes & Noble, and Borders, among others. In order to provide lower prices than its competitors, Wal-Mart has developed a unique relationship with its suppliers.

Suppliers

Wal-Mart's 1,600-member Global Procurement Services team, based in 23 countries, buys merchandise from suppliers in more than 70 countries, including 61,000 suppliers in the United States.[114] Leveraging its size, "Wal-Mart not only dictates delivery schedules and inventory levels but also heavily influences product specifications. In the end, many suppliers have to choose between designing goods their way or the Wal-Mart way."[115] In return, companies with a streamlined product and supply chain can benefit greatly. "If you are good with data, are sophisticated, and have scale, Wal-Mart should be one of your most profitable customers," says a retired consumer-products executive.[116] "Wal-Mart controls a large and rapidly increasing share of the business done by most every major U.S. consumer products company," about 28 percent of the total sales of Dial and almost a quarter of the sales of Del Monte Foods, Clorox, and Revlon.[117]

Customers

Wal-Mart attracts 175 million people to its stores each week.[118] According to ACNielsen (the world's leading marketing information company), the typical Wal-Mart shopper has an annual household income of $10,000 to $50,000.[119] These shoppers account for 54 percent of Wal-Mart's sales.[120] Wal-Mart also attracts an affluent segment (with household incomes of at least $75,000) that accounts for 26 percent of its customer base.[121] The affluent segment cross-shops the most with Costco (27 percent) and Target (28 percent).[122] These upscale shoppers likely have lower price elasticity, a relatively lower switching cost, but a higher sensitivity to brand reputation.

Even though Wal-Mart recently hired some well-known public relations experts and ended its relationship with its Ad Agency of 32 years in hopes of creating a more positive image, according to a 2004 study, "2 to 8 percent of Wal-Mart consumers surveyed have ceased shopping at the chain because of 'negative press.'"[123] Shoppers interviewed by the authors of this case have strong opinions about Wal-Mart (see Exhibits 17 and 18).

Wal-Mart's recent struggles with bad press and lawsuits have created urgency to find a way to protect its market share from potential entrants or substitutes.

Other Sources of Competition

Customers have many alternatives for each of the products and services that Wal-Mart provides, but few alternatives exist for the large-scale discount superstore or warehouse shopping experience. The same products can be purchased at different types of retailers, but it is difficult to replicate the convenience, price, and diversity of merchandise found at a Wal-Mart. Also, new potential market entrants with similar scale would have difficulty competing in any substantial volume on price across a wide array of merchandise. Other large incumbents such as Target and Costco have also built economies of scale that would be difficult for a start-up to replicate. Supply chains must be extensive and very efficient. Product differentiation is usually minor in discount store merchandise. However, switching retailers would be easy for customers in well-served areas.

Beyond these retail industry forces, more general external trends also influence Wal-Mart's competitive situation.

External Trends

Government. Wal-Mart has become a "poster company" on political issues related to trade, health care, the environment, discrimination, worker pay, and

Exhibit 17 Wal-Mart Shopper Profile

Income

	% of sales
<$50,000	54%
$50-$75000	20%
$75,000 +	26%

Education

	% of sales
Less than a High School Diploma	20%
High School Diploma (incl. some college)	57%
Bachelor Degree and above	23%

Leisure Pursuits—Typical Customer

	% of customers
Tend Their Garden	43%
Listen to Country Music	30%
Like Auto Racing	17%
Go Fishing	17%
Go Camping	19%

Leisure Pursuits—Affluent Customer

	% of customers
Listen to Talk Radio	34%
Go to a Theme Park	32%
Listen to Contemporary Music	25%
Go to the Museum	21%
Go to the Zoo	18%

Source: S. Kapinus, 2006, Rollback sushi and discount organics: What Wal-Mart's push to upscale consumers means to you, *ACNielsen Consumer Insight Magazine*, http://us.acnielsen.com/pubs/2006_q2_ci_rollback.shtml, Q2.

general anticorporate sentiment. Many activists even contend that Wal-Mart is breaking antitrust laws by using its "power to micromanage the market, carefully coordinating the actions of thousands of firms from a position above the market."[124] Concerns about Wal-Mart's handling of hazardous waste have prompted local, state, and federal officials in the southwestern United States to initiate official actions. In addition to activists and union groups, U.S. political figures are lashing out against Wal-Mart. Democratic presidential candidates are "denouncing Wal-Mart for what they say are substandard wages and health care benefits."[125] Wal-Mart's political action committee's contributions to candidates (even to a former board member) are being returned as a sign of protest.[126] This sentiment is not only surfacing nationally, but locally as well. Governments in Inglewood, California, Cedar Mill, Oregon, and Vancouver, Canada, have rejected Wal-Mart expansion plans.[127]

Exhibit 18 Interviewee Perspectives on Wal-Mart, 2007

The environment steps are baby steps at the moment. We hope they will take substantive and [significant] action around the critical issues of the environment. Sadly, in the past, much of their efforts have been about publicity and positive spin, not about substance. We will wait to see what level of real commitment they will make around the environment.

—ROBERT GREENWALD, PRODUCER/DIRECTOR,
WAL-MART: THE HIGH COST OF LOW PRICE (2007, E-MAIL INTERVIEW, MAY 22)

[Wal-Mart has] a problem with blight. They leave behind in some cases blight by opening a new Supercenter and leaving their old stores empty. They need to have a plan for communities and not leave those huge buildings empty. In Hood River, the community didn't want Wal-Mart to open a Supercenter because they would leave the old store vacant, and Wal-Mart listened. They didn't open the Supercenter.

—FRED G.,
55, SUBURBAN WAL-MART SHOPPER (2007, PERSONAL INTERVIEW, MAY 21)

[B]eing the low-cost provider loses some of the service, the pleasure of going shopping. Target has wider aisles, and less product on the shelf. In contrast, Wal-Mart bombards you with tons of products.

—OLIVER DAVIS,
TARGET SHOPPER (2007, PERSONAL INTERVIEW, MAY 21)

There was a long time I didn't shop at Wal-Mart, and that had to do with the store's image of ruthlessness when it came to destroying the competition. To be honest, I feel a certain amount of shame at shopping there. As a mother, though, I'm afraid budget and convenience rule. In other words, I've sold out.

—LILI N.,
34, AFFLUENT SHOPPER (2007, E-MAIL INTERVIEW, MAY 19)

I shop at Wal-Mart for convenience-type items, but if the item I need is over $100 or is something that I need of quality, I will shop elsewhere. . . . I do not believe that Wal-Mart is capable of becoming related to quality items in the near future like Target and I do not believe that they will be successful at both discount and high quality.

—ANDRE S.,
26, BUDGET-CONSCIOUS SHOPPER (2007, PERSONAL INTERVIEW, MAY 20)

The [Wal-Mart] store itself is a little overwhelming—too many people, parking is usually tight, and the lines at the check-out are long. Also, there are so many [unfamiliar] employees working in a single Wal-Mart, that my shopping experience has no personal touch. I enjoy going to my neighborhood HEB [grocery store] because I see familiar faces—both at the check-out and in the aisles. If Wal-Mart would be willing to downsize a bit and have more of a neighborhood feel to it, I might consider stopping in more often.

—ANGIE R.,
29, AFFLUENT SHOPPER (2007, E-MAIL INTERVIEW, MAY 20)

Wal-Mart . . . lets you stay in their parking lot overnight. Friends stay at the "Wally-World" when we go windsurfing in Hood River. You can use their facilities and treat the parking lot like a campground. I like to shop there because of that corporate policy.

—FRED G.,
55, SUBURBAN WAL-MART SHOPPER (2007, PERSONAL INTERVIEW, MAY 21)

I shop at Wal-Mart very infrequently because I find it hard to find things, [and the store is] often not very clean. There doesn't seem to be well-laid-out aisles like Target; it is more of a jumbled maze. However, one plus is the live fish they have. Kids love to go by and see them! And they usually have better prices. If I am looking for a particular item, like a kids' outdoor toy/sandbox, that is what usually gets me there, because you can find it cheaper.

—CRYSTAL B.,
35, AFFLUENT SHOPPER (2007, E-MAIL INTERVIEW, MAY 21)

Wal-Mart neighborhood grocery is OK if you just need staples—it'll be cheap. I won't go into the 24-hour Supercenter down here. I think that was the store that had a stabbing over a Black Thursday laptop deal or something like that. SuperTarget is almost as bad during midday Sunday, but at least the store is cleaner and the meat looks a little better.

—MICHAEL C.,
35, WAL-MART SHOPPER (2007, E-MAIL INTERVIEW, MAY 21)

(continued)

Exhibit 18 Interviewee Perspectives on Wal-Mart, 2007 *(Continued)*

When I was an Operations Manager for a Fortune 500 company, we were having a yearly employee appreciation picnic . . . [so] my secretary and I hopped into a company van, shot down to Sam's Club, loaded up four shopping carts of hamburgers, hotdogs, beverages, and all the fixings, got to the checkout, pulled out my Visa, and then found out that Sam's club didn't accept Visa. After a few minutes of arguing with an unhelpful and unsympathetic manager, I left all four carts at the checkout and have never been back since.

—Brian S.,
former Sam's Club member (2007, discussion-board posting, May 22)

Wal-Mart has been such a negative experience that it would be hard for me to go back. I have been hesitant to go to a neighborhood Wal-Mart because of my poor shopping experiences around the country at different big-box Wal-Marts. The Wal-Mart I am closer to is a lower socioeconomic neighborhood, and I drive past it to go to Target because I perceive it as being safer and I feel that I am getting a higher quality product.

—Oliver Davis,
Target shopper (2007, personal interview, May 21)

[Wal-Mart] will continue to grow, and will make many changes in that time. Some are for the better and some are not. Unfortunately, sometimes plans that are not well [thought-out] are implemented and mandated, which only causes frustration/irritation. Other times workers are stuck in [their] ways and don't want to change.

—Anonymous
Wal-Mart manager (2007, e-mail interview, May 21)

[Wal-Mart needs better] price marking, more UPC scanners in the store. I see something and the price is ambiguous. They don't mark the prices. They can also make checkout faster. Why is it so slow? I don't go to Kmart anymore because a lot of times the UPC of something doesn't ring up at the cash register. It isn't in their system. If it is on the shelf, the UPC should be in the computer. Wal-Mart is also getting worse at this.

—Fred G.,
55, suburban Wal-Mart shopper (2007, personal interview, May 21)

[Wal-Mart] does offer a big variety [of benefits for associates], some much better than other companies and some not so good in my opinion. Some examples of good discounts are 10% discount on most items (excludes grocery, clearance, and a few other items—biggest complaint on this is that tax in most areas eats up most of the discount), vacation (depends on variety of factors, but generally 2 weeks for full time and 1 week for [part-time] 1st year, and increases thereafter), personnel days (day off with pay—earned up to a certain # each year (average 2)), sick days, holiday pay, etc. On the other side of the coin, [I] think much more needs to be done to provide better health care for its workers, and a goal should be done to improve this every year. Many co-workers I know have dropped [their] coverage or rely on state assistance programs. Wal-Mart also did away with some of its [benefits], such as Christmas bonuses, unless you are grandfathered in (must have been hired before the change was made).

—Anonymous
Wal-Mart manager (2007, e-mail interview, May 21)

We have an Associates Fund that everyone chips into in case someone is in critical need. For example, if a cashier were to, heaven forbid, have their house burn down, the fund would immediately come to help out by supplying a place to stay, warm clothes, and food, pretty much everything that the associate would need to get back on her feet, up to and including a replacement house, if that's what it takes. . . . A happy associate is more productive.

Sergio Jimenez,
Wal-Mart store co-manager (2007, personal interview, May 20)

Wal-Mart takes care of their people in dire situations. When my friend's wife died, they brought them groceries and really took care of them.

—Wendy S.,
46, friend of Wal-Mart associate (2007, personal interview, May 20)

One thing the company does . . . every year is [to] hold [grassroots] meetings for associates to come and vent about things they don't like, in the hope that something will change. Sadly, most associates (workers) feel that they are allowed to vent, but not without [retaliation] any more, or at best [their] input will not change anything. I think the

(continued)

company should not just write down the input they are being given, but act on it when possible. If they would do so it would boost morale, and more effort would be given, [causing] customer satisfaction to go up and sales to boost as well.

—ANONYMOUS
WAL-MART MANAGER (2007, E-MAIL INTERVIEW, MAY 21)

If I [were] to change Wal-Mart, I would reduce product on the shelves and change the lighting, and widen the aisles. [T]he bouncing ball for Wal-Mart gives it a cartoon-ish edge, whereas Target does an ad that goes coast to coast, with a heavy CGI aspect that it isn't cartoon-y. It has a big-city feel whereas Wal-Mart has a small-town middle America feel. I am partial to bigger cities. . . . Smaller towns that have limited options [make] me feel constrained, which is one of the reasons I like Target, which has hip trends, whereas Wal-Mart just has the bouncy smiley face. [T]he smiley face reduces [Wal-Mart's] seriousness. I would go to more subtle references to being the low-cost provider, and pitch one-stop shopping, but push the option to have your own personal brand, and reduce the number of SKUs on the walls so you don't feel overwhelmed by the experience there.

—OLIVER DAVIS,
TARGET SHOPPER (2007, PERSONAL INTERVIEW, MAY 21)

I would LOVE a coupon for a certain amount off any item the store. Sort of what Michael's has (40% off any item) or Bed Bath and Beyond has (20% off). I also find Target's returns the most convenient I've ever experienced: they can locate the item you purchased by sliding your credit card through the reader so you don't have to go searching for your receipt. I appreciate that kind of convenience.

—LILI N.,
34, AFFLUENT SHOPPER (2007, E-MAIL INTERVIEW, MAY 19)

Legal. Class-action lawsuits against Wal-Mart have become commonplace. In *Savaglio v. Wal-Mart Stores, Inc.*, the "plaintiffs allege that they were not provided meal and rest breaks in accordance with California law, and seek monetary damages and injunctive relief."[128] A jury ruled in favor of those plaintiffs and awarded them a total of $198 million.[129] In *Dukes v. Wal-Mart Stores, Inc.*, currently pending on behalf of all present and past female employees in all of Wal-Mart's retail stores and warehouse clubs, Wal-Mart is alleged to have "engaged in a pattern and practice of discriminating against women in promotions, pay, training, and job assignments."[130] These lawsuits are providing ample fodder for Wal-Mart opponents to inflict ongoing reputation damage.

Global. The globalization trend that began in the 1990s persists. As trade barriers continue to come down around the world and as technology enables greater access to information, the world is becoming one mega-market of labor, capital, goods, and services. Bilateral and multilateral free trade agreements are continuing to shape markets.

Technology. The development of radio frequency identification (RFID) is expected to play a major part in the next evolution of supply chain management in the retail industry. This technology may better enable retailers to track inventory locations, store shelving status, packages en-route to and from suppliers, warehouses, shelves, and even shoplifting.[131] Recent developments in the technology include a movement toward "common standards and practices that could make RFID as ubiquitous as bar codes," and a push to lower the cost per RFID tag from the current 10-cent mark to the Wal-Mart target of 5-cents.[132] RFID chips are increasingly "able to hold much more information and fit into different shapes and sizes—woven inside clothing, slipped into a paper-thin tag or molded inside a key chain."[133]

Another technology development impacting the retail industry is the unabated growth of electronic commerce, and the increasing pervasiveness of broadband Internet access in most developed countries. As consumers at various socioeconomic levels come to rely more on the Web for information, entertainment, and shopping, retailers are discovering the need to use their online presence not just to spur online sales, but to drive traditional-format sales as well.

Demographics. Americans, like those in many developed nations, are getting older. The Census Bureau estimates the number of those aged 65 and up will rise from approximately 35 million in 2000 to 86.7 million by 2050. The age 65 and up cohort made up 12.4 percent of the total U.S. population in 2000; by 2050, it will make up 20.7 percent of a projected population of nearly 420 million.[134]

The country is also becoming more diverse.[135] Ethnic and gender diversity in the U.S. workforce is on the rise. In 1995, whites/non-Hispanics made up 76 percent of the workforce, but this is projected to decrease to 68 percent in 2020. According to the U.S. Department of Labor, women comprised 46 percent of the labor force in 2006.[136] The percentage of women over the age of 16 in the labor force has risen 23 percent in 44 years to 59 percent in 2004.[137]

The distance in America between the "haves" and the "have-nots" is growing. Increasing returns to education have created a bifurcation in income distribution.[138] The bottom quintile has seen its mean income increase 34.5 percent in real terms from 1967 to 2005, whereas the top income quintile had an increase in mean income of 80.8 percent over the same time period.[139] Average income growth for the bottom three quintiles was only 30.4 percent. The typical Wal-Mart customer is in the middle-income quintiles.

As Wal-Mart's competitive landscape continues to evolve, the company is taking its strategic cues from Sam Walton's words of wisdom: "Everything around you is always changing. To succeed, stay out in front of that change."[140]

Current Strategies

To manage its competitive environment, Wal-Mart is currently deploying a variety of strategies, most of which stem from its relentless core generic strategy of cost leadership, but some of which represent beyond-cost approaches. "Our everyday low price position is the basis for our business," wrote Rob Walton in Wal-Mart's 2006 annual report.[141] He added, "While this core principle is critical to our growth and business strategy, by itself it is not enough anymore."[142] According to Scott in this year's shareholder letter, Wal-Mart is confronting "a period of perhaps the most rapid and profound change in our Company's history. With our transformation plan, we are committed to staying 'Out in Front' of the changes around us."[143] The corporate plan, encompassing previous change initiatives as well as newer ones, rests on "five pillars": "broadening our appeal to our customers, making Wal-Mart an even better place to work, improving operations and efficiencies, driving global growth, and contributing to our communities.[144]

Strategies to Deal with External and Reputational Challenges. Wal-Mart is pursuing two key strategies that will help them overcome external issues affecting the company, including environmental and community-impact issues, among others. These strategies include sustainability efforts and localized charitable giving to help portray it as being a responsible corporate citizen and a good neighbor. Wal-Mart launched its global environmental sustainability initiative in 2004 and has since taken action toward several sustainability goals: sell 100 million compact fluorescent bulbs by 2008; reduce packaging by five percent by 2013; buy fish from certified fisheries; sell "more organic and environmentally friendly products"; and make company facilities and trucks more energy-efficient.[145] The Wal-Mart Foundation in 2006 gave "more than $415 million in cash and in-kind merchandise to 100,000 organizations worldwide," making it the "largest corporate cash contributor in America."[146] The Foundation "gave most of the money at the local level where [it] can have the greatest impact."[147]

Wal-Mart has beefed up pro-community, pro-sustainability, pro-health care information on its Web site, on its television ads, and in its annual report. The company recently launched *In Front with Wal-Mart*, a 30-minute television show airing on the Lifetime and USA networks that "gives [Wal-Mart] a chance to showcase [its] incredible associates and the variety of ways they give back to their communities, bettering the lives of America's working families" and "sheds light . . . on some of [Wal-Mart's] eco-friendly practices."[148] Wal-Mart created an interactive Web site on sustainability, dedicated a page of its 2007 annual report to sustainability, and will soon publish a separate Sustainability Report.[149]

In its public outreach, Wal-Mart also stresses its benefits to suppliers and communities, as well as its commitment to providing affordable health care and competitive wages for its associates.[150] These efforts tie into its supply-chain innovation and people strategies.

Supply-Chain Innovation and People Strategies

As previously mentioned, Wal-Mart creates value for customers with a highly efficient and innovative supply-chain management operation. This operation combines tough, low-cost procurement tactics, leading-edge information systems and "rocket-science" logistics.[151]

There's not much negotiation at all. The manufacturer walks into the room. I've been in these little cubicles, I've seen it happen. The buyer says, "Look, we want you to sell it to us for 5 percent on a dollar—at cost—lower this year than you did last year." They know every fact and figure that these manufacturers have. They know their books. They know their costs. They know their business practices—everything, you know? So what's a manufacturer left to do? They sit naked in front of Wal-Mart. You know, Wal-Mart calls the shots. "If you want to do business with us, if you want to stay in business, then you're going to do it our way." And it's all about driving down the cost of goods.

—**FORMER WAL-MART STORE MANAGER JON LEHMAN ON FRONTLINE IN 2004**[152]

All Wal-Mart suppliers must participate in Retail Link, a computerized system in which they "plan, execute, and analyze their businesses."[153] Along with electronic data interchange, suppliers receive purchase order information and supply invoices electronically, thereby lowering expenses and increasing productivity. Suppliers must meet Wal-Mart's strict lead-time and shipping requirements by using the technology and complying with operating procedures. The Wal-Mart logistics team uses an Internet-based Transportation Link system that complements a Backhaul Betty telephone voice-response system to help them move goods. In one year, Wal-Mart estimated nearly 1 million loads of general merchandise moved to Distribution Centers throughout the country.[154] Store-bound shipments travel by the company's 7,000 trucks, one of the largest fleets in the world.[155] The company relentlessly strives to develop its supply-chain process. For example, "[t]o ensure greater supply chain visibility, satellite-based tracking technology is being installed in the Company's entire fleet of over-the-road trailers. The data generated . . . increases productivity, reduces costs and enhances security."[156]

In the stores, Wal-Mart's legendary inventory management capability is driven by its advanced Texlon barcode system. In addition to tracking the sales price, inventory levels of each product, and a history of quantities sold, Texlon can record trends and predict future needs. Quantities sold can be traced to specific weeks, days, or even hours of each day. Seasonal projections can be documented, and shopping habits are noted. Information is sent daily at midnight to the warehouses, so depleted products are restocked the following night. Reliance on this kind of technology to drive the supply chain enables Wal-Mart's suppliers to use "pull production" instead of "push production." The barcode system will eventually be replaced by an RFID-based system, technology Wal-Mart is driving.

Wal-Mart's technological supply-chain sophistication is intended to provide "value for customers, associates, and shareholders."[157] The system depends on Wal-Mart's 1.8 million associates to provide the final link in the value chain to customers. Wal-Mart's people strategy involves "[g]iving our associates the tools and opportunities they need to be as productive as possible," which has enabled "workforce productivity gains in every quarter of the last two years."[158] Associates who feel overworked may create a weak link in the value chain.

I would say that some customers are happy, but most are not. . . . [M]any workers feel they are being overworked due to mainly understaffing issues, which causes workers to treat the customers worse, then causing customers to become upset. Many customers have at one time been [Wal-Mart] associates and understand how things are handled at each store level and can relate. Personally, [I] believe that overall morale a few years ago was much higher with workers, and that attitude was passed along to the customers. Today many customers feel that [Wal-Mart] only wants them for [their] money, and does not care about them."

—**ANONYMOUS WAL-MART MANAGER (2007, E-MAIL INTERVIEW, MAY 21)**

Reassuring its "valued long-term associates" that the company "is listening to them," Wal-Mart "again increased [its] average full-time hourly wage in the United States."[159] The company is against unionization of its associates.

Wal-Mart's operational effectiveness goals of improving return on investment, comparable-store sales, and working capital productivity are setting the agenda for its business-segment strategies.[160]

Wal-Mart Stores Segment Strategies

The Wal-Mart Stores segment is in its second year of a three-year strategic plan to improve ROI, people development, and customer relevancy.[161] Customers have become the prime focus since January 2007, when Wal-Mart Stores elevated its new marketing and merchandising chiefs and completed its management reshuffle.

In 2006, Wal-Mart Stores rolled out a $4 generic prescription program, a clear opening-price-point approach. Merchandising has been characterized by the product-focused "opening price point" strategy, which relied on attractive low prices on entry-level items in every category to set the stage for higher-margin prices on more desirable items.[162] This single strategy has served to focus each of the two dozen departments at a typical Wal-Mart Supercenter (see Exhibit 19). Wal-Mart stores often offer retail space to other vendors that provide services, such as nail salons, hair salons, coffee shops, food and beverage vendors (e.g., McDonald's and Subway), full-service banks, and even employment agencies in some locations.

Recently, Wal-Mart Stores "realigned [its] merchandising . . . around five key power categories—entertainment, grocery, health and wellness, apparel, and home."[163] Global Procurement meanwhile is "establishing groups of technical experts—specialists that focus on the many important dynamics of a particular category purchase."[164]

Exhibit 19 List of Departments in Wal-Mart

Wal-Mart Departments	
Grocery	Pharmacy
Bakery	Health & Beauty
Produce	Vision Center
Deli	Jewelry
Frozen Foods	Lawn & Garden
Apparel	Portrait Studio
Housewares	Photo Lab
Entertainment	Hardware
Electronics	Furniture
Tire & Lube Express	Sporting Goods
Automotive	Toys & Games
School Supplies	Office Products & School Supplies

Source: http://www.walmart.com.

The Wal-Mart Stores customer segmentation and merchandising strategies have been in flux over the past few years, with three different strategies in play to move Wal-Mart Stores toward a more customer-focused position.

The first customer-focused strategy—mimicking Target's upscale, fashion-forward appeal—flopped. "In working to broaden our appeal to our customers, we moved too quickly in the rollout of some of our fashion-forward apparel in the United States," according to Scott.[165] Wal-Mart Stores has at least partially retreated from this strategy.

The second customer-focused strategy—localizing selections based on store-neighborhood demographics—continues to drive various store changes, though it may be waning. In 2006, Wal-Mart "launched six different types of customized stores to attract different demographics, from inner-city residents, to affluent suburbanites, to rural shoppers."[166] With these stores, Wal-Mart attempted to target African-Americans, Hispanics, empty-nesters, suburbanites, rural residents, and the affluent. Wal-Mart expanded and empowered regional marketing teams, moving many executives away from headquarters into regions to better understand Wal-Mart's wide customer base.[167] These changes were inspired by localized merchandizing selection in Wal-Mart de Mexico stores aimed at different mixes of inventory for different income levels.[168] For example, the localization strategy expanded the mix of hip-hop, gospel, and R&B music in a store outside Chicago and led to plans for larger pharmacy sections and fewer children's clothes at a store geared toward empty-nesters.[169] In his March letter to shareholders, Scott wrote, "We continue to strive to make sure every Wal-Mart store is a 'Store of the Community'—one that reflects the individual needs of each neighborhood we serve."[170]

The third customer-focused strategy—appealing to the three universal types of low-price-seeking customers who currently shop at Wal-Mart—now guides merchandising and marketing decisions. According to Fleming and Quinn, the three types are "'brand aspirationals' (people with low incomes who are obsessed with names like Kitchen Aid), 'price-sensitive affluents' (wealthier shoppers who love deals), and 'value-price shoppers' (who like low prices and cannot afford much more)."[171] For these types, the Wal-Mart Stores segment is concentrating on developing unique, innovative products and providing distinguished brands (such as the recently added Dell desktop computers) to better appeal to its core customers as the low-price leader on well-known brands.[172]

This is a much better strategy for Wal-Mart than the store segmentation strategy path . . . they were going down before . . . because it aligns with their basic brand proposition (EDLP) and basic consumer rather than trying to attract a new consumer by adding high-end fashion and complicated assortments. For the same reason, it aligns better with Wal-Mart's supply chain strength. It's far easier to roll out a national brand in stores nationally than it is to ship different assortments to different stores within a region without disrupting the cost efficient supply chain that is Wal-Mart's core competitive advantage. I'm not sure what took them so long but it looks like Wal-Mart is back to a strategy that is sustainable and executable for them.

—**Forrester Research senior analyst Lisa Bradner**[173]

Sam's Club Segment Strategies

Sam's Club, meanwhile, is focused on three areas: "reinvigorating the brand" by broadening products and services; improving inventory management and other performance measures; and optimizing the "in-club experience."[174] Sam's Club stores offer members products such as frozen and dry food goods in bulk, electronics, computer equipment, clothing, books, electronic entertainment, and general merchandise. Sam's Club recently restructured its management layers to give stores additional flexibility and to boost service.[175] Rumors have circulated that Sam's Club may spin off from Wal-Mart, in part to set its own direction in attracting and retaining members and associates, two key groups who are generally less loyal to Sam's Club than to its rival Costco.[176]

Wal-Mart International Segment Strategies

Wal-Mart International's strategy is to prioritize "where the greatest growth and greatest returns exist," what the segment calls "majoring in the majors."[177] The majors appear to include the Americas primarily, followed by the United Kingdom and Japan, as well as China and India over the long term.[178] Wal-Mart International is labeling this strategy "focused portfolio execution."[179] Its second strategy is global leverage, or "taking full advantage of our worldwide assets, including formats, information systems, purchasing organizations, category expertise, and shared best practices."[180] In the past year, it has concentrated on turning around Asda in the United Kingdom through "improved execution in all phases of customer service, differentiation with competitors, and development of new channels and formats."[181] To better compete against U.K. leader Tesco, second-largest Asda reportedly may be considering acquiring the third-largest U.K. retailer, the J. Sainsbury chain of grocery and convenience stores.[182] Wal-Mart's international stores are varied in their mix of products and services, and they stick to the motto of "offering working families the things they need at the prices they can afford."[183]

Just as the business segments are looking to focus on the right challenges for their short- and long-term success in the marketplace, the company must ensure it is applying its greatest resources against its greatest strategic challenges across the enterprise.

Strategic Challenges

The challenges Wal-Mart faces today are actually not much different from what they have been for the past several years. These following quotes come from an article in April 2003: "Even though it is the nation's largest apparel retailer with more than 12 percent of the market, Wal-Mart could be doing better in this category"; "It would like to be a fashion retailer and take on Target with good quality at a low price-point, but it hasn't convinced the American consumer it should be a destination for casual fashion"; "Wal-Mart is . . . looking abroad for future sales growth"; "Wal-Mart will need to struggle against the urge to centralize operations and eliminate decision making from the frontlines where managers have face-to-face contact with customers"; and "The only area in which Wal-Mart has not been able to pummel its competition is against Costco."[184] One of the company's challenges may be to stop proliferating nearly identical sets of challenges

each year. Like the stock price, the challenges appear to be stuck in a holding pattern.

One key new challenge is the sluggishness of same-store sales relative to Wal-Mart's competitors. According to *BusinessWeek,* Wal-Mart faces "the diciest conundrum in retailing today . . . can it seduce . . . middle-income shoppers into stepping up their purchases in a major way without alienating its low-income legions in the process?"[185]

Another growing challenge is the difficulty of expanding in the domestic market, whether because of community opposition or geographic saturation (see Exhibits 20 and 21).

These and other strategic challenges are weighing on the minds of Wal-Mart's shareholders, especially on the two with the most responsibility for the company's fate.

Questions Wal-Mart Leaders Must Address

CEO Lee Scott and Chairman Rob Walton are grappling with some vexing questions as they head into the 2007 Wal-Mart Annual Shareholders' Meeting:

- How can Wal-Mart Stores and Sam's Club increase same-store sales?
- How should the company capture share of middle- and upper-income wallets?
- Should Wal-Mart Stores fully retreat from fashion-forward merchandising and marketing? Will its neighborhood-store-localization strategy increase sales enough to offset the associated costs? What should it do to make its new three-types-of-customers segmentation strategy work?
- Should the company spin off Sam's Club? If not, what should it do to compete more effectively against Costco?
- Is Wal-Mart expanding the right kind of new stores at the right pace and in the right places? How and where should the company continue to grow internationally? Should Asda buy J. Sainsbury?
- What will it take to restore the company's reputation in America?
- Should Lee Scott change Wal-Mart's course? If so, how?
- Should Rob Walton replace Lee Scott? If so, when and with whom?

Exhibit 20 Spread of Wal-Mart Stores, 1970–1995

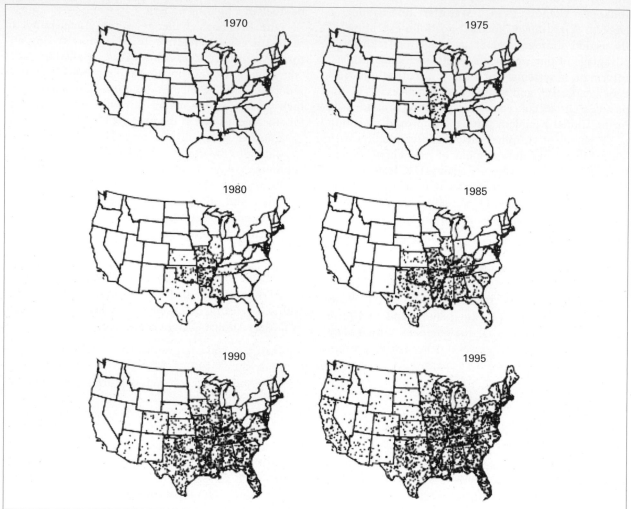

Source: E. Basker, 2004, Job creation or destruction? Labor-market effects of Wal-Mart expansion, University of Missouri, January, Figure 1, 28.

Exhibit 21 Number of Counties Having a Wal-Mart Store, 1963–2006

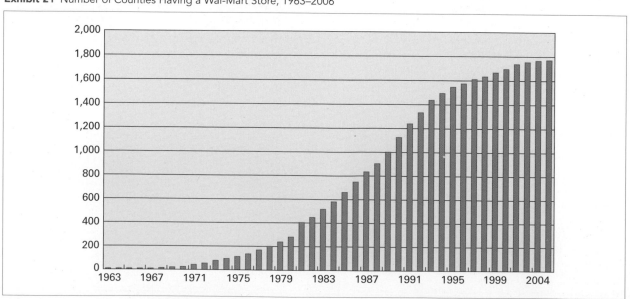

Source: 2005, The economic impact of Wal-Mart, Global Insight, Business Planning Solutions, Global Insight Advisory Services, November 2, Figure 4, 33.

NOTES

1. A. Bianco, 2006, The Bully of Bentonville: The High Cost of Wal-Mart's Everyday Low Prices, New York: Doubleday Publishing, 1.

2. 2007, 7 demands for change, Against * The * Wal, http://www.againstthewal.net/7demands.html, May 18.

3. 2007, Notice of 2007 Annual Shareholders' Meeting, DEF 14A, Proxy Statement, Wal-Mart Stores, Inc., U.S. SEC; April 19, 52–68.

4. A. Bianco, 2006, The Bully of Bentonville: The High Cost of Wal-Mart's Everyday Low Prices, 267; 2007, Yahoo! Finance, http://finance.yahoo.com/charts#chart6:symbol=wmt;range=20000103, 20070518;compare=cost+tgt;indicator=volume;charttype=line; crosshair=on;logscale=on;source=undefined, May 17.

5. 2007, Yahoo! Finance, http://finance.yahoo.com/charts#chart6:symbol=wmt;range=20000103,20070518;compare=cost+tgt;indicator=volume;charttype=line;crosshair=on;logscale=on;source=undefined, May 17.

6. A. Bianco, 2007, Wal-Mart's midlife crisis, BusinessWeek, April 30, 46–52.

7. 2007, Wal-Mart Data Sheet, http://walmartstores.com/Files/US_operations.pdf, February 8.

8. 2007, Wal-Mart Annual Report.

9. 2007, Wal-Mart Stores, Inc., Form 8-K, U.S. SEC, May 15; and 2007, Company Overview, Target.com, http://investors.target.com/phoenix.zhtml?c=65828&p=irol-homeProfile, May 25.

10. L. Michael Cacace & K. Tucksmith, 2007, Fortune 500 largest U.S. corporations, Fortune, April 30, F2.

11. Ibid.

12. A. Bianco, 2007, Wal-Mart's midlife crisis, 49–52.

13. A. Bianco, 2007, Wal-Mart's midlife crisis, 46.

14. 2004, Wal-Mart Tops Fortune's List of America's Most Admired Companies, Fortune, http://www.timeinc.net/fortune/information/presscenter/fortune/press_releases/02232004AMAC.html, February 23.

15. 2007, America's Most Admired Companies 2007, Fortune, CNNMoney.com, http://money.cnn.com/magazines/fortune/mostadmired/2007/top20/, May 18.

16. W. Zellner, 2004, Sam Walton: King of the discounters, BusinessWeek, August 9.

17. Ibid.

18. Ibid.

19. A. A. Thompson & A. J. Strickland, Strategic Management, Concepts & Cases, 10th ed., New York: Irwin/McGraw-Hill.

20. 2007, The Wal-Mart Timeline, Wal-Mart Facts, http://www.walmartfacts.com/content/default.aspx?id=3, April 1; D. Longo, 1998, Wal-Mart hands CEO crown to David Glass, Discount Store News, February 15, 1988.

21. 2007, Wal-Mart Annual Report, 19; 2007, The Wal-Mart Timeline, Wal-Mart Facts, http://www.walmartfacts.com/content/default.aspx?id=3, April 1.

22. A. Bianco, 2007, Wal-Mart's midlife crisis, 46–54.

23. 2007, Data Sheet, Wal-Mart Stores, http://walmartstores.com/Files/US_operations.pdf, February 8, May 25; and 2007, International Data Sheet, Wal-Mart Stores, http://walmartstores.com/Files/Intl_operations.pdf, February 8, May 25.

24. 2007, Wal-Mart Annual Report, 1.

25. A. Biesada, 2007, Wal-Mart Company Overview, Hoovers Online, http://premium.hoovers.com, May.

26. Ibid.

27. P. Engardio, 2007, Beyond the green corporation, imagine a world in which eco-friendly and socially responsible practices actually help a company's bottom line. It's closer than you think, BusinessWeek Online, January 29.

28. 2007, Wal-Mart Annual Report, 18-19.

29. 2007, Wal-Mart Annual Report, 31.

30. 2007, Wal-Mart Annual Report , 28.

31. Ibid.

32. Ibid.

33. 2007, Wal-Mart Annual Report, 31.

34. Ibid.

35. 2007, Wal-Mart Annual Report, 28.

36. 2007, Wal-Mart Annual Report, 36.

37. 2007, Wal-Mart Annual Report, 32.

38. 2007, International Data Sheet, Wal-Mart Stores, http://walmartstores.com/Files/Intl_operations.pdf, February 8.

39. 2007, Wal-Mart Annual Report, 32.

40. 2007, Wal-Mart Annual Report, 51-52.

41. 2006, IGD looks at Wal-Mart's decision to pull out of Germany, http://www.igd.com/CIR, March 8.

42. 2007, Wal-Mart Annual Report, 32.

43. 2007, Informe Annual 2006, Wal-Mart de Mexico, http://library.corporate-ir.net/library/19/194/194702/items/231792/AR06.pdf, May 21; and 2007, CIA World Fact Book, Mexico, https://www.cia.gov/library/publications/the-world-factbook/geos/mx.html#Econ, May 21.

44. 2007, Wal-Mart Facts: The Wal-Mart Story, http://www.walmartfacts.com/content/default.aspx?id=1, April 1.

45. 2006, CNBC Interview with Carter Cast, http://www.hoovers.com/global/co/interviews/player.xhtml, November 7.

46. 2007, About Sam's Club, Samsclub.com, http://pressroom.samsclub.com/content/?id=3&atg=524, March 1.

47. K. Hundson, 2007, Wal-Mart Pushes Financial-Services Menu, Wall Street Journal, June 6, A3.

48. 2007, The Wal-Mart Timeline, Wal-Mart Facts, http://www.walmartfacts.com/content/default.aspx?id=3, April 1; D. Longo, 1998, Wal-Mart hands CEO crown to David Glass, Discount Store News, February 15.

49. 2007, The Wal-Mart Timeline, Wal-Mart Facts, http://www.walmartfacts.com/content/default.aspx?id=3, April 1.

50. 2007, Wal-Mart Annual Report, 14; 2007, Senior Officers, Wal-Mart Stores, http://walmartstores.com/GlobalWMStoresWeb/navigate.do?catg=540, May 6.

51. 2007, S. Robson Walton, Wal-Mart Stores, http://walmartstores.com/GlobalWMStoresWeb/navigate.do?catg=540&contId=15, May 6; 2005. Forbes: America's richest 400, MSN Money, http://moneycentral.msn.com/content/invest/forbes/P129955.asp, September 23.

52. A. Bianco, 2006, The Bully of Bentonville: The High Cost of Wal-Mart's Everyday Low Prices, 61.

53. 2007, S. Robson Walton, Wal-Mart Stores.

54. 2007, Wal-Mart Annual Report, 13.

55. A. Bianco, The Bully of Bentonville: The High Cost of Wal-Mart's Everyday Low Prices, 104.

56. Ibid.

57. A. Bianco, The Bully of Bentonville: The High Cost of Wal-Mart's Everyday Low Prices, 79.

58. Ibid.

59. A. Bianco, The Bully of Bentonville: The High Cost of Wal-Mart's Everyday Low Prices, 80.

60. A. Bianco, The Bully of Bentonville: The High Cost of Wal-Mart's Everyday Low Prices, 81.

61. 2007, H. Lee Scott, Jr., Senior Officers, WalMartStores.com, http://walmartstores.com/GlobalWMStoresWeb/navigate.do?catg=540&contId=17, May 25.

62. Ibid.

63. 2007, Michael T. Duke, Senior Officers, WalMartStores.com, http://walmartstores.com/GlobalWMStoresWeb/navigate.do?catg=540&contId=22, May 25.

64. Ibid.

65. 2007, John B. Menzer, Senior Officers, WalMartStores.com, http://walmartstores.com/GlobalWMStoresWeb/navigate.do?catg=540&contId=19, May 25.

66. Ibid.
67. Ibid.
68. 2007, Eduardo Castro-Wright, Senior Officers, WalMartStores.com, http://walmartstores.com/GlobalWMStoresWeb/navigate.do?catg=540&contId=41, May 25.
69. 2007, C. Douglas McMillon, Senior Officers, WalMartStores.com, http://walmartstores.com/GlobalWMStoresWeb/navigate.do?catg=540&contId=33, May 25.
70. 2007, John E. Fleming, Senior Officers, WalMartStores.com, http://walmartstores.com/GlobalWMStoresWeb/navigate.do?catg=540&contId=42, May 25.
71. 2007, Stephen Quinn, Senior Officers, WalMartStores.com, http://walmartstores.com/GlobalWMStoresWeb/navigate.do?catg=540&contId=6396, May 25.
72. 2007, Wal-Mart Board of Directors, Walmart.com, June 28.
73. M. Halkias, 2007, Questrom nominated to Wal-Mart board, *Dallas Morning News*, http://www.dallasnews.com/sharedcontent/dws/bus/industries/retail/stories/042507dnbusquestrom.36b21ad.html, April 24.
74. Ibid.
75. S. Braun, 2007, At Wal-Mart, Clinton didn't upset any carts, *Los Angeles Times*, http://www.latimes.com/news/nationworld/nation/la-na-hillary19may19,0,5168474.story?coll=la-home-center, May 19.
76. 2007, Morningstar, Wal-Mart Stores (WMT), http://quicktake.morningstar.com/StockNet/powerbrokers.aspx?Country=USA&Symbol=WMT&stocktab=owner, May 6; 2007, Wal-Mart Stores Inc. (WMT), Major Holders, Yahoo! Finance, http://finance.yahoo.com/q/mh?s=WMT, May 6.
77. 2007, Wal-Mart Stores Inc. (WMT), Major Holders, Yahoo! Finance, http://finance.yahoo.com/q/mh?s=WMT; May 6; and 2005, Forbes: America's richest 400, MSN Money, http://moneycentral.msn.com/content/invest/forbes/P129955.asp, September 23; 2002, Proxy, Wal-Mart Stores, http://www.walmartstores.com/Files/proxy_2002/proxy_pg05.htm; M. Weil and M. Barbaro, 2005, John T. Walton, 58; Heir to Wal-Mart Fortune, *The Washington Post*, http://www.washingtonpost.com/wp-dyn/content/article/2005/06/27/AR2005062701471.html, June 28; 2007, Associated Press, *Washington Post*, Helen R. Walton; Philanthropic wife of Wal-Mart chief, http://www.washingtonpost.com/wp-dyn/content/article/2007/04/20/AR2007042002060.html, April 21.
78. 2007, Wal-Mart Stores Inc. (WMT), Insider Roster, Yahoo! Finance, http://finance.yahoo.com/q/ir?s=WMT, May 6.
79. 2007, Wal-Mart Stores Inc. (WMT), Major Holders, Yahoo! Finance, http://finance.yahoo.com/q/mh?s=WMT, May 6.
80. 2007, Morningstar, Wal-Mart Stores (WMT), http://quicktake.morningstar.com/StockNet/powerbrokers.aspx?Country=USA&Symbol=WMT&stocktab=owner, May 6.
81. 2007, Wal-Mart Annual Report, 64.
82. 2007, 2002 Wal-Mart Annual Reports.
83. Ibid.
84. 2007, Sam's Club vs. Costco: Battle of the brands, *BloggingStocks*, AOL Money & Finance, http://www.bloggingstocks.com/2007/04/12/sams-club-vs-costco-battle-of-the-brands/, April 12.
85. T. Otte, 2007, Spinoff in Bentonville revisited, Value Investing, MotleyFool.com, http://www.fool.com/investing/value/2007/05/07/spinoff-in-bentonville-revisited.aspx, May 7.
86. M. Wagner, 2003, Where's Wal-Mart: Wal-Mart's web revenue hardly registers on its ledger, *Internet Retailer*, http://www.internetretailer.com/internet/marketing-conference/70624-wheres-wal-mart.html, April.
87. D. Pinto, 2005, Mass market retailers, http://www.massmarketretailers.com/articles/Every_winner.html, May 16.
88. Ibid.
89. Ibid.
90. A. Bianco, 2007, Wal-Mart's, midlife crisis, 48.
91. D. Pinto, Mass market retailers.
92. M. Holz-Clause & M. Geisler, 2006, Grocery Industry, Grocery Retailing Profile, AgMRC, http://www.agmrc.org/agmrc/markets/Food/groceryindustry.htm, September.
93. 2007, Wal-Mart F1Q08 (Qtr End 4/30/07) Earnings Call Transcript, SeekingAlpha.com, http://retail.seekingalpha.com/article/35633, May 15.
94. Ibid.
95. 2007, Wal-Mart 1st Quarter 2008 Earnings Release, May 10.
96. Ibid.
97. 2007, Wal-Mart April Sales News Release, May 10.
98. R. Dodes & G. McWilliams, 2007, Fashion faux pas hurts Wal-Mart, *Wall Street Journal*, May 21, A8.
99. G. McWilliams, 2007, Wal-Mart net rises as weakness persists, *Wall Street Journal*, May 16, C6.
100. J. Covert, 2007, Retail-sales slide fuels concern: Decline of 2.3% in April among worst on record; even Wal-Mart slipped, Wall Street Journal, May 11, A3.
101. 2007, Target Corporation, Form 8-K, U.S. SEC, May 23; 2007, Company Overview, Target.com, http://investors.target.com/phoenix.zhtml?c=65828&p=irol-homeProfile, May 25.
102. Ibid.
103. 2006, Target Annual Report, 2.
104. Ibid.
105. 2007, Company Profile, Costco Wholesale Investor Relations, http://phx.corporate-ir.net/phoenix.zhtml?c=83830&p=irol-homeprofile, May 5.
106. 2006, Costco Annual Report, 9.
107. 2006, 2002, Costco Annual Report.
108. 2007, The Kroger Co., Form 10-K, U.S. SEC, April 4.
109. Ibid.
110. Ibid.
111. 2007, Carrefour profile, Hoovers, Lexis/Nexis Academic, May 8.
112. 2007, Tesco profile, Hoovers, Lexis/Nexis Academic, May 8.
113. Ibid.
114. 2007, Global Procurement, WalMartStores.com, http://walmartstores.com/GlobalWMStoresWeb/navigate.do?catg=337, May 26.
115. A. Bianco & W. Zellner, 2003, Is Wal-Mart too powerful? *BusinessWeek*, http://www.businessweek.com/magazine/content/03_40/b3852001_mz001.htm, October 6.
116. Ibid.
117. Ibid.
118. 2007, Wal-Mart Facts, http://www.walmartfacts.com/FactSheets/3142007_Corporate_Facts.pdf, March 14.
119. S. Kapinus, 2006, Rollback sushi and discount organics, *ACNielsen Consumer Insight*, http://us.acnielsen.com/pubs/2006_q2_ci_rollback.shtml, Q2.
120. Ibid.
121. Ibid.
122. Ibid.
123. Barney Gimbel, 2006, Attack of the Wal-Martyrs, http://money.cnn.com/magazines/fortune/fortune_archive/2006/12/11/8395445/index.htm, November 28.
124. B. C. Lynn, 2006, It's time to enforce antitrust law and break up Wal-Mart, *Harper's Magazine*, July.
125. A. Nagourney & M. Barbaro, 2006, Eye on election, Democrats run as Wal-Mart foe, *New York Times*, August 17.
126. Ibid.
127. 2006, Beaverton council rejects Cedar Mill Wal-Mart plan, *Beaverton Valley Times*, August 8; 2005, No Wal-Mart for Vancouver, *CBC News*, June 29; 2004, Inglewood Wal-Mart proposal defeated, http://www.laane.org/pressroom/stories/walmart/040407CityNewsService.html, April 6.
128. 2007, Wal-Mart Annual Report, 56.
129. Ibid.
130. Ibid.
131. C. Harrison, 2003, Commitment from Wal-Mart may boost tracking technology, *Dallas Morning News*, July 15.
132. Ibid.
133. Ibid.
134. 2004, U.S. Census Bureau, Interim Projections Consistent with 2000 Census, http://www.census.gov/population/www/projections/popproj.html, March.
135. Ibid.
136. 2007, U.S. Department of Labor, Women's Bureau: Statistics & Data, http://www.dol.gov/wb/stats/main.htm, May 14.

137. E. L. Chao & K. P. Utgoff, Women in the labor force: A databook, U.S. Bureau of Labor Statistics, May 2005, 1.

138. G. Becker & K. Murphy, 2007, The upside of income inequality, *The American*, May/June, 24–28.

139. 2007, U.S. Census Bureau, Historical Income Inequality Tables, http://www.census.gov/hhes/www/income/histinc/ineqtoc.html, May 21.

140. 2007, Wal-Mart "Out in Front," Fact Sheets, WalMartFacts.com, http://www.walmartfacts.com/FactSheets/4112007_Wal-Mart__Out_in_Front_.pdf, April 11.

141. R. Walton, 2006, Wal-Mart Annual Report, inside cover.

142. Ibid.

143. H. L. Scott, 2007, Wal-Mart Annual Report, 10.

144. 2007, Wal-Mart "Out in Front."

145. 2007 Wal-Mart Annual Report, 5, 12; and Wal-Mart Stores Overview, http://walmartstores.com/GlobalWMStoresWeb/navigate.do?catg=345, May 25.

146. 2007 Wal-Mart Annual Report, 8, 12.

147. Ibid.

148. 2007, In Front with Wal-Mart, Wal-Mart Stores, Inc., http://www.infrontwithwalmart.com/about.aspx, May 20.

149. 2007, Wal-Mart Annual Report, 5.

150. 2007, Wal-Mart Annual Report, 11.

151. 2003, Knowledge@Wharton, The Wal-Mart Empire: A Simple Formula and Unstoppable Growth, Research at Penn, http://www.upenn.edu/researchatpenn/article.php?631&bus, April 9.

152. 2004, FRONTLINE co-production with Hedrick Smith Productions, Inc., WGBH Educational Foundation, http://www.pbs.org/wgbh/pages/frontline/shows/walmart/etc/script.html.

153. 2007, Wal-Mart supplier requirements and processes, http://walmartstores.com/GlobalWMStoresWeb/navigate .do?catg=331, May 19.

154. Ibid.

155. 2007, Wal-Mart Sustainability, http://walmartstores.com/microsite/walmart_sustainability.html, May 19.

156. 2007, Wal-Mart Annual Report, 16.

157. Ibid.

158. 2007, Wal-Mart Annual Report, 11.

159. Ibid.

160. 2007, Wal-Mart Annual Report, 21.

161. 2007, Wal-Mart Annual Report, 18.

162. S. Hornblower, 2004, Always low prices: Is Wal-Mart good for America? *Frontline*, http://www.pbs.org/wgbh/pages/frontline/shows/walmart/secrets/pricing.html, November 23.

163. 2007, Wal-Mart Annual Report, 18.

164. 2007, Wal-Mart Annual Report, 17.

165. H. L. Scott, 2007, Wal-Mart Annual Report, 11.

166. B. Helm & D. Kiley, 2006, Wal-Mart leaves draft out in the cold, *BusinessWeek*, http://www.businessweek.com/bwdaily/dnflash/content/dec2006/db20061207_540888.htm?campaign_id=rss_innovate, December 7.

167. A. Zimmerman, 2006, To boost sales, Wal-Mart drops one-size-fits-all approach, *Wall Street Journal*, http://online.wsj.com/article/SB115758956826955863.html?mod=hps_us_pageone, September 7.

168. Ibid.

169. Ibid.

170. H. L. Scott, 2007, Wal-Mart Annual Report, 11.

171. M. Barbaro, 2007, It's not only about price at Wal-Mart, *New York Times*, http://www.nytimes.com/2007/03/02/business/02walmart.html?ex=1330491600&en=5a72ddc69030ce62&ei=5088&partner=rssnyt&emc=rss&pagewanted=print, March 2

172. 2007 Wal-Mart Annual Report, 17; P. Svensson, 2007, Dell to sell computers at Wal-Mart, Associated Press, Yahoo! Finance, http://biz.yahoo.com/ap/070524/dell_wal_mart.html?.v=11, May 24.

173. T. Ryan, 2007, From RetailWire: Wal-Mart classifies customers for growth, *Supply Chain Digest*, http://www.scdigest.com/assets/newsViews/07-03-27-2.php?cid=977, March 27.

174. 2007, Wal-Mart Annual Report, 19.

175. 2007, Wal-Mart cutting managers at Sam's Club, Reuters, http://www.reuters.com/article/businessNews/idUSN2628417520070426?feedType=RSS, April 26.

176. T. Otte, 2007, Spinoff in Bentonville revisited, value investing, MotleyFool.com, http://www.fool.com/investing/value/2007/05/07/spinoff-in-bentonville-revisited.aspx, May 7.

177. 2007, Wal-Mart Annual Report, 19.

178. Ibid.

179. Ibid.

180. Ibid.

181. 2007, Wal-Mart F1Q08 (Qtr End 4/30/07) Earnings call transcript, retail stocks, *SeekingAlpha*, http://retail.seekingalpha.com/article/35633, May 15.

182. 2007, Wal-Mart evaluating options in possible bid for the UK's J. Sainsbury chain, *Supply Chain Digest*, http://www.scdigest.com/assets/newsViews/07-03-27-3.php?cid=978, March 27.

183. 2007, Wal-Mart Retail Divisions, http://www.walmartfacts.com/articles/2502.aspx, April 4.

184. 2003, The Wal-Mart Empire: A simple formula and unstoppable growth, *Knowledge@Wharton*, http://www.upenn.edu/researchatpenn/article.php?631&bus, April 9.

185. A. Bianco, 2007, Wal-Mart's midlife crisis, 56.

Edward D. Hess

University of Virginia, Darden School Foundation

Room & Board was a privately owned home-furnishings retailer, offering products that combined classic, simple design with exceptional quality. Approximately $50 million of revenue a year was generated through Room & Board's fully integrated, multichannel sales approach, consisting of its eight national retail stores, an annual catalog, and a Web site. Based in Minneapolis, Minnesota, Room & Board's story is one of contrarian success as a company that had abandoned the standard retail-industry business model, disavowed debt and equity-growth financing, and embraced a unique multiple-stakeholder model that valued quality and relationships ahead of the bottom line while producing stellar financial results. That the company had achieved consistency and harmony between its values and actions also added to its uniqueness. Its culture supported an energized, positive growth environment for its employees that fostered high employee engagement and in turn, high customer engagement.

Room & Board was wholly owned by John Gabbert, who had created it more than 25 years earlier. Having reached the age of 60, Gabbert was now confronting his biggest challenge: how to institutionalize the unusual business model, culture, and employee environment he had built. His primary objective was to preserve and protect his "relationship" business model, which was the heart and soul of Room & Board's success.

History

Gabbert grew up working in a family retail business that sold traditional home furnishings; at the age of 24, he succeeded his father as the CEO. Family dynamics proved challenging, so when he was 33, he left the family furniture business to start his own furniture company initially based on IKEA's business model. He also diversified into other businesses. By the late 1980s however, feeling overextended and unfulfilled, he decided to focus all his energy on building a business with people he liked and on a model that represented quality. All this drew him into the design aspect of the furniture business.

To Gabbert, quality relationships were just as important as quality home furnishings. This belief helped shape Room & Board into a business focused on creating long-lasting relationships with customers, vendors, and employees, who were all fully integrated into the model of selling quality furnishings. At Room & Board, quality was also about providing value. That value was inherent in the firm's products, which lasted and whose style and design were timeless—furniture that customers could count on enjoying for many years. But Room & Board went further by believing that a customer's home should be a place where he or she can create a meaningful environment. This was made possible by offering customers a multitude of special-order products, ranging from fabric choices on throw pillows to customer-designed solid-wood storage pieces.

Supply Chain

The retail-furniture industry was generally controlled by large manufacturers that dictated style, product availability, and price, and that made many products overseas with cheaper labor than could be found in the United States. Room & Board decided early on that it did not want to compete by the traditional rules associated with the retail-furniture industry. In contrast, the firm created its own supply chain of approximately 40 different vendors, nearly all privately owned family businesses, many having grown alongside Room & Board over the years. Soon, more than 85 percent of the company's products were made in the United States—in places like Newton, North Carolina; Martinsville, Virginia; Minneapolis, Minnesota; Grand Forks, North Dakota; Shell Lake, Wisconsin; and Albany, Oregon—by craftsmen and artisans using high-quality hardwoods, granite, and steel. Most of these products were made exclusively for Room & Board, and more than 50 percent of the products were manufactured by 12 key vendors. Room & Board met with its vendors frequently to plan growth, discuss needs, and share financial data and results to ensure that everyone was making a fair living while creating high-quality, well-designed products.

These vendor relationships evolved over the years into true partnerships, which allowed Room & Board to set an annual goal of having 85 percent of its products in stock at all times, contributing to quick deliveries. Special-order products were programmed ahead of normal production with the aim of delivering the product as quickly as possible to the customer.

Under this model, Room & Board was more in control of its destiny; it had control over product quality, inventory availability, and the risk of supply-chain disruptions. This unique model carried its own risks however, as almost all of Room & Board's suppliers were private, family-owned businesses that shared the company's challenge of growing at a rate that sustained their economic health.

Culture

Room & Board had rejected common attributes of private-company culture: hierarchy, command and control from the top, information on a need-to-know basis, and, in the retail industry, high turnover resulting in customer-service challenges. Its culture was based on the principles of trust, respect, relationships, transparency, entrepreneurial ownership of one's job and career, and the importance of a balanced life. Room & Board eschewed rules, lengthy policy manuals, and elitism. Rather, it believed that individuals thrive in an environment where they are empowered to make decisions and everyone's view is heard and respected. These core beliefs were outlined in its *Guiding Principles,* partially based on the following expectation:

At Room & Board we hope you find meaning in your work. There is both tremendous productivity for the company and personal fulfillment for each staff member when someone finds their life's work. It's a wonderful circle of success.

Room & Board tried to achieve this "circle of success" by creating an environment of collaboration and engagement. This engagement was evidenced by deep relationships with customers, fellow employees, and suppliers. Respect for different views, openness to feedback, and responsibility for one's actions all drove the staff's behavior.

What worked for Room & Board as it tried to achieve balance was defined by Gandhi: Harmony exists when what you feel, what you think, and what you do are consistent. Many businesses talked a good game, but Room & Board actually tried to "walk the talk." In this company environment, there was a heightened sensitivity regarding the impact of actions across functions and an awareness of the real message being communicated.

Room & Board believed that success was rooted in shared accountability; therefore, there were no rules for personal leave or sick pay. All 670 employees were shown the company's annual strategy priorities and a complete detailed financial package every month so that they could understand the goals of the business. All financial and operating numbers were transparent to encourage responsibility for owning and, in turn, affecting Room & Board's success. In discussing the company's normal eight-hour day, Gabbert stated:

I learned a long time ago that most people only have so many productive hours a day—it is the number of productive hours that count, not the number of hours at work. We strive to have an environment which results in energy and productivity. That is why we have a full physical-fitness facility with classes going on during the workday, a masseuse, as well as a great kitchen for employees to prepare healthy lunches.

Room & Board also operated on the principle that people who have a balanced life, with a life outside work, were happier and dealt well with customers and with each other. Gabbert, who recognized that what set his company apart was its engaged employees who tried to make every customer experience special, said, "I never wanted to be the biggest. I never thought about size. I just wanted to be the best and to spend my time at work with good people doing something more meaningful than just making money or keeping score."

Employees

The retail industry is known for high employee turnover, with companies using many part-time employees to keep expenditures on employee benefits low and commission-based compensation to lower fixed costs. But Room & Board was proof that a very profitable, high-quality business could be built by not following any of those common retail practices.

Instead, Room & Board had very low employee turnover, mostly full-time employees, provided full benefits for part-time employees, and pay based on salary rather than on individual sales. The rejection of a commission-based structure, together with its integrated and multichannel purchasing options, allowed Room & Board customers to shop and purchase in the manner that made the most sense to them. "We want customers to rely on us for the best advice and to trust that we have their best interests in mind—sales commissions run against that type of trust," said Gabbert. The breakdown of Room & Board's employees by staff divisions is shown in Exhibit 1.

Room & Board stores more than five years old had average employee tenure of more than five years, which was very high for the retail industry. Delivery and warehouse personnel in delivery centers open for more than four years had an average tenure of five years. Employee tenure was 5.7 years for the central office, and total employee tenure for the company averaged nearly five years.

Room & Board also took a different approach to measuring employee satisfaction: The company tracked how many employees referred family and friends for jobs and how many employees participated in the company's 401(k) program. Room & Board believed that these measures truly contributed to long-term employee engagement. Following the philosophy that employees needed good physical, mental, and financial health, Room & Board offered an extensive physical-fitness facility, a healthy-lunch program, and personal financial-planning services and 401(k) investment advice from an outside financial consulting firm at no cost. In addition, all employees could buy Room & Board products at a substantial discount.

Leadership Team

Room & Board was led by a six-member advisory board made up of John Gabbert and the members (see Exhibit 2). The leadership team received generous bonuses if key company objectives were met.

Key Expectations for Employees and Leaders

Room & Board's *Guiding Principles* was the foundation for the company's expectations and also served as a tool to help employees understand their connection to the business. The document, which spoke primarily to

Exhibit 1 Room & Board Staff Divisions

Type	Number
Store personnel	237
Delivery personnel	220
Store and delivery leadership team	62
Central office staff	100

Exhibit 2 Leadership Team

Member	Title	Tenure
Bruce Champeau	Vice President of Distribution Delivery/Technology	16 years
Kimberly Ruthenbeck	Vice President of Retail Customer Experience & Vendor Managements	15 years
Mark Miller	Chief Financial Officer	11 years
Betsey Kershaw	Director of Brand Experience	5 years
Nancy McGough	Director of Human Resources	16 years

respect individual accountability and engaging the business, included the following statements:

- Respect is foundational to our work environment. Everyone is expected to build relationships based upon mutual respect and collaboration.
- Use good judgment when making decisions and apply principle, not rules, to each situation.
- The more you seek to understand how your role is related to our business objectives and tied to the broader success of the company, the more rewarding, enjoyable, and challenging the effort.

Just as all employees were expected to understand and embrace the core beliefs outlined in *Guiding Principles,* leaders were expected to adhere to their own additional roadmap. Room & Board set forth a number of leadership objectives for its central office, store, and delivery/distribution leadership team, including the following:

- You take ownership for your business—you're independent and therefore do not wait to be told what to do.
- You lead less with rules and rely more on principles.
- You value building relationships; collaboration is much more important to you than competition.
- You appreciate and desire longevity within your role. You do not seek to move from location to location or from department to department to get ahead; your growth occurs from richer experiences within your current role.

Financial Results

The Skokie, Illinois, store opened in 1986; the Edina, Minnesota, store in April 1989; the Denver store in 1991; and the Chicago store in 1993 (see Exhibits 3 and 4).

Exhibit 3 Room & Board Financial Results

Year	Sales (in millions [$])	New-Store Openings
1995	$33	
1996	$45	
1997	$53	Oakbrook, IL
1998	$67	
1999	$82	
2000	$98	
2001	$92	
2002	$95	South Coast, CA
2003	$110	
2004	$132	New York, NY; downtown Chicago store moves to Rush & Ohio location
2005	$173	San Francisco, CA
2006	$208	
2007	$229	

Source: Room & Board.

Exhibit 4 Room & Board Financial Results

Key Metrics	Goals
Sales growth	10% annual
Net profit	8% pretax
Customer satisfaction	>96%
Product in warehouse at time of sale	>85%
Vendor lead time	<7 weeks

Channels of Distribution	Approximate-Breakdown
Store sales	70%
Phone sales	2%
Web sales	18%

Markets	($ in millions)
Colorado	$18
Minneapolis	$24
Chicago	$44
San Francisco	$33
Southern California	$23
New York City	$46
National sales	$42

Main Product Lines	
Sofas and chairs	36%
Bedroom	17%
Dining room	12%

Source: Room & Board.

Delivery Centers

Another point of differentiation from other retailers was Room & Board's philosophy regarding deliveries. Many furniture chains outsourced their deliveries. Room & Board did not, operating its own delivery centers staffed by full-time Room & Board professionals. These teams delivered all the local products. For national deliveries, Room & Board had an exclusive relationship with a Minneapolis company. To ensure ongoing collaboration, a few employees from the national shipping company's office worked out of Room & Board's central location.

In addition, the company had dedicated delivery teams for just Room & Board products. It was not unusual for customers to assume that these delivery professionals were Room & Board employees, not just because of their Room & Board uniforms, but also because they adhered to the same principles that all Room & Board employees followed: namely, that the customer experience during every step of the process was hassle-free and treated as an opportunity to create long-lasting relationships. The individuals who had the last interaction with customers about purchases were viewed as brand ambassadors and acted as such.

Room & Board's goal of providing a great customer experience at every step of the buying-and-receiving process required delivery personnel to deliver and set up the product and leave the customer happy. Delivery times were scheduled to allow time for customer interaction, discussions, and the proper placement of the new purchases. If there was a problem, delivery personnel were empowered to solve it on the spot because they were trained to "leave the customer in a good place." The focus on interaction with the customer, from the beginning of the experience to the end, drove customer satisfaction, in terms of loyalty and referrals, to a rate of more than 95 percent.

Real Estate

To avoid the high rent typical in retail malls, Room & Board owned most of its locations and searched out freestanding sites with ample parking and easy access for customers. The company often chose to renovate an existing location, blending its store in with a particular environment rather than building a new one. This practice served as inspiration to customers who dealt with similar challenges when designing and furnishing their own spaces. Moreover, it prevented Room & Board from adopting a "cookie cutter" image for its stores and fostered the company's philosophy of unique design. The central-office facility was furnished with Room & Board products, so even employees who were not in customer-facing roles understood what the company sold, its quality, and its lasting design.

Pricing Model

Room & Board's pricing model was simple: no sales, no volume discounts, and no discounts for interior designers. Everyone paid the same price. As John Gabbert put it, "Nothing makes me madder than to buy something and then see it go on sale. I feel taken advantage of. That is why we have no sales, and we guarantee all prices for a year after purchase for each calendar year. If we sell a product within a year of your purchase for less than you paid, we will refund the difference."

Competition

Direct comparison with other retailers was impossible because Room & Board's exclusive designs, corporate structure, and long-lasting heirloom-quality products were not offered by any other company. Ultimately, Room & Board was competing for any of the dollars that customers spent on their homes no matter what the other retailer sold. Design Within Reach and Crate and Barrel were two companies that carried similar modern home furnishings and mid-century products.

Design Within Reach was a public company. In fiscal 2006, it had $110 million in sales through its 63 stores, which ranged in size from 1,100 square feet to 11,000 square feet. Although Room & Board stores were fewer in number, they were much bigger, at 30,000 square feet. Crate and Barrel had grown from a small family business, started in 1962, to a chain of over 160 mall-based stores owned by the private German company Otto, which also owned Spiegel and Eddie Bauer. More than 50 percent of Crate and Barrel products were imported from Europe.

Conclusion

Room & Board achieved the enviable market position of managing its growth and avoiding the capital-market pressures produced by debt financing and equity partners or by being a public company. It built a loyal and highly engaged workforce dedicated to its way of doing things, and managed to be a model of productivity and engagement without sacrificing quality. The company did not strive for the lowest operational costs, but instead embraced a vertically integrated business model and earned good net margins.

The beauty of the Room & Board success story was how it had created a consistent, seamless, self-reinforcing system that cut across culture, structure, execution philosophy, employee hiring, and benefits. The result was a company with a high-performance environment that manufactured 85 percent of its products in the United States, paid its people well, sold high-quality products, and made good profits.

Room & Board adhered to a multiple-stakeholder philosophy of capitalism, much like the European model and less like the sole-stakeholder model more common in the United States. It believed it would do well if its customers, employees, and suppliers did well. To create shareholder value had not been Room & Board's sole purpose. But now the company was looking at expanding—into Los Angeles, Seattle, Atlanta, Miami, and Washington, D.C.—but at its own pace and on its own terms. Room & Board's task was figuring out how to institutionalize its way of doing business beyond the life of its founder and how to strengthen its culture and high employee and customer engagement, while growing at a rate that sustained its economic health.

Ali Farhoomand

University of Hong Kong

China is a place where miracles are made.

JACK MA, FOUNDER AND CHAIRMAN OF ALIBABA GROUP[1]

On November 6, 2007, Alibaba.com debuted on the Hong Kong Stock Exchange, raising US$1.5 billion to become the world's biggest Internet stock offering since Google's initial public offering (IPO) in 2004. On the first trading day, frenzied purchases of the stock pushed prices up by 193 percent, the fourth-largest first-day gain in Hong Kong's stock exchange in three years. The closing price of US$5.09[2] per share gave Alibaba.com a value of about US$25.6 billion, making it the fifth-most-valuable Internet company and the largest in Asia outside Japan. It also made the company's stock among the most expensive on the Hong Kong exchange,[3] trading at 306 times its projected 2007 earnings of US$83.6 million.[4] In contrast, Yahoo!, a globally recognized "dot-com" brand that held a 39 percent stake in pre-IPO Alibaba.com, and Japan's SoftBank, which owned 29.3 percent of Alibaba.com prior to the IPO, traded at only around 60 times their projected earnings. In other words, shareholders had displayed extreme optimism about Alibaba.com's prospective earnings by paying a significant premium to own the company's shares.

Barely a week after the IPO, Alibaba.com was already reported to be in talks with SoftBank to set up a joint venture in early 2008 in Japan. Although the Japanese telecom giant disclosed no details regarding the proposed venture, it was likely that Alibaba.com would expand its service to mobile users in Japan, a market that had been impenetrable to the Chinese e-commerce company.[5] On its home turf, parent company Alibaba Group had already proven its mettle by topping EachNet, an older rival backed by global leader eBay.[6] Founder and Chairman Jack Ma had made it his aim to make the Alibaba Group one of three largest Internet companies in the world and a Fortune 500 company.[7] Could the IPO be the first step to Alibaba.com's global market dominance, or would it be overtaken just as quickly as it rose to regional pre-eminence?

Internet and E-Commerce in China

The world's most populous nation had 162 million Internet users as of June 2007.[8] Although the Chinese Internet-using population was second only to that of the United States,[9] China's Internet penetration rate of 12.3 percent significantly trailed those of the United States, Japan, and South Korea, whose penetration rates were all more than 65 percent.[10] Nevertheless, with the penetration rate growing at around three percentage points annually (see Exhibit 1), China was expected to experience even more rapid growth in the scale of penetration, having crossed the critical threshold of 10 percent and heading into the steep phase of the S-curve.[11]

Similarly, e-commerce was still in its infancy in China. Official figures estimated that only 25.5 percent of Internet users in China had engaged in online shopping, whereas the figure was 71 percent in the United States. The utilization rate of online sales and marketing was also very low—a mere 4.3 percent compared to 15 percent in the United States. The only exception to the trend was the rate of online stock transactions, which was 14.1 percent, narrowly beating the U.S. rate of 13 percent. The official explanation was the frenzy over the financial markets in China that started around 2006.[12]

Ricky Lai prepared this case under the supervision of Professor Ali Farhoom and for class discussion. This case is not intended to show effective or ineffective handling of decision or business processes.

Exhibit 1 China's Internet Penetration Rate

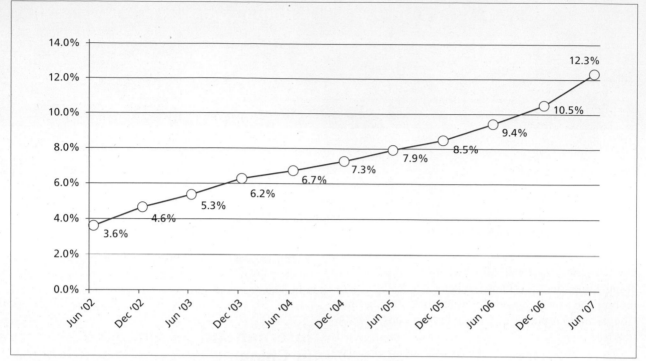

Source: China Internet Network Information Center, 2007, The 20th CNNIC Statistical Survey Report on the Internet Development in China, http://www.cnnic.net.cn/download/2007/20thCNNICreport-en.pdf (accessed November 19, 2007).

Chinese Internet media market researcher, iResearch Consulting Group, valued the Chinese online shopping market at US$1.5 billion in the first quarter of 2007. The online shopping market comprised the customer-to-customer and business-to-customer segments, with the former accounting for US$1.3 billion, or 89.7 percent of the market in China. Overall, the Chinese online shopping market recorded a 14.8 percent rise in the first quarter of 2007 compared to the preceding quarter and a massive 64.1 percent jump over the previous year (see Exhibit 2).[13] By comparison, the online business-to-business (B2B) market was much bigger, valued at US$65.7 billion in the second quarter of 2007, increasing 10.4 percent quarter-on-quarter and a staggering 69.8 percent year-on-year (see Exhibit 3).[14]

SMEs in China

Small and medium-sized enterprises (SMEs) have been a key driving force in the booming Chinese economy. In 2004, SMEs contributed 68.8 percent to the nation's gross industrial output (in current prices).[15] iResearch estimated that the number of SMEs in China would rise from 31.5 million in 2006 to 50 million in 2012 (see Exhibit 4).[16] Out of these 31.5 million Chinese SMEs, a mere 8.8 million, or 28 percent, utilized

third-party B2B e-commerce platforms. With the Chinese government's "11th Five-Year Planning for the Development of E-Commerce" encouraging SMEs to use third-party e-commerce platforms, however, the numbers were expected to rise to 41 million and 82 percent, respectively, in 2012 (see Exhibit 5).[17] The implication was that e-commerce had plenty of room for growth in China, at least among SMEs, where the market was expected to almost quadruple between 2007 and 2012.

The rising popularity of e-commerce among SMEs in China was fueled by several challenges in the traditional trade environment, including:

- Limited geographic presence restricting SMEs' ability to develop customer and supplier relationships beyond their immediate vicinity
- Fragmentation of suppliers and buyers, which made it difficult to find and communicate with suitable trading partners
- Limited communication channels and information sources through which to market and promote products and services or to find new markets and suppliers
- A relatively small scale of operation, limiting SMEs' resources for sales and marketing
- Absence of efficient mechanisms for evaluating the trustworthiness of trading partners[18]

Exhibit 2 Growth of the Chinese Online Shopping Market

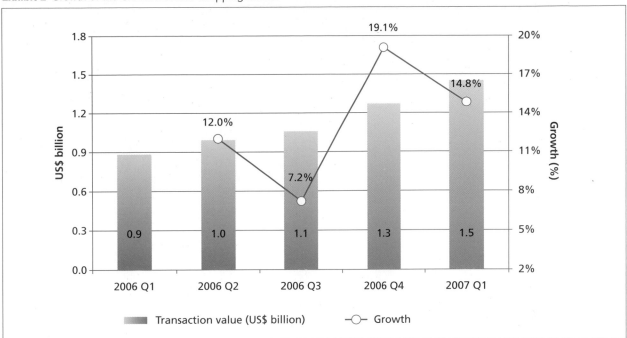

Source: iResearch Inc., 2007, China's online shopping market worth RMB 10.8 billion in Q1 of 2007, http://www.iresearchgroup.com.cn/html/Consulting/Online_Shopping/DetailNews_id_65929.html, June 18 (accessed November 20, 2007).

Exhibit 3 Growth of the Chinese B2B E-Commerce Market

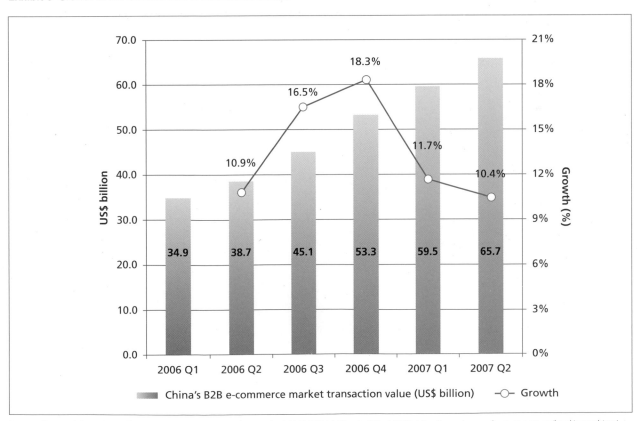

Source: iResearch Inc., 2007, China's B2B e-commerce market reached RMB 489.1 billion in Q2 of 2007, http://www.iresearchgroup.com.cn/html/consulting/B2B/DetailNews_id_72299.html, November 5 (accessed November 20, 2007).

Exhibit 4 Growth of Chinese SMEs

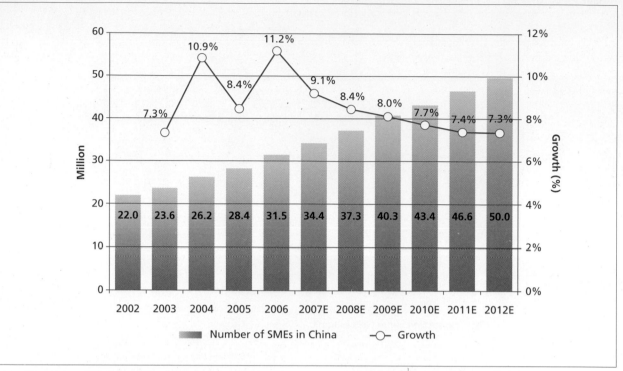

Source: iResearch Inc., 2007, China SME number to reach 50 million in 2012, http://www.iresearchgroup.com.cn/Consulting/others/DetailNews.asp?id=65361, June 6 (accessed November 22, 2007).

Exhibit 5 Usage of Third-Party E-Commerce among Chinese SMEs

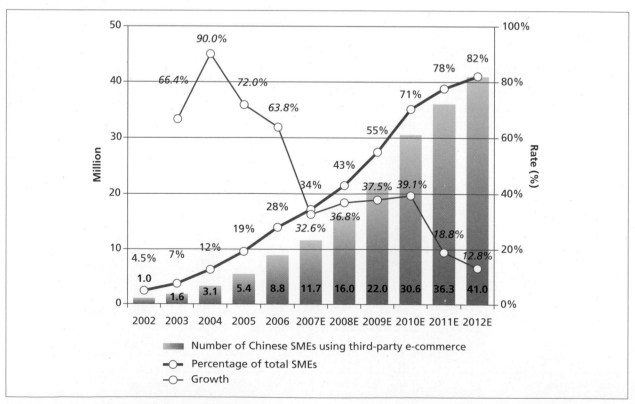

Source: iResearch Inc., 2007, B2B e-commerce should start with interest of SMEs, http://www.iresearchgroup.com.cn/html/Consulting/B2B/DetailNews_id_67225.html, July 12 (accessed November 22, 2007).

Alibaba.com

History

Alibaba's first online marketplace was launched as Alibaba Online in December 1998. Originally, the China-based Web site operated as a bulletin board service for businesses to post, buy, and sell trade leads. In June 1999, Jack Ma and 18 other founders formed the parent company, Alibaba Group, inaugurating its Web site in simplified Chinese to serve the Chinese mainland market. Three months later, a major operating subsidiary in China, Alibaba China, was established to carry out the business of operating B2B marketplaces. Within months, three more sites were launched: an English site for international users, a Korean site for Korean users, and a traditional Chinese site for Chinese users outside of China. In October 2000, Alibaba launched the Gold Supplier membership service for Chinese exporters, followed in August 2001 by the launch of International TrustPass, a membership service catering to exporters outside of China. China TrustPass was launched in March 2002 to serve SMEs engaged in domestic trade.

In September 2006, to facilitate the IPO of its B2B business, Alibaba underwent a restructuring of its B2B arm, Alibaba.com (see Exhibit 6). The principal company emerging from the restructuring, Alibaba.com Limited, became 17 percent–owned by public shareholders, with the remaining shares of the company held by the parent company, employees, and consultants.

Jack Ma

Lead founder and chairman of Alibaba Group, Jack Ma is a native of Hangzhou, located about 100 miles southwest of Shanghai, where the company's headquarters are located.

Exhibit 6 Corporate Structure of Alibaba.com Before and After Restructuring

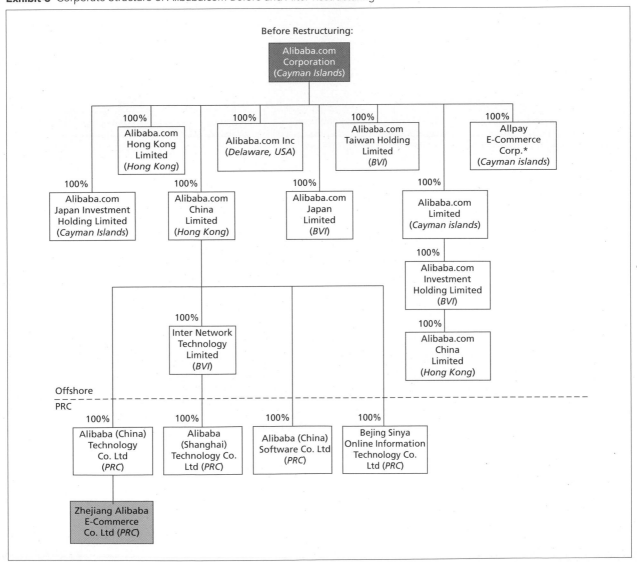

(Continued)

Exhibit 6 Corporate Structure of Alibaba.com Before and After Restructuring (*Continued*)

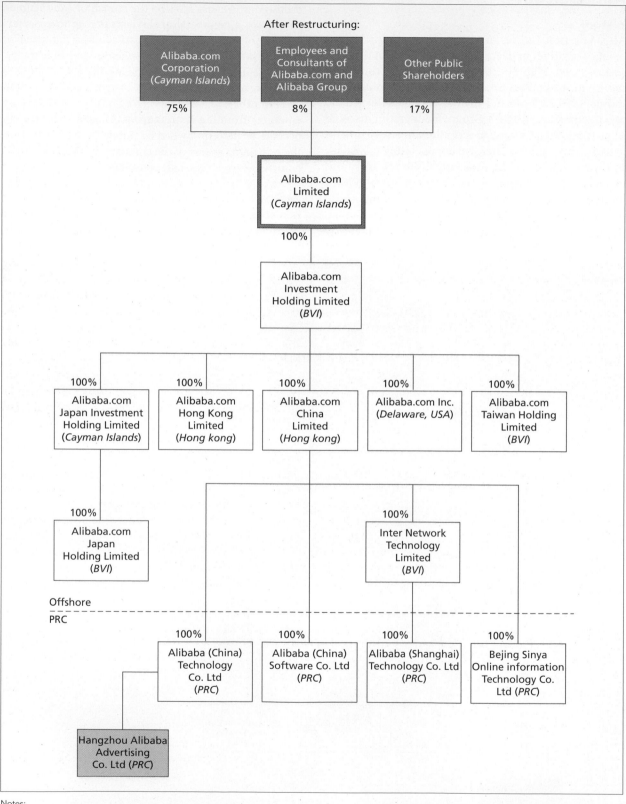

After Restructuring:

Notes:
_____ Denotes equity ownership
_ _ _ _ _ Denotes contractual relationship
* Formerly known as Alibaba.com E-Commerce Corp.

Source: Alibaba.com, 2007, Global Offering Prospectus, 63–64.

Growing up during China's Cultural Revolution, Ma became interested in learning English. Starting at age 12, and for the next 8 years, he rode his bicycle 40 minutes every morning to a hotel near the West Lake and worked on his English by giving free tours to foreigners. In spite of this effort, he failed his university entrance examinations twice before being accepted to a teachers' university.[19] The low-paying teaching job he was offered after graduation did not interest Ma, and in 1995 he found himself employed by the Chinese government to settle a dispute between a Chinese firm and its U.S. partner. Purportedly, Ma was held captive by the U.S. partner at gunpoint for two days before he regained his freedom by agreeing to become a partner in an Internet startup in China, even though he had no concept of the Internet at all.[20]

Although he never carried out his end of the deal, Ma came into his first contact with a computer and the Internet in Seattle, Washington, and was surprised to find nothing when he searched for "beer" and "China." He then returned to China, borrowed US$2,000, and started a company and Web site called China Pages. The Web site shared a strikingly similar ideology with Alibaba.com: to list Chinese companies on the Internet and help foreigners find their Web sites. Eventually, China Telecom would buy out Ma's stake and he would end up returning to civil service to promote e-commerce. Always looking for a chance to fulfill his dream of setting up his own e-commerce company, Ma stepped out of the civil service again in 1998 and resumed work on his vision to connect Chinese companies to the world through the Internet. This vision was realized in December of that year with the launch of Alibaba Online.

Business Model

By the second quarter of 2007, Alibaba.com was the largest online B2B e-commerce company in China, based on the number of registered users and market share by revenue.[21] The international marketplace was served by their English-language Web site, Alibaba.com, which focused on global importers and exporters. The Chinese marketplace was served by their Chinese-language interface, Alibaba.com.cn, which focused on suppliers and buyers trading domestically in China.

The two B2B marketplaces provided a platform to facilitate e-commerce between business sellers, whom Alibaba.com referred to as "suppliers," and wholesale buyers (see Exhibit 7 for Alibaba. com's value proposition). Suppliers and buyers used the marketplaces to establish their presence online, identify potential trading partners, and conduct business with each other. Suppliers and some buyers used the marketplaces to host their company profiles and catalogues in standardized formats known as "storefronts" and post "listings" such as products, services, and trade leads. Users could view storefronts and listings in over 30 industry categories and nearly 5,000 product categories by either searching for keywords or browsing through the online industry directory (see Exhibit 8 for a typical trading process). For many suppliers, their storefront or listing was their only presence on the Internet. As of June 30, 2007, there were more than 2.4 million storefronts. In the first half of 2007, users posted a monthly average of 2.9 million new listings on the marketplaces.

Through active listings, inquiry exchanges, instant messaging, discussion forums, and other user-friendly community features, suppliers and buyers formed large, interactive online communities on Alibaba.com's marketplaces. In June 2007, Alibaba.com registered more than 540,000 peak simultaneous online users of TradeManager, an instant messaging tool for trade communications. The two marketplaces collectively hosted more than 200 online forums and more than 4.2 million registered users.

To enhance the breadth and depth of the marketplaces, Alibaba.com offered basic features and services to all registered users free of charge. Revenue was generated from suppliers who purchased services, primarily membership packages that provided priority placement

Exhibit 7 Alibaba.com's Value Proposition

Suppliers	Buyers
• Access to active global buyer community	• Access to active global supplier community
• Targeted marketing to reach buyers	• Broad selection of listings
• Customer service and training	• Access to high-quality, organized information
	• Easy-to-use interface
• Always online	• Convenient, real-time medium
• Budget certainty through a fixed subscription fee model	• Authentication and trust profiles of suppliers

Alibaba.com

Source: Alibaba.com, 2007, Global Offering Prospectus, 78.

Exhibit 8 Typical Trading Process in the Alibaba.com Marketplace

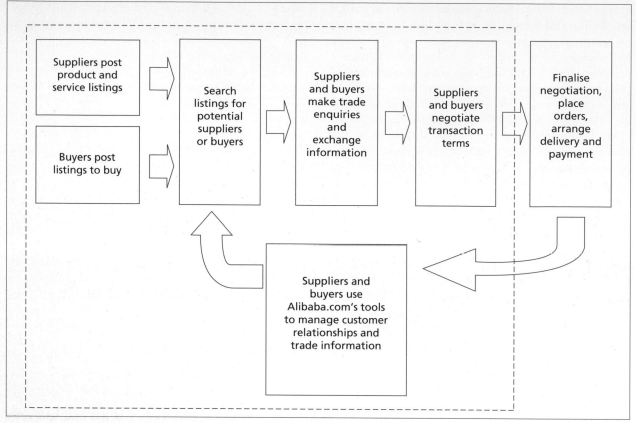

Source: Alibaba.com, 2007, Global Offering Prospectus, 83.

of storefronts and listings in the industry directory and search results. These paying members generated additional revenue by subscribing to value-added services, including purchases of additional keywords to improve their rankings in search results and premium placement on Alibaba.com's Web pages for enhanced exposure and visibility.

Results

Alibaba.com experienced significant growth in the number of registered users (Table 1) and in the number of paying members (Table 2) from 2004 to mid-2007.[22]

For the international marketplace, as of the end of June 2007, about 17.7 percent of users were based in the

United States, followed by 8.7 percent from the European Union (excluding the United Kingdom), 8.2 percent from India, 6.2 percent from the United Kingdom, and 2.7 percent from Canada.

For the Chinese marketplace, as of the end of June 2007, Guangdong led in the regional breakdown of registered users with a 21.5 percent share, followed by Zhejiang with 8.5 percent, Jiangsu with 6.6 percent, Shandong with 5.3 percent, and Shanghai with 4.6 percent.

Revenue increased at a staggering cumulative annual growth rate of 94.8 percent from US$48.3 million at the end of 2004 to US$183.2 million at the end of 2006. According to Alibaba.com's detailed financial data (see Exhibit 9), the international marketplace had been

Table 1 Growth in the Number of Alibaba.com's Registered Users

	End of 2004	End of 2005	Year-on-Year	End of 2006	Year-on-Year
Total registered users	6.0 million	11.0 million	+82.6%	19.8 million	+80.2%
International marketplace	1.2 million	1.9 million	+67.2%	3.1 million	+59.8%
Chinese marketplace	4.8 million	9.0 million	+86.3%	16.6 million	+84.6%

Table 2 Growth in the Number of Alibaba.com's Paying Members

	End of 2004	End of 2005	Year-on-Year	End of 2006	Year-on-Year
Total paying members	77,922	141,614	+81.7%	219,098	+54.7%
International marketplace	11,450	19,983	+74.5%	29,525	+47.8%
Chinese marketplace	66,472	121,631	+83.0%	189,573	+55.9%

Exhibit 9 Alibaba.com Financial Data, 2004–2007

	Year ending 31 December						Six months ending 30 June			
	2004		2005		2006		2006		2007	
	Amount	% of revenue	Amount	% of revenue	Amount	% of revenue	Amount	% of revenue	Amount	% of revenue
							(unaudited)			
				(in thousands of Rmb, except percentages)						
Revenue										
International marketplace	254,765	70.9	527,227	71.4	991,869	72.7	431,481	72.7	695,398	72.6
Chinese marketplace	104,670	29.1	211,070	28.6	371,993	27.3	162,156	27.3	260,965	27.3
Others	—	—	—	—	—	—	—	—	1,353	0.1
Total	359,435	100.0	738,297	100.0	1,363,862	100.0	593,637	100.0	957,716	100.0
Cost of revenue[1]	(62,569)	(17.4)	(126,509)	(17.1)	(237,625)	(17.4)	(109,131)	(18.4)	(122,717)	(12.8)
Gross profit	296,866	82.6	611,788	82.9	1,126,237	82.6	484,506	81.6	834,999	87.2
Sales & marketing expenses[1][2]	(194,773)	(54.2)	(393,950)	(53.4)	(610,198)	(44.8)	(299,034)	(50.3)	(307,428)	(32.1)
Product development expenses[1][2]	(19,151)	(5.4)	(35,678)	(4.8)	(105,486)	(7.7)	(47,256)	(8.0)	(58,278)	(6.1)
General and administrative expenses[1][2]	(57,639)	(16.0)	(101,082)	(13.7)	(159,969)	(11.7)	(59,820)	(10.1)	(88,432)	(9.2)
Other operating (loss) income, net	(426)	(0.1)	14,465	1.9	17,645	1.3	800	0.1	1,190	0.1
Profit from operation	24,877	6.9	95,543	12.9	268,229	19.7	79,196	13.3	382,051	39.9
Interest income	3,591	1.0	7,876	1.1	23,159	1.7	10,340	1.7	17,699	1.8
Profit before income taxes	28,468	7.9	103,419	14.0	291,388	21.4	89,596	15.1	399,705	41.7
Income tax credits (charges)	45,393	12.6	(32,965)	(4.5)	(71,450)	(5.3)	(28,253)	(4.8)	(104,543)	(10.9)
Profit for the year/ period attributable to equity owners	73,861	20.5	70,454	9.5	219,938	16.1	61,283	10.3	295,207	30.8

Notes:

(1) Includes share-based compensation expenses, which are allocated as follows:

(Continued)

Exhibit 9 Alibaba.com Financial Data, 2004,2007 (*Continued*)

	Year ending 31 December						Six months ending 30 June			
	2004		2005		2006		2006		2007	
	Amount	% of revenue	Amount	% of revenue	Amount	% of revenue	Amount	% of revenue	Amount	% of revenue
							(unaudited)			
			(in thousands of Rmb, except percentages)							
Cost of revenue	1,936	0.5	8,766	1.2	23,335	1.7	13,258	2.2	6,207	0.7
Sales & marketing expenses	5,259	1.5	26,920	3.6	50,068	3.7	21,975	3.7	21,517	2.2
Product development expenses	1,382	0.4	5,126	0.7	16,344	1.2	7,727	1.3	6,582	0.7
General and administrative expenses	2,838	0.8	8,079	1.1	24,157	1.8	10,442	1.8	20,183	2.1
Total share-based compensation expenses	11,415	3.2	48,891	6.6	113,904	8.4	53,402	9.0	54,489	5.7

(2) Includes expenses of Alibaba Group not related to the B2B business as follows:

	Year ending 31 December						Six months ending 30 June			
	2004		2005		2006		2006		2007	
	Amount	% of revenue	Amount	% of revenue	Amount	% of revenue	Amount	% of revenue	Amount	% of revenue
							(unaudited)			
			(in thousands of Rmb, except percentages)							
Sales & marketing expenses	—	—	35,959	4.9	83,186	6.1	58,661	9.9	—	—
Product development expenses	—	—	1,414	0.2	6,748	0.5	3,705	0.6	—	—
General and administrative expenses	9,594	2.7	29,972	4.0	47,573	3.5	18,818	3.2	—	—
Total	9,594	2.7	67,345	9.1	137,507	10.1	81,184	13.7	—	—

Source: Alibaba. Com, 2007, Globl Offering Prospectus, 102–103.

steadily contributing slightly more than 70 percent of revenue, while the Chinese marketplace brought in just short of 30 percent. Specifically, Alibaba.com derived around 71 percent of its revenue from Gold Supplier members of the international marketplace, who paid at least US$5,373.60 per year for a standard package and US$8,060.40 for a premium package. Alibaba.com indicated that it would merge the two tiers of membership beginning November 2007, with the new rate starting at US$6,717.00 per year.[23]

Strengths

Alibaba.com believed that it had certain competitive strengths to merit such moves as the membership merger, which would effectively produce more revenue.

First, Alibaba.com had built a premier brand in the e-commerce domain, boasting the highest traffic among all online B2B marketplaces. According to Internet statistics compiler Alexa.com, Alibaba.com was the most visited site in the e-commerce and international business and trade categories,[24] in addition to being the largest online B2B company in China. Alibaba.com attracted suppliers on the strength of the large number of potential buyers that used the marketplaces, which in turn attracted more buyers to sign up with Alibaba.com. Alibaba.com's breadth and depth in its marketplaces were difficult to replicate, thus creating an effective barrier to new entrants and a virtually insurmountable lead over competitors.

Second, Alibaba.com focused exclusively on the highly lucrative SME sector. Providing tools and solutions tailored to SMEs, Alibaba.com was confident in the value proposition of its service offerings. For example, Alibaba.com provided trust ratings for suppliers and buyers, thus facilitating the process of selecting potential trading partners. The fixed subscription fee model also gave budget certainty to SMEs, which were often budget-sensitive and averse to ad-hoc expenditures. Users and subscribers had responded positively, leading to the formation of interactive communities at the online marketplaces. Alibaba.com had also installed staff dedicated to enhancing the community experience of users to build up loyalty to and trust in the brand.

Third, Alibaba.com was confident about its sales force and customer service support in attracting and retaining users, especially those who paid for subscriptions. As of mid-2007, Alibaba.com maintained more than 1,900 full-time field salespeople in 30 cities across China, more than 800 telephone salespeople, and more than 400 full-time customer-service employees, all of whom were grouped into teams in direct, daily contact with current and prospective customers. The customer service arm provided customer feedback to the sales force which, in turn, made use of the findings and worked with the product development team to deliver services that more closely met customers' needs. For example, a number of services available to Alibaba.com users, such as e-mail and instant messaging, had initially been proposed by customers and later developed by Alibaba.com.

Strategy

Alibaba.com's mission was to make it easy to do business anywhere.[25] To accomplish this mission, Alibaba.com set forth a multi-pronged strategy to make its online marketplaces more effective for SMEs around the world.

First, Alibaba.com tried to increase the size of its marketplaces through the expansion of its user base and active listings. The company believed that the breadth and quality of users and listings were critical to the success of the marketplaces. To that end, Alibaba.com continued to leverage the networking aspect of its online marketplaces, its leading market position, and the "Alibaba" brand name to increase its user base worldwide. It also planned to conduct targeted marketing to potential users in specific industries and geographic locations.

Second, Alibaba.com planned to enhance community experiences to further improve user loyalty and activity through continued development and introduction of new features and tools. Specifically, it planned to invest further in the existing instant messaging service, online forums, and other communication services. Alibaba.com also planned to continue organizing regular meetings, training, and offline events for registered users and paying members to further build the sense of community.

Third, Alibaba.com was keen to monetize its user base after providing years of free service to the majority of its members. The company would strive not only to convert more users into paying members, but also to generate more revenue from existing paying members through sales of value-added services, such as additional keyword listing and premium listing placement.

Fourth, Alibaba.com planned to selectively expand its sales and customer service capabilities into international markets, either directly or through third-party agents, to acquire more paying members and sell premium services outside China. The company had already taken the first step by offering Gold Supplier membership packages to Hong Kong suppliers in 2007. Alibaba.com was already in talks with Japanese telecommunications giant SoftBank about a joint venture to tap the Japanese market, for which significant upgrades to Alibaba.com's Japanese language Web site were already in the pipeline.

Fifth, Alibaba.com believed that its online marketplace platform could be extended beyond pure trade marketing to address users' daily business processes, such as customer relationship management and internal operations. It aimed to enhance the loyalty of its users by providing business applications through the marketplace platform and becoming an integral part of users' business operations. For example, it launched an Internet-based business management application called Alisoft Export Edition, developed by sister company Alisoft, for users based in China.

Finally, Alibaba.com was set to expand its business through acquisitions, investments, licensing arrangements, and partnerships. The underlying objectives would be to expand its user and revenue base, widen geographic coverage, enhance content and service offerings, advance its technology, and strengthen its talent pool. Alibaba.com also considered leveraging its relationship with parent company Alibaba Group to seek cross-selling, cross-marketing, and licensing arrangements and other opportunities.

Competition from Global Sources

Despite Alibaba.com's dominance in the online B2B market in China, the company was not immune to competition from both domestic and international competitors (see Exhibit 10). Chief among Alibaba.com's competitors in the international marketplace was international B2B giant Global Sources, whose online directory was bolstered by the many other B2B services it offered, such as print business directories and exhibitions.

Founded in Hong Kong in 1971 as a monthly trade magazine for consumer products made in Asia for export to Western markets, Global Sources claimed to have a community of over 647,000 buyers and 160,000 suppliers as of the end of September 2007.[26] Global Sources also boasted the following:

- It enabled suppliers to sell to hard-to-reach buyers in over 230 countries.
- It delivered information on 2 million products annually.
- It operated 14 online marketplaces that delivered more than 23 million sales leads annually.
- It published 13 monthly magazines and over 100 sourcing research reports per year.
- It organized 9 trade-specific exhibitions that ran 22 times a year across seven cities.

In mainland China, Global Sources had over 2,000 staff members in 44 locations and a community of over one million registered online users and magazine readers of its Chinese-language media.

Global Sources clearly posed a threat to Alibaba.com because it was earning more and more of its revenue online, as evidenced by its 2006 annual report demonstrating that its online businesses generated more than 40 percent of its total revenue (Table 3).

Exhibit 10 Market Share of China's Online E-Commerce Market, by Revenue

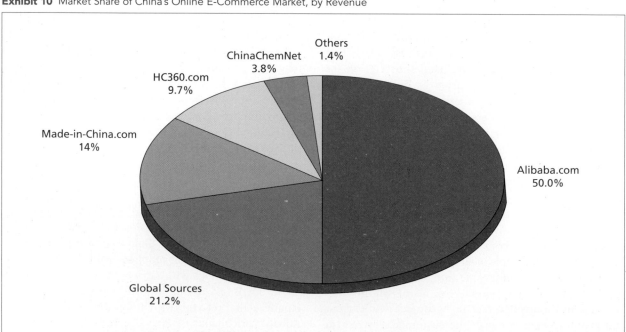

Source: iResearch Inc., 2007, China's B2B e-commerce market reached RMB 489.1 Billion in Q2 of 2007, http://www.iresearchgroup.com.cn/html/consulting/B2B/DetailNews it 72299 html, November 5 (accessed November 20, 2007).

Table 3 Contributors to Global Sources's 2006 Revenue[27]

	Revenue (US$ million)	% of total
Online	64.4	41.2
Print	48.7	31.1
Exhibitions	42.1	26.9
Miscellaneous	1.3	0.8
Total	156.5	

The growth strategy of Global Sources was built around four key foundations:[28]

- Market penetration through increasing revenue from exhibitions by selling more booths and increasing the average revenue per booth; cross-selling to clients not using online, print, or shows, particularly the large number of new clients patronizing only exhibitions; and expanding the online customer base by offering new services and pricing packages for the new Global Sources Online 2.0.
- New product development: Global Sources actively increased its online marketplaces, magazines, and exhibitions. In 2007, it added 11 new online marketplaces, monthly publications, and trade shows and announced eight new exhibitions to be launched in 2008 and 2009.
- Expansion into China's domestic B2B market: domestic trade in China was an attractive growth market and was synergistic with Global Sources's existing media serving China's export and import sectors. Global Sources launched new exhibitions in China in the hopes of attracting volume buyers as attendees. To complement these exhibitions and other vertical, industry-focused markets, the company launched China Global Sources Online to enable international suppliers to sell to China's domestic B2B market.
- Acquisitions and alliances: Global Sources, like Alibaba.com, was on the lookout for complementary businesses, technologies, and products that would help it to achieve and maintain leading positions in the markets it served. In 2007, in support of its plans to expand online business within China, Global Sources acquired the business and Web site assets of a Beijing-based online media company, Blue Bamboo China Ventures.

Given the similarities between the current positioning and growth strategies of Alibaba.com and Global Sources, competition between the two companies for the vast and growing Chinese market is bound to intensify.

Other Competition and Constraints

Competitors in Alibaba.com's Chinese marketplace include domestic B2B e-commerce platforms such as HC360.com, the Web site operated by HC International. As a generalized e-commerce platform, Alibaba.com also had to contend with specialized platforms that focused on vertical coverage of specific industries, such as ChinaChemNet, which catered to the chemical industry in China. Because Alibaba.com founded its success on the breadth of its horizontal coverage of industries, it would be tremendously difficult for it to pursue vertical coverage of a specific industry without upsetting its basic business model. In addition, there was indirect competition from other marketing service providers, such as Internet search engines and traditional trading channels, including exhibitions, trade magazines, classified advertisements, and outdoor advertising.

As Alibaba.com served mostly Chinese SMEs, it was also captive to the same problems that impeded offline commerce, ranging from China's credit and foreign exchange controls to the deficient national distribution network. Many procedures involved in a successful business deal, such as financing and shipping, were simply beyond Alibaba.com's scope. Alibaba.com also faced other issues with online commerce, such as fears about fraud, privacy, and trust that discouraged businesses from adopting the Internet as a medium of commerce.

Internally, Alibaba.com's executives regarded their charismatic and visionary founder and chairman Jack Ma as the company's cornerstone. However, Ma has indicated that his plan is to eventually exit to make room for the next generation of leadership. Despite the fact that many senior executives and potential future leaders of Alibaba.com were handpicked by Ma, questions remained over the issue of succession, especially with Ma's departure looming on the horizon.

At the end of 2007, Alibaba.com experienced a reshuffling of its senior management, with several executives going on study sabbaticals outside of China. Some industry watchers believed the move was a precursor to taking the company global by equipping its Chinese executives with international experience. Such speculation was heightened by reports that Alibaba.com had encountered difficulties in recruiting international business talent.[29]

The Way Forward

Four months into a record-breaking IPO that significantly raised both the capital and profile of the company, Alibaba.com's share price had slipped to around half of the launch value. Could investor optimism about

Alibaba.com be slipping? How could Alibaba.com best utilize the proceeds from the IPO to scale new heights in the B2B e-commerce industry and beyond?[30] Would it be able to emerge from the shadows of its totemic founder and mature into an international conglomerate? Would Alibaba.com thrive under a rising Chinese economy, or would its success only last for "One Thousand and One Nights"?

NOTES

1. R. Kwong & T. Mitchell, 2007, Alibaba shares soar on first day of trading, *Financial Times* (Asia Edition), November 7.
2. US$1 = HK$7.76425 on November 6, 2007.
3. R. Kwong & T. Mitchell, 2007, Alibaba shares soar on first day of trading, *Financial Times* (Asia Edition), November 7.
4. US$1 = RMB 7.4638 on November 6, 2007.
5. R. Kwong, 2007, SoftBank and Alibaba in Talks, *Financial Times* (Asia Edition), November 14.
6. B. Liu, 2007, US Giant eBay Loses Ground to Taobao, *China Daily*, April 17
7. J. Macartney, 2007, Workaholic's road to fortune "like riding on a blind tiger," *The Times, London*, November 7.
8. China Internet Network Information Center, 2007, The latest statistics, http://www.cnnic.net.cn/en/index/0O/index.htm (accessed November 19, 2007).
9. CIA, 2007, *The World Fact Book*, https://www.cia.gov/library/publications/the-world-factbook/rankorder/2153rank.html (accessed November 19, 2007).
10. China Internet Network Information Center, 2007, The 20th CNNIC statistical survey report on the Internet development in China, http://www.cnnic.net.cn/download/2007/20thCNNICreport-en.pdf (accessed November 19, 2007).
11. China Internet Network Information Center, 2007, The 20th CNNIC statistical survey report on the Internet development in China, http://www.cnnic.net.cn/download/2007/20thCNNICreport-en.pdf (accessed November 19, 2007).
12. China Internet Network Information Center, 2007, The 20th CNNIC statistical survey report on the Internet development in China, http://www.cnnic.net.cn/download/2007/20thCNNICreport-en.pdf (accessed November 19, 2007).
13. iResearch Inc., 18 June 2007, China's Online Shopping Market Worth Rmb 10.8 Billion in Q1 of 2007, http://www.iresearchgroup.com.cn/html/Consulting/Online_Shopping/DetailNews_id_65929.html (accessed 20 November 2007).
14. iResearch Inc., 2007, China's B2B e-commerce market reached RMB 489.1 billion in Q2 of 2007, http://www.iresearchgroup.com.cn/html/consulting/B2B/DetailNews_id_72299.html, November 5 (accessed November 20, 2007).
15. National Statistics Bureau of China, 2006, *China Statistical Yearbook*, Chapter 14–1.
16. iResearch Inc., 2007, China SME number to reach 50 million in 2012, http://www.iresearchgroup.com.cn/Consulting/others/DetailNews.asp?id=65361, June 6 (accessed November 22, 2007).
17. iResearch Inc., 2007, B2B e-commerce should start with interest of SMEs, http://www.iresearchgroup.com.cn/html/Consulting/B2B/DetailNews_id_67225.html, July 12 (accessed November 22, 2007).
18. Alibaba.com, 2007 Global Offering Prospectus, 74–75.
19. R. Fannin, 2008, How I did it—Jack Ma, Alibaba.com, *Inc.*, 30(1): 105.
20. C. Chandler, 2007, China's Web king, *Fortune*, December 10, 172.
21. iResearch Inc., 2007, Alibaba IPO Financial Research Report, http://www.iresearchgroup.com.cn/html/Consulting/B2B/Free_classi__id_1076.html, November 5 (accessed December 11, 2007).
22. Alibaba.com, 2007, Global Offering Prospectus, 102.
23. Alibaba.com, 2007, Global Offering Prospectus, 24.
24. Alexa, 2008, Browse: E-Commerce, http://www.alexa.com/browse?&CategoryID=298214; Alexa.com, 2008, Browse: International business and trade, http://www.alexa.com/browse?&CategoryID=42647 (accessed January 2, 2008).
25. Alibaba. com, 2007, Global Offering Prospectus, 80.
26. Global Sources, 2007, Investor Relations Factsheet, http://www.corporate.globalsources.com/IRS/IRFACT.HTM (accessed January 22, 2008).
27. Global Sources, 2006, Annual Report, 24–25.
28. Global Sources, 2007, Investor Relations Factsheet, http://www.corporate.globalsources.Com/IRS/IRFACT.HTM (accessed January 22, 2008).
29. S. So, 2008, Alibaba reshuffle a precursor to global expansion, *South China Morning Post*, January 29.
30. Alibaba.com stated its intention to allocate the net proceeds from the IPO as follows: 60 percent for strategic acquisitions and business development initiatives, 20 percent to increase the existing businesses both in China and internationally, 10 percent to purchase computer equipment and development of new technologies, and 10 percent to fund working capital and for general corporate purposes. Source: Alibaba.com, 2007, Global Offering Prospectus, 130.

CASE 5
eBay Inc.: Bidding for the Future

Kazi Ahmed, Phillip Feller, Tara Ferrin, Jeffrey Fletcher, Fidel Rodriguez, Juliet Taylor, Robin Chapman

Arizona State University

"Our purpose is to pioneer new communities around the world built on commerce, sustained by trust and inspired by opportunity."[1]

Introduction

John Donahoe took over as president and CEO of eBay Inc. in March 2008, during an unfavorable time for the company.[2] Since its inception in 1995, eBay has experienced revenue and earnings growth year after year, but the growth rate has slowed since 2006. For the first time, eBay's revenues fell from the previous year, down by 7 percent in the fourth quarter of 2008.[3] Although eBay is still the industry leader for online retailing with 17 percent market share, it has lost market share to innovative key competitors such as Amazon, Yahoo!, and Google. The expensive acquisition of Skype (a communications software company) did not have the outcome former CEO, Meg Whitman, expected. The company's venture into China failed, and changes in seller fees have not provided the results that eBay executives had anticipated. In addition, there have been lawsuits related to counterfeit products. In March 2008, Meg Whitman stepped down as CEO and was succeeded by John Donahoe, who has to confront the current situation. In a fast-cycle market such as online retailing, how can Donahoe discover new competitive advantages and regain eBay's market share and growth rate while confronting a more complex international and legal environment? In particular, Donahoe now faces a global economic downturn, a struggling e-commerce industry, and company shares trading between $10 and $11 below their prior year price of $40.

Company Leaders and Overview

In 1995, shortly after conducting a successful online auction for a broken laser pointer costing $14.83, Pierre Omidyar realized that the Internet enabled market efficiency by allowing millions of buyers and sellers to view products and conduct transactions. This inspired him to launch AuctionWeb, an online marketplace for buyers and sellers.[4] AuctionWeb officially became eBay in 1997 and hosted more auctions per month in that year than it did in all of 1996. Within four years and with the help of Meg Whitman, eBay grew from a programmer's experiment into a major publicly traded company, trading on NASDAQ with the symbol EBAY[5] (see Exhibit 1 for more details on eBay's history).

Meg Whitman was recruited as eBay's second president and CEO in 1998 and helped bring eBay public in September of that year. At the time eBay's registered users had grown six-fold, to over 2 million, from the prior year. Under Whitman's leadership the company grew to over 200 million users globally and over $7 billion in revenue. During her tenure, Whitman helped eBay enter China, integrated globally recognized brands like PayPal and Skype into the eBay portfolio, and most notably, successfully steered the company through the dot-com bust by staying focused on its core users and core competency—online auctions. She continues to serve on eBay's board of directors.

After a 20-year career at Bain & Company, Donahoe joined eBay in February 2005 as president of eBay marketplaces, where he served for three years. Donahoe's prior executive experience made him an ideal candidate to help expand marketplaces, eBay's core business. Under his leadership eBay acquired Shopping.com, StubHub, Gumtree, and LoQUo, giving it a strategic

The authors would like to thank Professor Robert E. Hoskisson for his support and guidance during the development of this case. This case is not intended to illustrate either effective or ineffective handling of managerial situations. The case is solely intended for class discussion.

Exhibit 1 eBay History

1995: Pierre Omidyar successfully conducted an online auction for a broken laser pointer which cost $14.83. Omidyar realized the Internet enabled market efficiency by allowing millions of buyers and sellers to view products and interact. It was this experiment that led Omidyar to found AuctionWeb, an online marketplace for buyers and sellers.
1996: AuctionWeb expanded greatly, with revenue topping which cost $10,000. In June Omidyar hired Jeff Skoll as president.
1997: AuctionWeb officially became eBay and hosted more auctions per month than it did in all of 1996.
1998: Meg Whitman joined as president and CEO and in September; eBay went public listing on NASDAQ under the symbol EBAY.
1999: eBay started its international expansion with marketplaces in the United Kingdom, Germany, and Australia.
2000: eBay became the number one e-commerce Web site, acquired Half.com to enter into the fixed price market, and continued international expansion with marketplaces in Austria, Canada, France, and Taiwan.
2001: eBay dramatically accelerated its international expansion through marketplaces in Ireland, Italy, Korea, New Zealand, Singapore, and Switzerland.
2002: eBay boosted revenues by acquiring Paypal.com, the primary payment method used on eBay.
2003: eBay expanded into Hong Kong; integrated PayPal Buyer Protection Services, protecting buyers and sellers in the eBay marketplace.
2004: eBay expanded into Malaysia and the Philippines, started strategic alliance in China, and acquired Rent.com. eBay purchased 28 percent ownership in online marketplace rival Craigslist.com for a reported $15 million.
2005: eBay diversified by acquiring Shopping.com, Skype, and foreign classified Web sites LoQUo and Gumtree while launching U.S. classified Web site Kijiji.com.
2006: Launched eBay express adding brand new fixed-price items to its marketplace, thereby further enhancing eBay as a primary shopping location.
2007: eBay acquired online ticket Web site Stubhub.com and Stumbleupon.com, which enhanced its Web presence while strategically partnering to enter India. eBay also partnered with Wal-Mart and Myspace.com to market Skype, and Northwest and Southwest Airlines to make PayPal a payment option. Major League Baseball named StubHub as its official provider of secondary tickets. In June, eBay cancelled its advertising on Google as a result of Google's push for Google Checkout as an eBay payment option.
2008: eBay announced that large-volume sellers with the highest feedback ratings will have preferential search locations and lower fees. eBay removed the option for buyers to receive negative feedback. On March 31, Meg Whitman stepped down as CEO and John Donahoe took over as president and CEO. On October 6, eBay announced a massive stream-lining process which entailed laying off 10 percent of its workforce and restructuring charges of $70 to 80 million. It acquired Bill Me Later and two Danish classified ad Web sites. In mid-2008 eBay signed a deal with Buy.com allowing some sellers to directly negotiate their seller fees, dramatically increasing its items listed, but angering many of its smaller "powersellers." On July 15, a U.S. District Court judge ruled that eBay did not bear legal responsibility for sales of counterfeit goods in its marketplace. On September 16, eBay lowered fees on fixed-cost auctions by more than 70 percent in an effort to better compete with Amazon.com while also eliminating the use of checks and money orders as payments, and shifted to PayPal as the sole payment option for most auctions.

Sources: 2008, eBay history, http://www.ebay.com, November 3; J. Swartz, 2008, eBay to lay off 1,600 employees, cites economy, *USA Today*, October 7, 2B; 2008, eBay 2007 Form 10-K, http://www.ebay.com, November 25, 51; 2008, eBay major direct shareholders, http://finance.yahoo.com, November 26; B. Stone, 2008, Buy.com deal with eBay angers sellers, *New York Times*, July 14, 1; C. Wolf, 2008, eBay cuts fixed-price sales fees by 70%, *Washington Post*, August 21, D03; J. Schofield, 2008, Technology, *The Guardian*, February 21, 3; J. Swartz, 2008, Listings down 13% in boycott of eBay, *USA Today*, February 28, 3B; D. Rushe, 2008, Silicon Valley culture clash as eBay sues Craigslist, *The Times (London)*, April 27, B9; 2008, Judge rules for eBay over fake Tiffany jewelry sales, *International Herald Tribune*, July 15, F12; 2008, Google cancels 'Freedom' party to appease eBay, http://www.techweb.com, June 14; 2008, eBay Fact Sheet, http://www.ebay.com, November 28; 2008, eCommerce marketsize and trends, www.goecart.com/ecommerce_solutions_facts.asp, November 30; 2008, World's most valuable general retailers, http://galenet.galegroup.com. November 30.

presence in the growing online comparison shopping industry, ticket sales, and classifieds. At the time of his transition to CEO, eBay's market share was declining and it had failed to gain in its number of unique visitors. In an attempt to reinvigorate growth, Donahoe shifted eBay's emphasis closer to other competitors by moving from auctions to fixed price listing, which has been the profit engine for Wal-Mart.com, Amazon.com, and Yahoo.com. He also streamlined the organization with a 10 percent workforce reduction and the acquisition of Bill Me Later, a transaction-based credit business with a total payment volume of over $1 billion, as a complementary payment method to PayPal.

Consisting of over 88 million active users in 39 global markets (see Exhibit 2 for eBay marketplace locations), eBay offers anyone the opportunity to be an entrepreneur.[6] The company's marketplace segment operates online auctions, classified ad sites, and other sites where people can conduct commercial transactions. Unlike other e-commerce companies, eBay does not operate the online equivalent of a store; it is more like an online mall or flea market. Its payment segment provides ways for individuals to transfer money to complete an e-commerce transaction. Its third segment, communications, offers technology that enables voice and video communications between computers, and from a computer to an ordinary telephone.[7]

The e-commerce industry is attractive because it is relatively simple to enter. Most of the major players in the industry, including Yahoo!, Google, and eBay, began as small entrepreneurial ventures with little more than an Internet connection and lines of code. Despite relatively low entry barriers, growth is difficult due to strong industry rivalry.

Competitors

Amazon.com Inc.

Amazon.com Inc. (Amazon) was founded in 1994 as an online bookstore. Over the years it expanded to include items ranging from books and CDs to clothing and electronics. This expansion occurred through partnerships with companies including Toys "R" Us, AOL, and Hoover's.[8] Amazon sells other companies' products on its Web site and uses its distribution network to ensure prompt and accurate delivery. After a relatively unsuccessful attempt to add an auction component, Amazon created the Amazon marketplace, which allows sellers to place used items on the site, featuring them alongside identical new items sold by Amazon.[9]

Amazon aims to be the low-cost leader in the e-commerce industry. In order to continue attracting new customers, Amazon continues to add innovative

Exhibit 2 Locations of eBay Marketplaces

Argentina	Malaysia
Australia	Mexico
Austria	Netherlands
Belgium	New Zealand
Brazil	Panama
Canada	Peru
Chile	Philippines
China	Poland
Colombia	Switzerland
Costa Rica	Singapore
Dominican Republic	Sweden
Ecuador	Taiwan
France	Thailand
Germany	Turkey
Hong Kong	United Kingdom
India	United States
Ireland	Uruguay
Italy	Venezuela
Korea	Vietnam

Source: 2008, eBay Web site, http://www.ebay.com.

value-added services such as "frustration-free packaging"—which eliminates difficult-to-open product containers—and the ability for customers to pay with installment payment plans.[10] Amazon is also attempting to vertically integrate as a supplier of kitchenware through its new division, Pinzon.

In 2008, even though third-quarter profit was up 48 percent, Amazon reduced fourth-quarter projections, citing expectations, along with the rest of the retail sector, for a bleak holiday season.[11]

Yahoo! Inc.

Originally known primarily as a search engine, Yahoo! Inc. ventured into the e-commerce industry in 1998 with the purchase of Viaweb. In addition to e-commerce services, Yahoo! products include advertising, e-mail, news and information, photo sharing, and Internet browser toolbars and add-ons.[12] Yahoo! has a presence in more than 20 countries. It appeals to advertisers by creating a Web site that users go to for all of their needs, thereby creating the most exposure for its ads.[13]

While the company currently operates a Yahoo! Shopping site, it discontinued its auction site in the United States and Canada in June 2007. However, Yahoo! still runs auction Web sites in Hong Kong, Singapore, and Taiwan.[14]

In recent years, Yahoo! was involved in a takeover bid by Microsoft. The software giant saw Yahoo! as a way to compete with Google for advertising dollars. After a friendly acquisition was rejected, Microsoft attempted and failed at an unsolicited takeover. Investors have criticized Yahoo!'s board for not dealing more effectively with Microsoft and for not acting in their interest.[15] Although Microsoft is reportedly no longer interested in a full takeover, it may still try to purchase the Yahoo! search engine segment.[16]

Google, Inc.

Google Inc. (Google) is a search engine site that was founded in 1998. It uses proprietary software to "understand exactly what you mean and give back exactly what you want" when searching on the Internet.[17] While Google continually adds applications, such as e-mail and file sharing, 70 percent of its resources are directed toward improving its search engine capabilities. This builds on Google's dominance in this industry, which is derived from its popularity as a search engine. Google also has a strong international presence, with its site available in 116 languages.[18]

From an e-commerce perspective, Google Product Search is an application that will search for items available for purchase on the Internet and display a side-by-side comparison. Google does not have an auction site available, although sellers do have the option of setting a negotiable price for their products. In order to compete with eBay's financial service segment, PayPal, Google launched Google Checkout in 2006 and began charging for its use in February of 2008.[19]

Craigslist

A successful new entrant in the e-commerce industry is Craigslist. A private company, Craigslist began in San Francisco as a way for local residents to list events and classified ads. Craigslist differentiates itself by not charging to list or sell products on its Web site.

All revenue comes from fees for job postings and brokered apartment listings in selected cities such as New York. Craigslist keeps its overhead low in many ways, such as by continuing to operate out of a house instead of an office building and by having a staff of only 25 employees.[20] While confirmed financials are not available, some experts estimate the value of Craigslist to be near $5 billion.[21] As part of eBay's growth and acquisition strategy it has *acquired* a portion, roughly 28 percent, of Craigslist (see Exhibit 3 and Exhibit 4 for competitors' financial data).

Acquisitions

eBay's revenue growth has come largely through acquisitions. The acquisitions have also allowed it to increase its geographic reach, move into related businesses such as online payments, and obtain technology that will strengthen its product differentiation.[22] eBay has completed many acquisitions, and some of the more noteworthy ones are discussed here.

Half.com was one of eBay's first acquisitions and allowed eBay to enter the fixed price marketplace. It was acquired in 2000 for $312.8 million. Half.com allows eBay users to sell used books, games, CDs, and DVDs at fixed prices. Sellers are paid directly by Half.com and eBay operates the Half.com Web site separately from eBay.com but allows eBay.com user profiles to be shared between the Web sites.

In 2002 eBay purchased PayPal for $1.5 billion, thereby enabling sellers of any size to receive online payments from a buyer's credit card or checking account. This greatly reduced the payment and shipment times and provided another source of revenue for eBay. PayPal's transaction fee for transactions less than $3,000 is 2.9 percent of the amount transferred.[23] Revenues for PayPal in 2008 were $2.4 billion, making up 28 percent of eBay's total revenue.[24] In September 2008, eBay announced that PayPal was the sole payment option for a majority of its marketplace listings.[25]

In 2004 eBay acquired Shopping.com, Rent.com, and 28 percent ownership of Craigslist. It purchased Shopping.com for $620 million. Shopping.com allows people to search for products and compare prices (similar to Google's product search formerly known as Froogle). This acquisition gave eBay a new channel for buyers and sellers to interact and a new medium for ad revenue.[26]

eBay acquired Rent.com for $415 million. Rent.com joins landlords with tenants online, charging property owners for each lease produced.[27] The acquisition of Rent.com gave eBay entry into the online classifieds market, while increasing revenue streams and online exposure.

Exhibit 3 Key Competitor Financials

	eBay	Google	Amazon	Yahoo!	Overstock	Craigslist
Annual Sales (in Billions)	8.69	20.92	18.14	7.32	0.873	N/A
Employees	15,500	16,805	17,000	14,300	844	25
Market Value (in Billions)	6.57	86.99	17.84	13.87	0.166	N/A
Total Cash (in Billions)	3.64	14.41	2.32	3.21	0.07	N/A
Beta	1.54	1.57	1.84	1.2	2.54	N/A
Gross Profit Margin (in Billions)	5.91	9.94	3.35	4.13	0.124	N/A
EBITDA (in Billions)	2.93	7.62	1.06	1.29	0.001	N/A
Net Income (in Billions)	1.94	5.05	0.627	0.933	−0.02	N/A
Return on Equity	18.0%	20.8%	38.1%	8.94%	−148%	N/A
Return on Assets	9.7%	14.4%	8.8%	2.51%	−9.03%	N/A
Total Debt/Equity	N/A	N/A	0.172	0.005	N/A	N/A
Market Capitalization (in Billions)	16.34	80.99	18.23	14.16	0.16	N/A

Sources: 2008, Yahoo! Finance, http://finance.yahoo.com, November 24; 2008, Craigslist Fact Sheet, http://www.craigslist.org/about/factsheet, November 24

eBay acquired its partial ownership of Craigslist for an undisclosed amount. eBay's relationship with Craigslist has always been somewhat icy. eBay purchased its shares from an owner that went against the other stockholders' wishes to not sell to a public company. Craigslist alleges that eBay placed a variety of excessive demands on it, such as giving eBay blocking rights on all forms of corporate transactions. In 2008 eBay accused Craigslist of diluting eBay's ownership interest by more than 10 percent; Craigslist countersued a month later accusing eBay of unlawful competition and copyright infringement because it launched the international classified-ad site Kijiji.[28] These lawsuits are yet to be resolved.

eBay acquired Skype in 2005 for $2.6 billion. Skype is an Internet phone provider, allowing users to make calls to almost every country with their computers using Voice Over Internet Protocol (VOIP).[29] eBay's plan for Skype was to integrate it to allow buyers and sellers to communicate prior to transactions.[30] Skype is a free service if both parties are using Skype, but it charges non-Skype users for in-and-out calls.[31] The number of Skype users has increased from 57 million in 2005 to 400 million in 2008.[32] In 2007, eBay declared a $1.4 billion asset impairment for Skype, meaning that either eBay overpaid for

Skype or that the strategic integration of Skype was not going as planned. Thus, to maximize Skype's potential, eBay has announced that it plans to make Skype a stand-alone business and will conduct an initial public offering in the first half of 2010.[33]

eBay acquired Stubhub.com in 2007 for $310 million. Stubhub.com is a secondary ticket marketplace that integrates guaranteed fulfillment and shipment using FedEx.[34] Stubhub partners with American Express for concert tickets and over 60 teams for sporting events.[35] In 2007 Stubhub was named the official secondary market for tickets by Major League Baseball.[36] Stubhub features a season-ticketholder option, encouraging customer loyalty, and an easy method for season ticketholders to resell tickets.[37] eBay operates Stubhub.com independently from eBay.com.

eBay's purchase of Fraud Sciences Ltd. for $169 million in 2008 adds to its technology portfolio. eBay has long operated on the notion that trust is the key to its success, and it has announced plans to improve the level of trust that it provides. Fraud Sciences has developed ways to detect fraudulent purchases and provides eBay with the technology that it needs but lacks the capability to develop.

Exhibit 4 Historical Financial Overview of eBay and its Competitors

eBay.com	2003	2004	2005	2006	2007	2008 Q1	2008 Q2	2008 Q3
Net Revenues	$2,165,096	$3,271,309	$4,552,401	$5,969,741	$7,672,329	$2,192,223	$2,195,661	$2,117,531
Cost of Net Revenues	416,058	614,415	818,104	1,256,792	1,762,972	525,412	562,103	560,963
Net Income (Loss)	441,771	778,223	1,082,043	1,125,639	348,251	459,718	460,345	492,219
Google.com	**2003**	**2004**	**2005**	**2006**	**2007**	**2008 Q1**	**2008 Q2**	**2008 Q3**
Net Revenues	$1,465,934	$3,189,223	$6,138,560	$10,604,917	$16,593,986	$5,186,043	$5,367,212	$5,541,391
Cost of Net Revenues	1,123,470	2,549,031	4,121,282	7,054,921	11,509,586	3,639,808	3,789,247	2,173,390
Net Income (Loss)	105,648	399,119	1,465,397	3,077,446	4,203,720	1,307,086	1,247,391	1,289,939
Amazon.com	**2003**	**2004**	**2005**	**2006**	**2007**	**2008 Q1**	**2008 Q2**	**2008 Q3**
Net Revenues	$5,264,000	$6,921,000	$8,490,000	$10,711,000	$14,835,000	$4,135,000	$4,063,000	$4,265,000
Cost of Net Revenues	4,007,000	5,319,000	6,451,000	8,255,000	11,482,000	3,179,000	3,096,000	3,266,000
Net Income (Loss)	35,000	588,000	359,000	190,000	476,000	143,000	158,000	119,000
Yahoo.com	**2003**	**2004**	**2005**	**2006**	**2007**	**2008 Q1**	**2008 Q2**	**2008 Q3**
Net Revenues	$1,625,097	$5,257,668	$6,425,679	$6,969,274	$6,969,274	$1,817,602	$1,798,085	$1,786,426
Cost of Net Revenues	358,103	2,096,201	2,675,723	2,675,723	2,838,758	755,083	765,911	772,227
Net Income (Loss)	237,879	1,896,230	751,391	660,000	660,000	542,163	131,215	54,348
Overstock.com	**2003**	**2004**	**2005**	**2006**	**2007**	**2008 Q1**	**2008 Q2**	**2008 Q3**
Net Revenues	$234,603	$490,621	$794,975	$780,137	$765,902	$202,814	$188,836	$186,855
Cost of Net Revenues	209,320	424,183	678,502	690,333	641,352	168,843	155,627	154,736
Net Income (Loss)	(11,981)	(4,414)	(25,212)	(106,762)	(48,036)	(4,724)	(7,359)	(1,589)

Sources: 2008, http://www.ebay.com; http://www.google.com; http://www.yahoo.com; http://www.overstock.com; http://finance.yahoo.com; http://www.amazon.com

Also, eBay has expanded into Europe and Asia through acquisitions. It increased its auction reach with Alando in Germany, iBazar in France, Tradera in Sweden, Internet Auction in South Korea, and Baazee in India. eBay incorporated international classified ad Web sites into its portfolio with purchases of Loquo in Spain, Gumtree in the United Kingdom, Marktplaats in the Netherlands, and Den Bla Avis in Denmark. Each international acquisition allows eBay to expand and diversify its revenue base by purchasing established Web sites that the local culture understands.[38] This is an extremely important element when developing any sort of presence in a foreign country as eBay learned through its experience in China (discussed in the Customer Demographics and International Experience subsection).

Alliances

In addition to acquisitions, eBay uses alliances with small entrepreneurs and large companies to increase revenues and enhance the number of items available in the marketplace.

In 2004, eBay established a certified provider program consisting of exams, references, and an annual fee.[39] Partners provide services and products that sellers might need and eBay itself does not wish to offer, such as inventory management software, outbound logistics, or a full consignment business.[40] This helps eBay to attract sellers that might not otherwise use its services, or who wish to conduct a high number of transactions but lack expertise in certain areas. Having these services and products available helps sellers move more product than they would otherwise.[41] Activia is one of the best-known certified companies, providing marketplace listing tools to sellers of multiple items.[42] This alliance allows entrepreneurs to use the eBay name to grow their business while providing eBay fee revenue.

In 2006, eBay aligned with Yahoo! in a marketing alliance to promote revenue growth for both companies. Under the alliance Yahoo! became the exclusive advertising provider on eBay, the companies have a co-branded toolbar, and PayPal became Yahoo!'s preferred payment provider.[43] eBay also aligned with Google in 2006, making Google the primary advertiser on eBay's Web sites outside of the United States.[44] Google has sought to integrate Skype into the alliance as a method to further sales from Web advertising.

In 2007, eBay aligned with Northwest and Southwest Airlines to enable PayPal as a payment option, and with Wal-Mart and Myspace.com to promote the growth of Skype.[45] The alliance with Wal-Mart will allow eBay to sell Skype phone equipment in 1,800 retail locations.[46] These alliances help expand the brand name of both PayPal and Skype while also increasing revenue for eBay.

Although initially many smaller sellers were angered by eBay's 2008 alliance with Buy.com because Buy.com does not pay listing fees and its volume, free shipping, and ability to take returns hurt smaller sellers, this alliance is one of the largest potential revenue generators for eBay. Buy.com is a middle-of-the-market tool that links retailers with buyers, and it immediately added five million fixed-price listings to the eBay marketplace.[47] eBay executives have responded to the objections about its alliance with Buy.com by stating, "eBay is aggressively using price as a lever to improve the value and selection on eBay.com. Consistent with our goals, we have entered into a partnership with Buy.com to bring their new-in-season merchandise onto eBay.com. We expect to learn a great deal from this partnership and we will build upon the results."[48]

It appears that eBay will continue to use partnerships as a large part of its growth strategy. Alliances with online competitors such as Yahoo! have allowed online exposure growth, and certified provider programs have given eBay the opportunity to fill the gaps that they are unable or unwilling to fill.

eBay also seeks growth through internal innovation. Product development accounts for almost 18 percent of the company's operating expenses.

Internal Innovation

eBay's early innovations include My eBay, the feedback forum, and final value fees.[49] My eBay is a personal account on eBay that allows users to track their buying and selling activity, send and receive e-mail, update personal information, and view feedback reports. The feedback forum is intended to form trust between buyers and sellers. Each eBay member has a feedback profile that consists of three main elements: the feedback score, the feedback percentage, and the feedback reports. The feedback score is a rating of a member's trade history—the number of good reports about a member minus the number of bad reports. The feedback percentage is the percentage of users that have reported a positive feedback experience with a seller in a given year. The feedback report displays both positive and negative reports from buyers and sellers who have traded with a member and includes information about each transaction. The final value fees are the portion that eBay takes when an item sells (or ends with a winning bid). For items less than $25, the final value fee is 8.75 percent; for items between $25 and $1,000, the final value fee is 8.75 percent of the initial $25 plus 3.5 percent of the remaining value; for items over $1,000, the final value fee is 8.75 percent of the initial $25 plus 3.5 percent of the initial $25 to $1,000 plus 1.5 percent of the remaining value.

In 2005, eBay unveiled Kijiji.com, an online classified Web site resembling Craigslist. By 2008, Kijiji attracted five million unique monthly visitors and was available in over 1,000 cities across the globe.[50] In 2006, eBay launched eBay Express in the United States, the United Kingdom, and Germany, providing buyers with the ability to buy multiple items, much like Amazon .com. However, due to feedback from both buyers and sellers, eBay closed eBay Express in all three markets in 2008 to focus more on its main eBay site.[51] David Hsu, a management professor at Wharton describes eBay's internal innovation as, "a poor job of identifying synergistic opportunities . . . eBay's research group has not been able to drive much growth by internal innovation. . . . [eBay] has to get that spark the company had in the early days."[52]

Economic Downturn

When it makes its acquisition, alliance, and innovation decisions, eBay first considers the environmental factors that may influence its success. The increasing unemployment rate and the mortgage crisis have also contributed to a decline in disposable income. This may increase the number of sellers on eBay as those who are unemployed seek ways to make extra money, but fewer people are buying, and those who are demand low prices.[53] Thus, in September 2008 eBay lowered fees on fixed-cost sales by more than 70 percent in an effort to better compete with Amazon.com;[54] and starting in June 2009 infrequent sellers will be able to offer up to five items every 30 days without paying a listing fee.[55]

Customer Demographics and International Experience

An aging population poses potential challenges. Currently, 50 percent of eBay buyers are over the age of 45, 53 percent are male, and 72 percent earn more than $50,000 per year; but as baby boomers age, the number of consumers in this age group will decline.[56]

Additionally, significant shifts in ethnic composition are occurring in the United States. For example, the Hispanic population is growing and is expected to triple over the next 40 years. This will likely alter the type of products desired for purchase on eBay.[57] Furthermore, as eBay continues to pursue international expansion, the products in demand will change and it will need to

broaden its understanding of business practices and levels of service that are required to attract consumers in specific countries.

eBay did not succeed in its first attempt to establish a presence in China, most likely because it lacked insight into the Chinese culture. eBay entered China in 2002 by purchasing a third of China's principal online auction site, Eachnet.com. In 2003, eBay purchased and became the sole owner of Eachnet.com, but by 2005 it had lost significant market share to Taobao, the consumer auction segment of China's largest ecommerce company.[58] eBay failed to understand that its popularity in the United States would not automatically make it successful in China. Some of the complaints were that eBay did not provide phone service or allow bartering, and it did not react quickly enough when Taobao entered the market without charging user fees.[59] Despite its failure with Eachnet.com, eBay is in China for the long haul, as Whitman said, "market leadership in China will be a defining characteristic of leadership globally," and failure to establish itself there would be an "astronomical" setback for the company as a whole.[60] Therefore in 2007 it established a partnership with a Beijing-based Internet company, Tom Online Inc., taking a 49 percent stake in the company and possessing administration rights. This allows eBay to have strong local management that understands the culture and consumer desires. Tom eBay has done much to win the trust of Chinese consumers such as using an escrow service to hold payments until the buyer confirms satisfaction with the product. Whitman stated, "Whatever we do elsewhere to assure trust and safety, in China we have to do more."[61] eBay has had some success in China with Skype; Skype has grown faster in China than anywhere else.[62]

Technology and Competitive Challenges

Various technological trends may pose challenges for eBay. Staying aware of the trends and responding quickly is essential—as eBay learned from its misfortune in Japan. eBay lost significant market share to Yahoo! and pulled out of Japan in 2002 mostly due to failing to be up to date with the technology that Japanese users expected to be available on an auction site.[63] Another possible issue is that Skype's technology may threaten eBay's profitability by giving buyers and sellers an opportunity to conduct the transaction without using eBay and thereby circumventing eBay's fees.

Another aspect of technology that poses a challenge is that retailers have put great effort into improving their Web sites to make online shopping easier for consumers. Stores such as Best Buy, Nordstrom, Target, and Wal-Mart carry items in four out of five of eBay's top volume categories (electronics, computers, clothing/accessories, and home/garden). Consumers may prefer these retailers over eBay because they have greater confidence in their ability to return items and to have some sort of recourse if a purchased item is never received or is broken upon receipt. However, eBay was founded on its judicious use of technology and it has recently developed some technology to help it limit the number of legal proceedings related to counterfeit products.

Legal Issues

Fashion fakes constitute a $600 billion industry worldwide[64] and despite eBay's efforts to crack down on counterfeit merchandise, some eBay users continue to sell it. This has led to lawsuits against eBay from companies such as Rolex, Tiffany & Co., Hermès, Louis Vuitton, and L'Oreal. Lawsuit results have been mixed. Rolex first instigated a trial against eBay in 2001. The original ruling was overturned by a German court in 2007 because the judge believed that eBay could not be held liable for damages, but it should monitor its site to prevent fakes from being sold. Again in early 2009 Rolex brought a case against eBay, but the judge ruled in favor of eBay.[65] In the case against Tiffany & Co. in July 2008, a U.S. District Court judge ruled that eBay did not bear legal responsibility for sales of counterfeit goods in its marketplace and that "it is the trademark owner's burden to police its mark."[66] However eBay was not as fortunate in the French courts in the cases against Hermès and Louis Vuitton. It was ordered to pay Hermès $30,000 in damages because "by failing to act within [its] powers to prevent reprehensible use of the site, both the seller and eBay committed acts of counterfeiting;"[67] eBay was also instructed to compensate Louis Vuitton $63 million for "culpable negligence," and an additional $20 million in damages for unauthorized sales of its perfume.[68] Most recently, though, courts in Paris have ruled in favor of eBay in a case against L'Oreal, stating that "preventing the sale of counterfeit goods on the eBay platform encounters major difficulties when it comes to perfumes and cosmetics."[69]

eBay is dedicated to thwarting the sale of counterfeit products on its site. It has developed a filter program that detects offerings that blatantly violate trademark rights, established a team that works closely with law enforcement agencies, and even launched an anti-counterfeit campaign that aimed to educate buyers on how to avoid counterfeit products.

Tax law also may present challenges for eBay. Currently, if a consumer orders merchandise from a company that does not operate in his or her state of residence, no sales tax is paid on the item.[70] However, there is a possibility that legislation will pass requiring Internet purchases to be taxed. The IRS has also proposed that certain types of Internet companies, including eBay, should be required to collect and report individuals' earnings, allowing the IRS to ensure income taxes are being paid.[71] If this legislation passes, eBay users may move their business to sites that are not required to adhere to this policy.

To this point, eBay has been able to successfully navigate the company through environmental obstacles; it will need to continue to do so in order to remain profitable.

Financial Results

eBay derives most of its income from transaction costs associated with online sales. The product category that brings in the most revenue for eBay is vehicles (see Exhibit 5). Revenues from its businesses outside of the main eBay auction marketplaces have grown to 44 percent of total revenue. In 2008, of its $8.5 billion total net revenues, PayPal made up $2.3 billion (27 percent), Skype made up $551 million (6 percent), and marketplace transactions made up $5.6 billion (66 percent); 46 percent came from the United States, and 54 percent came from international sources.[72] In recent years, more and more of eBay's revenue is generated from international operations (see Exhibit 6).

In 2008 eBay was ranked second among the world's most valuable retail Web sites, only trailing Amazon in unique visitors and year-over-year growth.[73] In annual sales, eBay trails Google ($20.92 billion) and Amazon ($18.14 billion), beating Yahoo! ($7.32 billion) and Overstock ($.873 billion) (see Exhibits 3 and 4). Craigslist is not a public company and thus its sales data is not public information.

Marketplace revenue depends on gross merchandise volume (GMV). eBay breaks down GMV into the number of listings multiplied by the conversion rate (the percentage of items that sold) multiplied by the average sale price.[74] New-listing and GMV growth in 2008 came primarily from the international marketplace (see Exhibit 6). In 2008 eBay marketplaces had 86.3 million active users and 140 million listings at any given time.[75] Vehicles, parts, and accessories made up 31.5 percent of the top 16 GMV categories for the years 2006–2008, while consumer electronics and computers composed 16.4 percent, clothing and accessories was 8.5 percent, and home and garden was 6.8 percent (see Exhibit 5). eBay's expansion into fixed-price sales is positive, as this area increased to 45 percent of total GMV in 2008.[76] Regardless of the positive financial results that eBay

Exhibit 5 eBay Categories and Trends

| | $1 billion categories trend data (in millions) | | | | | | | | | | |
	30-Sep-06	31-Dec-06	31-Mar-07	30-Jun-07	30-Sep-07	31-Dec-07	31-Mar-08	30-Jun-08	30-Sep-08
Vehicles	12,376	11,552	11,832	13,536	13,328	12,424	12,672	13,532	11,688
Parts and Accessories	3,764	4,172	4,680	5,016	4,596	4,768	5,348	5,392	4,620
Consumer Electronics	3,876	5,872	4,880	4,608	4,620	6,788	5,796	5,200	4,992
Computers	3,600	3,996	4,052	3,688	3,688	4,132	4,248	3,656	3,500
Clothing and Accessories	3,704	4,744	4,540	4,496	4,340	5,564	5,348	5,288	4,652
Home and Garden	3,036	3,496	3,584	3,640	3,700	4,120	4,244	4,184	3,840
Collectibles	2,208	2,804	2,684	2,388	2,380	2,948	2,772	2,468	2,232
Books/Movies/Music	2,780	3,032	3,124	2,720	3,000	3,288	3,456	2,952	2,864
Sports	2,496	2,668	2,584	2,892	2,836	2,884	2,940	3,232	2,992
Business & Industrial	1,752	2,012	2,232	2,220	2,140	2,300	2,584	2,452	2,212
Toys	1,700	2,564	2,136	1,940	1,940	2,748	2,396	2,144	1,952
Jewelry & Watches	1,644	2,184	1,972	1,960	1,924	2,508	2,332	2,216	1,988
Cameras & Photo	1,404	1,636	1,524	1,548	1,504	1,752	1,672	1,672	1,508
Antiques & Art	1,012	1,304	1,352	1,248	1,164	1,484	1,508	1,364	1,096
Coins & Stamps	900	1,044	1,320	1,068	1,028	1,192	1,428	1,188	1,032
Tickets & Travel	972	916	1,088	1,336	1,772	1,980	1,496	2,012	2,260
Total	47,224	53,996	53,584	54,304	53,960	60,880	60,240	58,952	53,428
Percentage Growth		14%	−1%	1%	−1%	13%	−1%	−2%	−9%

Source: 2008, eBay Annual Report, http://www.ebay.com

Exhibit 6 eBay Growth: U.S. vs. International

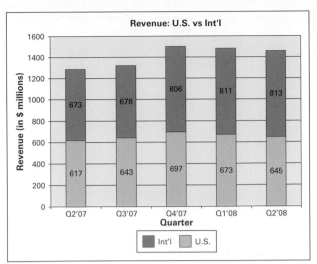

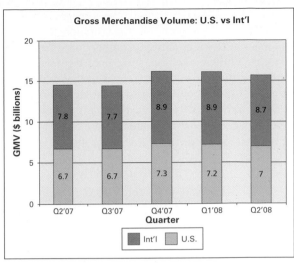

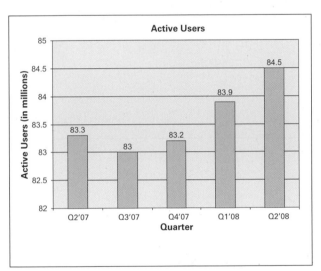

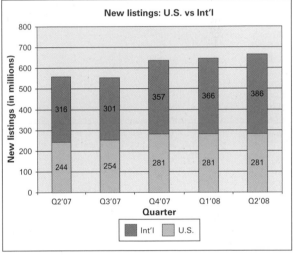

Source: 2008, Investor Relations, eBay company website, http:// www.ebay.com.

posted in 2008, there are some significant challenges for which the new CEO and other leaders must determine solutions.

Overview of Challenges

eBay is currently in a fast-cycle market, causing it to experience extreme external competitive pressure. This competitive pressure is from both dominant Internet companies such as Amazon, Yahoo!, and Google as well as small private companies such as Craigslist. eBay faces the challenge of differentiating itself from these competitors, while at the same time striving to attract

buyers and increasing revenues on each transaction. In an effort to attract more listings and higher revenues, eBay's alliance with Buy.com has sparked boycotts and a loss of some its core customers. eBay needs to find a balance between satisfying buyers and creating economically beneficial cost structures for large strategic alliance partners.

Given the current budget deficits of many states, they may push to overturn the 1992 Supreme Court ruling that liberated mail-order merchants from having to collect sales tax from a consumer in a state in which they do not have a physical presence. This would result in eBay having to ensure that sales tax is collected on each transaction, leading to increased costs and more book-keeping for eBay.[77]

Counterfeit merchandise affects eBay's image as a trust-worthy auction site and poses the threat of more time and money spent in lawsuits. Current competition is fierce in the fast-cycle VOIP marketplace and potential government regulations of the VOIP industry could further affect the Skype brand. Additionally, Skype's technology is licensed from third parties and although there are contracts in place, future license renewals could increase costs or make it illogical for eBay to use this third-party software.[78]

eBay is currently at a unique period in company growth as its acquisition strategy has created a large conglomerate of companies that intertwine within the online marketplace arena, while looking for new avenues to gain market share and revenue. The e-commerce industry as a whole is in a growth-stage and competitors are gaining market share as they innovate at a faster pace than eBay. With Meg Whitman's retirement and the company's recent shift toward focusing on the fixed-price marketplace, eBay has entered a defining phase of its business.

NOTES

1. 2008, eBay: The world's online marketplace, http://pages.ebay.com/aboutebay/thecompany/companyoverview.html, December 4.
2. A. Schmidt, 2008, eBay CEO Meg Whitman to retire, MSNBC, http://www.msnbc.com, January 23.
3. R. Waters, 2008, eBay revenue to decline for first time, Financial Times, October 16; F. Ross, 2009, eBay's 4th quarter earnings—The recession? All Business, http://www.allbusiness.com, February 14.
4. 2008, eBay History, http://www.ebay.com, November 3.
5. Ibid.
6. 2008, eBay Form 10-K, http://www.ebay.com.
7. 2008, eBay Form 10-K, http://www.ebay.com.
8. 2008, Hoover's Company Records: Amazon.com Inc., November 1.
9. T. Wolverton, 2000, Amazon, Sotheby's closing jointly operated auction site, Cnet News, http://news.cnet.com, October 10.
10. 2008, Amazon announces beginning of multi-year frustration-free packaging initiative, Forbes, http://www.forbes.com, November 3.
11. B. Stone, 2008, Profit is up at Amazon, but outlook is reduced, New York Times, October 23, B3.
12. 2008, Hoover's Company Records: Yahoo! Inc., November 25.
13. 2008, 2007 Yahoo! Inc. Form 10K, http://www.yahoo.com, February 27.
14. 2007, Yahoo! to close North American auction site, MSNBC, http://www.msnbc.msn.com, May 9.
15. A. Sorkin & S. Lohr, 2008, Pursuing Yahoo! again, Microsoft shows need for a Web franchise, New York Times, May 19, A1.
16. B. Stone, 2008, Now comes the hard part as Yahoo! wrestles with a question of direction, New York Times, November 18, B1.
17. 2008, Corporate information: Our philosophy, http://www.google.com, November 28.
18. Ibid.
19. 2007, Google Inc., Form 10-K, http://www.google.com.
20. 2008, craigslist fact sheet, http://www.craigslist.org, November 16.
21. J. Fine, 2008, Can Craigslist stay oddball? BusinessWeek, May 19, 75.
22. 2008, The Portfolio Story, http://ebayinkblog.com/wp-content/uploads/ThePortfolioStory_24Oct08.pdf, October.
23. 2008, Transaction fees domestic transactions, PayPal company Web site, http://www.paypal.com, December 3.
24. 2008, eBay 2007 Form 10-K, 51.
25. C. Wolf, 2008, eBay cuts fixed-price sales fees by 70%.
26. 2008, eBay to buy Shopping.com for $620 million, http://news.cnet.com, December 3.
27. 2008, eBay to buy Rent.com for $415 million, http://news.cnet.com, December 3.
28. 2008, eBay files corporate governance suit to protect its investment in Craigslist, eBay News, http://www.news.ebay.com, April 22; 2008, Craigslist-eBay suit details icy relationship, PC Magazine, www.pcmag.com, May 13; 2008, eBay goes public with Craigslist complaint, USA Today, http://www.usatoday.com, May 1.
29. 2008, About Skype, Skype company Web site, http://www.skype.com, December 3.
30. 2008, eBay to buy Skype in $2.6bn deal, http://news.bbc.co.uk, December 3.
31. 2008, About Skype.
32. 2009, Skype available on Apple App store, About Skype, http://www.skype.com, March 31; 2008, What to do with Skype, http://news.cnet.com, December 3.
33. 2009, eBay Inc. announces plan for 2010 initial public offering of Skype, About Skype, http://www.skype.com, April 14.
34. 2008, Is Stubhub the ticket for eBay, BusinessWeek, http://www.businessweek.com, December 3.
35. 2008, About Stubhub, Stubhub company Web site, http://www.stubhub.com/, December 3.
36. 2008, eBay 2007 Form 10-K.
37. 2008, About Stubhub.
38. 2008, The portfolio story.
39. Ibid.
40. 2008, eBay certified provider program, http://www.ebay.com, November 16.
41. 2008, Inside eBay's innovation machine—case studies, CIO Insight, http://www.cioinsight.com, November 16.
42. 2008, Certified providers program.
43. 2008, Yahoo!, eBay in Web advertising pact, MSNBC, http://www.msnbc.msn.com, December 3.
44. 2008, Google and eBay form an alliance to tailor adds to every customer, http://www.guardian.co.uk, December 3.
45. 2008, eBay 2007 Form 10-K, http://www.ebay.com, November 25, 51.
46. 2008, Wal-Mart to sell Skype phone gear, MSNBC, http://www.msnbc.msn.com, December 3.
47. B. Stone, 2008, Buy.com deal with eBay angers sellers, New York Times, July 14, 1.
48. R. Smythe, 2008, eBay partners with Buy.com, http://www.ebayinkblog.com, May 3.
49. A. Hsiao, 2009, Understanding the eBay feedback system, About.com, www.ebay.about.com, May 20; 2009, Final value fees, http://www.ebay,com, May 20; 2009, Using My eBay, http://www.ebay.com, May 20.
50. 2008, About Kijiji, http://bayarea.kijiji.com, December 3.
51. 2008, About eBay express, http://www.ebay.com, December 3.
52. 2008, eBay, After Meg, Forbes, http://www.forbes.com, December 3.
53. R. Waters, 2008, Add eBay to the cart, Financial Times, http://www.ft.com, October.
54. C. Wolf, 2008, eBay cuts fixed-price sales fees by 70%, Washington Post, August 21, D03.
55. R. Metz, 2009, eBay cuts auction listing fees for casual sellers, The Boston Globe, http://www.boston.com, May 12.

56. 2008, eBay Seller Central, http://www.ebay.com, November; 2008, The changing nature of retail: Planting the seeds for sustainable growth, *Deloitte Consulting*, http://www.deloitte.com, November 18.

57. 2005, Changing demographics result in shifting consumer habits, http://www.retailforward.com, November 4.

58. K. Hafner & B. Stone, 2006, eBay is expected to close its auction site in China, *New York Times*, http://www.nytimes.com, December 19.

59. Ibid., R. Hof, 2006, eBay's China challenge, *BusinessWeek*, http://www.businessweek.com, December 19.

60. K. Hafner & B. Stone, eBay is expected to close its auction site in China; B. Powell & J. Ressner, 2005, Why eBay must win in China, *Time*, http://www.time.com, August 22.

61. V. Shannon, 2007, eBay is planning to re-enter the China auction business, *New York Times*, http://www.nytimes.com, June 22.

62. Ibid.

63. B. Powell & J. Ressner, Why eBay must win in China; 2001, How Yahoo! Japan beat eBay at its own game, *BusinessWeek*, http://www.businessweek.com, June 4.

64. A. Szustek, 2009, eBay victorious over Rolex in latest counterfeiting lawsuit, *Finding Dulcinea*, http://www.findingdulcinea.com, February 27.

65. D. Woollard, 2009, Rolex loses eBay lawsuit, http://www.luxist.com, February 26.

66. 2008, Judge rules for eBay over fake Tiffany jewelry sales, *International Herald Tribune*, July 15, F12.

67. C. Matlack, 2008, Hermes beats eBay in counterfeit case, *BusinessWeek*, http://www.businessweek.com, June 6.

68. R. Waters, 2008, eBay wins court battle with Tiffany, *Financial Times*, http://www.ft.com, July 14; R.Waters, 2008, Moment of truth for eBay on luxury goods, *Financial Times*, http://www.ft.com, June 30.

69. I. Steiner, 2009, eBay fends off L'Oreal's counterfeiting lawsuit, *Auction Bytes*, http://www.auctionbytes.com, May 13.

70. A. Broache, 2008, Tax-free Internet shopping days could be numbered, *CNET News*, http://www.cnetnews.com, April 15.

71. 2008, Internet broker tax reporting, eBay Government Relations, http://www.ebay.com, November 20.

72. 2008, eBay 2007 Form 10-K, http://investor.ebay.com/annuals.cfm, 51, November 25.

73. 2009, eBay narrows the gap, but Amazon tops in traffic again, Nielsen says, *Internet Retailer*, http://www.internetretailer.com, February 27.

74. 2008, Q3 20008 Earnings Slides, eBay company Web site, http://www.ebay.com, November 16.

75. 2008, eBay 2007 Form 10-K, http://www.ebay.com, 51.

76. 2008, eBay Fact Sheet, http://www.ebay.com, November 28.

77. 2008, Sales tax on the Internet, http://www.nolo.com, December 4.

78. 2008, eBay 2007 Form 10-K, 29.

Ryan Gust, Brandon Barth, Joey O'Donnell, Drew Forsberg, Robin Chapman

Arizona State University

Introduction

In 1992 Boeing and Airbus parent, EADS, agreed to conduct a joint study on the prospects for a superjumbo airplane. With a forecasted 5 percent annual growth in air travel, both companies saw the need for a new aircraft large enough to support this growth. However, the world will not be permitted to see what the brain trust of the two aerospace industry giants could have produced. Airbus and Boeing reached different conclusions concerning market trends, and the joint effort was called off.

The average size of aircraft grew until the late 1990s; however, this trend began to change as carriers shifted their primary focus to profits as opposed to market share. Strong competition among airlines prompted ticket prices to fall in recent years. As a result, carriers dramatically reduced costs and aggressively expanded their networks. The assumption reached by many carriers was that in order to become more flexible, a smaller aircraft must be used to reach many regional airports rather than larger aircraft that can only access hub airports in major cities.[1]

As both companies considered which options to pursue in order to satisfy the growing market, Airbus speculated that the hub-and-spoke system would prove to be the future for airlines and decided to launch the A-380 project in December 2000. Boeing's aircraft, dubbed the 787, was launched in 2005. This aircraft represents a fundamentally different vision, one anchored in the belief that the point-to-point system is the most sensible growth platform.

What is at stake for Boeing and Airbus? Boeing invested more than $8 billion in development for the 787, while Airbus went over budget, investing more than $14 billion and experienced a two-year delay in delivery to its customers. Boeing received solid orders for the midsized 787 and is determined to deliver the 787 in May 2008 as promised to avoid the problems that have

plagued its competitor. Some manufacturing problems threatened to delay delivery, however, and are minimizing Boeing's margin for error.[2]

This case discusses the history of Boeing and the salient industry forces affecting the company, leading to the critical decisions faced by both competitors. The key strategic issues driving Boeing's competitive strategies are also outlined along with a discussion of strategies used to manage the competitive environment by both Boeing and Airbus, and the challenges facing both companies.

Boeing's History

William E. Boeing originally worked in the timber industry, and his knowledge of wooden structures led him to design and build an airplane, the B&W Seaplane. When the B&W was ready to fly, the test pilot was late and Mr. Boeing grew impatient, which prompted him to pilot the aircraft himself.[3] This example illustrates Mr. Boeing's level of determination, a key quality of his character, which was incorporated into his airplane manufacturing company.

Established on July 15, 1916, the company was originally called Pacific Aero Products Company. A year later Mr. Boeing changed the name to what is now the Boeing Airplane Company. Edgar Gott, William Boeing's first cousin, became president of the company in 1922.[4] Gott helped Boeing Co. obtain business contracts with the military; succeeding presidents, Philip G. Johnson and Clairmont L. Egtvedt, maintained this relationship with the government throughout WWII. Boeing became a powerhouse in large part due to its war effort, essentially because the military ordered numerous B-17 Bombers.

After the war many of the Bomber orders were canceled, so Boeing's management team tried to recover by

The authors would like to thank Professor Robert E. Hoskisson for his support and under whose direction the case was developed. The case solely provides material for class discussion. The authors do not intend to illustrate either effective or ineffective handling of a managerial situation. This case was developed with contributions from Hal Hardy and Emily Little.

diversifying its product offerings. Boeing began selling a luxurious four-engine commercial aircraft known as the Stratocruiser.[5] However, this aircraft was not the commercial success Boeing had hoped for and as a result, Boeing once again found itself at the drawing board.

William M. Allen took control of Boeing in 1945 and oversaw the building of the United States' first commercial jet airliner, the 707. The 707 had capacity for 156 passengers and helped the United States become a leader in commercial jet manufacturing. The 720 jet plane, which was faster, soon followed, but it had a shorter flying range. A demand for planes capable of flying long routes led Boeing to develop the 727.[6] This aircraft utilized one less engine than previous models and was thought to be significantly more comfortable and reliable than competitors' products.[7] Because most models are eventually discontinued to allocate resources to "new and improved models," the 727 was discontinued in 1984; however, by the beginning of 2000 almost 1,300 of these planes were still in service. Boeing achieved additional commercial success in 1967 and 1968 with the production of the 737 and 747. The 737 would become the best-selling commercial jet aircraft in history while the 747 would hold the passenger seating capacity record for 35 years. The 747 utilizes a double-decker configuration, allowing for a maximum of 524 passengers on board.[8]

In 1994, under the leadership of Frank Shrontz, Boeing developed the 777. This aircraft would actually be the first aircraft designed entirely by computer. "Throughout the design process, the airplane was 'pre-assembled' on the computer, eliminating the need for a costly, full-scale mock-up."[9] This aircraft became the longest range twin-engine aircraft in the world.

Thornton "T" Wilson became president of Boeing in 1968 and continued as CEO until 1986. Malcolm T. Stamper became president in 1972 and, in collaboration with Mr. Wilson, he led Boeing's development of the single-aisle 757 and the larger twin-aisle 767 in the wake of a new European competitor, Airbus. During these years Boeing also participated in space programs and military projects, such as the International Space Station and the development of new sophisticated missiles. Today, "Boeing is organized into two business units: Boeing Commercial Airplanes and Boeing Integrated Defense Systems," with the latter making Boeing the world's second-largest defense company.[10]

Philip M. Condit took over in 1996 but was quickly relieved of his position in 1997 because he underestimated Airbus's ability to compete with Boeing. Harry Stonecipher succeeded Condit and faced even more intense rivalry with Airbus. By 2003, Airbus had become the market leader, sending Boeing scrambling frantically to pursue new projects, such as the Sonic Cruiser. The Sonic Cruiser aimed to please customers with a faster, more comfortable ride for long-distance travel. The Cruiser would cut an hour off traditional travel time by flying at a higher elevation and a Mach speed of .98 (most aircraft fly at Mach .80).[11] When Lew Platt became board chair in December of 2003, Boeing abandoned the Sonic Cruiser project in order to focus its efforts on the 787 Dreamliner. Airlines were favoring planes that boasted fuel efficiency over those that offered faster speed. The Dreamliner, slated to fly in May 2008, is popular in the industry because of its potential fuel economy, one-piece composite fuselage sections, and eco-friendliness. It will cost slightly more than half of Airbus's complementary product, and currently has more than twice as much order-book value.[12]

Although each of Boeing's leaders sought to improve the organization during his tenure (for additional biographical information on Boeing's previous leadership, please refer to Exhibit 1), the rivalry with Boeing's key competitor is still intense.

Airbus: Boeing's Key Competitor

The industry for large commercial aircraft (LCA) is a duopoly composed of Boeing Co. and Airbus Industries. These two manufacturing giants have emerged in an unsteady industry whose fortune is based upon strategic timing and luck. Market share is overwhelmingly the most important consideration for each company when making strategic decisions. Essentially, market share determines success. Airbus, once considered a small player, swiftly emerged as an industry giant by focusing on the needs of the market, a standard product line, efficient production methods, and successful marketing ploys. Other players such as Douglas Aircraft Corporation and Lockheed Martin, who were successful and competitive corporations, fell from their positions due to failure in their demand forecast strategies and they merged with other competitors; especially significant was the merger between McDonnell Douglas and Boeing.[13]

Airplanes are grouped into families based on size, range, and technology. At the low end of the market are two single-aisle airplanes; the Boeing 737 and the Airbus A-320, which both seat about 190 people. These planes have each been extremely successful in generating sales, but fall short as revenue earners for both companies. The most profitable market segment has been the middle market, filled with the medium-sized aircraft, which seat from 200 to 300 passengers. Boeing's 757 and Airbus's A330-200 are the most popular planes in this segment. High-end jumbo airplanes fill the remaining segment of the market and are characterized by long-range flight capability, 300+ seats, and maximum use of technology. Each company attempts to develop its products to match the forecasted market demands by producing

Exhibit 1 Biographical Information on Boeing's Previous Leadership

Walter James McNerney Jr.
President, Chief Executive Officer, and Chairman of the Board of Directors of The Boeing Company, 2005–Present

McNerney received a BA from Yale University in 1971 and an MBA from Harvard in 1975. While receiving his education, Mc-Nerney played varsity baseball and hockey. McNerney started his executive career at General Electric in 1982. Over the next 19 years he held many positions including president and CEO of GE Aircraft Engines, GE Lighting, and GE Electrical Distribution and Control. He also spent time as president of GE Asia-Pacific and GE Information Services, and executive vice president of GE Capital. In 2001 McNerney joined 3M as CEO. After turning down two offers in two years, 3M CEO McNerney finally accepted the position as CEO and chairman of The Boeing Company in June of 2005. McNerney had already been a member of the board of directors at Boeing since 2001. He is the chair of the U.S.-China Business Council and serves on the World Business Council for Sustainable Development.

James A. Bell
Interim Chief Executive Officer of the Boeing Company, March 2005–June 2005; Chief Financial Officer, 2004–Present

James A. Bell received a BA in accounting from California State University. Mr. Bell started his career as an accountant at The Rockwell Company. He advanced through management at Rockwell, holding positions as senior internal auditor, accounting manager, and manager of general and cost accounting. When Rockwell's aerospace division was acquired by Boeing in 1996, Bell moved with it. At Boeing, Bell held positions as the vice president of contracts and pricing for the company's space and communications division, as well as senior vice president of finance and corporate controller. In 2004, following the firing of Michel M. Sears (due to a government contract scandal), Bell accepted the position as the chief financial officer of The Boeing Company. Bell also served as an interim CEO for a few months in 2005 between the time that Harry Stonecipher was forced to resign and James McNerney Jr. accepted the position.

Harry C. Stonecipher
President; 1997–2005; Chief Executive Officer of The Boeing Company, 2003–2005

Harry C. Stonecipher received a BS in physics from Tennessee Technological University in 1960. He began his career as a lab technician at General Motors. He then moved to GE's large engine division and worked his way up to become a vice president and then a division head. He left GE to go to Sundstrand where he became president and CEO after two years. After that he served as president and CEO of McDonnell Douglas until the merger with Boeing in 1997. At Boeing he served as the president and COO until 2003 when he filled the shoes of Philip M. Condit as CEO. In 2005, however, Stonecipher resigned at the request of the board after news of a "consensual relationship" with a female board member surfaced (violating Boeing's Code of Conduct).

Philip Murray Condit
Chief Executive Officer, 1996–2003; Chairman of the Board, 1997–2003 of The Boeing Company

Condit earned a Bachelor's degree in mechanical engineering from the University of California, Berkley; a master's degree in Aeronautical Engineering from Princeton; an MBA from the MIT Sloan School of Management; and a PhD in engineering from Science University of Tokyo. Condit started at Boeing in 1965 as an aerodynamics engineer, he then advanced to a lead engineer and soon after became a marketing manager. After a short break to earn his MBA he returned to Boeing, working through a myriad of leadership positions until he ascended to CEO in 1996 and board chair in 1997. His time as CEO and chairperson was characterized by a number of mergers and acquisitions as well as a struggle with increasing competition with Airbus. Condit was forced to resign in 2003 amidst corruption charges involving his freezing of a contract with the U.S. Air Force in 1997.

Thornton "T" A. Wilson
President, 1968–1972; Chief Executive Officer, 1969–1986; Chairman of the Board, 1972–1987; Chairman Emeritus of The Boeing Company, 1987–1993

Wilson received an aeronautical engineering degree from Iowa State University in 1943 and a master's degree in aeronautical engineering from the California Institute of Technology in 1948. Wilson begins his career with Boeing in 1943 and advanced rapidly. His first assignment of note was as project engineer on the B-52 and then was general manager of the proposal team for the Minuteman intercontinental ballistic missile program. Wilson became a vice president in 1963 and was put in charge of planning the Boeing corporate headquarters in 1964. He was named executive vice president in 1966 and president in 1968. Wilson became the CEO in 1969 and board chair in 1972.

Louis Gallois
Chief Executive Officer of Airbus, 2006–Present

Gallois graduated from both the Ecole Des Hautes Etudes Commerciales (where he received an education in economic science) and the Ecole Nationale de l'Administration. In 1972 Gallois started with the Treasury Department of the French government. During1982–1987, Gallois worked his way up at the Cabinet Office of the Ministry of Research. His appointment as the Head of Civil and Military Cabinet Office of the French Ministry of Defense took place in 1988. It was in 1989 that Gallois shifted his career from government to the private sector when be became board chair and CEO of SNECMA, an airplane engine manufacturer. He then moved to Aerospatiale, another aerospace manufacture, as board chair and CEO. Gallois was chair of the French National Railways from 1996 to 2006. In October 2006, Gallois became CEO of Airbus.

Source: Executive Biographies, Wikipedia, http://en.wikipedia.org; http://www.boeing.com.

an airplane that offers the appropriate size, range, fuel efficiency, and technology. These forecasts are based on huge uncertainties, such as what size of airplane will airlines need in order to carry an unknown amount of people to and from large hub airports or smaller regional airports. These variables make accurate short-term projections and assumptions key to long-term success in an industry that is constantly changing.[14]

Airbus became a competitive global manufacturer of LCAs with the help of "launch aid," a form of government subsidies implemented to help a company, such as Airbus, compete and survive in industries where competitive giants such as Boeing have established distribution networks and economies of scale. Airbus was able to establish a significant market share and a brand name by making airplanes that addressed the needs of the market. Airlines had been "crying" for midsized cost efficient airplanes, and Airbus answered by building the A-320. The "commonality" that the A-320 had with other Airbus airplanes was attractive to airlines because of its potential to reduce pilot and attendant training costs as well as improve airplane turnaround time.[15]

Despite Airbus's strategy, Boeing had not embraced commonality among its products because of the changes and high costs that would be incurred at its current stage. As a result, the manufacturing giant fell from its number one position. In order for Boeing to survive its newfound misfortune, it needed to make serious changes in its strategy and business processes. The first aspect considered for business-process change would be its relationships with suppliers.

Suppliers

The importance of suppliers to aircraft manufacturers has shifted with advancements in technology. Chuck Agne, a former director of supplier management for Boeing's Integrated Defense Systems, said in 2004 that Boeing's strategy was to "move up the value chain," meaning that Boeing was going to focus less on the many details and more on their core competence, integration, and assembly. As part of this strategy, Boeing consolidated its supplier list and managed relationships only with those that provide quality products with the best value. Agne said, "What we have found is, the suppliers we're sticking with are the ones who are able to move up that value chain with us."[16]

Traditionally, most manufacturers similar to Boeing completed all research and production in-house. Technological research and development is seen as a competitive advantage that must be closely guarded within the airplane production industry. Boeing's key technical expertise—such as wing technology and new lightweight materials such as composites—are considered its core competencies. Boeing traditionally believed that outsourcing these components to suppliers would give the suppliers control over manufacturing and ultimately place the supplier in control when determining its share of revenue. However, it is no longer a sensible option for Boeing to keep an entire production line in-house. Thus, a new trend emerged in the production of new aircraft, such as the 787 Dreamliner. For the first time Boeing announced it would "offload" (Boeing's term for *outsourcing*)[17] the design of it wings and parts of its fuselage to Japan, and also outsource its fuselage panel work to an Italian company. It is estimated that now 70 percent of the components of a given airplane are outsourced. As such, Boeing is responsible for plane assembly, assuming the title of "Systems Integrator."[18]

Boeing also sought strategic partnerships globally in an effort to reduce costs and perhaps generate sales. By outsourcing to countries such as China and India, Boeing entered what is called an "offset agreement," such that they obtain aircraft sales in return for manufacturing work. This arrangement allowed Boeing to gain more substantial entry into two of the largest and fastest growing airplane markets (China and India).[19]

One of the main attractions for establishing strategic partnerships is the ability to distribute some of the risk associated with the large investment required to build an airplane. By outsourcing, LCA manufacturers are able to share risks and focus their efforts on marketing and supplier relationships. By developing components of the 787 Dreamliner in Japan, Boeing also acquires support from Asian Airlines through the purchase of planes, aided by Japanese government incentives. Another indirect financial benefit to Boeing is the fact that the Japanese and Italian companies are all subsidized by their governments. If successful, the projects present multiple opportunities for Boeing to develop and market their product in an entirely new way.[20] However, risk sharing also equates to profit sharing.

In addition to diminished profits, other implications related to outsourcing are worth noting. First of all, many Boeing employees, including the engineers, are against the outsourcing for obvious reasons; they feel that their jobs are at stake and believe that Boeing has lost sight of its larger interests.[21] Former CEO Harry Stonecipher countered outsourcing concerns by stating, "We have to understand that the go-it-alone approach doesn't work in today's world. Companies will increasingly focus on their core competencies. As they do, they will outsource (a) where the markets are, and (b) where the best people to do the job are."[22] Eventually union leaders and employees were able to acknowledge that outsourcing is about more than just cutting jobs, it is about competing efficiently in a global industry.[23]

Additional controversy centers on whether Boeing is transferring knowledge vital to U.S. military security and commercial competitiveness. The United States has given Boeing's aerospace and defense divisions many subsidies to develop technology. Some of this technology has presumably been transferred to Boeing's aircraft manufacturing division. Japanese suppliers may use the technology shared by Boeing to eventually design their own airplanes. Over the past three years, "The Japanese government and its heavy industrial firms have openly sought to establish Japan as an aerospace power for generations."[24] A Japanese aerospace giant would pose a huge threat to both Boeing and Airbus because it would be able to capitalize on political and trade ties with the flourishing Asia-Pacific markets.[25]

Comparatively, Airbus has kept tighter control over the knowledge it shares with suppliers. In fact, in late 2005 Airbus tightened control over tier one suppliers, directing them to outsource only minimal amounts of work to Asian countries.[26] As such, most of their suppliers are associated with European Union countries, most of which have some ownership in Airbus's parent, EADS. Airbus models its relationship with suppliers after Wal-Mart and utilizes JIT, just-in-time delivery. To further develop efficiencies it follows the approach of the auto industry and requests that its suppliers deliver all components in prepackaged trays that can be loaded onto carts similar to a chest of drawers. Assembly line workers are able to get everything they need without having to leave their stations. As a result, some of Airbus's assembly lines have nearly doubled their efficiency in the past two years.[27]

Clearly, Airbus and Boeing are utilizing relatively different strategies concerning value chain logistics. Consequently, the question remains: Which strategic approach to value chain management will provide better efficiency and long-run strategic advantage? Boeing must continuously monitor and evaluate over time these key concerns in order to maintain positive relations with its stakeholders, specifically its customers and employees.

Customers

Boeing's mission statement signifies that one of its core competencies lays in "detailed customer knowledge and focus."[28] Customers have the choice of buying new or used planes and to license them or purchase them entirely. The customers for Boeing's commercial division are the airlines of the world, and governments are the customers for the defense division. For the commercial division, carriers in China and India are becoming valuable overseas customers, as income rises in these countries along with a forecasted air traffic growth of 8.8 percent in China through the year 2024, and 25 percent growth yearly in India.[29] Half of the orders for the Boeing 787 Dreamliner are from Asia-Pacific clients. Although it is early in the process, the Airbus A-380 currently has

not been purchased by any American carriers, which may suggest that Boeing will dominate the superjumbo aircraft market within the United States.[30] Australia's carrier, Qantas, has indicated it will purchase 115 of its 787 Dreamliners valued at more than $14 billion.[31]

United Airlines has traditionally been Boeing's largest domestic customer,[32] and low-cost airlines have also been key clients for Boeing. However, successful sales campaigns by Airbus resulted in some lost sales for Boeing with the low-cost airlines. JetBlue, when it first emerged in the low-cost industry, announced its decision to purchase Airbus's A-320 over Boeing's 737.[33] JetBlue liked the wider seats, more leg room, and more overhead storage that the A-320 could offer its passengers.

Through early 2004, a major problem seemed to lay in the fact that Boeing had a weak sales force and Airbus was consistently pricing its products below Boeing's prices.[34] These factors, coupled with superior technology in the A-320, won Airbus a considerable amount of Boeing's previous contracts. Boeing's list of lost deals was getting longer and longer, with notable losses to Airbus from United Airlines, AirBerlin, Air Asia, and Southwest. The situation became extremely alarming to Boeing, and in the latter half of 2004 and the beginning of 2005, numerous changes were made in Boeing's sales force. Senior executives and board members were sent into the field to garner sales, decision making was sped up, and the salespeople were empowered to take more risks in pricing.[35]

Frustration with the two-year delay in delivery of the Airbus A-380 (as discussed later in the case) allowed Boeing to acquire some valuable customers from Airbus, including FedEx. FedEx is experiencing growing demand for international freight shipments and needs more planes in its fleet sooner than Airbus can deliver, which resulted in a $2.3 billion loss for Airbus and a $3.6 billion gain for Boeing in new orders.[36] Virgin, also frustrated with the Airbus delays, canceled its order for the A-380 and partnered with Boeing, ordering 15 of its 787s.[37]

In addition to the battle for sales, Boeing and Airbus have been engaged in an ongoing dispute concerning the role that governments play in the success of the two companies.

Government Issues

Boeing attributes much of Airbus's success to its extensive financial support through subsidies called "launch aid" from Spain, France, Germany, and Great Britain, the four member countries that have ownership interests in EADS, the parent of Airbus. During the 1980s Airbus was able to create its multitude of products because of the financial support it relied on from these countries. Airbus still receives a debatable amount, thought to be $1.7 billion for the year 2005.[38]

Boeing was able to further its case against "launch aid" when Airbus released plans to develop the A-350 in response to Boeing's 787, which suspiciously will be developed despite the huge financial losses Airbus accumulated due the problems associated with its A-380 superjumbo jet.[39] Boeing sought protection from the World Trade Organization from these subsidies because they threaten its competitiveness in the global economy. Conversely, Airbus fired back, claiming that Boeing also receives subsidies from the U.S. government. This financial aid comes in the form of "federal research and development contracts from NASA and the Pentagon and, more recently, tax breaks from Washington State."[40] Those in support of Boeing counter with the argument that these contracts are business deals associated with its defense business (not its commercial airlines business) and for which other companies can compete and therefore are not defined as subsidies.[41] Nonetheless, Airbus argues that the government funded technology assists in commercial plane development because such technology is transferable.

For example, about half of the 787 will consist of composites of which knowledge can be directly drawn from Boeing's experience with the B-2 stealth bomber program. However, Airbus also has the ability to draw on military technology from its parent company EADS, so the true validity within this argument is uncertain. Both companies decided to file complaints with the WTO in 2004. The acceptance of government subsidies by global corporations, known as "extraterritorial income," is deemed illegal by the WTO. In reality both companies receive almost equal support from their governments, and tracking or even ending these funds is difficult. The WTO has little judicial power and really only provides leverage to settle disputes.

It is understood that WTO cases are fraught with risk and have uncertain outcomes and often last for years. Also, the European Union and the United States, the two sides in this dispute, are the strongest members in the WTO. The outcome is yet to be determined, but the ultimate conclusion is likely to have an impact on the finances of both firms.[42]

Financials

Boeing's revenue increased nearly 15 percent from 2005 to 2006 ($53,621 million to $61,530 million). In part, this extraordinary growth can be attributed to the record-breaking number of orders and a one-third increase in production capacity. Boeing's net profit on this revenue more than doubled from $464 million in 2005 to $980 million in 2006. This jump equates to net change of 111.2 percent. For investors it is great news. It allowed Boeing to increase its earnings per share (EPS) from $0.59 in 2005 to $1.28 in 2006 (see Exhibits 2, 3, and 4).

Boeing's financial margins indicate how well the organization is utilizing sales dollars. Boeing's gross margin increased at the end of 2006 to 17.6 percent from 14.6 percent in 2005. Gross margin provides insight into the profit available from the sales dollars. Generally, the higher the percentage of gross margin, the more flexible the organization can be in its operating decisions. The gross margin for the industry average is 13.8 percent for 2006 (see Exhibits 2, 3, and 4). Due to its increased flexibility Boeing increased its spending for R&D by nearly $1 billion.

Operating margin (or operating profit margin) increased 2.7 percentage points in 2006 from 2005, moving from 3.9 percent to 6.6 percent. This ratio is useful in determining the earnings before taxes (EBIT) on each dollar. The stronger the ratio, the better, and when coupled with growth year over year, this ratio equates to a favorable analysis. Net margin also increased from 2005 (3.3%) to 2006 (5.6%) for a net change of 2.3 percentage points, indicating that Boeing is doing a better job at controlling its costs and converting its revenue dollars into profit (see Exhibits 2, 3, and 4). Cash flow grew to be 12 percent of revenues, up $.5 billion from $7 billion in 2005 (see Exhibit 7).

Boeing is heavily leveraged compared to its industry; its debt-to-equity ratio is 2.01, compared to the industry average of 0.96. However, when building products with budgets discussed in terms of billions of U.S. dollars, leveraging perhaps allows for better use of assets. This rationale can be seen in Boeing's 2006 credit rating of A3, as provided by Moody's Investors Service.[43] Despite the positive credit rating it is especially important for Boeing to contain its debt levels and use its financial resources wisely in order to come out on top with its strategy versus Airbus's strategy. (For a broader picture of Boeing's financial condition and a comparison of Airbus's financials please refer to Exhibits 5, 6, 7, and 8.)

Opposing Strategies

In comparing the strategies of Boeing and Airbus, one analyst concluded the following: "In today's marketplace, distinct differences in the way competitive products work have become increasingly rare. But functional product differentiation is exactly what the rivalry between the Airbus A-380 and the Boeing 787 Dreamliner is all about: Two companies with fundamentally different products, based on diametrically opposite visions of the future."[44] Boeing maintains that increased fragmentation in the form of point-to-point travel will not only solve the problem of airport congestion, but also appeal to travelers. Airbus on the other hand believes that hub-to-hub travel, especially between major cities will continue to grow—with an emphasis on the Asian markets.

Exhibit 2 Boeing Financial Ratios with Contrast

Growth Rates %	Company	Industry	S&P 500
Sales (Qtr vs year ago qtr)	26.20	16.40	13.60
Net Income (YTD vs YTD)	−14.00	28.10	24.40
Net Income (Qtr vs year ago qtr)	111.20	57.40	80.80
Sales (5-Year Annual Avg.)	1.12	8.39	13.12
Net Income (5-Year Annual Avg.)	−4.83	58.28	22.42
Dividends (5-Year Annual Avg.)	12.03	11.41	9.95

Price Ratios	Company	Industry	S&P 500
Current P/E Ratio	33.1	22.2	21.9
P/E Ratio 5-Year High	65.3	88.0	61.3
P/E Ratio 5-Year Low	9.0	20.9	14.8
Price/Sales Ratio	1.20	1.28	2.77
Price/Book Value	15.63	7.46	4.06
Price/Cash Flow Ratio	19.80	16.10	14.80

Profit Margins %	Company	Industry	S&P 500
Gross Margin	18.0	13.8	36.8
Pre-Tax Margin	5.2	5.1	19.1
Net Profit Margin	3.6	2.7	13.4
5Yr Gross Margin (5-Year Avg.)	15.3	14.5	35.6
5Yr PreTax Margin (5-Year Avg.)	4.3	5.5	17.2
5Yr Net Profit Margin (5-Year Avg.)	3.5	4.0	11.8

Financial Condition	Company	Industry	S&P 500
Debt/Equity Ratio	2.01	0.96	1.32
Current Ratio	0.8	1.2	1.2
Quick Ratio	0.5	0.8	1.0
Interest Coverage	12.5	11.1	24.7
Leverage Ratio	10.9	5.5	4.6
Book Value/Share	6.01	18.51	19.14

Investment Returns %	Company	Industry	S&P 500
Return On Equity	27.9	24.5	21.6
Return On Assets	3.9	5.5	8.0
Return On Capital	8.2	9.8	10.5
Return On Equity (5-Year Avg.)	20.8	16.5	20.2
Return On Assets (5-Year Avg.)	3.5	4.0	6.6
Return On Capital (5-Year Avg.)	6.1	6.5	8.7

Management Efficiency	Company	Industry	S&P 500
Income/Employee	14,325	18,312	104,736
Revenue/Employee	399,546	315,545	856,844
Receivable Turnover	11.7	19.5	17.5
Inventory Turnover	6.3	9.6	8.9
Asset Turnover	1.1	1.1	0.8

Source: Boeing Company Financial Ratios, *Reuters*, http://stocks.us.reuters.com/stocks/ratios.asp?symbol=BA&WT.

Exhibit 3 Boeing Performance Summary, 10 years

	Avg P/E	Price/Sales	Price/Book	Net Profit Margin (%)
12/06	28.20	1.14	14.79	3.6
12/05	19.50	1.05	5.08	4.8
12/04	21.30	0.82	3.82	3.5
12/03	39.50	0.68	4.36	1.4
12/02	13.90	0.50	3.43	4.3
12/01	15.10	0.55	2.86	4.9
12/00	19.90	1.12	5.01	4.1
12/99	16.50	0.66	3.15	4.0
12/98	37.70	0.57	2.48	2.0
12/97	−286.40	1.04	3.68	−0.4

	Book Value/Share	Debt/Equity	Return on Equity (%)	Return on Assets (%)	Interest Coverage
12/06	$6.01	2.01	46.5	4.3	12.0
12/05	$13.82	0.97	23.2	4.3	9.3
12/04	$13.56	1.08	16.1	3.2	5.7
12/03	$9.67	1.77	8.4	1.3	NA
12/02	$9.62	1.87	29.8	4.4	10.9
12/01	$13.57	1.13	26.1	5.8	10.7
12/00	$13.18	0.80	19.3	5.0	6.7
12/99	$13.16	0.59	20.1	6.4	7.3
12/98	$13.13	0.57	9.1	3.0	3.6
12/97	$13.31	0.53	−1.4	−0.5	−0.4

Source: Boeing Company Financial Ratios, *Reuters*, http://stocks.us.reuters.com/stocks/ratios.asp?symbol=BA.

The solution for Boeing is the 787 Dreamliner, a midsized twin-engine airplane with long-haul capabilities, longer than any of Boeing's previous models. Boeing has championed the 787 as "revolutionary," encompassing major changes in all aspects of the airplane including design, production, and finance. Based on a decade of focus groups and scientific studies, the objective for the 787 has been to offer the passenger the most comfortable point-to-point travel experience with as few intermediate stops as possible. The 787 will have more standing room, larger windows and bathrooms, ambient light settings in the cabin to adjust to the time of day, and the cabin will also be set at a higher humidity level. For the airlines it is an attractive product because it is fuel efficient (burning 27 percent less fuel per passenger than the A-380[45]), made from lightweight composite materials, and simple to operate.[46]

Airbus's offering is dubbed the A-380, or commonly referred to as the "superjumbo." The A-380 will be the largest aircraft in the world, 35 percent larger than the current largest, the Boeing 747-400. The A-380 is 239 feet long and stands over 80 feet tall.[47] It can be configured with bars and specialty boutiques. With a wing span of almost 300 feet, the A-380 can transport 550 passengers in a typical three-class layout.[48] Airbus claims the A-380 will allow 10 million additional passengers per year to fly between airports with no increase in flights.[49] Despite a size that provides boasting rights, it also creates challenges because the A-380 will only be able to utilize the largest airports—most facilities are unable to accommodate this aircraft. Airports are having to spend millions of dollars to accommodate this new superjumbo plane. For example, London's Heathrow airport has already spent $909 million for upgrades to prepare for the A-380.[50] Thus, Boeing has the opportunity to exploit smaller airports. The success of Boeing's strategy will depend largely upon its marketing approach. (See Exhibits 9 and 10 to view the differences in features and success between the 787 and A-380.)

Marketing Approach

As a result of the billions of dollars already spent, and the future of the firm at stake, Boeing has marketed the 787 extensively. Boeing recognized that as its products became more sophisticated, it needed to revamp its marketing approach. Rob Pollack, vice president of branding at Boeing, said, "We realized that if you have the most

Exhibit 4 Financial Highlights

Financial Highlights

Sales	61.53Bil	Revenue/Share	78.68
Income	2.21Bil	Earnings/Share	2.85
Net Profit Margin	3.59%	Book Value/Share	6.01
Return on Equity	27.93%	Dividend Rate	1.40
Debt/Equity Ratio	2.01	Payout Ratio	43.00%

Revenue–Quarterly Results (in Millions)

	FY (12/06)	FY (12/05)	FY (12/04)
1st Qtr	14,264.0	12,681.0	12,903.0
2nd Qtr	14,986.0	14,684.0	13,088.0
3rd Qtr	14,739.0	12,355.0	13,152.0
4th Qtr	17,541.0	13,901.0	13,314.0
Total	61,530.0	53,621.0	52,457.0

Earnings Per Share–Quarterly Results

	FY (12/06)	FY (12/05)	FY (12/04)
1st Qtr	$0.91	$0.68	$0.77
2nd Qtr	−$0.21	$0.71	$0.75
3rd Qtr	$0.90	$1.28	$0.56
4th Qtr	$1.30	$0.62	$0.24
Total	$2.90	$3.29	$2.32

Qtr. over Qtr. EPS Growth Rate

	FY (12/06)	FY (12/05)	FY (12/04)
1st Qtr	47%	183%	—
2nd Qtr	NA	4%	−3%
3rd Qtr	NA	80%	−25%
4th Qtr	44%	−52%	−57%

Yr. over Yr. EPS Growth Rate

	FY (12/06)	FY (12/05)
1st Qtr	34%	−12%
2nd Qtr	NA	−5%
3rd Qtr	−30%	129%
4th Qtr	110%	158%

Source: Boeing Company Financial Highlights, *Reuters*, http://stocks.us.reuters.com/stocks/financialHighlights.asp?symbol=BA.

state-of-the-art products in the world, how you represent yourself has to be done with state-of-the-art marketing techniques." The new strategy presents Boeing as not just a manufacturer, but a "life cycle partner," providing its customers with business solutions through the full lifespan of its products.[51] "Trade shows are now more about creating an immersion than a spectacle. Media is designed to bring the brand to life. Press events strive to stamp an indelible message."[52] Prospective clients are now invited to Boeing's Customer Experience Center, a 30,000-square-foot facility that allows an interactive experience in which Boeing's sales force can address the needs, concerns, and challenges of its customers. "The studio is facilitating discussions that might never have taken place between Boeing and its clients."[53]

The effort taken to improve its marketing and sales approach will hopefully prove to benefit Boeing as it strives to overcome the challenges that lay ahead.

The Challenges Ahead

As previously mentioned, Airbus has experienced significant delays and other problems surrounding the A-380 project. Not only has Airbus run 50 percent over budget, but they also face hundreds of millions of dollars in penalties for delays. EADS's earnings will decrease by $6 billion over the next four years, and the share price has declined 21 percent in the past year (2006). Additionally, Christian Streiff was forced to quit after only three months in his position as CEO.[54] The problems started when mechanics spent weeks routing 348 miles of bundled electrical wiring in each plane, but came up short when attempting to connect one section to another. The cause was determined to be the fact that engineers in Hamburg were drawing on two-dimensional computer programs whereas engineers in Toulouse were using three-dimensional programs.[55]

Multiple redesigns of the proposed A-350 model intended to compete with Boeing's 787 Dreamliner have been delayed as well, resulting in more bad press for Airbus. Six years ago, Airbus executives said the company would need to sell 250 A-380s to break even on the investment. This number has now risen to more than 400 due to delays and cancelations. The company has ramped up production of its A-320 model, the single-aisle aircraft purchased by many low-cost carriers, in an effort to earn badly needed cash. This tactic could prove disastrous if suppliers are not able to keep up with

Exhibit 5 Boeing Income Statement

Boeing	2006	2005	2004	2003	2002
Period End Date	12/31/2006	12/31/2005	12/31/2004	12/31/2003	12/31/2002
Period Length	12 Months	12 Months	12 Months	12 Months	12 Months
Stmt Source	10-K	10-K	10-K	10-K	10-K
Stmt Source Date	2/16/2007	2/16/2007	2/16/2007	2/28/2005	2/28/2005
Stmt Update Type	Updated	Reclassified	Reclassified	Restated	Restated
Revenue	61,530.00	53,621.00	51,400.00	50,256.00	53,831.00
Total Revenue	**61,530.00**	**53,621.00**	**51,400.00**	**50,256.00**	**53,831.00**
Cost of Revenue, Total	50,437.00	44,984.00	43,968.00	44,150.00	45,804.00
Gross Profit	**11,093.00**	**8,637.00**	**7,432.00**	**6,106.00**	**8,027.00**
Selling/General/Administrative Expenses, Total	4,171.00	4,228.00	3,657.00	3,200.00	2,959.00
Research & Development	3,257.00	2,205.00	1,879.00	1,651.00	1,639.00
Depreciation/Amortization	0	0	3	0	0
Interest Expense (Income), Net Operating	−146	−88	−91	−28	49
Unusual Expense (Income)	571	0	0	892	−2
Other Operating Expenses, Total	226	−520	−23	−7	−44
Operating Income	**3,014.00**	**2,812.00**	**2,007.00**	**398**	**3,426.00**
Interest Income (Expense), Net Non-Operating	−240	−294	−335	−358	−320
Gain (Loss) on Sale of Assets	0	0	0	0	0
Other, Net	420	301	288	460	37
Income Before Tax	**3,194.00**	**2,819.00**	**1,960.00**	**500**	**3,143.00**
Income Tax, Total	988	257	140	−185	847
Income After Tax	**2,206.00**	**2,562.00**	**1,820.00**	**685**	**2,296.00**
Minority Interest	0	0	0	0	0
Equity In Affiliates	0	0	0	0	0
U.S. GAAP Adjustment	0	0	0	0	0
Net Income Before Extra Items	**2,206.00**	**2,562.00**	**1,820.00**	**685**	**2,296.00**
Total Extraordinary Items	9	10	52	33	−1,804.00
Accounting Change	0	17	0	0	−1,827.00
Discontinued Operations	9	−7	52	33	23
Net Income	**2,215.00**	**2,572.00**	**1,872.00**	**718**	**492**
Total Adjustments to Net Income	0	0	0	0	0

Source: Boeing Company Financial Statements, *Reuters*, http://stocks.us.reuters.com/stocks/incomeStatement.asp.

Exhibit 6 Boeing Balance Sheet

Boeing	2006	2005	2004	2003	2002
Period End Date	12/31/2006	12/31/2005	12/31/2004	12/31/2003	12/31/2002
Stmt Source	10-K	10-K	10-K	10-K	10-K
Stmt Source Date	2/16/2007	2/16/2007	2/28/2006	2/28/2005	2/27/2003
Stmt Update Type	Updated	Restated	Restated	Restated	Updated
Assets					
Cash and Short-Term Investments	6,386.00	5,966.00	3,523.00	4,633.00	2,333.00
Cash & Equivalents	6,118.00	5,412.00	3,204.00	4,633.00	2,333.00
Short-Term Investments	268	554	319	0	0
Total Receivables, Net	5,655.00	5,613.00	5,269.00	5,522.00	6,296.00
Accounts Receivable—Trade, Net	5,285.00	5,246.00	4,653.00	4,466.00	5,007.00
Accounts Receivable—Trade, Gross	5,368.00	5,336.00	0	0	0
Provision for Doubtful Accounts	−83	−90	0	0	0
Notes Receivable—Short-Term	370	367	616	857	1,289.00
Receivables—Other	0	0	0	199	0
Total Inventory	8,105.00	7,878.00	6,508.00	5,338.00	6,184.00
Prepaid Expenses	0	0	0	0	0
Other Current Assets, Total	2,837.00	2,449.00	2,061.00	3,798.00	2,042.00
Total Current Assets	**22,983.00**	**21,906.00**	**17,361.00**	**19,291.00**	**16,855.00**
Property/Plant/Equipment, Total—Net	7,675.00	8,420.00	8,443.00	8,597.00	8,765.00
Goodwill, Net	3,047.00	1,924.00	1,948.00	1,913.00	2,760.00
Intangibles, Net	1,426.00	671	955	1,035.00	1,128.00
Long-Term Investments	4,085.00	2,852.00	3,050.00	646	0
Note Receivable—Long-Term	8,520.00	9,639.00	10,385.00	10,057.00	10,922.00
Other Long-Term Assets, Total	4,058.00	14,584.00	14,082.00	11,447.00	11,912.00
Other Assets, Total	0	0	0	0	0
Total Assets	**51,794.00**	**59,996.00**	**56,224.00**	**52,986.00**	**52,342.00**
Liabilities and Shareholders' Equity					
Accounts Payable	16,201.00	16,513.00	14,869.00	13,514.00	13,739.00
Payable/Accrued	0	0	0	0	0
Accrued Expenses	0	0	0	0	0
Notes Payable/Short-Term Debt	0	0	0	0	0
Current Port. of LT Debt/Capital Leases	1,381.00	1,189.00	1,321.00	1,144.00	1,814.00
Other Current Liabilities, Total	12,119.00	10,424.00	6,906.00	3,741.00	4,257.00
Total Current Liabilities	**29,701.00**	**28,126.00**	**23,096.00**	**18,399.00**	**19,810.00**
Total Long-Term Debt	8,157.00	9,538.00	10,879.00	13,299.00	12,589.00
Long-Term Debt	8,157.00	9,538.00	10,879.00	13,299.00	12,589.00
Deferred Income Tax	0	2,067.00	1,090.00	0	0

Exhibit 6 Boeing Balance Sheet *(Continued)*

Boeing	2006	2005	2004	2003	2002
Minority Interest	0	0	0	0	0
Other Liabilities, Total	9,197.00	9,206.00	9,873.00	13,149.00	12,247.00
Total Liabilities	**47,055.00**	**48,937.00**	**44,938.00**	**44,847.00**	**44,646.00**
Redeemable Preferred Stock	0	0	0	0	0
Preferred Stock—Non Redeemable, Net	0	0	0	0	0
Common Stock	5,061.00	5,061.00	5,059.00	5,059.00	5,059.00
Additional Paid-In Capital	4,655.00	4,371.00	3,420.00	2,880.00	2,141.00
Retained Earnings (Accumulated Deficit)	18,453.00	17,276.00	15,565.00	14,407.00	14,262.00
Treasury Stock—Common	−12,459.00	−11,075.00	−8,810.00	−8,322.00	−8,397.00
ESOP Debt Guarantee	−2,754.00	−2,796.00	−2,023.00	−1,740.00	−1,324.00
Other Equity, Total	−8,217.00	−1,778.00	−1,925.00	−4,145.00	−4,045.00
Total Equity	**4,739.00**	**11,059.00**	**11,286.00**	**8,139.00**	**7,696.00**
Total Liabilities & Shareholders' Equity	**51,794.00**	**59,996.00**	**56,224.00**	**52,986.00**	**52,342.00**
Total Common Shares Outstanding	788.74	800.17	832.18	841.48	799.66
Total Preferred Shares Outstanding	0	0	0	0	0

Source: Boeing Company Financial Statements, *Reuters*, http://stocks.us.reuters.com/stocks/balanceSheet.asp.

Airbus's schedule. However, Airbus executives insist that losses will be recouped by 2010.[56]

Boeing also invested heavily in its 787 project and faced criticism over weight issues and composite construction materials. Although both firms experienced setbacks, Airbus has taken the brunt of these setbacks, as already noted. Boeing's challenges have more to do with potential production delays and meeting its massive order-backlog on time. In 2007, Boeing had already announced some delays. Boeing officials noted that "it is possible to overcome a nearly four-month delay in the 787 Dreamliner program and deliver the first jet on time in May [2008]."[57] However, "Industry observers and a number of the plane's suppliers say it would be the aerospace equivalent of hitting a hole in one on a golf course." The complexity of producing an aircraft is significant, but when you have to simultaneously bring together a large array of suppliers and the various parts that they produce to meet a deadline, the possibilities for error increase geometrically.

In the long term, Boeing must wonder whether it is going to create a new competitor in Japan and eventually in China, given its outsourcing strategy. Also,

Airbus countered Boeing's 787 product strategy with the A-350 in addition to the A-380 (Boeing does not have a comparable product, unless they can effectively update the 747). Thus, both Boeing and Airbus face significant strategic challenges.

Conclusion

Both Boeing and Airbus spent billions of dollars in developing their unique strategies. Airbus bet that the way to cope with increased customer demand is to offer a platform, namely the A-380, capable of moving mass amounts of people using the hub system. Alternatively, Boeing focused on the 787 to offer consumers long-range capabilities while at the same time using direct connections. Initial trends indicate support for Boeing strategies based on accumulated orders for the 787, numbering nearly 500, whereas Airbus's A-380 has not received the amount of orders originally forecasted. Airbus also experienced major setbacks with the two-year delivery delay while running nearly 50 percent over budget[58] and losing orders from frustrated customers. Thus, Boeing currently

Exhibit 7 Boeing Statement of Cash Flows

Boeing	2006	2005	2004	2003	2002
Period End Date	12/31/2006	12/31/2005	12/31/2004	12/31/2003	12/31/2002
Net Income/Starting Line	2,215.00	2,572.00	1,872.00	718	492
Depreciation/Depletion	1,445.00	1,412.00	1,412.00	1,306.00	1,362.00
Amortization	100	91	97	94	88
Non-Cash Items	1,552.00	1,807.00	1,538.00	1,737.00	2,907.00
Discontinued Operations	−14	12	−51	63	76
Unusual Items	344	−437	102	1,068.00	2,723.00
Other Non-Cash Items	1,222.00	2,232.00	1,487.00	606	108
Changes in Working Capital	2,187.00	1,118.00	−1,415.00	−1,079.00	−2,513.00
Accounts Receivable	−244	−592	−241	357	−155
Inventories	444	−1,965.00	535	191	1,507.00
Prepaid Expenses	−522	−1,862.00	−4,355.00	−1,728.00	−340
Other Assets	718	600	−425	−1,321.00	−2,038.00
Accounts Payable	−744	1,147.00	1,321.00	−132	−441
Accrued Expenses	114	30	214	311	67
Taxes Payable	933	628	1,086.00	320	322
Other Liabilities	1,677.00	3,086.00	705	876	−978
Other Operating Cash Flow	−189	46	−255	47	−457
Cash from Operating Activities	**7,499.00**	**7,000.00**	**3,504.00**	**2,776.00**	**2,336.00**
Capital Expenditures	−1,681.00	−1,547.00	−1,246.00	−836	−1,001.00
Purchase of Fixed Assets	−1,681.00	−1,547.00	−1,246.00	−836	−1,001.00
Other Investing Cash Flow Items, Total	−1,505.00	1,449.00	−200	896	−381
Acquisition of Business	−1,854.00	−172	−34	289	−22
Sale of Business	123	1,709.00	194	186	157
Sale of Fixed Assets	225	51	2,285.00	95	0
Sale/Maturity of Investment	2,850.00	2,725.00	1,323.00	203	140
Purchase of Investments	−2,815.00	−2,866.00	−4,142.00	−102	−505
Other Investing Cash Flow	−34	2	174	225	−151
Cash from Investing Activities	**−3,186.00**	**−98**	**−1,446.00**	**60**	**−1,382.00**
Financing Cash Flow Items	395	70	23	0	0
Other Financing Cash Flow	395	70	23	0	0
Total Cash Dividends Paid	−956	−820	−648	−572	−571
Issuance (Retirement) of Stock, Net	−1,404.00	−2,529.00	−654	18	67
Issuance (Retirement) of Debt, Net	−1,680.00	−1,378.00	−2,208.00	18	1,250.00
Cash from Financing Activities	**−3,645.00**	**−4,657.00**	**−3,487.00**	**−536**	**746**
Foreign Exchange Effects	38	−37	0	0	0
Net Change in Cash	**706**	**2,208.00**	**−1,429.00**	**2,300.00**	**1,700.00**
Net Cash, Beginning Balance	5,412.00	3,204.00	4,633.00	2,333.00	633
Net Cash, Ending Balance	6,118.00	5,412.00	3,204.00	4,633.00	2,333.00

Source: Boeing Financial Statements, *Reuters*, http://stocks.us.reuters.com/stocks/cashFlowStatement.

Exhibit 8 Airbus Select Financials

(Euro, million)	2006	2005	2004	2003
EBIT	(572)	2307	1919	1353
Total Revenue	25190	22179	20224	19048
Assets	33958	33226	35044	29290
Goodwill	6374	6987	6883	6342
Liabilities	24096	20553	17019	17501
Provisions	6272	4205	0	0
Capital Expenditures	1750	1864	2778	2027
Depreciation, Amortization	1140	1131	1088	1628
R&D	2035	1659	1734	1819
Exchange Rate	0.757855	0.844589	0.738788	0.793869

(U.S., million)	2006	2005	2004	2003
EBIT	(433)	1948	1418	1074
Total Revenue	19090	18732	14941	15122
Assets	25735	28062	25890	23252
Goodwill	4831	5901	5085	5035
Liabilities	18261	17359	12573	13894
Provisions	4753	3551	0	0
Capital Expenditures	1326	1574	2052	1609
Depreciation, Amortization	864	955	804	1292
R&D	1542	1401	1281	1444

Source: 2006, 2005, 2004, *EADS Annual Reports*, www.eads.com/1024/en/investor/Reports/Archive/Archives.html.

Exhibit 9 Dreamliner (787) vs. Superjumbo (A-380)

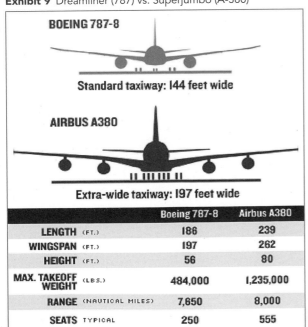

	Boeing 787-8	Airbus A380
LENGTH (FT.)	186	239
WINGSPAN (FT.)	197	262
HEIGHT (FT.)	56	80
MAX. TAKEOFF WEIGHT (LBS.)	484,000	1,235,000
RANGE (NAUTICAL MILES)	7,650	8,000
SEATS TYPICAL	250	555

Source: 2007, Dissecting the A-380's troubles, *Fortune*, http://www.fortune.com, March 5.

Exhibit 10 Boeing vs. Airbus Orders

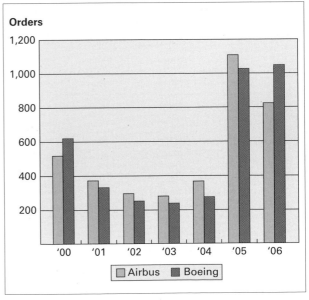

Source: 2007, Dissecting the A-380's troubles, *Fortune*, http://www.fortune.com, March 5.

holds the lead in the aerospace industry. However, the Asian markets are growing, and demand for large aircraft to meet air traffic increases is also likely to grow. Boeing may be confident in its strategy, but recent minor delays serve as a reminder that Boeing cannot get too comfortable. The first A-380 is slated to be delivered to Singapore Airlines on October 15, 2007.[59] Will this aircraft become a sensation? Will Airbus be able to recoup its costs by 2010 and flourish in the industry? Will Boeing realize continued strategic success, given Airbus's A-350 program, which was established to compete with the 787?

NOTES

1. 2001, Aviation competition: Regional jet service yet to reach many small communities, United States General Accounting Office, http://www.gao.gov, February, 5–10; D. Schlossberg, 2007, FAA fights proliferation of small planes, http://www.consumeraffairs.com, August 23.
2. J. L. Lunsford, 2007, Boeing's 787 faces less room for error: Dreamliner flight tests pushed by months, sticking to delivery date, Wall Street Journal, September 6, A13.
3. 2007, Boeing, Wikipedia, http://en.wikipedia.org/wiki/Boeing.
4. 2007, Boeing History, http://www.boeing.com/history/chronology.
5. 2007, Boeing History, http://www.boeing.com/history.
6. 2007, Boeing History: Beginnings—Building a company, Aviation History, http://www.wingsoverkansas.com/history/article.asp?id=404.
7. R. J. Gordon, 1983, Energy efficiency, user cost change, and the measurement of durable goods prices, The U.S. national income and product accounts: Selected topics, Chicago: University of Chicago Press, 235.
8. 2007, Boeing, Wikipedia, http://en.wikipedia.org/wiki/Boeing_747-8.
9. 2007, Boeing history, http://www.boeing.com/history/boeing/777.
10. 2007, Boeing, http://www.careerbuilder.com.
11. 2001, Boeing's Sonic Cruiser skirts the edge of the sound barrier, Popular Mechanics, http://www.popularmechanics.com, October.
2. L. Laurent, 2007, Boeing's Dreamliner, Airbus's nightmare, Forbes, http://www.forbes.com, July 9.
13. J. Newhouse, 2007, Boeing Versus Airbus, Toronto, Canada: Alfred A. Knopf.
14. Ibid.
15. Ibid.
16. J. Destefani, 2004, A look at Boeing's outsourcing strategy, Manufacturing Engineering, March.
17. Ibid.
18. Ibid.
19. 2006, Boeing's global strategy takes off: The aerospace titan is taking a measured approach to outsourcing, with help from local teams, BusinessWeek, http://www.businessweek.com, January 30.
20. Ibid.
21. Ibid.
22. Harry C. Stonecipher, 2004, Outsourcing, the real issue, Orange County Business Council Annual Meeting and Dinner, http://www.boeing.com/news/speeches, June 2.
23. 2006, Boeing's global strategy takes off.
24. E. F. Vencat, 2006, A Boeing of Asia? It could happen, now that Airbus and Boeing build planes in global factories, Newsweek International, http://www.msnbc.msn.com, May 15.
25. Ibid.
26. J. Newhouse, Boeing versus Airbus.
27. C. Matlack & S. Holmes, 2007, Airbus revs up the engines; to generate badly needed cash, it's boosting output of its popular A-320 to record levels, BusinessWeek, March 5, 4024: 41.
28. 2004, There where they're needed, Boeing Frontiers, http://www.boeing.com, December.
29. V. Kwong & A. Rothman, 2006, Boeing vs. Airbus: The next bout, International Herald Tribune, http://www.iht.com, February 16.
30. L. Wayne, 2007, Airbus superjumbo takes a lap around America, New York Times, http://www.nytimes.com, March 20.
31. A. Burgos, 2005, Qantas sets $14 billion order for Boeing planes, Forbes, http://www.forbes.com, December 14.
32. J. Newhouse, Boeing versus Airbus.
33. 1999, JetBlue chooses the Airbus A-320, Press Releases, http://www.jetblue.com, July 14.
34. L. Timmerman, 2004, Boeing sales to get new leadership, The Seattle Times, http://www.seattletimes.com, December 4.
35. D. Drezner, 2005, Competition has been good for Boeing, http://www.danieldrezner.com, April 13.
36. M. Schlangenstein, 2007, FedEx dumps Airbus for Boeing, The News Tribune (Tacoma, WA), http://www.thenewstribune.com, September 25.
37. P. Olson, 2007, Branson turns his back on Airbus, Forbes, http://www.forbes.com, April 25.
38. D. Ackman, 2005, Boeing, Airbus showdown at 40,000 feet, Forbes, http://www.forbes.com, May 31.
39. M. Adams, 2006, Airbus announces new jet to rival Boeing Dreamliner, USA Today, http://www.usatoday.com, July 18.
40. D. Ackman, Boeing, Airbus showdown at 40,000 feet.
41. Ibid.
42. J. Audley & K. Saleh, 2004, Boeing vs. Airbus: Trade fight could prove costly for everyone, The Seattle Times, http://www.seattletimes.com, December 6.
43. 2006, Moody's boosts Boeing's credit rating, International Business Times, http://in.ibtimes.com, March 15.
44. M. E. Babej & T. Pollak, 2006, Boeing versus Airbus, Forbes, http://www.forbes.com, May 24.
45. P. Olson, Branson turns his back on Airbus.
46. M. E. Babej & T. Pollak, Boeing versus Airbus.
47. 2007, Anatomy of an A-380, Fortune, March 5, 101–106.
48. J. Newhouse, Boeing versus Airbus.
49. Ibid.
50. R. Stone, 2007, Airbus A-380 promises less for big airports, Wall Street Journal, September 5, D7.
51. 2007, Ground Control, Event Marketer, http://www.eventmarketer.com, February 11.
52. Ibid.
53. Ibid.
54. N. D. Schwartz, 2007, Big plane, big problems, Fortune, March 5, 95–98.
55. 2007, Anatomy of an A-380.
56. G. Parkinson, 2006, Crisis at Airbus as chief quits after only 100 days, The (London) Independent, http://www.findarticles.com, October 10.
57. J. L. Lunsford, 2007, Boeing's tall order: On-time 787; suppliers say Dreamliner delivery could hit may target—if all goes right, Wall Street Journal, September 17, A8.
58. D. Michaels, 2007, More super, less jumbo for this carrier, Wall Street Journal, September 25, B8.
59. Ibid.

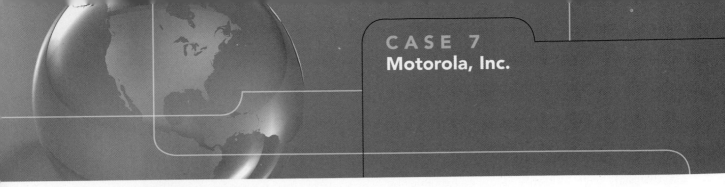

Aaron Christensen, Victor Delagarza,
Aric Griggs, Lubka Robertson,
Tamara Stuart, Michael Valverde

Arizona State University

In November 2008, Motorola announced the postponement of its highly publicized spinoff of the Mobile Device segment, a struggling business segment that is pulling down the results of the entire firm. In light of the challenging economy, Motorola faces the decision of if and when to spin off this division and which new market opportunities to explore in order to return to the profitable company it was for so many years.

Company History

In 1928, Paul and Joseph Galvin incorporated Galvin Manufacturing[1] after acquiring "battery eliminator operations"[2] from the bankrupt Stewart Storage Battery Company.[3] A battery eliminator is a device that allows "battery-powered radios [to] run on a standard household electric current"[4] instead of batteries. Galvin Manufacturing used the technology as the groundwork for its first car radio named Motorola.[5] The name Motorola is a combination of "'motor' (for motor car) and 'ola' (which implied sound)."[6] Galvin Manufacturing introduced its first Motorola car radio in 1930, the Motorola Police Cruiser radio in 1936,[7] and home radios in 1937.[8] By the end of 1937, B. F. Goodrich had partnered with Galvin Manufacturing to become the first national Motorola dealer.[9]

Starting in 1940, Galvin Manufacturing expanded its product line to include two-way communication devices.[10] The first product was the Handie-Talkie SCR536 AM Radio, which was used extensively by the military during World War II.[11] The success of the Handie-Talkie and a strong belief in the sustainable demand for its communication products led Galvin Manufacturing to create a separate product division and establish a sales subsidiary, Motorola Communications

and Electronics, Inc.[12] Leveraging its experience with military radios, Galvin Manufacturing introduced its first commercial line of Motorola FM vehicular two-way radio systems and equipment in 1941.[13] By the end of 1943, Galvin Manufacturing successfully completed its first initial public offering with its stock selling for $8.50 per share.[14] Building upon earlier success, Galvin Manufacturing produced the world's first portable backpack FM radio (SCR300), more commonly known as a "walkie-talkie."[15] In 1946, Galvin Manufacturing partnered with Bell Telephone Company to enable car radio-telephone service via Motorola communication equipment for the Chicago area.[16]

Galvin Manufacturing officially changed its name to Motorola, Inc. in 1947.[17] As part of a diversification strategy, Motorola acquired the car radio manufacturer Detrola, a supplier to Ford Motor Company, and entered the television market with the Golden View VT71.[18] Motorola sold more than 100,000 Golden View television units within the first year and became the fourth-largest U.S. television manufacturer.[19] Motorola illustrated its commitment to product development and innovation through the establishment of its R&D operations in Phoenix, Arizona, in 1949.[20] This R&D effort led to advances in semiconductor and transistor technology, including the germanium transistor technology Motorola used in its 1955 car radios.[21] The germanium transistor "was the world's first commercial high-power transistor . . . [and] Motorola's first mass-produced semiconductor."[22]

By 1954, Motorola had outgrown its existing organizational structure, causing Paul Galvin to decide to reorganize the company[23] into product-line divisions.[24] The following year, Galvin's son, Robert, became Motorola's president.[25] Robert Galvin continued to

Note: This case was written to be used as a basis for class discussion rather than to illustrate either effective or ineffective handling of an administrative situation. We would like to thank Robert E. Hoskisson and Robert E. White for useful feedback in writing this case. Data was collected from publically available sources.

lead the company by following its communication and television expertise but "shifted the company's strategy toward selling directly to government and business."[26] In 1958, Motorola introduced the Motrac vehicular radio that "enabled the radio to transmit without running the vehicle's engine."[27] Motorola also introduced a three-amp power transistor,[28] a small radio receiver used extensively in hospitals (more commonly known as a pager[29]) and color television sets[30] during the 1950s and 1960s. In 1969, Motorola's radio transponder on *Apollo 11* "relayed the first words from the Earth to the Moon . . . [and] transmitted telemetry, tracking, voice communications, and television signals from the Earth to the Moon."[31]

By 1968, frustrations over limitations concerning car-based communication technology led the Federal Communications Commission (FCC) to propose allocating bandwidth to new technologies that would address this problem.[32] Thus, Motorola pioneered the cellular phone industry by creating the first commercial cellular phone, the Motorola DynaTAC phone.[33]

Motorola continued its pioneering efforts in the world of manufacturing. In 1968, Motorola developed the Six Sigma quality improvement process.[34] Six Sigma is an analytical, statistical approach that is used to improve the quality of manufacturing processes and to eliminate defects.[35] Since its introduction, Six Sigma has become a global standard.[36]

During the 1990s Motorola extended its traditional product offerings into the digital arena. Motorola acquired General Instrument Corporation, the company that developed the all-digital high-definition television (HDTV) technical standard.[37] In 1991, Motorola developed the first digital cellular phone prototype[38] and by 1994 Motorola produced its Integrated Digital Enhanced Network (iDEN) digital radio, which combined paging data, cellular communications, and voice dispatch in a single radio network and handset.[39] Motorola continued to enhance product features and produce phones with more integrated features through the end of the 1990s.[40]

In 2000, Motorola partnered with Cisco Systems, Inc. to expand operations into the United Kingdom with BT Cellnet by supplying the "world's first commercial General Packet Radio Service (GPRS) cellular network."[41] Motorola then introduced the wireless cable modem which allowed computer networking, a 700-MHz high-speed data system for public safety, a cellular PDA handset that combined Linux and Java technology, and demonstration of the first WiMAX mobile hand-offs.[42]

In 2004, Motorola's introduction of the RAZR (see Exhibit 1) was a huge success as indicated by the facts that the firm sold more than 750,000 units in the first 90 days and held a 16 percent share of the cell phone

Exhibit 1 Motorola RAZR Phone

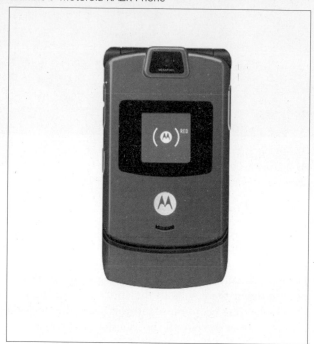

Source: 2009, http://www.motorola.com.

market until 2007.[43] Motorola tried to extend the RAZR's success by introducing the Q in 2005, but it ultimately failed to invoke the same response as its predecessor.[44] In 2006, Motorola expanded its international product offerings again by introducing the MING touch screen smartphone with advanced handwriting software and the Chinese alphabet targeted for the Asian market.[45] Despite continued efforts in the mobile device market segment, Motorola's market share decreased from 22.2 percent in 2006 to 12 percent in 2007.[46]

Edward Zander, the first non-Galvin CEO, was hired by the board of directors in January 2004 to replace Chris Galvin when he retired.[47] Zander steered the company toward products that focused on combining Internet technologies with wireless phone technologies.[48] In 2007, Motorola merged with Symbol Technologies in order to expand its product offerings in mobile computing, advanced data capture, and radio frequency identification (RFID).[49] Motorola also acquired Good Technology in 2007 to expand access to enterprise applications, intranets, and corporate applications for mobile employees.[50] Disappointing returns in 2007 led Motorola's second largest shareholder, Carl Icahn, to demand changes in the organization and the board of directors.[51] Greg Brown replaced Zander in January 2008.[52] Prior to being appointed as CEO, Brown held the president and COO positions. Brown possessed almost 25 years of high-tech experience and had been with Motorola since 2003.[53] However, his appointment did not help ease shareholder frustrations over Motorola's struggling mobile device business, and during his tenure there has been significant turnover in upper management positions, ultimately affecting the company.[54] Therefore, Motorola leaders have thoughtfully considered the direction the company should take, specifically which products it should offer, in order to resume successful operations.

Product Offerings

In 2007 when Motorola restructured the organization, it aligned its business into three operating segments: Home and Networks Mobility, Enterprise Mobility Solutions, and Mobile Devices.[55] The firm's product portfolio consists of wireless handsets, accessories, and access systems as well as digital entertainment devices, voice and data communications systems, and enterprise mobility products.[56]

The Home and Networks Mobility segment competes in the cable set-top box, broadband cable modem, cellular infrastructure, and wireless broadband systems industries.[57] In the third quarter of 2008, this division contributed 32 percent of Motorola's net sales.[58]

The Enterprise Mobility Solutions segment competes in areas such as two-way radio, wireless broadband systems, and private networks for both enterprise and government use.[59] Furthermore, Motorola provides broadcast interactive networks, third-party switching for broadband networks to include: Code Division Multiple Access (CDMA),[60] Global System for Mobile Communication (GSM), and Universal Mobile Telecommunications System[61] (UMTS), all of which are technologies used for mobile communication networking.[62] This division contributed 27 percent of Motorola's net sales in the third quarter of 2008.[63]

The Mobile Devices segment competes in the wireless handset industry. This segment manufactures and sells analog and digital two-way radios, voice and data communication products for private networks, and intellectual property in the form of licenses and patents.[64] This segment comprised 42 percent of Motorola's net sales in third quarter 2008.[65] In the same quarter Motorola held approximately 8.4 percent market share (25.4 million units) in the global handset market. There are several competitors that have taken market share from Motorola.

Competitors

In the wireless handset industry, Motorola's top competitors are Nokia, Samsung, and Sony Ericsson Mobile Communications. LG Electronics, Apple Inc., Research in Motion and HELIO are also competitors but do not pose as large a threat.

Nokia[66]

In 1998 Nokia became and has since been the leading cell phone manufacturer. In 2008 it had net sales of $70.5 billion from 468 million units shipped. This was a seven percent increase over 2007. In 2008 Nokia controlled 39 percent of the mobile communication device market. In 2008 alone Nokia introduced 26 different phones that were focused in five different categories. Smartphone sales made up 13 percent of total cell phones shipped, totaling 61 million units. Nokia is especially dominant in the European and Asian Pacific markets.

Nokia started a joint venture with Siemens in 2007 to provide industry leading consumer Internet service. Nokia has been actively acquiring other businesses to expand its dominance in the mobile phone industry. Since 2006, Nokia has acquired nine businesses in the consumer software field that range from file sharing and music services to advertising and security. Nokia has been affected by the global crisis that started toward the end of 2007; however, the firm has been able to reduce the negative effects of the crisis through its effective use of strategic acquisitions, partnerships, and industry-leading research and development.

Samsung Electronics[67]

Samsung produces and sells products ranging from televisions to home appliances to mobile devices. It is also a major supplier for both LCD screens and memory-based semiconductor chips. Samsung's Telecommunication Networks division, which manufactures and sells the firm's wireless handsets, generates approximately 23 percent of Samsung's sales revenue. With strong brand awareness, consumer-driven design, and aggressive expansion into developing markets, Samsung increased its net profit by 42 percent from 2006 to 2007.

Samsung has been able to launch premium products and rapidly penetrate emerging markets with its mid-range products. As such, it is currently the world's second-largest mobile phone maker, with a 14.3 percent market share. Its premium products, such as the Ultra Edition smartphone, have captured the attention of consumers with features such as a touchscreen, high megapixel cameras, and music capabilities. Samsung was voted "best brand" six years in a row in the United States and captured the number one market spot in France and Russia.

Sony Ericsson Mobile Communications[68]

With the joint venture between Sony and Ericsson in 2001, Sony Ericsson Mobile Communications was able to offer a variety of mobile handsets and other mobile devices that supported multimedia applications and other personal communication services. This is in line with the firm's vision to "be the prime driver in an all-communicating world … in which all people can use voice, text, images and video to share ideas and information whenever and wherever they want."

China, the United States, and India are Sony Ericsson's top three markets. However, by increasing the sales of lower-priced handsets in emerging markets such as Latin America, Sony Ericsson sold over 100 million handsets in 2007—an increase of 18 percent from the previous year. Sony Ericsson believes it is in a prime position to build on its recent strong performance and continues to develop its mid- to low-range products while establishing brand awareness with its high-end products.

LG Electronics[69]

The Mobile Communications division of LG Electronics (LG) is a global leader in the worldwide mobile market.[70] By strategically reallocating its resources, LG plans on becoming a member of the "Global Top 3." LG aims to anticipate customer needs and surpass them with products using the latest technology and presenting consumers with stylish product designs. This strategy seems to be effective as illustrated by a 13 percent increase in mobile handset sales worldwide and a 10 percent increase in global revenue in 2007.

Apple Inc.[71]

Most commonly known for designing and producing software, computers, computer peripherals, and portable music players, Apple Inc. entered the mobile communications devices market with the introduction of the iPhone through a partnership with AT&T Mobility LLC. The iPhone combines cellular communications, a portable music player, and Internet access using Wi-Fi into a single product, all through the control of a touchscreen. Many well-established companies have tried to imitate the capabilities of the iPhone in their respective smartphones.

For fiscal 2008, Apple generated annual revenue of $32 billion versus 2007 annual revenue of $24 billion. Profit margins increased from 14.6 percent in 2007 to 14.9 percent in 2008. Also, Apple's handset division revenue jumped up from approximately $250 million to $1.8 billion in 2008.

Research in Motion[72]

Founded in 1984, Research in Motion (RIM) is a leading designer and manufacturer of innovative wireless solutions.[73] RIM is best known for its telecommunication handheld device, the BlackBerry. It supports mobile telephony, text messaging, e-mail, and Web browsing.

By the end of fiscal year 2008, Blackberrys were available in more than 135 countries. Hardware generates 79 percent of RIM's revenue, which amounted to $6 billion in fiscal 2008, nearly double the revenue of 2007. Profit margins for 2008 were 21 percent versus 27 percent for 2007. The company plans on expanding its selection of mobile devices with several new smartphones as well as enhancing software and services to gain new market share.

HELIO, Inc.[74]

In January 2005, HELIO, Inc. was formed via a joint venture between EarthLink, Inc. and SK Telecom Co., Inc. with the purpose of developing wireless telecommunications services, including but not limited to handsets. Services that are included are integrated Imaging, an Ultimate Inbox, and other popular applications such as MySpace and YouTube.[75] A 282 percent increase in equipment sales and other revenue from 2006 to 2007 indicates that HELIO has successfully established itself in the U.S. market.

In addition to the main competitors in the handset market, Motorola is constantly faced with competition from emerging technologies such as Mobile Internet Devices (MIDs).

Mobile Internet Devices (MIDs)[76]

MIDs are devices that allow consumers to "communicate with others, enjoy [their] favorite entertainment, and access information on-the-go" by connecting to wireless hotspots around town. This new technology provides all of the Internet capabilities consumers want as well as the ability to have a conversation using Voice over Internet Protocol (VoIP). Industry-leading companies, such as Intel, are forming a Mobile Internet Device Innovation Alliance.[77] The MID Alliance is comprised of industry-leading original manufacturers as Asus, BenQ, Compal, Elektrobit, HTC, Inventec, and Quanta.[78] The members of the alliance are working together to solve engineering challenges with respect to power management, wireless communications, and software integration.[79]

Each of these firms is vying for business from the customers Motorola seeks to serve as it operates in its three business segments.

Motorola's Customers

Motorola's Mobile Device Segment has several large customers including Sprint Nextel, Verizon, China Mobile, AT&T, and America Movil. Motorola has stated that "the loss of one or more of [these companies] could have a material adverse effect on the Company."[80] Sales to these five companies accounted for 42 percent of total revenue in the Mobile Devices segment.[81]

Customers of the Home and Networks Mobility segment include Comcast, Verizon, KDDI, China Mobile, and Sprint Nextel. Sales to these five customers account for 43 percent of total net sales for this division. Similar to the Mobile Devices segment, the loss of any one customer could be detrimental.[82]

Enterprise Mobility Solutions segment customers include the U.S. government, Scansource, IBM, Ingram Micro, and Wal-Mart.[83] Sales to these customers generate 19 percent of the division's net sales. Other customers include resellers and distributors, who then sell to the commercial enterprise market.

Because of the late 2008 financial crisis and the tightening of credit, Motorola is concerned that customers will defer purchases, be unable to obtain financing, and submit more requests for vendor financing by Motorola.[84]

Motorola's Suppliers

Motorola's suppliers include Freescale, Qualcomm, ATI, Spansion, Texas Instruments, and STMicroelectronics. One drawback is that some of the inputs required to manufacture Motorola's products are only available from a single supplier. In 2003 and 2004, Motorola suffered from product delays due to supply shortages caused by a lack of a sufficient number of suppliers.[85] Also, with the current financial crisis, Motorola is concerned that its suppliers may become capacity constrained because of credit issues and thus cause possible product delays.[86]

However, Motorola actively works with suppliers to assist them in reducing lead times and improving efficiency. David Buck, the director of procurement, states "We look for opportunities for our suppliers to be more successful."[87] Motorola works with suppliers early in the design phase of a product, enabling a fast ramp-up of production. At times, "purchasers involved in design are co-located with designers."[88] These activities contribute directly to Motorola's bottom line since parts can be ramped up and delivered faster, with increased quality and lower cost.

Financial Performance

Motorola reported financial losses and a decline in annual sales in 2007 (see Exhibit 2). Net sales in 2007 totaled almost $36.7 billion, down 15 percent compared to net sales of $42.8 billion in 2006.[89] The Mobile Devices segment's net sales in 2007 were $19 billion, representing 52 percent of the Company's consolidated net sales, but experiencing a 33 percent decrease from the previous year. The Home and Networks Mobility segment's net sales in 2007 were $10 billion, representing 27 percent of the Company's consolidated net sales, a 9 percent increase from the previous year. The Enterprise Mobility Solutions segment's net sales in 2007 were $7.7 billion, representing 21 percent of the Company's consolidated net sales, a 43 percent increase in net sales from the previous year.[90]

Additionally, Motorola reported operating losses of $553 million (see Exhibit 2). In the previous year, the firm reported operating earnings of $4.1 billion.[91] Operating margins were 1.5 percent of net sales in 2007 compared to 9.6 percent in 2006—another substantial decline.[92]

Exhibit 2 Motorola, Inc. and Subsidiaries

Income Statement			
	Years Ended December 31		
(In millions, except per share amounts)	2007	2006	2005
Net sales	$ 36,622	$ 42,847	$ 35,310
Costs of sales	26,670	30,120	23,881
Gross margin	9,952	12,727	11,429
Selling, general and administrative expenses	5,092	4,504	3,628
Research and development expenditures	4,429	4,106	3,600
Other charges (income)	984	25	(404)
Operating earnings (loss)	(553)	4,092	4,605

Exhibit 2 Motorola, Inc. and Subsidiaries (*Continued*)

Income Statement			
	Years Ended December 31		
(In millions, except per share amounts)	**2007**	**2006**	**2005**
Other income (expense)			
Interest income, net	91	326	71
Gains on sales of investments and businesses, net	50	41	1,845
Other	22	151	(109)
Total other income (expense)	163	518	1,807
Earnings (loss) from continuing operations before income taxes	(390)	4,610	6,412
Income tax expense (benefit)	(285)	1,349	1,893
Earnings (loss) from continuing operations	(105)	3,261	4,519
Earnings from discontinued operations, net of tax	56	400	59
Net earnings (loss)	$ (49)	$ 3,661	$ 4,578
Earnings (loss) per common share			
Basic			
Continuing operations	$ (0.05)	$ 1.33	$ 1.83
Discontinued operations	0.03	0.17	0.02
	$ (0.02)	$ 1.50	$ 1.85
Diluted			
Continuing operations	$ (0.05)	$ 1.30	$ 1.79
Discontinued operations	0.03	0.16	0.02
	$ (0.02)	$ 1.46	$ 1.81
Weighted average common shares outstanding			
Basic	2,312.7	2,446.3	2,471.3
Diluted	2,312.7	2,504.2	2,527.0
Dividends paid per share	$ 0.20	$ 0.18	$ 0.16

Source: Motorola 2007 Annual Report, http://www.motorola.com.

The firm incurred a loss from continuing operations of $105 million which resulted in $0.05 per diluted common share.[93] This was down from the stated $1.30 per diluted common share in 2006 with continuing operations of $3.3 billion, as shown in Exhibits 2 and 3.

Another significant decrease from previous years occurred in the stated operating cash flow of $785 million in 2007 (see Exhibit 4). Generated operating cash flows from 2005 through 2007 are $4.3 billion, $3.5 billion, and $785 million, respectively, showing a continuation of a decreasing trend.[94]

The less-than-stellar financial situation has led management to consider different strategies that would best solve this predicament.

Exhibit 3 Motorola, Inc. and Subsidiaries

Balance Sheet		
	December 31	
(In millions, except per share amounts)	**2007**	**2006**
Assets		
Cash and cash equivalents	$ 2,752	$ 2,816
Sigma Fund	5,242	12,204
Short-term investments	612	620
Accounts receivable, net	5,324	7,509
Inventories, net	2,836	3,162
Deferred income taxes	1,891	1,731
Other current assets	3,565	2,933
Total current assets	22,222	30,975
Property, plant and equipment, net	2,480	2,267
Investments	837	895
Deferred income taxes	2,454	1,325
Goodwill	4,499	1,706
Other assets	2,320	1,425
Total assets	$34,812	$38,593
Liabilities and stockholders' equity		
Notes payable and current portion of long-term debt	$ 332	$ 1,693

Balance Sheet		
	December 31	
(In millions, except per share amounts)	**2007**	**2006**
Accounts payable	4,167	5,056
Accrued liabilities	8,001	8,676
Total current liabilities	12,500	15,425
Long-term debt	3,991	2,704
Other liabilities	2,874	3,322
Stockholders' equity		
Preferred stock, $100 par value	—	—
Common stock, $3 par value	6,792	7,197
Issued shares:	2,264	2,399
Outstanding shares:	2,236	2,397
Additional paid-in capital	782	2,509
Retained earnings	8,579	9,086
Non-owner changes to equity	(706)	(1,650)
Total stockholders' equity	15,447	17,142
Total liabilities and stockholders' equity	$34,812	$38,593

Source: Motorola 2007 Annual Report, http://www.motorola.com.

Exhibit 4 Motorola, Inc. and Subsidiaries

	Statement of Cash Flows		
		Years Ended December 31	
(In millions)	2007	2006	2005
Operating			
Net earnings (loss)	$ (49)	$ 3,661	$ 4,578
Less: Earnings from discontinued operations	56	400	59
Earnings (loss) from continuing operations	(105)	3,261	4,519
Adjustments to reconcile earnings (loss) from continuing operations to net cash provided by operating activities:			
Depreciation and amortization	903	558	540
Non-cash other charges	213	49	106
Share-based compensation expense	315	276	14
Gains on sales of investments and businesses, net	(50)	(41)	(1,845)
Deferred income taxes	(747)	838	1,000
Change in assets and liabilities, net of effects of acquisitions and dispositions			
Accounts receivable	2,538	(1,775)	(1,303)
Inventories	556	(718)	(19)
Other current assets	(705)	(388)	(721)
Accounts payable and accrued liabilities	(2,303)	1,654	2,405
Other assets and liabilities	170	(215)	(388)
Net cash provided by operating activities from continuing operations	785	3,499	4,308
Investing			
Acquisitions and investments, net	(4,568)	(1,068)	(312)
Proceeds from sale of investments and businesses	411	2,001	1,538
Capital expenditures	(527)	(649)	(548)

Exhibit 4 Motorola, Inc. and Subsidiaries (*Continued*)

	Statement of Cash Flows		
		Years Ended December 31	
(In millions)	2007	2006	2005
Proceeds from sale of property, plant and equipment	166	85	103
Proceeds from sales (purchases) of Sigma Fund investments, net	6,889	(1,337)	(3,157)
Proceeds from sales (purchases) of short-term investments	8	(476)	8
Net cash provided by (used for) investing activities from continuing operations	2,379	(1,444)	(2,368)
Financing			
Net proceeds from (repayment of) commercial paper and short-term borrowings	(242)	66	11
Repayment of debt	(1,386)	(18)	(1,132)
Net proceeds from issuance of debt	1,415	—	—
Issuance of common stock	440	918	1,199
Purchase of common stock	(3,035)	(3,826)	(874)
Excess tax benefits from share-based compensation	50	165	—
Payment of dividends	(468)	(443)	(394)
Distribution from (to) discontinued operations	(75)	(23)	283
Net cash used for financing activities from continuing operations	(3,301)	(3,161)	(907)
Effect of exchange rate changes on cash and cash equivalents from continuing operations	73	148	(105)
Discontinued Operations			
Net cash provided by (used for) operating activities from discontinued operations	(75)	(16)	297
Net cash used for investing activities from discontinued operations	—	(13)	(16)
Net cash provided by (used for) financing activities from discontinued operations	75	23	(283)
Effect of exchange rate changes on cash and cash equivalents from discontinued operations	—	6	2
Net cash provided by (used for) discontinued operations	—	—	—

Exhibit 4 Motorola, Inc. and Subsidiaries (*Continued*)

Statement of Cash Flows			
	Years Ended December 31		
(In millions)	**2007**	**2006**	**2005**
Net increase (decrease) in cash and cash equivalents	(64)	(958)	928
Cash and cash equivalents, beginning of year	2,816	3,774	2,846
Cash and cash equivalents, end of year	$ 2,752	$ 2,816	$ 3,774
Cash Flow Information			
Cash paid during the year for:			
Interest, net	$ 312	$ 322	$ 318
Income taxes, net of refunds	440	463	703

Source: Motorola 2007 Annual Report, http://www.motorola.com.

Motorola's Strategies

Motorola's current strategies are framed around efforts to return the firm to profitability. In the past couple of years there has been much discussion about spinning off the Mobile Devices segment as an independent company, similar to what Motorola had previously done with Free Scale. In a press release, Greg Brown stated the following: "Creating two industry-leading companies will provide improved flexibility, more tailored capital structures, and increased management focus—as well as more targeted investment opportunities for our shareholders."[95] However, as a result of the 2008 economic downturn, Motorola postponed the spin-off until the third quarter of 2009.[96]

Motorola is going to direct its efforts to better understand consumer demand.[97] In addition, it plans to pursue a product upgrade cycle and initiate operational changes to cut costs and make the company leaner.[98] This entails cutting approximately 3,000 jobs—2,000 of which will be from the handset division.[99] In addition, Motorola is considering reducing its emphasis on the European market.[100]

Motorola also invested heavily in the newly developed WiMax technology.[101] There are high expectations for WiMax as the next-generation wireless technology because it supports high-speed data transmission.[102] WiMax is capable of transmitting data at speeds from 1 to 5 megabits per second.[103] Furthermore, it works on

a radius of over 20 miles.[104] Motorola believes competing in this technological and product domain is crucial for its mobility strategy.[105] In November 2008, Motorola announced the deployment of its first trial network in Vietnam.[106] Dr. Ray Owen, head of Technology for Asia and general director of Motorola Vietnam, said: "Launching the trial network for Vietnam Datacommunications Company is another milestone in Motorola's long history of leading WiMAX development in the industry."[107]

Historically, Motorola has not limited the number of operating systems it supports in the Mobile Devices segment. However, recently the firm reduced the number of operating systems it supports to only P2K (Motorola's legacy platform for low-end devices),[108] Windows Mobile, and Android.[109] Motorola has been a featured partner with Google since the inception of the Android platform alliance.[110] Android will feature social networking applications such as Facebook and MySpace.[111] Moreover, analysts believe that social networking phones are expected to be a hit with the 16- to 34-year-old age segment, expected to comprise 23 percent of cell phone users by the end of 2012.[112]

Motorola's cost-reduction actions may expose the firm to additional risks.[113] Similar to most firms in this very competitive market, Motorola is confronted with an uncertain future.

Exhibit 5 Competitor Financials*

Key Numbers	Sony Ericsson Mobile	Nokia	Nokia (Mobile Phones)	Samsung	Samsung (Telecom)	RIM (2008)	RIM (Devices) (2008)	Apple (2008)	Apple (Headsets) (2008)	LG (Headsets)		
Annual Sales ($ mil.)	47.50	75,203.30	32,309.00	105,018	16,114	6,009.40	4,914	32,479	1,800	3,136		
Net Income ($ mil.)			5,434.00	8,446	2,407	1,294.00	370	4,834				
Employees		100,534	3,614		8,387			35,100				
Market Cap ($ mil.)				48,700								
Profitability											Industry	Market
Gross Profit Margin		33.90%									33.40%	52.70%
Pre-Tax Profit Margin		16.20%									0.50%	4.70%
Net Profit Margin	7.40%	14.10%	7.45%	8.04%	11.60%	21.53%	7.53%	14.88%		6%	−0.30%	2.70%

* Aside from Motorola, Nokia is the only publicly traded company on the U.S. exchanges; therefore, those companies traded on non-U.S. exchanges are not required by the Securities and Exchange Commission to report all necessary financials.

Source: 2008, http://hoovers.com; 2008, http://www.samsung.com; 2008, http://www.apple.com; 2008, http://www.lge.com; 2008, http://www.rim.net.

The Future for Motorola

Motorola has struggled to maintain pace with the change in technology that consumers desire. Indeed, the firm has struggled to have a top-performing product within the Mobile Devices segment since its introduction of the RAZR. Will a spinoff of this division help the rest of Motorola's business improve its financial performance? Can the new CEO and top-management team establish a positive reputation and limit the turnover that has taken place in upper management since he took over? These and other questions are at the forefront of the minds of the board of directors and stockholders alike.

NOTES

1. 2008, Motorola Inc Timeline, *Motorola Inc,* http://www.motorola.com.
2. 2008, Motorola – Early History, *Free Encyclopedia of Ecommerce,* http://ecommerce.hostip.info/pages/751/Motorola-Inc-EARLY-HISTORY.html.
3. Ibid.
4. 2008, Motorola Inc. Timeline.
5. 2008, Motorola Inc.—Early History.
6. 2008, Motorola Inc. Timeline.
7. Ibid.
8. 2008, Motorola Inc.—Early History.
9. Ibid.
10. 2008, Motorola Inc. Timeline.
11. Ibid.
12. 2008, Motorola Inc.—Early History.
13. 2008, Motorola Inc. Timeline.
14. Ibid.
15. Ibid.
16. Ibid.
17. Ibid.
18. 2008, Motorola Inc.—Early History.
19. Ibid.
20. Ibid.
21. 2008, Motorola Inc. Timeline.
22. Ibid.
23. 1990, Paul Galvin: Motorola, *American National Business Hall of Fame,* http://www.anbhf.org/laureates/pgalvin.html.
24. 2006, Illinois Hall of Fame; Paul Galvin, *Illinois Review,* http://illinoisreview.typepad.com/illinoisreview/2006/11/illinois_hall_o_2.html.
25. 2008, Motorola Inc. Timeline.
26. 2008, Motorola Inc., *Encyclopedia Britannica,* http://www.britannica.com, November 30.
27. 2008, Motorola Inc. Timeline.
28. 2008, Motorola Inc.—Early History.
29. Ibid.
30. 2008, Motorola Inc. Timeline.
31. Ibid.
32. 2008, Motorola DynaTAC—35th Anniversary, Motorola Inc., http://www.motorola.com.
33. 2008, Motorola Inc. Timeline, Motorola Inc., http://www.motorola.com/content.jsp?globalObjectId=7632.
34. 2008, Motorola Inc. Timeline, Motorola Inc., http://www.motorola.com/content.jsp?globalObjectId=7632.
35. 2008, Six Sigma: Motorola does it right, Motorola Inc., http://www.motorola.com.
36. 2008, Motorola Inc. Timeline.
37. Ibid.
38. Ibid.
39. Ibid.
40. Ibid.
41. Ibid.
42. Ibid.
43. 2008, 20 Moments in Motorola History, *ChannelWeb,* http://www.crn.com/networking/206906014;jsessionid=F0MYJEPAOMV5UQSNDLPCKH0CJUNN2JVN?pgno=3.
44. Ibid.
45. 2008, Motorola Inc. Timeline.
46. 2008, CCID Consulting reviews Motorola performance in the mobile phone market, *Reuters,* http://www.reuters.com, June 11.
47. 2008, 20 moments in Motorola history.
48. Ibid.
49. 2008, Motorola Inc. Timeline.
50. 2008, 20 moments in Motorola History.
51. Ibid.
52. Ibid.
53. 2007, Motorola names Greg Brown CEO, *BusinessWeek,* http://www.businessweek.com, November 30.
54. A. Dannin, 2008, Motorola Inc., http://library.morningstar.com.ezproxy1.lib.asu.edu/stocknet/MorningstarAnalysis.aspx?Country=USA&Symbol=MOT.
55. 2008, Motorola Inc. company description, *BusinessWeek,* http://investing.businessweek.com.
56. 2008, Motorola 2007 Annual Report, http://www.motorola.com.
57. 2008, Form 10-Q: Motorola, Inc., United States Securities and Exchange Commission, http://sec.gov/Archives/edgar/data/68505/000095015208008426/c47113e10vq.htm.
58. Ibid.
59. Ibid.
60. 2008, CDMA – Code Division Multiple Access, Birds-Eye.net, http://www.birds-eye.net/definition/c/cdma-code_division_multiple_access.shtml.
61. 2008, UMTS – Universal Mobile Telecommunications System, Birds-Eye.net, http://www.birds-eye.net/definition/u/umts-universal_mobile_telecommunications_system.shtml.
62. 2008, Motorola Inc. company description, *BusinessWeek.*
63. 2008, Form 10-Q: Motorola, Inc.
64. 2008, Motorola Inc. company description.
65. 2008, Form 10-Q: Motorola, Inc.
66. 2008, Nokia Annual Report, http://www.nokia.com; 2007, Nokia in 2007, *Nokia,* http://media.corporate-ir.net/media_files/irol/10/107224/reports/ann_acc_2007.pdf_.
67. Samsung Electronics 2007 Annual Report, http://www.samsung.com.
68. Ericsson Annual Report 2007, http://www.ericsson.com.
69. LG Annual Report 2007, http://www.lg.net.
70. 2008, About LG: Mobile communications, http://www.lge.com.
71. 2007, Apple Form 10-K, Securities and Exchange Commission, http://www.sec.gov, December 31.
72. Research in Motion 2008 Annual Report, http://www.rim.net.
73. 2008, RIM: Company, Research in Motion, http://www.rim.com.
74. 2008, Helio, Inc., and Helio LLC Exhbit 99.1, Helio, http://documents.scribd.com/docs/qk9y5wyxvrrcweuad2d.pdf
75. 2008, Don't call us a phone company, Helio, http://www.helio.com.
76. 2008, Mobile internet devices, Intel Corporation, http://www.intel.com.
77. Ibid.
78. Ibid.
79. Ibid.
80. 2008, SEC Form 10-Q: Motorola, Inc, *AOL Money and Finance,* http://finance.aol.com.
81. Ibid.

82. Ibid.
83. Ibid.
84. 2008, Motorola Form 10-Q.
85. T. Krazit, 2004, After delays, Motorola brings V400 to North America, *InfoWorld*, http://www.infoworld.com, January 16.
86. 2007, Motorola Form 10-Q.
87. P. Teague, 2007, The ABCs of spend analysis: Change the way you source, *Purchasing*, http://www.purchasing.com, May 3.
88. J. Carbone, 2007, Time-to-Market is key, *Purchasing*, http://www.purchasing.com, March 15.
89. 2008, Motorola 2007 Annual Report.
90. Ibid.
91. Ibid.
92. Ibid.
93. Ibid.
94. Ibid.
95. Ibid.
96. A. Dannin, Motorola Inc.
97. J. Zounis, 2008, Motorola Inc., http://library.morningstar.com.ezproxy1.lib.asu.edu/stocknet/AnalysisArchive.aspx?docId=234200&Year=2008&Country=USA&Symbol=MOT.
98. Ibid.
99. O. Kharif, 2008, Motorola's turnaround plans meet with skepticism, *BusinessWeek*, http://www.businessweek.com, October 31.
100. Ibid.
101. A. Dannin, Motorola Inc.
102. M. Reardon, 2005, Motorola, Intel team on mobile WiMax, CNET News, http://news.cnet.com, October 27.
103. Ibid.
104. Ibid.
105. Ibid.
106. Motorola Media Center, 2008, Motorola deploys its First WiMAX 802.16e trial network in Vietnam, http://www.motorola.com, November 27.
107. Ibid.
108. http://www.funambol.com/blog/capo/2008/10/motorola-focusing-on-android-why-it-is.html.
109. A. Dannin, Motorola Inc.
110. D. Gardner, 2008, Motorola reportedly trimming operating systems in favor of android, *Information Week*, http://www.informationweek.com, October 29.
111. O.Kharif, 2008, Motorola readies its own android social smartphone, *BusinessWeek*, http://www.businessweek.com, October 17.
112. Ibid.
113. Ibid.

James Francart, Harry Fry, Denis Grigorov,
Leonard Muhammad, Regina Pelkman,
Kyle Schlabach, Robin Chapman

Arizona State University

The worst sort of business is one that grows rapidly, requires significant capital to engender the growth, and then earns little or no money. Think airlines. Here a durable competitive advantage has proven elusive ever since the days of the Wright Brothers. Indeed, if a farsighted capitalist had been present at Kitty Hawk, he would have done his successors a huge favor by shooting Orville down.[1]

—WARREN BUFFETT IN A *2008* LETTER TO BERKSHIRE HATHAWAY SHAREHOLDERS

Some of the best minds in business have entered the commercial airline industry and failed. Included in this group is Warren Buffett, who invested in U.S. Air during the 1990s and was unsuccessful in saving the airline.[2] Since the inception of commercial flight, more than 200 airlines have tried and failed in the commercial airline industry.[3] These companies are a reminder that this business is tumultuous, complex, and in many cases, futile. Herb Kelleher, one of Southwest Airlines's founders, illustrates his awareness of how difficult it is to achieve any modicum of profitability in this industry with his comment, "If the Wright brothers were alive today Wilbur would have to fire Orville to reduce costs."[4]

Financial distress in the airline industry can be tied to the high costs incurred by the airlines to offer their services and low costs demanded by customers to travel. In an already extremely challenging industry, Southwest also faces dilemmas associated with its growth strategy, costs incurred to meet safety regulations on its aircraft, and a dispute with a labor union.[5]

These issues make the current and future decisions of the company more critical than ever. Fortunately for Southwest, the current president and CEO has a vast amount of experience within the company.

Key Leader

Gary C. Kelly replaced Herb Kelleher, one of the founders and chairman of the board, as president when he resigned in May 2008.[6] Kelly began his 22-year career with Southwest in the finance department as controller.[7] In that time, he has risen to the top of Southwest Airlines, holding positions such as vice president of finance, executive vice president, chief financial officer, and vice chairman.[8] Kelly, with such initiatives as fuel hedging, has been instrumental in Southwest's recent success.[9]

History of Southwest

Southwest Airlines, originally known as Air Southwest, was founded by Rollin King and Herb Kelleher. Southwest took its first flight in June 1971, serving three major cities: Dallas, Houston, and San Antonio.[10] Within the first two years Southwest suffered operating losses and was forced to make a difficult decision: lay off employees or sell one of its four aircraft. As an early indication of Southwest's loyalty to its employees, it chose to sell the aircraft.[11] This established the company's "no layoff policy" that is still in force.[12]

Southwest was able to sustain a four-aircraft schedule using only three aircraft by utilizing the "ten-minute turn."[13] Southwest turned its first annual profit in 1973. Southwest's expansion strategy flourished after 1973. By 1977 Southwest operated six airplanes and had transported five million customers.[14] New flight destinations were added such as Rio Grande Valley, Austin, Corpus Christi, El Paso, Lubbock, and Midland/Odessa.[15] Between 1979 and 1980, Southwest established its first interstate service to New Orleans and Albuquerque, followed by Oklahoma City and Tulsa.[16] Southwest expanded west in 1982, when it added service to Phoenix, Las Vegas, and San Diego.[17] In late 1984 the first 737-300 was added to its fleet and was used to service flights to Chicago Midway and St. Louis.[18]

In 1986, Southwest opened a new multi-million dollar training center for flight crews.[19] Since customer satisfaction was Southwest's main focus, it began a frequent flyer program, "The Company Club," in 1987. In 1988,

Southwest won its first monthly Triple Crown award for having the best on-time record, best baggage handling, and fewest customer complaints. All of its achievements allowed it to reach the billion-dollar revenue mark and become a major airline by 1989.[20] In 1990, Southwest created its corporate culture committee to take the lead in preserving the airline's unique culture.[21]

Southwest began to offer service to many new cities such as Nashville, Sacramento, Cleveland, and Columbus, and finally entered the east coast market in 1993 when it offered service to Baltimore/Washington International Airport.[22] With the acquisition and integration of Morris Air in 1994, the company was able to add service to seven new cities, including Seattle, Spokane, Portland, Salt Lake City, and Boise. That same year Southwest became the first airline to introduce Ticketless Travel in four cities, which eventually expanded system-wide in January of 1995.[23] Later in 1995, Southwest became one of the first airlines to have its own Web site, and the following year the Ticketless Travel system debuted online.[24]

After 25 years of service, Southwest owned a fleet of 243 aircraft and it saw an opportunity to introduce a fuel cost management program. The Asian market plummeted in 1998, causing jet fuel costs to drop to 35 cents per gallon. Southwest took advantage of this opportunity and hedged its fuel costs. Within two years fuel costs had increased as crude oil increased from $11 to $34 per barrel.

Further expansion, tangible asset improvements, and technology upgrades continued between 1999 and 2006. Southwest expanded to serve locations such as Long Island and Raleigh-Durham. It teamed up with IBM to introduce approximately 250 self-service check-in kiosks.[25] This project was "part of a nation-wide effort to reduce the amount of time Southwest customers spend in line and to improve the airport experience."[26] By 2004, Southwest was offering online boarding passes via its Web site, allowing passengers to go directly to the departure gates without having to stop at the ticket counter.[27] Customer convenience increased even more in 2005, when Southwest "extended online check-in to 24 hours prior to departure."[28] By 2006, Southwest was ranked number one among airlines in customer satisfaction.[29]

Southwest updated its boarding procedure in 2007. Passengers are now assigned a boarding letter and a number that assigns them a specific place in line.[30] Select fare increases aligned with continuous cost-cutting policies resulted in the year-end revenue of $9.8 billion and $645 million in profits.[31]

In November 2008, Southwest purchased one of its main competitors, ATA Airlines, which allowed it to obtain boarding slots at New York's LaGuardia Airport.[32]

Acquiring ATA has the potential to provide Southwest with means to connect to foreign destinations. Southwest also partnered with WestJet Airlines, a low-cost carrier, to synch flights between Canada and the United States.

Southwest followed other carriers in early 2009 by increasing fare prices $10 per leg in the domestic market and up to $40 per leg for international routes.[33]

Southwest's technological innovations, procedure changes, price increases, and recent acquisitions are attempts to overcome the looming challenges in the airline industry.

Industry Challenges

Factors such as increased fuel costs and other high operating expenses, a decrease in business travelers due to budget cuts, and increased regulation have placed strains on airline companies. Many airlines have subsequently been forced out of business or acquired by competitors. This is illustrated by the fact that the large group of airlines that made up the industry 30 years ago has narrowed to six major firms that control a majority of the market (see Exhibit 1). These six carriers constitute five traditional airline companies (American, Continental, Delta, United, and US Airways) and Southwest, the low-cost leader.

Additionally, many airlines have been forced to file for bankruptcy. From 2005 to 2007, US Airways, UAL Corporation (United Airlines), ATA Airlines, Northwest Airlines, and Delta Air Lines all emerged from bankruptcy proceedings.[34] In 2008, Frontier Airlines, Skybus Airlines, Inc., Aloha Airlines, and ATA Airlines (for the second time) filed for bankruptcy.[35] All of these

Exhibit 1 Airline Domestic Market Share (March 2009)

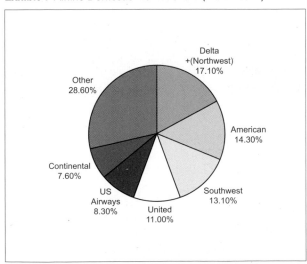

Source: 2008, Research and Innovative Technology Administration, http://www.transtats.bts.gov.

bankruptcies demonstrate the difficult and competitive nature of the industry.

Competitive Environment

Southwest considers any airline offering a flight on the same route it does a competitor, regardless of the overall size of that competitor's operation. Since Southwest now operates in many geographic markets throughout the United States, essentially every airline that offers service to domestic cities is viewed as a competitor.[36]

New companies still occasionally try to replace Southwest as the low-cost leader. Many of these new airlines have disappeared as fast and unspectacularly as they flashed into existence. For example, Skybus, founded by an ex-Southwest employee, copied Southwest's operating model and began its operations in May 2007. Within one year it discontinued operations, citing the weakened state of the economy and increasing fuel costs as the reasons for its ruin.[37]

Although it was able to sustain operations for a longer period of time, the final days of Frontier were no less tragic. When Frontier filed for bankruptcy in April 2008, six days after Skybus,[38] it was the fourth airline to close its doors that week.[39]

JetBlue, also founded by an ex-Southwest employee, emerged in 1999 and is one of the few new entrants to successfully become a principle competitor to Southwest both in terms of route coverage and low-cost, low-fare strategies.[40] It is currently the seventh-largest airline in the United States and holds 4 percent market share compared to Southwest's 13 percent. It operates mostly with point-to-point routes and reaches 52 destinations in 19 states as well as South and Central America and the Caribbean. It just opened its own terminal at JFK airport in New York and claims it has started a new airline category, the "value airline" based on service, cost, and style.[41]

Traditional carriers have recently also adopted cost-cutting practices to more effectively compete with their low-cost counterparts.[42] More than 200 aircraft were grounded in 2008, Continental cut 3,000 jobs, and airlines offered fewer flights.[43] Although the major carriers are still offering higher fares overall, their business models are beginning to mirror those of low-cost rivals. Thus, Southwest has to increasingly improve its marketing efforts to differentiate itself.

Marketing Strategy

Due to the industry-wide move to promote value, Southwest aims to differentiate itself from its competitors by utilizing quirky, humor-driven advertising.[44] One of its first ads, featuring the slogan, "How do we love you? Let us count the ways" illustrated that by offering many flights throughout the day to its first three destinations, Southwest loved its customers (see Exhibit 2).

Another example relates to the recent checked bags fees charged by most other airlines. In response, Southwest began promoting a "no fees" policy in its advertisements such as with its "The Other Side" ad, illustrating a desk clerk with two faces: one face offering only the competitor's airfare; the other face demanding additional fees.

To further develop its unconventional niche in the airline industry and achieve success as a low-cost provider, Southwest distinguishes itself using both quantitative and qualitative characteristics.

Low Costs

An efficiency technique that has consistently saved Southwest both time and expense is the standardization of its airline fleet. It was the first company to put into practice the "one-model-fleet" tactic,[45] meaning that it has focused on purchasing only one aircraft model. It started in 1971 with a fleet of Boeing 737-200s, and it has used the Boeing 737 model ever since, being one of the launch customers for the Boeing 737-700, 737-500, and 737-300 series.[46] This model has been deemed "the workhorse of the aviation industry" and has gained a reputation of being excellent in the areas of cost, reliability and flexibility.[47] "Having a single airplane model in a fleet also lowers inventory, record keeping and maintenance costs, and it minimizes the number of technical manuals, tools and spare parts. Also, fleet management is greatly simplified [and] maintenance crews do not have to modify their routines to service different models."[48]

Another tactic that Southwest employs to maintain its low costs is fuel hedging. Southwest began this practice in the late 1990s and it has played a major role in its 36 years of profitability.[49] Although Southwest is renowned for using this methodology, the idea of oil futures contracts is nothing new in the airline industry (see Exhibit 3). "All the major airlines have hedged fuel prices since the 1980s, but as the major carriers have run into financial difficulties in recent years, they have no longer had the cash—or the creditworthiness—to play the oil-futures market."[50] Nonetheless, Southwest has successfully hedged "at least 70 percent" of its fuel consumption, saving the company $727 million in 2007.[51] Fuel costs fluctuated significantly during 2008, starting out at $91, hitting $151 during the summer, and closing the year at $51. The significant change in oil prices did not provide Southwest with cost savings like those in 2007, but it

Exhibit 2 Southwest Advertisement

How do we love you?
Let us count the ways.

Dallas/Ft. Worth to Houston		Houston to Dallas/Ft. Worth	
Depart	Arrive	Depart	Arrive
7:30 a*	8:18 a	7:30 a*	8:18 a
8:45 a*	9:33 a	8:45 a	9:33 a
10:00 a	10:48 a	10:00 a*	10:48 a
11:15 a*	12:03 p	11:15 a	12:03 p
12:30 p	1:18 p	12:30 p*	1:18 p
1:45 p**	2:33 p	1:45 p	2:33 p
3:00 p	3:48 p	3:00 p**	3:48 p
4:15 p**	5:03 p	4:15 p	5:03 p
5:30 p	6:18 p	5:30 p**	6:18 p
6:45 p**	7:33 p	6:45 p	7:33 p
8:00 p	8:48 p	8:00 p**	8:48 p
9:15 p**	10:03 p	9:15 p**	10:03 p

Dallas/Ft. Worth to San Antonio		San Antonio to Dallas/Ft. Worth	
Depart	Arrive	Depart	Arrive
7:00 a*	7:50 a	8:15 a*	9:05 a
9:30 a	10:20 a	10:45 a	11:35 a
12:00 n	12:50 p	1:15 p	2:05 p
2:30 p	3:20 p	3:45 p	4:35 p
5:00 p	5:50 p	6:15 p	7:05 p
7:30 p**	8:20 p	8:45 p**	9:35 p

*Except Sunday.
**Except Saturday.

SOUTHWEST AIRLINES
The somebody else up there who loves you.

Source: 2008, Southwest Airlines Historical Advertising Gallery, http://www.southwest.com.

did allow it to secure a good hedging contract through 2013 based on the fourth quarter fuel prices ($51). This is expected to save $600 million in fuel costs annually compared to 2008.[52]

Southwest exercised other cost-saving measures concerning fuel consumption, such as the implementation of blended winglets on all of its 737-700s.[53] These blended winglets would "improve performance by extending the airplane's range, saving fuel, lowering engine maintenance costs and reducing takeoff noise."[54] (See Exhibit 4 for estimates on fuel savings.) Testing on the blended winglets demonstrated "gross fuel mileage improvement … in the range of 4 to 5 percent."[55] In 2003, Southwest announced that performance-enhancing "blended winglets" would be installed on all existing and future aircrafts, though this action was not carried out until 2007.[56]

In 2008, Southwest initiated a contract with Pratt & Whitney to use its EcoPower® engine wash services. EcoPower uses atomized water to wash aircraft engines and prevent potential contaminant runoff. This system is more efficient and effective than traditional engine washing processes and extends on-wing time for Pratt & Whitney, International Aero Engines, General Electric, Rolls-Royce, and CFMI engines. By using this engine wash, Southwest anticipates saving "more than $20 million in fuel costs [at 2008 prices]."[57]

The following measures not only help Southwest save on costs, but also to retain its reputation for being reliable and punctual.

Exhibit 3 Southwest Advertisement

Southwest's Profitable Bet

Percentage of each airline's fuel needs that are hedged against higher fuel prices and have been disclosed, with the price caps of their hedges.

	2007 4th quarter		**2008** full years		**2009**		**2010**	
	HEDGED	PRICE CAP	HEDGED	PRICE CAP	HEDGED	PRICE CAP	HEDGED	PRICE CAP
Alaska[1]	50%	$62	32%	$64	5%	$68	0	
American[1]	40	69	14	n.d.†	0		0	
Continental[2]	30	93	10*	93	0		0	
Delta[2]	20	99	0		0		0	
JetBlue[2]	47	83	0		0		0	
Northwest[1]	50	73	10*	84	0		0	
Southwest[1]	90	51	70	51	55	51	25%	$63
United[2]	18	93	0		0		0	
US Airways[1]	56	73	15	73	0		0	

[1]Price based on crude oil.

[2]Price based on heating oil, which is more expensive.

*First quarter only. †Price not disclosed.

Source: 2008, Southwest Airlines manages risk through oil price hedges. http://www.artdiamondblog.com/archives/energyenvironment/, March 18.

Exhibit 4 Improvements from Winglets

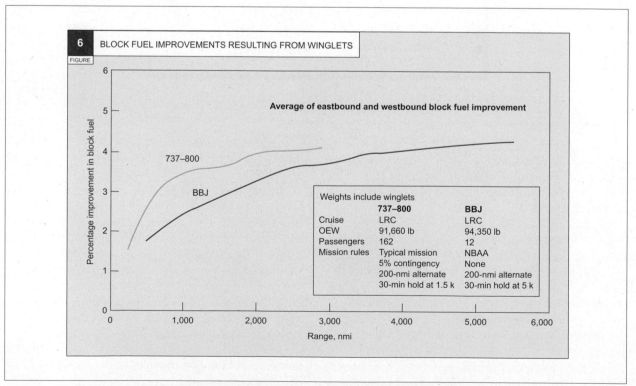

6 FIGURE

BLOCK FUEL IMPROVEMENTS RESULTING FROM WINGLETS

Average of eastbound and westbound block fuel improvement

737–800

BBJ

Weights include winglets		
	737–800	**BBJ**
Cruise	LRC	LRC
OEW	91,660 lb	94,350 lb
Passengers	162	12
Mission rules	Typical mission	NBAA
	5% contingency	None
	200-nmi alternate	200-nmi alternate
	30-min hold at 1.5 k	30-min hold at 5 k

Percentage improvement in block fuel (y-axis: 0–6)

Range, nmi (x-axis: 0–6,000)

Source: Aero 17 – Blended Winglets, fig. 6, http://www.boeing.com/commercial/aeromagazine/aero_17/winglet_story.

Punctuality

Timeliness has been a defining characteristic for Southwest since its beginning. In the 1970s, the company had a 10-minute turnaround time for aircraft while the industry average was four to six times longer.[58] Southwest's "turnarounds now average 23 minutes, but that's still . . . half the time it takes other airlines."[59] It is able to maintain this quick turnaround rate because it uses point-to-point service (curtailing connection times and luggage transfers) and secondary airports for the bulk of its flights (reducing potential congestion).[60] Instead of point-to-point service most legacy carriers use a hub-and-spoke system where small feeder airlines from smaller cities feed into larger international airports such as Delta's hub in Atlanta.

The boarding process with unassigned seating is another of Southwest's differentiating qualities, but one for which it has received mixed reviews from customers.[61] Although this tactic aids in quicker gate turnaround,[62] it is flawed from a customer service standpoint and has a reputation as "cattle call" check-in. It favors customers who are able to arrive at the gate early, no matter when the ticket was purchased (even with an "A" boarding pass—see Exhibit 5). In response to customer complaints Southwest initiated a new check-in process in 2007. Kelleher believes, "Customers are like a force of nature: You can't fool them, and you ignore them at your own peril."[63] The new method gives passengers a group letter (A, B, C) and a number (1 to 60) based on order of check-in, thus it reserves more of a semblance of a place in line than the previous process.[64] Even though this distinction creates perceived value for the customer in terms of time savings, there is still controversy about this method among Southwest customers. Recently, adjustments were made to accommodate families with small children, who did not receive priority seating when the change was first made.[65]

Exceptional Customer Service Begins at Home

A unique aspect of Southwest's customer service perspective is that the end-user is not the primary focus, the employees are; "If [Southwest] can effectively make employees feel good about what they're doing on a daily basis, satisfied employees will deliver [a] . . . sense of friendliness and care to Southwest passengers."[66]

In 2008, Southwest was the highest-rated airline in *Fortune's* list of "America's Most Admired Companies."[67] It ranked first in the categories "people management" and "quality of management." Southwest's reputation for being a great employer is further illustrated by the fact that in 2007, Southwest received 329,200 resumes from job seekers.[68] In 1973, the airline adopted the first profit-sharing plan in the U.S. airline industry, and employees now own at least 8 percent of the company stock.[69] It would be safe to assume that these factors are key contributors to the low employee turnover rate that Southwest enjoys.[70] However, there have been some recent issues related to union activities and contract negotiations that could possibly tarnish Southwest's reputation as an employer (see the Additional Challenges section).

Exhibit 5 Southwest's Boarding Process

How it worked before:

- Each passenger's boarding pass was assigned to Group A, B, or C, based on check-in.
- A and B groups had 45 passengers, with everyone else in Group C.
- Families with young children boarded before the groups were called.
- In the gate area, passengers in each of the groups lined up, often 30 to 45 minutes before boarding, in either the A, B, or C line.
- Passengers boarded by group letter.
- Seats were unassigned.

The new boarding drill:

- Passenger boarding passes will have a group letter (A, B, or C) and a number (1 to 60), based on order of check-in.
- In combination, the letter and number reserves passengers' places in line, leaving them free to relax or get something to eat.
- Groups A and B contain 60 passengers each; those remaining are in Group C.
- Families with young children must now wait until the A group has boarded, unless they hold A passes.
- At the gate, six stainless steel columns divide passengers into groups of five on each side. For example, the first column has passengers holding 1–5 passes on one side and those with 31–35 on the other. The second column has spaces for those holding 6–10 and 36–40.
- Electronic monitors indicate which group is boarding. Those with A passes standing on the first side of the column will board, followed by those on the other side. As the second half boards, Group B will assemble.
- Seats are still unassigned.

Source: S. Marta, 2007, Southwest launches streamlined boarding, *The Dallas Morning News*, http://www.dallasnews.com, October 15.

Reward Programs

Nearly every major airline has attempted to increase customer loyalty through reward programs. These programs offer repeat customers perks such as an accelerated check-in process, upgrades, and even free flights and hotel stays. However, it is debatable how effective these programs are. Leisure travelers may not travel enough to allow these programs to influence their purchasing decisions; and business and other frequent travelers, who are much more concerned about convenience and scheduling, are often members of many, if not all, frequent flyer programs from each airline. The end result is that Rewards programs have not had a major impact on Southwest's bottom line.

Financial Results

Southwest Airlines reported an operating profit of $449 million for the year 2008, despite rising operating expenses marking 71 consecutive quarters of profitability. Total operating expenses for the year increased 16 percent compared to 2007 and were driven primarily by higher fuel costs (44 percent), as well as ongoing maintenance costs (see Exhibit 6). However, Southwest did make 2008 its thirty-sixth consecutive year with annual operating profits.[71]

In 2008, Southwest boasted an operating profit margin (4 percent) much higher than its competitors such as Delta (−36 percent), JetBlue (3.2 percent),

Exhibit 6 Southwest Airlines—Consolidated Statement of Income

	Years Ended December 31		
	2007	2006	2005
	(In millions, except per share amounts)		
Operating Revenues:			
Passenger	$9,457	$8,750	$7,279
Freight	130	134	133
Other	274	202	172
Total operating revenues	9,861	9,086	7,584
Operating Expenses:			
Salaries, wages, and benefits	3,213	3,052	2,782
Fuel and oil	2,536	2,138	1,341
Maintenance materials and repairs	616	468	446
Aircraft rentals	156	158	163
Landing fees and other rentals	560	495	454
Depreciation and amortization	555	515	469
Other operating expenses	1,434	1,326	1,204
Total operating expenses	9,070	8,152	6,859
Operating Income	791	934	725
Other Expenses (Income):			
Interest expense	119	128	122
Capitalized interest	(50)	(51)	(39)
Interest income	(44)	(84)	(47)

Exhibit 6 Southwest Airlines—Consolidated Statement of Income (*Continued*)

	Years Ended December 31		
	2007	**2006**	**2005**
	(In millions, except per share amounts)		
Other (gains) losses, net	(292)	151	(90)
Total other expenses (income)	(267)	144	(54)
Income before income taxes	1,058	790	779
Provision for income taxes	413	291	295
Net income	$645	$499	$484
Net income per share, basic	$.85	$.63	$.61
Net income per share, diluted	$.84	$.61	$.60

Source: 2008, Southwest Airlines 2007 Annual Report, http://www.southwest.com.

United (−21.9 percent), and American (−7.9 percent).[72] This is an indication of Southwest's ability to control costs in an industry that has historically struggled in this area. Continued emphasis on cost cutting has allowed Southwest to avoid filing for bankruptcy, unlike many of its competitors (see Exhibit 7).

In the airline industry, a high ROA indicates a company's ability to generate high income proportionate to its held assets, which are primarily composed of aircraft and other flight equipment, property (including airport operating slots), and fuel hedge contracts. In 2008, Southwest operated with an ROA of 1.2 percent, double that of the next-closest competitor, JetBlue (−1.3 percent). This demonstrates Southwest's outstanding ability to avoid excess capacity and service outages.

Many airlines rely heavily on debt financing, since many investors avoid sinking cash into this industry. Southwest has been able to maintain low levels of debt and position itself with the lowest D/E ratio (77.6) among major airlines (the industry average D/E is 330). Southwest has been able to generate income, have positive profit margins, and maintain low debt levels because it puts great effort into wisely carrying out its strategies.

Part of Southwest's efforts to maintain positive operating margins and low debt levels is to expand its service to greater destinations.

Expansion Plans

Kelly has expressed a desire to expand Southwest beyond the 64 cities it currently serves, calling the airline "an adolescent" in the airline industry.[73] Although the airline

is cutting certain less profitable routes, the net result of the additional flights will increase the company's overall flights by nine.[74]

In March 2009, flights between Chicago and Minneapolis were added. "The people of Minnesota have been asking for Southwest Airlines' service for many years, and we can't wait to introduce them to our legendary customer service, as well as our low fares, on-time flights, and no hidden fees."[75] Even though its strategy is primarily limited to domestic expansion with a push into Denver, Southwest is exploring ways to launch services to the Caribbean and England.[76] It recently announced the addition of flights to Mexico through code-sharing with Volaris. "Volaris has a stellar reputation for being a highly efficient airline with a dedication to customer service, which makes it a natural fit for Southwest Airlines."[77] Growth initiatives also include possible acquisitions of flights once belonging to now defunct airlines such as Ted (United Airlines attempt at a lower cost approach).[78]

Additional Challenges

Technology

The airline companies' widespread integration of the Internet into the booking process acts as a double-edged sword. Customers value the ease provided by online booking, which in turn draws in customers. Southwest obtained first-mover advantage using this technology when it became the first airline to offer the service. However, now that this has become the industry

Exhibit 7 Financial Analysis of Southwest Airlines and Selected Key Competitors

	Southwest Airlines[1]	JetBlue Airways[2]	American Airlines[3]	Delta Air Lines[4]	United Airlines[5]
Period	2007	2007	2007	2007	2007
Annual Revenue					
Passenger	9,457	2,636	20,705	11,803	18,317
Freight and other	404	206	2,230	1,555	1,826
Total	9,861	2,842	22,935	13,358	20,143
Employees (FTE)	34,378	10,219	85,500	55,044	44,861
Operating Profit Margin	8.0%	5.9%	4.2%	6.0%	5.1%
Pre-Tax Profit Margin	10.7%	1.4%	2.2%	3.9%	3.5%
Net Profit Margin	6.5%	0.6%	2.2%	2.4%	2.0%
Return on Equity	9.6%	1.8%	49.1%	−18.0%	17.7%
Return on Assets	4.3%	0.3%	1.7%	1.2%	1.6%
Total Debt/Equity	1.42	4.40	9.75	2.21	9.02
12-month Revenue Growth	8.5%	20.3%	1.6%	nm	nm

[1] 2008, Southwest Airlines 2007 Annual Report, http://www.southwest.com.
[2] 2008, JetBlue Airways Corporation 2007 Annual Report, http://www.jetblue.com.
[3] 2008, AMR Corporation 2007 Annual Report, http://www.aa.com.
[4] 2008, Delta Air Lines, Inc. 2007 Annual Report, http://www.delta.com.
[5] 2008, UAL Corporation 2007 Annual Report, http://www.united.com.

standard, it has significantly increased consumer ability to apply some pressure on ticket prices. Travel search engine sites such as Expedia.com, Travelocity.com, Orbitz.com, Kayak.com, and others have further exasperated this issue for the airlines. Southwest has long refused to submit pricing information or allow the purchase of its tickets from these sites. Since there are many airlines and negligible switching costs, this is truly an industry that has long lacked customer loyalty.

Violations of Safety Requirements. Early in 2008, it was revealed that Southwest had flown at least 117 aircraft that were in violation of mandatory safety checks.[79] As a result, the airline had to temporarily ground 47 of its aircrafts for re-inspection, and the Federal Aviation Administration charged the airline with $10.2 million in fines.[80] Southwest claims, "[it] discovered the missed inspection area, disclosed it to the FAA, and promptly

reinspected all potentially affected aircraft in March 2007. The FAA approved our actions and considered the matter closed as of April 2007." FAA inspectors contest that Southwest continued to use the planes in question before inspections were complete, thus the airline did not take immediate corrective action.[81] Gary Kelly states, "Our interpretation of the guidance that we got from the FAA at the time was that we were in compliance with all laws and regulations … the important point is that at no time were we operating in an unsafe manner, and I think our history proves it."[82]

Union Walkout
The company that once enjoyed superior employee relations compared to its competitors ran into problems in 2008. Complaints of unequal pay for members of ground crew and no raises since 2005 prompted a walkout by the labor union on November 20, 2008.[83] In March

2009 an agreement was reached. The union president admitted that the negotiations were conducted with a spirit of cooperation that is part of Southwest's culture: "Southwest Airlines flight attendants have always been an integral part of the airline's success and it is great news that together they have negotiated a contract that recognizes their contribution."[84] Flight attendants will gain wage increases and a boost in 401k contributions, but only to the degree that such increases will allow Southwest to keep its low-cost advantage.

Questions to Address

As the airline industry as a whole suffers, due to threats from fuel price increases, ever-escalating operational costs, potential security threats, and the current global economic crisis, can Southwest maintain its 36-year streak of profitability? With fluctuating oil prices, can Southwest continue to depend on fuel hedging as an important source of cost control? As it expands its domestic flight operations, will "point-to-point" methodology still prove to be useful? As the major traditional airlines become more like their low-cost counterparts, will they ultimately become more of a competitive threat to Southwest? Using its current strategy, will Southwest be able to expand internationally? Can it maintain its positive relations with employees and avoid future union walkouts and negotiations? If the current economic crisis persists, how will the present expansion plans by Southwest fare? As environmental uncertainties mount, what overall strategies and as well as competitive tactics should Southwest consider to maintain it low cost position and perception of customer loyalty?

NOTES

1. Sykes, 2008, Buffett letter offers great lessons for investors, http://www.bloggingstocks.com, March 3.
2. 2008, Warren Buffett, airlines hasn't always been a successful marriage, *Local Tech Wire*, http://localtechwire.com, January.
3. 2008, Defunct airlines of the United States, http://en.wikipedia.org.
4. H. Kelleher, 1994, *USA Today*, June 8.
5. M. McSherry & M. Lewis, 2008, Southwest Airlines union pickets over wages, *Reuters*, http://www.reuters.com, November.
6. T. Maxon, 2008, Kelleher to preside over his last Southwest meeting Wednesday, *The Dallas Morning News*, http://www.dallasnews.com, May 20; 2008, Southwest officer biographies, http://www.southwest.com.
7. G. C. Kelly, 2008, *Forbes*, http://people.forbes.com/profile/gary-c-kelly/73447.
8. 2008, Southwest officer biographies, http://www.southwest.com.
9. S. Taylor, 2005, To provide the best customer service, put customers second, says Southwest President Colleen Barrett, *McCombs School of Business*, http://www.mccombs.utexas.edu, April 18.
10. 2008, Southwest Airlines, Wikipedia, http://en.wikipedia.org.
11. D. Koenig, 2008, Southwest leader Kelleher steps down, *USA Today*, http://www.usatoday.com, May 21.
12. 2003, What makes Southwest Airlines fly, *Knowledge@Wharton*, http://knowledge.wharton.upenn.edu, April 23.
13. 2008, About Southwest Airlines, http://www.southwest.com.
14. Ibid.
15. Ibid.
16. Ibid.
17. Ibid.
18. Ibid.
19. Ibid.
20. Ibid.
21. Ibid.
22. Ibid.
23. Ibid.
24. Ibid.
25. Ibid.
26. Ibid.
27. Ibid.
28. Ibid.
29. Ibid.
30. Southwest Airlines, Wikipedia.
31. About Southwest Airlines.
32. Ibid.
33. M. Schlangenstein, 2009, Delta, Southwest airlines raise most U.S. tickets $20, http://www.Bloomberg.com, June 17.
34. 2008, Southwest Airlines 2007 Annual Report, http://www.southwest.com..
35. J. Bunch & K. Yamanouchi, 2008, Frontier Airlines files Chapter 11, *The Denver Post*, http://www.denverpost.com, April 11; 2008, Southwest Airlines bids on 14 LaGuardia slots, *Queens Chronicle*, http://www.zwire.com, November; 2008, Skybus becomes third airline to close this week, CNN, http://www.cnn.com, April 4.
36. 2008, Southwest Airlines 2007 Annual Report.
37. Ibid.
38. J. Bunch & K. Yamanouchi, Frontier Airlines files Chapter 11.
39. Skybus becomes third airline to close this week.
40. 2008, America's most admired companies, *Fortune*, http://money.cnn.com, March 17.
41. 2009, JetBlue 2008 Annual Report, http://www.jetblue.com, June 17.
42. M. Maynard, 2008, As costs rise, airlines cut services and raise fares, *The New York Times*, http://www.nytimes.com, June 6.
43. Ibid.
44. 2008, Southwest Airlines historical advertising gallery, http://www.southwest.com.
45. 2002, The secret behind high profits at low-fare airlines, Boeing News Release, http://www.boeing.com, June 14.
46. 2008, Southwest Airlines Fact Sheet, http://www.southwest.com.
47. The secret behind high profits at low-fare airlines.
48. Ibid.
49. D. Reed, 2008, Can fuel hedges keep Southwest in the money? *USA Today*, http://www.usatoday.com, July 23.
50. E. Roston, 2005, Hedging their costs, *Time*, June 20.
51. Southwest Airlines 2007 Annual Report.
52. 2009, Southwest Airlines 2008 Annual Report, http://www.southwest.com, June 11, 9.
53. 2003, Southwest Airlines Boeing 737-700 fleet takes wing with sleek new look, Boeing News Release, http://www.boeing.com, June 17.
54. Ibid.
55. Ibid.

56. Ibid.
57. G. Brostowicz & J. Whitlow, 2008, Southwest Airlines to save millions in fuel costs and significantly reduce carbon dioxide emissions with Pratt & Whitney EcoPower® Engine wash services, *Pratt & Whitney*, http://www.pw.utc.com, June 11.
58. 2007, Something special about Southwest Airlines, CBS News, http://www.cbsnews.com,_September 2.
59. Ibid.
60. 2008, Southwest Airlines Company (LUV), Wikinvest, http://www.wikinvest.com.
61. D. Grossman, 2007, New Southwest boarding policy pits business travelers against families, *USA Today*, http://www.usatoday.com, October 28.
62. W. Haas, 2007, How Southwest Airlines plans for success, *Associated Content*, http://www.associatedcontent.com, February 2.
63. B. McConnell & J. Huba, 2001, The wild turkey, *Creative Customer Evangelists*, http://www.creatingcustomerevangelists.com, September 1.
64. S. Marta, 2007, Southwest launches streamlined boarding, *The Dallas Morning News*, http://www.dallasnews.com, October 15.
65. Ibid.
66. To provide the best customer service, put customers second.
67. America's most admired companies, *Fortune*.
68. Southwest Airlines Fact Sheet.
69. Ibid.
70. T. Tripp, Best practices case study: Best perks, Southwest Airlines, *Vault*, http://www.vault.com/nr/newsmain.jsp?nr_page=3&ch_id=402&article_id=19258&cat_id=1123.
71. Southwest 2008 Annual Report; 2008, Southwest Airlines reports third quarter financial results, http://www.southwest.com, October 16; 2008, Southwest Airlines reports fourth quarter earnings and 35th consecutive year of profitability, http://www.southwest.com, January 23.
72. 2009, Delta, Southwest, AMR, UAL, and JetBlue, *Reuters*, http://www.reuters.com, June 11.
73. J. Bottiglieri, 2008, Gary C. Kelly: Aspire to something greater; Southwest Airlines' CEO talks about sustaining profitability and mitigating risk, *Bnet Business Network*, March; R. Velotta, 2008, Southwest Airlines announces code share with Mexican airline, *Las Vegas Sun*http://www.lasvegassun.com, November 10.
74. 2008, Southwest Airlines cuts 31 flights, adds 40 flights, *DWS Aviation*, http://www.dancewithshadows.com, June.
75. 2008, Southwest Airlines announces schedule, fares for its new Minneapolis-Chicago service, *DWS Aviation*, http://www.dancewithshadows.com/aviation, November.
76. Ibid.
77. 2008, Southwest to partner with Volaris on international flights, *Austin Business Journal*, http://www.bizjournals.com, November.
78. 2008, Southwest Airlines bids on 14 LaGuardia slots, *Queens Chronicle*, http://www.zwire.com, November.
79. D. Griffin & S. Bronstein, 2008, Records: Southwest Airlines flew "unsafe" planes, *CNN*, http://www.cnn.com, March 6.
80. Ibid.
81. Ibid.
82. D. Griffin & S. Bronstein, 2008, Southwest Airlines CEO calls FAA's threats of fine "unfair", *CNN*, http://www.cnn.com, March 7.
83. Southwest Airlines union pickets over wages.
84. J. Horwitz, 2009, Arriving today, a tentative agreement for Southwest flight attendants that protects employees and the LUV airline's future, TWU News Room, http://www.twu.org, March 26.

Robin Chapman, Robert E. Hoskisson

Arizona State University

"This will go down in history as a turning point for the music industry," said Apple Computer CEO Steve Jobs. "This is landmark stuff. I can't overestimate it!"[1] Jobs was referring to the April 2003 debut of Apple's iTunes Online Music Store, the first legal online music service to have agreements with all five major record labels. Although initially available only for Macintosh users, iTunes sold more than 1 million songs by the end of its first week in operation. Not only did iTunes change the nature of the music industry, it also added greatly to Apple's revenues by way of promoting the purchase of the iPod—a portable digital music device that can store downloaded iTunes songs. In 2007, Apple controlled more than 70 percent of the digital music market,[2] and its net income was $3.5 billion (see Exhibits 1 and 2). Jobs hopes further that the success of iTunes will flourish with the launch of Apple TV and iPhone in 2007. In May 2007, Apple was named by *BusinessWeek* as the most innovative company for the third year in a row. Apple's focus on innovation has helped it maintain a competitive advantage and marketing prowess over other industry players that have historically been much stronger than Apple.[3] However, Apple must beat the competition on a number of levels. iTunes faces stiff competition from new and existing online music and video download services both legal and illegal. The iPod, Apple TV, and iPhone all face the threat of lower-priced rivals and possible substitutes. Apple's innovative ability and the quality of its marketing strategy will likely determine the outcome of the company's foray into the music, mobile phone, and video-on-demand businesses.

Early Company History

On April 1, 1976, Steve Jobs and Stephen Wozniak began the partnership that would eventually become Apple Computer. Both electronics gurus, Jobs and Wozniak had known each other since high school and had worked together previously on other projects.[4] In early 1976, Wozniak had been working on combining video monitors with computers. His idea was to invent a user-friendly computer that ordinary consumers could buy. Wozniak, who worked for Hewlett-Packard (HP) at the time, decided to approach his employer with his idea. HP, however, did not see a future for personal computers (PCs) and soundly rebuffed him. At that point, Steve Jobs told his friend Wozniak that they should go into business together and sell computers themselves.[5]

Their first computer, the *Apple I*, was built in the garage of Jobs's parents (see Exhibit 3). Known as a "kit computer," the original Apple consisted merely of a circuit board and did not even have an exterior casing. It was intended to be sold to hobbyists only. Jobs called the computer an "Apple" in honor of his days working at an orchard while seeking enlightenment—and because neither he nor Wozniak could come up with a better name.[6] The *Apple I* received mixed responses from hobbyists, and the duo decided it was time to expand the market for personal computers by building a more attractive and useful machine, the *Apple II*.[7]

Growth

After taking on new partners to fund expansion plans, the company officially became Apple Computer, Inc., in early

* This case is intended to be used as the basis for class discussion rather than to illustrate effective or ineffective handling of an administrative or strategic situation. We appreciate the previous input on an earlier case focused only on the music industry by Jeff Berrong, Marilyn Klopp, Max Mishkin, Jimmy Pittman, and Adrian Ray under the direction of Professor Robert E. Hoskisson.

Apple Computer, Inc., by Robin Chapman and Robert E. Hoskisson. Reprinted by permission of the authors.

1977.[8] Within months, the recapitalized company introduced the *Apple II*, the first computer to come with a sleek plastic casing and color graphics.[9] Annual sales increased dramatically to $10 million, and the company began to grow quickly in size, adding thousands of employees.[10] On December 12, 1980, Apple became a public company. On the first day of trading, its share price increased from an initial $22 offering to $29.[11] By the end of the year, Apple reached $100 million in annual sales.[12] The fledgling company, however, soon faced some experienced competition.

In 1981, IBM released its first personal computer. IBM's sheer size ensured its domination of the young PC market. Steve Jobs realized that Apple would have to move fast in order to remain a viable company. Over the next few years, the company released several new computer models, most notably the *Apple III* and the *Lisa*. Neither of these models sold particularly well.

In 1983, Jobs recruited Pepsi-Cola CEO John Sculley as Apple's president and CEO. Jobs hoped that this change would bring more structure and

Exhibit 1 Consolidated Statements of Cash Flows

(In millions)	Three Fiscal Years Ended September 29		
	2007	2006	2005
Cash and cash equivalents, beginning of the year	$ 6,392	$ 3,491	$ 2,969
Operating Activities: Net income	3,496	1,989	1,328
Adjustments to reconcile net income to cash generated by operating activities:			
Depreciation, amortization, and accretion	317	225	179
Stock-based compensation expense	242	163	49
Provision for deferred income taxes	78	53	50
Excess tax benefits from stock options	—	—	428
Gain on sale of Power School net assets	—	(4)	—
Loss on disposition of property, plant, and equipment	12	15	9
Changes in operating assets and liabilities:			
Accounts receivable, net	(385)	(357)	(121)
Inventories	(76)	(105)	(64)
Other current assets	(1,540)	(1,626)	(150)
Other assets	81	(1,040)	(35)
Accounts payable	1,494	1,611	328
Other liabilities	1,751	1,296	534
Cash generated by operating activities	5,470	2,220	2,535

Source: Apple's 2007 Fiscal Year 10K, www.apple.com/investor.

organization to the young company.[13] Apple's biggest computer achievement, the Macintosh (Mac), was released. After initially opposing it, Jobs had personally taken on the task of developing the Mac, which became the first PC featuring a graphical interface and a mouse for navigation. Apple first presented the now-famous Macintosh computer with a riveting January 1984 Super Bowl commercial. The memorable commercial featured an Orwellian *1984* world filled with stoic human zombies, all watching a large-screen image of "Big Brother." A young woman rushes into the room and dramatically destroys the screen. Apple used this *1984* imagery to depict IBM's computer dominance being destroyed by the new Macintosh.[14] With features that made the Mac easy to use for publishing and a marketing strategy that concentrated on universities, the new computer sold very well, pushing Apple's fiscal 1984 sales to an unprecedented $1.5 billion.[15]

Shake-Up

By 1985, however, Jobs and Sculley began to disagree over the direction they wanted the company to take. After Jobs's attempt to remove Sculley failed, Jobs left Apple in May to start his own new business, NeXT Computers. Meanwhile, Microsoft benefited from Apple's poor negotiation of a contract that cleared the way for successive versions of the Windows operating system to use graphical user interface (GUI) technology similar to that of the Mac. With this agreement, "Apple had effectively lost exclusive rights to its interface design."[16]

In 1990, Microsoft released Windows 3.0, the first universal software that could run on nearly every PC regardless of the manufacturer. Although Apple's worldwide sales had reached $7 billion by 1992, Apple soon found itself fighting an uphill battle against the movement toward standardized software. More and more businesses and consumers wanted compatible operating

Exhibit 2 Apple Computer, Fourth-Quarter Fiscal 2007 10Q Report

Net Sales (net sales in millions and unit sales in thousands)	Three Months Ended		
	12/29/07	12/30/06	Change
Net Sales by Operating Segment:			
Americas net sales	$ 4,298	$ 3,521	22%
Europe net sales	2,471	1,712	44%
Japan net sales	400	285	40%
Retail net sales	1,701	1,115	53%
Other segments net sales (a)	738	482	53%
Total net sales	$ 9,608	$ 7,115	35%
Unit Sales by Operating Segment:			
Americas Macintosh unit sales	841	625	35%
Europe Macintosh unit sales	705	491	44%
Japan Macintosh unit sales	91	70	30%
Retail Macintosh unit sales	504	308	64%
Other segments Macintosh unit sales (b)	178	112	59%
Total Macintosh unit sales	2,319	1,606	44%

(Continued)

Exhibit 2 Apple Computer, Fourth-Quarter Fiscal 2007 10Q Report (*Continued*)

Net Sales (net sales in millions and unit sales in thousands)	Three Months Ended		
	12/29/07	12/30/06	Change
Net Sales by Product:			
Desktops (c)	$ 1,515	$ 955	59%
Portables (d)	2,037	1,455	40%
Total Macintosh net sales	3,552	2,410	47%
iPod	3,997	3,427	17%
Other music-related products and services (e)	808	634	27%
iPhone and related products and services (f)	241	—	NM
Peripherals and other hardware (g)	382	297	29%
Software, service, and other sales (h)	628	347	81%
Total net sales	$ 9,608	$ 7,115	35%
Unit Sales by Product:			
Desktops (c)	977	637	53%
Portables (d)	1,342	969	38%
Total Macintosh unit sales	2,319	1,606	44%
Net sales per Macintosh unit sold (i)	$ 1,532	$ 1,501	2%
iPod unit sales	22,121	21,066	5%
Net sales per iPod unit sold (j)	$ 181	$ 163	11%
iPhone unit sales	2,315	—	NM

(a) During the third quarter of 2007, the Company revised the way it measures the Retail Segment's operating results to a manner that is generally consistent with the Company's other operating segments. Prior period results have been reclassified to reflect this change to the Retail Segment's operating results along with the corresponding offsets to the other operating segments. Further information regarding the Company's operating segments may be found in Notes to Condensed Consolidated Financial Statements at Note 7, "Segment Information and Geographic Data."

(b) Other Segments include Asia Pacific and FileMaker.

(c) Includes iMac, eMac, Mac mini, Mac Pro, Power Mac, and Xserve product lines.

(d) Includes MacBook, iBook, MacBook Pro, and PowerBook product lines.

(e) Consists of iTunes Store sales, iPod services, and Apple-branded and third-party iPod accessories.

(f) Derived from handset sales, carrier agreements, and Apple-branded and third-party iPhone accessories.

(g) Includes sales of Apple-branded and third-party displays, wireless connectivity and networking solutions, and other hardware accessories.

(h) Includes sales of Apple-branded operating system, application software, third-party software, AppleCare, and Internet services.

(i) Derived by dividing total Mac net sales by total Mac unit sales.

(j) Derived by dividing total iPod net sales by total iPod unit sales.

Source: Apple Company, 2007 4Q Form 10Q, hwww.apple.com/investor, 22.

Exhibit 3 Select Apple Product Releases

1976	Apple I
1977	Apple II
1980	Apple III
1983	Lisa
1984	Macintosh Graphical user interface (GUI)
1986	Macintosh Plus
1987	Macintosh II
1991	Macintosh Quadra PowerBook 100
1994	PowerMac 6100
1997	PowerBook G3
1998	iMac
1999	iBook
2001	iTunes iDVD iPod
2003	iLife suite iTunes 4 (online music store w/200,000 downloadable songs)
2004	iPod Mini eMac iPod (Click Wheel) iPod (U2 Special Edition) iPod Photo
2005	iPod Shuffle iPod nano iPod color iPod with video
2006	MacBook Mac mini
2007	Apple TV iPhone

Source: www.apple-history.com.

systems, but the Macintosh still ran exclusively on Mac OS, a system not available to other computers. By 1993, Apple's board of directors replaced Sculley as CEO. Apple moved through two CEOs over the next five years.

During this time, Apple partnered with IBM and Motorola to produce the PowerPC chip, which would run the company's new line of PowerMacs, allowing it to outperform computers powered by Intel microprocessors.[17] Despite this and Apple's attempts to reorganize, losses mounted in 1996 and 1997. In December 1996, Apple acquired NeXT, with the plan of using its technology as the basis for a new operating system. After being gone for more than a decade, Jobs returned to the company he had originally cofounded with Wozniak.

Jobs's Return

One of the first problems Steve Jobs moved to fix was the ongoing dispute between Apple and Microsoft over the Windows graphical user interface (GUI). Microsoft not only paid an undisclosed amount to Apple, but also made its Office 98 suite compatible with Macintoshes.[18] Jobs then proceeded to change the company's sales strategy in 1997 to encompass direct sales—both online and by phone. In a flurry of product releases, Apple introduced the new generation of PowerMacs, PowerBooks, and the highly anticipated iMac and iBook, which were less expensive computers aimed at the low-end computer market. After an entire year without showing a profit, the first quarter of 1998 began three years of profitable quarters for Apple.[19]

Jobs stated that he wanted to transform the company by making the Mac "the hub of [the consumers'] digital lifestyle." To do this, Apple introduced iLife in 2002, a software suite including applications such as iPhoto, iMovie, iTunes, and eventually the iPod. With the advent of Napster and peer-to-peer music sharing, Apple saw a way to capitalize on the emerging trend of cheap music downloads by creating a legal online music distribution network. iTunes would be the key to exploiting this market. Once downloaded by way of iTunes, music could then be transferred only to an iPod (due to encryption). With iTunes, Apple has quite possibly revolutionized the distribution of music and hopes to do the same with the distribution of movies on demand. Similar changes may be expected with the iPhone in the mobile or smartphone industry segments and with Apple TV in the mobile media and set-top box industry segments.

iTunes: Apple's Online Music Store

Apple ventured into the market of legal downloads with the introduction of its iTunes Music Store.[20] iTunes offers downloads at a specified price without requiring a subscription or monthly fees. Originally offered exclusively on Apple's own Mac, iTunes can now be installed on PCs as well. The idea behind iTunes was to provide a solution to the illegal pirating of music and software from rival sources such as Kazaa.

iTunes offers its users a selection of more than 6 million songs, with new songs continually added.[21] Titles are from just about every genre of music. Users can perform a search by type of music, artist name, or title of track or album. Each song available can be previewed without making a purchase. Purchasers have the option of purchasing an entire album or single songs. Each song is $0.99, and a complete album starts at $9.99. Downloads can be made not only to a Mac or PC, but also directly to an iPod. All new song additions are encoded in AAC format, which many say is superior to MP3, although iTunes does still carry the MP3 format on some of its older selections.

Once songs are downloaded, they are stored as a digital music library. As this collection grows, this list of songs can be arranged in many different ways. Songs can be arranged by personal rating, artist, or genre. This feature allows for a customizable playlist for playback or burning to a CD.

In addition iTunes offers a collection of more than 10,000 audiobooks ranging in price from $2.95 to $15.95, including many different language lessons. Also available are downloadable versions of public radio shows. Gift certificates are also available in different denominations and can be sent electronically through e-mail.

As previously mentioned, in its first week of existence, the number of downloads from iTunes surpassed the 1 million mark. This feat is amazing considering that at the time of iTunes' introduction, the download service was available only for the Mac. In addition, at that time, Mac users comprised less than 5 percent of U.S. computer users.[22] When iTunes became available for use on the PC, sales increased even more rapidly. iTunes PC downloads reached the 1 million mark in three days, less than half the time it took for the Mac version. But the success of iTunes is not measured in number of downloads sold per day or week, since after paying royalties, Apple makes only approximately 10 cents per song. iTunes is simply used as a means to boost the sale of iPods, iPhones, and Apple TVs, which generate a substantial profit per sale. For example, the iPod has been labeled "the profit machine" for Apple, as it tends to produce a 50 percent profit margin, per unit, before marketing and distribution costs.[23]

iTunes, iPod, iPhone, and Apple TV

iPod

For music lovers, the iPod is the greatest invention since the Walkman. With up to 160 GB of storage, it allows users to carry up to 40,000 songs or 200 hours of video wherever they go.[24] There are currently four different iPod styles: the iPod shuffle, iPod classic, iPod nano, and iPod touch. iPod owners can purchase accessories such as the armband, the radio remote, and the universal dock and remote to make using the iPod even more enjoyable. In 2007, with more than 100 million products sold, the closest competitor to Apple's iPod had only 8 percent of the market share, leaving Apple with the vast majority. While others are seeking to simply duplicate the complementary and innovative relationships between iPod and iTunes, Apple continues to innovate with new products such as the iPhone and Apple TV.[25] (See Exhibit 4 for more details about the iPod products.)

iPhone

In first-quarter 2007, Apple launched its "revolutionary" product, the iPhone. The iPhone combines three concepts popular with consumers: a mobile phone, a widescreen iPod, and an Internet communication device. The iPhone brags "an entirely new user interface based on a large multi-touch display and pioneering software," which users can control with just their fingers.[26] The iPhone's default Internet browser will be Apple's own Safari,** but it is open to other software as well.[27] The iPhone allows for 8 hours of talk time, 24 hours of audio playback time, and 10 days of standby time.[28] Apple sold 1 million iPhones less than three months after this product was available to consumers. Apple expects this trend to continue during 2008 and to reach sales of 10 million iPhones, stealing 1 percent of the mobile phone market share.[29]

Apple TV

In addition to the iPhone, Apple also introduced the Apple TV in 2007. With this product, Apple intends to revolutionize the Internet video industry, as it did with the music download industry. Users can download movies and TV shows via the iTunes online service or via YouTube as well as view digital photos and home videos.[30] Some negative hype claims that the Apple TV will be a flop just like the Apple III and the Power Mac

---

** Safari is Apple's Internet browser that was introduced in 2003. It is part of Apple's strategy to gain more market share by having both hardware and software products. Apple suggests that Safari is the fastest browser available. It blocks pop-up advertising and has a built-in text reader that reads the site pages aloud. In addition to being the default browser for the iPhone, it is the default browser for the iPod Touch and the Mac computer. Safari's user share was estimated to be 6 percent in early 2008. (P. Festa, 2003, Welcome to the browser jungle, Safari, CNET News, www.news.com, January 7; 2008, Wikipedia, http://en.wikipedia.org.)

Cube. Some of the features that made the first edition unpopular include the following:

- Users are not able to download a movie from iTunes directly to their TV; they have to download it to their PC first.
- It requires an HDTV, but the movies that can be downloaded are of such low resolution that the picture looks fuzzy and old-fashioned.
- It has no DVD drive.

Steve Jobs announced at the Macworld Conference & Expo in January 2008 that the upgraded version of Apple TV will allow owners to order movies directly from the TV rather than having to download to the PC.[31] Also, critics do compliment the fact that the Apple TV plays a slideshow of digital photos.[32]

The price to rent a movie using Apple TV is $2.99 for library titles, $3.99 for new releases, and $1 extra to view the movie in high definition.[33]

One key component that must be in place to have good media content for the three products mentioned is the relationship that Apple has with each of its media and phone service suppliers.

Service Suppliers: iTunes, Apple TV, and iPhone

iTunes

iTunes has agreements with all five major record labels (BMG, EMI, Sony Music Entertainment, Universal, and Warner Bros.) as well as more than 200 independent labels. These agreements allow iTunes to sell the music owned by these labels and pay the record label each time a song is downloaded. This deal is considered a reseller agreement, meaning that Apple is not licensing content from these labels, but rather buying it wholesale and reselling it to consumers.[34] Apple gets to keep its share, while the portion the label receives must be divided among many parties including artists, producers, and publishers. Labels earn approximately 70 cents per song sold on iTunes. This figure may seem small, but it is still greater than losing money to the millions of illegal downloads that nearly crippled the music industry.

The revenues for record label companies have been dropping in the past year due to tough market conditions, and Apple has introduced a strategy that may help increase revenues by at least a small percentage. It has already contracted with EMI to make its entire catalog available to iTunes' users in two formats, the traditional download option, which includes the Fairplay digital rights management (DRM) software and DRM-free versions. The DRM software limits the number of times a song can be copied, which decreases the quality of the song. The DRM-free versions would deliver greater quality music but would require a higher price tag. iTunes will start the DRM-free songs at $1.29 per song versus the traditional $0.99 per song. Other record labels may enter into the same agreement with Apple depending on how successful this strategy is with EMI.[35]

NBC recently cancelled its agreement with Apple to provide its TV shows on iTunes due to pricing disputes. Walt Disney Studios previously offered its new releases, and Paramount, Metro-Goldwyn-Mayer (MGM), and Lionsgate allowed older library titles to be purchased on iTunes, but the supplier agreements have changed with the launch of Apple TV.[36]

Apple TV

Apple did not have an easy time finalizing with movie studios contracts that will allow Apple to sell movies on iTunes for use on the iPod and Apple TV. Not only were the studios concerned about losing significant revenues from the sales of DVDs and Blu-ray discs, but some studios urged Apple to require a watermark on digital video for it to play on its devices. Their concern is heightened given the pirating experienced in the music download business. One movie-studio executive said, "Our position is, if you want our content, you have to protect our business." Apple, however, responded that it trusts its consumers not to play pirated movies.[37]

The limited number of movie downloads available on iTunes would significantly diminish the success of Apple TV. Thus, Apple's CEO was persistent in his negotiations with the movie studios. Jobs announced at the Macworld Expo in 2008 that Apple had reached agreement with each of the following major studios: Twentieth Century Fox, The Walt Disney Studios, Warner Bros., Paramount, Sony Pictures Entertainment, MGM, Lionsgate, and New Line Cinema.[38] Despite NBC's issues with Apple concerning TV shows, Universal Pictures (owned by NBC and General Electric) has agreed to allow Apple to rent its movies via iTunes.

The supplier agreement between Apple and the movie studios is that new movies will not be available for rent until 30 days after the DVD is distributed. Within a 24-hour period, customers will be able to watch a film as many times as they like once the movie is started. Movies that are downloaded but not started will not be available for viewing after 30 days.[39]

iPhone

Cingular was selected as the exclusive wireless carrier for the iPhone in the United States because, according to Steve Jobs, Cingular is the best and most popular carrier in the United States.[40] Together these companies

Exhibit 4 iPod Product Descriptions

	iPod shuffle		iPod nano		iPod classic		iPod touch	
Capacity[1]	1GB	Up to 240 songs	4GB	Up to 1,000 songs, up to 3,500 photos, up to 4 hours of video, or some of each	80GB	Up to 20,000 songs, up to 25,000 photos, up to 100 hours of video, or some of each	8GB	Up to 1,750 songs, up to 10,000 photos, up to 10 hours of video, or some of each
	2GB	Up to 500 songs	8GB	Up to 2,000 songs, up to 7,000 photos, up to 8 hours of video, or some of each	160GB	Up to 40,000 songs, up to 25,000 photos, up to 200 hours of video, or some of each	16GB	Up to 3,500 songs, up to 20,000 photos, up to 20 hours of video, or some of each
							32GB	Up to 7,000 songs, up to 25,000 photos, up to 40 hours of video, or some of each
Price	1GB 2GB	$49 $69	4GB 8GB	$149 $199	80GB 160GB	$249 $349	8GB 16GB 32GB	$299 $399 $499
Color display			2-inch		2.5-inch		3.5-inch Multi-Touch	
Wireless data[2]							Wi-Fi (802.11b/g)	
Battery life[3]	Up to 2 hours of audio		Up to 24 hours of audio Up to 5 hours of video		Up to 40 hours of audio Up to 7 hours of video		Up to 22 hours of audio Up to 5 hours of video	

1. 1 GB = 1 billion bytes; actual formatted capacity is less. Music capacity is based on 4 minutes per song and 128-Kpbs AAC encoding; photo capacity is based on iPod-viewable photos transferred from iTunes; video capacity is based on H.264 1.5-Mbps video at 640-by-480 resolution combined with 128-Kbps audio; actual capacity varies by content.

2. Internet access is required; broadband is recommended; fees may apply.

3. Testing was conducted by Apple in August 2007 using preproduction hardware and software. For audio playback, the playlist contained 358 unique audio tracks consisting of content imported from CDs using iTunes (128-Kbps AAC) and content purchased from the iTunes Store (128-Kbps AAC); all settings were default except that Ask to Join Networks was turned off for iPod touch. For video playback, video content was purchased from the iTunes Store; all settings were default except that Ask to Join Networks and Auto-Brightness were turned off for iPod touch. Battery tests are conducted with specific iPod units; actual results may vary. Rechargeable batteries have a limited number of charge cycles and may eventually need to be replaced (see www.apple.com/support/ipod/service/battery). Battery life and number of charge cycles vary by use and settings. See www.apple.com/batteries for more information.

Source: www.apple.com/ipod/whichipod.

developed the Visual Voicemail feature that allows users to listen to the voicemails they prefer rather than having to listen to all messages in succession. Since the agreement was made between Cingular and Apple, Cingular was acquired by AT&T. iPhone owners are required to sign a two-year service agreement with AT&T. AT&T offers four different plans, with monthly fees ranging from $59.99 to $119.99. All plans include the visual voicemail, unlimited access to the Internet, and roll-over minutes.[41]

Hardware

Concerning its hardware suppliers, Apple is usually not forthcoming with this information. However, a disassembled iPhone reveals that the microprocessor chip is supplied by Samsung; Philips, Texas Instruments, and Linear Technology all play a role in providing the batteries, and many other companies provide chips that are central to the camera, display, and motion sensor.[42]

Many companies have expressed frustration in working with Apple because Steve Jobs is very clear on his vision for his products and can tend to be controlling. Maintaining good supplier relationships and keeping enough control to provide the quality of products expected of Apple is a balance that Apple will have to find in order to stay ahead of its competitors.

Competitors

iTunes

Since the October 2003 launch of iTunes.com for Windows, Apple has faced a multitude of competitors. During the late 1990s, the emergence of music sharing came about with Napster, a freeware program offering free downloads using peer-to-peer transfers. Peer-to-peer transfers allow users to connect directly with other users without the need for a central point of management.[43] However, in recent years due to legal proceedings, Napster and all other competitors have become a subscription service similar to iTunes.

Napster. In May 1999, 19-year-old Shawn Fanning created Napster while studying at Northeastern University. The name Napster came from the Internet "handle" he had used as a programmer. He created a type of software that allowed music fans anywhere to "share" MP3s in one forum. During the first year of service, Napster was obtaining more than 250,000 new users a week while maintaining a free service.[44] This software creation led to the ever-growing controversy of the availability of MP3s on the Internet. Music sharing exploded in the late 1990s, and Napster's servers were overloaded with millions of requests a day for media downloads. Music artists considered this new "sharing" forum to be a continuous copyright violation. Fanning soon became the target of their animosity and became one of the most disliked people in the music industry.

During 2000, Napster was in and out of court and was finally slated to shut down on July 26, 2000. The decision was reversed two days later on July 28, 2000.[45] In 2001, Konrad Hilbers, a 38-year-old German, became

CEO of the rapidly declining music file-sharing site. In June 2001, Napster had more than 26 million users, but growth was declining fast, going from 6.3 billion to 2.2 billion minutes used a day. On March 7, 2002, Napster closed its servers while opting to implement a fee-based service to comply with the federal judge's decision. On June 3, 2002, Napster filed for Chapter 11 bankruptcy in an effort to secure court-ordered protection from creditors. This move was part of the overall financial restructuring strategy of Bertelsmann AG, which was proceeding with its takeover of the once popular file-sharing system. By July 2003, Roxio, Inc., had acquired Napster and was planning a Napster 2.0 launch for December 2003. Napster 2.0 is a successful, legal fee-based service.[46]

Through restructuring and quality legal representation, Napster finally has a legal base that is expected to stand. Currently, Napster 4.0 is online with content agreements from five major record labels and hundreds of independent labels; therefore, its library is made up of more than 5 million songs. Members have unlimited access to the library for $12.95 per month. Napster 4.0 now accommodates the use of its software for Mac and Linux users.

Kazaa. Sharman Networks Limited was founded in January 2002 as a private limited company. Sharman Networks develops and markets world-class Internet applications. Kazaa Media Desktop and Kazaa Plus are products of Sharman Networks. Sharman Networks earns revenue by soliciting companies to advertise on its software. Users that prefer ad-free use of the software can purchase an upgrade, Kazaa Plus for $29.95. This upgrade will also allow for greater search capabilities and more download sources.[47]

Being Australian-based, the company avoided legal intervention in allowing the file sharing, but in 2005, the Federal Court of Australia ruled that Kazaa had knowingly allowed users to illegally download copyrighted songs. The company was charged to change its software to prohibit copyrighted music or videos from being shared.[48] Kazaa owners agreed to pay the four major record labels (Universal Music, Sony BMG, EMI, and Warner Music) $100 million.[49]

Kazaa Media Desktop is a program rumored to be littered with spyware and ad-based programs that "infect" consumer systems; thus many users have become wary of accessing Kazaa's site.[50]

RealNetworks, Inc. RealNetworks, through its RealPlayer Music Store, sought a price war with Apple by dropping the price to $0.49 per song and $4.99 per album compared to Apple's price of $0.99 and $9.99, respectively. Analysts indicated that RealNetworks was pricing below the cost of purchasing the music from the record companies, and eventually it did increase its price to $0.99 per song; however, it still offers, select songs for $0.49 a track. As part of its battle to reduce Apple's market share, RealNetworks launched technology called Harmony, which allows RealNetworks users to translate songs purchased from RealPlayer Music Store into a format that can be played on an iPod. It also allows RealNetworks music to be played on Microsoft formats.[51] RealPlayer is a RealNetworks medium through which it competes in the video-on-demand market. Video can be downloaded from the Web to an iPod, PC, CD, and DVD. RealPlayer customers can subscribe to its SuperPass membership, which combines the benefits of RealPlayer and the RealPlayer Music Store. The $14.99 monthly fee provides subscribers with $10.00 worth of music downloads and full-length movies per month.

Sony. Sony started a music download service called Connect in the spring of 2004. Despite its efforts to compete in the music downloading market, it did not realize significant success; thus, Connect closed at the end of March 2008.[52] Instead, Sony is focusing its attention on gaining market share in the video download segment.[53]

Virgin Media. Virgin offers more than 15,000 record labels in addition to computer games and videos and Blockbuster movies. Similar to iTunes, customers can listen to a 30-second sample before purchase and download exclusive tracks through Virgin's V2 music label before the tracks are released to the general public.[54]

Wal-Mart. Wal-Mart launched its own online music store. It is currently the number-one music retailer in the nation, followed by iTunes.[55] Initially Wal-Mart offered music in MP3 format for $0.88 per song, $0.11 cheaper than Apple, but currently it offers songs for $0.94 and albums starting at $7.88.[56]

Yahoo! Music Unlimited. Subscribers to Yahoo! Music Jukebox have access to more than 2 million songs. Users can listen to 150 LAUNCHcast radio stations or download songs to any PC. After paying a monthly $6.00 fee, subscribers pay only $0.79 per song. Nonsubscribers can also download songs for $0.99 each.[57] At this time, Yahoo! offers only music on its site; video and TV shows are not available.

Apple TV

Amazon Unbox. The Amazon Unbox was introduced in 2006. Users download films or TV shows to the Amazon Unbox Player or on Windows Media Player. In addition, Amazon established a partnership with TiVo in 2007 that allows consumers to purchase movies or TV shows through Amazon's Unbox and send it to the TiVo machine to view. Amazon's service is similar to its competitors in that once a movie or show is downloaded, it must be viewed within 30 days and once it is started, it must be viewed within 24 hours. Amazon also has agreements with most of the major movie studios such as Paramount Pictures, Universal Studios, Warner Bros., CBS, and Fox.[58] NBC contracted with Amazon to offer its TV shows for download after NBC cancelled its agreement with Apple for the iTunes service.[59]

CinemaNow. This company seemed to have been ahead of the game, entering the video download market in 1999. It was the first to offer pay-per-view movies from the major Hollywood studios, the first to offer Download-to-Own services, and the first distributor of Burn-to-DVD movies. It is headquartered in Marina Del Rey, California, and its library consists of more than 10,000 movie titles, television programs, music concerts, and shorts. It has enabled users to download movies to the Microsoft Xbox 360 video game console as part of its strategy of providing multiple platforms on which to download movies. It has recently been creating joint ventures to differentiate itself in the industry. It originated as a distributor of videos via the Internet and has progressed most recently to wireless Internet "infotainment," a new feature available in select new car models. Its agreement with USTelematics, Inc. will allow it to offer a package of features and functions, including the creation of a mobile Wi-Fi Internet hotspot to enable online computer usage in the car, as well as DVD, movies, TV, Xbox, and other computer games.[60]

Disney. Disney, through an agreement made with Microsoft in 2007, offers movie download service for use on the Xbox 360. This service is one of the few that offers movies in high-definition format. Consumers have access to the Walt Disney Studios library, including titles from Walt Disney Pictures, Touchstone Pictures, Hollywood Pictures, and Miramax Films.[61]

HP. HP announced at the beginning of 2008 that it had reached an agreement with Sony Pictures Home Entertainment (SPHE) to deliver movies on demand. HP's manufactured-on-demand service will produce a DVD of any movie, TV show, or other content offered through SPHE. HP believes this service will aid movie studios in trying to match supply and demand for movies it sells on DVD. The current list of items available for order are classic TV shows never released on DVD, foreign movies, specialty cable programming, independent movies, specialty genres such as religion and education, and recently broadcast TV shows.[62]

Movielink. Recently acquired by Blockbuster, Movielink began in 2002 and was owned by five of the top movie studios: Universal Studios, Paramount Pictures, Sony Pictures, MGM, and Warner Bros. It operates as a subsidiary of Blockbuster and offers 3,300 movie titles.[63] Consumers who purchase a movie from Movielink must view it using a computer, a TV connected to a computer, or an Xbox 360 game console or via a set-top box company.

Netflix. Like many of its competitors, Netflix has teamed up with a technology company, LG, to become a stronger player in the video-on-demand market. In January 2008, Netflix announced that through LG's set-top box, customers can stream movies directly on their TVs. The device is expected to be available in the second half of 2008.[64] In the meantime, Netflix subscribers can stream to their PC an unlimited number of movies per month, unconstrained by hourly limits, for a monthly fee with plans starting at $8.99 per month. The on-demand library offers viewers the option of 6,000 titles of movies and TV shows.[65]

Sony. In the United Kingdom and Ireland, Sony offers video-on-demand service through its PlayStation Portable device. It has partnered with British Sky Broadcasting to provide the movies.[66] It also offers this service in Japan, but it is currently not available in the United States.

Vudu. Vudu, headquartered in Santa Clara, California, entered the video-on-demand market in April 2007.[67] Vudu's black box connects to the TV and Internet, and the built-in hard drive gives users the option of viewing 5,000 movie titles instantly. The box costs $400. The service has no monthly service charge, but a rental costs $2.00 to $4.00 per movie. As such, Vudu claims to be the cure-all for the movie rental business; it saves customers from running back and forth from the video store or waiting for the movie to come in the mail from Netflix or Blockbuster; it offers more movie titles than video-on-demand providers; and it is more functional than Internet download services because it does not require a PC. Similar to Vudu's competitors, once a movie is downloaded, it must be viewed within 24 hours.

Vudu offers movies from all major Hollywood studios. But since it is subject to the distribution windows, the time frame in which select movies are available may not match consumer demand. Only some movies have previews, and some are available only for purchase and not for rent.[68]

Wal-Mart. In December 2006, Wal-Mart entered the movie download segment of the entertainment industry, but only a year later it exited the business because it had not caught on with consumers. Raul Vasquez, Wal-Mart's CEO for walmart.com, stated that the download service was an experiment. "We want to understand what the customers want. And I think what we learned is that the initial experience of buying and downloading content needs to be better. We thought it was going to be easier for the customer to understand."

iPhone

Motorola. Motorola has been a long-time leader in mobile phone sales in the United States. However, since Apple's iPhone and Research In Motion's (RIM) Blackberry have been gaining ground, the leader is falling hard and fast. Motorola's RAZR phone has lost its popularity, and its smartphone made in partnership with Microsoft, the Motorola Q, has not performed as expected. Motorola announced in January 2008 that it is seeking alternatives for its handset business, most likely a divestiture.[69]

Palm. Despite the fact that Palm sold 689,000 Treos in the first quarter of 2007, a 21 percent increase from the previous year, Palm is struggling to remain a major player in the smartphone market amid the success of the Blackberry and the iPhone. The competition with the iPhone is especially fierce since AT&T is the phone service provider for both products. Palm introduced its Centro in October 2007 as a low-cost strategy to increase market share. Although the Centro sells for $99, it does not have all of the features of the iPhone. But cost-conscious consumers may choose it over the iPhone given the iPhone's $399 price tag.[70]

Research In Motion. The Blackberry created by Research In Motion (RIM) has been a popular product among corporate consumers who mainly needed e-mail service and a calendar. To stay in the competitive game, however, RIM has been adding features to make its product more appealing to users who want the fun features in addition to the features that aid in their work. Blackberrys now have cameras and can play music. There is a rumor that RIM is going to introduce a Blackberry 9000, which will have a touch-sensitive screen, making it similar to the iPhone.[71] Conversely, Apple has recently released tools that make its iPhone more corporate-user friendly, and it will now be compatible with Microsoft's Exchange platform.[72]

Exhibit 5 illustrates a comparison of the product features for the iPhone relative to its key competitors.

Exhibit 5 iPhone properties and its competitors

Apple iPhone - $499 to $599

- N/A
- **Bluetooth Wireless Technology v2.0 + EDR**
- N/A but most likely
- **Full QWERTY Soft Keyboard**
- N/A
- N/A
- **iSynch via Bluetooth or Wi-Fi Mac or PC**
- **Full Color Display 3.5" 320 x 480 Pixels at 160 ppi**
- **Multi Touch Screen**
- **Speakerphone**
- **Widgets**
- N/A
- N/A
- N/A
- **Predictive Text Entry with corrector**
- **Advanced Sensors for Rotation Detection**

Messaging & Internet Features
- **Safari Full Rich HTML Browser**
- N/A
- **SMS**
- **POP3/IMAP Push Email services**
- **Google Maps Built in**
- **Widgets**
- **Visual Voice Mail**
- N/A

Technical Specifications
- **OSX**
- **Data Download Speed - EDGE + WiFi (802.11 b/g)**
- **GSM Quad Band 850, 900, 1800, 1900**
- **Built-in Memory - 4GB or 8GB Available**
- None
- Dimension - 115 x 61 x 11.6mm
- Weight - 4.8 oz

Battery Life
- **Up to 300 Minutes Talk/Video/Browsing**
- N/A
- **Up to 16H Audio Playback**
- No

Moto Q - $499

- FM Radio with Software Sold Separately
- Bluetooth Wireless Technology v1.2
- Video Capture/Camcorder QCIF-quality
- QWERTY Keyboard Backlit with thumbwheel
- **Infrared Port**
- **Use Phone as Modem via USB Cable, Bluetooth, or IR**
- PC Synch via Cable: Infrared or Bluetooth: Active Sync
- Color Display 320 x 240 Pixels, 65K Colors, QVGATFT
- No
- **Speakerphone**
- To-Do List, Alarm, Calculator, Calendar, etc.
- **Voice Memo**
- Vibrate
- **Voice recognition**
- N/A
- No

Messaging & Internet Features
- Pocket Internet Explorer HTML
- MMS
- **SMS**
- Pocket Outlook Supports POP, IMAP, APOP, ESMTP
- No
- No
- No
- IM

Technical Specifications
- Windows Mobile 5.0 + BREW
- **Data Download Speed - EV-DO and 1xRTT**
- **GSM Quad Band 850, 900, 1800, 1900**
- Built-in Memory - 64 MB Available
- **SecureDigital (SD) Card Format Compatible Slot**
- Dimension - 116 x 63 x 11.5mm
- Weight - 6.40 oz

Battery Life
- Talk Time - Up to 240 Minutes
- Standby Time - Up to 192 Hours
- N/A
- **Removable**

BlackBerry Pearl - $299

- No
- **Bluetooth Wireless Technology v2.0**
- N/A
- QWERTY Keyboard
- No
- **Use This Phone as a Modem**
- PC Synchronization
- Color Display 240 x 260 Pixels, 65K Colors
- No
- **Speakerphone**
- To-Do List, Alarm, Calculator, Calendar, etc.
- N/A
- Vibrate
- **Voice-activated Dialing**
- **Predictive Text Entry**
- No

Messaging & Internet Features
- **Full HTML Web Browser**
- MMS
- **SMS**
- **Push Email POP3, IMAP, SMTP**
- No
- No
- No
- IM

Technical Specifications
- BlackBerry OS with Intel XScale Processor + Java
- Data Download Speed - EDGE
- **GSM Quad Band 850, 900, 1800, 1900**
- Built-in Memory - 64 MB Plus Online Photo
- **MicroSD Card Format Compatible Slot**
- **Dimension - 107 x 50 x 14.5mm**
- **Weight - 3.2 oz**

Battery Life
- Talk Time - Up to 210 Minutes
- Standby Time - Up to 360 Hours
- N/A
- **Removable**

Palm Treo 750 - $649

- FM Radio with Software Sold Separately
- Bluetooth Wireless Technology v1.2
- Video Capture/Camcorder QCIF
- QWERTY Keyboard Backlit
- **Infrared Port**
- **Use Phone as Modem via USB Cable, Bluetooth, or IR**
- PC Synch via Cable: Infrared or Bluetooth: Active Sync
- Color Display 320 x 320 Pixels, 65K Colors, TFT
- **Touch Screen**
- **Speakerphone**
- To-Do List, Alarm, Calculator, Calendar, etc.
- **Voice Memo**
- Vibrate
- No
- No
- No

Messaging & Internet Features
- Blazer Browser Supports
- MMS
- **SMS**
- Pocket Outlook Supports POP, IMAR, APOP, ESMTP
- No
- No
- No
- IM

Technical Specifications
- Palm OS 5.4 with Intel 312 Mhz XScale Processor
- Data Download Speed - EV-DO and 1xRTT
- **GSM Quad Band 850, 900, 1800, 1900**
- Built-in Memory - 123 MB Available
- **SecureDigital (SD) Card Format Compatible Slot**
- Dimension - 111.8 x 58.4 x 20.3mm
- Weight - 6.40 oz

Battery Life
- Talk Time - Up to 282 Minutes
- Standby Time - Up to 300 Hours
- N/A
- **Removable**

iPod

Some of the iPod's major competitors include Rio Karma, Dell Digital Jukebox DJ, Samsung Napster YP-910GS, and the Gateway Jukebox Player DMP-X20 (see Exhibit 6).[73] Some of the differences from the iPod include a longer battery life, such as a 16-hour battery life for the Dell MP3 player. The weight also varies from one competitor to the next, ranging from 7.7 ounces to 5.5 ounces. (For a detailed list of the major competitors' specifications, see Exhibit 7.)

The Microsoft Zune premiered in the fall of 2006. Due to its lack of tremendous success, in the fall of 2007, Microsoft exerted great energy in combating the success of the iPod with its improved Zune. The Zune offers options of 4, 8, or 80 gigabytes of storage with prices ranging from $150 to $300. The newest edition of the Zune is smaller, has a better viewing screen, and allows users to wirelessly synchronize the gadget with the music on their computers. It also includes a touch-sensitive pad that allows users to navigate through songs with more precise control than the iPod, according to Microsoft executives.[74] But critics suggest that the Zune does not pose a significant threat to the iPod because it does not offer any significant technological breakthroughs.[75] Only 1.2 million Zunes sold during 2007 while Apple sold more than 41 million iPods. Apple's success can likely be attributed to its marketing competency.

Marketing

Up until this point, Apple's marketing endeavors have earned it awards, product sales, and a devoted base of customers, both new and old. In 2003, Apple was awarded *Advertising Age's* Marketer of the Year for its upbeat, original, and (most importantly) memorable advertisements for both its iPod and iTunes.[76] Apple has been hailed as one of the best marketers by many different sources and has had a reputation over the years of being a brand that can gain customers through its well-thought-out and carefully executed marketing strategies.

Marketing has been one of Apple's strengths; however, staying on top of the game will become more difficult as Apple develops a broader range of products and markets them to the mainstream customer rather than just the "tech-savvy fanatics" in fields such as education and design.[77] "The customer base is now more diverse, including students and mainstream consumers, and it's harder to satisfy as a whole," says Lopo L. Rego, a marketing professor at the University of Iowa.[78] Business leaders today have a daunting job in balancing shareholder demands and running a successful company. Businesses want to market new products aggressively to try and ensure their products' success. Apple heavily promoted the iPhone when it was introduced in July 2007. Customer and investor expectations, due to Apple's reputation, boosted the stock price. But when customers don't believe that the marketing promises have been delivered, stock price, brand equity, and investor confidence are significantly affected.[79] Apple's success lies in a carefully thought-out plan.

Marketing Plan

A marketing plan begins with design of the product.[80] In an industry of low profit margins and cost cutting, Apple takes a different approach to the design of its products. While competitors are doing everything they can to keep costs down, Apple does what it can to make its product different. In 2007, for the third year in a row, Apple was named as the Most Innovative Company by *BusinessWeek*.[81] Its CEO, Steve Jobs is "a legend for his design sense."[82] Even employees of one of Apple's biggest competitors, Microsoft, have recognized Apple's dominance in the design of eye-catching products. The employees created a mock promotion for the iPod had it been created by Microsoft and circulated it on YouTube.[83]

Steve Jobs is essential to the public relations and promotional aspect of Apple, especially with the iPod.[84] He maintains relationships with the media and has been called the "public face and champion of the brand."[85] He is an expert when it comes to talking with the press, maintaining relationships with magazine editors, and continually creating new relationships.[86] Because of his dynamic, high-energy personality, he usually holds a new idea that he is energetic about and is always ready and willing to share the idea to gain exposure.

Jobs also takes action in response to customer feedback to show that he is listening and concerned. For example, three months after the iPhone was available in stores, Apple cut the price of this product by one-third. This was a strategic move to increase demand and meet sales goals; it was not the result of a faulty product. Consumers who had purchased the iPhone in the first three months for the higher price expressed great dissatisfaction. Jobs responded by promising these consumers a $100 Apple store credit.[87]

A more recent advantage in Apple's marketing strategy is its retail stores. Apple has opened more than 200 retail stores located worldwide. At the time that Apple opened its first retail store in 2001, analysts predicted that Apple would report huge losses and shut the store within two years. At the time, no computer manufacturer had proved profitable in running its own branded store.[88] However, Apple's retail stores contributed an estimated $200 million, 15 to 16 percent of its profits during the past two years (see Exhibit 8).[89] Apple's philosophy behind the stores is brand exposure. Apple believes that the more people can touch an Apple product

Exhibit 6 Products of Competitors to iPod

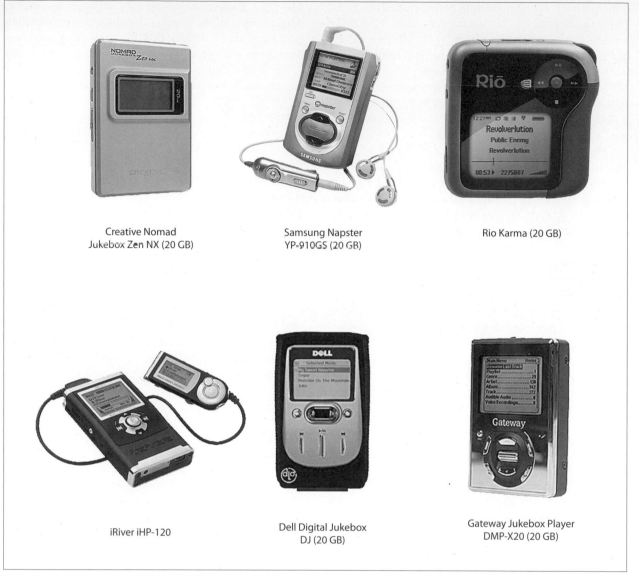

Creative Nomad
Jukebox Zen NX (20 GB)

Samsung Napster
YP-910GS (20 GB)

Rio Karma (20 GB)

iRiver iHP-120

Dell Digital Jukebox
DJ (20 GB)

Gateway Jukebox Player
DMP-X20 (20 GB)

Source: http://reviews.cnet.com/4520-6497-5093864.html.

and see what it can do with their own eyes, the greater the potential market share.[90] In addition, the stores provide free group workshops, personal training, and personal assistance for Apple customers.[91]

Apple offers a One-to-One program for an annual fee of $99; subscribers can attend a tutorial session with an Apple expert for an hour once a week for one year. Apple customers can also consult with the staff at the "Genius Bar" by appointment. The Genius Bar is where Apple product users meet face-to-face with Apple's "geniuses" for answers to technical questions and for problem troubleshooting. In addition, customers wanting to purchase a new computer or other equipment can schedule an appointment with a shopping assistant, who helps ensure that the customer selects the right equipment for his or her needs. Apple has apparently struck a chord with customers because its staff conducts more than 50,000 training sessions per week.[92] "Apple has become the new gathering place," said Steven Addis, chief executive of Addis Creson, a brand strategy and design firm in Berkeley. "You can't help but get caught up with it when you first walk in."[93]

As so eloquently stated in a *USA Today* article, "Apple's arsenal of attention-getting tools holds lessons for any company: design cool, innovative products. Have

Exhibit 7 Details of Products of Competitors to iPod

Basic Specs	Creative Nomad Jukebox Zen NX (20 GB)	Samsung Napster YP-910GS (20 GB)	Rio Karma (20 GB)	iRiver iHP-120	Dell Digital Jukebox DJ (20 GB)	Gateway Jukebox Player Product DMP-X20 (20 GB)
Product type	Digital player	Digital player / recorder / radio	Digital player	Digital player / voice recorder / radio	Digital player / voice recorder	Digital player / voice recorder / radio
PC interface(s) supported	Hi-Speed USB	Hi-Speed USB	Hi-Speed USB	Hi-Speed USB	Hi-Speed USB	Hi-Speed USB
Flash memory installed	8 MB	Info unavailable	Info unavailable	Info unavailable	Info unavailable	Info unavailable
Storage capacity	20 GB	20 GB	20 GB	20 GB	20 GB	20 GB
Digital formats supported	MP3	MP3	MP3	MP3	MP3	MP3
Weight	7.2 oz	6 oz	5.5 oz	5.6 oz	7.6 oz	7.7 oz
Resolution	132 × 64	Info unavailable	160 × 128	Info unavailable	160 × 104	160 × 128
Battery technology	Lithium ion	Lithium polymer	Lithium ion	Lithium polymer	Lithium ion	Lithium ion
Mfr estimated battery life	14 hour(s)	10 hour(s)	15 hour(s)	16 hour(s)	16 hour(s)	10 hour(s)
Software included	Creative MediaSource	Drivers & Utilities	Drivers & Utilities	Drivers & Utilities	Drivers & Utilities	Drivers & Utilities

Source: http://reviews.cnet.com/4520-6497-5093864.html.

a streamlined product line. Invest in memorable ads. Work your customer base to make customers feel special and create word-of-mouth agents. Most important: keep the world and media surprised, to generate gobs of attention."[94]

Finally, Apple has garnered major success for iPod and iTunes by way of strategic partnerships with other well-known brands. Apple has created marketing agreements with Volkswagen of America, Burton Snowboards, Nike, and Starbucks. By affiliating itself with different brands, Apple gains consumer confidence as well as exposure through marketing partner advertisements.

Strategic Agreements
All of the strategic agreements that are currently known by the public are agreements related to the iPod. It remains to be seen what alliances or joint ventures Apple enters in order to create awareness for the iPhone and Apple TV.

Volkswagen. In early 2003, Volkswagen of America (VW) offered a free iPod to customers who purchased a 2003 hardtop Beetle 10. The ad campaign was aptly named "Pods Unite."[95] The deal brought iPod enthusiasts (and people who just wanted to learn more about the iPod) into the Volkswagen stores, and both products benefited from the advertisement. For three months, iPods were shown in Volkswagen showrooms.[96] Also, the Volkswagen sold iPod connectivity wiring and a cradle for the iPod to be used in the new VW Beetle.[97] Because both brands are known for unique design, it is likely that the promotion brought in consumers who highly value the design aspect of a product, whether it is a car or a digital music player.

Exhibit 8 Retail Sales as a Contribution to Overall Apple Revenue

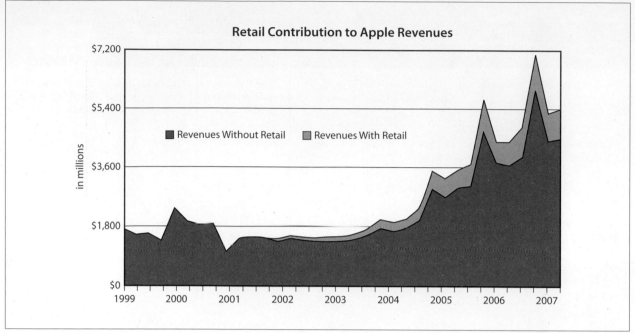

Source: 2007, Retail Stores' Importance Highlighted, http://ifoapplestore.com, August 17.

In the fall of 2007, rumors came out that Apple and VW were in discussions about furthering their relationship to create an iCar. This car would feature products that Steve Jobs fashioned. No details have been specified by either company's leaders.[98]

Burton Snowboards. In January 2004, Burton released a snowboarding/snow-skiing jacket made especially for use with the iPod (Exhibit 9). The jacket has a built-in iPod control electronic system on the sleeve of the jacket so that the wearer can operate the iPod without removing gloves, digging in pockets, or fumbling with zippers.[99] The iPod rests in a protected chest pocket in the inner lining of the jacket. With this jacket, Apple places a product into the hands of those who use iPods and creates exposure for the iPod by way of young snowboarders and skiers showing off and wearing the special jacket.

Nike. Nike and Apple have teamed up to create a smart running shoe. When runners combine a pair of Nike athletic shoes, an iPod nano, and the iPod Sport Kit, they are able to track their run in real time, with time, distance, pace, and calories burned displayed on the iPod. The iPod Sport Kit became available in 2006. Users' playlists can be selected based on the desired workout. If runners need a sudden burst of energy, they can press the Power Song button. An additional feature is the voice feedback that tells runners when they reach a personal best, whether it is in regard to pace, distance, time, or calories burned.[100] The personal data can be uploaded to Nike's Web site, and runners can compete virtually against one another.[101] The most recent partnership between Nike and Apple will shift to the gym. Teaming up with gym equipment makers and 24-Hour Fitness and Virgin Athletic Clubs, Apple and Nike will allow club members to plug their iPod nanos into the cardio equipment to track workouts, upload the information to Nike's Web site, and set goals based on personal history or to compete with others tracked on the Web site.[102]

Starbucks. In September 2007, Starbucks and Apple announced a joint venture that allows Starbucks customers to access (at no cost) the iTunes Wi-Fi Music store at more than 600 participating Starbucks locations. Customers can browse, search, and preview all songs available on the iTunes store, including the "Now Playing" service, which displays the name of the song playing at that moment in Starbucks. "Getting free access to the iTunes Wi-Fi Music Store and the 'Now Playing' service at Starbucks is a great way for customers to discover new music," said Steve Jobs.[103] If customers have to leave the Starbucks store before the download of a song is complete, their personal computer will complete the download automatically at a later time. Every song purchased in a Starbucks participating location syncs back to the users' computer the next time they connect.

In addition to these agreements with domestic companies, Apple is seeking opportunities to create demand for its products in the global market.

Exhibit 9 Complementary Product Advertised with iPods

Source: www.burton.com/Burton/gear/products.asp?productID=728.

Going Global

To stay on top of its game, Apple is pursuing opportunities to sell the iPhone globally. Apple has a goal of capturing 1 percent of the global cell phone business by the end of 2008. It already has partnership agreements with cell phone carriers in France, Germany, and Great Britain. It has also entered the Middle East and Africa regions, ranking fifth next to Nokia, Research In Motion, HTC, and Motorola.[104] Considering that Japan is one of the world's largest and most demanding mobile phone markets with almost 100 million mobile phone users, Steve Jobs has been meeting with officials in Japan in hopes of making a partnership agreement with some of the major telecommunications companies in Japan. This market will be difficult to penetrate, as many other foreign companies have tried unsuccessfully to compete with the 10 domestic handset makers in Japan. Some analysts wonder whether Apple will be able to develop a relationship with the Japanese carriers due to Apple's tight control over the design of the phone, but others believe Apple will succeed. Apple already has a positive brand image in Japan related to the Macintosh computer and the iPod and has seven Apple retail stores already in place.[105]

Stephen Kobrin, a Wharton Multinational management professor explained in a recent interview that companies that are high-tech and driven by technology that demands that they expand into many countries simultaneously are "born global." He clarifies by further stating, "Companies that are born global 'tend to have high-tech products that immediately find acceptance in many different cultures and societies.'"[106] Thus, it is likely that the iPhone will experience success in many different markets, as will the Apple TV and other new products that Apple may launch when they become part of its global strategy.

Future Opportunities and Challenges

As Apple tries to expand its product line to include media and software in addition to hardware and as it tries to reach many different consumers rather than its traditional niche of "cult followers," the tech-savvy consumers who work in fields such as education and design, the company will find it more difficult to keep a positive brand image among all consumers. The technology and entertainment industries are constantly and rapidly changing. Will Apple be able to keep its reputation related to innovative design and continually launch products that will be the "latest hit"? Competition has become extremely fierce in the technology sector, and Apple needs to be concerned not only about major competitors, but also about start-up companies. For example, in relation to the iPhone, GotVoice is a Web-based company that allows subscribers to record voicemail messages in MP3 format and send those messages to their e-mail account to view the subject line and the message length. This capability rivals Apple's Visual Voicemail on the iPhone, and the service is free unless users prefer to pay $10 to avoid ad pop-ups.[107]

Interestingly, GotVoice has an advantage over Apple's Visual Voicemail in that it works not only with cell phones, but also with home and work phones.[108] It will be a challenge for Apple to maintain its competitive advantage in new product hardware and to create strong relationships with powerful suppliers of media and other services as well as fend off startups such as GotVoice in software and other areas.

NOTES

1. D. Leonard, 2003, Songs in the key of Steve, *Fortune*, April 28.
2. D. Chmielewski & M. Quinn, 2007, Technology; Movie studios fear the sequel to iPod; They see risk that new Apple TV signals effort to control distribution, *Los Angeles Times*, June 11, C1.
3. R. E. Hoskisson, 2007, Strategic Focus: Apple: Using innovation to create technology trends and maintain competitive advantage, Hitt, Ireland, & Hoskisson, *Strategic Management: Competitiveness and Globalization*, 8th Edition.
4. Ibid.
5. Apple history, www.apple-history.com/frames.
6. Ibid.
7. L. Kimmel, 1998, Apple Computer, Inc.: A History, www.geocities.com/Athens/3682/applehistory.html.
8. Ibid.
9. http://apple-history.com.
10. Apple Computer History Weblog, http://apple.computerhistory.org.
11. L. Kimmel, 1998, Apple Computer, Inc.: A history.
12. Apple Computer History Weblog.
13. http://apple-history.com.
14. Ibid.
15. Apple Computer History Weblog.
16. http://apple-history.com.
17. Ibid.
18. Ibid.
19. Ibid.
20. http://www.apple.com/itunes.
21. 2008, iTunes store, www.apple.com/itunes/store/, January 8.
22. P. Hardy, 2003, Apple launches Windows-based iTunes, *Music & Copyright Magazine*, October 29.
23. A. Hesseldahl, 2005, Unpeeling Apple's Nano, *BusinessWeek*, www.businessweek.com, September 22.
24. 2007, www.apple.com.
25. R. E. Hoskisson, Strategic Focus: Apple.
26. 2007, Apple reinvents the phone with iPhone, Apple Inc. press release, www.apple.com/pr/library/2007/01/09iphone.html, January 9.
27. K. Allison, 2007, Apple encroaches on Window's turf, *The Financial Times*, www.ft.com, June 11.
28. 2007, iPhone delivers up to eight hours of talk time, Apple Inc. press release, www.apple.com/pr/library/2007/06/18iphone.html, June 18.
29. 2007, In three months, iPhone sales top a million, *New York Times*, www.nytimes.com, September 11.
30. Ibid.
31. M. Quinn & D. C. Chmielewski, 2008, Studios join Apple's movie-rental service, *Los Angeles Times*, www.latimes.com, January 16.
32. B. Schlender, 2007, The trouble with Apple TV, *Fortune*, June 11,155(11): 56.
33. 2008, www.apple.com/appletv/rentals.
34. W. Cohen, www.rollingstone/news/newsarticle.asp?nid =18075.
35. K. Regan, 2007, EMI revenue falls but DRM-free iTunes sales promising, *Ecommerce Times*, www.ecommercetimes.com, August 6.
36. M. Garrahan & K. Allison, 2007, Apple signs film deal with Fox studio, *Financial Times*, www.ft.com, December 27.
37. D. C. Chmielewski & M. Quinn, 2007, Technology; Movie studios fear the sequel to iPod; They see risk that new Apple TV signals effort to control distribution, *Los Angeles Times*, June 11, C1.
38. 2008, Apple premieres iTunes movie rentals with all major film studios, Apple press release, www.apple.com/pr/library, January 15.
39. M. Quinn & D. C. Chmielewski, Studios join Apple's movie-rental service.
40. 2007, Apple chooses Cingular as exclusive U.S. carrier for its revolutionary iPhone, Apple Inc. press release, www.apple.com/pr/library/2007/01/09cingular.html, January 9.
41. 2008, www.apple.com/iphone.
42. A. Hesseldahl, 2007, Take the iPhone apart, *BusinessWeek*, www.businessweek.com, July 2.
43. 2001, Napster's History, http://w3.uwyo.edu/~pz/nap2.htm.
44. 2001, The history of the Napster struggle, www.theneworleanschannel.com/news/457209/detail.html.
45. 2003, Napster 2.0 to launch by Christmas, www.roxio.com/en/company/news/archive/prelease030728.jhtml.
46. Ibid.
47. J. Ketola, 2003, Kazaa Plus service launched, www.afterdawn.com, August.
48. 2008, Wikipedia, http://en.wikipedia.org/wiki/kazaa.
49. 2006, Kazaa settlement, *BBC News*, http://news.bbc.co.uk., July 27.
50. 2003, Kazaa Usage Map, http://tools.waglo.com/kazaa.
51. N. Wingfield, 2004, Price war in online music, *Wall Street Journal*, www.wsj.com, August 17.
52. 2008, http://musicstore.connect.com.
53. Y. I. Kane, 2007, Sony to challenge Apple in TV, movie downloads, *Wall Street Journal*, www.online.wsj.com, September 4.
54. 2008, www.virgin.com/VirginProducts/Shopping/Musicdownloads.aspx.
55. 2008, iTunes now the number two music retailer in the United States, Apple press release, www.apple.com/pr/library.
56. 2008, http://musicdownloads.walmart.com.
57. 2008, http://music.yahoo.com.
58. B. Stone, 2007, Amazon and TiVo in venture to put downloaded movies on TV, *New York Times*, www.nytimes.com, February 7.
59. G. Sandoval, 2007, NBC says goodbye to Apple, hello to Amazon, www.news.com, September 4.
60. 2008, CinemaNow Inc., *BusinessWeek*, http://investing.businessweek.com, March 14; 2008, www.cinemanow.com; 2008, Wikipedia, http://en.wikipedia.org; A. Gonsalves, 2007, *Information Week*, www.informationweek.com, July 18.
61. 2007, The Walt Disney Studios to offer movie rentals on demand through Xbox Live starting now, *MicrosoftNews*, www.microsoft.com/presspass, July 10.
62. 2008, HP and Sony Pictures Home Entertainment announce manufactured-on-demand content licensing agreement, *HP News Release*, www.hp.com/hpinfo/newsroom, January 24.
63. 2007, Blockbuster acquires Movielink, *New York Times*, www.nytimes.com, August 9.
64. 2008, Netflix and LG unveil video-on-demand service, *Appliance Magazine*, www.appliancemagazine.com, January 7.
65. 2008, Netflix now offers subscribers unlimited streaming of movies and TV shows on their PCs for the same monthly fee, Netflix press release, www.netflix.mediaroom.com, January 14.
66. Leipzig, 2007, PSP (PlayStation Portable) video download service, Sony Computer Entertainment Europe press release, www.scei.co.jp/corporate/release, August.
67. 2008, Wikipedia, http://en.wikipedia.org.

68. D. Pogue, 2007, High-speed video store in the living room, *New York Times*, www.nytimes.com, September 6.

69. J. Goldman, 2008, Motorola hangs up on handsets, www.cnbc .com, January 31; A. Hasseldahl, 2008, Blackberry vs. iPhone: Who wins? *BusinessWeek*, www.articles.moneycentral.msn.com, January 3.

70. E. M. Rusli, 2007, Palm wilts, *Forbes*, www.forbes.com, October 2.

71. A. Hesseldahl, 2008, Blackberry vs. iPhone: Who wins?

72. J. Goldman, 2008, iPhone vs. Blackberry: Apple launches new software, www.cnbc.com, March 6.

73. www.reviews.cnet.com/html.

74. N. Wingfield, 2007, Microsoft tunes its Zunes to catch up with iPod, *Wall Street Journal Online*, www.wsj.com, October 3, D8.

75. Ibid.

76. A. Cuneo, 2003, Apple transcends as lifestyle brand, *Advertising Age*, December 15.

77. 2007, A bruise or two on Apple's reputation, *BusinessWeek*, www .businessweek.com, October 22.

78. Ibid.

79. J. Quelch, 2007, How marketing hype hurt Boeing and Apple, *Harvard Business*, http://discussionleader.hbsp.com, November 2.

80. Ibid.

81. J. Smykil, 2007, *BusinessWeek* names Apple most innovative, http://arstechnica.com, May 6.

82. L. Gomes, 2006, Above all else, rivals of Apple mostly need some design mojo, *Wall Street Journal*, May 24, B1.

83. Ibid.

84. Cuneo, Apple transcends as lifestyle brand.

85. Ibid.

86. Ibid.

87. 2007, In 3 months, iPhone sales top a million.

88. R. Stross, 2007, Apple's lesson for Sony's stores: Just connect, *New York Times*, www.nytimes.com, May 27.

89. Ibid.; 2007, Retail stores' importance highlighted, http:// ifoapplestore.com, August 17.

90. Cuneo, Apple transcends as lifestyle brand.

91. www.apple.com/findouthow/retail/.

92. J. Boudreau, 2008, Apple tutorial classes help create bond with customers, *The Mercury News*, www.mercurynews.com, March 3.

93. Ibid.

94. J. Graham, 2007, Apple buffs marketing savvy to a high shine, *USA Today*, www.usatoday.com, March 3.

95. Wong.

96. Ibid.

97. Ibid.

98. C. Campellone, 2007, Apple and Volkswagen team up for possible iCar, http://media.www.theloquitur.com, September 20.

99. Ibid.

100. www.apple.com/ipod/nike/run.html.

101. E.C. Baig, 2006, Apple, Nike exercise iPods to track workouts, *USA Today*, www.usatoday.com, May 23.

102. 2008, Nike, Apple plug iPods into gym equipment, *USA Today*, www.usatoday.com, March 4.

103. 2007, Apple and Starbucks announce music partnership, Apple press release, www.apple.com/pr/library, September 5; http://www .apple.com/itunes/starbucks.

104. N. Gohring, 2008, Apple beats Microsoft and Motorola in 4Q phone sales, IDG News Service, February 6.

105. Y. I. Kane & N. Wingfield, 2007, For Apple iPhone, Japan could be the next big test, *Wall Street Journal Online*, www.wsj.com, December 19, B1.

106. 2007, What makes a global leader? *India Knowledge at Wharton*, http://knowledge.wharton.upenn.edu/india, October 4.

107. M. S. Lasky, 2007, iPhone versus your phone: Tips to avoid iPhone envy, *PC World*, www.pcworld.com, June 27.

108. 2008, www.gotvoice.com.

Florence Nightingale,
Vara Vasanthi

ICFAI Business School

Blockbuster is committed to keeping pace with the changing needs of customers by offering them an expanding array of convenient ways to access entertainment content."[1]

— JAMES W. KEYES, CHAIRMAN AND CEO OF BLOCKBUSTER

Blockbuster Inc. is a leading global provider of in-home movie and game entertainment, with approximately 8,000 stores located throughout America, Europe, Asia, and Australia. The video rental market has undergone many changes and continues to constantly change with new product offerings from companies. The biggest change in the video rental market is the transition from store-based video rental to online video rental. To tackle the changes taking place in the industry, Blockbuster wanted to identify and implement initiatives designed to regenerate the company's activities and enhance its organizational structure to improve profitability. As part of these initiatives, in August 2007 Blockbuster acquired Movielink, a movie download service provider. This acquisition enabled Blockbuster to offer video downloading services to its customers. Blockbuster acknowledged that this acquisition was its next logical step in the planned transformation of the company.[2] It, however, remains to be seen if the acquisition will generate the expected synergies.

The Video Rental Market

In-home filmed entertainment includes video rentals and purchases of various video products such as DVDs with rentals being the most significant portion of this market. A key driver of this market is the affordability and improvement of high-quality DVD technology. Consumer spending on video rentals is nearly three times greater than the theatrical box office.[3] The home video market was the largest segment of consumer movie spending in 2007, generating just over $24 billion in revenue.[4] The breakdown for the revenue in the home video market was approximately $15.9 billion in sales and $8.2 billion in rentals.[5] Customer preferences are changing daily, making an exclusively bricks-and-mortar[6] approach to video sales and rentals unprofitable.[7]

In-home filmed entertainment is offered through various distribution channels such as the retail home video industry, the online video industry, movie downloads, the cable industry, and the satellite industry. Of these distribution channels, the retail home video industry includes the sale and rental of movies on DVD (including in the Blue-Ray format) and VHS by traditional video store retailers such as Blockbuster and other businesses. Online video retailers include Blockbuster Online, Movie Gallery, Netflix, Amazon.com, CinemaNow, and other retailers (Exhibit 1).

As home-viewing technology improves and becomes cheaper, downloading movies over the Internet and watching on wide-screen televisions at home is an emerging trend. By using a computer and a broadband link, movies can be downloaded from online video retailers for as low as $2 to $5 and watched by customers on their computers.[8] Online DVD rental services are convenient and allow customers to find, rent, and watch movies whenever they wish. Online video retailers such as Movielink and CinemaNow provide various methods of

This case was written by Florence Nightingale, ICFAI Business School, Chennai and Vara Vasanthi, ICFAI Business School Case Development Centre, under the direction of Doris Rajakumari John, ICFAI Business School, Chennai. It is intended to be used as the basis for class discussion rather than to illustrate either effective or ineffective handling of a management situation. The case was compiled from published sources.

Exhibit 1 Online Video Rental Companies

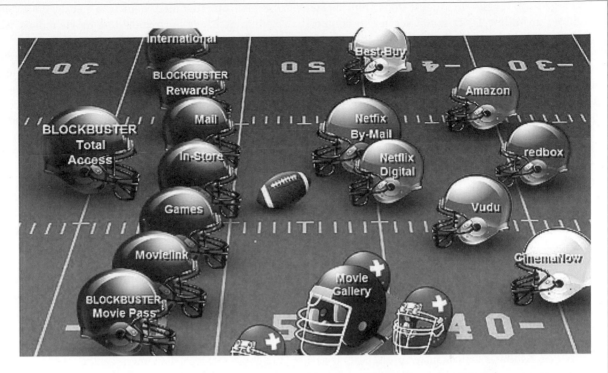

Source: Blockbuster's new paradigm and its impact on competitors, http://finance.paidcontent.org/paidcontent?Page=QUOTE&Ticket=Bbl, November 15, 2007.

access to customers for watching movies. Movielink, for example, offers two options to either buy or rent a movie. It provides a license to watch a movie and also allows for unlimited viewing. The movie can be stored on a hard disc.[9] The price to purchase a movie ranges between $8.99 and $19.99, and a movie rental from $0.99 to $4.99. As technology advances, it is likely to be easier to send a movie from a computer to a television. The major players in movie downloads are Sony, Universal, and Warner Bros., which embarked on a major endeavor to have movies transferred into digital designs. These companies also provide access to movies, similar to online video retailers. CinemaNow.com also provides free movie downloads and allows users to choose from a wide array of movies, ranging from major studio blockbusters to hard-to-find classics.

Despite the emergence of new technologies such as movie downloads and online movie purchases, the online rental business remains popular. The United States (the world's largest market for video rentals) and Europe generated more than $1 billion in consumer spending in this area in 2005.[10] By the end of 2005, there were about 6.3 million online DVD rental subscribers in the United States and Europe.[11] The United Kingdom dominates the European market, followed by Germany and thriving markets in France and Scandinavia. The online sector already accounts for more than 1 in 10 video rentals

in the United Kingdom.[12] According to recent research, 70 percent of Americans prefer watching movies at home, and Americans rented about 10 million movies in September 2007.[13] It is expected that by the end of 2009, more than half of the United Kingdom's rental transactions and rental spending will be online.[14]

The growth in the sector is further aided by customer-friendly strategies adopted by retailers. The retailers no longer insist on return dates or charge late fees for DVD rentals, thereby giving customers more freedom to keep the DVDs as long as they desire. The online rental companies allow customers to pay a monthly fee for access to unlimited rentals, which arrive and are returned by mail. In this fast-growing video rental market, Blockbuster Inc. was one of the early players and was the largest video rental chain in the United States.

The Blockbuster Business Model

Headquartered in Dallas, Texas, Blockbuster Inc. was founded by David Cook in 1982. In October 1985, Cook opened the first Blockbuster Video outlet in Dallas, with 8,000 tapes covering 6,500 titles. At the start of 1987, Blockbuster owned 15 stores and franchised 20 other stores. By the end of 1987, Blockbuster was operating 133 stores and had become the fifth-largest video chain in terms of revenue in the United States.[15] The company's basic revenues were from their stores and from late fees charged for rentals. In August 2004, Blockbuster introduced an online DVD rental service to compete with the established market leader, Netflix. Blockbuster offers services primarily through traditional retail outlets, online retailers, and cable and satellite providers. The company owns various trademarks such as Blockbuster, Blockbuster Video, "torn ticket" Logos, Blockbuster. com, Blockbuster Online, Blockbuster Night, Blockbuster GiftCards, Blockbuster Game Pass, Blockbuster Movie Pass word marks and logos, Blockbuster Rewards, related Blockbuster Family of Marks, Game Rush word mark and logo, and Life After Late Fees.[16]

Blockbuster's business model features a state-of-the-art distribution network and 41 distribution centers in the United States, which can reach most customers with one-day delivery, and an online recommendation system that lets customers select from 65,000 video titles. Blockbuster introduced a package that could travel as first-class mail, making it easy for customers to return DVDs at no charge to them. Blockbuster later launched a new online movie rental program to provide customers both Internet convenience and in-store benefits (see Exhibit 2). Blockbuster projects itself as a home entertainment enterprise with a diversified set of products and services, which includes an expanded games selection, DVD sales, online rentals, game trading, and various other businesses.

Later, the company introduced Blockbuster Total Access, a movie rental program that gives online customers the option of exchanging their DVDs through the mail or returning them to a nearby Blockbuster store in exchange for free in-store movie rentals, which was different from the existing model (Appendix I). In addition, most of Blockbuster's online subscribers had the option of exchanging their online movies for discounted in-store game rentals as well as free in-store movie rentals at more than 5,000 Blockbuster stores. Blockbuster reported, "We want to give consumers the most convenient access to media entertainment, whether that's through our stores or by mail, and are dedicated to doing that with flexible plans and pricing."[17] With more than 65,000 titles to choose from online, Blockbuster delivers DVDs to the subscribers' mailboxes in prepaid postage return envelopes. To increase its business, Blockbuster launched advertising campaigns and also undertook joint promotions with fast food outlets such as Domino's Pizza and McDonald's.

Blockbuster designed marketing and advertising campaigns to maximize opportunities in the marketplace, working closely with customers to connect and drive business. Blockbuster customized its stores' merchandise selection, quantity, and formats to meet the needs and preferences of local customers. As the new business was gaining ground, Blockbuster underwent several changes in its business-level strategy, focusing mainly on cost-cutting programs and selling products such as DVDs. This strategy made an impact, and the sales of DVDs increased as compared to DVD rentals. The popularity of online video rentals, however, was increasing with

Exhibit 2 Blockbuster Online Movie Rental Plan

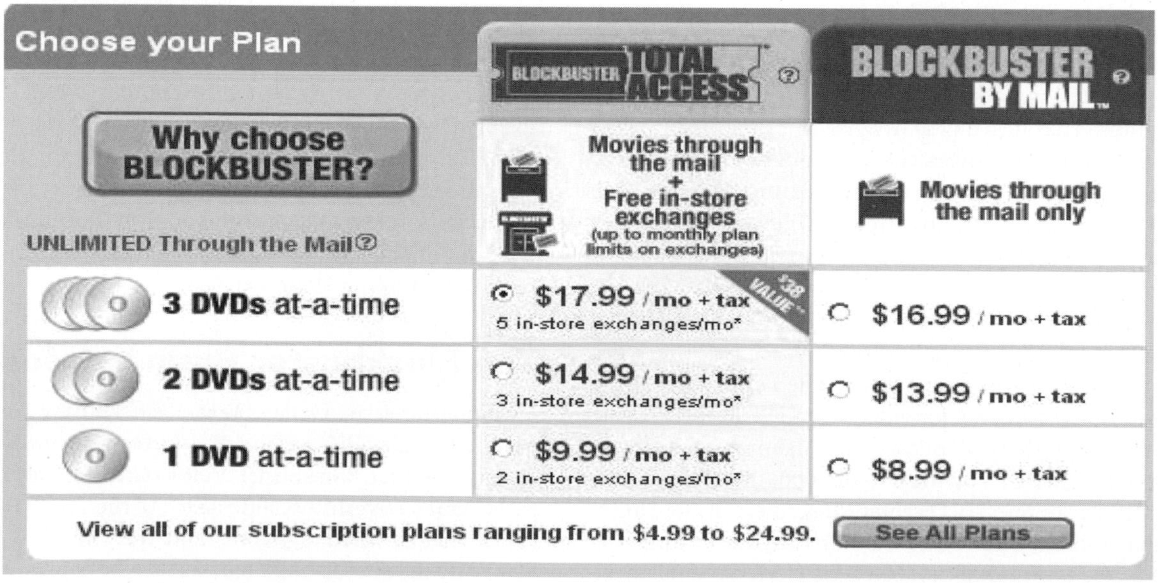

Source: Blockbuster Online, http://dvd-rental-review.toptenreviews.com/blockbuster-online-review.html.

video-on-demand (VoD) services gaining prominence. VoD services, in which video is streamed over the Internet, deviated from the firm's existing business model, which depended heavily on store ownership and increasing sales per store. Both VoD and online video-rental services diverted focus from the sale of DVDs.[18] Blockbuster developed a good understanding of how the online rental channel worked and what online customers were doing in their stores.

In 2005, as part of a comprehensive business transformation initiative, Blockbuster engaged Accenture, a global management consulting and technology services company, to develop the systems and processes and to launch the online business.[19] Both companies jointly built a network of distribution centers fully dedicated to service online customers. Blockbuster wanted to offer a "one-day" delivery to as many customers as possible. Working with Accenture, Blockbuster also identified sites for distribution centers that enhanced its customer service. The company's online rental program was unique and encouraged former customers to return to Blockbuster's stores.

Blockbuster reported worldwide revenues of more than $5.5 billion and a profit of $54.7 million in 2006.[20] In the same year, Blockbuster Online had about 1.4 million online subscribers.[21] To concentrate more on its online subscriber business, Blockbuster closed nearly 300 stores in the United States in 2006. Blockbuster continued to invest in its Total Access program and added more than 700,000 online subscribers[22] and more than 4 million total subscribers[23] in 2006. This action facilitated Blockbuster's efforts to compete with Netflix. Blockbuster reported, "We have invested heavily in Total Access during the first half of 2007 to capture market share in the overall video rental market and to set the stage for the expected future profitability of our online rental business."[24] Blockbuster's Total Access had a positive impact on its online movie rental revenue. In the first quarter of 2007, revenues reached about $108.9 million.[25] Total Access also helped Blockbuster generate more cross-channel sales and traffic. The average store had about 4,800 shoppers and 45,000 rentals per month. Blockbuster reported, "Growing the revenue of Total Access had helped to offset the in-store revenue decline."[26]

Michael Pachter, an analyst at Wedbush Morgan Securities,[27] said, "Under Keyes, Blockbuster will likely be looking for ways to maximize its customer base and leverage its chain of stores—the main differentiator with Netflix—all while also preparing for the fact that physical DVD rentals may not be its core business in just a few years."[28] Blockbuster focused on protecting its core rental business, developing new retail opportunities, and becoming the preferred provider of digital

entertainment.[29] In 2007, Blockbuster had 27 percent of the U.S. video rental market and served more than 87 million customers in the United States, its territories, and 25 other nations.[30]

While Blockbuster tried to make its mark in the online movie rental business, the firm encountered stiff competitions from Apple, Amazon.com, and Wal-Mart, as well as market leader Netflix. In 2007, Netflix was already an established player with 75 percent[31] of the market. Netflix's success was attributed to the firm's business model. Netflix's innovative subscription service, for example, allowed customers to keep videos as long as they wished. There are no due dates or late fees nor does the customer incur any shipping charges. Netflix's success inspired a number of other DVD rental companies both in the United States and abroad (see Exhibit 3).

Both Blockbuster and Netflix offer three movie rentals for a monthly fee of $17.99 (the price of this service changes in response to competitive challenges) and allow customers to return their rentals by mail. However, as part of the Total Access program, Blockbuster accepts returns at its stores and rewards subscribers with a free rental for each store return. Consumers were willing to pay a premium for convenience, and Blockbuster capitalized on that. As a result, Blockbuster gained subscribers from Netflix, which had no bricks-and-mortar presence and could not match with Blockbuster's Total Access plan.

Netflix, for its part, still posted a 36 percent increase in revenue to $305.3 million for the year 2007. Netflix was also investing more than $40 million in new digital download technology.[32] Blockbuster responded to these competitive actions by aggressively trying to take customers away from Netflix.[33] Reducing its prices and enhancing the layouts of its retail stores are examples of the competitive actions Blockbuster decided to initiate while competing against Netflix. Blockbuster also provides printable e-coupons for two free in-store movie or game rentals, and other special offers. Both companies were organized to focus on the key considerations such as selection, price, and customer satisfaction (see Exhibit 4).

Pachter said, "Netflix has tried to grab the lead in the digital distribution channel, but Blockbuster is signaling it's not going to give that up easily."[34] Blockbuster and Netflix offer similar plans and have repeatedly lowered prices or modified services in an effort to win customers. Blockbuster, in addition to the entertainment content provided through its stores and by mail, had taken an important step towards making movie downloading available to computers, portable devices, and directly to televisions in homes.

In 2007, Blockbuster introduced a wider range of subscription plans, including Blockbuster Total Access

Exhibit 3 Netflix—How it Works

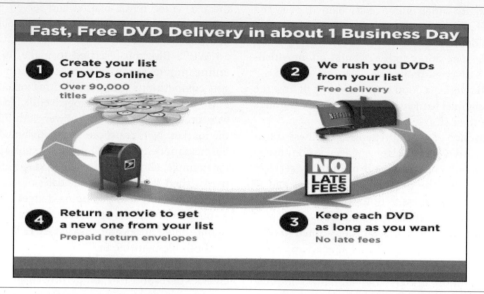

Source: Netflix—How it works, http://www.netflix.com/HowItWorks.

Exhibit 4 Comparison of Blockbuster Online DVD Rentals and NetFlix.com

	BLOCKBUSTER Online **Blockbuster Online** **DVD Rental**	**NETFLIX.** Netflix
No Late Fees	Keep the DVDs as long as you want **No Late Fees**	Keep the DVDs as long as you want **No Late Fees**
Selections	Over 40,000 titles	Over 40,000 titles
Turn-around Time	1 Day	1 Day
Unlimited DVD Rentals	YES	YES
Delivered to Your Mailbox	YES	YES
Free Shipping & Postage	**Free** first-class postage both ways	**Free** first-class postage both ways
No Return Dates	YES	YES
Distribution Centers	23 across the United States Will start using their **4,500** stores in coming year	35 across the United States.
Free In-Store Coupons	**YES** – Two e-coupons for **FREE** in-store movie or game rentals. Print coupons yourself.	**NO**
Gift Subscriptions	YES	YES
Special Offers	**$9.99 for First Month**	2-week free trial
$$ Cost $$	**$17.99 – 3 titles out** $29.99 – 5 titles out $37.49 – 8 titles out	$11.99, 4 DVDs a month, 2 titles out **$17.99 – 3 titles out** $29.99 – 5 titles out $47.99 – 8 titles out *Eight subscription plans offered*

Source: DVD Rental Services Comparison, http://www.acmetech.com/shopping/movies/dvd_rental.php.

Premium™, Blockbuster Total Access™, and Blockbuster® by Mail. The new subscription plans were available to all current and new subscribers to Blockbuster's online rental service with pricing as low as $4.99 a month[35] (see Appendix 2). Blockbuster's online movie rentals increased by 121.3 percent from $174.2 million in 2006 to $385.5 million in 2007.[36] Despite the increase in the online movie rentals, Blockbuster reported losses in 2007 (see Appendix 3).

According to the projected figures for 2008 in the Online DVD rental report published by *Online DVD Rental Reviews 2008*, Netflix ranked first, with Blockbuster second (see Appendix 4). To survive in the market, Blockbuster needed to increase its market share and establish its reputation in the online download business. According to PricewaterhouseCoopers, by 2010, annual revenue for the online video download business is expected to increase by $3.7 billion and DVD rentals and sales are expected to increase to about $29.5 billion.[37] For these reasons, Blockbuster decided to acquire Movielink.

Movielink Acquisition: The Strategic Rationale

When Blockbuster released its financial results for the year 2007, the firm's shareholders questioned the long-term sustainability of the company's current business model. In response to these concerns, company officials said, "Our goal is to continue to increase our membership base by providing even more ways for customers to get the entertainment they want through our stores, through the mail, and through new technologies."[38] As part of this goal, in August 2007, Blockbuster acquired Movielink, a leading movie downloading service.

Movielink offers movies for download through its video-on-demand Internet distribution service. Movielink was founded as a joint venture among five studios—Paramount Pictures, Sony Pictures Entertainment, MGM, Universal Studios, and Warner Bros.—who were responding to consumers' adoption of high-speed Internet access.[39] Movielink offers about 400 movies, which take 30 to 90 minutes to download, but the customers have the option of watching the movie after 10 minutes of downloading.[40] The Movielink Web site has two stores, a purchase store and a rental store, with a common home page. At the rental store, customers can browse the site and view trailers of movies without any charge. The customer can register with Movielink and pay for the rental by credit card.

Bruce Anderson, Movielink's vice president of engineering and operations, said, "As Movielink's business continues to grow, it is vital that our content delivery infrastructure continues to provide the quality of service our customers have come to expect."[41] Movielink has distribution agreements with the five studios that founded it, as well as Lionsgate and 20th Century FOX. Blockbuster's chief executive, James W. Keyes, said, "The acquisition immediately puts us in the digital download business. Clearly, our customers have responded favorably to having other convenient ways to access movies and entertainment."[42] The acquisition provided Blockbuster with a way to send movies straight to televisions and computers, complementing its store and movie-by-mail operations. Pachter stated, "The acquisition is a defensive move by Blockbuster to keep up with Netflix."[43]

Movielink CEO Jim Ramo said, "The studios' goal with the Movielink service has always been to make digital entertainment content more conveniently, more widely, and more securely available to consumers. This acquisition should further that goal."[44] He added, "With Blockbuster's ability to leverage its store network, online assets, and marketing expertise, Blockbuster should be able to grow the market for digitally-delivered entertainment content, and we believe that's good news for consumers and content providers alike."[45]

Blockbuster believed that the 1,400 movie titles in the Movielink catalog gave it a strong presence among firms offering movies for digital download via online capabilities. Customers are allowed to rent movies for $0.99, and they can store the movie for 30 days on their computers. Movielink announced that it was working on a plan that would allow customers to copy films to DVD.

Movielink's services, however, failed to catch on because the only way to watch films from Movielink on a television was to buy a set-top box. The company offered a network between a PC and television. Analysts felt the issue was that Movielink downloads could not be burned to discs.[46] Movielink did not provide a download-and-burn[47] service because of a misunderstanding between Movielink and the five studios.[48] In contrast, Blockbuster's competitor Netflix's movie download service was favorably received by customers. Movielink ended up failing to reach a wide audience and posted a net loss of $10.16 million in 2007.

Blockbuster's acquisition of Movielink failed to immediately expand the firm's business beyond the store-based movie-rental market. Competition from cable providers offering video-on-demand and DVD-rental services such as Netflix also posed problems for Blockbuster. Whether Blockbuster can use the Movielink acquisition to increase its market share and profitability in the video rental market and whether this acquisition offers Blockbuster an increased online presence remains to be seen.

NOTES

1. C. Metz, 2007, Blockbuster reels in MovieLink, http://www .theregister.co.uk/2007/08/09/blockbuster_buys_netflix, August 9.

2. K. Regan, 2007, Blockbuster chases online box office with movielink buy, http://www.ecommercetimes.com/story/58751.html, August 9.

3. EMA's 2007 Annual Report is now available, http://www.entmerch .org/annual_reports.html.

4. Ibid.

5. The Entertainment Merchant Association, http://www.entmerch.org/ annual_reports.html.

6. Companies that have a physical presence can offer face-to-face consumer experiences.

7. G. Millman, 2005, Blockbuster's bricks and clicks, http:// www.accenture.com/Global/Research_and_Insights/Outlook/ BlockbustersClicks.htm, June.

8. Blockbuster's bricks and clicks, op.cit.

9. D. Gynn, 2006, Download movies with Movielink/Optaros and reduce risk, http://opensource.syscon. com/read/256611.htm, August 8.

10. A. Wood & H. J. Davis, 2005, The outlook for online DVD rental: A strategic analysis of the U.S. and European markets, http://www .screendigest.com/reports/05onlinedvdrental/readmore/view.html, November.

11. Ibid.

12. The outlook for online DVD rental: A strategic analysis of the U.S. and European markets, op.cit.

13. 2007, Frost & Sullivan Commends DVDPlays Innovative Services in the Automated DVD Rental Machine Market, http://www.frost.com/ prod/servlet/press-release.pag?docid=110114449, October 23.

14. Ibid.

15. Blockbuster Inc., http://www.fundinguniverse.com/company-histories/Blockbuster-Inc-Company-History.html.

16. Blockbuster Inc., 2007, http://custom.marketwatch.com/custom/ nyt-com/htmlcompanyprofile. asp?MW=http://marketwatch. nytimes.com/custom/nyt-com/htmlcompanyprofile. asp&symb=BBI &sid=153477#compinfo, August 11.

17. 2007, Blockbuster announces expanded online subscription offerings, http://goliath.ecnext.com/coms2/summary_0199-6786323_ITM, July 26.

18. Diversity, http://www.blockbuster.com/corporate/diversity

19. Blockbuster's bricks and clicks, op.cit.

20. 2006, Blockbuster profit, 1.4 million online subscribers, http://www .hackingnetflix.com/2006/07/blockbuster_pro.html, July 27.

21. Ibid.

22. C. Spielvogel, 2007, Blockbuster Q4 income down, revenue up, http://www.videobusiness.com/article/CA6419949.html, February 27.

23. 2007, Blockbuster emphasizes its online program over stores, http://www.internetretailer.com/dailyNews.asp?id=22946, June 29.

24. Blockbuster profit, 1.4 million online subscribers, op.cit.

25. Ibid.

26. 2007, Blockbuster Q1 2007 Earnings Call Transcript, http://www .seekingalpha.com/article/34304-blockbuster-q1-2007-earnings-call-transcript, May 2.

27. It is recognized among securities professionals as a leading investment banking and brokerage firm.

28. Blockbuster chases online box office with movielink buy, op.cit.

29. 2007, Blockbuster reports third quarter 2007 results, new strategic initiatives and decisive actions taken to improve near-term profitability, http://www.b2i.us/profiles/investor/ ResLibraryView.asp?BzID=553&ResLibraryID=22067&Category=1 027, November 1.

30. Blockbuster Inc., op.cit.

31. J. M. Spool, 2006, Innovation is the new black, http://www.uie.com/ articles/innovation_from_experience_design/, June 1.

32. Blockbuster emphasizes its online program over stores, op.cit.

33. J. Love, 2006. E-retailing's brightest stars at IRCE 2007, http: //www.internetretailer.com/internet/marketing-conference/89902-e-retailings-brightest-stars-at-irce-2007.html, December.

34. Blockbuster chases online box office with movielink buy, op.cit.

35. Blockbuster announces expanded online subscription offerings, op.cit.

36. 2007, Blockbuster turns in a weaker third quarter performance, http://www.internetretailer.com/dailyNews.asp?id=24278, November 1.

37. Video download service, http://videodownloadservice.net.

38. A. Chowdhry, 2007, Blockbuster revenue drops 5.7 percent; focusing on membership gain, http://pulse2.com/category/ blockbuster, November 3.

39. Movielink, LLC Company Profile, http://biz.yahoo.com/ ic/106/106424.html.

40. Movielink, http://dvd-rental-review.toptenreviews.com/movielink-details .html

41. 2005, Equinix to provide connectivity infrastructure for Movielink video-on-demand service, http://findarticles.com/p/articles/mi_ m0EIN/is_2005_Jan_17/ai_n8694997, January 17.

42. 2007, Blockbuster acquires Movielink, http://www.nytimes. com/2007/08/09/business/09movie.html?_r=1&n= Toppercent2f Newspercent2f Businesspercent 2fCompanies percent2fBlockbu ste rpercent20Incpercent2e&oref=slogin, August 9.

43. Ibid.

44. Blockbuster reels in Movielink, op.cit.

45. Ibid.

46. G. Sandoval, 2007, Blockbuster acquires Movielink, http://www .news.com/2100-1026_3-6201609.html, August 8.

47. The service allows the consumers to purchase, download, and burn a complete DVD for instant gratification.

48. E. Bangeman, 2007, Is action better than inaction? Blockbuster buys Movielink for a song, http://arstechnica.com/news.ars/ post/20070809-is-action-better-than-inaction-blockbuster-buys-movielink-for-asong.html?rel, August 9.

Appendix 1 Blockbuster Business

SELECT MOVIES	**RECEIVE BY MAIL**	**MAIL BACK** OR **EXCHANGE IN-STORE**	**NEXT DVDS ON THE WAY**
Make your list online from over 75,000 titles.	Free shipping. Keep your online movies as long as you want.	Return by mail OR exchange in-store (up to monthly plan limits on exchanges) at a participating store*.	

Rent Online – Return by Mail Or In-Store with Blockbuster Total Access™

Only Blockbuster Total Access™ gives the convenience of renting movies online and the choice of how to return them: by mail or bringing them to participating Blockbuster store, where customers can exchange them for new movies or discounted game rentals on the spot (up to monthly plan limits on exchanges).*

In-Store Exchanges

For only $17.99 a month (plus taxes) customers can receive up to 3 DVDs at a time with up to 5 in-store exchanges for free movie rentals or discounted game rentals. When customers finish watching a DVD, they can send it back in the provided postage-paid envelope or return it to a participating Blockbuster store.

Special In-Store Monthly Offers

As a Blockbuster Online member, customers are eligible for exclusive deals and discounts each month at participating Blockbuster stores.

More than 75,000 Titles, Including New Releases

Online DVD library has more than 75,000 titles, and it is growing every week. Customers can find classic cinema, modern favorites, television shows, children's programming, health and fitness workouts, and of course, the hottest new releases from Blockbuster.

Delivered Right to the Mailbox

Renting DVDs is as easy as picking up the mail. DVDs usually arrive within 1–2 business days**. Return the DVD by placing the DVD in the provided postage paid envelope and send it back through the mail or return it to a participating store. Then, the next DVD will be on its way.

Free Shipping and Postage

Shipping is always free. Both ways. There are no postage charges.

No Return Dates on Online Rentals

Blockbuster online rental members can keep online rentals out as long as they want. There are never any due dates*. Watch the DVD when it is convenient for you, and send it back only when you are ready for a new selection.

No Extended Viewing Fees or Late Fees on Online Rentals

As a Blockbuster Online rental member, customers pay a flat monthly rate. There are no extended viewing fees or late fees on DVDs rented online.

* Separate, complimentary in-store membership required for in-store rentals. In-store movie rentals are subject to store rental terms and conditions, including due dates and charges which may apply to rentals not returned by the due date. See store for complete in-store rental terms and conditions. Free in-store rentals must be returned to the store where they were originally rented.

** One business day delivery for Blockbuster based on more than 90 percent of our subscribers being within one-day postal delivery zone. Certain subscribers may experience longer delivery times.

Source: Blockbuster Movies, https://www.blockbuster.com/signup/rp/howItWorks.

Appendix 2 Blockbuster Membership Plans

Blockbuster Online offers the following membership plans:

- $4.99 per month—offers 2 DVD rentals per month and allows 1 movie rental at a time.
- $8.99 per month—offers unlimited DVD rentals per month and allows 1 movie rental at a time.
- $13.99 per month—offers unlimited DVD rentals per month and allows for 2 movie rentals at a time.
- $16.99 per month—offers unlimited DVD rentals per month and allows for 3 movie rentals at a time.

Blockbuster Total Access offers the following membership plans:

- $7.99 per month—2 DVD rentals per month, allowing 1 movie rental at a time or 2 in-store exchanges 1 movie at a time.
- $9.99 per month—offers unlimited DVD rentals per month, allows 1 movie rental at a time and up to 2 in-store exchanges per month.
- $14.99 per month—offers unlimited DVD rentals per month, allows 2 movie rentals at a time and up to 3 in-store exchanges per month.
- $17.99 per month—offers unlimited DVD rentals per month, allows 3 movie rentals at a time and up to 5 in-store exchanges per month.

Blockbuster Total Access Premium plans include:

- $16.99 per month—offers unlimited DVD rentals per month, unlimited in-store exchanges, 1 movie at a time.
- $21.99 per month—offers unlimited DVD rentals per month, unlimited in-store exchanges, 2 movies at a time.
- $24.99 per month—offers unlimited DVD rentals per month, unlimited in-store exchanges, 3 movies at a time.

Source: Blockbuster Online, http://dvd-rental-review.toptenreviews.com/blockbuster-online-review.html.

Appendix 3 Blockbuster Income Statement – 2007

All amounts in millions except per-share amounts	Q3–2007 09/2007	Q2–2007 06/2007	Q1–2007 03/2007	Q4–2006 12/2006
Operating Revenue	1,238.20	1,263.20	1,473.00	1,463.10
Total Revenue	1,238.20	1,263.20	1,473.00	1,463.10
Adjustment to Revenue	0.00	0.00	0.00	0.00
Cost of Sales	396.30	441.00	531.60	536.90
Cost of Sales with Depreciation	570.40	627.70	711.00	699.90
Gross Margin	667.80	635.50	762.00	763.20
Gross Operating Profit	841.90	822.20	941.40	926.20
R&D	0.00	0.00	0.00	0.00
SG&A	603.20	624.30	654.50	610.70
Advertising	27.50	54.80	76.60	47.50
Operating Profit	−5.60	−13.70	−18.40	50.10
Operating Profit before Depreciation (EBITDA)	211.20	143.10	210.30	268.00
Depreciation	217.00	234.50	228.70	212.80
Depreciation Unreconciled	42.90	47.80	49.30	49.80
Amortization	0.00	0.00	0.00	0.00
Amortization of Intangibles	0.00	0.00	0.00	0.00
Operating Income After Depreciation	−5.80	−91.40	−18.40	55.20

Appendix 3 Blockbuster Income Statement – 2007 (*Continued*)

All amounts in millions except per-share amounts	Q3–2007 09/2007	Q2–2007 06/2007	Q1–2007 03/2007	Q4–2006 12/2006
Interest Income	1.30	1.90	1.90	2.60
Earnings from Equity Interest	0.00	0.00	0.00	0.00
Other Income, Net	−1.10	1.70	−0.40	1.60
Income Acquired in Process R&D	0.00	0.00	0.00	0.00
Interest Restructuring and M&A	0.20	77.70	0.00	0.00
Other Special Charges	0.00	0.00	0.00	−5.10
Total Income Available for Interest Expense (EBIT)	−5.40	−10.10	−16.90	54.30
Interest Expense	20.70	21.10	23.60	24.40
Income Before Tax (EBT)	−26.10	−31.20	−40.50	29.90
Income Taxes	8.70	3.00	8.50	10.30
Minority Interest	0.00	0.00	0.00	0.00
Preferred Securities of Subsidiary Trust	0.00	0.00	0.00	0.00
Net Income from Continuing Operations	−34.80	−34.20	−49.00	19.60
Net Income from Discontinued Operations	−0.20	−1.10	2.60	−6.70
Net Income from Total Operations	−35.00	−35.30	−46.40	12.90
Extraordinary Income/Losses	0.00	0.00	0.00	0.00
Income from Cumulative Effect of Accounting Change	0.00	0.00	0.00	0.00
Income from Tax Loss Carryforward	0.00	0.00	0.00	0.00
Other Gains (Losses)	0.00	0.00	0.00	0.00
Total Net Income	−35.00	−35.30	−46.40	12.90
Normalized Income	−35.00	−111.90	−49.00	24.70
Net Income Available for Common	−37.60	−37.00	−51.80	16.70
Preferred Dividends	2.80	2.80	2.80	2.90
Excise Taxes	0.00	0.00	0.00	0.00
Per-Share Data				

(*Continued*)

Appendix 3 Blockbuster Income Statement – 2007 (*Continued*)

All amounts in millions except per-share amounts	Q3–2007 09/2007	Q2–2007 06/2007	Q1–2007 03/2007	Q4–2006 12/2006
Basic Earnings Per Share (EPS) from Continuing Operations	−0.20	−0.19	−0.27	0.09
Basic EPS from Discontinued Operations	0.00	−0.01	0.01	−0.04
Basic EPS from Total Operations	−0.20	−0.20	−0.26	0.05
Basic EPS from Extraordinary Income	0.00	0.00	0.00	0.00
Basic EPS from Cumulative Effect of Accounting Change	0.00	0.00	0.00	0.00
Basic EPS from Other Gains (Losses)	0.00	0.00	0.00	0.00
Basic EPS Total	−0.20	−0.20	−0.26	0.05
Basic Normalized Net Income/ Share	−0.20	−0.62	−0.27	0.11
Diluted EPS from Continuing Operations	−0.20	−0.19	−0.27	0.09
Diluted EPS from Discontinued Operations	0.00	−0.01	0.01	−0.04
Diluted EPS from Total Operations	−0.20	−0.20	−0.26	0.05
Diluted EPS from Extraordinary Income	0.00	0.00	0.00	0.00
Diluted EPS from Cumulative Effect of Accounting Change	0.00	0.00	0.00	0.00
Diluted EPS from Other Gains (Losses)	0.00	0.00	0.00	0.00
Diluted EPS Total	−0.20	−0.20	−0.26	0.05
Diluted Normalized Net Income/ Share	−0.20	−0.62	−0.27	0.11
Dividends Paid per Share	0.00	0.00	0.00	0.00
Additional Data				
Basic Weighted Shares Outstanding	190.60	190.00	189.40	187.10
Diluted Weighted Shares Outstanding	190.60	190.00	189.40	189.00

Source: Blockbuster Inc. Income Statement, http://finance.google.com/finance?fstype=ii&q=BBI.

Appendix 4 Projected Figures – 2008 Online DVD Rental Report

Legend:
- ▪▪▪▪ Excellent
- ▪▪▪□ Very Good
- ▪▪□□ Good
- ▪□□□ Fair
- □□□□ Poor

	Netflix	Blockbuster Online	DVD Avenue	Gameznflix	CafeDVD.com	eHit.com	Intelliflix	Peerflix	Number Slate	iLetYou
Rank	GOLD	SILVER	BRONZE	4	5	6	7	8	9	10
Reviewer Comments	READ REVIEW	READ REVIEW	READ REVIEW	READ REVIEW	READ REVIEW	READ REVIEW	READ REVIEW	READ REVIEW	READ REVIEW	READ REVIEW
Lowest Price	BUY $4.99	BUY $4.99	BUY $9.99	BUY $8.99	BUY $14.95	BUY $13.99	BUY $24.95	BUY Varies	BUY $9.95	BUY Varies
Overall Rating	Very Good	Very Good	Good	Good	Fair	Good	Good	Fair	Fair	Fair
Ratings										
Inventory	Excellent	Excellent	Very Good	Very Good	Good	Fair	Excellent	Good	Fair	Fair
Membership Features	Very Good	Very Good	Very Good	Very Good	Fair	Good	Good	Fair	Very Good	Fair
Movie Arrival Time	Excellent	Excellent	Good	Good	Good	Fair	Good	Fair	Fair	Fair
Movie Information	Excellent	Excellent	Very Good	Excellent	Good	Good	Very Good	Fair	Good	Fair
Search Capabilities	Very Good	Very Good	Good	Very Good	Good	Good	Very Good	Fair	Fair	Fair
Inventory										
DVDs	✓	✓	✓	✓	✓	✓	✓	✓	✓	✓
Games				✓			✓			✓
TV Series	✓	✓			✓		✓	✓		✓
Movie Titles	85,000	75,000	25,000	28,000	13,000	5,000	60,000	unknown	5,000	unknown

Membership Features	Netflix	Blockbuster Online	DVD Avenue	Gameznflix	CafeDVD.com	eHit.com	Intelliflix	Peerflix	Number Slate	iLetYou
Unlimited DVDs per month	✓	✓	✓	✓	✓	✓	✓		✓	
Monthly Plans	✓	✓	✓	✓		✓	✓		✓	
Pay Per Movie				✓		✓	✓	✓		✓
No Due Date	✓	✓	✓	✓		✓	✓		✓	
No Late Fees	✓	✓	✓	✓		✓	✓		✓	
Free Two-Way Shipping	✓	✓	✓	✓		✓	✓			
Free Trial	✓	✓	✓	✓		✓			✓	
Number of Plans	4	11	4	4	4	4	4	1	1	1
Option to Purchase DVD	✓	✓		✓	✓			✓		
Download Movies	✓									
Average Days to Receive your DVD	1-2	1-2	2-5	2-5	2-4	2-4	1-3	varies	varies	varies
Movie Information										
Title	✓	✓	✓	✓	✓	✓	✓	✓	✓	✓
MPAA Rating	✓	✓	✓	✓	✓	✓	✓		✓	✓
Critic Rating						✓	✓			
Movie Synopsis	✓	✓	✓	✓	✓	✓	✓	✓	✓	✓
Actors	✓	✓	✓	✓	✓	✓	✓	✓	✓	✓
Director	✓	✓	✓	✓	✓	✓	✓	✓	✓	✓
Genre	✓	✓	✓	✓	✓	✓	✓	✓	✓	
Movie Studio	✓	✓		✓						
Awards	✓	✓	✓							
Movie Reviews (Critics)	✓	✓			✓		✓	✓		✓
Trailers/Previews	✓	✓			✓					

Appendix 4 Projected Figures – 2008 Online DVD Rental Report (*Continued*)

	Netflix	Blockbuster Online	DVD Avenue	Gameznflix	CafeDVD.com	eHit.com	Intelliflix	Peerflix	Number Slate	iLetYou
Search Capabilities										
Title	✓	✓	✓	✓		✓	✓	✓		✓
Actor	✓	✓	✓	✓		✓	✓	✓		✓
Director	✓	✓	✓	✓			✓	✓		✓
Year							✓			
Rating		✓		✓		✓				
Synopsis			✓				✓			
Genre	✓	✓	✓	✓	✓	✓	✓	✓	✓	✓
New Releases	✓	✓		✓	✓	✓		✓	✓	✓
Coming Soon				✓						✓
Production Studio				✓						
Screen Format				✓						
Language		✓		✓		✓	✓			
Subtitles				✓			✓			
Awards		✓					✓			
Support/Documentation										
Phone Support	✓		✓	✓						✓
FAQ	✓	✓	✓	✓	✓	✓	✓	✓	✓	✓
eMail/Online Form		✓	✓		✓	✓	✓	✓	✓	

Source: Top Ten Reviews, http://dvd-rental-review.toptenreviews.com/index.html#anchor, 2007.

X. U. Leiping

China Europe International Business School

It was the morning of October 18, 2007. In Beijing, the autumn air was clear and crisp. Zhang Lan, the founder and chair of the board of the South Beauty Group, sat in her office with her management team to discuss the future plans for her seven-year-old company.

As a successful player in China's catering industry, by September 2007 the South Beauty Group had expanded to a total of 20 plush restaurants in the most commercially valuable locations across Beijing, Shanghai, and Chengdu, with three different brands. South Beauty, the Group's flagship brand with 19 restaurants, targeted the upper-middle-class segment of businesspeople; LAN Club, the new luxury brand with two restaurants (one opened), targeted the upper-class dining segment; SUBU, the company's latest brand slated to shortly open its first restaurant in Beijing, would cater to health-conscious youth. All the restaurants were owned and operated by the group. Occupying more than 40,000 square meters in total, employing around 2,600 people, and registering more than 3.5 million footfalls a year, the South Beauty Group was regarded as an innovative and leading player

in the Chinese restaurant market. It won a prestigious contract to become a Food Service Partner of Chinese cuisine for the 2008 Beijing Olympics, which would provide more revenue than the group's estimated revenues in 2007.

However, as Zhang Lan sat with her team that morning, daunting challenges lay ahead for the company as it sought to expand its operations from the existing 20 restaurants in China to a total of 100 worldwide (35 in China and 65 in the international market) over the next three years. To achieve this scale of expansion, the company needed to make critical decisions on a number of issues: the standardization of the process of preparing the dishes to increase efficiency and quality, which was a tough task to achieve with Chinese cuisine; the prioritization of markets to enter (i.e., whether to focus on the local market to realize its full potential before venturing abroad, or to do both at the same time); entry into new businesses, such as airline catering and the supply of semi-processed food to retail outlets such as supermarkets; and the expansion model (i.e., through owned outlets,

This case was prepared by research fellow X. U. Leiping under the guidance of Prof. S. Ramakrishna Velamuri in collaboration with South Beauty Group for the purpose of class discussion, as opposed to illustrating either effective or ineffective handling of an administrative situation. Certain names and other identifying information may have been changed to maintain confidentiality.

Zhang Lan[1]

as had been the case until now, or through franchising). With so many areas to study, Zhang Lan realized that she and her team had their work cut out for them.

Zhang Lan: The Founder of South Beauty

Zhang Lan was born in Beijing. Her father was a professor of civil engineering at Tsinghua University. However, the Cultural Revolution in China shattered her carefree childhood. Her family was exiled to a farm in an impoverished mountainous area of the Hubei province, which was built to "reform" intellectuals through labor. Although moving to such an environment was devastating for a young girl, she secretly dabbled in drawing and music with her parents. Significantly, at the age of nine, she also learned to prepare simple meals for her parents, who returned exhausted after their daily toil on the farm.

At the age of 17, Zhang Lan and her parents returned to Beijing after the collapse of the Cultural Revolution. At that time, there was no opportunity for young people to study in universities. Her first job was as a worker in a factory. It was much later, in 1985, as a 27-year-old mother of a two-year-old boy, that Zhang Lan decided to study business administration at Beijing Business College[2] through an adult education program. When she graduated in 1987, she joined a civil engineering company as an office worker with a salary much higher than the average level at that time. But she was not content with things as they were, because her life was leisurely and carefree and she wanted something different. In early 1989, she obtained a visa to study in Canada with the help of her uncle, a Canadian resident. Once in Canada,

she worked part time in restaurants, hotels, and hair salons to support herself, working as many as four jobs at a time.

Following the Tiananmen Square protests in the summer of 1989, the Canadian government offered green cards to all Chinese students in the country. Zhang Lan was one of the few who rejected this opportunity. She was faced with the dilemma of staying in a prosperous country for the rest of her life or returning to an impoverished China to stay with her family. She finally decided to return to China as soon as her savings reached USD 20,000 (RMB 108,000 at that time).[3] Just four days before Christmas 1990, Zhang Lan's bank account met the target and she returned to China immediately.

When Zhang Lan reached Beijing with her substantial savings, she was brimming with ideas for possible business ventures—a pizza store, a dumpling-wrapping business, a frozen foods store, and even a paper production plant based on high-quality Canadian paper pulp technology—but soon realized that her savings could only support a business that required limited capital. During windy springtime in Beijing, with a gauze kerchief on her head, she rode a bicycle through the streets in search of business opportunities. She found that consumers' needs for dining out were increasing; however, many old and traditional restaurants could not meet this trend. Opening a small restaurant in Beijing seemed to be a relatively safe venture in that the total investment would be relatively low.

In April 1991, an attractive opportunity presented itself to open a small restaurant of only 96 square meters in Dong Si, Beijing's downtown area. Zhang Lan believed the restaurant business would help her realize her dream of doing something in China while enabling her to benefit from her extensive experience in several Canadian restaurants serving Chinese and Western food. She knew how to operate a Chinese restaurant, from the purchase of raw materials to customer reception. Her friends regarded the restaurant business as unsuitable for Zhang Lan; in spite of this, she remained adamant about pursuing her dream.

In the initial phase, Zhang Lan invested considerable time and effort to formulate her business plan. She selected Sichuan food as the restaurant's main cuisine. She believed that among the eight main Chinese cuisines, Sichuan food best expressed the Chinese culture. Sichuan food is known as "Bai Cai Bai Ge, Bai Cai Bai Wei," literally "a hundred dishes, a hundred flavors," which means that it is liked by people across the world.

Further, Zhang Lan wanted to provide a unique and comfortable ambience in her restaurant. In this pursuit, she traveled to Pi Xian, a county in Sichuan, to transport 13-meter-long bamboo shoots to Beijing by train. Three bamboo weavers designed her restaurant as a bamboo house. Zhang Lan named her restaurant

"A Lan," which sounded like her childhood nickname. "Lan" is the Chinese word for orchid or fragrance. Although bamboo was cheaper than other regular materials, by the time the restaurant was ready to open, Zhang Lan's savings were almost fully depleted.

In the early 1990s, China, especially Beijing, was staid and lacking in diversity because of slow economic and social growth. Zhang Lan's small restaurant was thus able to tap a large customer base as its unique style and offerings contrasted with the environment. Zhang Lan initially managed all operational issues (ordering dishes, purchasing, etc.) pertaining to the restaurant by herself. In a short time, A Lan Restaurant became known as a special small restaurant in Beijing.

In 1997, encouraged by the success of A Lan Restaurant, Zhang Lan opened a larger restaurant, Bai Niao Yuan Seafood and Shark's Fin Restaurant[4] in Beijing, which was quite different from the A Lan Restaurant (Exhibit 1). At that time, expensive shark's fin and abalone were popular in many Chinese cities. This popularity was influenced by Guangdong and Hong Kong cuisines. Zhang Lan capitalized on this business opportunity, seeking to exploit the demand for new tastes and accumulate profits from these relatively expensive dishes. At the same time, she was also occupied with other investments, including real estate, stocks, mobile phone retailing, and even a nightclub. In 1999, Zhang Lan sold all her restaurants and other assets and made a profit of RMB 60 million (USD 7.26 million).[5] She explained this surprising action afterwards: "I thought it was hard to earn high profits through cooking the dishes one by one in a traditional way. After selling out all my assets in 1999, I spent half a year to calm my mind and continuously ask myself … what activity should I pursue in the end?"[6]

After six months of hard and careful reflection, Zhang Lan realized that her heart was still in the restaurant business. Possessing a large cash reserve, she went to France to see her son, who was studying fashion design in Paris. While in Paris, she visited a few well-known restaurants and decided to do something different this time—start a restaurant to carry forward Chinese cuisine to the world, as opposed to the idea of opening an unoriginal restaurant in China. Zhang Lan explained the logic behind her decision:

When I was involved with the restaurant business, I felt that I should take up the responsibility of enhancing Chinese cuisine. Although China has a 5,000-year catering culture, Chinese cuisine is regarded as low-end. French cuisine, on the other hand, is regarded as high-end. I did not agree with this. However, I thought that it would take my whole life to do this job (to prove the detractors wrong). Moreover, it would also require several generations' efforts because the restaurant business is a difficult venture, which needs assiduousness, diligence, thriftiness, zealousness, earnestness, and willingness for undertaking hard work.[7]

The Birth of South Beauty

Zhang Lan took the second step in her journey as an entrepreneur. She discovered that there were only a few restaurants offering Guangdong cuisine in plush office buildings in Beijing. These restaurants were too expensive to attract average businesspeople and their potential buying power. These customers looked for a high-quality, stylish, and comfortable environment as well as hygienic and delicious food presented aesthetically at a reasonable cost. Therefore, she decided to build a top-notch Chinese restaurant brand by targeting these businesspeople:[8] "There is a big misunderstanding of Chinese cuisine in the world. A lot of foreigners regard Chinese cuisine as the Mapo Tofu and Sweet and Sour Pork that you find in Chinatown. In fact, there are deep cultural meanings inside Chinese cuisine. More and

Exhibit 1 Pictures of A Lan Restaurant and Bai Niao Yuan Restaurant

Zhang Lan in A Lan Restaurant, 1991

Mockup Pictures of Bai Niao Yuan Restaurant

Source: South Beauty Group provided the picture of A Lan Restaurant; the mockup pictures were selected from http://food.yoolink.com to simulate the environment of Bai Niao Yuan Restaurant at that time.

more foreigners and businesspeople are in Beijing now. But there are few Chinese restaurants with special and elegant atmosphere. I wanted to build a Chinese restaurant for global business people to understand Chinese catering culture in the shortest time."[9]

Zhang Lan selected a prestigious office building for her first new restaurant, located in the proximity of her target customers—white collar office workers—who were still an untapped niche market in China at that time.

In April 2000, she launched an upper-middle-class restaurant, "South Beauty" (in Chinese: Qiao Jiang Nan[10]), at Guomao (China World Trade Center), a high-end office building in Beijing. In those days, Chinese restaurants were acclaimed for their delicious offerings, while Western restaurants were credited for their ambience. But Zhang Lan had her own intuition: "People prefer visual pleasures to those offered to the taste buds. When customers walk into your restaurant, they first observe the ambience and only then decide what to eat. Therefore, the first glance at the restaurant is critical."[11]

Among 10 designers, Zhang Lan selected Jack Tam, a Chinese-American designer who graduated from Harvard University, to design her new restaurant. It was the first time that a Chinese restaurant in China was designed by a foreign artist. Zhang Lan believed that only Tam could understand both Western restaurant-styling practices and the Chinese catering culture. Once completed, Tam's work did not disappoint Zhang Lan. The targeted customers took to the restaurant almost instantly (see Exhibit 2).

Zhang Lan also decided to provide Sichuan food in her new restaurant, just as she had in her earlier

Exhibit 2 Pictures of the First South Beauty Restaurant at Guomao in Beijing

Source: Company internal information.

A Lan Restaurant. Sichuan food was regarded as a kind of low-middle-level cuisine in China due to its popular raw materials. However, South Beauty Restaurant introduced several innovations and improvements with regard to traditional Sichuan food, not only in terms of new raw materials, but also the process of preparing the dishes and the customer experience. For example, South Beauty launched a new Sichuan dish, "Stone-heated Tofu Congee," which was much appreciated by office workers. To prepare this dish, waiters poured cold liquid Tofu into a glass bowl, which contained three Sichuan-origin river stones heated to 200°C, in front of the customers. Then the bowl was covered. After five minutes, the Tofu congee was ready for customers to mix with various flavors. Zhang Lan also devised various creative ways to present Sichuan delicacies. For example, inspired by the countryside experience of washing clothes in the river after work and hanging them up under the setting sun, she created a new way to present a traditional Sichuan dish, "Cold Boiled Pork with Garlic Puree." In a highly innovative and visually impactful way, slices of meat were hung from a bamboo beam. In addition, she renamed this dish as "Hanging Meat." She had utensils of different shapes and colors in her office, allowing her to experiment with food presentation styles (see Exhibit 3).

With its unique positioning as an innovative Sichuan restaurant, providing businesspeople with pleasant ambience and located at prestigious office buildings, South Beauty was a success, although the initial four months were very difficult because of low market awareness. Zhang Lan once explained the difference between A Lan Restaurant and South Beauty Restaurant: "A Lan was just like other normal traditional Chinese restaurants and my purpose with that venture was just to earn money. South Beauty was different. South Beauty is a brand, actually."[12]

Some staff members of the A Lan restaurant moved to South Beauty in the finance and restaurant development divisions. Zhang Lan and her team also surmounted the SARS[13] crisis in 2003. Under a group of experienced managers, the company established a sound reputation and opened more restaurants successfully in other business buildings. Each restaurant was run autonomously and the role of the head office was minimal.

By mid-2007, the South Beauty Group had expanded to 19 restaurants, under the brand name of South Beauty, in three key cities: Beijing, Shanghai, and Chengdu. Zhang Lan also attempted to build new restaurant brands, LAN Club and SUBU. One LAN Club restaurant opened in Beijing in November 2006, a location of more than 5,000 square meters designed by the well-known designer Philip Stark with a total investment of over RMB 100 million. It was profitable from its first month. The Group expected to recover its investment on this first LAN Club in two years. Moreover, one new LAN Club restaurant was to open in Shanghai in April 2008, and one SUBU restaurant was scheduled to open soon in Beijing (see Exhibits 4–7). With estimated revenues of

Exhibit 3 Examples of Innovative Sichuan Dishes from South Beauty

Note: Top row (left to right) Stone-heated tofu congee; hanging meat; shredded chicken with spicy sauce; bottom row (left to right): four seasons; seasonal Williams pear aspic; spare ribs fried deeply with chili and spices; fried mandarin fish with Ziran and spicy sauce.

Source: Company internal information.

Exhibit 4 Coverage of South Beauty in China (2007)

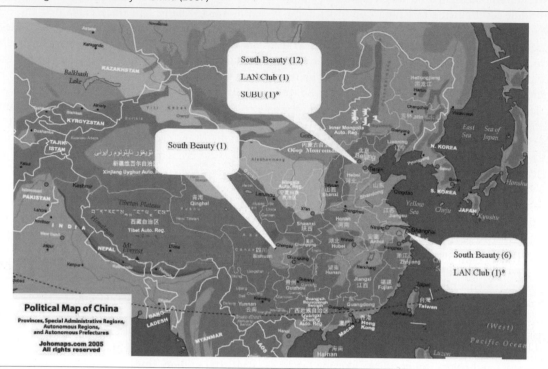

*SUBU and LAN Club's outlets in Beijing and Shanghai, respectively, are currently being furnished and are expected to open shortly.

Source: The map was copied from http://www.xxcha.com/All/449/8224_1.htm and company internal information.

Exhibit 5 Pictures of Various South Beauty Restaurants

Note: Names of these restaurants (top row, left to right): South Beauty at China World Trade Center in Beijing; South Beauty in Chengdu; South Beauty at Super Brand Mall in Shanghai; (bottom row, left to right) South Beauty at Beijing Yinzuo; South Beauty at Shanghai 881; South Beauty at Beida Resource in Beijing.

Source: Company internal information.

Exhibit 6 Pictures of LAN Club

The internal décor of LAN Club in Beijing

Source: Company internal information.

Exhibit 7 Design Effect of SUBU in Beijing

The design effect of SUBU Restaurant in Beijing, opening soon

Source: Company internal information.

RMB 384 million in 2007,[14] and around 10,000 footfalls every day, the Group became one of the benchmarks of the Chinese restaurant market (see Exhibit 8). Because of the highly fragmented nature of China's catering market, the market share of South Beauty in the total industry was less than 0.1 percent; however its market share in the Chinese dinner category[15] was an estimated two percent in 2006. In terms of the niche market of high-end Chinese dinner, South Beauty's share was more than 7 percent.[16] The company was also regarded as an innovative company, with 55 percent annual growth. The Group had also won the bid for providing food services for the 2008 Beijing Olympics. During the Olympic Games, South Beauty prepared food for around 150,000 people every day. It was the first time for Chinese food to be designated as one of the cuisines for the Olympic Games.

South Beauty's Business Model

From 2005 forward, the South Beauty Group slowed down its speed of expansion and started to develop functional management expertise at its head office with a view to coordinating the management of its restaurants, all of which were directly owned and managed by the Group. Under the recently adjusted structure, the Group had two divisions: one for head office functions and another one for restaurant operations (Exhibit 9).

The head office made decisions regarding the overall development of the Group, such as those pertaining to strategy, financial management, human resources, marketing, market expansion, engineering, R&D, and quality control of the food supply.

The three restaurant brands (South Beauty, LAN Club, and SUBU) had different missions. Within South

Beauty, each restaurant handled its own daily business operations. A new department was also set up to manage the franchising business in local and overseas markets, mainly for the South Beauty restaurant brand. Luo Yun, who was personal assistant to the board chairman, commented on the change in the management structure in the following manner:

To select the management direction, we spent two years considering how to conduct our business. Before 2005, we formulated operations for individual restaurants, not considering the overall company strategy. Later, we realized that we were not just a single restaurant business; in fact, we felt that we should use the company's central management to achieve greater synergies. Thus, we decided to move from single-restaurant-based operations to company-based management.

During the last two years, we have also been thinking about ways to differentiate ourselves from our competitors to capture greater market share. In China, we need to distinguish ourselves from numerous restaurants. We also set up the "Restaurant Chain Management Company" to try the franchising model to expand our business size.[17]

The size of a normal South Beauty Restaurant was between 2,000 and 3,000 square meters. In each restaurant, there were 100 to 150 workers, of which 30 to 40 percent worked in the kitchen. Usually, each restaurant offered more than 380 dishes, of which 60 to70 percent belonged to the Sichuan cuisine, while the remaining were Cantonese and other cuisines.

The unique features of South Beauty's business model were related to its brand positioning, menu innovation, location, pricing, interior decoration, IT application, and people management. With these

Exhibit 8 Chronology—South Beauty Group (2000–2007)

Year	Restaurants Number	Employees	Location and Number of Restaurants	Total Revenue (in RMB million)*
2000	2	200	Beijing (2)	10
2001	6	600	Beijing (6)	40
2002	8	800	Beijing (7); Shanghai (1)	60
2003	11	1,300	Beijing (8); Shanghai (3)	110
2004	16	1,900	Beijing (11); Shanghai (4); Chengdu (1)	200
2005	18	2,200	Beijing (12); Shanghai (5); Chengdu (1)	280
2006	20	2,600	Beijing (13); Shanghai (6); Chengdu (1)	350
2007	20	2,600	Beijing (13); Shanghai (6); Chengdu (1)	Est. 384

*Total revenue provided by company.

Source: Company internal information.

Exhibit 9 South Beauty's Organization Structure (2007)

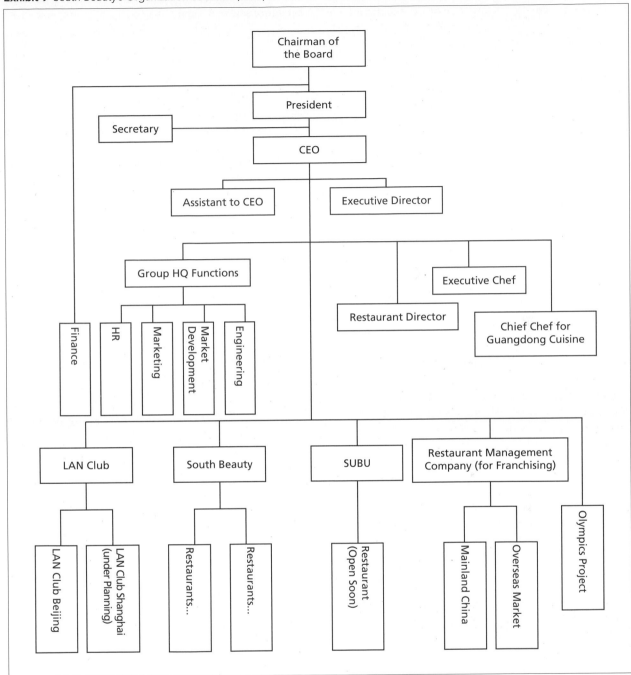

Source: Company internal information.

features, South Beauty could surpass almost all local competitors.

Positioning and Branding

With its positioning as an upmarket restaurant focused on office workers and businesspeople, South Beauty's occupancy rate was quite low during public holidays, such as the Golden Weeks,[18] because its target customers usually went on vacation at this time. In contrast, the business of other popular restaurants or fast food chains,

such as McDonald's, fared well during these holidays; this proved the correctness of the brand positioning of South Beauty.

Danny Wang, Zhang Lan's only child and executive director of the Group, was in charge of developing LAN Club and SUBU. He did his high school, university, and MBA education in France and Canada and visited upmarket restaurants all over the world. When he returned to China in 2004, Zhang Lan asked him to consider a multi-brand strategy for the Group. Danny

Wang mentioned the basic consideration of LAN Club brand and SUBU:

At the beginning, the company just wanted to build a flagship restaurant under the South Beauty Brand. But I did not agree with that. As a metropolis, Beijing lacks the attributes of a modern city. I think that Beijing needs a place for leisure with an international standard to provide the 360-degree experience of an exclusive and healthy lifestyle. It is the original positioning of LAN Club. LAN is the name of my mother and also means "orchid," a symbol of Chinese culture.

As the newest brand in the Group, SUBU was to be different from the luxury LAN Club and the business-segment-focused South Beauty. SUBU was to focus on innovative healthy food. Moreover, a special store was to be inside a SUBU restaurant to sell the SUBU-style CDs and tablewares, etc.[19]

In fact, no competitor in the Chinese restaurant market had such brand architecture. Almost all of them just operated their single brands without clear brand positioning, and their brand image was relatively inferior. Luo Yun explained the company's branding strategy thusly: "We focused on brand differentiation to cater to a wide range of customers. Thus, South Beauty targets businesspeople aged 30–45 years. LAN Club targets successful businesspeople aged over 45 years. SUBU targets younger and more fashionable office workers. We hope that our business would be like that of BMW, which rolls out 7-, 5-, and 3-series products at the same time."[20]

In order to promote these three brands systematically, the company built consistent brand identities and launched some outdoor and print advertisement. The company explored cooperation with certain international airlines, including Air France and KLM Royal Dutch Airlines, to provide business travelers flying between China and Europe with South Beauty–branded Chinese dishes (see Exhibit 10). In addition, it wanted to diversify into the business of partially cooked frozen foods—such as dumplings—for retail outlets.

Menu Innovations

The Group developed a range of innovations with regard to Sichuan cuisine. An independent R&D team was placed in charge of creating new dishes, and the executive chef was responsible for food quality. Under a strict assessment system, only 2 percent of all new dishes could be launched. Although many competitors copied the Group's dishes, Zhang Lan reminded her team to focus on continuous innovations to stay ahead of its followers instead of worrying about being copied by them. In addition, to enrich its variety and cater to the tastes of different people, the company also added certain

Cantonese cuisine and other flavors to its menu. As a brochure said:

The South Beauty Group primarily offers Sichuan flavors, but we also offer Cantonese and other dishes. We innovatively combine Chinese and Western cuisine that breaks with tradition and creates original new flavors. It is the first Chinese restaurant to offer Chinese food in a western style, and the first to mix food presentation with artistic elements.... For many years the Group has charged itself with the mission of developing the culture of Chinese cuisine and advocating a stylish and healthy lifestyle. It has always been focused on drawing from China's deep traditional culture while at the same time making bold innovations and improvements.... Some of the factors that make the Group's cuisine different from others are the strict requirements placed on raw ingredients, the innovation on traditional cuisine, the exacting criteria placed on a dish's nutritional value, and the strong emphasis on the visual appeal of each dish.[21]

Location and Pricing

In order to remain close to its targeted customer base, the Group's restaurants were located in top-notch office buildings in key cities. Although the operational costs were higher in comparison with those of other restaurants, meals could be more expensively priced to cover the costs. This combination of high-end location and high pricing was also helpful in developing the upper-middle-class brand image.

Interior Decoration

Each South Beauty restaurant had a different décor, designed by well-known artists in the field. Zhang Lan and her team insisted that people came to the restaurants not only for the food but also for the ambience. South Beauty never hesitated to invest in interior décor, and sought to combine both Chinese and Western designs in the restaurants. On average, the Group invested RMB 8 million (around USD 1 million) on the furniture, interior decoration, and in setting up the kitchen of a new South Beauty restaurant. Moreover, for the luxury LAN Club, the total investment on interior decoration was over RMB 100 million (around USD 13 million), including USD 2 million in design fees. In this way, the Group became unique in the Chinese restaurant market. In contrast, no competitor could invest so heavily in interior decoration.

IT Applications

In the South Beauty Group, advanced IT applications (e.g., portable order placement) were seen as potent tools to enhance the upper-middle-class image of the restaurant and to improve efficiency. Well before other Chinese restaurants constructed CRM systems, the Group built its own CRM system to record customer information

Exhibit 10 Branding Activities of South Beauty

(Left) Restaurant Signage in Shanghai; (Right) Outdoor Advertising in Beijing

Airline Food Cooperation between Air France and South Beauty

The Brand Logos of South Beauty, LAN Club, and SUBU

Source: Company internal information; the pictures of airline food cooperation with Air France were copied from http://www.cnsphoto.com/NewsPhoto/printNews.asp?ID=359106.

and use that information to provide tailor-made services and make promotional communications. An ERP system was established to control the key financial variables and the purchasing process. Meanwhile, the company tested its remote conference system to increase internal communication among various restaurants located at different places. These IT applications were quite innovative for the traditional Chinese catering industry, as most restaurants remain committed to their old ways of operating their businesses.

People Management

Zhang Lan believed that a dedicated workforce could surmount challenges pertaining to financial capital and market potential. In 2003, when the threat of the SARS virus had the population terrified and almost all other restaurants temporarily closed and dismissed their staffs, Zhang Lan resisted this course of action. She paid her more than 1,000 staff members their full salaries and provided them with proper accommodations to limit their risk of catching the disease.

The Group sought to apply performance management techniques with regard to the management team. At the same time, it worked with a consulting firm to design a new people management system to motivate its staff. Danny Wang regarded people management as a key part of the daily operation, stating: "Our industry is a labor-intensive business. Although the top management is critical (for efficient performance), it is the waiters who are the first point of contact with our customers. The process of training and managing these front-line people, who are young and inexperienced, is the most difficult issue. We initiated a large-scale training program for our staff last year."[22]

In 2006, waiters had to undertake a three-month course at a company training center, evaluated on metrics such as setting a table within three minutes. Restaurant managers, meanwhile, had to complete a two-year on-the-job training program. For two weeks each year, they were sent to tour restaurants in Europe, the United States, and Asia in order to compare service levels and bring back ideas. Zhang Lan also recruited Chinese executives who had previously managed the operations of McDonald's and Coca-Cola in China to work for South Beauty.

China's Restaurant Market

The Shandong, Sichuan, Guangdong, Fujian, Jiangsu, Zhejiang, Hunan, and Anhui cuisines, also known as the "Eight Cuisines," are the most popular in China. The essential factors that establish a particular cuisine are complex, and include history, cooking habits, geography, climate, resources, and lifestyles. A typical Chinese restaurant offers one or two cuisines.

Since the 1990s, China's catering industry had been booming with a compound annual growth rate (CAGR) of more than 15 percent. In 2007, the catering market size of RMB 1,200 billion (USD 155 billion) accounted for 4.87 percent of the gross domestic product (GDP) in China. This percentage was only 1.5 percent in 1978. In 2004, Eastern China contributed at least 50 percent of total industry revenue (see Exhibits 11 and 12).

Exhibit 11 Market Development—China's Catering Industry (1995–2007)*

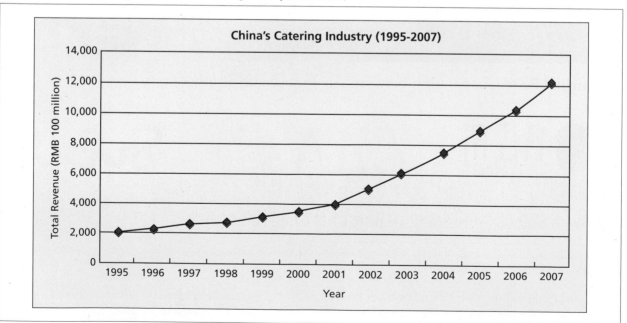

*The data for 2007 were estimated.

Source: Information from industry interviews.

Exhibit 12 Area Difference—China's Catering Industry (2004)

Area	Number of Provinces	Total Revenue of Restaurant Industry (in RMB billion)	% of Total	Annual Growth Rate (in %)
National Total	**31**	**748.6**	**100**	**21.6**
East China	11	418.3	55.7	22.0
Middle China	8	180.0	24.0	20.1
West China	12	152.0	20.3	23.8

Source: 2004, China catering industry analysis, *Economic Daily*, March 16, 2005.

There were three main sections in China's catering industry: breakfast stands, street hawkers, and restaurants. Although there were many breakfast stands and street hawkers, the restaurants section was especially significant (see Exhibit 13). In China, the restaurants section was divided into four subcategories: dinner (mainly Chinese cuisine), hot pot, fast food (Western and Chinese), and teahouses (including coffeehouses). Generally speaking, the growth of the Chinese dinner category was slower than that of the other three categories.

In 2006, the average profitability of the restaurant market was pegged at about 10 percent of total revenues; raw material costs were 43.6 percent of total revenues; labor costs were 11.92 percent; and rental costs were 8.75 percent. The labor costs in China were lower, while the overhead costs were higher, as compared with those in other developed countries.[23]

Beneath the prosperous surface, China's restaurant market faced critical problems. As a result of low entry barriers, thousands upon thousands of new restaurants emerged. However, the service quality, hygiene levels, and managerial capabilities of those in charge were often unsatisfactory.

Growth Dream

China's restaurant market was competitively challenging, not only in terms of the number of players, but also in terms of food varieties. This market was also affected by high rates of turnover (openings and closures) and fragmentation. Since 2001, half of the top 100 restaurant companies in China have been replaced by other emerging companies. In 2006, the sales revenue of the top 50 restaurant companies accounted for just 5 percent of the national restaurant market. In contrast, the sales revenue of the top 50 restaurant companies in the United States represented 20 percent of that market.[24] The global player, Yum! Brands, ranked at the top of China's catering industry, reaching annual revenues of more than RMB 11 billion; however, the revenue of the next biggest player in China was only around five billion, and that of the tenth biggest was less than one billion.[25]

Nevertheless, shocked by the success of Western fast food in China, the leading Chinese players explored how to expand their scale. It was believed that expanding the scale of the leading restaurants in China was critical for the market's healthy development. It was also believed that scaling required standardization. However, for traditional Chinese cuisine, standardization was difficult to implement. As an industry observer commented:

The features of Chinese catering culture are different from those of the Western one. Chinese cuisine has a wider range of raw materials, more varied consumption of dishes per meal, and more flexible ways of preparing dishes. It conflicts with the tenets of standardization, such as few product types, standardized processes and criteria,

Exhibit 13 Structure Difference—China's Catering Industry (2004)

Type	Number (in thousands)	Daily Revenue for Each Outlet (in RMB)	Est. Investment for Each Outlet (in RMB)	Estimated Employee Number
Breakfast Stander	1,900	<100	<500	1
Street Hawkers	1,000	300–400	2,000	2–3
Restaurants (100–400 seats)	600	5,000–10,000	300,000	20–50
Restaurants (400–800 seats)	200	15,000–30,000	2,000,000	150–200
Restaurants (800+ seats)	1	50,000–120,000	5,000,000	300–400

Source: Constraints on Chinese restaurant development: Reason and analysis; *Xinhua Daily*, April 27, 2005, and industry interviews.

etc. Comparatively speaking, it is easier for the sections of hot pot and Chinese fast food to explore standardization and expand scale through chain restaurants. However, for the Chinese dinner section, standardization is not an easy job. That's why the scaling of Chinese dinner restaurants is slower than that of the hot pot and Chinese fast food restaurants.[26]

Expanding Chains

The rapid development of many restaurant chains was notable, both in the hot pot and the Western fast food markets, especially with regard to the trend of franchising (see Exhibits 14 and 15). In 2006, the top 100 restaurants in China had 14,489 outlets, of which about 39 percent were directly owned while 61 percent were franchisees. In addition, the operational indicators of the dinner/hot pot restaurant chains were also distinct from those of fast food chains (see Exhibit 16).

Because expansion required significant investment, in 2006, at least 10 restaurant chains announced their intentions to launch initial public offerings (IPOs). Certain venture capital firms (VCs), which were normally in the business of technology, media, and telecom (TMT) deals, bought stakes in restaurant businesses. They expressed their increasing interest in this evolving traditional industry: "The restaurant business has better cash flow and lower risk than the TMT businesses. China is at the critical point of the booming consumption economy. There are many opportunities to foster leading companies in a traditional business. The VCs would like to select valuable companies who have the long-term dream to be great players in their industries."[27]

The restaurant chains' expansion was much quicker than the rate of economic growth and raised a great deal of issues. Besides the difficulties inherent in standardizing Chinese cuisine, the lack of human resources and management skills were bottlenecks as well. Although the franchising model became popular for chain expansion, the franchisees sometimes crept out of the control of the principal companies and gradually set up their own similar brands. In addition, a restaurant could quickly and easily copy any new dish created by another restaurant. Because of these issues, few Chinese restaurant chains could build their core competitiveness for the long term.

However, a few far-sighted restaurant chains were planning to avoid the potential risk of unplanned expansion and took actions to improve the quality of their business operations. For example, Little Sheep, which was the biggest hot pot chain and had received USD 25 million from venture capitalists, reduced its outlets from 721 to 326 in the summer of 2007. Even though the

Exhibit 14 Top 100 Restaurants—China's Restaurant Market (2006)

Type	Restaurant Chains	Restaurant Outlets	Total Revenue (in RMB billion)	% of Top 100
Hot Pot	22	6,682	30	36
Fast Food	15	4,375	23	27.8
Chinese Dinner	42	1,690	19.5	23.5
Tea/Coffee House	N/A	N/A	10.6	12.7

Source: The fast development of Chinese key restaurant companies, *China Business Newspaper*, June 15, 2007.

Exhibit 15 Restaurant Chains—China's Restaurant Market (2006)*

Type	Revenue (in RMB billion)			Restaurant Outlets		
	2005	2006	Growth (in %)	2005	2006	Growth (in %)
Western Fast Food	14.7	18.5	25.8	2,330	2,757	18.3
Chinese Fast Food	1.8	2.0	11.6	1,191	1,075	−10.8
Hot Pot	13.1	14.9	14	2,454	2,799	13.6
Chinese Dinner	139.0	151.0	9.5	1,507	1,545	2.25

*Because of various sampling, some data in Exhibit 15 are different from those in Exhibit 14; however, Exhibit 15 reveals the yearly difference between 2005 and 2006.

Source: *China Chain Store Business Year Book* 2007.

Exhibit 16 Dinner/Hot Pot Chains vs. Fast Food Chains in China (2006)

Index	Dinner/Hot Pot Chains		Fast Food Chains	
	2005	2006	2005	2006
Number of Restaurants	4,244	5,066	4,213	4,843
Total Size (10,000 m²)	338.2	426.6	123.6	140.7
Staff (10,000 people)	27.8	32.9	20.6	20.6
Seats (10,000)	191.6	212.6	49.2	55.7
Total Revenue (in RMB billion)	22.8	27.8	20.4	24.9
Purchased Product (in RMB billion)	9.5	11.24	7.35	8.43
By Central Distribution	3.99	4.74	6.74	7.75
By Owned Distribution Center	2.73	3.54	4.94	5.63
By Third-Party Distribution Center	1.26	1.19	1.79	2.10

Source: Adapted from *China Statistical Year Book 2007*.

majority of the closed restaurants were franchisees, only 30 percent of the remaining restaurants were directly controlled; the rest continued to be franchisees.[28]

Innovative Chinese Restaurants

Certain emerging, innovative Chinese restaurants, including South Beauty, sought to revamp the image of Chinese cuisine. For example, the appearance of the hot pot was considered unappealing and, therefore, it was not treated as refined food. However, the Hot Loft Restaurant in Beijing experimented with certain simple innovations in the dish, thereby elevating the image of the traditional hot pot.

Some of the innovative Chinese dinner restaurants also paid more attention to their brand statement, which dealt with the entire process of daily operations from raw material purchases to service delivery. These restaurants selected their menus carefully and limited customers' choices, although they had the capability to prepare a great variety of dishes in their kitchens. The founders of these restaurants realized the importance of innovative business ideas, a unique menu, and an impressive decoration style. They believed that unless such initiatives were undertaken, Chinese cuisine would not be able to catch up with the changing tastes of consumers. Paul Hsu, owner of Night Shanghai, suggested that "People only want to visit restaurants that have an impressive ambience. The food can be extremely simple, and they order a small number of dishes and enjoy them slowly."[29]

The most important innovation among Chinese dinner restaurants was the attempt to standardize raw material purchases, preparation of semi-cooked dishes, logistics, and customer service. For example, Jade Garden, with 11 top-grade Shanghainese Cuisine chain restaurants in Shanghai and Beijing, set up a central kitchen in 2002. At the beginning, its intention was just to manage various suppliers centrally for the quality control of raw materials. After a few years' operation, the central kitchen evolved into a production center for meals to be heated as well as to prepare dim sums and semi-cooked dishes with packs of well-mixed sauces. The chefs at each restaurant could prepare the food easily according to the required process. Li Jun, one of the founders of Jade Garden, shared her experience:

At the beginning, the Chief Chef was against the central kitchen, because he was worried that he had to make his cooking knowledge public. But I told him, with the central kitchen, he would be a Chief Chef supervising 500 chefs, not just 50 chefs at the current time. Then we separated the food preparing process into many steps, with each chef in the central kitchen just handling part of the entire process.

In this way, except the Chief Chef, nobody can grasp the whole process. But we are able to overcome the bottleneck of production and prepare Chinese dishes in a standardized way. Moreover, we also have unexpected results, such as lower stock of raw materials, and fewer chefs in each chain restaurant.

Operating several restaurants under the same brand does not necessarily constitute a real chain. A real chain requires a consistent business model and operation. With the standardized raw material purchases, food preparation and sauce mix, we believe that we are building a real restaurant chain. However, we would not request standardized interior decoration for each restaurant. We are not McDonald's, which makes simple standardized fast food; we are standardizing complex Chinese dishes to keep steady quality.[30]

Fast Food Players

The growth of international fast food brands such as KFC, McDonald's, and Pizza Hut in China have increased the food options available to consumers. For instance, since November 1987, KFC had launched 2,000 restaurants and covered more than 400 cities. The restaurant chain's next objective in China was to rapidly penetrate into smaller cities, with plans of opening one outlet every day. China had become the second-largest market for KFC, after the United States. Its main competitor, McDonald's, had 820 outlets and intended to reach 1,000 restaurants in 2008.

These Western fast food chains showed what standardization and logistics could achieve in the restaurant business. For example, by 2006, Yum! Brands, the parent company of KFC, Pizza Hut, and Taco Bell, established 16 distribution centers in China. Its newest East China distribution center, which was also the group's largest facility in Asia, was 15,500 square meters in area and nine meters high. It could manage more than 3,500 items to cover more than 300 restaurants and deliver at least five million cartons of food over three million kilometers every year. At the same time, in Shanghai, Yum! was testing its new brand, Dong Fang Ji Bai Chain Restaurant, focusing exclusively on Chinese fast food. This new brand had the same standardized operational system as KFC and showed encouraging results.

Local fast food chains, such as Kungfu, Ajisen Noodle, Malan Noodle, and Da Niang Dumpling, borrowed the best practices of these international brands. For example, Kungfu—a fast-growing local player with 200 restaurants—planned to establish three logistics centers in China to carry out the key functions of raw material procurement, food processing, and delivery. Kungfu also announced plans to open 2,000 restaurants by 2012. Most successful local chains had attracted foreign capital and also planned to offer IPOs to gain greater resources for scaling up their operations. However, they lagged far behind the international brands in some areas, especially food and process standardization and central logistics capability.

South Beauty's Competitors

Being positioned in the high-end Chinese dinner segment, South Beauty would not compete directly with fast food, hot pot, and "ordinary" restaurants. Among the top 100 restaurant companies in China in 2007, 10 were in this segment, including Shanghai Jingjiang (ranked No. 4), Beijing Shunfeng (No. 18), Guangzhou Jiujia (No. 28), Shanghai Xiaonanguo (No. 32), Shanghai Renjia

(No. 60), Shanghai Jade Garden (No. 88), Shanghai Shenjia Garden (No. 91), and South Beauty itself (No. 72). These competitors focused on various Chinese cuisines; for example, Beijing Shunfeng and Guangzhou Jiujia mainly served Guangdong cuisine, and Jingjiang, Xioananguo, Renjia, Jade Garden, and Shengjia Garden in Shanghai offered Jiangsu and Zhejiang dishes. Thus, South Beauty, which focused on Sichuan cuisine, did not compete with these restaurants directly in terms of cuisine. Normally, people selected the type of cuisine they were in the mood for first and the restaurant later.

The most crucial issue for South Beauty was that of restaurants claiming to be South Beauty franchises. In 2005, South Beauty found there were at least 16 "fake" restaurants in cities South Beauty had not penetrated, such as Nanjing, Xiamen, Tianjing, Qingdao, and Hong Kong. Generally speaking, the imposters used the same Chinese name as South Beauty (i.e., Qiao Jiang Nan), with one or two additional Chinese characters. The counterfeit logos enlarged the size of the "Qiao Jiang Nan" characters and minimized the other elements. In this way, these counterfeit restaurants attracted innocent customers and provided them with poor service and atmosphere. However, the unhappy customers complained to the "real" South Beauty. South Beauty attempted to use legal means to protect its brand, but because of the local protection the copiers enjoyed in some cities, the process was sometimes quite slow, and the results were not very encouraging.

Consumer Trends and Opinions

In recent years, as Chinese urban consumers' disposable incomes have increased, they have spent more on meals in restaurants. The annual expenditure per capita on restaurant meals increased from RMB 534 (USD 65) in 2004 to an estimated RMB 800 (USD 105) in 2007. However, compared with developed markets, there is still great potential for growth—the corresponding figure in the United States was USD 1,600 per capita, and, in France, USD 1,050.[31] Moreover, in more advanced cities, such as Shanghai, Guangzhou, and Beijing, this number was three to five times higher than the national average. In these cities, consumers had more choices of restaurants and made selections based on word of mouth. According to a Web site survey, 63 percent of consumers obtained restaurant information from word-of-mouth publicity, 15 percent from traditional media (newspaper, TV, radio, etc.), 12 percent from the Internet, and 10 percent from outdoor advertising.[32]

Since the 1990s, consumption in restaurants has evolved into various segments, such as office workers having lunches, family members dining out, friends gathering, lovers dating, and business-related meals. Different segments have different needs. The office workers select fast food (Western 30 percent and Chinese 70 percent) as their lunch for its convenience and quickness. This huge segment constituted one fourth of the total catering industry. The main consideration of families dining out is value for their money. The restaurant selection for a gathering of friends depends on the social status of the people; those with higher status select better restaurants. Lovers prefer a romantic restaurant for their dates.

Because of the booming economy in China, the business meals had more potential than the other segments because they could absorb higher prices. Also, businesspeople were not satisfied with simple eating and drinking—they required more in terms of the restaurant's atmosphere, food taste, location, and so on. These businesspeople were the target consumers of the South Beauty Group.

A popular restaurant review Web site stated:

Promoting "Refined or Improved Sichuan Food," South Beauty has elevated Sichuan food from the level of austerity to one fit for the nobility. The dishes have a unique taste, appearance, and preparation style. The ambience is also excellent—an elegant, grand, Western style—quite different from that offered by ordinary Chinese restaurants. The waiters and waitresses wear well-designed uniforms and are hospitable. It is a good place to entertain guests, although the charges are higher in comparison with normal restaurants.[33]

However, in Chengdu, the birthplace of Sichuan food, customers were of the opinion that the Sichuan food offered by South Beauty was not as spicy as the original cuisine. Others did not view South Beauty as a genuine Sichuan food restaurant. Nonetheless, they were pleased that South Beauty offered a range of innovative dishes that were presented elegantly (see Exhibit 17).

2008 Beijing Olympics Opportunity

The 2008 Olympic Games in Beijing were estimated to generate sales of RMB 18 billion for the catering industry in the city. Thirteen million meals would be provided for athletes, support personnel, media reporters, and other guests for three months. This revenue was divided between Western (estimated at 70 percent of meals) and Chinese cuisine (30 percent).

However, the mainstream international media challenged the food security situation in China. The Chinese government tried to ensure food supply safety for the Olympic Games. Following the completion of the bidding process based on strict food standards, six companies were selected as the food suppliers: South Beauty Group, along with three other local companies and two international ones, McDonald's and ARAMARK. Bian Jiang, the chief secretary of the China Restaurant Association, commented to the press: "The 2008 Beijing Olympic Games will facilitate the internationalization of the Beijing restaurant market. The food suppliers for the Olympic Games will suffer a critical technical transition,

Exhibit 17 Customer Ratings of South Beauty Restaurants (October 2007)

	Beijing (Among 420 customers)	Shanghai (Among 1,153 Customers)	Chengdu (Among 187 customers)
Rating (max. 30)			
Taste	18–21	17–18	17
Environment	24–27	21–26	27
Service	20–22	15–20	22
Consumption (RMB/per person)	**102–141**	**149–180**	**115**
Category Perception (%)			
Business Entertainment	34%	27%	41%
Sichuan Food	23%	18%	10%
Gathering of Friends	13%	8%	0%
Innovative Sichuan Food	0%	0%	33%
Dinner for Dating	16%	8%	16%

Source: Information collected from http://www.dianping.com in October 2007 based on customers' comments on a typical restaurant in each city.

especially in terms of the food and process standardization and logistics capacity, which will also lead to a change in the restaurant market. Restaurants that can upgrade their operations in response to the large-scale requirements of the Olympics are likely to fare well in China's catering industry in the future."[34]

Future Plans

Zhang Lan believed that the Chinese entrepreneurs of her generation should take greater responsibility to rejuvenate Chinese culture because they have access to better opportunities than previous generations:

I am thinking about how to develop Chinese cuisine to enter the mainstream restaurant market in Western countries as opposed to opening the kind of Chinese restaurants you find in Chinatown. The South Beauty Group has catered to more than 100,000 foreign guests from all over the world, and they all enjoyed our food. Thus, now is the time to expand. We have met success in China, and now we wish to build an international brand, which will have a presence in New York, Paris, London, Milan, Geneva, Tokyo, and other important international cities of the world.[35]

Undoubtedly, redefining Chinese cuisine and maintaining quality in the midst of rapid domestic and global expansion will not be an easy job. Luo Yun commented on the difficulties:

Having objectives and ambitions are not enough; we have to act to meet these objectives. Top management is thinking about the big picture. We also need to consider how to execute the tasks and foresee difficulties. For example, we should constantly improve the menu through R&D, improve people management practices, etc.; we also should train people to do things in a standardized way. It is difficult to do so, and until now, no one (in the China's dinner category) has been able to do it very successfully.[36]

The Challenges Ahead

The existing business of the South Beauty Group was flourishing, but the management team did not halt their efforts to improve the Group's operational efficiency through standardization, which was also the foundation for scaling up. To expand, the Group had to consider the prioritization of markets to enter (i.e., whether to focus on the local market to realize its full potential before venturing abroad, or to do both at the same time); entry into new businesses, such as airline catering and the supply of semi-processed food to retail outlets; the expansion model (i.e., through owned outlets as had been the case until now or through franchising); and the way to finance the expansion, which posed many challenges.

Seeking Standardization

It was easier for a fast food chain or a Western restaurant to standardize its food and processes—for example, McDonald's offered only 40 to 50 dishes and T.G.I. Friday's around 100. Each South Beauty restaurant carried 380 items on the main menu, excluding soft drinks and wines. Raw materials depended on local suppliers, and the quality of each dish relied on the experience of the chef. Although there was a team with three main chefs at the head office to develop new dishes and control the quality, the process of standardization was still in its nascent phase.

Jacy Yang, who joined the Group in July 2007 as executive director, had 25 years of experience in Western food companies such as McDonald's, T.G.I. Friday's, and Gino's. He was assigned the task of setting up a system to enhance operational efficiency. He described the challenges and the company's reactions:

In fast-food restaurants, such as KFC and Kungfu, it is easier to handle standardization. However, the same can be quite difficult to manage in high-end Chinese dinner restaurants. Before I came on board, the chefs did not define the inputs because these were regarded as their secrets, and some were even offended when asked to write down the recipes. Subsequently, I looked up the recipes, read the local menu, spoke to professional cooks, and studied the terminology to understand the entire process.

I think it is easy for a restaurant to elaborate on its two success factors. The first is service, which can be stipulated manually and standardized easily through training, rules, inspections, and the right incentive systems. The second is the menu. We are working on an idea for a central kitchen to prepare the main dishes and distribute them to each restaurant to ensure the same taste of key dishes at different times across various restaurants.

At present, in each restaurant, we have a kitchen that is 300–400 square meters in area. The function of a central kitchen that is 2,000 square meters in area is to prepare the main dish packets with uncooked raw materials and send them to the various company restaurants for cooking. The central kitchen will be set up in each city of operation. Currently, we are building two, in Beijing and Shanghai. In this way, we can achieve standardization and control the average cost. Our central kitchen will handle dishes prepared from expensive materials and the ones that can be easily standardized. However, the kitchens in individual restaurants will also prepare some dishes with fresh materials, such as vegetables, and other special requests, so they will still be required to make certain raw material purchases.[37]

Jacy Yang's other role was to standardize the Group's cost management. He explained his ideas this way:

Some people in our company say they have cut 30 percent of the cost, but I am not sure about it. They should provide data. I will set the standard, ask the chef, and nail down the recipe and the input cost, factor in the processing cost, and then arrive at a standard cost for each dish. Meanwhile, we will control the use of raw materials with computer software to calculate the number of dishes sold and the raw materials used, and check the stock situation to evaluate materials usage. In this way, we will be able to control the cost of raw materials, which constitutes the largest part of the cost structure.[38]

Venturing into Newer Markets

The South Beauty Group's domestic business was concentrated in Beijing and Shanghai. The city selection was a critical decision (see Exhibit 18). This same issue was raised with regard to international markets. In 2005, Zhang Lan planned to open two restaurants in Hong Kong, but little progress had been made on this front. Zhang Lan also wanted to test the market in the United Arab Emirates. Recently, the Group had communicated its ongoing projects to open restaurants in well-known international cities such as New York, Paris, and Tokyo, although the details of this plan have not been disclosed.

When Zhang Lan stated her scale expansion objectives, she projected the Group to have 30 restaurants in short term and 100 outlets in the next three years, of which 35 restaurants would be located in China and 65 in the international market in cooperation with strategic partners in Tokyo, New York, and other cities. The Group was also trying to expand its scale through entering into new product areas, such as airline catering in the global market and the supply of semi-processed food to retail outlets in the domestic market.

The scaling up of fast food restaurants has been achieved by several brands, both international and Chinese, but the expansion of upper-middle-class dinner restaurants posed a bigger challenge. Therefore, South Beauty Group's targets looked extremely ambitious and certain observers expressed their worries. According to a well-known international media publication, "There is no other successful national restaurant chain in this market segment, and South Beauty has still not covered all the major Chinese cities. Entering a mature (Western) market will involve working in a radically different operating environment."[39]

Expansion Model

The South Beauty Group was trying to develop a franchising system to expand its restaurant chain in China. There were two new restaurants at the stage of signing franchise contracts. The company also announced its plan to seek franchisees on its Web site and was flooded with questions from interested entrepreneurs. Luo Yun expressed his concerns:

It is a huge and extremely difficult transition for the company, because Chinese cuisine has not been standardized well with regard to operations. We studied the central management style, for example, of the McDonald's chain, which has 16 staff members in its financial division for 800 outlets. However, we recruited

Exhibit 18 Top 10 Cities—China's Catering Industry (2006)

Rank by Size	City	Total Revenue of Catering Industry (in RMB billion)	Rank by Growth	City	Annual Growth (in %)
1	Shanghai	45.2	1	Shanghai	29.0
2	Beijing	36.2	2	Jinan	21.8
3	Guangzhou	35.0	3	Qingdao	21.7
4	Tianjing	21.0	4	Chongqing	20.0
5	Chengdu	20.9	5	Zhengzhou	19.3
6	Chongqing	19.4	6	Hefei	19.1
7	Wuhan	17.7	7	Wuhan	17.9
8	Jinan	14.0	8	Hangzhou	17.9
9	Dalian	13.4	9	Tianjing	17.4
10	Zhengzhou	13.0	10	Changsha	17.2

Source: China's catering industry: Top 10 cities in 2006; *China Chain Store Business Year Book 2007.*

more than 80 people in the same department for only 20 restaurants. That is the big difference.[40]

However, in the international market, both owned and franchised restaurants might be risky models for expansion because of the lack of local market knowledge and the difficulties of managing the franchisees. The Group contacted local partners with complementary resources in target cities to seek cooperation. For example, Royal Company, a potential strategic partner for the group in Japan, controlled over 1,000 restaurants and provided airline food in the Japanese market. In addition, the requirements for the restaurant's size, style, and cuisine in the international market would be different from those in the domestic market. The Group had to adjust its plan accordingly.

Financing by IPO

In China, it was difficult for a private restaurant to apply for a bank loan because banks were hesitant to provide capital to restaurants because of the perceived risks involved in this industry. In addition, the government did not consider this industry as a priority area. The South Beauty Group funded its growth plans by reinvesting its profits. The company's cash flow was sufficient to maintain its current operations and to pursue moderate growth. However, the company needed external funding for its expansion plan and other projects related to standardization, new business development, and the Olympic Games contract.

Several private venture capitalists and investment banks, such as Citigroup and Credit Suisse, had expressed their wishes to cooperate with the South Beauty Group. In 2006, the Group announced the launch of a possible IPO in the international or domestic stock market, although a decision regarding the exact date of the IPO was not made. Zhang Lan discussed her company's IPO:

Our IPO is not just for funding. Our main objective is to build an open company with the supervision of the shareholders. I do not like the family company, because it is difficult to be a giant under family members' management. A long-life company could be built through a well-designed management system and a clear arrangement with the shareholders about their equity and responsibility.[41]

Dream Big but Do Small

At the break of the 2007 meeting with her management team, Zhang Lan looked out of her office window. She saw Beijing National Stadium (the "Bird's Nest") being built for the 2008 Olympics—the stadium's main body had already taken shape.[42] Zhang Lan sat back and pondered:

Should the Group scale up its size at a rapid pace? How can the company improve standardization of Chinese cuisine? Where should the targeted domestic and international markets be located? How can the company achieve the right balance between owned and franchised restaurants? What would be the correct time to invite external capital and launch an IPO?

Zhang Lan realized that she had to dream big for the future, but, at the same time, take small steps to keep everything on track. She knew that the road ahead was just like the Bird's Nest Stadium, which had an exciting outer shape and a complex inner structure as well.

NOTES

1. Picture of Zhang Lan from 2006, Zhang Lan: Planning to open South Beauty in New York and Paris, *China Entrepreneur*, December.
2. This school's name was changed to Beijing Technology and Business University in 1999.
3. Exchange rate in 1991: USD 1=RMB 5.4.
4. "Bai Niao Yuan" means a garden with a lot of birds.
5. Exchange rate in 1999: USD 1=RMB 8.27.
6. 2007, Boss town: Dialogue with Zhang Lan, http://www.sina.com.cn, January 19.
7. Ibid.
8. Businesspeople include entrepreneurs, professional managers, and some middle-level office workers.
9. 2008, LAN Club and its hostess, *Lifeweek*, February 4.
10. Qiao Jiang Nan: "Qiao" means beautiful and "Jiang Nan" stands for the area south of Yangtze.
11. 2006, South Beauty: Chinese food in a Western way, winning with details, *Eastern Entrepreneur*, March 2006.
12. Case writer's interview with Zhang Lan, October 16, 2007.
13. SARS is the acronym for Severe Acute Respiratory Syndrome.
14. This number was provided by the company. As a cautious private company that was contacting venture capitalists, South Beauty was sensitive about providing its financial data. However, some media (such as Zhang Lan: A woman behind South Beauty, *Money Talk*, April 17, 2008) estimated that the annual revenue of the South Beauty Group would be over RMB 1 billion in 2007, with 20,000 to 30,000 footfalls every day. According to another source, the company's actual revenue in 2005 was RMB 460 million, with an average annual growth of 55.6 percent in the past three years (*China Entrepreneur*, May 20, 2006).
15. Dinner is the main meal of the day, whether eaten at midday or in the evening. The Chinese dinner category includes Chinese restaurants that provide the main meals of Chinese cuisine, not fast food or hot pot.
16. The market share of the top player, Yum!, was around 1 percent. The market share of South Beauty was estimated by the case authors and industry observers.
17. Case writer's interview with Luo Yun, October 16, 2007.
18. Golden Week is a twice-yearly week-long Chinese holiday.
19. 2007, South Beauty promotes its multibrand strategy and plans the overseas market expansion, *China New Age*, October; case writer's interview with Danny Wang, October 16, 2007.
20. Case writer's interview with Luo Yun on October 16, 2007.
21. The brochure was printed by the South Beauty Group.

22. Case writer's interview with Danny Wang on October 16, 2007.

23. 2007, The out-of-order competition in China's catering industry," *Economic Policy Information*, January 15.

24. 2008, Who is the biggest in China's catering industry? *Lifeweek*, February 4.

25. 2007, China Catering Industry Report, Hu Nan Science and Technology Publishing Company, October.

26. 2008, Who is the biggest in China's catering industry? *Lifeweek*, February 4.

27. 2007, China's catering industry becomes a hotspot, *China Business News*, January 15.

28. 2007, Little Sheep Restaurant Chain: Plan an IPO in Hong Kong for HK$ 2 billion, *Oriental Morning Post*, August 3.

29. The features of Chinese restaurants, http://brand.hr.com.cn/html/40724.html.

30. 2008, Jade Garden: Dialectic of high end Shanghainese cuisine development, *Lifeweek*, February 4.

31. The data of personal consumption came from "China's catering industry is developing fast," *International Business Newspaper*, October 18, 2006, with adjustment based on *China Statistical Year Book 2004*. Exchange rate in October 2007: USD 1 = RMB 7.5; in 2004: USD 1 = RMB 8.27.

32. 2008, Restaurant consumer survey through Internet, *Pin Week*, March 15.

33. Adapted from the Web site: http://www.dianping.com.

34. 2007, Olympics 2008 will create RMB 18 billion business for China's catering industry, *Consumption Daily*, July 30.

35. Information combined from case interview and the media report, 2006, LV (Zhang Lan's South Beauty wants to be LV brand in the restaurant market, http://www.netease.com, January 26; China's 400 richest, http://www.forbes.com/global/2006/1113/098.html.

36. Case Writers' interview with Luo Yun on October 16, 2007.

37. Case Writers' interview with Jacy Yang on October 16, 2007.

38. Ibid.

39. China's 400 richest, http://www.forbes.com/global/2006/1113/098.html.

40. Case Writers' interview with Luo Yun on October 16, 2007.

41. 2008, LAN Club and its hostess, *Lifeweek*, February 4.

42. Please refer to http://en.wikipedia.org/wiki/Beijing_National_Stadium.

Steve Gove

Virginia Tech

Brett P. Matherne

Loyola University of New Orleans

If the motion picture industry's performance in 2007 were a feature presentation, the marquee would read "Massive Box Office: Smashing Records—the Sequel!" At $9.63 billion, box office revenue set another record in 2007, a full 5 percent above the record set in 2006.[1] An astonishing 1.4 billion tickets were sold in 2007. But beyond the headlines, the industry is a study in contradictions:

- The number of theaters is declining, but the number of screens is at an all-time high.
- Revenues are up, but attendance is largely flat—1.4 billion tickets sold is little improved from 1997, when 1.35 billion tickets were sold, and is a fraction of the 4 billion sold in 1946. In 1946, the average person attended 28 films a year. Today, it is 6.[2] (see Exhibits 1 and 2).
- The U.S. population is increasing, but the size of the market in the core demographic group is growing more slowly (see Exhibit 3).

- Americans spend more time than ever on entertainment—3,500 hours annually—but only 12 of those hours are spent at the movies.[3] The average person watches that much television every three days.

Movies remain as popular as ever, but opportunities for viewing outside the theater have greatly increased. While motion picture studios increased revenues through product licensing, DVD sales, and international expansion, the exhibitors—movie theaters—have seen their business decline. Movies are more available than ever, but fewer are venturing to the theater to see them. Many theaters have ceased operation, driven from the market by consolidation and a lack of patrons.

Will the marquee at the local theater soon change to: "A Horror Show at the Cinemaplex?" How has this come to be? What can exhibitors do to respond?

Exhibit 1 Domestic Tickets Sold and Box Office Gross

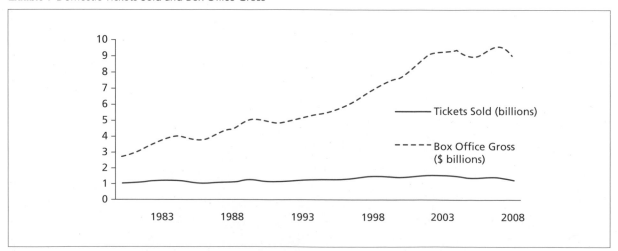

Source: http://boxofficemojo.com & U.S. Census.

Exhibit 2 Average Movie Ticket Price

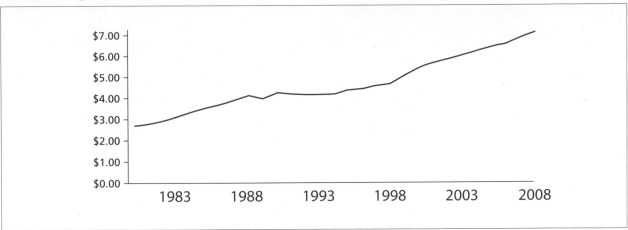

Source: http://boxofficemojo.com.

The Motion Picture Industry Value Chain

The motion picture industry value chain consists of three stages: studio production, distribution, and exhibition. All stages of the value chain are undergoing consolidation.

Studio Production

The studios produce the lifeblood of the industry; they create content. Films from the top 10 studios produce over 90 percent of domestic box office receipts (see Exhibit 4). Studios are increasingly part of larger corporations,

managed as any other profit center. Management is a challenge as investments are large and there is no one formula for success. Because of this, profitability swings wildly. The cost of bringing a typical feature to market is more than $100 million, up 25 percent in the past five years.[4] Typically, marketing expenses are a third of these costs.

Studios know their core audience is 12 to 24 years old. This age group purchases nearly 40 percent of theater tickets. Half are "frequent moviegoers" attending at least one movie per month. Profits are driven by the studios' ability to satisfy this fickle audience. In 2008, films based on two successful comic book characters met

Exhibit 3 Population Trend among 14 to 17 and 18 to 24 Age Groups (Millions)

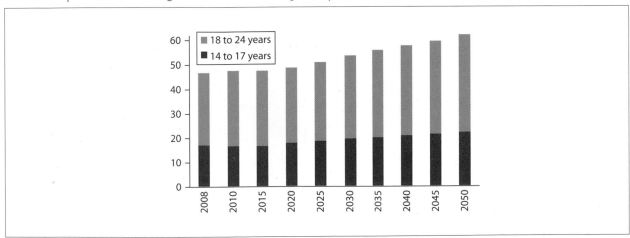

Source: U.S. Census.

Exhibit 4 Market Share of Film Production (2007)

Studio Parent & Label	2007 Combined Share (%)
Time Warner (Warner Brothers & New Line)	19.8
Sony (Sony & MGM)	16.7
Viacom (Viacom & Paramount)	15.5
Disney (Disney, Buena Vista Pictures, & Miramax)	15.4
Universal Studios	11.4
News Corp. (20th Century FOX)	10.5
Lions Gate	3.6
DreamWorks SKG*	0.0
	92.9

Note: *DreamWorks share in 2005 was 5.7%.

Source: Adapted from Mintel Report: Movie Theaters, United States, February 2008.

with wildly different fates.[5] Paramount's successful *Iron Man* was produced for $140 and grossed $318 million at the domestic box office. Warner Brothers's *Speed Racer*, produced for $20 million less and released the following weekend, was a flop, grossing just $44 million.

Demographic trends are unfavorable. The U.S. population will increase 17 percent by 2025, an increase of 54 million people. However, the number of 12- to 24-year-olds is expected to increase only 9 percent—just 4 million more potential viewers. Based on the current number of theaters and screens, this is an increase of less than 700 additional viewers per theater, or roughly 100 per screen.

Distribution

Distributors are the intermediaries between the studios and exhibitors. Distribution entails all steps following a film's artistic completion, including marketing, logistics, and administration. Exhibitors negotiate a percentage of gross from the studio or purchase rights to films and profit from the box office receipts. Distributors select and market film to exhibitors, seeking to maximize potential attendees. Distributors coordinate the manufacture and distribution of the film to exhibitors. They also handle collections, audits of attendees, and

other administrative tasks. There are over 300 active distributors, but much of this work is done by a few major firms, including divisions of studios. Pixar, for example, co-produced *Finding Nemo* with Disney and distribution was handled by Disney's Buena Vista.

Exhibition

Studios have historically sought full vertical integration through theater ownership, allowing greater control over audiences and capturing exhibition profits. A common practice was for the studio to use their ownership to reduce competition by not showing pictures produced by rivals. This practice ended in 1948 with the Supreme Court's ruling against the studios in *United States v. Paramount Pictures*. Theaters were soon divested, leaving them to negotiate with studios for film access and rental.

Theaters are classified according to the number of screens at one location (Exhibit 5). Single-screen theaters were the standard from the introduction of film through the 1980s. They have since rapidly declined in number, replaced by theater complexes. These include miniplexes (2 to 7 screens), multiplexes (8 to 15 screens), and megaplexes (16 or more screens). The number of theaters decreased more than 15 percent between 2000 and 2007, but the number of screens increased because of growth in megaplexes. Nearly 10 percent of theaters are now megaplexes, and the number of screens is at a historical high of 40,077.[6] Many analysts argue the industry has overbuilt and too many theaters and screens exist to make the business profitable.

Movie attendance usually increases as the economy declines. In 2008, there were rapid increases in gas prices, a large stock market decline, and significant layoffs. One summer movie patron commented, "There's not a whole lot you can do for $10 anymore."[7] Movies do remain a

Exhibit 5 Number of Theaters by Complex Size

	2000	2007	% Change
Single Screens	2,368	1,748	−26.18%
Miniplexes (2–7 Screens)	3,170	2,296	−27.57%
Multiplexes (8–15 Screens)	1,478	1,617	9.40%
Megaplexes (16+ Screens)	405	616	52.10%
Total	7,421	6,277	−15.42%

Sources: Developed by author from: Entertainment Industry, 2007 Report, Motion Picture Association of America, and Mintel Report "Movie Theaters, United States, February 2008."

Exhibit 6 Exhibition Market Leaders

Company	Theater Brands	# U.S Theater Locations	# U.S. Screens	Avg. Screens per Theater
Regal	Regal, United Artists, Edwards	526	6,355	12
AMC	AMC, Loews	315	4,585	14
Cinemark	Cinemark, Century	284	3,606	12
Carmike	Carmike	280	2,412	8
	Total for four leading companies	1,405	16,958	
	Industry total	7,421	40,077	

Source: Mintel Report "Movie Theaters, United States, February 2008," SEC filings and author estimates.

bargain in the entertainment business. Four tickets to a movie can cost under $27 (depending on the time of day and location) compared to $141 for an amusement park or $261 for a pro football game.[8] For many, the air-conditioned comfort of a dark theater and the latest Hollywood release offer a break not just from the summer heat, but from reality. "It's escapism, absolutely. It's probably a subconscious thing, and people don't realize it. But there's just so much going on, with people trying to pay their mortgages and get by. It's an escape for a couple of hours."[9]

Declining ticket sales and the increased costs associated with developing megaplexes led to a wave of consolidation among exhibitors. There are now four dominant exhibitors: Regal, AMC, Cinemark, and Carmike. While operating 1,405 theaters in the country (just 19 percent), these companies control 42 percent of screens. This market share provides these exhibitors with negotiating power for access to films, prices for films and concessions, and greater access to revenues from national advertisers.

There is little differentiation in the offerings of the major theater exhibitors—prices within markets differ little, the same movies are shown at the same times, and the food and services are nearly identical. Competition between theaters often comes down to distance from home, convenience of parking, and proximity to restaurants. Innovations by one theater chain are quickly adopted by others. The chains do serve different geographic markets and do so in different ways.[10] Regal focuses on mid-size markets using multiplexes and megaplexes. Regal's average ticket price of $7.43 is the highest among the leaders. AMC concentrates on urban areas with megaplexes and on large population centers, such as those in California, Florida, and Texas. Cinemark

serves smaller markets, operating as the sole theater chain in over 80 percent of its markets. Cinemark's average ticket price last year of $5.11 was the lowest of the majors. Carmike concentrates on small to mid-sized markets, targeting populations of less than 100,000 that have few other entertainment options. Carmike's average ticket price in 2007 was $5.89, but at $3.05, their average concession revenue per patron is the highest among the majors.

The different approaches of the companies are reflected in the cost of fixed assets per screens. These costs result from decisions made on how to serve customers, such as the level of technology and finish of the theater—digital projection and marble floors cost more than traditional projectors and a carpeted lobby.[11] Despite multi- and megaplex facilities, Regal's cost per screen is the highest at $430,000. Carmike, the rural operator, is the lowest at just $206,000. Cinemark is in the middle at $367,000. Data is not available for AMC, but costs are thought to be near or above those of Regal.

The Business of Exhibition

There are three primary sources of revenue for exhibitors: box office receipts, concessions, and advertising. Managers have low discretion; their ability to influence revenues and expenses is limited. Operating margins among exhibitors average a slim 10 percent. This is before significant expenses such as facility and labor costs. The result is marginal or negative net income. Overall, the business of exhibitors is best described as loss leadership on movies: the firms make money selling concessions and showing ads to patrons who are drawn by the movie.

Box Office Revenues

Ticket sales constitute two thirds of exhibition business revenues. The return on these receipts, however, is quite small. A power imbalance results in contracts that return the vast majority of box office receipts to the studios. The record-setting revenues at the box office have been the result of increases in ticket prices and have flowed back to the studios.

Concessions

Moviegoers frequently lament the high prices for concessions. Concessions average 25 to 30 percent of revenues. Direct costs are less than 15 percent of the selling price, making concessions the largest source of exhibitor profit. These are influenced by the three factors: attendance, pricing, and material costs. The most important is attendance: more attendees equal more concession sales. Sales per patron are influenced by prices. The $3.75 price point for a large soda is not by accident, but the result of market research and profit-maximization calculation. Costs are influenced by purchase volume, with larger chains able to negotiate better prices on everything from popcorn and soft drinks to cups and napkins.

Advertising

Exhibitors also generate revenue through pre-show advertising. Though this constitutes just 5 percent of revenues, it is highly profitable. Mintel reports that advertising revenues among exhibitors are expected to increase at a rate of approximately 10 percent over the coming decade.[12] Audiences signal consistent dislike for advertising at the theater. Balancing the revenues from ads with audience tolerance is an ongoing struggle for exhibitors.

Overall, the exhibitor has limited control over both revenues and profits. Box office receipts are the bulk of revenues, but yield few profits. Strong attendance numbers allow for profitable sales of concessions and advertisements, but there are significant caps on the volume of concession sales per person and selling prices seem to have reached their maximum. Advertising remains an attractive avenue for revenues and profits, but audiences loathe it.

The Process of Exhibition

The fundamentals of film exhibition have changed little since the early 1940s. To show a picture, each theater receives a shipment of physical canisters containing a "release print" from the distributor. Making these prints requires $20,000 to $30,000 in up-front costs and $1,000 to $1,500 for each print. Thus, a modern major motion picture opening on 2,500 screens simultaneously requires $2.50 to $3.75 million in print costs. This is borne by the studios, but paid for by movie attendees.

Each release print is actually several reels of 35-mm film, which are manually loaded onto projector reels, sequenced, and queued for display by a projector operator. The film passes through the projector, which shines intense light through the film, projecting the image through a lens that focuses the image on the screen. A typical projection systems costs $50,000, with one needed for each screen.

Digital cinema is becoming economically viable. Digital cinema involves a high resolution (4096 × 2160) digitized image projected onto the screen. Basic digital systems cost $150,000 to $250,000 per screen. Conversion of an existing eight-screen theater to digital thus involves an investment of $1.2 to $2 million. The costs for digital "release prints" are far lower than traditional film, but these costs savings most directly benefit the studio whereas the exhibitors must pay any costs to convert theaters. The number of digital theaters is expanding rapidly. In 2004, there were less than 100, and there are now approximately 4,600, or 12 percent of screens. Because of the cost involved, most theaters use a mixture of technologies, with a minority of screens in any one facility featuring digital projection.

The Theater Experience

For a significant number of moviegoers, the draw of the theater is far more than what film is showing. Moviegoers describe attending the theater as an experience, with the appeal based on:[13]

- the giant theater screen
- the opportunity to be out of the house
- not having to wait to see a particular movie on home video
- the experience of watching the movies with a theatrical sound system
- the theater as a location option for a date

The ability of theaters to provide more than what audiences can experience at home appears to be diminishing. Of the reasons why people go to the movies, only the place aspects—the theater as a place to be out of house and as a place for dating—may be immune from substitution. Few teenagers want to watch a movie and eat popcorn with their date at home with their parents next to them on the sofa.

The overall "experience" currently offered by theaters falls short for many. Marketing research firm Mintel reports the reasons for not attending the theater more frequently are largely the result of the declining experience. Specific factors include the overall cost, at-home viewing options, interruptions such as cell phones in the theater, rude patrons, the overall hassle, and ads prior to the show.[14] A recent *Wall Street Journal* article reported on interruptions ranging from the intrusion of soundtracks in adjacent theaters to cell phones. "The interruptions capped a night of moviegoing already marred by out-of-order ticketing kiosks and a parade of preshow ads so long that, upon seeing the Coca-Cola polar bears on screen, one customer grumbled: 'This is obscene.'"[15] Recounting bad experiences is a lively topic for bloggers. A typical comment: "I say it has gotten worse. I hate paying $9.00 for a ticket and the movie is 90–100 minutes long, people talking on the cell phone, the people who work at the theaters look like they are bored, and when you ask them a question, the answer is very rude. I worked as an usher in the late '60s and we had to wear uniforms and white gloves on Friday and Saturday nights, those days are long gone."[16]

A trip to the local cinemaplex can be eye opening even for industry insiders. In 2005, Toby Emmerich, New Line Cinema's head of production, faced a not-so-common choice: attending "War of the Worlds" in a theater or in a screening room at actor Jim Carrey's house. Said Emmerich in an *LA Times* article, "I love seeing a movie with a big crowd, but I had no idea how many obnoxious ads I'd have to endure—it really drove me crazy. After sitting through about 15 minutes of ads, I turned to my wife and said, 'Maybe we should've gone to Jim Carrey's house after all.'"[17]

The unique value proposition offered by movie theaters—large screens, the long wait for DVD release, and advantages of theatrical sound systems—also appears to be fading. Increasingly larger television sets, DVD content, and the adoption of high-definition technology are all part of this change. One blogger posts, "Whereas the electronics industry has been innovating to create immersive experiences from the comfort of our own home, the US theater industry has been dragging their feet."[18]

Home Viewing Technology

Home television sets are increasingly large, high-definition sets coupled with inexpensive, yet impressive audio systems. In 1997, the screen size of the average television was just 23 inches. Currently, almost half of LCD televisions sold have screens 36 inches or larger.[19] Because set size is measured as the diagonal screen size, increases in viewable area are greater than the measurement suggests. In recent years, the viewing area of sets doubled from 250 inches to 550 inches.

The FCC requirement that all broadcasters convert to digital broadcasts by June 12, 2009, is widely credited with starting a consumer movement to upgrade televisions. Since the 1950s, television transmissions were formatted as 480 interlaced vertical lines (480i) of resolution. The new digital format is high definition (HD), providing up to 1080 vertical lines of resolution (1080p).[20] Three quarters of all televisions sold since 2006 are HD capable.

As LCD technology became the standard for both computer and television screens, manufacturing costs declined. Wholesale prices for televisions fell 65 percent from the late 1990s to 2007.[21] In 2006, the average television retailed for $29 per diagonal inch of set size. This is expected to decrease to $22 within five years.[22] Consumers, however, are actually spending more on every television, consistently electing to purchase larger sets to achieve a better viewing experience. Sharp, a leading manufacturer of televisions predicts that by 2015 the average screen will reach 60 inches.[23]

Large screen televisions, DVD players, and audio and speaker components are commonly packaged as low-cost home theaters. The average DVD player now costs just $72[24] and high-definition DVD players are beginning to penetrate the market. Retail price wars during the 2008 Christmas season led to HD Blu-Ray players dropping below $200. These home theater systems offer a movie experience that rivals many theaters, all for $1,000 to $2,000. Says Mike Gabriel, Sharp's head of marketing and communications: "People can now expect a home cinema experience from their TV. Technology that was once associated with the rich and famous is now accessible to homes across the country."[25]

Content Availability and Timing

Even the best hardware offers little value without content for display. Rental firm Netflix advertises a selection of more than 100,000 titles extending well beyond new and classic films to include television shows, sports, and music performances. HD content is increasingly available to maximize the experience offered by those HD televisions. Satellite and cable television providers have engaged in a game of one-upmanship to provide the greatest percentage of HD content available to subscribers. By the end of 2009, 2,000 movies were available on Blu-Ray DVD.[26]

Movie fans no longer have to wait long for the summer's blockbuster to appear on DVD. The time period between theatrical and DVD release has declined 40 percent since 2000. The top five films in 2000 were released on DVD an average of 37 weeks after their box office opening. In 2007, the lag was just 23 weeks. And, studios are experimenting with simultaneous releases to theaters, pay per view, and DVD.

Overall, the visual and audio experience available in the home is rapidly converging with that available at the movie theater. As a blogger on the movie fan site Big Picture posted:

I used to go to the movies all the time—even my blog is called the Big Picture. Then I started going less—and then less still and now—hardly at all. My screen at home is better, the sound system is better, the picture is in focus, the floors aren't sticky and the movies start on time. My seat is clean. And there's no idiot chattering away 2 rows behind me, and (this is my favorite) THERE'S NO CELL PHONES RINGING. EVER.[27]

Is this a horror show at the cinemaplex?

NOTES

1. Motion Picture Association of America (MPAA), 2007, Entertainment industry market statistics.
2. A. Serwer, 2006, Extreme makeover: With big screens and high-def in more and more living rooms, movie theaters are taking radical new measures to woo filmgoers, *Fortune*, 153: 108–116.
3. Mintel Report, 2008, Movie theaters—U.S., February.
4. MPAA, 2007, Entertainment industry market statistics.
5. All data on these two films from http://www.boxofficemojo.com.
6. Developed by author from: Entertainment Industry, 2007 Report, Motion Picture Association of America.
7. J. Woestendiek & C. Kaltenbach, 2008, $10 is small price for a big escape: Movie box office figures are flourishing despite, or because of, economic worries, *Baltimore Sun*, July 8.
8. MPAA, 2007, Entertainment industry market statistics.
9. J. Woestendiek & C. Kaltenbach, 2008, $10 is small price for a big escape: Movie box office figures are flourishing despite, or because of, economic worries, *Baltimore Sun*, July 8.
10. Data on the firms, screen sizes, location, from Web sites and SEC filings.
11. All data is from SEC filings, based on net property, plant, and equipment reported in 2007 balance sheet and on the number of screens.
12. Mintel Report, 2008, Segment performance: cinema advertising, Movie theaters—U.S., February.
13. Mintel Report, 2008, Reasons to go to the movies over watching a DVD, Movie theaters—U.S., February.
14. Mintel Report, 2008, Reasons why attendance is not higher, Movie theaters—U.S., February.
15. K. Kelly, B. Orwall, & P. Sanders, 2005, The multiplex under siege, *Wall Street Journal*, December 24, P1.
16. Blog comment, Over the past years…, http://cinematreasures.org/polls/22/ (accessed December 11, 2008).
17. Incident reported in Patrick Goldstein, 2005, Now playing: A glut of ads, *Los Angeles Times*, July 12, E-1.
18. Designs of the week: The Movie Theater Experience, 2008, November 23, http://www.sramanamitra.com/2008/11/23/designs-of-the-week-the-movie-theater-experience/.
19. DuBravac, 2007.
20. DuBravac, 2007.
21. DuBravac, 2007.
22. B. Keefe, 2008, Prices on flat-screen TVs expected to keep falling, *Atlanta Journal-Constitution*, March 15.
23. Average TV size up to 60-inch by 2015, says Sharp, TechDigest, http://www.techdigest.tv/2008/01/average_tv_size.html (accessed December 11, 2008).
24. MPAA, 2007, Entertainment industry market statistics.
25. Average TV size up to 60-inch by 2015, says Sharp, TechDigest, http://www.techdigest.tv/2008/01/average_tv_size.html (accessed December 11, 2008).
26. http://www.movieweb.com.
27. The Big Picture, Why is movie theatre attendance declining?, http://bigpicture.typepad.com/comments/2005/07/declining_movie.htm (accessed December 11, 2008).

Theodore Bosley, Christopher Calton, Jeffrey Deakins, Tomoko Nakajima, Sally Orford, Robin Pohl, Robin Chapman

Arizona State University

Introduction

We're going to bring humanity back to air travel.
— **DAVID NEELEMAN**
FOUNDER AND CHAIRPERSON

David Neeleman, JetBlue's founder and chairperson, sought to "bring the humanity back to air travel."[1] Since launching operations in February 2000, JetBlue distinguished itself from its competitors by providing superior customer service at low fares. The JetBlue experience included brand new airplanes, leather seats, and personal satellite TV service. The firm experienced rapid early growth. In a period when most U.S. airlines struggled in the aftermath of the September 11, 2001, terrorist attacks, JetBlue reported 18 consecutive quarterly profits.

Then in 2005, JetBlue announced its first net loss of $20 million. The disappointing results were attributed to spiraling fuel prices, aggressive competition, and increasing operating costs. Global events such as war, political turmoil, and natural disasters contributed to the rise in fuel prices. The average price for a barrel of oil in 2003 was $30, by the summer of 2005 prices had climbed above $60 per barrel. The legacy airlines were becoming more competitive after exiting bankruptcy and streamlining their operations to benefit from economies of scale.[2] Analysts speculated that JetBlue was experiencing growth pains:, their maintenance costs on aging planes were increasing, employees were becoming more senior, and new profitable routes were harder to obtain.[3] The company continued to lose money in 2006. While major competitors, such as AMR, the parent company for American Airlines, and Continental, reported higher than expected returns, JetBlue announced a narrow third-quarter loss of $500,000. Following its third-quarter loss, JetBlue announced plans to slow down growth by delaying deliveries of some aircraft,

selling others, and eliminating some cross-country flights.[4] Despite these actions, in a recent interview Neeleman insisted, "We're still a growth airline."[5] It remains to be seen how JetBlue will continue to grow in the face of increasing strategic challenges.

History

Founding History of Jet Blue

David Neeleman founded JetBlue Airways Corporation in 1999, after raising $130 million in investment capital. Building on his past experiences, Neeleman hired talented executives, such as David Barger, previous vice president of the Newark, New Jersey, hub for Continental, and John Owen, previous vice president of Operations Planning and Analysis for Southwest.[6] JetBlue chose John F. Kennedy International Airport in New York as its hub and initially obtained 75 takeoff and landing slots.

Neeleman's vision was to provide "high-end customer service at low-end prices."[7] Although JetBlue imitated competitor Southwest Airlines with a single seat class, it did so with Airbus A-320 narrow-body jets instead of Boeing 737s. The A-320 provided wider cabins and wider seats for JetBlue passengers with more room for carry-on baggage.[8] JetBlue implemented innovative IT programs such as an Internet booking system that allowed customers to make reservations online or with a touch-tone phone, and a paperless cockpit to allow pilots to prepare for flight more quickly, helping planes to stay on schedule.[9] JetBlue also provided complementary, unlimited snacks and beverages, preassigned seating, and a selection of first-run movies available from Fox InFlight on flights longer than two hours. For further differentiation, JetBlue installed 36 channels of free DIRECTV programming.

The authors would like to thank Professor Robert E. Hoskisson for his support under whose direction the case was developed. The authors do not intend to illustrate either effective or ineffective handling of a managerial situation. The case solely provides material for class discussion.

Early in 2000, the first JetBlue flights departed from New York to Fort Lauderdale, with a fleet of two planes. JetBlue gradually increased its destinations during the year to include 12 additional airports in California, Florida, New York, Utah, and Vermont. By December, Neeleman announced the landmark of JetBlue's millionth customer and reported $100 million in revenues.

Rapid Growth in 2000–2004

The September 11, 2001, terrorist attacks on America resulted in a widespread fear of air travel, negatively impacting most of the airline industry. While other airlines announced millions in lost revenue following 9/11, JetBlue made a profit and within eight weeks expanded its network to include six more destinations and resumed IT spending to further improve services offered.[10] In February 2002, JetBlue won the 2002 Air Transport World "Market Development Award" for its successful first two years of service, and also was named "Best Overall Airline" by *Onboard Service* magazine.[11] On April 11, 2002, JetBlue announced its initial public offering (IPO) of 5.86 million shares of common stock at a price of $27 per share.[12] JetBlue grew steadily between 2003 and 2004, with annual operating revenues growing from $998.4 million in 2003, to $1.27 billion in 2004. Exhibits 1 through 3 show JetBlue's financial statements for the years 2001 to 2005.

Slowed Growth in 2005–2007

In November 2005 JetBlue decided to add nine new Embraer E190s to its fleet. JetBlue ordered the aircraft with a 100-seat configuration, bigger television screens than the Airbus A-320, and 100 channels from XM Satellite Radio. Also, in late 2005, JetBlue decided to fund $80 million of an airport expansion project at John F. Kennedy Airport, which had a total budget of $875 million. The expansion would allow for more than double the number of flights at JetBlue's hub airport within three years.[13]

Exhibit 1 Consolidated Statement of Income

JetBlue Airways Corporation (in $ millions, year ended December 31)					
	2006	2005	2004	2003	2002
Operating Revenues					
Passenger	$ 2223	$ 1620	$ 1220	$ 965	$ 615
Other	140	81	45	33	20
Total Operating Revenues	2363	1701	1265	998	635
Operating Expenses					
Salaries, wages, and benefits	553	428	337	267	162
Aircraft fuel	752	488	255	147	76
Landing fees and other rents	158	112	92	70	44
Depreciation and amortization	151	115	77	51	43
Aircraft rent	103	74	70	60	41
Sales and marketing	104	81	63	54	27
Maintenance materials and repairs	87	64	45	23	9
Other operating expenses	328	291	215	159	127
Total Operating Expenses	2236	1653	1154	831	530
Operating Income	$ 127	$ 48	$ 111	$ 167	$ 105
Other Income (Expenses)					
Interest expense	(173)	(107)	(53)	(29)	(21)
Capitalized interest	27	16	9	5	5
Interest income and other	28	19	8	8	5
government compensation				23	
Total other income (expense)	(118)	(72)	(36)	7	(10)
Income (Loss) before income taxes	9	(24)	75	174	95
Income tax expense (benefit)	10	(4)	29	71	40
Net Income (Loss)	$ (1)	$ (20)	$ 46	$ 103	$ 55

Source: JetBlue Airways Corporation 2006 Annual Report.

Exhibit 2 Consolidated Balance Sheet

JetBlue Airways Corporation
(in $ millions, except share data)

Assets	December 31				
	2006	2005	2004	2003	2002
Cash and short-term Investments	$ 699	$ 484	$ 450	$ 607.31	$ 257.85
Total receivables, net	77	94	37	16.72	11.93
Total inventory	27	21	10	8.3	4.84
Prepaid expenses	124	36	17	13.42	5.59
Other current assets, total	0	0	0	0	2.85
Total Current Assets	$ 927	$ 635	$ 514	$ 645.74	$ 283.06
Property/Plant/Equip, total	$ 3438	$ 2978	$ 2130	$ 1421	$ 997
Goodwill, net	0	0	0	0	0
Intangibles, net	32	43	54	62	68
Long-term investments	0	0	0	0	0
Note receivable long-term	0	0	0	0	0
Other long-term assets, total	446	236	99	57	30
Other assets, total	0	0	0	0	0
Total Assets	$ 4843	$ 3892	$ 2797	$ 2186	$ 1379

Liabilities and Shareholders' Equity	December 31				
	2006	2005	2004	2003	2002
Accounts payable	$ 136	$ 99	$ 71	$ 53	$ 46
Payable/Accrued	0	0	0	0	0
Accrued expenses	164	111	94	85	54
Notes payable/Short-term debt	39	64	44	30	22
Current port. of LT debt/capital	175	158	105	67	51
Leases					
Other current liabilities, total	340	243	174	135	98
Total Current Liabilities	$ 854	$ 676	$ 488	$ 370	$ 270
Long-term debt and leases	$ 2626	$ 2103	$ 1396	$ 1012	$ 640
Deferred income tax	136	116	121	99	39
Minority interest	0	0	0	0	0
Other liabilities, total	275	86	38	34	17
Total Liabilities	$ 3891	$ 2981	$ 2043	$ 1515	$ 964
Redeemable preferred stock	$ 0	$ 0	$ 0	$ 0	$ 0
Preferred stock-non	0	0	0	0	0
Common stock	2	2	1	1	1
Additional paid-in capital	813	764	581	552	407
Retained earnings	144	145	165	120	16
Other equity, total	(7)	0	7	(2)	(9)
Total Equity	952	911	754	671	415
Total Liabilities & Shareholders' Equity	$ 4843	$ 3892	$ 2797	$ 2186	$ 1,379

Source: JetBlue Airways Corporation 2006 Annual Report.

Exhibit 3 Consolidated Statement of Cash Flows

JetBlue Airways Corporation
(in $ millions)

	December 31				
	2006	2005	2004	2003	2002
Cash Flows from Operating Activities					
Net Income	$ (1)	$ (20)	$ 46	$ 103	$ 55
Operating Activities					
Deferred income taxes	10	(4)	29	69	40
Depreciation	136	101	67	45	25
Amortization	18	16	11	7	2
Stock-based compensation	21	9	2	2	
Changes in certain operating assets and liabilities					
Increase in receivables	(12)	(28)	(20)	(4)	7
Increase in inventories	(28)	(20)	(6)	(11)	(4)
Increase in air traffic liabilities	97	69	39	37	46
Increase in accounts payable and other accrued liabilities	33	54	21	38	35
Other, Net	0	(7)	10	1	11
Net Cash Provided by Operating Activities	274	170	199	287	216
Cash Flows from Investing Activities					
Capital expenditures	(996)	(941)	(617)	(573)	(544)
Predelivery deposits for flight equipment	(106)	(183)	(180)	(160)	(109)
Purchase of held-to-maturity investment	(23)	(5)	(19)	(26)	(11)
Proceeds from maturities of held-to-maturity investment	15	18	25	9	2
Purchase of available-for-sale securities	(1002)	(79)	76	(235)	(80)
Increase in restricted cash and other assets	(16)	(86)	(5)	(2)	(1)
Net Cash Used in Investing Activities	$ (1307)	$ (1276)	$ (720)	$ (987)	$ (744)
Cash Flows from Financing Activities					
Proceeds from:					
Issuance of common stock	28	178	20	136	174
Issuance of long-term debt	855	872	499	446	416
Aircraft sale and leaseback transactions	406	152		265	0.3
Short-term borrowings	45	68	44	33	150
Repayment of long-term debt	(390)	(117)	(77)	(57)	27
Repayment of short-term debt	(71)	(47)	(30)	(25)	(71)
Other, Net	−15	(13)	(19)	(9)	(34)
Net Cash Provided by Financing Activities	$ 1037	$ 1093	$ 437	$ 789	$ (5)
Increase in Cash and Cash Equivalents	$ 4	$ (13)	$ (84)	$ 89	$ 129
Cash and cash equivalent at beginning of period	$ 6	$ 19	$ 103	$ 14	$ 117
Cash and cash equivalent at end of period	$ 10	$ 6	$ 19	$ 103	$ 247

Source: JetBlue Airways Corporation 2006 Annual Report.

However, JetBlue's quarterly financial report started to show growth saturation. Quarterly growth records of operating revenue in 2005 were 29.5 percent, 34.5 percent, 40.2 percent, and –5.2 percent, respectively. JetBlue announced a fourth quarter net loss of $42.4 million, representing a loss per share of $0.25. It was JetBlue's first quarterly net loss.[14]

In 2006, the firm announced unstable earnings, and reported a loss of $32 million, a profit of $14 million, and a loss of $0.5 million in the first three quarters, respectively.[15] Even though JetBlue served 47 destinations with up to 470 daily flights, it decided to reduce its rate of growth over the next three years by delaying the delivery of additional planes.[16] Data for destination and service commenced

Exhibit 4 JetBlue's Destinations

Destination	Service Commenced
New York, New York	February 2000
Fort Lauderdale, Florida	February 2000
Buffalo, New York	February 2000
Tampa, Florida	March 2000
Orland, Florida	June 2000
Ontario, California	July 2000
Oakland, California	August 2000
Rochester, New York	August 2000
Burlington, Vermont	September 2000
West Palm Beach, Florida	October 2000
Salt Lake City, Utah	November 2000
Fort Myers, Florida	November 2000
Seattle, Washington	May 2001
Syracuse, New York	May 2001
Denver, Colorado	May 2001
New Orleans, Louisiana	July 2001
Long Beach, California	August 2001
Washington, D.C. (Dulles Airport)	November 2001
San Juan, Puerto Rico	May 2002
Las Vegas, Nevada	November 2002
San Diego, California	June 2003
Boston, Massachusetts	January 2004
Sacramento, California	March 2004
Aguadilla, Puerto Rico	May 2004
Santiago, Dominican Republic	June 2004
San Jose, California	June 2004
New York, New York (LGA Airport)	September 2004
Phoenix, Arizona	October 2004
Nassau, The Bahamas	November 2004
Burbank, California	May 2005
Portland, Oregon	May 2005
Ponce, Puerto Rico	June 2005
Newark, New Jersey	October 2005
Austin, Texas	January 2006
Richmond, Virginia	March 2006
Hamilton, Bermuda	May 2006
Sarasota-Bradenton, Florida	September 2006
Cancun, Mexico	November 2006
Island of Aruba	November 2006
Chicago, Illinois	January 2007
White Plains, New York	March 2007
San Francisco, California	May 2007

Source: JetBlue Airways Corporation Form 10-K, Fiscal year ending December 31, 2006.

are listed in Exhibit 4. Effort to slow the growth rate was intended to preserve cash, enabling JetBlue to remain stable among competitors.

The first quarter of 2007 did not get off to a great start for JetBlue. Bad weather in February resulted in many cancelled flights and stranded passengers. The climax of the crisis occurred when nine airplanes full of angry passengers sat on the tarmac for six hours, because JetBlue leaders had expected the weather to clear and did not cancel flights. CEO David Neeleman received bad press for his management of the situation. Neeleman responded by humbly admitting "that his company's management was not strong enough. [It] was the result of a shoestring communications system that left pilots and flight attendants in the dark, and an undersize reservation system."[17] Rapid efforts were made to regain its brand image such that a JetBlue Customer Bill of Rights was created, a customer advisory council was formed, plans were made to cross-train crew members, and new communication strategies were put in place.[18] In addition JetBlue waived change fees and fare differences to assist customers who may be affected by additional storms throughout the winter of 2007. Despite his sincere efforts to bounce back from this predicament, Neeleman eventually had to step down as CEO in order to appease shareholders. David Barger, former COO succeeded Neeleman as CEO and needed to establish a strong position against JetBlue rivals.

Competitive Environment

In 1978, the Airline Deregulation Act eliminated government control over fares and routes, opening up the industry to increased competition. The airline industry is now highly competitive, consisting of 43 mainline carriers and 79 regional airlines. The U.S. Department of Transportation (DOT) classifies airlines into three categories based on annual revenue: major (revenue more than $1 billion), national (revenue between $100 million to $1 billion), and regional/commuter (revenue less than $100 million).[19] With annual revenue of $1.7 billion, JetBlue is one of the smaller major carriers and competes primarily on point-to-point routes. Its major competitors are low-cost carrier Southwest Airlines and traditional carriers, AMR Corp, United Airlines, US Airways, Continental Airlines, and Delta Air.[20]

Southwest is JetBlue's most obvious competitor, but the traditional airlines are becoming more aggressive in the low-fare market. Following recent bankruptcies, legacy airlines are emerging with clean balance sheets and lower cost structures. As the major airlines become more competitive and expand their domestic businesses, the low-cost airlines struggle to find new markets.[21]

Competition also comes from the regional carriers, which typically partner with the major airlines to share routes, risk, and costs. For example, Mesa partners with United Airlines and operates as United Express, with Delta Airlines as Delta Express, and with US Air as US Air Express. In exchange for an agreed proportion of revenue, Mesa operates flights on select local routes, while its partners handle reservations and marketing. In recent years, the regional airlines fared better than most, growing twice as fast as the national carriers.[22] However, as the competitive environment toughens, many of the large airlines are renegotiating the agreements, and in some cases—such as Atlantic Coast, a former partner of United Airlines—regional airlines are deciding to operate independently.[23]

The major airlines also form alliances—with each other and international carriers—to share marketing and scheduling capabilities. American Airlines partners with British Airways, Quantas, and various European airlines to form the One World Alliance, which serves 135 countries and operates a shared frequent flyer program. The Star Alliance, spearheaded by United Airlines, with Lufthansa, Scandinavian Air System, All Nippon Airways, and Air Canada, serves 157 countries.[24] Such alliances increase the market power of their members, and research has shown they increase passenger volume by an average of 9.4 percent.[25] Although the benefit is more significant for global carriers seeking to expand their network abroad, researchers observed an average improvement in number of tickets booked by 7.4 percent on short-haul flights.

Although JetBlue does not currently participate in any alliances, it has had discussions about forming one with international airlines in an effort to leverage its power at the hub in JFK. JetBlue does not want to enter a traditional agreement with other airlines, because many of these agreements include increased overhead costs. JetBlue is hoping to create an agreement that will increase traffic without increasing costs.[26]

Fare pricing is an important competitive factor within the industry. For many years excess capacity posed a significant problem, causing airlines to either leave planes on the ground or fly planes with empty seats. In order to avoid this dilemma, carriers try to increase market share by discounting tickets. Even the legacy airlines slash fares in order to compete on low-cost routes. Although low-cost airlines, like JetBlue, still offer the greatest number of discounted fares, some of the cheapest tickets are now available from traditional airlines, such as American, Delta, and United.[27]

Rumors of consolidation in the industry could change the competitive landscape. US Airways made a hostile bid for bankrupt Delta Airlines in fourth quarter 2006, but withdrew its offer in January 2007 due to the inability to reach financial agreement with Delta creditors.[28] The merger would have created the largest airline in a fragmented industry and would likely have triggered further consolidations.[29] Even though a wave of consolidation may create a more efficient airline industry with fewer major players, consolidations affect ticket prices, usually leading to higher ticket prices, and complicate the flight paths offered by airlines. Therefore, consolidations affect all competitors within the industry.

Key Competitors

Southwest Airlines

Southwest is the leading low-fare, no-frills, U.S. carrier. The company was founded in 1967 as a Texas-based airline to serve Dallas, Houston, and San Antonio. The airline now flies to more than 63 cities across the United States. In 2006, Southwest reported a $499 million profit and net sales of $9.86 billion.[30] Exhibit 5 compares key financial data for the major airlines. In 2005, America West's CEO, Douglas Parker, described Southwest as follows: "They really were at one point the scrawny kid who was lifting weights in his basement. Now they come out and they're bigger than anybody else and stronger than anybody else."[31]

Southwest's strategy emphasizes low costs; the firm was the first to sell tickets online and to introduce unassigned seating. It operates a single aircraft fleet of 481

Exhibit 5 U.S. Major Airlines' Select Financials for Year Ended 2006 (in $millions)

	JetBlue	UAL	SWA	Delta	Continental	US Airways	AMR Corp.
Total revenues	$2,363	$ 19,340	$ 9,086	$ 17,171	$13,128	$11,557	$ 22,563
Cost of revenues	1,653	14,114	6,311	14,430	11,007	9,049	17,659
Gross profit	570	5,226	2,573	1,694	1,453	1,814	4,904
Profit as % of revenue	24%	27%	28%	10%	11%	16%	22%
Operating income (loss)	127	23,381	934	(6,148)	468	558	1,060
Net income (loss)	$ (1)	$ 22,386	$ 499	$ (6,203)	$ 343	$ 304	$ 231
Total assets	$4,843	25,369	$13,460	$ 19,622	$11,308	$ 7,576	$ 29,145
Current assets	927	6,273	2,601	5,385	4,129	3,354	6,902
Total liabilities	$3,891	$ 23,221	$ 7,011	$ 33,215	$10,961	$ 6,606	$ 29,751
Current liabilities	854	7,945	2,887	5,769	3,955	2,712	8,505
Total owner equity	$ 952	$ 2,148	$ 6,449	$ (13,593)	$ 347	$ 970	$ (606)

Source: 2007, MSN Money Central, http://moneycentral.msn.com/investor/research/welcome.asp, July 24.

Exhibit 6 Top 10 U.S. Airlines, Ranked by August 2006 Domestic Scheduled Enplanements

Passenger numbers in millions

August 2006 Rank	Carrier	August 2006 Enplanements	August 2005 Rank	August 2005 Enplanements
1	Southwest	8.7	1	8.1
2	American	6.5	3	6.8
3	Delta	5.4	2	7.0
4	United	5.1	4	5.0
5	Northwest	4.1	5	4.2
6	Continental	3.1	7	2.9
7	US Airways	2.6	6	3.1
8	America West	1.8	8	1.9
9	AirTran	1.8	9	1.5
10	JetBlue	1.7	13	1.3

Note: Percentage changes based on numbers prior to rounding.

Source: Bureau of Transportation Statistics, T-100 Domestic Market.

Boeing 737s. The company is also lauded for its unique and friendly culture and its high level of customer service.[32] However, evidence now indicates a shift in its strategy—from serving underserved routes, to competing in major markets such as Denver and Philadelphia. Southwest is now the largest U.S. airline in terms of number of passengers (Exhibit 6), and in order to continue to grow, Southwest is competing against United in its Denver hub, and US Airways, on routes out of Philadelphia.[33]

AMR Corp.

As the world's largest airline, American Airlines (AMR's main subsidiary) offers flights to 150 destinations throughout North America, Latin America, the Caribbean, Europe, and Asia. It has had its share of success and failures; two of its planes were hijacked during the September 11, 2001, terrorist attacks and the firm barely avoided bankruptcy in 2003.[34] In 2006, AMR Corp. reported net earnings of $231 million, an improvement over its net loss of $861 million in 2005 and other significant losses in preceding years.[35] In order to return to profitability, the firm streamlined costs and expanded its routes in Asia.

United Airlines

United also lost two planes on September 11, 2001, and after several years of financial difficulties, UAL eventually filed for Chapter 11 bankruptcy in 2002.[36] UAL emerged from bankruptcy as a more competitive firm. In February 2004, United launched its own low-cost off-shoot, Ted. The firm is now looking for new ways to expand and improve profitability. Global expansion is central to UAL's strategy; in July 2006, the firm announced plans to expand its Asia/Pacific routes.[37] Recent rumors report that UAL hired Goldman Sachs to assess possible merger options.[38]

US Airways

US Airways Group is the product of a merger between US Airways and America West. CEO Parker believes this acquisition strategy is successful; when comparing the firm's post-bankruptcy performance to United, he stated, "The big difference is we were able to generate synergies that United was not able to."[39] Shareholders experienced a 45 percent increase in stock price during the first full year after the merger.[40]

Delta Air

With an 11.8% domestic market share, Delta places third among traditional airline icons.[41] Delta is strongly focused on international expansion, adding 50 new international routes in 2005–2006. Delta now serves over 450 destinations in 95 countries. Delta filed for bankruptcy and was a target acquisition by US Airways just before it emerged from bankruptcy in April 2007.

Continental Airlines

Continental targets the business traveler by serving diverse U.S. and international routes.[42] Continental has a strong balance sheet, having recently retired $100 million in debt.[43] In the third quarter of 2006, Continental followed in the path of the other legacy airlines by reporting stronger than expected results. The positive results were attributed to greatly increased number of passengers, especially on Continental's regional and Latin American routes.[44]

As well as domestic competitors, the international airline market conditions are a factor that JetBlue must consider.

International Market Conditions

The demand for international travel has increased significantly over the past decade (see Exhibit 7). The international travel growth rate is more than double the domestic travel growth rate in the United States.[45] Travel to Southeast Asia and China increases every year by about 7.3 percent and 8.0 percent. Looking forward, the number of transatlantic plane tickets purchased is expected to grow by 4.6 percent annually. Global business transactions have contributed, as well as more discretionary income for consumers, and lower airfare resulting from greater efficiencies in international travel.

The international market is attractive to many airlines because they can include fuel surcharges in the ticket price and recover some of the costs associated with higher-priced fuel.

However, the airline industry is monitored more scrupulously by the government than any other industry conducting business internationally. The government has many regulations on when, where, and how airlines can fly, how much they can charge, and how they can market international travel.[46] Many lobbyist firms and politicians in the United States have been fighting for deregulation and less restrictions on international air travel so that the United States might be more of a force in the international market. The European airline industry, more specifically AirFrance/KLM, has taken the lead in revenues for international aviation.[47]

Not only is it important for JetBlue to consider its competitive environment, but it is also important to understand the companies/industries that supply the provisions necessary to remain competitive.

Key Suppliers

Fuel

Fuel is usually the second-highest expense for an airline next to labor.[48] Therefore, fuel price increases are a major contributor to rising operating costs in the airline industry. A Merrill Lynch analyst indicated that for every $1

Exhibit 7 U.S. Commercial Air Carriers Total U.S. Passenger Traffic

Fiscal Year	Revenue Passenger Enplanements (millions)			Revenue Passenger Miles (billions)		
	Domestic	International	System	Domestic	International	System
Historical*						
2000	641.2	56.4	697.6	512.8	181.8	694.6
2001	626.8	56.7	683.4	508.1	183.3	691.4
2002	574.5	51.2	625.8	473.0	158.2	631.3
2003	587.8	54.2	642.0	492.7	155.9	648.6
2004	628.5	61.4	689.9	540.2	177.4	717.7
2005	661	86.2	747.2	573.7	221.5	795.1
Forecast						
2006	660.9	89.7	750.6	577.6	232.5	810.1
2007	693.3	75.8	769.1	603.3	221.5	824.7
2008	713.8	79.8	793.6	624.6	234.5	859.0
2009	735.7	84.0	819.7	647.7	247.9	895.6
2010	758.9	88.3	847.2	671.9	262.1	934.1
2011	782.6	92.9	875.5	697.6	276.9	974.5
2012	807.7	97.6	905.2	724.5	291.9	1,016.4
2013	833.4	102.3	935.7	752.6	307.4	1,059.9
2014	860.5	107.2	967.7	782.2	323.5	1,105.7
2015	888.4	112.3	1,000.7	813.3	340.2	1,153.5
2016	917.7	117.6	1,035.3	846.1	357.5	1,203.6
2017	848.4	123.1	1,071.6	880.6	375.2	1,255.8
Average Annual Growth 2005–2017	2.9%	5.0%	3.1%	3.6%	5.5%	4.1%

Source: Forms 41 and 298-C, U.S. Department of Transportation.

increase in price for a barrel of fuel, the airline industry experiences a $450 million loss in pretax profits.[49] According to the FAA, jet fuel costs rose by 20.1 percent in 2004, 40.5 percent in 2005, and 30.4 percent in 2006.[50] In 2006, fuel costs became JetBlue's largest operating expense at 33.65 percent.[51] The FAA forecasts fuel costs will remain high for the next several years. Neeleman seriously considers fuel costs and is investigating alternative sources of energy, such as liquid coal. Because the United States has an abundant supply of coal, Neeleman is urging his customers to support a new bill to fund additional coal-to-liquid plants.[52]

Airlines engage in fuel hedging in order to manage unpredictable costs. However, the jet fuel commodities market is illiquid, and it is especially difficult for the large airlines to hedge sufficient quantities of fuel.[53] JetBlue is increasing its efforts to systematically hedge against future fuel needs. JetBlue also seeks more efficient fuel usage through the planes purchased and improved flight planning.[54]

Aircraft Manufacturers

The aircraft industry is dominated by two companies, Airbus and Boeing. Due to the weak economy following September 11, 2001, their orders for new commercial planes fell sharply. However, as commercial business improved, the large manufacturers profited from the buoyant space and defense markets. Embraer, the number four aircraft manufacturer, has seen lackluster commercial sales, but is benefiting from increased sales in the military sector.

Typically, the low-cost airlines operate few aircraft types, reducing their maintenance, scheduling, and training costs. JetBlue currently owns two airplane models, and its growth plans include the addition of 96 Airbus A-320s and 92 Embraer E190s.[55] Cost efficiencies would be lost if JetBlue switched suppliers, exposing the firm to any problems related to either of its aircraft suppliers. But currently more pressing for JetBlue are the challenges associated with the airline industry.

General Environment

A number of new trends are emerging in air travel. After September 11, 2001, the industry saw a drop in the number of corporate travelers, but five years later this trend appeared to be reversing. According to a survey by the National Business Travel Association, 65 percent of businesses expect employees to take more flights in 2007, and 75 percent predict an increase in the amount of business travel.[56]

Another factor in the environment of air travel is the characteristics of the airport and FAA density regulations. JetBlue experiences general performance setbacks by operating in high traffic areas such as the northeastern United States, and the airport congestion hampers performance statistics.[57] The FAA regulates airport slot (a slot is a time frame allotted for takeoff and landing)[58] allocations with the intent to ease congestion problems and enhance airport capacity. For example, recent measures at New York La Guardia airport include growth limitations, regulations encouraging use of larger aircraft, and a proposal for 10-year slot reallocation.[59]

Natural disasters and annual weather patterns also affect the performance statistics for air travel. Florida is quite popular during the winter months and the western states during summer months. Air travel is also affected by winter weather in the Northeast and tropical storms along the Atlantic and Gulf coasts.[60]

In the airline industry, more than 60 percent of employees are unionized.[61] Although JetBlue is non-unionized, it can be affected by the industry environment. In June 2006, the International Association of Machinists and Aerospace Workers campaigned to represent JetBlue's ramp service workers. The bid was unsuccessful; however JetBlue's management commented, "We can expect ongoing attempts by unions to organize groups of JetBlue crewmembers."[62]

As can be expected from the general environment, JetBlue is exposed to the widespread attraction of media coverage and negative press. One recent major incident appearing in headlines is the mechanical failure of Flight 292 landing in Los Angeles.[63] On September 21, 2005, JetBlue Flight 292 left Burbank, California, bound for JFK in New York City. Soon after takeoff, the pilot acknowledged problems with the landing gear. The decision was made to have an emergency landing at Los Angeles International Airport and after circling Orange County for three hours, to burn off fuel, Flight 292 landed safely. None of the 139 passengers or six crew members was injured during the landing. Upon landing it became certain that the nose gear had rotated 90 degrees and was locked in the down position[64] (see Exhibit 8). Although the outcome was ultimately favorable, had Flight 292 crashed or lives been lost, JetBlue's image would have

Exhibit 8 JetBlue Airbus A-320 Flight 292 with Its Nose Landing Gear Jammed

Source: JetScott, 2005, http://www.aerospaceweb.org/question/planes/q0245a.shtml, October 2.

suffered drastically. The perceived safety of air travel is important for all airlines.

Airlines also face a heightened sense of consumer information privacy. In 2002, JetBlue offered extensive passenger data to a data mining company, Torch, who in conjunction with the U.S. Army, tested a customer profiling system to identify high risk passengers that might threaten military installations.[65] According to the District Court, Eastern New York, Memorandum & Order 04-MD-1587, JetBlue was responsible for the release of "each passenger's name, address, gender, home ownership or rental status, economic status, social security number, occupation, and the number of adults and children in the passenger's family as well as the number of vehicles owned or leased."[66] With increased online purchases, all airlines are publicly pressured to protect passengers' identity.

JetBlue must make a conscious effort to rise above all of the setbacks associated with the general environment and ensure that all actions are in alignment with its corporate and business strategies.

JetBlue Strategies

Because many of the other airlines play a significant role in the low-cost carrier segment within the airline industry, JetBlue competes by differentiation. The goal is to achieve an image of far superior customer service.

Superior Customer Service

JetBlue delivers this service by offering additional pre-flight and on-board conveniences that other low-cost carriers do not provide as a whole package. Before traveling, customers benefit from JetBlue's simple-to-use reservation system, ticketless travel, and preassigned seating. The cabin features leather seats and an additional two inches of leg room than most carriers. As previously mentioned, on board JetBlue passengers receive free DIRECTV service, and its Embraer E190 planes have XM Satellite Radio.[67] To improve the customer experience, JetBlue added healthier snacks and, as of November 2006, offers a 100 percent transfat-free selection. All snacks are complementary and unlimited.

All passengers on "shut eye" flights receive a comfort kit from Bliss, which includes earplugs, lip balm, an eye mask, and hand lotion. Crewmembers wake customers with the smell of Dunkin' Donuts coffee and offer a hot towel service.[68]

It is valuable to customers to have their flight depart as planned. To provide customers with confidence, JetBlue focuses on its completion rate, even at the expense of its on-time rate. At the end of third quarter 2006, JetBlue had a 99.6 percent completion rate. In addition, customers want to be confident that they will have their bags at the end of the flight. At 2006 year-end, JetBlue was ranked number 1 out of the 15 busiest airlines in regard to the least number of lost or mishandled bags.[69]

A critical factor in achieving superior service is employee moral. As Neeleman has stated, the crewmembers are the "real secret weapon."[70] His philosophy is that if crew members are treated well, they will in turn treat the customers well.

Culture

Currently, David Neeleman, chairperson, and Dave Barger, CEO, are hands-on people who like to interact with employees and customers. Each week members of top management fly with 8 to 12 crew members and almost always attend new hire training to teach new crewmembers about JetBlue's brand, how the company makes money, and how crewmembers contribute to the bottom line. Whenever they fly, they help the crew clean the plane after the flight to ensure a quick turnaround time. In addition they have informal meetings with crewmembers to learn about issues and problems as crewmembers see them.[71] This management style continues to attract motivated new hires; JetBlue has a reputation as a great place to work, company profit sharing, high productivity of planes and people, and rapid advancements. In 2004 alone, JetBlue hired 1,700–1,800 people.[72]

The combined effort to provide exceptional service and instill a valued-employee culture will fulfill Neeleman's hope that JetBlue can "keep our folks fresh and keep our customers coming back."[73]

However, as proven by Delta's Song and the installation of leather seats in its planes, the "superior service" attributes can be imitated by competitors. What has also allowed JetBlue to remain one step ahead in its competitive environment is cost management.

Cost Management

JetBlue's cost-saving initiative includes electronic ticketing, paperless cockpits, and online check-in.[74] In order to achieve paperless cockpits, JetBlue supplied pilots and first officers with laptops to retrieve electronic flight manuals and make preflight load and balance calculations.[75] In the year following implementation of paperless cockpits, the company saved approximately 4,800 hours of labor.[76] One of JetBlue's more original strategies to cut costs is its telephone reservation system. Reservation agents work from their homes in Salt Lake City, using personal computers equipped with VoIP technology. VoIP stands for Voice over Internet Protocol and utilizes the Internet to make free phone calls.[77] This system gives JetBlue flexibility to handle varying call volumes without needing a costly call center.[78]

JetBlue also uses technology to manage its marketing costs. JetBlue employs Omniture software to increase efficiency of Internet searches, decreasing associated search conversion costs by 94 percent.[79] By using animation in its television ads with its advertising agency, JetBlue produced eight ads for the standard price of one.[80]

Another value-adding initiative is BlueTurn, the name for JetBlue's ground operations. In an effort to improve the overall on-time performance statistics, BlueTurn allows crewmembers to minimize ground time and decrease the turnaround time for aircraft.[81]

JetBlue operates two aircraft types and a single travel class. This simplicity reduces training, maintenance, and operating costs relative to competitors that operate multiple aircraft types.

These cost-cutting strategies follow the standard low-cost, low-fare business model, without sacrificing the ultimate strategy of providing superior customer service with happy employees.

In order to best market its services, JetBlue has carefully considered its marketing approach.

Marketing Strategy

Neeleman believes that marketing is best accomplished by word of mouth; therefore top management aims to make sure that customers are treated well and employees feel valued.[82] Yet, they have made concerted efforts to market in other ways. To establish a media campaign, JetBlue hired J. Walter Thompson (JWT) as its advertising agency.[83] To create a fresh identity, JWT found candid statements by customers on JetBlue service. Online sources were consulted such as Craigslist and Epinions. The statements, written as short stories, were used to create eight different animated ads as testimonials to JetBlue's customer service. Other forms of direct marketing were used such as leather benches and snack bins in serviced airports. JetBlue also created comical postcards and distributed to customers to mail back their comments.[84]

In order to record customers' opinions on JetBlue service, an interactive video installation called the "JetBlue Story Booth" was set up in Rockefeller Center, and is traveling around the country to other cities served by JetBlue.[85] In the one-week New York exhibit, an estimated 20,000 people participated in the installation.[86] A vehicle called Blue Betty was created to simulate an airplane cabin and showcase in-flight amenities. As it traveled to various events across the country, visitors could enter a contest (or lottery) for ticket giveaways. JetBlue also used direct marketing to target college students with a public relations team called CrewBlue. This group used unconventional methods of posters, flyers, and chalk art to educate students about various aspects of the airline's services. Other marketing efforts include "Blue Days," where students were encouraged to wear blue and were rewarded with airline tickets through drawings. A 2005 survey indicated this marketing campaign was successful and increased JetBlue awareness by 41 percent.[87]

In addition to marketing initiatives, JetBlue on a consistent basis updates its business strategy to increase growth and revenue.

Current Strategies

In the first quarter of 2006, due to operating losses, JetBlue executives announced a turnaround plan called "Return to Profitability." Items included in this initiative were revisions to fare structures, corrections to flight capacity, and reprioritizing of flight segments (short, medium, and long haul).[88]

The growth rate has been slowed. The company expects to grow between 14 and 17 percent over the next year versus the 18 to 20 percent originally forecasted.[89]

JetBlue plans to fuel this growth by adding a number of flights on existing routes, connecting new city pairs among the destinations already served, and entering new markets usually served by higher-cost, higher-fare airlines. To determine which cities JetBlue should include in its flight pattern, executives study information made available from the Department of Transportation, which outlines the historical number of passengers, capacity, and average fares over time in all city-pair markets within North America.[90] This information along with JetBlue's historical data allows them to predict how a market will react to the introduction of JetBlue's service and lower prices.

JetBlue expects to use the new Embraer fleet to create demand in many midsized markets that could benefit from its point-to-point service.[91]

In addition, as mentioned previously, JetBlue is in the midst of some discussions about creating a partnership to enter the international market. Due to the limited type of aircraft in JetBlue's fleet, an alliance is the only way for JetBlue to capitalize on the international market opportunities, because its aircraft are not large enough to fly overseas.

The firm is also optimistic that recent moves to expand distribution channels will increase revenue. In August of 2006, the company signed a five-year agreement with Sabre Holdings and Galileo International. This arrangement will allow more than 52,000 travel agencies to purchase tickets for JetBlue travelers with a single connection. These deals are an attempt to reach a broader customer base, especially business travelers.[92]

Moreover, JetBlue is constantly striving to introduce new methods of providing superior customer service. As of March 2007 the first 11 rows in the cabin feature four inches of legroom between each row rather than the previous two inches.[93] To augment its flight services, JetBlue has established complementary products and services.

Associated Products and Services

In addition to air travel, JetBlue sells combined flight and hotel packages, which it terms "JetBlue Getaways." When JetBlue Getaways launched in November 2005, Tim Claydon, vice president of Sales and Marketing, commented, "By working with the hotels directly, rather than through an intermediary, we are able to offer our customers only the finest properties at great prices. Using the latest technology to combine the lowest JetBlue airfare with the best hotel or resort rate, we are able to offer our customers a new level of value with vacations beginning and ending on JetBlue Airways—something not available on any other online travel site."[94]

An American Express card was issued in 2005 called the "JetBlue Card," which earns TrueBlue points for members.[95] Customers earn TrueBlue points when purchasing flights, movie tickets, sporting event tickets, and gym memberships. When a customer amasses 100 TrueBlue points (equivalent to approximately five medium-length round trips), the customer earns a free round-trip valid for one year. In 2006, award travel accounted for only 2 percent of JetBlue's total revenue passenger miles.[96]

In order to sustain its business and corporate strategies, JetBlue monitors its financial situation regularly.

Financial Condition

JetBlue's current financial situation is highlighted by its short-term liquidity, long-term stability, and company profitability. Stockholder profitability signals whether JetBlue is meeting its stockholders' expectations.[97]

Short-Term Liquidity

JetBlue's balance sheet over the past five years is shown in Exhibit 2. JetBlue has struggled with financial performance since 2005. The growth of current liabilities from

Exhibit 9 Liquidity Ratios

	2006	2005	2004	2003	2002
Current ratio	1.1	0.94	1.05	1.75	1.05
Quick ratio	1.05	0.91	1.03	1.72	1.03

Source: JetBlue Airways Corporation 2006 Annual Report.

Exhibit 10 Receivables and Payables

Receivables	2006	2005	2004	2003	2002
Receivable turnover	30.6	26	47.1	69.7	38.8
Days to collect	11.9	14.1	7.8	5.2	9.4

Payables	2006	2005	2004	2003	2002
Payable turnover	16.4	13.8	12.9	11.5	9.5
Days to pay		26.4	28.3	31.7	38.5

Source: JetBlue Airways Corporation 2006 Annual Report.

Exhibit 11 Stability Ratios

	2006	2005	2004	2003	2002
Debt/Asset ratio	0.8	0.8	0.7	0.7	0.7
Asset/Equity ratio	5.1	4	3.5	3.3	3.5
Debt/Equity (financial leverage)	4.1	3.3	2.7	2.3	2.3
Interest coverage ratio	0.7	0.7	2.7	8.4	7.1

Source: JetBlue Airways Corporation 2006 Annual Report.

Exhibit 12 Fuel Expenses

	2006	2005	2004	2003	2002
Operating revenue	$2363	$1701	$1265	$998	$635
Aircraft fuel	752	488	255	147	76
Aircraft fuel %	31	29	20	15	12
Other Costs % Revenue					
Salaries and benefits %	23	25	27	27	26
Aircraft rent %	4	4	6	6	6
Sales and Marketing %	4	5	5	5	7
Maintenance %	4	4	4	2	1

Source: JetBlue Airways Corporation 2006 Annual Report.

2003 to 2006 is significant, compared to the growth of current assets. However, the payables turnover ratio has been increasing, which indicates that JetBlue has been able to pay its suppliers at a faster rate even though it has not been as efficient in collecting receivables as in years past. (Liquidity ratios are shown in Exhibit 9 and turnover ratios are shown in Exhibit 10.)

Long-Term Stability

Long-term financial stability will be an issue as JetBlue toils to consistently turn a profit. JetBlue has maintained

Exhibit 13 Profitability

	2006	2005	2004	2003	2002
Gross margins	20%	27%	33%	40%	45%
Operating margins	5.4%	3%	9%	17%	17%
Net profit margins	0.4%	–1%	4%	10%	9%
Return on equity	0.97%	–2%	6%	19%	19%
Return on assets	2%	2%	3%	6%	6%

Source: JetBlue Airways Corporation 2006 Annual Report; 2007; http://www.finance.yahoo.com.

a fairly consistent debt-to-asset mix as most of the cash received from issuances has been invested in capital assets. The majority of JetBlue's issuances are floating rate bonds, exposing the firm to increases in the Federal Reserve's prime rate.[98] JetBlue's first quarter 2007 assets/equity ratio stood at 5.4 compared to the industry average of 3.[99] (See Exhibits 3 and 11 for details.)

Company Profitability

JetBlue's gross margins continued to decline in recent years, which can be mainly attributed to increasing fuel charges as shown in Exhibit 12. Salaries, landing fees, and other expenses remain fairly stable as a percent of revenues (most have actually decreased, see Exhibit 1). For 2006, gross margins remained 23 percent (see Exhibit 13). As stated earlier, interest expense has a negative effect on profitability.

Stockholder Profitability

In July 2007, the stock was trading at $11.01 versus $14.90[100] at the end of April 2002. In addition to the lackluster stock movement, JetBlue has never paid dividends, so the overall return for the past four years is 5.5 percent. According to moneycentral.com and Yahoo! Finance, the average analyst recommendation is "Hold" for JetBlue. The declining return on equity and inconsistency of net income appears to be having negative implications for JetBlue.

Strategic Challenges

JetBlue faces many challenges as it continues to operate in the highly competitive airline industry. The main challenges are maintaining JetBlue's culture as it grows, dealing with the surfacing complexities of two fleet types, managing maintenance expenses as airplanes and engines begin to age, and dealing with an increasingly senior labor pool. Although fuel prices are a concern, they affect the industry in the same way, and airlines have opportunities to mitigate these risks. Southwest hedged its fuel position more effectively than other airlines, but these hedges will expire and everyone will have a more level playing field when it comes to fuel prices.[101]

Maintaining the JetBlue culture will be difficult to do as the airline grows. The explosive increase in employees may hinder the ability to sustain high utilization and maintain a positive work environment. The time that top management has to interact with individual crewmembers will decrease. Neeleman stated that he would no longer be able to respond to every crewmember's e-mail.[102] This change will hinder a popular cultural component because the chairperson and CEO may no longer be seen as accessible.[103]

Multiple Aircraft Types

JetBlue will have a challenge as it continues to integrate two different types of aircraft. The firm suffered a setback when it incorporated the Embraer E190 into its fleet. JetBlue wanted to fly the new planes 14 hours a day, similar to its A-320s. However, the airplane characteristics were different from the Airbus.[104] Both pilots and mechanics needed additional time and training to understand the new plane. These factors caused flight delays and cancellations throughout the JetBlue system.[105] JetBlue had to reevaluate its plans.

Another issue associated with two types of aircraft is that JetBlue must staff two groups of pilots and flight attendants. The different aircraft require unique training and integration procedures. JetBlue will need separate inventories, training programs, and facilities to accommodate two fleet types.[106] In addition, the pay scales are different, which requires additional support from corporate employees.

Increased Maintenance Expenses

Maintenance expense will be a significant concern for JetBlue in coming years. As with a new car, new airplanes rarely need maintenance and when they do, they are covered under warranty. In 2004, JetBlue experienced a 94 percent increase in maintenance costs.[107] The increase in maintenance costs was not as significant in 2005 and 2006 at 36 percent and 42 percent, respectively (see Exhibit 1); however, as the large fleet of new planes comes due for heavy maintenance at the same time, JetBlue will experience a significant increase in maintenance costs.

Airplane operators have A, C, and D levels of scheduled maintenance and inspection intervals. A-checks occur every 400–500 hours and are similar to an oil change on a vehicle. C- and D-checks are more extensive, more expensive, and longer. The C-check schedule is every 18 months/6,000 hours/3,000 cycles.[108] Additionally, the fourth C-check consists of more inspections, and takes

10 days, compared to just 4 days for regular C-checks.[109] Furthermore, JetBlue decided to outsource maintenance to Air Canada Technical Services in Winnipeg, and Aeroman in El Salvador. Because these operations are not co-located with any of its scheduled service, JetBlue has to spend additional money ferrying planes and paying employees to work in these facilities. JetBlue spends "seven figures" each year in ferrying planes and as much as $700 per day extra for people to monitor the quality of work.[110] As JetBlue's planes enter more extensive service, the amount of time to ferry airplanes and actual maintenance will increase.

Engine expense is another huge maintenance cost for JetBlue. In July 2005, JetBlue signed a 10-year service agreement with a German company, MTU. It covers all scheduled and unscheduled repair for all A-320 engines.[111] At year-end 2006, JetBlue had more than 90 A-320 aircraft, and with two engines per plane and a healthy spares inventory, JetBlue has a significant number of engines to maintain (including its 23 E190 airplanes and engines).[112] Typical charges for a comparable engine overhaul range from $1 million to $1.5 million per heavy visit.

In addition to engines and airframes, airplane operators have additional equipment they must maintain and arrange for contract maintenance support. They have auxiliary power units, landing gear systems, environmental systems, avionics, and flight controls.

As the number of aircraft increases, the cost to maintain will increase. JetBlue may lose economies of scale because multiple aircraft types require multiple repair facilities, and they will have to employ and house multiple sets of inventory and people.

Increased Payroll Expenses

Payroll costs will multiply at JetBlue as the company ages. During 2006 salaries, wages, and benefits increased 29 percent, or $125 million, due primarily to an increased workforce (refer to Exhibit 1).[113] According to the Bureau of Transportation (see Exhibit 14), JetBlue experienced a 212 percent staff growth and ranks third among low-cost carriers for total number of employees in the United States.

Currently, all of the crewmembers are near the bottom of the pay scales, and JetBlue enjoys a relatively low-cost labor pool. However, as these people attain seniority with the company their pay level will increase.[114] Not only will salaried employees get annual pay raises, but crewmembers are paid for each hour flown, according to type of aircraft and depending on the number of years with the company (see Exhibit 15). A more senior staff means the company will start paying higher wages.

Exhibit 14 Low-Cost Carrier Full-Time Equivalent Employees, August 2002–2006

(Numbers in thousands)

Rank		2002	2003*	2004*	2005*	2006	Percent Change 2002–2006
1	Southwest	34	33	31	31	32	–4.5
2	America West	12	11	11	12	13	7.0
3	JetBlue	3	5	6	8	10	212.4
4	AirTran	5	5	6	6	7	56.9
5	Frontier	3	3	4	4	5	70.6
6	ATA	7	7	7	4	3	–61.5
7	Spirit	2	2	2	2	2	–14.4
8	Independence	N/A	4	4	3	N/A	N/A
	Total****	65	71	72	71	71	9.3

*Employment numbers in 2003, 2004, and 2005 for Independence Air, which changed its business model from a regional to low-cost carrier in mid-2004, are included with low-cost carriers. The carrier did not meet the standard for filing in previous years. The airline discontinued flights on January 5, 2006.

N/A = Not applicable because carriers did not meet the standard for filing.

Source: Bureau of Transportation Statistics.

Exhibit 15 Pay Scale Table

2004 Year	A-320 Captain	EMB190 Captain	A-320 FO	EMB190 FO
12	$126	$89	$76	$53
11	$126	$87	$76	$52
10	$126	$85	$76	$51
9	$125	$84	$75	$50
8	$124	$82	$74	$49
7	$123	$80	$74	$48
6	$122	$79	$73	$47
5	$121	$77	$72	$46
4	$118	$76	$67	$44
3	$116	$74	$61	$42
2	$113	$72	$56	$40
1	$110	$71	$51	$37

Note: Guarantee of 70 hrs/month; above 70 hours paid at 150%.

Source: 2006, Will fly for food, http://www.willflyforfood.cc/Payscales/PayScales.htm.

Because JetBlue desires to remain nonunionized, it will have to pay its employees well to ensure they do not become disgruntled and demand representation. Unions have not gained a foothold in JetBlue, but the Air Lines Pilot Association has JetBlue as a target. In addition to pilots, flight attendants, mechanics, ground crews, and gate agents will also receive pressure from other national unions for representation. If by chance the employees of JetBlue succumb to union pressure, union negotiators will then push for increased wages and other amenities—such as hotel requirements, time off, minimum number of flight hours per month, and so on—resulting in higher costs.

JetBlue's Challenge in Coming Years

David Neeleman started an airline based on previous experience and an entrepreneurial spirit. He knew what people wanted and how much they would pay for it. JetBlue attracted high-quality employees because of the unique culture that stressed customer service and differentiated offerings. Allowing at-home reservations agents, paperless cockpits, and crewmembers' easy access to executives has created an environment with which people want to associate. In addition, by purchasing brand new Airbus airplanes and having a junior staff, JetBlue has minimized labor and maintenance costs, both major operating expenses, for several years. As growth slows in the domestic market, its aircraft begin to age, and the workforce becomes more senior, the number of challenges will increase. Barger and Neeleman are faced with persistent questions about how to continue to grow the airline profitably. Does JetBlue attack Southwest, United, Delta, American, or Continental strongholds in the Midwest and/or smaller airports? Does it form an alliance in order to expand into international markets such as Europe and Asia? To minimize expenses related to airplanes, should JetBlue return to one airplane type? Finally, while unions are prevalent at every other airline, how can JetBlue maintain an environment where employees remain committed, dedicated, and satisfied?

NOTES

1. 2002, JetBlue Airways Corporation, *International Directory of Company Histories*, Vol. 44. St. James Press. 2006, Reproduced in Business and Company Resource Center. Farmington Hills, Mich.:Gale Group.

2. M. Trottman & S. Carey, 2006, Legacy Airlines may outfly discount rivals, *Wall Street Journal*, October 30, C1.

3. T. Fredrickson, 2006, Middle-aged JetBlue finds it's harder to fly; Ballooning fuel costs, intense competition turn it into a loser, *Crain's New York Business*, February 13, 22(7):4.

4. J. Bernstein, 2006, JetBlue posts quarterly loss, *Newsday*, October 25.

5. J. H. Dobrzynski, 2006, We're still a growth airline, *Wall Street Journal*, November 4, A6.

6. JetBlue Airways Corporation, http://galenet.galegroup.com. ezproxy1.lib.asu.edu/servlet/BCRC.

7. S. Overby, 2002, JetBlue skies ahead, *CIO Magazine*, http://www.cio.com, July 1.

8. 2006, Airbus, http://www.airbus.com/en/aircraftfamilies/a320/a320/.

9. S. Overby, JetBlue skies ahead.

10. Ibid.

11. 2002, JetBlue announces second quarter 2002 earnings—Low-fare carrier achieves record operating margin of 18.6%, JetBlue Airways Corporation press release, July 25.

12. 2002, JetBlue announces initial public offering of its common stock, JetBlue Airways Corporation press release, April 11.

13. 2005, JetBlue's New Terminal 5 will more than double airline's JFK capacity within three years, JetBlue Airways Corporation press release, December 7.

14. 2006, Fourth quarter of 2005, JetBlue Airways Corporation press release, February 1.

15. 2006, Third quarter of 2006, JetBlue Airways Corporation press release, October 24.

16. Ibid.

17. J. Bailey, 2007, JetBlue's C.E.O. is mortified after fliers are stranded, *New York Times*, http://www.nytimes.com, February 19; T. Keenan, 2007, JetBlue damage control, http://www.foxnews.com, February 27.

18. 2007, JetBlue announces the JetBlue Customer Bill of Rights, JetBlue Airways Corporation press release, February 20.

19. 2006, Air transportation, scheduled, *Encyclopedia of American Industries*, online ed., Thomson Gale.

20. 2006, Hoover's Company Records, JetBlue Airways Corporation, October 31.

21. R. M. Schneiderman, 2006, Legacy carriers fly back into favor, *Forbes*, http://www.forbes.com, October 20.

22. 2006, Air transportation, scheduled.

23. J. Schoen, 2006, Airline woes spark industry dogfight, http://www.msnbc.com, July 31.

24. 2006, Star Alliance, http://www.staralliance.com/en/travellers/index.html.

25. K. Iatrou & N. Skourias, 2005, An attempt to measure the traffic impact of airline alliances, *Journal of Air Transportation*, 10(3): 73–99.

26. C. Jones, 2006, JetBlue seeks international partnerships, *Deseret News*, Salt Lake City, March 16.

27. D. Rosato, 2006, How to score a cheap airline ticket, *CNNMoney*, http://www.cnnmoney.com, October 27.

28. 2007, US Airways withdraws offer for Delta Air Lines, press release, http://www.usairways.com, January 31.

29. C. Palmeri, D. Frost, & L. Woellert, 2006, Doug Parker wants to fly Delta, *BusinessWeek*, http://www.businessweek.com, November 16.

30. 2006, Southwest Airlines Co. Annual Report.

31. W. Zellner, 2005, Southwest: Dressed to kill . . . competitors, *BusinessWeek*, February 21.

32. R. E. Hoskisson, M. A. Hitt, & R. D. Ireland, 2003, *Competing for Advantage*, Mason, OH: South-Western, 24.

33. D. Reed, 2006, At 35, Southwest's strategy gets more complicated, *USA Today*, July 11.

34. 2006, Hoover's Company Reports: In-depth records, AMR Corporation, November 28.

35. 2006, AMR Corp Annual Report.

36. 2006, Hoover's Company Reports: In-depth records, UAL Corporation, November 28.

37. Ibid.

38. R. M. Schneiderman, 2006, Report: UAL looking to merge, *Forbes*, December 1.

39. C. Palmeri, D. Frost, & L. Woellert, 2006, Doug Parker wants to fly Delta.

40. 2006, USAirways Group, Inc. Annual Report.

41. 2006, Airline Domestic Market Share: September 2005–August 2006, *Bureau of Transportation Statistics—The Intermodal Transportation Database*, http://www.transtats.bts.gov/, December 6.

42. 2006, Hoover's Company Reports: In-depth records, Continental Airlines Inc., November 28.

43. R. Fozard, 2006, Continental's surprising ascent, *BusinessWeek*, July 31.

44. R. M. Schneiderman, 2006, Continental packs 'em in, *Forbes*, October 19.

45. 2006, Congressional testimony, *Congressional Quarterly, Inc.*, February 8.

46. Ibid.

47. Ibid.

48. E. Roston, 2005, Hedging their costs: Whether oil prices go up or down, smart airline companies are covered, *Time*, July 27.

49. 2005, Oil prices will prune revenue gains but Southwest, JetBlue look good, *Airline Business Report*, July 4, 23(12).

50. 2007, FAA aerospace forecast fiscal years 2007–2020, http://www.faa.gov/data_statistics/.

51. 2006, JetBlue Airways Corporation Form 10-K, Fiscal year ending December 31, 21.

52. C. Jones, 2006, JetBlue founder pushes for alternative fuel, http://www.timesdispatch.com, November 15.

53. K. Johnson, 2005, Fuel hedging gets tricky, *Wall Street Journal*, May 19.

54. 2005, JetBlue Airways Corporation Form 10-K, Fiscal year ending December 31, 4.

55. Ibid, 9.

56. 2006, *Wall Street Journal* (Eastern edition), November 22.

57. 2005, JetBlue Airways Corporation Form 10-K, Fiscal year ending December 31, 2.

58. 2000, http://www.house.gov/transportation/aviation/hearing/12-05-00/12-05-00memo.html.

59. D. Bond, 2006, The FAA's demand-management plans for LaGuardia call for bigger aircraft, market-based slot turnover, *Aviation Week & Space Technology*, September 4.

60. 2005, JetBlue Airways Corporation Form 10-K, Fiscal year ending December 31, 69.

61. S. Overby, 2002, JetBlue skies ahead.

62. S. Lott, 2006, IAM fails in first attempt to organize JetBlue ramp staff, *Aviation Daily*, July 20.

63. 2006, Significant safety events since 2000 for JetBlue Airlines, AirSafe, LLC, http://www.airsafe.com, May 6.

64. J. Scott, 2005, http://www.aerospaceweb.org/question/planes/q0245a.shtml, October 2.

65. R. Singal, 2003, Army admits using JetBlue data, Wired News, http://www.wired.com, September 23.

66. 2002, United States District Court Eastern District of New York, Memorandum & Order, JetBlue Airways Corp: Privacy Litigation: 04-MD-1587 (CBA), http://www.epic.org/privacy/airtravel/jetblue/decision_0705.pdf.

67. 2005, JetBlue Airways Corporation Form 10-K, Fiscal year ending December 31, 2.

68. 2006, JetBlue Announces 6.6 Percent Operating Margin for Third Quarter 2006, JetBlue Airways Corporation press release, October 24.

69. J. Miner, 2006, http://luxuryresorttravel.suite101.com/article/cfm./jetblue_airways_pros_and_cons, November 13.

70. S. Salter, 2004, And now the hard part, *Fast Company*, http://www.fastcompany.com, May, 82: 67.

71. Ibid.

72. Ibid.

73. B. Harrell, 2005, http://www.yaleeconomicreview.com/issues/fall2005/davidneeleman.

74. 2005, JetBlue Airways Corporation Form 10-K, Fiscal year ending December 31, 3.

75. S. Overby, JetBlue skies ahead.

76. Ibid.

77. R. Valdes, How VoIP works, http://electronics.howstuffworks.com/ip-telephony.htm.

78. S. Salter, 2004, Calling JetBlue, *Fast Company*, http://www.fastcompany.com, May, 82.

79. 2005, JetBlue soars with Omniture Research Center, Omniture, Inc., http://www.omniture.com, December 2.

80. D. Sacks, 2006, Rehab: An advertising love story, *Fast Company*, http://www.fastcompany.com, June, 106.

81. Ibid.

82. B. Harrell, http://www.yaleeconomicreview.com/issues/fall2005/davidneeleman.

83. 2005, JetBlue Airways Corporation Form 10-K, Fiscal year ending December 31, 3.

84. D. Sacks, Rehab: An advertising love story.

85. 2006, XS Lighting & sound lights JetBlue interactive kiosks, *Prism Business Media*, http://www.livedesignonline.com, June 7.

86. K. Prentice, Your client's ad, taking it to the streets, *Media Life Magazine*, Http://www.medialifemagazine.com, May 15.

87. Ibid.

88. 2005, JetBlue announces first quarter results, JetBlue Airways Corporation press release, April 1.

89. 2006, JetBlue announces 6.6 percent operating margin for third quarter, JetBlue Airways Corporation press release, October 24.

90. 2005, JetBlue Airways Corporation Form 10-K, Fiscal year ending December 31, 10.

91. Ibid.

92. R. M. Schneiderman, 2006, JetBlue courts Corporate America, *Forbes*, August 11.

93. D. Neeleman, 2006, http://www.jetblue.com/about/ourcompany/flightlog, December 14.

94. 2005, Introducing JetBlue getaways, JetBlue Airways Corporation press release, November 3.

95. 2005, JetBlue Airways Corporation Form 10-K, Fiscal year ending December 31, 1.

96. 2006, JetBlue Airways Corporation Form 10-K, Fiscal year ending December 31, 19.

97. Financial Accounting Module 3.

98. 2005, JetBlue Airways Corporation Form 10-K, Fiscal year ending December 31, 17.

99. 2006, Industry data from www.moneycentral.msn.com.

100. 2006, Yahoo! Finance, http://finance.yahoo.com/q/hp?s=JBLU&a=03&b=18&c=2001&d=10&e=30&f=2006&g=m.

101. K. Prentice, 2006, After backing away, some airlines turning to fuel hedging again, Associated Press State & Local Wire, September 4.

102. S. Salter, On the runway, *Fast Company*, http://www.fastcompany.com, May (82).

103. S. Salter, And now the hard part, 67.

104. D. Reed, 2006, Loss shifts JetBlue's focus to climbing back into black, http://www.usatoday.com, Feb 22.

105. Ibid.

106. M. Bobelian, 2003, JetBlue lands expansion plans, *Forbes*, http://www.forbes.com, June 10.

107. T. Reed, 2006, TheStreet.com, http://www.thestreet.com/stocks/transportation/10260392.html, January 6.

108. 2006, *Aircraft Technology, Engineering & Maintenance*, October/November, 99.

109. 2005, McGraw-Hill Companies *Overhaul & Maintenance*, Magazine for MRO Management, October 2.

110. Ibid, 5.

111. 2006, JetBlue Airways Corporation, Form 10-Q, October 24.

112. *Aircraft Technology Engineering & Maintenance*, 101.

113. 2006, JetBlue Airways Corporation Form 10-K, Fiscal year ending December 31, 41.

114. T. Reed, http://www.thestreet.com.

George Griffith, Tiffany Johnson, Rebecca Sebald,
Tracey Cowan, Nick Trotter, and Alfred Wong

Arizona State University

It's customers that made Dell great in the first place, and if we're smart enough and quick enough to listen to customer needs, we'll succeed.

—**MICHAEL DELL**

Dell Inc., founded in 1984 by present CEO and chairman of the board Michael Dell, is a leading technology provider that designs, develops, manufactures, and supports PCs, software and peripherals, storage and servers, and associated services. The public company is headquartered in Round Rock, Texas, with operations in three geographic regions: the Americas; Europe, the Middle East, and Africa (EMEA); and Asia Pacific–Japan (APJ). Additionally Dell has business centers and manufacturing sites in more than 20 locations around the world. Dell operates primarily on a direct customer sales business model that provides it with in-depth customer knowledge so that solutions can be effectively tailored to meet customer needs. Since its founding, Dell has expanded its core business model by broadening its product portfolio and adding distribution partners (retail, value-added resellers, and distributors) that allowed Dell to reach more than 24,000 retail locations worldwide in FY09.[1]

Over the past two decades, Dell has been very successful with the direct customer sales business model, with an average annual revenue growth of 10 percent annually. Dell shipped 43 million units in FY09 and held a 15.1 percent share of the worldwide computer systems market, enjoying 11.1 percent growth, which exceeded industry worldwide computer systems growth of 9.7 percent (in terms of sales). In April 2008, Dell was the top PC provider in the United States and second worldwide in terms of sales; however, the top position in the United States was overtaken by Hewlett-Packard (HP) in the first quarter of 2009.[2] Revenue growth has stalled, with fiscal year 2009 (FY09 ending January 30) revenues of $61.101 billion compared to FY08 revenues of $61.133 billion. PCs, their largest product revenue stream, experienced a 12 percent decline. Dell's average selling price (total revenue per unit sold) also decreased 7 percent year-over-year, which is attributed to changes in revenue mix from commercial to consumers, lower selling prices in retail, and an increasingly competitive environment. Amidst the economic downturn, corporate IT spending continues to weaken, with worldwide PC shipments declining 6.5 percent in the first quarter of 2009. With 80 percent of Dell's sales coming from corporate buyers, the scaled-back spending has directly impacted Dell's market share, with Dell shipping 16.7 percent fewer computers worldwide in Q1 2009 versus Q1 2008.[3]

On December 31, 2008, Dell announced it would reorganize its business units from regional segments to four globally operated areas—large enterprise, public sector, small and medium businesses, and global consumer—to better align with customer needs for "faster innovation and globally standardized products and services."[4]

History of Dell Inc.

In 1984, while still a student at the University of Texas and with only $1,000 to his name, Michael Dell founded PCs Limited, the original name of Dell Inc., and introduced its first computer, the Turbo, the following year. The company changed its name to Dell Computer Corporation in 1988 and ultimately to Dell Inc. in 2004 to recognize its expansion beyond a PC-only business. Dell's Web site began selling computers in 1996, and the company overtook Compaq as the largest seller of PCs in the United States in 1999. In 2006, Dell acquired computer hardware manufacturer Alienware and both ASAP Software Express Inc. and EqualLogic in 2008. Since its founding in 1984, Dell Inc. has grown to employ approximately 78,900 employees.

Note: This case was written to be used as a basis for class discussion rather than to illustrate either effective or ineffective handling of an administrative situation. We would like to thank Robert E. Hoskisson and Robert E. White for useful feedback in writing this case. Data was collected from publically available sources.

The early business model (1984–1990) was to assemble computers comparable to those of the more widely known IBM and target the price-conscious but tech-savvy consumer segment with lower prices. Dell was able to purchase parts and build their products in house, selling them at a fraction of the price that IBM could offer. It then took orders directly from customers (keeping advertising costs low), built the products to order (keeping inventory costs low), and provided a high level of customer service when delivering the end product.[5] Dell quickly moved into the top position in the direct-mail computer market, specializing in inexpensive PCs.[6] In 1984, Dell grossed $6 million in sales, increasing to $40 million the following year.

In order to sustain growth, the company brought the Tandy Group as consultants in 1987 to create a sales force focused on diversifying their customer base. While profits rose initially, Dell was unwilling to modify its direct customer sales business model to a more traditional sales approach with higher advertising spending and larger sales force, so most of the Tandy Group employees were released within the year. Around the same time, Dell opened new offices in London and Canada, allowing them to garner the attention of corporations, government, and educational consumers. This provided the foundation for the company to go public in June 1988, when they sold 3.5 million shares at $8.50 a share.[7]

Shortly after going public, Dell faced severe competition from several Japanese manufacturers offering similar products at lower prices. In response, Dell increased R&D spending and hired a computer scientist from IBM to manage the R&D staff and increase the technological sophistication of their product offerings. Dell also faced massive holding costs due to underestimating the change in demand the Japanese competition brought. Dell, in fact, had increased capacity substantially to accommodate the previously increasing demand, which resulted in unsold inventory.

To improve its management processes, Dell increased its emphasis on the corporate customer which resulted in a large increase in sales from the corporate segment, from 15 percent of sales in 1987 to 40 percent in 1990.[8] From 1990 to 2000, Dell opened new offices in Italy, France, and Ireland, allowing them to serve Europe, the Middle East, and Africa's larger corporations, offering powerful server solutions. At this time, they also worked to diversify their sales channels by introducing their products in large computer retail stores. As a result, Dell became the sixth-largest PC producer in the United States, and the focus on customer service earned them a #1 rating in J.D. Power and Associates's first survey of PC customer satisfaction.[9] By 1991, Dell had their first laptop PC available for purchase to cater to the fastest-growing segment of the PC market.

In response to the recession and ongoing price wars with PC makers Compaq, IBM, and Apple, Dell made steep price cuts, lowering their profit margins dramatically. Compaq, in particular, had released a lower-end PC that was priced competitively while offering increased customer service, which appealed to Dell's target consumers. Within the next few years, Dell also expanded their product portfolio to include fax machines and compact discs.

In the mid 1990s, "Dell introduced a line of network servers and was soon the fastest-growing company in the server sector."[10] Shortly thereafter, the company implemented an online channel for consumers to place their orders directly. They also strengthened their market position by opening a manufacturing plant in Malaysia. In the late 1990s, they began producing workstations and storage products as well as offering a leasing program that allowed customers to avoid maintaining a system as it became older and more obsolete. In 1998, they built a production and sales facility in China, further extending their global presence. Their final undertakings in the 1990s were to offer Internet access, Dellnet, to their customers as well as adding manufacturing plants in the United States and Brazil.[11] For the fiscal year ending in January 2000, Dell reported net income of $1.86 billion on total revenues of $25 billion.

In the first decade of the twenty-first century, Dell's strategy continued to develop. In late 2001, Dell introduced a new line of products, PowerConnect, which allowed consumers to network within a small business environment. In 2003, they launched their Axim line of handheld computers to compete with competitors' PDAs. In efforts to retain and attract new consumers, Dell set up kiosks in retail shopping malls, opened their first Dell location within a Sears store, created an online music service, and introduced their first line of printers.[12] Dell's diversification, coupled with large increases in shipments of high-profit-margin products such as servers, notebook computers, and storage equipment, propelled the company to new heights in 2004.[13] This diversification allowed annual net income to increase to $2.65 billion. Dell also had an interest in the growing Chinese market and began increasing their presence in rural Chinese areas, capitalizing on subsidies farmers received and has allowed Dell to weather the current tough economic times and boost sales.[14]

Despite the success of the direct sales model, Michael Dell realized the company must keep pace with shifting consumer sentiment and market conditions. Dell told *Forbes* in 2007 that "the old model ran its course, now it's time for a new course."[15] With eyes on the consumer market offering new channels of distribution, Dell brought on a new executive group to accomplish this goal.

Competitive Situation

Key Competitors

Dell faces stiff competition within the computer hardware industry. According to IDC, for Q1 2009, the top five PC shipment vendors worldwide are (in rank order): HP, Dell, Acer, Lenovo, and Toshiba (for U.S. PC shipments, Apple replaces Lenovo as fourth place).[16] For the enterprise market, Dell's standardized desktops and laptops remain the most popular among North American and European enterprises and are a clear leader over HP and Lenovo.[17] Market share data can be found in Exhibits 1 through 3 and competitor revenues from geographic regions can be found in Exhibit 4. The following key competitors will be discussed in order: Acer, HP, Apple, and Lenovo.

Acer Group. Founded in 1977, Acer Group is a Taiwanese company competing with Dell in the desktop PC, notebook computer, server, displays, and information technology (IT) solutions segments. Acer's portfolio of brands includes Gateway and eMachines, which were acquired in October 2007, as well as Packard Bell.

In the first quarter of 2009, Acer had sales of US $3.4 billion, which was down from $3.9 billion in the same quarter in 2008.[18] Their strongest sales came from the EMEA (Europe, Middle East, Africa), where they earned 49 percent of their revenue in the first quarter of 2009. They are the leading manufacturer of notebook computers in the EMEA, with a 26.6 percent market share. In the United States, Acer is the third-ranked maker of both PCs and notebooks with 13.6 percent and 16.8 percent market shares, respectively. Worldwide, for PCs and notebooks, they rank third and second,

Exhibit 1 Worldwide PC Shipments in 2008—Market Share

WW PC Shipments 2008		
PC OEM	Market Share	YoY Growth
HP	19.2%	12.7%
Dell	15%	11%
Acer	10.9%	53.3%
Lenovo	7.4%	8.3%
Toshiba	4.6%	25.1%
Others	43%	1.3%

Source: IDC

Exhibit 2 U.S. PC Shipments in 2008—Market Share

U.S. PC Shipments 2008		
PC OEM	Market Share	YoY Growth
Dell	29.5%	3.3%
HP	24.9%	1.8%
Acer	9.1%	62.1%
Apple	7.7%	25.7%
Toshiba	5.5%	7.6%
Others	23.4%	−16%

Source: IDC

respectively, with 12.8 percent and 19.6 percent market shares. Notebook sales accounted for 68 percent of their revenue in FY 09 Q1, while PCs accounted for 17 percent, displays 12 percent, and other segments 3 percent.[19]

Acer Group CEO J. T. Wang defines Acer's corporate sustainability as, "A successful global IT company which achieves in triple bottom lines, meaning, outstanding and balanced performance in the economy, environment and society."[20] Most recently, Acer has launched a set of new core values as described by CEO Wang: "The pillars on which we must base our actions include: value-creating, customer-centric, ethical and caring. The way we must act should be: innovative, fast and effective."[21]

Acer has been focusing on the execution of the October 2007 acquisition of Gateway and eMachines by positioning and uniquely segmenting each brand. Acer, which is not known for its direct customer selling, has been evaluating this strategy. However, Gateway has long had a similar direct-selling strategy to Dell but has failed to execute it as effectively. Acer's strategy is to segment their customers based on their needs and tailor one of their brands to meet those needs. Gianfranco Lanci, Acer's president and CEO, stated, "Our channel strategy will be very different from our competitors. The market is changing where users have different needs for our products. We do not want to confuse our customers and think that multiple branding is the future."[22]

Hewlett-Packard. Hewlett-Packard (HP), founded in 1936 and based in the United States, competes directly with Dell in almost every category.[23] HP holds the top position globally in the PC segment with 19 percent market share and recently overtook the top spot in the United States. HP's highest margin business

Exhibit 3 Enterprise Laptop and Desktop Market

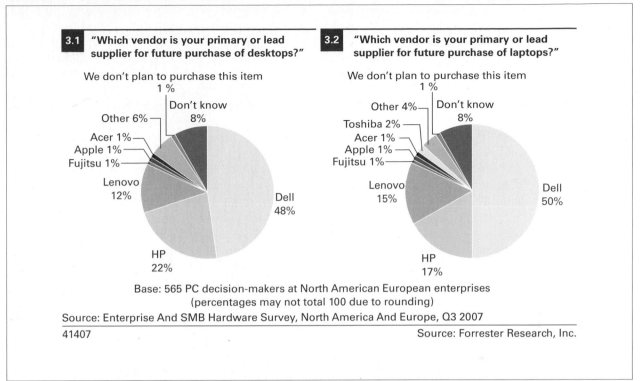

3.1 "Which vendor is your primary or lead supplier for future purchase of desktops?"

We don't plan to purchase this item 1%
Don't know 8%
Other 6%
Acer 1%
Apple 1%
Fujitsu 1%
Lenovo 12%
HP 22%
Dell 48%

3.2 "Which vendor is your primary or lead supplier for future purchase of laptops?"

We don't plan to purchase this item 1%
Don't know 8%
Other 4%
Toshiba 2%
Acer 1%
Apple 1%
Fujitsu 1%
Lenovo 15%
HP 17%
Dell 50%

Base: 565 PC decision-makers at North American European enterprises
(percentages may not total 100 due to rounding)
Source: Enterprise And SMB Hardware Survey, North America And Europe, Q3 2007

41407

Source: Forrester Research, Inc.

has been the imaging and printing business, which contributed 36 percent of earnings but only represented 25 percent of revenues.[24] Their 2008 revenues were $118.4 billion, up from $104 billion in 2007, and break down as follows among their core businesses: Personal

Exhibit 4 Percentage of Revenue by Global Regions and Competitor

Provider	% Sales by Region (2008)		
	Americas	EMEA	APJ
Dell[?]	47%	22%	12%
Lenovo	28%	22%	50%
HP	42%	42%	16%
Apple*	45%	23%	12%
Acer**	30%	49%	21%

[?]Dell's other operating segment, Global Consumer, accounts for 19% of sales and operates globally.

*Apple's other operating segment, Retail, accounts for 20% of sales and consists of locations in America and International.

**Acer figures based on Q1 2009 results and not annual due to limited availability of information.

Systems Group (PC and handheld devices segment) 35 percent, Imaging and Printing 25 percent, HP Services 19 percent, Enterprise Storage and Solutions 16 percent, HP Software 2 percent, HP Financial Services 2 percent, and Corporate Investments 1 percent.[25] By geographic regions, HP receives 42 percent of its revenue from the Americas (United States, Canada, Latin America), 42 percent from the EMEA, and 16 percent from Asia Pacific. EMEA shows the highest growth, with revenues up 22 percent in 2008 compared to 2007.[26]

In August 2008, HP acquired Electronic Data Services (EDS) for $13 billion, adding strength to their services business. EDS also expanded the breadth of products and services HP offers and gave potential customers, both businesses and at-home consumers, the ability to meet all of their needs. HP is currently going through a four-year restructuring project to improve its efficiency and seek financial savings through shared costs among its business units, and has released plans to cut 24,700 employees from its global workforce.[27]

HP's strategy moving forward is to serve as their corporate customers' only resource for everything IT related. As Mark V. Hurd, the chairman, CEO, and president of HP, stated in the 2008 annual report, "Enterprises are straining to meet ever-growing demand with aging, complex, proprietary and inefficient IT infrastructures. These dynamics are creating a massive disruption in the

IT marketplace and a massive opportunity for HP. With a comprehensive portfolio of hardware, software, and services, HP is well positioned to help customers manage and transform their IT environments."[28]

In their largest revenue business, the PC segment, they are trying to revamp stale sales by introducing new sleek touchscreen computers.[29] "HP is offering the assistance of hardware and software consultants from its services division to help customers come up with new uses for touch technology."[30] As part of this strategy, HP has partnered with Chicago's O'Hare airport and placed 50 touchscreens for patrons to use to access maps and local information. HP is hoping to increase sales from the 400,000 units sold in 2008.

Apple. Apple entered the computer industry in 1976 and has evolved its business strategies of brand loyalty, innovation, marketing advantage, and end-to-end user experience over the past 30 years. In 1998, Apple CEO Steve Jobs took note that their products integrated with very few of the industry standard peripherals, operating systems, and applications, threatening isolation. Jobs decided to adjust their business strategy to focus on product differentiation with offerings that were user friendly, attractively designed, well supported, and comprehensive using Apple products that address specific user needs. The iMac, introduced in 1998, had these qualities and was the catalyst for a turnaround in the company's performance.

While prices of Macs (Apple's computers) are generally more expensive than those of competitors, Apple's competitive strategy is basic: "make the best product possible, and rewards will follow."[31] Without the need to maintain a cost leadership position in the market, Apple is able to focus on differentiating its product, focusing on innovation to cater to the user experience.[32] On average historically, Apple spends 4 to 5 percent of its revenue on R&D, compared to 1 percent by competitors, including Dell.[33] Their current product portfolio now includes iPhones, Macs, notebooks, and iPods, as well as accessories for these core items. Diversification and user-centric design have allowed Apple to hedge the risk of substitutes and to enter markets without excessive marketing expenses traditionally required to target specific market segments or user groups. While Macs currently account for fewer than 5 percent of corporate desktops, many companies responding to an Information Technology Industry Council (ITIC) survey indicate that they are likely to let employees select Macs as business workstations within the next year.[34]

Apple continues to focus on controlling costs through efficient operations. In 2008, Apple outsourced much of its transportation and logistics management outside of the United States. This was done to control costs at the potential risk of losing direct control over production and distribution, potentially compromising quality and quantity of products, and limiting response flexibility to changing market conditions.[35] In 2008, Apple earned first place in the Supply Chain Top 25 ranking by AMR Research. AMR Research stated, "Behind-the-scenes moves like tying up essential components well in advance and upgrading basic information systems have enabled Apple to handle the demands of its rabid fan base without having to fall back on their forgiveness for mistakes."[36]

Apple's total net sales of domestic and international products increased 68 percent from FY06 to FY08 to $32.5 billion while cost of sales increased 50 percent to $4.8 billion.[37] The ratio between domestic and international sales has remained relatively consistent FY06 through FY08, with 43 percent of sales revenue being generated outside of the United States in 2008.[38] Despite strained economic times, Apple's earnings per common share continues to increase year over year. With 31,010 regular employees worldwide in 2008, Apple resource numbers continue to grow as well as research and development expenses (3 percent of net sales in 2008 which is below its historical average).[39]

Lenovo. Founded in 1984, Hong Kong–based Lenovo Legend Group is the largest computer producer in Asia and retains approximately 24,000 employees worldwide. Lenovo acquired IBM's personal computer business in 2005, creating the third-largest personal computer company in the world at the time. Lenovo has been listed on the Stock Exchange of Hong Kong since 1994 and currently controls 25 percent of the Asian computer market due to cost leadership and entry barriers to the Chinese market historically caused by high import tariffs.

Lenovo boasts a "worldsourcing" business model that distributes management, operations, and production into global "hubs of excellence." Strategies for growth in 2009 are outlined to include streamlining and improving the global supply chain and logistics network to control costs, growing customer intimacy to better understand consumer demands, PC focus on workstations and servers, increasing scale to appreciate benefits of economic efficiencies, and building brand recognition and loyalty.[40] Lenovo's product offerings are similar to Dell's (PCs, notebooks, servers, peripherals, and support services), however, it does not offer adjacent product lines (i.e., entertainment, telecommunications, TV), which competitors have begun to offer to hedge the risk of substitute products.

In 2008, Lenovo launched a backwards integration strategy into its supply chain in order to eliminate third parties from the manufacturing process.[41] This move into vertically shoring up its supply chain is aimed at reducing supplier power, thereby increasing control over quality and ability to implement design changes more quickly.

Lenovo sales decreased from FY07 to FY08 (FY ends March 31) by more than 20 percent while operating expenses decreased less than 9 percent.[42] Research and development expenses increased 17.1 percent, indicating a growing focus on innovation and product enhancements. The majority of sales, driven by China, account for nearly 40 percent of total sales while less than 30 percent of sales occur in the United States. Asia Pacific, Europe, Middle East, and Africa account for the remaining 30 percent of sales.

Customer Segments

As alluded to above, Dell serves four main customer segments—Home Users, Large Enterprise, Small and Medium Businesses (SMB), and Public Sector.[43] The segmentation is based on the different needs of each customer sector. As Michael Dell describes it, "Customer requirements are increasingly being defined by how they use technology rather than where they use it. That's why we won't let ourselves be limited by geographic boundaries in solving their needs."[44]

Home Users

The Home Users segment addresses all personal usage of computers and has traditionally been a smaller market than the commercial space. Of all computers shipped worldwide, approximately 75 percent are used professionally while 25 percent are for personal or home use.[45] Despite being a smaller market, the consumer segment "has the potential to expand faster than [Dell's] business with corporations and government agencies."[46]

Large Enterprise

Dell has identified Facebook, Microsoft, Amazon, Akamai, and Baidu as key customers in the corporate servers and data center business segment.[47] The needs of Large Enterprise customers vary from business to business across solutions for data storage, networking, security, or hardware procurement. Being the largest buyers in the IT industry, enterprise customers can demand customized solutions catered to their specific needs. However, with a large amount of resources invested with a specific IT vendor, it is not easy to switch to another vendor without incurring significant change and costs. Curiously, some of Dell's corporate customers also happen to be key vendors, which makes managing "these relationships [a] little challenging," according to

Dell's CIO Jerry Gregoire.[48] Enterprise IT spending is expected to remain flat for 2009.[49]

Small and Medium Business

Unlike large enterprises, SMBs do not have a large amount of resources dedicated for IT needs. In fact, the person responsible for IT is often "one of the founding members who is juggling many roles—CFO, sales manager, marketing guy, and so on."[50] Dell has traditionally been a strong player in the SMB market by comprehensively managing SMB's IT needs so the dedicated IT resource can focus on other roles. Dell understands that "SMBs are far more sensitive to cost issues because if their computers are down, that might be all of their systems," as opposed to large enterprises, which would have redundant backup systems with a dedicated IT staff resolving any issues.[51] By having multi-tier service offerings, Dell is able to potentially have more than 72 million SMB customers worldwide.[52] Analysts suggest that SMBs will spend double what big business spends in 2009. HP forecasts show that SMB is "one of the fastest growing IT market opportunities, with 4 to 7 percent growth expected in 2009 for a total available market opportunity of $68 billion."[53] Despite the economic slowdown, competitors such as HP, Lenovo, and Toshiba have all announced plans to target the SMB market in 2009.

Public Sector

In the Public Sector customer segment, Dell has identified government, education, and health care as areas of strategic focus.[54] For these customers, Dell is committed to providing simplified and standardized solutions to satisfy any of their IT requirements. Besides competing in the above segments, Dell is experiencing other competitive issues associated with these segments.

Additional Competitive Issues

Dell offers a broad range of product categories, including mobility products, desktop PCs, software and peripherals, servers and networking, services, and storage.[55] Due to the rapid technological innovations in computer electronics and the high level of dependency of many businesses and home users, there are no clear, direct substitute products for Dell's product portfolio.

While there are no imminent threats from substitute products, there is increasing competition from new entrants in the Home Users market segment. Witnessing the success of new entrants from Taiwan and Japan such as Acer, Asus, Toshiba, and Fujitsu in the late 1990s and early 2000s, many electronics manufacturers continue to attempt to enter the computer manufacturing market. For example, Micro Electronics Inc., the parent company of the computer retailer Micro Center, started selling an in-house line of laptops known as Winbook in 2004.[56,57] Other electronics manufacturers such as Archos, maker of portable DVD players, made its entry into the portable computing market in 2009 with its Archos 10 netbook.[58] Bigger brands such as Samsung, which is famous for its cell phones, LCD monitors, and TVs, also entered the Home User market with its line of laptops. It is expected that more electronics makers will try to leverage their brand name and enter the home computing market. Furthermore, as the younger population becomes more tech savvy, possible "new entrants" are home or small PC makers that purchase stock parts directly and assemble a customized machine themselves or for a small fee. Ironically, this is how Dell was first founded 25 years ago.[59]

On the other hand, the commercial and public sector markets are experiencing a wave of consolidation. This is evident through major strategic decisions in the industry such as HP's merger with Compaq, Acer's acquisition of Gateway, and IBM's decision to exit the hardware market and focus on IT services. However, there are new competitors in the server market, including producers of supplier products. For example, Cisco systems has signaled that it will enter the server market to more fully serve corporate data centers, which often require integrated solutions based on multiple products.[60]

Economic Downturn and Other Challenges

Dell faces significant challenges in the midst of the current economic recession. Gartner Research predicts the worst-case scenario for IT spending in 2009 will be no growth in the United States, and IT expenditures are expected to shrink in Europe.[61] Forrester Research analyst Andrew Bartels further predicts "the brunt of the slowdown in IT spending will hit servers and PCs,"[62] which is Dell's primary market. In the Home User market, households are reducing their discretionary spending and will opt for low cost PCs with the bare minimum number of features, which may impact Dell's product lineup.

In this difficult economic environment, supplier and customer insolvency is plausible and may result in product delays and reduced demand. Dell also faces risks on the global front due to its international exposure. In FY09, "sales outside the U.S. accounted for approximately 48 percent of [Dell's] consolidated net revenue." Changes in the U.S. monetary policy as well as economic policies around the world may lead to volatile exchange rates, exposing Dell to currency risks despite its foreign currency hedging program.

Also, government and environmental groups have called for corporations to become more "green" and energy efficient. Dell is an industry leader in this area, as it announced in August 2008 that it has "reached its goal of becoming 'carbon neutral' five months ahead of schedule."[63] While Dell's claim of "carbon neutrality" has been questioned by journalists, Dell is at least taking proactive steps to "set an example by reducing its environmental impact as responsibly and aggressively as it can."[64] Dell's reliance on renewable energy as well as being more energy efficient are estimated to save the company $3 million a year. Dell has also demonstrated itself to be a responsible corporate citizen by participating in programs such as (PRODUCT)RED™, where Dell contributes a part of the proceeds for each product sold associated with the program to a global fund to combat AIDS in Africa.[65]

Other regulatory and legal challenges remain. While Dell is not currently involved in any antitrust lawsuits, its suppliers, such as Microsoft and more recently Intel, have been fined for anti-competitive practices.[66] This can present challenges to Dell as these rulings may affect its pricing arrangements with suppliers as well as how Dell conducts its operations, particularly in Europe.

Finally, on the technological front, computer companies are watching the trend towards mobile computing. Analysts at IDC report that "laptops will overtake desktop PCs as the dominant form of computer in 2011."[67] Despite the economic downturn, IDC expects strong growth in the market of low-cost, small form-factor laptops known as netbooks. The proliferation of wireless infrastructure will also make "Portable PCs as part of a digital lifestyle, rather than just computing device, [which will] sustain growth in both Consumer and Commercial segments."[68] While Dell introduced the Dell Inspirion Mini series in the netbook market in September 2008, it is a follower in this market behind other companies such as Asus's EeePC and Acer's Aspire One.[69]

Dell's Segment Growth Strategies

Upon returning to Dell as CEO in January 2007, Michael Dell resumed control of a company showing signs of struggle in multiple areas including customer service, product quality, and the overall effectiveness of its direct sales model.[70] These issues caused Dell to lose market share to its major rivals. As a first step, Michael Dell identified five large growth areas with at least $5 billion of potential new revenue and reorganized the company around them.[71] The five focus areas for Dell's operations are "consumer business, mobile computers, emerging countries, enterprise, and small/medium business."[72] Dell has also identified and implemented additional company-wide strategic and cost cutting initiatives.

Dell's current strategic initiatives within the consumer market include providing technologically advanced differentiated products that can support price premiums in order to increase profit margins, rapidly detecting shifts in consumer preferences in order to reduce product development time, and increasing distribution via retail channels.

Within the consumer market, Dell is actively seeking to move upmarket to attract technologically savvy customers who are willing to pay a premium to have the newest and best technologies.[73] To support this migration, Dell's products must provide technological superiority compared to its competitors. Dell has increased research and development spending 39.1 percent in 2008 ($693M) versus 2007 ($495M) to facilitate the development of differentiated products.

Dell's historical direct sales model has provided the company with the potential to gather consumer sentiment information directly from consumers rather than through a third-party reseller. Dell is seeking to leverage its direct sales model to detect shifts in consumer preferences earlier than competitors in order to reduce new product development time. Both benefits increase Dell's pricing power and competitive advantage. CEO Michael Dell sees Dell's ability to sense rapidly changing consumer preferences as one of the company's largest potential strategic advantages.[74]

Dell is also seeking to diversify its distribution channels beyond direct sales in an effort to remain competitive as consumers increasingly show preference for shopping for computers at retailers where they can directly compare multiple models.[75] In addition, Dell is able to reach more customers worldwide than would otherwise be possible with a direct-only model. In 2007, Dell began offering its computers at retail outlets ranging from domestic retailers (i.e., Wal-Mart and Staples) to chains in Japan, China, Russia, and the United Kingdom. By 2009, Dell had expanded its retail operations to include 24,000 outlets worldwide. Dell's efforts have led to an 11 percent revenue growth within this segment from 2007 to 2008, a reversal from the 6 percent decrease Dell experienced in 2007. This turnaround in revenue suggests that Dell's efforts directed at the consumer market are having early success.

In regard to mobile computing, the entire computer market is undergoing a gradual transition to more mobility-based computing products. In Q3 of 2008, laptops outsold traditional desktop computers for the first time.[76] Dell's strategic efforts within the mobile computing market include creating new platforms to better meet new consumer and business-user needs in terms of performance, size, weight, and price. To do this, it has separated the product design function for consumer and commercial markets. This strategic change has enabled Dell to produce multiple new product platforms

specialized for both consumer and commercial markets, including the Inspirion Mini 3G that targets the rapidly expanding netbook consumer market, and the Latitude XT-2 tablet PC and new thinner and lightweight E-series Latitude laptop for the commercial markets.

In emerging markets, Dell's strategy is to focus on providing region-specific products to meet the needs of emerging markets, particularly in Brazil, Russia, India, and China (BRIC countries). Typically, customers in these markets need a low-cost PC that provides the basic PC functionality, including web-surfing, e-mail, and word processing.[77] Dell has introduced the Vostro-A line of desktop and laptop computers that are specifically focused on the needs of price-sensitive customers within the BRIC market. Dell's marketing and product development efforts targeting BRIC customers have led to 20 percent sales growth within the BRIC market.[78]

Dell provides value to its largest customers by helping them to "simplify their IT environments."[79] To reduce the cost and complexity of large enterprise IT systems, Dell seeks to partner with customers to provide customized solutions including servers, storage, software, and support services. In this way, Dell is potentially building long-term relationships with its most important customers. These complementary products, solutions, and services provide a consistent revenue stream in addition to Dell's traditional hardware lines.

Dell is also seeking to be an innovator in hardware and software products that enable Net 2.0 companies, such as Microsoft, Amazon.com, and Google, as well as "cloud computing" initiatives where companies deliver hosted services over the Internet, usually on a subscription or license basis.[80] These companies are building massive computer networks that require a significant number of servers and IT infrastructure to support their businesses.[81] Michael Dell believes that Dell has "created a whole new business just to build custom products for those customers."[82] He also goes on to state that "now it's a several-hundred-million-dollar business and it will be a billion-dollar business in a couple of years."[83] Supporting these companies with technologically advanced solutions is strategically important to Dell maintaining its leadership in this market.

Similar to the strategy for large enterprise, Dell's small/medium business strategy is to provide the "simplest and most complete IT solution customized for their [specific] needs."[84] To do this, Dell offers a complete line of fully customizable desktop and laptop computers and servers as well as consulting and support services for this market which provide additional revenue streams beyond traditional hardware lines.

In 2008, Dell acquired EqualLogic, Inc. an industry leader in iSCSI SAN storage devices, a key technology for small and medium business customers.[85] Dell executives expect this acquisition to allow them to offer a broader array of storage products specifically tailored for this market. Dell also launched the "Dell Download Store" to enable small and medium-sized businesses to directly obtain third-party software solutions from Dell's Web site.[86]

Dell offers a full set of consulting and support services to support small and medium businesses throughout the product life cycle, including "Dell Pro-Manage" services, which provide "a team that proactively monitors your entire Dell or non-Dell IT infrastructure to prevent downtime before it starts."[87] Dell also makes "a la carte" services available, including services to prevent or address technical problems or hardware failures, protection services for both hardware and data theft, and pre-sale consulting services and IT infrastructure installation.

Cost Initiatives

In addition to strategic efforts aimed at growth, Dell has undertaken a massive cost-cutting campaign to drive down costs while maintaining its supply chain and production cost advantages over its competitors. Dell's current cost-cutting initiative seeks to cut $4 billion in costs by end of FY 2011. They are focused on costs of goods sold (COGS) and Operating Expenses (OpEx), specifically "design-to-value" or designing products that optimize their manufacturing and logistics supply chain as well as reducing total headcount in its sales organization as more and more of its sales are originating from third-party retailers.[88] In design-to-value, "33 percent of the business client and 57 percent of the consumer platforms have been redesigned and cost optimized which now equates to more than 50 percent of [Dell's] total [product] volume."[89] These redesigns led to a 10 percent reduction in average cost per unit in the past 12 months. As Dell's competitors provide pressure to drive down prices, cost initiatives are critical to its competitiveness in the global market for computers and IT equipment.[90]

Changes in Supply Chain Management and Manufacturing

As a computer manufacturer, Dell's manufacturing plants perform computer assembly operations on parts supplied by other companies. These parts could range from instruction manuals to optical drives, which Dell procures and assembles into a final product for its customers. To provide a quality product to its customers, Dell interacts with a large number of suppliers for its many different needs.

To maintain supplier flexibility and manage supplier bargaining power, Dell maintains strategic partnership with a large number of suppliers, procuring parts from multiple sources. While some parts can be easily shipped, Dell requires suppliers of some parts, such as computer motherboards, to be located nearby.[91] Because Dell is often one of their largest customers, Dell's suppliers often open facilities within a 20-mile radius of Dell manufacturing plants. These include Eagle Global Logistics and Cerqa Copyright, which handle computer parts and components and manuals and software, respectively. Due to the oligopolistic/monopolistic nature of the high-tech industry, Dell is forced to contract exclusively with a few suppliers who have control over key capabilities in the value chain. For example, Dell deals almost exclusively with Intel and Microsoft as its suppliers of microprocessors and operating systems. However, Dell is also investigating opportunities with other suppliers. Dell has begun shipping servers equipped with the Linux operating system rather than Microsoft Windows, and while currently Dell only offers "one AMD (Advanced Micro Devices) desktop but no AMD notebooks ... a year from now, it's probably going to be different," states Darrel Ward, Dell's director of product management for its business client product group.[92]

As part of its business strategy, Dell has a Supplier Diversity program where "Dell relies on the diversity of its personnel, suppliers ... to maximize innovation, growth, competitiveness, and customer satisfaction."[93] This program has earned Dell the number two ranking on DiversityBusiness.com's list of Top 50 Organizations for Multicultural Business Opportunities, which cites, "supplier diversity is a global concern as the leading global systems and services company relies on a worldwide network of quality suppliers to help it build all the products it ships around the globe."[94] Dell also exemplifies industrial leadership in managing supplier relationship by recognizing and rewarding its top suppliers at its annual Worldwide Procurement Supplier Awards. Each year, six suppliers receive awards across the categories of Best Quality, Global Citizenship, Service, Diversity, General Procurement, and Best Overall Supplier.[95]

As noted, Dell has historically utilized a build-to-order approach to supply chain management with a just-in-time manufacturing model where unit pieces were manufactured and stored in inventory but were not pieced together until a consumer request was issued. While this methodology rarely affords the opportunity to maximize economies of scale, it does maintain a low inventory holding cost. In May 2007, Dell began its transition into the retail market when it began selling PCs through Wal-Mart and Sam's Club. Early in 2009, Mike Gray, supply chain director for Dell, made the decision to transition the build-to-order model over to an industry standard build-to-stock methodology to offset increasing manufacturing costs and logistical complexities.[96] This meant that PC units would be put together prior to a custom order in an attempt to decrease costs and compete with other companies selling stock items.

Dell is in the process of moving manufacturing operations from Ireland to Poland in order to better serve customers in Europe, the Middle East, and Africa. With the transition they will be able to automate work and reduce the necessary labor force by 1,900 employees.[97] Pieces of the historically integrated and tightly controlled manufacturing and supply chain process are being outsourced to continue to maintain profits as the profit margin decreases.

Product Lines and Services

Dell offers solutions for PCs, mobility, software, peripherals, storage, and networking servers as well as services. Dell's service offerings include infrastructure consulting, deployment service, asset recovery and recycling, product training, support, and IT management outsourced services. Dell also offers financial services for training and advising on consumer and enterprise financing opportunities. Exhibits 5 through 7 provide a detailed description of Dell's product and service offerings.

The desktop Personal Computer (PC), the flagship product line for Dell since 1984, has traditionally been their largest product revenue stream. Throughout the 1990s Dell continued to reinvent its PC line with bigger hard drives, faster processors, and better user experiences that cater to several different target market groups. Today, the PC product line includes:

Exhibit 5 Home Office/Consumer Product Comparison

Product Offering	Description	Target Market	Notebooks	Retail Price	Desktops	Retail Price (excludes monitors)	Sales Rep Notes
Inspiron Mini	Consumer Notebook	Cost Leadership, Travel and Portability	Mini9, Mini10, Mini12	$250–$400	None	—	Good for travel and highly portable. Very small screen with small memory but lightweight with good processing speed.
Inspiron	Consumer Desktop and Notebook	Mainstream Consumers	Inspiron13, Inspiron 14, Inspiron15	$350–$700	Inspiron530s, Inspiron 530, Inspiron 531, Inspiron 537s, Inspiron 537	$260–$350	Significantly slower than XPS and more for home use than office.
Studio	High Performance Desktop and Notebook	Enthusiast-Hi Tech Consumer	Studio15, Studio17	$600–$700	Studio Hybrid, Studio Slim, Studio Desktop, Studio One 19	$400–$500	Pre-loaded with antivirus and anti-spyware software.
XPS & Alienware	High end design with unique multimedia capability, high performance gaming systems rivaling HPs gaming division.	Gamers and Innovation Seekers	XPS M1730, XPS 1530, XPS M1330, Studio XPS 13, Studio XPS 16, M17, M15x	$750–$2,000	Studio XPS, XPS ONE, Studio XPS 435, XPS 625, XPS 630, XPS 730x, Alienware ALX X-58	$700–$3,700	Popular with gamers who especially respect the Alienware line. Very competitive against any Gateway and HP products. Great video cards with RunFast software. The newer XPS systems run the latest I7 processor technology.

Source: Dell Web site, http://www.dell.com/; Best Buy Interview performed May 26, 2009, with two customer specialists.

Exhibit 6 Business/Corporate Product Comparison

Product Offering	Description	Target Market	Notebooks	Retail Price	Desktops	Retail Price (excludes monitors)
OptiPlex	Office Desktop	Business, Government, Institutional Users	None	—	360, 740, 760, 960, 160	$300–$850
Vostro	Small Business Desktop and Notebook	Small Business	A90, A860, 1520, 1720, 1320, E5400	$300–$730	220 Mini Tower, 220s Slim Tower, 420 Tower	$300–$530
Latitude	Commercial Enterprise Notebooks	Business, Government, Institutional Users	E5400, E5500, D630, E6400, E6500, E4200, E4300, XT2, E6400 ATG, E6400 XFR	$750–$1,800	None	—
Precision	High performance Notebooks and Desktops	Working Professionals	M2400, M4400, M6400, M6400 Covet	$1,400–$3,400	T3500, T3400, T5500, T5400, T7500, T7400	$750–$1,800

Source: Dell Web site, http://www.dell.com/.

Exhibit 7 Network Server and Storage Solution Comparison

Product Offering	Description	Target Market	Model	Retail Price
PowerEdge Tower Server	Business Server	Cost Leadership	T105, T100, 840, T300, T605, 2900 III, T1610	$400–$1,000
PowerEdge Rack Server	Business Server	Cost Leadership	R200, R300, SC1435, 1950 III, R805, 2950 III, 2970, R905, R900, R710, R610	$650–$3,800
PowerEdge Blade Server	Business Server	Cost Leadership	M605, M600, M805, M905, M1000e, M710, M610	$1,000–$1,800
PowerEdge Rack Infrastructure	Business Server	Cost Leadership	2410, 2420, 4220	$600–$1,000
PowerVault	Direct Attach Storage and Some Network-Attached Storage	Limited Storage, Cost Advantage	MD 1000, MD 1120 DAS, MD 3000 DAS	$2,600–$5,500
PowerConnect	Network Switches	High Quality, Product Differentiation	>51 models	$300–$3,000
Dell/EMC	Storage Area Networks	Mid-level Enterprise Storage	>51 models	$2,000–$4,000

Source: Dell Web site, http://www.dell.com/.

- The **XPS™** and **Alienware** lines targeted at customers seeking innovative designs that cater to user experience.
- The **OptiPlex™** line, which was developed for business, government, and institutional users that are concerned with controlling costs while maintaining security.
- The **Inspiron™** line, which is designed for "mainstream PC users requiring the latest features for their productivity and entertainment needs."
- The **Vostro™** line, launched in July 2007, which caters to the needs of small businesses.
- **Precision™** workstations created for working professionals who demand exceptional performance from hardware platforms and software and application offerings. These professional users are less concerned with cost and are more interested in "three-dimensional computer-aided design, digital content creation, geographic information systems, computer animation, software development, computer-aided engineering, game development, and financial analysis."[98]

In mobile computing, two years after the first Dell laptop debuted in 1989, Dell jumped into the top five computer companies in the world in terms of unit shipments, sending shares skyrocketing. Apple PowerBook designer John Medica led the efforts to create the enhanced Dell Latitude notebook offering. As the industry frontrunner of lithium-ion battery production and the first to introduce a rapid notebook charger, Dell enjoyed financial benefits of a first-mover advantage. Today, the mobility product line includes:

- **XPS™** and **Alienware** laptop lines, which provide customers with the best design and user experience with a high level of gaming capacity. In 2008, the XPS M1330 was introduced with a 13-inch high-definition display with ultra-portable features that earned numerous awards for its unique design.
- **Inspiron™** laptops, which meet customer needs for innovation, style, and high performance at an affordable cost.
- **Latitude™,** developed for business, government, and institutional customers that are interested in security, product lifecycle management, and cost control.
- **Vostro™,** which serves small businesses, was introduced in July 2007.
- **Precision™** serves professionals with exceptional performance in running sophisticated applications that are offered within the line of mobile workstations.

Dell offers "a wide range of third-party software products, including operating systems, business and office applications, antivirus and related security software,

entertainment software, and products in various other categories."[99] The primary third-party software provider, ASAP Software Express Inc., historically licensed their software innovations to Dell. In 2008, Dell acquired ASAP and has since released products from more than 2,000 software publishers. Dell packages antivirus and antispyware software from McAfee, Webroot Software, Norton, PC Mover, and other third-party software solutions preloaded with their personal computer units using these software solutions to differentiate the notebooks and desktops.

In 2002, Dell chose to expand its product portfolio to include peripherals that could be value-added components for personal computers. Today, Dell's primary peripherals include printers, projectors, and displays. They first entered the projector segment, shortly followed by entrance into the printer market in 2004, and started using Blu-ray disc technology in 2006. Currently, Dell offers a variety of printers ranging from ink-jet to large multifunction devices for enterprise solutions. Their printers are differentiated by the Dell Ink and Toner Management System™ that streamlines the purchase process by displaying the ink levels of color and non-color cartridges during each print job. Dell offers both branded and non-branded display solutions. To maintain the same level of innovation as Acer and HP, in 2008 Dell introduced cameras and microphones into the external monitors. Since then, Dell has won several awards for "quality, performance, and value" for their monitors.

Dell also offers both network attached storage and peripheral storage. By offering "a comprehensive portfolio of advanced storage solutions, including storage area networks, network-attached storage, direct-attached storage, disk and tape backup systems, and removable disk backup," data can be stored and transitioned over to a new PC or network unit at the end of the prior unit's life cycle. The diversity in the storage options between Dell PowerVault™, Dell EqualLogic, and Dell/EMC storage systems caters to a wide variety of target segments. The options vary based on use, modularity, scalability, encryption options, and backup storage solutions.[100]

In 1994, both Dell and rival HP entered the network and server markets. Throughout the 1990s, Dell expanded their data center offerings to an enterprise solution utilizing the "high-end, fiber channel-based PowerVault™ 650F storage subsystem."[101] In 2004, Dell led a pioneering effort to develop the first Disk Data Format (DDF), a first attempt at a corporate data center server storage solution. By staying at the forefront of the industry and focusing on ease of use, Dell maintains a leadership position in the market. The products are known to be affordable, reliable, scalable, and customizable to meet client needs, demands, and level of understanding and requirement for use. The Dell networking solutions offer both managed and unmanaged connectivity. Current products include:

- The **PowerEdge™** line of servers competes in cost leadership and emphasizes scalability and reliability.
- **PowerConnect™** offers many high-quality features for very large data center customers, with switches that connect computers and servers in small to medium-sized networks.
- **PowerVault™** provides direct attached storage, common interfaces for internal and external storage, high capacity, and possible expansion.

From the time the first PC was introduced in 1985, Dell has relied on customer service as a corporate cornerstone and attributes its consistent success to this focus. In fact, in 2008, every *Fortune* 100 company did business with Dell.[102] Dell caters specifically to user needs in the areas of customer service, financing support, sales support, product support, and international

support. In the 2008 annual report, Dell outlined the importance of customer service—to listen to their customers, innovate, and then make the necessary changes In this way, Dell can drive innovation to meet market demands.[103] Businesses and users can call, chat, or e-mail service requests.

Financials

While operating in a very competitive industry, Dell has remained a fiscally stable company. In the last decade, Dell has increased revenues by 142 percent, with recent revenues of $61.1 billion in 2008 with a 10 percent compound annual growth rate (CAGR), and currently has roughly $9 billion in cash.[104] From 1999 to 2008, Dell's net income reached a high of $3.6 billion in 2005 and a low of $1.2 billion in 2001. However, as noted in the introduction, revenue growth has slowed with FY09 revenues of $61.101 billion compared to FY08 of $61.133 billion, with desktop PCs, their largest product revenue stream, experiencing

Exhibit 8 Dell Financial Performance (FY00–FY09)

Select Financial Details from Dell's Balance Sheet and Income Statement										
Income Statement ($M)	**FY09**	**FY08**	**FY07**	**FY06**	**FY05**	**FY04**	**FY03**	**FY02**	**FY01**	**FY00**
Revenue	$61,101	$61,133	$57,420	$55,908	$49,205	$41,444	$35,404	$31,168	$31,888	$25,265
Operating Income	$4,193	$4,344	$3,541	$4,740	$4,588	$3,807	$3,055	$2,510	$3,008	$2,613
Net Income	$2,478	$2,947	$2,583	$3,572	$3,043	$2,645	$2,122	$1,246	$2,236	$1,666
Effective Tax Rate	25.5%	22.8%	22.8%	21.9%	31.5%	29%	29.9%	28%	30%	32%
Balance Sheet ($M)	**FY09**	**FY08**	**FY07**	**FY06**	**FY05**	**FY04**	**FY03**	**FY02**	**FY01**	**FY00**
Cash	$9,092	$7,972	$9,546	$7,042	$4,747	$4,317	$4,232	$3,641	$4,910	$3,809
Total Assets	$26,500	$27,561	$17,791	$23,190	$23,215	$19,311	$15,470	$13,535	$13,435	$11,471
Current Liabilities	$14,859	$18,526	$17,791	$15,927	$14,136	$10,896	$8,933	$7,519	$6,543	$5,192
Long-Term Debt	$1,898	$362	$569	$504	$505	$505	$506	$520	$509	$508
% Long-Term Debt of Capitalization	30.8	8.6	11.4	10.9	7.2	7.4	9.4	10.0	8.3	8.7

Source: Dell Annual FY10 1Q Financial Tables, disclosed May 28, 2009.

Exhibit 9 Dell Revenue by Product Line (FY07–FY09)

Annual Revenue by Product Line (in millions, except %)								
	FY09 Fiscal Year Ending: 30 Jan 2009			FY08 Fiscal Year Ending: 1 Feb 2008			FY07 Fiscal Year Ending: 2 Feb 2007	
Product Line	Dollars	% of Revenue	% Change	Dollars	% of Revenue	% Change	Dollars	% of Revenue
Mobility	18,638	31%	7%	17,423	28%	13%	15,480	27%
Desktop PCs	17,244	29%	−12%	19,573	32%	−1%	19,815	34%
Software and Peripherals	10,603	17%	7%	9,908	16%	10%	9,001	16%
Servers and Networking	6,275	10%	−3%	6,474	11%	12%	5,805	10%
Services	5,715	9%	7%	5,320	9%	5%	5,063	9%
Storage	2,626	4%	8%	2,435	4%	8%	2,256	4%
Net Revenue	61,101	100%	0%	61,133	100%	6%	57,420	100%

Source: Dell Annual 10-K Report for FY2009, filed March 26, 2009.

a 12 percent decline. A breakdown of Dell's sales by product segment can be found in Exhibits 9 and 10.

In first quarter 2009 (reported as FY10 Q1), Dell released performance in the reorganized globally operating business segments. Large Enterprise, their largest commercial revenue stream, saw quarterly revenues down 31 percent to $3.4 billion (year to year) and operating margins of 5.7 percent. The public sector segment, which includes government, education, and health care, saw revenues down 11 percent to $3.2 billion from the previous year and operating margins of 9.2 percent. Growth in federal and national accounts was offset by the weak performance of remaining accounts. For SMB, revenue fell 30 percent from the previous year to $3 billion, with the strongest demand continuing to be from Asia. Operating margins remained relatively flat at 7.7 percent. The consumer segment saw growth in unit volume (a 12 percent increase) with notebook volume up 32 percent offset by desktop units, which were down 20 percent year to year. Revenues for the consumer segment were down 16 percent to $2.8 billion with operating margins at 0 percent.[105] Detailed financial results for Q1 FY10 can be found in Exhibits 10, 12, and 13.

Publicly traded on the NASDAQ, Dell has been a volatile stock over the past year with a high of $26.04

and a low of $7.84 per share. Dell's 12-month stock performance is −48.29%, which is due in large part to the global recession.[106] At the end of FY09, Dell had 29,542 stockholders, of which 69 percent were institutional owners. Dell has never paid a dividend in its history. In FY09, Dell's percentage of long-term debt to capitalization rose from a decade average of 11.3 percent up to 30.8 percent, earning Dell an A− S&P credit rating.

Dell continues to increase its investment in research and development to improve and expand their product lines in their five key areas (PCs, software and peripherals, servers and networking, services, and storage), spending $693 million in 2008. With the company expanding rapidly in international markets, their customer base is broad and no single customer accounted for more then 10 percent of their sales the last three fiscal years. Dell's sales breakdown by geographic region is available in Exhibit 11.

Key Strategic Leaders

Michael Dell is the youngest CEO ever to earn a ranking on the *Fortune* 500.[107] Dell has held the title of chairman since he founded Dell Inc. in 1984, and served as its CEO for the first 20 years of company history. Dell left his CEO role to Kevin Rollins in July 2004 to work with

Exhibit 10 Dell Revenue by Product Line (Quarterly Results–FY10 & FY09)

	Quarterly Results by Product Line (After Dec. 31st Organizational Announcement)												
	FY10			FY09									
Product Line	May 1, 2009			January 30, 2009		October 31, 2008		August 1, 2008		May 2, 2008			
	Dollars	% of Revenue	% Change Y over Y	Dollars	% of Revenue	Dollars	% of Revenue	Dollars	% of Revenue	Dollars	% of Revenue
Mobility	$3,875	31.4%	–20%	$3,999	30%	$4,861	32%	$4,895	30%	$4,849	30%
Desktop PCs	$3,163	25.63%	–34%	$3,538	26%	$4,091	27%	$4,954	30%	$4,781	30%
Software & Peripherals	$2,246	18.2%	–18%	$2,487	19%	$2,585	17%	$2,790	17%	$2,741	17%
Servers & Networking	$1,286	10.42%	–25%	$1,431	11%	$1,630	11%	$1,733	11%	$1,718	11%
Enhanced Services	$1,238	10.03%	–8%	$1,270	9%	$1,365	9%	$1,372	8%	$1,344	8%
Storage	$534	4.33%	–17%	$703	5%	$630	4%	$690	4%	$644	4%
Net Revenue	$12,342	100%	–23%	$13,428	100%	$15,162	100%	$16,434	100%	$16,077	100%

Source: Dell Annual FY10 1Q Financial Tables, disclosed May 28, 2009.

Exhibit 11 Revenue by Global Segments (FY07–FY09)

| | Annual Revenue by Business Unit (Prior to Dec. 31st Organizational Announcement) | | | | | | | |
| | FY09 Fiscal Year Ending: 30 Jan 2009 | | | FY08 Fiscal Year Ending: 1 Feb 2008 | | | FY07 Fiscal Year Ending: 2 Feb 2007 | |
Business Unit	Dollars	% of Revenue	% Change	Dollars	% of Revenue	% Change	Dollars	% of Revenue
Americas Commercial	$28,614	47%	–4.56%	$29,981	49%	5.98%	$28,289	49%
EMEA Commercial	$13,617	22%	0.07%	$13,607	22%	14.9%	$11,842	21%
APJ Commercial	$7,341	12%	2.43%	$7,167	12%	15.17%	$6,223	11%
Global Consumer	$11,529	19%	11.09%	$10,378	17%	–6.22%	$11,066	19%
Net revenue	$61,101	100%	–0.05%	$61,133	100%	6.47%	$57,420	100%

Source: Dell Annual 10-K Report for FY2009, filed March 26, 2009.

Exhibit 12 Revenue by Global Segments (Quarterly Results—FY10 & FY09)

	Quarterly Results by Global Segment (After Dec. 31st Organizational Announcement)												
	FY10					FY09							
Global Segment	May 1, 2009			January 30, 2009		October 31, 2008		August 1, 2008		May 2, 2008			
	Dollars	% of Revenue	% Change Y over Y	Dollars	% of Revenue	Dollars	% of Revenue	Dollars	% of Revenue	Dollars	% of Revenue		
Large Enterprise	$3,400	27.55%	–31%	$3,889	29%	$4,395	29%	$4,806	29%	$4,921	31%		
Public	$3,171	25.69%	–11%	$3,287	24%	$3,960	26%	$4,510	27%	$3,581	22%		
SMB	$2,967	24.04%	–30%	$3,043	23%	$3,647	24%	$3,958	24%	$4,244	26%		
Consumer	$2,804	22.72%	–16%	$3,209	24%	$3,160	21%	$3,160	19%	$3,331	21%		
Net Revenue	$12,342	100%	–23%	$13,428	100%	$15,162	100%	$16,434	100%	$16,077	100%		

Source: Dell Annual FY10 1Q Financial Tables, disclosed May 28, 2009.

the Michael and Susan Dell Foundation, which manages the family's philanthropic efforts. Amidst poor performance and scandals with accounting practices, Michael Dell returned as CEO in January 2007.

Dell attended the University of Texas but, much like other titans of the computer industry, dropped out of college and went on to found a company based on the idea of selling custom-made computers directly to customers, revolutionizing the way computers were sold.[108] Dell was the first company in the PC business services to offer toll-free technical support and on-site service, which is now considered standard practice throughout the industry. Dell also was able to reduce its inventory costs by ordering the computer parts from nearby suppliers only once an order has been received.

Steven Schuckenbrock joined Dell in January 2007 as Senior Vice President of Global Services, expanded his role to include CIO in September 2007 and currently serves as the president of the division. Schuckenbrock is responsible for all aspects of Dell's support services, which is a potentially quick-growing unit that is responsible for worldwide enterprise service offerings and technology infrastructure.[109] Schuckenbrock is responsible for pioneering Dell's recent "cradle-to-grave policy," offered to enterprise customers, where their systems are updated and maintained for them from the time the machines are purchased until they are retired.

Prior to Dell, Schuckenbrock was a client and competitor as co-COO and Executive VP of Global Sales and

Services for Electronic Data Systems Corporation (EDS), one of the largest IT consulting firms. He also brings previous experience as the COO of The Feld Group, an IT consulting organization, from 2000 to 2003 and the CIO for PepsiCo prior to that.

Prior to joining Dell, Ronald G. Garriques worked in Motorola through a number of executive positions, including Executive VP and President of the Mobile Devices Division. As the president of Dell's Global Consumer Group, Garriques is responsible for Dell's portfolio of consumer desktops, laptops, software, and accessories. Garriques is credited with the design of the Motorola RAZR that revived Motorola's line of cell phones in the North American market, and analysts expect Garriques to continue to design revolutionary products for the consumer market for Dell. Garriques holds an MBA degree from The Wharton School of Business at the University of Pennsylvania as well as a master's degree in Mechanical Engineering from Stanford University.

Alan Lafley is the Chairman and CEO of Procter & Gamble (P&G) and has served on the board of Dell since July 2006. When Michael Dell returned as CEO, he recognized the company had issues marketing its products to a consumer market, and utilized this board member connection to learn about consumer marketing from P&G. After spending a day with P&G's marketing group at its Cincinnati headquarters, Michael Dell recalled thinking, "We were doing everything wrong."[110]

Exhibit 13 Operating Performance by Global Segments (Quarterly Results – FY10 & FY09)

	Quarterly Results by Global Segment (After Dec. 31st Organizational Announcement)									
	FY10				FY09					
	May 1, 2009		January 30, 2009		October 31, 2008		August 1, 2008		May 2, 2008	
Global Segment	Operating Income ($M)	Operating Margin	Operating Income ($M)	Operating Margin	Operating Income ($M)	Operating Margin	Operating Income ($M)	Operating Margin	Operating Income ($M)	Operating Margin
Large Enterprise	$192	5.7%	$259	6.7%	$254	5.8%	$259	5.4%	$386	7.8%
Public	$293	9.2%	$289	8.8%	$361	9.1%	$331	7.3%	$277	7.7%
SMB	$230	7.7%	$239	7.9%	$374	10.3%	$330	8.3%	$330	7.8%
Consumer	–($1)	0.0%	$47	1.5%	$142	4.5%	$29	0.9%	$88	2.7%

Source: Dell Annual FY10 1Q Financial Tables, disclosed May 28, 2009.

Strategic Challenges

Michael Dell, with his newly reorganized business and five key areas of growth, is seeking to overcome the issues preventing its continued financial success. Shareholders and the technology world will be carefully watching how Dell and his leadership team deal with these issues. Internally, Dell will need to address operating costs while balancing the expansion into retail distribution channels other than through its traditional direct sales model. The corporate market, which Dell is accustomed to as its core source of revenue, is experiencing little to no growth worldwide, while the consumer market is growing slowly. Externally, the industry is reacting to the current economic downturn and price competition is intensifying. Competitors are aggressively taking market share by providing solutions that match or exceed Dell's technological offerings while meeting evolving customer needs. The globalization of the market is introducing opportunities to move manufacturing and operations to offset costs and open new potential customer markets, but it also exposes Dell to additional competition and risk associated with such emerging markets. With the success of competitors rising and growth in the corporate market declining, how should Dell change its corporate- and business-level strategies to enable growth and meet these challenges?

NOTES

1. 2009, Dell Inc Form 10-K for Fiscal Year 2009, http://i.dell.com/sites/content/corporate/secure/en/Documents/FY09_SECForm10K.pdf, filed March 26, 2009.
2. 2009, B. Charny, H-P dethrones Dell for top sales spot in U.S. Market, *Wall Street Journal* Online, April 16.
3. 2009, Gartner says Worldwide PC shipments declined 6.5 percent in first quarter of 2009, Gartner press release, http://www.gartner.com/it/page.jsp?id=939015, April 15.
4. 2008, Dell globalizes business groups around major customer segments, Dell press releases, http://content.dell.com/us/en/corp/d/press-releases/2008-12-31-00-global-business.aspx, December 31.
5. 2004, *International Directory of Company Histories*, Vol. 63, St. James Press, http://www.fundinguniverse.com/company-histories/Dell-Inc-Company-History.html.
6. 2003, BBC News Channel, Dell's diversification pays off, http://news.bbc.co.uk/1/hi/business/3269299.stm, November 13.
7. *International Directory of Company Histories*, Vol. 63, 2004, St. James Press, http://www.fundinguniverse.com/company-histories/Dell-Inc-Company-History.html.
8. Dell Inc., FY94, Form 10-K for year ending January 30, 1994, http://www.sec.gov.
9. Dell Company History, http://www.referenceforbusiness.com/history2/21/Dell-Computer-Corporation.html.
10. *International Directory of Company Histories*.
11. http://www.fundinguniverse.com/company-histories/Dell-Inc-Company-History.html.
12. 2007, B. Stokes, The history of Dell, http://www.articlealley.com/article_175455_10.html, June 16.
13. *International Directory of Company Histories*.
14. 2009, Bloomberg, Dell to push PCs to China rural areas to boost sales, http://www.bloomberg.com/apps/news?pid=20601080&sid=aJ3XJU_EvYzk&refer=asia, March 26.

15. C. Helman, 2007, The second coming, *Forbes*, December 10, 79–86.
16. http://www.idc.com/getdoc.jsp?containerId=prUS21797609.
17. B. Gray, 2007, How enterprise buyers rate their PC suppliers and what it means for future purchases, Forrester Research, http://www.dell.com/downloads/global/corporate/iar/2007112_Forrester_HowEnterpriseBuyersRate.pdf,_November 12.
18. 2009, Acer Inc. 2009 Q1 Investor Conference Presentation, http://www.acer-group.com/public/Investor_Relations/pdf/2009-4-29AcerQ1-2009-E.pdf, Presented April 29.
19. Acer Inc. 2009 Q1 Investor Conference Presentation.
20. Declaration from Management, http://www.acer-group.com/public/Sustainability/sustainability02.htm.
21. Acer Inc. 2009 Q1 Investor Conference Presentation.
22. Softpedia, 2007, Acer talks about its global strategy, http://news.softpedia.com/news/Acer-Talks-About-Its-Global-Strategy-66563.shtml, September.
23. Hewlett-Packard Web site, http://www.hp.com/hpinfo/abouthp/.
24. 2008, Standard and Poor's, Hewlett-Packard Stock Report, May 9.
25. 2008, Hewlett-Packard, 10-K Annual Report
26. Hewlett-Packard Web site, http://www.hp.com/hpinfo/abouthp/.
27. Ibid.
28. Ibid.
29. J. Scheck, 2009, H-P tries to revive PC sales with touch screens, *Wall Street Journal*, http://online.wsj.com/article/SB124234971369322195.html, May 15.
30. Ibid.
31. 2007, Welcome to planet Apple, *BusinessWeek* Online. http://www.businessweek.com/magazine/content/07_28/b4042058.htm, July 9.
32. L. Grossman, 2007, Invention of the year: The iPhone, http://www.time.com/time/specials/2007/article/0,28804,1677329_1678542,00.html.
33. D. B. Yoffie, 2004, Where does Apple go from here? Harvard Business School Working Knowledge, http://hbswk.hbs.edu/item/3877.html, February 2
34. J. Brodkin, 2009, Apple lacks broad corporate strategy but still sees gains, http://www.networkworld.com/news/2009/010609-apple-corporate-strategy.html, January 6.
35. 2008, Apple Inc, Form 10-Q, http://phx.corporate-ir.net/External.File?item=UGFyZW50SUQ9MzA4OHxDaGlsZElEPS0xfFR5cGU9Mw==&t=1.
36. S. Murphy, 2008, Apple's supply chain is tops, *Modenr Materials Handling*, http://www.mmh.com/article/CA6574253.html, July 1.
37. 2008, Apple 2008 Annual Report (10-K) filed November 5, http://www.apple.com/investor/.
38. Apple Inc., 2-Year Financial History, FY08/FY06, http://library.corporate-ir.net/library/10/107/107357/items/314467/AAPL_3YR_Q4FY08.pdf.
39. Apple 2008 Annual Report (10-K).
40. Lenovo 2007/2008 Annual Report, http://www.pc.ibm.com/ww/lenovo/pdf/07_08/Lenovo_2007-08_Annual_Report_Final_E.pdf.
41. A. All, 2008, Lenovo's strategy includes no global HQ, more vertical supply chain, *ITBusinessEdge*, http://www.itbusinessedge.com/cm/blogs/all/lenovos-strategy-includes-no-global-hq-more-vertical-supply-chain/?cs=10312, March 3.
42. 2009, Lenovo Interim Report 2008/2009. http://www.pc.ibm.com/ww/lenovo/annual-interim_report.html.
43. Dell Inc., 2009, Dell laptops, desktop computers, monitors, printers and PC accessories, http://www.dell.com/, May 13.
44. Dell globalizes business groups around major customer segments.
45. M. Kanellos, 2002, PCs: More than 1 billion served, CNET News, http://news.cnet.com/2100-1040-940713.html, June 30.
46. Ibid.
47. I. Fried, 2008, Dell racks up Microsoft as data center customer, CNET News, http://news.cnet.com/8301-13860_3-10111860-56.html, December 3.
48. R. Finney, 1999, Dell business strategy secrets (Part 1), The itmWEB Site, http://www.itmweb.com/f031099.htm, February 14.
49. S. Swoyer, 2009, IT spending to hold the line in 2009, Enterprise Systems, http://esj.com/articles/2009/01/20/it-spending-to-hold-the-line-in-2009.aspx, January 20.
50. 2009, Dell: Services targeting SMBs, seeking alpha, http://seekingalpha.com/article/130899-dell-services-targeting-smbs, April 14.
51. A. Patrizio, 2009, Dell targets SMBs with managed service, http://www.internetnews.com/infra/article.php/3815376/Dell+Targets+SMBs+With+Managed+Services.htm, April 15.
52. Dell Inc., 2008, Dell globalizes business groups around major customer segments, http://content.dell.com/us/en/corp/d/press-releases/2008-12-31-00-global-business.aspx, December 31.
53. J. Davis, 2009, More PC makers target SMBs as SMBs pull back IT spending, Channel Insider, http://www.channelinsider.com/c/a/News/More-PC-Makers-Target-SMBs-as-SMBs-Pull-Back-IT-Spending/, March 12.
54. 2008, Simplifying information technology, http://www.egovonline.net/interview/interview-details.asp?interviewid=321, January 3.
55. Ibid.
56. 2004, WinBook W360 Laptop Reviews, CNET Reviews, http://reviews.cnet.com/laptops/winbook-w360/4505-3121_7-30880951.html, May 10.
57. Wikipedia, 2008, Micro Electronics Inc., http://en.wikipedia.org/wiki/Micro_Electronics,_Inc., October 3.
58. J. Stern, 2009, Hands-on with the Archos 10 netbook, http://blog.laptopmag.com/hands-on-with-the-archos-10-netbook, January 14.
59. Wikipedia, 2009, Dell, http://en.wikipedia.org/wiki/Dell, May 12.
60. B. Worthen & J. Scheck, 2009, As growth slows, ex-allies square off in a turf war, *Wall Street Journal*, March 16, A1.
61. C. D. Marsan, 2008, 8 reasons tech will survive the economic recession, CIO.com, http://www.cio.com/article/462919/_Reasons_Tech_Will_Survive_the_Economic_Recession, November 13.
62. PC market continues to resist economic pressures with a boost from low cost portable PCs.
63. K. Johnson, 2008, Dell's green payday: Going carbon-neutral helps bottom line, *Wall Street Journal*, http://blogs.wsj.com/environmentalcapital/2008/08/06/dells-green-payday-going-carbon-neutral-helps-bottom-line/, August 6.
64. J. Ball, 2008, Green goal of "carbon neutrality" hits limit, *Wall Street Journal*, http://online.wsj.com/article/SB123059880241541259.html, December 30.
65. 2008, Introducing (RED) inspired Dell studio laptops, Product (RED), http://www.joinred.com/News/Articles/ArticleDetail/08-11-13/Introducing_RED_inspired_Dell_Studio_laptops.aspx, November 13.
66. Europa Press Release RAPID, 2009, Antitrust: Commission imposes fine of EU1.06Bn on Intel for abuse of dominant position; orders Intel to cease illegal practices, http://europa.eu/rapid/pressReleasesAction.do?reference=IP/09/745&type=HTML&aged=0&language=EN&guiLanguage=en, May 13.
67. BBC News, 2007, Laptops set to outsell desktops, http://news.bbc.co.uk/2/hi/technology/6474581.stm, Mar 21.
68. IDC, 2008, PC market continues to resist economic pressures with a boost from low cost portable PCs, http://www.idc.com/getdoc.jsp?containerId=prUS21420408, September 10.
69. Wikipedia, 2009, Dell Inspiron Mini Series, http://en.wikipedia.org/wiki/Dell_Inspiron_Mini_Series, May 12.
70. L. Lee & P. Burrows, 2007, Is Dell too big for Michael Dell?, *BusinessWeek*, http://www.businessweek.com/magazine/content/07_07/b4021052.htm, February 12.
71. O. Malik, 2008, GigaOM Interview: Michael Dell. Reprinted at Businessweek.com, http://www.businessweek.com/technology/content/jul2008/tc20080727_306498.htm, July 28.
72. PC market continues to resist economic pressures with a boost from low cost portable PCs.
73. A. Ricadela, 2009, Will this bold shakeup save Dell?, *BusinessWeek*, wwwbusinessweek.com, January 1.
74. PC market continues to resist economic pressures with a boost from low cost portable PCs.
75. 2009, Why the big dip at Dell in the first quarter, *Wall Street Journal*, http://blogs.wsj.com/digits/2009/04/15/why-the-big-dip-at-dell-in-the-first-quarter/?mod=crnews, April 15.
76. Suppli.com, 2008, Notebook PC shipments exceed desktops for first time in Q3, http://www.isuppli.com/NewsDetail.aspx?ID=19823, December 23.
77. C. Thompson, 2009, The netbook effect, *Wired*, http://www.wired.com/gadgets/wireless/magazine/17-03/mf_netbooks?currentPage=4, February 23.
78. Dell Inc Form 10-K for Fiscal Year 2009.

79. Ibid.

80. 2008, Michael Dell: A big second half, *BusinessWeek*, wwwbusinessweek.com, July 28.

81. J. Brandon, 2008, What does cloud computing mean for you? *PC Magazine*, http://www.pcmag.com/article2/0,2817,2320619,00.asp, June 23.

82. Why the big dip at Dell in the first quarter?

83. Ibid.

84. Dell Inc Form 10-K for Fiscal Year 2009.

85. Ibid.

86. Ibid.

87. 2009, Dell Web site, http://www.dell.com/content/topics/global.aspx/services/managed/managed_services_overview?c=us&cs=04&l=en&s=bsd.

88. A. Gonsalves, 2009, Dell cost cutting 1 billion as profits fall 48%, http://www.informationweek.com/news/hardware/desktop/showArticle.jhtml?articleID=214700011, February 26.

89. 2009, FY10 Q1 earnings call transcript, http://www.dell.com, May 28.

90. B. Einhorn, 2009, Acer boss Lanci takes aim at Dell and HP, *BusinessWeek*, www.businessweek.com, April 13.

91. M. Harrington, 2004, "Dell Suppliers could be key to deal," *The Business Journal*, http://www.bizjournals.com/triad/stories/2004/10/04/story1.html, October 1.

92. B. Crothers, 2009, Dell offers lesson in Intel-AMD rivalry, CNET News, http://news.cnet.com/8301-13924_3-10240294-64.html, May 13.

93. Dell Inc., 2009, Dell supplier diversity, http://www.dell.com/content/topics/global.aspx/corp/sup_diversity/en/index?c=us&l=en&s=corp, May 13.

94. J. Bowles, 2008, Supplier diversity in action: Best practices of the top organizations for multicultural business opportunities, *BusinessWeek*, advertisement.

95. 2005, Dell recognizes six suppliers in annual awards program, Servigistics press release, http://www.servigistics.com/news/press/2005/04-141.html, April 14.

96. M. Gray, 2008, Dell supply chain director, speaker introduction, http://www.supplychain.eu.com/speakers.asp, June 8.

97. 2009, Limerick, Dell to migrate manufacturing operations from Ireland to Poland and partners by early 2010, http://www.dell.com/content/topics/global.aspx/corp/pressoffice/en/2009/2009_01_08_rr_000?c=us&l=en&s=corp, January 8.

98. Dell Inc. Form 10-K for Fiscal Year 2009.

99. 2009, Dell, Inc. (DELL) description of business, http://www.hotstocked.com/companies/d/dell-inc-DELL-description-52599.html, May 26.

100. 2009, Dell Web site, Data storage and backup, http://www.dell.com/business/storage.

101. 2009, Dell Web site, History, Dell takes on servers and storage, http://www.dell.com/content/topics/global.aspx/about_dell/company/history/history?c=us&l=en&s=corp.

102. Dell Inc. Form 10-K for Fiscal Year 2009.

103. 2008, Dell fiscal year 2008 in review, http://content.dell.com/us/en/corp/d/corp-comm/ir-FY08-in-Review.aspx?c=us&l=en&s=corp&redirect=1, June 1.

104. Standard & Poor's, 2009, Dell stock report, May 9.

105. 2009, FY10 Q1 earnings call transcript.

106. Yahoo Finance, http://www.yahoo.com/finance.

107. Dell, 2009, Michael Dell, Dell executive team, http://content.dell.com/us/en/corp/d/bios/michael-dell-bio.aspx.

108. 2009, Michael Dell biography, A&E Television Networks, http://www.biography.com/articles/Michael-Dell-9542199.

109. Reuters, 2009, Officers and directors for Dell Inc., http://www.reuters.com/finance/stocks/companyOfficers?symbol=DELL.O&viewId=bio.

110. Helman, The second coming.

CASE 15
The Home Depot

Dan Phillips, Bo Young Hwang, Sarah Sheets, Tristan Longstreth

Arizona State University

Introduction

The succession of CEOs, presidents, and board of directors provides a challenge for businesses as they reform, reposition, and restructure. Although these successions may provide a company with beneficial results, many experience hardship. Top company officials leave due to a variety of reasons, but a common reason is conflict with employees related to executive leadership style and the culture it creates.

Robert Nardelli, former CEO of Home Depot Inc., resigned in January 2007. Numerous factors led to Nardelli's resignation: Shareholders experienced dissatisfaction with the performance of Home Depot's stagnating stock prices; Nardelli's militaristic leadership style and centralized organizational structure affected the performance of employees resulting in excessive layoffs; and the expansion of retail stores became unmanageable. The once successful and highly valued Home Depot culture had changed, affecting Home Depot's sales and customer loyalty. Along with the change in Home Depot's business culture, it faced challenges associated with the dramatic boom and fall in the housing market. These problems affected Home Depot's employee morale, stockholders, and customers. CEO successor Frank Blake has much to address in order to reposition Home Depot as the industry giant it has been for 20 years.

History

Bernie Marcus and Arthur Blank cofounded Home Depot on June 29, 1978, after being fired from Handy Dan, a small chain of home improvement stores. Their vision was to offer "warehouse stores filled from floor to ceiling with a wide assortment of products at the lowest prices" along with superior customer service provided by a knowledgeable staff.[1] This vision became a reality after acquiring sufficient capital from a New York investment banker. They opened two Home Depot stores on June 22, 1979, in the company headquarters, Atlanta, Georgia. Home Depot grew rapidly in a short period of time and went public in 1981. In 1986 Home Depot broke the $1 billion mark in sales with 50 stores that expanded into eight markets.

Home Depot revolutionized the home improvement industry by offering a wide selection of merchandise, low prices, and superior customer service to both the professional contractor as well as the do-it-yourself patron. In-store inventory contains premium products imported from more than 40 countries, including 40,000–50,000 different types of building materials, home improvement supplies, and lawn and garden products. An additional 250,000 products are available upon special order. In addition, merchandise is localized throughout each store to match the area's specific market needs.

Today Home Depot is the largest home improvement retailer in the world.[2] The 2,100 stores located throughout the United States, Canada, China, and Mexico employ roughly 335,000 people. Home Depot also operates 34 EXPO design centers, 11 landscape supply stores, and two floor stores.[3] In addition, Home Depot has become one of the leading diversified wholesale distributors in the United States due to its former HD Supply division. HD Supply Centers caters to the professional contractor for home improvement and municipal infrastructures with nearly 1,000 locations in the United States and Canada.[4]

Marcus and Blank implemented a decentralized structure with an entrepreneurial style of management, which consisted of a laid-back organization known for

The authors would like to thank Professor Robert E. Hoskisson for his support under whose direction the case was developed. The authors do not intend to illustrate either effective or ineffective handling of a managerial situation. The case solely provides material for class discussion. This case was developed with contributions from Kevin Holmberg.

the independence of its store managers.[5] Over time the changes in leadership, structure, and management style diverged from what the originators intended.

Strategic Leaders

Robert L. Nardelli acted as president, CEO, and chairperson of the board from December 2000 until January of 2007. Nardelli received his BS in business from Western Illinois University and earned his MBA from University of Louisville. Nardelli joined General Electric in 1971 as an entry-level manufacturing engineer and by 1995 became president and CEO of GE Power Systems.

After leaving GE he was quickly hired as CEO of Home Depot despite the fact that he lacked any retail experience. From GE he brought a new management strategy based on Six Sigma to Home Depot. Using Six Sigma principles he centralized the management structure of the company by eliminating and consolidating division executives, he initiated processes and streamlined operations, such as the computerized automated inventory system, and centralized supply orders at the Atlanta headquarters. He took the focus off the retail stores, moving beyond the core U.S. big-box business to conquer new markets by building up its Home Depot Supply division, and expanded into China.[6] Under Nardelli, Home Depot's sales over a five-year period went from $45.7 in 2000 to $81.5 billion in 2005,[7] and stock prices stagnated during Nardelli's six-year reign at just over $40 per share.[8] The weak financial profits and his results-driven management style, which allegedly affected the cherished culture of the company, led to a backlash and push for his resignation in January 2007.

Frank Blake succeeded Nardelli as chair and CEO of Home Depot in January of 2007. He earned his bachelor's degree from Harvard College and a jurisprudence degree from Columbia Law School. Blake originally joined the company in 2002 as executive vice president of Business Development and Corporate Operations.[9] His responsibilities included real estate, store construction and maintenance, credit services, strategic business development, special orders and service improvement, call centers, and installation services business. Prior to this role, Blake was deputy secretary for the U.S. Department of Energy and also a former GE executive. Blake also has public sector experience, serving as general counsel for the U.S. Environmental Protection Agency, deputy counsel to Vice President George Bush, and as a law clerk to Justice Stevens of the U.S. Supreme Court.[10] As Home Depot's new leader, Blake faces significant challenges, especially when it comes to rising above competition.

Competition

Competition fuels businesses to be efficient in almost every way. Competition forces companies to control their costs, develop new products, and stay at the forefront of technology. Companies that provide similar services are required to differentiate from the rest of the pack. All of these facets of competition exist in the home improvement industry. Home Depot has more than 25 direct competitors including Lowe's, Menards, True Value, Ace Hardware, Do It Best, Sears, Target, and Wal-Mart.[11] Only a select few pose a true threat to Home Depot.

Lowe's

Lowe's is Home Depot's largest competitor and holds a significant market share. Founded in 1946, Lowe's grew from a small hardware store in North Carolina to the second largest home improvement wholesaler in the world. It currently operates 1,375 stores in 49 states and ranks 42 on the *Fortune* 500 list. Lowe's can attribute its success to a philosophy similar to Home Depot's: "Providing customers with the lowest priced and the highest quality home improvement products."[12] However, Lowe's distinguished itself from Home Depot by targeting the individual customer, especially women, as Home Depot began to focus on contractors. Lowe's will continue to differentiate from competitors by promoting and expanding through exclusive private labels or select brands. Premium kitchen cabinets and stone countertops are a few new product lines that Lowe's is implementing within their stores. Much like Home Depot, Lowe's is looking to expand by pursuing interest in installing services, special orders, and commercial sales.[13]

Menards

Menards is Home Depot's second biggest competitor.[14] Although most competitors construct their stores in a compact fashion in order to adhere to real estate constraints, Menard's is moving ahead with an opposing strategy. The midwestern home center chain has started to build two-story urban stores. "We might be No. 3 as far as store counts go, but we are a regional player and we are innovative," said Menards spokeswoman Dawn Sands. Customers navigate the two-story stores using escalators that accommodate both the customer and their shopping cart. The stores also brag a unique customer experience, including a baby grand piano that provides in-store music, new boutique departments, upscale merchandise, specialty departments, wider aisles, and lower, more convenient merchandise shelves.[15]

Home Depot's competitive position is not only affected by the strategies used by the top two competitors, but also by the relationships it maintains with suppliers.

Suppliers

Home Depot relies on 10,000 to 12,000 suppliers to keep its shelves stocked, creating a tremendous challenge in regard to the process and coordination of the logistics.[16] During the reign of CEO Robert Nardelli, Home Depot expanded at a rapid rate and failed to take the additional supply requirements into consideration,[17] and thus found its brand image in jeopardy when suppliers were unable to keep up with the increased production demands.

When Robert Nardelli became CEO, he inherited a disorganized system of suppliers that relied on archaic accounting practices, including individual product order forms and fax-only lines of communication.[18] Nardelli placed increased emphasis on renovating the Home Depot supplier networks. The first thing he did was to gradually implement the Home Depot Online Supplier Center and the Cognos 8 Scorecarding software. The Center "features continuously updated information on how to do business with Home Depot, including the corporate performance policy, updates, news, information on events and training and scorecards."[19] The Cognos 8 system gathers data from warehouse management sources, purchase orders, and contract terms, and condenses it. The data is then analyzed and each supplier is rated on various aspects of the transaction. All the information is available online via the supplier center, allowing suppliers to see what areas they should improve to become more efficient.[20]

Nardelli also held workshops for specific groups of Home Depot suppliers. For instance, Nardelli hosted meetings with Home Depot's top 15 strategic suppliers four times a year to discuss plans for new products and store promotions. The suppliers toured a Home Depot Store and gave Nardelli input on product placement.[21] Because Home Depot has such a wide variety of suppliers, including suppliers from many different countries, it offers overseas workshops to educate prospective suppliers. The latest workshop took place in Shanghai and was conducted by native speakers in an effort to educate vendors on "how to do business with Home Depot, and be a better supplier overall."[22]

Another area of innovation is Home Depot's inventory and warehousing procedure. Home Depot prefers to receive products directly from their suppliers, eliminating the need for distribution centers, which are popular with many other retail organizations.[23] This system has serious benefits and drawbacks. First, it allows Home Depot to leverage the space it has and display a multitude of products in a warehouse setting. This capability is beneficial because customers are able to see the products available and purchase them in the same visit. The major drawback to this system is that each store must have an extremely efficient and organized warehouse supply chain operation. If a store runs out of a particular item, the customer will have to wait until the supplier can produce more of that item, which can take more time than transporting an out-of-stock item from a distribution center to a local store.[24] Finally, Home Depot has utilized a system of "less than truck load" store deliveries, which allows its trucking partners to carry inventories to Home Depot stores along with products destined for other customers to save on transportation costs. But as Home Depot expands, it may switch to a dedicated trucking system with full truck loads servicing multiple stores in a specific region.[25] Home Depot has developed many innovations to help make transactions with suppliers more efficient. One of Home Depot's biggest challenges is ensuring good interactions with its customer base.

Customers

Although Home Depot was originally designed as a home improvement superstore that would cater to both individual consumers and building contractors, throughout its tumultuous history, Home Depot has changed its focus a number of times. During Nardelli's reign, cost cutting was a key focus and the individual customer was neglected in lieu of professional contractors who purchased materials in bulk amounts. Many long-time Home Depot customers have switched to competitors, mainly Lowe's, because of constant inefficiencies at Home Depot. One customer explained that he had to wait three months to get his kitchen remodeled due to errors on Home Depot's behalf and he will now "go out of [his] way to go to Lowe's."[26] This customer's experience is not unique and new CEO Frank Blake has acknowledged the magnitude of this issue. Home Depot has sold its contractors supply division, which will allow them to resume the focus on the individual customer.[27] Due to the wide range of customers it caters to, Home Depot will likely face significant competition from other firms selling substitute services that match the information provided by Home Depot in the do-it-yourself segment.

Substitute Information Services for Do-It-Yourself Customers

Most companies focus on differentiating their products and services in order to combat rivalry, but also obtain enough loyalty to dissuade customers from switching to a substitute product. Not many substitutes can realistically threaten the success of Home Depot's product sales because they offer such a wide variety of products and people will always need to build houses and desire to improve existing homes. However, Home Depot's services, such as installation, may be hampered by substitutes. Today numerous Internet sites offer "How to" information as well as structured plans for various types of home improvement projects. HGTV and other home improvement shows may also deter customers away from Home Depot's services. One way to fend off threats from rivalry and possible substitutes is for Home Depot to expand its operations internationally.

International Operations

Home Depot is the largest home improvement retailer in the world and employs 335,000 people. In light of the industry trends that are occurring, Home Depot is reaching out to new markets, which may give them additional sources of revenue as well international business experience. Stores are opening in Canada and Mexico. In Canada, Home Depot acquired Canadian hardware store Aikenhead Hardware, and has ambitions to take over its biggest Canadian competitor Rona Hardware.[28] The most recent stage of expansion includes 12 stores in China, called "The Home Way."[29] This foothold in Asia will allow them access to markets that were previously inaccessible.

The Chinese home improvement industry is a refreshing niche market with a lot of potential for new sales for Home Depot. In China, when a consumer purchases a home from a contractor, they purchase an unfinished shell. The house itself is little more than four walls and floor.[30] In order to make the house livable, Chinese consumers must pay contractors, including electricians, plumbers, and drywall experts, to renovate the house. Home Depot plans to provide Chinese consumers with the hardware and skills to do much of the renovation work themselves. In order to meet this goal Home Depot will need to train an army of knowledgeable salespeople who can provide assistance and workshops for consumers.[31] Home Depot will face a number of challenges as they expand into China. It must contend with the bureaucratic communist government that rules China. There are relatively few safeguards against nationalization, if the government decides to appropriate Home Depot assets or property. In addition the Chinese consumers may not have the desire to renovate their homes by themselves. Upper management must decide which method of entry would be most appropriate, and the most effective way to appeal to the average Chinese consumer. In addition, given the recent domestic housing recession, upper management must decide whether expansion into China is the most effective use of the firm's money. Because of the diverse ventures Home Depot is involved in, Nardelli

and more recently Frank Blake adopted some basic strategies that can be applied in order to maintain the company's viability.

Strategies Used

As previously mentioned Home Depot historically used a decentralized organizational structure with an entrepreneurial management style, focusing on the retail stores. Store managers were given immense autonomy, and its stores were staffed with well-trained and knowledgeable employees who could offer advice and help customers find items they wanted quickly.[32] Home Depot used to place a huge emphasis on creating a customer-friendly atmosphere with clean aisles, organized shelves, and well-stocked inventory.

However, profit from the retail stores began to decrease as the home improvement retail industry matured and became saturated. Home Depot needed to find its next great idea that would sustain growth. Nardelli believed that the key to Home Depot's success was the acquisition and incorporation of existing business into Home Depot Supply, while simultaneously squeezing efficiencies out of its retail stores.[33]

Home Depot Retail

A critical part of Nardelli's strategy was to reshape Home Depot into a more centralized organization.[34] The centralization effort was evident in the management system that one journalist referred to as a "Command and Control Management system," with a goal to replace the old, sometimes random, management style with a strict one.[35] Management in corporate headquarters started to rank every employee on the basis of four performance metrics: financial, operational, customer, and people skills. Nardelli created an equation to measure effective performance. The equation is $VA = Q \times A \times E$: the value-added (VA) of an employee equals the quality (Q) of what the employee does, multiplied by its acceptance (A) in the company, times how well the employee executes (E) the task.[36]

Influenced by his military background, Nardelli often hired employees who had military experience. Of the 1,142 people who were hired into Home Depot's store leadership program, which consisted of a two-year training program for future store managers, 528 were junior military officers.[37] He also brought many militaristic ideas into managing Home Depot, which required his employees to carry out his "command." Home Depot began to measure everything from gross margin per labor-hour to the number of greets at its front doors to maintain better information, allowing the CEOs to improve control of the Home Depot operation. However, this lead to many underperforming executives being routinely pushed out of their positions. Since 2001, 56 percent of job changes involved bringing new managers in from outside the company.[38] This hiring trend is quite different from the past, when managers ran Home Depot stores based on the knowledge built through the years of internal experience in Home Depot operations.

In an effort to drive down labor costs, many full-time employees were replaced by part-time employees. But this approach did more than just cut costs; it damaged employee morale, diminished the knowledgeable staff available to customers, and led to many complaints about poor customer service and understaffing. As one customer from San Fernando, California, stated:

The Home Depot at 12960 Foothill Boulevard, San Fernando, California 91342, has virtually no customer service. First I thought I couldn't find any employees to help me because I used to go after work at around 5:00 P.M. Then I tried going during my lunch hour, then during off-work week days. To my surprise, no matter what time I go, there are no present employees out on the floor. The one or two that I've seen are obtained by hassling the cashiers. Try getting help from the guy out in the garden department and he answers with "I don't know, I'm not an expert. They didn't train me." What kind of answer is this, what kind of store is this? The commercials on TV make it almost seem like a mom and pop candy store. You go in and you're by yourself. You need a refrigerator? Tough. There's nobody there to sell it to you. You need a chandelier? Tough—no one in this department to help you. What about the next department? Oh, he replies he knows nothing about the department next door. Customers beware: shop elsewhere.[39]

According to the University of Michigan's annual American Customer Satisfaction Index released on February 21, 2006, with a score of 67, down from 73 in 2004, Home Depot scored 11 points behind Lowe's. Claes Fornell, a professor at University of Michigan, stated that the drop in satisfaction was one reason why Home Depot's stock price has declined at the same time Lowe's has improved.[40]

The general appearance of Home Depot retail stores was becoming a drawback for customers. They often complained that Home Depot had become more like a "warehouse" that was unclean, unorganized, and far from the enjoyable shopping experience it had been in the past.[41] This neglect of the Home Depot's retail stores may have been the result of Nardelli shifting his focus toward new ventures, including Home Depot Supply.

Home Depot Supply

The building supply market during the early 1990s was a growing yet fragmented market segment worth $410 billion per year.[42] Nardelli saw an opportunity to enter this new market because there were few large competitors. To reduce the cannibalization of sales from its existing retail stores, he announced that Home Depot would cut retail store openings by nearly half over a five-year period.[43] Using the money saved from cutting retail store construction, Home Depot spent about $6 billion acquiring more than 25 wholesale suppliers to build up Home Depot Supply (HDS). HDS was a wholesale unit that sold pipes, custom kitchens, and building materials to contractors and municipalities.

Because Home Depot had acquired so many wholesalers, HDS became one of the leaders in the building supply industry. For example, in 2005 Home Depot purchased National Waterworks and entered the municipal water pipe market. Home Depot's biggest purchase was that of the $3.5 billion acquisition of Hughes Supply in 2006, which made Home Depot a leading distributor of electrical and plumbing supplies. HDS expected to have 1,500 supply houses with revenues of $25 billion annually by 2010.[44]

Due to the fragmentation of the building supply market, many contractors were associated with their regional suppliers based on long-standing relationships. Those regional suppliers offered a highly trained sales staff and specialized service, whereas HDS stores worked much like the standard warehouse format.[45] Home Depot was challenged to satisfy a new range of customers' needs, which were different from do-it-yourself customers. Therefore, HDS encouraged its sales employees by rewarding them, primarily in commissions, to win contracts. Furthermore, Home Depot retained most of the management of acquired suppliers, realizing the importance of cultural continuity. Nardelli insisted that top management, salespeople, and internal cultures of the acquired companies maintain their corporate names and colors on stores and delivery trucks.[46] He believed that these efforts would help them keep existing long-term relationships with contractors. HDS was expected to earn 20 percent of the company's overall sales.

As mentioned, when Blake took over as CEO he saw the need to refocus Home Depot's vision and again cater to the retail market. Therefore, in June 2007 Home Depot announced the sale of Home Depot Supply for $10 billion to a group of private equity firms (Brian Capital Partners, Carlyle Group, and Clayton, Dubilier, and Rice).[47] The proceeds from the sale will be used to implement necessary changes in Home Depot such as increased capital spending, upgrading merchandise, and hiring trained and qualified staff and sales associates.[48] The latter is especially important because many employees were beginning to feel dissatisfied with their positions, leading to a dangerously volatile corporate culture.

Corporate Culture

Home Depot's corporate culture has changed drastically as a result of Nardelli's leadership style. Due to Nardelli's military background, many of the changes he implemented were designed to create a more vertically oriented management structure. Originally each Home Depot store enjoyed a sense of autonomy, as each store director was able to set prices and promote products within that store to match the needs of the community in which it was located. Under Nardelli, each executive and store director was responsible for various financial targets, and if these targets were not met, they were immediately terminated. This expectation created a general atmosphere of fear and distrust. Throughout Nardelli's tenure as CEO, 97 percent of top executives were removed and replaced.

To further cut costs, Nardelli implemented a part-time workforce and eliminated many of the full-time employee positions. This trend caused a great deal of resentment from employees who had previously worked full time for Home Depot, because they could no longer receive medical and dental benefits. When the part-time workforce was combined with a management system that only focused on the bottom line, no time was left for taking care of the customer.

The advent of new technology had a big impact on corporate culture, and ultimately customer service. Nardelli believed that by implementing automated checkout lines, customers would be able to pay for their purchases quickly and save time. This innovation would also cut down on employee hours, and checkout personnel would no longer be used. However, this plan backfired when the automated checkout machines malfunctioned more often than they worked correctly, and the few employees who were not laid off as a result of the innovation experienced a significant amount of stress due to having to fix the checkout machines, and answer customer questions at the same time. This frustration was mirrored by customers who were unable to find sales associates when they had specific questions. In addition to significant corporate culture problems, Home Depot's financial statements were beginning to show signs of trouble for the home improvement giant.

Financial Issues

Due to the housing and home improvement boom, sales soared from $46 billion in 2000, the year Nardelli took over, to $81.5 billion in 2005, with an annual average growth rate of 12 percent.[49] The Home Depot's gross margins increased 3.5 percent from 2000 to 35.5 percent in 2005.[50]

For fiscal 2006, net sales were $90.8 billion with earnings of $5.8 billion, an 11.4 percent increase from fiscal 2005. Fiscal 2006 net sales in the retail segment were $79.0 billion, a 2.6 percent increase from 2005, which was driven by the opening of new stores. The Home Depot Supply segment contributed $12.1 billion, an increase of 161.6 percent from 2005. This increase was driven by solid organic growth and sales from acquired businesses.[51] Although Home Depot remains one of the world's largest home improvement retailers in the world, results for fiscal 2006 were disappointing, according to Frank Blake, current chair and CEO.[52] Housing slowdowns have hurt the financial goals for the retail segment of Home Depot. In the third quarter of 2006, same-store sales at Home Depot's 2,127 retail stores declined 5.1 percent.[53]

Economic and current market conditions caused a slowdown in the residential and housing market and an overall market share decline. Analysts do not expect an improvement until late 2007 or early 2008. The company's main focus for fiscal 2007 will be on the retail segment of their business, with total investments of $2.2 billion of capital spending and investments.[54] For Home Depot's income statement, balance sheet, statement of cash flows, and key ratios, see Exhibit 1. For a comparison of January 2006 and January 2007 consolidated statement of earnings, balance sheet, and segment information, see Exhibits 2, 3, and 4, on pages 160, 161, and 162, respectively.

Shareholders

Even though Nardelli was helping Home Depot achieve drastic structural changes, stock prices were affected by the lack of focus of this retail organization. Home Depot's shares were down 7 percent while archrival Lowe's stock prices had soared more than 200 percent since 2000. The poor stock performance led to anger among many of the shareholders.[55] (For a comparison of Home Depot's top competitors and their industry and market, see Exhibit 5, on page 162.)

Investment bankers are currently working on different ways to solve the share price problem such as returning $1.4 billion in cash to shareholders through dividends paid.[56] The company's dividend payout ratio is now approximately 24 percent.[57] In addition, during fiscal year 2006, Home Depot returned cash to shareholders by spending $6.7 billion to repurchase 174 million shares, or 19 percent of its outstanding shares. A stock chart is provided in Exhibit 6, on page 163, which illustrates share prices between March 27, 2006, and March 27, 2007.

Exhibit 1 Highlights of Key Financial Statements and Ratios for Home Depot

Income Statement (in US$ millions, except for per-share items)	01/28/07	01/29/06	01/30/05 Restated 01/29/06	02/01/04 Restated 01/29/06	02/02/03
Net Sales	90,837.00	81,511.00	73,094.00	64,816.00	58,247.00
Cost of Goods Sold	29,783.00	27,320.00	24,430.00	20,580.00	18,108.00
Income Before Tax	9,308.00	9,282.00	7,912.00	6,843.00	5,872.00
Net Income	5,761.00	5,838.00	5,001.00	4,304.00	3,664.00

Balance Sheet	01/28/07	01/29/06 Restated 01/28/07	01/30/05 Restated 01/29/06	02/01/04 Restated 01/30/05	02/02/03
Assets					
Total Current Assets	$18,000.00	$15,269.00	$14,273.00	$13,328.00	$11,917.00
Net PP&E	26,605.00	24,901.00	22,726.00	20,063.00	17,168.00
Total Assets	52,263.00	44,405.00	39,020.00	34,437.00	30,011.00
Liabilities and Shareholders' Equity					
Total Current Liabilities	$12,931.00	$12,706.00	$10,455.00	$ 9,554.00	$ 8,035.00
Long-Term Debt	11,643.00	2,672.00	2,148.00	856.00	1,321.00
Total Liabilities	27,233.00	17,496.00	14,862.00	12,030.00	10,209.00
Total Shareholders Equity	25,030.00	26,909.00	24,158.00	22,407.00	19,802.00
Total Liabilities & Shareholders Equity	52,263.00	44,405.00	39,020.00	34,437.00	30,011.00

Cash Flow Statement	01/29/06	01/30/05	02/01/04 Restated 01/30/05	02/02/03 Restated 01/30/05	02/03/02
Net Cash Flows from Operations	$ 6,484.00	$ 6,904.00	$ 6,545.00	$ 4,802.00	$ 5,963.00
Net Cash Flows from Investing	(4,586.00)	(4,479.00)	(4,171.00)	(2,601.00)	(3,466.00)
Net Cash Flows from Financing	(1,612.00)	(3,055.00)	(1,931.00)	(2,165.00)	(173.00)

Key Ratios	As of 03/26/07
Price/Earnings (TTM)	$13.64
Annual Dividend	.90
Annual Yield %	2.36
Quick Ratio (MRQ)	.40
Current Ratio (MRQ)	1.39
Return on Equity (TTM)	16.22
Return on Assets (TTM)	11.92
Return on Investment (TTM)	16.22

Data provided by Marketguide. Shareholder.com, the producer of this site, and The Home Depot, Inc. do not guarantee the accuracy of the information provided on this page, and will not be held liable for consequential damages arising from the use of this information.

Source: Home Depot, 2007, http://ir.homedepot.com/summary_financials.cfm.

Exhibit 2 Statement of Earnings for Home Depot

THE HOME DEPOT, INC. AND SUBSIDIARIES
CONSOLIDATED STATEMENTS OF EARNINGS
FOR THE THREE MONTHS AND YEARS ENDED JANUARY 28, 2007 AND JANUARY 29, 2006

(Unaudited)
(Amounts in Millions Except Per Share Data and as Otherwise Noted)

	Three Months Ended		% Increase (Decrease)	Years Ended		% Increase (Decrease)
	1-28-07	1-29-06		1-28-07	1-29-06	
NET SALES	$20,265	$19,489	4.0 %	$90,837	$81,511	11.4 %
Cost of Sales	13,627	12,896	5.7	61,054	54,191	12.7
GROSS PROFIT	6,638	6,593	0.7	29,783	27,320	9.0
Operating Expenses:						
Selling, General and Administrative	4,594	4,132	11.2	18,348	16,485	11.3
Depreciation and Amortization	442	413	7.0	1,762	1,472	19.7
Total Operating Expenses	5,036	4,545	10.8	20,110	17,957	12.0
OPERATING INCOME	1,602	2,048	(21.8)	9,673	9,363	3.3
Interest Income (Expense):						
Interest and Investment Income	4	8	(50.0)	27	62	(56.5)
Interest Expense	(127)	(35)	262.9	(392)	(143)	174.1
Interest, net	(123)	(27)	355.6	(365)	(81)	350.6
EARNINGS BEFORE PROVISION FOR INCOME TAXES	1,479	2,021	(26.8)	9,308	9,282	0.3
Provision for Income Taxes	554	736	(24.7)	3,547	3,444	3.0
NET EARNINGS	$ 925	$ 1,285	(28.0)%	$ 5,761	$ 5,838	(1.3)%
Weighted Average Common Shares	1,993	2,119	(5.9)%	2,054	2,138	(3.9)%
BASIC EARNINGS PER SHARE	$0.46	$0.61	(24.6)%	$2.80	$2.73	2.6%
Diluted Weighted Average Common Shares	2,004	2,128	(5.8)%	2,062	2,147	(4.0)%
DILUTED EARNINGS PER SHARE	$0.46	$0.60	(23.3)%	$2.79	$2.72	2.6%

SELECTED HIGHLIGHTS

	Three Months Ended		% Increase (Decrease)	Years Ended		% Increase (Decrease)
	1-28-07	1-29-06		1-28-07	1-29-06	
Number of Customer Transactions (1)	304	308	(1.3)%	1,330	1,330	– %
Average Ticket (1)	$56.27	$57.20	(1.6)	$58.90	$57.98	1.6
Weighted Average Weekly Sales per Operating Store (000's) (1)	$617	$676	(8.7)	$723	$763	(5.2)
Square Footage at End of Period (1)	224	215	4.2	224	215	4.2
Capital Expenditures	$1,032	$1,028	0.4	$3,542	$3,881	(8.7)
Depreciation and Amortization (2)	$476	$445	7.0%	$1,886	$1,579	19.4%

(1) Includes retail segment only.
(2) Includes depreciation of distribution centers and tool rental equipment included in Cost of Sales and amortization of deferred financing costs included in Interest Expense.

Source: Home Depot, 2007, http://www.homedepot.com.

Exhibit 3 Consolidated Balance Sheets for Home Depot

THE HOME DEPOT, INC. AND SUBSIDIARIES
CONSOLIDATED BALANCE SHEETS
AS OF JANUARY 28, 2007 AND JANUARY 29, 2006
(Amounts in Millions)

	1-28-07 (Unaudited)	1-29-06 (Audited)
ASSETS		
Cash and Short-Term Investments	$ 614	$ 807
Receivables, net	3,223	2,396
Merchandise Inventories	12,822	11,401
Other Current Assets	1,341	665
Total Current Assets	18,000	15,269
Property and Equipment, net	26,605	24,901
Goodwill	6,314	3,286
Other Assets	1,344	949
TOTAL ASSETS	$52,263	$44,405
LIABILITIES AND STOCKHOLDERS' EQUITY		
Short-Term Debt	$ –	$ 900
Accounts Payable	7,356	6,032
Accrued Salaries and Related Expenses	1,295	1,068
Current Installments of Long-Term Debt	18	513
Other Current Liabilities	4,262	4,193
Total Current Liabilities	12,931	12,706
Long-Term Debt	11,643	2,672
Other Long-Term Liabilities	2,659	2,118
Total Liabilities	27,233	17,496
Total Stockholders' Equity	25,030	26,909
TOTAL LIABILITIES AND STOCKHOLDERS' EQUITY	$52,263	$44,405

Source: Home Depot, 2007, http://www.homedepot.com.

What Should Happen to Improve Home Depot?

Home Depot has been plagued by many problems in its recent history. Robert Nardelli's strategic approach of focusing on suppliers and improving efficiency demoralized much of the human capital in its retail business, and as a result seemingly reduced the effectiveness of Home Depot's cherished organizational culture. The approach left employees afraid of their own executives, which forced them to focus on maintaining their current positions through hyperefficiency and in effect to fall short in customer service. This bottom-line thinking had drastic implications for Home Depot's customer base as more customers left Home Depot to shop at other stores such as Lowe's and Wal-Mart to meet their home improvement needs. In addition, a cyclical market and international expansion are issues that will need to be addressed. Frank Blake as the new CEO faces the monumental task of making the home improvement giant profitable again and restructuring to repair the damaged aspects of the corporation. With Blake in command, Home Depot has a good chance of leveraging its core competencies in the retail market and becoming an excellent corporation for customers and shareholders. Shareholders and employees alike anxiously await the future to see what lies in store for Home Depot.

Exhibit 4 Segment Financial Information for Home Depot

THE HOME DEPOT, INC. AND SUBSIDIARIES
SEGMENT INFORMATION
FOR THE YEARS ENDED JANUARY 28, 2007, AND JANUARY 29, 2006
(Unaudited)
(amounts in $ millions)

Year Ended January 28, 2007

	HD Retail (a)	HD Supply	Eliminations/ Other (b)	Consolidated
Net Sales	$79,027	$12,070	$(260)	$90,837
Operating Income	9,024	800	(151)	9,673
Depreciation and Amortization	1,679	197	10	1,886
Total Assets	42,094	10,021	148	52,263
Capital Expenditures	3,321	221		3,542
Payments for Businesses Acquired, net	305	3,963	–	4,268

Year Ended January 29, 2006

	HD Retail (a)	HD Supply	Eliminations/ Other (b)	Consolidated
Net Sales	$77,022	$4,614	$(125)	$81,511
Operating Income	9,058	319	(14)	9,363
Depreciation and Amortization	1,510	63	6	1,579
Total Assets	39,827	4,517	61	44,405
Capital Expenditures	3,777	104	–	3,881
Payments for Businesses Acquired, net	190	2,356	–	2,546

(a) Includes all retail stores, Home Depot Direct and retail installation services.

(b) Includes elimination of intersegment sales and unallocated corporate overhead. Operating Income for the year ended January 28, 2007, includes $129 million of cost associated with executive severance and separation agreements.

Source: Home Depot, 2007, http://www.homedepot.com.

Exhibit 5 Industry Statistics and Comparisons

	Home Depot	Lowe's	Menard	True Value
Annual Sales	$81,511	$43,243	$6,500	$2,043
Employees	345,000	185,000	35,000	2,800
Market Cap ($ millions)	$77,488	$48,852.8	0	0

Comparison of Home Depot to Industry and Stock Market

Valuation	Company	Industry[1]	Stock Market[2]
Price/Sales Ratio	0.83	0.83	2.22
Price/Earnings Ratio	12.51	12.51	18.98
Price/Book Ratio	2.70	2.93	2.16
Price/Cash Flow Ratio	12.02	12.02	13.44

[1]**Industry:** Building Materials, Hardware, Garden Supply, and Mobile Home Dealers

[2]**Market:** Public companies trading on the NYSE, AMEX, and NASDAQ

Source: © 2007, Hoover's, Inc., All Rights Reserved, http://www.hoovers.com/home-depot/—ID__11470,ticker__—/free-co-fin-factsheet.xhtml.

Exhibit 6 Home Depot Stock Chart

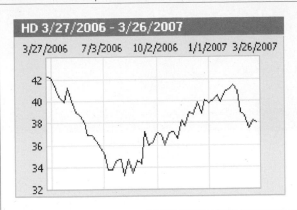

Source: Home Depot, Inc. (HD), http://moneycentral.msn.com/stock_quote?Symbol=HD.

NOTES

1. 2007, Home Depot, http://corporate.homedepot.com/wps/portal, March 28.
2. Ibid.
3. Ibid.
4. Ibid.
5. R. Farzad, D. Foust, B. Grow, E. Javers, E. Thornton, & R. Zegel, 2007, Out at Home Depot, *BusinessWeek,* http://www.businessweek.com, January 15.
6. Ibid
7. 2007, Home Depot, http://ir.homedepot.com/releaseDetail.cfm?ReleaseID=194738&ShSect=E, July 3.
8. Ibid.
9. 2007, Home Depot, http://corporate.homedepot.com/wps/portal, March 28.
10. Ibid.
11. 2007, http://www.hoovers.com, April 1.
12. 2007, Lowe's , http://www.Lowe's.com, April 1.
13. D. Howell, 2005, Lowe's hammers home growth objective: National in a year, http://findarticles.com/p/articles/mi_m0FNP/is_6_44/ai_n13726491.
14. 2007, HD: Competitors for Home Depot, *Yahoo! Finance,* July 10.
15. Ibid.
16. R. Bowman, 2006, Home Depot turns its attention to supplier performance management, *Global Logistics & Supply Chain Strategies,* http://www.glscs.com/archives/06.06.casestudy.htm?adcode=5, June.
17. Ibid.
18. Ibid.
19. Ibid.
20. Ibid.
21. Ibid.
22. Ibid.
23. R. Bowman, 2001, Global supply chain partnerships, *Global Logistics & Supply Chain Strategies,* http://www.glscs.com/archives/7.02.homedepot.htm?adcode=5, July.
24. Ibid.
25. Ibid.
26. B. Grow & S. McMillan, 2006, Home Depot: Last among shoppers, *BusinessWeek Online,* http://www.businessweek.com, June 19.
27. H. Weber, 2007, Home Depot undecided on supply business, *BusinessWeek Online,* http://www.businessweek.com, March 22.
28. 2007, Home Depot, http://en.wikipedia.org/wiki/Home_depot, accessed on April 17.
29. Ibid.
30. B. Grow & F. Balfour, 2006, Home Depot: One foot in China, *BusinessWeek Online,* http://www.businessweek.com, May 1.
31. Ibid.
32. D. Brady & B. Grow, 2006, Renovating Home Depot, *BusinessWeek,* http://www.businessweek.com, March 6, 50–56.
33. Ibid.
34. Ibid.
35. Ibid.
36. R. Farzad, D. Foust, B. Grow, E. Javers, E. Thornton, & R. Zegel, 2007, Out at Home Depot.
37. D. Brady & B. Grow, Renovating Home Depot.
38. Ibid.
39. 2004, http://www.complaints.com/directory/2004/june/14/15.htm.
40. D. Brady & B. Grow, Renovating Home Depot.
41. H. Weber, 2006, Home Depot needs makeover, *Washington Post,* http://www.washingtonpost.com, January 6.
42. 2006, Home Depot will buy building supply chain, *Winston-Salem Journal,* http://www.journalnow.com/servlet/Satellite?pagename=WSJ%2FMGArticle%2FWSJ_BasicArticle&c=MGArticle&cid=1128769238504&path=!business&s=1037645507703%20, January 11.
43. C. Terhune, 2006, Home Depot knocks on contractors' doors, *Wall Street Journal,* August 7.
44. P. Bond, 2006, Commercial wholesale division doubles Home Depot's supply business, *The Atlanta Journal-Constitution,* August 6.
45. C. Terhune, 2007, Home Depot knocks on contractors' doors, *Wall Street Journal Online,* http://online.wsj.com/article/SB115491714152328447.html, July 13.
46. Ibid.
47. M. Flaherty & K. Jacobs, 2007, Bids for Home Depot Supply due Friday, *BNET Today,* http://www.bnet.com/2407-13071_23-88489.html, July 5.
48. Ibid.
49. D. Brady & B. Grow, Renovating Home Depot.
50. Ibid.
51. Home Depot, 2007, The Home Depot announces fourth quarter and fiscal 2006 results, http://ir.homedepot.com, February 20.
52. Home Depot, 2007, The Home Depot announces fourth quarter dividend, http://ir.homedepot.com, February 22.
53. R. Farzad, D. Foust, B. Grow, E. Javers, E. Thornton, & R. Zegel, 2007, Out at Home Depot.
54. Home Depot, 2007, The Home Depot presents 2007 key priorities and financial outlook, http://ir.homedepot.com, February 28.
55. D. Brady & B. Grow, Renovating Home Depot.
56. Home Depot, 2007, The Home Depot announces fourth quarter dividend, http://irhomedepot.com, February 22.
57. Ibid.

Marit Loewer

Otto Beisheim School of Management

It was a Friday morning in May 2008 when Andreas Welsch, General Manager of the German department of Henkel Adhesives Technologies for Consumers and Craftsmen, arrived early at the Henkel site in Düsseldorf-Holthausen, Germany (see Exhibit 1).

The chimneys at the enormous production site were already bellowing smoke, even at this early hour. As Welsch walked to the impressive glass building where his office was located, he thought about his upcoming meeting with company marketing executives. A

Exhibit 1 Henkel site in Düsseldorf-Holthausen

gloomy forecast awaited him in the latest consumer report: Gasoline prices kept rising and further looming price increases caused German consumers to worry about their purchasing power. Concerns about price stability and uncertainty resulting from the financial crisis and the flagging U.S. economy fueled economic fears among German consumers. This news would certainly influence Henkel's business and increase the importance of today's meeting.

Upon his arrival at the conference room, he spoke to his marketing managers:

We are facing a challenging situation. As we already know, the growth of our markets has slowed down in recent years and the raw material price increase puts pressure on our margins. But even worse now, one of our competitors in the adhesives business is just about to enter one of our core categories with very low prices. This will certainly affect our sales numbers. The time has come where we have to develop a long-term strategy in order to escape the constant war for market share with our competitors. Competing for an ever smaller market is not a solution. This new strategy is of utmost importance for the adhesives business, if we want to stay put as market leaders in the long run. It has to be developed quickly as senior management expects it in two days!

Company Profile: Henkel AG & Co. KGaA

Based in Düsseldorf, Germany, Henkel AG & Co. KGaA was an international group with worldwide presence and listed on the London Stock Exchange. Its sales were €13,074 million (see Exhibit 2) and employed approximately 53,000 people in the fiscal year 2007. Henkel was among the most internationally aligned German-based companies in the global marketplace. Consumers in approximately 125 countries around the world trusted in brands and technologies that originated on the Henkel production line. The company was organized into three operational business sectors: Laundry & Home Care, Cosmetics/Toiletries, and Adhesives Technologies (see Exhibit 3). It was the umbrella company for well-known brands such as Persil, Schwarzkopf, Pritt, and Pattex.

History of Henkel

Founded in 1876 as Henkel & Cie in Aachen by 28-year-old merchant Fritz Henkel (see Exhibit 4), the company's first successful product was a washing powder based on water-glass. In contrast to all similar products, which were at that time sold loose, this heavy-duty detergent

Exhibit 2 Key Financial Data of Henkel AG & Co. KGaA for 2006–2007

Key Financials

Figures in mill. euros		2006	2007	Change
Sales		12,740	13,074	+2.6%
Operating profit (EBIT)		1,298	1,344	+3.5%
Return on sales (EBIT)	in %	10.2	10.3	+0.1 pp
Net earnings		871	941	+8.0%
Earnings after minority interests		855	921	+7.7%
Earnings per preferred share [1]	in euros	1.99	2.14	+7.5%
Return on capital employed (ROCE)	in %	14.5	15.4	+0.9 pp
Capital expenditures on property, plant, and equipment		431	470	+9.0%
Research and development expenses		340	350	+2.9%
Employees (annual average)	number	51,716	52,303	+1.1%

[1] basis: share split (1:3) of June 18, 2007

pp = percentage points

© Henkel 2008   1

Exhibit 3 Henkel Business Sectors

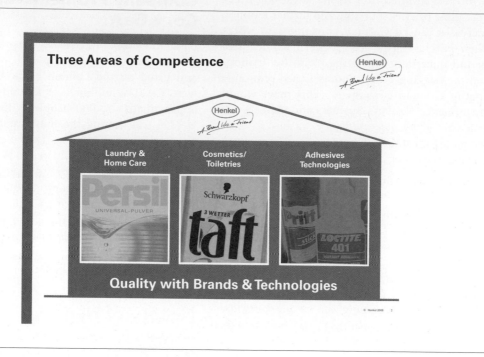

Exhibit 4 The Founder of the company

was marketed in handy packets. It was a huge success, and, two years later, Henkel relocated his company to Düsseldorf by the Rhine to take advantage of logistics and better sales opportunities. In the years to come, many innovations were developed at Henkel. In 1907,

Persil, the first self-acting laundry detergent, became the pillar for the company's growth and helped radically simplify the laborious and time-consuming household chore of doing laundry. However, Fritz Henkel did more than revolutionize laundry care. He was also a pioneer

of modern brand management. He systematically raised awareness about Persil in the general public by means of innovative and sensational advertising campaigns. Ever since then, the combination of outstanding product quality and intelligent brand management has been the cornerstone of Henkel's success. In 1922, the product range was extended to adhesives, and, in 1950, Henkel entered the cosmetics markets with the acquisition of TheraChemie (hair colorants). The Henkel brand grew very quickly as a result of international expansion.

Henkel's diverse product range and strengths that ranged from modern consumer products for everyday use to complex chemical and technical system solutions for industrial consumers influenced the company to concentrate on its corporate identity. Branded products and technologies were identified as strategic pillars for the future, and four business sectors were defined: Laundry and Home Care, Cosmetics/Toiletries, Consumer and Craftsmen Adhesives, and Henkel Technolgies (industrial and engineering adhesives, sealants, and surface treatments). The slogan "A Brand Like a Friend" was introduced to convince consumers to embrace the broad variety of Henkel products and facilitate the perception of Henkel as a brand, not a corporation. Henkel's intention was to suggest proximity to the customer and foster their trust in Henkel quality.

The latest major acquisition was completed in March 2008: Henkel took over the Adhesives and Electronic Materials business from Akzo Nobel, previously owned by National Starch. Following the integration, Henkel's Adhesive Technologies business sector was expected to increase to around €7.5 billion in annualized sales in 2008. By completing this acquisition, Henkel further strengthened its leading position in the global adhesives markets, particularly in the industrial segment.

Adhesive Technologies Business Sector

Effective April 1, 2007, the previously separately managed business sectors of "Consumer and Craftsmen Adhesives" and "Henkel Technologies" were merged to form the Adhesive Technologies sector. This enabled the adoption of a unified market approach with better utilization of core competencies of both businesses. The Adhesive Technologies business sector offered adhesives, sealants, and surface treatment products for use in household and office applications for the do-it-yourself populace, professional craftsmen, and for industrial and engineering applications. The new sector was the world leader in its segment, with about €5,711 million in sales in 2007, accounting for 43 percent of Henkel revenues overall (see Exhibit 5). In view of the heavily fragmented competitor landscape with over 1,500 vendors and a relatively small number of global players offering a comparable product portfolio, the business sector saw itself as market leader in each

Exhibit 5 Sales and EBIT by Business Sector

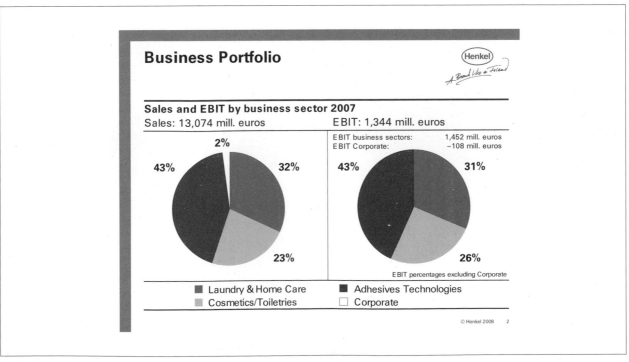

of its product categories. The variety of markets for adhesives was unmatched: the packaging industry, auto manufacturers, aircraft building, power plants, steel-mills, tin-can producers, and powerhouses were all customers of Henkel adhesives. Different competitors existed in each of these markets, and often each competitor only served a special niche and sector. Only very few companies were active in as many segments as Henkel, and this was the reason that Henkel was almost triple the size of its next best competitor.

Adhesive Technologies for Consumers and Professionals in Germany

The market catering to consumers and professionals for adhesive technology in Germany was also complex, with many different segments and sub-segments. Henkel was exceptional in that it offered so many different products under one corporate umbrella (see Exhibit 6).

Products were available for different customer segments. Consumers were divided into the two subgroups of households/offices, which were offered products for repair jobs and handcrafts, and "do-it-yourself" customers with products for renovation and repairing. On the other hand, there were professionals to whom Henkel offered products for construction and intensive usage, such as External Thermal Insulation Composite Systems. Sales channels for the customer segments were very different: products for consumers were sold in do-it-yourself (DIY) stores, specialist

shops, drugstores, and food retailing shops. Driven by the ever-growing discount channel, price had become a key parameter in all trade negotiations and even in the communication of the trade itself.

The products for professionals were sold in specialist stores, and producers had to follow a completely different approach in this channel. Sales representatives would contact the relevant craftsmen—painters, tilers, floorers, and so on—individually, as each one of them chose the products they would use and had to be convinced about the advantages of new products. The craftsmen were a rather conservative group who mostly trusted in products they already knew and worked with for a long time. Thus, they were difficult to convince about the advantages of new products, and it took the sales representatives about five to six visits per person to gain a new customer. Therefore, the quantity and quality of sales representatives were, understandably, key factors in how well a product sold. Professionals tended to stick with products with which they were familiar in order to avoid customer complaints. Craftsmen faced several challenges in earning new customers, including their high hourly wages and the challenge of showing, in advance, that their work was superior to that of others in the field and, as such, worthy of a higher salary. The most common way for customers to make their choice was through looking at ads for craftsmen in the Yellow Pages. No ranking system of any kind existed for craftsmen, and customers were often very hesitant

Exhibit 6 Sub-brands under the Henkel Brand

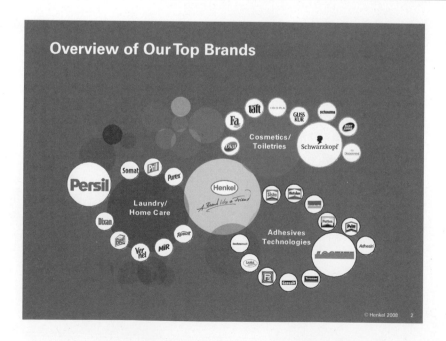

to order such professional services because they were unsure of the quality they would receive in return.

Henkel offered its customers (the do-it-yourself category and professionals) high-quality products (see Exhibit 7), as this was traditionally the way to differentiate the firm's products from the competition. Many customers were not familiar with Henkel brands, but instead knew the sub-brands, as Henkel did not invest in the overall Henkel name. The Henkel organization was built on these sub-brands because product managers for each sub-unit developed their own marketing strategy for the products of their sub-brand. Therefore, customer confidence had to be established for each sub-brand, and only some were already well known. Brands like Pritt, Pattex, and Ponal were the most popular brands in the DIY segment.

Adding new features to improve their products was another method Henkel used to outperform its competitors. Their product range was constantly expanding and different products had been developed for every possible area of application. However, in the DIY segment, this complexity did not make the task of choosing the "right" product easy for consumers. Information about renovation products in the DIY stores was not always sufficient, and qualified store personnel were sometimes difficult to find. Also, other supplementary information sources were rare. Customers could not access sufficient information about the proper application of a product, the required quantity for a certain renovation job, or new product information. Most women avoided DIY stores completely because the brand image and product descriptions were very technical. Traditionally, it was a man's task to maintain the house, and although many women were doing craftwork to decorate their homes, they felt less comfortable with renovation work. In addition, women preferred models and concrete samples of how a house would look after renovation so as to get some inspiration, but these samples were hard to come by. Even in the professional segment, the broad product range was not appreciated by all customers: some preferred to have a "universal" product for a certain task, since, from their point of view, many new products did not offer additional value.

Overall, it was difficult for Henkel to increase the number of products sold as its products had already achieved solid market positions. On the other hand, it was difficult to meaningfully influence the size of different markets in that each market was affected by trends associated with primary materials, such as tiles and wallpaper, as well as individuals' overall inclination to build and renovate.

The entire market had undergone a drastic downturn over the past 10 years. The reunion of East and West Germany in 1989 led to several years of strong growth. First, the population of East Germany entered the market and added another 13 million consumers. Second, East Germany was under-served by distribution channels for renovation products and many new DIY

Exhibit 7 Products of Henkel Adhesives Technologies

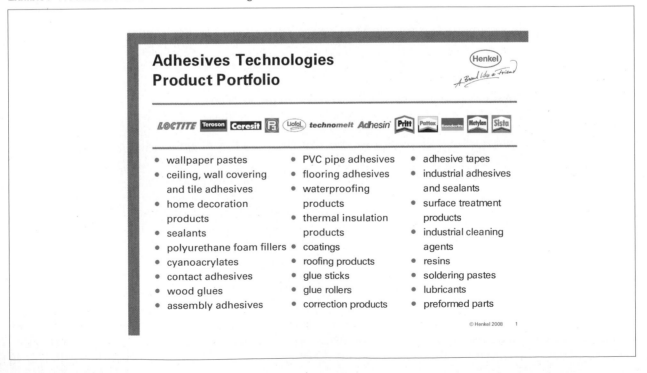

stores had to be set up. Third, the foundations of most houses in East Germany were very old and in need of renovation. Moreover, many new buildings were erected after the reunion, sponsored by the government through tax incentives. All these factors caused a boom in the industry that lasted until the late 1990s. There were few new competitors because of the entry barriers created by the need for significant capital investments to enter the industry. During the boom, many existing competitors built new capacities to be able to respond quickly and adequately to the high demand.

After 10 years of prosperity in the industry, the German DIY market became saturated with the 3,300 DIY stores that were built over the years and saw a decrease in public building licenses, which in turn reduced the demand for renovation material. Also, the percentage of homeowners in Germany was one of the lowest in Europe. Eventually the market began to shrink and competition intensified to secure and gain larger shares of a declining market.

The competition in the adhesives market for consumers and craftsmen was diversified among different product segments and target groups. In the adhesives segment for households and offices, UHU was the largest competitor in Germany. The company was part of the Bolton Group, a privately owned Italian business. UHU's product range was comparable to Henkel's in this segment. But UHU had one specific advantage—their adhesive "Alleskleber" was well known to every German since childhood and nearly synonymous with household adhesives. It was widely available and sold in supermarkets as well as stationery shops and malls, and, therefore, had the largest market share.

For the professional craftsmen target group, it was important to offer direct contact between the producer and client for support and product enhancements, technical advice, addressing complaints, and warranty support. Product innovations were another factor that companies used to attract customers. Henkel saw itself as an innovator in the industry and built its strategy around innovation. This positioned Henkel in the premium segment, but the strategy often deployed by competitors was to battle over price—the tighter the market, the fiercer the price war. This hurt every competitor. Henkel was very proud of its broad product range, which accentuated its unique image in the competitive landscape. Often, other companies tried to emulate Henkel's advantage by expanding their product portfolio to capture a share of the shrinking market, so as to reduce the factor of differentiation in competition.

Besides shrinking markets, increasing energy prices also cut into profitability. Henkel was highly dependent on energy prices in terms of product manufacturing and transportation. Since oil was the base for many of Henkel's products, oil prices directly influenced Henkel's profit margins. Employee salaries were also continuously rising. Henkel was a member of the IG Chemie, the industrial union for chemical companies that was very successful in negotiating higher wages.

In the long run, consumer markets were projected to stagnate. Low birth rates in Germany would lead to a lower population and a higher average age in the future. The typical age limit for doing DIY work was just 50 years, and this demographic development would lead to a shrinking target customer group.

The Business Situation for the Adhesives Technologies Department

The overall adhesives market influenced the business situation of Henkel's Adhesives Technologies department. Even if it was able to hold profits at the same level as the previous year, its profitability would be below expectations. In addition to the impact of high raw material costs and increasing salaries negotiated by the IG Chemie, it also had to compete successfully against its competitors in each business segment.

For example, in the tiler segment, the company PCI—a subsidiary of BASF—held a 28 percent market share and was the market leader, while Henkel's market share was at single digits. Even though PCI was the major player, it was not the most aggressive on price. These international companies entered the local market from outside Germany because Germany was still attractive: Requirements for quality standards for renovation work were comparably high. Local professional craftsmen appreciated high-quality products and product innovations offered by these international companies, as compared to other countries, in order to avoid customer complaints.

Italian producer Mapei entered the German market in 2006. It was number one internationally in the tiler segment with €1.3 billion turnover. It acquired several companies, including Soppro, which were already active in the German market and had local knowledge. These companies then received orders at such low prices that none of the local producers could compete with them. For these projects, they then assigned sub-contracts to tilers who had to use Mapei's products for their work. Henkel's strategy was different. It tried to gain market share by developing superior products. Henkel tried to convince tilers of the quality of its products with incremental product innovations. Henkel's developers had produced a "low dust" tile adhesive, which was healthier for tilers to work with. Another innovation was a "lightweight" tile adhesive. The product usage results of 25 kg

(55 lb) were comparative to jobs done with 80 kg (176 lb) of a conventional tile adhesive.

Nevertheless, Henkel's product innovations were not systematically based on current customer needs, but rather on technical feasibility. Market research completed by other departments recognized new trends in consumer behavior, such as the preference for wellness and health products and the awareness for eco-friendly goods. However, these trends were not incorporated during development of new adhesives products. Research and development was laboratory-driven rather than customer-driven. Therefore, products became increasingly specialized and equipped with new features that would allow them to be used with all possible materials and situations. The product range that served the same purpose widened.

In all, products became increasingly comparable throughout the industry. In the long run, incremental improvements would not assure business success because of the saturated market for adhesives. A further specialization in adhesives would not increase demand, but would only take away some market share from an existing product. It was a spiraling race with competitors trying to gain some temporary market share.

As a response to this development, Henkel's strategy was two-fold. First, Henkel strived to be better than its competition. It aimed to gain market share through innovation, POS excellence, distribution expansion, and better marketing concepts. Second, profitability was to be secured by cost-saving projects, simplification of processes, and improvements in the organization.

Andreas Welsch's introductory speech to his marketing executives included a presentation on the current business situation and the latest consumer report. It caused a lively discussion in the room about how to develop a long-term strategy for the department of Adhesives Technologies for Consumers and Craftsmen. Different possibilities were debated, which led to the conclusion that in the long run, the competition could not be beaten by incremental improvements of the existing products. A promising alternative would be to expand the existing market by creating new and uncontested market space where competition would be irrelevant. New target groups would expand the customer pool and alleviate the pressure of fighting with the competitors over the same customers.

Welsch was pleased with the direction the discussion was taking and announced that this meeting should be the kickoff for a Blue Ocean Strategy implementation. A creative but structured process to develop ideas for new markets and customer groups had to be started—and there was no time to lose.

Dr. Minyi Huang, Ali Farhoomand

The University of Hong Kong

In 2000, in response to intense competition and the dot-com boom, Citibank made a serious push to deliver integrated solutions that enabled its corporate customers to conduct business online. Citibank's e-business strategy ("connect, transform, and extend") was to Web-enable its core services, develop integrated solutions, and reach new markets. Citibank aimed to build a single Web-enabled platform for all customers with similar needs. Following the success of CitiDirect, a corporate banking platform which was developed in 2000 and strengthened in 2003, Citibank started to develop Treasury Vision as a replacement to suit the changing marketplace.

When developing its e-business, Citibank faced constant challenges in serving corporate customers with diverse needs. Sophisticated clients, such as multinational companies (MNCs), required custom-built host-to-host product interfaces. Other customers, such as small and medium-sized enterprises (SMEs), were more conservative and not ready for Web-based solutions. Meanwhile, Citibank was under increasing pressure to cut costs and improve efficiency. Following the outcry over subprime mortgages in October 2007, Citibank faced a very tough business environment.

How could Citibank build a flexible and agile e-business product that could capture its clients' total cash-management and trade-service needs, yet still lower costs and improve efficiency? Given Citibank's enormous global reach, how could it integrate Internet initiatives into its overall strategy and create sustainable competitive advantages?

Global Corporate Banking at Citibank

Citibank was incorporated in 1812 as City Bank of New York. The bank experienced several mergers after its inception. The name Citibank N.A. was adopted in 1976. Following its merger with Travelers Group in 1998, the holding company changed its name to Citigroup Inc. ("Citigroup"). In 2006, Citigroup employed 325,000 staff serving 200 million customers in over 100 countries and had an information technology expenditure of US$3,762 million.

Starting in the 1990s, Citibank's corporate banking activities became more centralized, with more attention focused on 1,400 large global corporations and institutional investors.[1] Citibank transformed from a geography-based organization into a multidimensional one. Customer needs became its first priority, while product types were given second priority.[2]

By most measures, Citibank was the most global U.S. bank. In 1997, Citibank was also one of the most profitable banks in the United States, with an annual profit of US$3.59 billion, of which global corporate banking accounted for US$2.56 billion. Citibank's global corporate banking business continued its healthy growth. The bank's Cash and Trade service was a core product offered to corporate customers. By 2000, Citibank's Cash and Trade division had already exceeded US$1 trillion in financial transactions for customers and counterparts around the world daily. These included foreign exchange transactions, equities, deposits, settlements of trade transactions, and payment of insurance policies. In 2006, the income from its global corporate and investment banking activities reached US$7.127 billion, a three percent increase over 2005.[3]

Citibank's target corporate client base included MNCs, financial institutions, government sectors, local corporations, and SMEs. Citibank differentiated itself from other banks through customer service by offering telephone hotlines, relationship managers who understood clients' needs, and product consultants who provided service expertise. Most importantly, Citibank made continuous investment in technology to support both the front-end and back-end electronic banking system.

For corporate customers, Citibank provided a full range of financial services, except for investment banking services in the United States. The core products were broadly grouped into three categories:[4]

- Transaction services, such as cash management, trade, and custody services
- Corporate finance services, such as working-capital finance, trade finance, and asset-based financing
- Treasury market services, such as hedging and foreign exchange

Citibank aimed to make the organization accessible to its corporate customers by using its unified platform and group-wide expertise. It used a team coverage approach, which allowed Citigroup to work closely with each function in a client's organization.

Cash Management[5]

The main focus of cash management was to find ways to move money around in the most efficient manner possible in order to meet customers' requirements. Two crucial aspects of a corporate treasurer's needs were accounts payable and accounts receivable. In 2000, Citibank focused on developing solutions to address three process areas: accounts receivable process management, accounts payable process management, and

liquidity management (Exhibit 1). By 2007, after continuous developments, Citibank's cash management products included Web-enabled payment and receivables solutions, vendor financing, commercial card solutions, and liquidity products designed to help customers to reduce financing costs and achieve greater returns on assets.

To help customers make payments, WorldLink Payment Services had been Citibank's cross-border banking solution for more than 20 years. Using WorldLink Payment Services, payments can be made in more than 135 currencies through a range of payment options including cash, cross-border Automated Clearing House (ACH)[6], checks, or electronic funds transfers. There was no need for multiple foreign currency accounts, and transactions were protected by sophisticated encryption technologies, access restrictions, and authentication procedures. Citibank's QuikRemit Service, a newer service, offered a robust software platform and global distribution network to process fund transfers effortlessly across borders. QuikRemit allowed corporate customers to offer both in-branch and Web-based money transfers to their own customers.

In terms of receiving payments, Citibank's Customer Initiated Payments offered an integrated solution enabling corporate customers to offer Web and telephone payment capabilities to their clients. Corporate customers were able to develop a tailor-made Internet payment application hosted on the Citibank Customer Initiated Payments system that provided one-time or automated

Exhibit 1 Citibank's Treasury and Cash Management Objectives

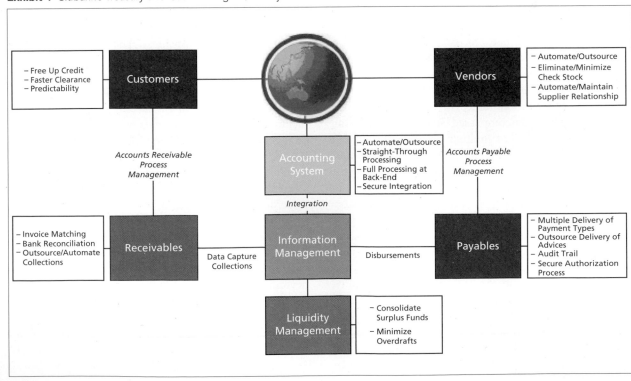

recurring payment initiation. This solution also included a touch-tone telephone payment application for one-time payment initiation as well as a customer service console to enable payment initiation by an operator.

Citibank's commercial cards offered a wide array of Web-based program management tools designed to streamline payment, reporting, spend analysis, global data consolidation, and other critical day-to-day processes. In Asia, commercial cards enabled corporate customers to receive consolidated spend data for all countries within Asia which could be easily leveraged during supplier negotiations. Corporate customers could also work with a single Citibank sales manager responsible for program implementation across all participating Asian countries. Therefore, clients could benefit from consistency in products, delivery, and services. By the end of 2007, Citibank remained the only bankcard issuer that was able to deliver local-currency and local-language programs to clients worldwide by using its own proprietary systems and customer service operations.

Citibank also offered an array of integrated investment options through multiple channels, including automatic orders, branch services, and online services. Through its network of Liquidity Desks, Citibank provided a central point of contact to facilitate investment transactions in every major region. Citibank's Online Investments was a global, secure, Web-based system allowing customers to access a variety of short-term investments using its award-winning electronic banking platform, CitiDirect Online Banking (which was later replaced by Treasury Vision) allowed customers to actively manage their short-term investment portfolios conveniently and efficiently.

Citibank also offered Target Balancing and Notional Pooling as integrated parts of its Global Liquidity and Investments product suite. Target Balancing was an automated process that concentrated end-of-day balances from a source account to a target account, while these services were maintained in-country, regionally, and globally, and encompassed structures operating within a single branch or multiple branches throughout the Citibank network. Notional Pooling was ideal for corporations with decentralized operational structures that wanted to preserve the autonomy of their subsidiaries and accounts. Pool participant accounts in a single currency were aggregated for interest compensation purposes. Funds were not physically moved, but were instead notionally combined. Notional Pooling enabled corporate customers to minimize interest expenses by offsetting debit and credit positions while preserving autonomy, control, and record-keeping. Customers were also able to benefit from offsetting without movement of funds, automating interest reallocation, reducing operating expenses, and concentrating balances. Notional Pooling was used

in conjunction with Target Balancing and Automated Investments to enable corporate customers to fully realize the benefits of a global liquidity structure.

Securities and Fund Services[7]

By 2008, Citibank had developed the financial industry's largest proprietary network, covering 49 markets with more than US$12.5 trillion in assets under custody. Citibank offered international securities trading and investment services to intermediaries. Citibank's Agency and Trust could provide support to help issuers raise short-, medium-, and long-term debts in all major markets. Additionally, Citibank's Depositary Receipts (DR) could provide a wide range of pre- and post-DR program services.

Trade Services and Finance[8]

Back in 2000, Citibank already offered Trade Finance, Trade Services, and Trade Support Services. These product offerings covered the banking service and financing needs of customers who conducted import or export trade transactions (Exhibit 2).

In 2007, Citibank was able to offer efficient services to both importers and exporters due to its global reach and ability to offer secure transactions. For importers, Citibank also provided an array of products to help conduct, monitor, and control international commercial transactions as well as mitigate the associated risks.

Citibank's global electronic banking service was a comprehensive system for initiating transactions and managing financial data activities. Customers could access information and manage all their banking transactions, trade services, cash management, and foreign exchange data from the multiple locations around the world where they conducted their business. They could control the entire trade process, including advising and confirming letters of credit, establishing direct export collections, initiating and tracking payments, retrieving timely status reports, communicating via an online customer service facility, retrieving real-time data worldwide, and customizing reports using data from different systems.

Pricing and Customer Service

Citibank set a standard price for each service, but price discrimination was discretionary based on client volume and value. While some banks competed on price, Citibank emphasized customer service (e.g., response time, technology and support), which gave customers more confidence. Citibank had moved beyond traditional boundaries of banking services by taking over some of the back-office functions of its customers. Customers could move away from the paper-based, labor-intensive payment and collection process, and instead focus resources on their core business of

Exhibit 2 Citibank's Trade Service Products

Letter of Credit Issuance

Collections

Standby Letters of Credit/Guarantees

Confirming Letters of Credit

Advising Letters of Credit

Trade Advisory

Risk Mitigation

Negotiation Export Letters of Credit

---

generating sales and revenue. The value to Citibank in offering outsourcing services was to lock in its corporate customers; when a customer outsourced all of its back-end processes to Citibank, Citibank not only secured all the businesses from the customer, but also gained a deeper relationship with the customer. Managing processes for a large number of customers also provided Citibank with economies of scale.

We have the economy of scale and it is viable for us to do all the back-end processes—because the more processes we do for more customers, the lower the unit cost. So our strategy is to get as many outsourcing customers as we can, and by providing the outsourcing, we get the total wallet of the client.

—*CAROLINE WONG, HEAD OF E-BUSINESS GROUP (CASH & TRADE), CITIBANK HONG KONG*[9]

Citibank also used technology to provide customers with better services at lower costs.[10] In 2006, for example, it invested in an electronic communications network that provided state-of-the-art technology for immediate access to liquidity.

A Changing Global Environment

Banks are always under the pressure of revenue and earnings growth to intensify cost-reduction efforts. In an era of tough competition, banks could not simply use head-count reduction and belt-tightening efforts and needed to find ways to increase operating efficiency while maintaining or even improving services to customers.[11]

Like most other businesses, banks need to increase their profit margins. Net interest margins were falling and fee income growth did not increase as expected. For example, for the 70 largest European banks, net interest margins fell from 2 percent in 2004 to about 1.8 percent in 2006.[12] Meanwhile, competition kept charges for credit cards relatively low; bank customers did not embrace brokerage or life insurance services. Moreover, regulators had made an effort to cap fees or require greater transparency of bank charges.

Between 2005 and 2006, Citigroup's revenue grew 8 percent; however, its operational expenses grew by nearly 15 percent. Therefore, in April 2007, Citibank announced an overhaul of its IT operations and cut 17,000 positions in order to save the company more than US$10 billion over the next three years. Charles Prince, then the company's chairman and chief executive, said that the goal was to identify and eliminate "organizational, technology, and administrative costs that do not contribute to our ability to efficiently deliver products and services to our clients."[13]

Moreover, as a result of the subprime mortgage crisis in the United States, a credit crunch[14] emerged in October 2007. The subprime market was focused on providing loans to those with limited or poor credit histories. During the U.S. housing boom between 2000 and 2006, this market expanded significantly, but a series of interest rate increases in 2006 and 2007 meant that many subprime borrowers could no longer afford their monthly payments, causing them to default on loans.

In November 2007, Prince had to resign after the full extent of Citigroup's subprime mortgage losses began to emerge. Vikram Pandit took up the top job at Citigroup in December 2007. Then, on January 15, 2008, Citigroup announced a US$9.83 billion net loss for the last quarter of 2007. Pandit explained that this loss was due to a US$18.1 billion exposure to bad mortgage debt and was "clearly unacceptable." The group announced that revenues during the fourth quarter had fallen 70 percent from a year earlier to US$7.2 billion.

Smarter and Tougher Customers

Citibank developed expertise and had specific coverage models to serve different market segments. However, as more of Citibank's clients expanded their businesses globally and became e-enabled, it became necessary for Citibank to shift to e-space. In particular, corporations that historically dealt largely through wholesale channels had found that the Internet allowed them to sell directly to customers. Sophisticated corporate customers began to look for an additional range of services. They wanted to collect payments online and have access to more efficient Web-enabled financial processes.[15]

Middle markets were also driving the growing need for Internet banking capabilities. A study by Greenwich Associates in May–June 2001 showed that over half of the middle-market companies in the United States and Canada were using their financial institutions' online banking facilities more often. Nearly 50 percent of respondents said online offerings represented an important component of their banking relationships, and cash management had the steepest gain in usage among mid-size companies.[16] Banks were therefore compelled to identify what companies were looking for and to keep up with the customers with whom they were supposed to develop consultative relationships.

The Business-to-Business (B2B) Market

Sophisticated clients were looking for ways to streamline and improve their traditional payment processes. They demanded electronic invoicing, automatic application of payments to accounts receivable, online payment guarantees, and non-repudiation of transactions that could be enabled by digital receipts stored in archives. On the payment side of transactions, businesses required multi-currency payment management and payment aggregation by invoice and currency. Most companies were interested in technological solutions that allowed them

to avoid paper disputes, which meant that the information flowing with a payment was deemed to be as important as the payment itself.[17]

TowerGroup, a research and consulting firm, predicted that payment activities would migrate to the Internet and that there would be US$4 trillion in B2B e-payment activities by 2010. TowerGroup also reported that in 2000, more than 90 percent of all B2B payments were made by check, with 7 percent occurring over the automated clearinghouse (ACH) network, a non-Internet system designed to handle large payments, and the rest using financial Electronic Data Interchange (EDI) services such as Fedwire.[18] The majority of small businesses used traditional payments such as checks; large companies that used ACH did not have the complete data that were necessary for a B2B payment. In addition to checks, various payment methods were available, with clearance time varying according to the method:

- Notes and coins: Notes and coins paid into an account did not require clearing; they had no particular attraction for banks, especially in large volumes, because they were a non-interest-bearing item.
- Banker's draft: This was a check drawn on a bank. Payment by banker's draft was guaranteed.
- Credit cards: Made by voucher or electronically, voucher payments were processed in a way similar to checks.
- Special presentation of checks: This payment method was taken only in cases of extreme doubt about a customer. For example, a payee company could ask its bank to make a special presentation of the check by posting the check to the paying customer's bank.
- Transfers: Funds were transferred from one bank account to another on receipt of instructions (through telephone, subsequently confirmed by writing, on paper, or sent by cable, telex, or an electronic processing center) by the paying bank to make the payment.

Bank-to-corporate connectivity was the biggest hurdle in enabling straight-through processing in treasury- and cash-management across borders.[19] In 1999, corporate customers could access SWIFTNet[20] to exchange confirmations with their banks through Treasury Counterparties. In 2002, access was enhanced by the Member Administrated Closed User Croup, where a company could join SWIFTNet if a member bank sponsored it. Though there were no limits on the messages that the corporate customer could exchange with the sponsoring bank, the communication was limited to the sponsoring bank and it was expensive and troublesome for corporate customers to reach an agreement with the banks.

Since the beginning of 2007, most large corporate customers had begun using a new legal model for accessing SWIFTNet: Standardized CORporate Environment (SCORE). Using the SCORE model, a corporate customer could access all participating banks with only one agreement in place. SCORE also laid down rules for the messages that could be sent within the SCORE framework. The only exception was for FileAct message, where the body of a FileAct message could contain any type of messages, such as an EDIFACT[21] or ISO 20022[22] format message. The introduction of SCORE was intended to make it easier, cheaper, and less risky for corporate customers to switch between banks because no technical or format changes were needed for corporate customers in switching banks.[23]

Many banks openly admitted that formats and connectivity were no longer a competitive space but instead a place for cooperation, using standards to reduce costs for their customers as well as themselves. The competition would be in the value-added services that banks sold to customers.[24]

Competition

Some MNCs could not wait for banks to develop Web-enabled financial products, so they started building their own systems and looking for ways to disintermediate banks. Other corporations approached the banks and announced their interest in participating in future developments. New technology, however, required major investments in people, risk, and technological services that some banks were not ready to make. The banking industry's trend toward consolidation meant that fewer banks were competing in the global transaction services marketplace. Deutsche Bank and Citibank were two leading banks that invested hundreds of millions of dollars in the infrastructure required to move and monitor cash balances online. ABN AMRO was also making a serious push to develop its product range.

In early 2001, Deutsche Bank sought to outdo its competitors by building a global payment system capable of accommodating many currencies, languages, and local business practices through its e-bills service. More large banks sought partnerships to provide global business solutions. In international cash management (ICM), companies either partnered with a lead bank that put together a solution for them, or dealt directly with local banks. The majority of companies used a lead bank to provide a solution in four ways: using correspondent banks, acting as an overlay bank, becoming a member of a banking club, or bringing together a network of standardized service providers (Exhibit 3).

Exhibit 3 The Main Trends in ICM in 2000 and 2008

Trends in 2000

- The centralization of cash management and the introduction of shared service centers continued in large companies and were spreading to medium-sized and small companies.
- There was a growing acceptance of the need to outsource ICM operations.
- Companies were realizing that the company-bank relationship was more important than whether or not a bank could offer Internet-based or e-commerce services.
- Companies increasingly wanted to understand and be comfortable with a bank's e-commerce strategy before they were prepared to award them business.
- The use of cross-border zero-balance accounts grew much faster than notional pooling because many companies had sophisticated in-house cash- and treasury-management systems to run them.
- There was a growing realization among some of the major banks that a network of standardized service-provider banks was not always enough; it was also important to have a local branch or branches in countries around the world.
- Banks were walking away from the ICM business where it had ceased to be profitable, producing a growing understanding and acceptance among large companies that banks needed to make reasonable returns; otherwise the standard and quality of services would inevitably suffer.
- As banks' ICM products and memberships of local clearings became similar, the key differentiator in the business became delivery.

Source: D. Danko, J. H. Godwin & S. R. Goldberg, 2002, How to profit from new trends in treasury management, *Journal of Corporate Accounting and Finance*, 14(1): 3–10.

Trends in 2008

- Banks and corporate treasurers were driving the move toward electronic payments in order to better integrate money and information flows.
- Corporate treasury was pushing to integrate the physical and financial supply chains, and there was a parallel convergence in international trade toward open-account, electronic financial supply chains.
- Corporate treasury was focusing on standardizing processes and strengthening internal controls in order to create transparency across a range of business activities to manage risk and ensure financial reporting integrity in compliance with Sarbanes-Oxley.[25]

Source: S. Wilder, 2008, The latest trends in North American cash management, JPMorgan Chase & Co.

Most Fortune 500 companies preferred Citibank when making international e-payments.[26] Although Citibank established itself as a strong contender, technology companies competed heavily by using their technological expertise and interests in providing new services.

Regulatory Scrutiny

Risk management and legal compliance were priorities for banks in 2008.[27] Regulators took an increasingly cross-platform view of risk and therefore expected banks to increasingly connect exposures across channels and payments, which put more pressure on bank architectures where risk management was usually buried at the platform level. For example, the implementation of Basel II[28] increased the pressure on information systems functions and encouraged banks to develop integrated information systems strategies and consequently amend their existing IT infrastructures.[29]

Regulators were also more cautious about privacy issues. They expected banks to be able to identify specific data breaches quickly in order to limit any damage as a result of fraud. In addition, with the growing number of nonbank processors in the marketplace who were generating numerous transactions within the banking systems, regulators scrutinized third-party arrangements much more closely to ensure that banks understood the underlying commercial purpose and ensure that a bank's operations were not hijacked for fraudulent purposes.

Citibank's E-Business Strategy

We are here to serve our clients: whatever our clients want us to do we'll do it for them. We're into e-business not because we're into the dot-com business; we're here because our clients want us to continue performing the basic banking functions for them on the web.

— *CAROLINE WONG, HEAD OF E-BUSINESS GROUP (CASH & TRADE), CITIBANK HONG KONG*[30]

Citibank's vision was to become the world's leading e-business enabler. It wanted to empower local, regional, and global customers and the business-to-business-to-consumer marketplace and provide solutions to help them take advantage of the efficiencies and opportunities created by e-commerce. Citibank's e-business strategy to "connect, transform and extend" was a means to deliver on its vision.

Meanwhile, with technology investments in the global financial service industry growing at a rate of 4.2 percent per year, Citibank tried to manage the overall costs of IT investments. The plan announced in April 2007 to overhaul IT operations included the consolidation of data centers; better use of existing technologies; optimization of global voice and data networks; standardization of its application-development processes; and vendor consolidation. As Citibank stated, "simplification and standardization of Citibank's information technology platform will be critical to increase efficiency and drive lower costs as well as decrease time to market."[32]

Citibank's E-Business Structure

In March 2000, Citigroup chief executive Sanford Weill announced the formation of the Internet Operation Group, a high-level committee charged with spreading

Citibank's E-Business Strategy[31]

CONNECT	TRANSFORM	EXTEND
Web-enable its core services to connect with its customers	Draw on the full range of Citibank's capabilities to deliver integrated solutions	Reach new markets, new customers, and new products

The Six Key Elements of Citibank's E-Business Strategy

- Embed Citibank as the trusted brand within communities
- Build a network of strategic partners
- Help customers to serve themselves
- Web-enable core services
- Create knowledge-based e-services
- 'e-Us'

Exhibit 4 Citibank's Global Transaction Services Awards in Asia, 2007

- Best Custodian in Asia; Best Fund Administrator in Asia (*Asia Asset Management*)
- Best Overall Cash Management Bank across all categories as voted by corporations; Best Electronic Banking Platform; Best at Understanding Business Strategies, Objectives, and Requirements as voted by financial institutions (*Asiamoney*)
- Best Transaction Bank in Asia; Best Cash Management Bank in Asia; Best Corporate Specialist in Asia (*The Asset*)
- Best Cash Management Bank; Best Cash Management Solutions (*FinanceAsia*)
- Asia's Best Investment Management Services; Best Corporate/Institutional Internet Bank in Asia (*Global Finance*)

responsibility for Internet activities more evenly between e-Citi, an incubator for Internet initiatives, and the bank's business units. In April 2000, the group announced the second phase of Citigroup's Internet activity, which involved the creation of two units aimed at infusing the Internet into all consumer and corporate banking activities: e-Consumer and e-Business. Both units were intended to complement e-Citi.[33] In May 2000, two new business units, e-Capital Markets and e-Asset Management, were added.

Jorge Bermudez, executive vice-president and head of Global Cash Management and Trade Services, was appointed to lead the e-Business unit.[34] Bermudez's e-Business unit was responsible for developing Internet software for corporate clients setting up B2B electronic commerce exchanges.

The new business units brought people from the business lines together with people from the Internet side of operations, which combined resources and eliminated duplication and competition. The new strategy of forming high-level committees reversed the centralized approach that Citigroup had pursued under John Reed, the driving force behind the formation of e-Citi.[35] Citigroup's new structure involved traditional business units in formulating Internet strategies and forming

committees to coordinate and synthesize an approach that mirrored that of other banks.[36]

In 2002, Global Transaction Services was created as a division of Citibank's Markets and Banking to integrate Cash, Trade, and Treasury Services and Global Securities Services. It offered integrated cash management, fund services, securities services, trade services, and finance to MNCs, financial institutions, and the public sector around the world (Exhibit 5). The objective was to help corporate customers gain greater control over financial positions both locally and globally, increase efficiency, and reduce costs.

Within just one year, Global Transaction Services was already tapped by 95 percent of Fortune 500 companies and profits grew 38 percent. With a global reach and local presence, Global Transaction Services had assets and businesses in several countries and regions. Its Internet-based cash management, electronic bill payment and online statements, reporting and analytics, securities processing, and other capabilities enabled corporate customers to re-engineer processes, manage working capital more effectively, and improve straight-through processing.

In 2006, Global Transaction Services already supported 65,000 clients, cleared an average of 752,000

Exhibit 5 Citigroup Organizational Structure

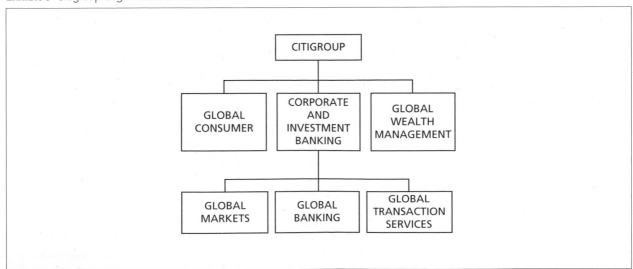

securities trades every week, and processed more than US$3 trillion in payments every day. On average, it held US$189 billion in liability balances under administration and US$10.4 trillion in assets under custody and trust, and had the world's largest commercial letter-of-credit portfolio, worth over US$7 billion.

Citibank's Alliance Strategy

Before 2000, Citibank had tried to excel at all facets of e-business—a strategy that failed. The company invested millions of dollars and tried to specialize in each area, including software development, systems development, and front-end services; however, clients and software technology were constantly changing and Citibank was struggling to keep pace with client needs. By 2000, Citibank's strategy focused on alliances and the use of its partners' strengths. Specifically, Citibank partnered with companies that had complementary technology, infrastructure, or access to markets. As Tom Edgerton, head of alliance for Citibank e-business, said, "In the future, it won't be what your company can do, but what the network of companies you work with can provide."[37]

Citibank's key technology players included Oracle, Commerce One Inc., SAP AG, Wisdom Technologies, and Bolero.net. In August 2000, four companies teamed up with Citibank to form FinancialSettlementMatrix.com, a company that connected buyers and sellers in e-marketplaces with payment processing, credit, and other services through multiple participating banks and financial service companies.[38] Citibank's challenge was managing the vendors and suppliers and ensuring that they understood Citibank's strategy and would not exploit the bank's existing strengths in the banking industry. Edgerton said of companies that had approached Citibank to partner with it: "Citibank brings considerable value to potential alliance partners. They're interested in our brand, our financial services expertise, our global presence, our strong customer relationships and position as a trusted provider, as well as our knowledge of specific industries and international markets."[39]

In 2004, Citibank acquired Lava Trading, a leader in electronic execution and sell-side order management systems. This acquisition enabled Citibank to offer institutional clients the benefits of the most sophisticated and robust electronic trading system in the market, with technology that complemented and enhanced their existing platforms and product ranges.

"Connect" in Citibank's E-Business Strategy

Customer convenience was the thrust of the continuous evolution of Citibank's products and services. Key to this goal was providing clients with more channels to access Citibank, and the Internet provided Citibank the flexibility to meet this demand. Jorge Bermudez, Citibank executive vice-president and head of e-Business, stated: "A core part of our e-business strategy is Web-enabling our current services. With CitiDirect, we are building the infrastructure that will serve as the foundation for many of the value-added services we are developing on the Internet."[40]

CitiDirect was designed for corporate customers to do full transactions online anywhere around the world.[41] It was a browser-based delivery channel designed to deliver all of Citibank's cash management and trade products and services online, enabling customers to make inquiries about their account balances, request statements, provide transaction initiation details, and request statement transaction reports online and in real time. CitiDirect allowed customers to perform these functions at any location with Internet access. This was particularly useful for global companies with operations spread out in many countries but wishing to maintain control at regional or global treasury centers.

CitiDirect was piloted in October 2000. In Asia, it was piloted in Singapore, Hong Kong, Australia, Japan, and Malaysia.[42] In 2000, CitiDirect was operating in 36 countries and available in five languages and was expected to be operating in 80 countries and 20 languages and doing a trillion U.S. dollars of business per day by 2002.[43] In May 2001, CitiDirect was already serving 1,000 corporate customers worldwide.

In 2003, Citibank upgraded CitiDirect Online Banking to offer complete payment, receivables, and trade capabilities in emerging markets. The service was made available in 90 countries and in 20 languages, and was awarded Best of the Web for 2003 by Forbes.com in the financial services category. In 2004 alone, this corporate banking platform processed more than 39 million transactions around the world. CitiDirect linked the back-office systems of 90 countries and allowed Citibank to replace its outdated and less-powerful systems and move training and customer services online.

In 2006, Citibank developed TreasuryVision, which was similar to CitiDirect. As Paul Galant, head of Global Cash Management for Citibank, noted, "We are putting a lot of energy behind it and TreasuryVision essentially meets the trends in the marketplace. It connects our clients not only to their internal systems, but it also connects to their enterprise resource planning systems."

TreasuryVision was staffed by world-class employees with expert knowledge of financial data. Once the data were proved by these experts, they would be put into a knowledge warehouse and provided to clients (i.e., corporate treasuries). Therefore, TreasuryVision would not only be an effective way of managing liquidity, but also be a useful channel for knowledge management.

"Transform" in Citibank's e-Business Strategy

Transaction processing, such as cash management, trade finance, and derivatives, was a back-office activity that was not at the forefront of customers' minds. Traditionally, transaction processing for a corporate customer (e.g., the transactional work involved in loan processing) was a function of the bank-customer relationship. Citibank's global presence translated to a huge transactional business and required supporting more than 200 data centers, which did basic, repeatable processes. In 1998, Citibank realized that, similar to any other factory product, this could be commoditized. At that point, Citibank began the transformation.

Regionalization
The transformation process involved consolidating all the data centers within each country and moving them to Singapore. Data were centralized and systems were developed to manage the automatic processing of transactions. By May 1999, the data centers were consolidated down to 60. On the operations side, Citibank began with the regionalization of cash and trade, which afforded Citibank a complete focus on the process. Approaches that Citibank used to decide the location for the regionalized centers were not mutually exclusive. It had considered the following in various combinations:

- Take the biggest infrastructure already existing (i.e., Singapore) and build it up to replace all the smaller centers.
- Ask where to get the best balance of all factors of production and start there from scratch (e.g., Penang)—Greenfield Approach.
- Rely on locally available people and skills (e.g., Sydney).
- Consider the pure cost of labor for lower-skilled areas such as voucher processing.

Singapore, which had back-office operations in several of the bank's business units, was the first processing center that was regionalized, followed by Penang[44] and Sydney's foreign-exchange and derivatives centers. The centers were time-zone-centric, so that decisions were based on the three continental time zones of Europe, Asia, and the Americas.

As a way to lower costs and improve efficiency, in 2006, Citibank reduced the number of data centers by 20 percent. In April 2007, in order to save the company more than US$10 billion, Citibank introduced a plan to overhaul its IT operations. It planned to further consolidate its existing data centers, better use its existing technologies, optimize its global voice and data networks, standardize its application development processes, and consolidate its vendor networks.

The regionalized and specialized processing centers provided Citibank scale and continual improvement opportunities. They reduced the cycle time for transactions, reduced error rates to nearly zero, and yielded new efficiencies for Citibank and its customers. As one manager noted:

We're now able to fragment the process and focus on the little pieces that make the difference, this also means that there's a lot of exchange of information and standardization of processes.

—VENRY KRISHNAKUMAR, CITIBANK VICE-PRESIDENT AND REGIONAL DIRECTOR, OPERATION AND TECHNOLOGY, ASIA-PACIFIC AND JAPAN[45]

Internalizing the Web
Within Citibank, there was a program to promote the e-workplace. The processing centers in particular had taken off through integrating the Web into their business processes. The transformations in the processing cycle focused on workflow automation; employees now had access to information without the need to make phone calls, check paper files, or send faxes. Processing centers had previously required millions of checks and huge reconcilement departments, which were paper-based and labor-intensive. The centralized and specialized processing locations made it easier for Citibank to integrate secure databases into the processing of a transaction. For example, signature-verification and digital-imaging systems were linked with the funds-transfer system.[46]

Straight-Through Automation
Citibank was continuously pushing the limits of straight-through automation by constantly deploying various initiatives. For example, Citibank conducted some artificial intelligence projects, such as prepopulating forms with historical data, which dramatically reduced error rates. It could select rejected transactions and take a look at a customer's history with similar transactions and try to predict what the customer would try to do.[47] The effective implementation of such projects was attributable to the qualified and experienced staff at Citibank.

The benefits of efficiency and cost savings also trickled down to Citibank's customers. In traditional transactions, customers deposited checks into ATMs or opened Letters of Credit by submitting the paperwork to banks, but they did not know when the banks would actually perform the task. With Citibank's straight-through processing, customers' expectations and need to know were matched because the processes took place online and in real time.

Achievements

Proof that Citibank was at the top of its league was the awards it received (Exhibit 4). Citibank was the first company in the financial services industry to receive a quality award for its cash-processing center or regional cash-process management unit (RCPMU).[48] Customer surveys showed that Citibank's RCPMU was rated higher than those of its competitors in the areas of accuracy, timeliness, accessibility, and responsiveness several years in a row. Processing was fast becoming one of Citibank's unique selling propositions. Citibank's commitment to excellence in its processing business translated to greater transparency of the process for customers, allowing them full access to information about the status of their transactions.

"Extend" in Citibank's E-Business Strategy

CitiDirect's roll-out was evidence of Citibank's vision of delivering transaction services online anywhere in the world at any time. Building a new global infrastructure gave Citibank the opportunity to deliver e-products at scale more quickly and efficiently, and any capability improvements in one region would be seamlessly deployed worldwide. Citibank expected CitiDirect to evolve constantly, which would give Citibank the flexibility to continuously enhance the system according to the changing needs of its customers. Other European banks focused mainly on providing pan-European solutions; very few banks wanted to deliver global services.

Citibank's priority was to move all its corporate customers onto CitiDirect because its main goal was to retire the legacy systems of electronic banking. Citibank had to contend, however, with difficulties in migrating customers from using traditional means to using the new products and services. Citibank's corporate clients included top-tier MNCs as well as SMEs. Previously, Citibank had not focused on SMEs; it was in 1997 that it started to consider the SME segment and introduced CitiBusiness.[49] While MNCs dealing in e-business knew what they wanted, SMEs that wanted an e-business presence were unsure how to move forward. Some were not even e-enabled and were still tied up with the legacy systems of the 1970s, 1980s, and 1990s. The greatest concern among most customers was security. Some

resisted making the transition because they were skeptical about security, and such behavior was entrenched. CitiDirect had already developed sophisticated security procedures using the latest encryption techniques. Its multilayered security architecture included public and private access keys, single-use passwords, and multiple authorization controls. Despite Citibank's readiness, customer concerns about security did somewhat hinder Citibank's roll-out of Web-based applications.

In 2001, Citibank still provided services using legacy systems for conservative SME customers, while at the same time serving global customers such as MNCs that demanded to transact through the Internet. Citibank was aware that building customers' trust in the Web took years of education. To encourage conservative customers to embrace CitiDirect, Citibank's plan was to build a strategy that included a pricing incentive scheme.

The Citibank Advantage

Global Reach

As part of a global financial institution that employed over 268,000 employees in 100 countries, Citibank was uniquely positioned to serve its customers' global needs. In emerging markets, where 86 percent of the world's population lived and which accounted for 43 percent of the world's purchasing power, Citibank implemented an "embedded bank" strategy. Through this strategy, Citibank established roots in a country as deep as those of any local indigenous bank by building a broad customer base, offering diverse products, actively participating in the community, and recruiting staff and senior management from the local population. This local commitment and history, together with Citibank's global reach and expertise, was a powerful combination that set Citibank apart from its competition. In 2002, Citibank celebrated its 100th year of operations in China, Hong Kong, India, Japan, the Philippines, and Singapore.

Continuous Investment in Technology

Citibank was committed to upholding its position as a premier supplier of cash-management and transactional banking services and invested heavily in technology to improve its services. The main goal was to provide corporate customers the most cost-effective, cutting-edge, reliable, and secure solutions. As a Citibank senior executive explained, "We continuously invest in technology and it's one of our competitive advantages. We've been around a long time, we have been able to invest year after year, and we have seen compounded value from that. A new entrant would have a difficult time investing all at once, but by spending money on infrastructure—not on salespeople or front ends—I think that's how you stay in the position we're in."[50]

Technology was used as a means to achieve a strategic objective for Citibank. With the need to lower costs and improve efficiency, its investment in IT provided better client services at a lower cost. Chuck Prince, former chief executive of Citigroup, said, "One of our goals is to have more common systems and standards across Citigroup so clients can transact with us more easily, no matter what business is serving them or where they're conducting business."[51]

Conclusion

The Internet affected many areas of banking and changed how institutions make strategic decisions. At the same time, technology changed customers' expectations and needs. It was a challenge for Citibank to translate its traditional strengths to the Internet in a way that would add value for its customers. Citibank responded to this challenge by:

- Deploying Web-enabling access points to allow customers to connect seamlessly to Citibank.

- Building a new global infrastructure to deliver products and services online.
- Integrating products in new ways.

In a business environment where change was inevitable and competition was tough, Citibank needed a distinctive strategic direction that would create competitive advantages that would not be easily replicated by its competitors. Citibank also needed to make transformations on a global scale to deliver its e-business strategy and create a business culture that would embrace the e-banking concept, a key element of a highly integrated e-business, within a reasonable budget.

A key question for Citibank is how can it continue to be successful and stay ahead of the competition as Web-enabled technology diffuses through the banking industry? Also, what future trends will emerge that Citibank will need to address in order to continue to be in the lead?

NOTES

1. D. Baron & D. Besanko, 2001, Strategy, organization and incentives: Global corporate banking at Citibank, *Industrial and Corporate Change,* 10(1): 12–14.
2. Ibid.
3. Citigroup 2006 Annual Report.
4. D. Baron & D. Besanko, 2001, Strategy, organization and incentives: Global corporate banking at Citibank, *Industrial and Corporate Change,* 10(1): 12–14.
5. This section adapted from Citigroup, 2008, Global Transaction Services: Cash Management, http://www.transactionservices.citigroup.com/transactionservices/homepage/cash/cash_mgmt.htm (accessed February 18, 2008).
6. Introduced in the 1970s as an alternative to traditional check payments, ACH is a secure network connecting banks to each other. Direct deposits, electronic payments, money transfers, debit-card payments, business-to-business payments, and even tax transactions may be processed through the ACH network.
7. This section adapted from Citigroup, 2008, Global Transaction Services: Securities and Fund Services, "http://www.transactionservices.citigroup.com/transactionservices/homepage/securitiesfunds.htm (accessed February 18, 2008).
8. This section adapted from Citigroup, 2008, Global Transaction Services: Trade Services and Finance, http://www.transactionservices.citigroup.com/transactionservices/homepage/trade/index.htm (accessed February 18, 2008).
9. Company interview in July 2001.
10. Citigroup 2006 Annual Report.
11. Deloitte, 2007, Global banking industry outlook: Issues on the horizon 2007, http://www.deloitte.com/cda/content/banking.pdf (accessed February 20, 2008).
12. Ibid.
13. J. Vijayan, 2007, Citigroup to lay off 17,000, overhaul IT operations, *ComputerWorld,* April 11.
14. A credit crunch is "a state in which there is a short supply of cash to lend to businesses and consumers and interest rates are high." Princeton University, 2008, Credit crunch, http://wordnet.princeton.edu/perl/webwn (accessed February 20, 2008).
15. C. Cockerill, 2001, Cash management takes to the Internet, *Euromoney,* 381(January): 105.

16. Greenwich Associates was an international research and consulting firm specializing in financial services. Greenwich Associates interviewed 500 corporate treasurers and other executives at middle-market companies in the United States and Canada in May–June 2001. See also: D. Rountree, 2001, Importance of on-line banking, *Bank Technology News,* 14(11): 86.
17. For example, if a company shipped a buyer 100 products at US$10 per piece, but five of the products were defective, the company might simply remit US$50 electronically without any information about the defective products. In such a case, there would be greater possibility of costly payment processes because of back-and-forth inquiries. The solution would be to send a paper explanation; however, this could translate to additional billing inquiries and disputes.
18. To use the ACH network, a company was required to have between US$10 million and US$50 million in annual revenues.
19. J. Jensen, 2007, Bank-to-corporate connectivity: The next stage, http://www.gtnews.com/article/6878.cfm, August 16 (accessed February 13, 2008).
20. SWIFTNet is a general-purpose, industry-standard solution for the financial industry. It provides an application-independent, single window interface to all the financial institutions around the globe.
21. EDIFACT is the international EDI standard developed by the United Nations.
22. ISO is a worldwide federation of National Standards Bodies. ISO20022 (UNIversal Financial Industry [UNIFI] message scheme) provides the financial industry with a common platform for the development of messages in a standardized XML syntax.
23. Ibid.
24. Ibid.
25. The Sarbanes-Oxley Act of 2002 is a U.S. federal law enacted in response to a number of major corporate and accounting scandals, which establishes new or enhanced standards for all U.S. public company boards, management, and public accounting firms.
26. P. Clark, 2001, No longer banking on exchanges, *B to B,* 86(13): 13.
27. S. DeZoysa, 2007, A strategy for future growth: Banking challenges and trends, http://www.gtnews.com/feature/201.cfm, August 16 (accessed February 12, 2008).

28. The Basel Accords are issued by the Basel Committee on Banking Supervision to make recommendations on banking laws and regulations. Basel II is the second of the Basel Accords, discussing how much capital banks need to put aside to prepare for the types of financial and operational risks they face.

29. A. Papanikolaou, 2007, Impact of Basel II on bank's IT strategies, http://www.gtnews.com/article/6875.cfm, August 16 (accessed February 13, 2008).

30. Company interview in July 2001.

31. 2001, CitiDirect online banking—a new era in business banking, *Asiamoney,* May, 84.

32. J. Vijayan, 2007, "Citigroup to lay off 17,000, overhaul IT operations, *Computerworld,* April 11.

33. Robert Willumstad was head of e-Consumer while Edward Horowitz was head of e-Citi.

34. Bermudez reported to Victor Menezes, chairman and chief executive of Citibank, and to the IOG.

35. Reed resigned from his co-CEO post on April 18, 2000.

36. For example, Wells Fargo & Co. and Chase Manhattan Corp. integrated their efforts on using the Internet more closely with their business units.

37. Citibank, 2000, Citibank seeks alliances to accelerate into the e-space, *The Citibank Globe,* http://www.citibank.com/e-business/, November–December (accessed December 3, 2001).

38. Citibank partner companies were Enron Broadband Services (a delivery platform), i2 Technologies (an integrated open-architecture solution), S1 Corporation (a provider of Internet-based payment processing), and Wells Fargo & Company (a provider of complementary services to the entire e-business market).

39. Citibank, 2000, Citibank seeks alliances to accelerate into the e-space, *The Citibank Globe,* http://www.citibank.com/e-business/, November–December (accessed December 3, 2001).

40. Ibid.

41. During the development of CitiDirect, Citibank asked its customers what they wanted from e-commerce and the Internet. Customers put a premium on security, stability, speed, accuracy, and user-friendliness.

42. 2001, CitiDirect online banking—a new era in business banking, *Asiamoney,* May, 83.

43. C. Power, 2000, Citibank deploys its Web troops into business lines, *American Banker,* 165(230), 1.

44. In Singapore, front-end securities processing was also regionalized; however, due to local settlement issues, the back-end processing of securities transactions still needed to be done in individual countries.

45. 2001, Processing comes to the fore, *Finance Asia,* May, 83.

46. A system similar to SWIFT and Forex systems.

47. 2001, Processing comes to the fore, *Finance Asia,* May, 83.

48. The center processed up to US$20 billion worth of transactions daily.

49. CitiBusiness was a one-stop financing solution offered to SME entrepreneurs. Products and services included: CitiBusiness Direct (Internet banking); Cash Management; Trade Services and Trade Finance (trade products); CitiCorp Commercial Finance (asset-based finance); treasury products such as Spot and Forward Foreign Exchange, Interest Rate Hedging, and Yield Enhancement Investment Products; and a customer center. The customer center provided CitiService (an integrated customer inquiry line for after-sales services), Document Collection (an express collection service), CitiFax (a convenient way to update account information) and CitiBusiness Direct (providing online access to account information and transaction initiation).

50. *Finance Asia,* 2001, Processing comes to the fore, May, 83.

51. Citigroup 2005 Annual Report.

Frank C. Barnes

University of North Carolina-Charlotte, Belk College of Business

Beverly B. Tyler

North Carolina State University, College of Management

Nucor was the classic American success story, rising on the world stage while "old steel" gave up. However, in 2009, Nucor and its CEO, Daniel DiMicco, faced challenges as great as any in the company's 54-year history. In December 2008, DiMicco announced earnings for the fourth quarter of 2008 would plunge and told Jim Cramer on CNBC how sales for the steel industry "went off the edge of a cliff." After three record quarters, capacity utilization "immediately" fell to 50 percent. The U.S. mortgage crises led to a global financial meltdown that affected the growth and economic health of both developed and developing economies. Iron ore and scrap metal prices, which had soared only months before due to the voracious demand for infrastructure projects in China and India, plummeted to bargain basement prices along with demand for steel and steel products. With the financial markets in disarray and governments working to bail out financial institutions, consumers who had spent freely on big ticket items suddenly became risk averse. Nucor, which had become the world's tenth largest steelmaker by 2005, dropped to the twelfth largest by 2007, as it and its competitors completed acquisitions around the world. DiMicco, who had led the company during the downs and ups of 2001 and 2005, had a big job ahead—to assess the threats and opportunities facing Nucor and to select the best strategies and structure for the company as it moved into the twenty-first century.

Background

The solid foundation of Nucor was built on the failure of several companies. The first failure involved Nuclear Consultants, a company formed after World War II to ride the wave of growth in "nuclear" technology. When this didn't happen, the renamed Nuclear Corp. of America moved on to the "conglomerate" trend popular at the time. Nuclear acquired various "high-tech" businesses, such as radiation sensors, semi-conductors, rare earths, and air-conditioning equipment. However, the company still lost money, and a fourth reorganization in 1966 put 40-year-old Ken Iverson in charge. The building of Nucor began.

Ken Iverson joined the Navy after high school and transferred from officer training school to Cornell's aeronautical engineering program. After graduation, he selected mechanical engineering/metallurgy for a master's degree to avoid the long drafting apprenticeship in aeronautical engineering. His college work with an electron microscope earned him a job with International Harvester. After five years in that company's lab, his boss and mentor prodded him to expand his vision by going with a smaller company.

Over the next 10 years, Iverson worked for four small metals companies, gaining technical knowledge and increasing his exposure to other business functions. He enjoyed working with the presidents of these small companies and admired their ability to achieve outstanding results. Nuclear Corp., after failing to buy the company Iverson worked for, hired him as a consultant to locate another metals business the firm could purchase. In 1962, Nuclear Corp. acquired a small joist plant in South Carolina that Iverson found. The purchase was completed with the condition that Iverson be allowed to run the operation.

Over the next four years, Iverson built up the Vulcraft division as Nuclear Corporation struggled. The president, David Thomas, was described as a great promoter and salesman but a weak manager. A partner with Bear Stearns actually made a personal loan to the company to keep it going. In 1965, when the company was on the edge of bankruptcy, Iverson, who headed the only successful division, was named president and moved the company's headquarters to Charlotte, North Carolina. He immediately began getting rid of the esoteric, but unprofitable, high-tech divisions and concentrated on the successful steel joist business. The company built more joist plants, and, in 1968, began building its first steel mill in South Carolina to "make steel cheaper than they were buying from importers." By 1984, Nucor had six joist plants and four steel mills, using the new "mini-mill" technology.

The original owner of Vulcraft, Sanborn Chase, was known at Vulcraft as "a scientific genius." He was a man of great compassion who understood the atmosphere necessary for people to be self-motivated. Chase, an engineer by training, invented a number of products in diverse fields. He also established the incentive programs for which Nucor later became known. With only one plant, he was still able to operate in a "decentralized" manner. Before his death in 1960, the company was studying the building of a steel mill using newly developed mini-mill technology. His widow ran the company until it was sold to Nucor in 1962.

Dave Aycock met Ken Iverson when Nuclear purchased Vulcraft and they worked together closely for the next year and a half. Located in Phoenix at the corporate headquarters, he was responsible to Iverson for all the joist operations and was given the task of planning and building a new joist plant in Texas. In late 1963, he was transferred to Norfolk, where he lived for the next 13 years and managed a number of Nucor's joist plants. In 1977, he was named the manager of the Darlington, South Carolina, steel plant. In 1984, Aycock became Nucor's president and chief operating officer, while Iverson became chairman and chief executive officer.

Aycock had this to say about Iverson: "Ken was a very good leader, with an entrepreneurial spirit. He is easy to work with and has the courage to do things, to take lots of risks. Many things didn't work, but some worked very well." For some companies, failure to take a risk is failure—this was the belief of the company's founder and reinforced by Iverson during his time at the helm. Nucor was very innovative in steel and joists. The firm's plant at Norfolk was years ahead of its time in wire rod welding. In the late 1960s, they had one of the first computer inventory management systems and design/engineering programs. They were very sophisticated in purchasing, sales, and managing, and they often beat their competition through the speed of their design efforts.

By 1984, the once-bankrupt conglomerate had become a leading U.S. steel company. It was a fairytale story. Tom Peters used Nucor's management style as an example of "excellence" while the barons of old steel ruled over creeping ghettos. NBC did a feature about Nucor, and *The New Yorker* serialized a book about how a relatively small American steel company built a team that led the whole world into a new era of steelmaking. Iverson was rich, owning $10 million in stock, but with a salary that rarely reached $1 million, a fraction of some other U.S. executives made. The 40-year-old manager of the South Carolina Vulcraft plant had become a millionaire. Stockholders chuckled and non-unionized hourly workers, who hadn't seen a layoff in 20 years, earned more than the unionized workers of old steel and more than 85 percent of the people in the states where they worked.

Nucor owed much of its success to its benchmark organizational style and the empowered division managers. There were two basic lines of business, the first being the six steel joist plants that made the steel frames seen in many buildings. The second line included four steel mills that utilized innovative mini-mill technology to supply the joist plants at first and, later, outside customers. In 1984 Nucor was still only the seventh-largest steel company in America, but it had established the organization design, management philosophy, and incentive system that led to the firm's continued success.

Nucor's Formula for Success, 1964–1999

In the early 1990s, Nucor's 22 divisions, one for every plant, had a general manager, who was also a vice president of the corporation. There were three divisions: joist plants, steel mills, and miscellaneous plants. The corporate staff consisted of less than 25 people. In the beginning, Iverson had chosen Charlotte "as the new home base for what he had envisioned as a small cadre of executives who would guide a decentralized operation with liberal authority delegated to managers in the field," according to *South* magazine. The divisions did their own manufacturing, selling, accounting, engineering, and personnel management, and there were only four levels from top to bottom (see Exhibit 1).

Iverson gave his views on keeping an organization lean:

Each division is a profit center and the division manager has control over the day-to-day decisions that make that particular division profitable or not profitable. We expect the division to provide a contribution, which is earnings before corporate expenses. And we expect a division to earn 25 percent return on total assets employed, before corporate expenses, taxes, interest or profit sharing. And we have a saying in the company—if a manager doesn't provide that for a number of years, we are either going to get rid of the division or get rid of the general manager, and it's generally the division manager.

Nucor strengthened its position by developing strong alliances with outside parties. It did not engage in internal research and development. Instead, it monitored others' work worldwide and attracted investors who brought them new technical applications at the earliest

Exhibit 1 Nucor Organization Chart, 1991

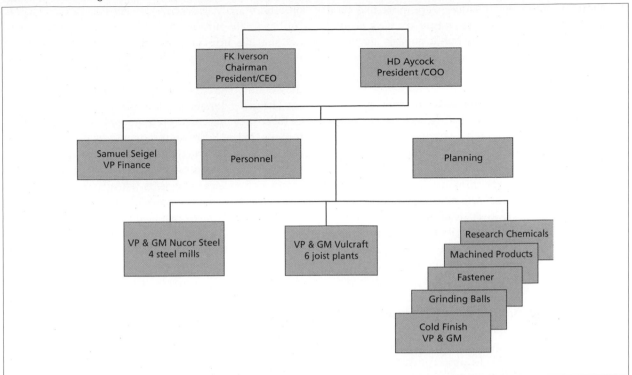

possible dates. Though Nucor was known for economically constructing new facilities, its engineering and construction team consisted of only three individuals. They did not attempt to specify exact equipment parameters, but asked the equipment supplier to provide this information and then held the manufacturer accountable. They had alliances with selected construction companies around the country who knew the kind of work Nucor wanted. Nucor bought 95 percent of its scrap steel from an independent broker who followed the market and made recommendations regarding scrap purchases. Nucor did not have a corporate advertising department, corporate public relations department, or a corporate legal or environmental department; however, it did have long-term relationships with outsiders to provide these services.

The steel industry had established a pattern of absorbing the cost of shipments so that, regardless of the distance from the mill, all users paid the same delivered price. Nucor broke with this tradition and stopped equalizing freight. It offered all customers the same sales terms—price plus actual shipping costs. Nucor gave no volume discounts, feeling that with modern computer systems, there was no justification. Customers located next to the plant guaranteed themselves the lowest possible costs for steel purchases. Two tube manufacturers, two steel service centers, and a cold-rolling facility were located adjacent to the Arkansas plant. These facilities accounted for 60 percent of the shipments from the mill.

The plants were linked electronically to each other's production schedules, thereby allowing them to function in a just-in-time inventory mode. All new mills were built on large enough tracts of land to accommodate collaborating businesses.

Iverson didn't feel greater centralization would be good for Nucor. Hamilton Lott, a Vulcraft plant manager, commented in 1997: "We're truly autonomous; we can duplicate efforts made in other parts of Nucor. We might develop the same computer program six times. But the advantages of local autonomy make it worth it." Joe Rutkowski, manager at Darlington steel, agreed: "We're not constrained; headquarters doesn't restrict what I spend. I just have to make my profit contribution at the end of year."

South magazine observed that Iverson had established a characteristic organizational style described as "stripped down" and "no nonsense." "Jack Benny would like this company," observed Roland Underhill, an analyst with Crowell, Weedon and Co. of Los Angeles, "so would Peter Drucker." Underhill pointed out that Nucor's thriftiness didn't end with its "spartan" office staff or modest offices. "There are no corporate perquisites," he stated, "No company planes, No country club memberships. No company cars."

Fortune noted, "Iverson takes the subway when he is in New York, a Wall Street analyst reports in a voice that suggests both admiration and amazement." The general managers reflected this style in the operation of their individual divisions. Their offices were more like plant offices or the offices of private companies built around manufacturing rather than for public appeal. They were simple, routine, and businesslike.

Division Managers

The corporate personnel manager described management relations as informal, trusting, and not "bureaucratic." There was a minimum of paperwork, a phone call was more common than memos, and no confirming memo was thought to be necessary.

A Vulcraft manager commented: "We have what I would call a very friendly spirit of competition from one plant to the next. And, of course, all of the vice presidents and general managers share the same bonus systems, so we are in this together as a team even though we operate our divisions individually."

The divisions managed their activities with a minimum of contact with the corporate staff. Each day disbursements were reported to corporate office. Payments flowed into regional lockboxes. On a weekly basis, joist divisions reported total quotes, sales cancellations, backlogs, and production. Steel mills reported tons rolled, outside shipments, orders, cancellations, and backlog.

Each month, the divisions completed a brief operations analysis, which was sent to all the managers. Its three main purposes were (1) financial consolidation, (2) sharing information among the divisions, and (3) corporate management examination. The summarized information and the performance statistics for all the divisions were then returned to the managers.

The general managers met three times a year. In late October they presented preliminary budgets and capital requests. In late February they met to finalize budgets and deal with miscellaneous matters. Then, at a meeting in May, they handled personnel matters, such as wage increases and changes of policies or benefits. The general managers, as a group, considered the raises for the department heads, the next lower level of management for all the plants.

Vulcraft: The Joist Divisions. One of Nucor's major businesses was the manufacture and sale of open web steel joists and joist girders at Vulcraft divisions located in Florence, South Carolina; Norfolk, Nebraska; Ft. Payne, Alabama; Grapeland, Texas; St. Joe, Indiana; Brigham City, Utah; and Chemung, New York. Open web joists, in contrast to solid joists, were made of steel angle iron separated by round bars or smaller angle iron (see Exhibit 2). These joists cost less, were of greater

Exhibit 2 Nucor's Vulcraft Group

BARTLE HALL
CONVENTION CENTER

Kansas City, Missouri

NUCOR
VULCRAFT - GROUP

strength for many applications, and were used primarily as the roof support systems in larger buildings, such as warehouses and shopping malls.

The joist industry was characterized by high competition among many manufacturers for many small customers. With a large percentage of the market, Nucor had been the largest supplier of joists in the United States since 1975. It utilized national advertising campaigns and prepared competitive bids on 80 to 90 percent of the buildings using joists. Competition was based on price and delivery performance. Nucor had developed computer programs to prepare designs for customers and to compute bids based on current prices and labor standards. In addition, each Vulcraft plant maintained its own engineering department to help customers with design problems or specifications. The Florence manager commented, "Here on the East Coast we have six or seven major competitors; of course none of them are as large as we are." He added, "It has been said to us by some of our competitors that in this particular industry we have the finest selling organization in the country."

Nucor aggressively sought to be the lowest-cost producer in the industry. Materials and freight were two important elements of cost. Nucor maintained its own fleet of almost 150 trucks to ensure on-time delivery all over the country, although most business was regional due to transportation costs. Plants were located in rural areas near the markets they served. Nucor's move into steel production was a move to lower the cost of steel used by the joist business.

On the basic assembly line used at the joist divisions, three or four of which might make up any one plant, about six tons of joists per hour would be assembled. In the first stage, eight people cut the angles to the right lengths or bend the round bars to the desired form. These were moved on a roller conveyer to six-man assembly stations, where the component parts would be tacked together for the next stage, which was welding. Drilling and miscellaneous work were done by three people between the lines. The nine-man welding station completed the welds before passing the joists on roller conveyers to two-man inspection teams. The last step before shipment was the painting.

The workers had control over and were responsible for quality. There was an independent quality control inspector who had the authority to reject the run of joists and cause them to be reworked. The quality control people were not under the incentive system and reported to the engineering department.

Daily production might vary widely, since each joist was made for a specific job. The wide range of joists made control of the workload at each station difficult; bottlenecks might arise anywhere along the line. Each workstation was responsible for identifying such bottlenecks so that the foreman could reassign people promptly to maintain productivity. Because workers knew most of the jobs on the line, including the more skilled welding jobs, they could be shifted as needed to avoid bottlenecks.

There were four lines of about 28 people each on two shifts at the Florence division. The jobs on the line were rated on responsibility and assigned a base wage, from $11 to $13 per hour in 1999. In addition, a weekly bonus was paid on the total output of each line. Each worker received the same percentage bonus based on their base wage. The Texas plant had a typical bonus of 225 percent, giving workers an average wage of $27 an hour.

The amount of time required to make a joist had been established over time. As a job was bid, the cost of each joist was determined through the computer program. The time required depended on the length, number of panels, and depth of the joist. At the time of production, the labor value of production, the standard, was determined in a similar manner. The general manager of the South Carolina plant stated, "In the last nine or ten years, we have not changed a standard." The Grapeland plant maintained a time chart based on the time jobs usually take, which was used to estimate the labor required on a job. The plant teams' bonuses were measured against this time.

Steel Divisions. Nucor moved into the steel business in 1968 to provide raw material for the Vulcraft plants. Iverson said, "We got into the steel business because we wanted to build a mill that could make steel as cheaply as we were buying it from foreign importers or from offshore mills." Thus, they entered the industry using the new mini-mill technology after they took a task force of four people around the world to investigate new technological advancements. A case writer from Harvard recounted the development of the steel divisions:

By 1967 about 60 percent of each Vulcraft sales dollar was spent on materials, primarily steel. Thus, the goal of keeping costs low made it imperative to obtain steel economically. In addition, in 1967 Vulcraft bought about 60 percent of its steel from foreign sources. As the Vulcraft Division grew, Nucor became concerned about its ability to obtain an adequate economical supply of steel and, in 1968, began construction of its first steel mill in Darlington, South Carolina. By 1972 the Florence, South Carolina, joist plant was purchasing over 90 percent of its steel from this mill. The Fort Payne, Alabama plant bought about 50 percent of its steel from Florence. Since the mill had excess capacity, Nucor began to market its steel products to outside customers. In 1972, 75 percent of the shipments of Nucor steel were to Vulcraft and 25 percent were to other customers.

Between 1973 and 1981, Nucor built three more bar mills and their accompanying rolling mills to convert the billets into bars, flats, rounds, channels, and other products. Iverson explained in 1984:

In constructing these mills we have experimented with new processes and new manufacturing techniques. We serve as our own general contractor and design and build much of our own equipment. In one or more of our mills, we have built our own continuous casting unit, reheat furnaces, cooling beds, and, in Utah, even our own mill stands. All of these to date have cost under $125 per ton of annual capacity—compared with projected costs for large integrated mills of $1,200-1,500 per ton of annual capacity, ten times our cost. Our mills have high productivity. We currently use less than four man-hours to produce a ton of steel. Our total employment costs are less than $60 per ton compared with the average employment costs of the seven largest U.S. steel companies of close to $130 per ton. Our total labor costs are less than 20 percent of our sales price.

In 1987, Nucor was the first steel company in the world to begin to build a mini-mill to manufacture steel sheet, the raw material for the auto industry and other major manufacturers. This project opened up another 50 percent of the total steel market. The first plant in Crawfordsville, Indiana, was successful, and three additional sheet mills were constructed in 1989 and 1990. During the next several years, these steel plants were significantly modernized and expanded. By 1999, their total capacity was three million tons per year at a capital cost of less than $170 per ton. Nucor's total steel production capacity was 5.9 million tons per year at a cost of $300 per ton of annual capacity. The eight mills sold 80 percent of their output to outside customers and the balance to other Nucor divisions.

The Steelmaking Processing

A steel mill's work is divided into two phases, preparation of steel of the proper "chemistry" and the forming of the steel into the desired products. The typical mini-mill utilizes scrap steel, such as junk auto parts, instead of the iron ore, which would be used in larger, integrated steel mills. The typical bar mini-mill had an annual capacity of 200 to 600 thousand tons, compared with the seven million tons of Bethlehem Steel's integrated plant in Sparrow's Point, Maryland.

In the bar mills, a charging bucket fed loads of scrap steel into electric arc furnaces. The melted load, called a "heat," was poured into a ladle to be carried by overhead crane to the casting machine. In the casting machine, the liquid steel was extruded as a continuous red-hot solid bar of steel and cut into lengths weighing some 900 pounds called "billets." In the typical plant the billet,

about four inches across and about 20 feet long, was held temporarily in a pit where it cooled to normal temperatures. Periodically, billets were carried to the rolling mill and placed in a reheat oven to bring them up to 2,000°F at which temperance they would be malleable. In the rolling mill, presses and dies progressively converted the billet into the desired round bars, angles, channels, flats, and other products. After cutting to standard lengths, they were moved to the warehouse.

Nucor's first steel mill, which employed more than 500 people, was located in Darlington, South Carolina. The mill, with its three electric arc furnaces, operated 24 hours per day, five-and-a-half days per week. Nucor made a number of improvements in the melting and casting operations. Thus, less time and lower capital investment were required at Darlington than at older mini-mills The casting machines were "continuous casters," as opposed to the old batch method.

Not all of Nucor's research projects were successful. The company spent approximately $2,000,000 in an unsuccessful effort to utilize resistance heating. Even more was lost from an effort at induction melting. As Iverson told *Metal Producing*, "That costs us a lot of money. Time wise it was very expensive. But you have got to make mistakes and we've had lots of failures."

The Darlington design became the basis for plants in Nebraska, Texas, and Utah. The Texas plant cost less than $80 per ton of annual capacity. Whereas the typical mini-mill at the time cost approximately $250 per ton, the average cost of Nucor's four mills was under $135. An integrated mill was expected to cost between $1,200 and $1,500 per ton.

The Darlington plant was organized into 12 natural groups for the purpose of incentive pay. Two mills each had two shifts with three groups: melting and casting, rolling mill, and finishing. In melting and casting there were three or four different standards, depending on the material. These standards had been established by the department manager years ago based on historical performance and were never adjusted. The caster, the key to the operation, was used at a 92 percent level—greater than the claims of the manufacturer. For every good ton of billet above the standard hourly rate for the week, workers in the group received a 4 percent bonus. Workers received a 4 to 6 percent bonus for every good ton sheared per hour for the week over the computed standard. A manager stated: "Meltshop employees don't ask me how much it costs Chaparral or LTV to make a billet. They want to know what it costs Darlington, Norfolk, Jewitt to put a billet on the ground—scrap costs, alloy costs, electrical costs, refractory, gas, etc. Everybody from Charlotte to Plymouth watches the nickels and dimes."

Management Philosophy

Aycock, while still the Darlington manager, stated:

The key to making a profit when selling a product with no aesthetic value, or a product that you really can't differentiate from your competitors, is cost. I don't look at us as a fantastic marketing organization, even though I think we are pretty good; but we don't try to overcome unreasonable costs by mass marketing. We maintain low costs by keeping the employee force at the level it should be, not doing things that aren't necessary to achieve our goals, and allowing people to function on their own and by judging them on their results.

To keep a cooperative and productive workforce you need, number one, to be completely honest about everything; number two, to allow each employee as much as possible to make decisions about that employee's work, to find easier and more productive ways to perform duties; and number three, to be as fair as possible to all employees. Most of the changes we make in work procedures and in equipment come from the employees. They really know the problems of their jobs better than anyone else.

To communicate with my employees, I try to spend time in the plant, and, at intervals, have meetings with the employees. Usually, if they have a question, they just visit me. Recently a small group visited me in my office to discuss our vacation policy. They had some suggestions and, after listening to them, I had to agree that the ideas were good.

In discussing his philosophy for dealing with the workforce, the Florence manager stated:

I believe very strongly in the incentive system we have. We are a non-union shop and we all feel that the way to stay so is to take care of our people and show them we care. I think that's easily done because of our fewer layers of management…I spend a good part of my time in the plant, maybe an hour or so a day. If a man wants to know anything, for example an insurance question, I'm there and they walk right up to me and ask me questions, which I'll answer the best I know how.

We don't lay our people off and we make a point of telling our people this. In the slowdown of 1994, we scheduled our line for four days, but the men were allowed to come in the fifth day for maintenance work at base pay. The men in the plant on an average running bonus might make $17 to $19 an hour. If their base pay is half that, on Friday they would only get $8 to $9 an hour. Surprisingly, many of the men did not want to come in on Friday. They felt comfortable with just working four days a week. They are happy to have that extra day off. About 20 percent of the people took the fifth day at base rate, but still no one had been laid off, in an industry with a strong business cycle.

In an earlier business cycle, the executive committee decided in view of economic conditions that a pay freeze was necessary. The employees normally received an increase in their base pay on the first of June. The decision was made at that time to freeze wages. The officers of the company, as a show of good faith, accepted a 5 percent pay cut. Management held meetings with the production workers to explain the economic crisis the company faced and to address any employee questions.

Personnel Policies

Nucor provided an incentive plan and job security. All employees at Nucor received the same fringe benefits and there was only one group insurance plan. Holidays and vacations did not differ by job. Every child of every Nucor employee received up to $1,200 a year for four years if they chose to go on to higher education, including technical schools. The company had no executive dining rooms or restrooms, no fishing lodges, company cars, or reserved parking places.

Jim Coblin, Nucor's vice president of human resources at the time, described Nucor's systems for *HR Magazine* in a 1994 article, "No frills HR at Nucor: a lean, bottom-line approach at this steel company empowers employees." Coblin, as benefits administrator, received part-time help from one of the corporate secretaries in the corporate office. The plants typically used someone from their finance department to handle compensation issues, although two plants had personnel generalists. Nucor plants did not have job descriptions, finding they caused more problems than they solved, given the flexible workforce and non-union status of Nucor employees. Surprisingly, Coblin found performance appraisal a waste of time. If an employee was not performing well, the problem would be dealt with directly. The key, he believed, was not to put a maximum on what employees could earn and pay them directly for productivity. Iverson firmly believed that the bonus should be direct and involve no discretion on part of a manager.

Employees were kept informed about the company. Charts showing the division's results in return-on-assets and bonus payoff were posted in prominent places in the plant. The personnel manager commented that as he traveled around to all the plants, he found everyone in the company could tell him the level of profits in their division. The general managers held dinners at least once a year with their employees. The dinners were held with 50 or 60 employees at a time, resulting in as many as 20 dinners per year for the general managers. After introductory remarks, the floor was opened for discussion of any work-related problems. There was a new employee orientation program and an employee handbook that contained personnel policies and rules. The corporate office sent all news releases to each division where they were posted on bulletin boards. Each employee in the company also received a copy of the annual report. For the last several years, the cover of the annual report contained the names of all Nucor employees.

Absenteeism and tardiness were not a problem at Nucor. Each employee had four days of absences before pay was reduced. In addition to these, missing work was allowed for jury duty, military leave, or the death of close relatives. After this, a day's absence cost the employee bonus pay for that week and lateness of more than a half-hour meant the loss of bonus for that day.

Safety was a concern of Nucor's critics. Nucor plants had 10 fatalities in the 1980s, but after safety administrators were appointed at each plant, safety improved in the 1990s. The company also had a formal grievance procedure, although the Darlington manager couldn't recall the last grievance he had processed.

The average hourly worker's pay was more than twice the average paid by other manufacturing companies in the states where Nucor's plants were located. In many rural communities, Nucor provided better wages than most other manufacturers. The plant in Hertford County illustrated this point. A June 21, 1998, article in The Charlotte Observer entitled "Hope on the Horizon: In Hertford County, Poverty Reigns and Jobs are Scarce" reported, "In North Carolina's forgotten northeastern corner, where poverty rates run more than twice the state average, Nucor's $300 million steel mill is a dream realized." The plant on the banks of the Chowan River saw employees earning up to three times the average local manufacturing wage. Nucor's desire to have other companies in the field close by to save on shipping costs led to four companies announcing they would locate close to Nucor's property, adding another 100 to 200 jobs. People couldn't believe such wages, but the average wage for these jobs at the Darlington plant was $70,000 and it was thought that this plant paid similarly. The plant CFO added that Nucor didn't try to set its pay "a buck over Wal-Mart" but instead went for the best workers. The article noted that steelwork is hot and often dangerous, and that turnover at the plant may be high as people adjust to the nature of the work and Nucor's hard-driving team system. He added, "Slackers don't last." The local preacher said, "In 15 years, Baron (a local child) will be making $75,000 a year at Nucor, not in jail. I have a place now I can hold in front of him and say 'Look, right here. This is for you.'"

In early 2009, Nucor's unique policies with its employees were still evident. Despite the economic crisis, performance in 2008 was excellent and $40 million in bonuses were distributed, with an extra bonus on top because of the extraordinary year. The company paid $270 million in profit sharing. Gail Bruce, the new vice president of human resources, explained how Nucor had avoided the layoffs other plants experienced. First, there was a history of open communications and a system designed to deal with the nature of the industry and educate workers about it. If plants were idled, pay automatically went to base pay, which was about half the usual total income with bonuses. No one was laid off and the well-paid workers could adapt, just like the company. He marveled, "The spirit in the operations is extraordinary." The cooperation extended to other solutions. BusinessWeek reported, "Work that used to be done by contractors, such as making special parts, mowing the lawns, and even cleaning the bathrooms, is now handled by Nucor staff. The bathrooms, managers say, [were] an employee suggestion." BusinessWeek reported that DiMicco and other managers received hundreds of cards and e-mails thanking them for caring about workers and their families.

The Incentive System

There were four incentive programs at Nucor, one each for (1) production workers, (2) department heads, (3) staff people, such as accountants, secretaries, or engineers, and (4) senior management, which included the division managers (VP/general managers of each division). All of these programs were based on group performance.

Within the production program, groups ranged in size from 25 to 30 people and had definable and measurable operations. The company believed that a program should be simple and that bonuses should be paid promptly. "We don't have any discretionary bonuses—zero. It is all based on performance. Now we don't want anyone to sit in judgment, because it never is fair…" said Iverson. Bonuses are based on roughly 90 percent of the historical time it takes to make a particular joist. If, for example, that week the joists are produced 40 percent faster than the standard time, workers get a 40 percent bonus in their pay the following week. The complete paycheck amount, including overtime, was multiplied by the bonus factor. A bonus was not paid when equipment was not operating. The foremen were also part of the group and received the same bonus as the employees they supervised.

The second incentive program was for department heads in the various divisions. The incentive pay here was based on division contribution, defined as the division earnings before corporate expenses and profit sharing are determined. Bonuses were reported to run between 0 and 90 percent (averaging more than 50 percent) of base salary. The base salaries at this level were set at 75 percent of industry norms.

There was a third plan for people who were not production workers, department managers, or senior managers. Their bonuses were based on either the division return-on-assets or the corporate return-on-assets, depending on their unit. Bonuses were typically 30 percent or more of a person's base salary for corporate positions.

The fourth program was for the senior officers. This group had no employment contracts, pension or retirement plans, or other perquisites. Their base salaries were set at about 75 percent of what an individual doing similar work in other companies would receive. Once return-on-equity reached 9 percent (slightly below the average for manufacturing firms) 5 percent of net earnings before taxes went into a pool, which was divided among the officers based on their salaries. For example, if the return-on-equity for the company reaches 20 percent, then senior officers can wind up with as much as 190 percent of their base salaries and 115 percent on top of that in stock. Half of the bonus was paid in cash and half was deferred. Individual bonuses ranged from zero to several hundred percent, averaging 75 to 150 percent.

However, the opposite was true as well. In 1982 the return was 8 percent and the executives received no bonus. Iverson's pay in 1981 was approximately $300,000 but dropped the next year to $110,000. "I think that ranked by total compensation I was the lowest paid CEO in the *Fortune* 500. I was kind of proud of that, too." In his 1997 book *Plain Talk: Lessons from a Business Maverick*, Iverson said, "Can management expect employees to be loyal if we lay them all off at every dip of the economy, while we go on padding our own pockets?" Even so, by 1986 Iverson's stock was worth over $10 million, and the former Vulcraft manager was a multimillionaire.

In lieu of a retirement plan, the company had a profit-sharing plan with a deferred trust. Each year 10 percent of pretax earnings were put into profit sharing for all employees below officer level. Twenty percent of this was set aside to be paid to employees the following March as a cash bonus, and the remainder was put into trust for each employee on the basis of a percentage of their earnings as a percentage of total wages paid within the corporation. The employee was vested after the first year. Employees received a quarterly statement of their balance in profit sharing.

The company had an Employer Monthly Stock Investment Plan into which Nucor added 10 percent to the amount the employee contributed to the purchase of any Nucor stock and paid the commission. For each five years of service with the company, the employee received a service award consisting of five shares of Nucor stock. Moreover, if profits were good, extraordinary bonus payments would be made to the employees. For example, in December 1998 each employee received an $800 payment.

According to Iverson:

I think the first obligation of the company is to the stockholder and to its employees. I find in this country too many cases where employees are underpaid and corporate management is making huge social donations for self-fulfillment. We regularly give donations, but we have a very interesting corporate policy. First, we give donations where our employees are. Second, we give donations that will benefit our employees, such as to the YMCA. It is a difficult area and it requires a lot of thought. There is certainly a strong social responsibility for a company, but it cannot be at the expense of the employees or the stockholders.

Having welcomed a parade of visitors over the years, Iverson became concerned with the pattern apparent at other companies' steel plants: "They only do one or two of the things we do. It's not just incentives or the scholarship program; it's all those things put together that results in a unified philosophy for the company."

Building on Their Success

Throughout the 1980s and 1990s, Nucor continued to take the initiative and be the prime mover in steel as well as the industries vertically related to steel. For example, in 1984 Nucor broke the industry pattern of basing the price of an order of steel on the quantity ordered. Iverson noted, "Some time ago we began to realize that with computer order entry and billing, the extra charge for smaller orders was not cost justified." In a seemingly risky move, in 1986 Nucor began construction of a $25 million plant in Indiana to manufacture steel fasteners. Imports had grown to 90 percent of this market as U.S. companies failed to compete. Iverson said "We're going to bring that business back; we can make bolts as cheaply as foreign producers." A second plant, which opened in 1995, gave Nucor 20 percent of the U.S. market for steel fasteners. Nucor also acquired a steel bearings manufacturer in 1986, which Iverson called "a good fit with our business, policies, and our people."

In early 1986, Iverson announced plans for a revolutionary plant at Crawfordsville, Indiana, that would be the first mini-mill in the world to manufacture flat-rolled or sheet steel, the last bastion of the integrated manufacturers. This market alone was twice the size of the existing market for mini-mill products. It would be a $250 million gamble on new technology. The plant was expected to halve the integrated manufacturer's labor cost of $3 per ton and save $50 to $75 on a $400-per-ton selling price. If it worked, the profit from this plant alone would come close to the profit of the whole corporation. *Forbes* commented, "If any mini-mill can meet the challenge, it's Nucor. But expect the going to be tougher this time around." If successful, Nucor would have the licensing rights to the next two plants built in the world with this technology. Nucor had spent millions trying to develop the process when it heard of some promising developments at a German company. In the spring of 1986, Aycock flew to Germany to see the pilot machine at SMS Schloemann-Siemag AG. In December the Germans came to Charlotte for the first of what they thought would be many meetings to hammer out a deal with Nucor. Iverson shocked them when he announced Nucor was ready to build the first plant of its kind.

Keith Busse was named general manager and put in charge of building the Crawfordsville steel sheet plant. The process of bringing this plant online was so exciting it became the basis for a best-selling book by Robert Preston, which was serialized in *The New Yorker*. Preston reported on a conversation during construction between Iverson and Busse. Thinking about the future, Busse was worried that Nucor might someday become like Big Steel. He asked, "How do we allow Nucor to grow without expanding the bureaucracy?" He didn't want to see Nucor end up like other companies with overlapping people doing the same job. Iverson agreed. Busse seriously suggested, "Maybe we're going to need group vice-presidents." Iverson's heated response was, "Do you want to ruin the company? That's the old Harvard Business School thinking. They would only get in the way, slow us down." He said the company could at least double in size before it added a new level of management. "I hope that by the time we have group vice-presidents I'll be collecting Social Security," he said.

The gamble on the new plant paid off, and Busse became a key man at Nucor. The new mill began operations in August 1989 and reached 15 percent of capacity by the end of the year. In June 1990 it had its first profitable month and Nucor announced the construction of a second plant in Arkansas.

The supply and cost of scrap steel to feed the mini-mills were an important future concern to Iverson. In 1993 Nucor announced the construction of plant in Trinidad to supply its mills with iron carbide pellets. The innovative plant would cost $60 million and take a year and a half to complete. In 1994 the two existing sheet mills were expanded and a new $500 million, 1.8-million-ton sheet mill in South Carolina was announced, to begin operation in early 1997.

In 1987, in what *The New York Times* called their "most ambitious project yet," Nucor began a joint venture with Yamato Kogyo, Ltd. to make structural steel products in a mill on the Mississippi River in direct challenge to the Big Three integrated steel companies. John Correnti was put in charge of the operation. Correnti built and then became the general manager of Nucor-Yamato when it started up in 1988. In 1991 he surprised many people by deciding to double Nucor-Yamato's capacity by 1994. It became Nucor's largest division and the largest wide-flange producer in the United States. By 1995, Bethlehem Steel was the only other wide-flange producer of structural steel products left and had plans to leave the business.

Nucor started up its first facility to produce metal buildings in 1987. A second metal buildings facility began operations in late 1996 in South Carolina and a new steel deck facility in Alabama was announced for 1997. At the end of 1997, the Arkansas sheet mill underwent a $120 million expansion to include a galvanizing facility.

In 1995, Nucor became involved in its first international venture, an ambitious project with Brazil's Companhia Siderurgica National to build a $700 million steel mill in the state of Ceara. While other mini-mills were cutting deals to buy and sell abroad, Nucor was planning to ship iron from Brazil and process it in Trinidad.

Nucor set records for sales and net earnings in 1997. Although sales for 1998 decreased 1 percent and net earnings were down 10 percent, the management made a number of long-term investments and closed draining investments. Startup began at the new South Carolina steam mill and at the Arkansas sheet mill expansion. The plans for a North Carolina steel plate mill in Hertford were announced. This would bring Nucor's total steel production capacity to 12 million tons per year. Moreover, the plant in Trinidad, which had proven much more expensive than was originally expected, was deemed unsuccessful and closed. Finally, directors approved the repurchase of up to five million shares of Nucor stock.

Still, the downward trends at Nucor continued. Sales and earnings were down 3 percent and 7 percent, respectively, for 1999. However, these trends did not seem to affect the company's investments. Expansion was under way in the steel mills and a third building systems facility was under construction in Texas. Nucor actively searched for a site for a joist plant in the Northeast. A letter of intent was signed with Australian and Japanese companies to form a joint venture to commercialize the strip casting technology. To understand the challenges facing Nucor, industry, technology, and environmental trends in the 1980s and 1990s have to be considered.

Evolution of the U.S. Steel Industry

The early 1980s were the worst years in decades for the steel industry. Data from the American Iron and Steel Institute showed shipments falling from 100 million tons in 1979 to around 85 million tons in 1980 and 1981.

A slackening in the economy, particularly in auto sales, led the decline. In 1986, when industry capacity was at 130 million tons, the outlook was for a continued decline in per-capita consumption and movement towards the 90 to 100 million-ton range. The chairman of Armco saw "millions of tons chasing a market that's not there: excess capacity that must be eliminated."

The large, integrated steel firms, such as U.S. Steel and Armco, which made up the major part of the industry, were the hardest hit. The *Wall Street Journal* stated, "The decline has resulted from such problems as high labor and energy costs in mining and processing iron ore, a lack of profits and capital to modernize plants, and conservative management that has hesitated to take risks." These companies produced a wide range of steels, primarily from ore processed in blast furnaces. They found it difficult to compete with imports, usually from Japan. They sought the protection of import quotas.

Imported steel accounted for 20 percent of the U.S. steel consumption, up from 12 percent in the early 1970s. The U.S. share of world production of raw steel declined from 19 percent to 14 percent during the period. *Iron Age* stated that exports, as a percentage of shipments in 1985, were 34 percent for Nippon, 26 percent for British Steel, 30 percent for Krupp, 49 percent for USINOR of France, and less than 1 percent for every American producer on the list. The consensus of steel experts was that imports would average 23 percent of the market in the last half of the 1980s.

By the mid-1980s, the integrated mills were moving fast to get back into the game: they were restructuring, cutting capacity, dropping unprofitable lines, focusing products, and trying to become responsive to the market. The industry made a pronounced move toward segmentation. Integrated producers focused on mostly flat-rolled and structural grades; reorganized steel companies focused on a limited range of products; mini-mills dominated the bar and light structural product areas; and specialty steel firms sought niches. There was an accelerated shutdown of older plants, elimination of products by some firms, and the installation of new product lines with new technologies by others.

The road for the integrated mills was not easy. As *Purchasing* pointed out, tax laws and accounting rules slowed the closing of inefficient plants. Shutting down a 10,000-person plant could require a firm to hold a cash reserve of $100 million to fund health, pension, and insurance liabilities. The chairman of Armco commented: "Liabilities associated with a planned shutdown are so large that they can quickly devastate a company's balance sheet."

Joint ventures were formed to produce steel for a specific market or region. The chairman of USX called them "an important new wrinkle in steel's fight for survival" and stated, "If there had been more joint ventures like these two decades ago, the U.S. steel industry might have built only half of the dozen or so hot-strip mills it put up in that time and avoided today's over-capacity."

The American Iron and Steel Institute reported steel production in 1988 of 99.3 million tons, up from 89.2 in 1987 and the highest in seven years. As a result of modernization programs, 60.9 percent of production was from continuous casters. Exports for steel increased and imports fell. Some steel experts believed the United States was now cost competitive with Japan. However, 1989 proved to be a year of "waiting for the other shoe to drop," according to *Metal Center News*. U.S. steel production was hampered by a new recession, the expiration of the voluntary import restraints, and labor negotiations in several companies. Declines in car production and consumer goods hit flat-rolled steel hard. AUJ Consultants told MCN, "The U.S. steel market has peaked. Steel consumption is trending down. By 1990, we expect total domestic demand to dip under 90 million tons."

The economic slowdown of the early 1990s did lead to a decline in the demand for steel through early 1993, but by 1995 America was in its best steel market in 20 years and many companies were building new flat-roll mini-mills. A *BusinessWeek* article at the time described it as "the race of the Nucor look-alikes." Six years after Nucor pioneered the low-cost German technology in Crawfordsville, competitors were finally gearing up to compete. Ten new projects were expected to add 20 million tons per year of the flat-rolled steel, raising U.S. capacity by as much as 40 percent by 1998. These mills opened in 1997, just as the industry was expected to move into a cyclical slump. It was no surprise that worldwide competition increased and companies that had previously focused on their home markets began a race to become global powerhouses. The foreign push was new for U.S. firms who had focused on defending their home markets. U.S. mini-mills focused their international expansion primarily in Asia and South America.

Meanwhile, in 1994, U.S. Steel, North America's largest integrated steel producer, began a major business process re-engineering project to improve order fulfillment performance and customer satisfaction on the heels of a decade of restructuring. According to *Steel Times International*, "U.S. Steel had to completely change the way it did business. Cutting labor costs and increasing reliability and productivity took the company a long way towards improving profitability and competitiveness. However, it became clear that this leaner organization still had to implement new technologies and business processes if it was to maintain a competitive advantage." The goals of the business process re-engineering project included a sharp reduction in cycle time, greatly decreased levels of inventory, shorter order lead times, and the ability to offer real-time promise dates to customers. In 1995, they successfully installed integrated planning/production/order fulfillment software, and results were very positive. U.S. Steel believed that the re-engineering project had positioned it for a future of increased competition, tighter markets, and raised customer expectations.

In late 1997 and again in 1998, the decline in demand prompted Nucor and other U.S. companies to slash prices in order to compete with the unprecedented surge of imports. By the last quarter of 1998, these imports had led to the filing of unfair trade complaints with U.S. trade regulators, causing steel prices in the spot market to drop sharply in August and September before they stabilized. A press release from William Daley, the U.S. Secretary of Commerce, stated, "I will not stand by and allow U.S. workers, communities and companies to bear the brunt of other nations' problematic policies and practices. We are the most open economy of the world. But we are not the world's dumpster."

The Commerce Department concluded in March 1999 that six countries had illegally dumped stainless steel in the United States at prices below production costs or home market prices. The Commerce Department found that Canada, South Korea, and Taiwan were guilty only of dumping, while Belgium, Italy, and South Africa also gave producers unfair subsidies that effectively lowered prices. However, on June 23, 1999, the *Wall Street Journal* reported that the Senate decisively shut off an attempt to restrict U.S. imports of steel despite industry complaints that a flood of cheap imports were driving them out of business. Reportedly President Clinton would have vetoed the bill anyway because it would violate international trade law and leave the United States vulnerable to retaliation.

The American Iron and Steel Institute reported that in May 1999, U.S. steel mills shipped 8,330,000 net tons, a decrease of 6.7 percent from the 8,927,000 net tons shipped in May 1998. They also stated that for the first five months of 1999, shipments were 41,205,000 net tons, down 10 percent from the same period in 1998. AISI president and CEO Andrew Sharkey III said, "Once again, the May data show clearly that America's steel trade crisis continues. U.S. steel companies and employees continue to be injured by high levels of dumping and subsidized imports … In addition, steel inventory levels remain excessive, and steel operating rates continue to be very low."

As the 1990s ended, Nucor was the second-largest steel producer in the United States, behind USX. The company's market capitalization was about two times that of the next smaller competitor. Even in a tight industry, someone can win. Nucor was in the best position because

the industry was very fragmented and there were many marginal competitors.

Steel Technology and the Mini-Mill

A new type of mill, the mini-mill, emerged in the United States in the 1970s to compete with the integrated mill. The mini-mill used electric arc furnaces initially to manufacture a narrow product line from scrap steel. The leading U.S. mini-mills in the 1980s were Nucor, Florida Steel, Georgetown Steel, North Star Steel, and Chaparral. Between the late 1970s and 1980s, the integrated mills' market share fell from about 90 percent to about 60 percent, with the integrated steel companies averaging a 7 percent return on equity, the mini-mills averaging 14 percent, and some, such as Nucor, achieving about 25 percent. In the 1990s, the integrated mills' market share fell to around 40 percent while mini-mills' share rose to 23 percent, reconstructed mills increased their share from 11 percent to 28 percent, and specialized mills increased their share from 1 to 6 percent.

Some experts believed that a relatively new technology, the twin shell electric arc furnace, would help mini-mills increase production and lower costs and take market share. According to the *Pittsburgh Business Times*, "With a twin shell furnace, one shell—the chamber holding the scrap to be melted—is filled and heated. During the heating of the first shell, the second shell is filled. When the heating is finished on the first shell, the electrodes move to the second. The first shell is emptied and refilled before the second gets hot." This increased production by 60 percent. Twin shell production had been widely adopted. Nucor Steel began running a twin shell furnace in November 1996 in Berkeley, South Carolina, and installed another in Norfolk, Nebraska, which began operation in 1997. "Everyone accepts twin shells as a good concept because there's a lot of flexibility of operation," said Rodney Mott, vice president and general manager of Nucor-Berkeley. However, this move toward twin shell furnaces was destined to affect scrap availability. According to an October 1997 quote in *Pittsburgh Business Times* by Ralph Smaller, vice president of process technology at Kvaerner, "Innovations that feed the electric furnaces' production of flat-rolled (steel) will increase the demand on high quality scrap and alternatives. The technological changes are just beginning and will accelerate over the next few years."

According to a September 1997 *Industry Week* article, steelmakers around the world were now closely monitoring the development of continuous "strip casting" technology, which many thought would prove to be the next leap forward for the industry. "The objective of strip casting is to produce thin strips of steel (in the 1-mm to 4-mm range) as liquid steel flows from a tundish—the stationary vessel which received molten steel from the ladle. It would eliminate the slab-casting stage and all of the rolling that now takes place in a hot mill." Strip casting was reported to have some difficult technological challenges but companies in Germany, France, Japan, Australia, Italy, and Canada had strip-casting projects under way. In fact, all of the significant development work in strip casting was taking place outside the United States.

Larry Kavanagh, American Iron and Steel Institute vice president for manufacturing and technology, said, "Steel is a very high-tech industry, but nobody knows it." The most-productive steelmaking facilities incorporate advanced metallurgical practices, sophisticated process-control sensors, state-of-the art computer controls, and the latest refinements in continuous casting and rolling mill technology. Michael Shot, vice president of manufacturing at Carpenter Technology Corp., a maker of specialty steels and premium-grade alloys, said, "You don't survive in this industry unless you have the technology to make the best products in the world in the most efficient manner."

Environmental and Political Issues

Not all stakeholders were happy with the way Nucor did business. In June 1998, *Waste News* reported that Nucor's mill in Crawfordsville was cited by the Environmental Protection Agency for alleged violations of federal and state clean-air rules. The Pamlico-Tar River Foundation, the North Carolina Coastal Federation, and the Environmental Defense Fund had concerns about the state's decision to allow the company to start building the plant before the environmental reviews were completed. According to the Charlotte *News & Observer,* "The environmental groups charge that the mill will discharge 6,720 tons of pollutants into the air each year."

Moreover, there were other concerns about the fast-track approval of the facility being built in Hertford County. This plant was to be located on the banks of one of the most important and sensitive stretches of the Chowan, a principal tributary to the Albemarle Sound and the last bastion of the state's once-vibrant river-herring fishery. North Carolina passed a law in 1997 that required the restoration of this fishery through a combination of measures designed to prevent overfishing, restore spawning and nursery habitats, and improve water quality in the Chowan. Another issue regarded the excessive incentives the state of North Carolina gave Nucor to build a $300 million steel mill there. Some questioned whether the promise of 300 well-paying jobs

in Hertford County was worth the $155 million in tax breaks the state was giving Nucor.

Management Evolution

Only five members of the board of directors were in attendance during their meeting in January 1999 due to the death of Jim Cunningham. Near the end of the meeting, Aycock read a motion, drafted by Siegel, that Ken Iverson be removed as chairman. It was seconded by Hlavacek and passed. This came as a surprise to Iverson. Prior to this time, in the spring of 1998, as Iverson approached his seventy-third birthday, he commented, "People ask me when I'm going to retire. I tell them our mandatory retirement age is 95, but I may change that when I get there." Now he was being forced out. It was announced that Iverson would be a chairman emeritus and a director, but after further disagreements, Iverson left the company completely. It was agreed, Iverson would receive $500,000 a year for five years. John Correnti succeeded Iverson in January 1999; but, he was voted out of this position in June 1999. At that time, David Aycock came out of retirement to become chairman, CEO, and president of Nucor.

All of this was a complete surprise to investors and brought the stock price down 10 percent. Siegel commented, "The board felt Correnti was not the right person to lead Nucor into the twenty-first century." Aycock assured everyone he would be happy to move back into retirement as soon as replacements could be found.

Aycock moved to increase the corporate office staff by adding a level of executive vice presidents over four areas of business and adding two specialist jobs in strategic planning and steel technology. When Siegel retired, Aycock promoted Terry Lisenby to CFO and treasurer and hired a director of IT to report to Lisenby (see Exhibit 3 for the organizational chart in 2000).

Jim Coblin, vice president of human resources, believed the additions to management were necessary, "It's not bad to get a little more like other companies." He noted that the various divisions did their business cards and plant signs differently; some did not even want a Nucor sign. Sometimes six different Nucor salesmen would call on the same customer. "There is no manager of human resources in the plants, so at least we needed to give additional training to the person who does most of that work at the plant," he stated. With these new additions there would be a director of information technology and two important committees, one for environmental issues and the second for audit.

Coblin believed the old system might have worked well when there was less competition. Aycock considered it "ridiculous." "It was not possible to properly manage,

Exhibit 3 Nucor Organization Chart, 2000

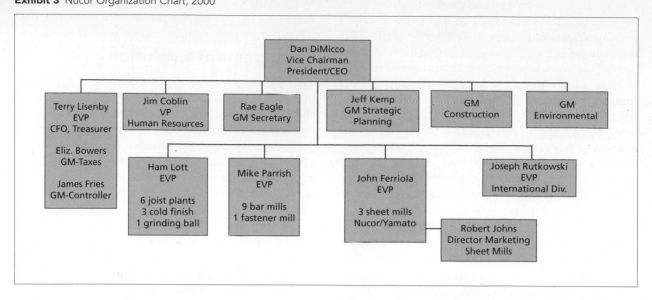

to know what was going on. The top managers have totally lost contact with the company." Coblin was optimistic the use of executive vice presidents would improve management. The three meetings of the general managers had slowly increased in length from about a day and a half to two-and-a-half days and became more focused. The new executive vice presidents would bring a perspective above the level of the individual plants. Instead of 15 individual detailed presentations, each general manager would give a short, five-minute briefing and then there would be an in-depth presentation on the group, with team participation. After some training by Lisenby, the divisions became pretty good with SWOT analysis. Coblin thought these changes would make Nucor a stronger global player.

To Jeff Kemp, the new general manager of strategic planning and business development, the big issue was how to sustain earnings growth. In the U.S. steel industry there were too many marginal competitors. The U.S. government had recently added to the problem by giving almost a billion dollars to nine struggling mills, which simply allowed them to limp along and weaken the industry. He was looking for Nucor's opportunities within the steel industry. His experience in the chemical industry suggested a need for Nucor to establish a position of superiority and grow globally, driving industry competition rather than reacting. He argued that a company should protect its overall market position, which could mean sacrifices for individual plants. Aycock liked Kemp's background in law and accounting and had specifically sought someone from outside the steel industry to head up Nucor's strategic planning. By June 2000, Kemp had conducted studies of other industries in the U.S. market and developed a working document which identified opportunities worthy of further analysis.

"Every company hits a plateau," Aycock observed, "You can't just go out and build plants to grow. How do you step up to the next level? I wouldn't say it's a turning point, but we have to get our strategic vision and strategic plans." Nucor had its first-ever strategic planning sessions. Aycock believed Nucor needed to be quick to recognize developing technology in all production areas. He noted the joint venture to develop a new strip caster. This new product could allow Nucor to build smaller plants closer to markets. This would be particularly helpful on the West Coast. Nucor would own the U.S. and Brazilian rights, their partners the rest. He was also looking forward to the next generation of steel mills and wanted to own the rights to them. He praised Iverson's skill at seeing technology and committing to it.

Aycock was very interested in acquisitions, but felt they must fit the company's strategic plans. A significant opportunity existed in pre-engineered buildings. Aycock intended to concentrate on steel for the next five to six years, achieving an average growth rate of 15 percent per year. In about seven years he wanted Nucor to be ready to move into other areas. He said Nucor had already "picked the low hanging grapes" and must be careful in its next moves.

Daniel DiMicco assumed the role of Nucor's president and chief executive officer in September 2000, when Aycock stepped down as planned. Peter Browning was elected chairman of the board of directors. Aycock retired from the board a year later.

Sales for 2000 increased 14 percent over 1999 to reach a record level. Earnings were also at record levels, up 27 percent over 1999. The year began strongly but business weakened by year's end. The good news was that Nucor had record profits while other steel companies faced bankruptcy. A Vulcraft plant was under construction in New York, their first northeastern operation. They were also attempting a breakthrough technological step in strip casting at Crawfordsville known as the Castrip process. They sold their Grinding Ball process and the Bearing Products operation because they were not a part of their core business.

In the company's annual report, DiMicco laid out their plans for 2000 and beyond: "Our targets are to deliver an average annual earnings growth of 10–15 percent over the next 10 years, to deliver a return well in excess of our cost of capital, to maintain a minimum average return on equity of 14 percent, and to deliver to return on sales of 8–10 percent. Our strategy will focus on Nucor becoming a 'Market Leader' in every product group and business in which we compete. This calls for significant increases in market share for many of our core products and the maintenance of market share where we currently enjoyed a leadership position." While pointing out that it would be impossible to obtain this success through the previous strategy of greenfield construction, he added, "There will now be a heavy focus on growth through acquisitions. We will also continue growing through the commercialization of new disruptive and leapfrog technologies."

Steel and Nucor in the Twenty-First Century

In early 2009, DiMicco reflected back on his nine-year tenure as CEO of Nucor with pride. These had been some of the steel industry's rockiest times, and yet under his leadership, Nucor had almost doubled in size (see Appendices 1, 2, and 3).

By October 2001, more than 20 steel companies in the United States, including Bethlehem Steel Corp. and LTV Corp., the nation's third- and fourth-largest U.S. steel producers, respectively, had filed for bankruptcy protection. Over a dozen producers were operating under Chapter 11 bankruptcy-law protection, which allowed them to maintain market share by selling steel cheaper than non–Chapter 11 steelmakers. On October 20, 2001, *The Economist* noted that of the 14 steel companies followed by Standard & Poor's, only Nucor was indisputably healthy. In the fall of 2001, 25 percent of domestic steel companies were in bankruptcy proceedings, although the United States was the largest importer of steel in the world. Experts believed that close to half of the U.S. steel industry might be forced to close before conditions improved.

In 2001, the world steel industry found itself in the middle of one of its most unprofitable and volatile periods ever, in part due to a glut of steel that had sent prices to 20-year lows. While domestic steel producers were mired in red ink, many foreign steelmakers desperately needed to continue to sell in the relatively open U.S. market to stay profitable. The industry was hovering around 75 percent capacity utilization, a level too low to be profitable for many companies. Three European companies—France's Usinor SA, Luxembourg's Arbed SA and Spain's Aceralia Corp.—merged to form the world's largest steel company. Two Japanese companies—NKK Corp. and Kawasaki Steel Corp.—merged to form the world's second-biggest steelmaker. These new mega-steelmakers could outmuscle U.S. competitors, which were less efficient, smaller, and financially weaker than their competitors in Asia and Europe. At this time, the largest U.S. steelmaker, USX-U.S. Steel Group, was only the eleventh-largest producer in the world. Furthermore, while in 1990 mini-mills accounted for 36 percent of the domestic steel market, by 2000 the more efficient mini-mill had seized 50 percent of the market and the resulting competition had driven prices lower for integrated steel as well as mini-mills.

The year 2001 turned out to be one of the worst ever for steel. There were the September 11th attacks, a recession, and a surge of imports. DiMicco broke with Nucor's traditional opposition to government intervention to make a major push for protective tariffs. He stated, "The need to enforce trade rules is similar to the need to enforce any other law. If two merchants have stores side by side, but one sells stolen merchandise at a vast discount, we know that it's time for the police to step in." In March 2002, President Bush, after an investigation and recommendation by the ITC, imposed anti-dumping tariffs under section 201 of the Trade Act of 1974. This restricted some imports of steel and placed quotas of up to 30 percent on others. The move was opposed by many, including steel users. Some criticized the president for abandoning free trade and pointed out that protection would hamper the necessary actions to restructure the steel industry in America by reducing excess capacity. The European Union immediately threatened reprisals and appealed to the WTO. In December, China imposed its own three-year program of import duties. Steel prices rose 40 percent in 2002 after the tariffs. Within a year, the price of hot-rolled steel increased to $260 per ton over the 20-year low of $210 during 2002. In November 2003, the WTO ruled against the tariffs and, under increasing pressure of retaliation, Bush withdrew them.

While many steel companies floundered, Nucor was able to take advantage of these conditions. In March 2001, Nucor made its first acquisition in 10 years, purchasing a mini-mill in New York from Sumitomo Corp. DiMicco commented, It's taken us three years before our team has felt this is the right thing to do and get started making acquisitions." In this challenged industry, he argued it would be cheaper to buy than build plants. Nucor made more purchases. They purchased the assets of Auburn Steel, which gave them a merchant bar presence in the Northeast and helped the new Vulcraft facility in New York. They acquired ITEC Steel, a leader in the emerging load-bearing light-gauge steel-framing market, and saw an opportunity to aggressively broaden its market. Nucor increased its sheet capacity by roughly one third when it acquired the assets of Trico Steel Co. in Alabama for $120 million. In early 2002, they acquired the assets of Birmingham Steel Corp. This $650 million purchase of four mini-mills was the largest acquisition in Nucor's history. However, 2002 also proved to be a difficult year for Nucor. While they increased their steelmaking capacity by more than 25 percent, revenue increased 11 percent, and earnings improved 43 percent over their weak numbers of 2001, their other financial goals were not met.

This did not stop Nucor from continuing its expansion through acquisitions to increase their market share and capacity in steel and by actively working on new production processes that would provide them with technological advantages. They acquired the U.S. and Brazilian rights to the promising Castrip process for strip casting. After development work on the process in Indiana, they began full-time production in May 2002 and produced 7,000 tons in the last 10 months of 2002. Moreover, in April, Nucor entered into a joint venture with a Brazilian mining company, CVRD, the world's largest producer of iron-ore pellets, to jointly develop low-cost iron-based products. Success with this effort would give them the ability to make steel by combining iron ore and coke rather than using scrap steel, which was becoming less available (as was once feared).

During 2003, prices of steel rose in the United States and Asia as global demand outpaced supply. China, with its booming economy, drove the market. World prices did not soar dangerously because the steel industry continued to be plagued by overcapacity, but steel-hungry China and other fast-growing nations added to their steel capacity to balance supply and demand.

In August 2003, imports of steel commodities into the United States fell 22 percent. A weakened dollar, the growing demand from China, and tariffs imposed in 2002 limited imports. Domestic capacity declined as producers consolidated, idled plants, or went out of business, which increased capacity utilization from 77.2 to 93.4 percent. Prices for iron ore and energy rose, affecting integrated producers. Mini-mills saw

their costs rise as worldwide demand for scrap rose. Thus, U.S. steelmakers boosted their prices. By February 2004, a growing coalition of U.S. steel producers and consumers was considering whether to petition to limit soaring exports of scrap steel from the United States, the world's largest producer of steel scrap. The United States had exported an estimated 12 million metric tons of steel scrap in 2003, a 21 percent increase from 2002. Moreover, the price of scrap steel had risen to $255 a ton. At the same time the price of hot-rolled sheet steel rose to $360 a ton. One result was that the International Steel Group (ISG) replaced Nucor as the most profitable U.S. steel producer. ISG was created when investor Wilbur Ross acquired the failing traditional steel producers in America, including LTV, Bethlehem, and Weirton. These mills used iron ore rather than scrap steel.

When 2003 ended, Nucor struck a positive note by reminding their investors that they had been profitable every single quarter since beginning operations in 1966. But, while Nucor set records for both steel production and steel shipments, net earnings declined 61 percent. While the steel industry struggled, Nucor increased its market share and held on to profitability. They worked on expanding their business with the automotive industry, continued their joint venture in Brazil to produce pig iron, and pursued a joint venture with the Japanese and Chinese to make iron without the usual raw materials. In February 2004, they were still "optimistic about the prospects for obtaining commercialization" of their promising Castrip process for strip casting in the United States and Brazil. The mini-mills could not produce sheet steel, a large share of the market. Moreover, Nucor was optimistic because trade laws were curtailing import dumping and Nucor expected higher margins.

Global competition continued. According to the *Wall Street Journal*, Posco Steelworks in Pohang, South Korea, enjoyed the highest profits in the global steel industry as of 2004. Moreover, *BusinessWeek* reported that the company had developed a new technology called Finex, which turned coal and iron ore into iron without coking and sintering and was expected to cut production costs by nearly a fifth and harmful emissions by 90 percent. They had also expanded their 80 Korean plants by investing in 14 Chinese joint ventures. By December 2004, demand in China had slowed and it had become a net steel exporter, sparking concerns of global oversupply.

Global consolidation also continued. In October 2004, London's Mittal family announced that they would merge their Ispat International NV with LNM Group and ISG, to create the world's largest steelmaker, with estimated annual revenue of $31.5 billion and output of 57 million tons. This would open a new chapter for the industry's consolidation, which had been mostly regional. Although the world's steel industry remained largely fragmented with the world's top 10 steelmakers supplying less than 30 percent of global production, Mittal Steel would have about 40 percent of the U.S. market in flat-rolled steel. Mittal, which had a history of using its scale to buy lower-cost raw materials and importing modern management techniques into previously inefficient state-run mills, was buying ISG, a U.S. company which already owned the lowest-cost, highest profit mills in the United States. In January 2005, Mittal also announced plans to buy 37 percent of China's Hunan Valin Iron & Steel Group Co.

In 2004 and 2005, Nucor continued its aggressive geographic expansion and introduction of new products. For example, Nuconsteel ("Nucon"), a wholly owned subsidiary of Nucor which specialized in load-bearing light-gauge steel-framing systems for commercial and residential construction markets, introduced two new low-cost automated fabrication systems for residential construction. In March 2005, Nucor formed a joint venture with Lennar Corporation, named Nextframe LP to provide comprehensive light-gauge steel framing for residential construction. Nucor's 25 percent joint venture with the Rio Tinto Group, Mitsubishi Corporation, and Chinese steelmaker Shougang Corporation for a HIsmelt commercial plant in Kwinana, Western Australia, started up in 2005. In 2004, Nucor acquired the assets of an idled direct-reduced iron (DRI) plant in Louisiana and moved them to Trinidad. By December 2006, construction was completed, and, in 2008, Nu-Iron Unlimited produced 1,400,000 metric tons of DRI from Brazilian iron ore for the United States.

By 2005, Nucor had 16 steel facilities producing three times as much as in 1999. The number of bar mills had grown to nine with capacity of 6,000,000 tons through the addition of Birmingham's four mills with 2,000,000 tons and Auburn's 400,000 tons. The sheet mills grew to four and increased capacity by one-third with the acquisition of Trico. Nucor–Yamato's structural steel capacity was increased by half a million tons from the South Carolina plant. A new million-ton plate mill, their second, had opened in North Carolina in 2000. Ninety-three percent of production was sold to outside customers.

By 2006, DiMicco had made many acquisitions while still managing to instill Nucor's unique culture in the new facilities. A May 2006 BusinessWeek article revealed that Nucor's culture and compensation system had changed very little since the 1990s. Michael Arndt reported that "Nucor gave out more than $220 million in profit sharing and bonuses to the rank and file in 2005. The average Nucor steelworker took home nearly $79,000 last year. Add to that a $2,000 one-time bonus to mark the company's record earnings and almost $18,000, on average, in profit sharing." He also noted that executive pay was still geared toward team building as "The bonus of a plant manager, a department manager's boss, depends on the entire corporation's return on equity. So there's no glory in winning at your plant if the others are failing."

Globally, steel mergers and acquisitions boomed during this time. This merger activity was due to a combination of low borrowing costs, high stock prices, and large amounts of cash. Another factor prompting mergers was a rise in the cost of raw materials. Despite all the transactions in 2006, 2007, and 2008, the industry remained fragmented, both domestically and internationally, and more mergers were expected.

Future merger activity was expected to differ slightly as steel companies attempted to become more vertically integrated. Examples included forward integration, such as combining Esmark's service center with Wheeling-Pittsburgh's steel production; and integration backward into scrap, such as the takeover of OmniSource by Steel Dynamics in 2007 and Nucor's acquisition of David J. Joseph Co. in 2008. These moves represented a trend toward becoming less dependent on outside vendors. This was due to the rising cost of scrap, which jumped from $185/ton in January 2006 to $635/ton in June 2008, and the highly concentrated nature of iron ore sources. BHP Billiton Ltd. based in Australia, Rio Tinto plc, headquartered in London, and Brazil-based Vale accounted for 75 percent of iron ore shipments worldwide.

Nucor was also active in mergers. In March 2007, Nucor acquired Harris Steel Group Inc. of Canada for $1.06 billion in cash, adding 770,000 tons of rebar fabrication capacity and over 350,000 tons of capacity in other downstream steel products. This acquisition showed that Nucor saw growth opportunities in finishing steel products for its customers and in distribution rather than additional steelmaking capacity. While many large steel companies were buying other primary steelmakers around the world, Nucor was focusing its investments largely in North America's manufacturing infrastructure such as reinforced steel bars, platform grating, and wire mesh for construction products ranging from bridges to airports and stadiums. According to Dan DiMicco, these moves "significantly advanced Nucor's downstream growth initiatives." Through the acquisition of Harris, Nucor also acquired a 75 percent interest in Novosteel S.A., a Swiss-based steel trading company that matched buyers and sellers of steel products on a global basis and offered its customers logistics support, material handling, quality certifications, and schedule management.

For the previous three years, Nucor had a joint venture with Harris, and in fact already owned a 50 percent stake in the company. Harris kept its name, as a Nucor subsidiary, and was led by the former chairman and CEO John Harris. However, the Harris board consisted of Harris and three Nucor representatives. This was the first time Nucor had broken from its non-union tradition, as about half of Harris's 3,000 employees were unionized. As steel analyst Timna Tanners said, "It's definitely a stretch for Nucor, culturally, since they have managed to keep its other operations non-union by offering higher salaries and production incentives. But there are not many non-union options left in North America when it comes to acquisitions and expansion."

The Harris team was operating as a growth platform within Nucor and had completed several acquisitions, including rebar fabricator South Pacific Steel Corporation in June 2007; Consolidated Rebar, Inc. in August 2007; a 90 percent equity interest in rebar fabricator Barker Steel Company, Inc. in December 2007; as well as smaller transactions. Nucor made several other acquisitions, which combined with the Laurel Steel, Fisher & Ludlow, and LEC businesses that came with the Harris acquisition and some internal organic growth, increased Nucor's cold finish and drawn products' capacity by more than

75 percent from 490,000 tons in 2006 to 860,000 tons at the end of 2007. In addition, it resulted in 90,000 tons of steel-grating capacity, and steel mesh capacity almost tripled, to 233,000 tons per year.

Nucor continued to invest in other downstream and upstream businesses (see Exhibit 4 for the organization chart in 2009). In the third quarter of 2007, they completed the acquisition of Magnatrax Corporation, a leading provider of custom-engineering metal buildings, for $275.2 million. The Magnatrax acquisition, when combined with their existing Building Systems divisions and a newly constructed Buildings Systems division in Brigham City, Utah, made Nucor the second-largest metal building producer in the United States, more than doubling their annual capacity to 480,000 tons of pre-engineered metal buildings.

In 2007, Nucor's seven Vulcraft facilities supplied more than 40 percent of all domestic buildings built using steel joists and joist girders. In both 2006 and 2007, 99 percent of its steel requirements were obtained from Nucor bar mills. Nucor's nine steel deck plants supplied almost 30 percent of total domestic sales in decking; six of these plants were constructed by Nucor adjacent to Vulcraft joist facilities and three were acquired in November 2006 as a wholly owned subsidiary called Verco Decking. These decking plants obtained 99 percent of their steel requirements from

Exhibit 4 Nucor Organization Chart, 2009

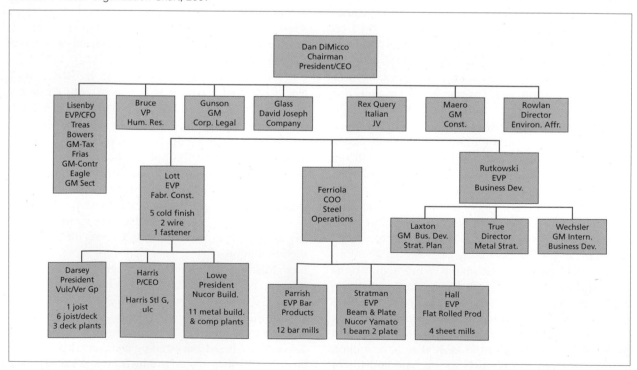

Nucor sheet plants in 2006, but only 76 percent in 2007.

In March 2008, Nucor completed the acquisition of the David J. Joseph Company (DJJ), the largest broker of ferrous and non-ferrous scrap in the United States and one of the nation's largest processors of ferrous scrap, for $1.44 billion. The company had been a supplier of scrap to Nucor since 1969. DJJ operated over 30 scrap-processing facilities. This acquisition expanded Nucor's scrap-processing capabilities from 500,000 to 4,000,000 short tons and provided them additional steelmaking raw materials through their brokerage operations, and rail services and logistics through its private fleet of some 2,000 scrap-related railcars. This allowed them to capture further margins in the steelmaking supply chain and to more closely control their raw-materials inputs. In May, they announced a plan to raise $3 billion for expansions and acquisitions, two-thirds to come from selling 25 million new shares.

U.S. steelmakers saw a major transition in 2008. In the first quarter, the combination of higher volume and increased prices led to a sizable gain in profits. Furthermore, data showed that the four leading domestic steel companies, AK Steel Holding Corp., Nucor Corp., Steel Dynamics Inc., and United States Steel Corp., which Standard & Poor's followed as a proxy for industry performance, collectively accounted for 45.5 percent of industry shipments in 2007. The rise in revenues for this proxy group reflected a 9.3 percent increase in revenue per ton, volume gained at the expense of imports, and the impact of acquisitions. At the end of July, major U.S. steelmakers' results were still supported by months of steel-price increases, which eased the burden of rising raw materials prices, as demand from emerging markets kept global steel supplies tight.

However, in September 2008, steelmakers in the United States experienced a sharp pullback from buyers who were concerned with the credit crisis and a slowdown in automobile and construction markets. This caused inventories to rise and prices on some key products to drop by 10 percent. The *Wall Street Journal* reported on November 17 that "Metals prices fell 35% in just four weeks last month—the steepest decline ever recorded, according to Barclays Capital." They also reported that big steelmakers worldwide were cutting production as much as 35 percent and that U.S. Steel planned to lay off 2 percent of its workforce. Chinese demand also slowed. This was a swift reversal in an industry that saw its profits increase 20-fold in five years. The pricing volatility was intensified by the global financial crisis as many hedge funds, pension funds, and other investors desperate to raise cash rapidly sold their commodities holdings. Still, the article said that ultimately the industry's problems were rooted in weakened demand, particularly in China, rather than the financial crisis.

So as 2009 began, with prices for steel, iron ore, and scrap metal plummeting, competition in the global steel industry was expected to increase. And further consolidation was expected as the major players sought to maintain their dominant positions (see Exhibit 5). In a December 2008 interview on CNBC, Cramer said to DiMicco, "Nucor's great CEO," that it was "amazing you can be profitable" with an overnight 40 percent drop in sales. DiMicco said it showed the success of their business model. He believed Nucor's acquisitions over the past 10 years, with their integration into steel products markets and raw materials, would position them to survive and even prosper—where there were threats there were also opportunities.

Exhibit 5 Top 12 Global Steel Producers, end 2007

2007 Rank	mmt	2006 Rank	mmt	Company Name
1	116.4	1	117.2	ArcelorMittal
2	35.7	2	34.7	Nippon Steel
3	34.0	3	32.0	JFE
4	31.1	4	30.1	POSCO
5	28.6	6	22.5	Baosteel
6	26.5	45	6.4	Tata Steel*
7	23.6	5	22.6	Anshan-Benxi
8	22.9	17	14.6	Jiangsu Shagang
9	22.8	9	19.1	Tangshan
10	21.5	7	21.2	U.S. Steel
11	20.4	16	15.1	Wuhan
12	20.0	8	20.3	Nucor

Note: *2007 figure includes Corus.
mmt = million metric tons.

Source: International Iron and Steel Institute, September 21, 2008.

Appendix 1 Balance Sheet 2000–2008 (in millions of U.S.[$])

As of 12/31	2008	2007	2006	2005	2004	2003	2002	2001	2000
Assets									
Cash	2,355	1,394	786	980	779	350	219	462	491
Receivables	1,229	1,612	1,067	1,001	963	572	484	331	350
Total Inventories	2,408	1,602	1,141	945	1,240	560	589	467	461
Other Current Assets	405	283	270	288	193	137	157	134	80
Total Current Assets	6,397	5,073	4,675	4,072	3,175	1,621	1,449	1,394	1,381
Property, Plant, & Equip.	4,132	3,233	2,856	2,856	2,818	2,817	2,932	2,366	2,329
Deposits & Other Assets	667	202	354	212	140	55	n/a	n/a	n/a
Goodwill, Other Intang.	2,679	1,318	n/a	n/a	n/a	n/a	n/a	n/a	n/a
Total Assets	13,874	9,826	7,885	7,139	6,133	4,492	4,381	3,759	3,711
Liabilities									
Accounts Payable	534	692	517	502	472	330	247	189	203
Curr. Long-Term Debt	180	n/a	n/a	n/a	n/a	n/a	n/a	n/a	n/a
Accrued Expense	352	431	478	384	565	300	319	295	355
Income Taxes	199	n/a	n/a	n/a	29	n/a	9	n/a	n/a
Other Cur. Liab., Salaries	580	436	455	369	n/a	n/a	n/a	n/a	n/a
Total Current Liabilities	1,854	1,582	1,450	1,256	1,066	630	592	484	558
Deferred Charges/Inc.	677	593	448	487	515	440	371	329	260
Long-Term Debt	3,086	2,250	922	922	924	904	879	460	460
Total Liabilities	5,945	4,713	2,820	2,665	2,504	1,973	1,841	1,274	1,279
Shareholder Equity									
Minority Interest	327	287	239	194	173	177	217	284	301
Preferred Stock	n/a	n/a	n/a	n/a	n/a	n/a	n/a	n/a	n/a
Common Stock	150	149	149	74	74	36	36	36	36
Capital Surplus	1,630	256	196	192	147	117	99	81	71
Retained Earnings	7,861	6,622	5,809	5,709	3,689	2,642	2,642	2,539	2,479
Treasury Stock	−1,521	−2,078	−1,332	−739	452	453	454	455	455
Total Shareholder Equity	7,929	5,113	4,826	4,280	3,456	2,342	2,323	2,201	2,131
Total Liability & Shareholder Equity	13,874	9,826	7,885	7,139	6,133	4,492	4,381	3,759	3,711

Source: Nucor annual reports.

Appendix 2 Income Statement 2000–2008

Period Ended	12/31/2008	12/31/2007	12/31/2006	12/31/2005	12/31/2004	12/31/2003	12/31/2002	12/31/2001	12/31/2000
Net Sales	23,663,324	16,592,926	14,751,270	12,700,999	11,376.83	6,265.82	4,801.78	4,333.71	4,756.52
Cost of Goods Sold	19,612,283	13,462,927	11,283,123	10,119,496	9,128.87	5,996.55	4,332.28	3,914.28	3,929.18
Gross Profit	4,051,041	3,130,049	3,468,147	2,581,503	2,247.96	269.28	469.5	419.43	827.34
R & D Expenditure	n/a	n/a	n/a	n/a	n/a	n/a	n/a	n/a	n/a
Selling G & A Exps	750,984	577,764	592,473	459,460	415.03	165.37	175.59	150.67	183.18
Depreciation & Amort.	n/a	n/a	n/a	n/a	n/a	n/a	n/a	n/a	n/a
Non-Operating Inc.	n/a	n/a	−37,365	−9,200	−79.3	−12.4	−49.57	−82.87	−150.65
Interest Expense	90,483	5,469	n/a	4201	22.35	24.63	14.29	6.53	n/a
Income Before Taxes	2,790,470	2,253,315	2,693,818	2,016,368	1,731.28	66.88	230.05	179.37	493.52
Prov. For Inc. Taxes	959,480	781,368	936,137	706,084	609.79	4.1	67.97	66.41	182.61
Minority Interest	313,921	293,501	219,121	110,650	80,840	n/a	n/a	n/a	n/a
Realized Investment	n/a	n/a	n/a	n/a	n/a	n/a	n/a	n/a	n/a
Other Income	n/a	n/a	n/a	n/a	n/a	n/a	n/a	n/a	n/a
Net Income	1,830,990	1,471,947	1,757,681	1,310,284	1,121.49	62.78	162.08	112.96	310.91

In thousands of USD

Source: Nucor annual reports.

Appendix 3 Nucor Valuation Rations, 2005–2008

	2008	2007	2006	2005
P/E(TTM)	7.38		11.76	7.38
Per Share Rations				
Divdend Per Share	1.31		0.67	0.47
Book Value Per Share	25.18		21.54	21.54
EPS Fully Diluted	5.98	4.94	5.68	7.02
Revenue Per Share	77.31		48.1	71.21
Profit Margins				
Operating Margin	13.95		18.26	16.23
Net Profit Margin	7.74	8.9	11.90	9.86
Gross Profit Margin	17.12		23.51	19.88
Dividends				
Dividend Yield	3.17		0.66	1.13
Dividend Yield -5-Year Avg.	3.21		2.17	1.28
Dividend Per Share (TTM)	1.31		0.6	0.52
Dividend Payout Ratio	35.94		37.32	6.66
Growth (%)				
5-Year Annual Growth	96.32		27.76	35.6
Revenue – 5-Year Growth	30.44		27.8	23.19
Div/Share – 5-Year Growth	45.63		71.5	12.57
EPS – 5-Year Growth	97.3		73.34	32.58
Financial Strength				
Quick Ratio	1.93		2.44	1.63
Current Ratio	3.45	3.2	3.22	2.98
LT Debt to Equity	38.92	44.01	19	26.72
Total Debt to Equity	42.09		19	26.72
Return on Equity (ROT) Per Share	27.91		38.61	38.57
Return on Assets (ROA)	16.19	16.62	23.4	25.4
Return on Invested Capital (ROIC)	19.91		29.58	33.33
Assets				
Assets Turnover	1.71		1.96	1.85
Inventory Turnover	9.51		10.82	9.7

Source: Thomson-Reuters Financial.

Jinxuan Zhang

We've been the No. 1 Web site in China for a number of years, and in fact we are the largest Web site outside of the U.S. When people get to know about the Internet, the first Web site they learn is about Baidu in China.

—ROBIN YANHONG LI, COFOUNDER, CHAIRMAN, & CEO, BAIDU[i]

We were late entering the China market, and we're catching up . . . . Our investment is working and we will eventually be the leader.

—ERIC SCHMIDT, CHAIRMAN & CEO, GOOGLE[ii]

By far China's most popular search engine, Baidu .com Inc. (Baidu) continued to dominate that market with a 60.4 percent market share in 2007,[iii] more than double that of Google Inc. (Google). In 2005, Google, the world's leading search engine, entered the Chinese market. While Google was catching up, Baida continued to grow. BNP Paribas observed: "Baidu and Google are winning at the expense of other search engines [in China] . . . Baidu gained market share at the expense of all players except for Google."[iv]

According to *BusinessWeek's* list of "The Best (and) Worst Leaders of 2006," Li was ranked third and his company was described as the "Best Answer to Google." Bill Gates and Steve Ballmer might want to have a sit-down with Chinese entrepreneur Robin Li. The founder and CEO of Baidu.com has achieved something that Microsoft's top brass have yet to manage—beating Google.[v]

On January 31, 2008, Ballmer made a proposal to Yahoo! to acquire outstanding shares of the company's common stock for per-share consideration of $31 in the hope of rapidly expanding Microsoft's presence in the online search advertising market dominated by Google.[vi]

On May 20, 2008,[vii] Baidu traded at a price to earnings ratio of 153. This is four times more than Google, over seven times more than Microsoft, and almost three times more than Yahoo! Was the price justified? Would it last?

Global vs. Local

Embarking on a Journey for Search

Google is a leading global Internet search and online advertising company. In January 1996, the company was founded by Larry Page and Sergey Brin, who started it as a research project when they were doctoral students at Stanford University. On September 7, 1998, it was formally incorporated as Google Inc. Google was able to win its audience because of the quality of its search results. Google's search algorithm[1] took into account relevance and other qualitative elements that other search engines did not.

Baidu—often referred to as "China's Google"—was incorporated in the Cayman Islands on January 18, 2000, by cofounders Robin Yanhong Li and Eric Yong Xu.[2] Both were Chinese nationals who had studied and worked overseas before returning to China. Baidu began as a provider of Internet search solutions to other Chinese portals. Then, it tapped into the unexplored Chinese online search market and gained a first-mover advantage by coming up with a search engine that provided information in local Chinese languages. Baidu initially became popular because of its multimedia content,

Research Associate Jinxuan (Ann) Zhang prepared this case under the supervision of Professor Didier Cossin as a basis for class discussion rather than to illustrate either effective or ineffective handling of a business situation.

This case was sponsored by the Securities Commission Malaysia (Suruhanjaya Sekuriti). Copyright © 2008 by IMD – International Institute for Management Development, Lausanne, Switzerland. Not be used or reproduced without written permission directly from IMD.

[1] In computer science, a search algorithm is an algorithm that takes a problem as input and returns a solution to the problem, usually after evaluating a number of possible solutions.

[2] Li earned a master's degree in computer science from the State University of New York at Buffalo and worked at search engine Infoseek for more than two years before returning to China. Xu, a biochemist who was well connected in the Silicon Valley, was not involved in the management of the company.

including MP3 music and movies, but was criticized for being "weak on piracy, strong on censorship."[viii]

A "1 followed by 100 zeros" vs. "Hundreds of Times"

The name Google originated from the mathematical term "Googol" for a 1 followed by 100 zeros. It reflected Google's mission "to organize the world's information and make it universally accessible and useful."[ix]

The literal meaning of Baidu is "hundreds of times." It was inspired by an ancient Chinese poem and represented a persistent search for the ideal. The name was chosen so that the world would remember Baidu's Chinese heritage. By focusing on what it knew best, Baidu aimed "to provide the best way for people to find information"[x] by applying an avant-garde technology to the world's most ancient and complex language.

Growing, But Not Yet on the Same Scale

Even though Baidu is growing quickly, it still remains tiny in comparison to Google's global size. Baidu earned about $86 million in net income in 2007 on $239 million in revenue,[xi] compared with Google's $4.2 billion in net income on $16.6 billion in revenue.

Products & Services

Baidu's homepage was strikingly similar to Google's—a search bar at the center of a mostly empty page (see Exhibit 1). Both Baidu and Google provided a wide range of products and services that gave users a better search experience with a view to increasing traffic and user stickiness. Their offerings could be placed into three categories: search, community, and other enhancements. While Google has started to experiment with other markets, such as radio and print publications, Baidu looked towards consumer-to-consumer (C2C) and mobile search.

Business Model

Baidu and Google essentially utilized the same business model—selling ads tied to user searches (see Exhibit 2). Both companies primarily derived their revenues from online marketing activities on their Web sites, principally auction-based pay-for-performance (P4P)[3] search advertisements.

Baidu introduced "pay-for-placement," which allowed companies to bid for search-result placement based on relevant keywords. Google believed that "you can make money without doing evil"[4,xiii] and did not allow ads to

be displayed on its results pages. Advertising produced by certain searches was clearly identified as a "sponsored link" and displayed above or to the right of the results.

In addition, Baidu and Google also expanded their search platforms to include a network of third-party Web sites that incorporated their search box or toolbar in a revenue-sharing model. This enabled both companies to use their advertising platforms to generate user traffic and enlarge their paid-search networks. According to BNP Paribas estimates, Baidu already derived 25 percent of its revenue from its partner Web sites,[xiv] while Google about 10% to 15% from such partner Web sites (see Exhibit 3 for the Google revenue breakdown).[xv]

Growth Strategy

Since 2001, Google has acquired some small startup companies with innovative teams and products—for example, Deja, Pyra Labs, and Sprinks. Since its IPO[5] in 2004, it also has entered into a wide array of products and services outside its sponsored-search domain. Google has attempted to keep pace with changing times and identify future growth opportunities both organically, by launching Gmail and Orkut,[6] and by acquiring YouTube and DoubleClick (see Exhibit 4 for a list of Google's major acquisitions). In April 2004, Google knocked on Baidu's door. Two months later, Google acquired a 2.6 percent stake in Baidu for $5 million (at the time, Baidu was not well known outside its homeland).

For its part, Baidu pursued strategic acquisitions of businesses, assets, and technologies that complemented its existing capabilities and business. In August 2004, it acquired the domain name hao123.com. Headquartered in Shanghai, hao123.com was Baidu's largest traffic contributor and its largest distributor of its P4P services.[7] Both companies also actively formed strategic alliances with market leaders in other business sectors to further broaden their customer bases and product and service offerings.

Geographic Expansion

Google has built up its international presence to the point that international revenues accounted for approximately 48 percent of Google's total revenue in 2007 and surpassed its domestic revenues in Q1 2008 (see Exhibit 3). More than half of its user traffic also came from outside the United States (see Exhibit 5 for a user traffic breakdown). Baidu, for its part, focused on offering searches in Chinese. However, on January 24, 2008, Baidu made

---

[3] P4P customers bid for priority placements of links to their Web sites among relevant search results.

[4] "Don't be evil" was the informal corporate motto or slogan for Google.

[5] Initial Public Offering.

[6] A social networking service run by Google and named after its creator—a Google employee.

[7] Baidu's ability for acquiring local companies was subject to foreign exchange regulations on mergers and acquisitions in China.

Exhibit 1 Homepages of Baidu and Google

Exhibit 2 Business System of a Search Engine

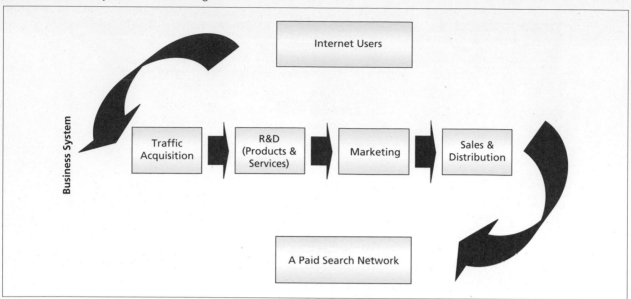

Source: IMD Research.

Exhibit 3 Google's Revenue Breakdown

By Source	2003	2004	2005	2006	2007	2008Q1
Revenues (in $ million)						
Google sites' advertising revenues	$792	$1,589	$3,377	$6,333	$10,625	$3,400
Google network advertising revenues	629	1,554	2,688	4,160	5,788	1,686
Total advertising revenues	1,421	3,143	6,065	10,493	16,413	5,087
Licensing and other revenues	45	46	74	112	181	99
Total revenues	$1,466	$3,189	$6,139	$10,605	$16,594	$5,186
As % of total revenues						
Google sites' advertising revenues	54%	50%	55%	60%	64%	66%
Google network advertising revenues	43%	49%	44%	39%	35%	33%
Total advertising revenues	97%	99%	99%	99%	99%	98%
Licensing and other revenues	3%	1%	1%	1%	1%	2%

Exhibit 3 Google's Revenue Breakdown *(Continued)*

By Source	2003	2004	2005	2006	2007	2008Q1
By Location (in $ million)						
U.S.	$1,038	$2,119	$3,757	$6,030	$8,629	$2,541
International	428	1,070	2,382	4,575	7,965	2,645
Total revenue	$1,466	$3,189	$6,139	$10,605	$16,594	$5,186
As % of total revenues						
U.S.	71%	66%	61%	57%	52%	49%
International	29%	34%	39%	43%	48%	51%

Source: Google's annual reports and quarterly results, dollar value in millions.

Exhibit 4 Google's Major Acquisitions

Acquisition Date	Company	Business	Country	Value	Derived Services
February 12, 2001	Deja	Usenet	USA		Google Groups
September 2001	Outride	Web search engine	USA		Google Personalized Search
February 2003	Pyra Labs	Web software	USA		Blogger
April 2003	Neotonic Software	Customer relationship management	USA		Google Groups, Gmail
April 2003	Applied Semantics	Online advertising	USA	$102 million	AdSense, AdWords
September 30, 2003	Kaltix	Web search engine	USA		iGoogle
October 2003	Sprinks (a division of Primedia)	Online advertising	USA		AdSense, AdWords
October 2003	Genius Labs	Blogging	USA		Blogger
May 10, 2004	Ignite Logic	HTML editor	USA		Google Page Creator
June 23, 2004	Baidu	Chinese language search engine	CHN	$5 million	Sold in 2006
July 13, 2004	Picasa	Image organizer	USA		Picasa, Blogger
September 2004	ZipDash	Traffic analysis	USA		Google Ride Finder
October 2004	Where2	Map analysis	USA		Google Maps

(Continued)

Exhibit 4 Google's Major Acquisitions *(Continued)*

Acquisition Date	Company	Business	Country	Value	Derived Services
October 27, 2004	Keyhole, Inc.	Map analysis	USA		Google Maps, Google Earth
March 28, 2005	Dodgeball	Social networking service	USA		Google Mobile, Google SMS
March 12, 2005	Urchin Software Corporation	Web analytics	USA		Google Analytics
July 2005	Reqwireless	Mobile browser	CAN		Google Mobile
July 7, 2005	Communications Group	Broadband Internet access	USA	$100 million	Internet Backbone
August 17, 2005	Android	Mobile software	USA		Google Mobile, Google SMS
November 2005	Skia	Graphics software	USA		Picasa
November 17, 2005	Akwan Information Technologies	Broadband Internet access	BRA		Internet Backbone
December 20, 2005	AOL	Broadband Internet access	USA	$1,000 million	
December 27, 2005	Phatbits	Widget engine	USA		Google Desktop
December 31, 2005	allPAY GmbH	Mobile software	GER		Google Mobile
December 31, 2005	bruNET GmbH dMarc	Mobile software	GER		Google Mobile
January 17, 2006	Broadcasting	Advertising	USA	$102 million	AdSense
February 14, 2006	Measure Map	Weblog software	USA		Google Analytics
March 9, 2006	Upstartle	Word processor	USA		Google Documents
March 14, 2006	@Last Software	3D modeling software	USA		Google Sketchup
April 9, 2006	Orion	Web search engine	AUS		Google Search
June 1, 2006	2Web Technologies	Online spreadsheets	USA		Google Spreadsheet
August 15, 2006	Neven Vision	Computer vision	USA		Google Maps
October 9, 2006	YouTube	Video sharing	USA	$1,650 million	Google Video
October 31, 2006	JotSpot	Web application	USA		Google Sites
December 18, 2006	Endoxon	Mapping	CHE	$28 million	Google Maps

Exhibit 4 Google's Major Acquisitions (*Continued*)

Acquisition Date	Company	Business	Country	Value	Derived Services
January 4, 2007	Xunlei	File sharing	CHE	$5 million	
February 16, 2007	Adscape	In-game advertising	USA	$23 million	AdSense
March 16, 2007	Trendalyzer	Statistical software	SWE		Google Analytics
April 13, 2007	Double Click	Online advertising	USA	$3,100 million	AdSense
April 17, 2007	Tonic Systems	Presentation program	USA		Google Documents
April 19, 2007	Marratech	Videoconferencing	SWE		Google Talk
May 11, 2007	GreenBorder	Computer security	USA		Internal Use
June 1, 2007	Panoramio	Photo sharing	ESP		Blogger
June 3, 2007	FeedBurner	Web feed	USA	$100 million	Google Reader
June 5, 2007	PeakStream	Parallel processing	USA		Server (computing)
June 19, 2007	Zenter	Presentation program	USA		Google Documents
July 2, 2007	GrandCentral	Voice over Internet Protocol	USA	$45 million	Google Mobile
July 9, 2007	Postini	Communications security	USA	$625 million	Gmail
July 20, 2007	Image America	Aerial photography	USA		Google Maps
September 27, 2007	Zingku	Social network service	USA		Google Mobile
October 9, 2007	Jaiku	Micro-blogging	FIN		Google Mobile

its first international move by launching its Japanese version—Baidu.jp[8]—with the primary objective of serving Chinese small and medium-sized enterprises (SMEs) doing business in Japan. Its focus remained on product development to meet the needs of Japanese users and operating costs and expenses of RMB30 million ($4.3 million) were incurred for Q1 2008 (no revenue was expected for fiscal year 2008).[xvii]

Google in China vs. "China's Google"

Google's Answer to Its Chinese Question
Google launched its Chinese language version in 2000 and its popularity quickly grew through word of mouth among Chinese Internet surfers. The company did well until September 2002, when Google was blocked by the "Great Firewall of China"[9]—a political rift over censorship with the Chinese government—and was denied rights to China. While Google's company Web site proclaimed, "Google—the closest thing the Web has to an ultimate answer machine," it did not have an answer to its one big China question: how can we go into China and yet not do evil?[xviii]

"They [Google] can't afford to not be in China . . . They are facing a hard choice. They really don't want to be seen as doing something that is evil, but no one goes into China on their own terms."[xix]

According to Eric Schmidt, Google actually did "an evil scale" and finally reached the decision that "not to serve [users in China] at all was a worse evil."[xx] It

[8] With four products only: a Web page, images, videos, and blogs.

[9] Also referred to as the "Golden Shield Project," a censorship and surveillance project operated by the Ministry of Public Security of China.

Exhibit 5 User Geographic Breakdown & Traffic Rank

| User Geographic Breakdown | | | | Traffic Rank | | | |
| Baidu.com | | Google.com | | Baidu.com | | Google.com | |
Market	%	Market	%	Market	Rank	Market	Rank
China	89.1%	U.S.	43.0%	China	1	U.S.	1
South Korea	2.8%	India	8.2%	South Korea	9	Algeria	1
U.S.	1.6%	Brazil	3.7%	Macao	9	Iran	2
Japan	1.0%	U.K.	3.2%	Hong Kong	14	India	3
U.K.	0.7%	Germany	3.0%	Singapore	14	South Africa	3
Taiwan	0.7%	Iran	2.8%	New Zealand	19	U.K.	4
Canada	0.6%	China	2.3%	Taiwan	22	Germany	4
Hong Kong	0.5%	Japan	2.3%	Malaysia	22	Spain	4
Australia	0.4%	Canada	1.8%	Australia	40	Australia	4
Malaysia	0.3%	Italy	1.7%	Canada	47	Indonesia	4
Germany	0.3%	Spain	1.4%	Nigeria	47	Pakistan	4
Singapore	0.3%	France	1.3%	U.K.	71	Saudi Arabia	4
Italy	0.1%	Australia	1.1%	Japan	125	Brazil	5
New Zealand	0.1%	Mexico	1.1%	U.S.	225	Italy	5
Indonesia	0.1%	Turkey	1.1%	Thailand	255	Turkey	5
Thailand	0.1%	Indonesia	1.0%	Indonesia	260	Netherlands	5
Macronesia	0.1%	Russia	0.9%	Germany	283	Canada	6
Spain	0.1%	Pakistan	0.8%	Netherlands	401	South Korea	6
Nigeria	0.1%	Algeria	0.7%	Italy	445	Mexico	9
India	0.1%	Saudi Arabia	0.7%	Spain	920	France	10
France	0.1%	South Africa	0.7%	France	1,024	Poland	10
Netherlands	0.1%	Netherlands	0.7%	Russia	1,226	Japan	11
Russia	0.1%	South Korea	0.7%	India	1,603	Russia	11

Exhibit 5 User Geographic Breakdown & Traffic Rank *(Continued)*

| User Geographic Breakdown | | | | Traffic Rank | | | |
| Baidu.com | | Google.com | | Baidu.com | | Google.com | |
Market	%	Market	%	Market	Rank	Market	Rank
Other markets	0.6%	Poland	0.5%			China	12
	100.0%	Argentina	0.4%			Argentina	12
		Other markets	14.9%				
			100.0%				

was finally granted the rights to open offices in China in January 2005, headed by Taiwan-born Kaifu Lee, a former Microsoft executive, who in 1998 was a founder of Microsoft Research Asia.[10] Several months later, Google introduced a new version of its search engine for the Chinese market by purging its search results of any Web sites of which the Chinese government did not approve.

"Gu Ge" in China

Consumer surveys showed that Chinese Internet users had a wide range of imaginative pronunciations of Google in English, including "gougou" (dog dog), "gugou" (ancient dog), "guoguo" (fruit fruit), and "gougou" (check check).[xxi] In fact, Google had been working on a Chinese name since 2002. After extensive internal debates, external consultations, and consumer surveys, in spring 2006 Google finally announced its Chinese name: Gu Ge. "Gu Ge" meant "song of the grain," expressing the abundance of harvest, or "song of the valley," a reference to the company's Silicon Valley roots.[xxii] This was the first time Google used a non-English name.

Because Google had now been able to enter China using its own name (or something like it), it decided to create on its own Web site there. In June 2006, Google sold its stake in Baidu for more than $60 million. Google spokeswoman Debbie Frost commented: "We have disposed of our modest investment in Baidu … It has always been our goal to grow our own successful business in China and we are very focused on that."[xxii]

Being Local, Understanding Local

Unlike Google, which offered multi-language search, Baidu focused on searches in Chinese. Interestingly, Chinese is one of the Asian languages based on syllables requiring two bytes to store each character while English only requires one byte. There were fundamental differences in algorithms and behavior between single-byte and double-byte searches. In addition, regular changes necessitated by these algorithms required manpower trained in the local language, which took time for outside companies to develop. CEO Robin Yanhong Li believed that Baidu's understanding of the Chinese language and culture gave it an advantage in that market over Google.[xxiv] On the other hand, Kaifu Lee, Vice President over Google's China operations, felt that his challenge was to help the leadership of Google understand the Internet in China—specifically, Chinese users.[xxv]

Channels

In China, most SME customers[11] were not accustomed to conducting business online. In addition, the payment and logistic infrastructure of e-commerce was far from perfect and required a lot of user education and support, at least initially, especially on how to navigate the Internet. Baidu had built up a direct sales force of more than 3,000 people located in seven major cities[12],[xxvi] to better serve its customers and assist in these areas. It also had a much higher penetration of distributors than Google (see Exhibit 6 for a comparison of channel strength in China), who only had one Chinese distributor in mid-2005 and also generally adopted its global model of customer self-service for China.

---

[10] Microsoft sued Google and Kaifu Li for the move but the case was resolved in a confidential settlement.

[11] Only 100 out of 161,000 of Baidu's online marketing customers were big advertisers as of Q1 2008, but their spending started to outpace its traditional SME customers, especially the financial services, IT, electronics, and automobile industries.

[12] Beijing, Shanghai, Guangzhou, Shenzhen, Taiyuan, Tianjin, and Pooshan by the end of 2007.

Exhibit 6 Comparison of Channel Strength in China

	Baidu	Google China
Number of distributors	~200[20]	24
Number of provinces covered	24	8
Number of direct sales force employees	~3,000	0
Revenue from distributors in Q3 2007 (%)	32	48
Number of paid advertisers in Q3 2007	143,000	38,00
Revenue from top 10 channel partners (%)	10	93

Source: BNP Paribas estimates according to industry sources.[xxxix]

Corporate Structure, Financial Performance, and Valuation

Corporate Structure

To comply with the foreign ownership restrictions on providing Internet content and advertising services in China, from the outset, Baidu operated its Web sites and provided online advertising services in China through contractual arrangements with its local subsidiary, Baidu Netcom. Baidu Netcom, set up on June 5, 2001, was wholly owned by Li and Xu[13] and had the necessary licenses and approvals to operate in China[14] (see Exhibit 7). Google.com operated under a license owned by Google's local partner, Ganii.com.[xxvii]

Financial Performance

Exhibits 8a through 9c provide detailed financial information for Baidu and Google for fiscal years 2003 to 2007. Exhibit 10 contrasts the financial performance and valuation of Baidu and Google across several indicators for fiscal year 2007.

Revenue Drivers

Exhibit 11 shows that Baidu's revenue growth was mainly driven by an enlarged active online marketing customer base effectively served by its direct sales force and third-party distributors and through increasing revenue per online marketing customer. Baidu started to improve its monetization algorithm in 2006 by implementing dynamic bidding and dynamic starting bid prices, and incorporating quality factors in ordering sponsored links as a way of improving its revenue per search.

Breakdown of Costs

Traffic acquisition costs (TAC) remained a key component of Baidu's and Google's cost of revenues. Baidu's TAC continued to rise, reflecting continued growth of revenue contribution from Baidu Union[15] member partners (faster growth than from its own platform).[16] About 70 percent of Google's cost of revenue was TAC. BNP Paribas estimated that Baidu's TAC would continue its upward trend and close the gap with Google worldwide (see Exhibit 12).[xxviii]

Impact of RMB Revaluation

Baidu's reporting currency was the RMB (China's currency). Its revenues and costs were mostly denominated in RMB while a significant portion of its financial assets were denominated in U.S. dollars. Considerable international pressure on the Chinese government to permit the free floatation of the RMB resulted in a significant appreciation of the RMB against the U.S. dollar (see Exhibit 13).

Taxation

As a foreign-invested enterprise registered in a high-tech zone and a "new or high-technology enterprise," Baidu enjoyed preferential tax benefits[17] and a much lower effective tax rate (in the single-digit range, around 4 percent in fiscal years 2004 to 2007 and 7 percent for Q1 2008[xxix]) than Google.

Financial Policies

Baidu relied entirely on dividends and other fees paid by its subsidiaries and affiliates in China. Like Google, it did not pay dividends to its common shareholders.[18]

---

[13] Baidu funded the initial capitalization of Baidu Netcom in the form of a long-term shareholder loan of RMB 2 million ($0.24 million) to Li and Xu.

[14] Under the current Chinese laws and regulations on advertising, P4P was not classified as a form of advertising. The company may not be operated through Baidu Netcom and/or would be subject to higher effective taxation if the laws and regulations were to be changed.

[15] Baidu Union was the network of third-party Web sites and software applications, with five categories: proprietary Web sites, software, Internet cafes, carriers, and other ad networks.

[16] Baidu had the flexibility to turn on or off of the Union traffic and partnerships based on its assessment of the ROI for customers and advertisers, and the return for its profitability and revenue growth.

[17] An exemption from enterprise income tax: 7.5 percent for the first three years and a further 15 percent as long as it maintained its status as a "new or high-technology enterprise." Eligibility for potential tax refunds for Baidu Online on revenues derived from its technology consulting services.

[18] In China, offshore remittance of dividends was also subject to foreign exchange control by the State Administration of Foreign Exchange (SAFE).

Exhibit 7 Ownership and Corporate Structure of Baidu

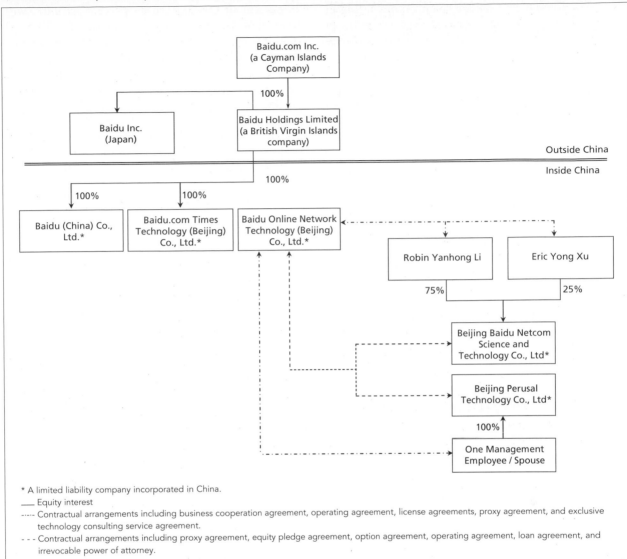

Source: Developed from Baidu IPO prospectus and SEC filings.

Valuation

IPO

While Baidu regarded its IPO more as a branding event to raise company profile, the outcome far exceeded expectations. When Baidu completed its IPO on NASDAQ on August 5, 2005, its share price soared to $122.54, up 354 percent from its IPO price of $27 on the first trading day, which made it immensely popular among investors. As one investor remarked:

"It's just been amazing. It could be over-enthusiasm, it could be the way Google charted, but there is obviously a lot of speculative buyers who think this could be an Asian Google."[xxx]

In December 2007 Baidu became the first Chinese company to join the NASDAQ 100 Index. Baidu traded at a much higher premium than Google—three times Google's P/E ratio (see Exhibit 14).

Equity Share Ownership

At the end of fiscal year 2006, Li still retained 21.5 percent ownership of the common stock of Baidu. Other directors and officers together owned 6.7 percent of the common stock shares.[xxxi]

Dual-Stock Structure

Like Google, Baidu had a dual-stock structure—two classes of ordinary shares with identical rights except for voting and conversion rights. As a result, it was reported that Baidu may not be in compliance with the listing rules in Hong Kong.[xxxii]

Secondary Listings

There was no clear timeline for Baidu's initial listing in Hong Kong after it was postponed. The goal of listing in Hong Kong would be to help raise the company profile and fund expansion into new areas, such as online auctions. Its plan for an IPO in Shanghai was unlikely due to regulatory huddles that effectively blocked foreign-owned firms (due to its listing on the NASDAQ) from selling stocks on Chinese exchanges.

Still Too Early to Declare A Winner...

On May 3, 2008, Microsoft withdrew its offer to acquire Yahoo! and chose not to pursue a hostile bid (see Exhibit 15). Microsoft had increased its offer to $33 per share (about $47.5 billion) but the two parties still could not reach an agreement. In addition, a recent successful Google–Yahoo! paid-search test and potential deal made the acquisition even more complicated for Microsoft. Two weeks after withdrawing its offer to purchase Yahoo!, Microsoft reopened the door to the possibility of a potential new investment in Yahoo! (not a total acquisition) while discussions were still ongoing between Yahoo! and Google.

Robin Yanhong Li, cofounder, chairman, and CEO of Baidu,[xxxiii] feels that Baidu will someday pose a similar threat, saying, "If he [Bill Gates] is worried about Google he will probably be more worried about Baidu somewhere down the road. . . . When the Chinese market stops growing faster than other countries in world, we will look outside. The reason we focus here now is that this is the fastest growing market we can access."

In recent years, the Chinese search ad market has grown quickly (see Exhibits 16a and 16b) and is also becoming more concentrated. The combined market share of the top three search engines increased from 78 percent in Q1 2006 to 95 percent in 2007 (with Baidu 60.4 percent, Google 21.2 percent, and Yahoo! China/Alibaba 13.8 percent[19]).[xxxiv] In November 2007 the Chinese search market already exceeded the United States in the number of search requests, and by February 2008 in the number of internet users. As Sukhinder Singh Cassidy, the vice president for Asia Pacific and Latin American Operations for Google has said, "We're in sort of inning one of a nine-inning game. . . . It is very early to call a winner in the China search market."[xxxv]

I had no intention of keeping Baidu inside China from the start. Now that we have won over 60 percent share [Q4 2007] in China, I think it's natural that we turn to overseas markets.

—**Robin Yanhong Li, Co-Founder, Chairman & CEO, Baidu** [xxxvi]

Whatever Baidu does, it does not matter to us. The internet is not the same as other IT businesses. [Between] Google and users will turn to whoever does the better, and they will change again when they find someone even better.

—**Kaifu Lee, VP and President for Greater Google China** [xxxvii]

Is it just a matter of time before there is a Baidu.us portal? In this regard Russia's search engine, Yandex, has operations in the United States near Google's headquarters. What will happen if Microsoft acquires (or fails to acquire) Yahoo!? What will Baidu's considerations be for its next choice of secondary listing? How should investors evaluate the stock? These decisions and events will help determine the global, regional, and country battle shaping up in the search engine markets.

---

[19] Alibaba, a leading Chinese e-commerce company, acquired the entire assets of Yahoo! China in 2005, including its search technology, the Web site, its communications and advertising business, and 3721.com (a real-name search engine) Web site. Alibaba also received a $1 billion investment from Yahoo! as well as the exclusive right of using the Yahoo! brand. In return, Yahoo! took 40 percent of Alibaba's shares but only 35 percent of voting rights.

Exhibit 8a Baidu: Consolidated Income Statement (Fiscal Year Ending December 31, 2007)

BAIDU FINANCIALS	RMB Million (except for share, per share information)					$ Million (except for share, per share information)				
INCOME STATEMENT	2003	2004	2005	2006	2007	2003	2004	2005	2006	2007
Exchange rate						8.2767	8.2765	8.072	7.8051	7.3041
Revenues										
Online marketing services	31.8	106.9	307.4	828.5	1,741.0	3.8	12.9	38.1	106.1	238.4
Other services	8.8	10.6	11.9	9.4	3.4	1.1	1.3	1.5	1.2	0.5
Total Revenues	**40.6**	**117.5**	**319.2**	**837.8**	**1,744.4**	**4.9**	**14.2**	**39.5**	**107.3**	**238.8**
Operating costs and expenses										
Cost of revenues	23.3	41.2	104.4	245.5	645.4	2.8	5.0	12.9	31.5	88.4
Business tax and surcharges	1.9	6.5	20.8	51.8	108.8	0.2	0.8	2.6	6.6	14.9
Traffic acquisition costs	10.6	10.9	21.2	75.2	204.7	1.3	1.3	2.6	9.6	28.0
Bandwidth costs	2.2	8.5	21.3	40.0	117.6	0.3	1.0	2.6	5.1	16.1
Depreciation costs	4.1	7.1	25.3	51.6	147.1	0.5	0.9	3.1	6.6	20.1
Operational costs	3.7	6.5	14.9	25.5	65.5	0.4	0.8	1.8	3.3	9.0
Share-based compensation expenses	0.6	1.7	1.0	1.4	1.7	0.1	0.2	0.1	0.2	0.2
Selling, general and administrative	19.6	50.7	134.8	250.2	411.2	2.4	6.1	16.7	32.1	56.3

Exhibit 8a Baidu: Consolidated Income Statement (Fiscal Year Ending December 31, 2007) (Continued)

BAIDU FINANCIALS	RMB Million (except for share, per share information)					$ Million (except for share, per share information)				
INCOME STATEMENT	2003	2004	2005	2006	2007	2003	2004	2005	2006	2007
Research and Development	7.0	14.5	44.2	79.2	140.7	0.8	1.8	5.5	10.2	19.3
Total operating costs and expenses	49.9	106.4	283.4	575.0	1,197.3	6.0	12.9	35.1	73.7	163.9
Operating profit	(9.3)	11.0	35.8	262.9	547.2	(1.1)	1.3	4.4	33.7	74.9
Other income (and expenses)										
Interest income	0.3	1.1	13.6	42.4	49.0	0.0	0.1	1.7	5.4	6.7
Foreign exchange loss, net	–	–	(0.7)	(0.1)	–	–	–	(0.1)	(0.0)	–
Other, net	0.1	0.3	0.8	4.2	20.1	0.0	0.0	0.1	0.5	2.7
Total other income (and expenses)	0.4	1.5	13.7	46.5	69.1	0.0	0.2	1.7	6.0	9.5
Net income before income taxes and cumulative effect of change in accounting principle	(8.9)	12.5	49.5	309.4	616.2	(1.1)	1.5	6.1	39.6	84.4
Income taxes	–	0.5	1.9	12.3	(12.8)	–	0.1	0.2	1.6	(1.7)
Income before cumulative effect of change in accounting principle	(8.9)	12.0	47.6	297.2	629.0	(1.1)	1.5	5.9	38.1	86.1
Cumulative effect of change in accounting principle	–	–	–	4.6	–	–	–	–	0.6	–

Exhibit 8a Baidu: Consolidated Income Statement (Fiscal Year Ending December 31, 2007) (Continued)

BAIDU FINANCIALS	RMB Million (except for share, per share information)					$ Million (except for share, per share information)				
INCOME STATEMENT	2003	2004	2005	2006	2007	2003	2004	2005	2006	2007
Net income	(8.9)	12.0	47.6	301.8	629.0	(1.1)	1.5	5.9	38.7	86.1
Net income per Class A and Class B ordinary shares										
Basic (prior to cumulative effect of change in accounting principle)	(0.87)	1.09	2.40	8.92	18.57	(0.11)	0.13	0.30	1.14	2.54
Basic (cumulative effect of change in accounting principle)	–	–	–	0.14	–	–	–	–	0.02	–
	(0.87)	1.09	2.40	9.06	18.57	(0.11)	0.13	0.30	1.16	2.54
Diluted (prior to cumulative effect of change in accounting principle)	0.43	0.43	1.49	8.62	18.11	0.05	0.05	0.18	1.10	2.48
Diluted (cumulative effect of change in accounting principle)	–	–	–	0.13	–	–	–	–	0.02	–
	0.43	0.43	1.49	8.75	18.11	0.05	0.05	0.18	1.12	2.48
Weighted average number of Class A and Class B ordinary shares outstanding										
Basic	10,188,850	10,983,478	19,808,058	33,290,696	33,872,611	10,188,850	10,983,478	19,808,058	33,290,696	33,872,611
Diluted	10,188,850	28,124,327	32,042,888	34,506,594	34,724,364	10,188,850	28,124,327	32,042,888	34,506,594	34,724,364

(Continued)

*2007 results were unaudited results.
Source: Baidu annual reports and quarterly results.

Exhibit 8b Baidu: Consolidated Balance Sheet (Fiscal Year Ending December 31, 2007)

BAIDU FINANCIALS		RMB Million						$ Million			
BALANCE SHEET	2003	2004	2005	2006	2007	2003	2004	2005	2006	2007
Exchange rate						8.2767	8.2765	8.072	7.8051	7.3041
ASSETS										
Current assets										
Cash and cash equivalents	62.8	200.2	900.6	1,136.3	1,350.6	7.6	24.2	111.6	145.6	184.9
Short-term investments	–	–	–	85.3	242.0	–	–	–	10.9	33.1
Accounts receivable, net of allowance	1.9	9.6	22.4	23.1	64.3	0.2	1.2	2.8	3.0	8.8
Prepaid expenses and other current assets	0.9	2.4	11.0	32.3	66.0	0.1	0.3	1.4	4.1	9.0
Deferred tax assets, net of valuation allowance	–	–	1.4	1.7	2.6	–	–	0.2	0.2	0.4
Total current assets	65.7	212.3	935.4	1,278.7	1,725.5	7.9	25.6	115.9	163.8	236.2
Non-current assets										
Fixed assets, net	11.0	35.9	96.4	191.7	678.9	1.3	4.3	11.9	24.6	92.9
Prepayment for land use rights	–	–	77.2	92.4	96.5	–	–	9.6	11.8	13.2
Intangible assets, net	–	13.0	13.3	44.4	40.5	–	1.6	1.6	5.7	5.5
Goodwill	–	–	9.3	47.3	51.1	–	–	1.2	6.1	7.0
Investments, net	–	–	2.0	–	15.4	–	–	0.3	–	2.1

Exhibit 8b Baidu: Consolidated Balance Sheet (Fiscal Year Ending December 31, 2007) (Continued)

BAIDU FINANCIALS	RMB Million					$ Million				
BALANCE SHEET	2003	2004	2005	2006	2007	2003	2004	2005	2006	2007
Deferred tax assets, net	–	–	2.8	5.8	15.7	–	–	0.4	0.7	2.2
Other non-current assets	–	1.1	–	7.7	32.3	–	0.1	–	1.0	4.4
Total non-current assets	11.0	49.9	201.1	389.3	930.4	1.3	6.0	24.9	49.9	127.4
TOTAL ASSETS	76.7	262.2	1,136.4	1,668.1	2,655.9	9.3	31.7	140.8	213.7	363.6
LIABILITIES AND SHARE-HOLDERS' EQUITY										
Current liabilities										
Customers' deposits	8.4	26.0	70.3	141.2	257.6	1.0	3.1	8.7	18.1	35.3
Accrued expense and other liabilities	3.8	21.9	53.1	153.1	359.3	0.5	2.6	6.6	19.6	49.2
Deferred revenue	7.5	6.3	7.7	2.6	11.8	0.9	0.8	0.9	0.3	1.6
Deferred income	–	–	0.1	4.1	2.5	–	–	0.0	0.5	0.3
Total current liabilities	19.6	54.2	131.2	301.0	631.2	2.4	6.5	16.3	38.6	86.4
Non-current liabilities										
Long-term payable for acquisitions	–	–	–	7.0	3.0	–	–	–	0.9	0.4
Deferred income	–	–	0.1	2.8	0.3	–	–	0.0	0.4	0.0
Total non-current liabilities	–	–	0.1	9.8	3.3	–	–	0.0	1.3	0.5

Exhibit 8b Baidu: Consolidated Balance Sheet (Fiscal Year Ending December 31, 2007) (Continued)

BAIDU FINANCIALS	RMB Million					$ Million				
BALANCE SHEET	2003	2004	2005	2006	2007	2003	2004	2005	2006	2007
Total liabilities	19.6	54.2	131.4	310.8	634.5	2.4	6.5	16.3	39.8	86.9
Commitments						0	0	0	0	0
Redeemable convertible preferred shares	91.622	211.4				11.1	25.5	0	0	0
Shareholders' equity										
Class A ordinary shares outstanding at year-end	0.004	0.004	0.004	0.009	0.01	0.0005	0.0005	0.0005	0.0012	0.0014
Class B ordinary shares outstanding at year-end	0	–	0.01	0.005	0.004		–	0.0012	0.0006	0.0005
Additional paid-in capital	24.046	43.3	1,009.5	1,088.2	1,171.6	2.9	5.2	125.1	139.4	160.4
Accumulated other comprehensive income (loss)	0	–	(5.5)	(33.7)	(82.0)	–	–	(0.7)	(4.3)	(11.2)
Retained earnings (accumulated losses)	(58.6)	(46.6)	1.0	302.8	931.7	(7.1)	(5.6)	0.1	38.8	127.6
Total shareholders' equity	(34.6)	(3.3)	1,005.1	1,357.3	2,021.4	(4.2)	(0.4)	124.5	173.9	276.7
TOTAL LIABILITIES AND SHAREHOLDERS' EQUITY	76.7	262.2	1,136.4	1,668.1	2,655.9	9.3	31.7	140.8	213.7	363.6

* 2007 results were unaudited.

Source: Baidu annual reports and quarterly results.

Exhibit 8c Baidu: Consolidated Cashflow Statement (Fiscal Year Ending December 31, 2007)

BAIDU FINANCIALS	RMB Million					$ Million				
STATEMENT OF CASH FLOWS	2003	2004	2005	2006	2007	2003	2004	2005	2006	2007
Exchange rate						8.2767	8.2765	8.072	7.8051	7.3041
Cash flows from operating activities										
Net income	(8.9)	12.0	47.6	301.8	629.0	(1.1)	1.5	5.9	38.7	86.1
Adjustments to reconcile net income to net cash generated from operating activities										
Depreciation of fixed assets	4.9	8.9	30.7	64.1		0.6	1.1	3.8	8.2	
Amortization of intangible assets	–	1.1	3.1	6.3		–	0.1	0.4	0.8	
Disposal of fixed assets	–	0.1	0.0	0.9		–	0.0	0.0	0.1	
Share-based compensation	5.1	16.5	33.6	48.3		0.6	2.0	4.2	6.2	
Provision for doubtful accounts	–	0.6	4.3	(0.3)		–	0.1	0.5	(0.04)	
Foreign exchange loss	–	–	0.6	0.1		–	–	0.1	0.01	
Impairment loss on investment	–	–	–	2.0		–	–	–	0.3	
Cumulative effect of change in accounting principle	–	–	–	(4.6)		–	–	–	(0.6)	
Change in operating assets and liabilities	n/a				n/a	–	–	–	–	n/a
Accounts receivable	(1.5)	(8.4)	(17.5)	(0.4)		(0.2)	(1.0)	(2.2)	(0.05)	
Prepaid expenses and other assets	0.3	(1.5)	(8.5)	(23.5)		0.0	(0.2)	(1.1)	(3.0)	
Customers' deposits	6.3	17.6	44.2	70.9		0.8	2.1	5.5	9.1	

Exhibit 8c Baidu: Consolidated Cashflow Statement (Fiscal Year Ending December 31, 2007) *(Continued)*

BAIDU FINANCIALS	RMB Million					$ Million				
STATEMENT OF CASH FLOWS	2003	2004	2005	2006	2007	2003	2004	2005	2006	2007
Accrued expenses and other liabilities	1.6	10.7	27.1	62.3		0.2	1.3	3.4	8.0	
Deferred tax assets, net	–	–	(4.3)	(3.2)		–	–	(0.5)	(0.4)	
Deferred revenue	5.0	(1.2)	1.4	(5.1)		0.6	(0.1)	0.2	(0.7)	
Deferred income	–	–	0.2	6.7		–	–	0.0	0.9	
Net cash generated from operating activities	12.7	56.5	162.4	526.1		1.5	6.8	20.1	67.4	
Cash flows from investing activities										–
Acquisition of fixed assets	(6.4)	(25.4)	(88.7)	(127.5)		(0.8)	(3.1)	(11.0)	(16.3)	
Acquisition of business	–	–	(10.5)	(43.3)		–	–	(1.3)	(5.6)	
Acquisition of intangible assets	–	(11.9)	(2.1)	(21.9)		–	(1.4)	(0.3)	(2.8)	
Capitalization of internal use software costs	(1.6)	(2.2)	(0.6)	(1.0)		(0.2)	(0.3)	(0.1)	(0.1)	
Acquisition of long-term investments	–	–	(2.0)	–		–	–	(0.3)	–	
Acquisition of marketable securities	–	–	–	(85.3)		–	–	–	(10.9)	
Prepayment for land use rights	–	–	(77.2)	(15.2)		–	–	(9.6)	(1.9)	
Net cash used in investing activities	(8.0)	(39.5)	(181.1)	(294.3)		(1.0)	(4.8)	(22.4)	(37.7)	
Cash flows from financing activities					n/a					n/a

Exhibit 8c Baidu: Consolidated Cashflow Statement (Fiscal Year Ending December 31, 2007) (Continued)

| BAIDU FINANCIALS | RMB Million | | | | | $ Million | | | | |
STATEMENT OF CASH FLOWS	2003	2004	2005	2006	2007	2003	2004	2005	2006	2007
Issuance of Series C convertible preferred shares	–	119.7	–	–		–	14.5	–	–	
Proceeds from initial public offering (IPO), net of expenses	–	–	716.3	–		–	–	88.7	–	
Payments for expenses in connection with IPO	–	–	–	(0.6)		–	–	–	(0.1)	
Proceeds from exercise of share options	0.1	0.6	8.0	32.8		0.0	0.1	1.0	4.2	
Net cash generated from financing activities	0.1	120.3	724.3	32.2		0.0	14.5	89.7	4.1	
Effect of exchange rate changes on cash and cash equivalents	–	–	(5.2)	(28.4)		–	–	(0.6)	(3.6)	
Net increase in cash and cash equivalents	4.8	137.4	700.4	235.7		0.6	16.6	86.8	30.2	
Cash and cash equivalents at the beginning of the year	58.0	62.8	200.2	900.6		7.0	7.6	24.8	115.4	–
Cash and cash equivalents at the end of the year	62.8	200.2	900.6	1,136.3		7.6	24.2	111.6	145.6	–
Supplemental cash flow information										–
Cash paid during the year for income tax	–	–	4.7	24.2		–	–	0.6	3.1	–
Insurance of ordinary shares in purchase of intangible assets	–	2.1	–	–		–	0.3	–	–	–

* 2007 results not available.
Source: Baidu annual reports.

Exhibit 9a Google: Consolidated Income Statement

GOOGLE FINANCIALS INCOME STATEMENT	Year Ended 31 December				
$ Million (except for share, per share information)	2003	2004	2005	2006	2007
Revenues					
Advertising revenues	1,420.7	3,143.3	6,065.0	10,492.6	16,412.6
Licensing and other revenues	45.3	45.9	73.6	112.3	181.3
Total Revenues	1,465.9	3,189.2	6,138.6	10,604.9	16,594.0
Operating costs and expenses					
Cost of revenues	634.4	1,469.0	2,577.1	4,225.0	6,649.1
Research and Development	229.6	395.2	599.5	1,228.6	2,120.0
Sales and marketing	164.9	295.7	468.2	849.5	1,461.3
General and administrative	94.5	188.2	386.5	751.8	1,279.3
Contribution to Google Foundation	–	–	90.0	–	–
Non-recurring portion of settlement of disputes with Yahoo	–	201.0	–	–	–
Total costs and expenses	1,123.5	2,549.0	4,121.3	7,054.9	11,509.6
Income from operations	342.5	640.2	2,017.3	3,550.0	5,084.4
Interest income and other, net	4.2	10.0	124.4	461.0	589.6
Income before income taxes	346.7	650.2	2,141.7	4,011.0	5,674.0
Provision for income taxes	241.0	251.1	676.3	933.6	1,470.3
Net income	105.6	399.1	1,465.4	3,077.4	4,203.7
Net Income per share					
Basic	0.77	2.07	5.31	10.21	13.53
Diluted	0.41	1.46	5.02	9.94	13.29
Number of shares used in per share calculations					
Basic	137,697	193,176	275,844	301,403	310,806
Diluted	256,638	272,781	291,874	309,548	316,210

Source: Google annual reports.

Exhibit 9b Google: Consolidated Balance Sheet

GOOGLE FINANCIALS BALANCE SHEET	Year Ended 31 December				
$ Million	2003	2004	2005	2006	2007
ASSETS					
Current assets					
Cash and cash equivalents	149.0	426.9	3,877.2	3,544.7	6,081.6
Marketable securities	185.7	1,705.4	4,157.1	7,699.2	8,137.0
Accounts receivable, net of allowance	154.7	311.8	688.0	1,322.3	2,162.5
Income taxes receivable	–	70.5	–	–	145.3
Deferred income taxes, net	22.1	19.5	49.3	29.7	68.5
Prepaid revenue share, expenses and other assets	48.7	159.4	229.5	443.9	694.2
Total current assets	560.2	2,693.5	9,001.1	13,039.8	17,289.1
Prepaid revenue share, expenses and other assets, non-current	17.4	35.5	31.3	114.5	168.5
Deferred income taxes, net, non-current	–	11.6	–		33.2
Non-marketable equity securities	–	–	–	1,031.9	1,059.7
Property and equipment, net	188.3	378.9	961.7	2,395.2	4,039.3
Goodwill	87.4	122.8	194.9	1,545.1	2,299.4
Intangible assets, net	18.1	71.1	82.8	346.8	446.6
TOTAL ASSETS	871.5	3,313.4	10,271.8	18,473.4	25,335.8
LIABILITIES AND SHAREHOLDERS' EQUITY					
Current liabilities					
Accounts payable	46.2	32.7	115.6	211.2	282.1
Accrued compensation and benefits	33.5	82.6	198.8	351.7	588.4
Accrued expense and other liabilities	26.4	64.1	114.4	266.2	465.0
Accrued revenue share	88.7	122.5	215.8	370.4	522.0

(Continued)

Exhibit 9b Google: Consolidated Balance Sheet *(Continued)*

GOOGLE FINANCIALS BALANCE SHEET	Year Ended 31 December				
$ Million	2003	2004	2005	2006	2007
Deferred revenue	15.3	36.5	73.1	105.1	178.1
Income taxes payable	20.7	–	27.8	–	–
Current portion of equipment leases	4.6	1.9	–	–	–
Total current liabilities	235.5	340.4	745.4	1,304.6	2,035.6
Long-term portion of equipment leases	2.0	–	–	–	–
Deferred revenue, long-term	5.0	7.4	10.5	20.0	30.2
Liability for stock options exercised early, long-term	6.3	6.0	–	–	–
Deferred income taxes, net	18.5	–	35.4	40.4	–
Income taxes payable, long-term	–	–	–	–	478.4
Other long-term liabilities	1.5	30.5	61.6	68.5	101.9
Commitments and contingencies					
Redeemable convertible preferred stock warrant	13.9	–			
Shareholders' equity					
Convertible preferred stock, $0.001 par value, 100,000 shares authorized; no shares issued and outstanding	44.3	–	–	–	–
Class A and Class B common stock at 31 December of each year	0.2	0.3	0.3	0.3	0.3
Additional paid-in capital	725.2	2,582.4	7,477.8	11,882.9	13,241.2
Note receivable from officer/stockholder	(4.3)	–	–	–	–
Deferred stock-based compensation	(369.7)	(249.5)	(119.0)	–	–
Accumulated other comprehensive income	1.7	5.4	4.0	23.3	113.4
Retained earnings	191.4	590.5	2,055.9	5,133.3	9,334.8
Total shareholders' equity	588.8	2,929.1	9,419.0	17,039.8	22,689.7
TOTAL LIABILITIES AND SHAREHOLDERS' EQUITY	871.5	3,313.4	10,271.8	18,473.4	25,335.8

Source: Google annual reports.

Exhibit 9c Google: Consolidated Cashflow Statement

GOOGLE FINANCIALS CASHFLOW STATEMENT	Year Ended 31 December				
$ Million	2003	2004	2005	2006	2007
Operating activities					
Net income	105.6	399.1	1,465.4	3,077.4	4,203.7
Adjustments					
Depreciation and amortization of property and equipment	43.9	128.5	256.8	494.4	807.7
Amortization of intangibles and other	11.2	20.0	37.0	77.5	159.9
Stock-based compensation	11.6	11.3	200.7	458.1	868.6
Excess tax benefits from stock-based award activity	229.4	278.7	433.7	(581.7)	(379.2)
Deferred income taxes	–	191.6	21.2	(98.5)	(164.2)
Other, net	–	201.0	22.0	12.5	(39.7)
Changes in assets and liabilities, net of effects of acquisitions					
Accounts receivable	(90.4)	(156.9)	(372.3)	(624.0)	(837.2)
Income taxes, net	(6.3)	(125.2)	66.2	496.9	744.8
Prepaid revenue share, expenses and other assets	(58.9)	(99.8)	(51.7)	(289.2)	(298.7)
Accounts payable	36.7	(13.5)	80.6	95.4	70.1
Accrued expenses and other liabilities	31.1	86.4	166.8	291.5	418.9
Accrued revenues share	74.6	33.9	93.3	139.3	150.3
Deferred revenue	7.0	22.0	39.6	30.8	70.3
Net cash provided by operating activities	395.4	977.0	2,459.4	3,580.5	5,775.4
Investing activities					
Purchase of property and equipment	(176.8)	(176.8)	(838.2)	(1,902.8)	(2,402.8)
Purchase of marketable securities	(316.6)	(316.6)	(12,675.9)	(26,681.9)	(15,997.1)
Maturities and sales of marketable securities	219.4	219.4	10,257.2	23,107.1	15,659.5

(Continued)

Exhibit 9c Google: Consolidated Cashflow Statement *(Continued)*

GOOGLE FINANCIALS CASHFLOW STATEMENT	Year Ended 31 December				
$ Million	2003	2004	2005	2006	2007
Investments in non-marketable equity securities	–	–	–	(1,019.1)	(34.5)
Acquisitions, net of cash acquired and purchases of intangible and other assets	(40.0)	(40.0)	(101.3)	(402.4)	(906.7)
Net cash used in investing activities	(314.0)	(314.0)	(3,358.2)	(6,899.2)	(3,681.6)
Financing activities					
Net proceeds from stock-based award activity	2.3	15.5	85.0	321.1	23.9
Net proceeds from stock-based award activity	–	–	–	581.7	379.2
Net proceeds from public offerings	–	–	4,287.2	2,063.5	–
Payment of note receivable from office/stockholder	–	–	–	–	–
Payments of principal on capital leases and equipment loans	(7.4)	4.7	(1.4)	–	–
Net cash flow by financing activities	8.1	1,194.6	4,370.8	2,966.4	403.1
Effect of exchange rate changes on cash and cash equivalents	1.7	7.6	(21.6)	19.7	40.0
Net increase (decrease) in cash and cash equivalents	91.2	277.9	3,450.3	(332.5)	2,536.9
Cash and cash equivalents at beginning of year	57.8	149.0	426.9	3,877.2	3,544.7
Cash and cash equivalents at end of year	149.0	426.9	3,877.17	3,544.67	6,081.59
Supplemental disclosures of cash flow information					
Cash paid for interest	1.7	0.7	0.2	0.3	1.3
Cash paid for taxes	247.4	183.8	153.6	537.7	882.7
Acquisition-related activities					
Issuance of equity in connection with acquisitions, net	73.5	25.7	22.4	1,173.2	–

Source: Google annual reports.

Exhibit 10 Selected Financial Indicators (fiscal year ending 31 December 2007)

Key Facts	$ Million (except for per-share data)	
	Baidu	Google
Sales	230.1	16,594.0
Operating income	72.2	5,084.4
Net income	83.0	5,268.4
Total assets	361.5	25,302.6
Total liabilities	84.7	2,612.9
EBITDA	100.7	6,642.8
Enterprise value	13,087.0	175,662.0
Headcount	5,200	16,805
Stock price year end	389.8	691.5
Shares outstanding (million)	34.1	312.9
Year-end market cap	13,305.0	216,375.3
EPS	2.5	13.3
Return on assets		
Operating margin (%)	31.4	30.6
Return on assets (ROA) (%)	28.9	19.2
Asset turnover	0.64	0.66
Operating margin (%)		
Costing of goods sold to sales	28.6	34.2
Depreciation	8.7	5.8
Research and development	8.4	12.8
Selling, general and administrative expenses	24.5	16.5
Operating income	31.3	25.6

(Continued)

Exhibit 10 Selected Financial Indicators (fiscal year ending 31 December 2007) *(Continued)*

Key Facts	$ Million (except for per-share data)	
	Baidu	**Google**
Asset turnover		
Days accounts receivable (relative to sales)	n/a	39.9
Days inventoried (relative to net cost of sales and services)	n/a	n/a
Asset turnover	0.64	0.66
ROE (rate of return on equity)		
Profit margin	36.1	25.3
Asset turnover	0.64	0.66
Financial leverage	1.3	1.1
Return on equity (ROE) (%)	36.9	21.2
Financial risk indicators		
Days accounts payables	n/a	23.0
Current ratio	2.7	8.5
Debt/equity	–	–
Times interest earned (EBIT/Interest expenses)	n/a	4,717.5
Cash flow/debt	n/a	n/a
Per share data		
Common stock price (close)	389.8	691.5
Common stock price (high)	389.0	747.2
Common stock price (low)	388.0	437.0
Equity shares	34.1	312.9
Earning per share	2.5	13.3
Book value of equity per share (end of year)	8.1	70.8
Stock market acceptance		
MVE/BVE (price/book)	48.1	9.8

Exhibit 10 Selected Financial Indicators (fiscal year ending 31 December 2007) *(Continued)*

Key Facts	$ Million (except for per-share data)	
	Baidu	Google
Price/earnings	148.1	52.0
Price/sales	57.8	13.0
Price/cash flow	129.0	50.2
EV/EBITDA	130.0	30.4
EV/EBIT	161.0	35.6
EV/cash flow	127.8	37.0
Relative equity risk of company ('Beta')	3.31	2.42
Common stock price (end of year)	389.9	691.5
Equity shares (millions)	34.1	312.9
Market value of equity (end of year)	13,305.0	216,375.3
Book value of equity (end of year)	276.7	22,079.1
Stern Stewart Performance Indicators		
Market value added (MVA)	13,028.3	194,296.2
After-tax return on invested capital (ROIC) (%)	n/a	21.17
Weighted average cost of capital (WACC) (%)	25.42	21.16
Economic value added (EVA)	(12.7)	(1,187.4)

Note: Figures here were taken mainly from Thomson Financials for comparison purposes, certain figures may be subject to change once Baidu's annual report becomes available.
Source: Thomson Financials, Company annual reports.

Exhibit 11 Baidu: Revenue Drivers

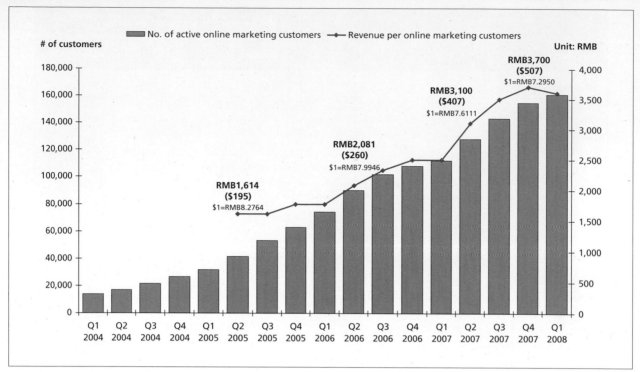

Source: Baidu's annual reports and quarterly results.

Exhibit 12 Comparison of Traffic Acquisition Costs

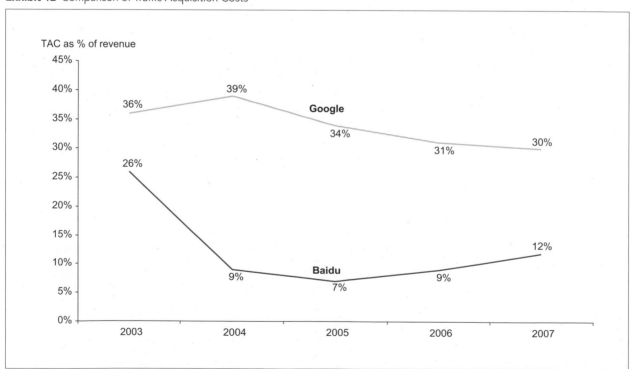

Source: Google's and Baidu's annual reports and quarterly results.

Exhibit 13 Evolution of USS vs. RMB Exchange Rate and Trend^{xl} (forward quotation for indication purpose only)

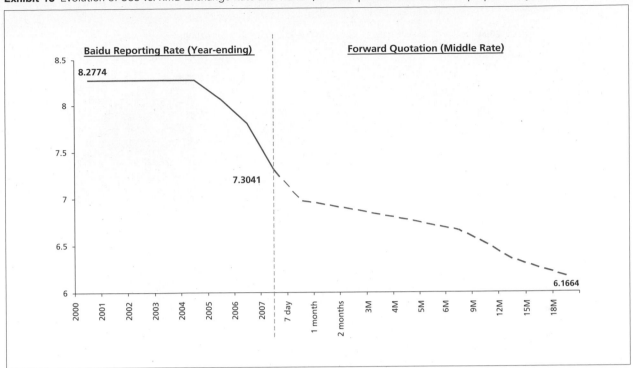

Source: Baidu's annual reports, quarterly results, and http://www.forex.com.

Exhibit 14 Share Performance and Selected Indexes

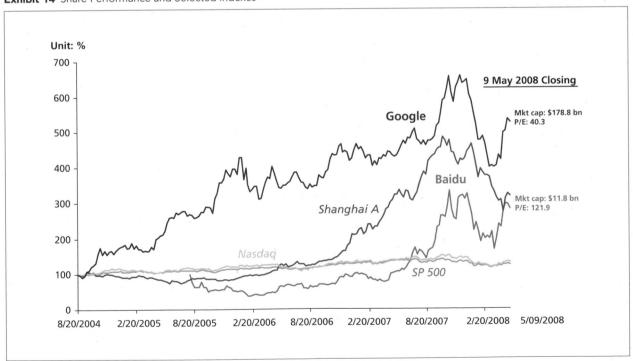

Source: Datastream.

Exhibit 15 U.S. Online Ad Market

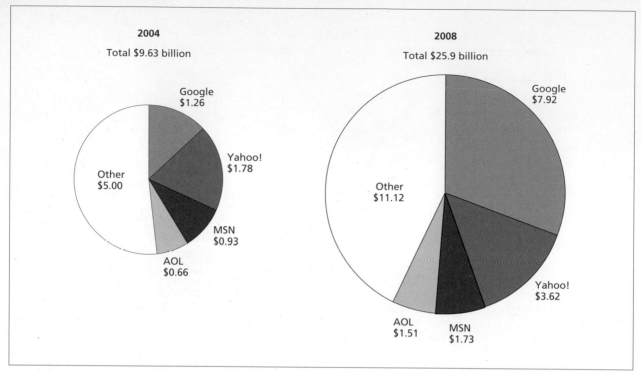

Source: *Wall Street Journal.*[xli]

Exhibit 16a China's Online Ad Market Size

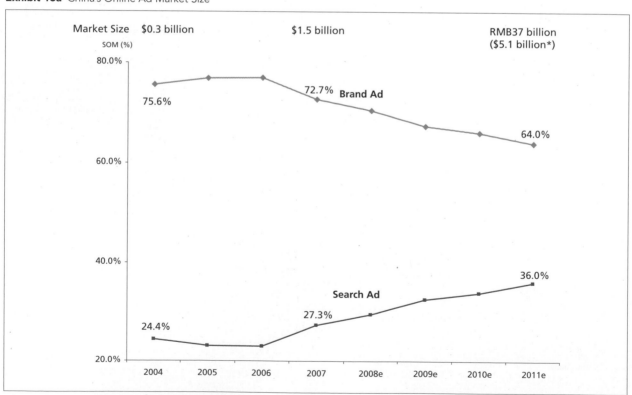

Note: Converted at the 2007 year-end rate: $1 = 7.3041, did not take into consideration the effect of RMB revaluation.

Exhibit 16b China's Search Ad Market Size

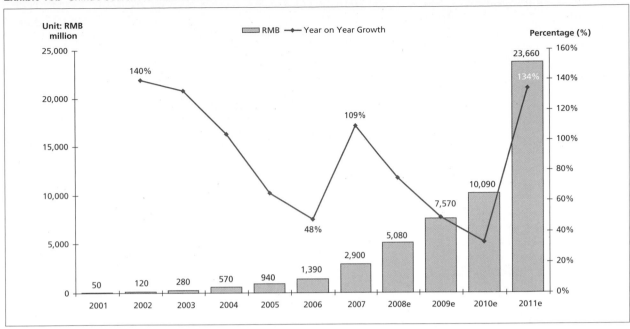

Source: iResearch.[xlii]

NOTES

i. L. Chao & E. Smith, New tune: Google aims to crack China with music push, *Wall Street Journal*, February 6, 2008.

ii. L. Chao & E. Smith, New tune: Google aims to crack China with music push, *Wall Street Journal*, February 6, 2008.

iii. iResearch China Online Search Annual Report 2007.

iv. BNP Paribas report, January 15, 2008.

v. Best Answer to Google, *BusinessWeek*, http://images.businessweek.com/ss/06/12/1207 bestleaders/source/4.htm (accessed May 17, 2008).

vi. Microsoft company press release. January 31, 2008, letter Microsoft sent to Yahoo! board of directors.

vii. Thomson Financials.

viii. Jonathan Watts in Beijing, 2005, Interview: Robin Li, founder of Baidu.com, *The Guardian*, December 8.

ix. Google company Web site.

x. Baidu company Web site.

xi. Baidu company press release.

xii. Google Web site.

xiii. Google Web site.

xiv. BNP Paribas report, January 15, 2008.

xv. Google annual reports.

xvi. BBC, 2006, Google offloads Baidu investment, http://news.bbc.co.uk/2/hi/asia-pacific/4715044.stm, February 15 (accessed May 12, 2008).

xvii. Preliminary Transcript: BIDU—Q1 2008 Baidu Earnings Conference Call, Thomson Street Events, April 24, 2008.

xviii. John Battelle, 2005, 2006, *The Search: How Google and Its Rivals Rewrote the Rules of Business and Transformed Our Culture*, London: Nicholas Brealey Publishing, 2005.

xix. John Battelle, *The Search: How Google and Its Rivals Rewrote the Rules of Business and Transformed Our Culture*, London: Nicholas Brealey Publishing, 2005, 208.

xx. Stacy Cowley, 2006, Google CEO on censoring: 'We did an evil scale,' IDG *News Service*, http://www.infoworld.com/article/06/01/27/74_874 HNgoogleceocensoring_ l html, January 27 (accessed May 16, 2008).

xxi. David Pescovitz, 2006, Chinese Google is song of the grain, http://www.boingboing.net/2006/04/14/chinese-google-is-so.html, April 14 (accessed May 11, 2008).

xxii. David Pescovitz, 2006, Chinese Google is song of the grain, http://www.boingboing.net/2006/04/14/chinese-google-is-so.html, April 14 (accessed May 11, 2008).

xxiii. A. Yeh, 2006, Google disposes of Baidu stake, *Financial Times*, http://www.ft.eom/cms/g/G/6756285a-026d-lldb-al41-0000779e2340.html7nclick_check=l, June 23 (accessed May 12, 2008).

xxiv. J. Watts, 2005, Interview: Robin Li, founder of Baidu.com, *The Guardian*, December 8.

xxv. Baidu 'not a great competitor," says Li Kaifu, *China Wire*, http://www.telecomasia.net/article.php?id article=6759 (accessed May 11, 2008).

xxvi. Baidu.com Q4 2007 Earnings Call Transcript—Seeking Alpha, http://seekingalpha.com/article/64687-baidu-com-q4-2007-earnings-call-transcript?page=-l (accessed May 17, 2007).

xxvii. 2006, Google defends China search site, BBC, http://news.bbc.co.Uk/2/hi/technology/4735662.stm, February 21 (accessed May 12, 2008).

xxviii. BNP Paribas report, January 15, 2008.

xxix. Preliminary Transcript: BIDU—Q1 2008 Baidu Earnings Conference Call, Thomson StreetEvents, April 24, 2008, and Baidu SEC Filings.

xxx. China's google Baidu soars in Nasdaq debut, ChinaDaily.com, http://www.chinadailY.com.cn/english/doc/2005-08/08/content_467140.htm (accessed May 12, 2008).

xxxi. Baidu annual report.

xxxii. 2008, Baidu was said not in compliance with the Hong Kong listing rules, Sina.com.cn, http://tech.sina.com.en/i/2008-05-20/l1522205926.shtml, May 20.

xxxiii. J. Watts, 2005, Interview: Robin Li, founder of Baidu.com, *The Guardian*, December 8.

xxxiv. iResearch, China Online Search Annual Report 2007.

xxxv. Q. Leheng, 2006Baidu vs. Google, r 2006, http://web2.commongate.com/post/Baidu_vs_Google/, December 6 (accessed May 11, 2008).

xxxvi. C. Hui & H. Kaneko, 2008, Baidu CEO talks about Japanese market, Tech-On!, February 5.

xxxvii. Baidu 'not a great competitor,' says Li Kaifu, *China Wire*, http://www.telecomasia.net/article.php?id_article=6759 (accessed May 11, 2008).

xxxviii. http://www.alexa.com/data/details/trafficdetails/baidu.com, http://www.alexa.com/data/details/traffic_details/google.com (accessed May 12, 2008).

xxxix. BNP Paribas report, January 15, 2008.

xl. Baidu IPO Prospectus, annual reports, and forward quotation from http://forex.hexun.com/2008-04-23/105491657.html (accessed May 13, 2008).

xli. K. J. Delaney, M. Karnitschnig, & R. A. Guth, 2008, Giving up on Yahoo!, Microsoft rethinks its Internet options, *Wall Street Journal*, May 6, 2008.

xlii. K. J. Delaney, M. Karnitschnig, & R. A. Guth, 2008, Giving up on Yahoo!, Microsoft rethinks its Internet options, *Wall Street Journal*, May 6, 2008.

Andrew Inkpen, Michael Moffett

Thunderbird School of Global Management

In July 2008, BP was embroiled in a dispute with the Russian shareholders of its TNK-BP joint venture. The Russian shareholders, a group led by billionaires Mikhail Fridman, Viktor Vekselberg, and Len Blavatnik, were demanding the removal of TNK-BP Chief Executive Robert Dudley. The Russian shareholders maintained that BP was not adequately controlling costs and was blocking efforts to expand TNK-BP outside of Russia because that would compete with BP's own operations. They also claimed that BP was employing too many highly paid expatriates in Russia. BP's response was that the venture's main area of operation was always meant to be Russia and Ukraine. According to Dudley: "The company's corporate governance is being tested and the fate of the company is a bellwether for Russia's progress in improving the way its companies are run … For five years, one of my roles has been trying to balance all the issues of shareholders. And I think the ability to keep this balance is important, and I will try to keep that balance."[1]

In comments made to the French newspaper, *Le Monde*, Russian Prime Minister Vladimir Putin said that he had warned both sides that the 50-50 structure would be problematic: "You shouldn't do this … Work it out between yourselves so someone has a controlling stake…There needs to be a boss … You see the result: There's always friction over who's in charge."[2]

With events escalating, Robert Dudley and BP senior management were faced with a challenging situation. Losing its stake in TNK-BP would have serious financial implications for BP. TNK-BP accounted for nearly one-quarter of BP's oil production, and close to one-fifth of its reserves. How the situation was resolved would have a lasting impact on BP and its presence in Russia. The resolution would also impact Russia's overall reputation for attracting and supporting foreign investment.

BP

BP, formerly British Petroleum, was the world's third-largest oil and gas supermajor. Originally founded as the Anglo-Persian Oil Company, BP went from a public company to a British state-owned entity, and then back to being publicly traded during the Thatcher years. BP made many acquisitions over the past century, including Standard Oil of Ohio, Amoco, Castrol, Aral, and Arco. BP's upstream business operated in various countries, including the United States, the United Kingdom, Australia, Angola, Azerbaijan, Canada, Egypt, Russia, Trinidad, Tobago, and Indonesia. The company also operated a diverse range of pipeline, refining, chemical, and retail assets around the world. In recent years, the company had adopted the tagline "Beyond Petroleum" as a way to distinguish itself from its hydrocarbon-based competitors.

Like its supermajor competitors, BP's biggest challenges were increasing oil and gas production and replacing reserves. Most host governments in oil-producing nations were looking for better contractual terms, and the so-called easy oil and gas discoveries were already made. Reserve replacement and equity ownership of new discoveries was becoming difficult. In 2003, then-CEO John Browne told analysts that BP's daily oil production would rise 1.0 million barrels to 4.5 million barrels per day by the end of 2007. The result was less than half the projection, and targets were scaled back to 4.3 million barrels per day by 2012. In 2008, the company planned to invest $15 billion in its upstream business. Relative to its competitors, BP's production growth was constrained by its mature oil fields. Thus, BP was aggressively looking for new reserves, and the stake in TNK-BP was a major part of expected production growth.

BP's financial performance in many areas lagged behind that of ExxonMobil and Shell, especially in the refining sector, which was planning 2,000 job cuts in 2008. The company was also planning about 2,500 head-office job cuts to eliminate bureaucracy and restructure the organization around global businesses rather than geographic sectors. In addition, BP's safety record was under close scrutiny after a recent series of incidents, the most serious being the 2005 explosion in Texas City (southeast of Houston, Texas) which killed 15 people.

The Oil and Gas Industry in Russia

Russia was the world's largest natural gas producer and second-largest crude oil producer. The share of oil and gas in Russia's GDP was believed by many analysts to have more than doubled since 1999 (although some reports, such as a 2007 report from Alfa Bank, said the oil and gas GDP share was declining). Oil and gas revenues made up about 50 percent of Russian budget revenues, 65 percent of exports, and 30 percent of foreign direct investment. According to *The Economist*, "The flow of petrodollars has created a sense of stability, masked economic woes, and given Russia more clout on the world stage."[3] Russia's proven reserves ranked number seven in the world, and there were huge opportunities for further exploration. To manage the windfall from high energy prices, the Russian government created a sovereign wealth fund that held almost $160 billion at the end of 2007.

The Russian oil and gas industry was dominated by six large firms: TNK-BP, Lukoil, Gazprom, Rosneft, Surgutneftegaz, and Tatneft (for comparable financial information see Appendix 4). The latter four were government controlled. Gazprom, with 436,000 employees, was Russia's largest company, the world's largest gas producer with about 93 percent of Russian gas production, and the dominant exporter of gas to Europe (Gazprom supplied about 25 percent of the European Union's gas). In recent years, Russia had been accused of using gas exports as a means of achieving foreign policy objectives. Gazprom had made many acquisitions of small Russian companies that had been privatized in the rigged auctions of the 1990s. Gazprom's oil subsidiary, Gazprom Neft, formerly the independent company Sibneft, was Russia's fifth-largest oil-producing company. Two oligarchs and former partners, Roman Abramovich and Boris Berezovsky, acquired Sibneft for US$100 million; in 2005, Gazprom paid $13 billion for majority control (an "oligarch" is a term for a small group of businessmen who acquired significant wealth and political influence in post-Soviet Russia). Gazprom announced that it planned to make major oil and gas investments outside Russia. Before becoming Russia's president, Dmitry Medvedev was chairman of Gazprom.

Rosneft, the largest oil producer, was a remnant of the Soviet Union's Ministry of Oil and Gas. Rosneft was broken up in the early 1990s and was left with few assets. After 2004, with the acquisition of assets from the now-defunct Yukos, Rosneft became a major firm. In 2006, Rosneft sold 15 percent of its shares in one of the world's largest IPOs. Surgutneftegaz was believed to be closely tied to the Kremlin. The controlling share-holder of Tatneft was the Russian Republic of Tatarstan. Ownership of Lukoil, the largest nongovernment-controlled oil company, included two oligarch share-holders with a 25 percent stake, and Conoco-Philips with 20 percent.

Despite the size and importance of the oil industry in Russia, all was not well. Production in 2008 was declining because of a combination of factors: (1) aging oil fields and poor maintenance; (2) a tax and regulatory regime that was increasingly viewed as confiscatory by oil companies; and (3) a dearth of Russian and foreign investment in exploration and development. The future of foreign investment was unclear. In May 2008, Russia's legislature approved a bill under which Gazprom and Rosneft would have exclusive rights to develop the country's offshore reserves in the Arctic and Far East (not the Caspian). This included the Sakhalin area, where Shell was forced in 2006 to transfer majority control of the Sakhalin II project to Gazprom. In May 2008, Russian President (and soon to be Prime Minister) Putin signed into law a bill limiting foreign investment in strategic industries, including major oil and gas fields. The law prohibited companies with less than 50 percent Russian ownership from bidding for strategic fields, allowing them to participate only as minority partners. The government retained the right to make a decision to issue a license to a foreign-controlled company in special cases.

BP's First Foray in Russia

In November 1997, BP paid $571 million to Uneximbank, one of Russia's most powerful financial and industrial groups, for a 10 percent ownership stake in Sidanco, Russia's fourth-biggest vertically integrated oil company. Sidanco owned three refineries and six production facilities. The deal gave BP 20 percent of the voting rights, a seat on the board, and the right to nominate chief operating and financial officers in the company. The intent was that BP and Sidanco would set up a joint venture to develop and operate Russian oil discoveries. The two companies would have an equal vote in how the venture was run. John Browne, CEO of BP, described the deal as a "major opportunity for BP in one of the great oil and gas provinces of the world … We believe the time is now right and, more importantly, that we have found in Sidanco a partner with a strong, established position at the heart of Russia's oil industry." Uneximbank said, "The agreement signed today is of great importance, both for Sidanco and the Unexim Group, which is the controlling shareholder of Sidanco. For successful development, Sidanco needs a strategic partner with considerable experience and a leading position in the international oil business. BP is this kind of partner."

In 1998, problems began to emerge with Sidanco's oil-producing subsidiary, Chernogorneft, in which Sidanco held 73 percent control. Although BP thought Chernogorneft was financially stable, oil sold to Sidanco had not been paid for, and large tax arrears had accumulated. This helped turn Chernogorneft's management against its parent, Sidanco. Also, the Russian financial crisis of 1998 undermined Uneximbank and sharply reduced oligarch Vladimir Potanin's political influence. Alfa, a rival conglomerate, became interested in Sidanco. As BP was drawn into daily management of Sidanco, Chernogorneft's debts continued to rise.

Alfa Access/Renova. In December 1998, Chernogorneft was driven into bankruptcy by Tyumen Oil Company (TNK), a company held 50–50 by a group known as Alfa Access/Renova, or AAR. TNK was created in 1997 from a cluster of 600 upstream and downstream companies in Russia and Ukraine acquired through various privatization auctions.

AAR was a complex alliance involving three private investment companies: Russia-based Alfa Group and Renova Group, and New York–based Access Industries. Each of the investment companies was headed by an oligarch:

- **Mikhail Maratovich Fridman**, president of Alfa Group Consortium, was born in 1964 in Lvov, on the western border of Ukraine. Fridman attended Moscow Institute of Steel and Alloys, where he had his first business ventures, including window washing, running a discotheque, and scalping Moscow theater tickets—all illegal under Soviet rule. In 1988, Fridman set up a photo cooperative, Alfa Foto, and subsequently ALFA/EKO, a commodities trading firm, which gave him the capital to establish Alfa Bank in 1991, which became one of Russia's largest banks. He hired a Russian foreign trade minister to head up the bank. As his wealth grew, Fridman was able to acquire significant oil interests in Russia. He was a member of a group that funded President Boris Yeltsin's 1996 re-election campaign. Alfa Group, one of Russia's largest privately owned financial-industrial groups, controlled Alfa Bank, Alfa Capital, several construction material firms (cement, timber,

glass), food processing businesses, and a supermarket chain. In 2008, *Forbes* listed Fridman's wealth as $20.8 billion, making him the twentieth richest person in the world.

- **Viktor Vekselberg** was born in 1957 in the Ukraine. He graduated from the Moscow Institute of Transportation Engineering and later went on to complete his master's degree and Ph.D. in mathematics. Vekselberg worked at the special design office of state-owned Rodless Pumps (OKB BN). He started as a technician and eventually became research manager. Vekselberg joined the world of business in 1990. In 1993, he became chairman of the board of directors of Renova Group, which became one of Russia's largest investment and business development companies. Through Renova, Vekselberg orchestrated Russia's first successful hostile takeover, acquiring the Vladimir Tractor Factory in 1994. He rose to prominence after Boris Yeltsin's re-election in 1996, when he started to purchase shares of oil companies, including Tyumen Oil (TNK). In 1997, he became a member of the board of directors of TNK. Vekselberg was ranked the sixty-seventh richest person in the world by *Forbes*, with a net worth of $11.2 billion.

- **Len Blavatnik** was born in Russia in 1958. After attending Moscow Institute of Transportation Engineering, he emigrated with his family to the United States in 1978. He received a master's degree in computer science from Columbia University and an MBA degree from Harvard Business School in 1989. In 1986, Blavatnik founded Access Industries, a privately held U.S.-based industrial group. After the fall of the Soviet Union, Access began making investments in Russia in industries such as oil, coal, aluminum, petrochemicals and plastics, telecommunications, media, and real estate. With his friend from university, Viktor Vekselberg, Access and Renova collaborated in various investments. Blavatnik was ranked the 113th richest person in the world by *Forbes* magazine with a net worth of $8.0 billion.

BP Writes off $200 Million. In February 1999, BP wrote off $200 million of its investment in Sidanco. In November 1999, Chernogorneft was sold out of bankruptcy for $176 million dollars to TNK. BP's director for external affairs in Russia commented: "The entire bankruptcy has been subject to major manipulations. We do not consider it to be valid. In many ways, this decision has damaging implications for foreign investors. BP Amoco will be very carefully reviewing its business position in Russia in the light of these events."[4]

Simon Kukes, chairman of TNK, said that his company had upheld "international standards of corporate governance and ethical behaviour," and stressed that "the purchase had been made in a competitive auction."[5] He offered BP the chance to enter a strategic alliance with him. Although TNK denied doing anything illegal, it appeared to most outside observers that the company used its political influence and the weaknesses of Russia's laws and judicial system to ensure that a succession of court cases went its way.

BP and TNK

In December 1999, TNK and BP announced an agreement under which Sidanco would regain Chernogorneft in return for TNK receiving a 25 percent stake in Sidanco. AAR, TNK's principal shareholder, would receive 25 percent plus one share in Sidanco. In exchange, TNK's shareholders would return Chernogorneft debt-free. The deal would cost TNK about $200 million, compared with $484 million paid by BP for its 10 percent stake. In 2000, after lengthy negotiations, AAR's controlling shareholders replaced Unexim Group as the dominant shareholders of Sidanco.

In February 2003, BP announced a major strategic alliance with the same companies with which it had battled for control of Sidanco. Under the terms of the alliance, BP and AAR would combine their interests in Russia to create the country's third-largest oil and gas business, in which both parties would have a 50 percent stake. The new company, TNK-BP, would be made up of various assets: TNK, Sidanco, and most of BP's Russian assets. BP's Russian assets included a retail network in the Moscow region, minority stakes in Sidanco Rusia Petroleum, and several other equity investments.

For its 50 percent stake, BP would pay AAR $3 billion in cash and three subsequent annual payments of $1.25 billion in BP shares. In describing the deal, BP CEO John Browne said that BP had instituted new governance mechanisms to protect the interests of all parties. He also said that changes in Russia's legal system and an increasing commitment to international rules of trade convinced BP that it was time to deepen its partnership with AAR. Browne called the experience with Chernogorneft and Sidanco a key learning experience in Russia. A BP executive said, "Of course, we had qualms, given the history. But sometimes you don't get the chance to choose your partners. It was the only deal available."[6]

When the JV was announced (see Exhibit 1), there was speculation that the Russian government had reservations about the desirability of foreign investment in energy reserves. There was also speculation that the speed with which the deal was done caught the government off guard.

Joint Venture Structure

The joint venture was legally created in August 2003. In 2004, a major restructuring simplified the complex TNK-BP holdings (a dozen subsidiaries and hundreds of legal entities). In 2005, further restructuring occurred. Three holding companies (TNK, Sidanco, and ONAKO) were merged into TNK-BP Holding. Approximately 70 percent (by value) of minority shareholders in 14 key TNK-BP subsidiaries exchanged their shares for shares in TNK-BP Holding through the voluntary share

Exhibit 1 Agreement on Structure of TNK-BP Holding Signed in London

TASS, Thursday, June 26, 2003

British Petroleum and the Russian Alfa Group (Access-Renova) signed an agreement in London on Thursday, determining the structure of a deal on establishing a TNK-BP joint venture. Under the agreement, all commercial and financial obligations of the sides are formalised, which opens a way for the final creation of a holding.

"The history of the TNK-BP Company starts from this moment," said chairman of the board of directors of the Alfa Group Mikhail Fridman. "I'm sure that this new unique entity will play a leading role in the Russian and, later, in the world oil industry." "We hope that merging trends in the Russian and world fuel and energy complex will not be limited to this deal," said, in turn, TNK board chairman Viktor Vekselberg. "This deal is an international recognition of rising political stability in Russia and its progress in the economic development," he noted.

Holding President Robert Dudley admitted in an interview with Tass that "it was not an easy thing" to take a decision on expanding BP business in Russia. The company carried out a painstaking assessment of assets over the past nine months, and spent enough time on making feasibility estimates. BP participated in a number of major deals over the past five years, and not a single one was concluded with greater carefulness than the present one: "this is true both of assets and obligations as well as legal formalities," the president said.

TNK-BP will have substantial assets in the most important oil-bearing areas of Russia: production will total 800,000 barrels a day in Western Siberia, and 370,000 barrels a day in the Volga-Ural area. Besides, Dudley continued, the company will continue the development of deposits, which was already conducted. There are now 8,000 mothballed wells, he went on to say, and the company mulls over a possibility of resuming their operation gradually. It will be necessary to restart several thousands of wells annually, the president stated. British Petroleum intends to use skilled Russian personnel and to bring machinery and methods from other areas of the world to organize production so as to optimize deposits, wells, and land infrastructure to boost efficiency of recovery, Dudley emphasized.

exchange program. Upon completion of the voluntary share exchange program, minority shareholders owned approximately 5 percent of publicly held TNK-BP Holding. An independent valuation by Deloitte & Touche put a value of $18.5 billion on TNK-BP Holding. See Exhibit 2 for the ownership structure in 2008.

Key elements of the joint venture agreement were as follows:

- Ten-member board with equal representation from BP and AAR.
- AAR nominates the chairman of the board and the chairman of the remuneration committee.
- BP nominates the vice chairman of the board and chairman of the audience committee.
- BP appoints the CEO and holds half the top management positions.
- The Russian shareholders have management control over government relations, legal affairs, and security.
- Dividends will be a minimum of 40 percent of TNK-BP's U.S. GAAP net income.
- The debt ratio must be kept at 25 to 35 percent.
- The business scope of TNK-BP is limited to oil and gas in Russia and Ukraine.
- Management is particularly focused on certain actions: to improve safety, focusing on reducing high-risk practices; to improve planning and forecasting, so that delivery can be assured and there are no surprises; to improve internal control systems and ethical conducts; to curb the chances of fraud,

illegal payments, and misjudgments; to improve the reporting of results, continuously diligent and appropriate disclosure; and, finally, to increase export and production, and reduce cost through the use of better technology.

- TNK-BP holds a 49.8 percent interest in Slavneft through TNK-BP International Ltd. Slavneft operates as a separate entity. TNK-BP and Gazprom Neft have equal representation on the Slavneft Board of Directors.
- The partners are not allowed to sell their interests in the venture until after December 31, 2007 (termed the "lock-in period").

BP appointed Robert Dudley as CEO. Dudley, an American and graduate of Thunderbird School of Global Management, was a veteran Amoco and BP executive. In the mid-1990s, Dudley worked for Amoco in Russia, and saw Amoco outmaneuvered on a deal by the Russian company Yukos.

Shareholder Comments about the JV Formation

At an analyst meeting in New York on October 17, 2003, BP Chairman John Browne made the following comments:

We regard this group of shareholders as one of the best in Russia, with a strong track record. We've built a strong relationship, tested by past difficulties, notably over Sidanco. We continued to build trust, and less and less viewed each other's motives with suspicion. AAR is a vital

Exhibit 2 TNK-BP Ownership Structure, 2008

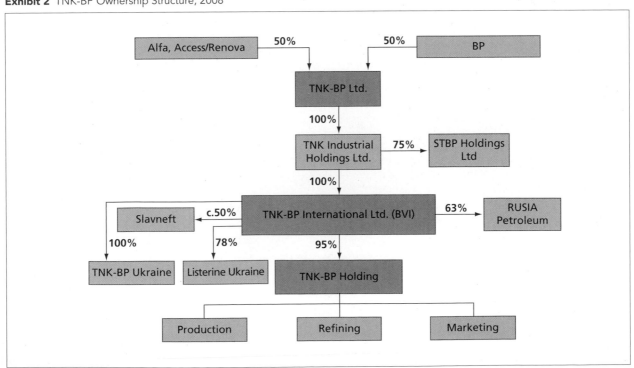

part of the future success of TNK-BP. It brings not only assets and people, but also experience and judgment on the right things to do in the Russian context. They've made it clear that they're committed to making TNK-BP not only a successful operation, but a company which can compare favorably with BP in terms of the quality of governance, transparency, safety, and ethics. In these matters, I know they are reinforcing President Putin's agenda for modernization. BP, as a powerful, globally connected company, brings not only technology to improve the business, but also credibility and experience in modern management. It is a partnership of mutual advantage. Finally, it's about people. And we've selected some of the very best people. Whether they've come from outside, or from TNK, or from Sidanco, or from BP.

At the same meeting, Mikhail Fridman (the lead oligarch shareholder) said:

Of course, we made quite significant profits from the deal but, frankly speaking, we've done this deal not because we just want to realize the profits, but because we do believe that the most important way for us as investors to increase our benefits and potential growth, we do believe that to create a joint venture with a company like BP at the end of the day, we'll benefit after all.

It is obvious to everybody here that the biggest challenge we have is probably the cultural gap between the Russian style of doing business and Western style of doing business. And it is not so easy to overcome that. And from this point of view, we are quite happy that we have a long story of relationship between us and BP. And this not very smooth story—not just, you know, [a] story of friendship and partnership that started from quite tough, you know, competition … We do believe that there are only two things we need as a shareholder. I think it's trust and, second, probably patience.

And it seems to me that both sides have enough of that. So, that's why I'm quite optimistic about the future of our company.

TNK-BP Assets

In 2008, TNK-BP was Russia's third-largest oil and gas company in terms of liquids production, and accounted for almost 20 percent of Russia's total oil production. TNK-BP employed about 65,000 people, including 85 foreign managers, many of whom had formerly worked for BP. The main oil production assets of TNK-BP were located in West Siberia and the Volga-Urals region (Exhibit 3), with new provinces being opened in East Siberia via the planned development of the Verkhnechonskoye oil field (concurrently with the construction of the Transneft-operated East Siberia Oil Pipeline) and in the south of the Tyumen region. The main gas business assets included the Rospan project in Novy Urengoi, which is 100 percent owned by TNK-BP, and the Yugragazpererabotka gas processing joint venture with SIBUR Holding in Nizhnevartovsk. TNK-BP owned 49 percent of Yugragazpererabotka. Some specific data on TNK-BP assets are as follows:

Exhibit 3 TNK-BP's Asset Map, 2008

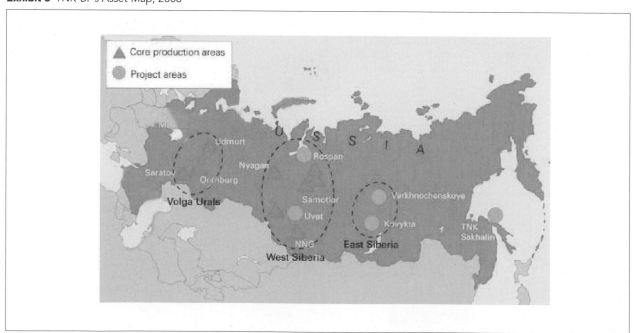

Source: BP.

- TNK-BP held approximately 200 exploration and production licenses.
- Twenty-seven new licenses were acquired in 2007.
- TNK-BP's top 10 fields delivered two-thirds of its production.
- Top 20 fields held 80 percent of proved reserves.
- Average well productivity was 15 tons per day.
- Approximately 25,000 km of infield gathering pipelines (following divestment of assets).
- TNK-BP had four refineries located in Russia (Ryazan Refinery, Saratov Refinery, Nizhnevartovsk Oil Refining Enterprize, and Krasnoleninsk Refinery) and one refinery in Ukraine (Lisichansknefteorgsintez), all close to production areas and export routes.
- The company operated approximately 1,600 retail outlets branded either as BP or TNK in Russia and Ukraine.

JV Financial Results

TNK-BP's revenues, profitability, assets, and cash flow grew substantially over its brief life span (see Exhibit 4; also see the various appendices). However, the revenue structure was heavily constrained by export duties (the Russian government captured about 90 percent of crude prices), and the domestic market prices earned were complex combinations of contracts and regulated rates.

TNK-BP Strategic and Financial Objectives

TNK-BP's strategic objective was to "become a world-class oil and gas group that is an industry leader in Russia, with a clear focus on the sustainability and renewal of its resources and the efficiency of its operations." The company was committed to being an integrated oil and gas company, but the partners were not in agreement as to the level of non-Russian growth. The company was also committed to growing its gas business and was involved in various different discussions with Gazprom.

The joint venture's financial objectives were as follows:

- To maintain a strong balance sheet providing flexibility, liquidity, and cost-effective borrowing.
- To target a gearing range of 25 to 35 percent (net debt/net debt + equity, U.S. GAAP basis).
- To maintain a conservative debt structure with a significant percentage of long-term debt.
- To maintain a dividend policy of at least 40 percent of net income.
- To attain an investment grade credit rating over time.
- To improve the timeliness and quality of financial reporting based on centralized financial management.

In 2008, TNK-BP accounted for about one-quarter of BP's total production, one-fifth of its reserves, and about one-tenth of net income.

Key Joint Venture Events 2003–2007

June 2003—Uncertainty

According to Robert Dudley, TNK-BP CEO: "With all due respect for BP, it had a fairly vague idea about what was going on in Russia. It knew about Russian risks, but it had never had to deal directly with tax authorities, customs officers, monopolies, and relationships with regions …This is more than just an oil deal. And if we fail, it will be more than just a setback for one foreign investor. It will be a setback for the whole country—and the Russian government understands that very well … We will insist on the same level of transparency and governance as in BP."[7]

June 2003—Russians Say the Expatriate Costs Are Too High

Victor Vekselberg commented on expatriate costs: "Bonuses and entitlement for expatriates has been one of the most hotly debated issues. Foreigners who come to Russia want to bring a piece of their own life here."[8]

May 2004—The Russian Partners Want the Deal Changed

The Russian partners informed BP that they wanted the payments for their share of the JV to be made earlier. BP made the following statement:

We have an excellent set of agreements. We expect all partners to stick to those agreements. As we announced in February last year, BP, under the terms of the agreement, will pay three annual tranches on the anniversary of completion of dollars 1.25bn in BP shares valued at market prices prior to each annual payment. What our partners do with those agreements is a matter for them. The agreements provide for AAR to be 50 percent owners of TNK-BP through 2007.[9]

August 2004—Yukos Is Dismantled

The Russian government began the process that would see the bankruptcy and dismantling of oil company Yukos, and the jailing of its prominent and outspoken CEO, Mikhail Khodorkovsky. Yukos was charged with tax bills and other claims of about $28 billion.

April 2005—TNK-BP Faces a Huge Tax Bill

Russian tax authorities announced a $1 billion tax claim relating to 2001 earnings. Viktor Vekselberg said, "We cannot possibly have such liabilities, and will therefore dispute them … There can be no risks, no parallels with Yukos."[10] A few months later, the tax liability was reduced.

Robert Dudley made the following comments:

The significance of this (tax claim) goes far beyond our company. Everyone will watch this as a test of whether

Exhibit 4 TNK-BP's Financial Results, 2002–2007

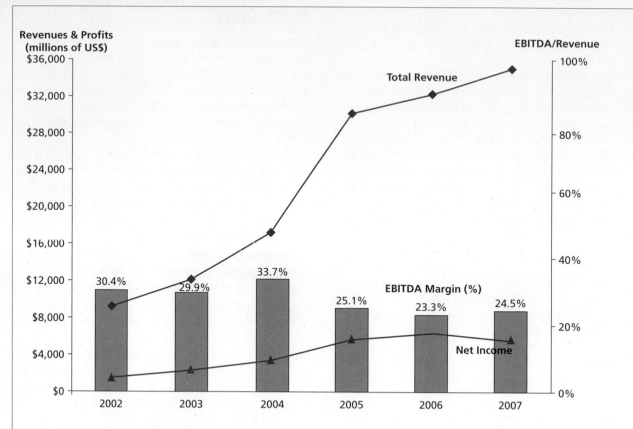

- Revenues grew from $9.2 billion in 2002 to $35 billion in 2007. Net income rose from $1.5 billion in 2002 (16.8 percent) to $5.7 billion in 2007 (16.1 percent).
- Total assets doubled between 2002 and 2007, from $12.6 billion in 2002 to $25.3 billion. The net debt/equity ratio (debt − cash/equity) decreased from 30.2 percent to almost zero in 2007 (0.1 percent). As a result, TNK-BP earned more in interest income than it paid in interest expenses in 2007.
- Operating cash flow grew from $1.385 billion in 2002 to $5.053 billion in 2007.
- The growth in cash flow was deployed between both the owners and the business. Capital expenditures (capex) rose from $595 million in 2002 to $2.23 billion in 2006, with another major jump to $3.285 billion in 2007.
- Dividends paid grew from $139 million in 2002 to $6.664 billion in 2006 and then down to $4.379 billion in 2007.
- Cash and liquid assets were $2.587 billion at end-of-year 2007.
- The share price for TNK-BP Holding fell from a high of $3.40/share in early 2006 to $2.00/share in mid-2008.

Russia can integrate with the world economy. I don't think it is in the interest of the Russian government to destroy TNK-BP. Russia is inadvertently becoming increasingly difficult to navigate for well-intentioned investors—Russian and foreign alike. The state has progressively asserted its influence over the commanding heights of the economy, and state-owned companies have begun to play an increasingly prominent role. At the time when Russia's economy is in need of knowledge and management skills, *it is becoming increasingly difficult to bring in managers and executives.*[11]

April 2005—TNK-BP May Not Be Allowed to Bid for New Oil Fields

A senior official in the Natural Resources Ministry said that that an auction for three major fields was canceled in March in order to exclude TNK-BP. Later in the month, Vladimir Putin told John Browne, BP CEO, "We were not mistaken when we supported your decision two years ago. The profits of the joint company have increased 20 times over. This is proof of the quality of management."[12]

October 2005—Foreign Oil Companies Cannot Participate in Auctions

Russia's natural resources minister announced that companies more than 50 percent foreign-owned will not be allowed to take part in 2006 auctions for new oil fields.

March 2006—TNK-BP in Major Dispute Over Gas Field

One of TNK-BP's most valuable assets was the Kovykta gas field in eastern Siberia. The license to develop Kovykta was held by Rusia Petroleum, 62.89 percent owned by TNK-BP and previously controlled by Sidanco. TNK-BP wanted to develop the gas for Asian markets, and Gazprom (the Russian government-owned natural gas company) said the gas should be developed for Russia. There was speculation that Rusia Petroleum's license for the field would be revoked. The Natural Resources Ministry accused TNK-BP of producing too little gas at the field. TNK-BP argued it could not produce the 9 billion cubic meters per year stipulated in the license since Gazprom had blocked construction of a pipeline to China, and local demand was insufficient. TNK-BP had been lobbying for years for the license to be amended.

October 2006—Robert Dudley Says TNK-BP Will Survive

Dudley stated, "We are confident there is a solid future for TNK-BP. Much has been written about the consolidation of the state … But I believe having companies like this is a good thing for the industry … As long as we continue to get good results, I think the company will more than survive, I think it will thrive. I have seen no evidence that they [the Russian partners] are working to sell their interest."[13]

An oil industry analyst had the following observation: "BP has found it is not only dancing with the wrong partner, but that the dance tune has changed, too. They got in at a good price, and they got in at a good time. It's better for the company to adjust rather than try to go against the tide."[14]

October 2006—TNK-BP Engineer Killed

The chief engineer for Rusia Petroleum, which held the license to develop the Kovykta gas field, was shot dead in Siberia. Rumors about a contract killing immediately began circulating.

June 2007—Putin Angry about the Kovykta Gas Field Dispute

In Germany for a G8 meeting, Putin said to reporters: "How long should we tolerate it if participants of that consortium do nothing to implement the license? This is not about BP, not about the foreign partner, but about all the shareholders that took the obligations to develop this field and, unfortunately, didn't meet the license terms … I won't even talk now about how the license was purchased. Let's leave this up to the conscience of those who did it a while ago, also in the early 1990s."[15]

Late June 2007—TNK-BP Sells Its Stake in the Kovykta Gas Field

TNK-BP sold its 62.89 percent stake in Rusia Petroleum to Gazprom for about $800 million, less than a third of its real value, according to some analysts. TNK-BP had invested about $450 million in developing the field. TNK-BP had the option to buy back 25 percent of the field at market price.

Gazprom Approaches BP about a Deal in 2007

In mid-2007, Gazprom initiated discussions with BP about a possible alliance. Gazprom's goal of becoming a global oil and gas company was being stymied by opposition from Western governments. Gazprom was interested in stakes in BP assets outside Russia. In return, Gazprom would contribute large stakes in its Russian oil business. A key element of the alliance would involve Gazprom buying AAR's TNK-BP stake, which would then allow BP and Gazprom to combine their various Russian oil assets and create the largest Russian oil producer.[16] Gazprom officials told BP privately that they believed AAR would sell. AAR said publicly that they had no intention of selling.

BP's country manager for Russia, James Dupree, handled most of the discussions with Gazprom. BP CEO Tony Hayward made several trips to Russia to meet with Gazprom CEO Alexei Miller. Based on the many meetings that were held, BP was confident that a deal would happen, and that the TNK-BP partner issues would be resolved.

2008: Can the JV Survive?

On March 19, 2008, Russian security services raided TNK-BP offices and detained an employee, Ilya Zaslavsky, on charges of espionage. On March 21, Russia's environmental agency announced an investigation of TNK-BP's largest oilfield. The investigation was to be led by the same official that investigated the Sakhalin II project operated by Shell. Shell was later forced to sell a stake in the project to Gazprom. On March 25, the Interior

Ministry said it was investigating a $40 million tax evasion case against Sidanco, a former TNK-BP subsidiary.

Expatriate Visa Problems for BP.

President Putin had complained about the dearth of Russians in top management positions in natural resource companies. In early 2008, BP had problems renewing visas for expatriate employees, allegedly because of a "lack of clarity." In May, a Siberian court refused to allow visas for 148 technology specialists seconded from BP. The court order was initiated by a Moscow brokerage, ZAO Tetlis, that owned a small stake in a publicly traded unit of TNK-BP, and alleged that the fees TNK-BP paid for the BP specialists amounted to an illegal dividend for BP. BP maintained that without the specialists, TNK-BP's production could be reduced. When the expatriates, already in the country, showed up for work, TNK-BP security refused to let them enter the office. Robert Dudley blamed a TNK-BP executive, German Khan (a billionaire investor and colleague of Mikhail Fridman), for orchestrating the visa issue, and sought his and two other executives' ouster from the venture for gross insubordination. BP said that Khan ignored instructions and applied for fewer than half the required visas. The Russian shareholders responded with a statement saying that TNK-BP should be allowed to expand outside Russia even if it would compete with BP's own operations, and called for reducing the venture's reliance on foreign specialists. The statement also called Dudley's recent comments about the visa issue deeply inappropriate.[17]

In July, immigration authorities approved only 71 visas, far fewer than the 150 BP requested. BP reassigned the 148 seconded employees to other BP units.

The Gazprom Deal Collapses.

Despite the various problems, BP remained hopeful that a deal with Gazprom would be worked out. In April 2008, BP CEO Tony Hayward visited Igor Sechin, a powerful Putin confidant and chairman of Rosneft (the following month, Sechin was promoted to deputy prime minister in charge of the energy industry). At the meeting, Hayward discussed BP's efforts to reach a deal with Gazprom. Sechin explained that Gazprom was not always able to deliver on its ambitions for making major international deals. In May, Hayward met with a former Kremlin official who informed him that his talks with Gazprom were "indecent" and that BP should be less confrontational with AAR. Hayward was also told that the Kremlin would not force AAR to sell. On May 14, 2008, Hayward met Gazprom officials in Manchester, England, at a football match. At this meeting, Gazprom was noncommittal and, in a surprise to BP, suggested holding off on any decisions for a month or so.

Partner Disagreements over JV Strategy.

In late May, the stakes escalated when the three Russian oligarchs met with Tony Hayward and demanded that Robert Dudley be removed as TNK-BP CEO. According to a statement released by the Russian shareholders, Dudley was favoring BP over the Russian shareholders. A spokesperson for the Russians said, "He [Dudley] is acting in the interests of only 50 percent of the shareholders. We want someone who will pursue the interests of all shareholders, not just run TNK-BP like a BP subsidiary."[18] The Russian shareholders were particularly upset with Dudley's five-year strategic plan forecasting lower shareholder returns in the coming years because of high taxes, increasing costs, and stagnant production. The Russian shareholders refused to approve the plan. They argued that Dudley was too focused on increasing reserves, and should be increasing the production of existing oil fields. They wanted the 2008 investment plan of $4.4 billion cut by $900 million and the money paid as dividends. BP argued that TNK-BP was the best-performing oil company in Russia. According to Mikhail Fridman: "There's a strategic conflict of interests between TNK-BP and BP itself. We had a company that was strong, energetic, and aggressive in the good sense of the word. BP turned it into a typical bureaucracy … We don't plan to leave, and I don't think that they plan to leave. So, ultimately, we're destined to come to some agreement.[19] The attempt to portray this conflict as a dispute between a respectable Western company and some Russian oligarchs who are trying to take control using dirty methods is completely cynical. It is our partners who are using methods from the 1990s. There is a good English word: arrogance … We sensed this condescending attitude towards what we were saying [for months] … This is about the type of foreign investors Russia needs. We don't need foreign investors who limit the development of the company."[20]

Hayward refused to remove Dudley. The Russian shareholders threatened legal action to strip BP-appointed directors of their powers. BP was contemplating its own lawsuit against the partners to recover a recently paid portion of back taxes. BP maintained that the taxes paid for the period prior to the formation of the JV should be borne entirely by the previous owners of TNK (which would include Fridman, Vekselberg, and Blavatnik) and its subsidiaries, and not BP.

BP Chairman Peter Sutherland expressed his frustration: "This is just a return to the corporate raiding activities that were prevalent in Russia in the 1990s. Prime minister has referred to these tactics as relics of the 1990s but, unfortunately, our partners continue to use them, and the leaders of the country seem unwilling or unable to step in and stop them. This is bad for us, bad for the company and, of course, very bad for Russia."[21]

"The Alfa Playbook." BP took several steps to deal with its partners. In early June, Tony Hayward met with Igor Sechin to discuss AAR's pressure tactics. BP moved Lamar McCay, an executive with Russia experience, from the United States to Russia to be executive vice president of TNK-BP. BP hired a consulting firm to study other foreign joint ventures involving AAR companies. The outcome of the study became known in BP as the "Alfa Playbook."[22] BP learned, for example, that other Alfa joint ventures had run into various difficulties. For example, Altimo, an Alfa subsidiary, had a joint venture with Norway's Telenor A/S. In 2007, Telenor accused Altimo of dirty tricks in the midst of a business dispute over a Ukrainian mobile phone company. Telenor accused Alfa of paying journalists in Ukraine to publish negative articles about Telenor. Altimo filed a lawsuit in Ukraine and received a favorable ruling. Telenor was never informed that the lawsuit was under way. The result of the lawsuit was sent to a Telenor address that was unoccupied, and by the time Telenor learned of the ruling, the Ukrainian judge on the case had disappeared (the day after giving the decision), and it was too late to appeal. According to BP officials, the Alfa Playbook was "playing out to the letter" in the TNK-BP dispute.

BP's Options

In late July 2008, it was looking increasingly likely that Robert Dudley would not be granted a visa and would have to leave Russia. There was also concern that Russia's Federal Labor and Employment Service would try to prosecute a group of TNK-BP managers for violating labor law. Because of the uncertainty, Dudley had not left Russia since March. The Russian partners maintained that his contract expired at the end of 2007, while BP said his contract was automatically renewed. In an interview, Dudley said: "Running the company now is like driving a car, and sometimes the brakes work and sometimes they don't. I spend a lot of time holding meetings out on the balcony of my office …. It's not me personally, it can't be performance; it's the role, the check and balance between the interests of the shareholders. I've got an obligation to hold the line for both sets of shareholders."[23]

Without a Gazprom deal to buy out AAR, Robert Dudley and his BP colleagues considered other options. One option was to take the dispute to the highest levels in the Russian government, perhaps even to Putin himself. The results of earlier meetings with Igor Sechin, deputy prime minister, suggested that this option would have limited value. A second option was to seek British government help, which had been offered. Prime Minister Gordon Brown was going to be in Russia in July for meetings with President Medvedev. A third option was legal action against AAR for violating the shareholder agreement. Finally, BP could sit tight, continue to run the business, and resist the Russian shareholders. Meanwhile, the Russian shareholders continued to push for Dudley's dismissal, with Victor Vekselberg calling for a July board meeting to discuss Dudley's infringement of Russian employment, immigration, and tax laws. Although BP said Dudley would keep his job, it was hard too see how he could remain CEO if he was outside Russia.

Appendix 1 TNK-BP Holding, Consolidated Statements of Income (millions of U.S. dollars)

	2002	2003	2004	2005	2006	2007
Sales revenue	$9,172	$12,114	$17,169	$30,106	$32,114	$34,995
Operating expenses	(6,381)	(8,497)	(11,390)	(22,536)	(24,684)	(26,399)
EBITDA	2,791	3,617	5,779	7,570	7,430	8,596
EBITDA margin	30.4%	29.9%	33.7%	25.1%	23.1%	24.5%
Depreciation & amortization	(580)	(814)	(1,039)	(1,206)	(1,250)	(1,341)
EBIT	2,211	2,803	4,740	6,364	6,180	7,255
Equity income					71	4
Net interest income					79	182
Interest expense	(273)	(177)	(29)	(111)	(210)	(167)

(Continued)

Appendix 1 TNK-BP Holding, Consolidated Statements of Income (millions of U.S. dollars) (*Continued*)

	2002	2003	2004	2005	2006	2007
Exchange gain (loss)					(104)	8
Gains on disposal of subsidiaries	133	189	—	766	2,677	105
Profit before tax	2,071	2,815	4,674	6,975	8,693	7,387
Income tax expense	(190)	(227)	(1,221)	(1,220)	(2,115)	(1,453)
Minority interest	(337)	(214)	(37)	(70)	(169)	(202)
Net profit	$1,544	$2,374	$3,416	$5,685	$6,409	$5,732
Return on sales	16.8%	19.6%	19.9%	18.9%	19.9%	16.4%
Weighted average shares (m)	15,448	15,448	15,448	15,448	15,448	15,448
EPS	$0.10	$0.15	$0.22	$0.37	$0.41	$0.37
DPS	$0.01	$0.04	$0.25	$0.25	$0.43	$0.16
Payout ratio	9.0%	25.0%	112.8%	68.6%	105.7%	42.2%
Export duties (part of operating expenses)					9,327	9,256

Source: TNK-BP Holding, TNK-BP, and author calculations.

Appendix 2 TNK-BP Holding, Consolidated Balance Sheet (millions of U.S. dollars)

	2002	2003	2004	2005	2006	2007
Cash and other liquid assets	1,083	869	477	485	827	635
Fixed assets	7,751	10,121	11,050	11,704	11,259	13,901
Long term investments	823	1,679	81	90	94	20
Other assets	2,948	3,445	4,826	6,609	9,530	13,348
Total Assets	12,605	16,114	16,434	18,888	21,710	27,904
Interest-bearing debt	3,167	2,755	1,669	1,811	1,515	1,859
Other liabilities	2,533	4,101	5,291	7,844	8,103	9,752
Total Liabilities	5,700	6,856	6,960	9,655	9,618	11,611
Shareholders' equity	5,099	8,530	8,958	8,606	11,488	15,585
Minority interest	1,806	728	755	866	604	708
Total Liabilities & Shareholders' Equity	12,605	16,114	16,434	18,888	21,710	27,904
Net debt	2,084	1,886	1,192	1,326	688	1,224
Net debt/equity	30.2%	20.4%	12.3%	14.0%	5.6%	7.8%
Change in working capital	(327)	661	(499)	(214)	2,453	3,369

Source: TNK-BP Holding and author calculations.

Appendix 3 TNK-BP Holding, Cash Flow (millions of U.S. dollars)

	2002	2003	2004	2005	2006	2007
Cash flow from operations	1,980	4,082	4,687	5,042	7,877	5,485
Net capital expenditures (capex)	(595)	(849)	(1,293)	(1,764)	(2,234)	(3,266)
Free cash flow	1,385	3,233	3,394	3,278	5,643	2,219
Dividends paid	(139)	(594)	(3,854)	(3,901)	(6,594)	(2,420)
Discretionary cash flow	1,246	2,639	(460)	(623)	(951)	(201)
Net change in borrowings	(472)	(807)	580	264	(2,026)	305
Equity capital raised, net	—	—	—	—	—	—
Other investing/financing activities	(72)	(2,111)	(338)	1,203	3,319	(296)
Net cash flow	702	(279)	(218)	844	342	(192)

Source: TNK-BP Holding.

Appendix 4 Public Comparables

Company	Country	Capitalization Million USD	Market Multipliers				Financial Multipliers				
			P/S	P/E	EV/ EBITDA	P/BV	ROE	ROA	ROIC	WACC	ROIC/ WACC
Gazprom	Russia	305,152	3.23	12.06	9.13	1.99	21.28%	12.70%	16.51%	8.89%	1.86
LUKOIL	Russia	64,090	1.06	8.50	5.62	1.69	25.07%	16.90%	21.97%	9.50%	2.31
Gazprom Neft	Russia	27,794	1.45	7.50	5.24	2.71	41.63%	29.59%	36.09%	10.15%	3.56
Surgut-neftegas	Russia	38,076	1.55	10.20	0.00	0.97	9.83%	9.15%	9.71%	10.84%	0.90
Tatneft	Russia	13,537	0.94	10.49	5.66	1.26	13.84%	9.90%	13.59%	11.30%	1.20
TNK-BP	Russia	29,634	1.27	4.38	0.00	2.44	73.96%	31.86%	60.87%	10.50%	5.80
Transneft	Russia	9,186	0.79	3.15	3.06	0.41	15.09%	10.38%	13.94%	9.86%	1.41
Rosneft	Russia	86,799	2.04	7.66	11.64	3.31	24.11%	9.20%	14.82%	9.86%	1.50
NOVATEK	Russia	23,531	9.91	34.44	21.34	7.20	22.42%	17.27%	20.78%	9.86%	2.11
Russia's Average			**2.47**	**10.93**	**6.85**	**2.44**	**27.47%**	**16.33%**	**23.14%**	**10.08%**	**2.29**
Petro-China	China	538,994	2.61	13.77	15.07	3.08	25.81%	17.24%	23.21%	17.20%	1.35
Petroleo Brasileiro SA	Brazil	253,141	2.29	17.58	9.83	3.39	29.39%	13.15%	19.85%	13.66%	1.45
Sasol	RSA	33,667	2.54	15.77		4.07	29.82%	15.33%	23.82%	14.09%	1.69
Sinopec	China	9,752	0.47	28.43	16.94	1.20	4.47%	3.11%	4.86%	17.49%	0.28

(Continued)

Appendix 4 Public Comparables (*Continued*)

Company	Country	Capitalization Million USD	Market Multipliers				Financial Multipliers				
			P/S	P/E	EV/ EBITDA	P/BV	ROE	ROA	ROIC	WACC	ROIC/ WACC
Emerging Markets Average			1.98	18.89	13.95	2.94	22.37%	12.21%	17.94%	15.61%	1.19
Murphy Oil	USA	15,409	0.83	18.85	11.15	3.16	16.99%	9.24%	14.32%	9.00%	1.59
Norsk Hydro	Norway	18,363	0.58	5.30		1.72	24.17%	11.16%	21.05%	13.13%	1.60
Occidental Petroleum	USA	64,736	3.48	14.91	6.29	2.85	25.67%	15.66%	24.14%	10.67%	2.26
Petro-Canada	Canada	24,295	1.11	9.96	3.66	2.00	24.50%	11.76%	19.69%	12.41%	1.59
Repsol YPF	Spain	42,498	0.54	8.73	4.37	1.51	18.54%	6.87%	12.30%	10.36%	1.19
Developed Markets Average			1.31	11.55	6.37	2.25	21.97%	10.94%	18.30%	11.11%	1.65
BP	Great Britain	205,892	0.73	10.03	5.94	2.20	23.38%	9.19%	18.64%	9.41%	1.98
Chevron Texaco	USA	186,271	0.92	10.25	5.68	2.49	26.04%	13.26%	22.56%	10.09%	2.24
Conoco-Phillips	USA	131,370	0.80	8.66	4.98	1.58	13.86%	6.94%	11.33%	10.09%	1.12
Exxon-Mobil	USA	488,394	1.36	12.28	6.91	4.12	35.11%	18.49%	33.43%	10.03%	3.33
Royal-Dutch	Holland	227,019	0.64	7.22	4.33	1.81	27.28%	12.41%	23.34%	9.18%	2.54
Total SA	France	182,004	0.83	8.61	4.33	2.52	30.95%	12.05%	22.81%	10.12%	2.25
Global Average			0.88	9.51	5.36	2.45	26.10%	12.06%	22.02%	9.82%	2.24

Source: Veles Capital, 2008, June 16, 17. Original data drawn from Bloomberg, Estimation, and Veles Capital.

NOTES

1. G. White, 2008, BP in Russia—plagued from start? Putin says venture structured poorly, clear boss is needed, *Wall Street Journal*, June 2, B2.
2. Ibid.
3. 2008, Trouble in the pipeline: Russia's oil industry, *The Economist*, May 10.
4. A. Jack, 1999, BP Amoco to review its Russian interests, *Financial Times*, November 27, 15.
5. Ibid.
6. G. White & G. Chazan, 2008, Boardroom brawl roils BP's Russia venture, talks break down; Kremlin's role murky, *Wall Street Journal*, June 12, A1.
7. C. Hoyas & A. Ostrovsky, 2003, Aiming to clean up in Russia with record deal: The success of BP's huge project will not only be judged in oil and money, *Financial Times*, June 26, 26.
8. Ibid.

9. C. Hoyas, A. Jack, & A. Ostrovsky, 2004, Russian partners seek to change BP deal, *Financial Times*, May 4, 1.

10. I. Gorst & A. Ostrovsky, 2005, TNK-BP hit by a dollars lbn tax bill, *Financial Times*, April 12, 21.

11. I. Gorst & A. Ostrovsky, 2005, TNK-BP chief attacks Russia's uncertain investment climate, *Financial Times*, April 13, 8.

12. C. Belton, 2005, Putin allays TNK-BP worries, *Moscow Times*, April 25.

13. C. Belton, 2006, Dudley dismisses talk of sale, *Moscow Times*, October 4.

14. Ibid.

15. A. Medetsky, 2007, An irritated president steps into Kovykta fray, *Moscow Times*, June 5.

16. G. White & G. Chazin, 2008, Misreading the Kremlin costs BP control in Russia venture, *Wall Street Journal*, December 16, A1, A6.

17. G. White & G. Chazan, 2008, BP venture is threatened as criticisms spill into the open, *Wall Street Journal*, May 28.

18. G. White & G. Chazan, 2008, Intrigue in Russia ensnares BP venture, *Wall Street Journal*, May 30, A1.

19. White & Chazan, Boardroom brawl roils BP's Russia venture.

20. C. Belton & E. Crooks, 2008, Fridman accuses BP of arrogance, *Financial Times*, June 17, 18.

21. R. Anderson, C. Belton, & E. Crooks, 2008, BP accuses Russians of corporate raiding, *Financial Times*, June 13, 1.

22. G. White & G. Chazan, 2008, BP is in the dark in struggle to save its Russian venture, *Wall Street Journal*, June 30, B4.

23. G. White, 2008, The bitter battle to lead TNK-BP: Dudley pushes back as Russian group seeks his ouster, *Wall Street Journal*, July 23, B1.

Mike Apostol, Jami Clement, Cory Edwards, Mairah Meller,
Sam Park, Phil Rogers, Doug Trucha, Robin Chapman

Arizona State University

The New York Times Company

Arthur O. Sulzberger Jr., chairman and publisher for The New York Times Company, left work on November 5, 2008, reeling from amazement over the events of the day. Although since the 1980s[1] print circulation had rapidly declined in the newspaper industry, this day had been very different. Thanks to the post-election front page headline declaring, "OBAMA – Racial Barrier Falls in Decisive Victory," *The New York Times* had flown off shelves at a rate not seen since November 11, 1918, when the newspaper, then owned by Sulzberger Jr.'s grandfather, announced the end of World War I.[2] Even more significant is the fact that copies of the Obama-headlined newspaper were selling on eBay for more than $600.[3]

However, Sulzberger Jr. did not dwell on the good fortune of this particular day. The excitement in the newsroom over the paper's interest did not erase or even ease the current crisis at The New York Times Company. In September 2008 total company revenues from continuing operations decreased 8 percent compared with the same month in 2007, and advertising revenues decreased 13 percent.[4] Unlike the challenges that his forebears had faced, today's challenges could not be solved simply by investing money in the company with the hope that high-quality journalism would prove more profitable.[5] The company was fast approaching the point where it would have to manage its business primarily to conserve cash (with only $46 million in cash on the books) and avoid defaulting on its debt (approximately $1.1 billion). Furthermore, Sulzberger Jr. realized that the situation would only worsen as advertising revenue was widely projected to keep falling.[6]

According to The New York Times Company's policy on ethics in journalism, the core purpose of the company is to "enhance society by creating, collecting and distributing high-quality news, information and entertainment."[7] For 100 years the company had been able to fulfill this purpose and has set the standard for print publications in the United States as well as around the world by spending big money not only on the addition of new sections and color illustrations but also on a highly gifted editorial staff (salaries are thought to exceed $300 million a year[8]).

Sulzberger Jr. pondered on how great it would be if the company could return to the "good old days," when the newspaper was a profitable business simply due to subscriptions and advertising income.

History

Former banker George Jones and journalist/politician Henry Jarvis Raymond founded *The New York Times* on September 18, 1851.[9] From 1851 to 1860 the newspaper was published Monday through Saturday. However, demand for daily news became so great during the Civil War that *The New York Times*, along with other major dailies, began publishing Sunday issues.[10] In the 1880s the newspaper moved from supporting Republican candidates to a more politically independent position (although the newspaper supported Grover Cleveland, a Democratic presidential candidate, in 1884, a decision that temporarily damaged readership).[11]

In 1896 *The New York Times* was purchased by Adolph Ochs, publisher of *The Chattanooga Times*, thus beginning the Ochs-Sulzberger family ownership of the newspaper. In 1897 Ochs coined the newspaper's slogan "All the news that's fit to print."[12] This motto, which can still be found on the front page of each daily issue of *The New York Times*, was a shot by Ochs at competing newspapers, which were known for downplaying legitimate news in favor of eye-catching headlines that sold more newspapers.[13]

The authors would like to thank Professor Robert E. Hoskisson for his support and guidance during the development of this case. This case is not intended to illustrate either effective or ineffective handling of managerial situations. The case is solely intended for class discussion.

Entering the twentieth century there were many "firsts" which allowed *The New York Times* (now called the "*Gray Lady*" by some due to its staid appearance and style), under Ochs's guidance, to achieve international scope, circulation, and reputation. In 1904 the newspaper received its first wireless transmission from a battle at sea during the Russo-Japanese war. *The New York Times* began its first regular air delivery to Philadelphia in 1910. In 1920 the newspaper made its first trans-Atlantic delivery.[14]

In 1935, in the midst of the Great Depression, Ochs passed away, leaving his son-in-law, Arthur Hays Sulzberger, as the newspaper's publisher.[15] Sulzberger got to work right away, pushing the newspaper's editors to begin an editorial barrage on President Roosevelt's plan to pack the Supreme Court with hand-selected individuals. This editorial crusade is still remembered as one of the most intense periods in *The New York Times'* history, and cemented the newspaper's commitment to "hard-hitting, ground-breaking journalism."[16]

During the 1940s, *The New York Times* extended its reach by introducing daily crossword puzzles and a fashion section. An international edition was published for the first time in 1946, and continued until the following year when *The New York Times* collaborated with the *New York Herald Tribune* and *The Washington Post* to publish the *International Herald Tribune* in France. In 1946, the newspaper also purchased a radio station (WQXR).[17]

The 1960s are remembered for the paper's involvement in the 1964 libel case, *The New York Times v. Sullivan.* This case resulted in one of the key U.S. Supreme Court decisions supporting freedom of the press.[18] In 1967 *The New York Times* went public and founded The New York Times Company.[19]

The company experienced a period of substantial change after going public. In the 1970s it acquired magazine publications such as *Golf Digest* and *Tennis Magazine*, book publishing companies like Cambridge, various daily newspapers, and even television stations.[20] Throughout the 1980s the company continued to aggressively acquire media outlets, and in the late 1980s investors were rewarded by two stock splits and many repurchases.[21]

Early in the 1990s, The New York Times Company began to advance its digital strategy, and in 1995 the company launched its domain, nytimes.com, on the World Wide Web. The New York Times Company has tried to exploit the Internet by spending more than $500 million on acquisitions and investments in new media from 2005 to 2008. 2005 saw The New York Times Company acquisition of About.com (an online consumer information provider), and in 2007 it acquired consumeresearch.com (an online aggregator and publisher of product reviews).

The New York Times Company also owns 53 percent of BehNeem (a Web-based software package that supports the day-to-day learning activities of students and faculty, including networking, object/file sharing, and storage and blogging), 14 percent of Indeed (a vertical meta-search for help-wanted listings), and less than 10 percent in several other new media companies.

The company's revenue stream changed during the first decade of the twenty-first century as advertising revenues declined in traditional print operations. In 2007 they created a new alliance with Monster.com to promote jobs on nytimes.com as a supplement to its declining classified revenues.[22]

In 2008, The New York Times Company announced a joint venture called quadrantONE with the Tribune Company, the Gannett Company, and the Hearst Corporation as an attempt to make it simpler for advertisers to do business with any of the four media groups. The challenge being that Internet giants such as Google, Yahoo!, and Microsoft are increasingly stealing advertising dollars through simple online advertising programs such as Google AdWords.[23]

As of 2008, The New York Times Company is a leading media company. It holds sole ownership of *The New York Times* (the third largest daily newspaper in United States, with a circulation of 1.1 million on weekdays and 1.6 million on Sundays[24]), *The International Herald Tribune*, *The Boston Globe*, 16 other daily newspapers, and a radio station.[25] *The New York Times* syndicate sells columns, magazine and book excerpts, and feature packages to more than 2,000 newspapers and other media to clients in more than 50 countries. It is the largest syndicate in the world specializing in text, photos, graphics, and other noncartoon features.[26] The New York Times Company also co-owns Discovery Civilization Channel[27] and has a 17.5 percent stake in New England Sports Ventures, which owns the Boston Red Sox and 80 percent of New England Sports Network, a cable network that televises Red Sox games.[28]

The company has also strived to put the right people in top leadership positions in order to meet the challenges facing the industry, but certain aspects of leadership have created some additional challenges.

Key Strategic Leaders

Arthur Ochs Sulzberger, Jr., Chairman & Publisher

Sulzberger Jr. became a correspondent for *The New York Times* in 1978. After serving in various reporting and business positions he was promoted to assistant editor in 1987, became publisher in 1992, and succeeded his father, Arthur Ochs Sulzberger, as chairman of the board of The New York Times Company in 1997.[29]

Due to the dual stock structure using Class A and Class B stocks to limit voting power, the Ochs-Sulzberger family has been able to maintain control of The New York Times Company since it went public in 1967. Prominent stakeholders such as Harbinger and Firebrand have been trying to change the dual stock structure, but six trustees must vote in favor of the change, which will not occur as long as the Ochs-Sulzberger family controls eight of the seats.[30]

Janet L. Robinson, President & CEO

Janet Robinson joined The New York Times Company in 1983. She became president and general manager in 1996, and was elected to the company's board of directors in December 2004. At that time she was also appointed to be the company's president and CEO.[31]

Since Robinson's appointment as CEO, traditional print media and the U.S. economy have endured significant losses. In 2004 the stock price was $47, down from a high of $53.80 in 2002. The price tumbled even further to around $6.65/share in November 2008. Robinson has attempted to offset the losses of traditional print media by placing emphasis on and expanding the company's new media operations. According to Robinson, expanding the company's Internet businesses is an "absolute priority."[32] Under Robinson, the company has grown its Internet businesses, but it has not liquidated assets as quickly as desired by some investors.

James Follo, Senior Vice President and CFO

Prior to taking his post as senior vice president and CFO in January 2007, James Follo was chief of finance at both Martha Stewart Living Omnimedia and General Media International.[33] Given the financial difficulties The New York Times Company is currently facing, Follo has publicly stated that with the exception of The New York Times, The New York Times Company is willing to sell any of its assets.[34] However, Follo recognizes that in the current economy, selling assets would do little to alleviate long-term financial troubles and has been negotiating with bankers to secure loans for the company.[35]

Vivian Schiller, Senior Vice President and General Manager

Vivian Schiller has been with The New York Times Company since May 2002. She was appointed as senior vice president and general manager of nytimes.com in May 2006. In this role she has led the day-to-day operations of the The New York Times most significant Web site overseeing product technology, marketing, classifieds, strategic planning, and business development. Schiller previously served as senior vice president of television and video for The New York Times and also executive vice president and general manager for the Discovery Times. In November 2008, Shiller announced that she would be leaving the company for the post of CEO at National Public Radio. This is a critical loss at a time when strategic Internet leadership is needed more than ever.

Dissident Investors and Harbinger Capital Partners

After enduring a loss of $29 per share, Morgan Stanley sold its 7 percent stake in The New York Times Company. However, many dissident investors are still on board and plan to make changes to return The New York Times to its once proud and profitable state. One of these investors, Harbinger Capital Partners, has a 19 percent stake in the company.[36] Philip Falcone, lead at Harbinger Capital Partners, "has a long record of buying into troubled firms and then relentlessly pushing for change despite the odds."[37] The primary complaints of investors are the dual stock system that limits their access to controlling votes, slower than expected online expansion, and unprofitable holdings such as The Boston Globe. They also do not like the Company's stake in the Boston Red Sox because, though profitable, it is an unrelated business.

The Harbinger Group aims to transform the company in five years from one that does about 10 percent of its business in digital to one that does most of its business in digital. However, friction within the board of directors impedes the company's ability to make quick decisions, and since the Ochs-Sulzberger family owns the majority of shares, it is believed that "the company is going to do what the family wants it to do."[38]

The board is influenced not only by the Ochs-Sulzberger family, but also by the actions that competitors take.

Key Competitors

The New York Times Company's competitors are primarily in the publishing industry. The company also competes in the "information collection and delivery" and "Internet content provider" sectors. Top competitors include Gannett Co., Inc.; News Corporation; and The Washington Post Company.[39]

Gannett Co., Inc.[40]

Founded by Frank Gannett in 1906 and made public in 1967, Gannett is not only the largest newspaper publisher in the United States (as measured by total daily circulation), but a leading international news and information company. Approximately 8,900 shareholders in the United States and several foreign countries hold the company's more than 230 million outstanding shares of common stock. Total revenues in 2007 were $7.4 billion. (See Exhibit 1 for Gannett Financials 2005–2007.)

Exhibit 1 Gannett Financials 2005–2007

Gannett Income Statement	2007	2006	2005
Revenue ($ mil.)	7,439.5	8,033.4	7,598.9
Gross Profit ($ mil.)	3,275.4	3,595.1	3,537.7
Operating Income ($ mil.)	1,650.9	1,998.2	2,048.1
Total Net Income ($ mil.)	1,055.6	1,160.8	1,244.7
Diluted EPS (Net Income)	4.52	4.90	5.05

Gannett Quarterly Statements	Quarter Ending Jun 08	Quarter Ending Mar 08	Quarter Ending Dec 07
Revenue ($ mil.)	1,718.0	1,676.9	1,856.5
Gross Profit ($ mil.)	729.5	690.4	828.8
Operating Income ($ mil.)	(2,133.6)	327.6	372.7
Total Net Income ($ mil.)	(2,290.8)	191.8	245.3
Diluted EPS (Net Income)	(10.01)	0.84	1.06

Gannett Financial Ratios	Company	Industry Median	MarketMedian[1]
Price/Sales Ratio	0.32	0.45	1.04
Price/Earnings Ratio	—	9.00	10.88
Price/Book Ratio	0.34	0.82	0.98
Price/Cash Flow Ratio	1.84	4.14	6.46

[1] Public companies trading on the New York Stock Exchange, the American Stock Exchange, and the NASDAQ National Market.

Source: 2008, Gannett, *Hoover's*, November 13.

In the United States, Gannett publishes 85 daily newspapers with a total circulation of 6.9 million, as well as nearly 900 nondaily publications. Major U.S. newspapers owned by Gannett include *USA Today* (the largest daily newspaper with a circulation of more than 2.2 million), *The Arizona Republic,* and the *Detroit Free Press*. In addition, Gannett owns 23 television stations in the United States that reach more than 20 million households, publishes periodicals and inserts, and operates approximately 150 news and Internet advertising sites customized to the markets they serve. In January 2008, Gannett's total U.S. Internet audience was 25.8 million unique visitors, reaching about 15.9 percent of the Internet audience.

Gannett's newspaper publishing operations in the United Kingdom, through its subsidiary Newsquest,

include 17 daily newspapers and approximately 300 weekly newspapers, magazines, and trade publications, as well as classified business Internet sites. In addition to its publishing and broadcasting businesses, in line with its mission "to successfully transform Gannett to the new environment,"[41] Gannett has also advanced in its digital strategy through business acquisitions including PointRoll (a provider of media marketing services to online advertisers) and Ripple6, Inc. (a social media services provider), partnerships with companies such as CareerBuilder (for employment advertising), ShopLocal (an online marketing solutions provider), and ShermansTravel (an online travel service).

Although Gannett has been aggressively cutting costs for some time and growing revenue from Internet sources, its newspaper advertising revenue decreased 14 percent in the first nine months of 2008 because of the movement of readers to the Internet as well as the weakening U.S. economy. In October 2008 Gannett reported that third-quarter profit fell 32 percent from the same quarter in 2007. In addition, the company announced that revenue and operating profit would likely experience double-digit percentage declines in 2009.[42] In response, Gannett planned to lay off 10 percent of its daily newspaper employees (up to 3,000 workers) by December 2008. These layoffs follow the elimination of more than 1,000 jobs since August 2008 in the company's most troubled division: U.S. publishing. However, Gannett is quick to point out that the layoffs amount to only 3 percent of the division's employees, and other publishers have made much more drastic eliminations (for example, since June 2008, the *Miami Herald* has carried out two rounds of 10 percent layoffs).[43] To further emphasize the company's dedication to cut costs, Gannett's chairman, president, and CEO Craig Dubow recently announced that he is taking a voluntary salary cut of $200,000 from now through 2009 as well as freezing the 2009 salaries of all company and divisional officers.[44]

News Corporation[45]

Created in 1980 by Rupert Murdoch, News Corporation is the world's third largest media conglomerate with total revenues of $33 billion in 2008. (See Exhibit 2 for News Corporation Financials 2006–2008.) The company is publicly traded and listed on the New York Stock

Exhibit 2 News Corporation Financials 2006–2008

News Corp. Income Statement	2008	2007	2006
Revenue ($ mil.)	32,996.0	28,655.0	25,327.0
Gross Profit ($ mil.)	12,465.0	10,010.0	8,734.0
Operating Income ($ mil.)	5,381.0	4,452.0	3,868.0
Total Net Income ($ mil.)	5,387.0	3,426.0	2,314.0
Diluted EPS (Net Income)	1.80	1.14	0.76
News Corp. Quarterly Statement	**Quarter Ending Jun 08**	**Quarter Ending Mar 08**	**Quarter Ending Dec 07**
Revenue ($ mil.)	8,589.0	8,750.0	8,590.0
Gross Profit ($ mil.)	3,361.0	3,298.0	(1,261.0)
Operating Income ($ mil.)	1,478.0	1,438.0	1,418.0
Total Net Income ($ mil.)	1,129.0	2,694.0	832.0
Diluted EPS (Net Income)	0.42	0.88	0.27
News Corp. Financial Ratios	**Company**	**Industry Median**	**Market Median[1]**
Price/Sales Ratio	0.46	0.48	1.06
Price/Earnings Ratio	4.60	10.41	11.20
Price/Book Ratio	0.53	1.01	1.03
Price/Cash Flow Ratio	3.84	4.79	6.54

[1] Public companies trading on the New York Stock Exchange, the American Stock Exchange, and the NASDAQ National Market.

Source: 2008, NewsCorp, *Hoover's*, November 13.

Exchange, the Australian Securities Exchange, and the London Stock Exchange. Nearly 40 percent of the company is controlled by Murdoch and his family.

News Corporation's newspaper and information services include News International (which publishes four national newspapers in the United Kingdom), News Limited (which publishes more than 110 national, capital city, and suburban newspapers in Australia), the *New York Post* (the fifth largest daily in the United States), and the *Wall Street Journal* (an English-language daily with a worldwide circulation of more than 2 million). Its publishing businesses include HarperCollins (a global English-language book publisher) and Dow Jones & Co. (a provider of global business news and information services). Additionally, News Corporation has operations in film, television, cable network, and direct broadcast satellite television segments. It owns Fox Filmed Entertainment (a global film and television production and distribution operation), Fox Broadcasting Company (the largest broadcasting network in the United States with more than 200 affiliate stations), the more than 30 television stations in the Fox Television Stations group, 23 percent of Premiere AG (a German pay-television company), 35 percent of British Sky Broadcasting (the U.K.'s largest digital pay-television platform), and nearly 100 percent of SKY Italia (Italy's most popular pay-television company).

New media properties held by News Corporation include Fox Interactive Media (an interactive services company including MySpace, a lifestyle and social-networking site which attracts 230,000 new users per day), NDS Group (a supplier of open end-to-end digital pay-television solutions), and News Outdoor (the largest outdoor advertising company in Eastern Europe). In November 2008, News Corporation announced that despite strong increases in first-quarter cable network operating income (31 percent) as well as newspaper and information services income revenue (37 percent, driven by the company's December 2007 acquisition of Dow Jones & Company), first-quarter profit fell 30 percent from the same quarter the previous year due to declining television and newspaper advertising revenue, a weaker performance by Fox Filmed Entertainment, and investment losses in Premiere AG. Additionally, the company announced that revenue and operating profit would probably see double-digit percentage declines in 2009.[46]

Although Murdoch has not provided much detail on cost-cutting techniques that will be employed, he has said that he is considering merging the back-office operations of the *Wall Street Journal* and the *New York Post* as well as closing 10 of the 17 U.S. printing plants that produce the *Wall Street Journal*.[47] Additionally, Murdoch has said that more emphasis needs to be placed on the

international expansion of Dow Jones & Company, as well as subscription-based businesses that have the benefits of twin revenues from subscribers and advertisers. "We will be looking to start new channels where there are opportunities, and we certainly see that on a big scale internationally."[48]

The Washington Post Company[49]

With a history dating back to 1877, The Washington Post Company is an education and media company publicly traded on the New York Stock Exchange since 1971. Apart from chairman Donald Graham and his family, who have voting control over the company, Warren Buffett and his Berkshire Hathaway corporation is also a substantial shareholder with 18 percent of the publicly traded shares. Total revenue in 2007 was $4 billion. (See Exhibit 3 for Washington Post Financials 2005–2007.)

Although The Washington Post Company is best known as the publisher of *The Washington Post*, the company also owns other media operations including *Newsweek*, six television stations, and the online publishing operations of Newsweek Interactive (WPNI) (a subsidiary whose products include washingtonpost.com, Newsweek.com, Slate, BudgetTravel.com, and Sprig.com). It owns nonmedia operations including Kaplan, Inc. (an international provider of educational and career services for individuals, schools, and businesses) and CableOne (a cable television and Internet service with approximately 700,000 subscribers in 20 U.S. markets).

In October 2008, The Washington Post Company reported an 86 percent decline in third-quarter profit compared with the same quarter in 2007. However, the company notes that if the $59.7 million goodwill impairment charge at some of its newspapers and the $12.5 million accelerated depreciation charge of *The Washington Post's* printing presses were to be excluded, its publishing division would be cash flow–positive with $3.8 million in profit for the quarter.[50]

At *The Washington Post*, advertising revenue fell 14 percent during the third quarter of 2008.[51] However, under Graham's leadership as well as that of his close advisors (namely Warren Buffet, who has publicly stated "The present model—meaning print—isn't going to work,"[52]) the company has been preparing for the industry's present crisis for some time. In addition to investing millions into its digital business (WPNI) since the mid-1990s, The Washington Post Company has labored to rebrand itself as a company associated with innovation in digital media and technology.

In March 2008 it announced that it would sponsor LaunchBox08, a global challenge for digital startups to submit innovative ideas in order to receive funding and

Exhibit 3 *Washington Post* Financials 2005–2007

Washington Post Income Statement	2007	2006	2005
Revenue ($ mil.)	4,180.4	3,904.9	3,553.9
Gross Profit ($ mil.)	2,297.4	1,862.5	1,644.3
Operating Income ($ mil.)	477.0	459.8	514.9
Total Net Income ($ mil.)	288.6	324.5	314.3
Diluted EPS (Net Income)	30.19	33.68	32.59

Washington Post Quarterly Statements	Quarter Ending Jun 08	Quarter Ending Mar 08	Quarter Ending Dec 07
Revenue ($ mil.)	1,106.2	1,063.1	1,125.5
Gross Profit ($ mil.)	598.2	572.0	596.9
Operating Income ($ mil.)	4.8	66.9	149.3
Total Net Income ($ mil.)	(2.7)	39.3	82.9
Diluted EPS (Net Income)	(0.31)	4.08	8.74

Washington Post Financial Ratios	Company	Industry Median	Market Median[1]
Price/Sales Ratio	1.17	1.44	1.56
Price/Earnings Ratio	31.16	19.02	15.82
Price/Book Ratio	1.51	2.99	1.52
Price/Cash Flow Ratio	8.84	13.62	9.88

[1] Public companies trading on the New York Stock Exchange, the American Stock Exchange, and the NASDAQ National Market.

Source: 2008, Washington Post Company, *Hoover's*, November 13.

participate in a business-building program with access to professional mentors and advisors.[53] Additionally, The Washington Post Company has steered away from investing in its print operations, but instead heavily investing in its nonmedia operations. Kaplan Inc. and CableOne now provide 53 percent and 16 percent, respectively, of total revenue.[54]

Nontraditional Media Competitors

While The New York Times Company has long fought its peers in the traditional print industry, the advent of the Internet created news opportunities for other companies beyond The New York Times Company and its traditional competitors. The second generation of the Internet brought with it new online mediums such as blogs, social networks, and online communities that allowed for anyone to self-publish for the world to see. With more than 112 million blogs now online, the avenues for advertisers to get their advertisements to niche audiences has risen dramatically. Bloggers add new blog entries with an astounding frequency of 1.6 million posts each day.[55] Recognizing the importance of the new online medium, *The New York Times* editor Bill Keller stated, "We must do whatever we can to strengthen our competitive position . . . [and ensure] among other things, that we are well equipped to navigate the passage to our digital future."[56]

Internet giants such as Google, Yahoo!, and Microsoft have increasingly encroached on the turf of traditional media by offering their own news sites. Sites such as Google News function without an editorial staff, instead leveraging an automated aggregation system that takes current, high-ranking stories and sorts them automatically into sections of the Google News page. "No human is involved in the altering of the front page or story promotion, beyond tweaking the aggregation algorithm.[57]"

The Google News site, which leverages more content from *The New York Times* than any other source (without paying for it), is said to be valued at more than $100 million, even though it generates no advertising revenue for Google directly.[58] Some have predicted a long drawn-out battle between Internet giants and the traditional print media.[59] The traditional print media has recognized this challenge and has suggested that perhaps partnering with Internet giants such as Google would be in their best interest. Jeff Jarvis, NYU journalist professor, and Edward Roussel, manager of digital content for *The Telegraph* said of print media's efforts to go online:

"It's hard to imagine a newspaper creating better technology than Google. And the service is proving to be brilliant at ad sales—so why not outsource those departments to Google so a paper can concentrate on its real job—journalism …. Ideally every newsroom would be able to think of Google and all its capabilities as their own.[60]"

Current Market Dynamics

Historically, The New York Times Company, like most of its primary competitors, has been deeply entrenched in the traditional print media industry where two consistent revenue streams exist: circulation unit sales and advertising related revenue. However, the Internet has truly become a disruptive technology in the information dissemination market. Internet subscriptions are replacing the daily newspaper expenditure in many households.

Unlike national newspapers such as *USA Today* and the *Wall Street Journal,* which have tended to hold their ground better, and for small-market dailies where competition from other media is not usually as intense, *The New York Times* has posted steep declines in circulation in recent years.[61] In October 2008 it was reported that its weekday circulation fell 3.6 percent from the previous year, and its Sunday circulation dropped 4.1 percent.[62] *The New York Times* has countered decreases in circulation with increases in subscription prices of more than 25 percent in recent years. As a result, it has not seen a decrease in circulation revenue. In fact, October 2008

circulation revenue increased 3.9 percent from the same period in 2007.[63]

As previously indicated, since the early 1990s the company has taken steps to profitably advance its digital strategy. In the past three years alone The New York Times Company has spent more than $500 million on acquisitions and investments in new media and the company's Internet operations. According to Nielsen Online, http://nytimes.com had 20 million unique visitors in September 2008, an increase of about 37 percent over the same period the previous year, and online advertising revenues climbed by approximately $10 million to $79 million. The popularity of the site stems not only from its content and format (which has benefited from the expertise of *The New York Times's* editorial staff), but also the reputation of *The New York Times* as a newspaper committed to "hard-hitting, ground-breaking journalism," something that cannot be easily replicated by competitors.

The New York Times Company also has the benefit of long-standing relationships with advertisers who may be wary of continuing a relationship with the company's traditional print media operations, but are eager to take advantage of the wide audience reached by the company's new media.

Despite the relationships *The New York Times* Company has maintained with advertisers and the reputation it has for employing great journalists, the financials indicate that the company has been more affected by its challenges than its assets.

Financials

Advertising revenues are typically elastic by nature. As the economy surges, companies advertising budgets expand. Unfortunately, economic challenges mean ad revenues generally decrease. Between October 2007 and October 2008, advertising revenues for The New York Times Company declined by 16.2 percent, with classified advertising revenue down 34.7 percent as offers for jobs, real estate, and automobiles each plunged at least 34 percent.[64]

The two major operating groups, News Media Group and the About Group, have seen divergent revenue paths during the past several years, with the About Group growing and becoming increasingly profitable while the News Media Group contracts and records net losses (see Exhibit 4 for New York Times Company Revenue Comparison by Segment).[65]

Advertising revenue for the About Group increased by 13.8 percent (see Exhibit 5) during the past year and has maintained double digit revenue growth since inception. However, this division of the company is

Exhibit 4 New York Times Company Revenue Comparison by Segment

Time Period	News Media Group Ad Revenue ($000s)	% Change	About Group Ad Revenue ($000s)	% Change	Circulation Revenue ($000s)	% Change
Q1–Q3 2008	1,231,411	−12.7	79,502	+16.5	676,486	+1.8
Q1–Q3 2007	1,410,208	−4.4	68,217	+28.2	664,539	+1.5
Q1–Q3 2006	1,474,408	−1.5	53,196	+102.4	654,994	+.01
Q1–Q3 2005	1,496,608		26,278		655,971	

Source: 2008, New York Times Company, http://morningstar.com, November 22.

Exhibit 5 New York Times Company Advertising Revenue Comparison 2007 v. 2008

The New York Times Company 2008 Q3 Advertising Revenues[a] ($ 000s)						
	September			Year to Date		
	2008	2007	% Change	2008	2007	% Change
News Media Group						
New York Times Media Group	$103,048	$116,753	−11.7	$781,607	$867,774	−9.9
New England Media Group	27,167	32,577	−16.6	240,591	289,414	−16.9
Regional Media Group	19,204	24,657	−22.1	209,212	253,020	−17.3
Total News Media Group	149,419	173,986	−14.1	1,231,410	1,410,208	−12.7
About Group[b]	8,739	7,878	+10.9	79,502	68,216	+16.5
Total Ad Revenues From Continuing Operations	$158,158	$181,864	−13.0	$1,310,912	$1,478,425	−11.3
Discontinued Operations: Broadcast Media Group[c]	0	0	N/A	0	45,745	N/A

(a) Numbers may not add due to rounding.
(b) Includes the Web sites of About.com, ConsumerSearch.com, UCompareHealthCare.com, and Calorie-Count.com.
(c) On May 7, 2007, the Company sold the Broadcast Media Group, consisting of nine network-affiliated television stations, their related Web sites and the digital operating center for approximately $575 million.

Source: 2008, New York Times Company, http:// www.nytco.com, November 22.

too small to make up for the decline in the traditional media group. As a result, total revenues for the company declined 8.9 percent in the third quarter of 2008, with circulation revenues up 1 percent because of the newspaper price increase (see Exhibits 6 and 7). Net income has decreased by 82.1 percent when compared to the same quarter in 2007, and net profit has decreased from $505 million in 1998 to $185 million in 2007 (Exhibit 8).

Total assets showed no growth at $3.5 billion in 2007, while total liabilities increased from $1.9 billion in 1998 to $2.4 billion in 2007 (see Exhibit 9). Debt-to-equity ratio increased from 0.39 in 1998 to 0.69 in 2007 (see Exhibit 10). At the end of third quarter in 2008, the company had $46 million in cash, $1.1 billion in debt, and a debt-to-equity ratio of 0.85. Of particular concern is the fact that $400 million of that debt is due in 2009.[66] Standard & Poor's threatened to downgrade the company's rating to junk status, causing insult to injury and raising the amount of interest expense The New York Times Company will be forced to pay on its debt.[67]

The company's quick ratio of 0.43 clearly shows the inability of the company to cover short-term cash needs. Further, the company's liquidity has decreased from the same period 2007, ironic given the fact that presidential election years typically create an advertising and circulation sales gain.

Exhibit 6 New York Times Company Revenue Comparison 2007 v. 2008

The New York Times Company 2008 Q3 Total Company Revenues[a] ($ 000s)			
	Third Quarter		
	2008	2007	% Change
Advertising Revenues			
News Media			
National	$188,666	$212,910	−11.4
Retail	86,507	97,191	−11.0
Classified	82,778	117,157	−29.3
Other Ad Revenue	13,658	14,423	−5.3
Total News Media Group	371,608	441,681	−15.9
About Group[b]	26,588	23,362	13.8
Total Ad Revenues from Continuing Operations	398,196	465,043	−4.4
Circulation Revenues	225,689	223,420	+1.0
Other Revenues[c]	63,157	65,896	−4.2
Total Company Revenues from Continuing Operations	$687,042	$754,359	−8.9
Discontinued Operations: Broadcast Media Group[d]	0	0	N/A

(a) Numbers may not add due to rounding.
(b) Includes the Web sites of About.com, ConsumerSearch.com, UCompareHealthCare.com, and Calorie-Count.com.
(c) Primarily includes revenues from wholesale delivery operations, news services/syndication, commercial printing, digital archives, direct mail advertising services, and rental income.
(d) On May 7, 2007, the Company sold the Broadcast Media Group, consisting of nine network-affiliated television stations, their related Web sites, and the digital operating center for approximately $575 million.

Source: 2008, New York Times Company, http://www.nytco.com, November 22.

Exhibit 7 New York Times Company Statement of Cash Flow 1998–2007

Cash Flow	As originally reported									
	1998	1999	2000	2001	2002	2003	2004	2005	2006	2007	TTM
Cash Flows from Operating Activities $Mil											
Net Income	278.9	310.2	397.5	444.7	299.8	302.7	292.6	259.8	(543.4)	208.7	(32.5)
Depr & Amort	135.2	197.5	228.0	194.0	153.4	47.8	146.8	143.8	169.9	189.6	155.1
Deferred Taxes	(12.6)	(44.6)	(28.2)	(52.9)	88.1	53.5	3.6	(29.6)	(139.9)	(11.6)	—
Other	49.9	138.1	(7.5)	(114.5)	(267.9)	(37.7)	1.1	(79.6)	935.8	(276.0)	103.2
Cash from Operations	451.5	601.1	589.9	471.2	273.3	466.3	444.0	294.3	422.3	110.7	225.8
Cash Flows from Investing Activities $Mil											
Cap Ex	(81.6)	(73.4)	(85.3)	(90.4)	(160.7)	(120.9)	(153.8)	(221.3)	(332.3)	(380.3)	(213.2)
Purchase of Business	0.0	—	(296.3)	(2.6)	(176.9)	(65.1)	0.0	(437.5)	(35.8)	(34.1)	(5.7)
Other	25.4	(9.5)	186.6	430.4	(23.3)	(60.0)	(38.4)	163.4	79.4	562.6	(2.7)
Cash from Investing	(56.2)	(82.9)	(195.0)	337.4	(360.9)	(245.9)	(192.2)	(495.5)	(288.7)	148.3	(221.6)
Cash Flows from Financing Activities $Mil											
Net Issuance of Stock	(441.9)	(395.8)	(543.1)	(591.4)	(62.7)	(175.3)	(252.1)	(43.0)	(52.3)	(4.0)	(2.7)
Net Issuance of Debt	222.5	103.9	331.3	—	195.1	49.9	107.4	658.6	61.1	0.0	—
Dividends	(69.6)	(72.0)	(75.4)	(77.0)	(80.3)	(85.5)	(90.1)	(94.5)	(100.1)	(125.1)	(133.1)
Other	(177.1)	(126.5)	(102.5)	(157.3)	20.5	(7.7)	(14.4)	(316.7)	(14.9)	(151.5)	122.8

(Continued)

Exhibit 7 New York Times Company Statement of Cash Flow 1998–2007 *(Continued)*

Cash from Financing	(466.1)	(490.4)	(389.7)	(825.7)	72.6	(218.7)	(249.2)	204.4	(106.2)	(280.5)	(13.0)
Currency Adj	—	—	—	—	—	—	—	—	—	—	—
Change in Cash	(70.8)	27.9	5.2	(17.1)	(15.0)	1.7	2.7	3.2	27.5	(21.6)	(8.7)
Free Cash Flow $Mil											
Cash from Operations	451.5	601.1	589.9	471.2	273.3	466.3	444.0	294.3	422.3	110.7	225.8
Cap Ex	(81.6)	(73.4)	(85.3)	(90.4)	(160.7)	(120.9)	(153.8)	(221.3)	(332.3)	(380.3)	(213.2)
Free Cash Flow	369.9	527.7	504.6	380.9	112.6	345.4	290.2	73.0	90.0	(269.6)	12.6

S&P Index Data: S&P 500 Copyright © 2008

Source: 2008, New York Times Company, http://morningstar.com, November 22.

Exhibit 8 New York Times Company Income Statement 1998–2007

Income Statement

As originally reported

	1998	1999	2000	2001	2002	2003	2004	2005	2006	2007	TTM
Revenue	2,936.7	3,130.6	3,489.5	3,016.0	3,079.0	3,227.2	3,303.6	3,372.8	3,289.9	3,195.1	3,042.6
COGS	1,461.6	1,378.8	1,458.1	1,362.9	1,352.6	1,428.8	1,475.6	1,540.4	1,529.5	1,341.1	1,325.4
Gross Profit	1,475.1	1,751.8	2,031.4	1,653.1	1,726.4	1,798.4	1,828.1	1,832.4	1,760.4	1,854.0	1,717.2
Operating Expenses $Mil											
SG&A	959.8	1,180.5	1,395.5	1,278.7	1,181.5	1,258.9	1,318.1	1,474.3	1,466.6	1,397.4	1,374.8
R&D	—	—	—	—	—	—	—	—	—	—	—
Other	0.0	NaN	0.0	0.0	NaN	0.0	(NaN)	(122.9)	814.4	229.1	194.7
Operating Income	515.2	571.3	635.9	374.4	544.9	539.6	510.0	481.1	(520.6)	227.4	147.7
Other Income and Expense $Mil											
Net Int Inc & Other	(9.70)	(32.80)	37.20	(34.60)	(53.50)	(31.50)	(33.60)	53.30	50.70	(39.80)	7.30
Earnings Before Taxes	505.50	538.50	673.10	339.90	491.40	499.90	476.70	446.10	(551.90)	185.00	(44.30)

(Continued)

Exhibit 8 New York Times Company Income Statement 1998–2007 *(Continued)*

Income Taxes	218.90	228.30	275.60	137.60	191.60	197.80	183.50	180.20	16.60	76.10
Earnings After Taxes	286.60	310.20	397.50	202.20	299.80	302.10	293.20	265.90	(568.50)	108.80
Acctg Changes	—	—	—	—	—	—	—	(5.90)	0.00	0.00
Disc Operations	—	—	0.00	242.50	0.00	0.00	—	—	24.70	99.80
Ext Items	(7.70)	0.00	0.00	—	—	—	—	—	—	—
Net Income	278.90	310.20	397.50	444.70	299.80	302.70	292.60	259.80	(543.40)	208.70
Diluted EPS, Cont Ops$	1.49	1.73	2.32	1.26	1.94	1.98	1.96	1.82	(3.93)	0.76
Diluted EPS$	1.45	1.73	2.32	2.78	1.94	1.98	1.96	1.78	(3.76)	1.45
Shares	192.00	179.00	171.00	160.00	154.00	152.00	149.00	145.00	144.00	143.00

S&P Index Data: S&P 500 Copyright © 2008

Exhibit 9 New York Times Company Balance Sheet 1998–2007

Balance Sheet										As originally reported	
Assets $Mil											
	1998	1999	2000	2001	2002	2003	2004	2005	2006	2007	Latest Qtr
Cash and Equiv	36.0	63.9	69.0	52.0	37.0	39.5	42.4	44.9	72.4	51.5	45.9
Short-Term Investments	—	—	—	—	—	—	—	—	—	—	—
Accts Rec	331.9	366.8	341.9	318.5	358.3	387.7	389.3	435.3	402.6	437.9	364.6
Inventory	32.3	28.7	35.1	31.6	23.3	29.0	32.7	32.1	36.7	26.9	27.5
Other Current Assets	121.8	155.7	164.8	157.8	144.5	147.2	149.6	145.5	673.3	148.1	139.3
Total Current Assets	522.0	614.9	610.8	559.9	563.1	603.3	613.9	657.8	1,185.0	664.5	577.3
Net PP&E	1,326.2	1,218.4	1,207.2	1,166.9	1,197.4	1,187.3	1,367.4	1,468.4	1,375.4	1,468.0	1,354.8
Intangibles	1,327.6	1,305.0	1,480.1	1,410.2	1,393.1	1,474.4	1,464.6	1,851.0	784.4	811.9	737.2
Other Long-Term Assets	289.4	357.5	308.7	301.7	480.3	539.8	504.0	555.9	511.2	528.7	552.4
Total Assets	**3,465.1**	**3,495.8**	**3,606.7**	**3,438.7**	**3,633.8**	**3,804.7**	**3,949.9**	**4,533.0**	**3,855.9**	**3,473.1**	**3,221.7**
Liabilities and Stockholders' Equity $Mil											
Accts Payable	163.8	191.7	178.3	171.0	177.7	176.6	190.1	201.1	242.5	202.9	160.7
Short-Term Debt	124.1	0.0	291.3	158.3	178.1	228.0	335.4	496.5	546.7	111.7	397.9
Taxes Payable	—	—	—	225.2	8.4	10.6	—	—	—	—	—
Accrued Liabilities	257.0	298.8	318.1	242.2	253.7	267.3	264.7	285.5	321.3	335.4	258.7
Other Short-Term Liabilities	82.9	183.0	89.7	64.2	117.9	77.9	329.6	83.5	187.5	325.7	131.8

Exhibit 9 New York Times Company Balance Sheet 1998–2007 (*Continued*)

Total Current Liabilities	627.8	673.5	877.4	860.9	735.7	760.4	1,119.8	1,066.5	1,298.0	975.7	949.1
Long-Term Debt	513.7	512.6	553.4	517.1	648.6	646.9	393.6	822.0	720.8	672.0	672.5
Other Long-Term Liabilities	792.1	861.0	894.7	911.1	980.2	1,005.2	1,036.0	1,128.3	1,017.3	847.1	803.0
Total Liabilities	1,933.6	2,047.1	2,325.5	2,289.0	2,364.5	2,412.5	2,549.3	3,016.8	3,036.1	2,494.9	2,424.6
Total Equity	1,531.5	1,448.7	1,281.2	1,149.7	1,269.3	1,392.2	1,400.5	1,516.3	819.8	978.2	797.1
Total Liabilities & Equity	3,465.1	3,495.8	3,606.7	3,438.7	3,633.9	3,804.7	3,949.9	4,533.0	3,855.9	3,473.1	3,221.7

S&P Index Data: S&P 500 Copyright © 2008

Source: 2008, New York Times Company, http://morningstar.com, November 22.

In comparison to industry competitors, The New York Times Company is underperforming in sales growth and net profit margin while capital spending is higher. Despite an effort to improve its financial situation, capital spending reached $213 million in 2008, up from $82 million in 1998 (see Exhibit 7).

Not unexpected with these financial results, the company's stock price has underperformed. In an effort to curb the steady stock devaluation, The New York Times Company announced in March 2007 that it would increase its dividend by 31 percent hoping that such a drastic increase in an already generous dividend would help stabilize, if not increase, the stock price.[68] It did not work. Since then the stock dropped from $24/share to just over $5/share in November 2008, when the company announced that it would need to cut its dividend by 74 percent.[69] Financial analysts have favorably viewed this dividend reduction, upgrading the stock and commenting that the move alone should recoup $100 million in annual revenue.[70]

The New York Times Company's market cap is just under $1 billion, an astonishingly low figure given that far smaller media companies have sold for far more. Earlier this year for example, CBS acquired the consumer

Exhibit 10 New York Times Company Liquidity Ratios 1998–2007

						Liquidity/Financial Health					
	1998	1999	2000	2001	2002	2003	2004	2005	2006	2007	Latest Qtr
Current Ratio	0.83	0.91	0.70	0.65	0.77	0.79	0.55	0.62	0.91	0.68	0.61
Quick Ratio	0.59	0.64	0.47	0.43	0.54	0.56	0.39	0.45	0.37	0.50	0.43
Financial Leverage	2.26	2.41	2.82	2.99	2.86	2.73	2.82	2.99	4.70	3.55	4.04
Debt/Equity	0.39	0.41	0.50	0.52	0.57	0.52	0.34	0.59	0.97	0.69	0.85

Source: 2008, New York Times Company, http://morningstar.com, November 22.

technology reviews company CNET Networks for $1.8 billion,[71] nearly twice The New York Times Company's market cap.

The company's financial condition makes it difficult for it to support growth at competitive rates, let alone to simply continue operations.

Strategic Challenges and the Future

The New York Times Company lacks any clear differentiators when compared to its market competitors. Moreover, its primary competitors are in stronger financial positions as the economy is in a period of turbulence and certain change is coming to the traditional print industry. In addition, the company lacks a defined strategic intent; clearly defined goals with respect to where

and how it intends to compete in the market. The New York Times Company will see significant headwinds as it enters various digital market segments. It will face a multitude of new (nontraditional) competitors, some with unique strategies and better capitalization to enter these markets and create new product offerings, vying for the same advertising dollars.

As Sulzberger Jr. looks beyond the momentary good fortunes of The New York Times owing to the Obama-headlined newspaper of November 5, 2008, he must address the serious challenges facing The New York Times Company. How can he influence the board of directors to act in unison? What long-term strategy should they implement? How can the company differentiate itself from competitors? How can it leverage the competencies of the new media outlets it has acquired to help improve its financial situation?

NOTES

1. L. Han, 2008, Newspaper circulation falls Again, Forbes, April 28.
2. 2008, Sulzberger Family, Wikipedia, November 20.
3. 2008, Guardian, November 6.
4. 2008, New York Times Company reports September revenue, Yahoo Finance, October 23.
5. 2005, The future of the New York Times, BusinessWeek, January 17.
6. H. Blodget, 2008, Cash crunch at the New York Times, Silicon Alley Insider, November 8.
7. 2008, New York Times Company: Press www.nytco.com, November 25.
8. A. Bianco, J. Rossant, & L. Gard, 2005, The future of the New York Times, BusinessWeek, January 17.
9. 2008, New York Times Company, Hoovers, November 18.
10. 2008, New York Times Company, Wikipedia, November 14.
11. Ibid.
12. New York Times Company, Hoovers.
13. New York Times Company, Wikipedia.
14. 2008, New York Times Company: Company Milestones 1981–1910, www.nytco.com, November 14.
15. 2008, New York Times Company: Company Milestones 1911–1940, www.nytco.com, November 14.
16. 2008, New York Times Company: Company Milestones 1941–1970, www.nytco.com, November 14.
17. 2008, New York Times Company: Company Milestones 1971–1980, www.nytco.com, November 14.
18. 2008, Times v. Sullivan, Cornell University, November 14.
19. New York Times Company: Company Milestones 1971–1980.
20. Ibid.
21. New York Times Company: Company Milestones 1981–1990.
22. R. Gavin, 2007, New York Times Co. partners with Monster, The Boston Globe, February 14.
23. L. Story, 2008, 4 news companies ally to sell ads on the Internet, New York Times, February 15.
24. New York Times, Wikipedia.
25. 2008, New York Times Company, www.nytco.com, November 20.
26. 2008, New York Times Company, www.answers.com November 25.
27. 2002, New York Times Company and Discovery Communications, Inc. announce joint venture in Discovery Civilization Channel, Business Wire, April 5.
28. L. Haul, 2008, New York Times CEO: Red Sox a good investment, Forbes, March 11.
29. 2008, Arthur Ochs Sulzberger, Jr., Wikipedia, November 15.
30. J. Yarow & J. Fine, 2008, How can the New York Times be worth so little?, BusinessWeek, July 25.
31. 2008, Janet L. Robinson, Wikipedia, November 15.
32. 2008, NY Times CEO: Focused on online growth, Forbes, March 11.
33. 2008, New York Times Company, www.nytco.com, November 20.
34. NY Times CEO: Focused on online growth.
35. C. Douglas, 2008, Globe shows red ink as Times faces cash crunch, Boston Business Journal, November 13.
36. R. Perez-Pena, 2008, Two funds raise their stake in Times Company to 19%, New York Times, February 26.
37. E. Hessel, 2008, Times Tussle, Forbes, February 15.
38. 2008, Dissident investors increase Times Co. stake, www.boston.com, February 21.
39. 2008, New York Times Company, Hoovers, November 13.
40. 2008, Gannett, www.gannett.com, November 14.
41. Ibid.
42. R. MacMillian, 2008, Gannett profit falls short on weak advertising, News Daily, October 24.
43. 2008, Gannett laying off 10% of newspaper staff; Dicky warns in memo: 'fiscal crisis is deepening,' http://Gannettblogspot.com, October 28.
44. 2008, Gannett Chairman Dubow takes $200,000 pay cut, Editor and Publisher, November 3.
45. 2008, NewsCorp, www.newscorp.com, November 13.
46. D. Wilkerson, 2008, News Corp shares plunge after outlook cut, MarketWatch, November 6.
47. R. MacMillian, 2008, News Corp slashes outlook, profits dive, Reuters, November 5.
48. D. Wilkerson, News Corp shares plunge after outlook cut.
49. 2008, Washington Post Company, www.washpostco.com, November 13.
50. F. Ahrens, 2008, Washington Post Co. earnings plummet in third quarter, washingtonpost, October 31.
51. A. Jesdanon, 2008, Ad sales drop squeezes 3Q earnings for Post, Belo, www.boston.com, October 31.
52. M. Gunther, 2007, Can the Washington Post survive?, http://money.cnn.com, July 26.
53. 2008, Washington Post Co. Sponsors LaunchBox08 Startup Competition, Business Wire, March 10.

54. Lin E., 2008, S&P: Washington Post Co. outlook negative, *Shaping the Future of the Newspaper*, October 28.

55. 2008, Technorati, www.technorati.com, November 26.

56. J. Koblin, 2008, Layoffs at The New York Times; Keller Says 'We Hope Worst is Behind Us,' *New York Observer*, May 7.

57. 2008, Google News, *Wikipedia*, November 18.

58. J. Fortt, 2008, What's Google News Worth? $100 Million, *Fortune Magazine*, July 22.

59. M. LaMonica, 2004, Googlezon: The Future of Media, *CNET*, December 27.

60. J. Jarvis, 2008, The Host With the Most, *Guardian*, July 21.

61. S. Sitel, 2008, New York Times Circulation Plummets, *The Huffington Post*, April 28.

62. R. Perez-Pena, 2008, Newspaper Circulation Continues to Decline Rapidly, *The New York Times*, October 27.

63. 2008, Internet Revenue At New York Times (NYT) Needs To Be Going Up 100%, But It's Not, *247wallst*, November 20.

64. 2008, New York Times Company: Investor Relations Financials, www.nytco.com, November.22.

65. Ibid.

66. C. Douglas, 2008, Globe Shows Red Ink as Times Faces Cash Crunch, *Boston Business Journal*, November 13.

67. J. Yarrow & J. Fine, How Can The New York Times Be Worth So Little.

68. Ibid.

69. D. Wilkerson, 2008, New York Times Co. Shares Tumble to New Low, *MarketWatch*, November 21.

70. M. Peer, 2008, NY Times' High Dividend Is Old News, *Forbes*, November 24.

71. M. Arrington, 2008, CBS to Acquire CNET for $1.8 Billion, *TechCrunch*, May 15.

Markus Kreutzer, Christoph Lechner

University of St. Gallen

Introduction

In 2008, the UK-based international food and general merchandising retailer Tesco reached a market share of about 30 percent in the United Kingdom, roughly the same as its rivals Sainsbury's and ASDA combined. In recent years, Tesco has greatly diversified, extending its business lines from food into non-food, clothing, financial services, and telecommunications. It ranks sixth in the international retail market behind Wal-Mart (United States), Carrefour (France), Home Depot (United States), Metro (Germany), and Royal Ahold (Netherlands).[1]

Tesco was not always the dominant player it is today. In 1990, it was a mid-sized food chain far behind its rival, Sainsbury's. Starting in the 1990s, it pursued a broad set of growth initiatives, steadily increasing its market share and gaining importance. In 1995, Tesco surpassed Sainsbury's to become the U.K. market leader. Today, Tesco is the clear market leader. How did that happen? Why was Tesco so successful in growing sales and profits, while Sainsbury's could not keep pace? Where did the competitive actions of these firms differ? Let us start with a close look at their origins.

Sainsbury's, Tesco, and the U.K. Retail Market in 1990

Sainsbury's was established in 1869 by John James and Mary Ann Sainsbury, making it the oldest food retailing chain in Britain. In 1922, J Sainsbury became a private company, with J Sainsbury plc acting as parent company of Sainsbury's Supermarkets Ltd, commonly known as Sainsbury's, a chain of supermarkets in the United Kingdom. In 1973, the company was floated as J Sainsbury plc in what was at the time the largest flotation on the London Stock Exchange. The family currently retains about 14 percent of its shares. The group is also engaged in property and banking, owning real estate worth about £8.6 billion. For much of the twentieth century, Sainsbury's was the market leader in the U.K. supermarket sector, but in 1995 it lost its place to Tesco; in 2003, it was pushed to third place by ASDA.

Tesco was founded by Jack Cohen in London's East End. From a modest background, Cohen began selling groceries in Well Street market, Hackney, in 1919. In the aftermath of World War I, food supplies were low, so he bought damaged goods from other stores and re-sold them at reasonable prices. The Tesco brand first appeared in 1924. The name originated after Cohen bought a shipment of tea from TE Stockwell. He made new labels using the first three letters of the supplier's name and the first two letters of his surname. The first Tesco store opened in 1929 in Burnt Oak, Edgware, Middlesex. Tesco was floated on the London Stock Exchange in 1947 as Tesco Stores (Holdings) Ltd. During the 1950s and 1960s, Tesco grew slowly, until it owned more than 800 stores. The company purchased 70 Williamsons stores (1957), 200 Harrow Stores outlets (1959), 212 Irwins stores (1960), 97 Charles Phillips stores (1964), and the Victor Value chain (1968) (sold to Bejam in 1986). In 1973, Jack Cohen resigned and was replaced as chairman by his son-in-law, Leslie Porter. Porter and managing director Ian MacLaurin abandoned the "pile it high and sell it cheap" philosophy of Cohen, which had left the company stagnating with a bad image. In 1977, Tesco launched "Operation Checkout," which included price reductions and centralized purchasing for all its stores. As a result, its market share rose by 4 percent within two months.

At the beginning of the 1990s, the U.K. retail market slowly became more competitive. Three players dominated the food market: ASDA[2] (which became Wal-Mart's largest overseas subsidiary in 1999), Sainsbury's, and Tesco. ASDA positioned itself as the price leader and held this position for some time, closely followed by Tesco. Sainsbury's targeted the upper price segment, positioning itself between mass market and high end.

In the mid-1990s, competition intensified as a price war among these players emerged, resulting in squeezed margins and cost cutting. It is not surprising that this also had an adverse impact on the service level these corporations provided.

In general, prices of standard brands and private labels at both Sainsbury's and Tesco came closer, while the two firms differed slightly in their discounting policies. Tesco emphasized its low-price private label ("Value") and continued to cut prices, while Sainsbury's emphasized price reductions on the standard private labels. The price cuts were prompted by the increased price pressure from the market entry of discounters. For example, Aldi entered the market in 1990, followed by Lidl in 1994. In 2005, these two hard discounters had acquired a market share of 2.2 percent and 1.9 percent, respectively.

Store Formats

In 1975, Sainsbury's launched the "Sainsbury's SavaCentre" hypermarket format as a joint venture with British Home Stores. This was the first attempt in the United Kingdom to launch supermarkets with a large non-food range. SavaCentre became a wholly owned Sainsbury's subsidiary in 1989. As the hypermarket format became mainstream, with rivals such as ASDA and Tesco launching ever-larger stores, Sainsbury's decided that a separate brand was no longer needed. Over the following years, these stores were converted to the regular Sainsbury's superstore format and, subsequently, Sainsbury's retreated from hypermarkets and changed its store formats. Now, Sainsbury's operates three formats: regular Sainsbury's stores, Sainsbury's local stores (convenience stores), and Sainsbury's central stores (smaller supermarkets in urban locations). For an overview of Sainsbury's U.K. store portfolio at the end of fiscal year 2005–06, see Exhibit 1.

While Sainsbury's retreated from hypermarkets, Tesco expanded Tesco Extra and strengthened its hypermarket formats.[3] Its overarching store strategy is reflected in its core marketing slogan adopted when Terry Leahy became CEO in 1997. "The Tesco Way" implies a shift from a focus on the corporation to a focus on people, both employees and customers. Tesco stores are divided into five formats, differentiated by size and range of products, and are customized to specific segments: Tesco Extra, Tesco Superstores, Tesco Metro, Tesco Express, and One Stop (see Exhibit 2). The approximately 500 One Stop stores are the smallest units. They stay open in the late evening and feature a differentiated pricing and offer system. Tesco Extra, launched in 1997, is the largest format, consisting mainly of out-of-town hypermarkets that stock Tesco's entire product range and offer free parking. Their number has increased about 20 percent annually, mainly by conversions of other formats. Tesco Superstores are the standard large grocery supermarkets, with a much smaller range of non-food goods than Extra. They are referred to as "superstores" for convenience, but not as part of the name. It is the standard Tesco format. Most are located in suburbs of cities or on the edges of large- and medium-sized towns. Tesco Metro stores are sized between normal Tesco stores and Tesco Express stores. They are mostly located in city centers and on the high streets of small towns. The first Tesco Metro was opened in Covent Garden, London, in 1992. Tesco Express stores are neighborhood convenience stores, stocking mainly food, with an emphasis on high-margin products alongside everyday essentials. They are found in busy city center districts, in small shopping precincts in residential areas, and in petrol station forecourts. As CEO Terry Leahy remarked in the company's 2000 annual report:

This obsession with our customers, their needs, and how these must be changing, means that you should not expect us to go on opening large edge-of-town superstores long after the need for new ones has passed. Expect . . . continual evolution: expect us to provide a mix of formats in different locations . . . to meet special needs of customers in each location.

Exhibit 1 Sainsbury's Store Portfolio in the United Kingdom (at the end of 2006)

Format	Number	Area (ft²)	Area (m²)	Percentage of Space
Supermarkets	455	15,916,000	1,467,000	95.1%
Convenience stores	297	821,000	76,000	4.9%
Total	752	16,737,000	1,543,000	100%

Exhibit 2 Tesco's Store Portfolio in the United Kingdom (at the end of 2007)

Format	Number	Total Area (m²)	Total Area (sq ft)	Mean Area (m²)	Mean Area (sq ft)	Percentage of Space
Tesco Extra	147	952,441	10,252,000	6,479	69,741	36.89%
Tesco	433	1,227,434	13,212,000	2,834	30,512	47.55%
Tesco Metro	162	177,073	1,906,000	1,093	11,765	6.85%
Tesco Express	735	145,114	1,562,000	197	2,125	5.62%
One Stop	506	62,988	678,000	124	1,339	2.44%
Tesco Homeplus	5	16,258	175,000	3,251	35,000	0.62%
Total	1,988	2,581,310	27,785,000	1,298	13,976	100%

Much of Tesco's sales increases occurred through increases in total square footage with the opening of new stores, including new formats such as Metro and Express. From 1994 to 1996, selling areas increased by 22 percent for Tesco and 10 percent for Sainsbury's. At the same time, Tesco managed to increase sales per square foot by 14 percent, while Sainsbury's gained only 3 percent. In addition, acquisitions and alliances complemented the organic growth strategy. Tesco, for example, purchased Adminstore in 2004, owner of 45 Cullens, Europa, and Harts convenience stores in and around London. In late 2005, it purchased the 21 remaining Safeway/BP stores after Morrison's dissolved the Safeway/BP partnership. In 1997, Tesco formed an alliance with Esso Petroleum Company Ltd (now part of ExxonMobil Corp.). The agreement included several petrol filling stations on lease from Esso, where Tesco would operate the store under the Express format. In turn, Esso would operate the forecourts and sell their fuel via the Tesco store. Ten years later, over 600 Tesco/Esso stores can be found across the United Kingdom.

Sainsbury's also expanded by acquisition. As part of the acquisition of Safeway Group by Morrison's, Morrison's was to dispose of 53 of the combined group's stores. In May 2004, Sainsbury's announced that it would acquire 14 of these stores, 13 Safeway stores, and one Morrison's outlet, all located primarily in the Midlands and the north of England. The first of these new stores opened in August 2004. In 2004, Sainsbury's also expanded its share of the convenience store market through other acquisitions. Bell's Stores, a 54-store chain based in northeast England, was acquired in February 2004. Jackson's Stores, a chain of 114 stores based in Yorkshire and the North Midlands, was purchased in August 2004. JB Beaumont, a chain of six stores in the East Midlands, was acquired in November 2004. SL Shaw Ltd, which owned six stores, was acquired in April 2005 for £6 million. On September 29, 2004, Sainsbury's established Sainsbury's Convenience Stores Ltd to manage its Sainsbury's local stores and the Bell's and Jackson's chains. The latter two are to be rebranded as Sainsbury's local stores by 2009.

Service Offerings and Distribution Systems

"An inclusive offer" is how Tesco describes its aspiration to appeal to upper-, medium-, and low-income customers in the same stores. According to Citigroup retail analyst David McCarthy, "They've pulled off a trick that I'm not aware of any other retailer achieving. That is, to appeal to all segments of the market." One plank of this program has been Tesco's use of its private label products, including the upmarket "Finest" and low price "Value." Other examples include organic, kids, British specialty food, and "free from" brands. As Edward Garner, the communications director of the TNS Superpanel, remarks: "Tesco's winning formula is largely due to its ability to be all things to all people. According to TNS, over 60 percent of British households shop in Tesco every four weeks. That's 20 percent more than its nearest rival. The store appeals to wide-reaching demographics across the country and has built up a heritage of reliability and trustworthiness, which keeps shoppers returning to its stores. These factors have enabled Tesco to gain close to a third of the British grocery market."

Sainsbury's has also invested in private labels. A large Sainsbury's store typically stocks around 50,000 lines, of which about half are private labels. These lines include, for example, "Basics" (an economy range similar to

Tesco's "Values"), "Taste the Difference" (a premium range similar to Tesco's "Finest"), "Different by Design" (a smaller range of premium non-food lines), "Kids," "Be Good to Yourself" (products with reduced calorific and/or fat content), "Free from," "Sainsbury Organic," "Fair Trade," and "Super Naturals™" (a range of ready-made meals with healthy ingredients).

While service offerings today are quite similar, the rivals' distribution strategies differ significantly. In common with most other large retailers, Tesco decided to draw goods from suppliers into regional distribution centers for preparation and delivery to stores. Tesco is extending this logistic practice to cover collection from suppliers (factory gate pricing) and input to suppliers in a drive to reduce costs and improve reliability.

In contrast, Sainsbury's has heavily invested in fully automated depots. On January 14, 2000, Sir Peter Davis was appointed Sainsbury's CEO. This decision was well received by investors and analysts, as in his first two years he raised profits above targets. By 2004, however, the group had suffered a decline in performance relative to its competitors and fell to third in the U.K. food market. Davis oversaw an almost £3 billion upgrade of stores, distribution, and IT equipment. Part of this investment included the construction of four fully automated depots, which, at £100 million each, cost four times more than standard depots.

Loyalty Programs

Retailers try to gain the loyalty of their customers in various ways. Tesco was the first to launch a Clubcard system. It was introduced in 1995 and has become the most popular card in the United Kingdom, with around 13 million active Clubcard holders. Customers collect one Clubcard point for every £1 (€1 in Ireland) they spend in a Tesco store, Tesco Petrol, or at Tesco.com. Customers also collect points by paying with a Tesco credit card or by using Tesco Mobile, Tesco Homephone, Tesco Broadband, selected Tesco Personal Finance products, or by using its Clubcard partners, Powergen or Avis. Each point is worth 1p in-store when redeemed or 4p when used with Clubcard deals (offers for holidays, day trips, etc.). Every three months, holders receive a Clubcard statement offering discount coupons that can be spent in-store, online (if opted into eVouchers), or on various Clubcard deals. The program has numerous partners (e.g., hundreds of British pubs), but the Clubcard belongs to Tesco alone. Tesco implemented the Clubcard rewards program to gather customer information, which is then used to cater to specific potential customer needs and wants. When shoppers sign up for the card, they automatically submit their ages, genders, and incomes.

Tesco segments their shoppers on the basis of these factors. As soon as the shopper uses the card online or in-store, product information is automatically uploaded into the Tesco database. Product information is used to cross-sell additional products and services, such as food delivery.

Tesco is the most customer-focused business that I have ever worked for. They are absolutely obsessed with the customer.

—JOHN HOERNER, NON-FOOD DIRECTOR, TESCO

Sainsbury's was "wrong-footed" in its original reaction to the Tesco Clubcard, showing "no immediate response apart from disdain."[4] It lost market share in subsequent years. In 2004, the *London Times* quoted a former executive and others who viewed this event as the start of the company's downturn due to management failures by David Sainsbury and his successors, Dino Adriano and Peter Davis. David Sainsbury, who in 1992 replaced his cousin, the long-time CEO John Sainsbury, first dismissed Tesco's Clubcard. After long internal debates, Sainsbury introduced the Sainsbury's reward card in 1996. A multiparty card program, "Nectar," was launched in the autumn of 2002. Nectar gives the customer a versatile and powerful point-gathering system to be used and redeemed at a variety of stores. In Nectar, Sainsbury's has strong partners such as Barclaycard, British Petroleum, and the department store chain Debenhams. The Nectar card was re-launched in summer 2007 to celebrate its fifth anniversary. The scheme was changed from a reward- to a treats-based program. In its early days, the Nectar scheme was criticized as being among the worst card schemes offered. At the time, it was said that some consumers who spent £5,000 on Barclaycard received as little as £12.50 in points to redeem, while Sainsbury's customers had to spend as much as £1,000 just to get two tickets to the cinema. Today, points on spending in-store are earned at a rate of two points per £1 spent (except 1 point per liter of fuel); 500 points can subsequently be exchanged for a voucher worth £2.50 to spend in Sainsbury's. The card scheme is run by a third-party company, Loyalty Management UK (LMUK), which collects information on behalf of the partner sponsors.

Online Sales Channels

Toward the end of the 1990s, both firms targeted online distribution channels that promised large growth potential. Non-store retailing growth rates were expected to be higher than store-based rates, as online usage gained popularity among British consumers (see Exhibit 3). Following these predictions, the United

Exhibit 3 Retailing: Growth in Value Sales by Broad Sector/Sector 2001–2006 (percentage of current value growth)

	2005–2006	2001–2006 CAGR	2001–2006 Total
Non-store retailing	13.3	13.8	91.2
Internet retailing	24.8	32.9	313.9
Vending	2.5	5.0	27.7
Home shopping	2.8	3.8	20.6
Direct selling	–1.0	–1.5	–7.4
Store-based retailing	2.4	3.7	19.8
Food retailers	3.0	4.0	21.7
Non-food retailers	1.9	3.4	18.3
Retailing	3.1	4.2	23.1

Source: 2007, Official statistics, trade associations, trade press, company research, trade interviews, Euromonitor International estimates; Euromonitor, U.K. Retail Market: Market overview.

Kingdom has evolved into a leader of Internet retailing in Europe, and growth is continuing.

Tesco[5] has operated on the Internet since 1994 and was the first retailer in the world to offer a robust home-shopping service in 1996. Tesco.com was formally launched in 2000. It also has online operations in the Republic of Ireland and in South Korea. Food sales are available within delivery range of selected stores, goods being hand-picked within each store, in contrast to the warehouse model followed by most competitors (e.g., Ocado[6]), which allows rapid expansion with limited investment. In 2003, Tesco.com's then-CEO, John Browett, received the Wharton Infosys Business Transformation Award for the innovative processes he used to support this online food service. Today, Tesco operates the world's largest food home-shopping service, as well as provides consumer goods, telecommunications, and financial services online. As of November 2006, Tesco was the only food retailer to make online shopping profitable.

Sainsbury's has been involved in e-business and home-shopping development since 2000, when it launched Sainsbury's to You in April of that year. Although some employees transferred from the traditional side of the business, Sainsbury's also hired new staff with Web and marketing skills. Specific training was provided on e-business, as well as cross-functional training. Sainsbury's to You did not completely spin off

but occupied a separate building, thereby combining entrepreneurial flexibility with the strength and security of a strong brand. Sainsbury's Online currently operates from 144 stores and uses two dedicated picking centers that are not open to the public. In addition to food, also available are flowers, wine, gifts, and electronics. In October 2007, Sainsbury's was receiving around 80,000 online orders per week. This represents quite strong growth, but is far less than Tesco, which processes weekly orders of 250,000. Sainsbury's did not release any e-commerce sales figures, but said it was still on track to expand its Web service to 200 stores by March 2010. Tesco.com captured two-thirds of all online food orders in the first seven months of 2007, generating sales of approximately £2.5 million per day. Sainsburystoyou .com took third place with 14 percent, behind ASDA with 16 percent. Customers of Sainsbury's, however, spent the most per order, averaging almost £90, compared to £80 for both Tesco and ASDA. ASDA and Sainsbury's online shoppers also bought more items per order, with both averaging 69 units per order compared to 58 for Tesco. Sainsbury's online customers incurred the lowest average delivery charge during the period, at just over £3. Tesco online customers paid over £4 per delivery, and ASDA online customers paid nearly £5.50.

Diversification into Non-Food

A number of retailers have created such sense of nearness with customers in terms of perception, safety and security that you can refer to them as brands.
—KAREL VUURSTEEN, CHAIRMAN & CEO, HEINEKEN

Originally specializing in food, Tesco began to diversify into areas such as discount clothes, consumer electronics, consumer financial services, DVD sales and rentals, compact discs and music downloads, Internet service, consumer telecoms, consumer health insurance, consumer dental plans, and budget software. In these new product segments, Tesco heavily built on its skills in private labels. For example, it introduced brands such as "Cherokee" and "F+F" in clothing, "Technika" and "Digilogic" in consumer electronics, and other labels ranging from DVD players to televisions and computers. Tesco used its food brands "Finest" and "Value" to expand into non-food items. In its Extra stores, Finest health and beauty, home, and clothing lines resulted.

In 1997, Tesco Personal Finance was launched as a fifty-fifty banking joint venture with the Royal Bank of Scotland. Products offered included credit cards, loans, mortgages, savings accounts, and several types of insurance, including car, home, life, pet, and travel. They are promoted by leaflets in Tesco stores and through its

Web site. All of its offers are simple, providing customers few but clear options and choices. Profits were £130 million for the 52 weeks prior to February 24, 2007, of which Tesco's share was £66 million. This move toward the financial sector has diversified the Tesco brand and provides opportunities for growth outside the retailing sector. For example, Tesco offers Clubcard points or free petrol when consumers purchase Tesco car insurance. The company is currently conducting trials at a finance center in the Glasgow Silverburn Extra store, providing free financial advice and quotes for insurance and loans; this service is staffed by trained Royal Bank of Scotland employees. The center also has a Euro cash machine providing commission-free Euros and a Bureau de Change run by Travelex. If successful, this service will be rolled out to more key and flagship stores.

Tesco also entered the telecommunications sector. Though it launched its Internet service provider in 1998, the company was not seriously active in telecommunications until 2003. Rather than purchasing or building its own telecom network, Tesco paired its marketing strength with the expertise of existing telecom operators. In autumn 2003, Tesco Mobile was launched as a joint venture with O2, and Tesco Home Phone was created in partnership with Cable & Wireless. In August 2004, Tesco Broadband, an ADSL-based service delivered via BT phone lines, was launched in partnership with NTL. In January 2006, Tesco Internet Phone, a Voice over Internet Protocol service, was launched in conjunction with Freshtel of Australia. Simple and clear offering logic is also evident in the strategic move into telecommunications. Tesco Mobile offers only four different pay-as-you-go tariffs: Value, Standard, Extra, and Staff (for employees). Tesco announced in December 2004 that it had signed up 500,000 customers to its mobile service in the 12 months since launch. By December 2005, one million customers were using its mobile service, and by April 2006, Tesco claimed over one and, one-half million telecom accounts in total, including mobile, fixed line, and broadband. On December 19, 2006, Tesco Ireland announced that it would enter into a joint venture with O2 Ireland to offer mobile telecommunications services, also under the Tesco Mobile brand.

Recently, Tesco entered the housing market with a self-advertising Web site, Tesco Property Market. Other strategic initiatives into non-food items include, for example, following a successful trial in 2006, "Apple" zones in 12 outlets, where the iPod range is sold alongside Mac computers and other Apple products.

Sainsbury's was much more reluctant to move into non-food retailing. Inspired by the success of its main rivals (ASDA had also moved strongly into the non-food

area) and the sheer size of the U.K. non-food retail market (in 2003, it was estimated at over £100 million), it launched 2,500 home and cookware products in September 2003. Copying Tesco, Sainsbury's also used its own food brands and transferred them to non-food items. For example, it extended its clothing range with an organic line. In addition to food and non-food items, Sainsbury's expanded into retail banking and property development. In 1997, Sainsbury's bank was established as a joint venture between J Sainsbury plc and the Bank of Scotland (now HBOS). Sainsbury's bank offers services similar to Tesco's, including travel (insurance and money), savings, and lending; it also offers a Sainsbury's credit card. By 2010, Sainsbury's expects to achieve sales of £3.5 billion, with 33 percent of its total sales coming from non-food businesses.

International Diversification

These results show that our new growth businesses—in international, in non-food and in services—have contributed as much profit as the entire business was making in 1997.

—CEO TERRY LEAHY, 2005

Tesco's international expansion[7] began in the late 1970s with the purchase of a small company in the Republic of Ireland. The small-scale nature of this first foray was seen as a weakness, and the company was eventually sold in the mid-1980s. In 1994, Tesco acquired the Scottish supermarket chain William Low. Tesco successfully fought off Sainsbury's for control of the Dundee-based firm, which then operated 57 stores. This paved the way for Tesco to expand its presence in Scotland, where it was weaker than in England. Inverness was recently branded "Tescotown" because well over 50p in every £1 spent on food is believed to be spent in its three Tesco stores. In March 1997, Tesco announced the purchase of the retail arm of Associated British Foods, which consisted of the Quinnsworth, Stewarts, and Crazy Prices chains in the Republic of Ireland and Northern Ireland, as well as associated businesses, for £640 million. This acquisition gave Tesco both a major presence in the Republic of Ireland and a larger presence in Northern Ireland than Sainsbury's, which had begun its move into the province in 1995.

In the 1990s, Tesco strongly expanded overseas by increasing investments in emerging markets such as Hungary, the Czech Republic, Thailand, and South Korea. Tesco was buying into successful companies, a strategy that resulted in strong positions in these markets. In 1997, the new CEO, Terry Leahy, enforced Tesco's international growth strategies beyond Great Britain. However, outside the United Kingdom the supermarket firm's position was far from dominant and remained in the shadow of larger, more high-profile international operators such as Wal-Mart and Carrefour. Tesco then analyzed countries for expansion, putting high emphasis on two dimensions: the market potential for growth and the competitive situation in the market. Only if a market was characterized by relatively high growth potential and relatively low rivalry was it considered a real target market and approached in an orderly fashion.

In 2002, Tesco purchased 13 HIT hypermarkets in Poland. In June 2003, Tesco purchased the C Two-Network in Japan. It also acquired a majority stake in the Turkish supermarket chain Kipa. Another acquisition was the Lotus chain in Thailand. In mid-2006, Tesco purchased an 80 percent stake in Casino's Leader Price supermarkets in Poland, which were subsequently reconfigured as small Tesco stores.

Many British retailers attempting to build international businesses have failed. Tesco has responded to the need to be sensitive to local expectations in foreign countries by entering into joint ventures with local partners, such as Samsung Group in South Korea (Samsung-Tesco Homeplus), and Charoen Pokphand in Thailand (Tesco Lotus), and by appointing a high proportion of local personnel to management positions.

In late 2004, the amount of floor space Tesco operated outside the United Kingdom surpassed its home market space for the first time, although the United Kingdom still accounted for more than 75 percent of group revenue due to lower sales per unit area outside the territory (for an overview of Tesco's international store portfolio, see Exhibit 4). Tesco regularly continues to make small acquisitions to expand its international businesses. For example, in the 2005–06 fiscal year, acquisitions were made in South Korea, Poland, and Japan.

In September 2005, Tesco announced that it was selling its operations in Taiwan to Carrefour and purchasing Carrefour stores in the Czech Republic and Slovakia. Both companies stated that they were concentrating their efforts in countries where they had strong market positions. Tesco entered China by acquiring a 50 percent stake in the Hymall chain from Ting Hsin of

Exhibit 4 Tesco's Store Portfolio "International"

Country	Entered	Stores	Area (m²)	Area (sq ft)	Turnover (£ million)
China	2004	47	392,422	4,224,000	552
Czech Republic	1996	84	381,459	4,106,000	807
France	1992	1	1,400	16,000	Note 3
Hungary	1994	101	448,164	4,824,000	1,180
Republic of Ireland	1997	95	205,780	2,215,000	1,683
Japan	2003	109	29,078	313,000	287
Malaysia	2002	19	174,750	1,881,000	247
Poland	1995	280	606,935	6,533,000	1,135
Slovakia	1996	48	225,475	2,427,000	498
South Korea	1999	81	473,340	5,095,000	2,557
Thailand	1998	370	698,166	7,515,000	1,326
Turkey	2003	30	102,936	1,108,000	256
United States of America	2007	6	Unknown	60,000 (est.)	Unknown

Note 1: The store numbers and floor area figures are as of February 24, 2007, but the turnover figures are for the year 2005, except for the Republic of Ireland data, which are for the year ending February 24, 2007, like the U.K. figures. This information is taken from the 2007 final broker pack.

Note 2: China: Joint venture in February 2006; now a 90 percent–owned subsidiary.

Note 3: France: Tesco owned a French chain called Catteau between 1992 and 1997. Its existing single store in France is a wine warehouse in Calais (opened in 1995 and targeted at British day trippers).

Note 4: Malaysia: Tesco Stores (Malaysia) Sdn Bhd was incepted on November 29, 2001, as a strategic alliance with local conglomerate, Sime Darby Bhd of which the latter holds 30 percent of total shares.

Taiwan in September 2004. In December 2006, it raised its stake to 90 percent in a £180 million deal, which was just after Tesco lost out to Wal-Mart to partner with the Indian group, Bharti, to develop a national retail chain in India.

In February 2006, Tesco announced its intention to move into the United States, opening a chain of convenience stores on the West Coast (Arizona and California), Fresh & Easy Neighborhood Market. The first store was opened in November 2007, with 100 more openings scheduled in the first year. By planning to open a new store in the United States every two-and-one-half days, Tesco intends to mimic the successful expansion of U.S. pharmacy chains such as Walgreens. Tesco's strategy and unorthodox tactics have not been without controversy. In 2005 and 2006, the company covertly sent an advance team consisting of executives in disguise to conduct intelligence on potential competitors. Like a James Bond movie, the company's agents sought to keep their plans secret by posing as Hollywood film producers making a movie about supermarkets, according to *BusinessWeek*. The bold operation collected intelligence on the U.S. market and on competitors such as Wal-Mart, Kroger, Safeway, Albertson's, Whole Foods, and Trader Joe's. The covert operation was so unusual and unsettling that some potential rivals hired security teams to infiltrate Tesco and obtain information about executives involved in the operation. In the end, Tesco did obtain the necessary information to proceed with its store openings. A Tesco senior manager said, "For me, it is remarkable that in five years Tesco has moved from being a U.K.-based supermarket chain to become an international mixed retail and services business. This rapid transformation is based on clarity at the top and a tremendous creativity and energy in making it happen quickly." Sainsbury's international strategy can be described as that of a fast follower, albeit with varying results and to a lesser extent. It expanded its operations into Scotland, opening a store in Darnley in January 1992. In June 1995, Sainsbury's announced its intention to move into the Northern Ireland market, which had until that point been dominated by local companies. Between December 1996 and December 1998, the company opened seven stores. Two others at Sprucefield, Lisburn, and Holywood Exchange, Belfast, would not open until 2003 due to protracted legal challenges. Sainsbury's move into Northern Ireland was undertaken in a very different way than that of Tesco. While Sainsbury's outlets were all new developments, Tesco (apart from one Tesco Metro) instead purchased existing chains from Associated British Foods (see Tesco Ireland). In 1999, Sainsbury's acquired an 80.1 percent share of the Egyptian Distribution Group SAE, a retailer in Egypt with 100 stores and 2,000 employees. However, poor profitability led to the sale of this share in 2001.

Management Teams

At the end of March 2004, Davis was promoted to chairman and was replaced as CEO of Sainsbury's by Justin King. Justin King joined Sainsbury's from Marks and Spencer plc, where he was a director with responsibility for its food division and Kings Super Markets, Inc, a subsidiary in the United States. King was also previously a managing director at ASDA, with responsibility for hypermarkets. In June 2004, Davis was forced to resign as chairman in the face of an impending shareholder revolt over his salary and bonuses. Investors were angered by a bonus share award of over £2 million, despite poor company performance. In July 2004, Philip Hampton was appointed chairman. Hampton had previously worked for British Steel, British Gas, BT, and Lloyds TSB.

King perceived Sainsbury's to be not sufficiently focused on its customers or its main competitors. King ordered a direct mail campaign to one million Sainsbury's customers, asking what they wanted from the company and where the company could improve. Results re-affirmed the commentary of retail analysts; that is, the group was not ensuring that shelves were fully stocked, partly due to the failure of the IT systems introduced by Peter Davis. In October 2004, King unveiled the results of the business review and his plans to revive the company's fortunes. This was generally well received by both the stock market and the media. Immediate plans included terminating 750 headquarters staff and recruiting around 3,000 shop floor staff to improve the quality of service and the firm's problem of stock availability. Another significant announcement was the decision to halve the dividend in order to increase funds available to offer price cuts and to improve quality. The company's fortunes have improved since the launch of this recovery program.

In 2004, King hired Lawrence Christensen, previously an expert in logistics at Safeway, as supply chain director. Immediate supply chain improvements included the reactivation of two distribution centers. In 2006, Christensen commented on the four automated depots introduced by Davis, saying, "[N]ot a single day went by without one, if not all of them, breaking down … the systems were flawed. They have to stop for four hours every day for maintenance. But because they were constantly breaking down you would be playing catch up. It was a vicious circle." Christensen felt that a fundamental mistake was to build four such depots at once, rather than building one and testing it thoroughly before building the others. In 2007, Sainsbury's announced an additional £12 million investment in its depots to keep pace with sales growth and to remove the failed automated systems from its depots.

The Competitive Landscape Today

The situation today is clear. Tesco has outpaced its closest rival in its local and international markets. Edward Garner, communications director of the TNS Superpanel, said, "TNS supermarket share information shows that the retailer's market share has grown consistently and strongly over the last decade and shows no sign of abating."

These events led to shifts in the competitive landscape. The U.K. retail industry has become highly concentrated. The top four store-based retailers—Tesco, Sainsbury's ASDA, and Morrison's Supermarkets—dominate the market; all are original food retailers. This illustrates the status of food retailers in the market (see Exhibit 5). All are British, except ASDA, which was acquired in 1999 by the U.S. retail giant Wal-Mart.

Discounters adapted to this less-favorable environment by slightly improving their meager U.K. presence by expanding their number of outlets and moving upscale. This was helped by the trend of consumers to increasingly combine bargain shopping with purchases of luxury products or services. This "schizophrenic" shopping behavior blurs previously separate boundaries. The traditional structure of upper, middle, and mass market has been more or less abolished.

Since the launch of King's recovery program, Sainsbury's has reported nine consecutive quarters of sales growth, most recently in March 2007, even outpacing Tesco, making the company's performance the best since its glory days of the 1980s and early 1990s. Sales increases were credited to solving problems with the company's distribution system. More recent sales improvements have been attributed to significant price cuts and the company's focus on fresh and healthy food. On October 4, 2007, Sainsbury's announced plans to relocate their Store Support Centre from Holborn to Kings Cross in 2011. This office, part of a new building complex, will allow both cost savings and energy efficiency.

Despite this positive news, according to the latest Taylor Nelson Sofres rankings published in March 2007, Sainsbury's market share in food retailing remains third in the United Kingdom at 16.37 percent compared to Tesco's 31.35 percent, ASDA's 16.83 percent, and Morrison's 11.08 percent (see Exhibit 6). Tesco remains the clear market leader. In the past, Tesco showed itself

Exhibit 5 Retailing: Company Shares by Value 2004–2006 (in percentage of retail value)

	2004	2005	2006
Tesco plc	10.2	11.0	11.4
J Sainsbury plc	5.4	5.8	5.9
Asda Stores Ltd	4.7	4.9	5.1
Wm Morrison Supermarkets plc	3.7	3.7	3.5
Marks and Spencer plc	2.7	2.7	2.7
Alliance Boots plc	—	—	2.1
Dixons Group plc	1.3	1.4	1.4
Argos plc	1.3	1.4	1.4
B&Q plc	1.5	1.5	1.4
Somerfield Ltd	1.7	1.7	1.3
Waitrose Ltd	1.0	1.0	1.2
Co-operative Group (CWS) Ltd	1.3	1.3	1.2
Next plc	1.0	1.0	1.1
Spar Ltd (UK)	0.8	0.9	0.9
Debenhams Retail plc	0.7	0.8	0.8

Source: 2007, Official statistics, trade associations, trade press, company research, trade interviews, Euromonitor International estimates; Euromonitor, U.K. Retail Market: Market overview.

to be the quickest at seizing expansion opportunities. Furthermore, it has succeeded in building an image of providing good value at low prices.

The recovery in the Sainsbury market share builds on the positive picture already established. This strong performance has been achieved in the face of relentless pressure from Tesco, which continues its recent run of double-digit turnover growth. . . .

Whilst Tesco remains dominant, there are signs that it is experiencing increased competition. It is still growing, but the year-on-year share increase is below the average we were seeing last year. Looking towards the future, Tesco will continue to face challenging competition from its nearest competitor Asda as well as the likes of Sainsbury's, which is showing positive growth trends and Morrisons once the Safeway store conversions are complete. Tesco will need to prove its ability to meet increasingly challenging consumer demands and stay a step ahead of the competition. . . .

Exhibit 6 Food Retailing: Company Shares by Sales 1990–2007 (in percentage of retail value)

	1990	…	1994	1995	…	2002	…	2004	2005	2006	2007
Tesco plc	9.7		11.4	13.4		16.7		27.5	29.8	31.1	31.35
J Sainsbury plc	11.0		12.3	12.2		11.7		15.5	15.9	16.0	16.37
Asda Stores Ltd	6.8		6.7	7.2		10.6		16.6	16.5	16.4	16.83
Wm Morrison Supermarkets plc (Safeway included)						7.5 (only Safeway)		14.4	12.2	11.3	11.08

Source: TNS (Taylor Nelson Sofres) World Panel market-share data released June 2007.

Future Internationalization: It has a long way to go before it overhauls Wal-Mart as the world's biggest grocer—but analysts said the same about overhauling Sainsbury's in the U.K. market 15 years ago and now Tesco is almost double its size.

—**EDWARD GARNER, COMMUNICATIONS DIRECTOR OF TNS SUPERPANEL, 2007**

New Challenges Ahead

After a relatively long period of economic growth during the review period, conditions may well stagnate in the coming years, thus dampening the forecast performance of store-based retailing. Consumer debt levels have reached record highs and, with the United Kingdom's negative saving rate, there is less room for continued growth in consumption. As a result, discounters (both food and non-food) are well placed to gain importance. Euromonitor predicts food retailers to outperform non-food retailers with a value compound annual growth rate of 1 percent. Recent trends, such as health and wellness and ethical concerns, have opened opportunities, even in the saturated food category; however, most food retailers' growth is expected to stem from non-food items.

Consolidation is expected to continue (see the Safeway takeover), with independent shops closing, being taken over, or joining larger chains. This is evident in the decline of the number of total outlets, particularly independent ones.

Sainsbury's might be the target of additional takeover bids, since family investment in the company is only 18 percent. A first private equity bid was considered by CVC Capital Partners, Kohlberg Kravis Roberts (which later left the consortium in order to focus on its bid for Alliance Boots), and Blackstone Group; in February 2007, this also included Goldman Sachs and Texas Pacific Group. The initial offer submitted in April 2007 of 562p a share was rejected after discussions between Sainsbury's top management and the two largest family shareholders. A subsequent offer of 582p a share was also rejected. As a consequence, the CVC-led consortium abandoned its quest, stating "[I]t became clear the consortium would be unable to make a proposal that would result in a successful offer." In April 2007, Delta Two, a Qatari investment company, bought a 14 percent stake in Sainsbury's (causing its share price to rise 7.17 percent); this stake was increased to 25 percent in June 2007. On July 18, 2007, BBC News reported that Delta Two had tabled a conditional bid proposal. On November 5, 2007, it was announced that Delta Two had abandoned its takeover bid due to the "deterioration of credit markets" and concerns about funding the company's pension scheme. Following the withdrawal of the interest of Qatari investment, shares in Sainsbury's dropped about 20 percent (115p) to 440p on the day of this announcement.

Appendix 1 Retail: Number of Employees: 2001–2006 (in thousands)

	2001	2002	2003	2004	2005	2006
Retail employees	3,048	3,077	3,136	3,308	3,329	3,316
% growth	—	1.0	1.9	5.5	0.6	−0.4

Source: 2007, Official statistics, trade associations, trade press, company research, trade interviews, Euromonitor International estimates; Euromonitor, U.K. Retail Market: Market overview.

Appendix 2 Number of Employees of Food Retailers (full-time equivalents)

Employees	2006	2007
Tesco	380,000	318,283
Asda	150,000 90,000 part-time 60,000 full-time	143,125
Sainsbury's	96,200 104,100 part-time 49,200 full-time	95,500 98,100 part-time 48,800 full-time

Appendix 3 Tesco's Financial Figures

52 weeks ended	Turnover (£m)	Profit before Tax (£m)	Profit for Year (£m)	Basic Earnings per Share (p)
2007	46,600	2,653	1,899	22.36
2006	38,300	2,210	1,576	19.70
2005	33,974	1,962	1,366	17.44
2004	30,814	1,600	1,100	15.05
2003	26,337	1,361	946	13.54
2002	23,653	1,201	830	12.05
2001	20,988	1,054	767	11.29
2000	18,796	933	674	10.07
1999	17,158	842	606	9.14
1998	16,452	760	532	8.12

Note: The numbers include non-UK and Ireland results.

Appendix 4 Growth Rates (Tesco vs. Sainsbury) 1990–2007

Growth Rates (%)	Sales	Operating Income	Net Income	Div. Per Share	Equity	Total Assets
Sainsbury's Y2007				21.88		
Tesco Y2007	8.08	5.88	20.51	11.70	12.00	9.86
Sainsbury's Y2006	5.65	7.55	−64.67	2.56	−0.21	9.24
Tesco Y2006	16.50	13.40	16.82	14.15	9.03	11.97
Sainsbury's Y2005	−10.10	−53.04	−84.60	−56.50	−15.48	−7.11
Tesco Y2005	10.26	12.47	24.18	10.53	13.76	10.12
Sainsbury's Y2004	−1.66	−2.03	−12.78	0.70	2.05	4.70
Tesco Y2004	17.00	19.78	16.28	10.32	22.50	12.68

Appendix 4 Growth Rates (Tesco vs. Sainsbury) 1990–2007 (*Continued*)

Growth Rates (%)	Sales	Operating Income	Net Income	Div. Per Share	Equity	Total Assets
Sainsbury's Y2003	1.56	11.46	24.73	4.99	3.30	8.76
Tesco Y2003	11.35	12.49	13.98	10.71	18.24	21.91
Sainsbury's Y2002	7.57	9.95	38.93	3.63	−1.31	6.85
Tesco Y2002	12.70	13.29	8.21	12.45	4.02	16.00
Sainsbury's Y2001	−1.95	−5.78	−24.93	—	3.23	−1.94
Tesco Y2001	11.66	12.55	13.80	11.16	12.05	18.80
Sainsbury's Y2000	−0.99	−25.32	−41.64	—	0.65	4.32
Tesco Y2000	9.55	7.92	11.22	8.74	9.58	13.88
Sainsbury's Y1999	13.33	8.48	22.79	3.02	12.89	10.13
Tesco Y1999	7.81	5.03	20.00	6.54	10.42	15.58
Sainsbury's Y1998	8.25	11.58	20.84	13.01	12.01	25.23
Tesco Y1998	14.60	18.09	−2.88	12.09	−0.36	12.32
Sainsbury's Y1997	6.08	−11.94	−17.42	1.65	3.88	7.88
Tesco Y1997	14.83	6.91	11.59	7.81	8.78	6.74
Sainsbury's Y1996	11.18	−4.09	−8.87	3.43	7.45	15.81
Tesco Y1996	19.73	17.34	22.63	11.61	15.21	5.01
Sainsbury's Y1995	7.31	13.36	278.18	10.38	8.21	6.22
Tesco Y1995	17.45	18.38	27.43	10.99	12.92	18.84
Sainsbury's Y1994	9.27	1.80	−71.84	5.99	0.36	3.95
Tesco Y1994	13.43	−5.53	−28.59	9.13	−0.15	9.82
Sainsbury's Y1993	11.39	17.48	14.74	14.29	14.68	12.26
Tesco Y1993	6.82	15.06	5.56	12.71	12.50	9.03
Sainsbury's Y1992	11.29	14.29	23.37	20.41	57.92	22.22
Tesco Y1992	11.84	20.48	30.69	20.00	13.29	13.01
Sainsbury's Y1991	12.74	23.83	13.23	20.50	18.98	14.75
Tesco Y1991	17.48	25.63	19.27	25.72	72.23	50.90
Sainsbury's Y1990	22.47	17.16	24.88	20.79	20.38	16.97
Tesco Y1990	14.50	20.50	36.23	22.86	21.60	19.75

Source: Thompson Database 2007.

Appendix 5 Financial Leverage and Return on Equity/Assets 1990–2007

Profitability (%)	Financial Leverage Tesco	Financial Leverage Sainsbury's	Return on Equity Tesco	Return on Equity Sainsbury's	Return on Assets Tesco	Return on Assets Sainsbury's
Y2007	42.41	45.42	18.81		8.62	
Y2006	41.59	30.62	17.50	1.67	8.11	1.02
Y2005	44.13	36.50	16.20	−1.10	7.86	1.56
Y2004	42.72	40.12	15.65	8.09	7.31	3.70
Y2003	39.29	41.16	16.17	9.49	7.37	4.59
Y2002	40.51	43.34	15.65	7.71	7.72	4.21
Y2001	45.18	46.92	15.62	5.60	8.30	3.34
Y2000	47.91	44.57	15.26	7.55	8.54	4.12
Y1999	49.78	46.20	14.99	13.71	8.56	6.94
Y1998	52.11	45.07	13.01	12.56	8.08	6.79
Y1997	58.74	50.38	13.98	11.21	8.74	6.63
Y1996	57.64	52.32	14.02	14.29	8.90	8.48
Y1995	52.54	56.39	13.00	16.88	8.08	10.04
Y1994	55.29	55.36	10.84	4.70	6.96	2.77
Y1993	60.81	57.34	16.07	17.74	10.58	10.39
Y1992	58.93	56.13	17.17	19.88	11.18	11.96
Y1991	58.79	43.44	19.36	23.11	11.12	12.05
Y1990	51.51	41.90	21.05	24.40	12.82	12.20

Source: Thompson Database 2007.

Appendix 6 Margins 1990–2007

Profitability (%)	Gross Margin Tesco	Gross Margin Sainsbury's	Op Profit Margin Tesco	Op Profit Margin Sainsbury's	Pretax Prof Margin Tesco	Pretax Prof Margin Sainsbury's
Y2007	7.60	6.83	5.02	3.00	5.91	2.78
Y2006	7.67	6.95	5.13	2.22	5.46	0.65
Y2005	7.77	7.20	5.89	2.21	5.49	0.10
Y2004	7.65	8.89	5.78	4.22	4.92	3.56
Y2003	7.50	8.20	5.64	4.24	4.96	3.83
Y2002	7.51	7.41	5.58	3.86	4.97	3.33

Appendix 6 Margins 1990–2007 (*Continued*)

Profitability (%)	Gross Margin Tesco	Gross Margin Sainsbury's	Op Profit Margin Tesco	Op Profit Margin Sainsbury's	Pretax Prof Margin Tesco	Pretax Prof Margin Sainsbury's
Y2001	7.53	6.69	5.56	3.78	5.01	2.72
Y2000	7.39	6.96	5.51	3.93	4.91	3.12
Y1999	7.77	7.87	5.60	5.22	4.87	5.33
Y1998	7.68	8.05	5.74	5.45	4.67	4.85
Y1997	7.27	7.43	5.57	5.29	5.40	4.40
Y1996	7.65	8.36	5.99	6.37	5.58	5.49
Y1995	7.70	9.29	6.11	7.38	5.45	7.07
Y1994	8.13	9.00	6.06	6.99	5.06	3.48
Y1993	9.33	9.68	7.28	7.50	7.66	7.57
Y1992	8.98	9.44	6.76	7.11	7.69	7.21
Y1991	8.46	9.21	6.27	6.92	6.87	6.63
Y1990	8.39	9.06	5.86	6.30	6.69	6.49

Source: Thompson Database 2007.

Appendix 7 Sales per Share, EPS, and Dividends 1990–2007

Profitability (%)	Sales per Share Data Tesco	Sales per Share Data Sainsbury's	EPS Tesco	EPS Sainsbury's	Dividend Tesco	Dividend Sainsbury's
Y2007	5.37	10.14	0.24	0.19	0.10	0.10
Y2006	5.04	9.57	0.20	0.04	0.09	0.08
Y2005	4.41	8.81	0.18	−0.03	0.08	0.08
Y2004	4.22	10.24	0.15	0.24	0.07	0.18
Y2003	3.77	10.42	0.14	0.27	0.06	0.18
Y2002	3.43	10.28	0.12	0.22	0.06	0.17
Y2001	3.09	9.59	0.11	0.16	0.05	0.16
Y2000	2.81	9.72	0.10	0.21	0.04	0.16
Y1999	2.59	9.84	0.09	0.36	0.04	0.16
Y1998	2.43	8.87	0.08	0.30	0.04	0.16
Y1997	2.14	8.34	0.08	0.25	0.03	0.14
Y1996	1.92	7.94	0.07	0.31	0.03	0.14
Y1995	1.68	7.22	0.06	0.34	0.03	0.13
Y1994	1.46	6.79	0.05	0.09	0.03	0.12
Y1993	1.30	6.27	0.07	0.33	0.02	0.11

(Continued)

Appendix 7 Sales per Share, EPSs and Dividends 1990–2007 (*Continued*)

Profitability (%)	Sales per Share Data Tesco	Sales per Share Data Sainsbury's	EPS Tesco	EPS Sainsbury's	Dividend Tesco	Dividend Sainsbury's
Y1992	1.22	5.83	0.07	0.29	0.02	0.10
Y1991	1.28	5.81	0.06	0.26	0.02	0.08
Y1990	1.13	5.19	0.05	0.24	0.01	0.07

Source: Thompson Database 2007.

Appendix 8 Retailing: Company Shares by Value 2004–2006 (in percentage of retail value)

Company	2004	2005	2006
Tesco plc	10.2	11.0	11.4
J Sainsbury plc	5.4	5.8	5.9
Asda Stores Ltd	4.7	4.9	5.1
Wm Morrison Supermarkets plc	3.7	3.7	3.5
Marks and Spencer plc	2.7	2.7	2.7
Alliance Boots plc	—	—	2.1
Dixons Group plc	1.3	1.4	1.4
Argos plc	1.3	1.4	1.4
B&Q plc	1.5	1.5	1.4
Somerfield Ltd	1.7	1.7	1.3
Waitrose Ltd	1.0	1.0	1.2
Co-operative Group (CWS) Ltd	1.3	1.3	1.2
Next plc	1.0	1.0	1.1
Spar Ltd (UK)	0.8	0.9	0.9
Debenhams Retail plc	0.7	0.8	0.8

Source: 2007, Official statistics, trade associations, trade press, company research, trade interviews, Euromonitor International estimates; Euromonitor, U.K. Retail Market: Market overview.

Appendix 9 Food Retailing: Company Shares by Value 2004–2006 (in percentage of retail value)

Company	2004	2005	2006
Tesco plc	23.0	24.4	25.2
J Sainsbury plc	12.5	13.1	13.3
Asda Stores Ltd	10.9	11.0	11.2
Wm Morrison Supermarkets plc	8.7	8.5	8.1
Somerfield Ltd	4.0	3.8	3.1
Waitrose Ltd	2.3	2.3	2.8

Appendix 9 Food Retailing: Company Shares by Value 2004–2006 (in percentage of retail value) (*Continued*)

Company	2004	2005	2006
Co-operative Group (CWS) Ltd	2.7	2.6	2.5
Spar Ltd (UK)	2.0	2.0	2.0
Musgrave Group plc	1.6	1.8	1.8
Lidl Ltd	1.0	1.1	1.1
Aldi Stores Ltd	0.9	1.0	1.1
Iceland Frozen Foods Ltd.	1.2	1.1	1.0
Others	26.6	24.8	23.6

Source: 2007, Official statistics, trade associations, trade press, company research, trade interviews, Euromonitor International estimates; Euromonitor, U.K. Retail Market: Market overview.

Appendix 10 Food Retailers: Value Sales by Sector 2001–2006 (in millions of pounds, current rsp)

Retailer Type	2001	2002	2003	2004	2005	2006
Supermarkets	40,502.8	42,591.0	43,106.1	44,356.0	45,198.8	46,284.0
Hypermarkets	22,766.5	24,677.2	27,569.9	31,698.9	35,521.1	38,175.9
Convenience stores	10,514.3	11,895.7	13,729.7	14,306.0	14,577.8	14,875.2
Food/drink/tobacco specialists	12,074.0	11,460.6	11,100.0	10,700.0	10,144.0	9,667.0
Independent grocers	8,563.0	8,135.0	7,647.0	7,119.4	6,592.5	6,203.6
Discounters	2,395.0	2,582.6	2,672.2	2,725.4	2,980.2	3,375.5
Other food retailers	2,365.7	2,395.0	2,218.9	2,159.0	2,129.0	2,088.0
Food retailers	99,181.2	102,737.0	108,043.9	113,064.6	117,143.4	120,669.1

Source: 2007, Official statistics, trade associations, trade press, company research, trade interviews, Euromonitor International estimates; Euromonitor, U.K. Retail Market: Market overview.

Appendix 11 Food Retailers: Growth in Value Sales by Sector 2001–2006 (percentage of current value growth)

Retailer Type	2005/2006	2001–2006 CAGR	2001/2006 TOTAL
Hypermarkets	7.5	10.9	67.7
Convenience stores	2.0	7.2	41.5
Discounters	13.3	7.1	40.9
Supermarkets	2.4	2.7	14.3
Other food retailers	−1.9	−2.5	−11.7
Food/drink/tobacco specialists	−4.7	−4.3	−19.9
Independent grocers	−5.9	−6.2	−27.6
Food retailers	3.0	4.0	21.7

Source: 2007, Official statistics, trade associations, trade press, company research, trade interviews, Euromonitor International estimates; Euromonitor, U.K. Retail Market: Market overview.

Appendix 12 Share Price Tesco vs. Sainsbury (1990–2007)

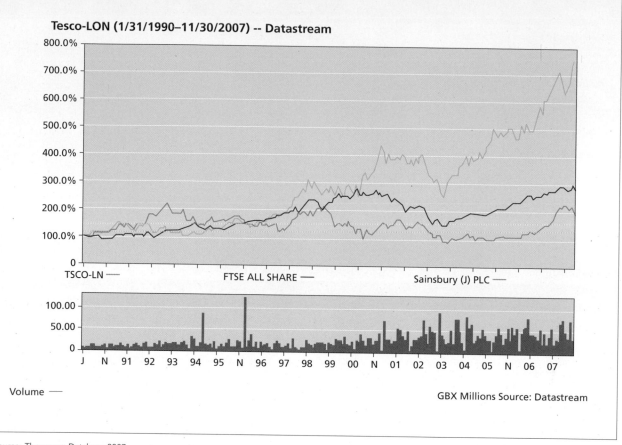

Source: Thompson Database 2007.

NOTES

1. The largest retailers in the world ranked by sales in 2005, http://www.chainstoreage.com.

2. For more information on ASDA and how the purchase of Asda by Wal-Mart in 1999 changed the competitive scenario of the U.K. retail industry, see, for example, Dhar & Sushma, 2005,: Tesco vs. Asda: UK's retailing battle, ECCH Case: 305-623-1.

3. For more detailed information on Tesco's store formats in 2003, see, for example, Padmini & Himansu, 2003, Tesco in 2003, ECCH Case: 304-173-1.

4. The article "Surpassing Sainsbury" describes Tesco's market-share dominance since the introduction of the Clubcard.

5. For Tesco's online sales strategy, see also Pole, 2007, Tesco's online sales strategy, ECCH Case: 507-024-1; Mukund, 2003, http://www.tesco.com: A rare profitable dotcom, ECCH Case: 903-034-1.

6. Ocado was launched in January 2002, in partnership with Waitrose and is today available to over 13.5 million households in the United Kingdom.

7. For Tesco's global expansion strategies, see also Bhavika & Phani Madhav, 2005, Tesco: The British supermarket chain's global expansion strategies and challenges, ECCH Case: 305-350-1.

Mark Brewer, Brandi Chauvin, Eric Mitchell,
Eric Partington, Mark Rade, Don Riddle,
Yinghong (Sara) Song, Robin Chapman

Arizona State University

Millions of people each year try to come up with a "million dollar" idea. Many believe that it requires an "unfathomable" idea, but sometimes going back to the basics is the key. That's what allowed Kevin Plank, the founder of Under Armour performance apparel, to find success. The task at hand was to simply make a superior T-shirt and nothing more. It all began in 1996 when the former University of Maryland football player wanted to create a shirt that would help control the temperature of an athlete's body, not just soak up the sweat during intense activities. He wanted a shirt that enhanced performance rather than detracted from it. As a result, Plank created a synthetic shirt made of high-tech material that had a snug fit designed to feel like a second skin.

The technology behind Under Armour's diverse product lines for men, women, and youth is complex, but the message is simple: wear HeatGear when it's hot, ColdGear when it's cold, and AllSeasonGear between the extremes. Under Armour's mission is to enhance the experience for all athletes by applying passion, science, and the relentless pursuit of innovation to create clothing with temperature control, comfort, and flexibility.[1]

Under Armour's stated goal is to be "a leading developer, marketer, and distributor of branded performance products." It has been able to successfully penetrate the sports apparel market by using the image and influence of: domestic and international professional teams, collegiate teams, Olympians, and individuals.

Utilizing broad-based, frequently free endorsements and well-received publicity, Under Armour has also reached regular athletes, active outdoor enthusiasts, elite tactical professionals, and active lifestyle consumers.

Under Armour is quickly becoming a leader in the sports apparel industry, and it could be argued that it is an opposing force to Nike in sports apparel, with its widespread popularity amongst top-name athletes and sports programs and teams. This is further evidenced by a 133 percent compound annual growth rate and an equally enormous increase in operating income from $5.7 million to $52.5 million between the years 2003 and 2007. As of 2007, Under Armour had $606 million in sales revenue, far surpassing its first year's revenue in 1996 of $17 thousand (see Exhibits 1 and 2).

Under Armour's products are sold worldwide, with the company's headquarters located in the United States and support offices in Hong Kong and Guangzhou, China. Primary sales are achieved through wholesale distribution and licensing to distributors. Products are offered through the company website and retailers, and company stores in the United States, Europe, Japan, Canada, South Africa, Australia, and New Zealand (see Exhibit 3). Under Armour operates in a highly competitive industry where the dominant competitors have significant breadth of market coverage that it is difficult to find an entry point. The main competitors have been advertising and establishing distribution channels, marketing agreements,

Exhibit 1 Under Armour Net Revenue: 2003–2007

	Year Ended December 31				
(In thousands, except per share amounts)	**2007**	**2006**	**2005**	**2004**	**2003**
Statements of Income data:					
Net revenues	$606,561	$430,689	$281,053	$205,181	$115,419

Source: 2008, Under Armour, Inc., Form 10-K 2007 Annual Report, December 31, 26.

Exhibit 2 Under Armour Income Growth from 2005 to 2007

Under Armour, Inc. and Subsidiaries Consolidated Statements of Income (In thousands, except per share amounts)	Year Ended December 31		
	2007	**2006**	**2005**
Net revenues	$606,561	$430,689	$281,053
Cost of goods sold	301,517	215,089	145,203
Gross profit	305,044	215,600	135,850
Operating expenses			
Selling, general and administrative expenses	218,779	158,682	100,040
Income from operations	86,265	56,918	35,810
Other income (expense), net	2,778	2,169	(2,836)
Income before income taxes	89,043	59,087	32,974
Provision for income taxes	36,485	20,108	13,255
Net income	52,558	38,979	19,719
Accretion of and cumulative preferred dividends on Series A Preferred Stock	—	—	5,307
Net income available to common stockholders	$52,558	$38,979	$14,412

Source: 2008, Under Armour, Inc., Form 10-K 2007 Annual Report, December 31, 46.

and recognition for many years. Thus the battle for Under Armour was much more uphill than most other new entrants to an established market. However, Under Armour has succeeded in breaking into a mature market and is no longer simply an amateur player in the sports apparel arena. The question is: "How does the company stay on top of its game?"

History of Under Armour

As previously mentioned, when Plank was a football player he grew tired of having to change his damp, heavy

t-shirt under his jersey, so he set out to create a unique product that would meet the needs of all athletes. His laboratory was his grandmother's basement in Maryland. After many prototypes, Plank created his first shirt; it was a shiny tight shirt made of high-tech fibers that wicked away moisture, keeping athletes cool, dry, and feeling "light."[2] Plank's shirts truly did regulate athletes' body temperatures, lending to improved performance.[3]

Starting Small

Plank believed that he could make a profitable apparel business with his advanced feature shirts, so he used

Exhibit 3 Net Revenue by Geographic Region

(In thousands)	Year Ended December 31		
	2007	**2006**	**2005**
United States	$562,439	$403,725	$266,048
Canada	23,360	16,485	9,502
Subtotal	585,799	420,210	275,550
Other foreign countries	20,762	10,479	5,503
Total net revenues	$606,561	$430,689	$281,053

Source: 2008, Under Armour, Inc., Form 10-K 2007 Annual Report, December 31, 68.

$20,000 of his savings and ran up $40,000 in credit card debt to launch Under Armour.[4] Success was initially slow in coming, but once Plank made his first big sale to Georgia Tech University,[5] Under Armour grew rapidly. Plank marketed his product by focusing on the value-added concept, and now many high school, college, and professional teams use Under Armour athletic gear.

At the end of its first year of operations, Under Armour had five lines of clothing made for every climate, and the company's operations were moved out of Plank's grandmother's basement into a manufacturing warehouse in Maryland.

Growing into a Recognized Brand

In the late 1990s, Under Armour achieved national recognition. By 1998, it was the official supplier of performance apparel to NFL Europe. In 1999, it signed a contract to feature Under Armour in Warner Brothers' movies. By 2000, Under Armour had become a globally recognized brand and was supplying performance apparel to the National Football League, National Hockey League, and Major League Baseball, USA Baseball, and the U.S. ski team as well as other professional leagues abroad.[6] Currently players from 30 of 32 NFL teams wear Under Armour products.

As of 2005, Under Armour was supplying over 100 NCAA Division 1A football programs and thirty NFL teams, but it was still looking for other areas to branch into within the performance apparel industry.[7] Consequently, Under Armour introduced a loose-fit clothing line and added women's clothing to its product line.[8] Also in 2005, the company went public, seeking to sell as much as $100 million in shares of common stock. Ben Sturner, president of Leverage Sports Agency, a New York–based sports marketing firm, said, "Under Armour is no longer an up-and-coming brand. [It] [has] positioned [itself] as a real player in the industry and in the eyes of consumers in only a few years' time."[9]

During 2007, Under Armour increased its marketing initiatives by opening self-owned retail and outlet stores. Plank recognized that "You can't be a world-class athletic brand without the ability to outfit the athlete head to toe,"[10] so Under Armour developed athletic footwear. As of the first quarter of 2008, Under Armour had 43 percent of the total U.S. performance apparel business sold through sporting goods stores, versus 32 percent for Nike and 5.1 percent for Adidas.[11] A marketing consultant has said, "Under Armour is identified with performance the way Starbucks is identified with better coffee, and that is a huge advantage in entering new categories."[12] Plank attributes the company's success to the fact that "[it] ha[s] grown and reinforced [its] brand name and image through sales to athletes and teams at all levels, from youth to professional, as well as through sales to consumers with active lifestyles around the globe."[13]

Current Product and Sales Profile

Geographic Distribution

Approximately 93 percent of sales in 2007 were in the United States. with the remaining 7 percent split between Canada [4 percent] and all other international markets [3 percent] (see Exhibit 3). Under Armour sells products in 13 countries, including in-house distribution in the United Kingdom, Germany, and France. Sales in other Western European and Asian countries are done through partnerships and third-party distributors. The limited sales outside of the North American market were primarily the result of an emerging international penetration plan that received new emphasis in 2006 with the opening of a European headquarters. In an effort to increase the geographic diversity of sales, these headquarters were opened to manage sales and distribution channels, and additional experienced industry talent was brought on board in 2007 (Exhibit 4 shows where offices and stores are located).

Exhibit 4 Geographic Diversity

Location	Use
Baltimore, MD	Corporate headquarters
Amsterdam, The Netherlands	European headquarters
Glen Bumie, MD	Distribution facilities, 17,000 square foot quick-turn, Special Make-Up Shop manufacturing facility, and 4,500 square foot retail outlet store
Denver, CO	Sales office
Ontario, Canada	Sales office
Guangzhou, China	Quality assurance & sourcing for footwear
Hong Kong	Quality assurance & sourcing for apparel
Various	Retail store space

Source: 2008, Under Armour, Inc., Form 10-K 2007 Annual Report, December 31, 20.

Product Segment Distribution

Under Armour's sales results are broken into apparel, footwear, accessories, and licensed products (see Exhibits 5 and 6). Apparel dominated in 2007 with 84 percent of total sales. Men's apparel made up the "lion's share" of Under Armour's business, representing 68 percent of apparel sales and 57 percent of total sales. The second largest apparel segment was women's with 23 percent of apparel sales and 19 percent of total sales, representing a significant growth and diversification opportunity. Youth products made up the balance of apparel sales.

Under Armour's non-apparel product segments made up the remaining 16 percent of sales: footwear (7 percent), accessories (5 percent), and licensed products (4 percent). Footwear is a new product line that was launched in fourth quarter of 2006. Initially this line only offered baseball, softball, and lacrosse cleats designed for high performance through a highly breathable and lightweight design. The footwear line now includes shoes for golf, football, running, and cross-training. In the near future it will likely introduce basketball shoes and soccer cleats. It captured 20 percent of the U.S. football

Exhibit 5 Net Revenue by Product Category

(In thousands)	Year Ended December 31		
	2007	2006	2005
Men's	$348,150	$255,681	$189,596
Women's	115,867	85,695	53,500
Youth	48,596	31,845	18,784
Apparel	512,613	373,221	261,880
Footwear	40,878	26,874	—
Accessories	29,054	14,897	9,409
Total net sales	582,545	414,992	271,289
License revenues	24,016	15,697	9,764
Total net revenues	$606,561	$430,689	$281,053

Source: 2008, Under Armour, Inc., Form 10-K 2007 Annual Report, December 31, 68.

Exhibit 6 Net Revenue by Product in 2007

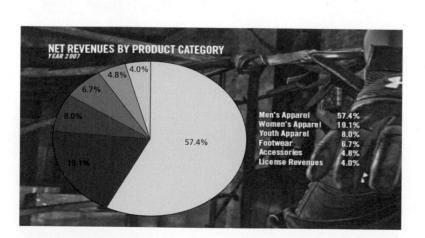

Source: 2008, Under Armour, Inc., Form 10-K 2007 Annual Report, December 31, Intro.

shoe market in the first year.[14] The company's 2009 first quarter earnings beat analysts' expectations, which the company attributes largely to the new running shoe.[15]

Under Armour's accessories category is developed and managed directly by Under Armour. The primary accessories products are performance gloves for football, baseball, running, and golf aligned to the Heatgear and Coldgear product lines with unique performance features.

Under Armour also licenses its brand name to independent manufacturers for other miscellaneous products such as bags, socks, headwear, eyewear, and watches. The company works with multiple licensees directly throughout the product development process to ensure that the products are aligned with its brand and quality expectations.

Seasonality

There appears to be a trend that sales are higher in the third and fourth quarters of each year, aligning with the football and basketball seasons and the traditional holiday gift-giving season in the United States. Under Armour has contemplated putting more emphasis on its baseball product line to improve the sales balance and reduce the seasonal variability in sales, inventory efforts, and distribution.

Operations and Distributions/Distributors

Under Armour possesses an efficient operations and distribution network. As with any corporation, this requires a blend of physical-location metrics and strategic qualities.

By leveraging its licensing partners (JR286, Inc. and USG), Under Armour can provide a wider range of branded products to its customers. This broader range of products adds value by reinforcing the brand and generating revenue without having to organically develop capabilities in these adjacent product categories. Through keen selection and effective partner relationships, Under Armour has developed unique products that consumers value.

For the first ten years of its existence, the company was able to sustain operations by using "off the shelf" software programs, but after it went public in 2006, Under Armour invested in a new SAP system. This system is key to the company's ability to add products to its list of offerings, as it allows Under Armour to manage a more diverse inventory and to ship directly to distributors.[16]

Under Armour does not have a patent on any of the materials[17] used in its products. Therefore, it needs to be cautious in its licensing agreements so companies do not steal its know-how and introduce their own versions. Though the materials and technology used to create its products are not exclusive, by implementing an effective corporate strategy Under Armour has been able to fashion itself as a profitable business and remain a key player among competitors.

Major Competitors

There is stiff competition in the athletic apparel industry with companies of various sizes employing different strategies in order to attract consumers to their product and brand. The athletic apparel industry is so diverse that some smaller companies may choose to target a specific area such as yoga; whereas the larger companies try to capture the whole market. The larger companies continuously increase the competition by spending large amounts of money on product innovation, advertising, and sponsorships. Under Armour's three largest competitors in the industry are Nike, Adidas/Reebok, and Columbia Sportswear.[18] There are also smaller competitors such as SportHill that could possibly break through to become larger threats.

Nike[19]

Nike was founded in 1964 by a University of Oregon track star, Phil Knight. Knight saw a need for better running shoes and began selling shoes imported from Asia out of the trunk of his car. By 1972 he severed his relationships with suppliers abroad because they had become strained and developed his first shoe branded as Nike. Nike over time became known as a high-quality, innovative product that consumers and athletes wanted to wear and were willing to pay a premium price to own.

By 1980, Nike had captured 50 percent of the athletic shoe market and in the 1980s began expanding into other areas of the market through acquisitions and product innovation. It produces its three main product segments (footwear, apparel, and equipment) mostly through contract manufacturers rather than operating its own plants. Nike has relationships with some 700 factories in 52 countries, with most in China, Vietnam, and India.[20] Nike is the leader in athletic shoes, apparel, and equipment and grossed $18.6 billion in fiscal year 2007. It sells products for every sport and climate and strives to be the best in every segment. Nike advertises its brand through high-priced endorsement deals, media advertising, event sponsorships, and partnerships and alliances. Nike currently has 30,000 employees spread across six continents and operates in 160 countries. Nike is an industry leader that is continually striving to stay ahead of the competition.

Adidas[21]

Adidas, combined with Reebok (through an acquisition), is the second largest athletic apparel manufacturer in the world. Adidas was founded in 1924 in Germany by Adolf Dassler. Dassler created the first running shoe made by hand without electricity in his mother's kitchen. Dassler's big break came in 1954 when the German soccer team beat Hungary in the World Cup wearing Adidas cleats. From that point forward, Adidas was the industry leader in soccer shoes and apparel.

Changes in leadership during the late 1980s led Adidas to branch out into other markets, but it struggled to find its niche. Through acquisitions and better management it was back on track by the mid-1990s. Adidas acquired three smaller companies: TaylorMade, Salomon Group, and Maxfli. These acquisitions gave it access to the golf and winter sports market segments. In 2006, it merged with athletic apparel and equipment giant Reebok making it the second largest athletic apparel manufacturer in the world. Today the Adidas product line includes shoes and athletic apparel for basketball, soccer, fitness, golf, and outdoor adventure. Adidas operates globally and has 25,000 employees worldwide with 80 subsidiaries and reported $15.6 billion in profits in 2007.

Columbia Sportswear[22]

Columbia Sportswear Company started in the 1930s as a family-owned and operated hat company in Portland, Oregon. Founder Paul Lamfrom grew tired of working with inadequate suppliers and decided to manufacturer his own products. Columbia quickly gained a reputation for its innovative, high-quality products.

Columbia's introduction of waterproof, breathable fabrics triggered the growth it has experienced since the 1980s from a small family-owned business to a billion dollar publicly traded company. Columbia continues to grow thanks to its innovative product development and the acquisitions of Sorel, Mountain Hardware, Pacific Trail, and Montrail. These acquisitions enabled the company to branch out into other market segments.

Columbia Sportswear is now one of the largest manufacturers and sellers of outdoor apparel specializing in skiwear, snowboard gear, and hunting, fishing, hiking, camping, and casual wear. Columbia currently operates in North America, Europe, and Asia, and its products are available in 90 countries. Columbia has 3,000 employees worldwide. In 2007, Columbia posted record net sales of $1.36 billion.

SportHill[23]

SportHill was founded in 1985 by a University of Oregon track runner who saw the need for cold weather track gear. His athletic apparel design concept merged the best American fabrics with European style to make unique athletic apparel. SportHill clothing is designed for use in any climate and for any sport. SportHill utilizes the expertise of elite athletes to perfect its design and innovate new products. It is well known for quality, comfort, and reliability. SportHill's clothing can be found globally in most major retailer stores and can be purchased online. The success of SportHill is apparent in the number of sponsorships it has, including many Olympic athletes and collegiate running teams; however, it is a privately held company so financial information is not available.

Under Armour has been able to remain successful among its competitors in large part due to the strength of character of its founder and other leaders.

Under Armour's Leaders

Under Armour's success may seem unbelievable at first, but it's no accident. Plank's drive to keep trying even during difficult times when it seemed the company might never flourish is what made it possible. In the beginning, when customers would request products that Plank had not created, he would respond, "Of course we make that!" and then immediately go to work with suppliers and contractors to deliver on his promise. Two such examples were when the equipment manager for the Atlanta Falcons wanted long-sleeve Under Armour shirts, and when the equipment manager for Arizona State wanted clothing for cold weather.[24]

"He's one of the hardest workers I've known in my life," says Plank's mother.[25] Plank's humble beginnings give him valuable insight into his business. He knows every aspect of it because at one time he actually did the work himself. Many of his first employees were his college classmates and teammates. Most of them are still with Under Armour and play important roles in management.

He spent five months driving round-trip from Baltimore to Moundsville at least twice a week to help Ella Mae Holmes produce and ship Under Armour products. He left Baltimore at 4 AM, arrived in Moundsville about 8 AM, and worked with Holmes and her boyfriend throughout the day. At 8 PM, Plank would take his shipment to the local FedEx office and drive back to Baltimore.[26]

Plank effectively uses his athletic experience and connections to help Under Armour's marketing and sales teams earn new business. In the athletic world, he is considered by his customers to be "one of them" rather than a CEO of a very profitable business. It frequently takes competitors years to develop a loyal customer, but Under Armour has been able to quickly earn loyalty after a customer has had one or two good experiences with their purchase. Most of the sports teams feel that Plank is truly helping them by providing a better product and not simply trying to sell his brand. Plank embraces and nurtures this connection respectfully and gracefully. He regularly seeks feedback regarding existing products and the need for new products.

Management Style

Having been part of a sports team, Plank manages his company with a unique team-driven style. "Under Armour is one team and my job is to help ensure we operate and execute as one team. Because there's a lot of noise and clutter surrounding our brand, I try to simplify our story and objectives for the team to help keep everyone running on the same wavelength and working towards the same goal: to become the world's number one performance athletic brand."[27]

To remind him of his critical role every day, Plank has written on a whiteboard in his office four things that define his job: (1) make a great product, (2) tell a great story about the product, (3) service the business, and (4) build a great team. Every morning when he arrives at the office and every evening before he leaves, he looks at the board. Plank said, "If I don't work toward those things, I'm not doing my job …. You can overcomplicate your job … It's important that you don't allow the clutter to grow too loud […] and distract you from your mission."[28]

International Leadership

In order to facilitate its international expansion, Under Armour hired several new executives with experience in international business, most notably Peter Mahrer. Mahrer was appointed as president and managing director for Under Armour Europe, B.V. Mahrer, a seasoned industry executive, will oversee Under Armour's European operations headquartered in Amsterdam. Mahrer previously served as head of international sales and general manager for Puma AG.[29]

Under Armour's Business Strategies

Ever since its inception in 1996, Under Armour's leaders have strived to achieve the company's vision of becoming the world's leading performance athletic apparel brand by employing a differentiation strategy through innovation. Under Armour attains physical differentiation through the value chain activities of technological development and procurement. As CEO Kevin Plank puts it, "The key driver is to offer products that are better than what is currently in the market, best in class."[30] Additionally, Under Armour is able to exploit psychological differentiation through its marketing campaign, which has hundreds of professional athletes that not only volunteer to wear Under Armour gear, but actually want to wear it. Most budding stars or wannabe weekend recreational athletes want to wear the gear the pros wear. Plank is fixated on maintaining differentiation from Nike, and uses "authenticity" as his guiding principal to grow or advertise the brand. Under Armour, for example, identifies itself with team sports, rather than individual sports and fashion. "Everything we do is centered on performance … we aren't ever going to develop products to fill up a sales table," says Plank. Specifically, Under Armour will never use cotton to produce its clothing.[31]

Under Armour's corporate level strategy consists of a low level of diversification. While it does offer more than one product, 84 percent of its revenue comes from athletic apparel and gear. Incorporating a shoe line is helping the company with its diversification efforts, but it is still highly dependent upon premium priced products that are closely related. There is obviously a degree of economic risk associated with the premium pricing and Under Armour is feeling the effects of the current declining retail consumer market that is affecting the broader economy. Additionally, Under Armour is exposed to a degree of risk by offering closely related, nonessential products that are, to a degree, subject to the fashion whims of its customers. Plank said Under Armour is "cautiously optimistic about 2009" and is looking at the year with the "appropriate degree of conservatism."[32]

Under Armour added new domestic sales channels by introducing its first independent retail sales outlet in 2007 in Annapolis, Maryland. However, due to the conservative approach to growth in 2009, no new retail stores will be opened during the year.

Under Armour has placed major emphasis on international expansion. In addition to creating a broader consumer base, "Researchers have found that international diversification can lead to greater operational efficiency, which ultimately leads to higher financial performance."[33] Because its product transcends cultural differences and is appealing to many athletes, regardless of nationality, Under Armour is pursuing a worldwide scope via regionalization. Over the past three years, revenues from foreign sales other than Canada have increased at a rate of 100 percent per year and are expected to increase even more quickly with the international growth emphasis (Exhibit 3). Under Armour is fortunate because performance sports apparel appears to transcend any jingoistic trends and exporting does not require an in-depth knowledge of local customer service. Additionally, Under Armour's products are already manufactured overseas in China; therefore, the new offices in Europe are primarily geared toward marketing and distribution and do not have to contend with the challenges associated with establishing manufacturing plants in foreign countries.

Marketing

Under Armour's marketing strength is twofold. First, its products have proven to be so effective that professional athletes want to use them. Second, Under Armour has become a master of product placement in movies, TV shows, and video games.

Plank believes that word-of-mouth advertising is the most effective method. Plank has said, "We always build a product for the athlete's needs." The customer is willing to pay the price because the Under Armour product has value in it. "Without value, our product is just an expensive t-shirt. But we have the technology in the fabric [and] the design and the features satisfy what the athlete needs."[34] "Our model is getting to the athletes—supplying them with great product that helps them perform better."[35]

Athletes are a valuable marketing resource and the mouthpiece for Under Armour. The company signed a five-year partnership agreement in April 2009 with Cal Ripken, Jr., a retired professional baseball player, to be their official uniform representative. Under Armour feels this is a great opportunity because Ripken previously was partnered with Nike.[36] The company has reached out to capture much of the youth sports industry by sponsoring recreational teams and major youth tournaments, including the Under Armour All-America high school football and lacrosse games (see Exhibit 7).[37]

Under Armour has initiated other sponsorships that help get its name out in public, such as the Baltimore Marathon, which is now named the Under Armour Marathon. In an effort to boost the women's clothing line, Under Armour sponsored the women's U.S. field hockey team and some of the U.S. women's softball and volleyball athletes during the 2008 Olympic Games.[38]

During the first three months of 2008, Under Armour apparel appeared in cable shows nearly 3,000 times, more than any other company, according to Nielsen Media.[39] Ironically, movie studios are asking to use Under Armour's products as opposed to Under Armour having to purchase product placement time. The desire of athletes and movie studios to use Under Armour's

products leads to a lower-cost, more effective, grass roots ad campaign. While Under Armour did sponsor its first Super Bowl commercial in 2008, the company will continue to use more guerrilla tactics than traditional expensive ad campaigns.

Strategic Challenges

Like most up-and-coming companies, Under Armour faces several issues and challenges. These challenges include the current economic downturn, competing against major rivals such as Nike and Adidas/Reebok, and maintaining a positive brand image despite setbacks, such as the recent recall of its men's protective athletic gear.[40] In addition, some of the most critical issues involve protection of the differentiation strategy, improvement of production and procurement capabilities, and continued implementation of a sound international expansion strategy.

Under Armour's differentiation strategy has been successful to date; however, the lack of proprietary product rights, intellectual property rights in foreign countries, and a heavy reliance on relatively few third-party suppliers and manufacturers could adversely affect the long-term sustainability of the firm. "The intellectual property rights in the technology, fabrics, and processes used to manufacture our products are generally owned by our suppliers and generally not unique to us."[41] The company's ability to obtain patent protection for its products is limited, and as previously mentioned it does not currently own any fabric or process patents.[42]

Intangible assets such as trademarks are very important to the Under Armour brand, as are licensing arrangements and other legal agreements. The intellectual property rights laws and regulations of countries in the global market vary dramatically. Under Armour relies heavily on suppliers and manufacturers outside of

Exhibit 7 Sponsorship and Other Marketing Commitments

(In thousands)	December 31
	2007
2008	$14,684
2009	14,660
2010	13,110
2011	10,125
2012 and thereafter	1,005
Total future minimum sponsorship and other marketing payments	$53,584

Source: 2008, Under Armour, Inc., Form 10-K 2007 Annual Report, December 31, 60.

the United States. Seventy to 75 percent of the fabric used in its products come from only six suppliers,[43] lending to Under Armour's weak position relative to its suppliers. Additionally, some of its supplies are commodities and thus are subject to price fluctuations; for example, petroleum-based materials are used in Under Armour's products and the petroleum industry has experienced significant swings in price and relative availability in recent months and years.[44]

Under Armour has achieved a level of success in the U.S. domestic market and limited foreign markets, but is relatively small in size and financial strength compared to its major competitors (Nike and Adidas) with similar or competing product offerings. Does Under Armour run the risk of diluting the brand relative to its competitors? Is an acquisition strategy feasible due to the company's current debt situation? Although a cooperative strategy may be beneficial to bridge barriers to entry into desirable markets such as China, how likely is it that Under Armour would pursue this option due to its emphasis on innovation and premium branding? Overall, has Under Armour done a good job in finding key strategic leaders with the experience necessary and does it have the right organization in place to help exe-

cute its international growth strategy? Going forward, how can it maintain the product quality that it has nurtured thus far?

Additional questions that Plank and other managers are pondering are: Can Under Armour maintain strong relationships with its suppliers so that it becomes the customer of choice? Should Under Armour pursue patents or strike agreements to limit the chance of competitors offering identical products? If so, will this effort actually be a defense or will counterfeit merchandise undermine such an investment? Does Under Armour possess appropriate supplier relationships and have an understanding of the inherent economic impacts on raw materials? If not, how will Under Armour acquire or develop these capabilities? What capabilities should Under Armour develop to ensure international success? What barriers to entry exist in additional markets, and is licensing or some other method the best approach based on its current cash position? Will the international strategy be different from Under Armour's overall differentiation and growth strategy? As its founder and CEO has stated, "Under Armour's success in 2010 and beyond will be significantly impacted by the decisions we make in 2009."[45]

NOTES

1. 2008, Investors Relations—About Under Armour, Inc., http://www.underarmour.com.
2. 2008, Five questions with Under Armour CEO, Kevin Plank, *Sports Business Journal*, http://www.sportsbusinessconferences.com/sss-pov/entries/2008/five-questions-with-kevin-plank, August 15.
3. Ibid.
4. Ibid.
5. S. Lyster, 2008, The history of Under Armour—A mastermind for performance apparel, http://www.ezinearticles.com, December 4.
6. 2008, Under Armour performance apparel, *Funding Universe*, http://www.fundinguniverse.com, December 4.
7. Ibid.
8. Ibid.
9. D. Rovell, 2005, Under Armour could offer up to $100 million in stock, http://sports.espn.go.com, August 26.
10. S. N. Mehta, 2009, Under Armour reboots: The sports apparel maker is sprinting into footwear—and trying to take on Nike—with the help of software and science, *Fortune*, http://www.money.cnn.com, March 5.
11. D. Kiley, 2008, Under Armour steps into footwear field: Sports apparel maker set to do battle with Nike and Adidas, *BusinessWeek*, http://www.businessweek.com, January 31.
12. Ibid.
13. 2008, Under Armour 10-K 2007 Annual Report, http://www.underarmour.com/annuals.cfm, February.
14. D. Kiley, 2008, Under Armour steps into footwear field.
15. A. K. Walker, 2009, New shoe helps Under Armour beat expectations, *Baltimore Sun*, http://www.baltimoresun.com, April 29.
16. S. N. Mehta, 2009, Under Armour reboots.
17. D. Kiley, Under Armour steps into footwear field.
18. 2008, Under Armour, *Hoovers*, http://premium.hoovers.com.ezproxy1.lib.asu.edu/subscribe/co/competitors.xhtml?ID=ffffrfjjfkrrrhkxsxh.
19. 2008, Nike history, http://www.nikebiz.com/company_overview/history, December 4.
20. 2009, Nike company overview fact sheet, http://www.nikebiz.com; 2009, Nike pulling production from four Asian factories, *Reuters*, http://www.reuters.com, March 24.
21. 2008, Adidas group history, Adidas Group, http://www.adidas-group.com/en/overview/history/default.asp. December 4.
22. 2008, Columbia Sportswear, *Funding Universe*, http://www.fundinguniverse.com/company-histories/Columbia-Sportswear-Company-Company-History1.html, December 4.
23. 2008, http://www.sporthill.com, December 4.
24. M. Hyman, 2003, How I did it: Kevin Plank: For the founder of apparel-maker Under Armour, entrepreneurship is 99% perspiration and 1% polyester, *Inc.*, http://www.inc.com, December.
25. S. Graham, 2004, Kevin Plank's drive makes Under Armour an industry overachiever, *Sports Business Journal*, http://www.sportsbusinessjournal.com/article/36213, January 19.
26. Ibid.
27. 2008, Five questions with Under Armour CEO, Kevin Plank.
28. 2008, How do you define your job? *Business Management Daily*, http://www.businessmanagementdaily.com, November 8.
29. 2007, Under Armour appoints Peter Mahrer as president & managing director, Europe; Experienced sporting goods industry executive to lead sport performance brand's European growth strategy, Baltimore, MD, Under Armour press release, http://www.underarmour.com, July 9.
30. T. Heath, 2008, In pursuit of innovation at Under Armour: Founder Kevin Plank says Super Bowl commercial has generated "buzz," *Washington Post*, February 25, D03.

31. D. Kiley, 2009, Under Armour steps into footwear field.

32. R. Sharrow, 2009, Plank: Under Armour eyeing '09 "with appropriate degree of conservatism," *Baltimore Business Journal*, http://www.baltimore.bizjournals.com, January 29.

33. R. E. Hoskisson, M. Hitt, R. Ireland, & J. Harrison, 2008, *Competing for Advantage*, Thomson Southwestern, 286.

34. 2007, I am, Video interview with Kevin Plank, *CNBC*, http://www.cnbc.com/id/25191722, September 11.

35. M. Hyman, 2003, How I did it: Kevin Plank.

36. R. Sharrow, 2009, Under Armour, Ripken Baseball swing for fences with sportswear pact, *Baltimore Business Journal*, http://www.baltimore.bizjournals.com, April 22.

37. R. Sharrow, 2009, Cal Ripken Jr. nears deal to promote Under Armour, *Baltimore Business Journal*, http://www.baltimore.bizjournals.com, March 20.

38. R. Sharrow, 2008, Under Armour entering an Olympic contest of its own, *Baltimore Business Journal*, http://www.baltimore.bizjournals.com, August 1.

39. A. K. Walker, 2008, Under Armour in public eye, *The Baltimore Sun*, July 24.

40. J. Alper, 2009, Under Armour recalls 200,000 cups: Injuries involve cutting and bruising, *NBC New York Sports*, http://www.nbcnewyork.com/sports, April.

41. 2007, Under Armour, Inc., Form 10-K Annual Report, http://investor.underarmour.com, December 31, 18.

42. Ibid.

43. 2008, Under Armour, Inc., Form 8-K, http://investor.underarmour.com, 6.

44. Ibid.

45. R. Sharrow, 2009, Plank: Under Armour eyeing '09 with appropriate degree of conservatism.

Mtina Buechel

IMD–International Institute for Management Development

Late October, 2001, Matt Barrett, CEO of Barclays, was preparing for a seminal event that was to take place the following week. After 24 months in office, he was comtemplating how best to introduce the Group strategy that he had developed with Marakon Associates to the wider organization.

According to Barrett, his key challenge in transforming Barclays was to move it from a large U.K. bank dabbling overseas to a global bank which happened to have a strong U.K. franchise. Barrett's aim was to improve Barclays's performance rapidly and significantly so it could be a predator and not a victim in the industry consolidation that he felt sure was coming.

From the start, he had worked on changing the mind-set and culture of Barclays. His next step was to try to convince the top 100 company executives that the current model for running the business was inadequate for reaching its goals. He passionately believed that a more fact-based, value-growth orientation to running Barclays was essential. This event was key to ensuring that Barclays's new management model would be widely used within the businesses across the Group.

Barclays History

The history of Barclays dates to 1690 when John Freame and Thomas Gould started trading as Goldsmith bankers on Lombard Street in London. In 1896, the company joined with 19 other private banking businesses to form a new joint-stock bank called Barclay and Company Limited. Almost 30 years later, Barclays began its global expansion. In 1981, it became the first foreign bank to file with the Securities and Exchange Commission in Washington, D.C.

After years of expansion, including the acquisitions of the stockbrokers De Zoete & Bevan in 1986 and Wells Fargo Nikko Investment Advisors in 1995,

Barclays faced a leadership challenge. Between 1995 and 1999, Barclays had five different CEOs. In October 1999, Barclays appointed Matt Barrett, a Canadian/Irish citizen who had been the CEO of the Bank of Montreal for the previous decade. Matt was enjoying his retirement when he received the invitation to run Barclays and saw it as a great opportunity. Having been in the financial services industry from the start of his career, Matt had deep vocational knowledge about how a bank, with its multiple businesses and functions, works.

Business Overview

In 2000, Barclays PLC was one of the four dominant retail and commercial banks in the United Kingdom. It was the ninth-largest bank in Europe by assets, with total assets exceeding £320 billion.

The Group consisted of four divisions, of which Retail Financial Services contributed 61 percent of earnings (see Exhibit 1). Its retail franchise included direct relationships with one in five personal customers in the United Kingdom.

In the corporate banking market, Barclays had a direct relationship with more than 25 percent of U.K. businesses, which it served via a network of more than 1,200 relationship managers.

In 1997, Barclays sold the cash, equities, and corporate finance businesses from its investment banking division—Barclays de Zoete Wedd—to Credit Suisse First Boston. As a result, by 2000, the rebranded Barclays Capital had become a collection of sub-scale businesses united by a focus on debt products.

In 2000, Barclays Global Investors (BGI) offered advanced active and indexed asset management services to about 1,800 institutional clients in 36 countries. It introduced the world's first index fund and was managing £529 billion of assets.

Professor Mtina Buechel wrote this case as a basis for class discussion rather than to illustrate either effective or ineffective handling of a business situation.

Exhibit 1 Barclays PLC Corporate Structure (2000)

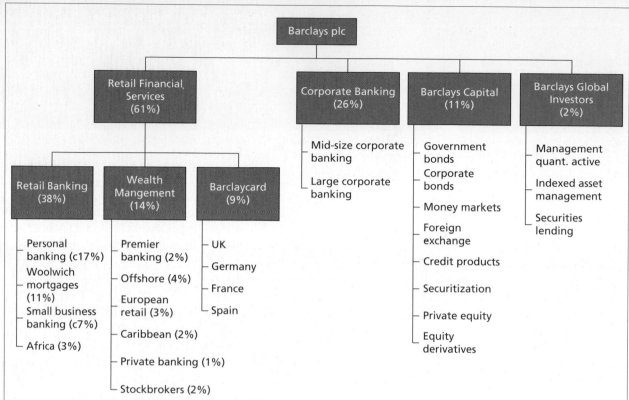

Note: Percentages represent estimated earnings contributions, including pro forma Woolwich.

Source: Company data and Credit Lyonnais Securities Europe estimates.

By 2000, 78 percent of Group revenue and 80 percent of Group profits came from the United Kingdom. Continental Europe generated 10 percent of sales and profits, primarily from high-net-worth retail banking operations in Spain, France, and Portugal. The United States and various African businesses generated the remaining balance.

Situation Assessment

When Barrett joined Barclays, he came across an organization that, according to him, had lost confidence due to years of underperformance and several significant corporate crises. During the 20 years leading up to Matt's arrival, the bank executed 57 divestitures and only two acquisitions. Barclays's global market capitalization rank had fallen from four in 1980 to 22 in 2000 (see Exhibit 2). As a result, predators were circling the company as a potential takeover target and the investor community was increasingly losing patience.

Barclays had lost its way—it had gone from "one of the best" to "one of the rest." Given a prolonged period of underperformance and revolving doors for CEOs, Barclays had become an easy target for the media. Institutional investors were unhappy, employees were demoralized, and the front-line and senior executives had lost confidence. There was at base, however, a great brand and reputation as well as a strong domestic franchise.

Exhibit 2 Barclay's Market Capitalization Rank*

	1980	1985	1990	1995	2000
Rank*	4	13	13	19	22
Mkt Cap (£ bn)	2.0	3.4	7.4	12.4	34.3

*Barclays's rank among the top 100 financial services players globally for any given calendar year.

Source: Marakon Associates.

The Group had no coherent strategic plan, ineffective performance standards and woefully inadequate MIS [management information systems]. We had very little indication where we were losing money and where value was being created. It was like flying a 747 without any controls—exhilarating but life-threatening.

—**MATT BARRETT**

One of Barrett's early discoveries was the excessive cost base. For more than 10 years, Barclays had struggled to make significant inroads into reducing its cost base. By 2000, its cost to income ratio was significantly higher than that of competitors (see Exhibit 3). Part of the reason for the excessive cost base was that divisions set up their own HR, IT, and finance divisions to protect themselves from erratic Group governance. Barrett quickly realized that he had a major task ahead of him—to clean up management incompetence and fix the core infrastructure. Indeed, he soon realized that the bank needed a shift in culture and mind-set, a new strategic direction, a structural overhaul, and an improved communications policy.

Building the Foundation

During his first three months in office, Barrett engaged with employees throughout the Group in what he termed "open forums." These were sessions of two to three hours where he would meet up to 1,000 employees from various functions and hierarchical levels. These sessions would typically start with Barrett summarizing his understanding of the current situation. He would then take questions from the audience. In an effort to prepare the organization for the changes he wanted to make, he would also pose provocative questions to his employees, such as "Do you feel that there are people in your area who do not pull their weight?" and "Is it fair that these people are paid the same as you are?" Barrett met approximately 10,000 employees during this initial three-month period to transmit the message that everyone was in this transformation together. There were no second-class citizens.

At the same time, Barrett developed his own vision for the bank—"earn, invest, and grow." He planned to double Barclays's economic profit in four years.[1] In order to finance growth, he planned to reduce costs by £1 billion (from a cost base of £5.5 billion). He emphasized that the money saved from cost reductions created an opportunity for people to shape their destiny, as they could decide which business areas were worth investing in.

In February 2000, six months after Barrett became CEO, the first top 100 executive event was organized in Brighton. Barrett spoke to the group about his vision for the future and explained the company's new financial and strategic goals. These goals were met with skepticism. As one top executive reflected, "I was initially thinking, if I keep my head down, this too will pass." To those who thought the challenge was too great, Barrett's approach was sympathetic but unyielding. Barrett said, "I recognized that it was a significant challenge, and I

Exhibit 3 Barclays Operating Expense as a Percentage of Income in Comparison with Competition

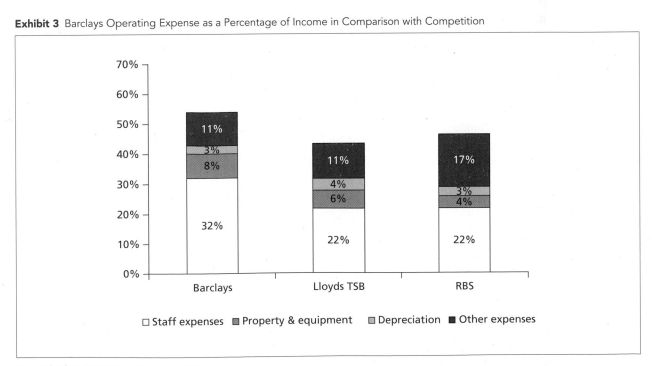

Source: Credit Lyonnais Securities Europe, 2000.

told them that each and every one could count on my support, but that the goal was non-negotiable."

A week later, Barrett publicly committed to these goals to ensure that there would be no scaling back of the commitments. The organization and the top team, while skeptical, were now on the hook to deliver. The goals were to apply equally to him, top management, and everyone in the organization.

Changes at the Top

Barrett started by focusing on his direct reports and spelling out what he believed in—sincerity, encouraging people to take risks, and learning from mistakes. He led as if he had to be reelected the next day. He had to show that he was deeply involved and that he cared.

Barrett quickly turned his sights to realigning the mind-set, and, ultimately, the composition of the top team. He felt that the executive committee (ExCo) was not performing as decision makers but as an administrative body. Each meeting seemed more like a series of bilateral discussions with the CEO than multilateral, high performance dialogues.

At an early ExCo dinner, while the team was having its appetizers, Barrett launched into a direct discussion. He suddenly said he was thinking of disbanding the ExCo meetings if he couldn't make them more productive. There was silence in the room. The team seemed shocked at the prospect of having a FTSE 100 firm that was no longer run by an ExCo (and of each potentially losing his seat at the top table). The team came out vocally against Barrett's proposal and immediately took up his challenge—from then on, their commitment to making the ExCo work became a shared goal. This was reflected in the decision to make co-managing the Barclays Group the primary task of the ExCo and managing their business unit responsibilities the second task. To reflect this change, Barrett realigned ExCo members' rewards, placing more weight on overall company results.

With respect to team composition, Barrett rapidly engineered significant changes on the ExCo. His aim was to undermine opposition to change by bringing in new perspectives and disconnecting existing members from their traditional power bases. Gary Dibb, who had worked for the Bank of Montreal, soon followed Barrett and became the chief administrative officer. John Varley was appointed Group finance director and given ExCo responsibility for delivering cost, productivity, and economic profit goals. This appointment, in particular, was an important step toward building broad organizational confidence in the Group's ability to deliver on its new goals. By spending significant time with the top 100, Barrett was also able to spot and promote young talent to the ExCo, including Gary Hoffman and David Roberts,

who in their late thirties, considerably reduced the average age of the top team.

From an investor's perspective, changes to the senior management team raised concerns about pace and velocity of change. It was, however, positively viewed by equity analysts, such as Credit Lyonnais: "Barclays is undergoing a significant process of change that requires a fresh look and innovative solutions. It can only be assisted by a new senior team."

Gaining Confidence

In October 2000, Barclays acquired Woolwich, a leading mortgage business in the United Kingdom, for £5.4 billion. The acquisition expanded Barclays's product and service portfolio and strengthened an area in which Barclays was weak—residential mortgages. As Barclays had primarily divested in the last 20 years, another purpose of this acquisition was just to show that Barclays could *grow*, not just divest. The Woolwich CEO, John Stewart, moved into Barclays to head Retail.

Value-Based Management Underpins Strategy Development

In the second half of 2000, Barclays Strategic Planning Group, on behalf of the ExCo, reviewed bids from potential advisors to accelerate both the understanding of value and the push for value growth. As Matt Barrett reflected afterwards: "We needed to have tools to make fact-based decisions. There was no cross-organizational discussion of value-adding activities. Barclays was run as four separate pillars and each had its own head office. I used to joke that I was never lonely at the top—there were dozens of 'CEOs.'"

After reviewing the proposals, Barrett and the ExCo decided to work with Marakon Associates, the advisory firm that pioneered "managing for value." Barrett knew Marakon well as he had worked successfully with the company when he was at the Bank of Montreal. Marakon and the ExCo set about looking at all businesses and activities from a value perspective, identifying where value was being created and where it was being destroyed. By assessing all businesses, the supertanker was broken down into a "flotilla of highly maneuverable speedboats," or 20 to 25 smaller value-creating entities, which could be analyzed and managed. The goal was to enable a thorough analysis of each business's potential contribution to the Group.

The value-based approach to developing and delivering strategy was applied within each business. At ExCo meetings, each of the four divisional heads was asked to present two or three alternatives for each business. Each of these strategic options was to be grounded in analysis of industry and company data. Varley characterized the environment as follows: "We are having to up our game, and that is pulling lots of us out of our comfort zones …. All the time we are asking: What makes money and what doesn't? Where are the weaknesses in the business? It had a profound effect— energizing and clarifying …."

As one of the outcomes, it was expected that every investment decision—whether a project, geographic expansion, or new product introduction—presented to the ExCo would have to be assessed using the new value-based management approach. Implicitly, this led to an evaluation of every manager and business unit leader in that sound reasoning had to be used as the foundation for every strategic decision. This method was wildly unpopular at first because it challenged the managers' beliefs. However, as Barnett noted, "We needed to institutionalize the approach. Every meeting we ran had to involve the same questions. Only then would it become part of the DNA."

In the analyst community, the change in management approach did not go unnoticed. As Commerzbank's James Alexander commented: "Value-based management depends on risks and expected profitability, bad debts, and your view of the economy. It's still an art rather than a science. It doesn't entirely help avoid mistakes, but it makes the decision-making process more rigorous."

Developing the Group Strategy

Under Barnett's leadership, and with the help of Marakon's systematic, fact-based approach, the ExCo developed a long-term strategic direction during the first half of 2001. Five full-day ExCo meetings were devoted to debating and agreeing upon a Group strategy. In addition, key opinion formers from across the organization were engaged to provide input and challenge. This resulted in a new strategic direction that called for change along multiple dimensions, including:

- Greater presence outside the United Kingdom, complementing continued strong growth within the U.K. market.

- Greater diversity of sources of economic profit across different product/customer markets, with a greater contribution from asset accumulation and capital markets.
- Growth driven by a more balanced combination of organic and acquisitive moves.
- Selected businesses with full global reach (e.g., Barclays Capital and Barclays Global Investors) leading the way and complementing strong "local" businesses (e.g., UK Retail/Commercial).
- Greater bias of Barclays's personal customer base toward the highly profitable affluent and high-net-worth segments.
- Strongly differentiated customer offers with clearly articulated value for clients, supported by a strong brand and improved distribution, sales, and information.

To drive change, a series of medium-term themes and near-term priorities were developed. As an example, one of the near-term priorities was to develop a "second home market" in continental Europe. This was part of a broader theme to change Barclays's European franchise. Another priority was to expand capital market activities as part of a broader theme to establish world-class global product/customer businesses.

Each of the near-term priorities had a value creation goal attached to it and was led by an ExCo sponsor who had full responsibility for delivering on expectations.

Implementing the Group Strategy

The work with Marakon led to the formal articulation of a Group strategy (see Exhibit 4). In October 2001, this Group strategy was disseminated at the "top 100" meeting in Canary Wharf. Barnett had achieved buy-in from the eight ExCo members, but how would the wider organization receive the Group strategy?

Exhibit 4 Group Strategy Framework

Objective of Our Group Strategy
Our overarching Group Strategy objective is to maximize the economic value of the Group. Accordingly, our Group Strategy has been developed using our value-based strategy development framework and standards.
Components of Our Group Strategy
Our Group Strategic Direction ("Where we are heading")   +Our View of the Future   +Long-Term Direction (5–10 years)   +Medium-Term Strategic Themes (next 2–5 years)   +Near-Term Priorities (next 12 months)

(Continued)

Exhibit 4 Group Strategy Framework (*Continued*)

Our Group Management Model ("How we will run the business")

Group Goals

Our aspiration is to deliver top quartile Total Shareholder Returns vs. our peers over time. However, we do not believe we will be able to continue to deliver against a four-year double-value goal over a 10-year period from our existing business portfolio. As a result, we expect to face a "value gap" in 2010 in the region of £40 billion (£16 billion in today's money) of incremental value creation (as opposed to market capitalization)—broadly equivalent to adding another business of the size of Barclays today over the next 10 years. We expect an economic profit gap of at least £1.5 billion in 2010.

Group Structure

The Group ExCo will have greater involvement in managing cross-Group synergies and "top-down" strategy development; the recent restructuring of the Group into the current model of Clusters, SBUs, and SSUs (Shared Service Units), and the acquisition of Woolwich reflect this evolution.

Group Mission, Beliefs, Practices, and Behaviors

We aspire to be one of the most admired financial services organizations in the world, recognized as an innovative, customer-focused company that delivers superb products and services, ensures excellent careers for our people and contributes positively to the communities in which we live and work. In addition, there are 18 beliefs and practices that outline more specifically the expected operating mode, e.g. Practice 14: We ensure all decisions are fact-based and value-maximizing through our strategy development and agenda management processes. The management team defined an acceptable set of behaviors for the Group. These were—Drive Performance, Build Pride and Passion, Delight Customers, Grow Talent and Capability, Execute at Speed, and Protect and Enhance our Reputation.

Group Decision Rules

Rule 1: Select the strategy/investment alternative which creates the highest economic value (EV).
Rule 2: Select the EV alternative if it meets or exceeds Group/SBU goals for EV, economic profit (EP),[1] and cosW savings.
Rule 3: Select the EV alternative if it is aligned with the Group Strategic Direction.
Rule 4: Select the highest EV if it is aligned with the Group Management Model.
Rule 5: Select the highest EV alternative if it complies with the Group operating policies and standards (e.g., brand, risk, compliance).

Source: Framework developed by Marakon Associates for Barclays.

NOTE

1. Economic profit = net profit after tax less the equity charge, a risk-weighted cost of capital.

Analia Anderson, Jake Johnson, Pauline Pham,
Adam Schwartz, Richard Till, Craig Vom Lehn,
Elena Wilkening

Arizona State University

Air transportation powers the U.S. economy—this is an industry that drives economic and social development. Air transportation is a critical part of our nation's infrastructure and should play a vital role in our country's economic recovery ... enabling our cities and smaller communities to connect and compete domestically and globally. It is, therefore, hugely ironic that we enable such economic and business development in the United States—to the tune of more than $1 trillion a year and contribut[ing] some 5 percent of GDP—but have historically and systemically been incapable of earning our cost of capital.

> —GLEN TILTON, CHAIRMAN, PRESIDENT, AND
> CEO OF UNITED AIRLINES[1]

In early 2009, the U.S. economy was mired in its worst recession since the Great Depression. With airline industry business cycles closely mirroring larger economic trends, United Airlines felt the effects of the downturn. United, the fourth-largest U.S. passenger airline, lost more than $5 billion in 2008 and reported further declines in both revenue and traffic in the first quarter of 2009.[2] Even before the economy soured, United managed only minimal profits in 2006 and 2007, which were considered great years for the U.S. airline industry. Prior to that, the company spent three years in Chapter 11 bankruptcy protection as a result of losses early in the decade. In addition, United encountered challenges related to expanding service internationally, introducing subsidiaries in an effort to compete with low-cost carriers (LCCs), and maintaining positive relations with its employees and the unions that represent its employees. Thus, more than just waiting for economic recovery, United is exploring tactics to become profitable again and reclaim the image and success it once experienced.

Early History

United Air Lines, Inc. came into existence in 1931 to provide mail service and passenger transport.[3] United was born uniquely national, with Eastern and Western subsidiaries, and diversified by virtue of its ownership of Boeing Air Transport, an aircraft manufacturer.[4] Early growth in the fledgling industry was funded largely by U.S. government payments for mail service. When accusations of collusion arose from the allocation of routes by the postal service, the government stepped in to regulate both the process and the industry.[5] The resulting Civil Aeronautics Act of 1938 transferred power over route allocation to the newly created Civil Aeronautics Authority,[6] which required United to divest Boeing and several airports it owned, but awarded the company "grandfather certificates on U.S. transcontinental and West Coast routes it was operating when the law took effect."[7]

Like most airlines, United prospered and grew under government regulation. Pricing was regulated, and approval from government regulators was required for an airline to enter or exit a particular route.[8] While the market for passenger travel grew significantly after World War II, artificially high prices limited air travel to wealthier travelers and businessmen. Under regulatory protection, carriers developed hub-and-spoke networks that allowed them to centralize operations and provide convenient connections to passengers. The beginnings of United's network can be seen in Exhibit 1, which shows the airline's route map in 1940. Hubs in Chicago, San Francisco, and Los Angeles were beginning to take shape. Eventually they would be joined by hubs in Denver and Washington D.C.[9] Larger airports often were dominated by one or two carriers, such as United in Denver and Chicago.[10] As a result of regulation

Exhibit 1 United Air Lines Route Map, 1940

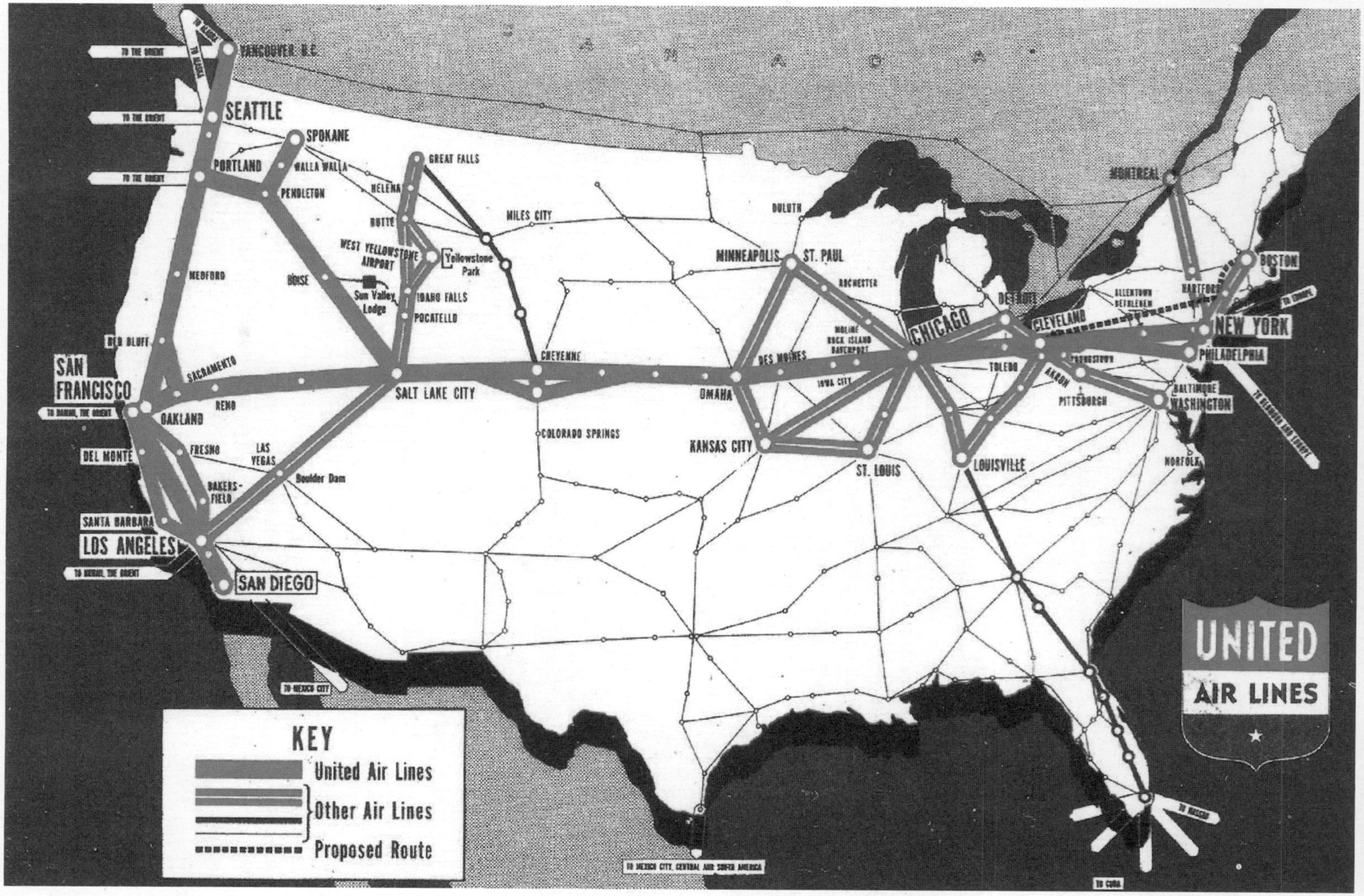

Source: United Air Lines Route 1940, Wikipedia, http://en.wikipedia.org.

and network distribution, competition was restrained, with carriers making small but reliable profits based on the uniqueness of their networks and the convenience of schedules and connections, but deregulation changed all of this.

Deregulation

In 1978, the passage of the Airline Deregulation Act eliminated government oversight of routes and fees, allowing carriers to compete along a much broader range of parameters.[11] Deregulation brought about a glut of new airlines "causing airfares to plummet 40 percent in real terms between 1978 and 1997."[12] For United and its competitors, business cycles have been much more dramatic under deregulation, with profits in years when the economy is strong and heavy losses when it is weak.[13] Along with the challenges came opportunities for expansion. United secured its first Trans-Pacific route in 1983 and subsequently purchased 13 additional Asian routes from the ailing Pan American Airways.[14] In 1990, the company launched service to Europe, and in 1992 it operated flights to South America.[15] By 1995, with the introduction of service to Mumbai, India, United could advertise that it offered "Round the World" service.[16]

Although United was taking advantage of the opportunities that deregulation made possible, the company was struggling with the higher oil prices that resulted from the Persian Gulf War and the emergence of successful low-cost carriers such as Southwest Airlines. By the early 1990s, United was losing money. In 1993, the company attempted to remedy its financial problems by exchanging $5.15 billion of salaries and benefits with its employees for a 53 percent stake in the company.[17] As a result, in 1994, United became the "largest majority employee-owned corporation in the world."[18] Also in 1994, United launched "Shuttle by United" to compete against the low-cost carriers in the western United States; however, in 2001 when air travel diminished and cost savings had not materialized, the Shuttle was assimilated back into the main business.[19] Business took a sharp turn for the worse at the beginning of the new millennium when United declared bankruptcy and confronted other challenges.

Bankruptcy and Beyond

At the end of 2001, United recorded a $2.1 billion loss, the largest in airline history. With losses continuing to mount, United, under newly appointed CEO Glenn Tilton, filed for Chapter 11 bankruptcy protection in December 2002.[20]

Under bankruptcy protection, the company restructured its labor contracts and defaulted on its employee pension plan. United took out a $3 billion loan from investment banks in order to gain approval to exit bankruptcy, which it did on[21] February 1, 2006.[22] The timing was auspicious for the company as the U.S. economy was once again on the rise and airlines, including United, earned profits in 2006 and 2007.[23] The good times came to an end in 2008, however, as the U.S. economy slipped into recession, and United posted its largest-ever loss of $5.2 billion.[24]

In an unusual move for a bankrupt company, United also formed a new business line called Ted, which was a second attempt at creating a low-cost subsidiary.[25] Ted failed to meet expectations and the company announced its closure in 2008.[26]

Company executives have tried to reposition the company since 2006. United bid to merge with Delta in 2007[27] and with both Continental[28] and US Airways in 2008, but none of these negotiations were successful.[29] United was forced to make significant cuts once again, and by June 2008 the company had announced plans to ground 70 planes, eliminate 950 pilot positions, and cut up to 1,600 salaried positions.

While United has suffered many trials since deregulation, it has managed to survive. Many airlines have not been so fortunate, as competition in the airline industry is intense.

Competition

Within the last 30 years the airline industry has undergone significant contraction, as healthier carriers acquired failing competitors or their assets. Exhibit 2 shows the 51 mergers and acquisitions that brought the airline industry to its current state.[30] Six airlines now control 71.4 percent of the U.S. market (see Exhibit 3). The top six carriers consist of five traditional carriers—American, Continental, Delta, United, and US Airways—along with Southwest, the most successful of the LCCs (Exhibit 4 shows relevant financial data).

Competition is becoming more intense among the traditional carriers because the amount of business travel is decreasing.[31] Among the factors contributing to the decline in business travel are the use of videoconferencing, e-mail, and other Internet-based interactive technologies that make it easy to convey information without a face-to-face meeting.[32] Even more significant, perhaps, are cuts in corporate expenditures and increased governance, which lead to fewer approved trips and more price sensitivity among business travelers. The end result of this shift is that "the leisure segment of demand now constitutes the dominant one in air transport today."[33]

The similarities between United and its major competitors (excluding Southwest Airlines) are far greater

Exhibit 2 The Evolution of the U.S. Airline Industry

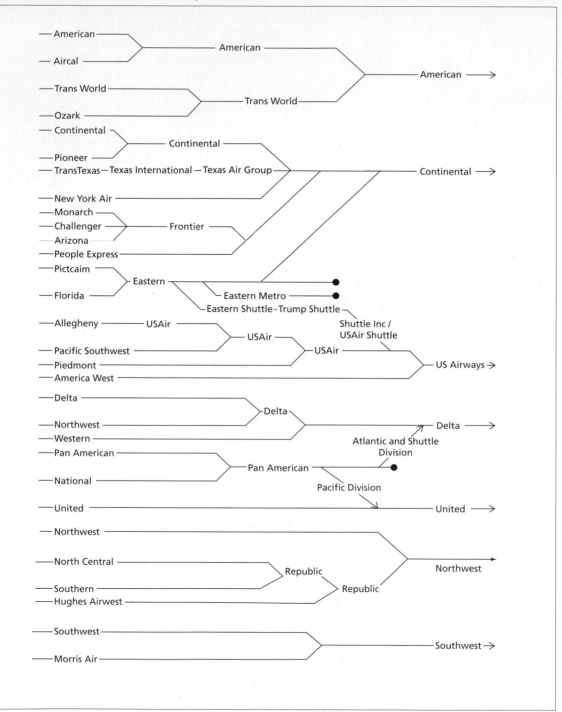

Source: B. Vasigh, K. Fleming, & T. Tacker, 2008, *Introduction to Air Transport Economics*, Ashgate Publishing, 16.

than their differences. All operate a hub-and-spoke route network, seeking to efficiently transfer passengers across the country. They all run a mainline service with large jets and extend their reach through networks of regional affiliates and global alliances. They all focus on the business traveler, offering service upgrades and frequent flyer loyalty programs to appeal to the business segment of the market. These companies differ, however, in their history, size, and hub locations.

American Airlines

Founded in 1934 as the Robertson Aircraft Corporation, American Airlines has grown from a small airmail service to one of the largest passenger airlines with 84,000

Exhibit 3 Airline Domestic Market Share, March 2009

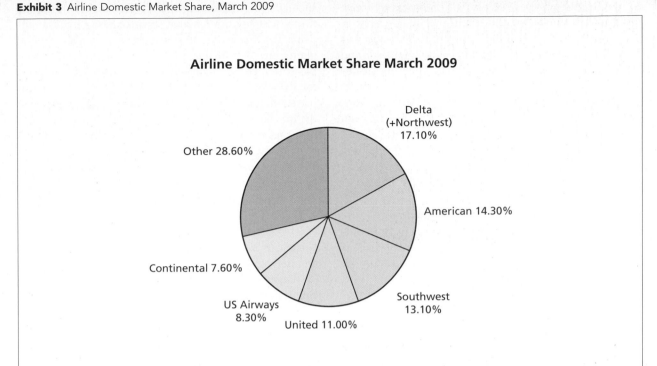

Source: 2009, Chart by authors, data from RITA, http://www.transtats.bts.gov.

Exhibit 4 Comparison of Net Profits between United and Top Competitors

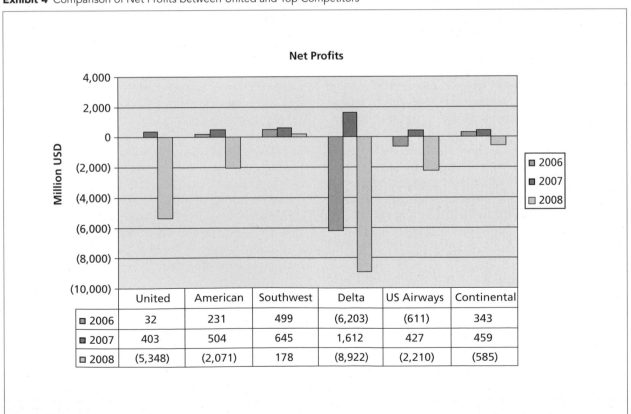

	United	American	Southwest	Delta	US Airways	Continental
2006	32	231	499	(6,203)	(611)	343
2007	403	504	645	1,612	427	459
2008	(5,348)	(2,071)	178	(8,922)	(2,210)	(585)

Source: 2009, Chart by authors using data from the 2008 10-K reports of each company.

employees and a fleet of 900 aircraft.[34] From its corporate headquarters in Dallas and additional major hubs in Chicago, St. Louis, and Miami the company transports 270,000 passengers on 3,300 flights to 250 domestic and international destinations every day.[35] Like most traditional carriers, American operates a mainline business serving larger cities and a regional affiliate network (American Eagle) serving smaller airports. American Eagle accounts for 300 of American's planes, flying 1,800 daily flights to 150 destinations in the United States and the Carribean.[36] American's network is further extended by its participation in the Oneworld global airline alliance.

American is the only large traditional domestic carrier that has not filed for bankruptcy, narrowly avoiding this fate in 2003.[37] In 2008, the company posted the fourth-largest loss among domestic carriers, just under $2.1 billion.[38]

Continental Airlines. Unlike American, Continental Airlines has filed for bankruptcy protection twice—once in 1983 and again in 1990.[39] Since the second bankruptcy, the company's fortunes have improved significantly, leading *Fortune* to name Continental, "The World's Most Admired Airline" for five years running.[40] While several competitors posted multi-billion dollar losses in 2008, Continental's loss was modest by comparison, $585 million.[41]

Continental and its regional affiliates, Continental Express, Continental Micronesia, and Continental Connection, fly more than 2,600 flights per day to 265 domestic and international destinations using a network based on hubs located in Newark, Houston, Cleveland, and Guam.[42] Continental has more than 42,000 employees, 44 percent of whom are covered by collective bargaining agreements.[43]

In 2007, Continental entered into merger talks with United Airlines. The talks subsequently failed to produce a merger, but did result in an alliance that involved Continental terminating its membership in the SkyTeam global alliance (anchored by Delta and Air France KLM) and becoming part of the Star Alliance dominated by United, Lufthansa, and US Airways.[44]

Delta Airlines. Founded in Georgia in 1924 by a cropduster named Huff Daland, Delta's first decades of operation were dominated by agricultural and public service flights, with the majority of its domestic flights dedicated to mail handling, and then for military purposes during World War II.[45]

From the 1940s through the late twentieth century, Delta aggressively pursued a differentiation strategy, known for its innovation and contribution to the art and science of aviation. There were many "firsts" for Delta,

such as being the first airline to offer night service, the first to employ interchange service among flight attendants, the first airline to transport living vegetables and plants, the first airline to use the Douglass DC-8 and DC-9 (which would become standard in the industry for decades), and the first to offer passengers an in-flight telephone system (Airfone). In 1962, Delta had the quickest flight time from coast to coast (Atlanta to Los Angeles); its record time of just less than three hours remains the fastest cross-country passenger flight to date. The hub-and-spoke system was Delta's innovation that improved passenger plane transfers with coordinated flight arrival and departure times.[46]

However, this airline giant has experienced financial trouble in recent years. In September 2005, Delta Airlines filed for Chapter 11 bankruptcy.[47] Goodwill and deferred tax asset write-offs, significant declines in passenger miles, and high fuel costs led management to conclude that "… these results underscore the urgent need to make fundamental changes in the way we do business."[48] A more fundamental shift in industry strategy, however, seemed to underlie the firm's demise. The continued growth of low-cost carriers, intense competitive rivalry within the industry (most notably increased price sensitivity), and increased customer use of the Internet for travel information challenged Delta's differentiation strategy that was framed around exceptional customer service and innovative aviation.

To counter the increasing threats to its firm, Delta finalized its merger with Northwest Airlines in October 2008. Although the combined organization lost $8.9 billion in 2008,[49] Delta hopes to obtain three major benefits from the merger: (1) larger market share by including Northwest's mid- and northwest U.S. routes, along with its Asia routes; (2) improved financial capacity to sustain cyclical downturns in the economy and associated volatility in fuel costs; and (3) synergy of resources created by the combination of the Delta SkyMiles and Northwest WorldPerks frequent flyer programs, facilitated by both airlines membership in the SkyTeam alliance (including over 20 other commercial carriers).[50] As a result of the merger, Delta offers the largest variety of domestic and international commercial routes (378 destinations in 66 countries) and is the largest commercial airline in the world.[51]

US Airways. Headquartered in Tempe, AZ, US Airways is the nation's fifth-largest airline. It employs over 33,000 people and has more than 3,000 departures a day using a fleet of 351 mainline and 299 express aircraft serving 155 domestic and 46 international destinations in 27 different countries from its major hubs in Phoenix, Charlotte, and Philadelphia.[52]

As a result of its acquisition by America West Airlines in September 2005, US Airways avoided filing a second bankruptcy in three years and inevitable liquidation.[53] The new US Airways (under the America West leadership team and CEO Doug Parker) was able to offer "more non-stop flights and better connecting service than either the West-Coast-oriented America West or the old, East-Coast-centric US Airways had before," and even "branded [itself] as 'America's largest low cost carrier.'"[54] The post-merger airline earned $427 million in profit on reported $11.7 billion in revenue in 2007 and $304 million on $11.6 billion in revenue in 2006. The firm reported a net loss of $2.2 billion on increased revenue of $12.1 billion in 2008.[55]

As with many of its competitors, US Airways relies on its regional affiliate, US Airways Express, to provide jet service to passengers traveling in and out of the smaller airports across the country, as well as flying during off-peak hours when it becomes inefficient to operate a larger jet.[56] In addition, US Airways is a member of the Star Alliance, which provides customers with even more access to various destinations across the globe without additional costs for the airline.[57]

US Airways competes on price, flight availability, and level of service provided with both low-cost carriers such as Southwest and AirTran, and full service traditional airlines such as American, Delta, and United.[58] The weakened state of the U.S. economy, a higher operating cost structure than that of true low-cost carriers, and fluctuations in fuel prices make it extremely difficult for the airline to earn profits on an annual basis. In fact, according to the airline officials, "one cent per gallon change in fuel prices will result in a $14 million increase/decrease in annual fuel expense."[59] However, US Airways is determined to be successful by providing the best customer service. But according to the 2008 American Customer Satisfaction survey conducted by the University of Michigan, the airline only scored 59 out 100 and thus has significant room for improvement in this regard.[60]

Southwest Airlines. Founded in 1971, Southwest Airlines introduced a new business model in the U.S. airline industry. It originally flew only intra-state routes in Texas, allowing it to operate outside the price and route regulations inter-state carriers faced.[61] Thus it was able to focus on providing low-cost no-frills travel to price-conscious consumers. When the industry was deregulated in 1978, Southwest began to expand beyond the borders of Texas. By 2007, Southwest had carried nearly 102 million passengers, more than any other airline in the world.[62] At the end of 2008, the company had a fleet of 500 Boeing 737 aircraft that flew 3,300 flights to 65 U.S. cities daily.[63]

Unlike its traditional competitors, Southwest does not rely on a hub-and-spoke network, using instead a point-to-point service between medium and large metropolitan areas.[64] Southwest minimizes costs by standardizing its fleet to reduce training and maintenance expenses, by using secondary airports that charge lower access fees, and by minimizing downtime for both aircraft and employees.[65] While traditional hub-and-spoke networks attempt to coordinate hub arrivals to facilitate shorter layovers for passengers, Southwest makes regular, frequent flights throughout the day. The result is a flatter demand for labor (less peaks and valleys) and higher aircraft utilization because of turnarounds that take half as long as the industry average.[66]

The customer experience on Southwest is described as "no-frills" because the company uses first-come, first-served seating and does not provide complimentary meal service. Southwest was also a pioneer in online bookings, e-ticketing, and self-check kiosks, reducing the cost of the ticketing and check-in process.[67]

Although "no-frills" might indicate a lack of commitment to service, industry statistics and surveys confirm that passengers feel otherwise. In fact, "Southwest Airlines has consistently received the lowest ratio of complaints per passengers boarded of all major U.S. carriers that have been reporting statistics to the Department of Transportation (DOT) since September 1987."[68]

The company earned profits during every year from 1975 to 2008, including recessionary periods in the early 1990s and 2000s when traditional carriers suffered losses.[69] In 2008, while every major traditional U.S. carrier posted a loss, Southwest turned a profit of $178 million.[70] The extent of the threat posed by Southwest and its model is evident in the number of low-cost carriers that have been launched around the world and the extent to which traditional carriers have tried to change their business models in direct response to the growth of low-cost airlines. Primarily, traditional carriers have tried combating low-cost carriers by creating "low-cost" subsidiaries of their own. American Airlines is the only major competitor to avoid this temptation.

Southwest has not posed a threat in regard to international travel because its operations do not yet extend beyond the borders of the United States.

International Transport

Generally speaking, an airline is permitted to carry passengers from a domestic airport to a foreign destination, drop them off, pick up passengers at that airport, and return to its country of origin.[71] Airlines are usually not permitted to carry passengers to other airports in other countries or within any country other than their home nation. Obviously, this situation presents problems for a traveler who wishes to go for example from a small airport in the United States to a small airport in Russia. This traveler would need to purchase separate tickets on a U.S. and a Russian carrier, transfer his or her own baggage, and assume the risks of missed connections between the carriers.

One obvious way around this dilemma is a merger of carriers with domestic rights in both countries. Unfortunately, "U.S. law limits the amount of foreign ownership in its domestic airlines to a maximum of 49 percent, with a maximum of 25 percent control."[72] Because other nations have similar restrictions, international airline mergers are essentially impossible at this time.

To circumvent the limitations related to international routes and restrictions on ownership, airlines have formed global strategic alliances.

Global Alliances

Alliances allow passengers to book end-to-end itineraries to a much larger pool of international destinations through airlines code-sharing on their joint networks.[73] In addition to extending a carrier's network, alliances also allow airlines to expand the value of their Frequent Flyer Programs (FFP) by providing passengers the opportunity to accumulate and redeem awards for other member airlines.[74] These alliances have extended beyond code-sharing and agreements on FFP programs to include food service agreements and maintenance contracts for each other's aircraft. There are three main airline alliances that compete against one another: Oneworld, SkyTeam, and Star. Exhibit 5 shows the airlines participating in each alliance as of June 2009, along with key statistics from 2008 for each alliance.

Star Alliance. The Star Alliance is the largest and the oldest formed by an agreement between United Airlines, Lufthansa, Air Canada, Thai Airways, and SAS (Scandinavian Airlines) in 1997.[75] In its 12-year existence, Star Alliance has grown to 21 member airlines and 3 regional members. The extent to which the alliance has been successful in covering the globe is evident in the combined route map shown in Exhibit 6.

Exhibit 5 Global Alliances

Global Alliances			
Alliance	**Oneworld**	**SkyTeam**	**Star**
Year formed	1999	2000	1997
Countries served	134	169	159
Unique airports	673	905	912
Daily departures	8,419	16,787	16,500
Passengers (thousands)	328,626	462,000	499,900
Lounges	550	447	805
Fleet (operated)	2,226	2,496	3,325
Employees	302,753	356,998	393,559
Full members	American Airlines	Aeroflot	Air Canada
	British Airways	Aeromexico	Air China
	Cathay Pacific Airways	Air France	Air New Zealand
	FinnAir	Alitalia	ANA
	Iberia	China Southern Airlines	Asiana Airlines
	Japan Airlines (JAL)	Continental Airlines*	Austrian
	LAN Airlines	CSA Czech Airlines	bmi
	Malev Hungarian Airlines	Delta Air Lines	EGYPTAIR
	Mexicana	KLM Royal Dutch Airlines	LOT Polish Airlines

Exhibit 5 Global Alliances (*Continued*)

Global Alliances			
Alliance	**Oneworld**	**SkyTeam**	**Star**
	Qantas	Korean Air	Lufthansa
	Royal Jordanian	Northwest Airlines	Scandinavian Airlines
			Shanghai Airlines
			Singapore Airlines
			South African Airways
			Spanair
			SWISS
			TAP Portugal
			THAI
			Turkish Airlines
			United Airlines
			US Airways
Associate/regional members	Air Nostrum	Air Europa	Adria Airways
	American Connection	Copa Airlines	Blue1
	American Eagle	Kenya Airways	Croatia Airlines
	BA Citiflyer		
	Click Mexicana		
	Comair		
	Dragonair		
	J-Air		
	JAL Express		
	JALways		
	Japan Transocean Air		
	Jetconnect		
	LAN Argentina		
	LAN Ecuador		
	LAN Express		
	LAN Peru		
	QantasLink		
	Sun-Air of Scandinavia		

* Continental is transitioning from SkyTeam to Star in 2009.

Source: 2009, Table compiled by authors using data from http://www.oneworld com, http://www.skyteam.com, and http://www.staralliance.com.

Exhibit 6   Star Alliance Route Network

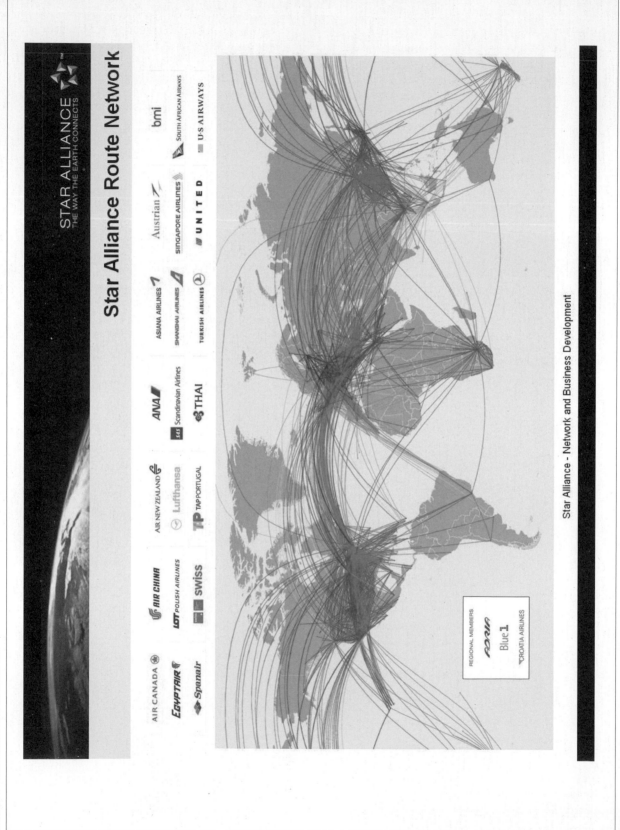

Star Alliance - Network and Business Development

Star Alliance exemplifies both the advantages and disadvantages of global airline alliances. Member airlines have been able to reduce costs and increase convenience for passengers through initiatives such as Star's dedicated terminals in Tokyo, Bangkok, Miami, and elsewhere.[76] Placing Star Alliance member airlines in a single terminal allows passengers to connect faster with shorter walks between gates. It also allows airlines to share lounges as well as personnel and resources used in check-in and ground handling activities.[77]

However, critics of alliances claim that code-sharing arrangements can lead to a reduction in competition, as "all the flights on a route carry the codes of [all] the 'competitors' and are jointly marketed by [all] the airlines."[78] Too many alliance members flying the same routes can also adversely affect the airlines involved, "as new airlines are added to the alliance, the importance of an existing airline may be reduced."[79]

Additionally, airlines face expenses when they join an alliance. Service levels must be standardized, information technology systems must be integrated, and costs are incurred for running the alliance itself.[80] Still, on the whole, there is general agreement that the benefits of alliances outweigh their drawbacks.

Oneworld. Oneworld is the smallest of the three major alliances. Offering the same basic benefits as Star, Oneworld also consolidated operations in dedicated terminals in Madrid, London Heathrow, Tokyo Narita, and elsewhere.[81] Oneworld seeks to distinguish itself from the Star and SkyTeam alliances by offering innovative fare structures that are designed to appeal to adventurous pleasure travelers as well as frequent business travelers.[82] In the United States, American is the primary Oneworld carrier.

SkyTeam. Formed in 2000, SkyTeam is the youngest of the major alliances. Like its competitors, SkyTeam is working to reduce member costs and "has opened more than 40 co-locations."[83] Member airlines are currently in the process of repainting some aircraft to emphasize the SkyTeam brand and de-emphasize the individual carrier brands.[84] Exhibit 7 shows a standard Delta branded plane and a new SkyTeam-Delta co-branded model. In 2007, the U.S. market was served by SkyTeam carriers Delta, Northwest, and Continental. Delta acquired Northwest in 2008 and Continental is scheduled to switch to the Star Alliance in 2009, leaving Delta as the sole U.S. airline in SkyTeam. Continental's defection is not surprising given Delta's acquisition of Northwest coupled with "Delta's and Continental's battle on transatlantic routes."[85]

Of the six largest U.S. airlines, Southwest is the only one that is not a member of a global alliance. In fact, no LCC is currently a member of any alliance. LCCs have traditionally avoided global alliances because of the service level requirements that membership places on them, although they do have some domestic code sharing agreements (Southwest had a code sharing agreement with ATA Airlines, for example, until ATA ceased service in 2008). A particularly enlightening case is Aer Lingus, which was in Oneworld, but quit the alliance as part of its attempt to restructure itself as an LCC.[86]

In addition to extending its network globally through the Star Alliance, United extends its network to smaller domestic airports through its regional affiliate, United Express.

United Express. The goal of this air carrier service is to transport passengers from smaller airports to United hubs for convenient connections to other United and Star Alliance flights.[87] United maintains agreements with regional carriers such as Chautauqua Airlines, Colgan Airlines, Go Jet Airlines, Mesa Airlines, Shuttle America, SkyWest Airlines, and Trans States Airlines, all of which fly planes bearing the United Express insignia; as such, passengers are generally unaware of the relationship and consider these flights to be United Airlines flights.[88] United Express conducts more than 2,000 flights daily and all of the same elements apply, such as acquiring points for the United frequent flier program.

Not only are alliances and networks important considerations for airline companies, but factors of production may be even more crucial.

Factors of Production

Aircraft Manufacturers. The most visible tangible asset of any airline is its fleet of aircraft. For large jet aircraft (more than 100 seats), Boeing and Airbus are currently the only two suppliers in the world.[89] The two companies are relatively evenly matched in terms of capabilities, and "since both manufacturers price their aircraft almost identically, competition occurs in the area of additional services, such as financing agreements or agreed buy-back of older aircraft."[90] Most airlines, including United, tend to maintain a relationship with both manufacturers to avoid becoming overly dependent on either supplier.

Fuel. With recent increases in the cost of oil, fuel has become the largest and most volatile expense for airlines.[91] In 2008 oil prices escalated to a high of $145 per barrel in July, then dropped to $70 a barrel in October, making it difficult for airlines to forecast expenses.[92] To smooth the variance, airlines routinely participate in fuel hedging, but this is not a foolproof practice. United lost $519 million in just the third quarter of 2008 when price decreases lowered the

Exhibit 7 Delta Planes with Traditional Delta Branding and New SkyTeam Branding

Source: 2009, Delta Air Lines N702DN and N844MH, http://www.flickr.com, March 30.

value of its hedges.[93] American, Delta, Continental, and even Southwest also posted losses due to fuel hedges.[94]

Airport Slots. The relationships between airlines and airports are quite complex. While airports generally have significant latitude with regards to the fees they charge airlines to use their facilities, the resulting

agreements give airlines significant power over gates, terminals, ticket counters, and slots for takeoffs and landings.[95]

Of particular interest is something called an "airport slot." Essentially, airport slots grant the holder "the right to land or take off from an airport at a given time."[96] Once these slots are granted, they exist in perpetuity as long as the owner uses the slot at least

80 percent of the time.[97] This provides a significant incentive to slot owners to continue flying in every slot they own to keep those slots from becoming available to other carriers.[98]

Labor. Labor relations can be challenging for any company, but for the airline industry, where a large percentage of airline workers are represented by labor unions, it is a very critical component of the business. Unfortunately for United, the firm's history of problems with the labor unions representing its workers continues to plague the company today.

After years of strikes and bitter negotiations, 1994 was something of a watershed moment for United's labor relations. As part of contract negotiations, it became the largest company in the world to be majority owned by its employees. Pilots bought 25 percent of the company, machinists, 20 percent and salaried and management workers, about 10 percent, and several seats on the board of directors were granted to union representatives.[99] It seemed that United and its unions were finally working together; however, that perception ended quickly. While the company's Employee Stock Ownership Plan (ESOP) provided job security for the so-called new "owners," there was little change in employee relations, airline efficiency, or customer satisfaction as workers still had little control over the critical decisions the company made. In retrospect, it seems that there was no intention to create an "ownership culture" by either side. Instead, union leaders "wanted to use ownership to prevent United from breaking up into regional carriers … and outsourcing work performed by union members," while the company's management saw ESOP "primarily as a way to get wage concessions."[100]

Results of a 2008 employee survey showed that a staggering 70 percent of United's employees remain dissatisfied working for the airline, and only 38 percent were proud of the company, "compared with the average *Fortune* 500 Company, where 84 percent of employees express pride in their employer."[101]

United's pilots, along with the Air Line Pilots Association (ALPA), criticized CEO Glenn Tilton based on the fact that his compensation package remains the highest in the industry by a considerable margin, even while his airline was reporting negative earnings, its employees are being laid off, and customers are being charged extra service fees.[102] Further, United's decision in June 2008 to eliminate 950 pilot jobs, lay off 1,600 salaried positions, and ground 70 aircraft was not received well by the ALPA community.[103] In fact, the union's pilots went on strike; in response, United sued the ALPA claiming it organized an illegal and disruptive "sickout" that caused hundreds of flight cancellations costing the airline millions of dollars in potential revenue and "damaging its reputation with the flying public and disrupting travel plans of about 36,000 passengers."[104] In November 2008, the federal court ruled against United's pilots, stating that their actions were illegal.[105]

Financial Results

During fiscal year 2008, five out of six major domestic carriers sustained losses on their income statements (see Exhibit 8a). Low-cost carrier Southwest Airlines was the only exception to this outcome. Most of these firms, because of liabilities that exceed their total assets, maintain a negative equity position (see Exhibits 8a, 8b, 8c). The extraordinarily high ROE shown simply demonstrates the significant amount of

Exhibit 8a Industry Financial Statistics 2008 (in millions except ratios and per-share figures)

Year Ending 2008	United	American	Southwest	Delta	US Airways	Continental
Income Statement						
Sales	20,194	23,766	11,023	22,697	12,118	15,241
Average daily sales	55	65	30	62	33	42
EBIT	(4,856)	1,348	383	(8,336)	(1,957)	(352)
Total interest	523	723	105	705	253	332
Lease obligations (capital leases)	1	1	25	473	752	195
Net income	(5,348)	(2,071)	178	(8,922)	(2,210)	(585)
Balance Sheet						
Current assets	4,861	5,935	2,893	8,904	2,418	4,347
Accounts receivable	977	811	574	1,844	293	669

(Continued)

Exhibit 8a Industry Financial Statistics 2008 (in millions except ratios and per-share figures) (Continued)

Year Ending 2008	United	American	Southwest	Delta	US Airways	Continental
Inventory	237	525	203	388	201	235
Finished goods	NA	NA	NA	NA	NA	NA
Fixed assets	10,312	15,735	11,040	20,627	3,286	7,327
Total assets	19,461	25,175	14,308	45,014	7,214	12,686
Current liabilities	7,281	9,374	2,806	11,022	3,044	4,474
Long-term debt	8,286	9,001	3,498	15,411	3,634	5,371
Total debt	21,926	28,110	9,355	44,140	7,719	12,581
Annual dividend per share	0	0	0	0	0	0
Current market price per share	12	10	9	12	9	19
After-tax earnings per share	(42)	(8)	0	(19)	(22)	(6)
Common shares outstanding	140	285	741	772	114	124
Owner's equity	(2,465)	(2,935)	4,953	874	(505)	(105)
Statement of Cash Flows						
Net change in cash	780	43	(845)	1,607	(914)	37
Profitability						
Profit margin	−26.48%	−8.71%	1.61%	−39.31%	−18.24%	−3.84%
Asset turnover	103.77%	94.40%	77.04%	50.42%	167.98%	120.14%
Return on assets	−27.48%	−8.23%	1.24%	−19.82%	−30.63%	−4.61%
Financial leverage	789.49%	857.75%	288.88%	5,150.34%	1,428.51%	12,081.90%
Return on equity	216.96%	70.56%	3.59%	−1,020.82%	437.62%	557.14%
Liquidity						
Current ratio	0.67	0.63	1.03	0.81	0.79	0.97
Quick ratio	0.64	0.58	0.96	0.77	0.73	0.92
Inventory to net working capital	−0.10	−0.15	2.33	−0.18	−0.32	−1.85
Leverage						
Debt to assets	1.13	1.12	0.65	0.98	1.07	0.99
Debt to equity	−8.89	−9.58	1.89	50.50	−15.29	−119.82
Long-term debt to equity	−3.36	−3.07	0.71	17.63	−7.20	−51.15
Times interest earned	−9.28	1.86	3.65	−11.82	−7.74	−1.06
Fixed-charge coverage	−9.26	1.86	3.14	−6.67	−1.20	−0.30
Activity						
Inventory turnover	NA	NA	NA	NA	NA	NA
Fixed assets turnover	1.96	1.51	1.00	1.10	3.69	2.08

Exhibit 8a Industry Financial Statistics 2008 (in millions except ratios and per-share figures) (*Continued*)

Year Ending 2008	United	American	Southwest	Delta	US Airways	Continental
Total assets turnover	1.04	0.94	0.77	0.50	1.68	1.20
Accounts receivable turnover	20.67	29.30	19.20	12.31	41.36	22.78
Average collecting period	17.66	12.46	19.01	29.65	8.83	16.02
Shareholder's Return						
Dividend yield on common stock	0.00	0.00	0.00	0.00	0.00	0.00
Price-earnings ratio	−0.28	−1.25	37.50	−0.63	−0.41	−3.43
Dividend-payout ratio	0.00	0.00	0.08	0.00	0.00	0.00
Cash flow per share	5.57	0.15	−1.14	2.08	−8.00	0.30

Source: 2009, Table compiled by authors using data from the 2008 10-K reports of each company.

Exhibit 8b Industry Financial Statistics 2007 (in millions except ratios and per-share figures)

Year Ending 2007	United	American	Southwest	Delta	US Airways	Continental
Income Statement						
Sales	20,143	22,935	9,861	19,154	11,700	14,232
Average daily sales	55	63	27	52	32	39
EBIT	1,337	1,398	1,127	2,471	707	922
Total interest	642	894	69	652	273	356
Lease obligations (capital leases)	1,106	846	39	526	765	183
Net income	403	504	645	1,612	427	459
Balance Sheet						
Current assets	6,095	7,229	4,443	5,240	3,347	4,561
Accounts receivable	966	1,027	279	1,208	374	865
Inventory	242	601	259	262	249	271
Finished goods	NA	NA	NA	NA	NA	NA
Fixed assets	11,359	17,153	10,874	11,701	2,488	6,558
Total assets	24,220	28,571	16,772	32,423	8,040	12,105
Current liabilities	7,979	8,483	4,838	6,605	2,434	4,449
Long-term debt	7,521	10,093	2,050	7,986	3,031	4,366
Total debt	21,431	25,914	9,831	22,310	6,601	10,555
Annual dividend per share	0	0	0	0	0	0
Current market price per share	32	13	12	13	13	20
After–tax earnings per share	3	2	1	5	5	4

(*Continued*)

Exhibit 8b Industry Financial Statistics 2007 (in millions except ratios and per-share figures) (*Continued*)

Year Ending 2007	United	American	Southwest	Delta	US Airways	Continental
Common shares outstanding	117	255	808	772	114	124
Owner's equity	2,418	2,657	6,941	10,113	1,439	1,550
Statement of Cash Flows						
Net change in cash	2,573	26	823	614	832	5
Profitability						
Profit margin	2.00%	2.20%	6.54%	8.42%	3.65%	3.23%
Asset turnover	83.17%	80.27%	58.79%	59.08%	145.52%	117.57%
Return on assets	1.66%	1.76%	3.85%	4.97%	5.31%	3.79%
Financial leverage	1,001.65%	1,075.31%	241.64%	320.61%	558.72%	780.97%
Return on equity	16.67%	18.97%	9.29%	15.94%	29.67%	29.61%
Liquidity						
Current ratio	0.76	0.85	0.92	0.79	1.38	1.03
Quick ratio	0.73	0.78	0.86	0.75	1.27	0.96
Inventory to net working capital	−0.13	−0.48	−0.66	−0.19	0.27	2.42
Leverage						
Debt to assets	0.88	0.91	0.59	0.69	0.82	0.87
Debt to equity	8.86	9.75	1.42	2.21	4.59	6.81
Long-term debt to equity	3.11	3.80	0.30	0.79	2.11	2.82
Times interest earned	2.08	1.56	16.33	3.79	2.59	2.59
Fixed-charge coverage	1.40	1.29	10.80	2.54	1.42	2.05
Activity						
Inventory turnover	NA	NA	NA	NA	NA	NA
Fixed-assets turnover	1.77	1.34	0.91	1.64	4.70	2.17
Total-assets turnover	0.83	0.80	0.59	0.59	1.46	1.18
Accounts-receivable turnover	20.85	22.33	35.34	15.86	31.28	16.45
Average collecting period	17.50	16.34	10.33	23.02	11.67	22.18
Shareholder's Return						
Dividend yield on common stock	0.00	0.00	0.00	0.00	0.00	0.00
Price–earnings ratio	9.58	7.30	14.29	2.49	2.79	4.94
Dividend-payout ratio	0.00	0.00	0.02	0.00	0.00	0.00
Cash flow per share	22.01	0.10	1.02	0.80	7.28	0.04

Source: 2009, Table compiled by authors using data from the 2008 10-K reports of each company.

Exhibit 8c Industry Financial Statistics 2006 (in millions except ratios and per-share figures)

Year Ending 2006	United	American	Southwest	Delta	US Airways	Continental
Income Statement						
Sales (millions USD)	17,880	22,563	9,086	17,171	7,117	13,128
Average daily sales	49	62	25	47	19	36
EBIT	511	1,232	867	(6,098)	(379)	752
Total interest	729	1,001	77	870	242	383
Lease obligations (capital leases)	1,350	927	51	387	956	200
Net income	32	231	499	(6,203)	(611)	343
Balance Sheet						
Current assets	6,273	6,902	2,601	5,385	1,413	4,129
Accounts receivable	942	988	241	1,317	252	747
Inventory	218	506	181	181	177	217
Finished goods	NA	NA	NA	NA	NA	NA
Fixed assets	11,463	17,763	10,094	12,973	3,370	6,263
Total assets	25,369	29,145	13,460	19,622	8,422	11,308
Current liabilities	7,945	8,505	2,887	5,769	2,383	3,955
Long-term debt	8,803	12,041	1,567	6,509	2,637	4,859
Total debt	22,860	29,751	7,011	33,215	8,856	10,961
Annual dividend per share	0	0	0	0	0	0
Current market price per share	46	32	15	20	54	45
After-tax earnings per share	197	1	1	(32)	4	3
Common shares outstanding	140	285	808	772	114	124
Owner's equity	2,148	(606)	6,449	(13,593)	(434)	347
Statement of Cash Flows						
Net change in cash	2,183	(17)	(890)	26	(191)	400
Profitability						
Profit margin	0.18%	1.02%	5.49%	–36.12%	–8.59%	2.61%
Asset turnover	70.48%	77.42%	67.50%	87.51%	84.50%	116.09%
Return on assets	0.13%	0.79%	3.71%	–31.61%	–7.25%	3.03%
Financial leverage	1,181.05%	4,809.41%	208.71%	144.35%	1,940.55%	3,258.79%
Return on equity	1.49%	–38.12%	7.74%	45.63%	140.78%	98.85%
Liquidity						
Current ratio	0.79	0.81	0.90	0.93	0.59	1.04

(Continued)

Exhibit 8c Industry Financial Statistics 2006 (in millions except ratios and per-share figures) *(Continued)*

Year Ending 2006	United	American	Southwest	Delta	US Airways	Continental
Quick ratio	0.76	0.75	0.84	0.90	0.52	0.99
Inventory to net working capital	–0.13	–0.32	–0.63	–0.47	–0.18	1.25
Leverage						
Debt to assets	0.90	1.02	0.52	1.69	1.05	0.97
Debt to equity	10.64	–49.09	1.09	–2.44	–20.41	31.59
Long-term debt to equity	4.10	–19.87	0.24	–0.48	–6.08	14.00
Times interest earned	0.70	1.23	11.26	–7.01	–1.57	1.96
Fixed-charge coverage	0.90	1.12	7.17	–4.54	0.48	1.63
Activity						
Inventory turnover	NA	NA	NA	NA	NA	NA
Fixed-assets turnover	1.56	1.27	0.90	1.32	2.11	2.10
Total-assets turnover	0.70	0.77	0.68	0.88	0.85	1.16
Accounts-receivable turnover	18.98	22.84	37.70	13.04	28.24	17.57
Average collecting period	19.23	15.98	9.68	28.00	12.92	20.77
Shareholder's Return						
Dividend yield on common stock	0.00	0.00	0.00	0.00	0.00	0.00
Price–earnings ratio	0.23	32.65	24.59	–0.63	15.38	13.72
Dividend-payout ratio	0.00	0.00	0.03	0.00	0.00	0.00
Cash flow per share	15.59	–0.06	–1.10	0.03	–1.67	3.23

Source: 2009, Table compiled by authors using data from the 2008 10-K reports of each company.

financial leverage that is commonplace in the airline industry.

Competition from low-cost carriers, recent emergence from bankruptcy, and intense competitive rivalry (because of high fixed costs and the need for high turnover) among carriers has forced United to contract its operations. With negative cash flows from operating and financing activities, United was forced to finance its activities by forgoing future investment and liquidating its assets (see Exhibit 9). In 2008, the firm permanently removed 100 aircraft from its fleet, reduced capital spending by $200 million, and cut 6,000 employees from its workforce.[106] In addition, in 2009 the company plans to eliminate 1,400 more workers, limit capital expenditures to $450 million, and reduce premium seats on domestic flights by 20 percent. Net sales of short-term investments accounted for the majority of United's liquidity in 2008 ($2.2 million of $2.7 million on the Statement of Cash Flows).[107]

Volatile fuel costs remain the most significant threat to financial stability for the airline industry as whole, but for United in particular. For the airline industry as a whole, fuel accounts for approximately 30 percent of total operating expenses. In 2008, United witnessed a 59 percent increase in the cost of fuel, leading to a $3.1 billion increase in overall costs related to hedging or direct fuel costs.[108]

United, along with competitors American, Continental, Delta, and Northwest, have implemented fees and reduced service in order to cope with rising fuel costs and decreased traffic. While charging fees for checked baggage seems intuitively counterproductive to increasing passenger traffic for United Airlines, according to CFO Kathryn Mikells, "a la carte pricing is proving to be a very large opportunity," and is expected to provide $700 million in additional income for 2009.[109] However, in many instances, such fees have caused an increase in public ire toward the airline industry. Thus, in an attempt to win back passengers and generate

Exhibit 9 UAL Statement of Cash Flows, 2006 to 2008

Period Ending	12/31/08	12/31/07	12/31/06
Net income	−5,348,000	403,000	22,876,000
Operating Activities, Cash Flows Provided by or Used in			
Depreciation	981,000	925,000	882,000
Adjustments to net income	3,374,000	496,000	636,000
Changes in accounts receivables	195,000	−59,000	43,000
Changes in liabilities	−591,000	638,000	1,447,000
Changes in inventories	—	—	—
Changes in other operating activities	150,000	−269,000	−1,411,000
Total Cash Flows from Operating Activities	−1,239,000	2,134,000	1,539,000
Investing Activities, Cash Flows Provided by or Used in			
Capital expenditures	−415,000	−658,000	−362,000
Investments	2,295,000	−1,951,000	−235,000
Other cash flows from investing activities	841,000	49,000	347,000
Total Cash Flows from Investing Activities	2,721,000	−2,560,000	−250,000
Financing Activities, Cash Flows Provided by or Used in			
Dividends paid	−253,000	—	—
Sale purchase of stock	96,000	24,000	10,000
Net borrowings	−702,000	−2,253,000	770,000
Other cash flows from financing activities	157,000	82,000	2,000
Total Cash Flows from Financing Activities	−702,000	−2,147,000	782,000
Effect of Exchange Rate Changes	—	—	—
Change in Cash and Cash Equivalents	$780,000	−$2,573,000	$2,071,000

Source: 2009, UAL Corporation cash flow, *Yahoo! Finance*, http://finance.yahoo.com.

brand loyalty, United has embraced several marketing strategies.

Marketing Initiatives

In 2008, United began its "Travel Options by United" program in an effort to provide passengers with greater choice and flexibility.[110] The program is comprised of six services that passengers can elect to add to their ticket price: economy plus, Premier Line, door-to-door baggage, travel insurance, award accelerator, and Red Carpet Club.[111] Through the Travel Options program, United is attempting to offer travelers services they will value—even if the service must be purchased by the passenger. The Premier Line, for example, was the result of market research aimed at uncovering customer needs and desires. Dennis Cary, senior vice president and chief marketing and customer officer, described the process as follows: "when we asked our customers what travel services were most important to them they told us the access to priority lines was something they value highly."[112] The Premier Line provides priority access at check-in, security, and boarding for a starting fee of $25.[113]

Another marketing strategy that United is using is its Premium Service, or p.s., flights. According to the company Web site, "in its essence, p.s. is about doing a few things extraordinarily well." The p.s. flights offer the only domestic lie-flat bed in first class, more leg room, laptop power, and a premium menu.[114] Currently, p.s. flights only service three cities: Los Angeles, New York, and San Francisco, providing special accommodations for a select few.[115] For United, p.s. flights are a confirmation of the belief that "to get business travelers to pay more and not simply shift to discount airlines, big airlines may have to find ways to offer premium service travelers will value."[116]

In addition to its marketing efforts to increase passenger transport, United Airlines maintains cargo service to supplement its revenues. United Cargo is the seventh-largest domestic freight company.[117]

Additional Revenue Streams

In 2008, cargo accounted for approximately 4 percent of the United's operating revenue, generating $854 million in freight and mail revenue.[118] While United and most of its competitors derive some revenue from the freight market, "competition in the freight market has grown steadily, and it is becoming less and less likely that airlines treating freight purely as a by-product will be successful."[119] The bulk of the market (which is expected to grow more rapidly than passenger service) is expected to fall to dedicated air freight companies.[120]

Despite all of United's attempts to improve its financial situation and future viability, it faces multiple challenges.

Strategic Challenges

Just three years removed from bankruptcy, United Airlines is suffering financially once again. The company's losses in 2008–2009 combined with its high levels of debt and low liquidity placed the company on shaky ground. The growth of LCCs, especially Southwest, and United's failed attempts at countering their influence are also troubling trends for the firm.

The company must decide how best to face the changing landscape of the passenger airline industry. Can United find a viable merger opportunity? If so, does a merger only postpone resolution of United's problems? Most importantly, can United neutralize the market erosion caused by low-cost carriers, or must it find a way to compete with them directly by lowering its own cost structure? Glenn Tilton and his executive team must find the most viable answers as the pathway for United Airlines to operate in ways that will satisfy all stakeholders, certainly including shareholders.

NOTES

1. 2009, Glenn Tilton remarks to the Phoenix Aviation Symposium, http://www.united.com, March 27.
2. 2009, UAL Corporation reports first quarter 2009 results, United Press Release, http://www.united.com, April 21; 2009, UAL Corporation 2008 Annual Report, http://www.united.com.
3. 2009, Era 2: 1926–1933 Timeline, http://www.united.com.
4. 2009, Era 3: 1934–1940, http://www.united.com.
5. R. Freeman, Walter Folger Brown: The postmaster general who built the U.S. Airline industry, U.S. Centennial of Flight Commission, http://www.centennialofflight.gov/essay/Commercial_Aviation/Brown/Tran3.htm.
6. E. Preston, The Federal Aviation Administration and its predecessor agencies, U.S. Centennial of Flight Commission, http://www.centennialofflight.gov/essay/Government_Role/FAA_History/POL8.htm.
7. Era 3: 1934–1940 Timeline.
8. S. Shaw, 2007, Airline Marketing and Management, 6th ed., Ashgate Publishing, 52.
9. 2008, Star Alliance Facts & Figures, Star Alliance, http://www.staralliance.com, December 11.
10. B. Vasigh, K. Fleming, & T. Tacker, 2008, Introduction to Air Transport Economics: From Theory to Applications, Ashgate Publishing, 227.
11. S. Shaw, Airline Marketing and Management.
12. B. Vasigh, K. Fleming, & T. Tacker, Introduction to Air Transport Economics, 308.
13. Ibid., 2.
14. 2009, Era 7: 1970–1989 Timeline, http://www.united.com.
15. 2009, Era 8: 1990–1993 Timeline, http://www.united.com.
16. 2009, Era 9: 1994–1999 Timeline, http://www.united.com.
17. 2002, United, CBS News, http://www.cbsnews.com, December 9.
18. Era 9: 1994–1999 Timeline.
19. 2009, Era 10: 2000–... Timeline, http://www.united.com.
20. United, CBS News.
21. Ibid.
22. Ibid.
23. 2009, UAL Corporation 2008 Annual Report, http://www.united.com.
24. Ibid.
25. Ibid.
26. M. Maynard, 2008, More cuts as United grounds its low-cost carrier, The New York Times, http://www.nytimes.com, June 5.
27. 2007, Delta, United deny being in merger discussions, MSNBC, http://www.msnbc.msn.com, November 14.
28. M. Maynard, 2008, United and Continental form alliance, The New York Times, http://www.nytimes.com, June 20.
29. United, CBS News; M. Maynard, United and Continental form alliance.
30. B. Vasigh, K. Fleming, & T. Tacker, Introduction to Air Transport Economics: From Theory to Applications, 51.
31. S. Shaw, Airline Marketing and Management, 37.
32. Ibid., 70.
33. Ibid., 37–39.
34. 2009, American Airlines History, http://www.aa.com, March; 2009, AMR Corporation 2008 Annual Report, http://www.aa.com, June.
35. 2008, AMR Corporation – American's Parent Company, http://www.aa.com, August.
36. 2009, American Eagle Airlines: At a glance, http://www.aa.com, May.
37. 2003, American Airlines avoids bankruptcy, BBC News, http://news.bbc.co.uk, April 1.
38. 2009, AMR Corporation 2008 Annual Report, http://www.aa.com.
39. A. Salpukas, 1990, Continental files for bankruptcy, The New York Times, http://www.nytimes.com, December 4.
40. 2008, Continental Airlines ranked No. 1 world's most admired airline by Fortune magazine, Reuters, http://www.reuters.com, March 11.
41. 2009, Continental Airlines 2008 8-K, http://www.continental.com, April, 24.

42. 2009, Continental Airlines facts second quarter 2009, http://www.continental.com; 2009, Continental Airlines 2008 Annual Report, http://www.continental.com, February.

43. Ibid.

44. 2009, Continental to join Star Alliance, Continental Airlines News Release, http://www.continental.com, April 16.

45. 2009, Delta through the decades, http://www.delta.com, April.

46. Ibid.

47. Ibid.

48. 2009, Delta Air Lines 2005 Annual Report, http://www.delta.com, April.

49. 2009, Delta Air Lines 2008 Annual Report, http://www.delta.com, April.

50. Ibid.

51. Ibid.

52. 2009, US Airways fact sheet, http://www.usairways.com, April; 2009, US Airways 2008 Annual Report, http://www.usairways.com, April.

53. 2009, US Airways chronology, http://www.usairways.com, April.

54. D. Reed, 2008, US Airways highlights drawbacks of consolidation, USA Today, http://www.usatoday.com, May 3; 2009, US Airways & America West Airlines combined route network map, http://www.airlineroutemaps.com, April; 2008, Is US Airways a low-cost carrier?, http://www.associatedcontent.com, February 14.

55. 2009, US Airways 2008 Annual Report, http://www.usairways.com, April.

56. Ibid.

57. Ibid.

58. Ibid.

59. Ibid.

60. S. McCartney, 2009, For the first time in awhile, airline customer satisfaction is up, Wall Street Journal, http://online.wsj.com, May 20.

61. We weren't just airborne yesterday, http://www.southwest.com.

62. 2008, Scheduled passengers carried, World Air Transport Statistics, http://www.iata.org.

63. 2009, Southwest Airlines Fact Sheet, http://www.southwest.com, April 27; 2009, Southwest Airlines Investor Relations, http://www.southwest.com.

64. Ibid.

65. B. Vasigh, K. Fleming, & T. Tacker, Introduction to Air Transport Economics, 309–318.

66. S. Shaw, Airline Marketing and Management, 96.

67. We weren't just airborne yesterday.

68. 2009, Southwest Airlines 2008 Annual Report, http://www.southwest.com, April.

69. S. Shaw, 2007, Airline Marketing and Management, 90.

70. Southwest Airlines 2008 Annual Report.

71. B. Vasigh, K. Fleming, & T. Tacker, Introduction to Air Transport Economics.

72. Ibid., 138.

73. S. Shaw, Airline Marketing and Management, 112.

74. Ibid., 255.

75. 2007, Backgrounder: 10 years Star Alliance from "The airline network for Earth" to "The way the Earth connects"—A chronological history, Star Alliance Press Office, May 14, 2.

76. Ibid., 3.

77. 2009, SkyTeam airline member benefits, http://www.skyteam.com, April.

78. S. Shaw, Airline Marketing and Management, 112.

79. B. Vasigh, K. Fleming, & T. Tacker, Introduction to Air Transport Economics, 173.

80. Ibid.

81. 2007, An introduction to Oneworld: The alliance that revolves around you, http://www.oneworld.com, July 11.

82. Ibid.

83. SkyTeam airline member benefits.

84. 2009, SkyTeam names managing director, introduces aircraft livery, http://www.skyteam.com, April 1.

85. B. Vasigh, K. Fleming, & T. Tacker, Introduction to Air Transport Economics, 173.

86. Ibid.

87. 2009, United Express, http://www.united.com, April.

88. 2009, United Airlines 2008 Annual Report, http://www.united.com, April.

89. B. Vasigh, K. Fleming, & T. Tacker, Introduction to Air Transport Economics, 212.

90. Ibid.

91. J. Lowy, 2008, Pilots: To cut costs, airlines forcing us to fly low on fuel, The Huffington Post, http://www.huffingtonpost.com, August 8.

92. M. Maynard, 2008, United, citing fuel hedging, loses $779 million in quarter, The New York Times http://www.nytimes.com, October, 21.

93. Ibid.

94. Ibid.

95. B. Vasigh, K. Fleming, & T. Tacker, Introduction to Air Transport Economics, 190.

96. Ibid., 191.

97. Ibid.

98. Ibid.

99. Era 9: 1994–1999 Timeline; 2003, United Airlines likely to lose employee ownership, USA Today, http://www.usatoday.com, January 16.

100. C. Rosen, 2002. United Airlines, ESOPs, and employee ownership, The National Center for Employee Ownership, http://www.nceo.org, November.

101. 2008, United Pilots: Leadership void costly for UAL in 2008, UPI, http://www.upi.com, December 29.

102. Ibid.

103. 2008, United Airlines to lay off 950 pilots—cuts in addition to those announced earlier, domain-b.com, http://www.domain-b.com/aero/unitedairlines/20080624_united_airlines.html, June 24.

104. 2008, United Airlines sues pilots' union, says it caused hundreds of flight cancellations, domain-b.com, http://www.domain-b.com/aero/unitedairlines/20080731_united_airlines.html, July 31.

105. 2008, Injunction halts United Airline's pilot strike, RoutesOnline, http://www.routesonline.com, November 19.

106. United Airlines 2008 Annual Report.

107. D. Koenig, 2008, Major airlines ready to cut more flights in 2009, Associated Press, http://www.news.yahoo.com, December 2; 2009, United Airways 2008 Annual Report, http://www.united.com; L. Stark, M. Hosford, & K. Barrett, 2008, Layoffs continue for airlines in crisis, ABC News, http://www.abcnews.go.com, June 5.

108. United Airlines 2008 Annual Report.

109. A. Karp, 2008, Downsizing United, Air Transport World, http://www.atwonline.com, November.

110. 2009, United Airlines, Wikitravel, http://wikitravel.org/en/United_Airlines, April.

111. 2009, Travel Options by United, https://www.united.com, April.

112. Ibid.

113. 2009, Travel Options by United—Premier Line, https://store.united.com; 2008, Take the fast track through the airport with United's new Premier Line service, http://www.united.com, December 8.

114. S. McCartney, 2008, A posher domestic first class; United sells space and comfy beds on "p.s." flights, Wall Street Journal, http://online.wsj.com, July 29.

115. 2009, p.s. Experience the comfort of our exclusive coast-to-coast service, http://www.unitedps.com, April.

116. S. McCartney, A posher domestic first class; United sells space and comfy beds on "p.s." flights.

117. Scheduled Freight Tonne—Kilometres, IATA Web site, http://www.iata.org/ps/publications/wats-freight-km.htm.

118. United Airlines 2008 Annual Report.

119. S. Shaw, Airline Marketing and Management, 40.

120. Ibid.

Amy Falter, Scott Thompson

Arizona State University

Netflix is one of the most recognizable online movie rental services in the world. Since the company's launch in 1998, its business model has revolutionized the movie rental business and the way U.S. viewers rent and watch movies. Netflix's service has captured approximately 6.7 million subscribers and offers a video library of more than 90,000 movies, television, and other entertainment videos on DVD.[1] The majority of Netflix subscribers pay about $18 per month and are allowed to keep up to three movies at a time.[2] Although Netflix was the first company to tap this new market of online movie rental, they would not be the last trying to capitalize on its potential.

In August 2004, Blockbuster countered Netflix's entry into the movie rental business with a strategic response by introducing Blockbuster Online, its own online rental service.[3] Blockbuster Online offered the same services as Netflix, putting the two companies in direct competition with each other for the first time. In late 2006, Blockbuster revamped the online rental service and renamed it "Blockbuster Online Total Access."[4] This new Blockbuster service gives the customer the option of either returning the video through the mail or dropping it off at a local Blockbuster store.[5] It does however, encourage customers to return videos rented online to the store by offering a voucher for a new in-store rental.[6] As Blockbuster boasts, "With this kind of access, you'll never have to wait to have a new movie to watch!"[7] The only caveat with the new in-store rental is that normal due dates and late fees typical of brick-and-mortar video rental stores are enforced.[8] Without any physical stores, Netflix executives now face the difficult challenge of finding a legitimate and value-adding way to compete with Blockbuster.

Netflix also faces the development of video streaming and downloads on PCs as well as mobile devices. "Computers, portable MP3 video players, and telephones are now options for watching downloaded TV shows and movies, especially among younger audiences."[9] Companies such as Amazon, Apple, and YouTube have all been looking at ventures in this market.[10] To stay atop the online rental market, Netflix must decide how to adjust its current business model in order to grow and adapt to the market's dynamic environment.

To better understand these salient strategic challenges, the following topics will be touched upon: Netflix's history, current strategic leaders, the competitive environment, supplier relationships, Netflix's current strategies and functional operations, and recent financial outcomes.

Brief History

Reed Hastings founded and incorporated Netflix in August 1997 as a more conventional rental service, with online offerings.[11] It was not until April 1998 that Netflix opened its Internet store for DVD rentals and then offered a subscription service in September 1999.[12] Netflix's rapid growth can be attributed to its early strategic relationships with leading DVD hardware and home theater equipment manufacturers (Sony, Toshiba, RCA/Thomson Consumer Electronics, Pioneer, and Panasonic) and marketing tactics (promotional techniques) to build brand recognition and acceptance among the growing DVD-rental consumer base.[13] In December 1999, Netflix announced the elimination of due dates and late fees, helping it to quickly become a popular rental service, as it also did not charge shipping and handling fees and per-title rental fees.[14] On May 22, 2002, Netflix made an initial public offering (IPO) of 5.5 million shares of common stock at $15 per share.[15]

Due to the overwhelming acceptance of and demand for Netflix services, it became necessary for Netflix to

The authors would like to thank Professor Robert E. Hoskisson for his support under whose direction the case was developed. The authors do not intend to illustrate either effective or ineffective handling of a managerial situation. The case solely provides material for class discussion. This case was developed with contributions from: Garret Lumley, Evan Mallonee, & Terri Phillips.

Exhibit 1 Monthly Plans

Movie Rentals	Cost
1 at-a-time (2 per month)	$ 4.99 per month
1 at-a-time (unlimited)	$ 9.99 per month
2 at-a-time (unlimited)	$14.99 per month
3 at-a-time (unlimited)	$17.99 per month
4 at-a-time (unlimited)	$23.99 per month
5 at-a-time (unlimited)	$29.99 per month
6 at-a-time (unlimited)	$35.99 per month
7 at-a-time (unlimited)	$41.99 per month
8 at-a-time (unlimited)	$47.99 per month

Source: http://www.netflix.com/MediaCenter.

build new distribution and shipping centers every year. In the 2003 fiscal year, Netflix recorded its first profitable year with record revenues of $272.2 million, up 78 percent from the 2002 fiscal year with earnings of $152.8 million.[16] As Netflix grew, it developed tailored service packages based on consumers' desired number of rentals per month (see Exhibit 1). In 2005, the number of subscribers grew to a record high of 4.2 million, 60 percent over the previous year.[17] Both 2005 and 2006 were also solid growth years, leaving CEO Reed Hastings optimistic about future growth and earnings potential: "Our accomplishments during the year [2006]—strong subscriber growth, continued improvement in the customer experience, and increased profitability—together with the recent launch of the first generation of our online video option, leave us better positioned than ever to achieve our long-term objective of being the movie rental leader."[18] In February 2007, Netflix celebrated the delivery of its one-billionth DVD by giving the recipient a free lifetime Netflix membership.[19]

Netflix recently offered new features to its subscribers. In January 2007, Netflix launched "Watch Now."[20] This feature allows subscribers not only to rent online and continue to receive DVDs through mail, but also watch more than 1,000 movies and television shows via their PCs.[21] Netflix hopes to eventually bring this type of technology to any device with access to the Internet.[22] Another new endeavor Netflix has launched is Red Envelope Entertainment; this new division "looks to leverage its proprietary technology to offer subscribers unique and original content to which they wouldn't otherwise have access."[23] The unique and original content includes independent films such as those found at the Sundance and Toronto Film festivals.[24]

At year end 2006 Netflix employed 1,300 full-time and 646 temporary employees at the corporate headquarters in Los Gatos, California, and in its shipping centers across the nation.[25] Many of Netflix's senior officers have been with the company for a majority of the company's lifespan. The current strategic decision makers of Netflix are six key individuals from the C-suite.

Netflix Strategic Leaders

Founder, CEO, and Chairperson. Reed Hastings has served as chairman since the company's inception.[26] Hastings studied mathematics at Bowdoin College in Brunswick, Maine, and was awarded the Smyth Prize in 1981 by the math department and received his BA in 1983.[27] To round out his education, Hastings went to Stanford University and received a master's degree in computer science.[28] A former Netflix director, Bob Pisano, said of Hastings "[he is] an engineer, is analytical and very charismatic . . . that's a rare combination."[29]

Hastings created the vision for Netflix and is in perpetual motion to evolve and sustain his business based on critical factors developed by other members of his management team.

Neil Hunt, Chief Product Officer. Neil Hunt created and manages the Netflix site. He has served in this capacity since 1999.[30] His job and decisions are of critical importance, because his output is the portal customers ultimately interact with via the company. Hunt's focus is "Customization and personalization [ensuring] every Netflix member [receives] a unique experience every time they visit the site. This includes the movies they see on each page, the recommendations they receive on movies, and the critical account management tools they use, such as their dynamic queue to order movies."[31] Mr. Hunt is a noteworthy scientist who has the leadership skills to inspire teams to be innovative, and create powerful software that is user-friendly.

Ted Sarandos, Chief Content Officer. Since 2000, Mr. Sarandos's role is to manage and cultivate relationships with studios, networks, film makers, and producers to gain access to films and distribution channels.[32] His most critical role is making sure customers' needs are satisfied through the current video selection and by staying abreast of new trends within the entertainment industry.

Leslie Kilgore, Chief Marketing Officer. Because Netflix is an online entity, Ms. Kilgore's responsibility is to find the most effective and cost-efficient methods to acquire new subscribers through various marketing approaches.[33] Her success is demonstrated in that "more than 90 percent of trial members convert to paying subscribers and more than 90 percent of those tell family and friends about the service."[34]

Barry McCarthy, Chief Financial Officer. Since 1999 Mr. McCarthy has overseen the financial and legal affairs for Netflix. Barry has vast experience in his field, including work with Credit Suisse First Boston. He has helped Netflix become a billion dollar revenue company within 7 years.[35]

Patty McCord, Chief Talent Officer. Ms. McCord has been with Netflix since 1998 and helps the company attract and retain high-talent employees. Having 16 years of human resources experience with high-tech companies, she plays a large role in establishing a culture in which employees are devoted to superior customer service. "She is adamant about keeping a lean organization in which openness, approachability, and honesty are valued above all else."[36]

The strategic leaders have directed Netflix to target three distinct customer segments: those who like the convenience of free home delivery, the movie buffs who want access to the widest selection of, say, French New Wave or Bollywood films, and the bargain hunters who want to watch 10 or more movies for 18 dollars a month. The challenge is to keep all segments happy at the same time.[37]

Netflix hopes that catering to the needs and desires of its different customer segments will help it remain a key player in this rapidly developing and competitive industry.

Competitive Environment

Until recently, Blockbuster Inc. dominated the movie rental industry, with few threatening competitors and drawing annual revenues of more than $3 billion.[38] Netflix challenged the traditional brick-and-mortar video rental chains. With the continual advent of new technology and widespread Internet adoption and usage, the Netflix business model appealed to many consumers, especially those who were frustrated with Blockbuster's late fees. With Netflix's entire business model focused on providing unique online rental, free delivery to households, no due dates or late fees, and movie recommendations to all its subscribers, Netflix appeared to have found a niche market.[39]

As a result of the short product life cycles in the technological sector, continual improvements in products, and lower costs in technology, it has become more common for consumers around the globe to own their own movie viewing devices and access the Internet from home. Thus, the online movie rental market base is expected to grow continuously. In 2005, the online movie rental industry had more than 6 million subscribers in the United States and Europe, and by the end of 2006 that number rose to more than 8 million subscribers.[40]

Emerging Competitors

Progress in technology is changing the competitive dynamics. The main impetus challenging movie rental companies is video on demand (VOD). Video on demand is gaining more attention and popularity, especially among cable/satellite companies, television networks, and dot-com companies. In contrast to buying or renting a video, VOD allows the user to download the entire movie to a computer or stream the video, where the movie is viewed in realtime.[41]

Downloadable movies are in an embryonic stage, with early adopters experimenting with the service, but are not yet widely utilized among Internet users.[42] A potential current pitfall of this product is that neither downloaded nor streaming videos come in high definition yet, and this could be a deal buster for many consumers who have recently bought into the high definition craze.[43] However, most of the key online rental industry players have sought relationships with video on demand providers to maintain a competitive advantage.

New entrants are crafting technology devices specifically designed to support these new services. One major player will be Apple; movies and television shows can be viewed on Apple TV, iPods, and Macs. Smartphones will also begin to offer the downloadable movie and television show service, acting as portable TVs.[44] The downloadable Amazon Unbox allows consumers to access DVD-quality movies and television shows for rent or purchase.[45] Wal-Mart joined the fight for market share by creating its own downloading movie business in February 2007.[46] Wal-Mart has gained the interest of studios such as 20th Century Fox, Lions Gate, Disney, MGM, MTV Networks, Paramount Pictures, Universal Studios, Sony Pictures Entertainment, and Warner Bros.[47] Wal-Mart currently offers approximately 3,000 titles for download purchase ranging in price from $14.88 to $19.88.[48]

Netflix is in its infancy stage of introducing streaming videos and television shows offered to current subscribers.[49] This new addition of streaming service was built upon the Microsoft infrastructure.[50] Over time, the company hopes to make Netflix's service available on other software combinations, portable devices, and televisions screens.[51] Netflix has also partnered with video recorder maker TiVo to allow TiVo customers access to DVDs on Netflix's Web site.[52] CEO Reed Hastings has stated, "We want to be ready when video on demand happens. That's why the company is [called] Netflix and not DVD-by-mail."[53]

Even though Blockbuster has been Netflix's strongest competitor, other companies are strengthening their competitive position to challenge these two giants and gain market share. These competitors seem to believe they can differentiate their service and product offerings in order to challenge Netflix in an entirely new dimension.

Key Competitors

Blockbuster Inc.

Blockbuster is the world's largest video and video disk retail chain today, with approximately 9,040 company-owned or franchised brick-and-mortar stores located in more than 25 countries (about 60 percent located within the United States).[54] Each year, Blockbuster rents more than a billion videos, DVDs, and video games through its retail outlets.[55] Blockbuster became a video giant through its foresight, acquisition strategy, and prime store locations.

History. In 1982, David P. Cook determined that "most [video] stores were relatively modest family operations that carried a small selection of former big hit movies."[56] Cook wanted to create a nationwide movie rental company chain with a vast selection of videos.[57] The biggest selling point to enter this industry was that he could use his computer skills to create an innovative computing system for inventory control and checkout; therefore, it would decrease manual labor costs and help eliminate high costs associated with theft.[58] Cook used the proceeds from the sale of his computer data services company to open a flashy video rental store that maintained the video catalog via computer bar code systems. He named his new company Blockbuster Entertainment, with the first store opening in Dallas, Texas, in 1985.[59]

Growth Strategy. Initially, Blockbuster's growth strategy included franchising and selling the Blockbuster name and proprietary computer system.[60] After being in existence for only one year, Blockbuster altered its strategy to horizontal acquisitions to spur rapid growth. Blockbuster desired to be the first-mover in the superstore video rental chain.[61] "Blockbuster's management continued to maintain that since the video 'superstore' concept was open for anyone to copy, it needed to grab market share as fast as possible in order to exploit its ground-breaking concept."[62]

Although Blockbuster rapidly expanded nationally and experienced astronomical growth (company earnings in 1988, 1989, and 1990 were 114%, 93%, and 48% respectively), the rental industry was beginning to reach maturity.[63] Blockbuster began to offer video game equipment and games for rental and purchase.[64] In addition, Blockbuster continued to expand globally with market entries in the United Kingdom, Japan, Australia, Europe, and Latin America.[65]

To further diversify its business portfolio, Blockbuster purchased Music Plus and Sound Warehouse, a music retail chain, from Shamrock Holdings in 1992, for $185 million and created Blockbuster Music.[66] Within the past 15 years, Blockbuster has entered into many agreements with movie production companies, communication companies, and other entertainment companies, many of which proved beneficial; but some relationships had to be severed, such as Blockbuster Music (1998), so as to not drain Blockbuster of all its financial resources.

Revenue Sharing Program. The current CEO, John Antioco, took the reins in the summer of 1997 with Blockbuster in a world of mess.[67] Not only was its stock 50 percent below its value from the previous year, but suppliers were not delivering newly released movies on time, and there was not enough qualified staff to allow for effective store operations.[68]

Antioco turned the company on its head. He scaled back on expansion and eliminated the nonrental operations (i.e., selling retail merchandise in Blockbuster stores).[69] He also implemented a revenue sharing program with major Hollywood movie studios. "Now instead of paying $65 for new tapes, Blockbuster paid $4 and turned over 30 to 40 percent of the rental income to the studio."[70] This arrangement allowed Blockbuster to stock more videos on its shelves with a lower cost structure. In 2007 Antioco announced his resignation as chairperson and CEO due to various disagreements with Blockbuster's board about salary.[71] The succeeding CEO James Keyes confronts the challenge of holding market share in a volatile industry.

Challenge to Netflix. As noted previously, in response to the success and popularity of Netflix, Blockbuster launched its Blockbuster Online service in 2004 "where members can rent unlimited DVDs online and have them delivered via mail for a monthly fee."[72] This service has evolved into its current state called Blockbuster Total Access, where DVDs are still ordered online and delivered to households, but now customers can return the DVDs for a free in-store rental.[73] Blockbuster also developed a subscription service called Blockbuster Movie Pass where customers can have 2 or 3 movies out at a time without any late fees.[74]

Most recently, Blockbuster and Weinstein Co. entered into an agreement where Weinstein Co.—an independent American film studio—will sell its titles such as *Sicko, Miss Potter, and Hannibal Rising* exclusively to Blockbuster outlets for a three-year period in exchange for the aforementioned revenue sharing program.[75] This strategic action will prohibit Netflix access to any of the titles produced by this studio. Netflix has pursued its own agreements with independent film producers, so it remains to be seen whether these relationships will prove beneficial for each company.

Also, Blockbuster recently acquired Movielink LLC, an online movie downloading company owned by major Hollywood studios, such as MGM, Paramount Pictures, Sony Pictures Entertainment, Universal Studios, and Warner Brothers.[76] In this agreement, Blockbuster will have long-term deals for content with the major film studios, which will significantly enlarge its current video library used by both the brick-and-mortar stores and online subscribers.[77] Blockbuster has also sought out a video download partner so its customers will have three ways to attain movies—in-store, mail order, or download. "While Blockbuster trailed behind in the online DVD rental business after entering it in 2004—five years after Netflix—it's not taking a wait-and-see attitude toward movie downloads."[78]

Movie Gallery, Inc.

Movie Gallery is the second-largest North American video rental retail chain, with more than 4,700 stores located in all 50 states, Canada, and Mexico.[79] Its growth strategy is internal growth and pursuing selective complementary acquisitions. "By focusing on rural and secondary markets, [Movie Gallery] is able to compete very effectively against the independently owned stores and small regional chains in these areas."[80] Movie Gallery's acquisition of Hollywood Entertainment in 2005 made the company stronger and more competitive with Blockbuster by challenging Blockbuster on its strength—owning stores in prime locations.

By acquiring Hollywood Entertainment, Movie Gallery inherited 74 automated movie vending machine kiosks similar to ATMs, which "provide around the clock availability of movies" for rent.[81] Because of the minimal overhead and fixed costs associated with the kiosks Movie Gallery intends to expand its fleet with a rollout of an additional 200 units through 2007.[82]

Joe Malugen, chairperson, president, and CEO of Movie Gallery, stated "While we firmly believe that our retail brick-and-mortar stores will remain the foundation of our business, over the past three years we have been diligently pursuing alternative delivery platforms to further complement our base business."[83] As such, in March 2007 Movie Gallery purchased MovieBeam, a movies-on-demand service, which was created and funded by Walt Disney Co., Cisco Systems, and Intel Capital.[84] Movies are "beamed" into consumer homes using MovieBeam's patented over-the-air data-casting technology to the set-top box.[85] Currently, this technology is limited to television set use only, but Movie Gallery plans to expand these services to video on demand capability over the Internet.[86]

Hastings Entertainment. Hastings Entertainment operates in approximately 20 midwestern and western states, focusing on small to medium-sized towns with underserved markets (towns with populations of 33,000 to 105,000).[87] This multimedia retailer "combines the sale of new and used CDs, books, videos, and video games, as well as boutique merchandise, with the rental of videos and video games in a superstore format."[88] Sales and rentals of videos and games account for the primary revenue stream (35 percent) with music sales pulling in the second highest amount (25 percent).[89] According to Hoover's Inc., "As is the case throughout most of the rental industry, Hastings video rental sales continue to drop in the face of mail-order rental houses like Netflix and video on demand services from cable companies."[90] Although Blockbuster, Movie Gallery, and Hastings Entertainment are the "Big Three" competitors for Netflix, other movie delivery methods exist and capture some of the market share.

Other Competitors

While movie rentals are the most common method for viewing newly released films or older pictures, other channels are available. These channels include movie retail stores (e.g., Best Buy, Wal-Mart, and Amazon.com); subscription entertainment services (e.g., Showtime and HBO); Internet movie providers (e.g., iTunes, Amazon.com, Movielink, CinemaNow.com, and Vongo); Internet companies (e.g., Yahoo! and Google); and cable and direct broadcast satellite providers.[91]

To remain a key player in the industry it is just as important for Netflix to consider the movie content providers as it is the competitors.

Content Providers

Netflix has exercised great effort in establishing strong relationships with a number of entertainment film providers. They have sought to ensure that the relationships are mutually beneficial. Netflix obtains content from the studios through either revenue sharing agreements or direct purchase. The revenue sharing program provides Netflix with a tremendous cost savings, and in return provides the studios a percentage of Netflix's subscription revenues for a defined period of time. This agreement also allows the studios an additional distribution outlet for new releases, television shows, and so on. Once the defined period for the revenue sharing has ended for a particular movie title, Netflix will destroy the title, purchase the title, or return it to the studio.

Netflix contracts movies offered through its instant-viewing feature with studios and other content providers on a fixed fee or per-view basis. The general arrangement is the same, but the specific terms are often unique to each provider.[92]

Netflix orders movies in two different formats: HD-DVD and Blu-Ray[93] through content providers such as Hollywood Film studios, 20th Century Fox, Walt Disney Studios, Columbia Pictures, Lions Gate Films, New Line Cinema, Paramount Pictures, Universal Pictures, Warner Bros. Pictures, and other independent film studios.[94]

The online rental industry has enjoyed large growth and success up to this point largely due to the distribution rules established by studios. Currently, DVDs are available for movie rental and retail sales three to six months before the movies are available on pay-per-view and VOD, nine months before satellite and cable, and two to three years before basic cable and syndicated networks. The studios have discussed either eliminating the distribution windows or shortening them, which would adversely affect Netflix.[95]

Netflix has been able to establish a relationship with content providers and differentiate itself among competitors through its strategic approach.

Netflix's Strategies and Functional Operations

Netflix is focused on continuous improvement and metrics to add value to the business and the customers' experience.[96] All these goals culminate into one overlying company strategic goal—to maintain a low-cost structure. Dillon states,

The Company's fulfillment costs are about half what Blockbuster's are, which enables profitability at a lower price. Every penny counts in a high-volume business. As we keep lowering our cost, we're able to lower our price. It's a very elastic market; so, the lower the price, the more our market grows.[97]

As mentioned previously, the company developed strategic alliances with sources in the film and television sectors.[98] These arrangements provided a significant cost savings, which freed up funds to use for other projects and investments, such as the continued investment and development of its proprietary software for inventory management, logistics, and shipping.[99]

Netflix has also carefully managed its payroll expenses to keep in line with the low-cost structure. "When the company first started in 1999, Netflix had 75,000 customers and was using 100 employees to package software for customer support."[100] Netflix cut that number roughly in half with just 45 current employees serving more than 6 million subscribers.[101] This dramatic cut in staffing is driven by an essentially self-service Web site and home-grown support software that enables representatives to handle higher volumes.[102] Tom Dillon, COO explains,

We firmly believe in building IT from scratch; this is a custom business. . . . If you want to get it done exactly the way you want, build it yourself. . . . IT is not a strategic weapon in most companies. But in our company, IT is the business. We live and breathe [the idea] that the way you get more competitive, lower your costs, and provide better service is through continuous improvement of the information technology.[103]

Netflix transcended the norms for IT use and will continue to rely on its information technology capabilities and resources. It has built a strong, reliable Web platform that is compatible with all kinds of portals and browsers in order to sustain a large number of users and maintain a positive "brand experience."[104]

Netflix is a company that competes on its strong foundation of mathematical, statistical, and data management expertise and uses these strengths to further distinguish itself from other competitors.[105] It uses analytics in two different ways. Internally created, algorithmically driven software makes movie recommendations for customers through a system called Cinematch.[106] This capability essentially led to the creation of personalized Web sites for each customer who visits Netflix and gives a customized interaction with every individual.[107] Netflix also uses a process called *throttling*. With this process, the company balances the frequent-use and infrequent-use distribution shipping requests of its customers.[108] Infrequent-use customers are given higher priority in shipping than frequent-use customers.[109] Some customers became disgruntled when they learned that Netflix uses the throttling process. Netflix's senior leaders did not seemed concerned about the complaints as shown in a statement by CEO Reed Hastings, "Few customers have complained about this 'fairness algorithm.' We have unbelievably high customer satisfaction ratings." In January, 1995 Netflix changed its "terms of use" to read "In determining priority for shipping and inventory allocation, we give priority to those members who receive the fewest DVDs through our service."[110]

Netflix's services provide value for its large customer base. The value provided has led Netflix to be almost four times larger than Blockbuster's in regard to subscribers for the online service, and to maintain this position, Netflix is continually reinvesting its money into marketing.[111]

Marketing Approaches

Marketing has been a key advantage for Netflix. Early on it established an agreement with Best Buy in that Best Buy set up a cobranded version of the online DVD rental service on its five online Web sites and instituted a joint-marketing program in the 1,800-plus retail stores. In return, Netflix directs its customers interested

Exhibit 2 Advertising Expenditures

As of	Blockbuster	Netflix
December 2006	$154,300,000	$225,524,000
December 2005	252,700,000	144,562,000
December 2004	257,400,000	100,534,000
December 2003	179,400,000	49,949,000

Sources: http://www.marketwatch.com; Netflix SEC10-K 2003, Netflix SEC10-K 2004, Netflix SEC10-K 2005, and Netflix SEC10-K 2006.

Exhibit 3 Historic Stock Price and P/E Ratios

	2006	2005	2004	2003	2002
High Price	33.12	30.25	39.77	30.50	9.10
Low Price	18.12	8.91	9.25	5.93	2.42
Year-End Price	25.86	27.06	12.33	27.35	5.51
High P/E	46.61	47.16	119.18	294.52	−12.25
Low P/E	25.50	13.89	27.72	57.21	−3.26
Year-End P/E	36.39	42.19	36.95	264.05	−7.41

Source: http://stocks.us.reuters.com/stocks/performance.asp?symbol=NFLX.O&WTmodLOC=L2-LeftNav-18-Performace.

in buying DVDs to Best Buy's Web sites.[112] It has a similar agreement with Wal-Mart; both companies have promoted one another since 2005 when Wal-Mart exited the online movie market.[113]

Other marketing efforts include online advertisements such as banner ads, paid search listings, pop-up advertisements, and text on popular Web portals—Yahoo!, MSN, and AOL.[114] Netflix was ranked as being the number two company to spend the most money on online advertisements.[115] Most online retailers face budget restrictions on advertising expenditures, as did Netflix in the beginning, and therefore are selective in the channels of advertising,[116] but as Netflix's subscriber base has grown, so has its advertising budget and expenditures (see Exhibit 2).

Netflix also targets a broad demographic in its advertising plan by running ads on the mainstream networks—ABC, NBC, FOX, and CBS, as well as radio advertisements.[117] Direct mail, print advertising, and promotions in certain consumer package goods are used as well in their marketing strategy.[118]

For online video rental, Netflix pioneered the use of database marketing to develop a personalized relationship with consumers. The database, possible because of Netflix's strengths in IT, allowed Netflix to understand individual customers, aggregate and predict behaviors, and then send customized e-mails informing customers of what new movies are available. Netflix has a strong culture of analytics and a test-and-learn approach to its business.[119] Metrics tracked include Web site users, advertising testing, data mining, subscriber satisfaction, segment research, and marketing material effectiveness.[120] Often, the effectiveness of its marketing endeavors can be assessed by reviewing the company's financials.

Financial Results

Stock Related Issues

Netflix's stock price has been highly volatile since its IPO on May 22, 2002. After adjusting for the eventual 2-for-1 stock split on February 12, 2004, its first year stock was valued anywhere between $2.42 and $9.10.[121] In the following three years, the stock price fluctuated even more until it started showing signs of stabilization in 2006 (see Exhibit 3). The earnings per share (EPS) for Netflix has been constantly on the rise (see Exhibit 4). Estimates for 2007 and 2008 suggest that this trend will continue at a reasonable rate, which can also be seen in Exhibit 4.

Also important to note is Netflix's P/E ratios. Netflix's 006 P/E ratio of 32.88 (2007) is showing a trend toward becoming more in line with the rest of the industry, which has a current P/E ratio of 29.17.[122] This high P/E ratio indicates that the market views Netflix as having a higher potential for future earning compared to others in the video rental industry. Netflix's P/E ratio has moved from an extremely high number in 2003 to its more stable current P/E ratio. Historic P/E ratios can be found in Exhibit 3.[123]

Company Liquidity

The current ratios for 2002–2006 can be found in Exhibit 6. Netflix has consistently had a high current ratio, always above 1.75.[124] As of December 2006, its current ratio was 2.20, while the rest of the industry had a less favorable ratio of .59.[125] At 2006 year end, the cash ratio was 2.09 and the debt ratio was .319. With all these ratios considered, Netflix seems to be in a favorable position. (See Exhibit 5 for balance sheet information.)

Company Profitability

Netflix has continued to increase revenues since its IPO at a significant rate.[126] The net profit margin has remained in the 4 to 6 range for the past three years and appears to be the most stable profitability ratio. This value is significantly lower than the industry's net profit margin at 14.80.[127] Return on assets, return on stockholders' equity, operating profit margin, and net profit margin have all been computed and listed in Exhibit 7.

Competitor and Industry Financial Ratios

See Exhibit 8 for a list comparing Netflix to its main competitors—Blockbuster, Hastings Entertainment, and Movie Gallery—and to other industry averages.

Exhibit 4 Income Statement

Income Statement
(in US$ thousands, except per share data)

	2002	2003	2004	2005	2006	2007 (est.)	2008E
Revenues	$150,818	$270,410	$500,611	$682,213	$996,660	$1,295,550	$1,595,890
Cost of revenues							
Subscription	77,044	147,736	273,401	393,788	532,621		
Fulfillment expenses	20,421	32,623	58,311	71,987	94,364		
Total cost of revenues	$ 97,465	$180,359	$331,712	$465,775	$626,985		
Gross profit	53,353	90,051	168,899	216,438	369,675		
Operating expenses							
Technology and development	$ 17,632	$ 21,863	$ 29,467	$ 35,388	$ 48,379		
Marketing	37,423	51,535	100,534	144,562	225,524		w
General and administrative	9,867	13,390	22,104	35,486	36,155		
Gain on disposal of DVDs	(896)	(1,209)	(2,560)	(1,987)	(4,797)		
Total operating expenses	$ 64,026	$ 85,579	$149,545	213,449	$305,261		
Operating income (loss)	$(10,673)	$ 4,472	$ 19,354	$ 2,989	$ 64,414		
Other income (expense)							
Interest and other income	1,697	2,457	2,592	5,753	15,904		
Interest and other expense	(11,972)	(417)	(170)	(407)	–		
Income (loss) before income taxes	$(20,948)	$ 6,512	$ 21,776	$ 8,335	$ 80,318		
Provisions for (benefit from) income taxes	–	–	181	(33,692)	31,236		
Net income (loss)	$(20,948)	$ 6,512	$ 21,595	$ 42,027	$ 49,082		
Net income (loss) per share:							
Basic	$ (0.74)	$ 0.14	$ 0.42	$ 0.79	$ 0.78	$ 0.79	$ 1.04
Diluted	$ (0.74)	$ 0.10	$ 0.33	$ 0.64	$ 0.71		
Weighted average shares outstanding							
Basic	$ 28,204	$ 47,786	$ 51,988	$ 53,528	$ 62,577		
Diluted	$ 28,204	$ 62,884	$ 64,713	$ 65,518	$ 69,075		
Year-end price per share	$ 5.51	$ 27.35	$ 12.33	$ 27.06	$ 25.86	$ 29.83	$ 21.79
Price/earnings ratios	(7.45)	273.50	37.36	42.28	36.42		

Sources: Netflix SEC10-K 2002, Netflix SEC10-K 2003, Netflix SEC10-K 2004, Netflix SEC10-K 2005, and Netflix SEC10-K 2006; http://stocks.us.reuters.com/stocks/estimates.asp?symbol=NFLX.

Exhibit 5 Balance Sheet

Balance Sheet (in US$ thousands, except share and per share data)					
	2002	2003	2004	2005	2006
Assets					
Current assets					
Cash and cash equivalents	$59,814	$89,894	$174,461	$212,256	$400,430
Short-term investments	43,796	45,297	–	7,848	4,742
Prepaid expenses	2,753	2,231	2,741	5,252	9,456
Prepaid revenue sharing expenses	303	905	4,695	13,666	3,155
Other current asses	409	619	5,449	4,669	10,635
Total current assets	107,075	138,946	187,346	243,691	428,418
DVD library, net	9,972	22,238	42,158	57,032	104,908
Intangible assets	6,094	2,948	961	457	969
Property and equipment, net	5,620	9,772	18,728	40,213	55,503
Deposits	1,690	1,272	1,600	1,249	1,316
Deferred tax assets	–	–	–	21,239	15,600
Other assets	79	836	1,000	800	2,065
Total assets	$130,530	$176,012	$251,793	$364,681	$608,779
Liabilities and Stockholders' Equity					
Current liabilities					
Accounts payable	$20,350	$32,654	$ 49,775	$ 63,491	$93,864
Accrued expenses	9,102	11,625	13,131	25,563	29,905
Deferred revenue	9,743	18,324	31,936	48,533	69,678
Current portion of capital lease obligations	1,231	416	68	–	–
Total current liabilities	40,426	63,019	94,910	137,587	193,447
Deferred rent	288	241	600	842	1,121
Capital lease obligations, less current portion	460	44	68	–	–
Total liabilities	$41,174	$63,019	$95,510	$138,429	194,568
Commitments and contingencies					
Stockholders' equity	45	51	53	55	69
Additional paid-in capital	260,044	270,836	292,843	315,868	454,731
Deferred stock-based compensation	(11,702)	(5,482)	(4,693)	–	–
Accumulated other comprehensive income (loss)	774	596	(222)	–	–
Accumulated deficit	(159,805)	(153,293)	(131,698)	(89,671)	(40,589)
Total stockholders' equity	$89,356	$112,708	$156,283	$226,252	$414,211
Total liabilities and stockholders' equity	$130,530	$176,012	$251,793	$364,681	$608,779

Sources: Netflix SEC10-K 2002, Netflix SEC10-K 2003, Netflix SEC10-K 2004, Netflix SEC10-K 2005, and Netflix SEC10-K 2006.

Netflix experienced some financial setbacks in the first quarter of 2007, most of which can be attributed to its key strategic challenges.

Key Strategic Challenges

Netflix faces a rapidly developing competitive environment with new technological innovations affecting product and service offerings among the various movie rental businesses, whether it be a brick-and-mortar store, click-and-mortar store, or online business. However, perhaps the main challenge Netflix will encounter is trying to figure out how to adjust its business model to the new technological pressures while staying true to the company's strengths and providing value to its subscribers.

Churn

Churn is the cancellation of a subscription service. Churn can be triggered by a number of factors: insufficient use of the service does not justify the expense; delivery is

Exhibit 6 Liquidity Ratio

	2002	**2003**	**2004**	**2005**	**2006**
Current ratio	2.65	2.20	1.97	1.77	2.20

Sources: Netflix SEC10-K 2002, Netflix SEC10-K 2003, Netflix SEC10-K 2004, Netflix SEC10-K 2005, and Netflix SEC10-K 2006.

Exhibit 7 Profitability Ratios

	2002	**2003**	**2004**	**2005**	**2006**
Return on assets (%)	−19.56	3.70	11.53	11.52	8.06
Return on stockholders' equity	−23.44	5.78	13.93	18.58	11.85
Operating profit	−13.89	2.41	4.35	1.22	8.06
Net profit margin	−13.89	2.41	4.31	6.16	4.92

Sources: Netflix SEC10-K 2002, Netflix SEC10-K 2003, Netflix SEC10-K 2004, Netflix SEC10-K 2005, and Netflix SEC10-K 2006.

Exhibit 8 Comparative Performance of Netflix and Key Competitors

	Blockbuster BBI	**Hastings Entertainment HAST**	**Movie Gallery MOVI.O**	**Netflix NFLX**	**Industry Median**
Profitability					
Gross profit margin	54.68%	67.62%	60.19%	37.09%	48.94%
Pre-tax profit margin	−0.15%	1.51%	−0.95%	8.06%	16.47%
Net profit margin	1.23%	0.59%	−1.01%	4.93%	14.82%
Return on equity	10.54%	5.22%	–	15.33%	11.84%
Return on assets	2.15%	1.26%	−2.03%	10.08%	6.37%
Valuation					
Price/Sales ratio	0.22	0.12	0.06	1.60	2.82
Price/Earnings ratio	21.43	13.99	–	32.92	18.97
Price/Book ratio	2.06	0.69	–	3.84	3.80
Operations					
Inventory turnover	7.57	3.28	7.30	–	27.08
Asset turnover	1.75	2.13	2.00	2.05	0.52
Financial					
Current ratio	1.12	1.63	0.89	2.22	0.63
Quick ratio	0.88	0.16	0.37	2.22	0.48
Total debt/Equity ratio	1.33	0.42	–	0.00	0.68

Sources: http://stocks.us.reuters.com/stocks/ratios.asp?symbol=NFLX.O&WTmodLOC=L2-LeftNav-16-Ratios; http://stocks.us.reuters.com/stocks/ratios.asp?symbol=BBI.N; http://stocks.us.reuters.com/stocks/ratios.asp?symbol=MOVI.OQ; http://www.investor.reuters.wallst.com/stocks/Ratios.asp?rpc=66&ticker=HAST.O.

too long; poor service; or competitive services provide better added value and/or experience to the consumer. These factors are critical to any online movie rental business, but especially for Netflix because its entire business model is based on attracting and maintaining subscribers (see Exhibits 9 and 10).

Some of the company's key competitors have more brand name recognition, experience, and financial resources to provide value to the customer. This makes it difficult for Netflix to compete at its existing price level or at lower price level structures in the future. Netflix needs to offer services that compete effectively.

Managing Growth

Finally, Netflix must have the ability and foresight to manage extensive growth to maintain its current service

Exhibit 9 Potential Growth for Netflix

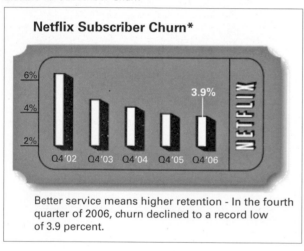

Total Online Subscribers
(in thousands)

37+% CAGR

20,000+

8,800

5,500

3,300

1,600

900

'02 '03 '04 '05 '06 '10 - 12E

NETFLIX

The overall market for online subscription rentals is still early in its growth cycle, according to estimates from Adams Media Research and internal Netflix estimates.

Exhibit 11 Subscriber Growth

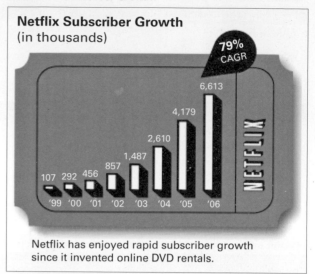

Netflix Subscriber Growth
(in thousands)

79% CAGR

6,613

4,179

2,610

1,487

857

107 292 456

'99 '00 '01 '02 '03 '04 '05 '06

NETFLIX

Netflix has enjoyed rapid subscriber growth since it invented online DVD rentals.

Exhibit 10 Subscriber Churn

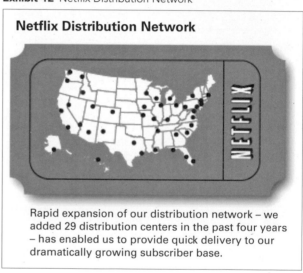

Netflix Subscriber Churn*

6%

4%

3.9%

2%

Q4'02 Q4'03 Q4'04 Q4'05 Q4'06

NETFLIX

Better service means higher retention - In the fourth quarter of 2006, churn declined to a record low of 3.9 percent.

Exhibit 12 Netflix Distribution Network

Netflix Distribution Network

NETFLIX

Rapid expansion of our distribution network – we added 29 distribution centers in the past four years – has enabled us to provide quick delivery to our dramatically growing subscriber base.

level. Since the company's launch in 1998, Netflix has seen phenomenal growth and profitability (see Exhibit 11). As the company grows, it must add additional distribution centers to its already existing infrastructure (see Exhibit 12). However, if the company does not properly prepare for a continual increase in clientele Netflix's managerial operations and financial resources could be spread too thin, which translates into orders not being met and customer satisfaction levels decreasing.

The Central Question

Reed Hastings started Netflix on the premonition that users would buy into his business concept of online movie rental without the hassle of late fees and due

dates while choosing a movie from the confines of their home. With Hastings's vision and charisma, along with his strong supporting cast of IT, marketing, and entertainment industry experts, Netflix set in motion a new wave of how consumers viewed the movie rental business. Netflix was the primary proponent of change in the movie rental business. Now, the key concern is how to cope with industry and technological trends that are evolving. Should Netflix transition from an online movie rental business to solely VOD or streaming services? Or can Netflix maintain its stronghold position with its current business model while making slight improvements to keep current with VOD and other new technologies? Should Netflix's strategic leaders and decision makers consider a merger or a joint venture with another company in order to offer a unique basket of services to consumers? Netflix must weigh its options carefully. It has established brand equity and delivered a distinctive solution during its short history. Now Netflix must realize how it can sustain its business livelihood in a cutthroat, highly competitive industry.

NOTES

1. 2006, Netflix Inc. Annual Report.
2. M. Helft, 2007, Netflix to deliver movies to the PC, *New York Times*, http://www.nytimes.com/2007/01/16/technology/16netflix.html?ex=1326603600&en=71618d2092f5b372&ei=5088&partner=rssnyt&emc=rss, January.
3. 2007, Hoover's Company Reports—Full Overview, Netflix, February 8.
4. 2007, Hoover's Company Reports—Full Overview, Blockbuster Inc., February 10.
5. 2007, Blockbuster Total Access—How It Works, http://www.blockbuster.com.
6. Ibid.
7. Ibid.
8. Ibid.
9. 2007, Netflix, Blockbuster competes for supremacy with new DVD services, *Pittsburgh Post Gazette*, January 30.
10. Hoover's company reports.
11. 2007, About Us, http://www.netflix.com, March.
12. 2007, First online DVD rental stores open, http://www.netflix.com/mediacenter, March.
13. 2007, Netflix's aggressive growth plan, http://www.netflix.com/mediacenter, March.
14. 2007, Netflix.com transforms DVD business eliminating late fees and due dates from movie rentals, http://www.netflix.com/mediacenter, March.
15. 2007, Netflix announces IPO, http://www.netflix.com/mediacenter, March.
16. 2004, Netflix announces Q4 revenue growth of 80% year over year and a 2-for-1 stock split, Netflix financial release, http://www.netflix.com, January 21.
17. 2006, Netflix announces Q4 2005 financial results, Netflix press release, http://www.netflix.com, January 24.
18. 2007, Netflix announces Q4 2006 financial results, Netflix press release, http:// www.netflix.com, January 24.
19. 2007, One billion and counting, http://www.netflix.com/mediacenter, March.
20. 2007, Netflix offers subscribers option of instantly watching movies on their PCs, http://www.netflix.com/mediacenter, March.
21. Ibid.
22. 2007, Netflix press release, http://www.netflix.com/MediaCenter, March 27.
23. 2007, http://www.netflix.com/mediacenter.
24. 2007, Netflix Hoover's Full Overview, http://premium.hoovers.com.
25. 2006 Netflix Inc. Annual Report.
26. 2007, Netflix board of director's committee composition, http://ir.netflix.com/committees.cfm.
27. J. Hopkins, 2006, Charismatic founder keeps Netflix adapting, *USA Today*, http://www.usatoday.com/money/companies/management/2006-04-23-exec-ceo-profile-netflix_x.htm, April 23.
28. Ibid.
29. Ibid.
30. 2007, Management, http://www.netflix.com/mediacenter.
31. Ibid.
32. Ibid.
33. Ibid.
34. Ibid.
35. Ibid.
36. Ibid.
37. P. Sauer, 2005, How I did it: Reed Hastings, Netflix, http://www.inc.com/magazine, December.
38. T. H. Davenport & J. G. Harris, 2007, Competing on analytics: The new science of winning, *The Nature of Analytical Competition*, http://harvardbusinessonline, 3.
39. Ibid., 4.
40. M. Kirdahy, 2007, Blockbuster takes on Netflix, *Forbes*, http://www.forbes.com, January 3.
41. 2007, Video on Demand (VOD): About Broadband Movies, Downloads and More, Broadbandinfo.com, http://www.broadbandinfo.com/got-high-speed/video-on-demand/default.html.
42. 2006, What's next for Netflix? *Financial Times*, http://www.ftpress.com/articles/article.asp?p=671844&rl=1, November 2.
43. 2007, The big picture, Hoovers.com, *Pittsburgh Tribune Review*, January 28.
44. Ibid.
45. 2007, Amazon.com, Amazon Unbox, http://www.amazon.com/gp/video/help/faq.html/ref=atv_dp_faq_dscvr/103-7381394-1357468#discover.
46. P. Gogoi, 2007, Wal-Mart enters the movie download wars, *BusinessWeek*, http://www.businessweek.com, February 6.
47. Ibid.
48. Ibid.
49. Ibid.
50. Ibid.
51. Ibid.
52. T. Krazit, 2004, Netflix, TiVo team up on broadband movie delivery, *PC World*, http://www.pcworld.com, September 30.
53. P. Sauer, How I did it: Reed Hastings, Netflix.
54. 2007, Blockbuster Inc., Netflix Full Overview, http://premium.hoovers.com, February 10.
55. Ibid.
56. Ibid.
57. Ibid.
58. Ibid.
59. Ibid.
60. 2000, Blockbuster Inc., Funding Universe—Company History, *International Directory of Company Histories*, http://www.fundinguniverse.com/company-histories/Blockbuster-Inc-Company-History.html.
61. Ibid.
62. Ibid.
63. Ibid.
64. Ibid.
65. Ibid.
66. Ibid.
67. Ibid.
68. Ibid.
69. Ibid.
70. Ibid.
71. 2007, Blockbuster CEO Antioco to leave company, *Yahoo! Finance*, http://www.finance.yahoo.com, March 23.
72. 2007, Blockbuster, Inc. Full Overview, Hoovers, http://premium.hoovers.com, February 10.
73. Ibid.
74. Ibid.
75. S. Ault, 2006, Blockbuster, Weinsteins sign exclusive deal, http://www.videobusiness.com.
76. M. Halkias, 2007, Blockbuster may buy downloading firm, *The Dallas Morning News*, March 1.
77. Ibid.

78. Ibid.
79. 2007, About Movie Gallery, Moviegallery.com, http://www .moviegallery.com, March 18.
80. Ibid.
81. 2007, Movie Gallery to introduce online video rental service and extend automated video vending machine program, *Movie Gallery* press release, http://phx.corporate-ir.net/phoenix .zhtml?c=85959&p=irol-newsArticle&ID=975465&highlight=, March 25.
82. 2007, Movie Gallery to launch online service, http://www .businessweek.com, March 19; R.C. Lim, 2007, Movie Gallery mayhem, *Motley Fool Stock Advisor*, www.fool.com/investing, July 24.
83. Ibid.
84. P. Sweeting & C. Spielvogel, 2007, Movie Gallery acquires MovieBeam, www.videobusiness.com, March 7; 2007, Movie Gallery News Release, http://www.moviegallery.com, March 7.
85. Ibid.
86. Ibid.
87. 2007, Hastings Entertainment, Hoovers.com, http://premium. hoovers.com/subscribe/co/overview.xhtml?ID=ffffctthjfcxryycrk, February 10.
88. 2007, About Hastings, Gohastings.com,http://www.gohastings .com/Investor/AboutHastings.stm, February 10.
89. 2007, Netflix Full Overview, http://premium.hoovers.com, February 10.
90. Ibid.
91. 2006, Netflix Inc. Annual Report.
92. Ibid.
93. Ibid.
94. 2007, Motion Picture access, major film studios in the U.S., http://ncam.wgbh.org/mopix/studios.html.
95. 2006, Netflix Inc. Annual Report.
96. Ibid.
97. Ibid.
98. Ibid.
99. Ibid.
100. Ibid.
101. Ibid.
102. Ibid.
103. Ibid.
104. M. Levy, 2002, Netflix analyzed via the value framework, http://www.valueframeworkinstitute.org/May2002/feature.article.htm, May.
105. T. H. Davenport & J. G. Harris, 2007, Competing on analytics.
106. Ibid.
107. Ibid.
108. Ibid.
109. Ibid.
110. 2006, Frequent Netflix renters sent to the back of the line, *Associated Press*, http://www.msnbc.msn.com/id/11262292/, February 10.
111. P. Sauer, 2005, How I did it: Reed Hastings, Netflix.
112. 2001, Best Buy and Netflix offer co-branded online DVD movie rental service, *Retailer Merchandiser*, http://www.allbusiness.com/retail, September 11.
113. P. Sauer, How I did it: Reed Hastings, Netflix.
114. 2006, Netflix Inc. Annual Report.
115. L. Punch, 2007, Advertising to the masses, http://www .internetretailer.com, January.
116. Ibid.
117. Ibid.
118. 2006 Netflix Inc. Annual Report.
119. Ibid.
120. Ibid.
121. 2007, Historical prices for Netflix Inc., *Yahoo! Finance*, http://finance .yahoo.com/q/hp?s=NFLX&a=00&b=5&c=2002&d=03&e=17&f=2 007&g=m.
122. 2007, Summary for Netflix Inc., *Yahoo! Finance*,http://finance.yahoo .com/q?s=nflx&x=0&y=0.
123. 2007, Netflix Inc. performance, http://stocks.us.reuters.com/stocks/performance.asp?symbol=NFLX.O&WTmodLOC=L2-LeftNav-18-Performace.
124. 2006, Netflix Inc. Annual Report.
125. 2007, Netflix Inc. ratios, http://stocks.us.reuters.com/stocks/ratios .asp?symbol=NFLX.O&WTmodLOC=L2-LeftNav-16-Ratios.
126. 2006, Netflix Inc. Annual Report.
127. Ibid.

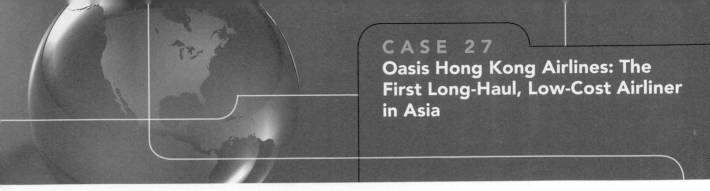

Gary Chan, Andrew Lee

The University of Hong Kong, Asia Case Research Centre

It was August 2006, and Stephen Miller, chief executive officer (CEO) of the newly founded Oasis Hong Kong Airlines, was busy rallying his management team for the purpose of launching Asia's first long-haul, low-cost carrier. Oasis intended to pioneer the concept of affordable business class and offer one-way economy-class fares between Hong Kong and London for as little as HK$1,000.[1] Miller was confident that with a unique business model, solid financial backing from a few entrepreneurial investors, and almost 30 years of experience in the aviation industry under his belt, he had what it took to make Oasis a success. Meanwhile, Miller stumbled upon a Singapore Airlines advertisement in the *South China Morning Post* offering a special round-trip fare from Hong Kong to London for HK$2,950 (US$378). As he glanced over the advertisement again, he decided that traditional airlines had thrown down the gauntlet and that the time had come for him to prove that his business model would prosper.

The Airline Industry

The International Airline Industry[2]

The shape of the international airline industry was largely the result of deregulation, privatization, liberal air traffic agreements, and economic downturns. The United States led the world in air traffic deregulation in 1977 when it deregulated its domestic air cargo market, allowing carriers the freedom to choose domestic routes and set fares. This was followed by deregulation in the passenger market, which started in 1978, relaxing restrictions on fares, routes, and mergers. By 1981, all restrictions on routes and services had been eliminated and, by 1983, all rate regulations were ended.

Within approximately 20 years after deregulation, the number of airlines operating in the United States had roughly doubled and passenger traffic had nearly tripled.[3] By one estimate, roughly 85 percent of passengers had a choice of at least two airlines in 2001. Meanwhile, air fares had fallen by 35 percent. Major airlines found themselves settling on a few major hubs as the foundation for connecting passenger and cargo traffic to other destinations. This structure came to be known as the hub-and-spoke.

As deregulation forced U.S. carriers to become more efficient and competitive, the competitive pressure was felt throughout the rest of the world and triggered a series of privatizations of flag carriers in Europe and Japan, many of which had been state-owned. British Airways, for instance, was restructured and floated in 1987. Similarly, in 2000, the Japanese government deregulated its domestic market and privatized Japan Airlines. Nonetheless, many European national carriers that sustained losses were still heavily subsidized by their respective governments, and other carriers outside of Europe and Japan, even if not state-owned, still maintained a very close relationship with their governments. For example, such flag carriers and listed companies as Singapore Airlines, China Airlines, and Air China were all majority-held by entities that could be traced back to their respective national governments.

International air traffic remained regulated by bilateral air services agreements that were negotiated between countries. These agreements were often very elaborate, detailing the granting of different traffic rights and specifying which airlines could fly which routes and at what capacity and frequency. Traffic rights described in these agreements were commonly known as Freedoms of the Air (see Exhibit 1). Since 1992, the United States had

Gary Chan and Andrew Lee prepared this case under the supervision of Dr. Venkat Subramanian for class discussion. This case is not intended to show effective or ineffective handling of decision or business processes.

Exhibit 1 Freedoms of the Air

First Freedom of the Air: The right or privilege, in respect of scheduled international air services, granted by one State to another State or States to fly across its territory without landing. This is also known as a **First Freedom Right.**

Second Freedom of the Air: The right or privilege, in respect of scheduled international air services, granted by one State to another State or States to land in its territory for non-traffic purposes. This is also known as a **Second Freedom Right.**

Third Freedom of the Air: The right or privilege, in respect of scheduled international air services, granted by one State to another State to put down, in the territory of the first State, traffic coming from the home State of the carrier. This is also known as a **Third Freedom Right.**

Fourth Freedom of the Air: The right or privilege, in respect of scheduled international air services, granted by one State to another State to take on, in the territory of the first State, traffic destined for the home State of the carrier. This is also known as a **Fourth Freedom Right.**

Fifth Freedom of the Air: The right or privilege, in respect of scheduled international air services, granted by one State to another State to put down and to take on, in the territory of the first State, traffic coming from or destined for a third State. This is also known as a **Fifth Freedom Right.**

   ICAO characterizes all freedoms beyond the Fifth Freedom as "so-called" because only the first five "freedoms" have been officially recognized as such by international treaty.

Sixth Freedom of the Air: The right or privilege, in respect of scheduled international air services, of transporting, via the home country of the carrier, traffic moving between two other countries. This is also known as a **Sixth Freedom Right.**

Seventh Freedom of the Air: The right or privilege, in respect of scheduled international air services, granted by one State to another State, of transporting traffic between the territory of the granting State and any third State with no requirement to include on such operation any point in the territory of the recipient State (i.e., the service need not connect to or be an extension of any service to or from the home State of the carrier). This is also known as a **Seventh Freedom Right.**

Eighth Freedom of the Air: The right or privilege, in respect of scheduled international air services, of transporting cabotage traffic between two points in the territory of the granting State on a service which originates or terminates in the home country of the foreign carrier or (in connection with the so-called "Seventh Freedom of the Air") outside the territory of the granting State. This is also known as an **Eighth Freedom Right** or **"consecutive cabotage."**

Ninth Freedom of the Air: The right or privilege of transporting cabotage traffic of the granting country on a service performed entirely within the territory of the granting country. This is also known as a **Ninth Freedom Right** or **"stand-alone cabotage."**

Source: ICAO, 2006, Freedoms of the air, http://www.icao.int/icao/en/trivia/freedoms_air.htm (accessed November 19, 2006).

been advocating and signing the so-called Open Skies agreements with foreign governments. These bilateral or multilateral agreements included unrestricted landing rights on each other's soil and unrestricted capacity and frequency; however, these agreements did not allow increased foreign ownership or control of airlines, nor did they grant cabotage freedom in the United States or U.S. domestic traffic rights, to foreign carriers. Meanwhile, the European Union (EU) was increasingly behaving like a single nation. In April 1997, the EU took a major step toward deregulation by allowing an airline from one member state to fly within another member's domestic market.[4] In 2000, the EU established the Common European Aviation Area, comprising all 15 member states and within which airlines of member states would have full traffic rights and ability to set fares.

Types of Carriers

There are three primary types of commercial carriers: scheduled airlines, charter airlines, and feeder airlines.

   Scheduled airlines, the most common type and the one with which most passengers are familiar, operate year-round on established schedules. International carriers of this type operate under the framework of the bilateral air services agreements described earlier. Any international carrier that obtains approval to operate under a bilateral agreement is a "designated carrier." Scheduled airlines sell their capacities directly to the public within specified fare levels, which must be filed with and approved by their respective governments.

   Charter airlines differ from scheduled airlines in that they do not operate on established schedules, but rather as ad hoc services, either to support the operations of scheduled airlines or to meet the demands of specific groups of customers. Charter airlines do not operate under the normal bilateral agreements, and each flight is separately approved by the respective governments. Some airlines that had started off as charter airlines eventually became scheduled airlines. From time to time, scheduled airlines also operate charter services.

   The third type of commercial carrier, feeder airlines, are mostly scheduled airlines operating smaller aircraft for the primary purpose of carrying passengers from smaller cities to larger air traffic hubs for connections with other flights. As the aviation industry evolved, many of these smaller feeder airlines either were bought out by their larger competitors or simply perished under the pressure of fierce competition. Because most feeder airlines operate domestic flights, their operations do not involve any bilateral agreements between nations.

Traditional and Low-Cost Carriers

A commercial scheduled airline could be either a traditional carrier or a low-cost carrier. While most commonly known airlines in 2006 (e.g., United Airlines, British Airways, Cathay Pacific Airways, and Singapore Airlines) were traditional carriers, the late 1990s and early 2000s saw a proliferation of low-cost carriers in almost every part of the world. Inspired by Southwest Airlines' impressive success, as indicated by the fact that Southwest was the only major U.S. airline in 2005 that had remained profitable since the September 11, 2001, terrorist attacks,[5] many attempted to replicate this firm's business model either in the United States or in other parts of the world. By 2006, examples of low-cost carriers could be found in all major regions of the world: Southwest and JetBlue in North America; Ryanair and easyJet in Europe; Kingfisher and Air Deccan in India; Tiger Airways, Jetstar Asia, and Valuair in Singapore; Air Asia in Malaysia; and Jetstar and Virgin Blue in Australia.

Traditional Carriers. Traditional carriers usually provide a full complement of options and services throughout the entire passenger experience, from the point when a booking is made to the end of the return flight. They allow passengers to book tickets through various means, including travel agents (usually via one or more global computer reservation systems) and directly with the airline (which could be by phone, in person, or online), and provide a choice of up to four classes of cabin service. Upon check-in, using the International Air Transport Association (IATA) interline system, a traditional airline can check passengers and their baggage through to connecting flights on other airlines and issue onward boarding passes. For premium-class passengers or members of loyalty clubs, a comfortable waiting lounge is provided with complimentary food and beverages, as well as other services. Once on board, passengers are provided with various in-flight amenities, reading materials, in-flight audio and video programs (on a broadcast or on-demand basis via personal TVs or cabin-based screens), and hot meals and beverages. For some overnight flights, lounges are also available for select passengers to freshen up upon arrival. Service agents are present at arrival gates to assist passengers with connecting flights. Most traditional carriers provide these services at no additional cost to passengers.

Operating on a scheduled basis with a hub-and-spoke model, traditional carriers have multiple origins of sales and multiple destinations. For example, Cathay Pacific Airways, a Hong Kong–based traditional carrier that offered service between Tokyo and Los Angeles via Hong Kong, would sell tickets in Tokyo for both the Tokyo–Hong Kong sector and the Tokyo–Los Angeles sector. At the same time, a portion of seats would be reserved to be sold in Hong Kong for the Hong Kong–Los Angeles sector of the same flight. The proportions of seats assigned to the Tokyo–Los Angeles, Tokyo–Hong Kong, and Hong Kong–Los Angeles sectors would vary from flight to flight, based on the forecasted yield and demand at any particular time of the year, with the overall objective of optimizing profit. There are also many different fare classes within each cabin class that carry different validities and restrictions.

Most traditional carriers serve a variety of long-, medium- and short-haul destinations with a variety of aircraft types. British Airways, for instance, serves destinations from its bases in the United Kingdom, ranging from other points in the United Kingdom that are flights shorter than one hour, to trips to New York, which would take 8 hours, and Hong Kong, which would take 14 hours. To serve such a broad range of destinations, British Airways's fleet at this time consisted of a wide variety of aircraft types: Boeing 737s, 747s, 757s, 767s, and 777s; Airbus A319s, A320s, and A321s; and a few other smaller aircraft types.[6]

Traditional carriers often use expensive primary airports as bases and hubs. The major advantage of this model is that airlines can schedule effectively and capture passengers from more origins to more destinations through the hubs. This additional revenue generation allows carriers to operate flights between cities where point-to-point demand alone does not justify the operation economically. By dominating a hub, airlines may also be able to limit competition on certain routes because the supply of slots at leading airports is limited. Nevertheless, any flight irregularities occurring at the hub can wreak havoc on an airline's entire network.

Traditional carriers usually offer loyalty clubs or frequent-flyer programs, which rewarded frequent travelers with such privileges as lounge access, upgrades, and free tickets. Typically, rewards are based primarily on mileage flown, though mileage could also be earned by purchasing from partnering companies or using airline-branded credit cards. To strengthen and expand their hub-and-spoke networks, traditional airlines have chosen to form alliances. These alliances link the networks of their various member airlines and offer alliance-wide loyalty clubs that provide passengers with privileges throughout an alliance's enlarged network. The world's three largest alliances are Star Alliance, Sky Team, and Oneworld. As of 2005, Star Alliance was the largest, with 18 full members (including Lufthansa Airlines, United Airlines, and Singapore Airlines), and an estimated 23.6 percent share of the international air travel market.[7] Sky Team was the second largest, with 10 full members (including Northwest Airlines, Air France-KLM, and Korean Airlines) and a world market share of 20.7 percent. Oneworld was the smallest among the top three, with eight full members (including American Airlines, British Airways, Cathay Pacific, and Qantas Airways) and a world market share of 13.5 percent.

Low-Cost Carriers.

The term "low-cost carriers" commonly refers to airlines that offer low ticket prices and limited services. However, when this term was first used, it referred specifically to carriers with lower operating-cost structures than traditional carriers. As competition and the overall business environment toughened, most airlines, traditional or otherwise, lowered their operating costs significantly, blurring the definition of the term. It was for this reason that low-cost carriers were later distinguished from traditional carriers by ticket prices and services rather than by cost structures.

Unlike traditional carriers, low-cost carriers tend not to use travel agents or computer reservation systems. Instead, they prefer to sell directly and limit their use of travel agents. Low-cost carriers usually provide a single-class cabin and very basic complimentary services such as soft drinks and peanuts. Southwest Airlines, for example, is well known for offering complimentary peanuts. Some also provide limited in-flight entertainment. One such example is JetBlue, which historically provided an in-flight entertainment system that broadcast satellite TV. Low-cost carriers commonly charge for additional services.

Low-cost carriers typically do not adopt the hub-and-spoke network business model. Instead, their networks consist of city pairs that support direct service, or point-to-point traffic. Many low-cost carriers believe that direct service is cheaper than the hub-and-spoke model. One industry observer even suggested that the cost of handling passengers in a hub-and-spoke system was as much as 45 percent higher than in a point-to-point system. With a simpler network, low-cost carriers also tend to have much simpler pricing systems and fewer fare classes than their traditional counterparts. To keep their costs low, low-cost carriers also fly to secondary airports. One example is easyJet, which, instead of flying in and out of London Heathrow, a major air transport hub in Europe, opted to base its London service out of London Gatwick.

Most low-cost carriers focus on short-haul services, flights of less than five hours. Because the type of operations of all the different flights is similar, low-cost carriers usually use just one type of aircraft. Since its inception, Southwest Airlines has flown only Boeing 737s. Although there were different versions of the 737 in the fleet, including the new generation 737, the commonality among the aircraft reduces the cost of both the spares inventory and the training of pilots, flight attendants, and maintenance personnel, and also facilitates quick turnarounds. Likewise, JetBlue adopted a similar model and flew only Airbus A320s, all with the same engine type.

Low-cost airlines were unlikely to be members of the IATA and did not value receiving feeder traffic or feeding traffic to other airlines. As a result, low-cost airlines do not complete interline check-ins or baggage transfers, nor are they members of an alliance. Indeed, Ryanair encourages passengers not to have any checked baggage[8] by reducing ticket prices by £2.5 for these passengers. In contrast, those with checked baggage have to pay £2.5 or £5.

Although typical low-cost carriers keep to themselves and do not collaborate with other airlines in the form of alliances, some are beginning to deviate a bit from this model. Southwest Airlines, which had an unprecedented 33 consecutive years of profit, is an example of a low-cost carrier doing so. In 2005, Southwest Airlines announced a code-sharing agreement[9] with ATA Airlines, allowing customers to book flights on ATA to fly to such destinations as Hawaii.[10] Some low-cost carriers also offer a simpler version of frequent-flyer programs. For example, Southwest Airlines operates a simple frequent-flyer program where points are accumulated based on the number of one-way trips, not mileage flown, and a free round-trip is rewarded for every 18 points accumulated. Similar to frequent flyer programs of traditional carriers, Southwest also allows spending on partner companies and through Southwest-branded credit cards to be converted into frequent flyer points.

Airline Economics

Airlines operate much like many other businesses in that the primary aim is to generate maximum revenue and incur minimum cost to maximize return on invested capital. For these firms, seats and cargo space, which travel at a particular time from one location to another, are the products. As products, passengers and cargo both have a very short shelf life (from the time the schedule is published to the time the gate closes for departure) and are perishable by nature (once an aircraft departs, any unsold products "perish").

To benchmark themselves against each other, airlines often examine their capacities in available seat kilometers (ASKs) for passenger service or available tonne kilometers (ATKs) for total capacity, including passenger and freight[11] (see Exhibit 2 for a glossary of airline terms). Two closely related benchmarks are

Exhibit 2 Glossary of Terms

Terms	Description
Available seat kilometer (ASK)	A measurement of an airline's passenger-carrying capacity, calculated by multiplying the number of seats available by the distance flown in kilometers. If miles are used, available seat mile (ASM) is used instead of ASK.
Available tonne kilometer (ATK)	A measurement of an airline's total capacity (including both passengers and cargo), calculated by multiplying the capacity in tonnes by the distance flown in kilometers. If miles are used, available ton mile (ATM) is used instead of ATK.
Block hours	The distance of a flight leg between two points, from the time when the aircraft is pushed back for takeoff to the time when the aircraft arrives at the gate. Compare with "flying hours."
Break-even load factor	The percentage load factor that represents the point at which an airline breaks even.
Cost per ASK	A unit cost measurement of an airline, calculated by dividing the total operating cost by ASK or ASM. This is regarded as an appropriate measurement for airlines with a predominant focus on passenger service.
Cost per ATK	A unit cost measurement of an airline, calculated by dividing the total operating cost by ATK or ATM. This is regarded as an appropriate measurement for airlines that provide only cargo service, or passenger as well as cargo service.
Cycle	A measurement of utilization, where one cycle equals one takeoff and landing.
Flying hours	The distance of a flight leg between two points, from the time when the aircraft lifts off the ground during takeoff to the time when the aircraft touches the ground during landing. Compare with "block hours."
Load factor	A measurement of capacity utilization in percentage, calculated by dividing RPK by ASK, or RTK by ATK.
Narrow-body aircraft or single-aisle aircraft	An aircraft that has a fuselage diameter of about 3 to 4 meters and has only one aisle in its seat arrangement.
Revenue passenger kilometer (RPK)	A measurement of passenger volume carried by an airline, calculated by multiplying the number of revenue-generating passengers by the distance flow in kilometers. If miles are used, revenue passenger mile (RPM) is used instead of RPK.
Revenue tonne kilometer (RTK)	A measurement of total volume carried by an airline, calculated by multiplying the revenue tonnage by the distance flown in kilometers. If ton and mile are used, revenue ton mile (RTM) is used instead of RTK.
Seat pitch	The distance between two rows of seats, typically in inches, measured from the back of one seat to the back of the seat directly behind it.
Sector	A sector is a direct flight between two cities and is usually represented by the city pair names. For example, Hong Kong–London is one sector and London–Hong Kong is another sector.
Sector length or stage length	The distance of a flight leg measured either in physical distance in kilometers (or miles) or time in hours. When it is measured in time, it can be represented in block hours or flying hours, depending on the purpose.
Wide-body aircraft or twin-aisle aircraft	An aircraft that has a fuselage diameter of about 5 to 6 meters and has only two aisles in its seat arrangement.

Sources: Adapted from http://moneyterms.co.uk, http://en.wikipedia.org, and industry sources.

revenue passenger kilometers (RPKs) and revenue tonne kilometers (RTKs); these benchmarks measure the number of seat kilometers or tonne kilometers that an airline sold during a particular period of time. To measure their financial performance, airlines published their unit costs in cost per ASK or ATK. The fraction of RPK over ASK yields the passenger load factor while the fraction of RTK over ATK shows the overall load factor.

For airlines focusing on passenger service, cost per ASK is used as a primary measure of unit cost. For airlines that also have a sizeable cargo service, a combined measurement, including cost per ATK, is used. Airlines also measure their ability to generate revenue with revenue per ASK and revenue per ATK.

Armed with these numbers and various other figures and forecasting tools, airlines employ sophisticated inventory management and pricing techniques to maximize revenue and profitability and to lower their breakeven load factors (see Exhibits 3 and 4 for the ASKs, ATKs, RPKs, RTKs, and related data of selected airlines).

Exhibit 3 Income Statements and Company Information of Two Low-Cost Carriers

	Southwest Airlines Year Ending December 31, 2005 (in US$ millions)	EasyJet Year Ending September 30, 2005 (in UK£ millions)
Total operating revenue		
Passenger	7,279	1,254
Freight	133	
Other	172	87
	7,584	1,341
Total operating expenses		
Salaries, wages & benefits	2,702[a]	267
Fuel & oil	1,342	260
Maintenance & repairs	430	119
Aircraft rentals	163	124
Landing fees & other rentals	454	339
Depreciation & amortization	469	37[d]
Other operating expenses	1,204	148
	6,764	1,293
Total operating income	820	49
Other expenses (income)		
Interest expense	122	8
Interest income	(47)	(27)
Other (gains) losses, net	(129)	0
	(54)	(19)
Profit before tax	874	68
Taxes	326	25
Net income	548	43

Exhibit 3 Income Statements and Company Information of Two Low-Cost Carriers *(Continued)*

	Southwest Airlines Year Ending December 31, 2005 (in US$ millions)	EasyJet Year Ending September 30, 2005 (in UK£ millions)
Other information		
Fleet size (averaged)	431[b]	94
Aircraft types	Boeing 737	Boeing 737, Airbus A319
Total trips flown	1,028,639	229,068
Average trips per aircraft per day	6.5[b]	6.7[b]
Average stage length (block hour)	1.84[b]	1.75
Average hours per aircraft per day	12.02[b]	11.70[b]
RPK (thousand)	96,356,960[c]	27,448,000
ASK (thousand)	136,276,472[c]	32,141,000
Passenger load factor	70.7 percent	85.4 percent
Passenger revenue per ASK	5.57 cents	4.17 pence
Operating cost per ASK	4.96 cents	3.97 pence[e]

Notes: Income statement items have been aligned for comparison purposes; [a] included handling charges; [b] estimated by case writer; [c] converted from ASM/RPM; [d] included goodwill amortization of £17.4 m; [e] before goodwill.

Sources: Southwest Airlines, 2005, Annual Report; easyJet, 2005, Annual Report.

Exhibit 4 Income Statements and Selected Information of Two Traditional Airlines

	British Airways Year Ending March 31, 2006 (in UK£ million)	Cathay Pacific Airways Year Ending December 31, 2005 (in HK$ million)
Total operating revenue		
Passenger	6,820	30,274
Freight	498	12,852
Other	1,197[a]	7,783
	8,515	50,909
Total operating expenses		
Salaries, wages & benefits	2,346	9,025
Fuel & oil	1,632	15,588
Maintenance & repairs	473	4,527
Aircraft rentals	112	4,893[e]
Landing fees & other rentals	559	6,947
Depreciation & amortization	717	790[f]
Other operating expenses	1,971[b]	4,996[g]
	7,810	46,766
Total operating income	705	4,143

Exhibit 4 Income Statements and Selected Information of Two Traditional Airlines *(Continued)*

	British Airways Year Ending March 31, 2006 (in UK£ million)	Cathay Pacific Airways Year Ending December 31, 2005 (in HK$ million)
Other expenses (income)		
Interest expense	221	1,605
Interest income	(93)	(1,161)
Other (gains) losses, net	(43)	(269)
	85	175
Profit before tax	620	3,968
Taxes	153	500
Net income	467	3,468
Other information		
Fleet size (averaged)	281[c]	93
Aircraft types	10 major types	4 major types
Total trips flown	368,000	84,000
Average trips per aircraft per day	3.6[c]	2.5[c]
Average stage length (block hour)	2.83[c]	5.06[c]
Average hours per aircraft per day	10.14	12.60
RPK	111,859,000	65,110,000
ASK	147,934,000	82,766,000
Passenger load factor	75.6 percent	78.7 percent
Passenger revenue per ASK	4.61 pence[d]	HK$0.37
ATK	23,106,000	17,751,000
Total revenue per ATK	31.67 pence	HK$2.87
Operating cost per ATK	28.62 pence	HK$2.19

Notes: Income statement items have been aligned for comparison purposes; [a] included fuel surcharge; [b] included selling cost of £449 m; [c] case writer's estimates; [d] before fuel surcharge; [e] for Cathay Pacific this category should be "aircraft depreciation and leases"; [f] for Cathay Pacific this category should be "non-aircraft depreciation and leases"; [g] included commission of HK$555 million.

Sources: British Airways, 2006, Annual Report; Cathay Pacific Airways, 2005, Annual Report.

Airline Cost Structure. Personnel, fuel, capital cost and maintenance cost of assets, selling expenses, and airport and landing fees are the major costs airlines incur. Personnel-related costs are among the largest of the incurred costs for major airlines. Typically, airlines employ large labor forces including pilots, flight attendants, engineers, mechanics, airport service agents, and support staff. Labor in the airline industry is highly unionized, especially in North America and Europe, though strong pilots' and flight attendants' unions were also found in Asia. In 2005, labor costs for a major airline represented 20 to 40 percent of total costs.

The cost of fuel is a major concern for all airlines due to the huge increase in oil prices in the first decade of the 21st century. In 2005 for example, fuel represented approximately 20 to 30 percent of an airline's operating costs in contrast to around 12 to 15 percent during most of the 1990s. A successful fuel hedge program could save an airline a significant amount of money. Southwest Airlines was renowned for its fuel hedging program. In 2005, fuel cost represented about 20 percent of Southwest's operating cost. In 2006, its fuel expenses were approximately 73 percent hedged at about US$36 per barrel, which translated into savings of hundreds of millions of U.S. dollars.

In addition to the costs of offices, fixtures, office equipment, and ticketing equipment, airlines incur substantial capital costs to purchase aircraft and the flight simulators that are used to train pilots. In 2006, the Boeing 737 and the Boeing 777 were the best selling families of the firm's commercial planes. At this time, the list price of a Boeing 737, a single-aisle, narrow-bodied aircraft, ranged between US$47 million and US$80 million. A Boeing 777, a twin-aisle, wide-bodied aircraft, was priced between US$180 million and US$260 million. Although the actual purchase price was usually at least 15 to 20 percent lower than the list price,[12] aircraft capital costs are substantial. Airlines typically finance their purchase of aircraft through a finance/lease[13] arrangement. An operating lease[14] is a viable alternative, but with a typical monthly lease rate of 1 percent of the purchase price for a long-term lease, the rental cost for a brand-new Boeing 737 was still around US$600,000 a year in 2006 while that of a Boeing 777 was US$2.64 million a year.

The cost of maintaining aircraft and engines is another major expense for an airline, accounting for about 6 to 10 percent of operating costs. Managing maintenance costs is interwoven with asset and fuel cost management. For instance, an airline needs to balance the average age of its aircraft (capital costs of older aircraft tended to be cheaper) with maintenance costs, which tend to be more expensive as aircraft age. Also, as aircraft and engines age and enter their heavy maintenance cycles, ground time of up to 45 days for aircraft and 90 days for engines is required, necessitating additional aircraft or engines to uphold schedule integrity. Fuel cost management also plays a part, as older assets are usually less efficient and consume more fuel.

Selling expenses are another category of operational costs for an airline. Traditionally, air tickets were bought through travel agents, who subscribed to global computer reservation systems where airlines made bookings and reservations available. Airlines incurred costs through paying agency commissions and charges for using global computer reservation systems. In the fiscal year ending March 2006, British Airways's selling cost was £449 million (US$829 million), amounting to 5 percent of its total turnover. However, as online bookings and direct sales increased, the cost of agency commissions also came

down, especially for low-cost carriers. In 2001, 25 percent of Southwest Airlines's ticket sales were through travel agents, while 24 percent came from reservation centers (where customers could call to make reservations directly) and 39 percent from the Internet. By 2005, Southwest's reliance on travel agents and reservation centers dropped to 11 percent and 15 percent, respectively, while sales generated through the Internet rose to 65 percent.

Operating aircraft incurs airport charges, landing fees, and route costs. For example, British Airways's landing fees and en-route costs amounted to £559 million (US$1.032 billion), or 6.6 percent of total turnover, in the fiscal year ended in March 2006. In stark contrast, easyJet, British Airways's low-cost counterpart, spent £438 million (US$808 million), or 25.2 percent of turnover, on airport charges and navigation expenses.

Airline Profitability. A report published by IATA in 2006,[15] which studied the fiscal performance of 85 of the world's major carriers who together accounted for 85 percent of worldwide passenger numbers and the vast majority of global freight volumes, found that eight of them made operating profits in excess of US$500 million each, among which three made more than US$1 billion. On the other hand, 20 of the carriers surveyed had incurred operating losses, with nine having lost more than US$100 million each. Asian and European carriers were among the highest profit generators, whereas 9 of the 20 who lost money were U.S. carriers. Only 14 carriers had operating margins of greater than 10 percent, many of which were low-cost carriers (see Exhibit 6).

Experience in the United States further suggested that low-cost carriers operating on a point-to-point model displayed higher aircraft utilization rates, lower unit operating costs, and higher staff productivity. For example, in 2004, JetBlue's A320 fleet had an average utilization rate of 13.6 block hours per day, 46 percent higher than Northwest's A320 fleet, and a unit operating cost of US$0.032 per available seat mile (ASM), compared to Northwest's US$0.051.[16]

In Asia, airlines such as Cathay Pacific Airways, Singapore Airlines, Qantas, and Emirates Airlines were among the most profitable commercial carriers in the world, yet they all operated on the traditional hub-and-spoke model. Collectively, these airlines generated over US$6.4 billion in net profits between 2003 and 2005, even after the severe acute respiratory syndrome (SARS) pandemic nearly caused the Asian air travel market to grind to a complete halt in 2003.

Asia also differed from the United States in that the majority of Asian countries did not have large domestic air travel markets, and there were a limited number of secondary airports, which low-cost carriers could use as operating bases. This meant that low-cost carriers were faced with high airport charges, which was contrary to

Exhibit 5 Operating Profits by Airline, Fiscal Year 2005 (* = fiscal 2004)

By Total Operating Profit			By Operating Profit Margin		
Rank	Airline	US$ (mil)	Rank	Airline	%
1	FedEx*	1.414	1	Gol Airlines	23.3
2	British Airways	1,330	2	Ryanair	21.8
3	Air France-KLM	1.200	3	Air Asia	18.9
4	Lufthansa	377	4	COPA	17.3
5	Southwest	820	5	Kenya Airlines	15.6
6	Emirates	786	6	Philippine Airlines	13.7
7	All Nippon	776	7	DHL International*	12.5
8	Qantas*	775	8	Kalitta Air	12.3
9	Singapore Airlines	590	9	Emirates	11.9
10	Cathay Pacific	533	10	Mesa Airlines	11.7
11	Ryanair	459	11	American Eagle	11.3
12	Air China	458	12	SkyWest	11.2
13	Iberia	457	13	Southwest	10.8
14	Air Canada	388	14	Jet Airways	10.3
15	UPS Airlines	293	15	Air China	9.6
16	Thai Airlines	269	16	Virgin Blue	9.6
17	Gol Airlines	266	17	TAM	9.5
18	TAM	232	18	Singapore Airlines	9.1
19	American Eagle	225	19	Royal Jordanian	9.0
20	SkyWest	220	20	Qantas*	8.9
21	Korean Airlines	207	21	Atlantic Southeast	8.5
22	Virgin Blue	184	22	British Airways	8.3
23	China Eastern*	179	23	Aer Lingus	8.2
24	LAN Airlines	142	24	Cathay Pacific	8.1
25	Asiana*	136	25	FedEx*	7.2

Source: IATA, 2006, IATA economic briefing, June 2006.

their basic operating principles. Recently, however, this situation began to change. In 2006, both Singapore's Changi Airport and Malaysia's new airport in Kuala Lumpur opened separate, no-frills terminals that catered to low-cost carriers' needs. However, the airport authority of Hong Kong showed no interest in following suit.

Front-End (Business- and First-Class) Traffic Revenue Contribution.

For a typically configured Boeing 747-400 aircraft flying on a popular transatlantic route between the United States and Europe, the revenue split between first, business, and economy classes would be roughly 20 percent, 60 percent, and 20 percent, respectively. In 2006, typical published fares for such a flight would be around US$14,000, US$7,000, and US$750, with the aircraft equipped with 14, 79, and 265 seats, respectively, for the three classes. Because of the differences between carriers in short-haul and long-haul mixes, primary target markets, load factors, aircraft types, and so on, the resulting revenue mix across the three classes could vary significantly.

In the first half of 2006, front-end traffic accounted for 11 percent of all international traffic and 15 percent of long-haul routes. During this period, the top five route areas accounted for 72 percent of all front-end traffic volume, falling from 82 percent in 2000. Routes within Europe accounted for around one-third of all international front-end traffic, while routes between Europe and East Asia contributed 14 percent (see Exhibit 6). Because of the strong rebounds in trade and investment after the decline triggered by the September 11th terrorist attacks in 2001, front-end traffic between Europe and Asia had grown faster than overall traffic, contributing to strong revenues for airlines in 2005 and 2006.[17]

The International Airline Industry in 2006.

In the five years following the September 11, 2001, terrorist attacks, the average financial performance of commercial airlines around the world improved substantially, except for the second and third quarters of 2003, when carriers operating in Asia were badly hit by the SARS pandemic. Between 2000 and 2006, total revenues increased from US$329 billion to a projected US$450 billion while the number of passengers carried increased from 1.672 billion to a projected 2.154 billion, representing an increase of 36.8 percent and 28.8 percent, respectively. Cargo volume grew from 30.4 million tonnes to 39.8 million tonnes, a 30.9 percent increase. Operating profit fluctuated from a high of US$10.7 billion in 2000 to a

loss of US$11.8 billion in 2001 due to the 9–11 terrorist attacks, but rebounded to a projected US$9.8 billion in 2006. However, as fuel expenses skyrocketed from US$46 billion to a projected US$115 billion (a 150 percent increase), airlines' net profit actually decreased from US$3.7 billion to a projected loss of US$1.7 billion. When broken down geographically, North American carriers incurred a US$4.5 billion loss, followed by African carriers at US$0.8 billion. European and Asian carriers earned net profits of US$1.8 billion and US$1.7 billion, respectively.[18]

The Airline Industry in Hong Kong.

Located in southern China and historically an important trade port between the East and the West, Hong Kong's catchment area (within five hours of flight time) included most of the urban centers in East Asia, whose cumulative population was about 2 billion in the late 1990s.[19] With flights connecting to over 40 cities in the Chinese Mainland, Hong Kong was also the leading gateway to the rapidly growing Chinese market. In 2005, over 78 scheduled airlines served the Hong Kong International Airport, providing about 5,300 scheduled passenger and all-cargo flights each week between Hong Kong and more than 140 destinations worldwide. In the same year, the airport handled some 40.7 million passengers and 3.4 million tonnes of cargo, making Hong Kong the fifth-busiest international passenger airport and the busiest airport for international cargo in the world. In 2005, the airport also saw more than 19.8 million passenger departures.[20] Among them, South-East

Exhibit 6 Distribution of Front-End Traffic Volume by Route, January–May 2006

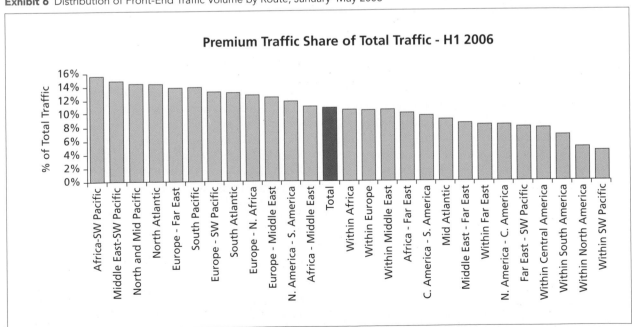

Source: IATA, 2006, IATA economic briefing, August 2006.

Asian destinations contributed 24 percent to the total, followed by mainland China at 21 percent and Taiwan at 19 percent. The remaining traffic was divided among Japan, Europe, North America, Australia, and others.[21]

According to the *Current Market Outlook 2005* published by Boeing,[22] passenger air travel would grow at an annual rate of 4.8 percent from 2005 to 2024, while cargo was forecast to grow at an annual rate of 6.2 percent. In Europe and North America, where the air travel market was mature, a slower growth of 3.4–5.5 percent was expected. The Asia-Pacific region was expected to be a major source of growth. Intra-regional traffic was expected to grow at an annual rate of 5.1 percent, while China was forecast to have an annual growth rate of 8.8 percent in this area. Traffic between Europe and Asia-Pacific was expected to grow 5.4 percent annually, while traffic between North America and Asia-Pacific, 6 percent.

Industry observers believed that Hong Kong, being a major air transport hub between the Far East and the Western world, was uniquely positioned to reap the benefits of this growing trend. However, they cautioned that the growing and rapidly improving mainland Chinese airports might challenge Hong Kong's position as a leading gateway to China. The Guangzhou Baiyun International Airport, Macau International Airport, Shenzhen Baoan International Airport, and Zhuhai Airport are all within 30 minutes by air from Hong Kong and the catchment area of the Pearl River Delta. In addition, direct traffic from Beijing's Capital Airport and Shanghai's Pudong International Airport to Europe and North America was also expected to increase during the 2008 Beijing Olympics and the 2010 Shanghai World Expo.

In response, Hong Kong had been extending its airport's market reach to serve the Pearl River Delta's population of 48 million, as well as the rest of China.[23] Since the early 2000s, Hong Kong International Airport has established multi-modal links that connect Hong Kong with other cities in the Pearl River Delta: the SkyPier provides frequent ferry connections to selected Pearl River Delta cities (including the four airports) and the SkyLimo provides coach services to and from major Pearl River Delta cities. Additionally, there were more than 170 daily coach trips operating between more than 40 Pearl River Delta cities and Hong Kong International Airport. In 2003, the Hong Kong Airport Authority (HKAA) signed a letter of intent with Shanghai Airport Authority to strengthen exchanges and facilitate closer cooperation between the two airports. In 2005, HKAA agreed to buy a major stake in the Hangzhou Xiaoshan International Airport.

Airlines in Hong Kong

In late 2006, seven airlines used Hong Kong as their home base. Among them, six were commercial airlines providing scheduled services to the public: Cathay Pacific Airways, Hong Kong Dragon Airlines, Air Hong Kong, CR Airways, Hong Kong Express Airways, and Oasis Hong Kong Airlines.

Cathay Pacific Airways. Founded in 1946 by American Roy C. Farrell and Australian Sydney H. de Kantzow, Cathay Pacific Airways was Hong Kong's largest airline and de facto flag carrier. The airline started with passenger service to destinations such as Shanghai, Manila, Singapore, Bangkok, and Guangzhou. In 1948, Butterfield & Swire (which later became the Swire Group) bought 45 percent of the airline and subsequently increased its stake to 5.2 percent. Since the 1960s, the airline has undergone significant expansion, both in fleet size and in the number of destinations served. By 2006, Cathay Pacific served 90 passenger and cargo destinations worldwide and had a fleet of 100 aircraft, including the Boeing 747 and 777 series and the Airbus A330 and A340 series. The average age of its fleet was seven years and the longest non-stop flight on its regular schedule was its Hong Kong–New York flight at 12,968 km and roughly 16 hours of flying time. It operated four daily flights to London's Heathrow airport, two using Airbus A340–300s and two using Boeing B747–400s, with all four offering three classes of service.

Cathay Pacific had a reputation as one of the industry's best airlines, with regular and frequent updates of seats, entertainment systems, meal options, and other in-flight amenities. Its latest first-class seats are equipped with 17-inch personal TVs with Audio-Video on Demand ("AVOD"), massage functions, extendable meal tables, and the largest pitch-flat beds available on a scheduled commercial airline, all enclosed within private areas. Meals could be selected and served at any time. Passengers also received preferential check-in service, access to exclusive lounge facilities, priority luggage handling, and other personalized services. Personal TVs with AVOD were also standard for its business-class service. Menus were created in cooperation with leading local fine-dining establishments and a broad wine selection was also available to passengers in both first and business class. Among its numerous industry awards, Cathay Pacific was named "Airline of the Year" by *Skytrax* in 2003 and 2005 and by *Air Transport World* in 2006.[24]

Cathay Pacific was a founding member of Oneworld. The airline had established a large number of code-share agreements with other carriers, including Air China, American Airlines, British Airways, Japan Airlines, Qantas, and Malaysian Airlines. Cathay Pacific had two loyalty programs: the Marco Polo Club, reserved exclusively for Cathay Pacific customers, and Asia Miles, where membership was available to customers of a number of participating airlines and other merchants, such as restaurants, hotels, and entertainment establishments.

Hong Kong Dragon Airlines.[25] In May 1985, Hong Kong Dragon Airlines ("Dragonair") was established as a wholly owned subsidiary of Hong Kong Macau International Investment Co. on the initiative of a local shipping tycoon, K. P. Chao. The airline, however, struggled under the one-airline-one-route policy of the then British colonial government of Hong Kong. In 1990, CITIC Pacific, the Swire Group, and Cathay Pacific acquired an 89 percent stake in Dragonair. As a result, Dragonair transitioned into a regional carrier with a focus on mainland Chinese destinations. In 1996, at the onset of the sovereignty change of Hong Kong from being a British colony to becoming a Special Administration Region of the People's Republic of China, the China National Aviation Corporation ("CNAC") purchased a 35.86 percent interest in Dragonair, becoming the largest shareholder. CITIC Pacific remained the second-largest shareholder, with a 28.5 percent stake, while the Swire Group and Cathay Pacific together held a 25.5 percent stake.

The new shareholding structure allowed Dragonair to develop outside the shadows of Cathay Pacific. The year 2000 marked a watershed for Dragonair, when it introduced its all-cargo service with a Boeing 747-200 special freighter, competing directly with Air Hong Kong, a wholly owned subsidiary of Cathay Pacific. The following five years saw Dragonair's passenger fleet double in size to 30 aircraft and its freighter fleet grow to four. Meanwhile, Dragonair established its own frequent-flyer program; rolled out a new cabin interior with lie-flat seats and personal TVs in the premium classes; competed with Cathay Pacific head-to-head on passenger services to Taipei, Bangkok, and Tokyo; and won numerous accolades for its outstanding service in the mainland Chinese market.

In June 2006, a joint announcement was made by Air China (the parent company of CNAC and China's flag carrier), CNAC, CITIC Pacific, the Swire Group, and Cathay Pacific about a shareholding realignment that resulted in a cross-shareholding between Air China and Cathay Pacific and made Dragonair a wholly owned subsidiary of Cathay Pacific.[26]

Air Hong Kong.[27] Founded in 1986 and initiating charter services in 1988 with a Boeing 707 freighter, Air Hong Kong was Hong Kong's only all-cargo operator. In 1994, Cathay Pacific bought a 75 percent stake in the company, strengthening Air Hong Kong's market and giving it access to Cathay Pacific's distribution system. In February 2002, Cathay Pacific acquired the remaining 25 percent stake in Air Hong Kong, making it a wholly owned subsidiary. In October 2002, Cathay Pacific and DHL Express announced a joint venture in which DHL Express acquired 30 percent of Air Hong Kong. Under the agreement, an initial investment of about US$300 million was to be committed by 2004 and a further US$100 million by 2010 to purchase a fleet of long-range, wide-body freighters to operate DHL Express's network connecting the major cities in the Asia-Pacific region. In March 2003, DHL Express acquired an additional 10 percent stake in Air Hong Kong from Cathay Pacific. By mid-2006, Air Hong Kong's fleet included eight A300-600GFs and one wet lease[28] Airbus A300-600F, and operated a freighter service network between Hong Kong and Tokyo, Osaka, Seoul, Taipei, Bangkok, Penang, Singapore, and Shanghai.

CR Airways and Hong Kong Express Airways. CR Airways was founded in 2001 and began service with Bombardier CRJ200 and CRJ700 regional jets.[29] In December 2005, it was reported that Hainan Airlines, a mainland Chinese carrier based on the island of Hainan, was interested in acquiring a 60 percent stake in CR Airways. In the same month, CR Airways announced the signing of a Memorandum of Understanding with Boeing to acquire thirty 737-800s and ten 787 Dreamliners. Hainan Airlines later revealed that it would reduce its stake in CR Airways to 45 percent to ensure that CR Airways remained a Hong Kong–based airline. In early 2006, the acquisition was given the green light by the government. CR Airways's service network changed rapidly as new routes were tested for viability and as the airline phased in the 737-800s, the first of which was delivered in early 2006 and coincided with the launch of services to Changsha and Tianjin. More destinations were slated to be added to the network in the second half of 2006, including Chengdu, Xian, Nanjing, and Fuzhou in China, as well as Seoul, Taegu, and Pusan in South Korea. CR Airways was also keen to begin long-haul service and was planning to operate Boeing 777s in the interim before the arrival of its Boeing 787s (which were expected to be delivered from 2010 onwards).

Hong Kong Express Airways Limited (formerly Helicopters Hong Kong Limited) was 51 percent owned by Macau casino tycoon Stanley Ho. Hong Kong Express wanted to take advantage of liberalization of air service between Hong Kong and the Chinese mainland. In September 2005, Hong Kong Express launched its first service to Guangzhou. As the fleet expanded, it added such destinations as Hangzhou, Ningbo, Chongqing, and Chengdu in China, as well as Chiang Mai in Thailand. However, six months after starting service to Guangzhou, they cancelled this route because the load factor fell short of the 30 percent target.[30] In May 2006, Hong Kong Express acknowledged that negotiations were under way regarding a possible capital injection from Hainan Airlines and a merger with CR Airways.[31]

Oasis Hong Kong Airlines

Oasis Hong Kong Airlines was founded by ex-Dragonair CEO Stephen Miller, with principal investment from property developer Raymond Lee and his wife Priscilla. Oasis had a definitive positioning as the only long-haul, low-fare airline operating out of Hong Kong. After developing the idea of a long-haul, low-fare carrier, Miller went to Lee with a proposal. Although initially skeptical, Lee eventually agreed to invest in the proposal Miller brought to him. The Lees provided the majority of the seed funding, which was supplemented by additional investments from Allan Wong, chairman and CEO of VTech Holdings (a multinational corporation), and Richard K. Lee, founder of Trinity Textiles.[32]

The Oasis Model

Oasis marketed itself as a long-haul, low-fare carrier that offered exceptional value with customizable options. It offered two classes of service, targeting both economy- and business-class passengers, whereas other low-cost carriers only offered economy-class service and competed primarily on price. While all other low-cost carriers served short-haul routes, Oasis would only serve long-haul routes. The initial network plan of Oasis included Oakland and Chicago in the United States, Berlin and Cologne in Germany, Milan in Italy, and London Gatwick in the United Kingdom, which would be the airline's launch destination.[33]

While Oasis did not position itself to be a low-cost carrier, competitive pricing was nevertheless one of its competitive advantages. Oasis only sold one-way tickets,

which, on the Hong Kong-London route, would sell for as low as HK$1,000 (US$128) for an economy class seat and HK$6,600 (US$846) for a business class seat, excluding taxes and surcharges. In the long run, at least 10 percent of seats would continue to be sold at these fares.[34] In contrast, for a Hong Kong–London round-trip economy-class ticket departing on October 31, 2006, and returning on November 10, 2006, Cathay Pacific's prices varied from HK$5,880 (US$754) to HK$9,550 (US$1,224), depending on the level of travel restrictions, while British Airways's prices ranged from HK$2,250 (US$288) to HK$4,525 (US$580), and Virgin Atlantic's fell between HK$5,532 (US$709) and HK$17,263 (U$4,525). At these prices, Cathay Pacific was 190 to 380 percent more expensive than Oasis, 112.5 to 130 percent more expensive than British Airways, and 180 to 760 percent more expensive than Virgin Atlantic. For business-class tickets, Cathay Pacific charged HK$44,952 (US$5,763), British Airways HK$21,350 (US$2,737), and Virgin Atlantic between HK$44,897 (US$5,756) and HK$46,813 (US$6,002). In addition to attractive prices, Oasis also had a relatively simple, easily understood fare structure, which the firm expected customers would find appealing (see Exhibit 7).

Operating long-haul flights would also allow the airline to have high average aircraft utilization and efficiency. It was expected that Oasis could achieve average aircraft utilization in excess of 15 hours per day. This would give Oasis a low operating unit cost on a per available seat kilometer basis. Furthermore, by spending a large proportion of time in cruise, an aircraft flying long-haul flights would have fewer takeoffs and landings than one flying short-haul, which would translate into

Exhibit 7 Oasis Hong Kong Airlines Fare Types

Fare Type	Description
Flexi Fare	• Available year-round • Reservation held for 72 hours before payment • Unlimited free changes to flight and date • Changes to passenger name allowed on payment of change penalty plus fare difference • Refundable subject to cancellation penalty
Advance Purchase Fare	• Booked 45, 21, or 14 days in advance • Payment must be made at time of flight confirmation • Changes to flight, date, and passenger name allowed with penalty and fare difference • Refundable subject to cancellation penalty
Value Fare	• Semi-flexible fare available year-round • Payment must be made at time of flight confirmation • Changes to flight, date, and passenger name allowed with penalty and fare difference • Refundable subject to cancellation policy
Hot Deal	• Discount value fare • Payment must be made at the time of flight confirmation • Changes to flight, date, and passenger name not permitted • Non-refundable

Source: Oasis Hong Kong Airlines, 2006, Fare types, http://www.oasishongkong.com/hk/en/services/faredetails.aspx (accessed November 19, 2006).

lower maintenance costs for the airframe and engines, as well as lower fuel consumption.

Another area where Oasis would save on costs was airport landing and parking fees because the airline would use secondary airports such as Gatwick instead of Heathrow in London and Oakland instead of San Francisco in California. Other secondary airports under consideration included Milan in Italy, and Berlin and Cologne in Germany. All these secondary airports were also major hubs of leading low-cost carriers: London Gatwick, Milan, and Berlin were hubs for easyJet; Cologne was the main hub for Germanwings; and Oakland was a hub for Southwest Airlines and a busy port for JetBlue. By flying into the hubs of major low-cost carriers, Oasis hoped to receive feeder traffic from them and feed traffic to these carriers. Doing so would require interline ticket sales, check-ins, and baggage transfers, which were not unusual among low-cost carriers.

Oasis's value proposition was to offer products and services that were not significantly inferior to those of the major competitors at a price that would be considered extremely competitive and of solid value. Oasis's two Boeing 747-400s were configured for 81 business-class seats and 278 economy-class seats.[35] All passengers in economy class would be offered standard complimentary hot meals. For business-class passengers, Oasis would offer standard upgraded meals with complimentary drinks. In-flight entertainment, such as video and audio programs with personal TVs and in-flight magazines, was a part of Oasis's standard offerings. Lounge access, if required, would be available at an additional cost.

On the distribution side, Oasis adopted the traditional carriers' model and relied on brick-and-mortar travel agents to sell tickets. Passengers would also be able to buy tickets directly on the company's Web site or through a call center.

The traditional model for low-cost carriers placed little emphasis on cargo revenue. However, because Hong Kong was a major air cargo hub for the Asia-Pacific region, demand for cargo space was consistently high, and hence the corresponding market prices, especially on routes to Europe and North America, were very high. Thus, Oasis was also looking at tapping into this revenue stream by filling the bellies of its aircraft with freight.

The Plan

Oasis planned to launch its inaugural flight to London Gatwick in late October 2006. It had purchased two Boeing 747-400s from Singapore Airlines. The first was to be delivered in September, just in time for the planned inaugural flight, and the second one was to be delivered in November. With just two aircraft, Oasis could only serve one destination, with over 12 hours of idle time at London Gatwick. As Lee admitted, load factors would have to be extremely high to be profitable.[36] With four

aircraft and the added service to Oakland, the break-even load factor would come down to around 85 percent. With six aircraft, the break-even load factor could come under 80 percent.

The airline's five-year plan called for aggressive growth of fleet size, amounting to 25 aircraft. The challenge was finding the right aircraft at the right price.[37] Oasis wanted the Boeing 747-400, but in 2005–2006, this aircraft was in high demand. With high fuel prices and the availability of more efficient aircraft types, many 747-400s were expected to cease being economical as passenger aircraft. However, with a healthy growth forecast for the air cargo market, many of these aircraft were destined to be converted into freighters. Singapore Airlines, for example, not only had sold or pre-sold 11 of its 747-400s to Cathay Pacific and Dragonair for freighter conversions, but also was planning to convert a few of its own into freighters. Meanwhile, some airlines, including Singapore Airlines, had originally planned to replace their 747-400s with Airbus's A380 super jumbos starting in 2006, but were caught off guard by Airbus's 22-month delay in its A380 program, forcing airlines to hold on to their 747-400s longer than they had planned. In 2005, the market value of a 747-400 manufactured in 1991 ranged from US$33 million to US$52 million (see Exhibit 8).[38]

Exhibit 8 Market Value of a Boeing 747-400 (in US$ millions)

	Value (market)	Future Value	
Vintage	2005	2009	2012
1989	33.9	19.5	13.7
1991	45.5	26.5	18.9
1993	56.9	33.9	24.5
1995	68.4	41.7	30.5
1997	79.9	50.0	37.1
1999	91.4	59.1	44.6
2001	103.0	68.1	52.5
2003	114.5	76.1	60.2

Source: Aircraft Value News, 2005, Semi-annual jet aircraft value listing, September 5.

Rental Cost per Month (in US$ thousands)

Vintage	2005
1989–1995	360–490
1996–2002	470–865

Source: Aircraft Value News, 2005, Widebody lease rates (dry) US$, October 2005.

Other possible aircraft types for Oasis included the Airbus A340-600 and the Boeing 777-300ER. Albeit slightly smaller than the 747-400, the A340-600 could work, but not many were available at this time. Similarly, the 777-300ER, which had been in service for only a few years, was not readily available on the second-hand aircraft market. In 2005, an A340-600 manufactured in 2002 was valued between US$102 million and US$111 million, whereas a 777-300ER manufactured in 2003 was worth between US$117 million and US$132 million. There was always the option of purchasing brand-new aircraft, but because of long production lead times and production slot availability, it would take 36 to 48 months before any new aircraft delivery. Oasis needed to increase capacity and add new services sooner rather than later.

Preparing for Takeoff

Oasis's potential to get off to a successful start depended to a great extent on the global economic situation at the time, as there is a strong positive correlation between gross domestic product growth and the amount of money businesses and individuals are willing to spend on travel and air freight. However, the biggest question was whether Oasis's target customers would readily embrace these services from a newcomer. On its inaugural route from Hong Kong to London, Oasis's service would be judged and compared to such reputable carriers as British Airways, Virgin Atlantic, Cathay Pacific, and Qantas. It was up to Miller and his management team to prove themselves in the marketplace.

NOTES

1. This price excluded surcharges and taxes.
2. This section is adapted from: P. Ferreira, 2001, Systems in transportation: The case of the airline industry, http://web.mit.edu/esd.83/www/notebook/Transportation%20-%20Airline%20Ind.ppt (accessed November 15, 2006); The airline industry and the World Trade Center disaster, Centre for Asian Business Cases, University of Hong Kong.
3. P. Ferreira, 2001, Systems in transportation: The case of the airline industry, http://web.mit.edu/esd.83/www/notebook/Transportation%20-%20Airline%20Ind.ppt (accessed November 15, 2006).
4. The airline industry, http://adg.stanford.edu/aa241/intro/airlineindustry.html (accessed November 15, 2006).
5. M. Schlangenstein, 2005, Southwest Airlines profit jumps: Lower fuel costs let carrier nearly triple its bottom line, Washington Post, April 15.
6. British Airways, 2005–2006 Annual report & accounts.
7. Wikipedia, 2006, Airline alliance, http://en.wikipedia.org/wiki/Airline_alliance (accessed November 20, 2006).
8. 2006, Ryanair turns screw to hold luggage, http://news.cheapflights.co.uk/flights/2006/01/ryanair_turns_s.html (accessed November 21, 2006).
9. A code sharing agreement is a cooperative agreement between two or more airlines whereby a flight operated and marketed by one airline is also marketed by its code share partner(s). In this case, the flight will have more than one flight number—one that is given to it by the operating airline and other one(s) given to it by the code share partner(s)
10. 2005, Southwest Airlines Annual Report.
11. In the parts of the world where the imperial system was prevalent (e.g., the United States), the equivalent terms were Available Seat Mile (ASM) and Available Ton Mile (ATM). Note that "ton" referred to the imperial ton equal to 2,000 pounds, whereas "tonne" in ATK referred to the metric tonne, which was equal to 2,000 kilograms.
12. This was due to the various discounts that aircraft manufacturers would offer to airlines or leasing companies.
13. A finance lease was basically a mortgage arrangement. Typically an airline would set up a special purpose company, which financed the purchase of the aircraft through a syndicate loan and would in turn lease the aircraft back to the airline.
14. As opposed to a finance lease, an operating lease was purely a leasing arrangement between the airline and a leasing company.
15. IATA. 2006, Profitability: Does size matter?, Economics Briefing, June.
16. The airline industry and current challenges, http://web.mit.edu/airlines/www/the-airline-industry/the-airline-industry.htm (accessed November 14, 2006).
17. IATA, 2006, Premium traffic, Economic Briefing, August, 3.
18. IATA Economics, 2006, Industry financial forecast briefing note, September, 4.
19. Trade Development Council, 2006, Air transport, http://logistics.tdctrade.com/ (accessed November 15, 2006).
20. Hong Kong Civil Aviation Department, 2006, Hong Kong International Airport Civil International Air Transport Movements of Aircraft, Passenger and Freight (1998–2006), http://www.cad.gov.hk/english/p-through.html (accessed November 21, 2006).
21. Airport Authority Hong Kong, 2006, Annual report 2006.
22. Boeing Commercial Airplanes, 2005, Current market outlook 2005, 3–5.
23. Airport Authority Hong Kong, 2006, The airport authority, http://www.hongkongairport.com/eng/aboutus/profile.html (accessed October 17, 2006).
24. Cathay Pacific Airways, 2006, Awards and honours, http://www.cathaypacific.com/cpa/en_INTL/aboutus/cxbackground/awardsandhonours (accessed November 29, 2006).
25. This section was adapted from: Hong Kong Dragon Airlines, 2006, History, http://www.dragonair.com/icms/servlet/template?series=98&lang=eng (accessed November 29, 2006).
26. Air China, Cathay Pacific, CNAC, CITIC Pacific, and Swire Pacific 2006, Changes in shareholding structure builds new aviation partnerships in Greater China, Joint Press Release, June 9.
27. This section was adapted from: Air Hong Kong, 2006, History, http://www.airhongkong.com.hk/ahk/en/F300/History/index.jsp (accessed June 21, 2006).
28. A wet lease was an aircraft leasing arrangement between two parties whereby the lessor provided not only the aircraft, but also the crew, maintenance, and insurance to the lessee.
29. Wikipedia, 2006, Hong Kong Airlines, http://en.wikipedia.org/wiki/CR_Airways (accessed November 29, 2006).

30. C. So, 2006, HK Express to drop Guangzhou service, *South China Morning Post*, February 9.

31. R. Barling, 2006, CR Airways and Ho carrier eye merger, *South China Morning Post*, May 9.

32. Asia Travel Tips, 2006, New low cost–long haul Hong Kong-based airline opens for reservations, http://www.asiatraveltips.com/news06/59-OasisHongKongAirlines.shtml (accessed November 23, 2006).

33. Wikipedia, 2006, Oasis Hong Kong Airlines, http://en.wikipedia.org/wiki/Oasis_Hong_Kong_Airlines (accessed November 22, 2006).

34. Wikipedia, 2006, Oasis Hong Kong Airlines, http://en.wikipedia.org/wiki/Oasis_Hong_Kong_Airlines (accessed November 22, 2006).

35. Wikipedia, 2006, Oasis Hong Kong Airlines, http://en.wikipedia.org/wiki/Oasis_Hong_Kong_Airlines (accessed November 22, 2006).

36. R. Barling, 2006, Oasis success still on a wing and a prayer to distant horizon, *South China Morning Post*, October 27.

37. Wikipedia, 2006, Oasis Hong Kong Airlines, http://en.wikipedia.org/wiki/Oasis_Hong_Kong_Airlines (accessed November 22, 2006.

38. Aircraft Value News, 2005, Semi-annual jet aircraft value listing, September 5.

Havovi Joshi, Samuel Tsang

The University of Hong Kong, Asia Case Research Centre

For some time we have believed the game industry is ready for disruption. Not just from Nintendo, but from all game developers. It is what we all need to expand our audience. It is what we all need to expand our imaginations.

— *SATORU IWATA*

    PRESIDENT OF NINTENDO CO. LTD[1]

In the 2008 *BusinessWeek*–Boston Consulting Group ranking of the world's most innovative companies, Nintendo Co. Ltd ("Nintendo") was ranked seventh, up from thirty-ninth the previous year.[2] This improvement was in recognition of Nintendo's transformation into an innovative design powerhouse that challenged the video game industry's prevailing business model.

In 2000, when Sony, Microsoft, and Nintendo (the "big three" of the video game console manufacturers) released their latest products, Sony's PlayStation 2 (PS2) emerged as the clear winner, outselling Microsoft's Xbox, and Nintendo's GameCube. In 2006, these players introduced a new generation of video game consoles, precipitating a new competitive battle in the industry. Microsoft and Sony continued with their previous strategy of increasing the computing power of their newest products and adding a more impressive graphical interface. However, Satoru Iwata, president of Nintendo, believed that the video game industry had been focusing far too much on existing gamers and completely neglecting non-gamers. In light of this belief, the company repositioned itself by developing a radically different console, the Wii (pronounced "we"). The Wii was an interesting machine that used a wand-like remote controller to detect players' hand movements, allowing them to emulate the real-life play of such games as tennis, bowling, and boxing.

The new console proved to be a runaway success. By September 2007, Nintendo had become Japan's most valuable listed company after Toyota, and its market value had tripled since the launch of the Wii. In spite of this initial success, however, it was not clear whether Nintendo had really disrupted the industry and significantly changed the dynamics of competition in it.

History of Nintendo, 1889 to 2002

Nintendo's[3] roots could be traced all the way back to 1889 in Kyoto, Japan, when Fusajiro Yamauchi, the founder of the company, started manufacturing playing cards. In 1907, the company began producing Western playing cards, and by 1951, it had become the Nintendo Playing Card Company. In 1959, it began making theme cards under a licensing agreement with Walt Disney Company; by 1963, the company had gone public and taken its current name. During the period 1970 to 1985, Nintendo began focusing on the manufacture of electronic toys and entered the emerging field of video games (see Exhibit 1).

Interestingly, 1991, the year Nintendo launched the highly popular Super NES in the United States, was also the year Nintendo's vision become Sony's opportunity—and the creation of what could be described as Nintendo's "greatest challenge" for over a decade—the Sony PlayStation (PS). Nintendo had wanted to incorporate CD-ROM into its Super NES, and Sony had agreed to create the PS for this purpose. However, over the next two years there were many conflicts of vision between Nintendo and Sony, and the two finally parted ways. Nintendo went ahead with Philips

Havovi Joshi and Samuel Tsang prepared this case under the supervision of Professor Ali Farhoomand for class discussion. This case is not intended to show effective or ineffective handling of decision or business processes. © 2009 by The Asia Case Research Centre, The University of Hong Kong. No part of this publication may be reproduced or transmitted in any form or by any means—electronic, mechanical, photocopying, recording, or otherwise (including the Internet)—without the permission of The University of Hong Kong.

Exhibit 1 The History of Nintendo, 1889 to 2002

1889	Fusajiro Yamauchi, the founder of the company, began manufacturing and selling Japanese playing cards.
1907	The company began producing Western playing cards.
1951	Begins using the name "Nintendo Playing Card Company Ltd."
1959	Nintendo began making theme cards under a licensing agreement with Disney.
1962–63	The company went public and took its current name.
1970	Nintendo began focusing on the manufacture of electronic toys and entered the emerging field of video games by licensing Magnavox's Pong technology.
1977	Nintendo developed its first home video game machines, Color TV Game 15 and Color TV Game 6.
1980	Nintendo established its U.S. subsidiary, Nintendo of America. Developed and started selling the first portable LCD video games with a microprocessor.
1981	One of Nintendo's most famous coin-operated games, "Donkey Kong," appeared and was an instant hit in both the United States and Japan.
1983	Nintendo expanded its product range from games and arcade machines to home consoles, and the company released Famicom, a technologically advanced home video game system, in Japan. With its high-quality sound and graphics, Famicom was a huge hit, dominating the Japanese market.
1985	Nintendo successfully launched Famicom in the United States as the Nintendo Entertainment System (NES). The company then marketed a follow-up version of "Super Mario Bros." for the NES, and this classic game helped the NES become a resounding success.
1989	Nintendo released a new console, the Game Boy. The Game Boy was the first major product in the handheld game console industry and became immensely popular because of its portability and accessibility.
1990–92	In 1990, Nintendo launched the Super Family Computer game system in Japan, which also did very well. A year later, the same product was launched as the Super NES in the United States. In 1992, Super NES was released in Europe.
1994	Nintendo formed design alliances with companies such as Silicon Graphics. Released the Super Game Boy, a peripheral for the Super NES, which enabled Game Boy software to be played on the TV screen.
1995	Introduced a 32-bit Virtual Immersion System, known as the "Virtual Boy."
1996	Nintendo launched its 64-bit N64 game system. It launched "Pokémon" on the Game Boy: the game involved trading and training virtual monsters and was the first in a hugely popular video-game series. The company also released another blockbuster video game, "The Legend of Zelda: Ocarina of Time." In just six weeks, 2.5 million units of the game were sold.
1997	It introduces the innovative "Rumble Pak" attachment for the N64 controller, which enabled the game player to feel vibrations while playing the game.
1998	Release of Game Boy Color. "Pokémon" is introduced overseas and becomes a smash hit.
2000	Nintendo acquired a 3 percent stake of convenience store operator Lawson in order to leverage Lawson's online operations and network to sell video games.
2001	Launched the new version of the Game Boy, with a 32-bit CPU. Nintendo GameCube is launched in Japan and the United States.
2002	GameCube is launched in the European and Australian markets.

Source: Nintendo Co. Ltd, 2008, Annual Report, http://www.nintendo.co.jp/ir/pdf/2008/annual0803e.pdf (accessed October 3, 2008).

technology,[4] and Sony was left with the PS, which the company decided to continue developing. Given Sony's clout and resources, when the PS and its wide range of games were finally released in Japan in 1994, the console was an instant success. In 1995, Sony released the PS in the United States, totally uprooting Nintendo's established name in the industry.

For many years, Nintendo was a dominant player in the video game industry. It had sold more than two billion games since 1985. Its top-selling series included nonviolent and easy-to-play games such as "Super Mario Bros." and "The Legend of Zelda." Its games were so successful largely because they appealed to all age groups across different cultures. The title of a book published in 1993 summed up Nintendo's supremacy: *Game Over: How Nintendo Zapped an American Industry, Captured Your Dollars, and Enslaved Your Children*. Suddenly, after the debut of the Sony PS, it was no longer the leader of the video game industry.

Nintendo tried various strategies to counter Sony. However, competition continued to intensify, and the PS2 also captured a significant portion of the video game market, maintaining a dominant position in the industry. In May 2001, Microsoft too entered the video game market by introducing the Xbox console, leaving Nintendo with an even smaller piece of the market.

In 2002, Nintendo appointed Satoru Iwata[5] as president of the company. It was hoped that, with his experience and deep insights into how the market evolved, Iwata would help the company develop a brand-new vision and approach.[6]

The Video Game Industry

History

The video game industry was born in the 1970s. In the early days, notable players such as Atari from the United States and Namco from Japan brought video games to teenagers in the form of arcade games found in malls and video game arcades. With the introduction of home consoles, video games began to make their way into households around the globe.

In the 1980s and early 1990s, many new players came to the market. With the increasing popularity of personal computers (PCs), gamers were no longer limited to playing their favorite video game titles on proprietary consoles. Although the market was affected by the introduction of PCs, video game makers achieved steady growth.

Nevertheless, the target customer group of video game consoles was narrowly confined to teenagers. Armed with insightful targeting and positioning, image-conscious branding, and superb graphics technologies, Sony introduced the PS in the mid-1990s. The Japanese electronics giant revolutionized the perception of video game consoles and successfully captured new players, thereby helping the industry grow substantially. Video gaming suddenly became the new popular entertainment. It was especially well received by young adults, mostly males in their late 20s or early 30s, and often with substantial disposable incomes. By the time Sony launched the PS2 in 2000, technology giant Microsoft realized that it could no longer ignore the runaway success of this product or the effect the booming video game market was having on its traditional PC and software domains. Thus Microsoft's video game console, the Xbox, was launched in 2001.

Since the early 2000s, the convergence of information technology, telecommunications, media, and entertainment has brought dramatic social and technological changes. With the new socio-technological movement and a wider audience base, the big video game console markers such as Sony and Microsoft began to realize that there were new opportunities for their video gaming and console product offerings, which would play a far greater role in people's lives than mere entertainment.

Trends in the Industry

With the broad availability of broadband Internet, increasing sophistication of high-definition (HD) video technologies, and decreasing cost of hard-drive storage, video game console manufacturers realized that their products no longer had to be for gaming only. In fact, many players such as Sony and Microsoft envisioned their game consoles as all-encompassing home entertainment centers. Further, given the increasing speed achieved by broadband connections, Internet users were increasingly able to access large quantities of data files, especially those containing HD audio and video. Consequently, these console producers developed and offered online libraries as a new service enabling users to download and stream a variety of movies, music, and television shows through their consoles.

As top-quality video materials became more readily available through HD broadcasting and Internet downloads, a new recording medium with increased storage capacity was required. Two formats, the Blu-ray format[7] developed by a consortium led by Sony, and the HD-DVD format developed by a consortium led by Toshiba, competed to become the standard in this area.

By offering online games based on new and existing titles, console makers could provide similar social-networking or virtual-world services to get online gamers to play, connect, and form loyal communities. Such communities were expected to help create a perpetual demand for services and products created by the video game makers and their alliance partners. In fact, in-game advertising had already started and offered a new revenue stream to video game developers.

Nintendo: Innovation and the Launch of the Wii

Traditionally, Sony, Microsoft, and Nintendo would enter a new cycle or a new competitive battle every five to six years, and in 2000, Sony's PS2 emerged as the clear winner.[8] Since then, the industry's focus turned even more to the technological advancement of the console hardware, particularly in terms of faster processing speed, higher definition of video quality, and increasing complexity of the games. The relentless pursuit of superior technologies became the driver of the industry's dynamics.

However, the former leader in the video game industry, Nintendo, adopted a vastly different viewpoint about the industry's future development. Some years before the battle that began in 2006, Iwata saw the potential threats facing the industry. He observed that the video game market in Japan was shrinking. Based on various market trends and data, the key factor causing this reduction appeared to be the increasing complexity of video games, which required players to invest a significant amount of their time to learn and play them using increasingly complicated controllers with combinations of buttons and joysticks. Consequently, occasional gamers with busy lives had stopped playing. Further, for novices and non-gamers, the time required to learn and play these games was a major deterrent for potential newcomers to join the camp. Iwata also saw that the video game industry had largely ignored non-gamers and was focused on the existing players. Armed with these insights, Iwata decided to devise a radically new strategy as the foundation for leading Nintendo down an unorthodox path.

The new strategy's objective was to reach out to non-gamers in order to create a bigger market. Iwata's mandate was for simpler games to be developed, targeting all customers, irrespective of age, gender, or gaming experience. These new games were to take no more than a few minutes to set up and play. In addition, they would require an easy-to-use controller. He also wanted the game scenarios to be largely based on real-life situations rather than fantasies.

In order to pilot Iwata's idea, Nintendo first developed a new handheld gaming device called the DS, which stood for "double screen." It was launched in 2004. The DS was positioned as "the machine that enriches the owner's daily life."[9] One of the key features of this device was a touch-screen that gamers could tap or write on with a stylus. This innovative design enabled gamers to play without using complicated sets of buttons or a mini-joystick. The company then launched the Nintendo Wi-Fi Connection, an innovative service that allowed DS system players to play with other users through a wireless network. The DS was a huge success, and by April 2008, more than 70 million units had been sold worldwide.[10]

Among the many DS game titles, the most popular was "Nintendogs," particularly among female gamers. Players of "Nintendogs" could interact with their virtual pets through the DS's built-in microphone and "touch" them via the touch-screen. They could take these dogs for walks, teach them tricks, and enter them into competitions. Another popular game was "Brainage," which featured brain-training games that were basically puzzles.

Following the success of the DS, Nintendo rolled out the DS Lite in 2006. With its mature Game Boy and innovative DS systems, Nintendo remained the leader in the handheld console segment and continued to retain well over 90 percent of the handheld device market that it had captured since 1989.

However, the deciding factor in Nintendo's success was the video game console segment. Since 2000, Nintendo had lost control of the fixed console market to Sony's PS. With its new strategy to capture non-gamers and expand the market, coupled with the lessons learned from the DS handheld device, Nintendo developed its new console, the Wii, which arrived about the same time as the rollout of Microsoft's Xbox 360 and Sony's PS3, and just in time for the 2006 holiday shopping season (see Exhibit 2 for a timeline).

Our goal was to come up with a machine that moms would want—easy to use, quick to start up, not a huge energy drain, and quiet while it was running. Rather than just picking new technology, we thought seriously about what a game console should be. Iwata wanted a console that would play every Nintendo game ever made.

—SHIGERU MIYAMOTO,
MEMBER OF THE WII DEVELOPMENT TEAM[11]

The Wii was an impressive, well-designed, tiny machine that was controlled with a wand-like controller that resembled a TV remote control. Without an elaborate joystick and wire, gamers could navigate the system simply by moving the controller. Motion detectors would then translate the movement of the wand into on-screen action, enabling simulation of real-life games such as tennis, bowling, and boxing. The games were sold on optical discs similar to DVDs. The Wii could also be connected to the Internet for online news and weather updates and to access Nintendo's classic game catalogue, which could be downloaded from the Web. To do this, players could access the Virtual Console service, whereby games originally released for the SNES and N64 could be downloaded from the Wii Shop Channel and accessed from the Wii.

Nintendo positioned the Wii as "a machine that puts smiles on surrounding people's faces," encouraging communication among family members as each of them found something personally relevant and were motivated to turn on the console every day in order to enjoy "the new life with Wii."[12] To promote the Wii, Nintendo adopted the same word-of-mouth strategy that had proven successful in promoting the DS. The company "recruited a handful of carefully chosen

Exhibit 2 Significant Milestones in the Video Game Console Industry

1967	German engineer Baer and co-workers designed the first video game console and developed the first set of games, the Brown Box.
1972	Magnavox approved of the Brown Box and developed Magnavox Odyssey, the first commercial video game console.
1975	Atari, a company founded by Bushnell in 1972, had its first major hit with the arcade game "Pong." "Pong" introduced at-home video games to the masses and Atari became hugely popular.
1977	With Warner Bros. having bought Atari in 1976, the Atari VCS, a cartridge-based system that played multiple games, was developed and released, and became a resounding success.
1980	Mattel entered the market and released Intellivision, a console featuring synthesized voices.
1983–84	Unlicensed games flooded the market and, with many new home systems such as the Atari 5200, the video game industry crashed. Nintendo launched Famicom in Japan.
1985	Nintendo released the NES in the United States.
1989	Nintendo released its second smash hit, the Game Boy.
1991	Nintendo released the Super NES in the United States, a year after its launch in Japan.
1995	Sony launched the PS.
1996	The N64, the last mass-market system to use cartridges, was released by Nintendo.
2000	Sony released the PS2.
2001	Microsoft released the Xbox.
2002	Nintendo released the Game Boy Advance.
2004	Nintendo launched the DS.
2005	In early 2005, Sony released the PSP. In November, Microsoft released the Xbox 360.
2006	Nintendo launched the Wii. Sony launched the PS3.

Source: *Time*, 2005, Video game console timeline—video game history—Xbox 360, http://www.time.com/covers/1101050523/console_timeline/ (accessed August 13, 2008).

suburban housewives to spread the word among their friends that the Wii was a gaming console the whole family could enjoy together."[13] The Wii was also featured in the gamers' self-made video, which was then shared through YouTube and social networking sites. This once-experimental approach was more effective than the traditional advertising or mass-media campaigns used by Sony and Microsoft.

In addition to becoming the home gaming system for the family, Wii also helped expand "exergaming," which was the combination of on-screen action with physical exercise. The origins of exergaming can be traced to 1989, when Nintendo released the Power Pad and Power Glove, two accessories for its gaming console. The Power Pad was a "large plastic platform that plugged into the console and contained pressure sensors on which gamers could step or jump to play sports games."[14] The Power Glove was a "glove-like controller that translated various gestures into on-screen movements."[15] However, these two accessories had not sold well. Now, with the introduction of the Wii into millions of households, boxing, tennis, bowling, golf, and baseball games would require players to act out the physical movements involved in these sports. Consequently, it was predicted that the Wii would spawn a whole new generation of exergaming that would go far beyond the existing games that used dance mats or video cameras to detect players' actions, as the Wii's controller could detect more subtle movements and could be used to record and analyze these movements through intelligent software to determine the players' physical fitness levels.[16]

The Wii proved to be a runaway success and by September 2007, Nintendo became Japan's most valuable listed company after Toyota, at US$72 billion in market value—nearly tripling in value since the launch of the Wii (see Exhibits 3 and 4).[17]

Exhibit 3 Nintendo's Income Statements, 2006 to 2008 (US$ Millions)

	March 31, 2006, Restated	March 31, 2007, Restated	March 31, 2008
Revenues	4,736.0	8,988.8	15,553.5
Cost of Goods Sold	2,735.4	5,289.1	9,043.0
Gross Profit	2,000.6	3,699.7	6,510.6
Selling, General and Administrative Expenses	850.4	1,219.0	1,602.0
R&D Expenses	284.5	350.7	344.1
Depreciation	16.4	24.8	31.7
Other Operating Expenses	1,151.3	1,594.4	1,977.8
OPERATING INCOME	849.3	2,105.2	4,532.8
Interest Expense	0.0	—	—
Interest and Investment Income	209.2	316.1	410.7
Currency Exchange Gains	423.3	239.4	−858.8
Other Non-Operating Income	22.3	28.7	16.5
Earnings before Tax (excluding unusual items)	1,504.1	2,689.3	4,101.1
Gain on Sale of Investments	32.8	5.2	−101.2
Gain on Sale of Assets	−0.2	−1.2	34.1
Other Unusual Items, Total	11.5	—	—
Earnings before Tax (including unusual items)	1,548.2	2,693.3	4,034.1
Income Tax Expense	633.7	1,072.7	1,641.7
Earnings from Continuing Operations	914.9	1,620.9	2,393.3
NET INCOME	914.9	1,620.9	2,393.3

Source: Adapted from *BusinessWeek*, 2008, Financial results for Nintendo Co. Ltd, www.investing.businessweek.com/research/stocks/financials (accessed August 4, 2008).

Key Players in the Video Game Industry

Video Game Hardware

Other than Nintendo, the video game hardware industry (essentially comprising the manufacture of consoles and devices) was dominated by Sony with its PS family, and Microsoft with the Xbox 360.

Sony.[18] For decades, Sony defined the leading edge in gadgetry, producing transistor radios in the 1950s, Trinitron TVs in the 1960s, and the revolutionary Walkman in the 1970s.[19] Similarly, when the company introduced the PS in Japan in March 1994 and in the United States in 1995, it brought the technology of video gaming to a whole new level (see Exhibit 5). With Sony's strategy of attracting older teenagers and young adults (who had significantly more disposable income)

by offering more sophisticated and often more violent games, the PS dominated the market.

In 2000, the PS2 was released and completely won over the video game market. The PS2 was not only backward-compatible with the PS, but could also be used to play CDs and DVDs. For most people who bought the PS2, it was their first DVD player. In July 2008, Sony announced that worldwide PS2 console sales exceeded 140 million,[20] making the PS2 the best-selling console in history.

In order to compete against Nintendo, the ruler of the handheld video game market, Sony introduced the PlayStation Portable ("PSP") in 2004. In the meantime, Sony continued to release other electronics, such as Sony Connect, an online music service; Vaio Pocket, a portable music player designed to compete with Apple's iPod; and Network Walkman, which was the first Walkman with a hard drive.

Case 28: Nintendo's Disruptive Strategy: Implications for the Video Game Industry

Exhibit 4 Nintendo's Consolidated Sales Information for the Six Months Ending September 30, 2007 (US$ Millions)

		Year Ending March 31, 2007	Six Months Ending September 30, 2006	Six Months Ending September 30, 2007
Hardware	Handheld	3,241	1,349	1,827
	Console	1,356	33	1,741
	Others	470	79	355
	Total	5,068	1,461	3,923
Software	Handheld	2,530	1,019	1,322
	Console	714	93	719
	Others	46	10	44
	Total	3,289	1,121	2,085
Total Electronic Entertainment Products Division		8,357	2,582	6,008
Others (playing cards, etc.)		19	7	13
TOTAL		8,376	2,589	6,021

(US$1 = ¥115.4 on March 31, 2008)

Source: Nintendo Co. Ltd, 2007, Consolidated financial statements for the six months ending September 30, 2007, http://www.nintendo.com/corp/report/ FY07FinanciaiP£SiiltsYdf, October 25 (accessed August 1, 2008).

Although the PS product line dominated the market, the sales of Sony's other electronics (e.g., DVD recorders, TVs, and computers) and music products dropped significantly. Consumer demand remained weak as there was a battle over prices, with Apple's iPod undermining the sales of Sony's CD and MiniDisc Walkmans, as well as their TV products. These challenges, in addition to the costs incurred in streamlining operations, significantly decreased Sony's market value, and in 2004 the company reported a loss. Sony, once acknowledged globally for its cutting-edge technological innovations, was coming to be perceived as a bureaucratic conglomerate.

In order to rectify the situation, in 2005 Sony brought in Sir Howard Stringer to replace Nobuyuki Idei as chairman and chief executive. Stringer was the first non-Japanese chief of the company and, prior to this post, had been the head of the company's U.S. and electronics divisions. After taking over, Stringer announced Project Nippon, a corporate restructuring plan designed to revamp Sony's electronics business and foster better collaboration between the company's divisions. His plan called for eliminating 10,000 jobs (the company had 150,000 employees) and closing 11 of Sony's 65 factories. Stringer also revealed plans for improved research-and-development (R&D) with a stronger focus on consumer demand, aiming to reestablish Sony's presence in Japan. Sony's emphasis became HD products for consumers and broadcasters, and semiconductors designed to improve performance in the company's products.

As one of the major weapons in Sir Stringer's grand plan, Sony planned to introduce and leverage the PS3 to regain its position in the electronics industry. The PS3 was designed to be a multimedia entertainment hub. Thus, people would buy the PS3 to watch movies in addition to playing games. Its computing power would also allow users to chat online, listen to music, and view high-quality animations. The machine would also be backward-compatible with games designed for previous PS consoles. Sony hoped that it would be able to utilize the Cell computer chip, jointly developed with IBM and Toshiba, in other products too, such as selling home servers broadband and high-definition television (HDTV) systems. This powerful chip would power the new PS3, whose games would also be the first mass utilization of the Blu-ray format.[21]

In November 2006, after several delays, Sony's PS3 was released nearly a year after Microsoft's Xbox 360 and within a week of the debut of Nintendo's Wii. However, the results were largely disappointing. Supply problems and the high price tag of the PS3 resulted in Sony losing its dominant position in the console market to Nintendo. To boost sales, the company slashed the price of the PS3 in mid-2007. Around the same time, because of continuous setbacks in terms of delays and inability to ramp up production, Sony fired Ken Kutaragi, who was the chief architect of the PS product line.

Exhibit 5 Evolution of Technology in the Video Game Console Industry's War for Supremacy

First Generation 1972–1977	Simple gameplay and basic visuals, such as Atari's "Pong."
Second Generation 1977–1984	Consoles such as the Atari 2600 were launched. The 8-bit cartridge appeared. This era ended with the video game market crashing.
Third Generation 1983–1987	The 8-bit cartridge continued. The first console war took place between Nintendo's NES and Sega's Master System, with Nintendo emerging as the leader. Games such as "Super Mario Bros." and "Metal Gear" were launched and became huge successes. The handheld market, allowing mobility while playing games, was introduced with Nintendo's Game Boy and Sega's Game Gear.
Fourth Generation 1987–1996	The 16-bit cartridge arrived. Graphics became increasingly well defined. Nintendo again won the war against Sega, with its SNES sales exceeding those of the Sega Mega Drive.
Fifth Generation 1995–2002	32-bit, 64-bit, and 3D graphics were introduced. In this era, Sony launched the PS and the CD format arrived—two events that completely revolutionized the industry. In the format war of CD versus cartridge, the cartridge just did not have the capacity of the CD to store games, which were increasingly complex and featured high-quality graphics. Further, while there was a possibility the CD could be pirated, it had the advantage of being cheaper than the cartridge. Nintendo's N64 was the last cartridge-based console to be produced.
Sixth Generation 1998–2004	The 128-bit era began. Sony launched the PS2, which used the DVD format and got exclusive licenses for games such as "Grand Theft Auto" and "Metal Gear Solid 2," making it the winner of this round of competition. Microsoft launched the Xbox and took second place. Nintendo's Game Cube trailed in third. Sega's Dreamcast lagged at fourth place.
Seventh Generation 2004–2008	The Xbox 360 and the PS3 introduced HD gaming and graphics. The PS3 had now moved ahead from the DVD to the Blu-ray format, and this combination of HD and Blu-ray implied far superior storage capacity and graphics. Nintendo's Wii had motion sensors.

Source: Adapted from D. Lero, 2007, A history of gaming, http://www.gamespot.com/pages/unions/home.php?union_id=Contributions, November 14 (accessed August 13, 2008).

In July 2008, 20 months after the release of the PS3, the console had barely achieved 10 percent of its sales target. At the end of Sony's fiscal year in March 2008, sales were 12.85 million, and the company expected to sell just about 10 million in the fiscal year ending March 2009.[22] Sony's more pressing need was to steer the PS3 to profitability, which was estimated to finally happen by 2009 (see Exhibits 6 and 7). Given the shaky situation, Sony had no plans to cease development of games for the older PS2 system and planned to continue rolling out titles specifically for it.[23]

Microsoft. Entering the video game business in 2001 was one of Microsoft's diversification moves when the company recognized the remarkable success of Sony's PS2 and the potential threat the video game market posed to its stronghold in the PC market. The Xbox was the company's first foray into the industry and was launched to compete directly with Sony's PS2 and Nintendo's GameCube. In November 2002, the company launched Xbox Live, allowing subscribers to play online Xbox games with other subscribers around the world. By mid-2005, the service had attracted about two million subscribers worldwide.

However, by May 2005, the software giant had sold only 21.3 million Xbox units, which put the company in a distant second place behind Sony's PS2 (which had sold 83.5 million units) and slightly ahead of Nintendo's GameCube (with sales of 18.3 million units).[24] By August 2005, Microsoft's Xbox division had cost the company US$4 billion.[25] Soon after, production of the Xbox was ended in favor of the Xbox 360.

Microsoft was determined to capture the top spot in the market with the launch of the Xbox 360 in November 2005, several months ahead of its rivals (Sony's PS3 appeared in the market in late 2006, about a week after Nintendo's Wii). Some believed that the previous success of Sony's PS2 was partly due to its advantage in reaching the market earlier than its rivals; thus, Microsoft imitated this marketing strategy and became the first game console in the new business cycle. Further, having learned a hard lesson from the flop of the original Xbox in Japan, Microsoft worked closely with the producers of Japanese games in an attempt to neutralize the traditional advantages of its two main rivals. The company also abandoned its previous approach of using off-the-shelf parts provided by Intel and NVIDIA to build its consoles because while such an approach was efficient, it lacked the flexibility that Microsoft's rivals enjoyed in reducing costs and increasing profit margins during a console's lifetime.[26] (For instance, Sony had gradually reduced the number of chips required by its

Exhibit 6 Sony's Income Statement, 2006–2008 (US$ Millions)

	March 31, 2006	March 31, 2007	March 31, 2008
Revenue	63,541.2	70,513.4	89,601.3
Cost of Goods Sold	43,786.9	54,652.4	68,885.3
Gross Profit	19,754.3	15,861.0	20,716.0
Gross Profit Margin	31.1%	22.5%	23.1%
Selling, General and Administrative Expenses	12,446.4	8,719.8	9,525.6
Depreciation	5,682.2	6,531.3	7,408.1
Operating Income	1,625.7	609.9	3,782.3
Operating Margin	2.6%	0.9%	4.2%
Non-Operating Income	1,054.6	489.3	1,159.1
Non-Operating Expenses	246.5	231.9	231.6
Income before Taxes	2,433.8	867.3	4,709.8
Income Taxes	1,500.4	458.0	2,055.1
Net Income after Taxes	933.4	409.3	2,654.7
Continuing Operations	1,050.7	1,073.8	3,731.3
Total Net Income	1,050.7	1,073.8	3,731.3
Net Profit Margin	1.7%	1.5%	4.2%

Source: Adapted from C. Colbert, 2008, Sony Corporation, Hoover's Company Information.

PS2 without sacrificing its performance.) Subsequently, Microsoft adopted a new design for its Xbox 360 in the hope that this would achieve a new degree of manufacturing flexibility that could help integrate various components and increase profitability in the future (see Exhibit 8).[27]

Video Game Software

The computer game industry, one of the biggest money-spinners in the global entertainment industry, routinely spent amounts ranging from US$12 million to US$20 million to develop each game. As the consoles became more expensive, the cost of developing games for them also increased. However, Nintendo turned its lower-cost hardware into another competitive advantage. By focusing on characters rather than special effects, developing Wii games cost the company about half what its competition was spending on Xbox and PS games, and thus the expense could be recouped at a much lower sales volume. Nintendo had also thrown in

Exhibit 7 Analysis of Sony's Income Statement for the Year Ending March 31, 2008

Sony's increase in revenues was largely due to the group's electronics segment, comprising televisions and digital cameras, which saw an 8.9 percent increase in sales. The video game segment increased sales by 26.3 percent to US$12.2 billion, largely due to an increase in sales of the PS3. In all, 9.24 million PS3 units were sold during the year, an increase of 5.63 million units over the previous year. With Sony increasing software sales to 57.9 million units (from 44.6 million) and reducing hardware costs, the losses in the PS3 segment declined to US$1.18 billion from US$ 2.21 billion in the previous year.

PSP sales increased by 4.36 million units to 13.89 million, and PSP software sales rose by 0.8 million to 55.5 million units. PS2 sales declined by 0.98 million units to 13.73 million, with PSP software sales decreasing by 39.5 million units to 154 million.

For the year ending March 31, 2009, Sony expected game segment sales to decline and the PS2 business to shrink. However, the company was optimistic that profitability would increase with more titles available for the PS3 and reductions in hardware costs. There would be an estimated 22 percent reduction in profits, taking into account the one-off increase in the March 2008 financials due to property sales and the floating of the group's financial services segment.

Source: Adapted from D. Jenkins, 2008, "Sony's game division sees 26% sales jump, http://www.gamasutra.com/php-bin/news-index.php?story=8638, May 14 (accessed August 11, 2008).

Exhibit 8 Microsoft's Income Statement, 2005–2007 (US$ Millions)

	June 30, 2005	June 30, 2006	June 30, 2007
Revenue	39,788	44,282	51,122
Cost of Goods Sold	6,200	7,650	10,693
Gross Profit	33,588	36,632	40,429
Gross Profit Margin	84.4%	82.7%	79.1%
Selling, General, and Administrative Expenses	18,172	19,257	20,465
Depreciation	855	903	1,440
Operating Income	14,561	16,472	18,524
Operating Margin	36.6%	37.2%	36.2%
Non-Operating Income	2,067	1,572	1,577
Income before Taxes	16,628	18,262	20,101
Income Taxes	4,374	5,663	6,036
Net Income after Taxes	12,254	12,599	14,065
Net Profit Margin	30.8%	28.5%	27.5%

Source: Adapted from S. Shafer, 2008, Microsoft Corporation, Hoover's Company Information.

five simple but highly addictive games, Wii Sports, with each console so that the buyer was getting a "complete" product at a great price. Sony and Microsoft, on the other hand, incurred losses on the consoles they sold, despite their high price. To compensate for these losses, they sold their games with high licensing royalties. As of July 2008, 6 of the 10 most popular games worldwide were for Nintendo consoles (see Exhibit 9).

Nintendo also focused on developing first-party titles. Nintendo had placed its top software designers at the helm of hardware design. Thus, while Sony and Microsoft relied heavily on third parties to develop titles,

Exhibit 9 Top 10 Games Worldwide, July 2008 (approximate number of units in thousands)

Rank	Console	Game	Publisher	Number of Weeks Since Launch	Sales for the Week Ending July 25, 2008	Sales Since Launch by July 25, 2008
1	Wii	Wii Sports	Nintendo	88	333	26,826
2	Wii	Wii Fit	Nintendo	35	206	6,010
3	DS	Dragon Quest V	Square Enix	2	181	861
4	Wii	Mario Kart Wii	Nintendo	16	167	6,604
5	Wii	Wii Play	Nintendo	87	144	13,840
6	DS	Pokemon Mysterious Dungeon 2	Nintendo	46	117	2,919
7	DS	Guitar Hero: On Tour	Activision	3	116	740
8	Wii	Super Smash Bros. Brawl	Nintendo	26	95	6,430
9	PS2	Powerful Pro Baseball 15	Konami	1	88	88
10	Xbox 360	NCCA Football 09	Electronic Arts	2	84	374

Source: Adapted from VGChartz, 2008, "Worldwide chart for week ending July 25, 2008, http://www.vgchartz.com (accessed August 4, 2008).

Nintendo's consoles were designed to suit the concepts of the games that would run on them, allowing the creation of early first-party titles that really showcased the hardware, including low-profit and offbeat games like Brainage. Such games would have been impossible on another company's hardware.[28]

The sales of hardware consoles such as the Wii, Xbox, and PS were highly correlated to the launch and sale of the video games that could be played on them. For instance, in March 2008, Nintendo launched its exclusive hit game "Super Smash Bros. Brawl" for the Wii and, in that month, along with selling 2.7 million copies of the game, the company sold more video game consoles in the United States than Sony and Microsoft combined.[29]

The Battle Begins

Until the launch of the Wii at the end of 2006, competition in the video game market was straightforward. The leader was the company that introduced a wider array of games with high-quality graphics and increasingly complex gameplay. Then Microsoft introduced the Xbox 360 in November 2005, and Nintendo and Sony followed about a year later with the Wii and PS3. It was apparent that the rules of competition had changed.

Sony continued to claim success in selling the aging PS2 console. Given its long history in the market, the PS2 had outsold both the Xbox 360 and the Wii. Microsoft also remained confident about its Xbox 360. As of May 2008, Microsoft announced its Xbox 360 game machine had beaten the Wii and PS3 to reach 10 million units in U.S. sales.[30] The head start of several months in selling the Xbox 360 gave Microsoft an edge over Sony's PS3 and Nintendo's Wii. The lead time also helped Microsoft and its partners build a vast library of games, which was a major factor for consideration when gamers chose a particular console.

However, within a month of Microsoft's announcement that it was the leader in the U.S. console war, the June 2008 figures were released and it was evident that the Wii had usurped the Xbox 360 as the leader. A total of 10.9 million Wiis were sold in the United States since its launch in November 2006, whereas a total of 10.4 million Xbox 360s were sold since its launch a year earlier.[31] The PS3 came in a distant third with 4.8 million units sold. In the United States, which was Nintendo's largest market,[32] the Wii had taken off the fastest by selling 600,000 units in the first eight days, generating US$190 million in sales.[33] In fact, because of its high demand and market buzz, many consumers found it difficult to get their hands on the machine even months after the launch (see Exhibit 10). The same story about demand existed

Exhibit 10 Sales Figures of Wii, PS3, and Xbox 360 in the United States (approximate number of units in thousands)

	Xbox 360	Nintendo Wii	Sony PS2	Sony PS3
September 2006	259	0	300	0
October 2006	217	0	235	0
November 2006	511	476	664	197
December 2006	1,132	604	1,400	491
January 2007	294	436	299	244
February 2007	228	335	295	127
March 2007	199	259	280	130
April 2007	174	360	194	82
May 2007	155	338	188	82
June 2007	198	382	270	95
July 2007	170	425	222	159
August 2007	277	404	202	131
September 2007	528	501	215	119
October 2007	366	519	184	121

Exhibit 10 Sales Figures of Wii, PS3, and Xbox 360 in the United States (approximate number of units in thousands) (*Continued*)

	Xbox 360	Nintendo Wii	Sony PS2	Sony PS3
November 2007	770	981	496	466
December 2007	1,260	1,350	1,100	798
January 2008	230	274	264	269
February 2008	254	432	352	281
March 2008	262	721	216	257
April 2008	188	714	124	187
May 2008	187	675	133	209
June 2008	220	667	189	406
TOTAL	8,079*	10,853	7,822	4,851

*Cumulative sales of the Xbox 360 from the launch date in November 2005 to September 2006 equaled 2,414 units, bringing the total from launch to June 2008 to 10.5 million units.

Source: Adapted from PVC Forum, 2008, "Games sales chart—monthly console hardware sales in America, www.forum.pcvsconsole.com, July 17 (accessed August 11, 2008).

in other parts of the world, and Nintendo emerged as the clear month-on-month leader with the outstanding success of its new console (see Exhibit 11).

In terms of profitability, Nintendo was in an enviable position of making a profit on each Wii console sold from the first day (see Exhibit 12). Sony, on the other hand, had already slashed the price of the PS3 by US$100 to US$499 to help boost sales of the console. This was still US$20 more than Microsoft's most expensive version of the Xbox 360 and about twice the price of Nintendo's Wii.[34]

Exhibit 11 Worldwide Sales Figures of Wii, PS3, and Xbox Units (approximate number of units in thousands)

	Xbox 360	Nintendo Wii	Sony PS2	Sony PS3
September 2006	446	0	859	0
October 2006	431	0	793	0
November 2006	1,263	1,068	2,016	516
December 2006	2,028	2,418	3,282	843
January 2007	692	1,308	981	546
February 2007	648	1,315	954	389
March 2007	438	900	708	954
April 2007	395	1,060	648	530
May 2007	482	1,522	746	418
June 2007	392	1,245	647	298
July 2007	350	1,371	735	419

	Xbox 360	Nintendo Wii	Sony PS2	Sony PS3
August 2007	636	1,612	882	609
September 2007	837	1,149	754	428
October 2007	1,007	1,234	699	632
November 2007	1,516	2,698	1,334	1,525
December 2007	2,215	4,267	2,456	2,389
January 2008	1,064	2,961	1,271	1,480
February 2008	648	1,606	830	948
March 2008	710	1,730	765	929
April 2008	886	2,545	668	1,189
May 2008	796	2,331	488	939
June 2008	618	1,921	499	995
TOTAL	18,498	35,596	23,015	15,981

Source: Estimated data adapted from VGChartz, July 2008, World hardware sales—weekly comparison, http://www.vgchartz.com/aweekly.php (accessed August 16, 2008).

Exhibit 12 The Economics of the Game: Wii, PS3, and the Xbox 360

Microsoft and Sony were prepared for initial losses in producing their Xbox 360 and PS3 in the hopes that there would be a long-term profit from software sales. However, by integrating hardware and software development, Nintendo made profits on both from the very start. In the United States and Europe, where the Wii's retail price was higher than in Japan and it came bundled with Wii Sports, it was estimated that it made a healthy gross profit margin per console of US$49 in the United States and US$74 in Europe, factoring in currency conversions.[37]

Nintendo also outsourced nearly all production of the Wii and the DS. Its strategy of having more than one supplier for the same part meant that it got the parts cheaper and increasing production was not difficult. Sony, on the other hand, produced an estimated 40 percent of its components in-house.[38] The massive costs of investing in the game console, which was equipped with a Blu-ray player and the powerful Cell chip, meant that Sony continued to incur a loss on each PS3 sold.[39] Electronics supply chain researcher iSuppli's analysis in November 2006 showed that Sony's selling price of US$499 per 20GB PS3 resulted in a unit loss of about US$306.85, not including packaging, controller, and cables.[40]

As for Microsoft, at launch the Xbox 360 was estimated to be losing about US$125 per console.[41] By November 2006, the company streamlined processes and reduced manufacturing costs by almost 40 percent, thereby making an estimated profit of US$75.70 on the retail price of US$399.[42] However, the year ending 2007 remained difficult for the company's Xbox 360 division, which managed both hardware and software sales. The division posted a net loss of US$2 billion. This was primarily due to Microsoft incurring costs exceeding US$1.1 billion by extending the warranty on the product from one year to three years, mainly due to "red ring o' death" issues (a problem that arose due to a defective graphic chip and which caused the console to die while in use). It was only for the year ending June 30, 2008, that a yearly operating profit—amounting to US$426 million—was reported.

Finally, unlike Sony's and Microsoft's reliance on third-party development of games, Nintendo's focus on in-house titles had a pronounced impact on revenues. These were far more profitable than third-party titles, for which the console manufacturer might get only 10 to 15 percent of the price of the game.[43]

It was becoming clear that, in this latest battle between the Xbox 360, PS3, and Wii, the Wii was the clear winner of the game.

Nintendo's Disruptive Strategy

It was not just the video game industry that had felt the impact of the innovative Wii. With the December 2007 release of Wii Fit (an extension of the Wii for exercise activities utilizing the Wii Balances Board peripheral), the potential for capturing yet another class of non-gamers was significantly increased. Wii Fit aimed to integrate health and entertainment and featured approximately 40 different activities, including yoga, pushups, and other exercises. It was described as a way to help get families to exercise together. Within six months of being released, the product had sold two million copies in Japan and had long queues waiting for its delivery in many parts of the world. Its effect on the health industry was already evident, with doctors and therapists recommending it for various purposes, such as body balance, strength training, keeping patients interested in performing repetitive and tedious exercises, and for the elderly to enjoy expanding their range of motion.

Nintendo's business model was also exciting for small, independent software producers. In May 2008, Nintendo made the strategic move of loosening its traditionally tight control over content by launching WiiWare in the United States and Europe. WiiWare, an online channel for distributing downloadable games, enabled users to download new games by independent developers. Reggis Fils-Aime, president of Nintendo of America,[35] said, "Independent developers armed with small budgets and big ideas will be able to get their original games into the marketplace to see if we can find the next smash hit. WiiWare brings new levels of creativity and value to the ever-growing population of Wii owners."

While it was still too early to predict the final results, Nintendo's Wii has revolutionized and changed the nature of competition, and not just in the video-game industry. Would this disruptive transformation of the video game industry leave the competitors in the cold? What course of action was available to them?

Appendix
Disruptive Technology

The term "disruptive technology" was coined by Clayton M. Christensen, a professor at the Harvard Business School. Christensen believed that leading companies, despite having followed all the right practices (i.e., keeping a close watch on competition, listening to their customers, and investing aggressively in new technologies), still lost their top positions when confronted with disruptive changes in technology and market structure. He suggested that, while keeping close to customers was critical for current success, it was paradoxically also the cause for companies' failure to meet the technological demands of customers in the future.

To remain at the top of their industries, managers must first be able to spot disruptive technologies. To pursue these technologies, managers must protect them from the processes and incentives that are geared to serving mainstream customers. And the only way to do that is to create organizations that are completely independent of the mainstream business.[36]

Disruptive technology is an innovation that uses a "disruptive strategy'" rather than a "sustaining" strategy (one which improved the performance of an established product) or a "revolutionary" strategy (one which introduced products with dramatically improved features). Christensen argued that following good business practices could ultimately weaken a great company because truly important breakthrough technologies were often rejected by mainstream customers because they could not immediately use them. Companies with a strong customer focus would thus reject those strategically important innovations. As a result, it was left to the more nimble, entrepreneurial companies to pursue those disruptive opportunities, which might result in worse product performance in the short term, but in the long run were of strategic importance in creating new markets and finding new customers for future products.

NOTES

1. S. Iwata, 2006, GDC keynote address, *Nintendo World Report*, http://www.nintendoworldreport.com/newsArt.cfm, March 23 (accessed July 31, 2008).
2. J. McGregor, 2008, The world's most innovative companies, *BusinessWeek*, http://www.businessweek.com/magazine/content/08, April 17 (accessed July 10, 2008).
3. "Nintendo," loosely translated from Japanese, means "leave luck to heaven."
4. Under this deal, Philips, one of Sony's principal rivals, would produce an add-on device for Nintendo game players allowing them to use optical compact discs with greater storage capacities than game cartridges.

5. Iwata joined HAL Laboratories in 1982 and shortly after became the company's coordinator for software production, where he helped create video games such as "Kirby." In 1993, he became president of HAL, a post he held until 2000, when he joined Nintendo as head of the corporate planning division. When Yamauchi retired in 2002, Iwata became president of Nintendo.

6. C. Colbert, 2007, Nintendo Co. Ltd, Hoover's Company Information; M. Sanchanta, 2007, Nintendo market cap rockets, *Financial Times*, September 26; 2006, Playing a Different Game, *The Economist*, October 26.

7. Blu-ray was a new DVD format derived from the blue laser, which had a short wavelength of 405 nm. Blu-ray discs could store substantially more data than the DVD format, which was derived from red-laser (650 nm) technology.

8. The PS2 had been updated since introduction and was available in a much smaller format than the original.

9. Nintendo, 2007, Consolidated financial statements for the six months ending September 30, 2007, http://www.nintendo.com/corp/report/FY07FinancialResults.pdf, October 25 (accessed August 1, 2008).

10. Data sourced from VGChartz.com (week ending April 5, 2008), Hardware table, http://www.vgchartz.com (accessed August 1, 2008).

11. K. Hall, 2006, The big ideas behind Nintendo's Wii, *BusinessWeek*, http://www.businessweek.com/technolgy/content/nov2006, November 16 (accessed June 25, 2008).

12. Nintendo, 2007, Consolidated financial statements for the six months ending September 30, 2007, http://www.nintendo.com/corp/report/FY07FinancialResults.pdf (accessed August 1, 2008).

13. 2007, "Building buzz: Marketing, 2007, *The Economist*, 383(8525): 64.

14. http://www.wordspy.com/words/exergaming.asp?r=16.9423217396108&svr=9&lang=en_us& (accessed August 1, 2008).

15. Ibid.

16. C. Colbert, 2007, Nintendo Co. Ltd, Hoover's Company Information; 2007, Let's get physical, *The Economist*, March 8.

17. K. Takenaka, 2007, Nintendo becomes Japan's second most valuable company, *Reuters*, http://www.reuters.com/article/technology-media-telco, September 25 (accessed August 1, 2008).

18. This chapter contains excerpts from A. Farhoomand & S. Tsang, 2006, Microsoft's diversification strategy, Asia Case Research Centre, The University of Hong Kong.

19. L. Stahl, 2006, Sir Howard Stringer: Sony's savior? *CBS News 60 Minutes*, http://www.cbsnews.com/stories/2006/01/06/60minutes/main1183023_page3.shtml, January 8 (accessed June 25, 2008).

20. C. Nutall, 2008, Sony sets 150m sales target for PS3, *Financial Times*, http://www.ft.com/cms/s/0/1c46ad2e-5678. July 20 (accessed August 14, 2008).

21. Sony joined Matsushita and Samsung, plus a few other companies, to jointly develop the Blu-ray format. The alliance, formed in 2004, aimed to establish the new DVD format for optical storage media. In late 2004, Disney agreed to use the Blu-ray format.

22. C. Nutall, 2008, Sony sets 150m sales target for PS3, *Financial Times*, http://www.ft.com/cms/s/0/1c46ad2e-5678, July 20 (accessed August 14, 2008).

23. C. Colbert, 2007, Nintendo Co. Ltd, Hoover's Company Information.

24. Data sourced from http://vgchartz.com, 2005, Hardware table, May 28 (accessed July 30, 2008).

25. V. Murphy, 2005, Microsoft's midlife crisis, *Forbes*, http://www.forbes.com/2005/09/12, September 13 (accessed August 1, 2008).

26. Lifetime refers to the complete stages of the product's life cycle: from conception, through design and production, to its service and, finally, disposal.

27. This chapter contains excerpts from A. Farhoomand & S. Tsang, 2006, Microsoft's diversification strategy, Asia Case Research Centre, The University of Hong Kong.

28. R. Ehrenberg, 2007, Game console wars II: Nintendo shaves off profits, leaving competition scruffy, *Seeking Alpha*, http://seekingalpha.com/article/34357-game-console-wars-ii-nintendo-shaves-off-profits-leaving-competition-scruffy, May 3 (accessed August 14, 2008).

29. P. McDougall, 2008, Nintendo Wii sales trounce Xbox 360, Playstation 3, *Information Week*, http://www.informationweek.com/news/hardware/, April 18 (accessed July 15, 2008).

30. D. Wakabayashi, 2008, Xbox 360 sales surpass Wii, PS3, *Reuters*, http://www.reuters.com/article/technologyNews, May 15 (accessed June 25, 2008).

31. T. Ricker, 2008, NPD: Wii usurps Xbox as best selling U.S. game console, pulling away, *Engadget*, http://www.engadget.com/2008/07/18/npd-wii-usurps-xbox-360-as-best-selling-us-game-console, July 18 (accessed August 11, 2008).

32. The United States comprised 36 percent of Nintendo's total sales for the year ending March 2007, followed by Japan with 34 percent.

33. C. Colbert, 2007, Nintendo Co. Ltd, Hoover's Company Information.

34. CNN, 2007, Sony slashes PS3 price tag by about $100, http://www.cnn.com/2007/TECH/fun.games/07/09/sony.prie.reut/index, July 9 (accessed August 11, 2008).

35. J. L. Bower & C. Christensen, 1995, Disruptive technologies: Catching the wave, *Harvard Business Review*, http://www.hbsp.harvard.edu/b01/en/common/item_detail.jhtml, January 1 (accessed August 11, 2008).

36. M. Sanchanta, 2007, Nintendo Wii success helps component makers score, *Financial Times*, http://ft.com/cms/s/0/4f9a9108-6467-11dc-90ea-00009fd2ac.html, September 16 (accessed August 14. 2008).

37. Ibid.

38. C. Nutall, 2008, Sony sets 150m sales target for PS3, *Financial Times*, http://www.ft.com/cms/s/0/1c46ad2e-5678. July 20 (accessed August 14, 2008).

39. Edge Online, 2006, iSuppli: 60GB PS3 costs US$840 to produce, http://www.edge-online.com/news/isuppli-60gb-ps3-costs-840-produce, November 16 (accessed August 14, 2008).

40. Ibid.

41. J. Mann, 2006, Microsoft makes tiny profit on Xbox 360 hardware, *TechSpot News*, http://www.techspot.com/news/23612-microsoft-makes-a-tiny-profit-on-xbox-360-hardware.html, November 20 (accessed August 14, 2008).

42. R. Ehrenberg, 2007, Game console wars II: Nintendo shaves off profits, leaving competition scruffy, *Seeking Alpha*, http://seekingalpha.com/article/34357-game-console-wars-ii-nintendo-shaves-off-profits-leaving-competition-scruffy, May 3 (accessed August 14, 2008).

43. R. Ehrenberg, 2007, Game console wars II: Nintendo shaves off profits, leaving competition scruffy, Seeking Alpha, http://seekingalpha.com/article/34357-game-console-wars-ii-nintendo-shaves-off-profits-leaving-competition-scruffy, May 3 (accessed August 14, 2008).

IVEY

Richard Ivey School of Business
The University of Western Ontario

"I am working harder and longer hours than ever before and making less money," thought Kevin Wilson as he drove his van to work one morning in Knoxville, Tennessee. Wilson was the sole owner and manager of Pro Clean LLC, a carpet cleaning business. He was still the first one to arrive at work and the last one to leave. As a result, he had been neglecting his family lately and the first tensions in his marriage were becoming visible.

The issue was fast becoming not one of working harder and longer and making less money but that of survival. Looking back at his decision to expand his business, he was now close to admitting that he had made a mistake. But was there a chance to rectify his mistake or would his business spiral ever faster to bankruptcy?

Knoxville

Knoxville was the third largest city in Tennessee. It was located in a broad valley between the Cumberland Mountains to the northwest and the Great Smoky Mountains to the southeast.[1]

Knoxville had a population of 183,546 in 2007 and the population had grown by 4.6 per cent since 2000. The estimated median household income in 2005 was $30,473 (it was $27,492 in 2000) and the estimated median house/condo value in 2005 was $100,400 (it was $78,000 in 2000). Knoxville had a land area of 92.7 square miles.[2]

Knoxville had a highly diversified economy with no over-reliance on any industry. The local economy had seen substantial growth in the areas of trade, transportation, utilities and financial activities recently.

The Market

The residential house cleaning market in Knoxville was serviced predominately by independent companies. There were also a few large franchises competing for market share. Residential house cleaning services were divided into different categories: maid or house cleaners, carpet cleaners, window cleaners and a variety of other service providers. The carpet cleaning market consisted of approximately 60 cleaners. The figure was close to 80 if one took into account the cleaners in the distant Knoxville counties. Roughly 90 per cent were owner/operators that had one van. There was one large national franchise, which had seven vans and 18 to 20 employees. The remaining companies operated with two or three vans (see Exhibit 1). The market grew an approximate five per cent per year, which was what Wilson averaged. Pro Clean had built up a respectable five per cent market share in Knoxville.

The commercial cleaning market was serviced by janitorial service providers that offered a one-stop service to commercial businesses and offered diverse services such as general office cleaning, carpet cleaning, window cleaning, etc.

Regardless of the saturated marketplace, a number of national janitorial cleaning and carpet cleaning chains were advertising aggressively to establish new franchises in the city.

Pro Clean

Wilson was an old-timer in the carpet cleaning business. He had run his own carpet cleaning business as an owner/operator in Chicago, Illinois, for seven years and had moved to Knoxville, Tennessee, eight years ago when his wife had gotten an offer to run a medical clinic (the average American family relocated every 12 years). He had worked hard to establish himself in Knoxville and what had worked for him in Chicago had also worked in Knoxville and he was making $75,000 a year as an owner/operator. They had settled in well in Tennessee and had two young children, who were now in elementary school.

Wilson offered both steam cleaning and dry cleaning options to his customers but the method of choice was steam cleaning (see Exhibit 2).

As an owner/operator, Wilson managed the following daily functions:

- Scheduling
- Estimates
- Cleaning
- Inventory management
- Training
- Ordering
- Payroll
- Marketing
- Customer care management
- Van and equipment maintenance
- Accounting

Wilson used QuickBooks software to do his accounting and was not good with numbers. He also was not good at selling and avoided public speaking at all cost. After 15 years of hard work, long hours and incessant back pains he had finally decided that it was time for him to hang up his overalls and leave the cleaning to others.

Business Expansion

He had long envied the high prices that one of his competitors, King Rug, charged and had tried to emulate the business model of that company. Two years ago he had hired three workers to do the cleaning, (see Exhibit 3), moved the business out of his home to a newly rented commercial facility and purchased two new vans on lease. Upon the suggestion of a fellow member of the Knoxville Chamber of commerce who designed web sites, he had also invested in a basic web site.

He had thought "With four employees, three vans and a web site, Pro Clean is now ready to take on even the best in Knoxville." Wilson had targeted to become the new King Rug of Knoxville.

Expansion Pains

The expansion process had been exhilarating at first. A new Pro Clean logo had been designed. He had trained the new employees to clean and had outfitted his employees with Pro Clean-branded overalls. The Pro Clean logo had also been painted on the sides of all the vans to complete the branding effort.

At the onset of the expansion, the business had started to churn cash as a result of the increased payroll expense and the lease payments for the new vans. Cash flow had quickly become a problem, one that Wilson was not used to and he had had to resort to using his business and personal credit cards' overdraft facility to finance his business.

His return on investment, however, was dismal. Increasing capacity threefold had not increased business threefold as originally foreseen and cleaning technicians and their assigned vans were spending at least two thirds of the day idly at the new office.

Looking for answers to get him out of his predicament, he had tried to get help from peers at the Chamber of Commerce, but to no avail. As a last resort, he had sought help online and had found a carpet cleaning guru in Memphis, Tennessee, who went by the title of "King of Klean." The King of Klean had promised guaranteed results and Wilson had enrolled in the program, paying for the $20,000 workshop and tutorials over the duration of a year with his already overextended credit card.

He had tried to the best of his knowledge to enact the standardized marketing templates that had brought fame and glory to the King of Klean. What had worked for the King of Klean and turned him into a millionaire had unfortunately not worked for Wilson, as he was not able to replicate the great man's success.

Restructuring

Accepting that his expansion plans had run into trouble, he had laid off Jeremy Turner, one of his cleaning technicians. Desperately in need of new business and in response to one of the remaining cleaning technicians, who had problems adapting to the rigor of cleaning and the ensuing back pains, he had temporarily transformed the cleaning technician position to that of sales and office administration. The change in position had been made permanent shortly thereafter, along with a pay rise and new title of sales and office manager.

The Restructured Pro Clean Organization

Initially, the new sales/office manager had spent a lot of time stuffing envelopes with direct mail material, answering phones, giving estimates, etc. After six months of spending most of his time in the office and with little additional business to show for, he had started to visit real estate agents and business owners to garner referrals and do in-home estimates for residential prospects that called in. He had also started to visit current business clients to build stronger relationships.

The sales/office manager had now been routinely visiting real estate agents and other referral sources for half of the day and spending the remainder of the day in the office, usually when Wilson was out. He had also seemingly been doing a lot of work from his home, with full online access to the Pro Clean computer network and claimed that he clocked-in at least 60 hours a week. The two men had established a good rapport and Wilson regularly conferred with him before making business decisions.

The other cleaning technician had not been available to clean after hours or on weekends and Wilson himself was back to cleaning on one of the vans for overflow work for after-hours and weekend cleaning jobs. The rest of Wilson's time had been spent trying to develop the business and at the office dealing with administrative and clerical tasks.

Marketing Strategy

Pro Clean's strategy was to target all potential residential customers in Knoxville without bothering to focus on demographics. A paying customer was a paying customer. In the past year, it had done some commercial cleaning and hoped that it could build on that in the present year, targeting small businesses with carpets of not larger than 10,000 square feet/930 square meters. The commercial business was not a cash business and required receivables follow-up and payments were usually late. Pro Clean tried to stay in touch with all its customers by sending out quarterly newsletters.

Pro Clean Customer Profile

- Income greater than $250,000 per year
- Mostly single-income families
- Most homes had pets/young children
- Stay-at-home spouse made the purchasing decision
- Mostly paid in cash
- Want a safe, healthy, quality service
- Want to protect their investments with regular maintenance

Purchasing Patterns

- The average Pro Clean customer had their carpets cleaned every 12 months
- Frequent-use customers had their carpets cleaned every six months

- Frequent-use customers made up approximately 20 per cent of the business
- Most carpet owners cared for their carpets themselves regularly on a weekly or bi-monthly basis using standard household vacuum cleaners

Source of Business

Pro Clean had a loyal and satisfied customer base which provided most of the business. 60 per cent of Pro Clean's business was repeat business, with marketing accounting for 10 per cent, referrals 8.5 per cent, other sources like walk-ups and calls from people that saw the van accounting for 19.5 per cent and internet-based sales for three per cent. The Pro Clean website had not lived up to expectations and Wilson himself had tried to upgrade the website himself with the help of a high school student.

Source of Revenue

Carpet cleaning was the main source of revenue for Pro Clean and accounted for 77 per cent of its revenue. The other service offerings did not bring in that much revenue. Upholstery cleaning accounted for nine per cent, area rug cleaning five per cent, tile and grout cleaning five per cent, carpet and fabric protection three per cent and drapery cleaning a mere one per cent.

Wilson suspected that his competitors generated considerable extra revenue by up-selling customers extra services in addition to carpet cleaning. It was a well-known fact in the carpet cleaning industry of Knoxville that King Rug derived a substantive portion of its revenue from rug cleaning at its place of business and did well with cross selling and up-selling. Pro Clean, however, did not, or as he sometimes admitted to himself, could not, successfully upsell.

Sales Incentives

Pro Clean had a commission system in place for its technicians that paid 10 per cent of each new job. After each job, technicians were encouraged to distribute flyers to the two to three houses across the street and one on each side of the house they were cleaning. The technicians, however, rarely bothered to distribute flyers, as their previous efforts had yielded no results.

Scheduling

Pro Clean had divided Knoxville into zones and tried to schedule cleaning jobs on a one-zone-a-day basis to save fuel. More often than not, trucks would have to service two or more zones a day.

Customers were given time options to accommodate their own schedules. The size of the cleaning job was not prioritized unless it affected Pro Clean's punctuality. Scheduling became even more complicated because the new vans had faster setup and cleaning times versus the older van.

Vans

The new vans gave Pro Clean a better return on investment versus the old van:

- The new vans averaged 40 per cent better fuel efficiency than the old van
- Van setup for each job was faster
- New equipment required less fuel
- New equipment cleaned faster

New Service Offering

Wilson was thinking of offering a new service to his clients. He had carefully studied the competitive landscape and seen that only one company offered hardwood floor cleaning. He planned to introduce the new service as soon as he had been trained for it.

Sales and Cleaning Process

New Customers

See Exhibits 4, 5 and 6.

Potential customers would call to get information and prices as a result of interest sparked by Pro Clean's marketing effort. The sales/office manager would prequalify the sales leads and visit the prospective customer at the agreed day and time and prepare an on-site estimate after measuring the areas to be cleaned. Potential customers would usually take a couple days to come to a decision. Most of them would contact other carpet cleaners and ask for estimates. Once the job was given to Pro Clean, a cleaning technician would be dispatched to clean at the agreed day and time. The technician would also collect the cash payment upon completing the job.

Existing Customers

Existing customers' details were stored on the Pro Clean computer. The price estimate would be given over the phone unless the customer required additional spaces to be cleaned or asked for new services. A technician would then be dispatched at the agreed day and time to clean (see Exhibits 4, 5 and 6).

On-Site Estimates versus Phone Estimates

Only King Rug and Pro Clean made on-site estimate visits. Wilson thought that doing on-site estimate calculations was one way to impress customers and was just one more way to emulate King Rug. At times, he had watched the young, professional King Rug technicians' interactions with customers and admired the way they managed the customer interaction process in a standardized way. The only other cleaner that had a similar level of standardized proficiency was D-Cleaner.

All other cleaners gave approximate estimates over the phone and followed up with a detailed price once they were on-site to clean. This was when the inevitable up-selling began and greatly increased the low estimate given over the phone.

Wilson was not very good at selling and it was Andrew Scott that did most of the visits for Pro Clean. Alexander Martinez preferred just to clean and his closing ratio on the few times that he had made on-site estimate visits was dismal. Scott had a higher closing ratio with elder customers, with whom he claimed he was able to "connect" better. His approach did not work as well with other age groups or with commercial buyers.

The Pro Clean estimate kit consisted of a tape measure, calculator and pre-printed estimate form of which a copy was given to the customer. Wilson had taught Scott and Martinez how to do the calculations and fill out the estimate form in their first week at work after showing them how to clean.

Competitive Field

Pro Clean had more than 80 direct competitors in Knoxville providing carpet cleaning services. The market was very price-competitive and there was a large national chain, D-Cleaner, with high brand recognition that advertised aggressively at the national and local levels. D-Cleaner had successfully acquired a good portion of the market with a standard low price for standard cleaning services. D-Cleaner advertised prices by area rather than by square feet and a favorite ploy was to advertise a $199 all-inclusive price for five areas of a standard home, which was usually upsold by at least 50 per cent by aggressive point of sale bait and switch tactics.

The exception to price-based competition was King Rug, which was able to attract a wealthier clientele. King Rug had 20-plus years of business presence in the Knoxville area, operated four top-of-the-line vans and equipment and worked out of a nice building with a warehouse where oriental rugs were treated. King Rug charged on average 50 to 100 per cent higher for its services than its competitors.

At the bottom of the price spectrum was Kleen Clean, run by Kim Lee, a Korean-American, which offered low-cost dry/chemical cleaning services (see Exhibit 7).

Exhibit 1 Map of Knoxville, Tennessee

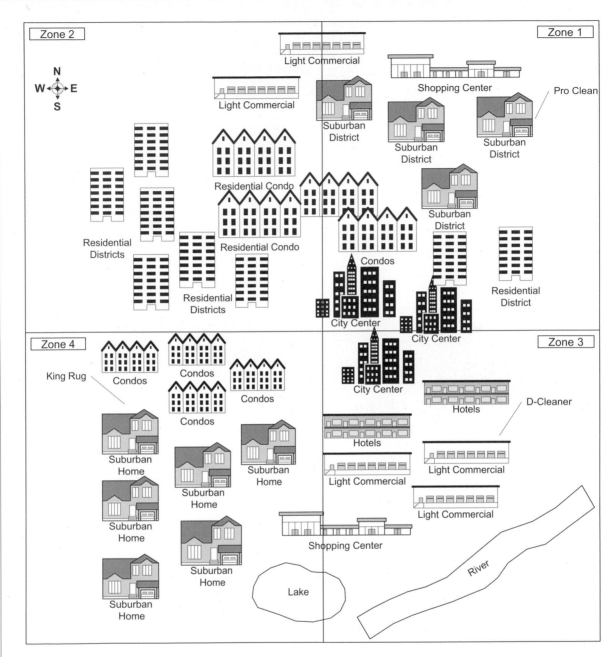

Source: Author.

Exhibit 2 Cleaning Methodology

There were two methods of carpet cleaning available in the market:

- Steam cleaning
- Low moisture/chemical cleaning

Steam Cleaning

- 85 per cent of the professional carpet cleaning business in the United States was steam cleaning
- Steam cleaning done with the right equipment and trained technicians dried within three to fours hours of application and dried in full within 12 to 16 hours
- Steam cleaning flushed the carpet with hot water piped in from the van with a long retractable hose at 180 to 220 degrees (steam was the term used to help buyers visualize the service better)
- Carpet manufacturers required steam cleaning every 12 to 16 months to keep maintenance warranties valid

Steam cleaning advantages:

- Preferred by clients as cleaning method of choice
- Required by carpet manufacturers
- Best deep down cleaning (fibers were flushed and extracted to remove all contaminates)
- Better overall results

Steam cleaning disadvantages:

- Average truck-mounted cleaning system started at $17,000 and went up to $40,000 (not including van)
- Longer setup time
- Longer cleaning time
- Longer dry time
- Longer training time for new technicians
- More equipment maintenance and downtime
- More fuel costs to operate equipment

Dry Cleaning/Chemical Cleaning

The cleaning process consisted of using a chemical compound to treat the carpet and then using a cotton bonnet spinning on a rotary machine, with the bonnet absorbing the dirt into the cotton pad.

Low moisture/chemical cleaning advantages:

- Faster dry times — 30 to 60 minutes after initial application
- Faster setup and cleaning time
- Faster learning curve
- No fuel costs to run machines
- Low equipment cost ($700–1000)

Low moisture/chemical cleaning disadvantages:

- Limited to surface cleaning of fibers
- Did not rinse carpet of contaminants
- No extraction
- Most consumers did not prefer it for fear of chemicals

Exhibit 3 Pro Clean HR Data

1. Kevin Wilson – Owner

   - Age: 48
   - Education: Some community college
   - Past Experience: 15 years of experience in the carpet cleaning industry

2. Andrew Scott – Sales/Office Manager

   - Age: 47
   - Education: High school diploma
   - Past Experience: Had owned and operated a limousine rental service for eight years in Kansas before moving to Knoxville (company went out of business); had started work in Knoxville as a call center operator handling customer service complaints for a large national appliance manufacturer
   - Had started out as a cleaning technician before making the switch to sales/office manager
   - Wilson had hired him because of his business experience and his ability to deal with people

(Continued)

Exhibit 3 Pro Clean HR Data (*Continued*)

3. Alexander Martinez – Technician

- Age: 51
- Education: High school diploma
- Past Experience: 20 years' experience in air conditioning installation (company went out of business)
- Had a wife, who had a serious health problem and needed constant care
- Wilson had hired Martinez because he was very eager to work for him (due in part to the good health benefits) and was mechanically inclined

4. Jeremy Turner – Technician

- Age: 27
- Education: High school diploma
- Past Experience: Five years of experience working in different janitorial cleaning service companies in the Knoxville area
- Hired because he had good references, was a hard and reliable worker, and knew the Knoxville area well

Exhibit 4 New Residential Customer Sales, Cleaning, and Collection Process

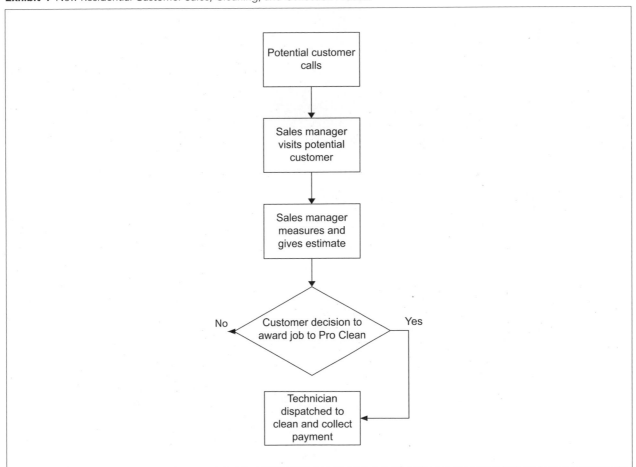

Exhibit 5 Existing Residential Customer Sales, Cleaning, and Collection Process

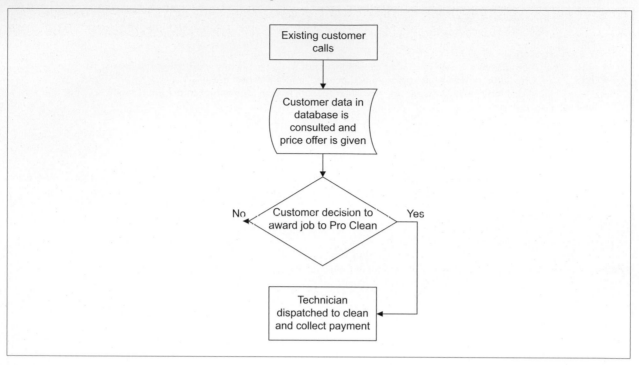

Exhibit 6 New Commercial Customer Sales, Cleaning and Collection Process

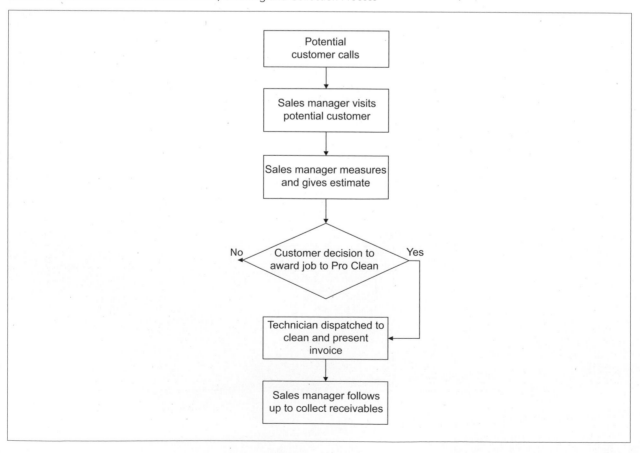

Exhibit 7 Competitive Analysis

Competitive Analysis	Pro Clean	D-Cleaner	King Rug	Green Clean	Right Clean	Kleen Clean
BUSINESS BASICS						
Number of vans	3	7	4	2	2	1
Number of employees	3	18–20	5	3	5	1
Number of years in business	15	50	20	8	18	5
MARKET FOCUS						
Residential	Y	Y	Y	Y	Y	Y
Commercial	N	N	N	N	N	N
CLEANING METHOD						
Steam	Y	Y	Y	Y	Y	N
Chemical	Optional	N	N	N	N	Y
CLEANING SERVICES						
Carpets	Y	Y	Y	Y	Y	Y
Upholstery	Y	Y	Y	Y	Y	Y
Rugs	Y	N	Y	N	N	N
Tiles	Y	Y	Y	Y	Y	N
Drapery	Y	Y	N	Y	Y	N
Air ducts	N	Y	N	Y	Y	N
Odor treatment	Y	Y	Y	Y	Y	Y
Natural stone car	Y	N	Y	N	N	N
House exteriors	N	N	N	N	N	N
RVs, trailers	Y	Y	Y	Y	Y	Y
Hardwood floor restoration	N	Y	N	N	N	N
Hardwood floor cleaning	Y	Y	N	N	N	N
MARKETING						
Carpet cleaning packages	N	Y	N	Y	Y	Y
Referral program	Y	N	Y	N	N	N
Coupons	N	Y	N	Y	Y	Y
Newsletter	Y	N	Y	Y	N	N
Advertising	N	Y	N	Y	Y	N
Loyalty program	N	N	Y	N	N	N
Unconditional guarantee	Y	N	Y	Y	Y	N
Good web page	N	Y	Y	N	N	N

(Continued)

Exhibit 7 Competitive Analysis (*Continued*)

Competitive Analysis	Pro Clean	D-Cleaner	King Rug	Green Clean	Right Clean	Kleen Clean
PRODUCT SALES						
Flooring goods	N	Y	N	N	N	N
GEOGRAPHICAL FOCUS						
Focus on metro Knoxville	Y	Y	Y	Y	Y	Y
Focus on other counties	N	N	N	N	N	N
Close to customer base	Y	Y	Y	Y	Y	Y
PRICING						
Carpet	$0.27 per sq. ft.	$36 per room	$0.60 per sq. ft.	$36 per room	$30 per room	$33 per room
Sofa upholstery cleaning (per piece)	$85	$80	N	$75	$60	N
Love seat cleaning (per piece)	$60	$60	N	$55	$50	N
Chair cleaning (per piece)	$55	$50	N	$35	$30	N
Rug cleaning (sq. ft.)	$2.00	$1.50	$3.00	$1.75	$1.50	$1.50
Tile cleaning (sq. ft.)	$0.90	$0.65	$1.25	$0.75	$0.75	N
Drapery cleaning (per pleat)	$1.75	N	N	N	N	N
Upholstery cleaning (by linear foot)	N	N	$15	N	N	N

NOTES

1. http://www.cityofknoxville.org/about/history.asp.
2. http://www.city-data.com/us-cities/The-South/Knoxville-Population-Profile.html.

Case Title	Manu-facturing	Service	Consumer Goods	Food/Retail	High Tech-nology	Internet	Transportation/Communication	International Perspective	Social/Ethical Issues	Industry Perspective
Biovail			●		●			●	●	
Wal-Mart Stores				●				●	●	
Room and Board				●					●	
Alibaba		●				●		●		
eBay, Inc.		●			●	●		●		●
Boeing	●							●		●
Motorola, Inc.	●		●					●		●
Southwest Airlines		●					●			●
Apple Computer, Inc.	●	●			●	●	●			●
Blockbuster			●	●		●				●
South Beauty Group		●		●				●		
Cinemaplex		●		●						●
JetBlue		●					●	●		●
Dell	●		●		●	●				●
Home Depot		●		●				●		
Henkel	●		●					●		
Citibank		●			●	●		●		
Nucor	●						●	●		●
Baidu		●				●		●		
TNK-BP	●							●		
The New York Times Company		●				●	●			●
Tesco versus Sainsbury's			●	●				●		
Under Armour			●					●		●
Barclays		●						●		
United Airlines		●					●	●		●
Netflix		●		●						
Oasis Hong Kong Airlines		●					●	●		
Nintendo			●		●	●		●		●
Pro Clean		●		●